shakespearean criticism

"Thou art a Monument without a tomb,
And art alive still while thy Book doth live
And we have wits to read and praise to give."

Ben Jonson, from the preface to the First Folio, 1623.

MR. WILLIAM

SHAKESPEARES

COMEDIES,
HISTORIES, &
TRAGEDIES.

Publiſhed according to the True Originall Copies.

LONDON
Printed by Iſaac Iaggard, and Ed. Blount. 1623.

Frontispiece to the First Folio (1623). By permission of the Folger Shakespeare Library.

ISSN 0883-9123

Volume 32

Shakespearean Criticism

Yearbook 1995

A Selection of the Year's Most Noteworthy Studies of William Shakespeare's Plays and Poetry

Advisers

Ralph Berry, *University of Ottawa*
Graham Bradshaw, *Kyoto University*
William C. Carroll, *Boston University*
S. P. Cerasano, *Colgate University*
Sidney Homan, *University of Florida*
MacDonald P. Jackson, *University of Auckland*
Randall Martin, *University of New Brunswick*
T. McAlindon, *University of Hull*
Yasuhiro Ogawa, *University of Hokkaido*

GALE

DETROIT • NEW YORK • TORONTO • LONDON

STAFF

Marie Lazzari, *Editor*

Dana Ramel Barnes, *Associate Editor*

Susan Trosky, *Managing Editor*

Marlene S. Hurst, *Permissions Manager*
Margaret A. Chamberlain, Maria L. Franklin, Kimberly F. Smilay, *Permissions Specialists*
Diane Cooper, Edna Hedblad, Michele Lonoconus, Maureen Puhl, Susan Salas,
Shalice Shah, Barbara A. Wallace, *Permissions Associates*
Sarah Chesney, Margaret McAvoy-Amato, *Permissions Assistants*

Victoria B. Cariappa, *Research Manager*
Barbara McNeil, *Research Specialist*
Alicia Biggers, Julia Daniel, Tamara C. Nott, Michele P. Pica,
Tracie A. Richardson, Cheryl Warnock, *Research Associates*

Mary Beth Trimper, *Production Director*
Deborah Milliken, *Production Assistant*
Sherrell Hobbs, *Macintosh Artist*
Randy Bassett, *Image Database Supervisor*
Mikal Ansari, Robert Duncan, *Imaging Specialists*
Pamela A. Hayes, *Photography Coordinator*

∞™ This book is printed on acid-free paper that meets the minimum requirements of American National Standard for Information Sciences—Permanence Paper for Printed Library Materials, ANSI Z39.48-1984.

Library of Congress Catalog Card Number 86-645085
ISBN 0-8103-9978-4
ISSN 0883-9123

Printed in the United States of America

10 9 8 7 6 5 4 3 2 1

Gale Research

Contents

Tragedies

Romances and Poems

Preface

Shakespearean Criticism (SC) provides students, educators, theatergoers, and other interested readers with valuable insight into Shakespeare's drama and poetry. The critical reactions of scholars and commentators from the seventeenth century to the present day are reprinted in the series from hundreds of periodicals and books. Students and teachers at all levels of study will benefit from *SC,* whether they seek information for class discussions and written assignments, new perspectives on traditional issues, or the most noteworthy analyses of Shakespeare's artistry.

Scope of the Series

Volumes 1 through 10 of the series present a unique historical overview of the critical response to each Shakespearean work, representing a broad range of interpretations. Volumes 11 through 26 recount the performance history of Shakespeare's plays on the stage and screen through eyewitness reviews and retrospective evaluations of individual productions, comparisons of major interpretations, and discussions of staging issues. Beginning with Volume 27 in the series, *SC* focuses on criticism published after 1960, with a view to providing the reader with the most significant modern critical approaches. Each of these volumes is organized around a theme that is central to the study of Shakespeare, such as politics, religion, or sexuality.

The *SC* Yearbook

SC compiles an annual Yearbook, collecting the most noteworthy contributions to Shakespearean scholarship published during the previous year. The essays are chosen to address a wide audience, including advanced secondary school students, undergraduate and graduate students, and teachers. Each year an advisory board of distinguished scholars recommends approximately one hundred articles and books from among the hundreds of valuable essays that appeared in the previous year. From these recommendations, Gale editors select examples of innovative criticism that represent current or newly developing trends in scholarship. The 38 essays in the present volume, *SC-32,* the *1995 Yearbook,* provide the latest assessments of the Shakespeare canon.

Organization and Features of the *SC Yearbook*

Essays are grouped on the basis of the genre of the Shakespearean work on which they focus: Comedies, Histories, Tragedies, and Romances and Poems. An article examining the relationship between pastoralism and *The Winter's Tale,* for example, appears in the Romances and Poems section of the yearbook.

- Each piece of criticism is reprinted in its entirety, including the full text of the author's footnotes, and is followed by a complete **Bibliographical Citation.**

- The *SC Yearbook* provides a **Cumulative Index to Topics.** This feature identifies the principal topics in the criticism and stage history of each work. The topics are arranged alphabetically, and the volume and starting page number are indicated for each essay that offers innovative or ample commentary on that topic.

Citing the *SC Yearbook*

Students who quote directly from the *SC Yearbook* in written assignments may use the following general forms to footnote reprinted criticism. The first example pertains to material drawn from periodicals, the second to material reprinted from books.

[1]Michael Neill, "Unproper Beds: Race, Adultery, and the Hideous in *Othello,*" *Shakespeare Quarterly,* 40 (Winter 1989), 383-412; reprinted in *Shakespearean Criticism,* Vol. 13, Yearbook 1989, ed. Sandra L. Williamson (Detroit: Gale Research, 1989), pp. 327-42.

[2]Philip Brockbank, "*Julius Caesar* and the Catastrophes of History," in *On Shakespeare: Jesus, Shakespeare and Karl Marx, and Other Essays* (Basil Blackwell, 1989), pp. 122-39; reprinted in *Shakespearean Criticism,* Vol. 13, *Yearbook 1989,* ed. Sandra L. Williamson (Detroit: Gale Research, 1991), pp. 252-59.

Suggestions Are Welcome

The editors encourage comments and suggestions from readers on any aspect of the *SC* series. In response to reader recommendations, several features have been added to *SC* since the series began, including the topic index and the sample bibliographic citations noted above. Readers are cordially invited to write, call, or fax the editors: *Shakespearean Criticism,* Gale Research, 835 Penobscot Bldg., Detroit, MI, 48226-4094. Call toll-free at 1-800-347-GALE or fax to 1-313-961-6599.

Acknowledgments

The editors wish to thank the copyright holders of the excerpted criticism included in this volume and the permissions managers of many book and magazine publishing companies for assisting us in securing reprint rights. We are also grateful to the staffs of the Detroit Public Library, the Library of Congress, the University of Detroit Mercy Library, Wayne State University Purdy/Kresge Library Complex, and the University of Michigan Libraries for making their resources available to us. Following is a list of the copyright holders who have granted us permission to reprint material in this volume of ***SC.*** Every effort has been made to trace copyright, but if omissions have been made, please let us know.

COPYRIGHTED EXCERPTS IN *SC,* VOLUME 32, WERE REPRINTED FROM THE FOLLOWING PERIODICALS:

Cahiers Elisabethains, April, 1995. Reproduced by permission of the publisher.—***Criticism,*** v. 37, Fall, 1995 for "*Edward III* in *Henry V*" by E. Pearlman. Copyright, 1995, Wayne State University Press. Reproduced by permission of the publisher and the author.—***ELH,*** v. 62, Summer, 1995 for "(Dis)embodied Letters and 'The Merchant of Venice'." Copyright © 1995 by The Johns Hopkins University Press. All rights reserved. Reproduced by permission of the publisher and the author.—***English,*** v. 44, Spring, 1995. © The English Association 1995. Reproduced by permission of the publisher.—***English Literary Renaissance,*** v. 25, Winter, 1995. Copyright © 1995 by *English Literary Renaissance*. Reproduced by permission of the publisher.—***Essays and Studies,*** v. 48, 1995. © The English Association 1995. All rights reserved. Reproduced by permission of the publisher.—***Essays in Criticism,*** v. 45, July, 1995 for "The Shapeliness of 'The Tempest'" by Peter Holland. Reproduced by permission of the Editors of *Essays in Criticism* and the author.—***Journal of English and Germanic Philology,*** v. 94, July, 1995 for "Loyal Fathers and Treacherous Sons: Familial Politics in *Richard II*" by Sharon Cadman Seelig. © 1995 by the Board of Trustees of the University of Illinois. Reproduced by permission of the publisher and the author.—***The Modern Language Review,*** v. 90, July, 1995 for "The Integrity of 'King Lear'" by Sidney Thomas. © Modern Humanities Research Association 1995. Reproduced by permission of the publisher and the author.—***New Literary History,*** v. 26, Autumn, 1995. Copyright © 1995 by *New Literary History*. Reproduced by permission of the publisher.—***Philological Quarterly,*** v. 74, Winter, 1995 for "*King John* and *The Troublesome Raigne:* Sources, Structure, Sequence" by Brian Boyd. Copyright 1995 by The University of Iowa. Reproduced by permission of the publisher and the author.—***Renaissance Quarterly,*** v. XLVIII, Autumn, 1995. Copyright © 1995 by the Renaissance Society of America, Inc. Reproduced by permission of the publisher.—***Representations,*** v. 41, Summer, 1995 for "*The Merry Wives of Windsor:* Sharing the Queen's Holiday" by Leslie S. Katz. © 1995 by The Regents of the University of California. Reproduced by permission of the publisher and the author.—***Review of English Studies,*** v. XLVI, 1995. Reproduced by permission of Oxford University Press.—***Shakespeare Bulletin,*** v. 13, Winter, 1995. Reproduced by permission of the publisher.—***Shakespeare Quarterly,*** v. 46, Winter, 1995; v. 46, Fall, 1995. © The Folger Shakespeare Library 1995. Both reproduced by permission of the publisher.—***Shakespeare Studies,*** v. XXII, 1995 for "Lucrece's Gaze" by Stephen J. Carter; v. XXIII, 1995 for "Interlinear Trysting and Household Stuff: The Latin Lesson and the Domestication of Learning in 'The Taming of the Shrew'" by Thomas Moisan. © 1995 by Associated University Presses, Inc. All rights reserved. Both reproduced by permission of the respective authors.—***Shakespeare Survey: An Annual Survey of Shakespeare Studies and Production,*** v. 48, 1995 for "'The Tempest' and Cultural Exchange" by Jean-Marie Maguin; v. 48, 1995 for "Holy War in *Henry V*" by Steven Marx; v. 48, 1995 for "Pilgrims of Grace: *Henry IV* Historicized" by Tom McAlindon; v. 48, 1995 for "Venetian Culture and the Politics of 'Othello'" by Mark Matheson. © Cambridge University Press, 1995. All reproduced with permission of Cambridge University Press and the respective authors.—***Shakespeare Quarterly,*** v. 47, Spring, 1995. © The Folger Shakespeare Library 1995. Reproduced by permission of the publisher.—***Studies in Philology,*** v. XCII, Fall, 1995 for "The Sequence of Posterity: Shakespeare's *King John* and the Succession Controversy" by Robert Lane. Copyright © 1995 by The University of North Carolina Press. Used by permission of the publisher and the author.—***Texas Studies in Language and Literature,*** v. 37, Fall, 1995 for "Katherine of 'The Taming of the Shrew': A Second Grissel" by Carolyn E. Brown; v. 37, Fall, 1995 for "Spectator Seduction: 'Measure for Measure'" by Louis Burkhardt; v. 37, Fall, 1995 for "Nashe as 'Monarch of Witt' and Shakespeare's 'Romeo and Juliet'" by Joan Ozark Holmer. Copyright © 1995 by the University of Texas Press. All reproduced by permission of the publisher and the respective authors.

COPYRIGHTED EXCERPTS IN *SC,* VOLUME 32, WERE REPRINTED FROM THE FOLLOWING BOOKS:

Dessen, Alan C. From ***Recovering Shakespeare's Theatrical Vocabulary***. Cambridge University Press, 1995. © Cambridge University Press 1995. Reproduced with the permission of the publisher and the author.—Hall, Jonathan. From ***Anxious Pleasures: Shakespearean Comedy and the Nation-State***. Associated University Presses, 1995. © 1995 by Associated University Presses, Inc. All rights reserved. Reproduced by permission of the publisher.—Kernan, Alvin. From ***Shakespeare, The King's Playwright: Theater in the Stuart Court, 1603-1613***. Copyright © 1995 by Yale University. All rights reserved. Reproduced by permission of the publisher.—Kolin, Philip C. From "'Come Down and Welcome Me to This World's Light': 'Titus Andronicus' and the Canons of Contemporary Violence," in ***Titus Andronicus: Critical Essays***. Edited by Philip C. Kolin. Garland Publishing, Inc., 1995. Copyright © 1995 by Philip C. Kolin. All rights reserved. Reproduced by permission of the publisher.—Laroque, François. From "Tradition and Subversion in 'Romeo and Juliet'," in ***Shakespeare's 'Romeo and Juliet': Texts, Contexts, and Interpretation***. Edited by Jay L. Halio. University of Delaware Press, 1995. © 1995 by Associated University Presses, Inc. All rights reserved. Reproduced by permission of the publisher.—Liebler, Naomi Conn. From ***Shakespeare's Festive Tragedy: The Ritual Foundation of Genre.*** Routledge, 1995. © 1995 Naomi Conn Liebler. All rights reserved. Reproduced by permission of the publisher.—Shapiro, James. From ***Shakespeare and the Jews***. Columbia University Press, 1995. Copyright © 1995 Columbia University Press, New York. All rights reserved. Reproduced with the permission of the publisher.—Westlund, Joseph. From "Idealization and the Problematic in 'The Tempest'," in ***Subjects on the World's Stage: Essays on British Literature on the Middle Ages and the Renaissance***. Associated University Presses, 1995. © 1995 by Associated University Presses, Inc. All rights reserved. Reproduced by permission of the publisher.

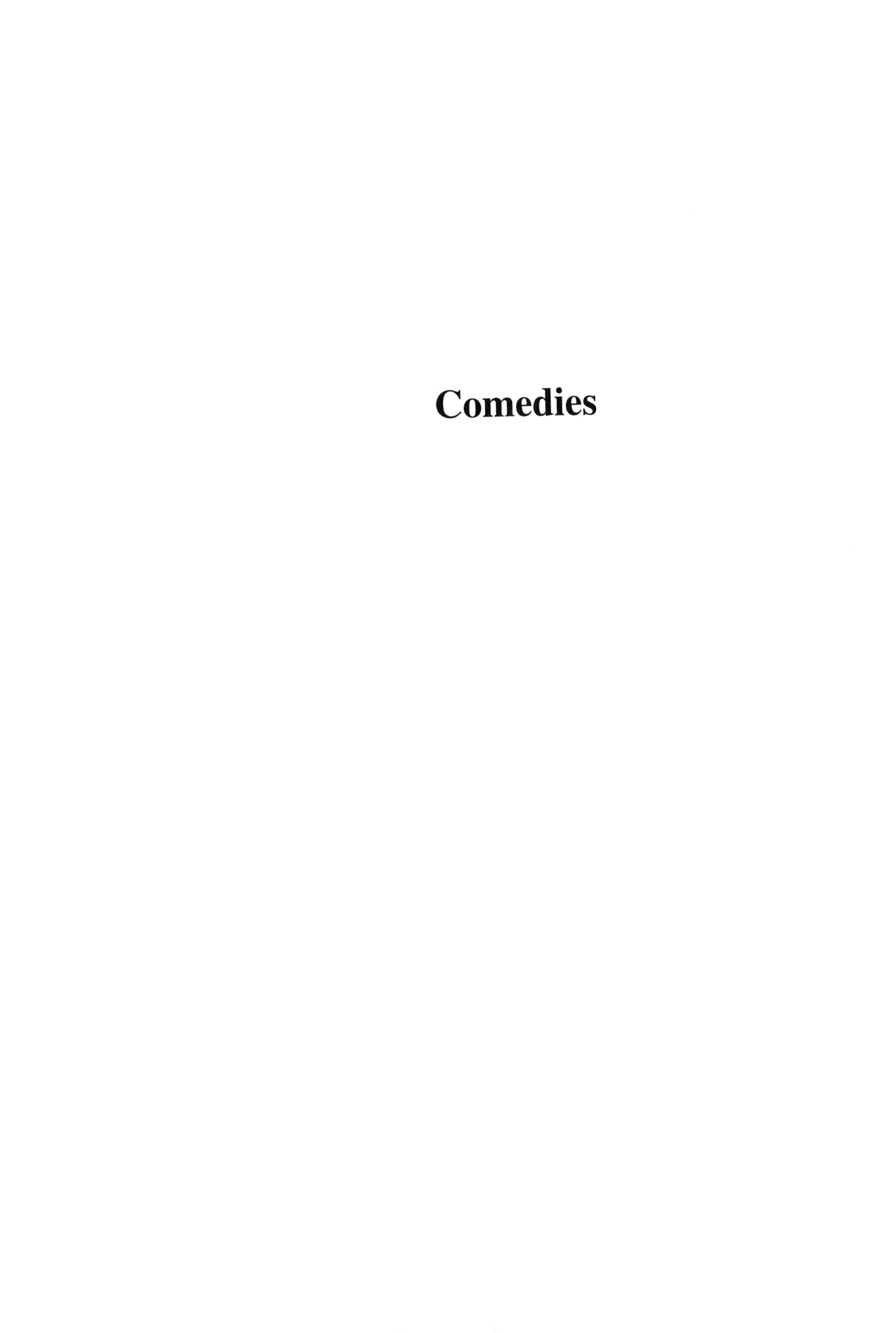

Comedies

Katherine of *The Taming of the Shrew*: 'A Second Grissel'

Carolyn E. Brown, *University of San Francisco*

Shakespeare wrote *The Taming of the Shrew* within the genre of shrew literature, popular in medieval and Renaissance times. Shrews appeared in almost every form of literature—written and oral—in these periods. And Shakespeare composes his play subtly enough that it can be read as written within the tradition, and he makes Katherine "spirited" enough that she can be read as a shrew, who finds a wise and courageous man with the skills to mold her into a peaceful, loving wife. Numerous critics have compellingly interpreted the play and the protagonists in these terms.[1] But some critics contend that Shakespeare put his own special touch on the tradition, modifying it in some important ways. These critics see Katherine, for example, as not quite fitting the mold of the traditional shrew. Most traditional shrew literature panders to misogynistic portrayals of women and clearly favors the male—typically a rational husband tormented by a loquacious, scolding, railing, irrationally violent, tricky woman. Shakespeare seems to have done something different with Katherine, who does not embody these characteristics. She has been shown to be too silent, too sympathetic, too tortured, too compliant to Petruchio's "taming strategies" to be a typical shrew. Camille Wells Slights, for example, notes that "Shakespeare's Kate—probably the most famous shrew of all—seems to elude the categories of literary history." Charles Brooks calls Katherine a "romantic shrew" and claims that Shakespeare humanizes his heroine. Robert Ornstein notes that Katherine is "more sensitive and tormented" and "more sympathetic and more psychologically complex than the [patently shrewish] heroine of *The Taming of a Shrew*"—either a bad quarto of Shakespeare's play, a source play, or a play derived from the same source that Shakespeare used.[2] Critics have argued, in fact, that Katherine is not a shrew at all and that her seeming shrewishness is only a defense mechanism against the hurt inflicted on her by a misogynistic world.[3]

Shakespeare has also been read as having conceived Petruchio in terms different from those of the traditional shrew tamer: a patient man who usually wants a loving, mutually nurturing relationship with his spouse but who is forced to resort to violent measures in order to counteract the uncontrollable, destructive violence of his shrewish wife. In many ways, Shakespeare makes his male protagonist more problematic. At times Petruchio behaves like a bully and a brute, and his tactics with Katherine can be read as gratuitously severe and prolonged tormenting of her. Some critics express reservations about him. For example, George Bernard Shaw condemns Petruchio for his "domineering cruelty." Mark Van Doren argues that we must "confess" that Petruchio is "torturing" Katherine during his "taming" of her. J. Dennis Huston derides Petruchio's "courtship" of Katherine as "nothing less than psychological rape" and suggests that Petruchio "touches upon the 'low,' the bestial, in man's nature." Robert Ornstein argues that "Shakespeare's version of the wife-tamer is both coarser and less attractive as a dramatic figure than his counterpart in *The Taming of a Shrew*." And Jeanne Addison Roberts claims that "there have been some overtones of the monster in Petruchio right from the start" of the play and that "Kate's journey with him to his country house is for her a descent into hell."[4] The reading of the play that I offer argues that these differences in the portrayal of the protagonists result from Shakespeare's modifying the shrew tradition in order to merge it with another equally dominant genre of the period—the story of Patient Griselda. Certainly the image is contained within the play itself when Petruchio states that everyone has "talk'd amiss" of Katherine, for she is not a shrew but "for [her] patience she will prove a second Grissel" (II.i.284, 288).[5] Shakespeare lodges some truth in Petruchio's statement and allows for the reading that Katherine has been misjudged and is more similar to a Griselda than a shrew figure.[6]

Alfred L. Kellogg explains that the "roots of the Griselda story go back into pagan antiquity."[7] One of its most noteworthy appearances is in Chaucer's "Clerk's Tale," "a retelling of a popular medieval tale," that "circulated in Italian, Latin, French, and English versions in the Middle Ages."[8] Although sometimes modified and enhanced, the basic plotline appears in such works as Boccaccio's tenth day of *The Decameron* (1353); Petrarch's *De Obedientia ac Fide Uxoria Mythologia* (1373-74); John Phillip's play *The Commodye of Pacient and Meeke Grissill* (1565); and Thomas Dekker, Henry Chettle, and William Haughton's *The Pleasant Commoedye of Patient Grissill* (1599).[9] These works begin with a powerful lord deciding to marry a poor maiden, whom he subjects to torturous tests, despite her honorable behavior. Soon after the birth of each of Griselda's two children, her husband takes them from her, lying to her by telling her that he is going to have them killed when secretly he has his relatives care for them. After he throws her out of his household, he orders her back to his estate and has her make preparations for his new marriage, forcing her to serve his new bride. Once Griselda passes all of the tests with extraordinary patience and fortitude, her husband reveals the deception to her—that her children are alive and that he is not marrying another woman, since his supposed bride-to-be is actually their long-lost daughter. He glories in her well-tested virtue, and she glories in finding that her children are alive and well. The Patient Griselda figure appears in many other works, especially plays, in the early seventeenth century, some of which have little in common with the basic plot other than a heroine who patiently endures mistreatment from the men in her life. In many cases, the Patient Griselda works are meant to be, as Linda Woodbridge argues, "a male wish-fulfillment fantasy appropriate to historical periods when few living wives behaved like Patient Grissill."[10] Indeed, many of them are written from a misogynistic point of view and perpetuate the ideal of wifely obedience, subservience, and unquestioning submission to the often cruel whims of husbands. And, in fact, some of the Griseldas love their husbands even more after all of the persecution.

But some of these works appear to be much more than patriarchal endorsements of female servitude and more than "wish-fulfillment fantasies" for men about female subjugation. Some of them are unconventional and respond to what Louis Wright calls "intelligent thinking upon women's status in a new commercial society"[11] and to the medieval and Renaissance debate over woman's nature. While the women are subservient and ever suffering, our attention is drawn not so much to female submission as an ideal but to male cruelty as an evil. Boccaccio and Petrarch direct negative judgments toward the husbands and make their works different from traditional tales. It is Chaucer, however, who heightens the criticism. Harriet Hawkins clarifies that Chaucer "consistently alters his sources, on the one hand, to make Walter's [Griselda's husband's] behavior toward Griselda infuriating and reprehensible and, on the other hand, to make Griselda's uncritical acceptance of unnecessary suffering painful and pitiable"—an observation that some critics make about Shakespeare's depiction of Petruchio and Katherine. Hawkins goes on to state that Chaucer "criticized Walter far more powerfully, frequently, and severely than his predecessor" and enlists us on the side of his victim "by confronting us with cosmic and social injustices so cruel, so extreme, that we cannot but join in the protest."[12] Chaucer has been shown to use the Griselda figure to uncover the "treachery of daily domestic life" for women.[13] Shakespeare, as well as other Renaissance writers (such as Phillip in his *The Commodye of Pacient and Meeke Grissill* and Dekker, Chettle, and Haughton in their *The Pleasant Commoedye of Patient Grissill*), followed Chaucer's lead and transformed genres typically associated with misogynistic portrayals of women into explorations of marital abuse of women.

The two traditions of shrew and Griselda literature seem to be diametrically opposed to each other, for one concerns itself with a patient, self-effacing, ever-suffering female figure who follows her husband's every command, while the other portrays a vocal, demanding, aggressive woman who refuses to follow commands and, instead, gives them herself. One seems the best of wives; the other, the worst. But the plot dynamics can be quite similar, and with just a few modifications, the two traditions can be made to resemble each other. Both begin, for example, with a man who, for various reasons, is looking for a wife. The men decide on the least appropriate choice: although a man of power and influence, the lord of the Griselda story chooses the daughter of the poorest man of the village; the man of the other tradition chooses, of course, the undesirable shrew, whom all other men shun. Both genres include a wedding and a reception, which are followed by the testing of the wives. In the shrew plot, the husband attempts to tame or stamp out the intolerable shrewishness of his new wife; in the Griselda plot, the husband tests his wife's patience or wifely virtue. Although the husbands enlist different strategies, they are both trying to make their wives into models of womanly submissiveness and obedience. Both stories can end with a banquet, with the husbands calling their wives to come to them. Much of shrew literature, like that of the Griselda genre, is clearly misogynistic propaganda against women, teaching the pitfalls of husbands not keeping their wives in subservience. But if in shrew literature the taming is needless and excessive, and the woman has been mislabeled a shrew and is portrayed sympathetically, then the shrew can become a Chaucerian Griselda figure, and the shrew tamer can become a kind of Chaucerian lord, who is doing something far more menacing than merely testing or taming a wife.

It is my contention that Shakespeare in *The Taming of the Shrew* is integrating the two traditions, which bear striking resemblances to each other. Shakespeare's framework of the play is in the shrew format, and on one level he allows Katherine to be read as a shrew and the play as a festive comedy. Jan Harold Brunvand in his study of the folktale background of the shrew story has thoroughly clarified the elements from the shrew tradition that Shakespeare incorporates into his play.[14] But Shakespeare also subtly interweaves elements of the Griselda plotline that flesh out the shrew framework and transform the play into a dark study of domestic abuse—like that of Chaucer—permitting Katherine on another level of meaning to be read as a Patient Griselda.[15]

Shakespeare's play does not begin as traditional shrew tales usually do; rather, it starts in a fashion similar to that of stories of sympathetic Griseldas. Since writers of traditional shrew tales are not interested in creating sympathy for the scold, they see no need to personalize her; she remains little more than an inanimate object. These tales usually begin with the wedding or soon after. But in Shakespeare's play and in Griselda literature like that of Chaucer, Boccaccio, and Petrarch, we are allowed to meet the protagonists before marriage plans are officially made. And in both, the woman is portrayed in a more sympathetic fashion than is the man, who shows signs of the brutal nature that only intensifies as the works proceed. These Griselda plots predispose us to admire the heroine for her virtue and fortitude in adversity. Because she comes from humble beginnings, her inner worth is overlooked, and she is not valued in society, but we are allowed to appreciate what others cannot see. These works present a dutiful, chaste, diligent, honorable daughter, who shows reverence for her father. She never seeks regard but, rather, lives unassumingly. From the very beginning of these tales, though, we are encouraged to be suspicious, even to disapprove, of the lord, who seems selfish and irresponsible. Chaucer, in fact, has his Clerk begin his tale by casting "blame" on the Lord:

> I blame hym thus, that he considered noght
> In tyme comynge what myghte hym bityde.
> But on his lust present was al his thoght,
> As for to hauke and hunte on every syde.
> (78-80)[16]

Although he is a lord with responsibilities to his lieges, all he cares about is his own pleasure or "lust." He is so self-consumed that his lieges are forced to approach him and remind him of his duties—that he should marry and provide a rightful successor for them so they can avoid "wo" should he die (139). All of the tales give indications of a peremptory, tyrannical nature in their male protagonist by the way he interacts with his men and by the way they respond to him. Chaucer heightens the oppressive nature of his lord over that of Boccaccio and Petrarch's lords: "In the very meticulousness of the decorum with which the people approach their 'lord,' there is more than a suggestion that there is indeed in Walter something to fear."[17] Chaucer's lord's people seem reluctant to approach him and are repeatedly described as loving their lord but also "dred[ing]" him (181). Griselda's father, in fact, is "al quakyng" (317) when the lord approaches him to arrange to marry his daughter, and we detect that the father is feeling something more than the awe of the lord's majestic presence. The lord is shown constantly giving "commands," which his men rush to "obey." They are to do his "lust" at all times. Later when Chaucer's lord threatens to strike off his sergeant's head (586) if he does not perform his duty to the letter, we begin to sense the danger and imperiousness of this lord and are allowed to interpret his later testing of his wife as another manifestation of his brutal temperament.

Shakespeare makes us feel uncomfortable with Petruchio as well. He permits us to get an especially revealing insight into Petruchio's character when we first see him alone with his servant Grumio. This kind of scene is not to be found in any of the shrew literature, not even in the similar play *The Taming of a Shrew*. Just as in the Griselda stories, the male protagonist's treatment of his servants and their reaction to him help to reveal much about Petruchio's true nature. And the man we meet bears all the markings of a bully and a tyrant, obsessed with control. Petruchio seems to savor seeing Grumio jump upon command, refusing even to knock on the gate of his friend's house himself and demanding that his man do it for him: "Now knock when I bid you, sirrah villain" "or I'll knock your knave's pate" (I.ii.19, 12). Looking for an excuse to beat Grumio, he wrings his ears for no reason. In fact, Grumio seems to have been so chronically abused that he is looking for a legal way to end his servitude with Petruchio and hopes this incident will prove to be "a lawful cause for [him] to leave his service" (I.ii.29). Later, on the trip home after the wedding, Petruchio is just as unjustifiably abusive, as he duplicates his earlier actions with Grumio and jumps at any opportunity to beat his servant again: Grumio complains that his master "beat [him] because [Katherine's] horse stumbled" (IV.i.69). At the dinner at his home, he barks commands at his servants, dissatisfied with the most prompt service, threatening to batter and actually striking any servants within his reach, and throwing food and dishes. The servants' behavior is similar to that of Griselda's lord's servants, who respond to him obsequiously and obey his commandments for fear of his cruelty. The repetitiveness of Petruchio's abusive behavior and the fact that some of it occurs before he even knows of Katherine's existence suggest that violence is a permanent part of his character, not a contrived method to tame a shrew.

Shakespeare can be read as making Katherine's initial situation as pitiable as he makes Petruchio's offensive. Critics have noted that Shakespeare from the very beginning has Katherine evoke our sympathy and regard for her, just as authors of unconventional Griselda literature do for their heroines.[18] While Katherine does not come from a background of poverty as Griselda does, she is like Griselda in that she is poor in reputation and public regard. None of the characters at the beginning of the play can appreciate the woman of worth that Shakespeare—like Chaucer, Boccaccio, and Petrarch—allows his audience to see. Shakespeare presents a painful scene of everyone mocking Katherine, taunting that she will never find a "mate." Despite all of the nasty name-calling, Katherine addresses the men and her father as "sirs," showing them a deference and respect that they do not deserve. When Hortensio cruelly taunts her with her undesirability, she tries to protect herself from the hurt by projecting the defensive posture of indifference and callousness:

> I'faith, sir, you shall never need to fear [that
> she will choose him as a mate]
> Iwis it is not half way to her heart.

> But if it were, doubt not her care should be
> To comb your noddle with a three-legg'd
> stool,
> And paint your face, and use you like a fool.
> (I.i.61-65)

Shakespeare shows us a woman treated deplorably by everyone, a woman whose patience is certainly put to the test. And yet she responds with great aplomb.

Because Shakespeare first has us experience Katherine's torment, he predisposes us not to judge her harshly when she later lashes out at her tormentors. Katherine's reactions allow Shakespeare to make her look like a shrew on one level of meaning, yet like a woman much abused on another level. He permits us to feel that the heckling has been chronic and that it has a cumulative effect on Katherine, forcing her to strike out when her patience can no longer endure the abuse. Shakespeare allows us to read her responses as warranted, much different from the violence of Petruchio, who resembles a raucous bully who strikes out without provocation. Coppelia Kahn notes that Katherine responds only "because of provocation or intimidation."[19] Shakespeare, moreover, encourages us to view Katherine's behavior as understandable when later even her uncaring father justifies it, saying he "cannot blame" her, "for such an injury would vex a saint" (II.ii.27-28). And, indeed, even a "saint" or a Patient Griselda can be provoked to the point of anger if vexed enough. Dekker, Chettle, and Haughton's Grissill, for example, snaps at her husband's servant when he threatens to take her children from her: "Come, come Ile chide, / In faith you cruell man, Ile chide indeede, / If I growe angrie" (IV.i.115-17).

The next step in the Griselda plotline involves the lord choosing the woman he will marry. The tales of Chaucer and Boccaccio reinforce the lord's self-centered and peremptory nature and, conversely, Griselda's dutiful and compliant nature. The lord is not interested in a wife as a lifetime marital companion but as a vessel to provide him with heirs. He views the woman as a means to a desirable end and is concerned solely with his own "lust" or wishes. The lord shows himself to be a shrewd bargainer who decides on his choice and gets what he wants, even if the maid he chooses is not willing. Typically, he goes to Griselda's father before he even meets Griselda and maneuvers the old man into giving him his daughter in marriage, for example, using his power and influence and intimidating the "quakyng" (317) father as in Chaucer's version, or simply determining to have the maiden and announcing his intentions to the father as in Boccaccio. The lord speaks for the father and even for Griselda: Chaucer's lord tells the father "And al that liketh me, I dar wel seyn / It liketh thee" (311-12); and he gives Griselda no voice at all in her future—"It liketh to youre fader and to me / That I yow wedde, and eek it may so stonde, / As I suppose, y wol that it so be" (345-47). He never asks her if she wishes to marry him, but tells her, and certainly does not wait for a reply from her. He decides on the day of the marriage and proclaims that she will "rule hire after me" (327). He instructs her that she must be "redy with good herte / To al my lust" (351-52). In Phillip's version and that of Dekker, Chettle, and Haughton, the lord proposes to Griselda, and although she rejects him, he traps her by convincing her father to give him Griselda in marriage. Phillip's Griselda laments her situation—"Alas poore sillie girle increased is thy smart" (751)—and addresses her complaint to her father, who tells her to "lament no more, distill no teares, though thou departe mee froe" (765). In all versions, Griselda obeys her father's wishes. We see a woman trapped and forced into marriage and are encouraged to sympathize with her plight.

Traditional shrew literature does not contain the element of an enforced marriage, for the marriage arrangements are not an issue, or the shrew is already married when the tale begins, or she wishes to marry and establish sovereignty over her husband. A shrew is not forced to do anything against her will, especially not to marry. But Shakespeare veers from the shrew tradition to evoke a situation similar to that of the enforced marriage of Griselda literature. Like Griselda's lord, Petruchio is not interested in a wife as a human being or a companion; rather, he sees the woman as a source of financial security and cares only about himself. Petruchio also makes arrangements with the father without having even met his prospective mate. He displays the same domineering, intransigent nature of the lord in that he is so determined to have his way and marry Katherine that, although Baptista expresses reservations, Petruchio will hear none of them: "I am as peremptory as she proud-minded" (II.i.131).

Katherine, on the other hand, acts like a Griselda: obedient to her father's wishes, she goes unaccompanied to meet with the suitor whom her father has ordered her to entertain. During their first meeting, Petruchio is "rough and woo[es] not like a babe" (II.i.137), for there are indications that he physically holds her against her will. Once he resorts to some obligatory wooing and forestalls her leaving the scene, he, like the lord of the Griselda story, tells her that he is going to marry her and that he will tolerate no dissension: "Your father hath consented / That you shall be my wife; your dowry 'greed on; / And will you, nill you, I will marry you" (II.i.262-64). When Baptista and the other men enter the scene, Petruchio gives Katherine instructions about how to behave—"Never make denial; / I must and will have Katherine to my wife" (II.i.272-73)—and misrepresents the situation by acting as if Katherine has privately expressed her love for him and only feigns disgust for him in public. Like Chaucer's lord, Petruchio proclaims that she will be ruled by him because he knows that if she were allowed to rule her own life, she would not marry him. Like some of the Griseldas, Katherine futilely pleads with her father, asking him how he could marry her to such a brute—"You have show'd a tender fatherly regard / To wish me wed to one half lunatic" (II.i.279-80)—and wishing rather to see Petruchio "hang'd" (II.i.292) than to wed him. Shakespeare evokes the situation found in Griselda literature and has Petruchio trap Katherine, resorting to any measures necessary to get his way. She has nothing left to do but patiently obey—which she does. Baptista notes that she is "in [the] dumps" (II.i.277), depressed and mournful, almost in a death state, left to "go sit and weep" (II.i.35) by herself and endure her pain alone—as a Patient Griselda does. And as in the Griselda tales, we are permitted to sympathize with her.

While the lord in these Griselda tales is shown to be a potential bully and tyrant, he has one saving grace: an astute ability to perceive Griselda's real nature. He is able to see what no one else can—that despite her lowly condition, Griselda is actually an embodiment of virtue and honor. Chaucer has his lord commend her "wommanhede / And eek hir vertu" (239-40), explaining that "thogh the peple hath no greet insight / In vertue, he considered ful right / Hir bountee" (242-44). Petrarch praises his lord for "his swift intuition [that] had perceived in her a virtue, beyond her sex and age, which the obscurity of her condition concealed from the eyes of the common throng" (142). Shakespeare, too, has Petruchio speak highly of Katherine. This is a deviation from shrew tales. Since traditional shrew literature is directed against women, a shrew is never spoken of favorably. Critics who see Katherine as the shrew and Petruchio as her wise therapist suggest that Petruchio's favorable delineations of Katherine are part of his therapy and are meant to show her the mild woman she can become if she modifies her behavior.[20] But Shakespeare allows for another reading as well, one similar to that of Griselda tales.

Shakespeare models Petruchio after the lord of these tales in that only Petruchio can see the goodness in Katherine. After being alone with her for just a short while and detecting her embarrassment at his bawdy and crass talk, Petruchio discerns that she is not what she is reported to be—a shrew: "I find you passing gentle. / 'Twas told me you were rough, and coy, and sullen, / And now I find report a very liar" (II.i.236-38). He contends that she has been "slander[ed]" (II.i.247) and tells her father that he "and all the world / That talk'd of her have talk'd amiss of her" (II.i.283-84). He is able to see that the world has misjudged her, that it has misinterpreted her spiritedness as shrewishness and has missed her true worth. Petruchio's characterization of Katherine, unlike that of her detractors, poignantly captures the woman we have been allowed to appreciate—a woman who is "pleasant, gamesome, passing courteous, / But slow in speech" (II.i.239-40), "modest as the dove" and "temperate as the morn," indeed a "Roman Lucrece for her chastity"—descriptions that befit a "second Grissel" (II.i.286-89). As with the lord in Griselda tales, Petruchio seems attracted to Katherine partly because of her gentleness and poor reputation, detecting a woman he can dominate.

The next stage in the Griselda story involves the day of the marriage. In Petrarch's and especially Chaucer's version, there is another suggestion of the lord's love of control and power, for he will tell no one which maiden he has decided to marry until the last minute. The sense of suspense and wonder is heightened. Petrarch declares that "no one knew whence the bride would come, and there was no one who did not wonder" and that "universal bewilderment had risen very high" (142). Chaucer underscores the lord's love of power games as his men stand in wonder and suspect him of "bigyl[ing]" them (252). Once the lord holds everyone in suspense to his satisfaction, he comes forward, peremptorily announcing his choice. In the Boccaccio and Chaucer versions, he has Griselda "stripped naked" in the presence of all his company before he marries her so that he can clothe her in more elegant attire, suitable to her new station as the wife of a lord. The emphasis, though, is on his degrading her in public. Norman Lavers clarifies that Chaucer means for his lord to "humiliate" her and demonstrate her "abjectness,"[21] as he begins to establish his control over her in a manner that shames her the most. Griselda's misery is underscored in Phillip's version when she expresses that her "harte is much pained" (828) to leave her home and marry a man whom she does not love. Nonetheless, she obeys her father's and then her husband's commands.

Shakespeare's Katherine, likewise, is pained yet obedient. She arrives on time for the wedding, dutifully following her father's "will," and waits for the groom. Shakespeare underscores her misery and the enforced condition typical of Griseldas, allowing his audience to sympathize with his heroine as she laments being "forc'd / To give [her] hand, oppos'd against [her] heart" (II.ii.8-9). Although Katherine's heart is not in the marriage, she endures her fate, not making a scene, not refusing to do what is contrary to her own wishes, not being disrespectful to her father. She goes off once again to be alone and bewail a fate she dreads. She is honest and dutiful—just like a Griselda. Petruchio's arriving late on an old nag is derived from the shrew tradition, but the sense of suspense and control that Petruchio derives from holding up the proceedings until he arrives is similar to that of the lord in Chaucer's and Boccaccio's Griselda stories: nothing happens until he is ready. He must control everything, and everyone must abide by his "lusts." While Petruchio does not literally strip Katherine of her clothes as the lord does to Griselda, Shakespeare suggests that his groom gears all of his behavior to stripping Katherine of her pride and humiliating her, especially with his "stripped down" clothing. Petruchio makes what should be one of the most glorious days for Katherine into one of the most humiliating, as Katherine expresses her sense of being made into a laughing stock: "No shame but mine" (II.ii.8); "Now must the world point at poor Katherine / And say 'Lo, there is mad Petruchio's wife, / If it would please him come and marry her'" (II.ii.18-20). Shakespeare has Katherine, like the shamed Griselda, feel debased, not knowing which is worse—to marry a brute who is dressed in base attire and whom she does not love or to be a public spectacle of a bride stood up at the altar. On a festive level, Shakespeare allows us to surmise that Petruchio's behavior before, during, and after the wedding ceremony is meant in some way to be part of his taming strategy. But in not clarifying Petruchio's purpose, Shakespeare on a darker level allows that Petruchio is simply a man obsessed with power, violence, and control—like the lord of Chaucer's Griselda tale.

Like Shakespeare's Katherine, Griseldas, who start the works being either unrecognized for their inner goodness or lowly regarded, begin to win other characters' admiration once others are allowed to know them. The people begin to recognize the Griseldas' inner beauty, to which they were initially blinded. Griseldas win this regard by their virtue and their concern for the lord's subjects, often serving as peacemakers and protecting the subjects. Dekker, Chettle, and Haughton's Griselda behaves much as Shakespeare's Katherine when she ignores her own misery and intercedes for her lord's servant, Furio, trying to dissuade her husband from murdering him: "Temper your wrath I beg it on my knee, / Forgiue his fault though youle not pardon me" (II.ii. 112-13). Furio and others begin to see the sweet nature in Griselda that they had not recognized before: "Shees a saint sure" (II.ii.124). Chaucer's Griselda also makes others reevaluate her:

> [She was] so discreet and fair of eloquence,
> So benygne and so digne of reverence,
> And koude so the peples herte embrace,
> That ech hir lovede that looked on hir face.
> (410-13)

Her peace-loving nature makes her highly valued: "Ther nas discord, rancour, ne hevynesse / In al that land, that she ne koude apese, / And wisly brynge hem alle in reste and ese" (432-34). The lord's subjects begin to believe that "she from hevene sent was" in order "peple to save and every wrong t'amende" (440-41). While the people may praise the lord for seeing her hidden virtue when they could not, their estimation of him begins to falter when he treats Griselda poorly. In Boccaccio, the lord's vassals "blamed him greatly, accounting him a barbarous man, and had the utmost compassion for his wife" (786). Chaucer has the lord's subjects begin to reevaluate his lord's reputation and to see him as being "wikked" and having a "cruel herte" (723): "For which, wher as his people ther bifore / Hadde loved hym wel, the sclaundre of his diffame / Made hem that they hum hated therfore" (729-31).

Shakespeare clearly has Katherine behave like a Griselda in trying to appease rancor and save the unfortunate from abuse. Shrews, in contrast, never assist others; rather, they are the cause of misfortune to others. For example, although the horse falls on Katherine on the ride home after the wedding, she does not complain. Rather she extricates herself from under the horse to rush to Grumio's aid: Grumio reports that she "waded through the dirt to pluck [Petruchio] off" of him (IV.i.69-70). She does not think of her own misfortune but, instead, helps to relieve another's misery. When Petruchio throws food and dishes and hits servants during the meal at his home, Shakespeare once again has Katherine try to placate the raging master and makes her the embodiment of patience and compassion for others. She advises Petruchio to be more understanding, more humane toward others, telling him not to hit the servant for a mere accident: "Patience, I pray you, 'twas a fault unwilling" (IV.i.143). Although Petruchio only rages more and becomes more violent, Katherine maintains her aplomb and tries yet again to intervene and save the servants from their master's violence: "I pray you, husband, be not so disquiet. / The meat was well, if you were so contented" (IV.i.155-56). In many senses, Petruchio's description of her as his "most patient, sweet and virtuous wife" (III.ii.193) most accurately portrays the Griselda, not the shrew, figure that Shakespeare presents as Katherine.

Shakespeare models his play after these Griselda tales by having characters, some of whom are predisposed to favor Petruchio, begin to change their estimation of him and Katherine once they experience how deplorably Petruchio behaves and how patiently Katherine responds to this shameful treatment. As in the Griselda tales, they begin to condemn Petruchio and praise, even sympathize with, Katherine. This certainly deviates from traditional shrew literature, where the readers' sympathies and respect are clearly enlisted for the husband and their derision is reserved solely for the shrew. Gremio is the first to articulate his disgust with Petruchio's behavior at the wedding—behavior that so shocks and embarrasses Gremio that he leaves the ceremony as quickly as he can. Gremio tries to set Tranio straight by telling him that Petruchio was not a "bridegroom," a respectful participant in the ceremony, but a "groom," a crude fellow,[22] a "grumbling groom," "a devil, a devil, a very fiend" (III.ii.151, 153). Once Gremio gets beyond the gossip and rumors about Katherine and actually meets and observes her, his perceptions of her begin to change as well: he suggests that Petruchio is "curster" (III.ii.152) than Katherine, that, in fact, she is not at all what she is portrayed to be but "a lamb, a dove" (III.ii.155). His designations of her all suggest gentleness, meekness, patience, and humility—characteristics typically associated with Griseldas. Chaucer, in fact, associates his Griselda with a lamb: "as a lamb she sitteth meke and stille" (538). The lamb and the dove also have religious significance, as Shakespeare, like Chaucer, suggests a kind of religious nuance to Katherine and her suffering. After Curtis, another servant of Petruchio, experiences his master's treatment of Katherine, he, likewise, feels sorry for her, describing her plight as piteous: "She, poor soul, / Knows not which way to stand, to look, to speak" (IV.i.171-72). Even Hortensio, whom Petruchio calls his "best beloved and approved friend" (I.ii.3), is so shamed and pained by Petruchio's mistreatment of Katherine that he censures him to his face: "Signor Petruchio, fie! You are to blame. / Come, Mistress Kate, I'll bear you company" (IV.iii.48-49). Hortensio tries to distance himself from Petruchio and sides with Katherine, offering her his company and his consolation. By having the least perceptive and sophisticated characters—like Gremio and Curtis—as well as the least sensitive to Katherine's plight—like Baptista and Hortensio—begin to feel compassion for Katherine and reservation, if not dislike, for Petruchio, Shakespeare intimates the danger of Katherine's situation and encourages his more astute audience to reassess Katherine's so-called shrewishness and Petruchio's civility.

Like Griselda, Katherine shows herself to be "ever good." Shakespeare has her act admirably again and again: she obediently arrives for the wedding; she weds Petruchio without any remonstration; she endures his outrageous behavior during the ceremony, Gremio never suggesting that she speaks one word of disgruntlement; she behaves graciously once they arrive at his home for dinner, expressing "content" with the service and food. Despite the fact that both Petruchio and Griselda's lord have proof of their wives' goodness and have personally attested to the women's virtues, they test and tame them nonetheless. Petrarch puts it this way: the lord "was seized with a desire more strange than laudable—so the more experienced may decide—to try more deeply the fidelity of his dear wife, which had been sufficiently made known by experience" (145). Chaucer's Clerk searches for a motivation for the lord's testing, but he cannot arrive at a satisfactory one and repeatedly calls it "nedelees": "He hadde assayed hire ynow bifore, / And fond hir evere good; what neded it / Hir for to tempte" (456-58). In IV.i.175-98, Petruchio officially announces his scheme for taming Katherine. Scholars have tried to explain and justify Petruchio's actions, resorting to elaborate and sophisticated readings. But Chaucer's Clerk's judgment can as easily apply to scholars' defenses of Petruchio as they do to Griselda's lord's defenders: "Som men preyse it for a subtil wit. / But as for me, I seye that yvele it sit / T'assaye a wyf whan that it is no nede" (459-61). Perhaps scholars give Petruchio too much credit for "subtil wit." Even if we feel Petruchio is actually trying to tame Katherine, Shakespeare allows for Petruchio's actions to be blameworthy not just for their severity but also for their needlessness—just as Chaucer's Clerk says of the lord's strategies. Shakespeare, indeed, permits the reading that Katherine does not need to be "tamed," just as Griselda does not need to be "tested."

Petruchio's tactics of taming a shrew are different from those of other shrew tamers. Brian Morris, for example, states that "no one has discovered a version in which the tamer goes to work in the way in which Shakespeare's Petruchio does."[23] In traditional shrew literature, the taming tactics are typically violent as the husband tries to modify his shrewish wife's behavior by combating her violence with some of his own. Critics have praised Petruchio for not resorting to such physically brutal measures and have argued that Shakespeare is attempting to make his protagonist sympathetic.[24] But Shakespeare largely models Petruchio's tactics after those of Griselda's lord, whose methods may not be physical but are just as torturous, if not more so, than the cruelty of shrew tamers. The lord and Petruchio practice mental games: they are more interested in mind control than in behavior modification.[25] Chaucer's lord, for example, is not testing Griselda so much as he is breaking her spirit. The lord means to wear Griselda down mentally, to take away her self-will, to make her agree with whatever he does, no matter how barbarous. Many of the lord's tactics smack of mental torture, as our attention is drawn to their cruelty.

The lord accomplishes the annihilation of Griselda's self by resorting to various methods. He first removes her from contact with her family and friends, isolating her from almost everyone except for himself. In commenting on Chaucer's lord's treatment of Griselda, Deborah Ellis argues that although Griselda "is never physically far from her first home, her marriage is a spiritual and emotional exile."[26] Once the lord has Griselda under his sole influence, he begins his testing: he methodically wrenches from her arms her first child and then her second, depriving her of what is most precious in her life and making her think he intends to have the children killed. This action is meant to have various effects. His depriving her of some of the greatest comforts of life—contact with friends, family, and her own children—increases her dependency on him and her subjection to his whims. The lord intimidates her with his power and apparent ruthlessness, making her scared of a husband who seems capable of committing the horrific acts of killing his children. Chaucer has his Clerk proclaim that the lord "nedeless, Good woot, he thoughte hire for t'afraye" (455) and highlights that his Griselda lives in fear and trembling: she is "quakyng for drede" (358). Scaring her makes her more pliant, as she is terrified not to obey. He also means his actions, as the Clerk says, to cause her mental "angwyssh" (462) by depriving her of her children almost from their birth and proclaiming he has ordered their slaughter. Elizabeth Salter claims that Chaucer has his male protagonist display "malice indulged to the point of luxury,"[27] and at times he seems clearly sadistic. These methods are meant to intimidate Griselda, to provoke her to the point of protestation and yet not to allow her such a release, to torment her until she loses the will to object. The lord wants Griselda to beg him for mercy, to be completely at his disposal, to realize she is dependent on him for her life. Chaucer's lord brings his wife to the point of begging that she might kiss her child before it is killed and that the child might be buried so that wild animals will not devour the corpse. And in forcing her to beg, he divests her of her dignity and humiliates her. Several critics clarify the lord's intentions: Ellis argues that Chaucer's lord "takes over Griselda's will so completely that she loses even her autonomy"; John P. McCall clarifies that the lord aims for "complete abnegation of her will"; and Harriet Hawkins compares Chaucer's lord to a "neurotic power seeker" who cannot be satiated.[28]

Shakespeare has Petruchio's tactics resemble those of the lord in these Griselda tales and allows us to see him as not taming Katherine so much as he is breaking her spirit. Although Shakespeare does not have Petruchio duplicate the lord's precise method of testing his wife, Petruchio means it to have the same effect—to torment his wife and to crush her self-will. Petruchio also exiles Katherine from familiar surroundings. He takes her to his home in the country and will not let her return to her family home until he is satisfied with her submission. In order to tame her, a process that he compares to the taming of a falcon, he "mews" her up as one would a hawk, constricting her to her chamber and not allowing her any human contact, making her dependent solely on him. What he does is to isolate her and deny her sleep, food, and basic human comforts such as adequate clothing and warmth—just as Griselda's lord denies her the emotional sustenance of life. The element of fright has also been present from the very beginning of her exposure to Petruchio. His behavior at the wedding, on the ride home, and at the dinner at his home frightens Katherine and everyone who witnesses it. Grumio reports that Katherine "prayed that never prayed before" (IV.i.70-71), implying that she is so frightened that she prays to God to protect her from her husband's violence. By IV.iii we begin to see the effects of this so-called taming: Katherine describes herself as "famish[ed]" (3), "starv'd for meat, giddy for lack of sleep" (9), and "as cold as can be" (37). While Katherine is suffering physical pain, it is the mental torment that Shakespeare emphasizes: her physical state makes her "giddy" or mentally confused, incapable of serious thought or steady attention (OED 2a;3). What Petruchio is trying to do is not "pluck up" (IV.iii.38) her spirits but "pluck" them out. His tactics, like those of Griselda's lord, are similar to brainwashing strategies, for he degrades her physically and mentally until she becomes completely dependent on him for the most basic human needs.[29]

Part of his plan to break her spirit involves making her so hungry, so disoriented, and so downcast that she will do anything for food, including begging. Both Griselda and Katherine are brought to the point of desperation. Part of the process of degradation and humiliation is to make the wife subject to the whims of the lowest servant. Dekker, Chettle, and Haughton's lord tells his wife that he "will haue [her] stoope, / And kneele euen to the meanest groome I keepe" (II.ii.79-80). Katherine clarifies just how much Petruchio degrades her in making her beg the servant Grumio for food, for her situation is worse than that of a beggar, who at least gets hand-outs: "But I, who never knew how to entreat, / Nor never needed that I should entreat, / Am starv'd for meat, giddy for lack of sleep" (IV.iii.7-9). What Shakespeare has Petruchio do to Katherine is to torment her, to induce her to "entreat" for any "wholesome food" (IV.iii.16), and to give her little more than a crumb, just as Griselda's lord forces her to beg for some compassion toward her children and shows her none. Petruchio is debasing her, treating her like an animal, who gets a reward for obeying her master's commands. He is making her "stoop" or bow to his will completely, and yet even this is not enough. The attack is on her integrity and her self-sufficiency until she loses the "spirit to resist." Like Chaucer, Shakespeare alienates his readers from his male protagonist when Petruchio displays "malice indulged to the point of luxury" and prompts them to take the victim's side when they experience the heroine's misery.

Petruchio continues the assault on Katherine's spirit and her resistance by tantalizing and tormenting her even more, cataloging a great wardrobe he intends to lavish on her and inducing her to beg, and then telling her she must go home to her father's house in her tattered clothes, in "mean habiliments" (IV.iii.167). Although Petruchio tells her not to "account'st it shame" (IV.iii.178), this is exactly the effect he means the poor clothing to have on Katherine—to humiliate and shame her, to divest her of her integrity, worth, and identity. During the Renaissance, clothing importantly defined a person's social status and worth. Brunvand notes that this incident over the clothing and the sending Katherine forth in mean garb are not present in any other shrew tales.[30] But it is present in Griselda stories. For the lord, after telling his wife that he intends to marry another woman, divests her of her fine clothing and threatens to send her back home naked, inducing Griselda to beg for a less humiliating proposal. After she begs, he finally gives her a simple smock. The father of Griselda in Phillip's play clarifies just what the lord means to accomplish in denying Griselda decent attire: she is "of dignitie thus cleane depriued" (1749). Salter argues that in Chaucer the paltry clothing "symbolise[s] the extremity of her suffering."[31]

To complete the process of controlling their wives' every thought and movement, Griselda's lord and Petruchio, who can both be seen as neurotic power seekers rather than wife tamers, do more than dictate their wives' dress and actions. To complete the mind control, they silence their wives' voice, making their wives always agree with them and never express a thought of their own. Petrarch's lord, for example, demands that his wife "agree with [him] in all things" and "dispute [his] wish in nothing, and permit [him], with mind consenting, and without remonstrance of word or look, to do whatever [he] wills with" her (143). Chaucer's lord requires that Griselda do as he commands whether it is right or wrong and more specifically that she never contradict him in her words:

> [She must be] redy with good herte
> To al [his] lust, and that [he] frely may,
> As [he] best thynketh, do [she] laughe or smerte,
> And nevere [she is] to grucche it, nyght ne day
> And eek whan [he] sey[s] "ye" ne sey nat "nay,"
> Neither by word ne frownyng contenance.
> (351-56)

Kellogg clarifies the kind of control Chaucer's lord requires, a characterization that could just as easily apply to Shakespeare's Petruchio: the lord requires "not only obedience but obedience performed with a willingness which admits of no question as to the ultimate rightness of the thing willed."[32] Other scholars explain how tyrannical Chaucer's lord is: he wants "not simply her passive submission . . . but the death of her own desires"; he wants "submission beyond reason" and "demands total and unconditional obedience."[33]

Petruchio demands that he control Katherine's tongue as well—probably her greatest and most vital asset. Katherine articulates the importance to her of speaking her mind: "I will be free / Even to the uttermost, as I please, in words" (IV.iii.79-80). It is this last shred of freedom that Petruchio wants to squelch. He refuses to go to her father's house, for example, unless Katherine agrees to the incorrect time—that it is seven o'clock in the morning when it is actually two o'clock in the afternoon, that it is the moon that shines when it is actually the sun. Shakespeare has Petruchio sound very much like the lord of the Griselda tales, demanding that she never "cross" or contradict him in word or thought, even though he may be wrong: "It will be what o'clock I say it is" (IV.iii.192); "It shall be moon, or star, or what I list / Or e'er I journey to your father's house" (IV.v.7-8). Shakespeare has Petruchio force Katherine to agree to incorrect statements of time to suggest that his male protagonist means to impose his own sense of reality on his wife, to make himself the center of her existence; he is her new "sun." As soon as Katherine agrees with his incorrect statements, he then contradicts her and makes her agree to his new assertions. He is making her agree with him unconditionally. Katherine astutely perceives that Petruchio treats her like a "child," like a "babe" (IV.iii.74), and assaults her integrity.

One of the crucial issues of both Shakespeare's play and the Griselda stories is that the wives consistently pass the so-called tests and taming, yet the husbands refuse to cease their grilling of their wives and, in fact, only intensify their efforts. Chaucer has his Clerk repeatedly express puzzlement about the lord's motivations, since Griselda is never anything but obedient: "O nedeless was she tempted in assay! / But wedded men ne knowe no mesure, / Whan that they fynde a pacient creature" (621-23). This judgment could as easily apply to Shakespeare's Katherine and Petruchio, for although she is consistently patient, Petruchio will not moderate his gruelling strategies. Shakespeare impresses us again and again with Katherine's ability to behave admirably under the greatest duress. For example, when Petruchio displays the meat before his famished and "amort" wife, Katherine, despite her desperate condition and the preceding taunting by Grumio, remains polite and patient, begging him to not take the food away: "I pray you, let it stand" (IV.iii.44). When he tells her she must thank him for the meat, she obeys and expresses gratitude: "I thank you, sir" (IV.iii.47). In making Katherine's responses curt and noncommittal, Shakespeare, however, allows for some equivocation. He permits a performative edge to Katherine's words under the surface obedience, a potential for a sarcastic subversiveness, for Katherine's "I thank you, sir" can be said with a snide inflection. But, certainly, the surface Katherine is submissive, and the only freedom she salvages is a covert irony in her words.

While Petruchio is contrary and refuses to be pleased with any article of clothing, Katherine, unlike a shrew who can never be pleased, is easily satisfied with every piece and tries to reason with Petruchio to accept the cap: "I'll have no bigger. This doth fit the time, / And gentlewomen wear such caps as these" (IV.iii.69-70). Although Petruchio means the statement "all [his] pains is sorted to no proof" (IV.iii.43) to mean that Katherine is unappreciative of all he has done for her, Shakespeare makes the statement equivocal: it seems that, indeed, Petruchio is "pain[ing]" his wife "to no proof" or for no reason. Ornstein claims that Petruchio "proceeds despite Kate's reasonableness."[34] The question that Chaucer's Clerk poses to his audience could just as easily be posed to Shakespeare's audience:

But now of wommen wolde I asken fayn
If thise assayes myghte nat suffise?
What koude a sturdy housbond moore devyse
To prove hir wifhod and hir stedfastnesse,
And he contynuynge evere in sturdynesse?
(696-700)

Shakespeare allows for the reading that Katherine has endured enough trials and that she has proven her steadfastness.

Despite Katherine's gentle behavior, Petruchio persists in his taming strategies, which like the lord's testing of Griselda, get only worse with each new step. Shakespeare allows us yet again to ask the same question that Chaucer's Clerk asks when he wonders "if these assayes myghte nat suffise." When Petruchio insists that the sun is the moon, Katherine submits her voice to Petruchio:

Forward, I pray, since we have come so far,
And be it moon, or sun, or what you please.
And if you please to call it a rush-candle,
Henceforth I vow it shall be so for me.
(IV.v.12-15)

Instead of becoming more adamant in her contrary stance or putting up repeated resistance, as shrews typically do, Katherine behaves as a Griselda, who, as Petrarch clarifies, with "each day [becomes] more devoted and more obedient to [her husband's] wishes" (147). Although he needlessly continues his "taming," she offers him no resistance:

Then, God be blest, it is the blessed sun.
But sun it is not, when you say it is not,
And the moon changes even as your mind.
What you will have it nam'd, even that it is,
And so it shall be so for Katherine.
(IV.v.18-21)

Once again, her language has the potential to evoke a snide subtext with Katherine alluding to Petruchio's "moon" madness and intimating that Petruchio's calling the sun the moon is as ludicrous as calling a "rushcandle" the sun. But her subversiveness is concealed with her adroit use of language, and on a literal level, she is obedient. Shakespeare suggests the gratuitousness of Petruchio's tactics by having even Petruchio's friend Hortensio express annoyance at Petruchio's unnecessary "taming": "Petruchio, go thy ways, the field is won" (IV.v.23). While Hortensio may be applauding his friend for his success, there is also a tone of exasperation as he tells Petruchio that enough is enough. Shakespeare has Hortensio articulate the sentiment that Chaucer's Clerk repeatedly poses: "If these assayes myghte nat suffise?"

Shakespeare has Katherine sound very much like Griselda, who makes her husband's will her own: Petrarch's Griselda reassures her lord that "I have said, and I say again, that I can have no wishes save yours . . . Whatever you wish to do, therefore, about anything whatsoever, that is what I wish too" (146); Chaucer's Griselda similarly states that "ther may no thyng, God so my soule save, / Liken to yow that may displesen me" (505-06). Hawkins's description of Chaucer's Griselda's situation can apply to that of Shakespeare's Katherine: she is "denied any voice in the decisions that most affect her life"; "she must never express her own thoughts or feelings about his actions."[35] Like Griselda, Katherine is being forced to become what she feared the most—a "puppet" (IV.iii.103)—a mere shell of a woman, whose actions and words are suggested and controlled by another. The only way she can "be free" (IV.iii.79) is through a well-concealed subtext. Chaucer has Griselda clarify just how much she has lost since her marraige: she has lost her "wyl and al [her] libertee" (656)—exactly what Petruchio demands of his new wife.

Shrew and Griselda literature can end in similar ways: tales about shrews sometimes end at a banquet with husbands wagering on their wives' obedience; Griselda tales also end at a banquet with the lord continuing to test his wife's steadfastness. The major difference is that while the shrew's husband subjects his wife to a test, Griselda's lord makes his wife endure repeated and more humiliating tests and requires that she give a speech of submission. After pronouncing that his marriage to Griselda is ended, the lord sends Griselda to her father's home and announces his intention of marrying a more suitable woman. He then commands that Griselda come to him from her father's house in the same rags in which he sent her away and perform a servant's duties, such as making preparations for his upcoming marriage. Dekker, Chettle, and Haughton have their lord heighten Griselda's humiliation by making her bear wood, clothe the new bride, and present the bride to him. Griselda comes obediently to the lord's call and fulfills his commands. Chaucer intensifies Griselda's submissiveness and humiliation by having her bow on her knees "and reverently and wysly" (952) address her lord. On the wedding day, the guests arrive for the banquet, and before the assemblage the lord calls Griselda to come to him again. She responds with alacrity and obedience. He then asks her what she thinks of his new bride and invites her to speak. Petrarch, in particular, suggests his lord is playing a kind of game that involves displaying his wife's servitude before his guests: "Just as they were to sit down at the tables, Walter turned toward her and said before them all, as if he were playing game of her, 'What think you, Grisildis, of this bride of mine? Is she pretty and worthy enough?'" (150). Chaucer has his Clerk underscore that this testing has gone beyond all rational bounds and that it is superfluous and cruel: "What neded it / Hir for to tempte, and alwey moore and moore?" (457-58). Once Griselda has proven her constancy far more times than is necessary, finally the lord proclaims "this is ynogh" (1052) and reveals the extent of his game playing.

For his ending, Shakespeare borrows ingredients from both genres as he has throughout his play, but his emphasis is on the Griselda story. Since there is no indication that Katherine gets a new set of clothing for her trip to her father's house, she most likely is in rags, just as Griselda appears in the basest attire. Like Griselda's lord, Petruchio is playing a kind of game, betting on and flaunting his wife's obedience. Petruchio, too, calls Katherine to come on command, another test she passes. Like Griselda's lord, Petruchio, though, is not satisfied, and he subjects her to more trials, all of which are unnecessary, since she has already proven her meekness in both this scene and in earlier scenes—again and again. He now commands her to throw off her cap, and not satisfied with that, he orders her to deliver a speech to the other wives on the "duty they do owe their lords and husbands" (V.ii.132). Once again Katherine obeys each command, but Petruchio never stops. Reminiscent of Chaucer's lord, Petruchio continues "hir for to tempte, and alwey moore and moore." Right up to his last words, he is still proving Katherine's obedience, ordering her to kiss him in front of the whole assemblage—an indecorous act. Like Griselda's lord's last commands to his wife, Petruchio's tactics can be read as meaning to humiliate Katherine. He takes away her dignity and disgraces her by making her come on command, perform a servant's duties of retrieving guests, and fawn over him whenever he orders.

In all of the tales during the lord's last set of tests, the Griseldas are excessively submissive and dutiful—on the surface, at least. But in all of the Griselda stories, there are intimations that Griselda is actually miserable and that she is forced to suppress her agony under the opposite pose of wifely contentment in order to appease her husband. Chaucer's Clerk, for example, remarks that he "deme[s] that hir herte was ful wo" (753), although Griselda shows no obvious outward signs in her countenance or behavior. The Griselda tale, thus, contains a tension between the feigned public profession of submission and the concealed torment. Chaucer, especially, finds a way to have his Griselda give voice to this tension, making his heroine speak in ambiguous terms. In the envoy to the tale, Chaucer advises wives not to let "humilitee [their] tonge nayle" (1184) but to "stondeth at defense" and "beth egre as is a tigre" (1195, 1199). He goes on to advise wives to fight back with the subtlety of words:

> Ne dreed [husbands] nat, dooth hem no
> reverence,
> For thogh thyn housbond armed be in maile,
> The arwes of thy crabbed eloquence
> Shal perce his brest, and eek his aventaile.
> (1202-04)

And, indeed, under her extreme submissiveness, Chaucer's Griselda harbors resentment and pierces her husband with her "crabbed eloquence." She is adroit at making her words lament her state and condemn her husband while seeming to express selfless devotion to him. When the lord asks her in public if she thinks his new wife is beautiful and virtuous, she compliantly agrees word for word. But she adds a few words that celebrate her fortitude and, conversely, deride his brutality:

> O thyng biseke I yow, and warne also,
> That ye ne prike with no tormentynge
> This tendre mayden, as ye han do mo;
> For she is fostred in hir norissynge
> Moore tendrely, and, to my supposynge,
> She koude nat adversitee endure
> As koude a povre fostred creature.
> (1037-43)

Elaine Tuttle Hansen explains that Griselda responds "to her banishment with the longest, most pathetic speech" and that she exercises the "powers of subversive speech."[36]

Shakespeare places Katherine in a situation similar to that of Griselda during her last trials. Like Griselda, she delivers a speech—a characteristic not found within the tradition of shrew literature.[37] Katherine, too, speaks and behaves compliantly, vowing utter obedience to her husband, spouting patristic doctrine about a wife's duties to her husband, and even offering to place her hand beneath Petruchio's foot as token of her surrender to his will, just as Chaucer's Griselda bows on her knees before her lord. She seems the embodiment of wifely servitude and dependence, and, indeed, Shakespeare allows her to be read as such. There are indications, however, especially in Katherine's last speech, that she is miserable and that she suppresses her torment to avoid her husband's oppressive temperament. But Katherine, like Chaucer's Griselda, can be read as not nailing her tongue completely and as adroitly using her language as a weapon: she wounds Petruchio with her "crabbed eloquence."

Just as her earlier responses to Petruchio seem compliant on the surface yet are equivocal enough to suggest a snide subversion, Katherine's last seemingly meek words contain a submerged tone of mockery and irony. The lengthiness of her speech, like that of Griselda, suggests that under the guise of submission she is assuming dominance and drawing attention to her misery and Petruchio's cruelty. Her words covertly allude to her resentment toward her "lord": "Fie, fie! Unknit that threatening unkind brow, / And dart not scornful glances from those eyes, / To wound thy lord, thy king, thy governor" (V.ii.137-39). While Katherine is addressing the other wives present—Bianca and the Widow—she is also speaking about and to herself, as the speech comes to resemble a kind of soliloquy. Her speech is addressed to angry and hurt women, of which she has been a member throughout the play, and advises them to conceal their murderous thoughts—as she is doing with her "crabbed eloquence." Katherine speaks of wives secretly wanting to "wound" and harm their husbands but having to project the opposite pose of patience and kindness: "It blots thy beauty as frosts do bite the meads, / Confounds thy fame as whirlwinds shake fair buds, / And in no sense is meet or amiable" (140-42). Her speech continues with more references to women's (and implicitly her own) anger, comparing "a woman mov'd" to a "fountain troubled" (143). If a woman is troubled, she must appear as clear, tranquil water—at least on the surface—and let the agitation well beneath the surface—a description that befits the subversive subtext of her speech. A few lines later in the speech, Katherine again underscores other wives' and her own discontent, speaking of "froward, peevish, sullen, sour" women (158).

She ridicules Petruchio by imitating his exaggerated bravado, making her listing—"Thy husband is thy lord, thy life, thy keeper, / Thy head, thy sovereign" (147-48)—as excessive as his speech of self-enhancement: "She is my goods, my chattels, she is my house, / My household stuff, my field, my barn, / My horse, my ox, my ass, my any thing" (III.ii.228-30). Her tributes to male dominance are overwrought and inflated and, thus, are allowed to mock Petruchio's inflated and unwarranted sense of greatness. By making her language devoid of references to love and affection and, instead, surfeited with references to domination, power, and authority, Shakespeare has her suggest that Petruchio is more like a despot than a loving husband and she more like a frightened subject than a devoted wife. The language she uses to describe Petruchio's treatment of her applies more to a prison warden or an animal trainer than a husband: he is her "keeper," who "cares" for her and provides her with "maintenance" (147-49). Katherine's word choice suggests Petruchio does no more for her than an animal keeper does for his pet or a warden does for a prisoner held in confinement. She is merely kept alive by his providing her with the basics of life, although we have seen that in starving her and denying her sleep and warmth Petruchio does not do even this. And in return for the most meager day-to-day maintenance that one would allow for an animal, for example, she must give him everything: she gives him her life, "love, fair looks, and true obedience; / Too little payment for so great a debt" (154-55). Once again Shakespeare has Katherine speak equivocally: if we read "too little payment" as referring to the wife's actions, then Katherine is lauding husbands for their solicitude, which a wife can never adequately repay. But if we read the phrase as referring to the husband's actions, then Katherine is suggesting that women sacrifice much more than they ever get in return.

Her language continues to present her relationship with Petruchio as more like a battle that she has lost than a loving union:

> I am asham'd that women are so simple
> To offer war where they should kneel for
> peace,
> Or seek for rule, supremacy, and sway,
> When they are bound to serve, love and obey.
> (162-65)

She implies that she would like to "rebel" (160) and be a "traitor" (161) to Petruchio, but she is forced to kneel, like a captured prisoner of war, "bound" or shackled in prison. Her language contains no references to affection but rather to governorship, as she portrays herself as a conquered "subject," who is dutiful to her "prince," not out of devotion but out of compulsion: "Such duty as the subject owes the prince / Even such a woman oweth to her husband" (156-57). While she seems to suggest female inferiority, she acknowledges that women have inner "strength" (175) but that they are so weak with respect to physical prowess and political power in a patriarchal world that their strength does them little good. Katherine's subversive message suggests that men rule and women obey not because of men's innate superiority but because men use physical might to oppress women—as Petruchio has used to oppress her. The men win the battle because they have the stronger "lances": their gender gives them more political clout over the "lance-[less]," powerless women; and they can always use their "lances" or penises[38] to rape and victimize women. Katherine, in fact, intimates that women are treated little better than "worms" (V.ii.170), just as Chaucer's Griselda accuses her husband of treating her like a worm: he lets her "lyk a worm go by the weye" (880). She ends the speech with the same advice with which she started: she tells herself and other women to "vail [their] stomachs" (177), an expression meaning to conceal one's temper and anger[39] as she does in her speech.

Despite the subversive message, both Shakespeare's play and the Griselda tales end happily. But the endings can be read as only superficially happy, as all of the works end on a troublesome, ambivalent note. While Griselda is reunited with her children and we are told Griselda and her husband are happy, we are not allowed to experience this happiness for ourselves. Chaucer's Griselda embraces her children, not her husband, and swoons so many times and expresses the desire to die that she seems near death. Because Chaucer does not convince us that his lord is a changed, loving husband, he distresses us when we realize, as Hansen clarifies, that Griselda faces a "permanent union with a man whom the Clerk has carefully characterized as a sadistic tyrant, worst of men and cruelest of husbands."[40]

On one level, Shakespeare's play, likewise, seems to end harmoniously, and Shakespeare allows for a festive reading, with the shrew being transformed into an obedient wife and with Petruchio and Katherine ending the play by kissing and leaving to consummate their union. But, like Chaucer's tale, there is a disturbing, ambivalent tenor that allows the ending to be read differently. Although Katherine can vent her anger through her "crabbed eloquence," in some senses her fate is worse than that of Griselda, for Petruchio never says "this is ynogh," as Chaucer's lord does. There is no indication, as there is for Griselda, that her situation will ever improve. For example, Chaucer's Griselda is dressed in fine clothing at the tale's end, an action that signals the elevation of her condition. But Shakespeare does not suggest that Katherine obtains any finer attire, an indication that her abjection and humiliation are never to end. By having Petruchio test Katherine more and more right up to the very end, Shakespeare suggests that Petruchio will never be satisfied and that Katherine will have to endure these humiliating tests for the rest of her life. Considering the many references throughout the play to Petruchio's proclivity for violence and the pained, if not "amort," future for Katherine, Shakespeare writes a subtext that makes his audience feel uncertain and troubled about Katherine's future safety. Like Chaucer's heroine, Katherine can be read as being in a "permanent union" with a man who has seemed a "sadistic tyrant, worst of men and cruelest of husbands." But her situation seems even more grieved, for on a subtextual level, we are allowed to wonder if she will "survive" him (II.i.124).

Notes

[1] The following are a sampling of the critics who have read Katherine as constructed within the traditional outlines of a shrew and Petruchio as her successful tamer: Robert Heilman, "The Taming Untamed; or The Return of the Shrew," *Modern Language Quarterly* 27 (1966): 147-61, calls Petruchio a "remarkable therapist"; Hugh M. Richmond, *Shakespeare's Sexual Comedy: A Mirror for Lovers* (New York: Bobbs-Merrill, 1971), 83-101; Joan Hartwig, "Horses and Women in *The Taming of the Shrew*," *Huntington Library Quarterly* 45 (1982): 285-94, esp. 294, sees Katherine as being transformed "from unhappy shrew into graceful woman, creating 'wonder' in her world"; Maurice Hunt, "Homeopathy in Shakespearean Comedy and Romance," *Ball State University Forum* 29 (1988): 45-57, esp. 46, argues that Petruchio helps his "patient to achieve a truer self, one freed, for instance, from . . . the trap of shrewishness"; Ruth Nevo, "Kate of Kate Hall," in *Modern Critical Interpretations of "The Taming of the Shrew,"* ed. Harold Bloom (New York: Chelsea House, 1988), 29-39; Joel Fineman, "The Turn of the Shrew," in *Modern Critical Interpretations of "The Taming of the Shrew,"* 93-112; Tita French Baumlin, "Petruchio the Sophist and Language as Creation in *The Taming of the Shrew*," *Studies in English Literature* 29 (1989): 237-57, esp. 237, 247, praises Petruchio as a "sophistic rhetorician" who transforms "an isolated, selfish, dysfunctional personality into a socially integrated woman at peace with herself and the world."

[2] Camille Wells Slights, "The Raw and the Cooked in *The Taming of the Shrew*," *Journal of English and Germanic Philology* 88 (1989): 168; Charles Brooks, "Shakespeare's Romantic Shrews," *Shakespeare Quarterly* 11 (1960): 351-56; Robert Ornstein, *Shakespeare's Comedies* (Newark: University of Delaware Press, 1986), 72, 68.

[3] Consult, for example, the following: John Masefield, *William Shakespeare* (New York: Henry Holt, 1911), 108-09; Harold C. Goddard, *The Meaning of Shakespeare,* vol. 1 (Chicago: University of Chicago Press, 1960), 69-70, contends that Katherine is "lovely and sweet by nature" and that her "shrewishness is superficial, not ingrained or congenital"; Nevill Coghill, "The Basis of Shakespearian Comedy," in *Shakespeare Criticism,* 1935-60, ed. Anne Ridler (London: Oxford University Press, 1963), 208, calls Katherine a "girl of spirit" who has "developed the defensive technique of shrewishness"; George R. Hibbard, "*The Taming of the Shrew:* A Social Comedy," in *Shakespearean Essays,* ed. Alwin Thaler and Norman Sanders (Knoxville: University of Tennessee Press, 1964), 23-24, contends that Katherine's "shrewishness is not bad temper, but the expression of self-respect"; Anne Barton, introduction to *The Taming of the Shrew,* in *The Riverside Shakespeare,* ed. G. Blakemore (Boston: Houghton Mifflin, 1974), 107; Coppelia Kahn, "*The Taming of the Shrew:* Shakespeare's Mirror of Marriage," in *The Authority of Experience: Essays in Feminist Criticism,* ed. Arlyn Diamond and Lee R. Edwards (Amherst: University of Massachusetts Press, 1977), 84, argues that Shakespeare's heroine is "trapped in the self-destructive role of shrew by her male guardians"; Marilyn French, *Shakespeare's Division of Experience* (New York: Ballantine, 1981), 77; Brian Morris, introduction to the New Arden *The Taming of the Shrew* (New York: Methuen, 1981), 114, argues that Katherine's shrewishness is a "disguise" "forced on her by a neglectful father, a sly sister, and an unsympathetic society."

[4] George Bernard Shaw, *Shaw on Shakespeare,* ed. Edwin Wilson (London: Cassell, 1961), 178; Mark Van Doren, *Shakespeare* (New York: Henry Holt, 1939),

50; J. Dennis Huston, "'To Make a Puppet': Play and Play-Making in *The Taming of the Shrew,*" *Shakespeare Studies* 9 (1976): 74, 76; Ornstein, 65; Jeanne Addison Roberts, "Horses and Hermaphrodites: Metamorphoses in *The Taming of the Shrew,*" in *Modern Critical Interpretations of "The Taming of the Shrew,"* 60-61.

[5] All quotations will be from the New Arden edition of *The Taming of the Shrew,* ed. Brian Morris.

[6] A few critics allude to the connection between Katherine and a Griselda figure but do not develop the comparison: Roberts states that Petruchio's "comparison of Kate to Lucrece and Grissel [is apt]; he proceeds to treat her like each of these women in turn" (59); David M. Bergeron, "The Wife of Bath and Shakespeare's *The Taming of the Shrew,*" *University Review* 35 (1969): 279, states that "Katharina evolves into a type of Griselda in the play" and that "Petruchio's passing remarks" about her being a "second Grissel" remind us of Chaucer.

[7] Alfred L. Kellogg, "The Evolution of the 'Clerk's Tale': A Study in Connotation," in *Chaucer, Langland, Arthur: Essays in Middle English Literature* (New Brunswick: Rutgers University Press, 1972), 277.

[8] Deborah S. Ellis, "*The Color Purple* and the Patient Griselda," *College English* 49 (1987): 188.

[9] Giovanni Boccaccio, "The Tenth Story of the Tenth Day," of *The Decameron,* vol. 2, trans. John Payne (Berkeley: University of California Press, 1982), 780-91; Francis Petrarch, *De Obedientia ac Fide Uxoria Mythologia,* trans. R. D. French, in *Chaucer: Sources and Backgrounds,* ed. Robert P. Miller (New York: Oxford University Press, 1977), 140-52; John Phillip, *The Commodye of Pacient and Meeke Grissill* (London: Malone Society Reprints, 1909); Thomas Dekker, Henry Chettle, and William Haughton, *The Pleasant Commoedye of Patient Grissill,* in *The Dramatic Works of Thomas Dekker,* vol 1, ed. Fredson Bowers (Cambridge: Cambridge University Press, 1953), 208-98. All textual references will be to the aforementioned editions.

[10] Linda Woodbridge, *Women and the English Renaissance: Literature and the Nature of Womankind,* 1540-1620 (Chicago: University of Illinois Press, 1984), 211.

[11] Louis Wright, *Middle-Class Culture in Elizabethan England* (Chapel Hill: University of North Carolina Press, 1935), 507.

[12] Harriet Hawkins, "The Victim's Side: Chaucer's *Clerk's Tale* and Webster's *Duchess of Malfi,*" *Signs* 1 (1975): 345, 341.

[13] Deborah S. Ellis, "Domestic Treachery in the Clerk's Tale," in *Ambiguous Realities: Women in the Middle Ages and Renaissance,* ed. Carole Levin and Jeanie Watson (Detroit: Wayne State University Press, 1987), 111.

[14] Jan Harold Brunvand, "*The Taming of the Shrew*": *A Comparative Study of Oral and Literary Versions* (New York: Garland, 1991).

[15] Valerie Wayne, "Refashioning the Shrew," *Shakespeare Studies* 17 (1985): 161, contends that Shakespeare uses the "shrew to raise issues about women and marriage without simply endorsing customary and conservative attitudes." Harriet A. Deer, "Untyping Stereotypes: *The Taming of the Shrew,*" in *The Aching Hearth: Family Violence in Language and Literature,* ed. Sara Munson Deats and Lagretta Tallent Lenker (New York: Plenum Press, 1991), 77, argues that the play "does indeed exploit spouse abuse as a major source of action and humor. But it does not encourage such behavior; rather it reveals how destructive and widespread is its hold on society."

[16] All quotations will be from Geoffrey Chaucer, *The Clerk's Tale,* in *The Tales of the Clerk and the Wife of Bath,* ed. Marion Wynne-Davies (New York: Routledge, 1992), 71-117.

[17] Kellogg, 297.

[18] Hibbard, 23, claims that when we first see Katherine, she is "being grossly insulted" by the men and "her vigorous complaint to Baptista is fully justified"; H. J. Oliver, introduction to *The Taming of the Shrew* (Oxford: Clarendon Press, 1982), 51, argues that Katherine's first words are "deserving of sympathy"; Slights, 171, says Katherine is being "publicly humiliated" and "understandably reacts with resentment toward her father."

[19] Kahn, 91.

[20] See, for example, the following: Maynard Mack, "Engagement and Detachment in Shakespeare's Plays," in *Essays on Shakespeare and Elizabethan Drama in Honor of Hardin Craig,* ed. Richard Hosley (Columbia: University of Missouri Press, 1962), 280; Cecil C. Seronsy, "'supposes' as the Unifying Theme in *The Taming of the Shrew,*" *Shakespeare Quarterly* 14 (1963): 19; Morris, 124; Ann Thompson, introduction to *The Taming of the Shrew* (Cambridge: Cambridge University Press, 1985), 32, 34.

[21] Norman Lavers, "Freud, the Clerkes Tale, and Literary Criticism," *College English* 26 (1965): 185.

[22] *The Compact Edition of the Oxford English Dictionary,* 2 vols. (New York: Oxford University Press,

1971), "groom" sb.[1] 2. All further citations will be noted in the text as OED.

[23] Morris, 75. Richard Hosley, "Sources and Analogues in *The Taming of the Shrew,*" *Huntington Library Quarterly* 27 (1964): 299, also argues that Petruchio's tactics with his wife appear "to be Shakespeare's original contribution to the literature of shrew-taming."

[24] Barton suggests that in comparison to traditional shrew tamers, Petruchio "is almost a model of intelligence and humanity" (106); Wayne labels Petruchio's tactics a "more humane and artistic way to 'tame' a shrew" (174); Slights argues that Petruchio "gives no evidence of the sadism . . . in earlier versions of the shrew story" (178).

[25] Deer, 74, agrees that "wanting to civilize Kate is one thing; wanting to displace her independence and vitality with a mere echo of himself is quite another. . . . We wonder whether controlling another person's imagination may not be the worst abuse that one spouse can inflict on another."

[26] Ellis, "Domestic Treachery in the *Clerk's Tale,*" 110.

[27] Elizabeth Salter, *Chaucer: The Knight's Tale and The Clerk's Tale* (New York: Barron's Educational Series, 1962), 60.

[28] Ellis, "Domestic Treachery in the *Clerk's Tale,*" 105; John P. McCall, "The *Clerk's Tale* and the Theme of Obedience," *Modern Language Quarterly* 27 (1966): 263; Hawkins, 350.

[29] Lawrence Danson, "Continuity and Character in Shakespeare and Marlowe," *Studies in English Literature* 26 (1986): 229, allows for the possibility that Petruchio subjects his wife to something "comparable to brainwashing or cult-indoctrination." See also French, 77.

[30] Brunvand, 187.

[31] Salter, 47.

[32] Kellogg, 297-98.

[33] The quotations belong respectively to McCall, 264, 265, and J. Mitchell Morse, "The Philosophy of The Clerk of Oxenford," *Modern Language Quarterly* 19 (1958): 18.

[34] Ornstein, 68.

[35] Hawkins, 346.

[36] Elaine Tuttle Hansen, "The Powers of Silence: The Case of the Clerk's Griselda," in *Women and Power in the Middle Ages,* ed. Mary Erler and Maryanne Kowaleski (Athens: University of Georgia Press, 1988), 235.

[37] Brunvand, 187.

[38] Eric Partridge, *Shakespeare's Bawdy* (1947; rpt. New York: Routledge, 1990), 132.

[39] Thompson, 153.

[40] Hansen, 232.

Source: "Katherine of *The Taming of the Shrew:* 'A Second Grissel'," in *Texas Studies in Literature and Language,* Vol. 37, Fall, 1995, pp. 285-313.

Spectator Seduction: *Measure for Measure*

Louis Burkhardt, ***University of Colorado, Boulder***

Vice is a monster of so frightful mien,
As, to be hated, needs but to be seen;
Yet seen too oft, familiar with her face,
We first endure, then pity, then embrace.
—Alexander Pope, "An Essay on Man"

1

The magisterial achievement of *Measure for Measure* is also its nemesis: it provokes intolerance. By mirroring virulent desires in its characters, it mediates similar desires to the offstage spectators (audiences and readers).[1] Often, as soon as critics note the intolerance displayed by certain of the play's characters, the critics themselves become intolerant.[2] This critical intolerance signals the influential role played by "desire": a category by which I refer to motivational impulses in humans, including forces of repulsion as well as attraction. Desire includes both erotic or binding emotions such as love, pity, and affection and violent or alienating emotions such as fear, hate, and disdain. While the play portrays sexual desire, it privileges intolerance as a dominant form of desire that is both represented in its action and reproduced by its performance. At times, characters and critics alike attempt to eliminate a surplus of desire through the selection of a victim, animate or inanimate. Far from purging spectators of desire according to the Aristotelian ideal, therefore, the play contaminates them with fear and, more often, pitilessness.

One especially useful framework for analyzing this affective power of *Measure* is provided by René Girard's work on mimesis. While Girard's hypothesis, which extends far beyond the concerns of this article, has been expounded in relation to Shakespeare, it has not been applied at length to *Measure*, nor has it found a fully favorable reception among Shakespeare scholars. In his review of Girard's *A Theater of Envy: William Shakespeare* (1991), Robert Adams (*New York Review,* 16 July 1992, 51-52) finds it both "an old-fashioned book" and a book with "a fresh slant" and "a fresh angle"—appropriate metaphors for the theme of mimetic, triangular relationships. However, according to Adams, the book pays "relatively little attention" to *Measure for Measure* (among other neglected plays), it gives little attention to critical commentaries and hurts itself methodologically by resorting to a "two-play-two-audience" theory.[3]

Picking up Adams's gauntlet, I would like to adapt certain Girardian insights and apply them to *Measure* in a manner that answers Adams's objections. My argument neither neglects the play's critical commentaries nor relies upon a dual-audience theory. Whether my use of Girard satisfies Adams's reservations, the theory of mimetic desire fits the play better than any psychological theory yet applied. It is at once broad enough to account for responses of dramatic characters *and* human spectators, yet specific enough to remain faithful to the thematic fields of the play itself. Girard's conception of monstrous doubling (i.e., that subjects who define themselves in opposition to each other increasingly resemble each other in the most negative ways) provides a rationale for the irrational behavior of the characters. Furthermore, the theory closely links the play's title (taken from Christ's Sermon on the Mount) to the play's action. It helps us understand how and why the play redefines judgment as desire and justice as forgiveness.

Because Girard's work is often misunderstood, the theory as I adapt it merits some introduction.[4] Following the third book of *Things Hidden from the Foundation of the World,* Girard's magnum opus, I refer to the study of intersubjective mental conflicts as "interdividual psychology."[5] The major premise of interdividual psychology is that human desires result from human relationships instead of the reverse. Desire thus understood is model-oriented, and its mode of communication is imitational (or mimetic). This approach runs contrary to object-oriented theories, such as Freudianism (which privileges the mother as an object of desire). According to this model-oriented theory, both objects of desire and types of desire are determined by the subject's relationships within his or her society. Therefore, in the drama of human life, objects and types of desire shift constantly within the web of social relations. For obvious reasons, such a psychological perspective lends itself readily to the analysis of drama, a genre formulated to represent the flux of human conflict. Because interdividual psychology assumes that external, relational conflicts precede and structure inner, psychical conflicts, it provides the basis for a character analysis that explicitly focuses on visible, audible events rather than on invisible, postulated instinctual entities.

The primary paradigm of mimetic desire describes the bonds among the *model, disciple,* and *object*. The individual who exhibits a desire functions as a *model* who, for whatever reason, impresses the *disciple* as imitable. The disciple who unknowingly imitates that desire attempts to appropriate either the same *object* as the model (which turns the model into a rival) or the same sort of object (which makes the disciple a double of the model in certain respects). If we ask how the disciple recognizes a desire as such in the first place, Charles Peirce's categories prove useful. The signs that make a model's desire evident may be nondiscursive, either through an *index,* such as a woman's pregnancy that attests to a man's (previous) desire for her, or through an *icon,* such as a nun's habit that suggests that the Church has laid claim to that woman. Or the evidence may be discursive, through *full symbolicity,* such as Angelo's statement of desire, "Plainly conceive, I love you" (2.4.140).[6] In these examples, the man, the Church, and Angelo function as models. Generally the mediation utilizes both modes of communication, discursive and nondiscursive, and most often the disciples remain ignorant of the sources of their desires.

Desire creates conflict. On one hand, mediated desire masks its source, convincing the disciple that his or her desire is original and necessary, an authentic extension of the "inner self" or, in Renaissance terms, "soul." On the other hand, the desire, being borrowed, leads the disciple into the path of the model. Upon colliding, the two subjects perceive each other as rivals. Violence follows. In the interval during which the model becomes a rival, the type of desire motivating the disciple alters. What began as a desire for a given object becomes a desire for reprisal. This stage of violent interaction marks the movement from "acquisitive mimesis" to "conflictive mimesis."[7] According to this schema, conflictive mimesis occurs when the importance of gaining the object is superseded by the importance of supplanting the model-obstacle.

However, in *Measure*'s array of sexual propositions, the disciple and the object are often identical. No sooner is an acquisitive intention expressed than conflict occurs. Thus appropriative desires carry their own violence, however subtle it may appear. For example, Isabella (rightly) interprets Angelo's "I love you" as a form of extortion that entails rape. Therefore, she opposes and alters the desire rather than endorsing it—but this reaction does not free her from Angelo's influence as a model. An unwilling "disciple" in Isabella's situation fiercely struggles to escape the model yet reciprocates the model's gestures and words until the two relate as enemy twins. In such situations, the emotional intensity easily escalates; misunderstandings abound; and each rival feels the injustices of the other impinging upon his or her own course of desire.

This self-blinding reciprocity pervades the play and its spectators' reactions. While it is a form of conflictive mimesis, it constitutes a specific type of imitation that involves a developed moral consciousness—as is hinted by the play's title. Only creatures who have obtained a definition of "righteousness" can be swept away by self-righteousness. In the Judeo-Christian tradition, this consciousness is traceable to the Jewish reception of the Law and gains fairly clear articulation during David's reign. By way of parable, Nathan rebukes David for adultery with Bathsheba and the murder of her husband. David, however, fails to recognize himself as the greedy shepherd. Instead, he condemns the shepherd, saying he should die. Nathan then unveils the allegory, telling David, "You are the man!" Judging another, David actually judges himself and soon regrets his failure to show mercy (2 Sam. 11-12). The psychological implications of inadvertently judging oneself further unfold in the Sermon on the Mount: "Ivdge not, that ye be not iudged. For with what iudgement ye iudge, ye shal be iudged, and with what measure ye mette, it shal be measured to you againe" (Matt. 7:1-2, Geneva version). The violence or mercy one directs to others inescapably affects one's self.

Building on this perspective, my argument interprets "judgment" as a kind of desire that distorts reality and at the same time reveals itself through ethical statements. Judgment is the imitative moment during which one character distances and/or differentiates him- or herself from another.[8] The moment is imitative because it would not occur apart from another character, and it distorts reality by exaggerating existing differences or creating imaginary ones. As the protagonist judges (differentiates) with increasing passion, he or she inevitably perceives the rival as a sort of monster yet at the same time begins to speak and act like the rival. This doubling, this hallucinatory self-righteousness, is the punishment that Christ's injunction threatens. By using the passive voice ("ye shal be iudged" and "it shal be measured to you againe"), the sermon refuses to designate an external agency of judgment. It insinuates that judgment, measurement, punishment, *and* reward are all self-reflexive. Because these judgments structure relationships according to binary oppositions, they lend themselves to formulaic, antithetical expressions, the *locus classicus* of which belongs to the Pharisee in Christ's parable: "I thanke thee that I am not as other men" (Luke 18:11). In English, the future tense and the subjunctive voice better intimate an unrealized intention of moral superiority. Thus, for my purposes, echoes of the Pharisee's statement, such as "I'll never be like that person" or "I would never do *that,*" adequately capture the psychological implications, and such echoes can be heard throughout *Measure.*

Because judgments are overdifferentiating, exclusionary evaluations, they constitute a form of negative desire, a desire by which one seeks to distance him- or herself from an object (and its model). Judgment persuades the subject that he or she is above or beyond the transgression or personality type being judged. The actual act of passing judgment assures the subject that he or she is establishing that distance. Ironically, the subject who passes judgment becomes absorbed with the other. Thus the subject will experience erratic behavior and emotions but will not identify them with their source precisely because the subject has (over)differentiated him- or herself from that source. Through its dialogue, *Measure* tersely mocks this act of overdifferentiation. What is said of Lucio and a Gentleman applies to all: "There went but a pair of shears between" the characters, although they cannot see their similarities (1.2.27). When Abhorson complains that Pompey "will discredit our mystery," the Provost replies: "Go to, sir, you weigh equally: a feather will turn the scale" (4.2.26-29). Such is the fate of most of the characters. At the moment they articulate their unlikeness to other characters, they are most similar: a feather will turn the scale.

Outside of purely comic situations, this overdifferentiation ultimately leads toward victimization. The victim, in this context, deflects attention from the disparity between what the victimizer claims to be and what the victimizer is. Of course, the victim can be either the rival or a third party. Only forgiveness can arrest a situation of escalating rivalry and eventual victimage. Put differently, forgiveness turns even deadly serious situations toward comic ends. An act of forgiveness breaks the bond of reciprocity by focusing on similarities between the rivals and halting the desire for differentiation. True to the etymology of the word (αφιημι) translated "forgiveness" from the Sermon on the Mount (Matt. 6:12, 14-15), forgiveness requires the offended individual to *untie* or *release* the enemy. Otherwise, the two remain tied together through reciprocity. Overriding all differences, forgiveness alone admits the mutual need for mercy. This need for mercy is mutual, not because all moral offenses are equally destructive or equally malicious—nor even because both parties are offenders—but because the refusal to offer mercy subjects the offended party to an unwanted model which will continue to mediate unwanted desires, mostly for revenge. All offenses must be forgivable in order to break the chain of reciprocity.

To stress the seductive dynamic of judgment that structures the play, I conclude this theoretical sketch by remarking on the conventional readings of *Measure* as they have privileged external agencies of judgment over internal ones. Although the title of this play, *Measure for Measure,* is often remarked upon, the judicial and theological dimensions generally obscure the psychological.[9] The mention of the Sermon on the Mount and its injunction for listeners to "Iudge not" conjures up images either of a divine judge enforcing his laws or of an earthly vicar enforcing them with divine authority. In both cases, that of the juridical state and that of the vindictive god, transcendental powers intervene in human affairs to establish justice. According to my reading, *Measure* ultimately supplants such agencies of justice, as well as the conception of justice as a fair distribution of punishment. Even in the final act of the play, when Duke Vincentio is perceived as a "power divine," he refuses to mete out punishment according to the crime. Nothing in his actions executes such "justice," just as nothing in the biblical injunction insists on an external judge. The "measure" he applies to Angelo is one of mercy, whereas the reciprocal "measure" demanded by Angelo (and many critics, including Johnson and Coleridge)[10] is a death for a death. The lack of severity in Duke Vincentio, therefore, shifts the focus from external judgment to internal, interdividual judgment.

If the above assumptions are correct, *Measure for Measure* assigns the source of judgment and vindictiveness to humans, not to institutions or to a divine power. The immanence of reciprocal human relationships precludes the need of a transcendental power. Instead of a divine judge who threatens judgment, human relationships enforce the threat. Thus, the reciprocity of judgment that governs *Measure*'s characters (and spectators) can be accounted for in strictly psychological terms. This human proclivity toward judgment and against forgiveness is registered in a failure among critics to understand "measure for measure" as a neutral descriptor, one that is as accurate in describing merciful, loving transactions as in describing vilifying, vindictive ones. These critics, who insist on poetic justice, understand "measure for measure" only in its punitive sense. For example, Charlotte Lennox writes, "Thus it should have been, according to the Duke's own Judgment to have made it *Measure for Measure;* but when *Angelo* was pardoned, and restored to Favour, how then was it *Measure for Measure?*"[11] Similarly, William Lawrence writes, "The title 'Measure for Measure' is, however, contradicted by the final decisions of the Duke, who concludes that mercy should temper justice, and that the strict letter of the law should not be enforced."[12] Finally, Jocelyn Powell considers "measure" as applicable to only "the judicial deputy, who metes out measure for measure."[13] As I hope to show, the play offers a broader concept of "measure for measure," one by which characters are punished or rewarded according to their own standards.

2

More clearly than any other characters in the play, Angelo and Isabella discover themselves to be puppets of desire. They mediate "righteous" indignation to spectators. With less prominence, Claudio functions as a model-rival to these two characters, although he himself is conspicuously susceptible to models. While both Angelo and Isabella exhibit the full effects of passing judgment, Isabella's role makes the progression from judgment to doubling more perceptible. In addition, two of her speeches comment on the theme of mimetic bondage. While I do not examine the comic characters in this article, many of them, particularly Lucio, undergo mimetic oscillations similar to their graver counterparts. In contrast to these reluctant disciples, Duke Vincentio, who avoids unwanted models, is minimally imprisoned in psychological judgment. He functions rather to turn our attention to the play's spectators and their desires.

Angelo's response to Vienna's antifornication statute marks the undoing of a personality that thrives on overdifferentiating responses.[14] What appears as a legal judgment unveils the reciprocity of a moral judgment. The statute Angelo enforces eventually governs him, unleashing forces that transform him from lifelong frigidity to newly awakened concupiscence. This degeneration reveals the underlying moral logic of the play. In his first soliloquy (2.2.162-87), he remarks that his chastity, up to meeting Isabella, has come easily. He has not been pretending sexual purity:

> Never could the strumpet
> With all her double vigour, art and nature,
> Once stir by temper: but this virtuous maid
> Subdues me quite. Ever till now
> When men were fond, I smil'd, and wonder'd how.
> (2.2.183-87)

Shakespeare carefully registers this change in Angelo as shocking not only to himself but also to other characters. Claudio is taken by surprise. Hearing about Angelo's sexual extortion of Isabella, Claudio exclaims, "The precise Angelo!" (3.1.93). Duke Vincentio, also, is surprised: "but that frailty hath examples for his falling, I should wonder" (3.1.185-86). Finally, Lucio's explanation of Angelo's birth reinforces the unlikelihood of an outbreak of passion: "Some report, a sea-maid spawned him. Some, that he was begot between two stock fishes. But it is certain that when he makes water, his urine is congealed ice; that I know to be true. And he is a motion ungenerative; that's infallible" (3.2.104-08). This polyphony of voices, each surprised by Angelo's fall, warrants our attention. Intentionally, it seems, we are asked to ask, "How is it that now, for the first time in his life, Angelo feels passion for a woman?"

Whereas the psychoanalytic answer would focus on the object of that (hitherto repressed) passion, interdividual psychology looks at Angelo's circumstances and discovers a significant model. Before Isabella, Claudio is. Although Shakespeare allows Angelo to claim he is merely carrying out his duty to enforce the law that "hath slept" (2.2.91), the play indicates how tendentious is the selection of Claudio. Vienna is teeming with sexual transgressions. The contrast between Claudio and the play's innumerable overlooked candidates for arrest raises the question of Angelo's motivation. If, as I propose to argue, Angelo is attracted to Claudio as a model and entrapped by Claudio as an obstacle, which traits in Claudio attract Angelo and which traits entrap him? Claudio's sensuality piques Angelo's interest, while Claudio's engagement to a dowerless woman causes Angelo to stumble. The sensuality provides the basis for Angelo's overdifferentiating judgment (which takes the guise of a legal judgment). The engagement makes Claudio an inimitable model of enduring commitment to one's fiancée. Judgment against Claudio's sensuality brings Angelo face to face with Claudio's integrity; recognition of Claudio's integrity makes Angelo sensual. Angelo fails to see that whether he attempts to imitate "enduring commitment" or brute sensuality, his stoicism will frustrate either course he chooses, causing him finally to find victims who might bridge the inevitable gap between desire and fulfillment.

On the surface, Angelo judges Claudio because of their dissimilarities. Claudio, like a rat, pursues lechery, whereas Angelo, until meeting Isabella, would smile "when men were fond" and wonder "how?" The confidence with which Angelo arrests Claudio depends upon a difference whose importance Angelo overestimates: he has never slept with a woman. His mental act of overdifferentiation might be expressed thus: "I would never be like Claudio—without self-control, wanton, carnal." At one point in the dialogue, Angelo says something suspiciously similar. Refusing Isabella's request for mercy, Angelo says, "I will not do't" (2.2.51). Do what? Pardon? Fornicate? For Angelo, the two are inextricably bound. To refuse pardon (in light of Angelo's motivations) locks him into a trajectory that points toward extortion, fornication, slander, and intended murder. Thus the original difference between Angelo and Claudio necessarily disappears.

In spite of their initial differences, a similarity unites these male characters. Both men have been engaged to dowerless women. They, of course, wear their discontent with a difference: a slanderous breaking off for Angelo, a premature consummation for Claudio. But it is this similarity that sustains Angelo's overdifferentiating reaction. The past celibacy that permits Angelo to distance himself from Claudio is inseparable from the broken engagement that attests to Angelo's bad faith. Consequently, his moral grounds for sentencing Claudio argue at the same time for Claudio's pardon. Worse, his judgment of Claudio eventually foregrounds Claudio's relatively superior treatment of his fiancée. Whereas Claudio's "sin" mediates sensuality to Angelo, Claudio's fidelity mediates a desire for a lost integrity to Angelo. When we recall that Angelo is a character who takes "pride" in his "gravity" (2.4.9-10), a character who must have the endorsements of others in order to (mimetically) value his own piety, we can see the propensity for rivalry between him and Claudio.

Thus, while the arrest of Claudio gives Angelo immediate moral and political distinction ("'tis surely for a name," 1.2.160), it subjects Angelo to a disturbing desire and a scandalous rival. Contaminated by Claudio's concupiscence, Angelo experiences a desire he has never known. Because Angelo has concealed his failure with Mariana by fashioning himself as a stoic, he cannot imitate Claudio. Unable to follow Claudio's steps without relinquishing his gravity, Angelo cannot get beyond the rival-obstacle in his path. Where the path toward acquisitive mimesis is blocked, the way of conflictive mimesis remains open. Angelo's authorization to put Claudio to death is perfectly convenient because, in one legal action, he can memorialize Claudio's moral lapse and at the same time eliminate a living rival. These motivations of course are unrecognized by Angelo, which is why, later, his passion toward Isabella mystifies him.

Although Claudio is Angelo's model of desire, the moral backlash in Angelo's life need not be sexual. He could simply become colder and still be chained reciprocally to Claudio. But Shakespeare makes the mirroring explicit by making Angelo hot. The smallest trickle of desire will reduce his difference/distance from Claudio. Physiologically, the passion in Angelo is simply awakened. Structurally, the passion is re-created, passion for passion, because he has judged or condemned a man for yielding to his passions. Angelo's judgment supplies the form (which is imitation); Claudio's predicament supplies the content (which is fornication). Both as a model of conjugal love and as an object of differentiation, Claudio becomes the basis for Angelo's life. No matter the particulars of Isabella's beauty, purity, personality, or dress, Angelo is already destined to experience unwanted desire when he meets this character who reminds him of Claudio.

Arriving soon after Angelo's legal and moral judgment against Claudio, Isabella unintentionally precipitates his fall in two ways. First, she provides an object for the desire he has unknowingly borrowed from Claudio. Second, she reinforces Angelo's slavery through a second mimetic triangle. She has what Angelo wants: gravity. Apparently, she possesses it in a purer form, one that does not require public recognition, one that allows her to seek a life of seclusion in the convent. Therefore, not only is Isabella an object of desire to precise Angelo, but she also is a model of desire to the fallen Angelo, who still desires his reputation. Being both object of a lascivious desire and model of an austere desire endows Isabella with extraordinary influence upon Angelo. While he wants to satisfy his carnal yearnings, he cannot do so without encountering Isabella's gravity. He must have her unlawfully in order to sever her beauty from her integrity. As with Angelo's rivalry with Claudio, so is the case with Isabella: if he cannot possess what she possesses, he can at least lower her as a rival, robbing her of her virtue. The act of fornication, then, satisfies both Angelo's acquisitive mimesis toward Isabella as object and conflictive mimesis toward her as rival. The more she protests, the more intent he will be on destroying her. Words avail nothing. Whether she commends the mercy with which Claudio would treat Angelo if their positions were reversed (2.2.64-66), or more directly commands Angelo, "Go to your bosom, / Knock there, and ask your heart what it doth know / That's like my brother's fault" (2.2.137-39), it is too late. The doubling has been completed. Engrossed by Claudio as model-obstacle and mesmerized by Isabella as rival-object, Angelo's "sense breeds with" her words (2.2.143). He will "raze the sanctuary / And pitch our evils there" (2.2.171-72).

The play would be interesting, but not nearly so alarming if Angelo were the only victim of his own judgment. No sooner does Isabella diagnose Angelo's error as one of overdifferentiation, than she falls into the same trap. Critics often explain Isabella's likeness to Angelo in terms of the two saints' relatively fixed characterological and religious traits. Although such similarities are at moments striking, these essentialist comparisons stultify the drama. Interdividual psychology offers a less reductive explanation that is anticipated thematically in the play. Whatever Isabella supposedly shared in common with Angelo prior to their first meeting is nothing compared to the dynamic imitation that follows their second meeting. Early in that interview when Angelo is unmoved by her pleas, she judges him:

> I would to heaven I had your potency,
> And you were Isabel! Should it then be thus?
> No; I would tell what 'twere to be a judge,
> And what a prisoner.
>
> (2.2.67-70)

She would never be as he . . . never as ruthless and inflexible. Formulaically, she binds herself to Angelo with the consequence that she will imitate his violent intentions, finding herself entangled in conflictive mimesis, not only with Angelo but also with Claudio, who himself desires her body, though differently.

This mimetic entanglement accounts for both her anger and her eroticized language. Angelo's alarming proposition that she copulate with him in exchange for her brother's pardon causes her to seek Claudio's support in the rapidly altering situation. The ensuing scene is over-charged with conflictive mimesis. In turning toward Claudio, she yields to her mimetic dependency upon another for approval and thus opens the door wide for the expression of unwanted desires. Looking to Claudio to authenticate her decision, she soon imitates Angelo's style, controlling the dialogue with Claudio, just as Angelo controlled the dialogues with her.

Initially, she assures Claudio of her desire to see him set free, though not at the cost of her virginity:

O, were it but my life,
I'd throw it down for your [Claudio's] deliverance
As frankly as a pin.
(3.1.103-05)

At the outset, Claudio agrees that she should not consider Angelo's proposition. However, as Claudio begins to consider the uncertainty of his existence after death, he alters his tack and begins to reconsider Angelo's proposition. Within moments he recognizes Angelo as an ally. This "model" of virtue in Vienna—"he being so wise" (3.1.112)—becomes for Claudio a model of desire. Angelo's desire for Isabella's cooperation is appropriated by Claudio, so much so that Claudio's speech echoes Angelo's. Whereas Angelo earlier said, "Might there not be a charity in sin / To save a brother's life" (2.4.63-64), Claudio pleads:

What sin you do to save a brother's life,
Nature dispenses with the deed so far
That it becomes a virtue.
(3.1.133-35)

When Claudio aligns himself with Angelo, Isabella undergoes two radical changes. First, she sees Claudio no longer as her brother, the offspring of her father, but as Angelo's double, someone of his stock and quality. Second, and even more significant, she reacts to Claudio as mercilessly as Angelo had reacted to her. Even her speech replicates Angelo's. She says to her brother,

Take my defiance,
Die, perish! Might but my bending down
Reprieve thee from thy fate, it should proceed.
I'll pray a thousand prayers for thy death;
No word to save thee.
(3.1.142-46)

Just as Angelo has claimed he would condemn his own brother to death, so Isabella does condemn her brother, refusing even to bend down to save him. She echoes Angelo's "You but waste your words" with her line, "I'll pray . . . no word to save thee." Thus she is transformed. Her renunciation of any effort to save Claudio, even if it requires only "bending down" (3.1.143), contrasts darkly with her earlier appeals for mercy and her willingness to throw her life down "as frankly as a pin." The plot provides a sympathetic context in which we might place Isabella's change, but the dialogue indicates that she has become, in addition to a Roman Catholic novice and a victim of sexual harassment, an imitator of Angelo.

Isabella and Angelo are doubles in their rigid judgment against Claudio, and, similarly, she becomes split within herself in her response to fornication. Regarding acts of fornication, she remains inflexible as we have seen ("Take my defiance, / Die, perish"), yet she inadvertently intimates erotic interests—although these have been distorted in some psychoanalytic critiques.[15] Only in the heat of conflictive mimesis does she use eroticized language, such as "Hark, how I'll bribe you" (2.2.146). By the second interview, her intimations become even more detailed:

Th'impression of keen whips I'd wear as rubies,
And strip myself to death as to a bed
That longing have been sick for, ere I'd yield
My body up to shame.
(2.4.101-04)

As many commentators note, she casts her repulsion in terms that psychoanalytic theory readily accepts as deferred desire.[16] Rather than attributing the sexual metaphor chiefly to her own resources of libidinous desire, however, the mimetic hypothesis traces it to Angelo, from whom she unwittingly borrows it. The difference, according to my argument, is the difference between the play depicting a bestiality that is only masked by morals and revealing a rationality that is easily demoted to the level of the nearest model.

In spite of Isabella's captivity to Angelo, two of her speeches thematize the dynamics of mimetic desire. During their second interview, Angelo states, "Nay, women are frail too" (2.4.123). While he intends this statement to deflect her accusations of his likeness to Claudio, she takes it as a cue to expostulate on the vulnerability of women to bad (male) models. She theorizes how women, being constructed through relationships mediated by men, depend on external, mimetic examples to establish their identity. Women are

. . . as the glasses where they view themselves,
Which are as easy broke as they make forms.
Women?—Help, heaven! Men their creation mar
In profiting by them. Nay, call us ten times frail;
For we are soft as our complexions are,
And credulous to false prints.
(2.4.124-29)

Within her admission that women are "soft," she tucks another accusation: that men deliberately abuse this frailty. Her claim that men mar their source as divine creations by "profiting" from women has as its subtext the successive failures of three central male models in her life (a dead father, weak brother, and corrupt magistrate). All have been removed or corrupted. She can think only of Heaven as a means to deliver her from the mediation of false prints. On a more generalized level, this speech is as applicable to men as to women. It describes the human susceptibility to mimetic desire. An individual's character is "as easy broke" through conflictive mimesis as an individual's emotions "make forms" for desire through acquisitive mimesis.[17] Because the models of desire are themselves contingent, being disciples of other models, almost every major character in the play turns out to be "credulous to false prints." As Shakespeare represents the situation, the more a character denies his or her susceptibility, the greater the damage that occurs. Acquisitive and conflictive mimesis have monstrous effects, especially upon the "proud"—another name for those who imagine themselves to be beyond mimesis.

This generalized interpretation of women's frailty is borne out by an earlier speech. During their first interview, Isabella sums up the mimicry of desire as it confounds the proud. On this occasion, "man," not "women," is the specified subject:

> But man, proud man,
> Dress'd in a little brief authority,
> Most ignorant of what he's most assur'd—
> His glassy essence—like an angry ape
> Plays such fantastic tricks before high heaven
> As makes the angels weep.
> (2.2.118-23)

Paraphrased, the first lines might state that those who think themselves least susceptible to the influence of others prolong this illusion under the guise of political power. Their blindness increases according to their misplaced self-confidence, a confidence that is necessarily misplaced because their nature is mimetic. What better phrase to sum up the mimetic nature of humans than "glassy essence"? The enduring quality of this species is its mirrorlike, reflective, protean propensity. It leads to duplicitous, reciprocal, and sporadic character traits that *Measure* portrays.

Duke Vincentio serves the playwright as an antidote to these "fantastic tricks" of monstrous doubling. He is not, however, completely immune to judgment. He judges others for their need to marry. His lines, "Believe not that the dribbling dart of love / Can pierce a complete bosom" (1.3.2-3), might be paraphrased, "I will never marry like these. I will only enforce marriages." Like Angelo, who seeks to put fornicators to death, the duke seeks to put them together. Concerning the duke's own marriage proposal, critics frequently comment that it appears to be a Shakespearean afterthought. With more accuracy, we might imagine that Shakespeare designed the proposal as an unavoidable ducal afterthought.[18] In spite of this small instance of reciprocity, Duke Vincentio exhibits little of the mimetic oscillation and slavery to desire that the other main characters do. His detachment sets him apart from the violence adhered to by most of the characters and by many spectators who grow impatient with his pacifism. He resists the procedure of finding a victim for Vienna's "sacred" institutions, both secular and religious. He is unable to kill anyone, even after inclining himself toward violence by appointing Angelo in his place. The play's one sacrificial death suggests his repulsion toward violence. If all the victims of the world were like Ragozine—already dead—the Girardian thesis would be irrelevant.

By scripting much of *Measure*'s action, Duke Vincentio remains above most of the mimetic contamination in Vienna. This insular position makes him incredible by comparison to the other, struggling characters. While he remains one of the characters within his own drama, he transcends them by plotting their courses according to his craft, maintaining a concern for the whole and not just the part. Having initiated a crisis of degree both through his neglect of Viennese law and through his temporary absence, he must intervene in the affairs of Vienna without becoming trapped in reciprocal relations. He therefore attempts to stage corrective desires in order to achieve what Stephen Greenblatt calls "salutary anxiety."[19] Lucio's description of him as "the old fantastical duke of dark corners" (4.3.156) aptly describes the marginalized, histrionic role he fills. Not his political power, but his dramaturgy protects him from the implacable throes of mimetic desire into which Angelo, Claudio, and Isabella fall.

The playwright within the play—the duke—is endowed with a moral impunity that seems unfair. His function is well defined by Cynthia Lewis, who asserts that "the Duke's efforts to bring 'dark deeds' to light can easily awaken our own private feelings of guilt and our own sense of vulnerability to sudden, unexpected castigation."[20] Like my reading, Lewis's insists upon the interpenetration of literary figures with spectator psyches. "Unexpected castigation" relates most directly to parental anger, often paternal wrath. According to Lewis's scenario, our judgments against fathers (and other authority figures) color our perceptions of the duke, re-creating him as a much more malicious figure than he is. From Lewis's point of view, by opposing ourselves to the duke, we become little Angelos:

> But if we allow our impression of the Duke to be conditioned too much by these subjective fears and—out of self-protection and under the mask of anger—project these fears back onto the Duke, then we will miss the experience in which Shakespeare invites us to participate, with the Duke, as he becomes a vital part of Vienna's body politic. And having done so, we will remain nervous, suspicious, and repressed, as does Angelo, who, in dreadful and guilty anticipation of Vincentio's return, hastily transfers his own "distraction" onto the Duke: "pray heaven his wisdom be not tainted!" (IV.iv.4-5)[21]

If our reactions to Duke Vincentio lock us into moral judgment of him instead of into participating in civic judgment with him, we become that much more petty—that much more like the duke we create. In this function, the figure of the duke turns our attention from the representations of desire on stage to the overshadowing reproduction of desires among spectators.

3

Perhaps of all Shakespeare's plays, *Measure for Measure* causes spectators, both present and past, male and female, to side most intensely with or against its characters. Most spectators have a vested interest in desires that are clustered around activities that begin life (sexuality), degenerate life (compromise and lying), renew life (forgiveness), and end life (death). Moreover, these desires are presented vividly through the characters' dialogue and soliloquies. Except for Duke Vincentio, these characters are not staging desire but instead are desperately struggling with desires, often against their wills and beyond their understanding. This lack of theatricality in the play makes the incarnation of its themes within its characters more insistent. The characters' struggles become ours.[22]

According to my thesis, the verbal and behavioral doubling that occurs among the characters is mirrored by the emotional doubling that occurs between the characters and *Measure*'s spectators. Unfortunately, the most compelling evidence for "live" doubling is seldom documented, remaining available primarily to those who have led open discussions of the play among students.[23] The most available source of evidence is the commentary of literary critics, who, especially through their unresisted asides, supply the most durable evidence of the play's effects. A secondary source, studies of live productions, offers only limited help because most productions use cut texts and deploy "modern" significance by suggesting parallels to contemporary social and political concerns. These production studies tell us as much about the "spin" of a particular production as about the Shakespearean text.

Throughout approximately two centuries of recorded responses to the play, every generation is sharply divided among itself. Although every critical period uniquely uncovers aspects of the play, including dramatic, textual, religious, political, and psychological ones, historical boundaries do not define or delimit the judgments that the play evokes. A brief survey of critical antipathy directed toward Angelo, Isabella, and Duke Vincentio will sufficiently document the influence of conflictive mimesis in spectator responses.[24] The commentary on Isabella is the most interesting and detailed because although she is not an obvious villain as is Angelo, she is often perceived as one. The way to read these responses is, of course, to note moments when the critic resembles the object of criticism. The pervasive emotional tones are those of intolerance, repulsion, and condescension—the very responses censured in the characters.

While many critics realize Angelo is no model of virtue, those who are worth quoting imply that Angelo is categorically worse than they. For example, Charlotte Lennox (1753) claims that by Shakespeare's treatment of "the vicious and hypocritical *Angelo,*" the playwright "shews Vice not only pardoned, but left in Tranquility." She recommends that Shakespeare should have treated his source plot quite differently, so that Angelo, "deprived of his Dignity, in Disgrace with his Prince, and the Object of Universal Contempt and Hatred, to compleat his Miseries, he should feel all his former Violence of Passion . . . renewed, and falling into an Excess of Grief . . . stab himself in Despair." Samuel Johnson (1765) similarly believes "every reader feels some indignation when he finds [Angelo] spared," and Samuel Taylor Coleridge (1800) concurs that "our feelings of justice are grossly wounded in Angelo's escape." William Hazlitt (1820) writes, "Mariana is also in love with Angelo, whom we hate." Early in the twentieth century, Agnes Mackenzie (1924) finds Mariana as well as Angelo reprehensible: "But it is to be hoped they had no children." According to Una Ellis-Fermor (1936), Angelo's "impudence leaves the beholder breathless." Wilbur Dunkel (1962) finds him, "So despicable . . . that only Mariana could forgive him."[25]

Isabella evokes the strongest and most significant denunciations. One of the earliest and most quoted detractors of Isabella is Lennox, who claims that Isabella "is a mere Vixen in her Virtue . . . [whose] coarse and unwomanly Reflexions on the Virtue of her Mother [and] exulting Cruelty to the dying Youth, are the Manners of an affected Prude." Denouncing Isabella, Richard White (1854) manages to stereotype and malign a number of women: "Such is Shakespeare's marvellously truthful portraiture of a type which, sad to say, does exist among womankind. . . . *Isabella* is a woman with too much brain or too little heart [who] becomes unfeminine, repulsive, monstrous." Continuing into the twentieth century, we hear Brander Matthews (1913) labeling her "deficient both in feeling and in intelligence." Arthur Quiller-Couch (1922), one of her severest critics, first detaches himself from comment. He admits "the critics can make nothing of her" and urges that we let "the opinions of two of her own sex" assist our assessment. He chooses two detractors, Mrs. Jameson (Isabella is "less attractive and more imposing" than Portia) and Charlotte Lennox (whom I have quoted above). Then, unable to leave the matter in these women's words, he begins to rail: "Still, it has to be admitted that [Isabella] is something rancid in her chastity; and, on top of this, not by any means such a saint as she looks. To put it nakedly, she is all for saving her own soul, and she saves it by turning, of a sudden, into a bare procuress." He continues, authoritatively, "She is chaste, even fiercely chaste, for herself, without quite knowing what chastity means."

Finally, he concludes his imaginary relationship with her thus: "In effect, Isabella disappoints."[26]

Another critic, Jacqueline Rose, has already commented on G. Wilson Knight's (1930) reactions to Isabella.[27] She remarks how in Knight's essay, Isabella quickly moves from being considered "more saintly than Angelo" to being a "fiend." Knight's appreciation of the play and of (at times) the character Isabella is belied in his commentary by emotional oscillations similar to those undergone by characters in the play. In addition to Rose's citations, we read in Knight that "she is cold. . . . Isabella's self-centered saintliness is thrown . . . into strong contrast with Lucio's manly anxiety for his friend" and that "it is significant that [Isabella] readily involves Mariana in illicit love: it is always her own, and only her own, chastity that assumes, in her heart, universal importance."

Unlike Knight's ambivalent estimate, Ellis-Fermor's assessment is univocally harsh, maintaining that the character of Isabella "seals our impression of a world-order ineradicably corrupted and given over to evil." Weak as Claudio is, "his self-indulgence cannot stand comparison with hers, with the pitiless, unimaginative, self-absorbed virtue which sustains her." According to H. B. Charlton (1949), "She makes herself unattractive," speaking at times as a "self-possessed hussy." E. C. Pettet (1949) cannot understand how "such a shallow, cold-blooded creature as Isabella, aware only of an abstract and formal virtue" could "utter lines like those [2.2.114-22 'Merciful heaven . . . angels weep'], so warm, pitiful and extensive in vision." Bertrand Evans (1960) speaks of Isabella's "snow-broth," "outraged inhumanity," and "frozen humanity." An interesting take, impassioned yet methodically distanced, is presented by Patrick Swinden (1973), who claims, "The main point about her is neither her frigidity nor her inhumanity, but her ridiculousness." Anne Barton (1974), by contrast, finds her frigid: "Beneath the habit of the nun there is a narrow-minded but passionate girl afflicted with an irrational terror of sex which she has never admitted to herself."[28]

Following psychoanalytical currents, twentieth-century directors disarm Isabella's threat to their audience's ethos by accentuating her sublimation of aggression and eroticism beneath a religious exterior. John Barton's 1970 Royal Shakespearean Company production was colored by religious skepticism, presenting an Isabella whose "defense of virtue conceals an intense spiritual pride and selfishness." Keith Hack's 1974 RSC Isabella was valuable to Vienna primarily because of "her ability to manipulate male desire." Following a Freudian model of desire more explicitly, Robin Phillips, in his 1975 Stratford, Ontario, production, portrayed an Isabella who vacillated between an absolute repulsion of sex and an avid, even incestuous appetite.[29]

Duke Vincentio shares with Isabella the severest condemnation, and often the two are indicted together. According to Lennox, "the Character of the Duke is absurd and ridiculous." Johnson, perhaps recording his response before reading the final lines of the play, writes, "After the pardon of two murderers, Lucio might be treated by the good duke with less harshness; but perhaps the poet intended to show, what is too often seen, *that men easily forgive wrongs which are not committed against themselves*." White anticipates much of twentieth-century criticism: "The Duke, a well-meaning, undecided, feeble-minded, contemplative man, needed somebody to act for him and govern him." Such reactions continue into recent criticism, including that of Marco Mincoff (1966), who calls the duke "an excrescence who ruins the play," and that of Marcia Riefer (1984), for whom "the 'savior' in *Measure for Measure* turns out to be a villain as well."[30]

Stage productions of *Measure* during this century capitalize on representations of Duke Vincentio as politically incompetent and, at times, sexually incontinent. In the 1906 Oscar Ashe production, "The character of the Duke is criticized as 'idiotic,' and reviewers complain that 'we cannot like a Duke who deserts his post just to see how a substitute will behave in his place.'" According to Michael Scott, Barton's 1970 RSC production presented an "impotent ruler" who, according to Bock, was "completely deluded about his power to correct and instruct his subjects." More extreme than Barton's in its "subversion" of the duke was Hack's 1974 RSC production. Duke Vincentio's manipulation was "a conscious, vicious exercise of absolute power carried out by a sociopathic ruler who is intoxicated by the joys of exploitation." According to Berry, this "demoniac Duke" had, according to Bock, a "delight in sleazy sexuality," which, according to Scott, was evidenced by the duke "fondling Isabella whilst pretending to comfort her, lustfully encompassing her in the folds of his cloak." According to Berry, a similar emphasis on lechery was achieved in Phillips's 1975 Stratford, Ontario, production. The interest in staging a sexually deviant duke imitates, of course, Lucio's slander in the play, and it reciprocates the duke's notorious employment of Angelo to uncover promiscuity in Venice.[31]

4

As I argued in the introduction, *Measure* succeeds exactly where it fails: it catches spectators in a web of partisan character judgments. Referring to all drama, but particularly to *Measure for Measure,* Harriett Hawkins writes, "There are certain moments in the drama when most members of any audience—Christian or pagan, Elizabethan, modern, or, for that matter, Greek—are virtually forced to join the devil's party, perhaps without knowing it."[32] If the devil is another name for the forces of mimetic desire as they shape humanity, then my analysis wholeheartedly supports Hawkins's description. The harsh commentaries on Angelo, Isabella, and Duke Vincentio indicate reactions in the critics that are similar to those represented by Angelo when, out of all Vienna, he arraigns Claudio. Such reactions are both defensible and precarious. All the above-cited critics mimic on a verbal level the dramatic characters that they oppose. No one is immune to interdividual doubling. Those who enter into character evaluation, no matter their theoretical underpinnings, reveal themselves more deeply than they would like to admit. And, of course, not every impassioned mental event is recorded, especially in post-Bradleyan criticism.

Critical engagement with fictitious characters is a specter that refuses to die in spite of our postmodernist condition.[33] For example, Harold Bloom describes two comic characters as "the obsessive slanderer" and "the dissolute." Duke Vincentio, Claudio, and Isabella, according to Bloom, "descend even lower in our esteem."[34] As Bloom's language suggests, the verbal constructions in a play stimulate emotional—even personal—reactions within readers. This phenomenal response evidences the potency of the human imagination to construct coherent, animated wholes from clusters of signs, whether the signs are purely linguistic (as in literature) or both linguistic and nonlinguistic (as in one's neighbor). Every play elicits the kind of moral judgments that I cited from *Measure*'s critical commentaries. This universality only urges that literature adequately represents something that affects us much the same way as do our social interactions. However, the power of conflictive mimesis envelops productions of *Measure for Measure* as it does few of Shakespeare's other plays.[35]

The most common label attached to the faults of Angelo, Isabella, the duke, and, to a lesser extent, Claudio is "hypocrisy." And hypocrisy results directly from reciprocity, from individuals trying to be one thing while their judgments bind them to being another. In this hypocritical (i.e., both duplicitous and subcritical) fashion, spectators vehemently reject the characters they have passed judgment upon. What I have called judgment leads to what Girard calls sacrifice. The ultimate result of reductive, judgmental responses is the expulsion of one or more elements of the society or text—depending on the situation.[36] This expulsion convinces its agents that they are justified in their activities. Benign or malignant, imaginary or politically acted out, this act of expulsion is something few of us would take pride in: a scapegoating.

Often the term is applied to literary activities. Characters, texts, interpretations, and interpreters are scapegoated for a critic's convenience. Speaking of those who address structural problems with characterological solutions, E. M. Tillyard writes, "Some earlier critics felt justified in making the Isabella of the first half of the play the scapegoat of the play's imperfections."[37] Alfred Harbage sees the process in many of Shakespeare's plays, writing that the "fierce disputes . . . mean that the plays, purposely laden with moral stimulus, have achieved their purpose of inducing moral excitement."[38] The fierce disputes that seem to begin and stop in critical quarters register desires and judgments that potentially depict and/or determine the condition of the critics.

One of the clearest examples of critical scapegoating occurs in Carolyn Brown's criticism of *Measure*. She explicitly argues that both Angelo and Claudio are Isabella's victims.[39] Arguing like a defense lawyer in a rape case, Brown asserts that Isabella "slyly provokes her partner [Angelo] to assault her." Then "she begins a concentrated 'seduction of the aggressor,' Rudolph Loewenstein's description of a masochistic ploy that attracts the aggressor to the victim—often in a sexual way." Finally, "Angelo is sabotaged into bringing his sadism out of hiding and proposing the rape that Isabella unconsciously provokes." When Brown turns her attention to Isabella's victimization of Claudio, she claims that Isabella "subjects Claudio to more heartless, ruthless taunting than she did her first victim." Isabella's "depictions of brutal onslaughts and the writhing of victims betray the intense, almost over-powering attraction of her sadomasochistic longings." Her ultimate goal is to "sabotage [Claudio] into proposing rape." Brown thus succeeds in transferring the guilt from Angelo to Isabella in a manner worthy of Hawkins's "devil's party." The signifier is victim for Brown, in a way she does not comment upon.[40]

If the play invites or encourages scapegoating, it also demystifies it—or at least it invites interpretations that do. In an article that is more penetrating than most Christian-allegorical interpretations of *Measure,* Carole Diffey explains why Angelo's pardon both infuriates and satisfies (often the same) spectators. Among other reasons, it infuriates because it opposes our "desire not for justice but for revenge." It satisfies because "we know Angelo almost in the same way that we know ourselves." Not only Angelo, but almost every character in the play foregrounds our self-contradictory ethics, so that the play

> foreshadows the notion of justice that we are beginning to arrive at today and which is making us wary, even in our criminal courts, of the idea of judging others, increasingly conscious of our ignorance of factors that ought to be taken into account, and doubtful of the efficacy of punishment, as in the cases of Lucio and Barnadine [sic], to reform or even to deter, without that recognition of his fault on the part of the offender which renders it superfluous, as it is finally rendered for Angelo.

According to Diffey, the play neither affirms our overdifferentiating, judgmental tendencies, nor does it relinquish morality to a "kind of universal forgiveness which, eliminating moral distinctions rather than accentuating them, would plunge us into the moral vaccum of Lear's 'None does offend, none, I say, none' (IV.vi.170)." Instead, it has the potential for "awakening the sensibility of the culprit until he is capable of judging himself."[41] To Diffey's vision of this play, I would add that the themes of reciprocity and mercy so consciously hammered out in five acts invite the spectator to admit that he or she is "the culprit," or at least is capable of becoming one.

In *Measure for Measure,* therefore, desire is put on display directly and violently. *Measure,* a masterpiece of mediated desire, could never have been Shakespeare's most popular play because it does something to spectators that they are reluctant to admit: it *scandalizes* them. The scandal of mimetic desire is not one person's offense but the invariable complicity of offenses that result from attempts to rid a society or a play of offense. On an imaginary plane, the play provides for spectators one or another character that functions as a scandal, as that which, according to Robert Hamerton-Kelly, "has the sense of a hindrance that one needs to keep desire alive. The scandal is the model/obstacle or the victim that desire cannot live with and cannot live without."[42] Such has been the reception of *Measure for Measure*. Not only the characters, but the play itself has maintained an uneasy but indispensable place in the reevaluations of Shakespeare's canon. While *Measure*'s increased popularity over the last three decades owes much to its topicality of women and their bodies, it also owes much to our culture's sensitivity to the victim. Our understanding of our complicity in the things we hate is increasing, making our interpretations of *Measure* not necessarily deeper, but more circumspect. Through the play, we are able to see the dangers of overdifferentiation and still respond viscerally to what we define as its detestable elements. In the end, however, the playwright, like Duke Vincentio, smooths our complicity over with an ending more comic than tragic. Like some critics, we may sigh a breath of relief that the play is a comedy, however strange. Or like other critics, we may remain unconvinced by the fifth act, concluding that the play's dramatic potential is unfortunately undermined by this puzzling shift. In either case, our attention remains fixed on the generic form rather than on the form of mimesis to which we were exposed. All the while, forgetting what we felt, we also forget to be thankful it was *just* a play.

Notes

[1] Whenever permissible, I use "spectators" to include both audiences and readers. The sort of reactions of interest to this article result from both dramatic productions of *Measure* and from imagined productions. From the eighteenth century to the present, both scholarly responses and audience responses echo each other in concerns about the ambiguous moral standing of the characters, particularly Isabella and Duke Vincentio.

[2] Several essays take up the topic of the play as a critical mirror, among which are Willard H. Durham, "*Measure for Measure* as Measure for Critics," *Essays in Criticism: University of California Publications in English* 1 (1929): 111-32; A. J. Franklin, "Changing Critical Attitude toward *Measure for Measure,*" *Journal of English Studies* 3 (1980): 13-18; and Jonathan R. Price, "*Measure for Measure* and the Critics," *Shakespeare Quarterly* 20 (1969): 179-204. My essay follows in this vein, although instead of emphasizing the play's power to elicit reactions consistent with critical trends, as they do, mine stresses the play's power to generate within critics (and by extension, live audiences) similar desires and attitudes to those represented in the play. Generally the effects of the play motivate analysis of the play, rather than analysis of the audience. Critics frequently focus on specific arguments about characters instead of focusing on the character of their arguments, which is that they are deeply troubled by the play to the extent that their reactions are not only cognitive but emotional.

[3] The two-play-two-audience theory contends that a playwright encodes his play with a double message: a simple message directed toward the simpletons of the audience and an ironic, more sophisticated message directed toward the sages. This duplicitous structure allows the playwright to simultaneously please both the uncritical masses and the more thoughtful members of an audience. In recent exchanges, the controversy over the two-audience theory overlaps with the contention that a production and a reading of Shakespeare yield significantly different experiences. Harry Berger, Jr.'s, article, "Text against Performance in Shakespeare: The Example of *Macbeth,*" *Genre* 2-3 (1982): 49-79, elaborates ways in which a text creates ironies to which characters remain oblivious. Richard Levin responds to Berger in "The New Refutations of Shakespeare," *Modern Philology: A Journal Devoted to Research in Medieval and Modern Literature* 2 (1985): 123-41.

[4] The most notable (but by no means the only) misreading of Girard occurs in Hayden White's review of *Violence and the Sacred,* published as "Ethnological 'Lie' and Mythical 'Truth,'" (*Diacritics* 8 [1978]: 1-9). At one point, White writes, "Take, for example, the case of Nazi Germany. Here surely is a society which meets Girard's criteria of healthiness. . . . Is Nazi Germany then to be taken as a model solution for the problems of 'modernity'?" (8). This alleged alliance between Girard's theory and *any* justification of vio-

lence is thoroughly discredited by Girard's *Things Hidden from the Foundation of the World,* published first in France as *Des choses cachées depuis la fondation du monde*—the same year as White's review. For a response to White's interpretation, see Cesáreo Bandera's review of Girard's major works (*Modern Language Notes* 93 [1978]: 1007-14, esp. 1011).

[5] For the fullest account, see Book III, "Interdividual Psychology," of René Girard's *Things Hidden from the Foundation of the World* (Stanford: Stanford University Press, 1987), 281-431. See also chap. 1 of Robert G. Hamerton-Kelly's *Sacred Violence* (Minneapolis: Fortress Press, 1992), 13-39, and Raymond Schwager's *Must There Be Scapegoats?* (San Francisco: Harper and Row, 1987), 8-18. See also Jean-Michel Oughourlian's *The Puppet of Desire: The Psychology of Hysteria, Possession, and Hypnosis,* trans. Eugene Webb (Stanford: Stanford University Press, 1991).

[6] Charles Peirce, *Peirce on Signs: Writing on Semiotic by Charles Sanders Peirce,* ed. James Hoopes (Chapel Hill: University of North Carolina Press, 1991), 239-40. All quotations from *Measure* are from the New Arden *Measure for Measure,* ed. J. W. Lever (London: Routledge, 1965).

[7] These terms pervade discussions of mimetic desire. Sometimes "appropriative" is used in place of "acquisitive," and "conflictual" in place of "conflictive."

[8] I am indebted to John and Paul Sandford's *The Transformation of the Inner Man* (South Plainfield, N.J.: Bridge, 1982) for its sensitivity to the psychology of judgment. While my conception of "judgment" does not alter Girard's major contentions about human behavior, it takes them to a more "microscopic" level of analysis.

[9] For examples of judicial readings, see John W. Dickinson, "Renaissance Equity and *Measure for Measure,*" *Shakespeare Quarterly* 13 (1962): 287-97, and Wilbur Dunkel, "Law and Equity in *Measure for Measure,*" *Shakespeare Quarterly* 13 (1962): 275-85. For examples of theological readings, see C. J. Sisson, *The Mythical Sorrows of Shakespeare,* Annual Shakespeare Lecture of the British Academy, 25 April 1934; R. W. Chambers, *The Jacobean Shakespeare and "Measure for Measure,"* Annual Shakespeare Lecture of the British Academy, 1937; Roy Battenhouse, "*Measure for Measure* and Christian Doctrine of the Atonement," *PMLA* 61 (1946): 1029-59; G. Wilson Knight, "*Measure for Measure* and the Gospels," in *The Wheel of Fire* (London: Methuen, 1949), 80-106; and Nevill Coghill, "Comic Form in *Measure for Measure,*" *Shakespeare Studies* 8 (1955): 14-27.

[10] According to Johnson, "Angelo's crimes were such as must sufficiently justify punishment, whether its end be to secure the innocent from wrong or to deter guilt by example; and I believe every reader feels some indignation when he finds him spared" (*Samuel Johnson on Shakespeare.,* ed. W. K. Wimsatt, Jr. [New York: Hill and Wang, 1960], 76). Similarly, Coleridge remarks, "The pardon and marriage of Angelo not merely baffles the strong indignant claim of justice (for cruelty, with lust and damnable baseness, cannot be forgiven, because we cannot conceive of them as being *morally* repented of) but it is likewise degrading to the character of woman" (*Coleridge's Writings on Shakespeare,* ed. Terence Hawkes [New York: Penguin, 1959], 249-50).

F. R. Leavis, writing "If we don't see ourselves in Angelo, we have taken the play very imperfectly," rightly diagnoses these symptoms: "One has, then, to point out as inoffensively as possible that the point of the play depends upon Angelo's not being a certified criminal-type, capable of a wickedness that marks him off from you and me: 'Go to your bosom; / Knock there, and ask your heart what it doth know / That's like my brother's fault'" (*The Common Pursuit* [London: Chatto and Windus, 1958], 171-72).

[11] Charlotte Lennox, *Shakespeare Illustrated* (1753; New York: AMS, 1973), 35.

[12] William Witherle Lawrence, *Shakespeare's Problem Comedies,* 2d ed. (New York: Frederick Ungar, 1960), 121.

[13] Jocelyn Powell, "Theatrical *Trompe l'oeil* in *Measure for Measure,*" in *Shakespearian Comedy,* ed. Malcolm Bradbury and David Palmer, Stratford-upon-Avon Studies 14 (London: Edward Arnold, 1972), 184.

[14] This series of differentiating responses begins in the text with Angelo's separation from Mariana. The play and contemporary civil laws make clear that the lack of dowry did not necessitate his slanderous means of putting Mariana away (see Lever, liii-liv, and Victoria Hayne, "Performing Social Practice: The Example of *Measure for Measure,*" *Shakespeare Quarterly* 44 [1993]: 1-29, esp. 3-8). Throughout the play, he obtains emotional distance by constantly walking out on other characters, including Escalus, Froth, and Pompey (2.1.137); Isabella (in both interviews); and, figuratively, the entire city, begging for "Immediate sentence, then, and sequent death" (5.1.371). He prefers distinctive death over communal life.

[15] In an article that contains a useful bibliography on psychoanalytic readings of *Measure,* Carolyn Brown states that Isabella's sexual desire and pain are conflated under the rubric of spiritual discipline and that the "subterranean" sexuality of all the protagonists is aroused "not by affection but by abuse" ("Erotic Religious Flagellation and Shakespeare's *Measure for*

Measure," *English Literary Renaissance* 16 [1986]: 141). In another article, Brown directs the "unconscious" hypothesis toward Isabella's displaced pleasure: "She choreographs her flagellation scene with the sound of beating. The fantasizer's onomatopoetic words imitate the sounds produced during the whipping. Like these fantasizers, Isabella reiterates the key word "thunder,' chanting the word as though savoring the sound" ("*Measure for Measure*: Isabella's Beating Fantasies," *American Imago* 43 [1986]: 72). Similarly, Harriet Hawkins asserts, "Moreover, Isabella's fiery refusal to yield to [Angelo] is charged with an erotic power of its own" and raises the question whether "Isabella's initial desire for 'more severe restraints' within the convent suggest[s] that there is something to restrain? Why her emphasis on woman's frailty?" (*The Devil's Party* [Oxford: Oxford University Press, 1985], 69, 70). Contrary to this vein of analysis, my argument contends that the froth of eroticized language and imagery in *Measure* is incidental to the core of the protagonists' problems. Their error is not repression that emerges as sadomasochistic desire but judgment that brings reciprocal effects. The form of the dysfunction (measure for measure) is far more fundamental than the content (sexual desire).

[16] On Isabella's eroticized description of death, Lever writes, "Isabella expresses her readiness to die in erotic terms" (lxxxvi). Hawkins shares his opinion ("'The Devil's Party': Virtues and Vices in *Measure for Measure*," *Shakespeare Studies* 31 [1978]: 107). Freud, in "The Dream Work," writes that there is not "any doubt that all weapons and tools are used as symbols for the male organ"; thus Isabella's reference to "keen whips." Furthermore, he writes, "Since `bed and board' constitute marriage, the latter often takes the place of the former" (*The Interpretation of Dreams,* trans. James Strachey [New York: Avon, 1965], 391). Isabella's reference to "a bed"—rather than "board"—being more explicit, demonstrates less displacement. Finally, a sense of disgust (Isabella's "That longing have been sick for") is frequently mentioned by Freud as a response to sexual desire, and the redness of "rubies" might suggest the hymen (i.e., cherry) or menstruation.

[17] *Between Men,* Eve Sedgwick adapts interdividual psychology to illuminate the asymmetrical patterns of power and sexuality that emerge through her study of male-male relationships in English literature, beginning with Shakespeare. While she seeks to recover the "hidden obliquities" that Girard's transcultural, non-gender-specific method does not of itself recognize, she notes that Girard's "transhistorical clarity" has its place (*Between Men: English Literature and Male Homosocial Desire* [New York: Columbia University Press, 1985], 22). In this essay, I clearly follow the scope of Girard's method rather than that of Sedgwick's, particularly because the "sexual" conflicts I find in *Measure for Measure* are always rooted in violence. While the shows of power are expressed according to specific sexual roles, the mechanisms through which the appropriations and expropriations of desire occur are not gender dependent.

[18] Similarly, Cynthia Lewis comments: "Judgment in *Measure* is ultimately a collective activity. It is of no small consequence, for instance, that just as Claudio becomes penitent, the Duke turns amorous. By the play's end, in fact, Claudio seems to have had more effect on the Duke's way of life than the Duke has had on Claudio's" ("'Dark Deeds Darkly Answered': Duke Vincentio and Judgment in *Measure for Measure*," *Shakespeare Quarterly* 34 [1983]: 286).

[19] Stephen Greenblatt, "Martial Law in the Land of Cockaigne," in *Shakespearean Negotiations* (Berkeley: University of California Press, 1988), 135.

[20] Lewis, "'Dark Deeds Darkly Answered,'" 285.

[21] Ibid.

[22] Harriet Hawkins notes this power of *Measure* in contrast to its absence in similar plays: "Where *The Malcontent* and *The Tempest,* for their individual and proper dramatic reasons, subordinate their emotional impact for the sake of and by means of other kinds of effects, the first half of *Measure for Measure* makes a direct assault on the emotions" (*Likenesses of Truth in Elizabethan and Restoration Drama* [Oxford: Oxford University Press, 1972], 57). The "emotional impact" sustained by the play compels the spectators to identify with the characters—and not always sympathetically. As a result of assaulting the characters and spectators with a matrix of ethical concerns, Shakespeare achieves an unreflective mediation of desire upon the spectators.

[23] In my classroom, the outbursts of emotion have been incredibly vivid and unpredictable. Students of both sexes denounce and defend Isabella, Duke Vincentio, and Angelo with such intensity that they sometimes leave their seats. On one occasion, two students turned the matter into a personal issue and had to seek reconciliation with each other at a latter date. On another occasion, one woman issued her verdict, "Isabella makes a shitty martyr," without remembering afterward what she had said (when asked permission for quotation).

[24] Claudio, being more a placeholder than an instigator of action in the play, is generally dismissed with little critical reaction. A few remarks deserve mention. Coleridge states, "Claudio is detestable" (*Coleridge's Writings on Shakespeare,* 250). Una M. Ellis-Fermor finds him "selfish and self-indulgent" (*The Jacobean Drama* [London: Methuen, 1936], 261). And William Empson (1951) attributes his repulsion to Shakespeare:

"This [alteration in plot, reducing Claudio's role] seems good evidence that [Shakespeare] found the behaviour of Claudio disgusting" ("Sense in *Measure for Measure*," in *The Structure of Complex Words* [Ann Arbor: University of Michigan Press, 1967], 280).

[25] Lennox, 25-26; Samuel Johnson, *Samuel Johnson on Shakespeare,* ed. W. K. Wimsatt, Jr. (New York: Hill and Wang, 1960), 76; Coleridge, *Coleridge's Writings on Shakespeare,* 250; William Hazlitt, *Characters of Shakespeare's Plays,* ed. J. H. Lobban (Cambridge: Cambridge University Press, 1915), 233; Agnes Mure Mackenzie, *The Women in Shakespeare's Plays* (London: William Heinemann, 1924), 243; Ellis-Fermor, *Jacobean Drama,* 261; Wilbur Dunkel, "Law and Equity in *Measure for Measure*," *Shakespeare Quarterly* 13 (1962): 284.

[26] Lennox, 32-34; Richard Grant White, *Shakespeare's Scholar* (New York: D. Appleton, 1854), 149-50; Brander Matthews, *Shakespeare as a Playwright* (New York: Charles Scribner's Sons, 1913), 229; Arthur Quiller-Couch, intro. *Measure for Measure,* by William Shakespeare (Cambridge: Cambridge University Press, 1922), xxvii, xxviii, xxx, xxxii.

[27] Jacqueline Rose, "Sexuality in the Reading of Shakespeare: *Hamlet* and *Measure for Measure*," in *Alternative Shakespeares,* ed. John Drakakis (London: Methuen, 1985), 95-118; Knight, Wheel of Fire, 101, 102.

[28] Ellis-Fermor, 262, 263; H. B. Charlton, *Shakespearian Comedy,* 4th ed. (London: Methuen, 1949), 254; E. C. Pettet, *Shakespeare and the Romance Tradition* (London: Staples, 1949), 160; Bertrand Evans, *Shakespeare's Comedies* (Oxford: Oxford University Press, 1960), 196, 197, 207; Patrick Swinden, *An Introduction to Shakespeare's Comedies* (New York: Barnes, 1973), 144; Anne Barton, intro. *Measure for Measure,* in *The Riverside Shakespeare,* ed. G. Blakemore Evans (Boston: Houghton Mifflin, 1974), 546.

[29] Judith L. Bock, "*Measure for Measure:* The Duke and Isabella on Stage at the RSC, 1950-1987" (Ph.D. diss., University of Colorado, 1989), 98, 126; Ralph Berry, "*Measure for Measure* on the Contemporary Stage," *Humanities Association Review* 28 (1977): 246.

[30] Lennox, 31; Johnson, 76-77; White, 150; Marco Mincoff, "*Measure for Measure:* A Question of Approach," *Shakespeare Studies* 2 (1966): 149; Marcia Riefer, "'Instruments of Some More Mightier Member': The Constriction of Female Power in *Measure for Measure,*" in *William Shakespeare's "Measure for Measure,"* ed. Harold Bloom (New York: Chelsea, 1987), 133-34. For similar judgments, see Quiller-Couch, xxxiii; Harold Goddard, *The Meaning of Shakespeare* (Chicago: University of Chicago Press, 1951), 438; and Empson, 280.

[31] Bock, 21; Michael Scott, *Renaissance Drama and a Modern Audience* (London: Macmillan, 1982), 62; Bock, 108, 114; Berry, 246; Scott, 65; Berry, 244.

[32] Hawkins, "'The Devil's Party,'" 109.

[33] Hawkins writes: "Modern criticism, which frequently argues that such characters [as Hamlet and Falstaff] have no right to any existence apart from their immediate dramatic context, tends to imply that this phenomenon does not or should not exist. But whether or not it should, it does. The passionate adoration which individual critics accord to their own, private, saintly, or lovable Isabellas, and the equally passionate revulsion which other critics express towards their own smug, vixenish, intolerant, selfish Isabellas, testify to Isabella's after-life in the heavens or hells assigned to her by individual imaginations" (*Likenesses of Truth,* 58).

[34] Bloom, 1-2, 4.

[35] Perhaps *The Merchant of Venice* comes closest to evoking such intensely divided responses, although the ideological concerns of *Merchant* would necessarily outrage spectators, independent of the dramatist's efforts toward that end.

[36] Girard writes, "I fully agree that, in the case of plays like *Richard III* or *The Merchant of Venice,* an infinite number of readings is possible, and this infinity is determined by 'the play of the signifier.' I do not agree that this play is gratuitous, and that it is in the nature of all signifiers as signifiers to produce such infinite play. The literary signifier always becomes a victim. It is a victim of the signified, at least metaphorically, in the sense that its play, its *différence,* or what you will, is almost inevitably sacrificed to the one-sidedness of a single-minded differentiated structure *à la* Lévi-Strauss" ("'To Entrap the Wisest': A Reading of *The Merchant of Venice,*" in *Literature and Society,* ed. Edward W. Said [Baltimore: Johns Hopkins University Press, 1981], 119).

[37] E. M. W. Tillyard, *Shakespeare's Problem Plays* (London: University of Toronto Press, 1950), 123. Interestingly, Tillyard has been recognized as a scapegoat himself for his monolithic political stance: "taking Tillyard as their primary scapegoat, making him stand as the representative of almost four hundred years of liberal-humanist critical illusions . . . frees cult-historicists to recuperate the Elizabethan world picture" (Carol Thomas Neely, "Constructing the Subject: Feminist Practice and the New Renaissance Discourses," *ELR* 18 [1988]: 12).

[38] Alfred Harbage, *As They Liked It: A Study of Shakespeare's Moral Artistry* (Gloucester, Mass.: Torchbook, 1961), 16.

[39] Brown, "*Measure for Measure:* Isabella's Beating Fantasies," 70-77.

[40] Similarly, Harry Jaffa argues extensively that "Isabella has, unknown to herself, seduced Angelo" ("Chastity as a Political Principle: An Interpretation of Shakespeare's *Measure for Measure*," in *Shakespeare as a Political Thinker,* ed. John Alvis and Thomas G. West [Durham, N.C.: Carolina Academic Press, 1981], 208). He blames Isabella for Angelo's fall, arguing that Angelo no longer trusts the law as a result of Isabella's antinomianism: "In a sense, Angelo is taking a proper revenge upon Isabella: she has destroyed his dignity as a judge; he will do the same to her saintliness. She has put him on a level with fornicators; he will treat her as a prostitute. Here too we find a measure for measure" (211). If Isabella has victims, they are not sexual but sacrificial victims. As Lewis notes, in 3.1.231-33, Isabella thinks both Angelo and Mariana would be better off dead. In Lewis's words, "At the bottom of [Isabella's] reasoning lies an escapist impulse to ignore human problems" ("'Dark Deeds Darkly Answered,'" 283).

[41] Carole T. Diffey, "The Last Judgment in *Measure for Measure*," *Durham University Journal* 66 (1974): 236-37.

[42] Hamerton-Kelly, *Sacred Violence,* 71.

Source: "Spectator Seduction: *Measure for Measure,*" in *Texas Studies in Literature and Language,* Vol. 37, No. 3, Fall, 1995, pp. 326-63.

The Merry Wives of Windsor: Sharing the Queen's Holiday

Leslie S. Katz, *Amherst College*

I

The Merry Wives of Windsor is a spin-off: in it, Shakespeare resituates Falstaff in Windsor, where the well-known scoundrel causes mischief by wooing the wives of two prominent townsmen, Master Ford and Master Page. Perhaps the play's identity as sequel or appendage contributes to its minor reputation; but Merry Wives has also suffered (in the annals of twentieth-century criticism) for being an "occasional" play, trivialized by its connection to a ceremonial occasion—much as Charles Dickens's *Christmas Carol* has become irreversibly connected to the Christmas theater season in the United States. By historically reconstituting the occasion and establishing its relationship to the play's composition, we can reclaim the interest of *Merry Wives,* not only as Shakespeare's memorialization of Falstaff within Queen Elizabeth's private theater, but, more generally, as Shakespeare's meditation on the afterlife of dramatic characters.[1] The play reflects on how theatrical events, leaping the boundaries of court performance, penetrate an everyday network of conversation, recollection, and daydream: the "stuff" of imaginative interchange on a local level. *Merry Wives* has much to show us about the interior archaeology of Shakespeare's dramatic canon: about how plays, as well as characters, can live in the minds of an audience, and how, inversely, as a result of that habitation, the audience can find itself situated back inside the canon's imaginative interstices.

According to theater historians, *The Merry Wives of Windsor* was probably commissioned by George Carey to be performed in 1597 on St. George's Day at a feast honoring Queen Elizabeth and her Garter knights.[2] To mark the holiday, Shakespeare performed a restaging of Falstaff—relocating the fat rogue from the history plays in the theatrical milieu of civic comedy. Thanks to the Henry plays, Falstaff had become a distinct entity in the imagination of a popular audience, a character sufficiently known that he could cross genres as well as the boundaries of individual plays. Testimony to Falstaff's long and independent afterlife is the eighteenth century's claim—in disagreement with the theory that Carey commissioned the play—that Elizabeth "was so well pleased with that admirable character of *Falstaff,* in the two parts of *Henry the Fourth* that she commanded [Shakespeare] to continue it for one play more, and to shew him in love."[3] This claim can be traced to several sources, but T.W. Craik, deepening its romantic flavor, warns that any one of the informants "may have invented it."[4] What is interesting is how the lore spins out, creating a separate drama of cultural recollection. The legend of the Queen's commission aspires not only to give Shakespeare a retrospective motive for eroticizing Falstaff in *Merry Wives* but to interpret that motive as one of satisfying the Queen's desire, as if in a comic inversion Shakespeare were to pay suit to Elizabeth through a lascivious Falstaff—a Falstaff who, at any rate, had grown more lascivious in his passage from the court of Henry IV to that of the Queen. Thus two historical universes intersect in the context of Elizabeth's holiday, coming together in the plot of *Merry Wives* and, in particular, Falstaff's wooing of Mistress Ford.

The Queen's Garter ceremony created an occasion to assemble the English nobility, as well as foreign kings and dukes, who had been honored by inclusion in her royal Order. The garter emblem signified each knight's oath to defend the virtue and resplendence of the Queen. André Favyn, in his history of chivalry (*The Theater of Honour and Knighthood* [1619]), traced the origins of the Order to an anecdote about Edward III "picking up a lady's garter and reproving the lascivious thoughts of bystanders with the famous words *Honi soit qui mal y pense* (evil be to him who evil thinks)"[5]—or more precisely, "shame be to him who, with evil motives, thinks on shameful things." This, at any rate, was the popular (as opposed to official) legend, which, in the course of the sixteenth century, spawned a host of fashionable derivatives, many involving Edward III's Queen. In Holinshed, for instance, "the Queen drops her garter on the way to her lodging and Edward orders it to be brought to him and vows to make all men reverence it."[6] Every version of the tale ends with the same chivalric moral—of lust shamed and virtue encircled—not in the knight so much as in the bystanders who imagine that the knight entertains anything but virtuous intentions. That moral is variously communicated through the garter emblem or motto, or both, as in yet another permutation, where the fallen garter, belonging this time to one of the Queen's maids of honor, serves as the model for a blue velvet copy, embroidered with the words "Honi soit. . . ."[7]

Through the vehicle of the tale, Elizabeth acquires two roles: she is both Edward, royal host of the Order, and the Queen, whose chastity—or, under whose watchful eye, the chastity of the attending maids—is reverenced.[8] The character of Falstaff, emerging from the world of Shakespeare's history plays, brims over with lecherous designs, and thus threatens to violate the meaning of the Garter. We need to remember, however, that Falstaff, like Elizabeth, assumes a double role thanks to his insinuation in the Garter holiday. Acting as "lord over men" (Bardolph, Pistol, Nym), he parallels Elizabeth's role as patron.[9] If Falstaff exploits this role, requiring improper service of his men—in return for which they, once dismissed from his service, "correctly" plot revenge—does he become an image of the anti-patron, serving as a clownish foil to the monarch? I would say no, arguing instead that Falstaff's part is consistently written to "play out" the fantasies of Windsor's (implicitly male) citizens; in other words, to mediate—or entertain—the desires aroused in the occasion's onlookers. Put another way, Falstaff stands in for the Queen, pandering, as it was the clown's business to pander, to the vulgar portion of the audience, or to the lascivious portion of any viewer's mind. Here, at the farther reaches of "hideous imagination," hovered fantasies of violation, of choosing an Order of looting ravishers over one of chaste knights loyal in their service to God and the Queen.[10]

Let us return to the question of what it meant for Shakespeare to ignore genre boundaries, introducing a historical Falstaff into a comic Windsor at the same time that he placed this comic Falstaff at the center of the Queen's holiday. Falstaff was not only known to the audience, but known for his role in a play (*1 Henry IV*) that "remembered" England's historical past. Disengaged from the context of one play and translated to another, Falstaff gained a spiraling momentum. The associations attached to his character migrated into the audience's memory and continued to unfold there, constituting the kernel of a collective fantasy. The one I have sketched out here, of Falstaff's obliquely amorous connection to the Queen, is one among many possible scenarios. Shakespeare himself calls attention to the complexities of audience reception by placing *Merry Wives* in Windsor, the traditional setting of the Garter celebration. Apprised of the holiday's structure, its workings, and its lore, Shakespeare translated certain of the holiday's elements—such as its anachronistic and memorial character—into the dramatic design of *Merry Wives,* marking the comedy with his own awareness of what it meant to embed a play, not only in a multilayered celebration, but also in the material structures through which the celebration would be remembered.

Commemorative objects that have survived from Elizabeth's actual Garter Day celebrations include a portrait of the Queen holding a Badge of St. George, a portrait of her knights "in slightly updated medieval cloaks and bonnets," as well as numerous paeans remembering the procession of participants: "O knightly order, clothed in robes with Garter: / The Queen's Grace, thy mother, in the same. / The nobles of thy realm, rich in array, after . . . ," and so on.[11] Roy Strong writes, "Like so much else in the age of Elizabeth . . . [the holiday's observance] represents a deliberate cult and reinvigoration of archaisms."[12] The pageant of Queen and knights, dressed in fourteenth-century attire, passing by a stand of sixteenth-century onlookers, inspired the type of language we find in this description: "Under the glorious spreading wings of Fame, / I saw a virgin queen, attired in white, / Leading with her a sort of goodly knights, / With garters and with collars of Saint George";[13] in other words, language that stops at the surface of the pageant, indulging the illusion of a fantastical past, even as it processes (palpably) through the streets of London.

The Order of the Garter, founded in the fourteenth century by Edward III and intermittently resuscitated by certain of his successors, like Edward IV and Henry VII, was maintained in its original trappings during Henry VIII's reign. Garter reform, initiated by Edward VI, was reversed by Mary in 1553, waiting for Elizabeth to use the apparatus of the old Order as a means of reconciling Catholic imagery to Protestant readings:[14] in Strong's words, a way of giving visual form to the Queen's "religious ambiguity."[15] While Protestant reforms required using the English Litany in the procession, as well as a vernacular communion service in place of the High Mass,[16] the knights continued to array themselves in the collars of the medieval Order and arrange themselves in tableaux vivants of the archaic Catholic ceremony. Holding the pose for painters and poets to record, the knights became the subject matter for a body of new icons that collapsed the actual occasion into its legendary antecedents. In these representations, contemporary eyes did not peer anachronistically from the peepholes of an ancient scene; rather, the contemporary and ancient were compressed into a single surface, "embodiments of an identical [and timeless] power."[17]

Under Edward IV, St. George's Chapel at Windsor was rebuilt and the Garter ceremony resumed there "on a splendid scale. . . . [As they had in Edward III's reign], the Knights sat, like canons, in the choir stalls, each with his achievement hung above him."[18] From 1559 to 1572, the Elizabethan procession and feasts duly took place in Windsor but after 1572 were moved to Whitehall or Greenwich.[19] Nevertheless, an engraving executed by Marcus Gheeraert in 1576 depicts the procession as taking place at Windsor, suggesting that the Windsor site, like the origins of the holiday itself, had already sunk into mythology, becoming part of the repertoire of emblems through which the Elizabethan rituals were played out and afterwards recorded: "[At Whitehall] the Knights descended through the Great Chamber and Hall to the Chapel, which was arranged *like* the Chapel at Windsor."[20] But as the holiday produced an official way of being remembered, the ceremonies themselves, as physically enacted, came more fully into public view. "By 1592 the crush of people was so great that the ceremonies were held up awaiting the arrival of Knights who had failed to penetrate the throng. . . . [In 1595, the] Chapel Royal was packed with visitors, and the magnificent procession made its way not once but three times around the courtyard so that all might see the Queen."[21] Although we, scrutinizing the event, cannot see *into* the ceremony, that is, cannot see past the surface where quotidian rhythms were frozen into ritual formations, we can nonetheless try to imagine the bustle of the crowd at the periphery.

It is here that Shakespeare's play affords an enlarged perspective by placing the Queen's holiday at the periphery of *Merry Wives* and the holiday onlookers' digressive intrigues at its center. Indeed, as the play opens, the Inn at Windsor is filling up with guests who have come to see the Garter proceedings, a fact that explains the presence of foreign emissaries, like Sir Evans and Doctor Caius.[22] A representative of medieval aristocracy shows up in the figure of Anne Page's suitor, Fenton, while *imaginary* courtiers buzz in the fantasies of Dame Quickly, who describes a fictive procession of noble suitors begging Mistress Ford's attentions: "Yet there has been knights, and lords, and gentlemen, with their coaches—I warrant you, coach after coach, letter after letter, gift after gift—smelling so sweetly, all musk, and so rushling . . ." (*Merry Wives,* 2.2.60-63). Metatheatrically, *Merry Wives* is staged "inside" the Garter holiday, serving to entertain the ceremony's principals, that is, the Queen and her knights, as well as the surrounding ranks of courtiers and clergymen. But the psychology of characters in the play lies at the periphery of the event, with the members of the public audience who watch at a remove, consuming the sights, gossiping about the finery, the gestures, and the secret lives of the courtly participants, in short, employing their imaginative powers to elaborate outlandish scenarios in which members of the court come, as Falstaff does in *Merry Wives,* to participate in their fantasies.

II

> *Ask me no reason why I love you, for though Love use Reason for his precisian, he admits him not for his counsellor. You are not young, no more am I; go to then, there's sympathy. You are merry, so am I; ha, ha! then there's more sympathy. You love sack, and so do I; would you desire better sympathy? Let it suffice thee . . . —at least if the love of soldier can suffice—that I love thee. . . .*
>
> . . . John Falstaff.
> (*Merry Wives,* 2.1.4-19)

Mistress Page and Mistress Ford receive identical love letters from Falstaff. The adulterous ambition that the letters announce is menacing, not because it intrudes on an otherwise tranquil domestic order, but because it gives voice to a perverse desire festering already in the civic imagination, epitomized by Ford's desire to see his wife's reputation cheapened:

> She dwells so securely on the excellency of her honour that the folly of my soul dares not present itself; she is too bright to be looked against. Now, could I come to her with any detection in my hand, my desires had instance and argument to commend themselves; I could drive her then from the ward of her purity, her reputation, her marriage-vow, and a thousand other her defences which now are too too strongly embattled against me.
>
> (2.2.233-42)

Falstaff's lechery serves not as proof of Mistress Ford's dishonor but, rather, as the articulation of her husband's desire. In the reading Falstaff gives to Mistress Ford's actions, he delivers the lines that Ford himself would like to speak:

> I spy entertainment in her: she discourses, she carves, she gives the leer of invitation; I can construe the action of her familiar style.
>
> (1.3.41-43)

The play's comic intrigue derives from Ford's determination to heighten the pleasure of his fantasy by imaginatively switching places with Falstaff: first he disguises himself as a would-be suitor, and then he pays off the knight to make a liaison—under Ford's assumed name—with Mistress Ford:

> There is money; spend it, spend it, spend more; spend all I have, only give me so much of your time in exchange of it as to lay an amiable siege to the honesty of this Ford's wife. Use your art of wooing; win her to consent to you; if any man may, you may as soon as any.
>
> (2.2.223-28)

By borrowing material from Shakespeare's history plays and, in particular, building his fantasies around Falstaff, Ford identifies himself not only as a resident of Windsor—the play world—but also as a resident of London—the extradramatic world—and specifically as a member of Shakespeare's audience. If a man like Ford wishes, for whatever reason, to concoct scenarios of *being* cuckolded, how could he choose a more celebrated cuckolder than Prince Henry's fat knight, whose far-ranging reputation would give the scandal a seductive universality? The choice, moreover, plays on the prodigious body of Will Kemp, the clown who probably played the part of Falstaff: the unnatural proportions of his physique would simultaneously have maximized and minimized the fantasy's danger, giving it, on the one hand, more power to titillate and, on the other, more leeway to transform itself into a joke.[23] Now it is Ford, rather than Shakespeare, who ignores genre boundaries, introducing the historical Falstaff into

Windsor, indifferent to the transtemporal, translocative nature of his project. By becoming the property of their audience, characters in plays, and by extension the actors who play them, fuel a universe of private daydreams beyond the playwright's power or ken. This range of imaginative products (or "dreams") issues from what Michel de Certeau, in *The Practice of Everyday Life,* calls "the multiform labor of consumption. . . . The enigma of the consumer-sphynx. His products are scattered in the graphs of . . . urbanistic production. . . . They are protean in form, blending in with their surroundings, and liable to disappear."[24]

Ford sends "Falstaff" (that is, Falstaff playing pander to Ford's illicit desires) to a place where Ford can find him—to a mental image of the Ford household, where everything is known to Ford already: as Mistress Ford says, "Neither press, coffer, chest, trunk, well, vault, but he hath an abstract for the remembrance of such places and goes to them by his note" (4.2.53-56). The catalog of places includes a nook in the upper chambers where Ford, in his vicarious fantasy, has imagined that Falstaff will try to hide himself. As Ford runs along, both on stage and in his own mind, to catch his wife and Falstaff in the act, he collects a party of Page, Caius, and Evans to witness the climax. To them, he cries, "Gentlemen, I have dreamed to-night; I'll tell you my dream. Here, here, here be my keys; ascend my chambers; search, seek, find out. I'll warrant we'll unkennel the fox" (3.3.148-52). When Ford reaches the warren assigned to Falstaff in his "dream," however, he finds it empty and realizes with the force of a gestalt switch that he has broken into the wrong interior, that this is not his fantasy at all, that he has become, in fact, an actor in someone else's imaginative field.

The movement of the scene might be read this way: that Mistress Ford triumphs over her husband by compassing his fantastical construction with another that corresponds point by point to his—with the exception that Falstaff, stuffed the first time around in a "buck-basket," the second time in the woman of Brainford's clothes, has disappeared from the location he was supposed to occupy in Ford's version. The change is invisibly effected so that Ford does not suspect a scheme coterminous with his. That Mistress Ford is rearranging the stuff of his imagination, albeit in material form on stage, is made explicit in the pun on his name, "Brainford," as well as in this exchange:

> MRS FORD: Shall we tell our husbands how we have served Falstaff?
> MRS PAGE: Yes, by all means—if it be but to scrape the figures out of your husband's brains.
> (4.2.200-203)

But something remains to be said about how these imaginative configurations physically overlap in the act of staging them. The plan that Mistress Ford has prearranged with Mistress Page involves the latter arriving, out of breath, to warn Mistress Ford, "Your husband's coming hither, woman, with all the officers in Windsor, to search for a gentleman that he says is here now in the house. . . . You are undone" (3.3.97-101). Mistress Page's lines are *not* supposed to signal Ford's actual arrival but merely to serve as a cue for tossing Falstaff ignobly out of the house. Mistress Ford is equally taken by surprise, then, when her husband actually pushes through the door, followed by a train of men, wide-eyed and eager to share in the scandal. Shakespeare illustrates in this scene how plots-within-plots work: how when one person's play pushes through another's, the first (that is, Ford's fantasy of being cuckolded) materializes the imaginative gaps in the other (Mistress Ford's plot to punish Falstaff's desire to cuckold, which never—in its own right—imagined Ford's literal cuckolding). Ford's arrival brings an "extra joke" to the scene, an added physical dimension that gets shuffled into the layers of collective fantasy through which Falstaff in Windsor circulates.

Can we say, returning to the way Shakespeare positions the play with respect to Garter Day, that Falstaff pushes at the seams of the Queen's holiday, giving voice, on the one hand, to lascivious desires, which would otherwise find expression only in the negative ("Honi soit qui mal y pense"), while at the same time deflecting those desires into *Merry Wives*' spiral of comic intrigues? There is more to it. For if, as I am suggesting, Shakespeare locates the source of these desires at the boundary of court ceremony, in a public audience's voyeuristic impulse to share in the proceedings by borrowing (or taking home) pieces of the event to fit into their daydreams, he points out how such borrowing violates unities of time and place, yielding a train of imaginative associations that might pluck a character from here, insert him there, imagine him now as a fantastical personage, now as the actor who embodies that personage. On one level, then, *Merry Wives* portrays the construction of a piecemeal popular mythology, as such a mythology might be experienced by a playgoing public. On another level, the play draws a parallel between this activity and that in which the actors putting on *Merry Wives* are engaged, that is, participating in the construction of a national mythology that, in its own way, inserts contemporary personages into archaic backdrops, squeezes its official meanings into the symbology of a popular legend like the Garter story, and, in sum, pilfers as much from what lies at its periphery as, in turn, it is plucked and borrowed from. Even as I talk about the transactions that pass between these two sectors—the court and the popular stage—it is important to remember that Shakespeare's theater lies in the middle, mediating the commerce. This is because Shakespeare's company had been putting on a version of English history all along (from the Henry VI plays forward) that, in the very portable figure of Falstaff, could be recalled economically to court and public audiences alike without importing the whole history play apparatus. This is where Shakespeare's play most suggestively presses at the boundaries of St. George's Day, taking the work (like Emilia in *Othello*) "out" of the Queen's embroidered Garter, and stitching the inscription "Honi soit . . ." back into the moral universe of *1 & 2 Henry IV*.

III

A set of poetic associations travels via Falstaff between the world of Windsor and Shakespeare's history plays. Taken together, these associations imagine a fantastical relationship among kingship, theatricality, and lecherous desire. The relationship depends, in turn, on the doubleness that the history cycle invests, beginning with *Richard II,* in kingship and the crown. Commanding the onstage audience to watch as he uncrowns himself—"With mine own tongue deny my sacred state,/ With mine own breath release all duteous oaths" (4.1.209-10)—Richard strips his earthly body of the arcane mantle of the "body politic."[25] This "pompous body," however, belongs to a fiction that Richard himself scarcely believes, having learned already that "a little pin" can collapse that body's claim to inviolability. To defend against this knowledge, the circlet of rule, like the Garter itself, admits neither mortality nor its consort, shame, as intrinsic properties, but, rather, refers them endlessly back into an arena of exchange.

The crown, as Richard composes the sign, contains a mute message of inner purgatory, which it is the wearer's burden to articulate *for* his audience.[26] Thus when Hal is caught at his father's deathbed, in premature possession of the crown, his defense takes the form of a dialogue with the object:

> Thinking you dead,
> And dead almost, my liege, to think you were,
> I spake unto this crown as having sense,
> And thus upbraided it: "The care on thee depending
> Hath fed upon the body of my father;
> Therefore thou best of gold art worst of gold.
> Other, less fine in carat, is more precious,
> Preserving life in med'cine potable;
> But thou, most fine, most honour'd, most renown'd,
> Hath eat thy bearer up."
> (*2 Henry IV,* 4.5.155-64)

The speech recalls its counterpoint in *1 Henry IV* when Hal, playing his father in the Boar's Head Tavern scene, describes Falstaff as a disease that "feeds" on the kingdom, and scolds the prince for consorting with him.

> Why dost thou converse with that trunk of humours, that bolting-hutch of beastliness, that swollen parcel of dropsies, that huge bombard of sack, that stuffed cloak-bag of guts, that roasted Manningtree ox with the pudding in his belly, that reverend vice, that grey iniquity, that father ruffian, that vanity in years?
> (*1 Henry IV,* 2.4.442-49)

Hal's emphasis on "old" Falstaff, parading at life's outer limits, highlights Falstaff's resemblance to Henry IV. The improvisation of king unbraiding son, "across" Falstaff, turns into a glimpse of son berating father for the father's iniquities: for Richard's murder ("reverend vice") and for Bolingbroke's unlawful seizure of the crown ("father ruffian, . . . vanity in years"). Falstaff's lifeline is consequently stretched to compass son *and* father, setting the "old bag" up to inherit the legacy of shame, which properly belongs to Bolingbroke and to Bolingbroke's line. Describing the kingdom over which Falstaff is to "monarchize," Hal says, "Thy state is taken for a joint-stool, thy golden sceptre for a leaden dagger, and thy precious rich crown for a pitiful bald crown" (2.4.375-77). Falstaff is thus placed in the confines of the morality play that Richard II originally attached to the crown ("and there the antic sits, / Scoffing [the king's] state and grinning at his pomp, / Allowing him a breath, a little scene, / To monarchize, be fear'd, and kill with looks" [*Richard II,* 3.2.162-65]). But through the manipulation of kingly pretensions into Falstaff, Hal transfers the potentiality of the crown symbol—the crown shape even—into the formal compass of Falstaff's body, which, on the logic of both crown and garter, reads the audience's shameful desire back to itself.[27]

By risking the volatile circuiting of his desire through a fantasy of Falstaff, Master Ford finds himself spoken through by patterns of situation and speech belonging to this associative maze. When John and Robert, for instance, drag the buck-basket across his path, Ford responds to it as having a magical relevance. As if both he and the buck-basket were part of the Falstaff legend, Ford fixes compulsively on the word "buck," saying it over and over until it seems that his vocal cords themselves have stuck in a place from which accumulated shame cries out.

> FORD: How now? Whither bear you this?
> JOHN: To the laundress, forsooth.
> MRS FORD: Why, what have you to do whither they bear it? You were best meddle with buck-washing!
> FORD: Buck? I would I could wash myself of the buck! Buck, buck, buck! Ay, buck; I warrant you, buck; and of the season too, it shall appear.
> (3.3.140-47)

Reading this scene *through* the Garter motto ("Honi soit qui mal y pense"), I find that the "y" (or shameful things) marks the snare into which Ford unwittingly steps. By paying a fantastical Falstaff to make love to his wife, Ford aims both to buck and be bucked, unaware of the power of the word "buck" to raise Falstaff, not only as he will appear in the denouement of *Merry Wives*, crowned with horns, but also, in new and invigorated form, from the death he feigned in the final act of *1 Henry IV*.

Going back to the scene at Shrewsbury Field, we find Hal, standing over Falstaff's body, comparing it to Percy's, in an elegy that begins the process of punning conversion:

> Poor Jack, farewell! . . .
> Death hath not struck so fat a *deer* today,
> Though many *dearer,* in this bloody fray.
> Embowell'd will I see thee by and by,
> Till then in blood by noble Percy lie.
> (*1 Henry IV,* 5.4.102-9, my emphasis)

The speech implies that a dead Falstaff is both "deer" and "dearer" than a living one. The prince has, in fact, been looking forward to this conversion since 2.4:

> PRINCE (to Peto): We must all to the wars. . . . I'll procure this fat rogue a charge of foot, and I know his death will be a march of twelve score.
> (2.4.537-40)

> PRINCE (to Falstaff): Say thy prayers, and farewell. . . . thou owest God a death.
> (5.1.124-26)

> PRINCE (to Falstaff): [Percy is sure] indeed, and living to kill thee.
> (5.3.49)

A dead Falstaff can be more easily disembowelled and made hollow; at the same time, he can be removed from the stage and left to settle into public memory and imagination. In both capacities, Hal would use him as a repository for the disrepute of his own past, a strategy revealed at Shrewsbury, where just as the prince intends to absorb the breadth and range of Percy's honors

> I shall make this northern youth exchange
> His glorious deeds for my indignities.
> Percy is but my factor, good my lord,
> To engross up glorious deeds on my behalf.
> (3.2.145-48)

he also means to embowel and bury the sum of his indignities in Falstaff. The double name (deer/dear) fulfills a certain promise: although it does not conclusively kill Falstaff, it becomes an emblem—like the garter and its motto—of mortal flesh shot through with shame.

This emblem also tinges the tavern escapades of *2 Henry IV*. Mingling with the play's erotic Falstaff, it helps explain the mixed signals that emanate from a more mature version of Sir John, whose "day's service at Shrewsbury" has caused him to be decorated with a figurative death's head, an obliquely visible *memento mori* reflected in Doll Tearsheet's words at 2.4:

> DOLL: Thou whoreson little tidy Bartholomew boar-pig, when wilt thou leave fighting a-days, and foining a-nights, and begin to patch up thine old body for heaven?
>
> FALSTAFF: Peace, good Doll, do not speak like a death's head, do not bid me remember mine end.
> (2.4.227-32)

But Doll's grisly endearments are mixed with kisses that come from "a most constant *heart*" (267, my emphasis), and as Falstaff leaves a second time for the wars, she says, "I cannot speak; if my *heart* be not ready to burst" (376, my emphasis). By evoking Falstaff's "dear-ness" in terms of "heart," she generates a different pun, "hart/heart," which signals the capacity of *2 Henry IV* to absorb the indignities of "deer/dear" (as if steering intentionally clear of it) and to push its morbid flavor around until Falstaff is reestablished in his hart-like prime. In the tavern ambience, the nostalgia of "twenty-nine years, come peascod-time" sweetens the eroticism and makes the approach of death ("Come it grows late. . . . Thou't forget me when I am gone" [273-74]), like so many other moments in the play, into an occasion for reminiscence. The Hostess's parting words, "but an honester and truer-*hearted* man" (380-81, my emphasis), replace Falstaff with a name that restores him to the relatively shameless youth of the Eastcheap community. In its likeness to a death token, the "deer's head" becomes an aural alternative to Shakespeare's visual pun on Richard II's crown: "For within the hollow crown / That rounds the mortal temples of a king / Keeps Death his court" (3.2.160-62). That the crown is no more than a circlet to shame any mortal's aspiration "to monarchize" is a message that Richard has embedded already in the shape of the object, making it into a constrictive band and perpetual reminder to Bolingbroke of his kingly—not to mention usurper's—vanity. In Bolingbroke's seizure of Richard's crown, there is a taint of political cuckoldry—a whiff of illegitimate ascension—that plays out the morphological pun, elaborated above, connecting crowns and garters across the plays.

This is to say that when Ford reads his fantasy of cuckoldry (couched in the popular imagery of horns) into Falstaff, he figuratively assumes the antlers of Falstaff's emblematic shame. In other words, Ford's fantasy of local scandal is consumed in a mire of national shame, a kingly purgatory obliquely embedded, through the vehicle of Falstaff, in the Garter Day/ Windsor imagery of sexual appetite and violation. Not only does Ford become the object of his own ridicule ("'Tis my fault, Master Page, I suffer for it" [202]) and

Page's mockery ("Let's go in gentlemen—[aside] but, trust me, we'll mock him" [212-13]) but, charged with an "excess" of shame, he becomes "crowned" with the pinching, burning phantoms of Shakespeare's English histories. Put in the form of a more general thesis, Shakespeare's plays are constructed to remember each other: by incorporating parts of one another—fragments, echoes, or maturations of poetic imagery—individual plays in the canon spur a recollective process shared by the audience. In *Merry Wives,* the playwright sets forth the hypothesis, what if a sector of that audience, raised on his history plays, borrowed one of the more memorable characters and wrote that character into a chapter of its own local history, or, better yet, into a fantasy of scandal and intrigue on the local level? Could the local drama defend itself from incorporating, or rather being incorporated by, the "background" system of associations structuring the national history? If not, at what point would the local drama begin to remember, or be remembered by, the other history? Shakespeare's answer seems to be that the usurpation—or consumption—of one history by the other happens at the level of poetic image or device: where sixteenth-century knights strap on fourteenth-century garters, and citizens in a fantastical Windsor are cuckolded by characters from history; where Edwards turn into Elizabeths, and deer are resurrected as bucks; where time, in short, ceases to unfold linear plots, but moves, as images in language do, through metaphoric declension, or what Roland Barthes has called "flexional forms."[28]

What interests me is how the product created by Shakespeare's hypothesis, the play put on, differs from the artifacts or souvenirs generated by and around the official Garter Day ceremony, whose surfaces are made to deflect the gaze of onlookers. For one thing, the fluid connection running from *Merry Wives* back to Shakespeare's history plays travels by way of the punning name, a signifying sound that catches in the ear or throat, fixing identity only momentarily, and then at the place where imaginative worlds aurally overlap. Shakespeare's icons—if word pairs like dear/deer, heart/hart, buck/bucked can be thought of as constituting an aural iconography[29]—dissolve into the dramatic characters whom, like coats of arms, they name, tinging how those characters act on an audience's desire, and determining how, when members of the audience take them home, those characters will reshape private fantasy or local legend. To enter a role, even mentally—as Ford imagines himself to act through Falstaff's lust—involves entering an interiority that, like the circlet of the garter, instantly inverts itself, becoming a condition that compasses the actor, determining him from an external point of view as a name might. "Putting on" Falstaff, then, as opposed to "putting on" the Queen's garter, involves an act of playing *for* an audience, that is, obliging as well as putting off or shaming its desire.

In the final scene of *Merry Wives*, the men and women of Windsor commune to cast out what Falstaff, not to mention his host of iconic nicknames, officially stands for. To this end, they "put Falstaff together again," this time out of found materials—a chain, a pair of horns, a host of fairies—seeking to transform Prince Hal's deer into an effigy of Herne (half man, half deer; a hybrid of hunter and quarry), the closest that folk tradition comes to approximating Hal's intimately imagined rogue. The final act of *Merry Wives* is not unlike a rite of exorcism that tries to draw the spirit of Falstaff out of its historical dispersion into concrete form. What is compelling about this final ceremony, though, is its resemblance to a court masque, or rather how, built into a play of comic urges, it "slurs" over courtly conventions and almost instantly pulls the expurgated figure back into its circle:

> PAGE: Yet be cheerful, knight. Thou shalt eat a posset to-night at my house, where I will desire thee to laugh at my wife, that now laughs at thee. Tell her Master Slender hath married her daughter.
>
> (5.5.171-74)

By this time, Page has forgotten Falstaff's crimes, giddy in an oblique plot to "punish" his wife by marrying their daughter off, against Mistress Page's wishes, to Slender, who has his directions that Anne Page "shall be [at the masque] in white" (4.6.34). Mistress Page is equally preoccupied with taking revenge on her husband, by marrying their daughter to Caius, who, in turn, believes that Anne "in green . . . shall be . . . enrob'd" (4.6.40). In the course of the masque, Slender trips away with a boy-actor dressed in white, Caius with a boy in green, while Fenton takes Anne, dressed in neither white nor green, and marries her against the will of either parent. Like Master Ford's arrival, erupting with corporeal vigor into the frame of Mistress Ford's plot, the physical presence of the boy-actors, planted as decoys, provides the extra joke in the finale. They shame the expectation of male lust, or, rather, fill its imaginative gap by showing that a boy-actor's body always fleshes out the robes of the female stage character. Insides are once again turned out, in the form of a leftover laugh. Likewise, Dame Quickly's folk ceremony, which claims, through the vehicle of emblematic, floral script to "write out" the characters of the Garter motto:

> Meadow fairies, look you sing,
> Like to the Garter's compass, in a ring . . .
> And *"Honi soit qui mal y pense"* write
> In em'rald tuffs, flow'rs purple, blue, and white,
> Like sapphire, pearl, and rich embroidery,
> Buckled below fair knighthood's bending knee:
> Fairies use flow'rs for their charactery.
>
> (5.5.66-74)

Thus embodied, the motto is swallowed up in a turmoil of actors in petally costumes, dissolving altogether when, at the sound of the deer horn, the dancers disperse, leaving "nothing" inscribed on the empty stage. Like the body of Richard's king undecked, the pompous body of court ceremony fades into a blank surface, making the platform itself into a *memento mori* of the court holiday.

IV

The 1602 Quarto of *Merry Wives* states that the play was acted "'divers times,' both for the Queen 'and elsewhere.'"[30] A public performance would have served as a metatheatrical realization of the relationship implied within the play, of courtiers arriving to attend a Garter ceremony (and by extension the production of *Merry Wives* embedded in that ceremony) as well as the citizens at the periphery, assembling, in their turn, to watch the arrival of the court, and later, the grand procession of the Queen and her Order. In other words, the popular audience received the play itself as a thing produced for the court and, accordingly, went to the theater to see what the court *saw*. This factor introduces another extradramatic dimension into the performance history of *Merry Wives,* in which a popular audience played at being in attendance at an official, court production. The production would have come "smelling so sweetly" from the private hall, carrying the scent of "musk" into the public playhouse. What the public audience shared was the material experience of a production, whose elements—actors, situations, routines—crossed palpably from one performance setting to another. The point was not to reenact the significance of embodied gestures to English history, but to facilitate the appropriation of these embodiments by a public audience.

Notes

I owe my thanks to Paul Alpers, Joel Altman, Daniel Baird, Ben Avner Hecht, and Louis Suarez-Potts among the friends and mentors who have helped this essay evolve into its present form.

[1] For a recent argument retracing the commission of *Merry Wives* for the occasion of the Garter Feast, see David Wiles, *Shakespeare's Almanac* (Cambridge, 1993), 19-27. Taken as a whole, the book responds in a comprehensive way to what Wiles terms the "occasionalist" controversy.

[2] T.W. Craik outlines the dating argument in his introduction to *The Merry Wives of Windsor* (New York, 1989), 1-13; Edmond Malone (1790) inferred a connection to the Garter ceremony from Dame Quickly's order to the fairies (5.5.60) to scour "the several chairs of order" in preparation for the Installation at Windsor Castle; Leslie Hotson (1931) set the date of performance at 23 April 1597, on evidence that rumors were circulating in Elizabeth's court as early as February 1597 that George Carey, patron of the Lord Chamberlain's Men, would be elected to the Order of the Garter, leaving sufficient time for Carey to commission a play to be performed on St. George's Day "as his special contribution to the festivities"; ibid., 3.

[3] Cited from Nicholas Rowe's edition of *Merry Wives* (1709) by Craik, in ibid., 4-5.

[4] Ibid., 13; Craik says that the ascription travels from John Dennis back to John Dryden "who may have got it from Davenant." Ibid., 5; that the Queen would wish to see Falstaff "in love" (4-5) is consistent with the legend's assertion that she had already seen *2 Henry IV,* the play that most fully realizes Falstaff's erotic character. It is equally possible—if, as critics like H. J. Oliver propose, Shakespeare wrote *2 Henry IV* in the following year (1598)—that the legend developed retrospectively after this secondary incarnation had fully entered the social imagination of theatergoers.

[5] Roy Strong, *The Cult of Elizabeth: Elizabethan Portraiture and Pageantry* (London, 1977), 179.

[6] Ibid.

[7] Ibid.

[8] For an account of the imagery through which Elizabeth managed the transmission of her identity as "king and queen both," see Leah S. Marcus, *Puzzling Shakespeare* (Berkeley, 1988), 53-66.

[9] George Carey, whose election to the Garter provided the occasion for the play, had only the previous year succeeded his father as patron of the Lord Chamberlain's Men. Falstaff's transgression raises questions about the proper boundaries of patronage in general; his negative example might be construed as giving merry warning to the company's new patron, counsel rendered safely comic by the enormity of Falstaff's improprieties. The treatment Falstaff receives at the hands of Mistress Ford and Mistress Page inverts the Installation rite (which would take place the following month on 24 May) by calling to mind its antithesis: "the degradation ceremony in which an expelled Knight's heraldic achievements were thrown down from his stall in Saint George's Chapel and kicked into the castle ditch"; Craik, *Merry Wives*, 28; Strong, *Cult of Elizabeth,* 174. Falstaff fears that he will be mocked if news of his humiliation gets back "to the ear of the court" (4.5.89).

[10] Leah Marcus relates the story of a Catholic conspirator whose intention to assassinate the Queen was by his own report "appalled and perplexed" when he be-

held in her female form "the very likeness and image of King Henry the Seventh"; *Puzzling Shakespeare,* 58. The supernatural shield of the Queen's bi-fold gender could, on the one hand, act like the garter to deflect aggressive desire, or, on the other, inspire perverse fantasies of violation. In "Shaping Fantasies: Figurations of Gender and Power in Elizabethan Culture, *Representations* 2 (1983): 61-94, Louis Montrose points to a diary entry (written 23 January 1597) in which Simon Forman relates a dream in which he is walking with Elizabeth "through lanes and closes," carrying the train of her dress. "I told her she should do me a favor to let me wait on her, and she said I should. Then said I, `I mean to wait *upon* you and not under you, that I might make this belly a little bigger to carry up this smock and coats out of the dirt'"; A. L. Rowse, *The Case Books of Simon Forman* (London, 1974), 62-63. In this "familiar" (in the liberty-taking sense) dream of impregnating the Queen, we find a fantasy of violation couched in what would have passed more innocently as a national fantasy of the Queen producing an heir.

[11] Strong, *Cult of Elizabeth,* 164-65.

[12] Ibid., 185.

[13] Ibid., 164.

[14] Ibid., 165-67.

[15] Ibid., 185.

[16] Ibid., 167-68.

[17] Stephen Greenblatt, *Renaissance Self-Fashioning* (Chicago, 1980), 224.

[18] Strong, *Cult of Elizabeth,* 165.

[19] According to Craik, the Installation, at which only the newly elected knights were required to be present, continued to be conducted at Windsor by three commissioners specially appointed by the Queen; Craik, *Merry Wives,* 4.

[20] Strong, *Cult of Elizabeth,* 168, my emphasis.

[21] Ibid., 172.

[22] Craik notes Shakespeare's topical allusion to Frederick, Duke of Wurttemberg, who, although elected to the Order in 1597, failed to attend the proceedings; Craik, *Merry Wives*, 5-6. Caius says to the Host, "it is tell-a me dat you make grand preparation for a duke de Jarmany. By my trot', dere is no duke that the court is know to come" (4.5.80-81). All citations to Shakespeare texts are from the *Arden Shakespeare,* ed. Richard Proudfoot (New York).

[23] My argument returns to the question of whether Falstaff's erotic identity was fixed in the social imagination prior to or following his appearance in *Merry Wives*. Ford's fantasy indicates, in any case, that Shakespeare was interested (as fait accompli or future possibility) in what it would mean for a reputation of sexual conquest to attach itself to the Falstaff character. To determine Will Kemp's "sex appeal," we can look to *Nine Daies Wonder* (1600) in which the clown, in giving an account of his (in)famous dance from London to Norwich, testifies to having a magnetic pull on "corpulent" women. Having defeated "a lusty tall fellow" in dance, Kemp wins the admiration of a "lusty Country lasse" who says she will dance a mile at his side. "The Drum strucke, forward marcht I with my merry Maydemarian: who shooke her fat sides: and footed it merrily to Melfoord"; G.B. Harrison, ed., *Nine Daies Wonder* (Edinburgh, 1966), 14. Whether Kemp's claim to "prowess" grows out of his morris dancing or out of his connection to the Falstaff role, his erotic powers are clearly an essential (if self-mocking) part of his professional persona.

[24] Michel de Certeau, *The Practice of Everyday Life,* trans. Steve Rendall (Berkeley, 1984), 31. While de Certeau's remark is grounded in the metaphors of a twentieth-century consumer culture (and in particular of the television screen "grids" by which images reach into and mingle with the daydreams of contemporary consumers), the question he raises about "imaginative consumership," in other words, the active role played by audience imagination in transforming commercial products, has informed my reading of Shakespeare's Ford. De Certeau places a unique emphasis on consumer *production* ("Once the images broadcast by television and the time spent in front of the TV set have been analyzed, it remains to be asked what the consumer *makes* of these images and during these hours"; ibid., (31)] and does not let the fact that such production seldom leaves a concrete trace dissuade him from thinking through its implications. Even if the common Elizabethan "consumer" did not leave a record of what he (or less frequently she) "made" with material "gotten" from plays, the period offers proof that playhouse celebrities enjoyed, in literary representation at least, an afterlife in their public's dreams. In *Tarltons Newes Out of Purgatorie,* published anonymously in London in 1590, the narrator identifies himself as an avid fan of Richard Tarlton (the clown whose popularity reached "national" levels in the 1580s). After Tarlton's death, the narrator enters a period of mourning, marked by abstinence from playgoing, after which Tarlton visits him in a dream and takes him on a tour of Purgatory. See Jane Belfield and Geoffrey Creigh, eds., *Tarlton's Newes Out of Purgatorie* (Leiden, 1987), 144-85. The pamphlet collapses two types of consumership (going to plays and reading Boccaccio) together, providing an interesting example of the tendency of consumer production to override genre's boundaries.

[25] "The fiction of the oneness of the double body breaks apart. Godhead and manhood . . . both clearly outlined with a few strokes, stand in contrast to each other." For Ernst Kantorowicz's reading of *Richard II,* see *The King's Two Bodies* (Princeton, 1957), 24-41.

[26] For another reading of Richard II's manipulation of the crown image, see Harry Berger Jr., *Imaginary Audition: Shakespeare on Stage and Page* (Berkeley, 1989), 47-48: "[Richard seems] intent on the interpretative tease value of the image, which he manipulates with the same coyness as the crown [itself]" (48).

[27] Remember that the sign bars access to the interior of the person who wears it. By buckling on the garter, the knight announces his virtue to onlookers while shaming their suspicion of unchaste designs in him.

[28] Roland Barthes, "La métaphore de l'oeil," *Critique* (August-September 1963): 770-77.

[29] For a related discussion of the role of aurality in Shakespeare's *written* text, see Joel Fineman, "Shakespeare's Ear," *Representations* 28 (1989): 6-13. Pointing out the "exceptionally pornographic [and vulva-like] ear" embroidered on Elizabeth's robes in the "Rainbow Portrait" (c. 1600), Fineman notes that it falls "over Queen Elizabeth's genitals, in the crease formed where the two folds of her dress fold over on each other" (10). Fineman goes on to say that there are reasons to link the "bifold" erotics of the ear (as icon) "with a specific and historically determinate Renaissance sense of textuality" (11).

[30] Craik, *Merry Wives,* 53.

Source: "*The Merry Wives of Windsor:* Sharing the Queen's Holiday," in *Representations,* Vol. 51, Summer, 1995, pp. 77-93.

(Dis)embodied Letters and *The Merchant of Venice*

Howard Marchitello, ***Texas A & M University***

> The concept of the historical progress of mankind cannot be sundered from the concept of its progression through a homogeneous, empty time. A critique of the concept of such a progression must be the basis of any criticism of the concept of progress itself.
>
> —Walter Benjamin, "Theses on the Philosophy of History"

In recent years the practices and ideologies of modern textual criticism have come under significant review and critique. Our understanding of the linguistic instability of texts, informed by post-structuralism, together with recent re-theorizations of modern subjectivity, have produced a concern for the material or, more to the point, the *textual* nature of culture and its productions—what Jerome McGann recently has called "the textual condition."[1] The practices of this new textual criticism have been theorized in McGann's project, begun with *Romantic Ideology* (1983) and continued in *A Critique of Modern Textual Criticism* (1983) and *The Textual Condition* (1991), which is in part intended to heal "the schism between textual and interpretive studies, opened so long ago."[2] McGann's call for a reimagining of the bibliographical study of texts is predicated upon the identification of texts as "fundamentally social rather than personal."[3] This identification retrieves texts from both the misguided essentialist (and humanist) fiction of the wholly autonomous author and the related discourse of intentionality that are thought to determine the production of texts outside or beyond both culture and history.

The field of Renaissance studies has proven to be fertile ground for such inquiry. In particular, revisionist work on Shakespearean texts offers us powerful ways to theorize the question, "What is a text?" (even before we can begin to formulate answers to it); new ways of understanding the multiple, often divergent and yet nevertheless equally authentic texts we do have; fresh insights into the materiality of texts and textual production (printing house practices, for instance); and increasingly thorough and sophisticated accounts of early modern conceptions of publishing, collaboration, and the complex issues of authorship.[4] These newly articulated critical and theoretical interests and inquiries have served to redefine the nature of textual criticism. This practice of "unediting," as Randall McLeod and Leah Marcus have called it, has produced a long list of recovered texts—texts (quartos, copies) that traditional textual theory and criticism have consistently dismissed as "bad," "corrupt," or otherwise inferior to their own texts: the two versions of *King Lear,* or the equally valid versions of the much-disputed *Doctor Faustus,* to name two prominent examples.[5]

My use here of the terms "produced" and "recovered" is somewhat ironical: it has been the object of traditional textual criticism to produce authoritative texts in the absence of authorial script, which is itself imagined as recoverable because final authorial intention resides in the extant texts, even if it becomes visible (present) only in reconstructed texts, or, more frequently, in texts that are more or less hypothetical. "Unediting" *produces* no new texts, and can even be said to resist the entire notion of such production. Rather, "unediting" insists upon the integrity of textual productions without recourse to claims for the authorial status of these texts, and therein cannot be said either to produce or to recover texts—at least not in the conventional senses of these terms as they come to us through traditional textual criticism.

In discussing the composite nature of the two versions of *Doctor Faustus,* Leah Marcus argues that while both can claim aesthetic integrity on their own perhaps divergent terms, neither can claim a greater proximity to "the absent authorial presence we call Marlowe":

> It is time to step back from the fantasy of recovering Marlowe as the mighty, controlling source of textual production and consider other elements of the process, particularly ideological elements that the editorial tradition has, by the very nature of its enterprise, suppressed. I would like to second [Michael] Warren's call for a separation of the two texts of *Doctor Faustus,* but carry his argument further by contending that for *Faustus,* and for Renaissance drama more generally, a key element of textual indeterminacy is ideological difference.[6]

Marcus argues that "we can learn something about the vagaries of Renaissance authorship and mark out new areas for interpretation if we wean ourselves from the ingrained habit of regarding textual 'accidentals' as insignificant,"[7] and asks us to reconsider "accidentals"—such as the A text's "Wertenberg" and the B text's "Wittenberg"; A's empty stage at the play's end and B's stage littered with the fragments of Faustus's body—as significant in establishing markedly "different configurations of religious experience" in the two plays.[8] "Accidentals" such as those reflecting divergent religious experience are in fact substantial and consequential elements of both plays, attributable to revisions—Marlovian or post-Marlovian—of the play in history.[9]

As has been suggested above, the case for reconsidering our editorial determinations concerning texts and their relative authority has gone a long way in helping create the very possibility of this argument: in our relationship to texts we are no longer so strictly bound to the desire to recover—or, for that matter, the very faith in—the lost original. Indeed, as post-structuralist theory has taught us, the idea of the original is not only misleading, but wholly illusory; "we have no originals," Jonathan Goldberg reminds us, "only copies."[10]

Marcus's discussion of "accidentals" allows us access to nonauthorial elements that survive in or help to determine play-texts—evidence, as it were, for textual (and bibliographical) traces of nonauthorial agency. At the same time, however, Marcus's argument—while perhaps controversial in its revisionist claims for the two texts of *Faustus*—is nevertheless dedicated to the discussion of agency within texts, whether that agency is authorial or non-authorial, and as such offers only a restricted critique of textual criticism and traditional practices of editing. This is analogous to what Jonathan Goldberg has identified as "the combination of textual audacity and critical conservatism" to be found even in as bold an intervention in Shakespearean studies as *The Division of the Kingdoms:*

> There are two *King Lears,* we are told, but we are assured that the Quarto derives from Shakespeare's manuscript and that the Folio represents an authoritative revision. The kingdom has been divided, but Shakespeare reigns supreme, author now of two sovereign texts.[11]

As audacious as it is, Marcus's argument—perhaps like that of *The Division of the Kingdoms*—returns in the end to texts as instantiations of agency. I would like to extend the radical critique of traditional textual criticism and the traditional practices of text-editing implicit in the project of "unediting" by suggesting that while texts have historically been understood as instruments of agentiality *par excellence,* they nevertheless embody traces of nonagential writing. Goldberg argues that the "Shakespearean text is a historical phenomenon, produced by ongoing restructurations, revisions, and collaboration; by interventions that are editorial, scribal, theatrical; by conditions that are material, occasional, accidental."[12] New textual theory and practice, such as Marcus's, have indeed revised our notions of these material and occasional conditions. Following Goldberg's extension of the radical instability of the text to include "the typographical character" that stands as "one further sign—literally, a reminder of the compositor—that points to the composite nature of every Shakespearean text," however, and his explicit call ("since it is all that we have") for a "return to the letter," I propose to focus here on the accidental conditions of Shakespearean textuality, and to suggest that there are ways in which we can understand these significant traces of non-agency, these "accidentals" that are precisely *accidental.*[13] To argue for the value of true textual accidents (misspelled words, evident compositor's errors, textual obscurities or incoherences) and their availability to critical inquiry is to offer a fundamental revision of the philosophical underpinnings of traditional textual criticism that is founded upon the suspect epistemology of presence, and as such constitutes an elaborate discourse of causality: a complex set of theories and practices dedicated to the description and reconstitution of texts.[14] Traditional textual criticism, then, is nothing less than a form of historiography, fundamentally conservative in nature and essentially narrative in form, dedicated to the preservation of presence and historical continuity, and in which the text is construed as the site where historical progress is believed to be materially evident.

In his *Critique,* McGann discusses this notion of the text in history, especially as it is reflected in the ideas of the copy-text and the critical edition produced through the practice (I will want to say the historical practice) of collation, and the critical apparatus that "displays the 'history' of the text."[15] These practices, it is important to note, are both produced within an entirely historical epistemological framework and at the same time are intended to reproduce the text in its historical development. And yet, the effect of the critical text that has so thoroughly given itself over to the historical reconstruction of a hypostatized originary presence, is to evade history, to posit its own existence as transcendental, beyond temporality and outside history: "The critical edition embodies a practical goal which can be (within limits) accomplished, but it equally embodies an illusion about its own historicity (or lack thereof)."[16]

McGann finds the terms of this understanding problematical, especially as the long history of modern textual criticism is predicated upon the notion of development or progress:

> This view of scholarship and program of general education are based upon a paradigm which sees all human products in processive and diachronic terms. The paradigm has controlled the work of textual criticism from its inception, and it operates to this day.[17]

Like McGann, I want to return the text more fully to history. But unlike McGann, however, I do not understand history to be fully meaningful, or wholly caused. My desire is to renounce the Hegelian philosophy of history that determines historicism in the model of traditional bibliographical or textual studies. Textual study has always been informed by an implicit philosophy of history, even when it claimed to be managing a wholly positivistic set of operations and maneuvers. One of the explicit premises of this study is that the textual criticism it advocates is thoroughly historical and resolutely non-Hegelian. I will not argue that any current embodiment of a particular text represents the culmination of its teleological evolution, but rather that the text can be said to exist only within history so long as it (the text, our relationship to the text, history itself) is not merely inserted in a narrative that presupposes a paradigm of progress. I hope by this to extricate the following discussion of texts and textual embodiment from the appropriative claims of traditional textual criticism that imagines the text as existing *for us;* I want to argue, instead, that texts—like history—exist in spite of us.

In the first part of the essay I turn to *The Merchant of Venice* and its narratives of reading and writing—the first of a series of such narratives that extends from Shakespeare to the practitioners of traditional textual criticism. These narratives are predicated upon an implicit science of presence-in-writing and are, moreover, conceived as progressive and wholly inscribed within the world of essential agency. The metaphysical notions of writing, editing and textuality that authorize modern editorial practices indeed underlie *Merchant,* a play in which presence (body) is imagined as immanent in the letter. But the actual text (or texts) of *Merchant* and recent critiques of the practices of textual criticism belie these assumptions. Scenes of reading and writing, as Goldberg argues,

> do not allegorize a notion of the text itself. Rather, they point to a textuality that is radically unstable, upon which plots move, characters are (de)formed, language and observation is (improperly) staged. They point, that is, to historical and cultural demarcations, to what passes for essences, desires, knowledge, and the like.[18]

Presence-in-writing is always merely the dream of writing (even if an enabling dream), and texts do not finally exist in an entirely deterministic universe void of accidents; accidents abound, and they are meaningful precisely because they are uncaused. Accidents are signs forever detached from any system of signification, but the meaning of accidents is specific and absolute: accidents "mean" the absence of meaning. But this is an argument against which *Merchant* offers its considerable resistance.

The particular textual accident I will discuss in the essay's second part is the problem involving the characters Solanio, Salerio and Salarino, and the editorial decision (suggested by John Dover Wilson in the 1926 Cambridge edition and adopted almost universally by subsequent editors) to consider the name "Salarino" as simply an error, a textual mistake that should be replaced by "Salerio." Wilson's evidence supporting his emendation, however, is problematical, especially as it is generated by the idea of a unitary and authoritative text that depends upon a science of presence that produces both the notion of the authorial text and the unmistakable anxiety manifest in certain readers occasioned by its apparent aberrations and incoherences. Wilson's decision to eliminate Salarino offers a striking instance of a wilful intervention of nonauthorial agency into the Shakespearean text (however we construe that term) precisely at a moment in which the text marks an instance of nonagentiality.

The essay concludes with a discussion of the matter of textual accidents and the imperative evident in traditional textual criticism to over-write them. It is against these practices (of textual criticism and of a certain historicism) that a theory of radical unediting must stand.

I

A letter from Antonio is brought to Bassanio. In this letter, writing is understood as both an act of inscription and as an act of incision, as an act of construction and of destruction, as a hopeful act of preservation and at the same time as an act of absolute violence:

> Sweet Bassanio, my ships have all miscarried, my creditors grow cruel, my estate is very low, my bond to the Jew is forfeit, and (since in paying it, it is impossible I should live), all debts are clear'd between you and I, if I might but see you at my death: notwithstanding, use your pleasure,—if your love do not persuade you to come, let not my letter.[19]

Here is the hope for presence-in-writing, the hope for the body made immanent in the letter. And yet, at the same time—and as Bassanio understands—this is the letter that kills:

> Here is a letter lady,
> The paper as the body of my friend,
> And every word in it a gaping wound
> Issuing life-blood.
>
> (3.2.262-65)

Writing's dream of presence always inscribes its double: erasure. Commenting on the verse line, "Your penknife as stay in left hand let rest," that prefaces *A Booke Containing Divers Sortes of Hands,* Jonathan Goldberg discusses this double-nature of writing:

> "Stay" suggests that the knife is the support of writing (it keeps the place, marks the line, sharpens the quill, smooths the paper: there can be no act of writing without the knife); but "stay" also suggests that the knife impedes the quill (erasure lies within its domain). As Derrida has argued, what is true of the knife is true of the quill: these are the writer's weapons for a scene in which the production of script also effaces such production to produce the writer's hand—to produce the illusory presence of

> writing. "Stay" re-marks the double structure of the mark, and the scriptive domain that (dis)locates the writer.[20]

Antonio is similarly (dis)located by the letter he has sent to Bassanio. In the letter he identifies his imminent death as embodied in the bond to Shylock; he also both proclaims and rejects Bassanio's debt to him, and uses the letter to request, indeed virtually to command, Bassanio's presence, even as he rejects the notion of such efficacy in a mere "letter": "if your love do not persuade you to come, let not my letter." This is precisely Antonio's predicament in his forfeited bond (the letter) that situates him even as it guarantees his erasure: he stands, as he says, prepared to die.

This assertion—that Antonio's letter manifests both the desire for and the impossibility of presence-in-writing—is also clear on a material level in the Hayes Quarto. Dover Wilson recognized that the letters and scrolls in *Merchant* are "bibliographically speaking, textually distinct" from the rest of the play-text.[21] While I disagree with Wilson's argument that such distinctness serves to identify the letters as either scribal or playhouse additions, their bibliographical distinctness does stand as a material manifestation of the impossibility of the dream of presence-in-writing: these texts that seek to embody or to locate characters are themselves radically disembodied and dislocated from the surface of the play-text. Antonio's letter (which we can now see was mis-quoted above) actually appears in the 1600 Quarto thus:

> [*Por.*] But let me heare the letter of your friend.
> *Sweet* Bassanio, *my ships have all miscarried, my Creditors growe cruell, my estate is very low, my bond to the Jewe is forfaite, and since in paying it, it is impossible I should live, all debts are cleerd betweene you and I if I might but see you at my death: notwithstanding, use your pleasure, if your love do not perswade you to come, let not my letter.*
> *Por.* O love! dispatch all busines and be gone.[22]

The text of Antonio's letter is clearly distinct from the rest of the passage: it stands materially apart from the rest of the text most obviously by virtue of its use of italic typeface. At the same time, it separates itself from the rest of the text—and from the rest of the text's normal grammar—by virtue of being unassigned: Portia is given a speech tag both before and after the text of the letter, and there is no speech tag for the letter itself.[23]

In his discussion of Hamlet's letter to Claudius, especially the signature that either does (in the Folio) or does not (in the second quarto) accompany it, Jonathan Goldberg discusses a similar instance of a letter and its typographical relationship to the rest of the play-text in which it occurs:

> In the Folio [as compared to the second quarto], Hamlet's signature is printed in the same type as the rest of the text of the play and the same type as the names "Horatio," "Rosincrance," and "Guildensterne" that appear in the letter; save for them, the entire body of the letter as well as the subscription is in italics. Do italics therefore mark the letter as not part of the play, or not part of the script produced by the hand that wrote the rest of the text? But in that case, to whom does the letter belong when the signature is not in the same hand as the letter, but instead marked the same way as the hand that produces the rest of the text?[24]

Unlike the Folio Hamlet's letter, Antonio's letter is both unassigned and unsigned; it has no voice (that Portia or Bassanio voices the letter on stage is either purely conjectural or merely convenient), and the signature that would authorize it exists only under erasure. Though this is the letter that claims to be the body of its author, it is, finally, the letter that inscribes instead the impossibility of presence-in-writing. This is the disembodied letter.

The appearance of Antonio's letter represents a violent eruption of tragedy into the scene of romance surrounding Bassanio's choice. But before we see Portia's Belmont as wholly idyllic, it is important to recognize the ways in which Portia's world is in fact organized around a central but unstaged scene of writing/violence: her father's will mandating the test of the three caskets—the very thing that introduces further instances of violence or its implicit threat.

If we can speculate on the nature of this specular scene of writing/violence—as indeed the play invites us to do, particularly in those moments in which Portia herself contemplates her father's mandate (his will and his writing) and its effects on her: "I may neither choose who I would, nor refuse who I dislike, so is the will of a living daughter curb'd by the will of a dead father" (1.2.22-25)—Portia's father's will stands as an exemplary instance of a profound faith in the metaphysics of writing, its supposed ability to figure the presence of the body as immanent in writing itself.[25]

There is little doubt that Portia's father's will has more to do with Portia's father than it does with Portia herself, as is clear in Nerissa's early comment on the test of the three caskets: "Who chooses his meaning chooses you" (1.2.30-31). What is at stake, then, in the suitor's choice is the father's meaning—and the father's wealth, all of which Portia gives over to Bassanio, "Myself, and what is mine, to you and yours / Is now converted" (3.2.166-67). Portia signifies in this economy of male desire merely as the embodiment of wealth and as heir to her father's seemingly limitless fortune, as Bassanio's prioritized list of Portia's characteristics perhaps intimates: "In Belmont is a lady richly left, / And she is fair" (1.1.161-62). To the materialistic Bassanio (or Morocco, or Arragon), the correct casket holds the license to assume the position of the father, as well as his possessions marked by the representation of its "real world" signifier: Portia's portrait. The logic of Portia's father's will is predicated upon an informing faith in the myth of presence-in-writing executed across the figure of Portia as its signifier. It is this logic (with which I take exception) that was read so influentially by Freud in his famous essay "The Theme of the Three Caskets."[26]

Freud read well the intentions informing Portia's father; he understood, that is, that the caskets really do *for him* represent Portia herself. But there is no reason that we need to see the same thing in the three caskets. The caskets can be said to hold different versions of the preserved paternal will—that is, different versions of that will, or, even, of the father himself. What is more (and quite unlike the caskets in the source tale of the *Gesta Romanorum*), these caskets contain two sorts of material representations of the suitors's fates: the death's head, the "portrait of a blinking idiot," and Portia's portrait constitute the first sort, while writing constitutes the second.

Morocco had earlier announced another test to determine true from false love, the worthy from the unworthy:

> Mislike me not for my complexion,
> The shadowed livery of the burnish'd sun,
> To whom I am a neighbour, and near bred.
> Bring me the fairest creature northward born,
> Where Phoebus' fire scarce thaws the icicles,
> And let us make incision for your love,
> To prove whose blood is reddest, his or mine.
> (2.1.1-7)

Morocco's boast (and it is perhaps more than a mere boast; it may speak earnestly to the very prejudice of which Portia seems to be a mouthpiece—"Let all of his complexion choose me so" [2.7.79], she says upon Morocco's "thus losers part") displays an understanding of the ways in which truth is aligned with writing, or, as he says, inscribing. Much as a writer cuts into a page with the quill/knife, Morocco imagines that the resolution of the racial obstacles he faces lies in incising his body, in a writing both on and of the body—a writing that will embody or make present a truth (his virtue as equal to and deserving of Portia) symbolized for him in the redness of his blood.

It is a faith in real bodies, and their persistence even in absence—their immanence, that is, in the dream of presence-in-writing—that motivates Portia's father and his will. At the same time, a faith in real bodies motivates Shylock's passionate pursuit of the forfeiture of the bond, underwriting, as it were, Shylock's much-discussed adherence to "the letter of the law." Shylock very clearly understands there to be an intimate relationship between the body and writing, even as he hopes to kill Antonio by inscribing upon his body the costs of both the forfeited bond and the wages of Antonio's anti-semitism. At the same time, Shylock understands that there is an equally intimate relationship between the body and the state, which are mutually dependent and discursively figured: Antonio's fate lies in Shylock's hands to the extent that Venice as a political entity lies embodied in its laws, hence Shylock's repeated appeals to law and justice. The Duke necessarily finds this argument compelling and is left no choice but to endorse what he thinks is the young doctor's sentence against the merchant. Antonio, for his part, seems to accept the inevitability of his death at Shylock's hands; in fact, Antonio recognizes that Shylock's execution of the forfeiture constitutes a writing on his body that will inscribe a specific meaning:

> I am a tainted wether of the flock,
> Meetest for death,—the weakest kind of fruit
> Drops earliest to the ground, and so let me;
> You cannot better be employ'd Bassanio,
> Than to live still and write mine epitaph.
> (4.1.114-18)

For Antonio, the antidote to death is a kind of immortality in writing: his epitaph. He later invokes this imagined presence in his farewell to Bassanio:

> Commend me to your honorable wife,
> Tell her the process of Antonio's end,
> Say how I lov'd you, speak me fair in death:
> And when the tale is told, bid her be judge
> Whether Bassanio had not once a love:
> Repent but you that you shall lose your friend
> And he repents not that he pays your debt.
> For if the Jew do cut but deep enough,
> I'll pay it instantly with all my heart.
> (4.1.269-77)

Antonio's faith in presence-in-writing, like Portia's father's and Shylock's, construes the body as the ultimate ground of writing, whether that writing literally occurs on the body (Morocco's incision, Antonio's pound of flesh) or is understood as immanent in writing itself (Portia's father's will, Shylock's bond). In both instances, writing promises presence in absence and articulates its promise on the level of letteral configurations within the play.

Another significant instance of this is Portia's embodiment as Balthazar, the young doctor of laws. Portia's disguise as Balthazar is of particular interest because it is, like Jessica's and Nerissa's corresponding changes, a cross-gender embodiment: by virtue of the letter (first

Portia's letter to Bellario and then, in turn, Bellario's letter to the Duke), Portia and Nerissa will both appear as men ("accomplished / With what we lack" [3.4.61-62]) before the Venetian court.[27]

In her transformed shape, Portia manifests a profound ability to exploit the hypostatized relationship between the body, writing, and the state by recasting the narrative of embodiment Shylock and the others have imagined. Portia intervenes in Shylock's narrative (and Antonio's, too, as he projects his embodiment in Bassanio's epitaph) by appropriating Shylock's linguistic practice: he has insisted upon the letter of the law (the logic, that is, of presence-in-writing) and it is precisely this literalism ("letteralism") that Portia turns upon him:

> This bond doth give thee here no jot of blood,
> The words expressly are 'a pound of flesh':
> Take then thy bond, take thou thy pound of flesh,
> But in the cutting it, if thou dost shed
> One drop of Christian blood, thy lands and goods
> Are (by the laws of Venice) confiscate
> Unto the state of Venice.
>
> (4.1.302-8)

While the outcome perhaps startles—it is Shylock and not Antonio who will die by the violence of the letter—the logic of that violence is no surprise as it has in fact underwritten the entire play, even here in the moment of its evident reversal.[28]

Portia draws the play toward its conclusion with a final letter telling Antonio of the safe return of his ships.[29] But if this letter represents the moment of comic closure in which even the failure of Antonio's merchant venture (by now perhaps a moot issue) is recuperated, it also represents a profound mystification of the letter and all that it is held to signify:

> Antonio you are welcome,
> And I have better news in store for you
> Than you expect: unseal this letter soon,
> There you shall find three of your argosies
> Are richly come to harbour suddenly.
> You shall not know by what strange accident
> I chanced on this letter.
>
> (5.1.273-79)

Though this final letter carries a certain signifying and sensational content, like Antonio (and perhaps like Portia) we cannot account for its presence. The play forecloses any such accounting; the letter simply exists as the final sign of comic resolution. While this letter may stand emblematically for the various operations of the letters we have encountered throughout the play—particularly the desire for presence-in-writing upon which they are founded—this letter comes from nowhere and from no one's hand. It serves, then, to destabilize the very philosophy of the letter and its epistemology of presence; it betrays the mystical or, more aptly, the *theological* nature of the letter. In the end, the letter inhabits the realm of the conjectural, not the contractual, and our confidence in the letter is actually our profound and desperate faith in it. Rather than serving to guarantee desire and anchor it in the material, the mystical letter affords only the vision of such grounding always just beyond reach. And its only pleasures are the pleasures of the dream of immanence that the letter inscribes as the condition of its, and perhaps our own, ontology.

II

This dream informs *Merchant* in another instance of the conjectural letter—or conjectural letters—and a putative relationship to presence. The critical textual moment for the Salerio/Salarino/Solanio issue occurs within the play's most important staging of the scene of reading—in 3.2, the moment (discussed above) just after Bassanio has made the correct choice of the lead casket, and a character arrives carrying Antonio's letter. It is the identity of this character that has caused considerable debate. The 1987 New Cambridge Shakespeare edition, edited by M. M. Mahood, identifies the three characters in its "List of Characters" thus:

> Solanio
> *gentlemen of Venice, and companions with Bassanio*
> Salarino
>
> . . . . .
>
> Salerio, *a messenger from Venice*

The entry for Salarino is noted at the bottom of the page: "He may very probably be the same character as 'Salerio'," and we are asked to consult the "Textual Analysis" that supplements the text.[30] In the pages of the "Textual Analysis" devoted to a discussion of these characters, Mahood offers a careful review of the parameters of this textual problem and the solutions to it offered by various editors:

> Earlier editors of the play were reluctant to believe that Shakespeare, after naming two characters "Salarino" and "Solanio" . . . would have made confusion worse confounded by bringing on a third character called "Salerio." To have created so superfluous a character would have violated "dramatic propriety," put the actors to unnecessary expense, and shown a singular lack of inventiveness in the choice of names. . . . In the New Shakespeare edition of 1926, [John Dover] Wilson concurred with Capell in making Salarino and Salerio one and the same person but decided that Shakespeare's name for him must be "Salerio" since this occurs five

> times in the dialogue. He therefore substituted "Salerio" for "Salarino" or its variants in all previous stage directions and speech headings. All subsequent editors have followed Wilson in this, and Salarino has not put in an appearance for the past sixty years. On a number of grounds, I have restored him to the text of this edition. (M, 179)

Mahood argues there is "no *prima facie* case against Shakespeare having had three different personages in mind. On the other hand, the positive evidence in favour of three characters is admittedly slight" (M, 179). After a lengthy discussion of the various arguments both for and against the eliding of Salarino and Salerio, Mahood decides to maintain the distinction between these characters within the text, while noting in the textual apparatus the possibility that this decision may be untenable. This decision is underwritten, however, not by an argument for one character over the other, but is instead guaranteed by an appeal to a reputed authorial intention or the (lost, conjectural or—at the very least—the specular) authorial script:

> It is always open to the director to identify Salarino with Salerio, thereby economising on minor parts and very probably fulfilling Shakespeare's final intention into the bargain. But the printed text must, I believe, retain three Venetian gentlemen with similar names because, whatever his intentions, Salarino, Solanio, and Salerio all figured in the manuscript that Shakespeare actually gave to his actors as *The Merchant of Venice*. (M, 183)

Embedded within this final comment are a number of crucial issues. To begin with, Mahood accepts a fundamental distinction between the play as it is performed and the play as a text: in the first instance, the textual stand taken vis-à-vis Salarino/Salerio simply doesn't signify; in the latter, the textual becomes occasion for taking a stand. In other words, this textual matter finally doesn't matter if the play is imagined in performance—as spoken language—, but matters a good deal more if it is instead imagined as a text—as written language.

This constitutes a performative version of the logocentrism described by Derrida: spoken language is imagined as prior to and more immediate than the written, with the consequences in this particular instance being that in production the play is substantially different in such a way as to allow an editorial emendation that in print would be inadmissable. At the same time, Mahood suggests that whatever the decision in performance, in print the three characters must nevertheless still appear. The performed play, then, enacts yet another splitting, reifies the posited distinction between performed and textual play, as an actor may be—in performance—Salerio while in print he may (still) be Salarino.[31]

There is another issue at stake in Mahood's double-vision of a single version of the play, and it is an issue relevant to our understanding of *Merchant* more generally. In the above paragraph Mahood identifies the three characters as "three Venetian gentlemen," while in the "Textual Analysis" she suggests that their status as "gentlemen" is perhaps open to some question, and that, moreover, Salerio may not be a gentleman at all, as his nomination "a messenger from Venice" may well suggest:

> *a messenger from Venice* (3.2.218 SD) could imply that not only is Salerio not to be confused with the two men-about-town, but that his social status is rather different. Gratiano's "My old Venetian friend *Salerio*" (218) need not imply equality; it can be a condescending form of address and also an explanatory phrase such as the audience would not need if it had met Salerio four times already. Salerio . . . can be seen as a kind of state functionary. . . . This would accord with his role in the trial, where he is a kind of gentleman usher. (M, 181-82)

But Salerio's social status is not the only one at stake: while the "social nuances of four hundred years ago are not . . . something on which we can speak with confidence today," Mahood suggests, "it would be quite easy to make out a case, in the play's first scene, for a social difference between Solanio and Salarino on the one hand and Bassanio's more immediate group of friends on the other" (M, 182). Mahood clearly brings certain notions of class and class distinction to the play, and just as clearly suspects Shakespeare to have done so as well.

While Mahood's decision to retain Salarino seems to depend in part upon his presumed class-based differences from Salerio, it is in fact underwritten by an unquestioned adherence to the tenets of traditional textual criticism—particularly the faith in authorial intentionality. In this regard, then, Mahood's inclusion of Salarino is effectively no different from Wilson's exclusion of him.

Wilson's discussion of what he calls "the muddle of the three Sallies" (W, 100) is a careful analysis of this textual problem and has stood as the almost universal "resolution" reproduced by every editor of the play until Mahood. Wilson's argument—that "Salarino" is a repeatedly misrecognized or misprinted version of "Salerio"—is heavily indebted to a complex textual genealogical argument in which the copy-text for the 1600 Hayes Quarto is believed to have been pieced together not from prompt-books or manuscript (the latter is the argument favored by recent editors), but from what Wilson calls "secondary theatrical manuscripts" (W, 105). Wilson finds corroborating evidence for this conclusion in a number of the play's more striking textual characteristics: the evident addition of texts into the play—specifically, the letters read aloud in 3.2 and

4.1 and the three scrolls of the casket scenes—, the play's stage directions, the related matter of the "three Sallies," and what Wilson deems the evident playhouse additions to the play.

Wilson notes the curious textual features associated with the letters and the scrolls—that they are bibliographically "marked off" within the Quarto, and that for each a speech heading is missing. This bibliographical distinctness, Wilson claims, is "a textual fact of capital importance":

> For the absences of prefixes before the letters and the duplication of prefixes in the speeches afford clear evidence that both letters and scrolls are, bibliographically speaking, textually distinct from the rest of the copy, or in other words, insertions. . . . Any text, therefore, in which letters, songs or scrolls are seemingly insertions, is to be suspected of being derived, not from the original "book," but from some secondary theatrical source, composed of players' parts. (W, 97-98)

The "frequent vagueness" of entry directions ("Enter Bassanio with a follower or two" [2.2.109], one of whom later turns out to be Leonardo; the entry for the "man of Portia's" whom we later learn is Balthazar, and the "Messenger" [5.1.24] who "is discovered four lines later to be Stephano, one of Portia's household") prove that, as Wilson had argued earlier in the New Shakespeare edition of *The Comedy of Errors,* "the dialogue had been copied out (from the players' parts) by one scribe and the stage-directions supplied by another . . . who possessed very vague ideas of the text he was working on" (W, 100). It is precisely this "scribe responsible for the stage-directions" whom Wilson holds accountable both for the "muddle of the three Sallies" and for the general textual state of the entire Quarto.

In his argument for resolving the Salerio/Salarino crux, Wilson lays the responsibility for the problem entirely at the hands of the scribe, reconstructing, based upon his sense of evidence, what must have happened in the scribe's production of the text:

> Whence then came this curious "Salarino"? If we assume, as we have already found ourselves entitled to assume, that the text before us was made up of players' parts strung together, transcribed and then worked over by a scribe who supplied the stage-directions, the reply is not difficult.... This scribe had before him at the outset, we must suppose, a transcript from the parts containing only the bare dialogue and the abbreviated prefixes, so that he would be obliged to rely upon his memory of the play upon the stage for the full names of those characters which were not mentioned in the dialogue itself. Now the form "Salarino" is found, apart from the stage-directions, nowhere in the dialogue and in only one prefix, which occurs at 1.1.8. The prefix "Salari" (which is of course a variant spelling of "Saleri") is, on the other hand, fairly frequent. The beginning of all the muddle, we suggest, was that the scribe found the prefix "Salari" in his text at 1.1.8, took it as a contraction for "Salarino," added "no" to it, and framed his entry-direction accordingly. It accords with this theory that the only time we get the erroneous "Salanio" in the prefixes is at 1.1.15. . . . Clearly, we think, the meddling scribe made the two changes at the same time. (W, 103-104)

From this description of an imagined scene of scribal intrusion and disruption of the Shakespearean text, Wilson constructs an entire narrative of the scribe's work and his absolute consistency in his erroneous and meddling ways:

> "Salarino" (or "Salerino") marches happily along in the stage-directions hand in hand with "Salanio" (or "Solanio") up to the end of 3.1, by which time the former name had become such a habit with the scribe that when he comes upon "Salerio" in the dialogue of 3.2 he quite fails to recognize his identity and puts him down as "a messenger from Venice." (W, 104)

The final evidence for Wilson's theory of the "assembled text" is what he identifies as the playhouse additions to the play itself, arguing that "texts derived from secondary theatrical manuscripts are likely to preserve traces of actors', or at least of playhouse, additions." Wilson identifies an early section of 5.1 as such a trace—a "piece of 'fat,' as the modern actor would call it, [that] has clearly been inserted in the text": the prose lines introduced by Lancelot's repeated "sola's" and concluded with what Wilson conjectures is the misassignment of "sweete soule" (W, 105). In his analysis of the significance of the textual irregularities he finds in this brief passage, Wilson has recourse to the assistance of W. W. Greg ["whose authority on matters of this kind is unrivalled" (W, 106)]; when asked by Wilson what he made of the "sweete soule" matter, Greg theorized a version of the assembled text argument:

> I think it is pretty clear that the preceding passage was an insertion in the margin, or more probably on a slip, ending up, as was usual, with a repetition of the *following* words to show where it was to come. The sense shows that the insertion must have begun with the Messenger's words: "I pray you is my Maister yet returnd?" I suppose that the printer finding the words repeated in the MS, omitted the second occurrence. The compositor would not be very likely to do this, but a proof-reader might—or there may have been an intermediate transcript. (qtd. in W, 106)

Authorized by Greg's words, Wilson continues his argument by wondering why there should be this addition at all—especially as "the passage . . . might be omitted without any injury to the context." The answer, Wilson declares, is simple: "to give the clown who played Lancelot an opportunity of making the theatre ring with his 'sola!'." "Evidently," Wilson concludes, "the clown in Shakespeare's company, Will Kempe presumably, was fond of caterwauling tricks" (W, 106-7).

Let us for a moment consider the rhetoric of this derisive passage which manifests a certain ideological bias brought to bear not only on the passages under review, but to the editing of the entire play, and, moreover, to that play's meaning.[32] In this passage Wilson makes the small but serious mistake of referring to Will Kempe not as the comedian of Shakespeare's company, but as its clown. To confuse or conflate the two is to eradicate any distinction between actor and the part an actor might play upon the stage; the consequences of this confusion are significant. In Wilson's rhetoric, Kempe literally is a clown, and as such occupies the same position in the space of the social world that a clown does in the space of the theater. So Kempe's addition here—his "piece of 'fat'"—is pure clowning, but clowning with serious ramifications. For Wilson, Kempe's addition represents nothing less than the eruption of chaos and disorder into the otherwise decorous and high-aesthetic world of the Shakespearean play. Kempe becomes the sign of both social and aesthetic disruption and literal (letteral) textual corruption.

Wilson's vision of Kempe as the figure of radical instability does not end here, however, for as Wilson says, "if an addition was made to this 'assembled' prompt-book at one place, why not at others?" (W, 107); the text stands hopelessly vulnerable to the pernicious effects of Kempe as the socially and aesthetically disenfranchised figure of instability and subversion. Wilson identifies a second "prose-patch, this time of a ribald nature," in 3.2:

> It is pretty certainly a textual addition, and we suspect that it was made by the same hand as wrote the 'sola' slip. Indeed, we are inclined to go even further and to attribute a whole scene to this unknown scribe. (W, 107)

The passage under review here—the opening 59 lines of prose—includes Lorenzo's famously obscure charge, "the Moor is with child by you Lancelot!" (3.5.35-6), and ends when Lancelot exits to prepare dinner. Wilson argues that not only is this so-called prosepatch an addition, but that the entire scene was (again) instigated by Kempe:

> It is the verse with which the scene closes that seems to provide the clue we are seeking. The first five and a half lines of this verse are a tribute to Lancelot, or rather to the actor who played him, while the reference to "A many fools that stand in better place" is obviously intended as a hit at some successful rival. In a word, we suggest that Shakespeare had no hand whatever in the composition of 3.5, which might be omitted altogether without loss to the play; that it was added to the "assembled" prompt-book at the same time as the insertions at 5.1.39-49 and 3.2.214-18; and that while 3.5.60-5 was written by some second-rate poet as a compliment to William Kempe, Kempe himself may have been responsible for the very dull fifty-nine lines of prose with which the scene opens. (W, 108)

Wilson concludes his discussion of the copy for the Hayes Quarto by suggesting that Kempe not only presumed to write in Shakespeare's hand, but, also that it was he who was the "unknown" and "meddling" scribe Wilson's theory of the text had posited:

> To sum up, our contention is that the manuscript used as copy by Roberts' compositors in 1600 contained not a line of Shakespeare's handwriting, but was some kind of prompt-book made up from players' parts, to which a theatrical scribe (maybe Kempe himself) had added stage-directions and additions of his own devising. (W, 108)

For Wilson, Kempe's intrusive and radically disruptive acts of destabilizing self-promotion are complete, but at a material cost to the integrity of the Shakespearean hand and text. Wilson's theory of the production of *Merchant* attributes virtually everything that is of uncertain authority and authorship—and therefore everything that is deemed aesthetically bankrupt—fully to the hands of Will Kempe.[33]

These suspicions of Kempe's destabilizing presence in *Merchant* betray Wilson's fundamental distrust—not to say fear—of the lower class of which Kempe is made to stand as the embodiment. Wilson's "aristocratic" position, in turn, stands in steadfast opposition to such a disruption, as it seeks to guarantee the "sovereignty" of the Shakespearean texts against dissent, disruption or subversion "from below." This is precisely the sort of political and critical conservatism Terence Hawkes has so brilliantly analyzed in Dover Wilson's career as a "social" writer on Russia and its revolution, and as a literary critic.[34] Hawkes describes Wilson's conservatism (like Tillyard's) as "a version of what, by the time of the second world war, had become a standard British response to national crisis: the construction of longpast, green, alternative worlds of percipient peasants, organic communities, festivals, folk art, and absolute monarchy to set against present chaos."[35] Such a vision imposes a radical reconstruction of "peasant" and "folk" culture as happily acquiescent to the absolute monarch. This is an Edenic vision of folk culture that fails to see in it any potential source of subversive energy, any potential for misrule.

But this vision is not imagined, however, as necessarily natural. In fact, it takes the very deliberate and careful intervention on the part of people such as Wilson (and their appropriation of figures such as Shakespeare) to produce it, to identify potentially disruptive people such as Will Kempe, and re-create them as docile (royal) subjects. This is achieved, in Wilson's view, through both a well-regulated and maintained aesthetic and nationalistic education.[36]

Wilson's political conservatism (like his critical and editorial conservatism) is dedicated to the preservation of so-called traditional values: Nation, high-aesthetic value, and the sovereign individual—whether that individual is Shakespeare or Tsar Nicholas II. And these transcendental values are themselves underwritten by a Hegelian philosophy and historiography that understands human activity not merely as diachronic, but as processive and, finally, teleological.

It is precisely against this teleological or exclusively linear model that Hawkes offers *Telmah*. For Hawkes, *Hamlet* is structured on the model of recursivity: events, words and phrases appear and then are replayed again. Hawkes warns us, however, not to be deceived by this recursivity and its symmetries:

> It would be wrong to make too much of "symmetries" of this sort, and I mention them only because, once recognized, they help however slightly to undermine our inherited notion of *Hamlet* as a structure that runs a satisfactorily linear, sequential course from a firmly established and well defined beginning, through a clearly placed and signaled middle, to a causally related and logically determined end which, planted in the beginning, develops, or grows out of it.
>
> Like all symmetries, the ones I have pointed to suggest, not linearity, but circularity: a cyclical and recursive movement wholly at odds with the progressive, incremental ordering that a society, dominated perhaps by a pervasive metaphor of the production line, tends to think of as appropriate to art as to everything else.[37]

The metaphor of the production line bespeaks a deep-rooted notion of (historical) progress and it is this philosophy of progress that authorizes and determines Wilson's editorial practices and produces his version of *Merchant*. Moreover, this philosophy of progress and the epistemology of presence together have powered traditional textual criticism, regardless of local responses to textual problems. Mahood's decision, for instance, to retain or restore Salarino to the play is a good one, though I disagree with her traditionally-determined reasons for doing so. Our current understandings of (Shakespearean) textuality no longer require or endorse the appeal to authorial intention or authorial script. My argument is more concerned with the untenable nature of traditional editorial practice typified by Wilson than with evidential weight behind retaining Salarino. In fact, it seems to me not much to matter how there came to be three characters with such names in the Hayes quarto, but simply that there came to be these three "letteral" configurations we have decided to call characters. The matter of the three Sallies is important here not because it stands as yet another site for our intervention in the attempt to solve a textual crux, but rather precisely because it marks the eruption—inexplicable and yet undeniable—of the accidental.

. . . . .

In the anticipated aftermath of the collapse of traditional textual criticism, can we theorize a textual practice and a theory of textuality not determined by a Hegelian processive philosophy?

III

> To the interpreter, texts often appear as images of time; to the makers of texts, however, they are the very events of time and history itself.
>
> —Jerome McGann, *The Textual Condition*

I begin this concluding section with the above quotation in part because it strikes me as an apt characterization of the various ways in which the relationship between texts and history is frequently construed: for some readers and critics, texts often are imagined as fully self-present representations of the past, while for their creators texts simply are, one might say, "the stuff of history." In criticism texts are typically implicated in history only to the extent that they either 1) represent (embody) a particular historical moment, or 2) can themselves stand as historical fields. The latter is precisely what happens in traditional textual criticism that posits the eclectic text as its interpretive paradigm. The model of the eclectic text (the text produced historically) construes the text as a historical field, the place of history, and, moreover, as the site of historical evolution and progress—that "homogeneous, empty time" Benjamin identifies as the "foundational" conceit so much in need of what we might today call deconstruction.

To imagine the text not in time but as time; this is the tendency of traditional textual criticism, powered, as it is, by an underlying Hegelian conception of history as the gradual exfoliation of a master-narrative. Thus traditional editorial practice emerges as a kind of historiography predicated upon an essentially teleological model of progress. For Dover Wilson, it is the progressive narrative of an aristocratic or monarchical political and class conservatism that seeks in archaic forms of absolutism the redemption of traditional aesthetic and national value against the threat of proletarian political struggle and revolution. Wilson's is a redemptive vision of the social place of high literary culture: it is in this high literary culture, Wilson suggests, that we can find transcendent liberation and salvation.

The appeal to these putative redemptive and salvational powers has been characteristic of our cultural appropriation of Shakespeare, and literary and aesthetic "genius" more generally. But if it is true that texts do not necessarily embody or imply a politics of redemption or liberation, what, then, can texts be said to embody?

In truth, this is a misleading question. Since embodiment as a textual property depends on the manifestly untenable hope of presence-in-writing, we cannot legitimately say that texts *embody* anything. We can say, however, that texts occur, and as such they stand not as objects but rather as events. As McGann suggests, "Properly understood . . . every text is unique and original to itself when we consider it not as an object but as an action."[38] Texts happen in a way analogous to the happening of events (historical, social, political, accidental) outside our anachronistically imposed narratives of authorship, textuality, causality, diachronicity, history, nationalism, liberation, and so on. This is a way of reading that goes entirely against the grain of a play such as *Merchant,* which articulates the very faith in and philosophy of presence-in-writing and embodiment I have tried to critique here. In place of this theory of reading predicated upon the metaphysics of presence, let us put in place a non-appropriative theory and practice of reading and historiography that allows the texts to exist more purely in history, rather than as latter-day reconstructions of our own self-interested narratives.

And what of accidents?

To the extraordinary extent that they are routinely subjected to narrative strategies dedicated to the explanation or discovery of meaning (the establishment of chronology, the articulation of significance—in short, the demonstration of absolute causality and accountability), textual and historical accidents (the two seem almost indistinguishable) have always been subjected to a reactive practice of over-writing. Corrected, emended, or re-defined out of existence, accidents have almost universally been construed as sites for the contestation of the subject (the author, or—more likely—the critic) against error, confusion, and meaninglessness, and seldom as mere instances of the uncaused—that great bugbear to systems of the production of meaning. Accidents are important precisely because as accidents they mark eruptions of phenomena for which we simply cannot account. It is the accident that gives the very notion of causality the lie, and as such accidents can be said to delimit the domain of agency. Traditional textual criticism (like most other forms of historiography) is motivated by a relentless desire to articulate—in some instances, to manufacture—causality, and as such is dedicated to the description and, more importantly, the extension of the domain of agency. We can see this is the paradigm of the eclectic text in which every word is entirely caused, and in which nothing is allowed to remain accidental. To clean up accidents in a text is to construct a narrativized world of total causality and accountability, a purely rational world in which everything is under control. This is Dover Wilson's practice, for example, in his construction of a wholly meaningful text of *Merchant,* or in his meaningful description of Russian absolutism. And there are accidents within the narrative of *Merchant* that the play clearly attempts to over-write: the "accident" of a Jew's domination of a Christian that Portia overwrites, for example, or the accident of the loss of Antonio's merchant ships which is redeemed through the mystification of the letter. And there are legion over-writings of accidents in criticism of the play—whether textual or interpretive in nature.

The three Sallies, then, are certainly part of the play. Or, to be more precise, the multiple Sallies are all of them part of the play: the quartos and Folio present, Wilson remarks, not only Salerio, Solanio, and Salarino, but "Salerino," "Salari," and "Saleri," and Mahood lists the cornucopic variety of textual incarnations of these "characters": Salaryno, Salino, Slarino, Salerino, Sala, Salan, Salanio, Salarino, Salanio, Salar, Sola, Sal, Solanio, Salari, Saleri, Sol.[39]

Mahood's list of the Sallie "characters" is emblematic not only of the radical instability of the text, or the proliferation of accidents in that text, but also of our sheer inability to account for these "characters," our inability to construct a narrative (of a story or of a text) in which they all have a truly meaningful place. Unediting, then, of the most radical sort—unediting, that is, dedicated to the domains of both agency and non-agency—returns the text more fully to history, and at the same time understands texts as more fully historical, and as such demonstrates the limits of agency. In spite of our collective insatiability for meaning, there is, as it happens, a world apart—an *accidental* world.

Notes

[1] Jerome McGann, *The Textual Condition* (Princeton: Princeton Univ. Press, 1991): "Both the practice and the study of human culture comprise a network of symbolic exchanges. Because human beings are not angels, these exchanges always involve material negotiations. Even in their most complex and advanced forms—when the negotiations are carried out as textual events—the intercourse that is being human is materially executed: as spoken texts or scripted forms. To

participate in these exchanges is to have entered what I wish to call here 'the textual condition'" (3).

[2] Jerome McGann, *A Critique of Modern Textual Criticism* (Chicago and Charlottesville: Univ. of Chicago Press and Univ. of Virginia Press, 1992), 11.

[3] McGann (note 2), 8.

[4] The growing list of such works is extensive; what follows is not intended to be exhaustive, but rather suggestive of the range and depth of this work. Margreta De Grazia and Peter Stallybrass, "The Materiality of the Shakespearean Text," *Shakespeare Quarterly* 44 (1993): 255-83; Stephen Orgel, "The Poetics of Incomprehensibility," *Shakespeare Quarterly* 42 (1991): 431-37; Leah S. Marcus, *Puzzling Shakespeare: Local Reading and Its Discontents* (Berkeley: Univ. of California Press, 1988); Paul Werstine, "Narratives About Printed Shakespearean Texts: 'Foul Papers' and 'Bad' Quartos," *Shakespeare Quarterly* 41 (1990): 65-86; Marion Trousdale, "A Second Look at Critical Bibliography and the Acting of Plays," *Shakespeare Quarterly* 41 (1990): 87-96; Randall McLeod (Random Cloud), "'The very names of the Persons': Editing and the Invention of Dramatik Character," in *Staging the Renaissance: Reinterpretations of Elizabethan and Jacobean Drama,* ed. David Scott Kastan and Peter Stallybrass (New York: Routledge, 1991), 88-96; Margreta De Grazia, *Shakespeare Verbatim: The Reproduction of Authenticity and the 1790 Apparatus* (Oxford: Clarendon Press, 1991). See also the important critical work by Steven Urkowitz, Michael Warren, Gary Taylor, and Stanley Wells.

[5] For theoretical and practical discussions of "unediting," see Randall McLeod, "UnEditing Shakespeare," *Sub-Stance* 33/34 (1982): 26-55 and Leah Marcus, "Textual Indeterminacy and Ideological Difference: The Case of *Doctor Faustus,*" *Renaissance Drama* n.s. 20 (1989): 1-29.

[6] Marcus, "Textual Indeterminacy" (note 5), 3.

[7] Marcus, 24.

[8] Marcus, 12. Marcus also notes, "The A text could be described as more nationalist and more Calvinist, Puritan, or ultra-Protestant, the B text as more internationalist, imperial, and Anglican, or Anglo-Catholic—but each version places the magician at the extreme edge of transgression in terms of its own implied system of values" (5).

[9] Marcus discusses these revisions: "The 1602 revisions worked to keep *Doctor Faustus* on the thrilling/unnerving edge of transgression by inscribing the play with a new set of national priorities and anxieties. A theatrical company and its hired 'hack' writers transformed what was then extant as 'Marlowe' in order to keep the 'Marlowe effect' alive, to keep Marlowe sounding like himself even decades after his physical demise. In the curious case of *Doctor Faustus,* nonauthorial revision functioned to heighten, not to destroy, an aura of authorial 'authenticity' in the theater" (15).

[10] Jonathan Goldberg, "Textual Properties," *Shakespeare Quarterly* 37 (1986): 214. Goldberg continues, "the historicity of the text means that there is no text itself; it means that a text cannot be fixed in terms of original or final intentions. At best, Shakespearean practice authorizes the dispersal of authorial intention" (214). De Grazia and Stallybrass (note 4) also discuss the illusory nature of the "original": "Return to the early texts provides no access to a privileged 'original'; on the contrary, for the modern reader it bars access. The features that modernization and emendation smooth away remain stubbornly in place to block the illusion of transparency—the impression that there is some ideal 'original' behind the text" (256).

[11] Goldberg, "Textual Properties" (note 10), 214; *The Division of the Kingdom: Shakespeare's Two Versions of King Lear,* ed. Gary Taylor and Michael Warren (Oxford: Clarendon Press, 1983).

[12] Goldberg, 215.

[13] Goldberg, 216.

[14] Goldberg discusses the Shakespearean text in which, now, "no word . . . is sacred." Moreover, he continues, with this "radical instability" of the Shakespearean text, "all criticism that has based itself on the text, all forms of formalism, all close reading, is given the lie" (215).

[15] McGann, *A Critique* (note 2), 24.

[16] McGann, 93-94.

[17] McGann, 119.

[18] Goldberg, "Textual Properties" (note 10), 217.

[19] *The Merchant of Venice,* ed. John Russell Brown (London: Methuen, 1955), 3.2.314-20. All references are to this edition and are cited parenthetically in text by act, scene and line.

[20] Jonathan Goldberg, *Writing Matter: From the Hands of the English Renaissance* (Stanford: Stanford Univ. Press, 1990), 78.

[21] *The Merchant of Venice,* ed. John Dover Wilson (Cambridge: Cambridge Univ. Press, 1926), 97. Subsequent references to Wilson appear parenthetically in the text in the text and are cited by W.

[22] *The Merchant of Venice, 1600,* Shakespeare Quarto Facsimiles (Oxford: Clarendon Press, 1957).

[23] There are two further differences between the modern and the Quarto versions of the letter and its physical/material presentation. In our modern editions we are accustomed to the addition of two linguistic items not found in the Quarto text: the parentheses around "since in paying it, it is impossible I should live," and the insertion of a comma after the phrase "all debts are cleared between you and I." In the first instance, the addition of the parentheses serves to make Antonio's recognition of the cost of the forfeiture subordinate to the act of forgiveness within which it occurs, a highly intrusive editorial decision that alters the sense of the passage. As punctuated in the Quarto, the passage makes perfect sense, though not the sense we have ascribed to it (or to Antonio, for that matter) in our modern editions. The letter may well want to register linguistically the equivalence of Antonio's death and Bassanio's debts; the subordinating effect of the parentheses suppresses such a reading. In the second instance—the instance of the comma—the Quarto's syntax makes rather explicit that there is a causal relationship between the forgiveness of the debt and Bassanio's appearance at Antonio's death: the former is more explicitly conditional upon the latter. The editorial addition of the comma serves to mitigate the force of Antonio's determination. Again, such an editorial decision is intrusive and in a way revises the sense of the letter.

[24] Jonathan Goldberg, "Hamlet's Hand," *Shakespeare Quarterly* 39 (1988), 324.

[25] This is the same faith that can be said to underwrite drama as a genre: a belief in presence-in-writing is given the extraordinary dimension and expression in the representational embodiments of characters in the figures of the actors who portray them on stage before our very eyes. Drama is, perhaps, the expression of the metaphysics of writing *par excellence.*

[26] Freud's essay begins by reading the caskets as symbols for women: if the scene of the three caskets from *Merchant* appeared in a dream, Freud says, "it would at once occur to us that caskets are also women, symbols of the essential thing in woman, and therefore of a woman herself, like boxes, large or small, baskets, and so on" ("The Theme of the Three Caskets," in *Sigmund Freud: The Collected Papers,* ed. Joan Riviere, 5 vols. [New York: Basic Books, 1959], 4:245-56). Then, by way of a circuitous path through various national mythologies, folk-tales, and *King Lear,* Freud arrives at his perhaps predictable conclusion that the theme of the three caskets allegorically represents "the three inevitable relations man has with woman": "That with the mother who bears him, with the companion of his bed and board, and with the destroyer. Or it is the three forms taken on by the figure of the mother as life proceeds: the mother herself, the beloved who is chosen after her pattern, and finally the Mother Earth who receives him again" (256).

[27] In a discussion of letters and their circulation in Shakespearean texts, "Shakespearean Inscriptions: The Voicing of Power" [in *Shakespeare and the Question of Theory,* ed. Patricia Parker and Geoffrey Hartman (New York: Methuen, 1985), 116-137], Jonathan Goldberg argues that Portia's position in court and her ultimate success there—and in the fifth act drama of the ring—depend upon the sheer impossibility of the "self-sameness" of the letter: "The 'turn' that Portia takes calls into question the differences upon which the play rests, male and female, Jew and Christian, letter and spirit, for the lewdness of the play that she initiates—sending the letter and donning the disguise (the device)—rests upon equivocations within the letter, differences within the self-same. Portia's 'whole device' involves filling a place—the place of Bellario, the place of the law—through an act of replacement that calls into question the possibility of duplication (the repeatability and self-sameness upon which the law rests)" (122).

[28] This reversal also manifests the play's fundamental dependence upon Christian historiography that posits two related phases of post-lapsarian history—the Mosaic or Old Testament articulation of life under the law, and the New Testament life of the spirit. In this vision of history, the Christian progresses from the first phase to the second in a movement that is suggested by Christ's example and guaranteed by virtue of the spirit's redemption of the law and its letter. Portia leads the Christians of the play in this progress toward redemption and salvation; Shylock, on the other hand, is its clear victim.

[29] Portia's and Nerissa's taunting of Bassanio and Gratiano over the matter of the rings has special significance as well, in part because their laughter—and their husbands' initial consternation—are explicitly linked to the politics of embodiment and textuality. Portia can assure Bassanio that she will welcome the doctor to her bed ("Know him I shall, I am well sure of it" [5.1.229]) because of her embodiment as both "herself" and as "the doctor." In fact, the moment Portia produces the ring—"I had it of him: pardon me Bassanio, / For by this ring the doctor lay with me" (5.1.258-59)—she stands, as it were, as both herself and the doctor. This crisis is averted not simply with Portia's announcement that she was the doctor and Nerissa the clerk, but only when she produces the letter as evidence:

> you are all amaz'd;
> Here is a letter, read it at your leisure,—
> It comes from Padua from Bellario,—

There you shall find that Portia was the doctor,
Nerissa there the clerk.
(5.1.266-70)

[30] *The Merchant of Venice,* ed. M. M. Mahood (Cambridge: Cambridge Univ. Press, 1987), 56. Subsequent references to Mahood occur parenthetically in text and are cited by M.

[31] Jonathan Goldberg discusses a similar manifestation of logocentrism in Shakespeare's second tetralogy: "The subsequent plays are haunted too by what is put on deposit in the deposition scene [of *Richard II*]: the alliance of kingship with the repression of textuality, and the ways in which the play both supports that logocentrism and undermines it." ("Rebel Letters: Postal Effects from *Richard II* to *Henry IV," Renaissance Drama* n.s. 19 [1988]: 10).

[32] It is interesting to note that in the 1939 Clark Lectures at Trinity College, Cambridge (later published as *The Editorial Problem in Shakespeare: A Survey of the Foundations of the Text,* 2d ed. [Oxford: The Clarendon Press, 1951]), Greg rejects both the conclusions drawn by Dover Wilson on the textual genealogy of *Merchant* and its production from assembled promptbook, and his own evident participation in the argument: "I do not regard the presentation of the promptbook for registration [in the Stationers' Register] as involving its use as copy. Like Chambers 'I see no clear reason why the copy used . . . should not have been in Shakespeare's hand'—and foul papers at that, at least in the technical sense, for the text itself is remarkably good. . . . A prompt copy would surely have straightened out the tangle of ambiguous prefixes that according to Wilson led to the creation of a ghost character in Salarino. *It appears that I once argued that a passage at the foot of sig. 12 was an insertion probably written on a separate piece of paper.* Wilson and Chambers allow the possibility: but the addition might have been made in foul papers as easily as in the prompt-book" (123; emphasis added).

[33] In Goldberg's discussion of the important textual crux in *1 Henry IV* regarding the identity of the character that actually reads aloud the paper taken from the sleeping Falstaff's pocket, he discerns a similar class-based agenda on the part of traditional textual critics: "Dover Wilson and Bowers indulge fantasies about restoring Shakespeare's lost original text. . . . Bower's elaborate argument about stage history and its role in shaping Q1 is quite clearly bent on saving Hal from being sullied with low companions like Peto. . . . The Petos of the world, Bowers insists, cannot read without being risible. Shakespeare cannot originally have wanted the Prince to have ended the scene in his company. Modern editors, on the whole, are willing enough to leave Peto there, and reading, as he does in F1; but they, too, share similar suppositions. The Prince must not read. And perhaps the editorial emendation in F1 is a result of the ideological construction of scenes of reading in the play; rebels read, but royalty do not" ("Rebel Letters" [note 31], 23).

[34] Hawkes identifies Dover Wilson's political conservatism in his renunciation of the Bolsheviks and his explicit endorsement of Tsarism in the article, "Russia and Her Ideals," in which he writes: "[Autocracy] still has a long life before it and much work to perform in Russia. It is therefore wiser to face the facts and to recognize that the Tsardom is after all Russia's form of democracy. . . . it is the kind of government the people understand and reverence, and it is their only protection against the tyranny of an aristocratic clique. . . . when the will of the autocrat is clearly and unmistakably expressed, it has always been found to correspond with the needs of the people" (quoted in Hawkes, "Telmah" [note 27], 323).

[35] Hawkes, 324.

[36] Hawkes discusses Dover Wilson's participation in this pedagogic regime as it was articulated in the famous Newbolt Report of 1921 (*The Teaching of English in England*). Wilson's contribution falls into the category of "Literature and the nation," asserting, Hawkes suggests, that "teaching literature to the working class is a kind of 'missionary work' whose aim is to stem the tide of that class's by then evident disaffection." In this manifestly political vision, "literature is offered as an instrument for promoting social cohesion in place of division": "The specter of a working class, demanding material goods with menaces, losing its national mind, besmirching its national character, clearly had a growing capacity to disturb after the events of 1917, particularly if that class, as Dover Wilson writes in the Newbolt Report, sees education 'mainly as something to equip them to fight their capitalistic enemies.' . . . To Dover Wilson . . . the solution lay quite clearly in the sort of nourishment that English literature offered: the snap, crackle and pop of its roughage as purgative force of considerable political power" (Hawkes, 326-27).

[37] Hawkes, 311-12. Hawkes offers the curtain call—"that complex of revisionary ironies"—as yet another theatrical practice that marks the emergence of the counter-current of recursive movement: "Here [in the curtain call] . . . any apparent movement in one direction of the play halts, and it begins to roll decisively in the opposite direction (if only towards the next performance, when its 'beginning' will emerge from these smiling actors). In short, the sense of straight, purposive, linear motion forward through the play—the sense required by most 'interpretations' of it—evaporates at the curtain call, and we sense an opposing current" (313).

[38] McGann, *The Textual Condition* (note 1), 183.

[39] Mahood (note 29), 180-81.

Source: "(Dis)embodied Letters and *The Merchant of Venice,*" in *ELH,* Vol. 62, No. 2, Summer, 1995, pp. 237-65.

Interlinear Trysting and 'Household Stuff': The Latin Lesson and the Domestication of Learning in *The Taming of the Shrew*

Thomas Moisan, *Saint Louis University*

Sly. Is not
a comonty a Christmas gambold, or a
tumbling-trick?
Page. No, my good lord, it is more pleasing
stuff.
Sly. What, household stuff?
Page. It is a kind of history.
Sly. Well, we'll see't.
(*Taming of the Shrew*, Induction 2.137-42)[1]

. . . . .

Titus. Soft, so busily she turns the leaves!
Help her.
What would she find? Lavinia, shall I read?
This is the tragic tale of Philomel,
And treats of Tereus' treason and his rape—
And rape, I fear, was root of thy annoy.

. . . . .

Demetrius. What's here? a scroll, and written
round about.
Let's see:
[Reads] *"Integer vitae, scelerisque purus,*
Non eget Mauri jaculis, nec arcu."
Chiron. O, 'tis a verse in Horace, I know it
well,
I read it in the grammar long ago.
(*Titus Andronicus,* 4.1.45-49, 4.2.18-23)

That there are advantages to knowing one's Ovid, and that there are, conversely, considerable disadvantages in having forgotten one's Horace, and that there is dramatic capital to be made out of both facts are all truths Shakespeare put to use in *Titus Andronicus,* and from which in contexts and with consequences less grim, he derives profit in other plays, where characters operating from positions of linguistic inequality negotiate unevenly with each other along the linguistic and cultural frontier of translation. We have a celebrated example of the political uses of such inequality and translation in Henry's courtship of Katherine in Henry V (5.2.98-280), a memorably comic Latin grammar-cum-Welsh pronunciation lesson in *The Merry Wives of Windsor* (4.1.7-85), and a less celebrated but no less interesting tutorial in the scene that provides the locus of this paper, the Latin lesson of 3.1 in *The Taming of the Shrew,* the exchange between Lucentio and Bianca in which Lucentio, scion of the conventional "devious lover" figure Shakespeare inherited from his putative source Gascoigne and through him Italian and Roman comedy,[2] is disguised as a Latin tutor and seeks to court Bianca both under the increasingly anxious surveillance of his disguised rival and pseudomusic tutor Hortensio and, literally, "between the lines" of the Ovidian text he pretends to be teaching her. It is a scene less notable for what happens than for what does not happen: for the language instruction not given, for the translation of Ovid not made, and for the seduction of Bianca that gets at least partially deflected and deferred; and it derives a good measure of its humor from our sense of it as an exercise in pedagogical harassment and manipulation thwarted, manipulation of a literal sort if, following the suggestion of at least one editor, we include Hortensio's overly zealous fingering exercises as part of what gets thwarted,[3] manipulation of a more subtle and intellectual kind in the form of Lucentio's attempt to exploit his position as tutor, not only to gain access to Bianca, but to use the very foreignness of the Latin text, and the powerful license of the translator both to disregard what the text says and make it say what he wants it to say, as a mask and vehicle for his overture to Bianca, interpolating seduction both between and in place of the lines.

In what is to follow I would suggest that precisely for all that does not happen in it, the "translation" scene offers an illumination of the play of which it would seem but a marginal moment and of the social issues and tensions that traverse that play. When read against the backdrop of contemporary concerns over the uses and abuses of learning, particularly classical learning, and especially when applied to the education of women, the scene presents a travesty of what happens when learning and what Sly calls "household stuff" collide,[4] when Latin becomes a part of Baptista's domestic decor and an extension of his attempt to keep his daughters a part of that decor. At the same time, in a play set so self-consciously in a "foreign" land, the Latin lesson exemplifies the uses of things foreign, and in particular the domestication of foreign language, throughout the play, offering a comic peek at the acculturating power of translation, and a comic rehearsal of that process of cultural expropriation in which Nietzsche would assign translation a central part, whereby a culture *"vergangene Zeiten und Bucher sich einzuverleiben sucht,"* "seeks to embody past epochs and books into its own being."[5]

Above all, however, in the degree to which it could be argued that the translation scene contributes to Bianca's social development, it evokes contemporary critics' worst fears about the corruptive potential of learning in general and theater in particular, and recalls other moments in the *Shrew* in which the play seems at once to embrace a didactic function only to allegorize its own didactic insufficiency and insincerity,[6] its very indebtedness to the conventions of Roman comedy a cheerful affiliation with a form cited by detractors and apologists of the stage alike in debating the role of plays, and plays in translation, in propagating "family values." So it is, for example, that in the Prologue to his "prodigal son" play, *The Glasse of Gouernement* (1575), George Gascoigne, whose *Supposes* is commonly taken as one of the sources of Shakespeare's *Shrew*, simultaneously proclaims his play a morally instructive "tragicall Comedie" and renounces the very tradition by which a play like *Supposes* had been nourished:

> A comedie, I meane for to present,
> No *Terence* phrase: his tyme and mine are twaine:
> The verse that pleasde a *Romaine* rashe intente,
> Might well offend the godly Preachers vayne.[7]

On the other hand, in the Dedication of the 1598 printing by John Legate of Terence's translated plays, Terence, presented as "a Latin author taught to speake English," is alliteratively hailed as "a comicall Poet pithie, pleasant, and very profitable," whose "fraudulent flatterer," "grimme and greedie old Sire," "royst-ing ruffian," "minsing mynion," and "beastly bawd" were all intended by their creator, and translated into English, to show us how "to avoid such vices, and learne to practise vertue," so that the readers of these plays may safely "vse them, & not as most doe such autors, abuse them."[8]

Indeed, purveying seduction under the cloak of learning, the translation scene might be taken to epitomize what Philip Stubbes saw as the peculiarly pedagogical mendacity of theater, which Stubbes derides with incantatory vehemence, not simply for its failure to inculcate the good it pretends to teach, but for its success in teaching "al kinde of sinne and mischeef": "if you will learne cosenage: if you will learne to deceiue: if you will learne to play the Hipocrit: to cogge, lye and falsuffie: if you will learne . . . to sing and talke of bawdie loue and venery . . . you neede to goe to no other schoole, for all these good Examples, may you see painted before your eyes in enterludes and playes."[9] In short, in a play the central fable of which concerns and celebrates the "taming of a shrew," the domestication of learning in the translation lesson might well be "constered" as a practicum and frame for the training of a shrew.

And, to be sure, read simply as a piece of dramatic action, the scene stands as a "defining moment" in the relationship of Lucentio and Bianca and in the representation of Bianca's character, with the dynamics of the exchange an adumbration of what Lucentio will and, more significantly, will not gain by the end of the play, and with Bianca's behavior the first clear indication that she is not the passive "blank" her name suggests and everyone, or, rather, every male, seems to suppose. In turn, the scene has invited interpretive comment as but exhibit "A" in a reading of the play that would take the relationship of Lucentio and Bianca as but a transparent foil for and vindication of the relationship of Petruchio and Katherina, and, pace Stubbes, would "conster" Bianca's education as mis-education and license for connubial corruption, her classroom a school for the wrong kind of wife.[10]

Nor, though, does the significance of the scene end there. For in a play that, as Marianne L. Novy has put it, "gives lip service to patriarchy and victory to youth,"[11] the genuinely undercover advances of Lucentio, bearing a text intoning the ruination *Priami regia celsa senis* (3.1.29), of "the lofty palace of Priam the *ancient*" [italics mine],[12] "beguile" and subvert the intentions of two representatives of the older set: the patriarch Baptista, whose professed and self-congratulatory desire to be "liberal" in his daughters' upbringing leads him to bring "[s]choolmasters" into his house in the first place (1.1.91-99); and the "old pantaloon" Gremio, who funds his own amatory undoing by providing his rival Lucentio with both the access and the erotic instructional materials through which to court Bianca in his employer's stead (1.2.144-47). So too, in its use of a Latin lesson as camouflage for Lucentio's pursuit of Bianca, the translation scene epitomizes the uses, or misuses, to which education and formal "learning" are put throughout the play, with educational projects and the value of learning invoked only to be genially disregarded, subordinated to other plans, or simply, and just as genially, trashed, the ridicule to which they are subjected personified in the stock figure of the hapless, and perhaps spurious "Pedant" who fecklessly wanders into the play just in time to provide fodder for one of the "wily servant" Tranio's schemes.[13] "O this learning, what a thing it is," the deluded Gremio exclaims as the disguised and newly hired Lucentio promises to use all of the "words" at his scholarly disposal, and in the books Gremio has provided, to "plead" love to Bianca; "O this woodcock," notes Grumio in editorial aside, "what an ass it is" (1.2.159-60). Let's not be "so devote to Aristotle's checks / As Ovid be an outcast quite abjured" (1.1.32-33), the canny Tranio admonishes his master, Lucentio, upon their arrival in Padua at the outset of Act 1, as the latter declares his commitment to study with a becoming junior-year-abroad zeal and comparable credibility:[14] "In brief, sir, study what you most affect" (40), and Bianca's Latin lesson, with Ovid as primer, is the result.

Indeed, and much to our purpose here, in the degree to which the translation scene brings briefly to the foreground the treatment of education and formal learning in the *Shrew,* it reminds us of the prominence in the play of more practical educational projects and brings into metonymic focus the curiously synergetic, and ultimately, I would argue, parasitic relationship in the play of the educational and domestic. Now, at a glance, the vectors in this relationship seem to go decidedly in one direction, with much of the "bounded" or domestic space we encounter in the play employed as classrooms of one sort or another, and with many of the "things" we encounter, the semiology of which Lena Cowen Orlin has exhaustively parsed,[15] from books and musical instruments, to clothing and even quasi-, or not so quasi-, pornographic paintings, deployed as materials in broadly defined exercises in pedagogical outreach, in teaching lessons and—with a nod to the humanist elision of intellectual and moral formation—inculcating and modifying certain behaviors.[16] One obvious effect of this association in the play is, of course, the conversion of the domestic, and particularly its localization as domicile, into an arena for the care, feeding, and augmentation of masculine and patriarchalist control. Hence, Petruchio's house becomes the location of his "taming-school," to which Kate is taken, most unwillingly, to matriculate and, as Petruchio had threatened earlier, to domesticate her, "to bring her from a wild Kate to a Kate / Conformable as other household Kates" (2.1.277-78); and it is Petruchio's house to which Hortensio, a failed suitor and soon-to-be failed tamer, resorts as a not terribly apt auditor and would-be "patriculator" (4.2.50-58), while the banquet over which Lucentio presides at the end of the play reconstitutes itself as a public *examen* for the three new wives, the ultimate pass-fail, no-partial-credit test in which the only lesson for which the wives are responsible is that of obedience. In contrast to Gaston Bachelard's "topophiliac" reading of bounded space as "protective" and intimate,[17] the *Shrew* comically dramatizes the domestic as a site for contestation and an apparatus for indoctrination, a decidedly unprotective and vulnerable space, its atmosphere embodied in the cryogenic cold which Grumio brings into Petruchio's house from outside, but which the interior of Petruchio's house neither repels nor soon, or soon enough for Grumio, at least, dispels (4.1.1-45).

At the same time, though educational projects of a practical and social nature have a way of encroaching upon domestic space in the *Shrew*, it is also true that what the play, or what Sly calls in that interesting elision, the "comonty," transacts is the domestication, not only of Kate as one more, as Petruchio punningly classifies her, "household Kate,"[18] but of learning itself, with the simultaneous commodification and transformation of the objectives and processes of education into "things," and "things" for the home. We get a socially satiric hint of this "reifying" commodification—and its corruptive potential—in the Induction, when the meddling Lord, having ordered his men to carry the inert Sly to his "fairest chamber," instructs them to deck out the room with "all my wanton pictures," the better to persuade Sly that he really is a lord (Induction 1.46-47). And the hint is amplified in the play proper when Gremio, who seems to hope that Bianca will prove the sort of bibliophile who does, indeed, judge a book by its cover, insists that the books—"[a]ll books of love"—which he is going to have the disguised Lucentio use as his texts be "very fairly bound" and "very well perfum'd" (1.2.144-45, 151-52). "O this learning, what a thing [italics mine] it is!"

No less a "thing" is language instruction, and in representing Baptista's attempt to include it among his "household stuff," the play could be said simply to reflect what R. C. Simonini, Jr. described some time ago as the "vogue of foreign language study" cultivated in aristocratic and middle-class households from the middle of the sixteenth century[19]—though with a distinctly satiric lens. For, to extrapolate from the evidence of the translation scene, Latin instruction domesticated is traditional Latin instruction traduced, and offers little to allay the misgivings of the age about the wisdom of educating women—Roger Ascham's paean to the scholastic virtues of his star pupil Elizabeth notwithstanding[20]—and much to underscore the truth in the contemporary William Vaughan's truism that "A tutor should not be overfriendly with his student."[21] "Proposterous ass," Lucentio, the fake classics tutor, chides Hortensio, the fake music tutor, at the outset of the scene, in an attempt to browbeat his rival into letting him deliver his Latin "lecture" to Bianca before her music lesson (3.1.9-14), and in doing so strikes the keynote for the genuinely "preposterous"[22] inversions of decorum that mark the ensuing "lesson." "I am no breeching scholar in the schools," Bianca declares, arrogating to herself the authority to dictate the order and schedule of her lessons, and dropping a hint, in the process, of the terms to which she would expect any subsequent, nonacademic relationship to adhere. "I'll not be tied to hours nor 'pointed times, / But learn my lessons as I please myself" (3.1.18-20), an echo, we will recall, of the hedonistic notion of curriculum Tranio had recommended to Lucentio, but also a fundamental contravention of the role of the student and of the conditions by which students were expected to abide, the severity and regimentation of which have been amply documented by T. W. Baldwin and, quite recently, by J. W. Binns.[23] Moreover, in pointedly reminding her pseudotutors of what, in the dramatic context, one would imagine should have been quite obvious, namely that she is "no breeching scholar," which most editors have glossed as meaning "a schoolboy liable to be flogged,"[24] Bianca exempts herself from the culture of violence which, as Roger Ascham's pleas in *The Schoolmaster* for more gentle tactics only confirm,[25] was integral to Latin instruction and, of course, to the upbringing of children in general. "[I]f you forget your *qui*'s, your *quae*'s, and your *quod*'s," Sir Hugh Evans admonishes his student William in *The Merry Wives of Windsor*, "you must be preeches" (4.1.77-78); or, as Vaughan much more menacingly declares, "[R]ods are expedient for the chastisement of the corruptions of the soul."[26] Dictating the conditions of her tutelage, Bianca simultaneously prescribes its form and adopts a rhetorical posture far more like that of the pedagogue than pupil as she interrogates Lucentio as to the place in the text where they left off and commands him to "conster" it (3.1.26-30).

And if, as Walter J. Ong has argued, the normative conventions for the inculcation of Latin functioned as a masculine puberty rite, reinscribing masculine dominance in the authority and exclusionary eloquence of Latin discourse,[27] then Bianca's inversion of the roles of teacher and student has inevitable gender implications as well, and alerts us to the hints of gender inversion that inflect the characterizations of Lucentio and Bianca at various moments in the play, hints lodged inconspicuously and untranslated in various bits and pieces of classical reference with which the verbal surface of the *Shrew* is laden. One instance, and, perhaps, a comic warning of the power of classical learning to inculcate incorrect, or culturally inappropriate lessons, especially in weak minds, comes very early in the play when Lucentio tries his hand at classical analogy by way of Vergil to demonstrate the extremity of his immediate infatuation with Bianca, "confessing" to Tranio,

> That art to me as secret and as dear
> As Anna to the Queen of Carthage was,
> Tranio, I burn, I pine, I perish, Tranio,
> If I achieve not this young modest girl.
> (1.1.150-53)

Moreover, Lucentio's association of himself with one of Renaissance authors' favorite classical avatars of female victimization is interestingly underscored in the First Folio text of the play when, quoting, or misquoting, a theatrical progenitor in Terence, Tranio invokes the reassuring tag, "*Redime te captam quam queas minimo*" (1.1.159), with the feminine form "*captam,*" which in the dramatic context modifies Lucentio, appearing in place of the masculine accusative form, "*captum*"—though most modern editors "correct" the Folio and restore the masculine form.[28] And if classical analogy has provided Lucentio with a feminine association, symmetry demands reciprocity for Bianca, which is what she may receive at the end of the translation scene, when the spurned Hortensio, sensing that he has been bested by his Latin teacher rival, follows misogynist tradition in directing his deepest resentment at the woman, vowing renunciation if Bianca has "cast thy wandering eyes on every stale" (3.1.88); though generally taken as a hawking reference in which Bianca plays the hawk to Lucentio's decoy pigeon, the image, particularly with its epithet "wandering," also evokes the figure of the peregrine hero of classical lore, Dido's "pious" victimizer, Aeneas, for example, or, more likely, in the context of this scene, the wandering worthy who figures so prominently in the text Lucentio has not been translating, Ulysses, a reading that brings the slighting reference to Lucentio as a "stale" into proximity with another "common" contemporary valence of the word, that of "prostitute."[29]

At the same time, to give ear to such possibilities in the classical periphery is to find more equivocal and ludic the representation of gender at the heart of the translation scene. For even as the *Shrew*, as a number of critics in recent years have compellingly argued, calls attention to its own theatricality,[30] so does it make it more difficult for its audience to differentiate the female character Bianca from the boy actor and theatrical apprentice playing her, and, thus, a more complex matter to accept unblinkingly Bianca's assertion that she is "no breeching scholar." Heard in this way, Bianca's remark bears a double resonance and two-fold blatancy: a blatant defiance of the prevailing rules for young scholars, and a blatant lie, since it is clear to everyone that the actor uttering this line has, in fact, much more in common with the "breeching scholar" than with the young woman Bianca. The hint that Bianca is not precisely what she seems only echoes, of course, the duplicity in which Lucentio and Hortensio are engaged in the scene and infuses it with the sort of liberating, transgressive energy which one associates with a *fabliau,* and that percolates throughout the *Shrew*, providing an insurgent counternote to the socially prescriptive and patriarchalist fantasy that is its central fable. In a play which, we have become accustomed to acknowledging, absorbs as a central motif the image of "supposing" from its source in Gascoigne's play, *Supposes,*[31] the intramural contention of the Latin lesson reminds us of the recurrence in the play of a more transgressive variation on "supposing" in the image of "facing," assuming a mask or pose and defiantly maintaining a lie, "braving," or "facing the matter out," as Katherina accuses Petruchio of doing in the previous scene when he insists to Baptista and all of the assembled suitors that Katherina has given her consent to have him as a husband (2.1.289). "Where is that damned villain, Tranio, / That fac'd and braved me in this matter so" (5.1.108-9), demands Lucentio's father, Vincentio, after Tranio had, to his master's face, clung to his assumed identity as Lucentio, thus denying his own servitude and his master's mastery (5.1.63-111). "Sirrah, I will not bear these braves of thine," the outfaced Hortensio tells his rival tutor at the outset of the Latin scene, momentarily dropping his own mask as just another hired music tutor to assume the posture of social superiority scorned (3.1.15). In the "in-your-face" domestic anomie of the Latin lesson scene, where the exercise of translation becomes a vehicle for misrepresentation, Bianca's interlinear skepticism, "I trust you not" (3.1.43), affords the aptest rendering of and gloss upon the text Lucentio is purveying.

And, of course, Bianca's distrust might be affected by her familiarity with the language that is not being taught her. To be sure, part of the comically transgressive energy released in this scene arises both from our sense that we cannot be certain who knows more, or less, about Latin here, the tutor or the "tutee," or whether, to paraphrase Casca, the Latin in question is equally Greek to both, and also from the possibility that we as audience, and as critics, are being teased and "braved" as much as the characters onstage. In, for example, his compendious assault upon the questions of how much Latin Shakespeare could have known and how and when he was likely to have learned it, T. W. Baldwin speculates in passing that the selection of the first epistle in Ovid's *Heroides* as Lucentio's text would imply that in her Latin competence Bianca was at the level of a fifth or sixth former,[32] a plausible surmise *if* we assume that finding a text appropriate to Bianca's grade level was important either to Lucentio or to his employer Gremio, whose mix of priorities seems to comprise "small Latine," more eros. Still, even if Bianca can translate little or nothing of her Latin text, and is impervious both to the possible corruptions, textual, that is, which editors have noted in the Ovidian text Lucentio is using and to possible lapses in Lucentio's erudition,[33] it is clear that she does at least know enough about the rhetoric of learned disputation to be a credit to Baptista's humanist educational pretensions and to be able to translate her own suspicions and resistance into the patter of academic discourse. Seizing upon what may in fact be a questionable piece of commentary by Lucentio in identifying the grandson of Aeacus as Ajax rather than Achilles,[34] Bianca employs the rhetoric of academic quibbling to express her emotional suspicions:

> I must believe my master; else, I promise you,
> I should be arguing still upon that doubt.
> (3.1.54-55)

Evincing no hard evidence that either mentor or pupil knows much about the language, or text, in question, the Latin lesson may offer the most immaculate demonstration of the license of translation, translation so unfettered as to owe nothing to its original at all!

In this respect, however, the translation exercise stands as but the most sustained example in the *Shrew* of the role and treatment generally accorded the various snippets of foreign language that dot especially the early portions of the play. If, as Benjamin observes, "translation is only a somewhat provisional way of coming to terms with the foreignness of languages,"[35] the non-translation and not infrequently incorrect transcriptions in the *Shrew* of foreign language have the effect of italicizing that foreignness, of rendering the language quoted less important for what it communicates than for the use to which its "foreignness' and failure to communicate can be put. In part, the invocation of foreign expressions provides a conventionally comic instrument of social intimidation and oneupmanship, a means of asserting an otherwise inconspicuous or non-existent superiority, and as such plays its part in detonating the class and generational rivalries that define the subtext of the *Shrew*. "Therefore *paucas pallabris*" (Induction.1.5), commands the debt-evading Sly in "facing" down his creditor, the Hostess, underscoring his bogus claim to nobility and descent from "Richard Conqueror" (sic) with an equally bogus command of Spanish,[36] while the rich "pantaloon" Gremio, certifying his kinship with stock *senex* figures, summons a stock piece of comically pretentious faux latinity in a futile attempt to assert the dignity of his age and wealth against the importunate advances of Petruchio, who has jumped the courtship queue in his haste to claim Katherina: "Backare! you are marvellous forward" (2.1.73).[37] On the other hand, we have those gratuitous interjections in Italian which seem so much a sort of linguistic "dress-ups," and which in calling attention to themselves as interjections make their grammatical imperfections seem all the more evident, as in Tranio's First Folio remark, *"Me pardonato,"* which a number of editors sedulously correct and print as *"Mi perdonato"* (1.1.25). Now, one editor, H. J. Oliver, in allowing the First Folio readings of this and other pieces of incorrect Italian to stand, notes that such interventions, errors notwithstanding, are still "good enough to give the illusion that the speakers are Italian";[38] I would suggest, however, that, quite to the contrary, they serve to show that the speakers are *not* Italian, and that their linguistic forays only accentuate their English-ness and the robustly domestic agenda of this play, which acknowledges its "foreign" setting and theatrical pedigree only to distance itself from them, even as the discourse of classical learning and allusion is at once translated into and domesticated by the "household stuff" of the abortive Latin lesson.

Still, notable as the translation scene may be for what does not occur and what does not get translated, the text it leaves largely ignored and encased within its un- or mistranslated Latin looms nonetheless large over it, complicating our sense of what the scene does transact, and, indeed, becoming more conspicuous in it the more it is "effaced" by Lucentio's interlinear glosses and Bianca's deflections of them. What significance that text has is open, of course, to some question. For though in bringing Ovid into Baptista's home, Lucentio would seem to be satisfying both his own amorous designs and his employer's specifications concerning the content of Bianca's instructional materials, yet the particular text Lucentio selects here, the First Epistle of the *Heroides,* is probably not the sort of Ovid which Gremio had in mind, or from which sprang Ovid's lurid reputation among sundry Renaissance commentators, such as Vives, who warns women in particular to shun the corruptions, nontextual, of Ovid's more licentious books "like as of serpents or snakes."[39] Instead, for Erasmus, at least—whose colloquy, *A Mery Dialogue, Declaringe the Propertyes of Shrowde Shrewes, and Honest Wyves,* has been cited as "either a source or an analogue" for the *Shrew*—[40] "the *Heroides* are more chaste," and offer matter more suitable for "callow youth" than Ovid's *"amatoriae,"* and Erasmus even singles out "the epistle of Penelope to Ulysses," the very one Lucentio pretends to translate, as "wholly chaste."[41] In fact, at a glance, a text centered on the proverbially patient and faithful Penelope might seem intended simply to provide an ironic counterpoint to the rather less patient and coolly uncommitted Bianca.

Yet behind such incongruities lie interesting congruencies between the Latin lesson and the text it does not teach, and with them a demonstration of some interesting uses of literary domestication. To have occasion to juxtapose Penelope and Bianca is, of course, to recognize an obvious if comic parallel between their dramatic situations, and in the degree to which Bianca's deft negotiation of the "lessons" of her imported and self-appointed tutors evokes Penelope's deft deflection of the advances of her self-invited suitors, it also permits us to recall the genuine interweaving of art and domesticity that forms the "fabric" of Penelope's delaying strategy, with Penelope's daily weaving followed by nightly unweaving a paradigmatic example of the commodification of art and of the uses to which one can put even a text that isn't there. Indeed, in the only lines from Ovid's text that actually surface in the Latin lesson scene, art and the domestic literally commingle, with the recollected description of Troy and Priam's ruined palace the effluence of dinner-table conversation, and a picture outlined with a little wine:

> *atque aliquis posita monstrat fera proelia mensa,*
> *pingit et exiquo Pergama tota mero:*
> *'hac ibat Simois; haec est Sigeia tellus;*
> *hic steterat Priami regia celsa senis.*
> (31-34)

> ["And someone about the board shows thereon the fierce combat, and with scant tracing of wine pictures forth all Pergamum: 'Here flowed the Simois; this is the Sigeian land; here stood the lofty palace of Priam the ancient."]

Still, what this detail only serves to underscore and metonymize is the larger act of literary domestication that turns the heroic into the *Heroides,* distilling and framing the epic narrative of *The Odyssey* within the rhetorical agenda of Epistle I and Penelope's writing chamber, and ostensibly giving voice to Penelope's point of view. Yet domestication can be an instrument of manipulation, and, to recall an earlier speculation, did Bianca actually know Latin and the Heroides, all the more might she be inclined to say, "I trust you not," in part, perhaps, because of Lucentio's handling of the Ovidian text, but in part because of the text itself. For one thing, though Ovid's poem enables Penelope to tell Ulysses what life has been like in Ithaca without him, the only part of her epistle that Lucentio chooses for translation is, as we have seen, a mere piece of scenery, a part of Penelope's account of an account of the ruined Troy, significant in its new context at most, as we have noted, as a humorous hint of the subversion of the patriarch's best laid plans. Decontextualized, the excerpt helps to deconstruct its original. For in a play that culminates in Katerina's bet-winning celebration of a domestic order that envisions the husband committing "his body / To painful labour both by sea and land," while his wife lies "warm at home, secure and safe (5.2.149-51), Lucentio's selection has the effect of silencing and suppressing a radically different and far unhappier perspective on the domestic arrangement Katherina's exposition dutifully idealizes.

On the other hand, the decontextualization produced by Lucentio's excerpt is but an extension of the decontextualization and deconstruction that mark Ovid's expropriation of epic history, and reminds us that Troy domesticated is Troy miniaturized and trivialized, with all of Pergamum inscribed on a table with, and within, a little wine, the circumscription of its boundaries mirrored by the linguistic framing of Ovid's word order: *"exiquo Pergama tota mero"* (32). With the field of epic exploits reduced, the focus on Penelope's domestic sufferings is intensified, though it is surely debatable whether Penelope profits from the scrutiny and from having her sufferings and endurance translated into a one hundred and sixteen line letter of concentrated complaint. Given a voice, Penelope is also given all of the rhetorical dexterity at Ovid's disposal with which to be made to appear to "lay a guilt trip" on her errant husband, as when she poses a rhetorical question laced with praeterition to give an ironic pointedness to her enumeration of some of the most oppressive results of Ulysses' being "shamefully absent," *"turpiter absens"*:

> *quid tibi* Pisandrum Polybumque Medontaque dirum
> *Eurymachique avidas Antinoique manus*
> *atque alios referam, quos omnis turpiter absens*
> *ipse tuo partis sanguine rebus alis?*
> (91-94)

> ["Why tell you of Pisander, and of Polybus, and of Medon the cruel, and of the grasping hands of Eurymachus and Antinous, and of others, all of whom through shameful absence you yourself are feeding fat with store that was won at cost of your blood?"]

In the process of Ovid's "translation," that is, the patient, prudent Penelope of Homer emerges as someone distinctly more petulant, and in the degree to which she is both possessed of considerable rhetorical sophistication and an inclination to use it to upbraid her husband, she is invested with a kinship with a character-type who for Elizabethan readers would have been a most recognizable domestic literary commodity, the querulous wife.

And, indeed, that kinship is amplified in the translation of the *Heroides* with which it is generally agreed that Shakespeare would have been familiar, George Turbervile's, first published in 1567, and republished several times before the period most often assigned to the composition of the *Shrew*.[42] In part, that amplification could be attributed to the sheer amplitude and, as Frederick Boas notes in his edition of Turbervile's translation, the characteristically Elizabethan taste for pleonasm that mark Turbervile's style, doubling the one hundred and sixteen lines of complaint Penelope recites in Ovid, and turning the rhetorical question cited above (91-94) into two sentences and twice the number of lines.[43]

More important, while staying close to Ovid's language, with "renderings" that are, as Boas expresses it, "comparatively seldom wrong,"[44] Turbervile nonetheless exploits the license of the translator to editorialize, and nudges his readers towards seeing the story of the epistle as one of wifely jealousy. As Deborah Greenhut has contended,[45] such are the thrust, and almost literally, the "bottom line" of the "Argument" Turbervile appends to his translation (2), and he reinforces the point in translating the pseudo-Ovidian "Replie" by Ulysses, noting in the "Argument" of that piece the judgment that in the "Replie" Ulysses "quittes himselfe of all such blame / As by his wife imputed was," and that "[w]hat so she did object to him, / The Greeke reanswered very trim" (310.5-8). And if, again, Turbervile augments the suggestion of complaint in Penelope's rhetorical question simply by lengthening it, he simultaneously leaves untranslated the participial phrase in Ovid that gives Penelope's lament its bite, namely, "*turpiter absens*" (93), thus suppressing any reminder that the "absent" Ulysses may by being absent have done something, not only to occasion Penelope's distress, but to warrant her censure, while excising from Penelope's conjugal grief its implicit appeal to conjugal justice.

"Familiarizing" Penelope, Turbervile, in turn, conceives of the process of translation in the language of domestic consumption, repeatedly invoking the conventional rhetoric of self-effacement, with the odd effect, on the one hand, of accentuating the distance between the Ovidian original and his own rendering of it, while, at the same time, making his own product seem more modest, more familiar, more accessible, more, again, in Petruchio's punning words, "[c]onformable as other household Kates" (2.1.278). So it is that, in a fit of literary anorexia, Turbervile hopes that his patron, Sir Thomas Howard, will prove the sort of lord who is willing to accept "slender gyfts," seeks Howard's protection for "my slender Muse" (v-vi), concedes in defending his translation against "the Captious Sort of Sycophantes" that his translation is a "thing but slender" (342), and invites his "Reader" to join him in a "slender" and "base banquet" (ix).

As an example, then, of the ways in which literary translation interacts with the pressure of cultural domestication, Penelope's Epistle hovers conspicuously about the translation scene of the *Shrew* as its unvoiced lesson, as one more intrusive, albeit invisible, tutor. And though in leaving this text untranslated and its lesson unvoiced, the scene would seem to resist the pressure of domestication, in fact, it could be argued that that pressure is simply deflected and comically displaced onto the very next scene, the wedding scene, where Petruchio mockingly dons the "face" of heroic rescuer in order to justify his determination to yank the unwilling Katherina peremptorily away from Baptista's wedding banquet:

> Grumio,
> Draw forth thy weapon, we are beset with thieves,
> Rescue thy mistress if thou be a man.
> —Fear not, sweet wench, they shall not touch thee, Kate;
> I'll buckler thee against a million.
> (3.2.235-39)

Here, of course, in one of the moments that illuminate the antipaternalist subtext of the play, Petruchio disrupts the domestic rites of the father in order to assert his own rights as husband, though in doing so he parodically supplies the ending Penelope's Epistle in the *Heroides* lacks, in effect restoring the epic version of the ending, with its classically violent restoration of domestic tranquility through the thieving-guest-slaughtering return of Odysseus.

Indeed, far from resisting the pressure of domestication, the translation scene could be said to signal a total capitulation to it, with the lessons it teaches having nothing to do with "learning" as such and everything to do with the configurations of behavior that define the relations and circumscriptions of the sexes—and, more precisely, the circumscription of the female sex—in this insistently domestic play. And if, as we have seen, the scene travesties some of the norms of instruction and seems to invert the roles of student and teacher, in doing so it also translates the student into the studied, leaving us on our own to speculate on what Bianca may have learned from the behavior of Lucentio, while italicizing, rather as a piece of *ekph-*

rasis, what Hortensio, at least, as we have noted above, has learned from his observation of Bianca.

> Yet if thy thoughts, Bianca, be so humble
> To cast thy wandering eyes on every stale,
> Seize thee that list; if once I find thee
> ranging,
> Hortensio will be quit with thee by changing.
> (3.1.89-92)

Not for Hortensio is it to think with detachment about the parallels between Bianca and the classical personage whose letter does not get translated, any more, of course, than it would have been for Medon, Eurymachus, Antinous, and their *confrères* to compliment Penelope on her pluck and inventiveness, so that Hortensio's inability to read the analogue this scene at once evokes and evades ironically brings the analogue closer. In fact, if he were inclined at this point to cast his disillusionment and growing misogyny into a position on educational policy, Hortensio might well count himself among those "manye" critics of women Vives invokes, "who sayth, the subtiltie of learning should bee a nourishment for the maliciousnesse of nature."[46] As it is, however, for Hortensio, Bianca's domestic education has utility, not for what Bianca may learn but for what may be learned about her.

In this way, and in its harnessing of learning to a domestic agenda, the translation scene lesson merely illuminates the permeable boundary shared by learning and domestication throughout the play, where, from the moment of Bianca and Kate's first appearance (1.1.48 ff.) and culminating in their last (5.2.65 ff.), women's behavior and potential as domestic partners become the stuff of male speculation, in both the ordinary and root meanings of the word, and public examination. Still, in turning Bianca's lessons into tableaux in which Hortensio observes her and grades her on criteria decidedly nonintellectual, the translation scene reminds us, not only of the way in which the definition of female character in the play is very much a male construction, but of how restrictive the males' choice of building materials is, with women construed in dichotomous terms and with a precariously fine line dividing the two, and separating "sweet Bianca" from Bianca the potential shrew. At the same time, in a play that ostensibly—even ostentatiously—concerns itself with domestic management, the translation scene offers a subversive interlude that suggests that a play may be especially instructive in dramatizing its own instructional limitations, and, above all, reminds its audience of what a malleable, and manipulable, a thing learning, for all of its patriarchalist prescriptions, is.

Notes

[1] Unless otherwise stated, citations of Shakespeare's plays are taken from *The Riverside Shakespeare,* ed. G. Blakemore Evans (Boston: Houghton Mifflin, 1974).

[2] See Geoffrey Bullough, *Narrative and Dramatic Sources of Shakespeare,* (London: Routledge and Kegan Paul, 1957), vol. I.; also, *The New Cambridge Taming of the Shrew,* Ann Thompson, ed. (Cambridge: Cambridge University Press, 1984), 9-17.

[3] See the note on 3.1.s.d, by Brian Morris, ed., *The Taming of the Shrew, The Arden Shakespeare* (London: Routledge, 1989), 218.

[4] In its note on Sly's comment, *The Riverside* text, 113, warily glosses "household stuff" as "house furnishings" or "domestic goings-on"; see also Lena Cowen Orlin's comment that "[t]hrough the term 'household stuff', the performances of things, of persons, and of plays are suggestively analogized," in "The Performance of Things in *The Taming of the Shrew,*" *The Yearbook of English Studies* 23 (1993): 183.

[5] Friederich Nietzsche, *The Joyful Wisdom, II,* trans. Thomas Common, *The Complete Works of Friedrich Nietzsche,* ed. Oscar Levy, 18 vols (New York: Russell & Russell, 1909-11; rpt. 1964), 10, 115.

[6] Though one senses, for example, that the audience is being teased, the players in the Induction of the Quarto *Shrew* claim, at least, to see the play they are about to perform as exemplary, "a good leson for us my Lord, for us that are married men" (Induction 1.64), in *A Pleasant Conceited Historie, called The Taming of a Shrew As it hath beene sundry times acted by the right Honourable the earle of Pembrooke his seruants* (London: Nicholas Ling, 1607), STC 23669. This claim does not surface in the Folio *Shrew*, where the players place emphasis on the therapeutic value of a "pleasant comedy," with its "mirth and merriment" (Induction 2.129-36).

[7] George Gascoigne, *The Glasse of Gouernement* (London: 1575).

[8] Publius Terentius Afer, *Fabulae Comici Facetissimi et Elegantissimai Poetae* (Cambridge: 1598), STC 23890.

[9] Philip Stubbes, *The Anatomie of Abuses: Contayning A Discouerie, or Breife Summarie of such Notable Vices and Imperfections, as now raigne in many Christian Countreyes of the Worlde: but (especiallie) in a verie famous Iland called AILGNA of late, as in other places, elsewhere* (London: 1583), STC 23376, f. L5, L8-M1.

[10] In such homologous terms, for example, has the scene been scanned quite recently by Dennis S. Brooks, who in "'To show scorn her own image': The Varieties of

Education in *The Taming of the Shrew," Rocky Mountain Review of Literature* 48 (1994): 18, declares that "the pupil's mastery of the tutor . . . foreshadows the wife's mastery of the husband."

[11] Marianne L. Novy, "Patriarchy and Play in *The Taming of the Shrew.*" *English Literary Renaissance* 9 (1979): 279; see also Jeanne Addison Roberts, *Shakespeare's English Comedy: The Merry Wives of Windsor in Context* (Lincoln: University of Nebraska Press, 1979), 122.

[12] Citations of the *Heroides* will be inserted in parentheses and are, until otherwise stated, from Publius Ovidius Naso, *Heroides and Amores*, trans. Grant Showerman (1914; rev. Cambridge: Harvard University Press, 1986). In George Turbervile's translation, with which it is not unlikely that Shakespeare was familiar, the reference to Priam's age is rendered no less forcibly: "aged Priam's Hall / and Princely house"; see Turbervile, trans., *The Heroycall Epistles of the learned Poet Publius Ovidius Naso* (1567), ed. Frederick Boas (London: Cresset Press, 1928), 5.

[13] In his note on 4.2.63, Morris, Arden *Shrew*, 255, offers instances of the comic uses to which schoolmasters are put in Shakespeare's early plays.

[14] In "The Lord-Treasurer's Advice to his Son," Sir William Cecil, Lord Burghley, exhorts his son to "suffer not thy Sons to pass the Alpes, for they shall learn nothing there but Pride, Blasphemy and Atheism; and if by Travelling they get a few broken Languages, that will profit them no more, than to haue the same Meat served in divers Dishes," in *Instructions for Youth, Gentlemen and Noblemen by Sir Walter Raleigh, Lord Treasurer Burleigh, Cardinal Sermonetta, and Mr. Walsingham* (London: Randall Minshull, 1722), 50.

[15] Orlin, "The Performance of Things," esp. pp.171 ff.

[16] See Morris, Arden *Shrew*, 133; Thompson, Cambridge *Shrew*, 34-35; and Brooks, "To Show Scorn," passim.

[17] Gaston Bachelard, *The Poetics of Space,* trans. Maria Jolas (Boston: Beacon Press, 1969), xxxi-ii, 149-50.

[18] That the "taming" of Katherina needs to be read in financial terms and as a financial investment is central to the thesis of a paper by Donald Hedrick, "Commodity Kate: Shakespeare's Shrew and the Domestication of Money," delivered at the meeting of the Shakespeare Association in Atlanta in April, 1993.

[19] R. C. Simonini, Jr, "Language Lesson Dialogues in Shakespeare," *Shakespeare Quarterly* 2 (1951): 319. Indeed, in a paper written for the meeting of the Shakespeare Association of America, in Albuquerque, April, 1994, "'Loytering in Love': Ovid's *Heroides,* Pleasure, and Household Stuff in *The Taming of the Shrew,*" 21, and n. 38, Patricia Phillippy cites the pretensions exemplified by Baptista's educational plans for his daughters as the very sort of "parental mismanagement" of female children castigated by contemporary continental and English educators and conduct book writers.

[20] Roger Ascham, *The Schoolmaster* (1570), ed. Lawrence V. Ryan (Charlottesville: University Press of Virginia, 1967), 56, 87.

[21] William Vaughan, *The Golden-grove, moralized in three books A worke very necessary for all such as would know how to governe themselues, their houses, or their countrey* (London: Simon Stafford, 1600), STC 24610, f. X2v. In addition to being far too friendly with his student, Bianca, Lucentio might also qualify simply as bad company, or the sort of temptation Richard Pace feels students should abstemiously avoid; see Richard Pace, *De Fructu Qui Ex Doctrina Percipitur* (1517), ed. and trans. Frank Manley and Richard Sylvester (New York: Frederick Ungar Publishing Company, 1967), 114-15.

[22] In "Preposterous Events," *Shakespeare Quarterly* 43 (1992): 198-99, Patricia Parker argues that the epithet "preposterous" here serves to link the action of this scene with a long list and significant subtext of "preposterous events," inversions of what should come first with what should follow, that create a pattern of upheavals throughout Shakespeare's plays.

[23] T. W. Baldwin, *William Shakespeare's Small Latine, Lesse Greeke,* 2 vols. (Urbana: University of Illinois Press, 1944), 1 passim; J. W. Binns, *Intellectual Culture in Elizabethan and Jacobean England: The Latin Writings of the Age* (Leeds: Francis Cairns, 1990), 292.

[24] *Riverside,* 124; Morris, Arden *Shrew*, 219; see also the glosses on this word by Barbara Mowatt and Paul Werstine, ed., *The Taming of the Shrew, The New Folger Library Shakespeare* (New York: Washington Square Press, 1992), 108, and H. J. Oliver, ed., *The Taming of the Shrew, The Oxford Shakespeare* (Oxford: Oxford University Press, 1984), 158.

[25] Ascham, 37-38, 60.

[26] Vaughan, *The Golden-grove,* f. X5v; on the culture of violence in which boys studied Latin, see Walter J. Ong, S. J., *Fighting for Life: Context, Sexuality, and Consciousness* (Amherst: University of Massachusetts Press, 1989), 131-4.

[27] Ong, "Latin Language Study as a Renaissance Puberty Rite," *Rhetoric, Romance, and Technology* (Ith-

aca: Cornell University Press, 1971), 113-41; see also Ong, *Fighting for Life,* 129-39; and Parker, "Preposterous Events," p. 199.

[28] Allowing the reading of *"captam"* from the First Folio to stand, "uncorrected," H. J. Oliver in the Oxford *Shrew,* 114, accepts the inappropriate feminine form as but one of a number of mistakes in transcriptions of foreign words and expressions that punctuate the early parts of the play.

[29] Noting the possibility that the reference is to hawking, Oliver, Oxford *Shrew,* 162, comments, "Perhaps that is the sense here, but the word came also to mean anyone who allures to deceive (and so particularly a prostitute, especially one serving as a decoy)."

[30] See Karen Newman, "Renaissance Family Politics and Shakespeare's *The Taming of the Shrew,*" in *Fashioning Femininity and English Renaissance Drama* (Chicago: University of Chicago Press, 1991), 35-50, an earlier version of the article, with the same title, appearing in *English Literary Renaissance* 16 (1986): 86-100; Juliet Dusinberre, "*The Taming of the Shrew:* Women, Acting, and Power," *Studies in the Literary Imagination* 26 (1993): 67-84; Michael Shapiro, "Framing the Taming: Metatheatrical Awareness of Female Impersonation in *The Taming of the Shrew,*" *Shakespeare Yearbook* 23 (1993): 143-66.

[31] See Cecil C. Seronsy, "'Supposes' as the Unifying Theme in *The Taming of the Shrew,*" *Shakespeare Quarterly* 14 (1963): 15-30; and Thompson pp. 31-32.

[32] Baldwin, *William Shakespeare's Small Latine,* 1.589.

[33] See Oliver's speculation on the possibly intended corruptions and questionable commentary, Oxford *Shrew,* 158-159.

[34] See Oliver's note on 3.1.50, *Ibid.*, 159

[35] Walter Benjamin, "The Task of the Translator: An Introduction to the Translation of Baudelaire's *Tableaux Parisiens,*" *Illuminations: Essays and Reflections,* trans. Harry Zohn (New York: Schocken Books, 1969), 75.

[36] See Morris, Arden *Shrew,* 153; Oliver, Oxford *Shrew,* 89.

[37] See Morris's note on 2.1.73, Arden *Shrew*, 200, on the comic pedigree of *backare;* see also Morris's reference in the same note to John Lyly's *Midas* (1592), 1.2, for a very comparable use of *backare* as a comically maladroit gesture of social pretense.

[38] Oliver, note on 1.1.25, Oxford *Shrew* 107. Simonini, "Language Lesson Dialogues," 323-24, argues that such expressions typify the "kind of polite conversation that was taught in the dialogue manuals for learning Italian, such as Florio's *First Fruites* and *Second Frutes* (1591)."

[39] Juan Vives, *A Very Fruitfull and pleasant booke, called the instruction of a Christian woman,* trans. Richard Hyrde (London: 1585), STC 24862, 37-39; see also Thomas Lodge, *The Complete Works of Thomas Lodge* (Glasgow, Scotland: 1883), 1:19; and William Prynne, *Histriomastix* (1633), ed. Arthur Freeman (New York: Garland Press, 1974), 912.

[40] Richard Hosley, "Sources and Analogues of *The Taming of the Shrew,*" *The Huntington Library Quarterly* 27 (1963-4): 298-9.

[41] Cited in Baldwin, *William Shakespeare's Small Latine,* 1.239.

[42] Frederick Boas, Introduction to Turbervile's *Heroycall Epistles of the learned Poet Publius Ovidius Naso,* xv-xvi.

[43] *Ibid.,* xvii.

[44] *Ibid.,* xviii.

[45] Deborah S. Greenhut, *Feminine Rhetorical Culture: Tudor Adaptations of Ovid's Heroides* (New York: Peter Lang, 1984), 81-2.

[46] Vives, *A Very Fruitfull and pleasant booke,* 18.

Source: "Interlinear Trysting and 'Household Stuff': The Latin Lesson and the Domestication of Learning in *The Taming of the Shrew,*" in *Shakespeare Studies: An Annual Gathering of Research, Criticism, and Reviews,* Vol. XXIII, pp. 100-19.

The Pound of Flesh

James Shapiro, *Columbia University*

> What a matter were it then if I should cut of his privy members, supposing that the same would altogether weigh a just pound? *—spoken by the Jew in the English translation of Alexander Silvayn's* The Orator, 1596

> I hope I shall never be so stupid as to be circumcised. I would rather cut off the left breast of my Catherine and of all women. *—Martin Luther, c. 1540*

Perhaps the least explicable feature of the ritual murder accusations was the charge that Jews first circumcised their victims before killing them. In some ways it must have made perfectly good sense. After all, it was well known that Jews circumcised young boys, and it was not all that difficult to imagine this practice as part of a more complex and secretive Jewish ritual ending in human sacrifice. In other ways, however, it made no sense at all, for as Menasseh ben Israel justifiably wondered, "to what end he was first circumcised" if "it was intended that shortly after this child should be crucified?" The confusion is understandable, since the ritual significance of what is described in the Bible as cutting the "foreskin" of the "flesh" remains poorly understood even by Jews and other peoples who have long practiced this rite. In the twentieth century we stand doubly removed from appreciating the effect of circumcision upon cultural identity. Even as circumcision is now routinely practiced in Western cultures for hygienic and aesthetic reasons, an awareness of its symbolic meanings (aside from psychoanalytic ones) has been virtually lost. Current debate about circumcision has focused almost exclusively on the pain it might cause the child, or on its effects upon reducing the spread of certain diseases. A very different situation prevailed in early modern Europe, where there was an intense curiosity about the often unnerving implications of a ritual bound up with theological, racial, genealogical, and sexual concerns. I am interested here not only in restoring a sense of the fascination and importance circumcision held for Elizabethans but also in arguing that an occluded threat of circumcision informs Shylock's desire to cut a pound of Antonio's flesh. Before turning to the presence of circumcision in *The Merchant of Venice* and its sources, it is important to consider what this ritual might have meant to Elizabethans, what their understanding of it was based on, and what light this casts on their cultural beliefs.

I. Elizabethan ideas about circumcision

In the twentieth century circumcision has often been described as a symbolic form of castration or emasculation. This association has undoubtedly been influenced by the theories of Sigmund Freud, who, in an argument that bears a striking resemblance to Maria Edgeworth's ideas about childhood trauma and the wellsprings of anti-Jewish feelings, writes in *Little Hans* that the "castration complex is the deepest unconscious root of anti-semitism; for even in the nursery little boys hear that a Jew has something cut off his penis—a piece of his penis, they think—and this gives them a right to despise Jews. And there is no stronger unconscious root for the sense of superiority over woman."[1] For Freud, the symbolic act of circumcision proves a vital source of both misogyny and antisemitism.[2] The notion that circumcision could easily slide into the more definitive cut of castration did not originate with Freud and in fact had long circulated in English culture. D'Blossiers Tovey, in his account of instances in medieval England in which Jews were charged with being "emasculators," cites a case from the reign of King John in which "Bonefand a Jew of Bedford was indicated not for circumcising, but totally cutting off the privy member" of a boy named Richard.[3] And Shakespeare's contemporaries used circumcision as a metaphor for castration: the poet Gabriel Harvey, for example, implores God to "circumcise the tongues and pens" of his enemies.[4]

For early modern English writers, though, the threat of circumcision did not begin and end with emasculation. In the sixteenth century circumcision was more than a cut, it was an unmistakable sign. But of what, exactly? When the Elizabethan preacher Andrew Willet tried to answer this question he found himself describing circumcision as not only a "a sign of remembrance or commemoration of the Covenant . . . made between God and Abraham" but also as a sign "distinguishing the Hebrews from all other people." To this genealogical, Jewish association, he added a few more that are distinctly Christian: circumcision prefigured "baptism" and demonstrated "the natural disease of man, even original sin."[5] To these Willet might have added yet another: that through circumcision, one "is . . . made a Jew,"[6] a troubling thought for a Christian who might find himself threatened with such a cut.

One such individual was Thomas Coryate, the celebrated Elizabethan traveler. Coryate describes how his efforts to convert the Jews of the Venetian ghetto soured, leading him to flee from the hostile crowd. Though this specific detail is never mentioned in the narrative itself, a picture of Coryate pursued by a knife-wielding Jew is included in a series of scenes illustrating the title page of his travel book, *Coryats Crudities*.[7] For those who wrote commendatory poems to Coryate's book—including Laurence Whitaker—this Jew threatens not death but circumcision: "Thy courtesan clipped thee, 'ware Tom, I advise thee, / And fly from the Jews, lest they circumcise thee." Hugh Holland, too, draws attention to the danger to Coryate's foreskin: "Ulysses heard no Syren sing: nor Coryate / The Jew, least his prepuce might prove excoriate." Coryate's conversionary effort backfires, and instead of turning Jews into Christians he finds himself in danger of being religiously transfigured by means of a circumcising cut.[8] Holland, comparing Coryate to Hugh Broughton, the evangelizing Elizabethan Hebraist, makes this symmetrical relationship between baptism and circumcision explicit:

> He more prevailed against the excoriate Jews
> Than Broughton could, or twenty more such
> Hughs.
> And yet but for one petty poor misprision,
> He was nigh made one of the circumcision.[9]

With the exception of a handful of infants circumcised by the radical Puritan group led by John Traske around 1620, and a few self-circumcisors like Thomas Tany and Thomas Ramsey thirty years later, there is no evidence that circumcisions took place in early modern England. Nonetheless, the same post-Reformation interest that led to this Judaizing impulse also inspired a broader curiosity about a ritual not only central to the Old Testament accounts of the patriarchs but also crucial to the theological position maintained by the apostle Paul in that central text of the Protestant Reformation, Epistle to the Romans. One result of this new interest was that English travelers eagerly sought out invitations to circumcisions and recorded what they witnessed for the benefit of their contemporaries. As noted earlier, the resilient Coryate, who in the course of his extensive travels had long desired to observe a circumcision, finally had his wish granted in Constantinople, at the "house of a certain English Jew called Amis" [i.e., Ames]. The fact that Ames and his two sisters spoke English no doubt made it easier for Coryate to have various details of the ritual explained to him. Coryate describes how the Jews

> came into the room and sung certain Hebrew songs, after which the child was brought to his father, who sat down in a chair and placed the child being now eight days old in his lap. The whole company being desirous that we Christians should observe the ceremony, called us to approach near to the child. And when we came, a certain other Jew drawing forth a little instrument made not unlike those small scissors that our ladies and gentlewomen do much use, did with the same cut off the prepuce or foreskin of the child, and after a very strange manner, unused (I believe) of the ancient Hebrews, did put his mouth to the child's yard, and sucked up the blood.[10]

English observers were particularly struck by how the rite symbolically enacted the male child's passage from his mother to the community of men.[11] Coryate observes that at the conclusion of the rite, the "prepuce that was cut off was carried to the mother, who keepeth it very preciously as a thing of worth," and Fynes Moryson, describing a circumcision he had witnessed in Prague, was alert to the fact that women were "not permitted to enter" the room and that they "delivered the child to the father" at the door. Like Coryate, Moryson records his surprise at witnessing another practice for which Scripture had offered no precedent, *metzitzah,* the part of the ceremony in which the circumcisor sucks the blood from the glans of the circumcized "yard" or penis of the infant. Moryson writes that "the rabbi cut off his prepuce, and (with leave be it related for clearing of the ceremony) did with his mouth suck the blood of his privy part."[12] Apparently, this innovative practice, introduced during the Talmudic period, though not universally practiced by Jews, must have seemed to these English observers to have sodomitical overtones.[13]

Coryate, Moryson, and other Elizabethan observers express surprise at the discrepancy between the ceremonies that they witnessed and that which they had expected to see based on the divinely ordained precepts set forth in the Bible.[14] There was also disagreement over whether the Jews were the first people to have practiced circumcision. At stake in this debate was whether circumcision should be viewed as something peculiarly Jewish. On one side there were those like Samuel Purchas, who had read too many accounts from too many foreign lands to accept the argument that all peoples who practiced circumcision had learned this rite from the Jews. Purchas insisted that the "ceremony and custom of circumcision hath been and still is usual among many nations of whom there was never any suspicion that they descended from the Israelites."[15] Opposing this minority view were those like Andrew Willet, who maintained that "circumcision was a peculiar mark of distinction for the Hebrews" and further urged that "some nations among the Gentiles retained circumcision by an apish imitation of the Hebrews, but they did abuse it superstitiously and did not keep the rite of institution as the Lord had appointed it."[16] Writers who sided with Willet's position used this as a basis for substantiating claims about the discovery of the ten lost tribes of Israel. When Thomas Thorowgood, for example, writes that "many Indian nations are of Judaical race," he offers as evidence that the "frequent and constant character of circumcision, so singularly fixed to the Jews, is to be found among them."[17]

While it was widely accepted that others—especially Turks—practiced circumcision, there was still considerable resistance to abandoning the idea that it was a distinctively Jewish rite. An unusual story regarding Turkish circumcision—and murder—made its way to

England in February 1595 when John Barton, the English ambassador in Constantinople, forwarded to Lord Burghley a report describing the events surrounding the accession of the Turkish monarch Mohamet III. The narrative, written in Italian by a Jew named Don Solomon, describes how Mohamet consolidated his power by inviting his nineteen brothers, the eldest eleven years old, to greet him: Mohamet "told them not to fear, he meant no harm to them but only to have them circumcised according to their custom. . . . As soon as they kissed his hand, they were circumcised, taken aside by a mute, and dextrously strangled with handkerchiefs. This certainly seemed strange and cruel, but it was the custom of this realm."[18] The story offers yet one more instance, in the year preceding the first staging of *The Merchant,* of the association of circumcision with ritualistic and surreptitious murder.

II. Romans and the theological meanings of circumcision

This unprecedented interest in the physical act of circumcision was directly related to some of the theological preoccupations of post-Reformation England. Elizabethans knew that circumcision had caused something of an identity crisis for early Christians, especially Paul. Paul, who was himself circumcised and had circumcised others,[19] directed his epistles to communities for whom to circumcise or not to circumcise was a matter of great concern. But Paul's remarks on circumcision went well beyond approving or disapproving of the act itself: they offered a revolutionary challenge to what defined a Jew, and by implication, a Christian. Luther and Calvin both devoted themselves to explicating Paul's often cryptic remarks on circumcision, and a host of English translators, commentators, theologians, and preachers enabled the widespread circulation of these interpretations to the broadest community possible. More than anything else in the late sixteenth century—including firsthand reports like the ones described above—Paul's ideas about circumcision saturated what Shakespeare's contemporaries thought, wrote, and heard about circumcision. At times confusing and even contradictory, Paul's remarks, and the extraordinary commentary produced to explain and resolve various ambiguities contained in them, had an immeasurable impact on Elizabethan conceptions of Jews. This body of commentary, much of it gathering dust in a handful of archives, richly repays close examination.

The first problem confronting a Christian explicator of Paul's Romans was a fairly simple one. Since God had first ordered Abraham to undertake circumcision as a sign of the Covenant, what justified abandoning this practice? And what were the consequences of such a break? The immediate answer was that the Jews had misunderstood that this Covenant, like the Law, was not changed or abolished by Jesus, "but more plainly expounded . . . and fulfilled." "Surely," Philippe de Mornay wrote, in a text translated by Sir Philip Sidney, "in this point . . . we [Christians] be flat contrary to them." And sounding a bit like a modern deconstructive critic, Mornay adds, that the "thing which doth always deceive" the Jews is that "they take the sign for the thing signified," since circumcision was merely a "sign or seal of the Covenant, and not the Covenant itself."[20]

For John Calvin, the "disputation and controversy" over circumcision similarly masked a more consequential debate over "the ceremonies of the Law," which Paul "comprehendeth here under the particular term of circumcision." By equating circumcision with the Law and its supersession by faith, English Protestants drew an analogy between Paul's rejection of circumcision and their own repudiation of Catholicism's emphasis on justification through good works: it is "not circumcision, but faith [that] makes us wait for the hope of righteousness; therefore not circumcision but faith justifies."[21] Calvin's interpretation of Paul had made it clear that "circumcision" had lost its "worth,"[22] having been replaced by the sacrament of baptism. No longer even "a sign," it was "a thing without any use."[23]

But such an outright rejection of circumcision seemingly contradicted Paul's own assertion that "circumcision verily is profitable, if thou do the Law."[24] Confronted with such a claim, commentators had to work hard to show that Paul's words actually meant quite the opposite of what literalists might mistakenly imagine. In order to achieve this end, the gloss to the Geneva Bible takes Paul's wonderfully concise and epigrammatic phrase and turns it into a ponderous argument: "The outward circumcision, if it be separated from the inward, doeth not only not justify, but also condemn them that are circumcised, of whom indeed it requireth that, which it signifieth, that is to say, cleanness of heart and the whole life, according to the commandment of the Law."[25]

The commentator's overreading is enabled by the fact that Paul in the verses that follow introduces a crucial distinction between inward and outward circumcision. It is a distinction central to his redefinition of Jewish identity in a world in which circumcision has been superseded: "He is not a Jew which is one outward, neither is that circumcision, which is outward in the flesh. But he is a Jew which is one within, and the circumcision is of the heart, in the spirit, not in the letter, whose praise is not of men, but of God."[26] Paul here attacks Jewish identity at its genealogical root.[27] If he can deny that outward physical circumcision alone defines the Jew from generation to generation, he can insist on a figurative reading of the Law in all other matters as well. For Joseph Hall, Paul's message is unambiguous: "He that would be a true Israelite or Jew indeed must be such inwardly" and must be "cleansed from all corrupt affections and greed." Moreover, this "circumcision must be inwardly in the heart and soul and spirit (in cutting off the unclean foreskin thereof) and not a literal and outward circumcision of the flesh."[28]

Before turning to the symbolic circumcision of the heart touched on here by Paul and his explicators—the most striking feature of his argument and the most relevant to a reading of *The Merchant of Venice*—it is important first to emphasize that Paul and his followers were reluctant to abandon the outward, physical implications of trimming the foreskin, in part because this surgical act so perfectly symbolized the cutting off of sexual desire. Andrew Willet, drawing on the work of Origen, remarks that even if "there had been no other mystery in circumcision, it was fit that the people of God should carry some badge or cognizance to discern them from other people. And if the amputation or cutting off some part of the body were requisite, what part was more fit then that . . . which seemed to be obscene?"[29] The gloss to the Geneva Bible reads this puritanical perspective back into Genesis 17.11, explaining there that the "privy part is circumcised to show that all that is begotten of man is corrupt and must be mortified." And the 1591 Bishops' Bible similarly stresses the connection between circumcision and the curbing of sexual desire, explaining that Deuteronomy 30.6—"And the Lord thy God will circumcise thine heart"—means that God will "cut away thy ungodly lusts and affections." These commentaries effectively rewrite Old Testament allusions to circumcision, infusing them with Paul's deep discomfort with human sexuality.[30]

John Donne was particularly drawn to this line of thought. In his New Year's Day sermon preached in 1624 commemorating the Feast of the Circumcision, Donne imagines himself in Abraham's place after having been commanded by the Lord to circumcise himself and all the men in his household. Given that it was to be done "in that part of the body," Donne surmises that this command must have struck Abraham as too "obscene a thing to be brought into the fancy of so many women, so many young men, so many strangers to other nations, as might bring the promise and Covenant itself into scorn and into suspicion." Why, Abraham must have wondered, "does God command me so base and unclean a thing, so scornful and misinterpretable a thing, as circumcision, and circumcision in that part of the body?" The answer, of course, is that in "this rebellious part is the root of all sin." The privy member "need[s] this stigmatical mark of circumcision to be imprinted upon it" to prevent Abraham's descendants from "degenerat[ing] from the nobility of their race."[31] Willet, Donne, and like-minded commentators never quite acknowledge that insofar as the cutting off of the foreskin effectively subdues that rebellious and sinful part of men's bodies, circumcision once again veers perilously close to the idea of a (partial) sexual castration and emasculation.

It was also clear to Christian theologians that for the Jews who literally circumcised the flesh, the Covenant could only be transmitted through men.[32] This helps explain why Jewish daughters like Jessica in *The Merchant of Venice* and Abigail in *The Jew of Malta* can so easily cross the religious boundaries that divide their stigmatized fathers from the dominant Christian community. The religious difference of Jewish women is not usually imagined as physically inscribed in their flesh, and the possibility of identifying women as Jews through some kind of incision never took hold in England, though for a brief time in the fifteenth century in northern Italy the requirement that Jewish women have their ears pierced and wear earrings served precisely this function. In her investigation of this sumptuary tradition, Diane Owen Hughes cites the Franciscan preacher Giacomo della Marca, who in an advent sermon said that earrings are jewels "that Jewish women wear in place of circumcision, so that they can be distinguished from other [i.e., Christian] women."[33] One wonders whether Pauline ideas about circumcising desire also shaped this bizarre proposal. Though this method of marking Jewish women was shortlived (other women also wanted to wear earrings) and apparently not widespread, a trace of it may possibly be found in *The Merchant of Venice,* when Shylock, upon hearing that Jessica has not only left him but also taken his money and jewels, exclaims: "Two thousand ducats in that and other precious, precious jewels. I would my daughter were dead at my foot, and the jewels in her ear!"[34] Shylock fantasizes that his converted daughter returns, and through her earring is reinscribed at last as a circumcised Jewess.

The problems that circumcision raise for issues of gender and sexuality persist into our own more secular age. To cite an unfortunate instance of this, modern medicine, when confronted with the extremely rare cases of botched circumcisions, has found it advisable to alter the gender of the child by reconstructing female rather than male genitalia.[35] Does this procedure confirm the kind of anxieties we have been exploring about the underlying castrating and feminizing threat of circumcision? Or does it suggest that doctors are perhaps so influenced by such deeply embedded cultural beliefs as to translate them into scientific practice? In either case it underscores how provisional the assignment of gender is, a point familiar enough to Shakespeare's audiences confronted in *The Merchant* with cross-dressing women and a hero who describes himself as a "tainted wether," or castrated ram. Circumcision, then, was an extraordinarily powerful signifier, one that not only touched on issues of identity that ranged from the sexual to the theological but, often enough, on the intersection of the two. The threat of Shylock's cut was complex, resonant, and unusually terrifying.

II. Circumcision in the sources of The Merchant

The foregoing analysis may help explain why *The Merchant of Venice,* more than any other depiction of Jews in this period, has continued to provoke such controversy and has also continued to stir long-buried prejudices against the Jews. I want to be careful here about being misunderstood. I am not proposing that Shakespeare is antisemitic (or, for that matter, philosemitic). *The Merchant of Venice* is a play, a work of fiction, not a diary or a polygraph test; since no one knows what Shakespeare personally thought about Jews, readers will continue to make up their own minds about this question. *The Merchant of Venice* is thus not "about" ritual murder or a veiled circumcising threat any more than it is about usury, or marriage, or homosocial bonding, or mercy, or Venetian trade, or cross-dressing, or the many other social currents that run through this and every other one of Shakespeare's plays. Plays, unlike sermons, are not reducible to one lesson or another, nor do they gain their resonance from being about a recognizable central theme. Surely, in the hands of a talented dramatist, the less easily definable the social and psychological currents a play explores, the greater its potential to haunt and disturb. We return again and again to Shakespeare's plays because they seem to operate in these depths and tap into the roots of social contradictions on a stunningly regular basis, leaving critics with the task of trying to explain exactly what these are and how Shakespeare's plays engage them. With this in mind, I offer the following interpretation of the pound of flesh plot.

Those watching or reading *The Merchant of Venice* are often curious about what part of Antonio's body Shylock has in mind when they learn of Shylock's desire to exact "an equal pound" of Antonio's "fair flesh, to be cut off and taken" in that "part" of his body that "pleaseth" the Jew. Those all too familiar with the plot may forget that it is not until the trial scene in act 4 that this riddle is solved and we learn that Shylock intends to cut from Antonio's "breast" near his heart.[36] Or partially solved. Why, one wonders, is Antonio's breast the spot most pleasing to Shylock? And why, for the sake of accuracy, wouldn't Shylock cut out rather than "cut off" a pound of flesh if it were to come from "nearest" Antonio's "heart"? Moreover, why don't we learn of this crucial detail until Shylock's final appearance in the play?

It is not immediately clear how for an Elizabethan audience an allusion to a Jew cutting off a man's "fair flesh" would invoke images of a threat to the victim's heart, especially when one calls to mind the identification of Jews as circumcisors and emasculators. On a philological level, too, the choice of the word flesh here carries with it the strong possibility that Shylock has a different part of Antonio's anatomy in mind. In the late sixteenth century the word *flesh* was consistently used, especially in the Bible, in place of *penis*. Readers of the Geneva Bible would know from examples like Genesis 17.11 that God had commanded Abraham to "circumcise the foreskin of your flesh," and that discussions of sexuality and disease in Leviticus always use the word *flesh* when speaking of the penis.[37]

Not surprisingly, popular writers took advantage of the punning opportunities made available by this euphemism. Shortly before writing *The Merchant of Venice* Shakespeare himself had played on the sexual possibilities of *flesh* in *Romeo and Juliet.* In the opening scene of that play the servant Samson, boasting of his sexual prowess, tells Gregory: "Me [the maids] shall feel while I am able to stand, and 'tis known I am a pretty piece of flesh." Playing on the contrast between erect flesh and flaccid fish, Gregory responds: "'Tis well thou art not fish." Mercutio returns to the same tired joke about the loss of tumescence when he says of Romeo's melancholy: "O flesh, flesh, how art thou fishified."[38] *The Merchant of Venice* is similarly replete with bad jokes about trimmed male genitals. As noted above, Antonio in the court scene speaks of himself as "a tainted wether" best suited to suffer the exaction of Shylock's cut.[39] In addition, Salerio's jibe about Jessica having Shylock's "stones," that is, testicles, "upon her" and Gratiano's tasteless joke about "mar[ring] the young clerk's pen" (i.e., penis) offer two other instances from the play of men's obsessive anxiety about castrating cuts.[40] It should also be noted that in Elizabethan England such a cut was not merely the stuff of jokes. As a deterrent to crime, convicted male felons were told at their sentencing to prepare to be "hanged by the neck, and being alive cut down, and your privy members to be cut off, and your bowels to be taken out of your belly and there burned, you being alive."[41]

Scholars have long recognized that Shakespeare drew upon a well established tradition in his retelling the story of the pound of flesh. Among the printed sources Shakespeare may have looked at were Giovanni Fiorentino's *Il Pecorone* and Alexander Silvayn's *The Orator*. Other scholars have uncovered a range of analogues and antecedents, including popular English ballads like "Gernatus the Jew" and medieval works like the *Cursor Mundi* that bear a strong resemblance to Shakespeare's plot. Surprisingly little attention has been paid, however, to what part of the body the pound of flesh is taken from in these sources and analogues. In fact, when Shakespeare came to one of the main sources that we are pretty confident he consulted, Silvayn's *The Orator,* he would have read about a Jew who wonders if he "should cut of his [Christian victim's] privy members, supposing that the same would altogether weigh a just pound?" Before turning to this story and its curious reception, I want to consider another first, one that is even more revealing about the significance of the pound of flesh: Gregorio Leti's *The Life of Pope Sixtus the Fifth.*

Leti was a popular Italian historian, born in the early seventeenth century, who left Italy and took up residence in Northern Europe after converting to Protestantism. For a brief period in the early 1680s he lived and wrote in England. Although there are no recorded performances of *The Merchant of Venice* during his stay there, Leti may well have become familiar with the printed text of Shakespeare's play in the course of the extensive research he undertook on Elizabethan England.[42] The earliest edition of his biography of Sixtus V, first published in Lausanne in 1669, omits any reference to the celebrated pound of flesh story; the anecdote was only introduced in the revised version, published in Amsterdam after Leti's visit to England,[43] which may suggest that Leti drew on English sources for this addition.

After 1754, when Ellis Farneworth translated Leti's story,[44] those unable to read the Italian original could learn how in the days of Queen Elizabeth I it was "reported in Rome" that the great English naval hero, Sir Francis Drake, "had taken and plundered St. Domingo, in Hispaniola, and carried off an immense booty. This account came in a private letter to Paul Secchi, a very considerable merchant in the city, who had large concerns in those parts, which he had insured." Leti then relates that Secchi then "sent for the insurer, Sampson Ceneda, a Jew, and acquainted him with it. The Jew, whose interest it was to have such a report thought false, gave many reasons why it could not possibly be true; and, at last, worked himself up into such a passion, that he said, "'I'll lay you a pound of my flesh it is a lie.'" Secchi replied, "If you like it, I'll lay you a thousand crowns against a pound of your flesh, that it's true." The Jew accepted the wager, and articles were immediately executed betwixt them, the substance of which was "that if Secchi won, he should himself cut the flesh, with a sharp knife, from whatever part of the Jew's body he pleased."

Leti then relates that "the truth of the account" of Drake's attack "was soon after confirmed by other advices from the West Indies," which threw the Jew "almost into distraction, especially when he was informed that Secchi had solemnly sworn [that] he would compel him to the exact literal performance of his contract, and was determined to cut a pound of flesh from that part of his body which it is not necessary to mention." We move here from a cut "from whatever part of the Jew's body he pleased" to the more precisely defined "part of his body which it is not necessary to mention." The original Italian version conveys even more strongly a sense that only modesty prevents specifying that Secchi's intended cut will come from the unmentionable genitals of the Jew ("e che la modestia non vuo che io nomine").[45] The circumcised Jew faces a bit more surgery than he reckoned for.

The rest of the story should be familiar to anyone who has read Shakespeare's play, except, of course, that this time it is the Christian who is intent on cutting the flesh of the Jew. The Governor of Rome referred the tricky case to the authority of Pope Sixtus V, who tells Secchi that he must fulfill the contract and "cut a pound of flesh from any part you please, of the Jew's body. We would advise you, however, to be very careful; for if you cut but a scruple, or a grain, more or less than your due, you shall certainly be hanged. Go, and bring hither a knife and a pair of scales, and let it be done in our presence." This verdict led both Secchi and the Jew to agree to tear up the contract, though the affair was not fully settled until Sixtus V fined both of them harshly to serve as an example to others.[46]

Farneworth, in a note appended to his translation, states the obvious: the "scene betwixt Shylock and Antonio in Shakespeare's *Merchant of Venice* seems to be borrowed from this story, though the poet has inverted the persons and decently enough altered some of the circumstances."[47] Farneworth's comment that Shakespeare "decently enough . . . altered some of the circumstances" presumably alludes to the threatened castration of the Jew. And while we don't know why Leti in the version of the story has "inverted the persons," there is little likelihood that he did it out of love of the Jews. In his book on Great Britain published in England shortly before his departure, Leti reveals his familiarity with London Jewry, describes the services at the Bevis Marks Synagogue in London in somewhat mocking terms, and makes fun of the ridiculous gestures of the Jewish worshippers.[48] We can only speculate about the original source of Leti's seventeenth-century story. Did it antedate Shakespeare's play, and was Shakespeare familiar with versions in which the Jew was the victim? Or did it emerge out of a tradition that was itself influenced by *The Merchant of Venice?* Did turning the tables and having the Christians threaten to castrate or symbolically recircumcise the Jew ultimately prove more satisfying to Christian readers?

Farneworth's translation of Leti's story made a strong impression on eighteenth-century English interpreters of *The Merchant of Venice*. Edmond Malone reproduced this passage in his influential edition of Shakespeare's works in 1790,[49] and David Erskine Baker, though he does not acknowledge his source, wrote that Shakespeare's story "is built on a real fact which happened in some part of Italy, with this difference indeed, that the intended cruelty was really on the side of the Christian, the Jew being the happy delinquent who fell beneath his rigid and barbarous resentment." Tellingly, he adds that "popular prejudice, however, vindicates our author in the alteration he had made. And the delightful manner in which he has availed himself of the general character of the Jews, the very quintessence of which he has enriched his Shylock with, makes more than amends for his deviating from a matter of fact which he was by no means obliged to adhere to."[50] Again, we are left with a set of difficult choices: is it "popular prejudice" that "vindicates" Shakespeare reassigning the "intended cruelty" to Shylock? Or is it Shakespeare's play that by the late eighteenth-century is influential enough to perpetuate and channel this "popular prejudice"?

Familiarity with this inverted version of the pound of flesh story was given even broader circulation by Maria Edgeworth in her novel *Harrington,* where she allows the Jew, Mr. Montenero, to present what he believes to be the historically accurate version of the facts in his response to Harrington, who had recently attended a performance of Shakespeare's *Merchant of Venice.* Edgeworth, too, sees the issue of "popular prejudice" as a central one, and has Mr. Montenero politely acknowledge that while "as a dramatic poet, it was" Shakespeare's "business . . . to take advantage of the popular prejudice as *a power,*" nonetheless "we Jews must feel it peculiarly hard, that the truth of the story should have been completely sacrificed to fiction, so that the characters were not only misrepresented, but reversed." Harrington "did not know to what Mr. Montenero meant to allude." He politely tried to "pass it off with a slight bow of general acquiescence," before Mr. Montenero went on to explain that in "the true story, from which Shakespeare took the plot of *The Merchant of Venice,* it was a Christian who acted the part of the Jew, and the Jew that of the Christian. It was a Christian who insisted upon having the pound of flesh from next the Jew's heart." Seeing how struck Harrington is by this revelation, Mr. Montenero magnanimously offers that "perhaps his was only the Jewish version of the story, and he quickly went on to another subject." Edgeworth adds her own authority to Montenero's when she provides a footnote to the words "true story" directing readers to "Steevens' Life of Sixtus V and Malone's Shakespeare," where the Farneworth translation appears. Strikingly, though, at the very moment that she insists on the original version, Edgeworth herself either misremembers or swerves away from a key features of Leti's "true story" in favor of Shakespeare's version of the events when she substitutes the words "having the pound of flesh from next the Jew's heart" for Farneworth's translation of Leti's original: "from that part of his body which it is not necessary to mention."[51]

Once nineteenth-century Shakespearean source-hunters like Francis Douce and James Orchard Halliwell-Phillipps pointed out that Leti's version could not have antedated Shakespeare's play, and, moreover, that this episode in Sixtus V's life was probably fictional, interest in Leti's narrative rapidly declined. H. H. Furness, in his still influential variorum edition of *The Merchant of Venice,* includes Farneworth's translation but then invokes the authority of those who dismiss it as a source. And though he quotes Farneworth's observation that Shakespeare's plot "is taken from this incident," he cuts off the quotation at the point where it leads Farneworth to point out that Shakespeare has also made the Jew the victim and left out indecent details.[52] Interest in pure sources—rather than near contemporary versions that might cast light on various aspects of the story—has been influential enough in Shakespeare studies in this century to account for the virtual disappearance of Leti's story from editions or even from collections of Shakespeare's sources.[53] Nowadays, Leti's version is no longer cited, mentioned, or even known to most Shakespeareans.

When we turn to Alexander Silvayn's *The Orator,* which these same source-hunters agree is one of Shakespeare's primary sources for the pound of flesh plot, we find a clear precedent for the argument that a Jew considers the possibility of castrating the Christian. The ninety-fifth declamation of *The Orator,* translated into English in 1596 shortly before the composition of *The Merchant,* describes "a Jew, who would for his debt have a pound of the flesh of a Christian."[54] In his appeal to the judge's sentence that he "cut a just pound of the Christian flesh, and if he cut either more or less, then his own head should be smitten off," the Jew insists that in the original agreement the Christian was to hand over the said pound:

> Neither am I to take that which he oweth me, but he is to deliver it me. And especially because no man knoweth better than he where the same may be spared to the least hurt of his person, for I might take it in such a place as he might thereby happen to lose his life. What a matter were it then if I should cut of his privy members, supposing that the same would altogether weigh a just pound?[55]

While Shakespeare's eighteenth-century editors included this source in unadulterated form,[56] a century later it would be partially suppressed, apparently proving too obscene for Furness to reprint in unexpurgated form. In a strange act of textual castration and substitution, Furness alters the line to read "what a matter were it then, if I should cut of his [head], supposing that the same would weigh a just pound."[57] This makes little sense, no matter how light-headed the victim might be, since in the next sentence the Jew continues, "Or else his head, should I be suffered to cut it off, although it were with the danger of mine own life,"[58] and in the sentence after that wonders if his victim's "nose, lips, his ears, and. . . . eyes . . . make of them altogether a pound."[59] Furness's textual intervention immediately influenced subsequent editions of the play; a year after his edition was published, for example, Homer B. Sprague wrote "head" (without brackets) in his popular school edition of the play.[60] The bowdlerization of this source, and the lack of interest in Leti, have effectively deflected critical attention away from aspects of the play that touch upon ritual Jewish practices.

III. The circumcision of the heart

> Why this bond is forfeit,
> And lawfully by this the Jew may claim
> A pound of flesh, to be by him cut off
> Nearest the merchant's heart.
> —*The Merchant of Venice,* 4.1.227-30

When Paul declares that "the circumcision is of the heart" and is "in the spirit, not in the letter," we are presented with a double displacement: of the physical by the spiritual and of the circumcision of the flesh by the circumcision of the heart. Elizabethan commentators were well aware that Paul's metaphorical treatment of circumcision builds upon a preexisting tradition in the Old Testament, expressed particularly in Deuteronomy 10.16 and 30.6: "Circumcise the foreskin of your heart," and "The Lord thy God will circumcise thine heart."[61] Mornay, in Sidney's translation, also notes that when the Old Testament prophets "rebuke us, they call us not simply uncircumcised, but uncircumcised of heart or lips,"[62] and Peter Martyr simply confirms that "Paul borrowed" this "phrase touching the circumcision of the heart . . . out of the Old Testament."[63]

Hugo Grotius understood that this substitution of heart for flesh neatly defined the relationship between Christian fellowship and the genealogical Judaism it replaced, since the Covenant "should be common to all people." He even argued that the Old Testament prophets recognized this "mystical and more excellent signification contained" in "the precept of circumcision," since they in fact "command the circumcision of the heart, which all the commandments of Jesus aim at."[64] John Donne is particularly eloquent on this symbolic displacement: "The principal dignity of this circumcision was that it . . . prefigured, it directed to that circumcision of the heart." For Donne, "Jewish circumcision were an absurd and unreasonable thing if it did not intimate and figure the circumcision of the heart."[65]

The unexplained displacement of Shylock's cut from Antonio's "flesh" upward to his heart is now considerably clearer. Viewed in light of this familiar exegetical tradition, Shylock's decision to exact his pound of flesh from near Antonio's heart can be seen as the height of the literalism that informs all his actions in the play, a literalism that when imitated by Portia leads to his demise. Also echoing through the trial scene of *The Merchant* are the words of Galatians 6.13: "For they themselves which are circumcised keep not the Law, but desire to have you circumcised, that they might rejoice in your flesh," that is to say (as the gloss to this line in the Geneva Bible puts it), "that they have made you Jews." Shylock will cut his Christian adversary in that part of the body where the Christians believe themselves to be truly circumcised: the heart. Shylock's threat gives a wonderfully ironic twist to the commentary on Paul's Romans that "he is the Jew indeed . . . who cuts off all superfluities and pollutions which are spiritually though not literally meant by the law of circumcision."[66] Psychoanalytically inclined readers will immediately recognize how closely the terms of this Pauline displacement correspond to the unconscious substitution central to Freud's secular theories. Theodore Reik, a disciple of Freud's, interpreted Shylock's bond in just these terms, arguing first that the "condition that he can cut a pound of flesh 'in what part of your body pleaseth me'" is "a substitute expression of castration." Reik adds that when it is later decided that "the cut should be made from the breast, analytic interpretation will easily understand the mechanism of distortion that operates here and displaces the performance from a part of the body below to above."[67]

In repudiating circumcision, [Paul] sought to redirect the Covenant, sever the genealogical bond of Judaism, distinguish Jew from Christian, true Jew from false Jew, and the spirit from the flesh (while retaining in a metaphorical sense the sexuality attendant on the flesh). Yet his actual remarks about circumcision are enigmatic and confusing. It is only mild consolation that they proved no less puzzling to the sixteenth-century theologians who tried to untangle the various levels of Paul's literal and symbolic displacements. Take, for example, the Geneva Bible's gloss to Romans, which reaches new depths of convolution in its attempt to iron out these difficulties by asserting that "Paul useth oftentimes to set the letter against the spirit. But in this place the circumcision which is according to the letter is the cutting off of the foreskin. But the circumcision of the spirit is the circumcision of the heart. That is to say, the spiritual end of the ceremony is true holiness and righteousness, whereby the people of God is known from profane and heathenish men." In their frustration, Paul's interpreters often turned against one another. Andrew Willet, for example, chastised Origen for misreading Paul and "thus distinguishing the circumcision of the flesh; that because there is some part of the flesh cut off and lost, some part remaineth still. The lost and cut off part (saith he) hath a resemblance of that flesh, whereof it is said, all flesh is grass. The other part which remaineth is a figure of that flesh, whereof the Scripture speaketh, all flesh shall see the salutation of God." Willet is sensitive to Origen's conflation of the two kinds of circumcision here, spiritual and fleshly—"Origen confoundeth the circumcision of the flesh and the spirit, making them all one"—but it is hard to see how to maintain hard and fast divisions when, on the one hand, commentators drive a wedge between the spiritual and the physical, while, on the other, they show how even in the Old Testament circumcision was used both literally and metaphorically. For Willet, then, the correct interpretation, and one that seems to require a bit of mental gymnastics, requires that we think not of the circumcision of the flesh and the circumcision of the heart "as though there were two kinds of circumcisions" but as "two parts of one and the same circumcision which are sometimes joined together, both the inward and the outward."[68]

IV. Uncircumcision

If the distinction between inward and outward circumcision were not confusing enough, Paul further complicated matters by introducing the concept of reverse, or *un*circumcision. Even if a faithful Christian were circumcised in the heart, what if one's body still carried (as Paul's did) the stigmatical mark that revealed to the world that one was born a Jew? The seventeenth-century Scottish preacher John Weemse recognized that the early Christians were embarrassed by this Judaical scar: "When they were converted from Judaism to Christianity there were some of them so ashamed of their Judaism that they could not behold it; they took it as a blot to their Christianity."[69] Uncircumcision, then, was the undoing of the seemingly irreversible physical act that had been accomplished through the observance of Jewish law, and it was a topic that Paul would return to obsessively (in large part because it was a pressing issue within the new Christian communities he was addressing). Paul asks in Romans "if the uncircumcision keep the ordinances of the Law, shall not his uncircumcision be counted for circumcision? And shall not uncircumcision which is by nature (if it keep the Law) condemn thee, which by the letter and circumcision art a transgressor of the Law?"[70] In Galatians he writes in a similar vein that "in Jesus Christ neither circumcision availeth anything" nor "uncircumcision, but faith, which worketh by love."[71] His remarks in Corinthians on the irrelevance of this mark are even more forceful: "Is any man called being circumcised? Let him not gather his circumcision. Is any called uncircumcised? Let him not be circumcised. Circumcision is nothing, and uncircumcision is nothing, but the keeping of the commandments of God."[72]

Paul's shifts between literal and figurative uncircumcision in these key passages are dizzying, and the commentators had to scramble to keep up with him. Thomas Godwyn voices the question that must have been on many readers' minds: "Here it may be demanded how it is possible for a man, after once he hath been marked with the sign of circumcision, to blot out that character and become uncircumcised?"[73] He is responding to Paul's warning that one should not "gather" or reverse one's circumcision. The gloss to this line in the Geneva Bible also takes Paul in the most literal sense imaginable, explaining that this "gathering" is accomplished with "the help of a surgeon" who undoes the effect of the cutting of the foreskin by "drawing the skin with an instrument, to make it to cover the nut" or glans of the penis. The Geneva Bible even directs readers to the medical source for this procedure, the seventh book of Celsus's *De Medicina*.[74] Other writers explained that Paul forbids this literal uncircumcision in his letter to the Corinthians "because some that were converted to Christianity from Judaism did so renounce all their Judaical rites that they used means to attract the preputia again, which was an act of too much superstition and curiosity, and so is censured here."[75] It also needs to be stressed here that uncircumcision, like circumcision, was understood by Paul's commentators to operate both spiritually and literally; Andrew Willet reminds his readers that "as there are two kinds of circumcision, so there is also a twofold uncircumcision, "an uncircumcision of the heart, and another of the flesh."

The belief that one could be uncircumcised, could have one's irreducible Jewish identity replaced with a Christian one, is also a fantasy that powerfully shapes the final confrontation between Shylock and Antonio in *The Merchant of Venice*. Antonio's consummate revenge upon his circumcised adversary, whose actions symbolically threaten to transform not just his physical but his religious identity, is to ask of the court a punishment that precisely reverses what Shylock had in mind for him. When Antonio demands that Shylock "presently become a Christian," a demand to which the Duke readily agrees, the "christ'ning" that Shylock is to receive will metaphorically uncircumcise him. The new covenant has superseded the old, as the sacrament of baptism, which has replaced circumcision, turns Jew into Christian.[76] In his commentary on Romans Peter Martyr offers up a summary of Paul's treatment of the Jews that ironically foreshadows Antonio's victory over Shylock at the end of the trial scene: "In civil judgments, when any is to be condemned which is in any dignity or magistrateship, he is first deprived of his dignity or office, and then afterward condemned. So the apostle first depriveth the Jews of the true Jewishness, and of the true circumcision, and then afterward condemneth them."[77]

Antonio and Shylock, who fiercely insist on how different they are from each other, to the last seek out ways of preserving that difference through symbolic acts that convert their adversary into their own kind. Paradoxically, though, these symbolic acts—a threatened circumcision of the heart and a baptism that figuratively uncircumcises—would have the opposite effect, erasing, rather than preserving, the literal or figurative boundaries that distinguish merchant from Jew.[78] It is just this fear of unexpected and unsatisfying transformation that makes *The Merchant of Venice* so unsettling a comedy, and that renders the even more deeply submerged and shadowy charge of ritual murder such a potent one. The desire to allay such fears produces a fantasy ending in which the circumcising Jew is metamorphosed through conversion into a gentle Christian. While this resolution can only be sustained through legal force in the play (Shylock's alternative, after all, is to be executed), its power was sufficiently strong for this spectacle of conversion to be reenacted in a number of English churches in late sixteenth- and early seventeenth-century England, as a handful of Jews were led to the baptismal font.

Notes

Epigraph sources are as follows: Geoffrey Bullough, *Narrative and Dramatic Sources of Shakespeare,* 8 vols. (New York: Columbia University Press, 1957-75), vol. 1, p. 483; and Leon Poliakov, *A History of Anti-Semitism,* 3 vols. (New York: Vanguard Press, 1974), vol. 1, p. 223. Poliakov does not provide the source of this quotation.

[1] Sigmund Freud, *The Standard Edition of the Complete Works,* trans. James Strachey et al., 24 vols. (London: Hogarth Press, 1953-1974), vol. 10, p. 36. See, too, his *Leonardo da Vinci* (1910), where Freud notes that "here we may also trace one of the roots of the anti-semitism which appears with such elemental force and finds such irrational explanation among the nations of the West." For Freud, "circumcision is unconsciously equated with castration. If we venture to carry our conjectures back to the primaeval days of the human race we can surmise that originally circumcision must have been a milder substitute, designed to take the place of castration" (vol. 11, p. 95). He added this footnote in 1919. In his *Introductory Lectures on Psychoanalysis* he similarly writes that there "seems to me no doubt that the circumcision practiced by so many peoples is an equivalent and substitute for castration" (vol. 15, p. 165). Sander Gilman's penetrating studies—*The Case of Sigmund Freud,* and *Freud, Race, and Gender* (Princeton: Princeton University Press, 1993)—discuss in great detail the historical and medical issues that informed Freud's ideas about circumcision; see especially the chapter on "The Construction of the Male Jew" in *Freud, Race, and Gender,* pp. 49-92.

[2] In Freud's own analysis of Shakespeare's play he avoids Jewish questions, focusing not on the pound of flesh plot but on the tale of the three caskets. Marjorie Garber, turning Freud's psychoanalytic approach against him, brilliantly argues that by "turning *The Merchant of Venice* into *King Lear,* Freud occludes Portia and her own scene of choice, when, dressed like a man, she chooses between two men, two symbolic castrates, Antonio the 'tainted wether of the flock' (4.1.114) and Shylock 'the circumcised Jew.'" Garber wonders whether Freud, by focusing on this issue, is able to avoid confronting his own patriarchy and misogyny by failing to address the more disturbing "problem of the two things he does not want to think of, the two last things that remain on the periphery of the essay on 'The Three Caskets,' discreetly offstage and off-page, the two figures central to *The Merchant of Venice:* the cross-dressed woman and the Jew?" (Marjorie Garber, *Shakespeare's Ghost Writers: Literature as Uncanny Causality* [New York: Methuen, 1987], p. 187, n. 63).

[3] Tovey, *Anglia Judaica,* p. 65. Bonefand, we learn, "pleaded not guilty, and was very honourably acquitted," raising the interesting question of how, given the medical evidence, the case could ever have been successfully prosecuted.

[4] Gabriel Harvey, *Works,* ed. Alexander Grosart, 3 vols. (London, 1884-1885), vol. 1, p. 203.

[5] Andrew Willet, *Hexapla: That Is, a Six-fold Commentarie Upon the Most Divine Epistle of the Holy Apostle S. Paul to the Romanes* (Cambridge, 1611), p. 203.

[6] As Purchas puts it in his *Pilgrimage* (1613), p. 158.

[7] While this woodcut no doubt relates to his reputed escape from a crowd of hostile Venetian Jews whom he sought to convert, there is no evidence anywhere in Coryate's book that these Jews bore weapons against him. Coryate himself explains that "that some forty or fifty Jews more flocked about me, and some of them began very insolently to swagger with me, because I durst reprehend their religion. Whereupon fearing least they should have offered me some violence, I withdrew myself by little and little towards the bridge at the entrance into the ghetto" (Coryate, *Coryats Crudities* [London, 1611], pp. 236-37).

[8] Coryate is subsequently imagined as facing the danger of circumcision in his travels through Islamic nations. A poem written in 1615 to Coryate by John Brown, an English merchant residing at the time in India, warns Coryate to "have a care (at Mecca is some danger) / Lest you incur the pain of circumcision." Coryate published the poem in his *Thomas Coryate, Travailer . . . Greeting . . . from the Court of the Great Mogul* (London, 1616), p. 34.

[9] Coryate, *Coryats Crudities,* sigs. D7v, E1r, and A2r.

[10] Coryate adds: "All his privities (before he came into the room) were besprinkled with a kind of powder, which after the circumcisor had done his business was blowed away by him, and another powder cast on immediately. After he had dispatched his work . . . he took a little strong wine that was held in a goblet by a fellow that stood near him, and poured it into the child's mouth to comfort him in the midst of his pains, who cried out very bitterly; the pain being for the time

very bitter indeed, though it will be (as they told me) cured in the space of four and twenty hours. Those of any riper years that are circumcised (as it too often commeth to pass, that Christians that turn Turks) as at forty or fifty years of age, do suffer great pain for the space of a month" (Coryate, *Coryate's Crudities; Reprinted from the Edition of 1611. To Which Are Now Added, His Letters from India,* vol. 3, sig. U7r-U8v.

[11] See Daniel Boyarin's essay in which he notes that "at a traditional circumcision ceremony the newly circumcised boy is addressed: 'And I say to you [feminine pronoun!]: in your [feminine] blood, you [feminine] shall live,'" and offers as a possible interpretation that "circumcision was understood somehow as rendering the male somewhat feminine," or alternatively, "that there is here an arrogation of a female symbol that makes it male, and that circumcision is a male erasure of the female role in procreation as well" (Boyarin, "'This We Know to Be the Carnal Israel': Circumcision and the Erotic Life of God and Israel," *Critical Inquiry* 19 [1992], p. 496, and n. 64).

[12] Charles Hughes, ed., *Shakespeare's Europe: Unpublished Chapters of Fynes Moryson's Itinerary,* 2 vols. (London: Sherrat and Hughes, 1903), vol. 2, pp. 494-95.

[13] Cf. John Evelyn, who reports in his diary entry for January 15, 1645, in Rome, that when "the circumcision was done the priest sucked the child's penis with his mouth" (as cited in A. Cohen, *An Anglo-Jewish Scrapbook, 1600-1840* [London: M. L. Cailingold, 1943], p. 292). Charles Weiss notes that *metzitzah* "was probably introduced during the talmudic period," and that "its practice never became universal" ("A Worldwide Survey of the Current Practice of *Milah* [Ritual Circumcision]," *Jewish Social Studies* 24 [1962], p. 31). See too Bernard Homa, *Metzitzah* (2d ed., London, n.p., 1966), where the relevant Midrashic texts that are the source of the authority for this practice are cited. Michel de Montaigne also found an opportunity to observe and describe "the most ancient religious ceremony there is among men," which he "watched . . . very attentively and with great profit." He too was struck by the practice of *metzitzah:* "As soon as this glans is thus uncovered, they hastily offer some wine to the minister, who puts a little in his mouth and then goes and sucks the glans of this child, all bloody, and spits out the blood he has drawn from it, and immediately takes as much wine again, up to three times." After bandaging the child, the "minister" is given "a glass full of wine. . . . He takes a swallow of it, and then dipping his finger in it he three times takes a drop of it with his finger to the boy's mouth to be sucked. . . . He meanwhile still hath his mouth all bloody" (Michel de Montaigne, *Montaigne's Travel Journal,* trans. Donald M. Frame [San Francisco: North Point Press, 1983], pp. 81-82. The event was recorded by one of Montaigne's servants, assigned to compile the journal).

[14] The Bible also failed to prepare English travelers for what they would witness in Africa: female "circumcision." Samuel Purchas, anticipating the skepticism of his readers, writes of one of the voyages into Ethiopia: "Let no man marvel which heareth this, for they circumcise women as well as men, which thing was not used in the old Law." He also notes that both in Cairo and "Abassine" they "circumcise not only males, but with a peculiar rite females also" (Purchas, *Pilgrimage,* pp. 1040, 841, and 1134). The Islamic practice of delaying circumcision until sexual maturity struck Elizabethan writers, versed in a scriptural tradition of circumcision occurring on the eighth day, as unusual. Richard Jobson's description of his trip to "Gambra" in 1620, provided readers in England with considerable details of the practice—locally known as the "cutting of pricks"—experienced by brave adolescent boys in Africa: "Hither we came in season for that solemnity, hearing before we came, shouts, drums and country music. The boy knew the meaning, and told us it was for cutting of pricks, a world of people being gather[ed] for that purpose, like an English fair. . . . We saw our black boy circumcised, not by a marybuck [that is, a priest], but an ordinary fellow hackling off with a knife at three cuts his praepuce, holding his member in his hand, the boy neither holden nor bound the while" (As cited in Purchas, p. 925). See, too, a later narrative where Richard Jobson speaks of the local African custom concerning circumcision: "It is done without religious ceremony, and hath no name but the cutting of pricks, the party stripped naked and sitting on the ground, and the butcher pulling the skin over very far, and cutting it, not without terror to the beholder" (As cited in Purchas, p. 1573).

[15] Purchas, *Pilgrimage,* p. 121.

[16] Willet, *Hexapla,* p. 204.

[17] Thorowgood, *Jews in America,* pp. 13, 15. Similarly, when Queen Elizabeth's ambassador to Russia, Giles Fletcher, declared that the Tartars were the ten lost tribes of Israel, he too found confirmation in the fact that they "are circumcised, as were the Israelish and Jewish people" (Giles Fletcher, "The Tartars or, Ten Tribes," first published sixty-six years after his death in 1611, in Samuel Lee, *Israel Redux: Or the Restauration of Israel* [London, 1677], p. 22).

[18] *List and Analysis of State Papers: Foreign Series, Elizabeth I,* vol. 6 (January to December 1595), ed. R. B. Wernham (London: HMSO, 1993), p. 269. For a facsimile and transcript of Don Solomon's letter, see H. G. Rosedale, *Queen Elizabeth and the Levant Company* (London: Henry Fraude, 1904), pp. 19-33.

[19] See Acts 16.3. Unless otherwise noted, scriptural passages are quoted from the 1589 edition of the Geneva Bible, published in London (I have modernized spelling and orthography here as well).

[20] Philippe de Mornay, *A Woorke Concerning the Trewnesse of the Christian Religion, Written in French, Against Atheists, Epicures, Paynims, Jewes, Mahumetists, and Other Infidels,* trans. Sir Philip Sidney and Arthur Golding (London, 1587), pp. 581-82.

[21] William Perkins, *A Commentarie or Exposition, Upon the First Five Chapters of the Epistles to the Galatians* (Cambridge, 1604), p. 380.

[22] Jean Calvin, *Sermons of M. John Calvine Upon the Epistle of Saincte Paule to the Galatians,* trans. Arthur Golding (London, 1574), fol. 325r.

[23] John Calvin, *A Commentarie upon S. Paules Epistles to the Corinthians,* trans. Thomas Timme (London, 1577), fol. 82v. Others offered an evolutionary model that would explain the different attitudes the earliest Christians held toward circumcision. For example, the Scottish preacher John Weemse writes that in the "first period," Christians "might only circumcise; in the second period, circumcise and baptize; (for they had yet more regard to circumcision than to baptism); in the third period they baptized and circumcised (now they had more regard to baptism than circumcision); in the fourth period, they only baptized" (Weemse, *The Christian Synagogue,* 4 vols. [London, 1633], vol. 1, p. 129).

[24] Romans 2.25.

[25] *The New Testament of Our Lord Jesus Christ Translated Out of the Greek. By Theod. Beza,* trans. Laurence Tomson (London, 1596). Different editions offer slightly different wording. The first edition of Tomson's revision of the Geneva New Testament (based on Beza's 1565 Latin text) appeared in 1576. It was subsequently published both independently and as part of the larger Geneva Bibles. This was the final and popular form of the Geneva Bible.

[26] Romans 2.28-29.

[27] For this aspect of Paul's thought, see Daniel Boyarin, who astutely observes that Paul's problem with circumcision was that it "symbolized the genetic, the genealogical moment of Judaism as the religion of a particular tribe of people. This is so both in the very fact of the physicality of the rite, of its grounding in the practice of the tribe, and in the way it marks the male members of that tribe (in both sense), but even more so, by being a marker on the organ of generation it represents the genealogical claim for concrete historical memory as constitutive of Israel." Thus, by "substituting a spiritual interpretation for a physical ritual, Paul was saying that the genealogical Israel 'according to the Flesh,' is not the ultimate Israel; there is an 'Israel in the Spirit'" (Boyarin, "'This We Know to Be the Carnal Israel,'" p. 502).

[28] See Joseph Hall, *A Plaine and Familiar Exposition by Way of Paraphrase of All the Hard Texts of the Whole Divine Scripture of the Old and New Testament* (London, 1633), p. 160.

[29] Willet, *Hexapla,* p. 142. Origen's own position may have been qualified by the possibility (according to Eusebius) that he had castrated himself in his youth in order to work unconstrained with female catechumens.

[30] It should also be noted that there is a Jewish tradition that values circumcision because it curtails male desire. Daniel Boyarin cites the observation of Maimonides that circumcision was instituted "to bring about a decrease in sexual intercourse and a weakening of the organ in question, so that this activity be diminished and the organ be in as quiet a state as possible" (in Moses Maimonides, *The Guide of the Perplexed,* trans. and ed. Shlomo Pines (Chicago: University of Chicago Press, 1963), p. 609, cited in Boyarin, "'This We Know to Be the Carnal Israel,'" p. 486, note 37. Boyarin also notes the Platonic, allegorizing view of circumcision in Philo as well. Some of the complex ways in which circumcision was understood symbolically in Jewish exegetical traditions are explored by Elliot R. Wolfson in "Circumcision, Vision of God, and Textual Interpretation: From Midrashic Trope to Mystical Symbol," *History of Religions* 27 (1987), pp. 189-215, and "Circumcision and the Divine Name: A Study in the Transmission of Esoteric Doctrine," *The Jewish Quarterly Review* 78 (1987), pp. 77-112.

[31] Donne concludes, "God would have them carry this memorial about them, in their flesh," in "A Sermon Preached at Saint Dunstan's Upon New-Years-Day, 1624," *Sermons,* vol. 6, pp. 190-92.

[32] The gendering of the act had long been a problem for Christian interpreters of the Bible, some condemning the Jews for leaving women out of the Covenant, others answering the objection "that circumcision was an imperfect sign, because it was appointed only for the males, the females were not circumcised," by saying that "the priviledge and benefit of circumcision was extended also unto the females, which were counted with the men, the unmarried with their fathers, the married with their husbands" (Willet, *Hexapla,* p. 205).

[33] Diane Owen Hughes, "Distinguishing Signs: Ear-Rings, Jews, and Franciscan Rhetoric in the Italian City State," *Past and Present* 112 (1986), p. 24.

[34] Shakespeare, *The Merchant of Venice,* 3.1.82-84.

[35] This problem is usually due to excessive electrocautery used in some hospitals, which burns off too much of the infant's penis to warrant reconstructing the organ. The surgeons perform a "feminizing genitoplasty," that is, reconstructing female rather than male genitalia (and at the age of puberty performing a second operation, a vaginoplasty, supplemented by estrogens). See John P. Gearhart and John A. Rock, "Total Ablation of the Penis After Circumcision with Electrocauter: A Method of Management and Long-Term Follow-up," *Journal of Urology* 142 (1989), pp. 799-801. The authors note that the "successful adaption and normal sex life of our 2 older patients are a tribute to early gender reassignment, the involvement of a complete team of specialists, including a medical sexology expert, and extensive familial counseling from the time of injury" (p. 801). I am indebted to Dr. Franklin Lowe of Columbia Physicians and Surgeons for making this scholarship available to me. I am also grateful to Patricia E. Gallagher, of Beth Israel Medical Center, for providing me with material on circumcision procedures.

[36] Shakespeare, *The Merchant of Venice,* 1.3.146-48, and 4.1.249. The first hint appears in act 3, when Shylock says to Tubal "I will have the heart of him if he forfeit" (3.1.119-20).

[37] "Whosoever hath an issue from his flesh is unclean because of his issue," Leviticus 15.2. Biblical anthropologists have traced the practice of using the euphemism *basar* (flesh) when referring to the penis to the priestly redactors (rather than the Jahwist, who did not use this euphemism). See Howard Eilberg-Schwartz, *The Savage in Judaism: An Anthropology of Israelite Religion and Ancient Judaism* (Bloomington: Indiana University Press, 1990), pp. 170-71.

[38] Shakespeare, *Romeo and Juliet,* 1.1.29-30, and 2.4.37.

[39] Shakespeare, *The Merchant of Venice,* 4.1.113. Antonio's next lines—"the weakest kind of fruit / Drops earliest to the ground, and so let me" (4.1.114-15)—may connect back to the recurrent biblical identification of fruit trees with circumcision. In his chapter on "Uncircumcised Fruit Trees," Howard Eilberg-Schwartz notes the frequent comparison in biblical literature between "fruit trees and male organs" (p. 149; see, for example, Leviticus 19.23-25), and concludes that "the symbolic equation of an uncircumcised male and a young fruit tree rests on two, and possibly three, associations. The fruit of a juvenile tree is proscribed like the foreskin of the male organ. Furthermore, a male who is uncircumcised and not part of the covenantal community is infertile like an immature fruit tree. Finally, this symbolic equation may draw part of its plausibility from an analogy between circumcision and pruning," Eilberg-Schwartz, *The Savage in Judaism,* p. 152. See, too, his "People of the Body: The Problem of the Body for the People of the Book," *Journal of the History of Sexuality* 2 (1991), pp. 1-24.

[40] Shakespeare, *The Merchant of Venice,* 2.8.22, 5.1.237.

[41] As cited in J. H. Baker, "Criminal Courts and Procedure at Common Law, 1550-1800," in *Crimes in England, 1550-1800,* ed. J. S. Cockburn (Princeton: Princeton University Press, 1977), p. 42.

[42] Before he had to leave in 1683—having run afoul of the Duke of York and England's Catholic community—Leti had even been elected to the Royal Society and asked by Charles II to write a history of England from its origins to the Restoration. See the introduction to Nati Krivatsy, *Bibliography of the Works of Gregorio Leti* (Newcastle, Delaware: Oak Knoll Books, 1982).

[43] Gregorio Leti, *Vita di Sisto V,* 3 vols. (Amsterdam, 1693), vol. 3, pp. 134ff. Since the first English translation of Leti's biography—*The Life of Pope Sixtus the Vth* (London, 1704)—was based on the 1669 text, it does not contain the pound of flesh story.

[44] Gregorio Leti, *The Life of Pope Sixtus the Fifth,* trans. Ellis Farneworth (London, 1754). A subsequent edition of this translation was published in Dublin in 1766.

[45] Leti, *Vita di Sisto V* (1693), vol. 3, p. 136.

[46] And, conveniently, to pay for a hospital that he had recently founded. See Leti, *Sixtus the Fifth,* trans. Farneworth, pp. 293-95.

[47] Leti, *Sixtus the Fifth,* trans. Farneworth, p. 293, n. 19.

[48] Leti writes of their "gesti ridicolosissimi." For his remarks about London's Jews, see Leti, *Del Teatro Brittanico o Vero Historia dello Stato, Antico e Presente . . . della Grande Brettagna,* 2 vols. (London, 1683), esp. vol. 1, pp. 251-52, 549-50, as cited in Jonathan I. Israel, "Gregorio Leti (1631-1701) and the Dutch Sephardi Elite at the Close of the Seventeenth Century," in *Jewish History: Essays in Honour of Chimen Abramsky,* ed. Ada Rapoport-Albert and Steven J. Zipperstein (London: Peter Halban, 1988], p. 269).

[49] Edmond Malone, *The Plays and Poems of William Shakespeare* (London, 1790), vol. 3, pp. 111-13.

[50] David Erskine Baker, *Biographia Dramatica or a Companion to the Playhouse Containing Historical and*

Critical Memoirs, 3 vols. (London, 1812), vol. 3, p. 34. First published in 1782.

[51] Edgeworth, *Harrington,* p. 96.

[52] Furness, ed., *The Merchant of Venice, A New Variorum Edition,* pp. 295ff.

[53] For one of the few twentieth-century citations of Leti's story in relationship to Shakespeare's play, see Berta Viktoria Wenger, "Shylocks Pfund Fleish," *Shakespeare Jahrbuch* 65 (1929), esp. pp. 148-50.

[54] Bullough, *Sources,* vol. 1, p. 483.

[55] Bullough, *Sources,* vol. 1, p. 484. In other sources the cutting is to be done to the eyes (as in Anthony Munday's *Zeluto*), or is left ambiguous or unspecified, in the words of Fiorentino's *Il Pecorone* (1558), "wheresoever he pleases."

[56] Malone, ed., *Plays and Poems of Shakspeare,* vol. 3, p. 114.

[57] Furness, ed., *The Merchant of Venice, A New Variorum Edition,* pp. 311-12.

[58] Bullough, *Sources,* vol. 1, p. 484.

[59] Furness, ed., *The Merchant of Venice, A New Variorum Edition,* p. 312.

[60] Sprague, ed., *The Merchant of Venice* (New York: Silver, Burdett, 1889).

[61] See Willet's gloss on this passage in *Hexapla.* Elizabethan editions of the Bible constantly read Pauline doctrine back into the Old Testament passages. Thus, for example, the Bishops' Bible gloss explains: "That is, let all your affections be cut off. He showeth in these words the end of circumcision"; and "Cut off all your evil affections."

[62] Mornay, *Trewnesse of the Christian Religion,* pp. 581-82.

[63] Peter Martyr [Vermigli], *Most Learned and Fruitfull Commentaries of D. Peter Martir Vermilius, Florentine . . . Upon the Epistle of S. Paul to the Romanes* (London, 1568), p. 49v. Andrew Willet also cites the prophet Jeremiah, who proclaims that "all the nations are uncircumcised, and all the house of Israel are uncircumcised in the heart" (9.26).

[64] Hugo Grotius, *True Religion Explained and Defended* (London, 1632), p. 274.

[65] Donne, *Sermons,* vol. 6, p. 193.

[66] Henry Hammond, *A Paraphrase and Annotations Upon All the Books of the New Testament* (London, 1653), p. 475.

[67] For this psychoanalyst (who had first witnessed Shakespeare's play as a young boy at the turn of the century in antisemitic Vienna), only "one step is needed to reach the concept that to the Gentile of medieval times the Jew unconsciously typified the castrator because he circumcised male children." The "Jew thus appeared to Gentiles as a dangerous figure with whom the threat of castration originated." Theodore Reik, "Psychoanalytic Experiences in Life, Literature, and Music," in *The Search Within* (New York: Farrar, Strauss and Cudahy, 1956), pp. 358-59; first printed as "Jessica, My Child," *American Imago* 8 (1951), pp. 3-27.

[68] Willet, *Hexapla,* pp. 130-31.

[69] Weemse, *The Christian Synagogue,* vol. 1, p. 127. There is considerable medical evidence for uncircumcision or reverse circumcision as far back as classical antiquity. See, for example, J. P. Rubin, "Celsus' decircumcision operation: medical and historical implications," *Urology* 16 (1980), p. 121; and B. O. Rogers, "History of External Genital Surgery," in *Plastic and Reconstruction Surgery of the Genital Area,* ed. C. E. Horton (Boston: Little, Brown, & Co., 1973), pp. 3-47. Willard E. Goodwin's "Circumcision: A Technique for Plastic Reconstruction of a Prepuce After Circumcision," *Journal of Urology* 144 (1990), pp. 1203-1205, offers a helpful overview of both the history of and the procedures for reversing circumcision.

[70] Romans, 2.26-27.

[71] Galatians, 5.6. He would return to this idea again shortly, when he states that "in Christ Jesus neither circumcision availeth any thing, nor uncircumcision, but a new creature" (Galatians, 6.15).

[72] Corinthians, 7.18-19.

[73] Thomas Godwyn, *Moses and Aaron: Civil and Ecclesiastical Rites Used by the Ancient Hebrewes,* 4th ed. (London, 1631), p. 242.

[74] The same information was also made available in the margin of the Geneva Bible, where Elizabethans, who had no need of this procedure themselves, were nonetheless informed that "the surgeon by art draweth out the skin to cover the part circumcised." The Geneva Bible also cross-references 1 Maccabees 1.16, which describes how the Jews followed the "fashions of the heathen" and "made themselves uncircumcised, and forsook the holy Covenant." The table of contents to the 1589 Geneva Bible (which usefully cites all biblical passages that mention circumcision) cites this pas-

sage as one in which the "Jews did uncircumcise themselves, and became apostates," indicating that the act carried with it associations of abandoning one religion for another.

Those curious enough to follow up the medical reference would have read in the Latin text of A. Cornelius Celsus (the first English translation, from which I quote, was not published until 1756) that this procedure requires that "under the circle of the glans, the skin" is "to be separated by a knife from the inner part of the penis." Celsus explains that this "is not very painful, because the extremity being loosened, it may be drawn backwards by the hand, as far as the pubes; and no hemorrhage follows upon it." Next, the "skin being disengaged, is extended again over the glans; then it is bathed with plenty of cold water, and a plaister put round it of efficacy in repelling an inflammation." Celsus offers as postoperative advice that "the patient is to fast, till he almost be overcome with hunger, lest a full diet should perhaps cause an erection of that part." Finally, when "the inflammation is gone, it ought to be bound up from the pubes to the circle of the glans; and a plaister being first laid on the glans, the skin ought to be brought over it" (A. Cornelius Celsus, *Of Medicine. In Eight Books,* trans. James Greive [London, 1756], pp. 438-39).

[75] Hammond, *A Paraphrase,* p. 565. Hammond also describes the "practice of some Jews, who under the Egyptian tyranny first, then under Antiochus, and lastly under the Romans, being oppressed for being Jews, of which their circumcision was an evidence, used means by some medicinal applications to get a new praeputium. And these were called by the Talmudists *mishuchim*" (I transliterate the Hebrew here). Following the Geneva Bible gloss, Hammond cites as a medical authority "the famous Physician" Celsus, and, unusually, also invokes Talmudic antecedents, citing Rabbi "Aleai of Achan," who "made himself a praeputium."

[76] Shakespeare, *The Merchant of Venice,* 4.1.383, 4.1.394. Cf. Reik, who argues that if "Shylock insists upon cutting out a pound of flesh from Antonio's breast, it is as if he demanded that the Gentile be made a Jew if he cannot pay back the three thousand ducats at the fixed time. Otherwise put: Antonio should submit to the religious ritual of circumcision." In addition, at "the end of the 'comedy' Antonio demands that Shylock should 'presently become a Christian.' If this is the justified amends the Jew has to make for his earlier condition, it would be according to poetic justice that the Jew be forced to become a Christian after he had insisted that his opponent should become a Jew" (*The Search Within,* pp. 358-59).

[77] Martyr, *Most Learned and Fruitfull Commentaries,* p. 48r.

[78] See the fascinating discussion of the philosophical implications of Shylock's circumcising cut in Stanley Cavell, *The Claims of Reason: Wittgenstein, Skepticism, Morality, and Tragedy* [(New York: Oxford University Press, 1979], pp. 479-81). Marjorie Garber notes that both "Reik and Cavell predicate their insights upon an assumption of doubling or twinship, a moment of perceptual equipoise that enforces the disconcerting confusion of identities. . . . Cavell, with 'skepticism with respect to other minds' and the epistemological uncertainty of identity. Each reader appropriates Shylock's scene, persuasively, to his own theoretical project, and finds the twinship of Shylock and Antonio in the courtroom a theatrical hypostasis, an onstage crux that reifies his own perceptions" (Garber, p. 187, n. 63). See also Marc Shell, *Money, Language, and Thought* (Berkeley: University of California Press, 1982), pp. 47-83.

Source: "The Pound of Flesh," in *Shakespeare and the Jews,* Columbia University Press, 1995, pp. 113-30.

Questionable Purpose in *Measure for Measure*: A Test of Seeming or a Seeming Test?

David Thatcher, *University of Victoria*

The notion that Duke Vincentio is deliberately leaving Vienna in order "to find out whether Angelo is all that he appears,"[1] or "to test the validity of Angelo's pious puritanism"[2] is by now commonplace in criticism on *Measure for Measure*. This "test" theory goes back at least as far as Charlotte Ramsay Lennox's *Shakespear Illustrated* (1753), and echoes down the centuries in countless commentaries on, and editions of, the play as if it were a self-evident truth hardly worth the trouble of argument and demonstration. G. Wilson Knight is an influential supporter of it: "[The Duke] performs the experiment of handing the reins of government to a man of ascetic purity who has an hitherto invulnerable faith in the rightness and justice of his own ideals—a man of spotless reputation and self-conscious integrity, who will have no fears as to the 'justice' of enforcing precise obedience. The scheme is a plot, or trap: a scientific experiment to see if extreme ascetic righteousness can stand the test of power."[3] According to Nevill Coghill, the play, like *The Book of Job,* some of Chaucer's tales, and (he might have added) the medieval play *Everyman,* shows "the human world as a testing-ground": "[It] pictures the world as a place where all are continually liable to tests, and some to tests increasingly severe, that they may show their virtues. Isabella and Angelo are tested to the core."[4] Coghill discerns a pervasive "pattern of testing" running through the narrative design of the play, a pattern which involves even minor characters[5] like Pompey, Barnardine and Mistress Overdone: "We have seen who the tested are. Who is the tester? In all cases, sometimes directly and sometimes at one or two removes, it is the Duke. He is the *primum mobile* of the play."[6]

Louise Schleiner has recently endorsed Coghill's allegorical view by developing a full-blown version of the "test" theory: she depicts the Duke as "a man of tests, a character modeled on the absentee-master figure in a group of parables from the synoptic gospels"; she habitually refers to him as "the testing master" who tests not only Angelo and Isabella but also minor characters "by observing their conduct from his absentee perspective and then determining appropriate judgments"; in fact, she regards the Duke as a unifying factor in a play often regarded as structurally divided, since he is "the testing master from beginning to end," contriving "the opening situation to test Angelo, Escalus, and the government he expects of them."[7] And, as one final example, T. F. Wharton (1988) has linked Marston's *The Malcontent* with *Measure for Measure* as plays of "moral experiment": "It is impossible not to treat the entire leave-of-absence ploy as Vincentio's experiment on Angelo's virtue: to discover either that his virtue is a fraud, and the true self will be revealed, or that his virtue is real, but that power will corrupt it" (p. 37).[8] Among the better known twentieth-century critics (besides Knight, Coghill, Schleiner, and Wharton) who unquestioningly subscribe to the "test" or "moral experiment" theory are F. R. Leavis, Peter Ure, and Anne (Barton) Righter.[9]

Conventional wisdom is always worth challenging, and, since no one ever seems to have challenged this particular tenet of critical orthodoxy, perhaps it is time to take up the gauntlet. As Eliot has said about Shakespeare criticism, "it is probable that we can never be right; and if we can never be right, it is better that we should from time to time change our way of being wrong," and "it is certain that nothing is more effective in driving out error than a new error."[10] Perhaps I offer a new error by suggesting that there might be an alternative reading of the text, preferable to the one which has been unanimously adopted, and, further, that even if the text were believed to support the theory of a "test" (which I do not think it does), the theory itself suffers from serious deficiencies of logic, coherence, and plausibility.

II

In the opening scene of *Measure for Measure* Duke Vincentio is curiously reticent about divulging his motives for leaving Vienna in such haste. The urgency of immediate departure is, in fact, invoked as the reason that there is no time even for the briefest explanation, and Angelo and Escalus receive their several "commissions" (the warrants confirming their new authority) very much in doubt as to the nature and extent of their delegated powers. A little later, speaking privately to Friar Thomas (who, it is implied, has insinuated that the Duke is seeking an opportunity for a clandestine love-affair) the Duke says Angelo supposes him travelled to Poland, for that is the destination he has "strewed . . . in the common ear";[11] his hidden agenda or real purpose, he confides, is to permit Angelo ("a man of stricture and firm abstinence") to enforce the "strict statutes and most biting laws" (1.3.12, 19) which he, the Duke, reproaches himself for having allowed to fall into desuetude. We should note that he has invested Angelo with his full ducal power, telling him "Mortality and mercy in Vienna / Live in thy tongue and heart" (1.1.43-44), and repeating the point by advising Angelo that he may "enforce or qualify the laws / As to your soul seems good"

(1.1.64-65). His words to the Friar, however, indicate that he fully expects, and even hopes, that Angelo will be far less lenient and permissive than he had been and will, in the "ambush" of the Duke's name, "strike home," that is, impose the law to the letter. When he later learns of Angelo's "severity" toward rampant sexual transgression, the Duke approves of it, and calls it necessary (3.3.100-01). It may also be that the "commission" Angelo received from the Duke explicitly commanded him to be strict. When he gives Escalus his "commission" the Duke directs him not to deviate from it (1.1.13-14), suggesting that it contains written instructions.[12]

Taking the Friar even further into his confidence, the Duke promises to give him "moe reasons" for his departure (although he never actually does so in the course of the represented stage action), and offers what appears to be an additional reason:

> Lord Angelo is precise,
> Stands at a guard with envy; scarce confesses
> That his blood flows, or that his appetite
> Is more to bread than stone. Hence we shall see,
> If power change purpose, what our seemers be.
>
> (1.3.50-55)[13]

These lines, the focal point of this essay, have been widely interpreted as providing not simply a refinement of motive but a second and an altogether different motive: that the Duke is leaving in order to test Angelo. In Wharton's view the words "confesses" and "seemers" seem to imply that Angelo "is at best repressed, at worst a hypocrite, and that his appetites are indeed as strong as other men's." Wharton continues: "When [Vincentio] goes on to speak of seeing if power will change purpose, he is directly speaking of an experiment on Angelo. Having placed this suspect character in a position of influence he will test the proposition that all authority corrupts" (1989, p. 63). One's first response is that Vincentio would have had ample opportunity to test whether "all authority corrupts" during his own years in office. At first glance, however, there seems little reason to doubt the apparently interdependent notions that the Duke is contriving a test for Angelo, that he is testing him because he suspects him of hypocrisy, and that his hypocrisy takes the form of some kind of sexual fallibility perspiring under the mask of frigid puritanism and punctiliousness.

The idea of a "test" seems to announce itself at the outset. In the first scene the Duke tells Angelo that "spirits are not finely touched / But to fine issues" (1.1.35-36), a line which, although ambiguous, may be interpreted as meaning that the quality of a man can be tested by his actions as the purity of gold is tested by a touchstone or refined in a cupel (known technically as a "test").[14] In his diffident and self-deprecating response Angelo takes up the metaphor of testing gold coins. "Let there be some more test made of my mettle," he implores the Duke, "Before so noble and so great a figure / Be stamped upon it" (1.1.47-49).[15] Other images of testing occur later in the play: the Duke-as-Friar assures Claudio, rather mendaciously, that Angelo "had never the purpose" to corrupt his sister and was only making "an assay" of her virtue in order "to practice his judgment with the disposition of natures" (3.1.161-62)[16] (exactly what most critics think the Duke is "assaying" with Angelo). It might be granted that the Duke is testing both Claudio (by concealing from him the possibility he may be saved from execution) and Isabella (by keeping her unaware that her brother is still alive). Even Juliet, we might agree, is being tested by the Duke when he seeks to discover whether her penitence is sincere or feigned. Neither is it difficult to regard Angelo as a "seemer"[17] or hypocrite, since three major characters denounce him as being one. Isabella reproaches him for his "Seeming, seeming!" (2.4.149), and for being "an outward-sainted deputy" (3.1.88); during her public accusation of him, she labels him "an hypocrite" (5.1.41, 52-59). The Duke refers to "this well-seeming Angelo" (3.1.222), and his convoluted (and possibly corrupt) lines, "That we were all, as some would seem to be, / From our faults, as faults from see[m]ing, free!" (3.2.39-40) may be glossed as a reference to Angelo. He is certainly alluding to Angelo when he comments, octosyllabically: "O, what may man within him hide, / Though angel on the outward side!" (3.2.271-72). Even Angelo admits to his own "false seeming" (2.4.15).[18]

It is also undeniable that the word "purpose" often has an unambiguously sexual connotation in this play[19]: Escalus asks Angelo to consider whether "the resolute acting of your blood / Could have attained th'effect of your own purpose" (2.1.12-13); "My words express my purpose," Angelo says to Isabella, who replies, belatedly catching the drift, "And most pernicious purpose" (2.4.147, 149); Angelo, the Duke tells Claudio, "had never the purpose" to "corrupt" Isabella (3.1.160-61); and finally Isabella, pretending that she had yielded to Angelo, states that "the next morn betimes, / His purpose surfeiting, he sends a warrant / For my poor brother's head" (5.1.101-03).[20] With these connotations in our ears it is no wonder that so many critics have read "purpose" in "if power change purpose" as referring implicitly to Angelo's aim to remain chaste.[21]

Despite the cumulative weight of such presumptive evidence, however, I think that the theory of a "test," on closer examination, has very little solid ground to stand on. Based almost exclusively on an exiguous portion of text and a good deal of conjecture, it fails to take satisfactory account of the ambiguity of the phrase "if power change purpose," of the non-sexual connotations of "purpose" also present in the play, and perhaps most tellingly, of the stubborn intractability of the plural word "seemers." Yet such stumbling blocks do not deter critics from asserting, particularly on the basis of lines 53 and 54 ("Hence shall we see, / If power change purpose, what our seemers be") that the Duke is deliberately testing Angelo, or testing the validity of a hypothesis about him. Of course it would be manifestly absurd to argue that Angelo is not undergoing a test—all major characters in Shakespeare, like people in real life, are continually being tested insofar as all experience is a kind of test of a human being's mettle. The Duke frankly acknowledges that, as a result of his designs on Isabella, the "corrupt deputy" will be "scaled" or weighed in the balance, judged, tested (3.1.255). What can and should be denied is the suggestion that the Duke is *deliberately* or *purposely* setting out to test his deputy. Granted, Shakespeare often represents characters testing each other for serious or trivial purposes: for example, in *The Taming of the Shrew* Kate, wishing to test whether Petruchio is a gentleman, strikes him to see if he will retaliate (2.1.217-21); in *Hamlet* Polonius devises tests to confirm his theory that Hamlet's "transformation" sprang from Ophelia's rejection of him; in *The Tempest* Prospero tests Ferdinand lest Miranda be won too easily. Examples could be multiplied further. Whether these tests succeed or fail, and whether or not they are reliable, whether or not they are justified, the fact remains that they are set in motion explicitly and deliberately—the "test" of Angelo, on the other hand, is purely circumstantial and fortuitous. There is no hint of a deliberate test of Angelo in any of Shakespeare's sources for *Measure for Measure,* if only for the simple reason that they contain no character whose role corresponds closely to that of Shakespeare's Vincentio.[22]

In his function as "contriver," the Duke admittedly spends much of his time directing the actions and destinies of other characters, although not, I think, with quite the magisterial authority of Prospero, let alone (*pace* G. Wilson Knight and others) of providence or God.[23] Mesmerized by the lure of establishing a neat and unifying teleological pattern, critics like Knight exaggerate the significance of the element of testing in *Measure for Measure;* although undeniably present in the play, it is not as omnipresent as they make out, and is certainly no more important than the "testing" which runs through other Shakespeare plays. To regard the Duke as considerably more than a purely incidental tester, as Knight, Coghill, Schleiner, and Wharton do, is to succumb to a very general and imprecise use of the word "test" and thereby distort the play in the interest of a thematic pattern or theological paradigm. The unstated syllogism at the back of their minds might run something like this: God is the supreme tester, Duke Vincentio acts as a kind of God, therefore the Duke is a supreme tester. Unlike Time, which is presented in Shakespeare as the most persistent and formidable tester of all,[24] the Duke deals only intermittently and opportunistically with characters, like Claudio and Juliet, in a way which will illuminate what kind of people they are. The main "testing," if we retain the question-begging term, is not carried out by the Duke, but by Angelo: after all, it is he who orchestrates the situation in which Claudio and Juliet are forced to confront the consequences of their past actions, and it is he (together with Claudio) who confronts Isabella with a terrible choice—the "tests" of her chastity, her courage, and her integrity are not instigated by the Duke, who intervenes after they have been set in motion. And even if Angelo is seen as instigating tests of Claudio and Isabella, testing them is not his main purpose: his main purpose is to punish the one and violate the other—the "tests" are inevitable concomitants of Angelo's actions, not their major objectives. Far from being the *primum mobile,* the Duke is not even as instrumental as Angelo is: he is limited, for the most part, to improvising methods of "damage-control," that is, trying to remedy or palliate situations unilaterally brought about by Angelo, and trying to extricate those entangled in them. In fact, the Duke's supposed role as principal "tester" is sometimes transmogrified into that of an occasional and disgruntled "testee," particularly at the ungentle hands of Lucio, who doesn't readily concur with his inflated estimate of himself or, like the uncooperative Barnardine, who resists being cajoled into being hanged: "I swear I will not die today for any man's persuasion" (4.3.59-60). It is salutary to remember that on leaving Vienna the Duke expressed no intention of being either a "tester" or a "testee"—his purpose of adopting disguise was, as he informs Friar Thomas, for visiting "both prince [=Angelo] and people," "to behold [Angelo's] sway" (1.3.43-45).[25] Although he initially intended simply to be a detached observer, the Duke is forced by events to intervene in the affairs of his subjects. Compelled intervention is a curious position for a *primum mobile* to find itself in.

III

Let me return to the nub of my inquiry, the so-called "test" of Angelo. According to Wharton, the "initial experiment" is over once Isabella has told him of Angelo's designs: "The Duke has discovered what he imagined he would discover: that a priggish but also suspect man placed in a position of absolute power would be corrupted by it" (1989, p. 69). But if the Duke is engineering a test, what might the Duke supposedly be testing Angelo *for?* Is virtue, like gold, being assayed, or (Wharton's reading) is vice or the propensity to vice being exposed? Four major answers present themselves, two pertaining to Angelo as governor (virtue), and two pertaining to his private life and personal conduct (vice).

The first two are political considerations which apply equally well to Escalus, who is also being entrusted with a position of authority. Angelo is being tested for his capacity to govern well, to discharge his responsibilities fairly and conscientiously, but also for his incorruptibility. According to Coghill, Angelo "*of course* falls at the first fence" [italics mine]: "He falls at the test of faithfulness in elementary matters of justice, when he is to adjudicate in the case of Mr. Froth and Pompey Bum; instead of doing his duty he exhibits the insolence of office, refuses the tedium of sifting evidence and departs with a pun and a flick of cruelty, leaving the patient Escalus to do his work for him" (Coghill, p. 19). Even if this is as serious a dereliction of duty as Coghill makes out, the Duke, absent from this scene, never comes to learn of it—it is a very odd kind of "testing-master" who sets tests without being privy to the test results. Moreover, despite Isabella's threat to "discover his government" (3.1.193-94) and his own reference to "the corrupt deputy" (3.1.254-55), the Duke takes relatively little notice of Angelo's abuse of authority and does not punish it at the end of the play. If he, admittedly in pretense, can think of discharging the provost from his office for failing to obtain a special warrant for Claudio's execution, surely Angelo deserves (in addition to the suffering he feels) some formal punishment for his corrupt abuse of authority. It would seem, then, that if anything is deliberately being tested, it is not Angelo's fitness to govern.

The other two aspects of Angelo that might be tested concern his private life. As I have noted, the Duke's "Hence shall we see / If power change purpose, what our seemers be" is cited as evidence that Angelo is a "seemer" or "dissembler" by critics who remind us that Angelo jilted Mariana when her dowry was lost in a shipwreck in the Duke's version of events, "by pretending in her discoveries of dishonour" (3.1.227).[26] In the words of Coghill: "Of course the Duke knows, before the play begins, that there is some reason to suspect Angelo's integrity; indeed he gives him the strongest possible hint that he knows of his not wholly creditable past when he tells him that one who has observed his history could unfold his character. ['There is a kind of character in thy life, / That to the observer doth thy history / Fully unfold' (1.1.27-29).] The hint wears a polite veil of ambiguity, but it is a warning to him none the less" (p. 19).[27] It is likewise perceived as ironic that Isabella should say to the Duke-Friar: "But O, how much is the good duke deceived in Angelo! If ever he return and I can speak to him, I will open my lips in vain, or discover his government" (3.1.191-94). The irony, as Wharton rightly points out, is that "she is already speaking to the Duke and disclosing Angelo's government." But a further irony Wharton detects ("that the Duke was not deceived in Angelo in the least") lacks foundation (1989, p. 69). If the Duke is *already* convinced that Angelo is a dissembler, isn't it redundant to put him to trial again?[28] Wharton finds this "a troubling question" and answers it by a rather tendentious and exaggerated argument without textual support: "The Duke wants stronger proof of Angelo's worthlessness, wants him to commit some outrage, wants to see him break moral limits. He puts him in the ideal position for these things to happen" (1988, p. 38). I cannot accept either that Angelo is "worthless" or that the Duke thinks he is; nor can I accept that Angelo's being in a position of authority will necessarily expose his "worthlessness."

A more moderate approach might be to say that the Duke is seeking to expose Angelo as a dissembler and to subject him to public humiliation. But even this he is not entitled to do because Angelo is not a dissembler: callous, selfish and even immoral as his behavior may have been, it was not sinful or criminal, nor (although out of expediency rather than natural predisposition an element of pretense was involved) was it demonstrably hypocritical: a hypocrite, according to a typical definition, is "a person who pretends to have desirable or publicly approved attitudes, beliefs, principles, etc. he does not actually possess." Only if Angelo had publicly claimed to be a man who treated women honorably, and who said he always abided by his words and commitments, could his actions be construed as hypocritical. Pretending to be better than one knows oneself to be, and pretending that a woman is worse than one knows her to be, are horses of a very different color—indeed, damaging a woman's reputation by falsely accusing her of promiscuity may well be thought more shamefully immoral than any kind of hypocrisy. Angelo's *initial* account of his relationship with Mariana is, in some respects, very different from the Duke's and Mariana's: there was, according to him, not a marriage contract, but only "some speech of marriage" between them, and it was (unilaterally?) broken off, partly because she could not provide the full dowry she had first promised, but chiefly because "her reputation was disvalu'd / In levity" (5.1.217-22). "Disvalu'd" by whom? we might ask. Believing in a rumor about Mariana's promiscuity (or using it as a convenient pretext) is not the same as putting such a rumor in circulation. Even if the contract were a binding one, and later Angelo admits having been "contracted" to Mariana (5.1.376-78), Angelo would have had every right to dissolve it on suspicion of promiscuity.

Angelo's supposed lack of "integrity" in his cruel desertion, and slandering, of Mariana cannot be the object of a test in any sense: in deciding to appoint Angelo his deputy the Duke could not have anticipated that Angelo's past conduct would become a matter of public knowledge (if that was what the Duke wished to happen), and if he wanted it to happen he could easily have done so without making Angelo his deputy. Equally, he could not have anticipated that Angelo's breach of promise to Mariana would be replicated in breaking his word to Isabella that Claudio would live if she yielded to him. It is a crucial mistake to ironize the Duke's initial declaration of confidence in Angelo by invoking his knowledge of the jilting—the two episodes are, thematically and temporally, quite discrete—and it would be impossible for any audience, on learning about the jilting after a lapse of more than an hour of stage time, to ironize the opening scene in the light of this fresh knowledge. The jilting of Mariana is likely to recall the bed-trick stratagem, not the issue of Angelo's competence to govern, or any doubt about that competence on the part of the Duke.

IV

Wharton raises the possibility that "Mariana is a spur-of-the-moment invention, the mere objective correlative of a plot device" (1989, p. 38), only to dismiss it out of hand: seeking to "put two and two together" to show that in trusting power to Angelo, the Duke "was licensing a man of known ruthlessness and inhumanity," Wharton has come up not with four but with nothing. Despite the obvious verbal echo, the connection between "seemer" and "well-seeming" is too tenuous to bear the weight of interpretation Wharton places upon it (for one thing, as I shall argue, the Duke's "seemers" may not apply to Angelo at all). It is not the case that the Duke "already knows Angelo to be more than 'well-seeming'." Far from having his supposed doubts about Angelo's integrity confirmed, the Duke seems, in this context (3.1.223) as in others, to be genuinely surprised at his deputy's scandalous conduct. "But that frailty hath examples for his falling," he says to Isabella, "I should wonder at that Angelo" (3.1.185-86). And again in his soliloquy at the end of Act III, the Duke, far from congratulating himself on being right about Angelo's corruptibility, seems taken aback by developments: "O, what may man within him hide, / Though angel on the outer side." If some kind of test has revealed the correctness of the Duke's diagnosis of Angelo's moral character, surely it is here, or in the denouement of the play, that we should look for a reference to such a test, but no such reference is offered in either place. If the Duke's motive was to resurrect strict moral laws, one critic finds it "odd" that the Duke "put the task in the hands of a man known to be unscrupulous."[29] But even if the Duke had judged Angelo's conduct toward Mariana to be "unscrupulous" it might not have prevented him from thinking Angelo the ideal man to enforce sexual morality—Angelo was not "unscrupulous" in the sense of being unjust to many, or in the sense of being sexually promiscuous. An isolated moral lapse does not cast doubt on a man's qualifications for political office. The same critic also finds it "odd" that the Duke was prepared "to risk the well-being of his subjects"[30] at the hands of such an "unscrupulous" man, but does not stop to consider this as a significant objection to the theory of a "test."

The second possibility is that the Duke is setting out to test the genuineness of what he describes as Angelo's "precise" rectitude and his "holy abstinence" (4.2.83).[31] As one commentator has written: "The virtues which have so far appeared in Angelo's precise life of contemplation are now to be tried in the active world of government—and the Duke implies that they will be found to be mere 'seeming' or false show."[32] However, as in the revelation of Angelo's treatment of Mariana, he could not anticipate that Angelo's chastity would necessarily be put to a severe trial or that, when it was, the attempt on Isabella's chastity would become known to the populace at large. Modern critics, looking askance at the long and hallowed tradition of Christian (as well as non-Christian) self-abnegation, are inclined to fault Angelo, as the sneering Lucio does, for seeking to "rebate and blunt his natural edge / With profits of the mind, study and fast" (1.4.60-61).[33] If we don't approve of Angelo's continence, so this line of thinking goes, neither does the Duke, and his purpose is to compel Angelo to abandon his self-denying ways. If the enforcement of the laws is the Duke's primary concern, then according to one argument, the Duke's explanation for his delegation of authority is "sadly inadequate, especially since the close of the play looks forward to no continued severity in those laws" (Coles, p. 24). If, on the other hand, "the testing of Angelo and the puritan style of life is the Duke's main interest, his actions become more acceptable"—what underlies the test is "the need to return Angelo to humanity," to make him learn "that he has human appetites, [and] that his blood can flow with passion" (Coles, p. 24). There are three objections to this line of reasoning: first of all, as I have shown, the Duke can have no prior guarantee, nor is there any logical reason, that giving Angelo political power will lead to a situation which will induce Angelo to recognize his own latent sexuality, to become aware, in Arthur Symons' striking words, "of the fire that lurked in so impenetrable a flint";[34] second, the sexuality which Angelo does come to recognize has more to do with lust (which the Duke wishes to eradicate) than with other-directed, mutual love; and finally, just as Lucio protests being compelled to marry Kate Keepdown, so Angelo, far from being "returned to humanity," is still asking to be put to death even after being compelled by the Duke to marry Mariana (5.1.476-79). An alleged objection to considering enforcement as the major theme is that the play ends with nothing having been done to amend the lax sexual laws, yet the play also ends with Angelo far from regenerate, so by the same token the "test" of him, if it exists, can hardly occupy the central position assigned to it.

V

Whether the "testing" is thought to relate to political or to sexual matters, semantic analysis of the Duke's lines at 1.4.50-54 casts serious doubt on the theory of a "test." The five lines can be broken down into a description of Angelo's temperamental coldness in which the Duke elaborates on his earlier one-line depiction of him as "a man of stricture and firm abstinence," and a deduction ("hence"=therefore), or prediction ("hence"=henceforward), of what will happen once Angelo assumes the reins of power. To those who maintain that Angelo is being tested, the conditional phrase "if power change purpose"[35] means that the possession of power might change Angelo's purpose—that he might take advantage of his position to satisfy his repressed sexual urges. But there is no reason for the Duke or for us to think that Angelo will abuse his authority in this way. It is more likely, given that his interest in Mariana was more an interest in her dowry, that he would use his office for financial gain.[36] Like every other Viennese citizen, Angelo would have had every opportunity for sexual activity and the concealment of such activity during the period of lax enforcement of the laws.

A better meaning of the phrase "if power change purpose" would be "if the laws are more stringently enforced," so that Angelo is to be seen as the agent or instrument of harsher measures, not as the subject of a change in his personal conduct. "What our seemers be" is elliptical for "what our seemers might be," the auxiliary "might" being omitted,[37] and the relative pronoun "what" can be construed either as a substitute for "who" or as an ellipsis for "what kind of persons." For advocates of the moral experiment, "seemers" (=hypocrites) should constitute a problem, for if the Duke is testing Angelo specifically it is hardly appropriate for the word to be in the plural. If he means that Angelo and Escalus may turn out to be "seemers," only *seeming* to possess the capacity to govern well, why does he preface his reference to "seemers" with an irrelevant allusion to Angelo's cold and unsexual nature while saying nothing, relevant or irrelevant, about Escalus? At this early stage of the play, despite his knowledge of Angelo's despicable conduct towards Mariana, the Duke does not and cannot suspect Angelo of being a "seemer." Even his later punning exclamation "O, what may man within him hide, / Though angel on the outward side" (3.2.272-73), although it is spoken after the Duke has learnt of Angelo's dishonorable intentions toward Isabella, is not accurate as an accusation of hypocrisy. Doesn't Isabella accuse Angelo of being a hypocrite? Yes, she does, but that is part of her rhetorical strategy to bring him to justice. Later, in a different context when she is imploring the Duke to spare Angelo's life, she cannot bring herself to accuse him of downright, inveterate hypocrisy: "I partly think," she says, "A due sincerity governed his deeds / Till he did look on me" (5.1.447-49). Until the encounter with Isabella there is no shred of evidence that Angelo has been a hypocrite in the sense of practicing vice while preaching virtue; were this the case, Angelo's cool and controlled reply to Isabella's threat to expose him ("Who will believe thee, Isabel?"[38]) would lose much of its dramatic force: the encounter with Isabella has simply revealed him to be a fallible man who has, against all expectation (including his own), felt irresistible sexual desire for the woman least likely to excite or accommodate it. As already indicated, the Duke evinces surprise at Angelo's sexual misdemeanour,[39] and Escalus is equally shocked: "I am, more amazed at his dishonor / Than at the strangeness of it" (5.1.332-33).[40] Angelo is not so much a practitioner of hypocrisy (which involves habitual and active deceit) as a victim of self-deception.[41]

So, if *in this speech* Angelo is not being referred to as a "seemer," who is? Not, we can agree, the comic characters in the play, for they "avoid all 'seeming' or pretence to a virtue they do not possess."[42] The "seemers" the Duke is alluding to are, I suggest, those citizens of Vienna who have managed during the old dispensation to engage in pre- or extramarital sex while maintaining an untarnished reputation for virtue; it is these people, the Duke concludes, who will be exposed as hypocrites if Angelo, as he confidently expects and has perhaps commanded in his written "commissions," chooses to exercise the full weight of the law. Given that Angelo "scarce confesses / That his blood flows,"[43] he is just the man, the Duke thinks, to expose and suppress sexual offences and the kind of hypocrisy which habitually attends them.[44] It would be easier to make a case that Claudio and Juliet have been exposed as "seemers" (that is, not chaste lovers) as a direct result of the new rigidity that Angelo is imposing. The "wise burgher" (1.2.103) who saved the brothels in the city (by means of intercession, purchase, or bribery) may also have been a "seemer."

Another candidate is the Duke himself. It is an abiding comic irony that the man who is anxious for "seemers" to be exposed is himself, in his masquerade as friar-confessor, an unequivocal "seemer." "We should note," writes Leech, "that he claims to know Angelo's mind by virtue of being Angelo's confessor. One does not have to be deeply religious to be affronted by this piece of impertinence" (Leech, p. 70). What is most offensive is not his false pretences, but the implied willingness to betray the secrets of the confessional: he is similarly indiscreet when, after having doffed his disguise, he says: "Joy to you, Mariana. Love her, Angelo; / I have confessed her, and I know her virtue" (5.1.528-29). In a way (although not as a result of appointing Angelo his deputy) he is also exposed as being a "seemer"[45] in the sense that critics think Angelo is. After all, the man who unctuously tells Friar Thomas not to believe that "the dribbling dart of love / Can pierce a complete bosom," maintaining that his departure "hath a purpose / More grave and wrinkled than the aims and ends / Of burning youth" (1.3.2-6), and who repudiates Lucio's accusations that "he had some feeling of the sport" by declaring that "he was not inclined that way" (3.2.120, 123), ends up by suddenly proposing to the same novitiate who had involuntarily thawed Angelo's icy blood. To see the Duke as "testee" rather than "tester" also exonerates him from any charge of wilful irresponsibility in choosing Angelo as his deputy, and obviates what might otherwise appear as inconsistencies or contradictions in the conduct of the plot.

VI

The theory of a "test" is, I conclude, highly suspect: each part of it has been arrived at by extrapolating, retrospectively, elements which occur at a later stage of the play. One of these is the revelation about Angelo's conduct toward Mariana; another is the prominence given to Angelo and the effects of his actions on other characters, a prominence which usurps the stated aim of the Duke's departure: to facilitate the clampdown on sexual license in Vienna. Perhaps what has most misled critics is the impression that in his words to Friar Thomas, the Duke is offering not just a refinement of a motive but an additional one. I take him to be saying, first, that Angelo, being the kind of man the Duke thinks he is, is the right man to prevent future offenses from occurring, and second, as an elaboration of his first position, that Angelo is also the right man to detect and punish offenses committed in the past and since concealed. However arbitrary and unfair we may think it to be, the arrest of Claudio and Juliet is an example of this course of action. But it is only one in a play which could have seen far more: taking "seemers" to refer to Angelo deflects attention away from the fact that the promise (and premise) of moral and social regeneration with which the play started has not been followed through—as so often in Shakespeare, character conflict has pushed thematic concerns into the background. Furthermore, at no point in the play does the Duke make it clear that his main or even subsidiary purpose is to test Angelo. And, although it would be foolhardy to base an argument solely on as botched an ending as that of *Measure for Measure,* there is no acknowledgment in the denouement of any such a test having taken place, or that the moment is ripe to evaluate it. It may be, as Rosalind Miles has said, that the whole idea of "testing" is "alien, even repugnant,"[46] to modern sensibility. But that is not a compelling reason to resist it—a better reason is that it is spurious. For those like myself who remain unconvinced of the centrality or even the existence of the theme of a "test," Angelo is, or rather is not, a test case.

Notes

A shorter version of this paper was presented in May 1992 at a session of the Canadian Society for Renaissance Studies at the Annual Conference of Learned Societies, Charlottetown, P. E. I.

[1] Clifford Leech, "The Meaning of *Measure for Measure,*" *Shakespeare Survey* 3 (1950), 67-68.

[2] Coles Editorial Board, *Measure for Measure* (Toronto, 1987), p. 24. What helps to make this source representative is that it is explicitly designed for students' use.

[3] "*Measure for Measure* and the Gospels," in *The Wheel of Fire* (London, 1930), p. 79. Cf. T. F. Wharton: "The idea of law-enforcement is simply [the Duke's] device to entrap and break Angelo," *Moral Experiment in Jacobean Drama* (London, 1988), p. 41. Long before Knight and Wharton, Richard G. Moulton had claimed that by withdrawing from Vienna the Duke "is designedly contriving special conditions in which he will be able to study the workings of human nature." See *The Moral System of Shakespeare* (London, 1903), pp. 148-49.

[4] "Comic Form in *Measure for Measure,*" *Shakespeare Survey* 8 (1955), p. 19. Like Ernest Schanzer, *The Problem Plays of Shakespeare* (New York, 1963), pp. 126-27, I find no evidence for any test of Isabella.

[5] With the exception of Lucio, who "is the only major character who is not tested; no assay is made on whatever virtue he may be thought to have" (p. 22). Ernest Schanzer has pointed out that Angelo is the very opposite of Lucio, "the lapwing and jester, the reckless scandalmonger, the debauchee, and the loving friend" (p. 84).

[6] Coghill, pp. 24, 21.

[7] "Providential Improvisation in *Measure for Measure,*" PMLA, 97 (1982), 227, 228, 229. Schleiner's essay was thought sufficiently important to be included in the "Modern Critical Interpretations" series on the play, ed. Harold Bloom (New York, 1987). Coghill's was reprinted in an earlier casebook, *"Measure for Measure": Text, Source, and Criticism,* ed. Rolf Soellner and Samuel Bertsche (Boston, 1966).

[8] Wharton offers the same view in his monograph entitled *Measure for Measure* (London, 1989).

[9] F. R. Leavis, *"Measure for Measure,"* in *The Common Pursuit* (London, 1952), pp. 160-72; Peter Ure, *William Shakespeare: The Problem Plays* (London, 1961), p. 30; Anne Barton, *Shakespeare and the Idea of the Play* (London, 1962), p. 178.

[10] "Shakespeare and the Stoicism of Seneca," in *Elizabethan Essays* (New York, 1964), pp. 33, 34.

[11] *Measure for Measure* (1.3.35), ed. S. Nagarajan, in *The Complete Signet Classic Shakespeare* ed. Sylvan Barnet (New York, 1963). All references to Shake-

speare are to this edition. Lucio, for one, does not believe the rumor, telling Isabella that he has it on good authority that the Duke's "givings-out were of an infinite distance / From his true-meant design" (1.4.54-55). See also 2.2.84-95, 131-36.

[12] For evidence that a "commission" can convey "an exact command," see *Hamlet* 5.2.18-25.

[13] "Both reasons cannot be true: if, as the last lines seem to imply, Angelo is not going to be a good magistrate, because of personal failings of one kind or another, then the Duke cannot be serious in expecting him to administer the laws harshly but scrupulously. Neither the Duke, nor the play in which he appears, attempts to reconcile these flagrantly different statements of intent; nor is it clear whether the inconsistency is a hit at the Duke or simply an oversight." A. L. French, *Shakespeare and the Critics* (Cambridge, Eng., 1972), p. 14. Leech makes a similar point, p. 68.

[14] Shakespeare is very fond of the "touchstone" idea—he uses it again in *Measure for Measure* (2.2.150), and in a number of other plays: *Richard III* (4.2.8-9); *King John* (3.1.25-26); *The Merchant of Venice* (2.7.52-53); *I Henry IV* (4.4.9-10); *Timon of Athens* (3.3.6, and 4.3.390), and *Pericles* (2.2.36-38). An alternative reading of 1.1.35-36, and one consistent with the lines that follow, is: "A human being is never endowed with fine qualities unless he is intended to be exercised in matters requiring the finest powers of discrimination and judgement."

[15] "But the Duke, reversing the usual sequence, prefers to test his metal after the figure is stamped upon it, in order to see 'if power change purpose, what our seemers be'. . . . His handing over to Angelo could have been sufficiently motivated, as it partly is, by his desire to test and watch him" (Schanzer, pp. 96, 114).

[16] In the same scene the Duke tells Isabella that Angelo "will avoid your accusation: he made trial of you only" (196-97). Perhaps there is an ellipsis here and the words "he will defend himself by saying that" should be inserted after the colon to complete the sense.

[17] Shakespeare never uses this word in the singular, and his one use of "seemers" occurs in *Measure for Measure*.

[18] He may even be accusing Isabella of "seeming" (see 2.4.77-80, and 158-66).

[19] See under "purpose" in Franklin Rubinstein, *A Dictionary of Shakespeare's Sexual Puns and Their Significance,* 2nd ed. (London, 1989).

[20] In his edition of 1854 James O. Halliwell suggested that "purpose" here "may simply be" his purpose of releasing my brother now cooling, quoted in *Measure for Measure,* New Variorum Edition, ed. Mark Eccles (New York, 1980), p. 243.

[21] As, e.g., Oscar James Campbell does in his gloss: "if power change its aim, whether he is what he seems to be." See *The Living Shakespeare* (New York, 1949).

[22] Norman N. Holland has argued that in four respects (including the test on Angelo) the "underlying situations" in *Measure for Measure* and the story of Remirro de Orco in Innocent Gentillet's so-called "Anti-Machiavel" of 1576 are substantially the same. However, I cannot see that Gentillet's "pious hope" that "Iudges be not suspected nor passionat" implies a reason for appointing and testing Angelo. See Holland's *"Measure for Measure:* The Duke and the Prince," *Comparative Literature* II (1959), 16-20.

[23] Nagarajan hesitates to accept the Duke as Providence: "Providence never had such a narrow escape from defeat at human hands" (p. 1141).

[24] Cf. *As You Like It* (4.1.198), and *The Winter's Tale* (4.1.1).

[25] He never visits Angelo unless we believe him when he says that he is "confessor to Angelo" (3.1.165-66). He may have confessed Angelo even though his report of that confession is totally fabricated. In any case, what Angelo allegedly told the Duke (about only making "an assay" of Isabella's virtue) is not strictly a confession, since there is nothing sinful about it.

[26] Henry Hallam complained as long ago as 1839: "It is never explained how the Duke had become acquainted with this secret, and being acquainted with it, how he had preserved his esteem and confidence in Angelo." Quoted in Eccles, p. 397.

[27] Cf.: "[The lines] 'Hence we shall see, / If power change purpose, what our seemers be' offer a clear indication that the Duke already knows Angelo to be a dissembler, and the revelations in 3.1 about his treatment of Mariana, which can scarcely rest on freshly acquired knowledge, establish that this is so." *Measure for Measure,* ed. J. M. Nosworthy (Harmondsworth, 1969), pp. 38-39 (see also p. 157). And also: "The Duke knows about Mariana, suspects that Angelo is a 'seemer,' and appoints him because he suspects him." Darrel Mansell, Jr., "'Seemers' in *Measure for Measure," Modern Language Quarterly* 27 (1966), 271.

[28] "If the Duke knew all along that Angelo had jilted Mariana . . . he would hardly have needed to test for flaws in the facade." Harriet Hawkins, *Likenesses of Truth in Elizabethan and Restoration Drama* (Oxford, 1972), p. 62.

[29] Wharton (1989), p. 38. The same point is made by Leech (p. 68): "We will not stay to consider whether, in view of these suspicions, the appointment of Angelo should have been made."

[30] Wharton (1989), p. 38. Hawkins notes that the Duke's motive for leaving Vienna "hardly entitles him (morally or dramatically) to put Angelo to a test, or to cause unnecessary suffering for a number of his subjects merely to find out what might lie behind Angelo's stony exterior" *Likenesses*, p. 62 (see also p. 71). On these grounds Robert Ornstein (one of the few critics to deny Angelo's integrity is being tested) denies that a test is underway: "No intelligent ruler tests his subordinates by giving them power of life and death when he knows beforehand their lack of simple humanity." See *The Moral Vision of Jacobean Tragedy* (Madison, 1960), p. 255.

[31] Escalus tells Angelo he believes him to be "most straight in virtue" (2.1.9).

[32] Nigel Alexander, *Shakespeare: "Measure for Measure"* (London, 1975), pp. 41-42. Cf. Leavis' remark that Angelo "was placed in a position calculated to actualise his worst potentialities" (p. 172).

[33] There is a similar (very modern) reluctance to grant Isabella the right to choose a life of chastity.

[34] Cited in Eccles, p. 398.

[35] Note Shakespeare's characteristically strict use of the subjunctive for something hypothetical, not necessarily true or uncertain. Regarding "if" as equivalent to "whether" A. E. Thiselton places a colon after "purpose" to make "what our seemers be" a second object of the verb "see." *Some Textual Notes on "Measure for Measure"* (London, 1901), p. 12. Following Thiselton, J. W. Lever objects to the "fatuousness" of the commas Rowe placed after "see" and "purpose." *Measure for Measure* (London, 1965), p. 22n. Contentious issues of punctuation do not, I think, affect my argument.

[36] It is even doubtful that Angelo would have accepted money for services rendered—although he misunderstands the tenor of Isabella's words, he angrily repudiates the suggestion he might be open to a bribe (2.2.146-47).

[37] In Elizabethan English, writes N. F. Blake, "almost any part of speech may be omitted." *Shakespeare's Language: An Introduction* (New York, 1983), p. 126. As an example of an auxiliary being omitted, "may" is omitted before "Thy" in the Countess' blessing on Bertram: "Thy blood and virtue contend for empire in thee" (*All's Well That Ends Well,* 1.1.66-67).

[38] Angelo continues by saying that his "unsoiled name" and the "austereness" of his life will vouch against her (2.4.153ff.).

[39] I cannot agree with Mansell (p. 272n.) that the Duke is only pretending amazement at Angelo's fall from grace.

[40] That is, "more amazed at his lapse from virtue in trying to possess a nun, than at the bedtrick which revealed the lapse." Later Escalus turns to Angelo directly, expressing regret that "one so learned and so wise . . . [s]hould slip so grossly" (5.1.472,474). "Slip" in Shakespeare is often a sexual slip—see Isabella's use of "slipped" (2.1.65) and *The Winter's Tale* (1.2.85, 273).

[41] I am aware that critical opinion is sharply divided over the issue of whether or not Angelo is to be regarded as a hypocrite. See Eccles, pp. 420-27, esp. p. 426.

[42] Herbert Weil, Jr., cited in Bloom, p. 70.

[43] Cf. Lucio's "a man whose blood / Is very snow-broth" (1.4.57-58).

[44] Since the Duke oscillates between the first person singular and the royal (or ducal) "we," it is difficult to ascertain whether "hence shall we see" and "our seemers" refers to private or public knowledge.

[45] The point has been made by M. C. Bradbrook, who adds: "The difference between the Duke's seeming and that of Angelo is of course that the Duke's is purely an external change." Cited in Bloom, pp. 16, 17.

[46] The Problems of "Measure for Measure" (London, 1976), p. 279.

Source: "Questionable Purpose in *Measure for Measure:* A Test of Seeming or a Seeming Test?" in *English Literary Renaissance,* Vol. 25, No. 1, Winter, 1995, pp. 26-44.

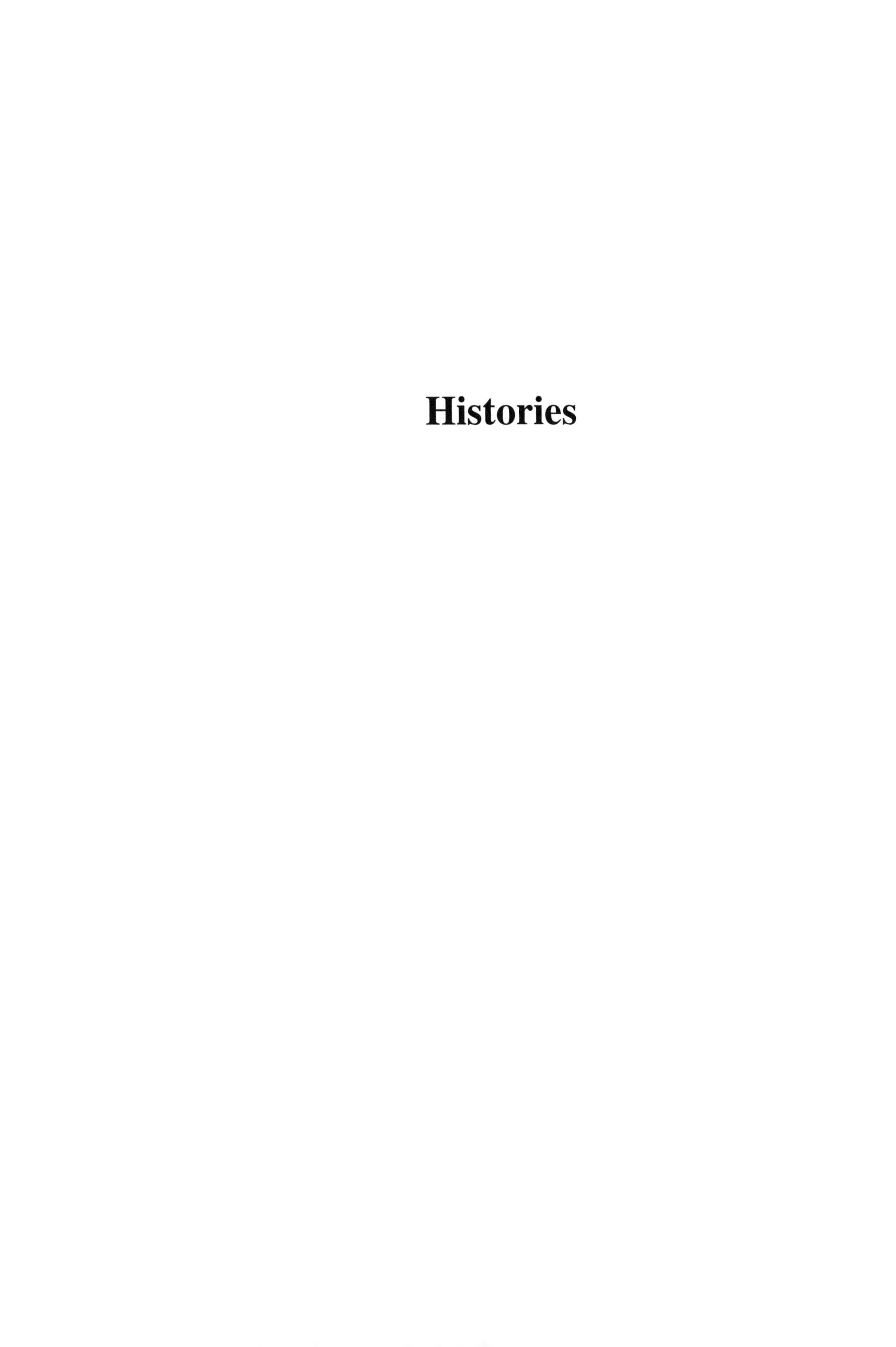

Histories

King John and *The Troublesome Raigne*: Sources, Structure, Sequence

Brian Boyd, ***University of Auckland***

The debate goes on: is Shakespeare's *King John* a source or a derivative of the anonymous *The Troublesome Raigne of King John* (1591)? In 1989 "the 'orthodox' opinion that *The Troublesome Raigne* precedes *King John*" seemed to one critic "now . . . so strong as to need no further elaboration or support."[1] A year later, another made the best case yet for the "unorthodox" position that *King John* spawned rather than sprang from *The Troublesome Raigne*.[2]

Everyone concurs that *The Troublesome Raigne* is intimately related to and manifestly inferior to *King John,* but there agreement ends. To some, a writer with the merest fraction of Shakespeare's talent could not have followed *King John* almost scene for scene and often speech for speech and yet have repeatedly substituted his own awkward limp for the forceful stride Shakespeare's language has throughout this play.[3] To others, a writer with so little talent would never have been able to reshape Holinshed and other historical sources so well that Shakespeare could work from it, again, almost scene for scene and often speech for speech.[4]

Although both conclusions sound plausible, the first can be set aside if, as Suzanne Gary and L. A. Beaurline suggest, the author of *The Troublesome Raigne* was working from a mere scenario of *King John,* perhaps in the form of an "author's plot" such as we know were made in the Elizabethan theater.[5] If someone with little experience as a dramatist had access to an outline of Shakespeare's scenes but not to the details of his language, he could easily have produced what we find in *The Troublesome Raigne*.

The second conclusion, however, becomes more and more difficult to dislodge. All participants in the debate agree that "the author who worked first from the chronicles undertook a massive reorganization of historical material" (Smallwood, p. 367). John's reign naturally falls into three periods: 1199-1206, dominated by the disputes with King Philip of France and Prince Arthur over John's claim to the Angevin territories in France; 1207-1213, the confrontation with the Pope; and 1213-1216, the barons' rebellion and the French invasion. One of the two authors makes these three crises coalesce by dint of a daring rearrangement of events. In the long sequence outside Angiers, he even fashions a single stylized day[6] from the destruction of Angiers (1206),[7] the marriage between Blanche and Louis (1200), the papal excommunication of John (1207-1211), the battle of Mirabeau (1202), the killing of Limoges (1199), the abortive French invasion prompted by the Pope (1213) and the Dauphin's invasion (1216).[8] So boldly and brilliantly has history been reshaped that even those who argue for the priority of *The Troublesome Raigne* sometimes feel that nobody but Shakespeare could have moulded the material so well, that somehow or other he must at least have had a hand in *The Troublesome Raigne* before rewriting it as *King John.*[9]

No one doubts that Shakespeare had the imagination and skill to reconstruct the chronicles, since throughout his career he radically rearranged and recombined sources. So thoroughgoing indeed are his transformations of his material, historical and dramatic, in the rest of the canon that it is difficult to suppose that in this one instance he would have meekly followed a mediocre novice. Shakespeare already had to his credit not only his first comedies and tragedy but four English history plays that had opened up the possibilities of the genre, whereas the author of *The Troublesome Raigne* appears to have written nothing else.[10] As even supporters of *The Troublesome Raigne's* priority admit, the play shows him to be—*apart* from the reinvention of John's reign—"an insipid versifier and an uninspired journeyman playwright" (Dover Wilson, p. xxxix), whose "construction is loose" and whose "working-out in detail . . . is clumsy" (Bullough, 4:9), and who can even be capable of outright "imbecility" (Hamel, p. 43). The one isolated strength *The Troublesome Raigne*'s author has, apparently, is the kind of superb structural imagination that allows him to reshape Holinshed—yet curiously, as we will see, not to structure his own scenes.

It is not enough to point to the mere fact that the chronicles have been so rigorously reworked. We must also ask *why.* For decades critics have agreed that Arthur provides a focus for *King John.*[11] As some also point out, Arthur's claim to the throne and John's attempt to extinguish it by ordering him killed also underlie the reconstruction of the chronicles in *The Troublesome Raigne:* "This is the selective principle for the actions of both plays: nearly everything done by John, King Philip, and their entourage seems contingent upon Arthur."[12]

Regardless of their position on sources, critics have also agreed that *The Troublesome Raigne* is "a play with a consistently anti-Catholic thrust" (Smallwood, p. 369). This in fact "forms the main theme" (Dover Wilson, p. lviii) of the play, announced in the prefatory "To the Gentlemen Readers"

> A warlike Christian and your Contreyman.
> For Christs true faith indur'd he many a storme,
> And set himself against the Man of *Rome*[13]

and insisted upon by an anti-papal outburst on average at least every hundred lines. The play aims to show John as a Christian warrior, a precursor of Henry VIII:[14]

> From out these loynes shall spring a Kingly braunch
> Whose armes shall reach unto the gates of *Rome,*
> And with his feet treade downe the Strumpets pride.
>
> (2.1084-86)

Now it seems strange in the extreme that a play that aims to exalt John for his defiance of the Pope should take extraordinary pains to refocus Holinshed's materials around the death of Arthur, the one event most widely held against him, since although his subjects resented the possibility that John may have arranged the boy's death, their grumbings in fact had little effect on his reign.

John Bale, in the fiercely anti-papal polemics of his *King Johan* (written 1538-1560), simply ignores the death of Arthur.[15] Of course Bale's play, being more a morality than a history, functions in quite a different way from its later non-allegorical counterpart, but *The Troublesome Raigne* too could easily have omitted Arthur's death altogether and certainly need not have structured itself around the prince.

In Holinshed, John's role is mitigated by several factors. Once he has captured Arthur, John asks him "to forsake his freendship and aliance with the French king, and to leane and sticke to him being his naturall vncle. But Arthur like one that wanted good counsell, and abounding too much in his owne wilfull opinion, made a presumptuous answer, not onelie denieing so to doo, but also commanding king John to restore vnto him the realme of England, with all those other lands and possessions which king Richard had in his hand at the houre of his death" (Holinshed, 2:285), a claim he had not made before and according to Holinshed, he had no real grounds for making. It was not on his own initiative but "through persuasion of his councellors" (2.286) that John ordered Arthur to be blinded. And though Arthur disappeared from view, it was not clear whether he jumped to his death, pined away in captivity, or was murdered at John's command, "but verelie king John was had in great suspicion, whether worthilie or not, the lord knoweth" (2:286). Avoiding the option of omitting Arthur's death altogether, *The Troublesome Raigne* also fails to avail itself of the extenuating circumstances Holinshed provides, and chooses only, like *King John,* to discredit the suspicions of John's responsibility by showing Arthur jumping to his own death.

Now the mere fact that *The Troublesome Raigne* is "permeated by a fanatical Protestant spirit" (Elson, p. 185) need not rule out on the part of its author an attempt to present a rounded image of John, as a king heroic but not unflawed. Indeed it would be difficult to exclude every shadow from the portrait of a monarch who earned the disaffection of so many of his subjects and who had to kneel abjectly to the Pope he once proudly spurned.

But where it can, *The Troublesome Raigne* exonerates John. In handling the submission to the Pope, for instance, the play strives to eliminate blame, in a way quite unlike Bale, Holinshed, or Shakespeare. When John yields his crown up to the Pope's legate, Shakespeare's Bastard roundly chastises him, for the one time in the play:

> Shall we, upon the footing of our land,
> Send fair-play orders and make compromise,
> Insinuation, parley, and base truce
> To arms invasive?
>
> (5.1.66-69)

The Troublesome Raigne by contrast offers no criticism of John at this point, but presents him as a shrewd politician, resorting in an emergency to an unpalatable but necessary tactic, consciously dissembling, unable to hide his contempt even after he first kneels to Pandulph ("Accurst indeed to kneele to such a drudge," he tells himself, "And get no help with thy submission, / Unsheath thy sword, and sley the misprowd Priest, / That thus triumphs ore thee a mighty King: / No *John,* submit againe, dissemble yet, / For Priests and Women must be flattered," 2.300-5), deciding on submission at last without realising that it involves handing over the crown, recoiling from that humiliation ("What? shall I give my Crowne with this right hand? / No: with this hand defend thy Crowne and thee," 2.325-26), only to be forced into capitulation when a messenger arrives with news that the French invasion fleet is about to land.

Arthur's death proves more awkward. In general *The Troublesome Raigne* seems by comparison with *King John* to downplay John's role in his nephew's death and to lower the price he must pay for his evil intent. Three memorable sequences in Shakespeare, John's reticent order to Hubert to kill Arthur, Constance's laments over the loss of her son, and Pandulph's shrewdly cynical suggestions to Lewis that he exploit popular discontent at Arthur's death, all recur in *The Troublesome Raigne* but in such drastically curtailed form that as Beaurline comments an audience could easily fail to realise what has happened in the first and last of these key exchanges (Beaurline, p. 203). All three sequences seem an echo of Shakespeare's, without any real understanding of their structural role, and certainly without any notion of the centrality of Arthur.

In Shakespeare it is Arthur's death that, quite unhistorically, leads to the barons' rebellion and the French invasion. In *The Troublesome Raigne,* too, the play's structure stresses Arthur's death as the cause of John's misfortunes while the language tries, if not to suppress entirely its baleful role, at least to shift the blame elsewhere, especially on to Rome. As in Shakespeare but not in Holinshed, the lords leave John after Hubert's report of Arthur's death, and then, when they see him dead, immediately settle on rebellion against John and collusion with France. But in explaining their decision to serve a foreign invader, they adduce two other reasons—Chester's banishment, never mentioned previously, not explained here, never referred to again, and "Our private wrongs," not elaborated upon—before citing as the third "His Cosens death, that sweet unguilty childe" (2395-406). But Essex concludes his speech implying that even without these three factors the Pope's denunciation would have sufficed by itself to provoke rebellion:

> Only I say, that were there nothing else
> To moove us but the Popes most dreadfull
> cursse,
> Whereof we are assured if we fayle,
> It were inough to instigate us all
> With earnestnesse of sprit[e] to seeke a mean
> To disposses *John* of his regiment.
> (2.414-19)

Even in the scene where the genuine news of Arthur's death has just reached John, the Bastard reports that "The Nobles, Commons, Clergie, all Estates, / Incited chiefely by the *Cardinall,*" have united against him (2.186-88). "This is the cursed Priest of *Italy,*" the Bastard sums up, that "Hath heapt these mischiefes on this haplesse Land." Addressing himself, John concurs:

> The Pope of *Rome,* tis he that is the cause,
> He curseth thee, he sets thy subjects free
> From due obedience to their Soveraigne:
> He animates the Nobles in their warres,
> He gives away the Crowne to *Philips* Sonne,
> And pardons all that seeke to murther thee:
> And thus blind zeale is still predominant.
> (2.254-73)

But if *The Troublesome Raigne* obscures the lead-up to and the flow-on from Arthur's death, the play briefly places John's role in the death under a harsh spotlight at the point where it becomes the immediate subject. In Shakespeare, Hubert lies to John, aside, that the orders are completed and Arthur is dead; in *The Troublesome Raigne,* Hubert enters and blithely announces in public: "According to your Highnes strickt commaund / Yong *Arthurs* eyes are blinded and extinct. / . . . of the extreame paine,/ Within one hower gave he up the Ghost" (1.1661-65). When his noblemen, appalled, storm away, John in Shakespeare immediately asks himself what he has done, but in *The Troublesome Raigne* he harshly denounces the departing lords

> Proud Rebels as you are to brave me so:
> Saucie, uncivill, checkers of my will.
> Your tongues give edge unto the fatall knife:
> That shall have the passage through your
> traitrous throats
> (1.1681-84)

before he realizes the cost of his command.

And at the end of play, Arthur's death, after having been minimized since this point, becomes the reason John does not succeed in freeing England from the papal yoke:

> Since *John* did yeeld unto the Priest of *Rome,*
> Nor he nor his have prospred on the earth:
> Curst are his blessings, and his curse is blisse.
> But in the spirit I cry unto my God,
> As did the Kingly Prophet *David* cry,
> (Whose hands, as mine, with murder were
> attaint)
> I am not he shall buyld the Lord a house,
> Or roote these Locusts from the face of earth:
> But if my dying heart deceave me not,
> From out these loynes shall spring a Kingly
> braunch
> Whose armes shall reach unto the gates of
> *Rome*. . . .
> (2.1075-85)

Arthur's death here offers *The Troublesome Raigne* a convenient way to explain John's failure to liberate his country permanently from Rome: it allows the play to skirt the resubmission to Rome for which other Protestant writers reproached him, and even as it assigns him blame glorifies him by the comparison to David, who despite his errant personal life stood as the Bible's model of a monarch under God.

The Troublesome Raigne's handling of Arthur's death seems much more an ad hoc use of someone else's prior decision to focus on the prince than an original plan to realign Holinshed around Arthur. The play appears not to realize the centrality of Arthur to its own structure, and often prefers to diminish the importance of his death, but where it is inescapable exploits it for its dramatic value or as a means of admitting to flaws in John that do not challenge his role as Henry

VIII's precursor. John is as troubled a king in *The Troublesome Raigne* as in Bale or Foxe's *Actes and Monuments of Martyrs,* but even more unequivocally in the heroic vanguard of the Reformation.

Not only is it inexplicable, if *The Troublesome Raigne* derives directly from Holinshed, that an author so committed to what Virginia Mason Carr calls "the drama of propaganda" should take great pains to reshape the chronicle material around the very event most likely to mar the image of John as proto-Protestant hero, and then try to minimize the damage; but it also makes no sense that he should eschew the anti-papal ammunition Holinshed offers. [16] John's resistance to the Pope's choice of Stephen Langton as Archbishop of Canterbury provoked the confrontation between London and Rome that lasted from 1207 to 1213. Accordingly, in Bale's *King Johan,* Langton becomes the villain, interchangeable with the chief Vice, Sedition. Although *The Troublesome Raigne* operates on different principles, it too could have easily furthered its anti-Catholicism by focusing on Langton, not as the equivalent of a moral abstraction, but as a concrete historical figure from the chronicles. In Holinshed, John appeals to English national pride when he writes to Pope Innocent III in 1207 "that he would neuer consent that Stephan which had beene brought vp & alwaies conuersant with his enimies the Frenchmen, should now enioy the rule of the bishoprike and dioces of Canturburie" (2:296). In 1211 the Pope sends Pandulph with Stephen Langton to visit King Philip "and to exhort the French king to make warre vpon [John], as a person for his wickednesse excommunicated" (2:303). Holinshed also stresses the Archbishop's role between 1213 and John's death in "setting on" the "lords and peeres of the realme" (2:313) to press the king for their rights. As Holinshed phrases it on one occasion: "The archbishop coueting to extinguish the sedition (whereof he himselfe had beene no small kindler) which was like to grow, if the Nobilitie were not pacified the sooner, talked with the king . . ." (2:319).

Stephen Langton in other words could have provided an anti-papist playwright drawing on Holinshed with a way of combining all the elements he needed—all the elements Bale had needed—from John's reign: the feud with the Pope, the hostilities with the French, the rebellion of the nobility. A focus on Langton required no complex realignment of historical sequences, and would have allowed the play to avoid Arthur's death, rather than, as in *The Troublesome Raigne,* to exaggerate its implications. But *The Troublesome Raigne* assigns Stephen Langton a mere two lines. Pandulph asks John why does he "disanull the election of *Stephen Langton,* whom his Holines hath elected Archbishop of *Canterburie*" (1.972-74), in a speech that exactly corresponds to Shakespeare's Pandulph asking John

> Why thou against the church, our holy mother,
> So wilfully dost spurn, and force perforce
> Keep Stephen Langton, chosen Archbishop
> Of Canterbury, from that holy see.
> (3.1.141-44)

In both *The Troublesome Raigne* and *King John,* this is Pandulph's first speech in the play, spoken to John at the marriage of Louis and Blanche, and with Arthur present, although in fact Arthur died in 1203, Stephen Langton was chosen by the Pope in 1207, the papal interdiction pronounced in 1208, and Pandulph sent to John only in 1211. No one extolling *The Troublesome Raigne*'s reconstruction of Holinshed has explained why the play should minimize Langton and maximize Arthur, whose near-death at John's command dominates the next several scenes.

As it does also, of course, in *King John.* But in *King John* Arthur serves as a focus throughout. Even at the cost of violating historical fact, Shakespeare expands Arthur's and diminishes John's right to succeed Richard I. He focuses on Arthur's claims and on his fate to call into question John's legitimacy as a monarch, first in a formal, then in a moral sense. As Bonjour points out (p. 259) and many have reiterated, John's ordering Arthur's death is the turning point of the play. When we next see him, after Hubert almost blinds Arthur, John has already begun to lose both his subjects' loyalty and his own sense of purpose.

To increase the pathos of Arthur's plight and the depth of John's guilt, Shakespeare makes the prince younger and more helpless than in Holinshed. For the same reason, he makes Constance a lonely widow, fixated on her child, when in fact by the time of Arthur's death she had remarried not once but twice (cf. Holinshed 2:278). Why does the author of *The Troublesome Raigne* make Constance a solitary, unsupported widow, unless he is following Shakespeare, who had a purpose in presenting her thus?

There seems to be no reason why the insistently anti-Catholic author of *The Troublesome Raigne* should—and every reason why he should not—wrestle arduously with Holinshed so as to reconfigure John's reign around Arthur. Nor is there any indication in any other aspect of the play that he has the literary skill and strength to perform such a complex and subtle task. But where he has neither means nor motive, Shakespeare has both.

Although Shakespeare's restructuring of John's story does not suit the polemical purposes of *The Troublesome Raigne,* the play's author seems ready to accept as a foundation for his own play this brilliant rationalization and dramatization of Holinshed. After all, he is an inexperienced dramatist and Shakespeare is already established as, if not the inventor, at least the foremost creator of the English chronicle play. Shakespeare's only weakness, the anonymous author seems to have felt, was his failure to stress John's glorious role in defying the power of the Pope. He therefore builds on an outline of Shakespeare's structure, consulting the chronicles to eke out what he cannot understand from the scenario, [17] and adds whatever anti-papal flourish he chooses. This alone seems to explain why a virulently anti-Catholic author serves up a version of John's reign that inadvertently organizes itself around Arthur—and that, as Beaurline shows, then fails to realise the implications of that choice. [18]

If both plays rearrange history around Arthur, both also add a major character almost entirely without historical basis: the Bastard Faulconbridge, illegitimate son of Richard Coeur de Lion. Again, regardless of their positions on priority, critics accept the Bastard as *the* "striking novelty" in the plays, the proof of "remarkable inventiveness" on the part of at least one of their authors (Hamel, pp. 42, 43).

Why and how would the author of *The Troublesome Raigne* have invented a bastard son of Richard Coeur de Lion? The Bastard we find in this play is indeed buoyantly anti-Catholic, amused by the nun in the friar's trunk and the friar in the nun's. But it is still John who carries the burden of hostility against the church, John, not the Bastard, who gloats about his abbots, monks and friars: "Ile rowze the lazie lubbers from their Cells, / And in despight Ile send them to the Pope" (1.1022-23). Perhaps the dramatist does need to provide John with an agent to ransack the monasteries, but why does he need to make such a person a bastard son of Richard Coeur de Lion?

One critic who particularly admires the ingenuity of the author of *The Troublesome Raigne* in creating the Bastard especially eulogizes the Bastard's role in the opening scene of the play, comparing it to "the thematic elaboration, the dramatic expansion, and the energy conventionally provided by the comically reflective underplot of Tudor drama" (Hamel, p. 43). Now these comments are perfectly justified as they apply to the Bastard in Shakespeare's opening scene, but in *The Troublesome Raigne,* what relevance does the inheritance squabble between the Bastard and his brother have to the anti-Catholic thrust of the play?[19]

In *King John,* by contrast, Arthur and his claim to inherit Richard I's lands are central to the play. In *The Troublesome Raigne,* no credence whatever is given to the French envoy's claim, which seems no more than opportunism on King Philip's part. But in Shakespeare's opening scene Arthur's right appears at least as strong as John's, so that when later in the scene the two Falconbridge boys argue out their respective cases, there is real point to the ironic juxtaposition of high and low. John inadvertently compounds the irony when he insists on the strict law of primogeniture in the Bastard's case—whoever his father is, he is the elder son, born within wedlock, and therefore the rightful heir—for this seems to rule against his own position, since if primogeniture were applied in his case, Arthur as the son of Richard's next eldest brother would inherit all. And that the person in whose favour John rules according to the principle of primogeniture is himself the eldest son of Richard Coeur de Lion deepens the already profound ironies of this first scene.

Although the author of *The Troublesome Raigne* has been praised for inventing the structural balance between the two inheritance disputes, he in fact badly skews the shape of his scene. The younger brother, Robert, insists that Philip, the elder, must be the son of the former king:

> looke but on *Philips* face,
> His features, actions, and his lineaments,
> And all this Princely presence shall confesse,
> He is no other but King *Richards* Sonne.
> (1.168-71)

A young man from Northamptonshire might know the dead king's profile from the coin of the realm, but it is never explained how he can be so sure of Richard Coeur de Lion's manner, or why he should suppose that the King and the Queen Mother can find it in the bland conduct of the Bastard in this scene. In Shakespeare, of which this seems a confused echo, it is of course Richard's mother and brother who immediately see the likeness between the features and the obstreperous spirits of Richard Plantagenet and Philip Falconbridge.

In Shakespeare, that suffices to clinch the case for Eleanor, who offers her grandson a place in her service. In the anonymous play, John admits to the resemblance, but tries to settle the facts of the case by "a contrivance from folk stories: he devises an *ad hoc* ceremony requiring the mother and the older brother to swear thrice to Philip's legitimacy" (Hamel, p. 52). This "naïve"[20] stratagem would of course settle nothing, were it not that on the third question to Philip,[21] he conveniently flips into a trance in which he discovers and simultaneously declares his certainty that he is Richard's son.

After this embarrassing ploy, there is still worse to come as the author of *The Troublesome Raigne* tries to follow Shakespeare but cannot quite reconstruct the sequence. Shakespeare's opening scene ends with the arrival of the Bastard's mother. Before she comes he has already, regardless of his paternity, renounced his rights to the Falconbridge inheritance. Now he asks his mother who his father was. Since he has already disclaimed his official lineage, she soon divulges the truth.

But in *The Troublesome Raigne* Lady Falconbridge is present during the Bastard's trance, which plays a decisive role in settling the inheritance dispute precisely because it leaves him and everyone who overhears it certain of the truth of his vision. Yet now, at the end of the scene, he tries to badger his mother into telling him who his father was. As in Shakespeare, she resists at first but then gives in. In Shakespeare, that makes perfect dramatic sense. In *The Troublesome Raigne,* it becomes nonsense, as the playwright wastes over a hundred lines in making the Bastard plead for an answer he already has and his mother resist telling him what in fact she knows and we know he already knows.

Perhaps this scene is a structural masterstroke by someone responsible for the "remarkable inventiveness" behind the Bastard himself—although for all his supposed resemblance to Richard Coeur de Lion, the Bastard cuts a lifeless figure in this scene.[22] Or perhaps the muddled and naive structure of the scene merely reflects a garbled attempt to capture what worked so well in Shakespeare's opening.

If there seems no particular reason for a play with the announced aim of presenting John as a "warlike Christian" to introduce the Bastard at the start, is there some reason to feature him in the play's conclusion? Bullough suggests (4:7) that the Bastard shows "that despite the failure of the erring monarch the spirit of his brother Richard I—that is, the true spirit of England—still survives." Like Hamel's Bastard as "thematic elaboration," this describes what we find in Shakespeare, but not in *The Troublesome Raigne*. In the anonymous play there is none of the immediate animation that proves the Bastard's likeness to Richard Coeur de Lion. And as many have commented, his role at the end of the play is markedly less prominent than in *King John.* He is not present in the scene of the discovery of Arthur's body, where in *King John* his poised but resolute judiciousness and his outrage at the possibility of Arthur's murder establish him as the only morally dependable character in the play. In Shakespeare, a panic-stricken John responds to the Bastard's patriotic fire by assigning him command of the English resistance to invasion: "Have thou the ordering of this present time" (5.1.77). When all the odds are against the King's forces, only the Bastard's efforts prevent a French victory: "That misbegotten devil Falconbridge, / In spite of spite, alone upholds the day" (5.4.1-5). In *The Troublesome Raigne,* by contrast, the Bastard is never assigned leadership, and as Gary shows is treated by the rebel lords with a deference he has not earned. As if the author cannot decide whether to follow Shakespeare or Holinshed, he at one moment (2:831-38) supposes the Bastard in charge of the troops swept away in the Washes, at another moment (2:965-69) assumes John was leader.[23]

Although Shakespeare's ending implies that the spirit of England once embodied in Richard Coeur de Lion lives on in the Bastard, the author of *The Troublesome Raigne* has no such design. For him, what matters is not that the Bastard harks back to Richard, but that John looks forward to Henry VIII. Robert Smallwood argues (pp. 370-71) that "the whole demotion of the importance of the Bastard, the sharp reduction in the number of his lines (set against the overall increase in the length of the play), the failure to reflect the central focus that Shakespeare gives him in Acts 4 and 5, argue strongly against the possibility that *The Troublesome Raigne* derives from" *King John.* Surely his evidence leads more naturally to the opposite conclusion. If the Bastard contributes so little to *The Troublesome Raigne,* why does the author go out of his way to invent this one major ahistorical figure?

Although the Bastard adds nothing to the plot of *The Troublesome Raigne,* perhaps his personality accounts for his large share in the play? But David Womersley rightly notes that it must strike us as odd when *The Troublesome Raigne's* Chatillion "describes the Bastard to King Philip as 'A hardy wilde head, tough and venturous'; the play has so far not displayed this aspect of his character."[24] By this point in the action, of course, Shakespeare's play had amply justified such a comment, and Chatillion's line in *The Troublesome Raigne* seems no more than an echo of the theatrical impression the Bastard creates in the first scene of *King John.* Robert Ornstein observes that in *The Troublesome Raigne* John is the only character "whose speech is memorable, the only one whose personality is vivid, the only one with some stamp of individuality," whereas in *King John* the Bastard "absorbs the audience's attention from his first entrance on stage."[25] Why then would the author of *The Troublesome Raigne* depart from history to concoct as the second most prominent role in his play a character with almost no personality or effect on the plot?

If a bastard son of Richard Coeur de Lion makes no special sense in *The Troublesome Raigne,* he makes perfect sense in *King John,* with its pointed focus on Arthur, another Plantagenet son who at least in the world of this play appears to have a better right than John to Richard Coeur de Lion's throne. The Bastard's is the largest role in *King John,* and over the last half-century critics have shown various ways of describing his structural role: his fortunes ascending as John's descends, his stature rising as John's falls (Bonjour); the contrast between three different kinds of claim to Richard's throne: possession (John), right (Arthur), character (the Bastard);[26] the clearing the stage in the final scenes of everybody but the Bastard who might seem fitted to lead England, until in the last scene the unmentioned Prince Henry emerges and the Bastard shows his true quality by submitting to him rather than seeking power for himself (Calderwood, p. 355; Matchett, pp. xxiv, xxxvi; Smallwood, p. 41).

Hamel comments on the similarity of the Bastard's role to that of the Elizabethan underplot. He is wrong about the Bastard of *The Troublesome Raigne,* but right about Shakespeare's character. In fact as I show elsewhere Shakespeare again and again creates from nothing or from the barest hint in his sources a character I call the "verso," who, like the underplot, stands in—and is constructed from—a series of pointed contrasts to the characters and situations of the original story.[27] In this case Shakespeare first sets John and Arthur, locked into a tense inheritance dispute, against the Bastard's high amusement at his brother's attempt to have him disinherited. Once John has confirmed him in possession of his lands, the Bastard blithely relinquishes them to his brother, in striking contrast to John, who of course after being doubly confirmed in *his* lands once he has captured Arthur, orders his rival's death. After this key decision, Shakespeare shows John collapsing into powerlessness as the Bastard steadily gains in authority. As everyone else flees John, the Bastard proves resolutely loyal, the only character in the play to remain constant in a world of catastrophic inconstancy.[28]

Shakespeare's first verso is Aaron, who clearly derives via Barabas from the Vice figure of late Tudor morality plays. The next, the Bastard, with his obstreperous stage presence, his satiric asides to the audience, and apparent self-dedications to villainy like "Gain, be my lord, for I will worship thee," owes a lesser but still considerable amount to the Vice, as Julia Van De Water has stressed in lamenting and David Womersley in lauding his characterization.[29] In later versos, the individuality of the character—Bottom, Jaques, Malvolio, Caliban—will often be all that remains, but even in some of the most vital of the later versos—Falstaff, Parolles, Autolycus—the Vice ancestry still shows through.

The Bastard, then, who seems not to justify his invention in *The Troublesome Raigne* if he were original there, not only warrants his place in *King John*'s structure, but seems to be a typical Shakespearean addition to his source material, although just as one would expect he stands at an early stage in the development of this device. Although *King John*'s Bastard is almost entirely fictional, he is nevertheless constructed from hints in the chronicles as well as from the structural needs of the play.[30] As Holinshed's account of John's reign relates, Richard I did indeed have a bastard son named Philip, who like the Bastard in Shakespeare's play kills Limoges in revenge for the killing of his father. But he takes up only a sentence in Holinshed and his revenge only four lines in Shakespeare. The ebullient interloper of the play's first scene, who happily prefers being the bastard son of Richard Coeur de Lion to being the legitimate son of the unprepossessing and undistinguished Sir Robert Falconbridge, derives from Jean, Count Dunois, the Bastard of Orleans, who when asked by the judges adjudicating his right to inherit the estate of the Lord of Cawny, declared, according to Edward Halle: "I am the sonne of the noble Duke of Orleaunce, more glad to be his Bastarde, with a meane livyng, than the lawfull sonne of that coward cuckolde Cauny, with his foure thousande crounes" (Bullough, 4:55). A third bastard, a vigorous soldier and a loyal supporter of John in his last years, was Faukes de Brent, who features late in Holinshed's account of John's reign, and he in turn seems to have suggested by his name yet another valiant and unruly bastard, who at last supplies the play's character with a surname: "Thomas Neuill, bastard sonne to that valiant capteine the lord Thomas Fauconbridge. . . . The bastard Fauconbridge . . . thought himself a man ordeined to glorie" (3:321-22).

The revealing thing about this quartet of bastards is that although two of them, Philip and Faukes de Brent, feature in Holinshed's record of John's reign, the other two, Dunois and Falconbridge, appear in parts of Halle's and Holinshed's accounts of a much later time—two and half centuries later, in fact—that Shakespeare had just used as sources for *1 Henry VI* and *3 Henry VI.* The kind of synthetic imagination at work in creating a bastard son of Richard Coeur de Lion defiantly proud of his true father (Dunois), ready to avenge his death (Philip), and an aggressive and loyal supporter of John (Faukes de Brent), for all that he had seemed he might prove a dangerously ambitious figure in his own right (Falconbridge), is the kind of imagination that had recently fused the comic tradition of the shrewish wife, Ariosto, and a story derived from the *Arabian Nights* in *The Taming of the Shrew,* and Kyd, Ovid, Seneca and Livy in *Titus Andronicus*.[31]

To sum up: if *The Troublesome Raigne* were the source of *King John,* it would require us to believe in a wholesale and daring reorganization of Holinshed's material by an otherwise unknown writer with otherwise poor literary and structural skills, an anti-Catholic partisan trying to celebrate John as a heroic precursor of Henry VIII but choosing by his restructuring of the chronicle material to maximize the death of Prince Arthur in captivity, the very event that most discredits his purpose, and to minimize the very parts of John's reign that would further his cause. It would also require us to imagine Shakespeare following this unheralded writer with unprecedented timidity.[32]

If on the other hand *King John* is the source for *The Troublesome Raigne,* the powerful reorganization of the material around the death of Arthur becomes perfectly explicable, since it matches Shakespeare's practice elsewhere. He shapes John's reign around the contrast between John's initial power and Arthur's powerlessness, just as he had imposed order on *1 Henry VI* by setting Talbot against Joan of Arc, and would design *1 Henry IV* around the opposition between Hal and Hotspur at Shrewsbury. The deliberate focus on Arthur also explains the invention of the Bastard in pointed parallel and contrast to Arthur and John, in a process that is a hallmark of Shakespeare's work throughout his career and that depends in this case on a conflation of the very sources Shakespeare is known to have consulted for his recent work.

We do not know what kind of outline of Shakespeare's plot the author of *The Troublesome Raigne* had in his possession, but that he worked from some such foundation, with the help of the chronicles, to build the anti-Catholic play we know, seems the natural conclusion to draw from comparing *King John, The Troublesome Raigne,* and the chronicles.

Notes

[1] Guy Hamel, "*King John* and *The Troublesome Raigne*: A Reexamination," in Deborah T. Curren-Aquino, ed., *King John: New Perspectives* (U. of Delaware Press, 1989), 41-61, p. 41.

[2] L. A. Beaurline, in his New Cambridge edition (1990), 194-210. Citations from *King John* are to this edition.

[3] See for instance John Dover Wilson, Cambridge edition (1936); Geoffrey Bullough, ed., *Narrative and Dramatic Sources of Shakespeare* (London: Routledge and Kegan Paul, 1962), 4; R. L. Smallwood, New Penguin edition (1974), 365-74; Kenneth Muir, *The Sources of Shakespeare's Plays* (London: Methuen, 1977), 79-85; A. R. Braunmuller, Oxford edition (1989), 2-19.

[4] A. S. Cairncross, *The Problem of Hamlet* (London: Macmillan, 1936), 137-43; E. A. J. Honigmann, Arden edition (1954), xi-xxxiii; Peter Alexander, *Shakespeare* (Oxford U. Press, 1964), 167-72; William H. Matchett, Signet edition (1966); Suzanne Tumblin Gary, "The Relationship Between *The Troublesome Reign of King John of England* and Shakespeare's *King John,*" unpub. doctoral diss., U. of Arizona, 1971; Honigmann, *Shakespeare's Impact on His Contemporaries* (London: Macmillan, 1982), 56-66, 78-88; Beaurline, op. cit.

[5] Gary, 20-28; Beaurline, 206-9. This answers the point made by Alice Walker, in her review of Honigmann's Arden edition (*RES* n.s. 7 [1956]: 421), that "there must be some documentary link between the two plays on the evidence of their stage directions," and elaborated by Sidney Thomas, "'Enter a Sheriffe': Shakespeare's *King John* and *The Troublesome Raigne,*" *SQ* 37 (1986): 98-101.

[6] Shakespearean double-time is at work here. From 2.1 to 3.3 the action is continuous, but the beginning of 3.4 implies a lapse of a week or so since the end of 3.3, only to suggest later in the scene that it takes place on the same day as the preceding scenes: cf. Pandulph's "What have you lost by losing of this day?" (3.4.116)

[7] The razing of Angiers in 1206, and John's remorseful rebuilding of the city from which "he was descended" (*Holinshed's Chronicles of England, Scotland, and Ireland,* 6 vols. [1807 ed., rpt. New York: AMS, 1976], 2:294) seem to provide the reason for basing this sequence at Angiers, though the main battle in 3.2-3 is closer to that of Mirabeau.

[8] Honigmann (1954: xxxi) shows that Shakespeare's 4.2 (which *The Troublesome Raigne* stretches over several consecutive scenes) similarly fuses events from, in this order, 1202, 1216, 1204, 1201, 1213 and 1200.

[9] W. J. Courthope, *A History of English Poetry* (London: Macmillan, 1903), 4:466; E. M. W. Tillyard, *Shakespeare's History Plays* (London: Chatto and Windus, 1944), 216-17; Hamel, 43.

[10] Assuming, since *The Troublesome Raigne* was published in 1591, that he wrote *King John* in 1590 or early 1591. Those who think *The Troublesome Raigne* Shakespeare's source tend to date *King John* 1595-1596. Honigmann 1982: 53-90 shows that if *King John* is proved to be prior to *The Troublesome Raigne* there is nothing to conflict with and much to favor an early (1586?) start to Shakespeare's career. Sidney Thomas, "On the Dating of Shakespeare's Early Plays," *SQ* 39 (1988): 187-94, takes issue with Honigmann but attacks only the weakest points in his argument. *Pace* Thomas, an early start makes for a much more even spread of Shakespeare's plays in the first half of his career. Allowing from seven to ten months per play (less for *Merry Wives of Windsor*) could yield a sequence like this for the first half of Shakespeare's career: 1586, *Two Gentlemen of Verona;* 1586-87, *Taming of the Shrew;* 1587-1588, *1 Henry VI;* 1588, *2 Henry VI;* 1588-1589, *3 Henry VI;* 1589, *Titus Andronicus;* 1590, *Richard III;* 1590-1591, *King John;* 1591, *Comedy of Errors;* 1592, *Love's Labour's Lost;* 1592, *Venus and Adonis;* 1593, *Rape of Lucrece;* 1593, *Love's Labour's Won*(?); 1594, *Richard II;* 1594-1595, *Romeo and Juliet;* 1595, *Midsummer Night's Dream;* 1595-1596, *1 Henry IV;* 1596, *Merchant of Venice;* 1597, *2 Henry IV;* 1597, *Merry Wives of Windsor;* 1598, *Much Ado.*

[11] Since Adrien Bonjour's "The Road to Swinstead Abbey: A Study of the Sense and Structure of *King John,*" *ELH* 18 (1951): 253-74.

[12] Beaurline (1990), 202. Even "selective principle" here understates the case, for events like the ex-

communication of John, the rebellion of the barons, and the French invasion at the end of the reign had nothing to do with the death of Arthur at the beginning, and had to be wrenched from context and sequence to forge the links with the prince in the plays. Cf. also John Elson, "Studies in the King John Plays," in James G. McManaway, et al., eds., *Joseph Quincy Adams Memorial Studies* (Washington: Folger Shakespeare Library, 1948), 183-97. Elson, who considers *The Troublesome Raigne* the earlier play, thinks the author's "greatest dramatic success, albeit one which does violence to history, is making the death of Arthur motivate the secession of John's barons"; he considers the play "constructed around the plot-unifying element of Arthur's death" (185).

[13] Bullough, 4:72. Future citations by part and line number of this edition.

[14] The facts of his reign—above all his inability to command the allegiance of his countrymen, and his capitulation to the Pope—make it impossible for him to be seen as anything but flawed, but in admitting his flaws the playwright still manages to exalt him by comparing him to another mighty precursor, "the Kingly Prophet *David*" (2.1079).

[15] Peter Happé, ed., *Four Morality Plays* (Harmondsworth: Penguin, 1979).

[16] *The Drama of Propaganda: A Study of* The *Troublesome Raigne of King John* (Salzburg: Institut für Sprache und Literatur, 1974), esp. p. 40.

[17] Elson shows conclusively that the author of *The Troublesome Raigne* has independently consulted Holinshed, Foxe's *Actes and Monuments of Martyrs,* and Matthew Paris.

[18] Beaurline demonstrates (202-3) that in *The Troublesome Raigne* John's instructions for Arthur's murder, Constance's grief, Pandulph's role in inciting Louis to invade, and the pathos of Arthur's pleading for his life, are all so severely understated that they seem the work of someone who did not quite know why he was including them.

[19] Carr, a champion of *The Troublesome Raigne,* remarks, apropos of *King John:* "The problem of deciding who shall inherit the Faulconbridge estate is an ingenious sub-plot. . . . The author of *TR* does nothing with this." (p. 80)

[20] Hamel, p. 52. This description comes from the critic who wants to make the greatest claims for the artistry of the author of *The Troublesome Raigne.*

[21] The playwright forgets to have John put the second and third questions to Lady Falconbridge.

[22] Nevertheless, even he has more personality than Robert, on whom the dramatic weight nevertheless falls for 160 lines, although he never appears after this scene. Another masterstroke? "Remarkable inventiveness": Hamel, 43; Frank O'Connor, *The Road to Stratford* (London: Methuen, 1948), astonishingly calls this scene (as conjecturally re-edited by himself to remove its clumsy repetitions) "one of the greatest things in English dramatic literature" (p. 76).

[23] Gary 67-69 and 129-30 points out the inconsistencies in the Bastard's role and the degree to which such prominence as he has at the end of *The Troublesome Raigne* is unexplained within the play.

[24] "The Politics of *King John,*" *RES* n.s. 40 [1989]: 497-515, p. 513.

[25] *A Kingdom for a Stage: The Achievement of Shakespeare's History Plays* (Harvard U. Press, 1972), 89.

[26] John F. Danby, *Shakespeare's Doctrine of Nature: A Study of "King Lear"* (London: Faber, 1949) p. 77; Muriel C. Bradbrook, "Virtue is the True Nobility: A Study of the Structure of *All's Well That Ends Well,*" *RES* n.s. 1 (1950), 289-301, p. 293; Matchett, xxiii; Smallwood, 20.

[27] *Shakespeare Shapes Here* (forthcoming).

[28] "Constancy and Change: The Bastard in *King John*" (forthcoming).

[29] "The Bastard in *King John,*" *SQ* 11 (1960): 137-46; Womersley 503 ff.

[30] See Dover Wilson, pp. xxxix-xl and Bullough, 4, 7-8. Jaqueline Trace, "Shakespeare's Bastard Faulconbridge: An Early Tudor Hero" (*Shakespeare Studies* 13 [1980]: 59-69) has found another bastard Faulconbridge, but no proof that Shakespeare knew of him or that his life was close enough to the image of the Bastard to have contributed to the character.

[31] This presumes, as recent criticism accepts, that *The Taming of A Shrew* is (like *The Troublesome Raigne*) not a Shakespearean source play but a derivative, and that, as scholarly opinion is now beginning to appreciate, the prose *History of Titus Andronicus* is also a derivative of the ballad derived from Shakespeare's play rather than the source of the other two versions. For the latter, still controversial, position, see Marco Mincoff, "The Source of *Titus Andronicus,*" *N&Q* 18 (1971): 131-34; G. K. Hunter, "Sources and Meanings in *Titus Andronicus,*" in J. C. Gray, ed., *Mirror up to Shakespeare: Essays in Honour of G. R. Hibbard* (U. of Toronto Press, 1984), 171-88; MacDonald P. Jackson, "The Year's Contributions to Shakespeare Study: 3. Editions and Textual Studies," *Shakespeare*

Survey 38 (1985): 248-50 and "*Titus Andronicus:* Play, Ballad and Prose History," *N&Q* n.s. 36 (1989): 315-17; Jonathan Bate, ed., *Titus Andronicus* (London: Routledge, 1995), 83-92; and Brian Boyd, "The Blackamoor Babe: *Titus Andronicus,* Play, Ballad and History" and "Kind and Unkindness: Aaron in *Titus Andronicus*" (forthcoming).

[32] Cf. Ornstein, 86: "In no other instance does Shakespeare use a source play as he uses *The Troublesome Reign*. . . . Only in *King John* does he accept the authority of another man's plotting; and only in *King John* does he plod patiently along in the footsteps of his source, scene by scene."

Source: "*King John* and *The Troublesome Raigne*: Sources, Structure, Sequence," in *Philological Quarterly,* Vol. 74, No. 1, Winter, 1995, pp. 37-56.

Carnival and Plot in *King Henry IV*

Jonathan Hall, *University of Hong Kong*

Bakhtin's concept of the carnival is useful for tracing out the inner conflicts in the discourse of *King Henry IV* Parts 1 and 2. But, in itself the idea of the indebtedness of Shakespeare to the forms of popular festivity is by no means new. Bakhtin's contribution lies in the way in which the popular forms themselves are thought out in terms of a *semiotic conflict* between "monologism" and "dialogism," and this, in my view, forces us to attend to the unconscious aspect of ideological misrecognition which Louis Althusser has called "interpellation."[1] Bakhtin himself avoided these problems, even though a major thrust in his theory is concerned with the historical suppression of popular, carnivalesque "dialogism" at the hands of the rationalistic "monologism" of the centralizing nation states. A helpful starting point for rethinking both history and the unconscious together is the definition of the sign given by Bakhtin's co-thinker, the Marxist Voloshinov:

> [This] social *multiaccentuality* of the sign is a very crucial aspect. By and large it is thanks to this intersecting of accents that a sign maintains its vitality and dynamism and its capacity for further development. . . .
>
> In actual fact, each living ideological sign has two faces, like Janus. Any current curse word can become a word of praise, any current truth must inevitably sound to many other people as the greatest lie. This *inner dialectic quality* of the sign comes out fully in the open only in times of crises or revolutionary changes.[2]

As it is a field of conflict, the sign can be "reaccentuated," and this challenge to established power within the sign underlies all of Bakhtin's arguments on the discourse of the carnival. The carnival practices, whose inversions of social, sexual, and religious proprieties had been noted earlier by many anthropologists, are important for Bakhtin because they can be seen as a form of discursive resistance to the dominant order. Therefore, the carnival figures and signs are also, like the literary text, a scene of dialogical encounter. Bakhtin develops a link between his own historical poetics and the anthropological accounts of carnival, when he argues for its laughter as a collective resistance to both primal terrors (the fear of death and supernatural forces), and the social agents of oppression together with their legitimizing ideologies. So popular resistance (which already presupposes a fairly differentiated society), creates a counterdiscourse, that of the "grotesque body," to oppose to the hegemonic discourse, with its hierarchical, sublimating, and "spiritual" values. The carnival celebration of the dispersed and collective body, in words, gestures, costume, and rituals, he argues, represents an ancient and enduring tradition. This version of the production of popular laughter is already thoroughly "dialogic" in structure, because it is constituted out of a relationship of opposition to the hegemonic discourse. Bakhtin himself does not call it "dialectical" (unlike Voloshinov) because in his view part of the negation of the hegemonic discourse turns upon an opposition to teleology, to linear history, and even to "use value," in the name of cyclicality, consumption, and, above all, celebration of the visceral, excretive, and reproductive organs independently of all law. What needs to be added for the main argument of this chapter is that the displacement of bodily appetites into the "scopic drive" is an agency of deferral and sublimation. Therefore the tendency to the theatricalization of the carnival is the activity of a desire opposed to participation. Furthermore, I will argue that the deferral of satisfaction in the viewing subject is closely involved with that subject's interpellation by a purposive national narrative.

The "grotesque body," whose celebration enables the people to negate the idealizing sublimations of the dominant order, is, of course, itself *socially produced.* Bakhtin writes of this body as a collective mobilization of signs. As a recent commentator points out:

> A severing of meaning from the body or the separation of matter and semiotic value is [thus] not possible in Bakhtin's conception, and it is precisely this interplay of matter and sign, of *soma* and *sema,* the play of a somatic semiotic, that constitutes culture for Bakhtin. Every coalition of matter and sign (i.e. every form of ideological creation, has its own language and its own techniques. It is the description of their specific morphology that becomes the focus of Bakhtin's approach.[3]

The "grotesque body" of Bakhtin's reading of the carnival traditions is historical and social because of the dialectic of resistance built into its every gesture and word. One consequence of this operation across the line conventionally drawn between *soma* and *sema* (i.e., between bodily drives and social meaning, or in more banal and familiar terms, between nature and culture), is that Bakhtin is investigating the same area which Freud calls instinct:

> We regard instinct as being the concept on the frontier-line between the somatic and the mental, and see in it the psychical representative of organic forces.[4]

Bakhtin's understanding of the somatic as always social and semiotic points irresistibly in that same linguistic direction of Freud's thought concerning the unconscious which has been highlighted by Lacan in particular, as opposed to the biologistic trend inherited from the nineteenth century. In this reading, the drives are not fully explicable in terms of energy and flow but are always already inscribed in a semiotic, i.e., social order. But Bakhtin himself eschewed the emergent discipline of psychoanalysis, largely on the grounds of the scientistic "monologism" which he and his fellow thinkers thought they found in it.[5] This marks a turning away from some important implications of his own theory of the "inward dialogism" of the sign.

Bakhtin's historical narrative tells how the festive traditions are overwhelmed by the centralizing, rationalistic, and ultimately bourgeois hegemony in Europe, from the mid-seventeenth century onwards. From that point, it is largely no longer a question of relativizing interplay, but of appropriation by the hegemonic order. Thus there is a second aspect to his utopian materialism, a familiar historical narrative of the fall from a prior situation, in which the social signs of the carnival are said to have corresponded to a natural truth, which resisted social falsehood. Within this narrative of a secular fall, the "grotesque body" is an original truth, present to the consciousness of the people, and resisting, as befits a *vox populi,* the sublimating and oppressive lies of the ruling order. The natural presence of this body to consciousness, as a truth by which all social lies were measured and resisted, is recognizable now as a myth of plenitude anterior to the present order where the monological is said to be dominant. The historical fall in this narrative is not the supremely naive one of the fall from an actual paradise, but rather from a state of active and aware resistance to existing power in the name of a Paradise of alternative values. What Bakhtin celebrates is conscious resistance to power; what his historical narrative mourns is the loss of the possibilities of conscious resistance to the power of monologism.

It is not that Bakhtin was totally mistaken in his history of the triumph of monological discourses in the service of centralism. Although his estimation of the nature of repressed carnival laughter is almost certainly too utopian, the real issue seems to me to be the need to theorize a textual unconscious, towards which his theory of the "*inward* dialogism" of the literary text, and of the carnival construction of the body as cultural text, makes a powerful thrust. For if the epoch prior to the triumph of centralism is marked by dialogism precisely because the festive, dramatic, and literary practices are a medium for intense struggles, it follows that the triumph of the centralizing hegemonic discourse is either an absolute (and impossible) obliteration of all oppositional "voices," or else their displacement into silence and "inwardness." Bakhtin's discovery of the "*inwardness*" of the dialogism of the sign, his denunciation of the illusion of the sign's singularity as precisely an effect of the discourse of power, is what makes his thought such a powerful tool for the reading of the texts of the bourgeois epoch. . . . Such "inwardness" is not a literal interiority in the subject (people have always had their secrets), but a discursive effect of monological control as it conceals the normal dialogical encounters, clashes and contradictions, in the subject and the social order alike. It is therefore impossible to understand "inward dialogism" except in terms of misrecognitions and displacements. But, at the same time this means that the "inwardness" by which the presence of the other within the subject's every utterance is concealed from the subject him/herself, is an effect of the subject's adherence to the monologizing discourses of his/her society. Thus a history of centralism is also a history of the internalization of discursive conflicts under the pressure of powerful *negations.*

. . . . .

It is not particularly new to identify Hal as the Lenten figure in the agon between himself and Falstaff as the representative of carnival, and to say that the traditional struggle between carnival and Lent provides Shakespeare with a way of organizing the historical narrative. The main issue, for my purposes, arises from Hal's triumphant demonstration that *he* has engineered the outcome of the plot, which he announces proleptically to the audience in the famous soliloquy about his future "reformation" in *Part 1:* "I know you all, and will awhile uphold / The unyok'd humour of your idleness," etc. (*1.2.190ff.*) In this speech, Hal theatricalizes even his own participation in the carnivalesque action by appropriating it to his intended plot. This raises exactly the same question as is raised by Bakhtin's history of the triumph of monological discourse in the service of centralism. For, as we will see, Hal makes the claim to be able to write the future narrative of the kingdom without the anarchic desires of the "grotesque" body. The question remains, however: do these disappear from history, so that "monologism" would be really "monological," or is the ancient public agon of the carnival merely displaced into the less visible public space of the audience's divided response to Hal's triumph? Isn't "monologism" really another word for the *silenced agon,* transformed into the space of a schizophrenia that is all the more intense because of its silence? And finally, isn't the production of the body as "grotesque" partly a retroactive justification of its repudiation?[6]

There is another issue here too. The carnival practices can certainly be seen in terms of semiotic resistance to the idealizing legitimations of the ruling order. But they were also part of the organization of a seasonal rural economy. Bakhtin himself spends considerable space in describing the agon between carnival and Lent, and the massive consumption of the Winter Festivals, in terms of the requirements of an economy without the means to accumulate surpluses. In this respect, carnival practices, including the December liberties, were also ways in which individuals and collectives were inscribed libidinally into a political economy, although it could not yet be called that because "political economy" is not yet differentiated from a whole range of other social practices. Indeed, it is arguable that the resistance to hegemony within carnival celebration becomes exacerbated precisely when the "monetarization" of society was destroying the settled cyclicality of the rural order, making the accumulation of surpluses not only possible but imperative. The task facing royal centralism in this epoch of dispersal was not a simple and impossible return to a feudal economy. The absolutist state may indeed be aristocratic and landed in the last resort, but it had to manage an emergent capitalism in its own interests. And it also had to reinscribe the libidinal identifications of its subjects into a national center in the form of the royal personage. In terms of *1 and 2 Henry IV,* the libidinal identifications of the audience with the participatory and carnivalesque figure of Falstaff must be shifted into the scopic deferred gratifications of Prince Hal's "theater." For one object of the play itself is the reorganization of audience desire in terms of deferral. And yet, in the course of doing that, it constructs a strong sense of loss around the repudiation of the anarchic drives of the "grotesque body." The gratifications and the corresponding anxious inner split which this entails will be the subject of the rest of this chapter.

Shakespeare's linkage of carnival and civil war as metaphorical equivalents in the Henriad should not be thought of as an "original" figure but as the reaccentuation of a familiar mode of discourse. Earlier literary examples can be found.[7] And, moving outside the purely literary to the social text, Ladurie's admirable *Le Carnaval de Romans* shows how an actual popular uprising of 1579-80 developed entirely in accordance with the forms of the Mardi Gras Carnival.[8] The town of Romans became a theater of war in the most literal sense; both the insurrection and the counterrevolution by the local nobility took place through the established forms of the rivalry of the *reynages,* i.e., through the carnival version of what revolutionary theory calls "dual power." Admittedly, it was exceptional for the street theater of the carnival to become so completely merged with the historical class struggle. But what was exceptional was that the participants were conscious of its politics and therefore took them beyond normal bounds. Ladurie's study suggests that the carnival forms were already an available discourse for channeling and containing social struggles, and that in Romans the containment momentarily broke down into dual power. Shakespeare shows the same thing happening in the Cade rebellion in his early *Henry VI* trilogy. There the comic is also a scene of national danger, and therefore the laughter tends, but not without "dialogical" ambivalences, towards a mockery of the feared rebellion.

Frazer and many others have argued that the European carnival had its roots in ritual and the cyclical conception of time. However, Bakhtin's more persuasive view is that the affirmation of cyclical renewal, in its carnival form, was not pure ritual but *parodied* ritual. It did not merely blot out history through ritual, but provided a means of dealing with it. Mircea Eliade's argument tends in the same direction when he says that the cyclical view of time served to protect men from the "terror of history" which arises from an awareness of history's linearity. This striking phrase is actually a chapter title in *The Myth of the Eternal Return.*[9] Eliade offers a historical schema in which the conception of linear history is superimposed upon earlier cyclical versions of time. This is not the familiar "progressive" idea that cyclical time gives way to linear time, but rather that the cyclical persists in a transformed way within the linear. As a form of resistance to the "terror of history," it is submerged within the linearity that it resists. Actually, I would argue that the cyclical conception as a form of resistance could only be produced (perhaps nostalgically) from within an epoch newly conscious of the "terror" of linearity. In this sense the carnival, as it becomes theatricalized, would have represented in cultural practice a complex interaction of an awareness of history and a relativizing refusal of it. This doubleness is similar to the joke's disruptive resistance to narrative structure, and has a great bearing on Shakespeare's use of carnival motifs in *Henry IV.*

Henry IV is a historical play in a much deeper sense than in being a mere chronicle. The rift between Prince Hal and Falstaff is momentous, for the plot is concerned with the emergence of the new linear historical outlook, with its stern national purposiveness. In part this is pitted against feudal divisiveness, but it also struggles against the other side of the feudal economy, the "grotesque body" and the relativizing, cyclical concept of time. Falstaff is the embodiment of those values which offer protection, in Eliade's striking phrase, against the "terror of history." His ultimate casting off is therefore deeply serious.

It is remarkable how Falstaff is first introduced as a carnivalesque body which denies time:

> *Prince.* What a devil hast thou to do with the time of day? Unless hours were cups of sack and minutes capons, and clocks the tongues of bawds, and dials the signs of leaping-houses and the blessed sun himself a fair hot wench in flame-coloured taffeta, I see no reason why thou couldst be so superfluous to demand the time of day.
>
> (*1 Henry IV; 1.2.6-11*)

The sexual transformation of the sun leads on to reversals of order under the governance of the moon. This is Falstaff's domain, and in this context he brings up the carnival theme of the reversal of official Justice:

> *Falstaff*. . . . but, prithee, sweet wag, shall there be gallows standing in England when thou art king, and resolution thus fubb'd as it is with the rusty curb of old father antic, the law? Do not thou, when thou art king, hang a thief.
>
> *Prince*. No; thou shalt.
>
> *Falstaff*. Shall I? O rare! By the Lord, I'll be a brave judge!
>
> *Prince*. Thou judgest false already: I mean thou shalt have the hanging of the thieves, and so become a rare hangman.
>
> (*1.2.56ff.*)

Prince Hal's joke concerns a social reversal that was commonly enacted in carnivals, as well as in carnivalesque literature. Falstaff claims as part of his sway the abolition of execution, whereas Prince Hal reinstates it. Although Hal is participating verbally in a joking carnivalesque reversal, he is nonetheless making judgments that presage its end. It is on a similarly sinister note that the most overtly carnivalized scene of the whole play ends, the scene in the Boar's Head Inn which parodies royal authority but at the same time anticipates the actual banishment of Falstaff. The main issue then, as when it is enacted later in the encompassing play, is the incompatibility of Falstaff with the social order. Falstaff in this early comic scene pleads against the banishment that will become "real" at the end of *Part 2*. That is to say, the comic cyclical banishment of the Fat Man of the carnival is overlaid already with an intimation of its future irrevocability.

Within the Boar's Head scene, it is Falstaff who first impersonates the king in order to praise himself and his values. Here he is the traditional carnival king, played by himself, extolling the virtues of the body and of misrule. Then he is discrowned in accordance with the norms of carnival. And in the role of the Lenten Thin figure it is Prince Hal, the real legitimate heir, who mounts the mock throne. Later he will mount the real one to cast down Falstaff at the height of his comic *hubris*. Here, in this play within a play, both figures are joking, but Hal closes the scene with a grim prophecy:

> *Falstaff*. If sack and sugar be a fault, God help the wicked! If to be old and merry be a sin, then many an old host that I know is damned: if to be fat be to be hated, then Pharoah's lean kine are to be loved. No, my good lord; banish Peto, banish Bardolph, banish Poins—but for sweet Jack Falstaff, kind Jack Falstaff, valiant Jack Falstaff, and therefore more valiant, being as he is old Jack Falstaff, banish not him thy Harry's company, *banish plump Jack, and banish all the world.*
>
> *Prince. I do, I will.* [Emphases added]
>
> (*2.4.464ff.*)

The prince's reply, though still uttered as a carnivalesque parody of his father, has turned to royal command in a highly significant passage from present to future tense. Equivocation persists, but its end is within earshot. Falstaff's defense of "sack and sugar" against the lean representative of order is the same as Sir Toby Belch's riposte to Malvolio: "Dost thou think because thou art virtuous there shall be no more cakes and ale?" (*Twelfth Night, 2.3.114ff.*) But here Shakespeare places the traditional carnival combat at the center of a play about the emergence of purposive, linear historical consciousness. However, Part 1 ends on yet another scene of carnival resistance, the cyclical resurrection of the Fat Man of the carnival from his "death" and the reenactment of the struggle with the Thin, as Falstaff arises and stabs the already dead Hotspur. For the ethics of heroism this is mere lying, but Falstaff's words still stand affirmatively against such ethics:

> *Falstaff*. 'Sblood twas time to counterfeit, or that hot termagant Scot had paid me scot and lot too. Counterfeit? I lie, I am no counterfeit: to die is to be a counterfeit; for he is but the counterfeit of a man who hath not the life of a man; but to counterfeit a dying, when a man thereby liveth, is to be no counterfeit, *but the true and perfect image of life indeed.* [emphasis added]
>
> (*5.4.112ff*)

Falstaff speaks for the cyclical logic of the carnival, and for the truth of "lies." When he "kills" the dead Hotspur, Prince Hal plays along with this carnival appropriation of his own heroism. But Falstaff's denial of the heroic and the historical is nonetheless itself denied at the end of *Part 2* by Prince Hal. And audiences have found this disturbing ever since.

Shakespeare's *Henry IV* does not simply employ carnival motifs within a historical play. The play is not historical in the mere sense of being about past events, however momentous they were. It is more importantly about a major development enacted within its own present discourse, namely the divorce of the popular and traditional carnival outlook (with its relativizing, comic, bodily anti-heroism and cyclical view of life) from the linear, historical and heroic purposiveness of the new forms of royal power and ideology. The dialogue between Prince Hal and Falstaff exists to give full dramatic measure to the break. The historical break, moreover, becomes a *psychic split*. It divides the audience against its own responses and forces an identification with new "necessities" (i.e., new desires which serve the demands of the emergent national ideology). Thus the carnivalesque in Shakespeare's play is not in simple continuity with the past. The carnival motifs and discourse function differently in the dramatic work by pointing to the historical impossibility of their actual continuance. Shakespeare's version of history registers a serious loss within the triumph, and that brings about the audience confrontation with its own divided response. Its gratification in the fulfillment of Prince Hal's early promise to be a true son and heir to heal the kingdom, which is a real pleasure, becomes the locus of a new anxiety and sense of loss.

Michael Bristol points out that "the Battle of Carnival and Lent is an explicit structuring device in the two parts of *Henry IV*." However, the Lenten figure, Prince Hal, does not intend to submit to the traditional destitution and thrashings which would place him on a par with the Fat figure:

> Hal's project . . . is eventually to break the rhythmic alteration between the abundance of the material principle embodied in Carnival and the abstemious social discipline embodied in Lent by establishing a permanent sovereignty of Lenten civil policy.[10]

This policy, "the permanent suppression of misrule," in fact corresponded to the policies of established central power throughout Europe from the mid-seventeenth century onwards. As in so much else, the bourgeoisie continued a process begun by absolutism. When Hal urges the necessity of limiting holidays, he is not merely describing a commonplace truth of a psychological need for contrast but is anticipating a new kind of social discipline:

> *Prince*. If all the year were playing holidays,
> To sport would be as tedious as work.
> But when they seldom come, they wished-for come,
> And nothing pleaseth but rare accidents.
> (*1 Henry IV, 1.3.199*ff.)

Lenten abstinence here takes the form of *work*, so that the work/holiday opposition becomes prominent, and this is a small but significant shift of the rule/misrule opposition which governs the rest of the play. Hal briefly aligns the work ethic with rule itself. In addition, this statement is part of his early monologue in which he announces to the audience his policy of pretense and his intention to throw it off at the appropriate moment. It is a meditation, offered to the audience themselves, upon the manipulation of spectators through the calculated procurement of their pleasure. His calculated construction of the plot will lead via delay to the pleasures of "clarification":

> *Prince*. So when this loose behaviour I throw off,
> And pay the debt I never promised,
> By how much better than my word I am,
> By so much shall I falsify men's hopes;
> And like bright metal on a sullen ground,
> My reformation glitt'ring o'er my fault,
> Shall grow more goodly, and attract more eyes,
> Than that which hath no foil to set it off.
> (*1 Henry IV, 1.2.203*ff.)

Prince Hal announces his policy as one designed to construct and then gratify the desires of *onlookers*. The emergence of a brighter self "better than my word" will be offered as ocular gratification. The audience that he has in mind is the realm itself, which must be captivated by the staged revelation. (And the proleptic announcement of the triumph of his policy is important because it is Prince Hal's claim to control the plot of history itself *via* this theatricalization.) He is playing with the desires of the realm, and creating the conditions of a future gratification, which will be the emergence of this golden self to pay the debt incurred by its contrived absence. His understanding of desire as that which is produced out of a lack will enable him to manipulate the desires of his subjects, so that loyalty will be freely given. This is Petruchio on a national scale.

It is striking that both King Henry and Prince Hal consider the art of kingship as the theatrical art of public appearance. However, this theater, which is offered as a spectacular "feast" for the eyes, must avoid any suggestion of the leading actor being consumed. When Henry reproaches his son in Part 1 with cheapening himself by too much mingling with the low, he talks of the strategy by which he won men's allegiance away from Richard II. Like his son in the earlier soliloquy, the king too describes his manipulations of his spectator subjects in terms of a holiday within an economy of scarcity and withdrawal:

> *King*. Thus did I keep my person fresh and new,
> My presence, like a robe pontifical,
> Ne'er seen but wonder'd at, and so my state,
> Seldom, but sumptuous, show'd like a feast,
> And wan by rareness such solemnity.
> (*1 Henry IV, 3.2.55*ff.)

For Henry Bolingbroke the essential part of his defeat of Richard took place through this calculated theatricality. The "presence" and "person" of the king are like the clothes of popish ceremony, surface appearances presented to create appetite, but not to satisfy and glut like Richard. Thus Richard's debasement in the public theater consisted in his being consumed. It is remarkable how the metaphors of consumption and scarcity double those of appearance and essence, and underlie this crucial statement of manipulable desire. Royal power depends upon spectacle, a feast for the eyes that must never satisfy the appetite. But there is always a risk for the monarch, because it is a public theater, frankly carnivalesque in the sense that the power relations in the sign are dangerously reversible. Royal dominance demands the perpetual deferral of satisfaction because satisfaction equalizes and destroys distance and authority. King Richard, says Henry Bolingbroke, is the negative example because he:

> Enfeoff'd himself to popularity,
> That, being daily swallow'd by men's eyes,
> They surfeited with honey, and began
> To loathe the taste of sweetness, whereof a little
> More than a little is by much too much.
> So, when he had occasion to be seen,
> He was but as the cuckoo is in June,
> Heard, but not regarded; seen, but with such eyes
> As, sick and blunted with community,
> Afford no extraordinary gaze,
> Such as is bent on sun-like majesty
> When it shines seldom in admiring eyes,
> But rather drows'd and hung their eyelids down,
> Slept in his face, and render'd such aspect
> As cloudy men use to their adversaries,
> Being with his presence glutted, gorg'd, and full.
>
> (*1 Henry IV, 3.2.69*ff.)

Henry defines the spectacle for the eyes as a feast, but one in which satisfaction or the end of desire must be avoided at all costs because it entails a loss of authority on the part of the desired object. The unity of belly and eyes as organs of appetite is a threat to the "scopic arrangement" of this order. Bakhtin's "grotesque body" is felt here as precisely that, i.e. *grotesque,* a body with engulfing orifices, to be manipulated at a distance but not yielded to.

What the audience grasps through Prince Hal's early soliloquy, but which the king, his father, cannot know, is that Hal's strategy also is founded in the same understanding of the need to operate through deferred gratification. Hal too is strategically using the public theater of the realm. But it is a risky strategy, and the audience is alerted to the risk by the King's comparison of Hal's conduct to that of Richard II. The risk is that the monarch as spectacle might be consumed by the collective body. This is extremely important for the evocation of the audience's anxieties *against* the kinds of pleasurable liberation which Falstaff engenders. For the audience the remembered terrors of feudal war are dissuasively linked to the pleasures of carnival participation which threaten Royal authority:

> *King.* And in that very line, Harry, standest thou,
> For thou hast lost thy princely privilege
> With vile participation. Not an eye
> But is a-weary of thy common sight,
> Save mine, which hath desir'd to see thee more,
>
> . . . . .
>
> *Prince* I shall hereafter, my thrice gracious lord,
> Be more myself.
> *King* For all the world
> As thou art to this hour was Richard then
> When I from France set foot at Ravenspurgh,
> And even as I was then is Percy now.
>
> (*1 Henry IV, 3.2.85*ff.)

Theatricality is necessary to Royal power but this theatricality must be freed from the risk of "vile participation," where the spectators' eyes are glutted. "Vile participation" clearly refers to the theater of carnivalesque debasement feared by Henry Bolingbroke, which the royal theater of distanced spectacle must struggle against. The audience anxiety is focused here upon the possibility of the cyclical repetition of history as the horror of civil war. Set against this anxiety is Hal's promise to "be more myself," which means to play the theatrical strategy of kingship to the limit. To "be more myself" is inescapably ironic because it means to play the role of a future King, and to defer the consumption of the royal personage by the subject's eyes. For the actual audience the immediate gratifications of the prince's participation in Falstaff's festive version of the public theater are played off against the delayed gratifications of the prince's stage-managed plot, and the banishment of Falstaff. Or, to put it in other terms, the shift to theatricality and the displacement of bodily appetites onto the "scopic drive" is absolutism's response to the carnivalesque threat of "vile participation."

The banishment of Falstaff appears in this play as a kind of self-repression by Hal, which is at the same time also a liberation of the whole realm from anarchic bodily desire. Before that moment the prince's relationship with Falstaff appears as a kind of self-permission to play. But it is also an occasion to study the language of his subjects, who can then be made to admire the appearance of kingly virtues. This does not mean that they are not *real* virtues; in fact from the point of view of the new ruling ideology which emerges with increasing emotive force, these virtues are all the more desirable because they are willed, intentional, and rationally controlled. Hal's plot is a *desirable* plot. The audience is brought to desire "Lenten civil policy," or scopic deferral of appetite. Satisfaction is a threat to the political order, just as it was in fact to the emergent economy of accumulation. Thus, an analysis of the contradictory audience responses set up by this play leads towards the goal of "schizoanalysis" as defined by Deleuze and Guattari, which is to show

"how desire can be brought to wish for its own repression in the desiring subject." [11]

At the same time it is essential to note how these redefined kingly virtues are sharply differentiated from the vice of hypocrisy (to which they are uncomfortably close) by being merged with the feudal codes of chivalry which they were in fact replacing. Thus, the audience is brought to admire the emergence of true chivalry in the prince, so that the obvious difference between himself and Hotspur (a historically crucial difference between the figure of feudal independence and the political intelligence required by centralism) is actually blurred. An outstanding example is his generous speech over the dead Hotspur, his rival in single combat. The new virtues appear rooted in feudal modes of conduct which serve to give them legitimacy. It is the Prince's character which enables the historical contradiction to be transcended. That is to say, "character" functions like a myth to reconcile a contradiction in social discourses. It is no accident that the battle in *Henry IV* Part 1 is represented as a series of knightly duels culminating in the combat between Hal and Hotspur. The prince's generosity is also exemplified in his intercession for the Earl of Douglas. Even in Part 2 the prince is carefully distanced from the calcualted treachery by his brother towards the rebellious nobles, though this is what ensures his succession.

Central to this display of ideal feudal behaviour is Prince Hal's reconciliation with his father. Early in the play, King Henry regretfully says that the paragon of feudal virtue, Hotspur, is more like a true son of his than his own looseliving real son. This means that Hotspur's rebellious claim to the throne is almost recognised as legitimate by the very holder of the throne himself. After all, what haunts the king is that he had actually inherited the throne, not by succession but by usurpation and murder. In painfully recognising Hotspur as more like his son than Prince Hal, the king is not only guiltily confronting the past; he is also bringing up the terrible alternative of succession through violence instead of succession through inheritance. Succession through violence is on the brink of being recognised as the truth of all legitimacy. This is crucial for the audience's emotional reaction, for it is much more important than the private conscience of a long-dead king. Though the play is distanced into the past, for an Elizabethan audience the issues were very close. Succession through inheritance may be a pretense involving a certain hypocritical repression of the real facts of the origins of royal power; legitimacy may well be a cloak thrown over history; but it is nonetheless preferable to an open and perhaps more honest eruption of succession through violence. That is why the prince's declaration of himself as the true son is so emotionally powerful. It is a pledge, to the audience, that the age of murder is over. And if the condition for the end of the age of succession by murder is that you must not look too closely into the actual foundations of legitimacy, that is a gratifyingly small price to pay. But, of course, Shakespeare's histories, *do* bring up the buried nightmares of feudal history. They do so in order to transform them into pleasure through a new legitimizing discourse.

From this point of view, if the regeneration of Prince Hal is studied and intended, so much the better. The virtue of this 'hypocrisy' is that it knows what it is doing. The prince must match Hotspur in valor and chivalry, but he must not be carried away like Hotspur. Hotspur sees the world as a stage in which men prove themselves by their deeds. Actions, publicly recognised by a world of warriors, close up any gap between appearance and being. The prince subscribes to the fundamentally feudal notion that deeds guarantee the connection between words and "self," and therefore for him too the battlefield is a theater for the display of that connection. But for the prince the display can be manipulated; the "proving" of the "self" can be managed by the "self." The gap between being and appearance is internalized as an ambiguity in the discourse and gestures of the ruler. The move beyond spontaneity, which in other contexts can be extremely sinister, is legitimized here because in the future ruler it marks an end to feudal divisiveness. Cool self-control is a better pledge for the general good in a centralized kingdom. The virtues of self-repression in the very ruler himself is the guarantor of a new national purposiveness and an imperial expansion. Hal's theatricality gratifies and inscribes its spectating subjects in a new centralizing power (particularly the offstage spectators), after confronting them with the destructive consequences which their libidinal identification with Falstaff would entail.

The plot of *Henry V* is the carrying out of Henry IV's advice to overcome dissension at home by wars abroad. In fact we know that Elizabeth hesitated over just such a policy but withdrew, fearing the expense, and the threat that foreign war would spread dissension at home. But the question I am touching on here is the wider one concerning the reasons why self-repression is an imperial virtue. It has a very long history ahead of it in English culture, and its heroic emergence can be seen in this play. Repression is not just exercised externally over others, as crude interpretations of ideology tend to assume. It acquires legitimacy because it is first and foremost internalized in the ruling circles or class. Centralized national purposiveness did not just happen; it emerged out of the internecine struggles of feudalism, and it replaced them as a "higher" alternative. ("Higher" here means from the standpoint of the emergent ideology and its own narrativization of history.) In this play, the triumph of the purposive Prince Hal over the spontaneous divisiveness of Hotspur and the bodily appetites of Falstaff is the heroic triumph of the new ethics. It is also the triumph over spontaneity and the submission of appetite to law in the ruler himself. This does not take the form of a "personal" crisis overcome; it takes the more public form of the overcoming of the anxieties in the audience. These anxieties can be specified. They are the desire for the fulfilment of the prince's early promise to abolish forever his own engagement with the Falstaffian world of the collective body of the carnival to the level of mere appearance, so that the real being of the future ruler is a transcendant directing will in control of all "appearances" including his own. But these "appearances" that are overcome are really not mere appearances but memories of an earlier libidinal economy. They are memories of an unrecoverable time, when direct satisfaction was not subject to deferral and scopic sublimation. Falstaff is the name of a powerful nostalgia for a time when appetite was unchanneled by the royal ego. It is this which permits the psychological readings in which the "grotesque body" is the "abjected" body of the mother, represented as grotesque precisely in order to achieve a psychic separation from its desires through a sense of disgust. [12] From the standpoint of the superintending ego, the "grotesque body" (or Falstaff) is the name of an always possible disaster.

. . . . .

The historical anxieties over the cyclical repetition of civil war are mediated through a structure which Freudian psychology easily recognises as "Oedipal." And the important point to note is that the audience is repeatedly gratified by a negation of the Oedipal pattern of parricidal desire. Towards the end of *Henry IV Part 2,* the pathos of the dying king repeats with a final intensity a mistake that has been made repeatedly throughout the whole play. Prince Hal makes his famous speech on the heavy burden of the crown, and takes it up as a gesture of filial acceptance, not of eagerness to replace his father. (This makes the usual assumption that the soliloquy as address to the audience, however ambiguous on occasions, is never deliberately deceptive). But the king then awakes to have his old suspicions about his son's parricidal desire reconfirmed. This "misunderstanding" is followed by a restoration of trust which carries enormously powerful emotional connotations for the audience. The most important point is that this is not an essentially new event, but a repeated one. The same pattern is to be found early in *Henry IV Part 1.* Just prior to their marching off to face Percy's rebellion, the king's trust is restored after a similar speech from the prince. Again, in the battle the king joyfully welcomes Hal's action in saving his life as proof that his son does not desire his death, as the rumors report. Hal's action repeatedly underwrites his words, but nonetheless the counterversion of Hal's desires continues to weigh upon the king. When the king on his deathbed regains consciousness, the powerful final talk between father and son opens:

> *Prince.* I never thought to hear you speak again.
> *King.* Thy wish was father, Harry, to that thought.
>
> (*2 Henry IV, IV.5.91*ff.)

As always the audience "knows" the truth that this is not so. But such scenes can legitimately be called "Oedipal" because through their repetition they point, beyond the single event of a misunderstanding being cleared up, to a structure of regular "misunderstanding." The audience gratification lies in the public affirmation of its untruth (though this will be drastically qualified below). So far then, the audience perceives that it is the father who imputes the murderous desire to the son. On each occasion there is gratification in the confirmation of the audience's knowledge (which is also a desire) that the father is wrong in the judgment of his son, and is brought to acknowledge this truth. One might say, then, that the guilty Henry Bolingbroke has a Laios complex, as it were, producing an Oedipal projection upon the son. This projection does not have a mysterious primeval or "psychic" origin; it corresponds directly to Henry's experience of history and the normal conditions of competitive power and succession. His fears are identical to the audience's fears. The gratification is strong because the anxiety is strong. The merely *familial* Oedipal formulation is misleading. The real issue is the stability of the kingdom and the strong desire that succession must no longer rest on usurpation *even at the level of desire.* Correspondingly, the audience gratification at the end depends upon the perception of a historic shift away from the pattern of competitive murder. At the end Hal, now Henry V, publicly (and again very theatrically since his intentions are known to the audience in advance) renounces private revenge on the Chief Justice and twice addresses him as "father." That is to say that the personal rule of kings, together with private desire, is subordinated to the rule of Law, which actually guarantees his rule as father and king. The audience welcomes this rule of Law insofar as it accepts that Law alone guarantees that the historical epoch of feudal competitive desire is over.

Prince Hal does not establish himself as a "true inheritor" by the normal feudal criterion of blood lineage alone. His father, like the audience, knows that such claims are hopelessly entangled in previous crimes, and it is precisely such knowledge that has led him to impute parricidal desire to his son. Prince Hal establishes his status as a "true inheritor" by displaying the absence of parricidal desire through submission to the Law. The play makes this test of the future king's subjectivity the crucial test of legitimacy, now that the previously objective criterion of lineage has broken down into competitive chaos. Hal talks of his unwilling grasping of the crown:

> *Prince*. Accusing it, I put it on my head,
> To try with it, as with an enemy
> That had before my face murder'd my father,
> The quarrel of a true inheritor.
> But if it did infect my blood with joy,
> Or swell my thoughts to any strain of pride,
> If any rebel or vain spirit of mine
> Did with the least affection of a welcome
> Give entertainment to the might of it,
> Let God for ever keep it from my head,
> And make me as the poorest vassal is,
> That doth with awe and terror kneel to it.
> (*2 Henry IV, 4.5.165*ff.)

It is worth remarking that Richard of Gloucester, when he seeks a spurious legitimacy, *simulates* the very same conditions of refusal as his strategy (*Richard III, 3.7*). In that case it is a grim and grotesque joke. And indeed the step from the sublime theater to its grotesque parody is very small. There is a modern joke which runs: "Anybody who wants to be President of the United States strongly enough to campaign for the job is manifestly unsuited for it." And in Genêt's play *Le Balcon,* the bishop muses similarly that elevation to his post demands the display of virtues which should lead him not to desire to be bishop. These jokes all refer to the impossibility of an ideal subjectivity in the ruler (from the standpoint of the ruled at least), given the competitive conditions out of which all rule proceeds. Bourgeois democracy generally attempts to overcome this by *impersonal* rule, contradictorily combined with carefully regulated conditions of personal competition. And the feudal political order engendered the fantasy of the just ruler, who would be able to transcend the competitive conditions of actual power. Hal's theatricality is irreducible to such ideal simplicity, but nonetheless, his speech cited above contains this promise: "true" inheritance will replace the conditions of *actual* inheritance. On the surface the speech is addressed to his father. But there is a more powerful address to the audience. Prince Hal says that the only condition that should separate him from the lowest vassal is his subjective condition of sublimated desire. Like his father, the prince knows that legitimation proceeds from the gratification of his audience, but unlike the king, Prince Hal seems able to present an incontrovertible picture of sublimation.

And yet audience gratification requires just that evocation of anxiety that could be called "Oedipal" from the father's standpoint but which is politically much wider from the standpoint of the audience. The "Oedipal" repression is inscribed, in this play, as a gratifying escape from the anarchy of civil war *and* from the anarchic pleasures of carnival laughter. Rebellion is always equivocally there in rumors about Hal's ambitions, in his father's suspicions and accusations, and above all in Hal's youthful revel (etymologically close to "rebel", as we are reminded by Shakespeare's treatment of the Cade rebellion in the *Henry VI* trilogy). Falstaff represents an appetite for what power promises to provide directly, but Hal renounces appetite in favor of the Law. In this play, "Oedipal" anxieties are evoked repetitively, but with ascending intensity, in order to be denied. That denial is the gratification afforded by Prince Hal's strategic narrativization of his own participation in history. But what is denied by deed and word (Hal's) cannot really be denied as psychic potential. Such denial cannot appeal to words and acts as facts, because words and deeds are always staged to a certain extent, and Henry IV and V are the supreme masters of the postfeudal art of staging their own deeds. Only Hotspur naively acts his own character. Insofar as they are staged (i.e., always to a certain extent), words and deeds are *negations,* testifying to the force of what is denied. Even Prince Hal's subordination of himself to the Chief Justice at the end is powerful because it is an overcoming of potential private desire, for revenge. Thus the earlier carnivalesque usurpation of his father's authority in the Boar's Head Inn (which stands for so much else throughout) could indeed be read and felt by the audience as the truthful enactment of a normally unconfessable desire. It is precisely *because* the scene is carnivalesque, and therefore has the special fictional status accorded to a joke, that it is able to express truths which in "real" life (the surrounding play) would be totally disruptive.

The casting-off of Falstaff and the sublimation of Hal's disruptive desires are dramatic equivalents. In this sense Falstaff is a scapegoat. The audience's gratification also testifies to the truths within that which is cast off. Hal can *say* that the king's suspicions are all based on rumor and misunderstanding, a factual matter to be cleared up in the clear light of day by words underwritten by deeds. But the gratification speaks of anxieties which also arise from the facts, truths of desires whose very characterization as "lies" is reassuring, given that the alternative is continuing political mayhem. *Henry IV* traces the replacement of the public agon of the carnival as a mode of dealing with political anxiety by the construction of an exemplary Oedipal subjectivity. This is what links the ideal figure of the new Henry V and the new forms of gratification in the audience.

The triumph of Hal's "monological" plot is not the "last word" (in Bakhtin's sense). Falstaff is displaced, negated, but persists as a counterclaim threatening, or denouncing, the idealizing purposiveness that would abolish him forever to a former life. His abolition from the court and the king's own person is a legal fiction in the form of a willed forgetting. This staged forgetting, so necessary to the monological narrative, haunts the moment of "clarification" and relevation of the king's true nature as its negated underside. The monological narrative exists only by denying the silent schizophrenia that it installs in place of the overt public agon of the carnival. However serious the issues are, the structure of the desired closure is that of the joke. Not only does it offer itself to critical reevaluations: it seems almost to provoke them. But even a critical rereading could never fully restore the laughter. At most there is room here for a sardonic smile of recognition.

Notes

[1] For some theories of the carnival, see [m.m. Bakhtin, *Rabelais and his World,* 1968. Works on the carnival abound. For a concern with the practices of the European carnival as millennial tradition, see Julio Caro Baroja, *El Carnaval* (Madrid: Taurus, 1965); Peter Burke, *Popular Culture in Early Moderr Europe* (London: Temple Smith, 1978); and Claude Gaignebet and Marie-Claude Florentin, *Le Carnaval: Essais de Mythologie Populaire* (Paris: Fayot, 1974). In Shakespearean studies, C. L. Barber, *Shakespeare's Festive Comedy: A Study of Dramatic Form and its Relation to Social Custom* (Princeton: Princeton University Press, 1965) is still indispensable. For a more contemporary Bakhtinian reading of the carnival as a sociopolitical practice which shapes the theatrical, see Michael D. Bristol, *Carnival and Theater: Plebeian Culture and the Structure of Authority in Renaissance England* (New York and London: Methuen, 1985). For the politics of its social containment and repression, see Yves-Marie Bercé, *Fête et Révolte: des Mentalités Populaires du XVle au XVllle siécle* (Paris: Hachette, 1976). And for an account of the relationship of Bakhtin's "grotesque body" of carnival discourse to bourgeois self-perceptions from the eighteenth century to the present, see Peter Stallybrass and Allon White, *The Politics and Poetics of Transgression* (Ithaca: Cornell University Press, 1986)]; and for Louis Althusser on ideology as "interpellation," see [his *"Lenin and Philosophy" and Other Essays,* trans. Ben Brewster, 1971].

[2] V. N. Voloshinov, *Marxism and the Philosophy of Language* [1930], trans. by L. Matejka and I. R. Titunik (New York: Seminar Press, 1973), 23. The argument that Voloshinov's work is essentially Bakhtin's is to be found in Katerina Clark and Michael Holquist, *Mikhaïl Bakhtin* (Cambridge, Mass., and London: Harvard University Press, 1985). A summary of the counterarguments, in my view persuasive, is to be found in the Introduction to *Rethinking Bakhtin: Extensions and Challenges,* ed. Gary Saul Morson and Caryl Emerson (Evanston, Ill.: Northwestern University Press, 1989). In any case, nobody disputes the strong mutual influence in the dialogue between the non-Marxist Bakhtin and his Marxist colleagues like Voloshinov and Medvedev.

[3] Renate Lachmann, "Bakhtin and Carnival: Culture as Counter-Culture," *Cultural Critique,* no. 11 (Winter 1988-9): 136.

[4] Sigmund Freud, "Psycho-Analytic Notes on an Autobiographical Account of a Case of Paranoia" [1911], *Standard Edition,* volume 12, ed. James Strachey (London: Hogarth Press, 1958), 74. See also "Instincts and their Vicissitudes" [1915], *Standard Edition,* volume 14.

[5] See I. R. Titunik's introduction to his translation of V. N. Voloshinov's *Freudianism: A Marxist Critique* [1927] (New York and London: Academic Press, 1976).

[6] I explore this issue further in "Unachievable Monologism and the Production of the Monster" in *Bakhtin: Carnival and Other Subjects,* ed. David Shepherd (Amsterdam: Rodopi Press, 1993).

[7] Chief among these would be the thirteenth-century poem "The Fight of Lent with the Meat Eater," cited by Bakhtin in *Rabelais and His World,* 289; and the famous "De la Pelea que ovo don Carnal con la Quaresma" in Juan Ruiz's *Libro de Buen Amor* [1343]. In this mock epic poem of about 300 pages in length, the warrior Don Carnal is supported by sausages, hams, etc., but thin Lady Lent summons the fish from the various coasts of Spain and Don Carnal is defeated and his sausages are hanged. He then stages a Spring counteroffensive in alliance with Don Amor, and Lady Lent is exiled to Rome, appropriately enough.

[8] Emmanuel Le Roy Ladurie, *Le Carnaval de Romans* (Paris: Gallimard, 1979).

[9] Mircea Eliade, *The Myth of the Eternal Return, or, Cosmos and History* trans. William Trask (Princeton: Princeton University Press, 1971).

[10] Michael D. Bristol, *Carnival and Theater: Plebeian Culture and the Structure of Authority in Renaissance England* (New York and London: Methuen, 1985), 204-206.

[11] See [note 1].

[12] See [Gilles Deleuze and Félix Guattari, *L'Anti-Oedipe: Capitalisme et Schizophrénie,* trans. R. Hurley et al., as *Anti-Oedipus: Capitalism and Schizophrenia,* 1984].

[13] See Julia Kristeva, *Pouvoirs de l'Horreur* (Paris: Seuil, 1980), 80-105 in particular, for her use of Mary Douglas' *Purity and Danger: an Analysis of Concepts of Pollution and Taboo* (Harmondsworth: Penguin, 1970).

Source: "Carnival and Plot in *King Henry IV,*" in *Anxious Pleasures: Shakespearean Comedy and the Nation-State,* Associated University Presses, 1995, pp. 215-34.

"The Sequence of Posterity": Shakespeare's *King John* and the Succession Controversy

Robert Lane, *North Carolina State University*

> Thus you see, this crown is not like to fall to the ground for want of heads that may claim to wear it, but upon whose head it will fall is by many doubted.
>
> —*Thomas Wilson*[1]

> This matter doth rather require the mouth of all England, then of anie one man.
>
> —*Peter Wentworth*[2]

When Parliament convened in February, 1593, the queen was 59 years old, her age intensifying public concern over that "uncertain certainty,"[3] the as-yet unsettled succession on her death. This apprehension had persisted since early in her reign, the succession issue having been the focus of domestic politics as early as the 1560s, especially after Elizabeth's serious illnesses in 1562 and 1564.[4] Despite, or rather because of, the decisive importance of this question, it remained largely invisible on the landscape of public discourse. Elizabeth's government was determined to see that this preoccupation had no outlet. Public discussion of the succession was forbidden, declared treasonous by parliamentary statute.[5] Authors of pamphlets on the subject on 1564 and 1568 were imprisoned, even though in the latter instance the author advocated what was the government's own position.[6] Despite Parliament's active participation in the question of succession during her father's reign,[7] Elizabeth consistently refused its counsel, "reserv[ing]" this prerogative, according to the French Ambassador, "for herself."[8] Elizabeth was adamant in refusing to name her successor, fearful that a rising sun would eclipse her, relegating her to lame-duck status.[9] The result was a population largely cowed into silence on this "notoriously taboo" question,[10] for, as Edmund Plowden declared in 1566,

> in dealing in tytles of kyngdomes there is mutche danger . . . and in these cases I thinke the surest waie is to be sylent, for in silence there is saufftie but in speache there is perill, and in wryting more.[11]

Despite the danger, however, there continued to be notable protesters against the government's position, whose treatment at the hands of the Crown punctuated its policy of enforced muteness. Most prominent among these was Peter Wentworth, who was imprisoned from 1593 until his death in 1597 for discussing the succession with a few of his parliamentary colleagues.[12] Wentworth had also been incarcerated in 1591 for his efforts to have the queen resolve this issue.[13] At that time the Lord Chancellor upbraided him before the Privy Council for prompting discussion of the succession in "cobblers' and taylors' shops."[14] The aim of the Crown's policy was wholly to remove the question of royal lineage from discussion by subjects, since the discussion itself implied their capacity to render judgment on the legitimacy of monarchs, a dangerous contradiction of the Crown's self-representation as immune from all judgment except God's.[15]

With Wentworth's example in front of it the 1593 Parliament refused to deal with the succession.[16] Its failure prompted the publication of the most famous of the 1590s succession tracts, the Jesuit priest Robert Parsons' *Conference About the Next Succession to the Crowne of Ingland* (1594).[17] Parsons' exhaustive work—together with responses to it by Henry Constable and John Hayward, Wentworth's two pamphlets on the subject, and Thomas Wilson's summary of the claims of the various contestants—define the issues surrounding the determination of Elizabeth's successor as they took shape after 1590.[18] Defying censorship in an effort to "influence a politically conscious reading public,"[19] they indicate the intense national interest in the question.

It has been recognized that Elizabethan drama addressed that interest, providing a forum for examination of the issue in a manner sufficiently oblique to avoid government retaliation. Marie Axton, for example, referred to Elizabethan drama as "the medium for speculation and protest, as testing ground for political ideas and situations."[20] What has not been acknowledged, however, is how thoroughly, almost systematically, Shakespeare in *King John* engages the specific issues entailed in the succession crisis of the 1590s, the issues the pamphleteers devoted so much attention to because their resolution would determine the next monarch of England. Indeed, it is more than plausible that Shakespeare chose King John's reign because its legitimacy—the fundamental focus of the play—turned on strikingly similar issues. The elements of Shakespeare's play are shaped to emphasize that similarity, underscoring three questions:

1. the effect of a monarch's will in naming the successor;
2. the propriety of a foreigner acceding to the throne; and
3. the process by which a successor would be chosen, in particular the role of the people in that determination.

A play about King John would have been self-evidently

topical, since his reign figured as a precedent (positive or negative) in the succession debate as to the first two of these issues.[21] Shakespeare's fashioning of the historical material intensifies its pertinence not only by highlighting the third, but by the way that he shapes and combines various elements in the play's own succession controversy. While the official representation of John emphasized the religious dimension, portraying him as wholly justified in resisting the illegitimate incursion of papal Rome,[22] Shakespeare significantly toned down the religious conflict in order to highlight those matters that pertained more directly to the succession.[23] Further, by farming the issues in a way that pits important principles and values against one another, rather than as all neatly aligned behind a single figure, Shakespeare's drama creates in his audience what Phyllis Rackin calls "divided allegiances."[24] This effect forces the audience to consider the relative weight to be given each of these principles in determining a prince.

When Philip the Bastard rails against the "scroyles [scoundrels] of Angiers" who

> [S]tand securely on their battlements
> As in a theatre, whence thay gape and point
> At [the kings'] industrious scenes and acts of death,
> (2.1.373-76)

he means to derogate the citizens' role as frivolous and impudent. But the simile ("As in a theatre") points up the relative security of the playhouse audience to take up contested political questions, albeit in veiled form, a security that encouraged the theater's role in critically examining those questions. The audience for the play is aligned with the citizens in it as judges of the respective claims of the competitors to the throne.[25] By his presentation Shakespeare provokes precisely what the Crown's policy precluded—the exercise of critical judgment on the part of his audience—casting them as participants in the process of determining the successor. In so doing he constitutes the theater as a deliberative forum where that judgment can be stimulated and nurtured.

"By Will Bequeath'd": The Monarch's Power to Fix the Succession by Will

In Elizabethan England continuity with the past was a potent source of legitimacy (hence the use of charges of "novelty" and "innovation" to discredit religious and political claims or activities). But in the 1590s discontinuity was unavoidable: the English people were facing, in Elizabeth's impending death without an heir, a radical disjunction in their history. The arguments over the succession were a contest, not just between candidates, but over which of the competing historical narratives could best restore that breach and re-align the monarchy, and the nation, with its antecedents.[26] The historical project of bringing past and present into a coherent relationship, one productive of a sense of collective identity, was at the heart of the contest over legitimacy.

Shakespeare's play offers several links to the reign of the deceased Richard I. Most important as far as John's title is concerned is the conflict pitting testamentary disposition of the Crown—a narrative that binds past and present through the exercise of the deceased monarch's will (in both senses)—against the operation of the laws of primogeniture—a narrative forging that link through the legal plotting of lineage. Though John's claim to the throne resides largely in his "possession." of it (1.1.38), we learn later that he was named as heir in Richard I's will, which Elinor claims "bars the title" (2.1.192) of John's nephew Arthur—the better claim under the rules of primogeniture in effect in both John's and Elizabeth's reigns.[27] The validity of what was historically a death-bed instrument is put in question by Elinor herself, with her acknowledgment of doubt about John's title (1.1.40), and by the denunciation of Arthur's mother Constance:

> A will! a wicked will,
> A woman's will, a cank'red grandam's will!
> (2.1.193-94)

A will like Richard I's purporting to fix succession to the Crown was central to the 1590s debate. Henry VIII by his will (also a death-bed instrument) had contravened primogeniture by designating the heirs of his *younger* sister Mary Tudor (the Suffolk line), rather than those of his *older* sister Margaret Tudor (the Stuart line) as the royal bloodline in the event Elizabeth died childless. If the will was valid, then the sons of Lady Catherine Grey would be next in line, instead of James VI of Scotland.[28] The will was challenged on technical grounds as well as for Henry's mental incapacity and was "for a time mislaid,"[29] but supporting its validity was the parliamentary authorization for the instrument,[30] as well as precedent. That precedent was Richard I's will, giving the succession dispute in *King John* a direct relevance to the Elizabethan debate.

Shakespeare both intensified and complicated its resonance, however, by the ways in which he shaped the Faulconbridge inheritance dispute that is the centerpiece of Act 1, altering it from the earlier anonymous play, *The Troublesome Raigne of King John* (1591; herein *TR*).[31] At the very outset of Shakespeare's play, John's legitimacy is put squarely in issue when the French ambassador snidely refers to his "borrowed majesty" (1.1.4).[32] John tacitly acknowledges the cloud on his title when he demurs, silencing his mother's protest (1.1.5-6).[33] Her objection appears to have been for the Ambassador's benefit, for she soon confides in John that the foundation of his reign lies in "[y]our strong possession much more than your right" (1.1.40).[34] With the equivocal status of John's title thus planted firmly in the audience's mind, the scene immediately shifts to the Faulconbridge controversy. This dispute revolves around the legal effect of the will of Sir Robert Faulconbridge (also a death-bed instrument [1.1.109]), which had attempted to disinherit his illegitimate son, Philip, conceived by Richard I in his absence. The issue, so to speak, is crystallized by Sir Robert's legitimate son, who argues for the will's validity:

> Shall then my father's will be of no force
> To dispossess that child which is not his?
> (1.1.130-31)

These lines have no analogue in *TR*. In fact, there is no mention of a will at all in the earlier play; it is wholly Shakespeare's invention.

Shakespeare makes another decisive change in the dispute from *TR,* namely its outcome. In *TR* John decided in favor of the legitimate son Robert, while in Shakespeare, though Robert's arguments are more compelling than those in the earlier play, John decides in favor of his older, though illegitimate, brother. In doing so, John repudiates the will of the deceased Faulconbridge. This judgment was apparently in accordance with feudal law and might seem to urge rejection of Henry's will.[35] But John's decision is contrary to his own title, resting as it did on the will of Richard I. By putting John, in a sense, at odds with himself, Shakespeare's play virtually forces its viewer to consider the effect of Henry's will, and thus to engage the larger question it posed about monarchical power: to what extent should the prince be able to dispose of the Crown as if it were his/her own property, thereby superseding the historically sanctioned rules of succession?

The Faulconbridge dispute raises another issue current in the succession debate: the significance of bastardy. The narrative of continuous bloodline was premised on the preservation and transmission of lineage through legally valid marriages. Birth outside that context was universally regarded as interrupting that line; bastardy "[c]ut off the sequence of posterity" (2.1.96) in a way fatal to any claim to the throne. Showing illegitimacy was thus the most effective way to defeat such a claim.[36] But Shakespeare's play problematizes this disqualification because, unlike *TR,* Philip's illegitimacy does not bar him from inheriting his father's land. Furthermore, outside the Faulconbridge family context, Philip's birth confers on him legitimacy from yet another narrative of continuity—biological inheritance—the power of which is expressed in physiognomy, Richard's visible presence in the Bastard.[37] John says of him: "Mine eye hath well examined his parts, / And finds them perfect Richard" (1.1.89-90). Casting Philip as the physical image of Richard draws attention to the simple fact that he is by far Richard's closest relative in the play, his only son.

But the circumstances of Philip's birth force him to a choice; he can either be a (legitimate) Faulconbridge or an (illegitimate) Plantagenet (1.1.134-37). Both contexts confer status on him which is at odds with his biological lineage: in the Faulconbridge family he succeeds to the position of a man who was not his father. In the royal family by the king's fiat he can be knighted and acquire the Plantagenet name (1.1.160-63), which accords with his embodiment of the "very spirit" of Richard (1.1.167). The lineal proximity imaged by the "trick of Cordelion's face" in him (1.1.85) cannot, however, give him a claim to the throne because the sanctioning narrative did not rest on the biological fact of patrilineage alone, but on marital legitimacy. By forcing Philip to choose between what are presented as mutually exclusive alternatives, Shakespeare invites appraisal of each of these circumstances of birth in determining succession.

"STRANGER BLOOD": THE CAPACITY OF A FOREIGNER TO INHERIT LAND OR CROWN

By juxtaposing John's dubious title with the Faulconbridge controversy Shakespeare's play poses the question of how inheritance and succession are related. Implicit in the disposition of the throne by will is the analogy between the demise of the crown and the devolution of property. But is the analogy a sound one? To what extent do the legal principles governing the inheritance of property apply to the succession?[38] Because English law precluded foreigners from inheriting land,[39] this question bore significantly on a central issue in the succession debate: whether a foreigner could accede to the English throne. John's reign was a central interpretive crux on this point: did his tenure affirm the principle that no foreigner can sit on the throne (i.e., was Arthur barred by having been born in France?), or was it simply a usurpation by John that deprived the rightful king?[40]

The bar cast a dark cloud over James's hopes to succeed to the throne on Elizabeth's death. Though he favored James, Thomas Wilson reports that "some thought [Arabella Stuart] more capable then he, for that she is English borne (the want whereof, if our Lawyers opinions be corant, is the cause of his exclusion)."[41] James took steps to remove this blemish from his claim by attempting to establish his right to the so-called Lennox lands which had been the property of his paternal grandparents, the Earl and Countess of Lennox. Establishing this right would have bolstered his claim to the throne precisely because of the importance of the analogy between inheritance and succession. Borrowing the Bastard's phrase we could say that James attempted to ground his title to the crown "upon the footing of [English] land" (5.1.66).

Elizabeth also well understood the significance of this property to the Scottish king, justifying her refusal to resolve the question because "some consequences which depende therupon hath made us forbare to dispose of [this matter] one way or the other."[42] She used those "consequences" to her best advantage, promising the lands to James in 1588 when the approaching Spanish fleet cast its shadow, but later reneging, hinting that James's rival Arabella had a colorable claim to them while never expressly rejecting James's.[43] On his part, James sought judicial recognition of his claim, but also continued to press it with the queen—most forcefully in 1596 and again in 1601—even trying to cast the annual pension he received from Elizabeth as compensation for the loss of this property.[44]

Shakespeare's play gives dramatic impetus to the arguments in the succession debate over foreign influence on the English throne. Shakespeare's portrayal of Arthur, emphasizing his youth (everyone repeatedly refers to him as "boy" or "child"), underscores his dependence on the King of France. Arthur himself acknowledges his subservient status when he refers to his own "powerless hand" (2.1.15). His youth and temperament raise grave questions about his capacity to govern. Unlike the character in *TR,* Shakespeare's Arthur does not speak in his own behalf or otherwise actively pursue his own claim (he is even embarrassed about the fight over it—"I am not worth this coil that's made for me" [2.1.165]).[45] His role is symbolized by his absence from the stage during negotiations over the peace pact between the kings.[46] Arthur's relative impotence enhances the power of the French king, who describes himself as Arthur's "guardian" (2.1.115). Philip's announcement of himself to the people of Angiers—"'Tis France, for England" (2.1.202)—bluntly dramatizes the spectre of alien intrusion. Shakespeare shapes the contest more sharply as one between the countries rather than between John and Arthur, with the French king's ascendancy graphically depicting the disturbing possibility of foreign dominion over the English throne.

At the same time that Shakespeare's Arthur is portrayed as more submissive than his counterpart in *TR* (and many historical sources),[47] he is personally treated more symphathetically and his claim to the throne more favorably, all of which casts John in a much more doubtful light in Shakespeare's play than in *TR*.[48] Arthur's status as a royal rival has a continuing, decisive impact on the action of the play, his irrepressible claim haunting John and impelling him toward Arthur's murder. Pandulph articulates the pressure Arthur's very existence exerts on John's dubious title:

> A sceptre snatch'd with an unruly hand
> Must be as boisterously maintain'd as gain'd;
> And he that stands upon a slipp'ry place
> Makes nice of no vild hold to stay him up.
> That John may stand, then Arthur needs must
>   fall. . . .
>
> (3.4.135-39)[49]

Unlike *TR,* Arthur's youth and innocence render his death in Shakespeare's play a much more lamentable scene and its link to the barons' defection is much more direct and firm (4.3.111-13). Underscoring the pathos of the event Shakespeare adds the Bastard's denunciation of the "cruel act" (4.3.126) and his apotheosis of Arthur as "[t]he life, the right, and truth of all this realm / [Who has] fled to heaven" (4.3.144-45).[50] Pitting the appropriation of Arthur's claim by hostile powers against the record of John's perfidy forces Shakespeare's audience to assess whether the native born John was indeed preferable to his immature, encumbered victim. Once again framed to admit no easy resolution, the question prompts evaluation of the categorical bar against accession by a foreigner.

Shakespeare further amplifies the issue in the figure of the French Dauphin Lewis, who also asserts a claim to the English throne. As with his treatment of Arthur, Shakespeare makes the issue here a subtler question than in *TR* by rendering Lewis in a much more favorable light than the earlier play, which depicts his villainy at every possible turn.[51] In Shakespeare there is even some sympathy for Lewis's firm resolve in the face of bad news (5.5.21-22; much qualified in *TR,* Pt. 2, 977-82), especially, in lines without counterpart in *TR,* for his ringing declaration of independence from the Pope—"Am I Rome's slave?" (5.2.97)—echoing John's own earlier affirmation (3.1.147-60). Even while opposing him in arms, the Bastard applauds Lewis's resolve: "The youth says well" (5.2.128). The split within Catholic Christendom which Lewis's speech represents echoed a historical reality. Some Catholic rulers (and the Pope himself) opposed the Hapsburgs' claim to the English throne because of the disproportionate power it would give Spain.[52] In England, too, Catholic subjects were split, with some ("the Appellants") actually negotiating with the Crown's representatives, not for a Catholic king, but for religious toleration under a Protestant one.[53]

Perhaps most striking is the difference in the way Lewis's claim is handled. In *TR* it is repeatedly compromised by being framed as "[t]riumph in conquest" (Pt. 2, 942), his express aim that of French dominance: "The poorest peasant of the Realme of Fraunce / Shall be a maister ore an English Lord" (Pt. 2, 949-50).[54] In Shakespeare, though, Lewis spells out the substantive basis for his claim, through Arthur, in his union with Blanche ("by the honor of my marriage bed / After young Arthur" [5.2.93-94]), the deal struck by Philip and John in 2.1. Unlike *TR* where the Bastard repudiates Lewis's "fained claime" (Pt. 2, 686), the legal validity of this claim is never challenged. Through Lewis Shakespeare's play replicates the intertwined lineages of the royal houses of Europe. "The centuries of dynastic marriage," according to the historian Joel Hurstfield, "had indeed created a situation in which most of the crowned heads of Europe could claim each others' thrones with some degree of plausibility."[55] Because in Lewis's case it is through just such a marriage that the English crown is exposed to a foreigner's claim, the play prompts scrutiny of exactly how that union came about. Specifically, how did it come to be proposed, not by any of the contestants for the throne, but by the citizens of Angiers?

"SPEAK, CITIZENS, FOR ENGLAND": THE PROCESS OF DETERMINING THE SUCCESSOR

At the very outset of Shakespeare's play, war is introduced as the readiest means for resolving succession disputes. When John asks the French Ambassador "what follows" if he rejects Arthur's claim to the throne, Chatillion declares, "The proud control of fierce and bloody war, / To enforce these rights so forcibly witheld" (1.1.17-18). Virtually all the pamphleteers invoked the spectre of war in urging alternatives for determining Elizabeth's successor.[56] Wentworth warned the queen that "[t]o leave [that designation] quyte without establishment, to whomever can catch it" would lead to civil war, "so that presentlie, the whole Realme wil be rent into as many shivers, as there be competitors .... And, thus, while the title to the crowne is in trying in the fielde by the dint of bloodie sword, one part will consume & devoure another."[57] The threat was far from fanciful; by 1599 James was taking concrete steps to arm his subjects to defend his claim.[58]

Both James and the French Ambassador offer violence as a means of *enforcing* legal rights—"[s]hadowing . . . right under . . . wings of war" (2.1.14). But the soldier in Parsons' work articulates the more realistic view of force as *supplanting* considerations of right:

> [W]hen this matter must come to trial . . . not you lawyers, but we souldiars must determyne this title. . . . [W]e should admit [the competing claimants'] causes to examination, and perhapps give sentence for him, that by your lawes would sonest be excluded, for when matters come to snatching, it is hard to say who shal have the better part.[59]

What the soldier affirms is the legitimating power of successful violence. John invokes the same function when he declares that he will "verify our title with [his soldiers'] lives" (2.1.277). His challenge, echoing the assumption of the medieval trial by combat that physical strength correlates with legal validity and moral purity, may strike modern ears as at least naive, if not barbaric, accustomed as we are to regarding might and right as categorically distinct.[60] But in fact their relationship was more complex than first appears, for possession of the Crown was itself regarded as conferring legitimacy. The historian William Camden, for example, in defending Elizabeth's title against her detractors, stated: "[T]he Lawes of *England* many yeeres agoe determined . . . [t]hat the Crowne once possessed, cleareth and purifies all manner of defaults or imperfections."[61] It is thus not merely self-serving hyperbole when John asks rhetorically, "Doth not the crown of England prove the King?" (2.1.273), but an allusion to this principle. The premise of the doctrine is that coronation, as the sign of free acclamation by the secular and religious authorities of the realm, cuts off any competing claims (an obvious effort to bring closure—and peace—to the theoretically endless and potentially lethal succession disputes). In practice, of course, the endorsement was frequently tained by the force used to acquire the Crown and even more frequently ineffective to subdue rival factions. The limitations of reliance on the doctrine are exposed by John's misplaced effort to use "double coronation" (4.2.40) to blot out Arthur's title, the self-destructive quality of which the nobles' speeches emphasize (4.2.9-34): it "doth make the fault worse by th'excuse" (4.2.31).[62]

While the prospect of violence raised the stakes for all English citizens, it simultaneously revealed the absence of any effective institutional means for authoritatively determining the succession. The issue of *who* would succeed to the throne necessarily entailed the question of *how* that person would be selected from the dozen or so candidates. Adopting the terms of Wentworth's declaration quoted as my epigraph, who should be heard on this question? Specifically, what role should the people play in this decision?

Most of the tracts dealing with the succession addressed this question.[63] The most scandalous aspect of Parsons' pamphlet was not its conclusion that the Infanta of Spain had the best claim to succeed Elizabeth but its tenet that the monarch not be determined by lineage alone, that election should play a role. Election worked to "remedy the inconveniences of bare succession," namely, "that some un-apt impotent or evel prince may be offered some times to enter by priority of blood" (Pt. 1, 130). But Parsons stopped short of advocating election as the sole determinant of succession because he felt it was "[s]ubject to great and continual dangers of ambition, emulation, division, sedition, and contention." These threats, Parsons believed, could be neutralized by giving substantial weight to lineage, "for that great occasions of strife and contention are ther by cut of" (Pt. 1, 126). In this way each of the determinants—succession and election—would be "salved [by the other], & the one made a preservative and treacle to the other" (Pt. 1, 130).

To assert even a partial role for the people in determining Elizabeth's successor was a radical proposal, and Parsons embedded his in a farreaching discussion of the relationship between the sovereign and the people. He conceived of that relationship in contractual terms,

> for as much as not nature, but the election and consent of the people, had made their first Princes from the beginning of the world . . . they were not preferred to this eminent power and dignity over others, without some conditions and promises made also on their parts, for using wel this supreme authority given unto them. (Pt. 1, 81)

The monarch's responsibilities, as well as those of the people, were spelled out at the coronation:

> [T]his agreement, bargayne and contract betwene the king and his common wealth, at his first admission, is as certayne and firme (notwithstanding any pretence or interest he hath or maye have by succession) as any contract or mariage in the world can be. (Pt. 1, 119)

In what was a significant extension of this theory, Parsons endowed the populace with the power to depose even a legitimate prince for breach of these obligations, "to dispossesse them that have bin lawfully put in possession, if they fulfil not the lawes and condicions, by which and for which, their dignity was given them" (Pt. 1, 32).[64]

Henry Constable's response to Parsons' work provides an index of how inflammatory its arguments for popular participation in governance were considered to be. He denigrates Parsons for "treadinge the steps of popularitie" by flattering "the phansies & conceits of people who ever delyghte in change" (21). Where Parsons had repeatedly referred to the people acting collectively as "the commonwealth," Constable derides them as "disordered multitudes, beinge no common wealthes indeed, but prodigious monsters of manye heads" (24), the latter image the common epithet used to express contempt for and deny political capacity to the populace.[65] The apocalyptic horror with which Constable greets Parsons' ideas is reflected in the following passage, its form as a rhetorical question declaring Parsons' proposal beyond the pale: "[W]ho seethe not those horrible scandals, & steepe downe falls, threatninge present ruyne to all obedience, humilitie & Civil order" should the people acquire the power to "lawfully place & displace kinges and Soveragnes . . . ?" (48-49). In Constable's view Parsons' "popular doctrine" (21) reduces the king to "a soveraigne upon souffrance" (50), his reign subject to the whim of a fickle rabble.

Amidst his tirade Constable does make one telling point: "how, & by what authoritye, that multitude is to be assembled, & other circumstances most expedient and necessarye, thies lawyers neyther define, nor regarde" (23). There was no discussion in Parsons of the exact means by which the voice of the people speaking as a commonwealth would be institutionalized. Wentworth had proposed that Parliament be the forum wherein "all titles and claimes to the Crowne of England after [Elizabeth's] decease, throughlie . . . be tried & examined" (5), and the recurrent parliamentary involvement in fixing the succession to Henry VIII created pressure to expand participation in the process.[66] It was, of course, the absence of a recognizably authoritative institution for judging among competing claims that produced the high premium on possession of the Crown by coronation, as well as the virulent threat of war to secure that position.

Given the proscription on public discussion of succession, and the sensitivity over the political capacity of the citizenry, it is not surprising that Shakespeare's treatment of the people's role in *King John* is oblique and muted. But it palpably touched on these troubling questions nonetheless. The effort to elaborate on how it did so must begin with a textual anomaly, namely the abrupt shift in the middle of 2.1 in the Folio from the "Citizen" to "Hubert" as the speaker on the walls of Angiers. The designation of this speaker is crucial to an interpretation of his role.

Most editors conclude there is a typographical error and that the Citizen and Hubert were intended to be the same character; some further conclude that Hubert is that character. But there are compelling reasons based on textual analysis alone for treating the designation of "Hubert" as spurious and his speeches in this scene as the continuation of the Citizen's. Contrary to the prevalent Shakespearean practice Hubert is never named in the dialogue, undermining any claim that there is dramatic significance either to the shift of characters in the scene, or to Hubert's reappearance much later (3.3) as John's righthand man.[67] There is simply no persuasive rationale for identifying this scrupulously neutral figure with the later Hubert who is John's ally and confidant.[68] On the contrary, the perspective and tone of "Hubert" reiterates precisely that of the Citizen earlier in the scene—the consistent use, for example, of the first person plural—reflecting this figure's continuing status as spokesman for the people of Angiers, the office the text repeatedly underlines.[69]

Given the weak textual basis, the editorial preference for Hubert over the Citizen signals a reluctance to grant a significant role to an unnamed, untitled figure who speaks for a body of the king's subjects. The choice may well evince a sense of political decorum that would downplay, if not altogether rule out, participation by the people in the selection of the monarch, even though this was a critical issue in the 1590s succession controversy. For in the Citizen the voice of the subjects becomes, as it was in the historical debate, a salient element in the contest over succession. The need both kings feel to actively solicit their consent gives that voice substance and weight. "[L]et us hear them speak," King Philip says, "Whose title they admit" (2.1.199-200).[70] Not only is the citizens' opinion as to the rightful prince treated as within their competence, at least initially it is portrayed as integral to the royal title. In this scene the consent of the public becomes the foundation for legitimate rule. Its authority here is visually depicted by the Citizen's placement on the wall *above* the two kings and their assembled armies.[71] Philip's declaration initiates a dialogue between prince and subject which contains in embryonic form the kind of mutual exchange Parsons theorizes, a conversation in which, however brief their speeches, the people are represented (in both senses) as vital participants.

Instead of straightforwardly rendering judgment on who should succeed, however, the people, by "hold[ing] the right from both" candidates (282) and calling upon them to "prove[] the King" (270), foreground the question of the basis for this decision. While the Citizen's demurral seems a refusal of political agency, its most salient effect is to expose the simplistically militaristic impulses of the kings. He calls upon them to "*compound* whose right is worthiest" (281; my emphasis), the word implying the settlement of a dispute through negotiation and compromise rather than its unrestrained prosecution by violence. Without pausing for consideration of alternatives, however, the royals move impetuously to armed conflict, determined to "arbitrate" the question "[w]ith fearful bloody issue" (1.1.37). The futility of that carnage—"blood hath bought blood" (2.1.329) of such equal quantity that this effort "verifies" (277) nothing—amounts to a repudiation of war on both pragmatic and moral grounds as a credible means of trying title.

The citizens' refusal to be drawn into an alliance with one or the other faction, an alliance that would surely result in the town's destruction, is impressively astute. Their prudent resolve contradicts Wentworth's prediction that the common people, "at their wits end, not knowing what part to take," nonetheless "shal be driven to followe" rivals among the competing claimants, producing civil war.[72] Their diplomacy nearly proves unavailing, however, for when the royals' further entreaties for acclamation prove unsuccessful, the Bastard spurs the kings' resentment toward these unmalleable subjects. His comments focus on the impertinence of the town ("these scroyles," "this contemptuous city" and "peevish town," "these saucy walls" [373, 384, 402, 404]), reproaching the people for their presumption in arrogating to themselves the power to render judgment in this dispute, even in the neutral form that they do.[73] But his rebuke is undercut, both by the fact that the town has been put into this position by the royals themselves, and even more so by the Bastard's own proposal, which the kings eagerly agree to,[74] that they conclude a military pact to "lay this Angiers even with the ground" (399). They thus conspire to destroy the city in order to rule it.[75]

This sequence exposes the potentially tragic divergence between the interests of the people and those of the competitors for the throne, a divergence which, without the institutional means of enforcing the will of the populace, leaves the realm vulnerable to violence.[76] Significantly, war here is *not* the product of a factionalized citizenry, for the subjects remain united and steadfast; the play rejects Parsons' fears of the people as divided and contentious. Rather, the threat comes from the ambition of the two contenders for the crown, portrayed here as extreme to the point of self-defeating absurdity: the destruction of the very substance of the kingdom that crown represents—its subjects.[77]

The neutrality of the Citizens up to this point thus is rendered not as spineless passivity or indecision, but as prudential adherence to a non-violent resolution of this question, for it is their lives and property which are jeopardized by any war that ensues. Their commitment to a peaceful determination becomes more active when, faced with the kings' united armies, they offer a peaceful way out of the conflict, one that satisfies the dynastic aims of both John and Philip, even at the price of Arthur's claim. They propose "peace and fair-fac'd league" (2.1.417) through the marriage between the Dauphin Lewis and John's niece Blanche. Not surprisingly, the Bastard rails against the proposal, in lines absent from *TR,* dwelling on the very fact of the Citizen's participation in the process:

> He speaks cannon-fire, and smoke, and bounce,
> He gives the bastinado with his tongue;
> Our ears are cudgell'd—not a word of his
> But buffets better than a fist of France.
> 'Zounds, I was never so bethump'd with words
> Since I first call'd my brother's father dad.
> (2.1.462-67)

His rant reiterates the Citizen's audacity he earlier denounced, but adds the imposition he feels, a discomfort that grows from the very *force* of the Citizen's speech itself (the Citizen's words are weapons that "cudgel" and "bethump"). What offends him is that the voice of the people carries weight with the kings, so much that it is effective in actually re-directing royal power.

The creativity of the Citizen's contribution—a "union [that] shall do more than battery can" (446)—lays bare the reflexively violent character of the royal rivals. That the pragmatic character of his proposal leaves matters potentially unstable because it does not resolve Arthur's claim is hardly the responsibility of the Citizens who acted "to keep [their] city" (2.1.455), to spare themselves and their polity the destruction of war. Though that instability has its occasion in the existence of a rival claimant to the throne, it is needlessly and fatally exacerbated by John's misplaced efforts to immunize his reign from that claim through his repeated coronation and Arthur's murder.

But John is no simple villain, nothing like Richard in *Richard III* in his calculated strategies for eliminating the numerous prior claimants to the throne. Resort to the character of John, as either hero or villain, fails to provide any secure vantage from which to determine the issues the play so insistently poses. Instead, Shakespeare distributes legitimacy among the various claimants,[78] especially by endowing the young Arthur with doubtful fitness, thus witholding the prospect of a neat resolution. By refusing any single criterion as the standard to be mechanically applied in fixing the successor Shakespeare's play demands that its audience "work, work [its] thoughts" (*Henry V,* 3.Chor.25). It calls upon its viewers, like the citizens of Angiers to decide "whose title they admit" (*King John,* 2.1.200), to mediate among the various candidates by assessing the sanction each invokes. This demand for the audience's active, if only imaginative, participation in determining the monarch is echoed and affirmed by the portrayal of the popular representative in the play, the Citizen. While the precise scope and form of public participation was not to be explicitly addressed for another half century, this play registers the potency of that question, already palpable in Elizabeth's England.

Notes

[1] Thomas Wilson, *The State of England, Anno Dom. 1600, Camden Miscellany* XVI (3rd. Series, 1936), 5.

[2] Peter Wentworth, *A Treatise Containing M. Wentworths Judgment concerning the Person of the True and Lawfull Successor to these Realmes of England and Ireland* (1598), 6.

[3] Wallace T. MacCaffrey, *Elizabeth I: War and Politics, 1588-1603* (Princeton: Princeton University Press, 1992), 453.

[4] John Guy, *Tudor England* (Oxford: Oxford University Press, 1988), 269.

[5] 13 Eliz. I, c.1.

[6] Mortimer Levine, *The Early Elizabethan Succession Question, 1558-1568* (Stanford: Stanford University Press, 1966), 89-90; John E. Neale, "Peter Wentworth, Part II," *EHR* 39 (1924), 185-86.

[7] It passed succession acts in 1534, 1536, and 1544.

[8] Quoted in Marie Axton, *The Queen's Two Bodies* (London: Royal Historical Society, 1977), 11. "[T]hose [in Parliament] who had wished to revive the question [in the 1576 session] had been silenced, and in [1581] . . . the lord keeper had forbidden its discussion in his opening speech" (Neale, "Peter Wentworth," 178).

[9] MacCaffrey, 545.

[10] John E. Neale, *Elizabeth I and Her Parliaments, 1584-1601* (New York: St. Martin's Press, 1958), 251.

[11] Quoted in Axton, 20.

[12] Neale, "Wentworth II," 186-205.

[13] Neale, "Wentworth II," 184-85.

[14] Quoted in Edward P. Cheyney, *A History of England From the Defeat of the Armada to the Death of Elizabeth* (New York: Peter Smith, 1948), 2: 280.

[15] The government's posture is aptly characterized by the rhetorical question of Shakespeare's Bishop of Carlisle: "What subject can give judgment on a king?" (*Richard II,* 4.1.121). All passages from Shakespeare's plays are from *The Riverside Shakespeare,* ed. G. Blakemore Evans (Boston: Houghton-Mifflin Co., 1974).

[16] The exclamation of James Morice, M.P., may express his colleagues' attitude: "Succession! What is he that dare meddle with it?" (quoted in Neale, *Elizabeth I,* 258).

[17] Parsons, writing under the name of R. Doleman, identifies Wentworth's suppression as the occasion for his work. It was prompted, he said, "when at length newes was brought, that nothing at al had bin done [in the 1593 Parliament concerning succession], but rather that one or two (as was reported) had bin checked or committed for speaking in the same" (*Conference About the Next Succession to the Crowne of Ingland* [1594], Part I, B.1r-B.1v).

[18] The works were Henry Constable, *A Discoverye of a Counterfecte Conference Helde At A Counterfecte Place, etc.* (Collen, 1600); John Hayward, *An Answer to a Conference, Concerning Succession* (London, 1603); Peter Wentworth, *A Pithie Exhortation to Her Majestie* (1598) and his *Treatise* cited above; and Thomas Wilson's work cited above. There was also a 1592 pamphlet by Richard Verstegen, *A Declaration of the True Causes of the Great Troubles, etc.* (1592), that addressed the succession at length.

[19] Levine, 89-90.

[20] Axton, ix. Axton believes that "[o]f all the media—lawsuit, parliamentary debate, political pamphlet, stage-play—the stage offered the freest forum for speculation about the succession to the throne and the issues related to it" (x).

[21] Axton, 32; Lily B. Campbell, *Shakespeare's "Histories": Mirrors of Elizabethan Policy* (San Marino, CA:

The Huntington Library, 1968), 142-44.

[22] Thus the *Book of Homilies:*

> The Bishoppe of Rome did picke a quarrell to King John of England, about the election of Steven Langton to the Bishopricke of Canterburie, wherein the King had ancient right, being used by his progenitors, all Christian Kinges of England before him, the Bishops of Rome having no right, but had begunne then to usurpe upon the Kinges of Englande, and all other Christian Kinges, as they had before done against their Soveraigne Lordes the Emperours. . . .
>
> (*Certaine Sermons or Homilies Appointed to Be Read in Churches in the Time of Elizabeth,* eds. Mary Ellen Rickey and Thomas B. Stroup [Gainesville, FL: Scolars' Facsimiles & Reprints, 1968], 315).

[23] "Shakespeare largely forewent," according to A. R. Braunmuller, "the obviously dramatic conflict with Rome because the dynastic struggle itself guaranteed contemporary attention" (William Shakespeare, *The Life and Death of King John,* ed. A. R. Braunmuller [Oxford: Clarendon Press, 1989], 60). Lily Campbell sees Shakespeare's play as a straightforward mirror of the troubles of Protestant England with the Catholic Church, and, more specifically, regards the figure of Arthur as a stand-in for Mary Stuart (Campbell, 126-67). This perspective grows out of a model of one-for-one correspondence (not uncommon in earlier historicist criticism) that overlooks important features of *King John,* such as the *reduced* role of religion, and the sympathy generated for Arthur by John's mistreatment. Together with the retrospective posture Campbell attributes to the play as largely a transcription of earlier historical events, her approach saps the play of much of its contemporary vitality, a potency augmented by the work's resistance to simple historical allegorization.

[24] Phyllis Rackin, *Stages of History: Shakespeare's English Chronicles* (Ithaca: Cornell University Press, 1990), 182. "[T]he ethical and political ambivalences" of the play make it, in her view, "the most disturbing of all Shakespeare's English histories" (182).

[25] See Rackin, 53.

[26] The importance of history to the succession reinforced the Crown's jealous protection of its prerogative to determine Elizabeth's heir. It was committed to what Annabel Patterson characterizes as "the belief that the history of the realm, not only in terms of access to state documents but in terms of interpretation, belonged to the monarch" (Annabel Patterson, *Censorship and Interpretation: The Conditions of Writing and Reading in Early Modern England* [Madison, WI: University of Wisconsin Press, 1984], 129).

[27] Because he was the son of John's deceased older brother, Arthur's title was superior by reason of "representation," "the principle which allows the children or remoter descendants of a dead person to stand in that person's stead" (Braunmuller, 56). Perhaps the best-known example of the operation of this principle is the accession, on the death of Edward III, of Richard II instead of his uncles.

[28] Levine, 63.

[29] Joel Hurstfield, "The Succession Struggle in Late Elizabethan England," in *Elizabethan Government and Society,* eds. S. T. Bindoff et al. (London: Atheneum Press, 1961), 372. Hurstfield comments that "the whole issue was criss-crossed with uncertainties" (372). See Parsons, Part II, 115-16; Wilson, 8-9.

[30] The latter two of Parliament's succession acts—28 Henry VIII, c. 7 (1536) and 35 Henry VIII, c. 1 (1544)—gave Henry limited right to settle the succession by will (Levine, 37).

[31] Critics disagree over whether Shakespeare's work antedated or followed *The Troublesome Raigne.* In the Introduction to his edition, Braunmuller ably compares the two works and summarizes the evidence for the possible relationships (2-15), concluding that *King John* postdates *TR* (15). His conclusion is further confirmed by the topical references discussed here, references whose allusiveness to the succession debate would have been amplified by the dissemination of Parsons' work in and after 1594. For that reason I believe Shakespeare's play came long enough after that work's publication for him to read and absorb it.

[32] In contrast *TR* begins with the declaration of John's succession to Richard and his acceptance of the burdens of office (the text of *TR* is that in *Narrative and Dramatic Sources of Shakespeare,* ed. Geoffrey Bullough [London: Routledge and Kegan Paul, 1962], 5: 72-151).

[33] In *TR* he responds sarcastically to the Ambassador's demand that he vacate the throne (Pt. 1, 35-44).

[34] There are no comparable lines in *TR.*

[35]George W. Keeton, *Shakespeare's Legal and Political Background* (New York: Barnes & Noble, Inc., 1967), 121, 127. "Only with legal statutes passed under Henry VIII could a will disinherit a lineal heir" (Virginia M. Vaughan, "*King John:* A Study in Subversion and Containment," *King John: New Perspectives,* ed. Deborah T. Curren-Aquino [Newark: University of Delaware Press, 1989], 66).

[36]It is for this reason that Elinor accuses Arthur of bastardy (2.1.122-23; a charge with no counterpart in *TR*). Such accusations abounded in the succession debate. Charges, for example, that James's grandmother was illegitimate because her father was already married when he married her mother, Margaret Tudor, were urged both in support of and against James's claim to the throne. The illegitimacy would break the line from Margaret Tudor to James that descended through his father, Lord Darnley, but, since James's link to her could also be established through his mother, Mary Stuart, the charge did not completely defeat his claim. It would, however, have broken the line from Margaret to Arabella, her granddaughter, James's closest lineal rival. (See Wentworth, *Treatise,* 11-12; and Wilson, 2, 6). The accusation of bastardy was also pivotal to the claim of Edward, Lord Beauchamp, son of Lady Catherine Grey, because he was next in the Suffolk line. His status was widely regarded as doubtful and "Elizabeth steadfastly refused to recognize [his parents'] marriage" (Helen G. Stafford, *James VI of Scotland and the Throne of England* [New York: Appleton-Century Co., 1940], 27). Questions were also raised about the legality of the marriages of Catherine's mother and grandmother (see Levine, 126f.; Wilson, 6; and Parsons, Part II, 130f.).

[37] The French king Philip also uses physiognomy, to reinforce Arthur's claim and undermine John's ("Look here upon thy brother Geoffrey's face" [2.1.100; see also 101-2]), opposing Arthur's "living blood" (2.1.108) of Geoffrey, John's older brother, to John's empty title ("How comes it then that thou art call'd a king?" [107]).

[38] See Parsons, Part II, 91.

[39] A statute during Edward III's reign condified the medieval common law principle precluding inheritance by a foreigner, the rule having originated in response to the loss of Normandy in 1204 as a way of depriving Frenchmen of their English land (25 Edward III, c. 1; see Frederick Pollock and F. W. Maitland, *The History of English Law* [Cambridge: Cambridge University Press, 1968], 1: 458-67; Levine, 99). The act barring aliens contained an exception for children of the king, the scope of which became a disputed issue in the succession controversy, namely, did it extend to more remote descendants? For discussion by the pamphleteers of this rule and its application to succession see Wilson, 7; Parsons, Part II, 5, 111f., 194f., 199f., and 214; and Wentworth, *Treatise,* 9f. and 43f.

[40] Levine, 102. A succession tract from 1565 cited John as precedent for its argument against Mary Stuart, asserting that Arthur was excluded by his foreign birth (Axton, 25).

[41] Wilson, 2.

[42] Quoted in Stafford, 250.

[43] Axton, 76-77; Stafford, 22.

[44] Stafford, 39-40, 175, 250-51.

[45] Contrast *TR,* Pt. 1, 440-51, 525-27. Shakespeare's King Philip gets the lines Arthur speaks in *TR* challenging the Citizens of Angiers to decide who their king will be (2.1.199-200, 362; *TR,* Pt. 1, 718-19).

[46] Shakespeare's Arthur only tries to quiet his mother's objections to the agreement; in *TR* Arthur himself pointedly objects to negotiations over his status (Pt. 1, 765-67).

[47] Holinshed, for example, pointedly describes Arthur's response to John's solicitous appeal to ally with him ("his naturall uncle"): "[L]ike one that wanted good counsell, and abounding too much in his owne wilfull opinion, [Arthur] made a presumptuous answer" (W.G. Boswell-Stone, *Shakespeare's Holinshed: The Chronicle and the Plays Compared* [New York: Dover Publications, 1968], 59).

[48] In contrast to *TR,* Shakespeare dwells on John's giving Hubert the order to kill Arthur (3.3); he renders the exchange between Hubert and Arthur over John's order to blind Arthur in much less philosophical and more personal terms (4.1); he more closely links the backlash from the self-defeating second coronation with Arthur, his imprisonment, and the report of his death (4.2); and he makes Arthur's death the axis around which the five moons prophecy and the reaction of the people revolve (4.2).

[49] These lines have no counterpart in *TR*. Though more inclined to John's point of view, Holinshed confirms Pandulph's logic: "[S]o long as Arthur lived, there would be no quiet in those parts" (60).

[50] In similar fashion Parsons questions what he regards as "but a common vulgar prejudice . . . against strangers" by laying out the tyrannical performance of several native English monarchs (Part II, 197-98, 214f.).

[51] In *TR,* for example, Lewis's hypocrisy toward the English lords is enacted at length in front of the audience, while in Shakespeare it is only briefly reported (*TR,* Pt. 2, 503-631; *King John* 5.4.10-39).

[52] Hurstfield, 378.

[53] Hurstfield, 373-74, 384-87.

[54] His right is rendered more doubtful in *TR* by his admission that he could win England only "by treason" (Pt. 2, 1167-71), the term implying John's legitimacy.

[55] Hurstfield, 372. Just how this condition was perpetuated, and how fraught with political implications, is evidenced by the case of James's rival the Scottish Arabella of the Stuart line. In the years just before Elizabeth's death there were various plots, all foiled, to marry her to one or another descendant of the Suffolk line in a last ditch effort to shore up both their claims. After James's accession, in 1610, she finally succeeded, secretly marrying William Seymour of the Suffolk line. Their imprisonment upon discovery of the union by the Crown testifies to the continuing threat competing claims represented to James, claims that could be solidified and enhanced by marriage. Except for a brief escape, Arabella languished in jail until her death in 1615.

[56] The contemporary bearing of the threat of violence in the play is urged by the anachronistic references to cannon (e.g., 1.1.26, 2.1.37 and 210), not invented until long after John's reign.

[57] Wentworth, *Exhortation,* 21 and 25. He viewed the prospect as imminent on Elizabeth's death: "[T]he breath shall be no sooner out of your body (if your successor be not setled in your life-time) but that al your nobility, counsellors, and whole people will be up in armes with all the speede they may" (101-2). Like others, he cited the Wars of the Roses as precedent for the "mercilesse shedding of rivers of innocent blood" and "the endlesse bloodie battailes" he foresaw (20, 104).

[58] Stafford, 196-97, 213. In that year he told his Parliament he was prepared to resort to arms, that he knew his right and would venture all for it (Hurstfield, 393).

[59] Parsons, Part I, B.3r-B.3v. Thomas Wilson echoes this view:

> [W]ell I wot that a slender tittle oftentime sufficeth for clayming and gayning of a Kingdome where there is power and opportunity to gett the possession once, as hath been seen often in that poor Island, first by William the Conqueror, and often since that in the struggling of the houses of Lancaster and Yorke, where many times Might hath overcome Ryght. (5)

[60] Elinor recognizes the distinction when she quips that John's title turns on "[y]our strong possession much more than your right" (1.1.40).

[61] William Camden, *Annales, The True and Royall History of the Famous Empress Elizabeth, Queene of England France and Ireland* (London: Benjamin Fisher, 1625), Book I, 14. The principle, of course, reflected pragmatic considerations growing out of the immediate need for a king. As the legal historians Pollock and Maitland comment about John's accession: "Those barons who had not rejected John did the obvious thing, chose the obvious man as their leader. It was not a time for constitutional dissertations" (Pollock and Maitland, 1: 523).

[62] *TR* handles the double coronation very briefly (Pt. 1, 1480-96, and 1538f.), omitting the negative reaction Shakespeare dwells on.

[63] Writers' views about the process were, of course, inextricably intertwined with their advocacy of specific candidates: those who favored claimants more distant in blood were much more likely to advocate opening up the process to allow for other considerations (see Axton, 92). For example, Wentworth's *Pithie Exhortation,* probably written in 1587 when, from a Protestant point of view, the succession was clouded by the Catholic Mary Stuart's claim and the uncertain religious posture of her son James, advocates much greater power for Parliament than does his *Treatise*—written 7 or 8 years later, by which time James's Protestantism had been established—downplaying Parliament's role and emphasizing James's right to succeed.

[64] One measure of the continuing influence of these ideas in Parsons' work is the republication of parts of it in disguised form in 1648 and 1655 as part of the debate over republican government in England.

[65] See Christopher Hill, "The Many-Headed Monster," in his *Change and Continuity in Seventeenth-Century England* (Cambridge: Harvard University Press, 1975), 181-204.

[66] That involvement, according to the historian Mortimer Levine, "made it almost impossible for Elizabeth, no matter what she felt her authority should be, to settle the succession without Parliament" (Levine, 196; see also 147-151). Almost, but Elizabeth, as we have seen, was successful in keeping the discussion of her successor, let alone its determination, out of the representative public forum, Parliament. By the time Elizabeth's death finally occurred, Parliament was wholly excluded from naming the successor, that denomination officially accomplished by a Proclamation signed by but fifteen nobles and privy councillors (Guy, 454).

[67] While it is overstating it to say that important characters are always named in the dialogue, here there is a complete absence of any *spoken* textual link between the Citizen and Hubert, and thus no reliable way for the audience witnessing a performance to recognize and make meaning out of Hubert's identification with the Citizen. Such connections as are offered are instead the product of editorial speculation.

[68] In a pithy summary of the distinction between the two figures, Deborah T. Curren-Aquino remarked that

"the voice in Angiers suggests a front-of-the-walls person, while the Hubert of subsequent episodes is more of a behind-the-scenes individual" (private correspondence).

[69] See the careful and detailed analysis of this point in William Shakespeare, *King John,* ed. L. Beaurline (Cambridge: Cambridge University Press, 1990), 188-92.

[70] Shakespeare omits the disclaimer of the Citizen in *TR* that "we comptroll not your title" (Pt. 1, 627-28).

[71] Act 3, scene 7 of *Richard III* employs the same visual logic of priority, though reversing its terms ("*Enter Richard [of Gloucester] aloft* . . . " [s.d., 3.7.94]). In both, the vertical superiority of the party whose consent is sought punctuates how decisive that consent is to the nomination of the monarch.

[72] Wentworth, *Exhortation,* 25.

[73] His rebuke has no counterpart in *TR*. In a similar vein Constable accused Parsons of "meddlinge in these matters above your reache and capacitye" (4). Elizabeth's punitive policy was premised on the same charge.

[74] The kings' alliance is Shakespeare's addition; it is not in *TR*.

[75] Their posture, which causes "slaughter [to be] coupled to the name of kings" (2.1.349), is echoed in the Vietnam War era justification that "we had to destroy the town to save it."

[76] It is also a Citizen in Shakespeare's *Richard III* who, on the death of Edward IV, marks the danger of such ambition in competing claimants:

> For emulation who shall now be nearest
> Will touch us all too near, if God prevent not.
> (2.3.25-26)

[77] Verstegen points out that the extraordinary character of the prize they seek impels the contestants to extreme measures: "[W]ho of them is it, that will not dare to venture the uttermost of his meanes, for the gayning of no lesse a thing, then is this kingdom of England" (51).

[78]See Rackin, 185.

Source: "'The Sequence of Posterity': Shakespeare's *King John* and the Succession Controversy," in *Studies in Philology,* Vol. XCII, No. 4, Fall, 1995, pp. 460-81.

Holy War in *Henry V*

Steven Marx, *California Polytechnic State University*

Joel Altman calls *Henry V* 'the most active dramatic experience Shakespeare ever offered his audience'.[1] The experience climaxes at the end of the final battle with the arrival of news of victory. Here the King orders that two hymns be sung while the dead are buried, the 'Non Nobis' and the 'Te Deum'. In his 1989 film, Kenneth Branagh underlines the theatrical emphasis of this implicit stage direction. He extends the climax for several minutes by setting Patrick Doyle's choral-symphonic rendition of the 'Non Nobis' hymn behind a single tracking shot that follows Henry as he bears the dead body of a boy across the corpse-strewn field of Agincourt. The idea for this operatic device was supplied by Holinshed, who copied it from Halle, who got the story from a chain of traditions that originated in the event staged by the real King Henry in 1415. Henry himself took instruction from another book, the Bible.[2]

The hymns which Henry requested derive from verses in the psalter. 'Non Nobis' is the Latin title of Psalm 115, which begins, 'Not unto us, O lord, not unto us, but unto thy Name give the glory . . .' This psalm celebrates the defeat of the Egyptian armies and God's deliverance of Israel at the Red Sea. It comes midway in the liturgical sequence known as The Egyptian Hallelujah extending from Psalm 113 to 118, a sequence that Jesus and the disciples sang during the Passover celebration at the Last Supper and that Jews still recite at all their great festivals.[3] Holinshed refers to the hymn not as 'Non Nobis' but by the title of Psalm 114, 'In exitu Israel de Aegypto' ('When Israel came out of Egypt').[4] The miraculous military victory commemorated in the 'Non Nobis' is the core event of salvation in the Bible, the model of all God's interventions in human history. That event is recalled and recreated in other psalms, in accounts of military victories like Joshua's, David's, the Maccabees', and archangel Michael's, and in stories of rescue from drowning like Noah's, Jonah's, and Paul's. Most scholars agree that the original source of these tales of deliverance is found in what they identify as the earliest biblical text, 'The song of the Sea' in Exodus 15: 'I will sing unto the Lord, for he hath triumphed gloriously . . . The Lord is a man of war, his name is Jehovah. Pharaoh's chariots and his host hath he cast into the sea . . . Thy right hand Lord, is glorious in power: thy right arm Lord hath bruised the enemy.'[5] Like 'The Star Spangled Banner', this song defines national identity by commemorating a miraculous underdog battle victory.

The place of the Agincourt story in Shakespeare's English history cycle resembles the place of the Red Sea victory in the Bible: it fixes the central moment both remembered and prefigured: 'Just as the first tetralogy looks back to *Henry V* as emblem of lost glory that shows up the inadequacy of his son's troubled reign, the second looks forward to his glorious accession . . . The progress of the two tetralogies, then, is a progress back in time to a dead hero . . .'[6] Agincourt creates a national hero like Moses, but more importantly it testifies to the intervention of God on our side: 'O God thy arm was here, / And not to us, but to thy arm alone, / Ascribe we all . . . Take it God, / For it is none but thine' (4.8.106-12), says Henry, once again quoting scripture: 'For they inherited not the land by their own sword: neither did their own arm save them. But thy right hand and thine arm . . .' (Psalm 44, 3-4). Under penalty of death, all the euphoria and relief of victory must be channelled toward God: 'be it death proclaimed through our host / To boast of this, or take that praise from God / Which is His only' (4.8.114-16).

Henry is known as both the most religious and the most warlike of English kings. In this essay, I will explore some of the relationships between war, religion and politics that connect Shakespeare's play to the depiction of holy war in the Bible. After a discussion of Henry the Fifth's pious fashioning of foreign policy from biblical models, I will examine Shakespeare's treatment of Henry's Machiavellian uses of religion to gain political power. Then I will reconcile the contradiction between pious and cynical understandings of holy war with references to Machiavelli's own interpretation of biblical history and politics. I will go on to show that this reconciliation stems from the inner holy war in Henry's personal relationship with God, a conflict illuminated by the notion of the Mystery of State developed by seventeenth-century French apologists for Machiavelli. I will conclude by comparing the rhetorical strategies of biblical and Shakespearian holy war narratives and their effects on later audiences.[7]

Alone in prayer, Henry addresses his deity as 'God of battles' (4.1.286). In the Hebrew Bible, God is referred to more than fifty times with the formula, 'Yahweh Sabaoth', the Lord of Hosts. This title was derived from earlier Canaanite and Babylonian deities who were described as leaders of battalions of followers warring against enemy gods or monsters to bring forth creation. Biblical usage of 'Lord of Hosts' at some times refers to God at the forefront of troops of angels and at others as the chief of the armies of the Israelites.[8] Yahweh's war god manifestations range from miraculous interventions as a destroyer of Israel's enemies to mundane advice on logistical procedures.

In the latter four books of the Torah, God functions as the king of the emergent Israelite nation and is so addressed. In the later books of Samuel and Kings, the role of kingship descendes to anointed human rulers like Saul, David and Solomon. Yet in the language of address and in the manifestations of royal behaviour, the demarcations separating these two levels of kingship are often blurred. No matter what level, the essence of kingship is sovereignty or rule, and rule is conceived as the exercise of military power. 'King' is synonymous with 'general' or 'warlord'. Yahweh's power is established by his victory in battle.

Miller, following von Rad, labels this underlying principle of biblical holy war as 'synergism': 'at the center of Israel's warfare was the unyielding conviction that victory was the result of a fusion of divine and human activity . . . while might of arms and numbers were not the determining factors . . . It was yet possible for the people to see themselves as going to the aid of Yahweh in battle (Judges 5: 23). Yahweh fought for Israel even as Israel fought for Yahweh . . . Yahweh was general of both the earthly and the heavenly hosts.'[9] Shakespeare's opening chorus proclaims this elision of god, king and general in a blithely syncretic mixture: 'O . . . should the warlike Harry, like himself, / Assume the port of Mars, and at his heels, / Leashed in like hounds, should famine, sword and fire / Crouch for employment' (1.0.1-8). The chorus specializes in such rhetoric of deification, referring to Henry as 'The mirror of all Christian kings', suggesting a 'King of Kings' godlike supremacy and instructing us to 'cry, "Praise and glory on his head." ' Exeter employs similar hyperbole when he warns the French King of Harry's approach, 'in fierce tempest is he coming, / In thunder and in earthquake, like a Jove . . .' (2.4.99-100). Mixing pagan and biblical references to a storm god, Exeter here alludes to the Yahweh of Psalm 29: 3-5: 'The voice of the Lord is upon the waters; the God of glory maketh it to thunder . . . the voice of the lord breaketh the cedars.'

In addition to being Godlike, like Moses or Joshua or Saul, the King claims God's authorization and backing for what he does. The Archbishops assert that 'God and his angels guard your sacred throne.' As opposed to the French who only use God's name to swear, Henry continually invokes His help and blessing, and his war cry in battle is 'God for Harry! England and St George!' (3.1.34). Specific biblical references and proof texts are offered as justification for his decisions. The Book of Numbers, the only biblical text mentioned in all of Shakespeare, provides support for the priests' interpretation of the Salic Law, and the rules for siege warfare in Deuteronomy 20 provide the guidelines for Henry's threat against and subsequent treatment of Harfleur.[10]

The attack against France is by implication a substitution for his father's oft-repeated intention to lead a holy crusade to liberate Jerusalem from the Turks: Crusade is a form of holy war that involves a different variation of the synergistic collaboration between God and humans. Rather than manifesting God's support of man, it is the human enactment of God's will on earth. Crusade undertakes to right wrongs, re-establish justice, punish evildoers and express God's wrath through human agency. It is waged by the faithful against those who have rebelled against God.[11] In addressing the French king, Exeter casts Henry in this role of God's agent: 'He wills you, in the name of God Almighty, / That you divest yourself and lay apart / The borrowed glories that by gift of heaven, / By law of nature and of nations, 'longs / To him and to his heirs, namely the crown . . . ' (2.4.77-81). 'Henry Le Roy' represents the King this way to Williams, Bates and Court: 'War is his [God's] beadle. War is his vengeance. So that here men are punished for before-breach of the King's laws, in now the King's quarrel' (4.1.167-70). His war is holy not only because it collectively punishes his evil-doing opponents, but because it individually mortifies his sinful subjects. This notion of war as the Scourge of God justifies unlimited brutality against those who resist but insists on mercy to those who accede and beg mercy. It is this principle that not only authorizes but requires Henry's cruel threats to French noncombatants in his initial declaration of war and at Harfleur.

However, though the King insists that the victory of Agincourt is not his but God's, Shakespeare's depiction of Henry and of the way events unfold suggests otherwise. Henry follows his father Bolingbroke's footsteps in thinking and behaving as if the outcome of events is decided by his own courage and cleverness. The elder Henry plans a holy war against the Turks as a means to quell civil war at home and to ease his conscience for usurping the throne, and his dying words include the advice to his son to 'busy giddy minds with foreign quarrels' to solidify his shaky régime (*2 Henry 4* 4.3.342-3). And immediately following the Chorus's opening invocation of Henry's divine mission, we eavesdrop on a backroom conversation revealing that he has secured the Archbishop's sanction for the invasion of France in return for his agreement to block the bill in Commons that would force the church to pay taxes to support the sick and indigent.

Incidents like these suggest that Shakespeare exposes holy war as a device manipulated by Kings for political ends, confirming what Stephen Greenblatt calls ' . . . the most radically subversive hypothesis in his culture about the origin and function of religion'.[12] That hypothesis was formulated by Machiavelli in his account of the ancient Roman practice of securing popular support for the state with the pretence of piety. The wisest leaders, Machiavelli claimed, are those who 'foster and encourage [religion] even though they be convinced that it is quite fallacious. And the more should they do this the greater their prudence and the more they know of natural laws.'[13]

The most popular critical solution to the apparent contradiction between Henry as holy warrior and as Machiavellian Prince is what Harry Berger labels 'the historico-political approach'. This explains Henry's manipulation of religion as the outcome of '" . . . a passage from the Middle Ages to the Renaissance and the modern world", . . . the familiar story of disenchantment in which religious attitudes toward history and politics give way to secular and humanistic attitudes . . . a fall from sacramental kingship to a Machiavellian conception of kingship . . .'[14] But as Berger points out, such a reading fails to take account of the genuine spiritual conflicts and concerns experienced by Henry—and, one might add, by his father, by Falstaff on his deathbed, and by all of those who continued religious warfare throughout the seventeenth century. Rather than demonstrate opposing biblical and humanist perspectives in *Henry V,* it may be more instructive to show how the Bible itself provided both Machiavelli and Shakespeare with a model for ambivalent attitudes toward holy war, kingship and the relationship between politics and religion.

Like *Henry V,* the biblical text is itself a 'site of contestation'.[15] The God of Deuteronomy through 2 Kings rewards those who obey His commandments and punishes those who don't. The God of Job states that assuming this, as the comforters do, is punishable heresy. Jesus states we should turn the other cheek, but also that he comes to bring the sword. Such inconsistencies are largely attributable to conflicting outlooks of previous 'traditions' or documentary sources of the final canonized text: priestly vs. prophetic, tribal vs. centrist, rural vs. urban, Northern vs. Southern Kingdoms.[16] Similarly, Shakespeare's histories are redactions of layers of documentary sources from Froissart to Halle to Holinshed, each the expression of different ideologies.

One of the contradictions most relevant to Shakespeare's histories is the Bible's dual view of kingship. The Henriad alternates between propounding the Tudor myth of divine ordination and royal infallibility and acknowledging 'that the crown is always illegitimate, that is, always an effect of social relations and not their cause, and therefore must (and can) endlessly be legitimated by improvisations of each wearer'.[17] Likewise, in the Bible, the institution of kingship was a gift of God to the Israelites—'I will send thee a man . . . to be governor over my people Israel, that he may save my people out of the hands of the Philistines: for I have looked upon my people and their cry is come unto me' (I Samuel 9: 16)—or an expression of the people's rebellion against God: ' . . . they have cast me away, that I should not reign over them . . .', a rebellion in face of the warning that the king will exploit and manipulate them for his own purposes: 'He will take your sons, and appoint them to his chariots and to be his horsemen . . . he will appoint him captains over thousands and captains over fifties; and to ear his ground and to reap his harvest and to make his instruments of war . . . And ye shall cry out that day because of your King whom ye have chosen and the Lord will not hear you at that day' (I Samuel 8: 7-18). And like all of Shakespeare's kings, the individual kings of the Bible are portrayed under profoundly ambivalent judgement. Saul is a charismatic general who succeeds in securing territory by uniting the tribes against the Philistines, but he arrogates too many powers to himself and is driven insane. He is succeeded by David, God's favourite and beloved by the people, but after displaying the self-abnegating loyalty to his master, the brilliance in battle, and the genius in diplomacy to build a great empire, he is punished for betraying God and his subjects in a scandalous sexual intrigue. David's son, Solomon, builds on his father's achievements and attains distinction as the wisest of men, turning the Empire into a showpiece of wealth and culture, but his glory is eclipsed when his sons once again divide the kingdom and plummet it into civil wars which eventually result in foreign conquest. An analogous reversal is reported in the epilogue of *Henry V*:

> The star of England. Fortune made his sword,
> By which the world's best garden he achieved,
> And of it left his son imperial lord . . .
> Whose state so many had the managing
> That they lost France and made his England bleed.
>
> (6-12)

The approach to Shakespeare's histories with a providential-historical or religious-secular dichotomy also breaks down when one notes how Renaissance humanists discovered that the Bible contained a political history as rich and revealing as those written by Romans and Greeks. Machiavelli himself found a precedent for his own remorseless value judgements in the Bible's often brutal portrayal of authority, rebellion and war. In the Moses of the Pentateuch, Machiavelli discovered an ideal hero, a model of the qualities that inhered in those who founded durable institutions: 'Of all men that are praised, those are praised most who have played the chief part in founding a religion. Next come those who have founded either republics or kingdoms.'[18] Moses was the only one in Machiavelli's history who did both. 'But to come to those who have become princes by their own virtue and not by fortune, I say that the most excellent are Moses, Cyrus, Romulus, Theseus and the like . . .' In common with all those political leaders who form new states, Moses faces a dual challenge: he must defeat enemies and maintain unity and support among followers. This is foreshadowed in the biblical story of Moses killing the Egyptian taskmaster who was beating a Hebrew slave (Exodus 2: 11-14). Next day, when he returned to try to get two Hebrews to stop fighting each other, they denied his authority and asked whether he planned to kill them as well. The only way that Moses can take control to achieve God's purpose of forming a nation strong enough to beat the Egyptians and conquer their own territory is by producing belief—in enemies, credibility; in followers, faith. This is also the task of Henry the Fifth as he takes the throne in an England on the edge of invasion and civil war, and reluctant to accept his rule. The means to succeed in this endeavour are enumerated both in the works of Machiavelli and in the Bible.

One such means is to supply legal justification for the appropriation of territory. This is provided to the Hebrews by the contractual agreement Moses reports that God made with their forefather Abraham to grant his seed the promised land. The Archbishops provide Henry with a similar covenant in 'the Law Salique', which 'proves' that he can 'with right and conscience make this claim' (1.2.96) of the territory of France. Such legal justification is largely for home consumption, since it is unlikely to be persuasive to those who presently occupy the land, but the next means—that of intimidation—is addressed equally to followers and opponents. Threats must be rendered convincing with terror tactics, both to weaken enemy morale and to buttress one's own side's confidence. God tells Moses to punish Pharaoh with plague after plague to demonstrate the strength of the Israelites and he repeatedly hardens Pharaoh's heart to make him responsible for the suffering of his own people: 'Then there shall be a great cry throughout all the land of Egypt, such as was never one like, nor shall be. But against none of the children of Israel shall a dog move his tongue neither against man nor beast, that ye may know that the Lord putteth a difference between the Egyptians and Israel' (Exodus 11: 6-7). After justification, Henry also resorts to intimidation, in a series of threats against the French which emphasize the suffering of noncombatants. First he instructs the ambassadors to ' . . . tell the pleasant Prince . . . his soul / Shall stand sore chargèd . . . for many a thousand widows / Shall this his mock mock out of their dear husbands, / Mock mothers from their sons . . .' (1.2.281-6). Through Exeter he bids the French king 'in the bowels of the Lord, / Deliver up the crown . . . take mercy / On . . . the widows' tears, the orphans' cries, / The dead men's blood, the pining maidens' groans . . .' (2.4.102-7). And finally he utters directly to the citizens of Harfleur the familiar litany of lurid atrocities which brings about the town's surrender (3.3.7-43).

Brutalizing of one's opponents like this also addresses the problem of 'murmurings' among one's followers that constantly troubles Moses—the 'lukewarmness' that Machiavelli observes in citizens of new states. Henry also uses intimidation among his own men to enforce discipline, letting them all know that he is willing to hang his former friend Bardolph for unauthorized plundering, and at the same time claiming that such rigour is mercy rather than cruelty: 'We would have all such offenders so cut off . . . none of the French upbraided or abused in disdainful language. For when lenity and cruelty play for a kingdom, the gentler gamester is the soonest winner.' (3.6.108-14) The king agrees with Machiavelli who insists that cruelty is merciful: 'A prince . . . so as to keep his subjects united and faithful, should not care about the infamy of cruelty, because with very few examples he will be more merciful than those who for the sake of too much mercy allow disorders to continue . . .'[19] Rather than contrasting this cynicism with biblical morality, Machiavelli substantiates his claims with the example of Moses: 'He who reads the Bible with discernment will see that, before Moses set about making laws and institutions, he had to kill a very great number of men who . . . were opposed to his plans.'[20] Here he refers to incidents of rebellion, like worship of the Golden Calf, or Korah's revolt which Moses responded to with mass executions. It is these God-sanctioned actions that validate the Machiavellian maxim that the end justifies the means.[21]

One of the most effective of such means is dissimulation: 'The princes who have done great things are those who have taken little account of faith and have known how to get around men's brains with their astuteness . . . it is necessary to know well how to . . . be a great pretender and dissembler.'[22] The Bible approves countless examples of such shifts: Abraham and Isaac's deception of Pharaoh and Abimelech, Jacob's deception of his father and uncle, Joseph's protracted deception of father and brothers, Ehud's assassination of the Moabite King, Eglon, David's feigned insanity, Nathan's entrapment of David into confessing his own guilt. Jesus himself tells his disciples they must proceed with the wariness of serpents (Matthew 10: 16) and constantly dissimulates his own weakness. Trickery is a skill that Henry learns from both his father figures, Bolingbroke and Falstaff. Henry IV feigns loyalty to the king he deposes and then solicitude for the one he executes, and he triumphs over his enemies in battle not by valour but with the stratagem of dressing many in the king's coats. Falstaff is the father of lies and disguises. Likewise, just as he robs the robbers and confuses his father's spies, Hal deceives the whole kingdom both with appearances of prodigality and of holiness.

Dissimulation serves to disorient and confuse those over whom one wishes to gain power, but it also serves as a device to gather intelligence. Moses is commanded to send spies into the promised land to report on enemy strength; Joshua sends spies into Jericho to recruit Rahab to spy for them; David constantly spies on Saul, and his general Joab maintains surveillance in all camps. God spies on his enemies in Babel and Sodom and on his subjects, like Adam and Eve, Abraham, Jacob and Job, as he tests their loyalty with temptations and ordeals. So Henry V spies on his subjects in the Boar's Head tavern, on his captains and foot soldiers on the night before battle, and on his close friends, Cambridge, Scroop and Grey, at the outset of the French campaign.

According to Machiavelli, to produce the belief required for political rule, it is as important to be sceptical oneself as to manipulate the faith of others. Religious deceptions are required because most people are not rational enough to accept the real truths which such deceptions support: 'Nor in fact was there ever a legislator, who in introducing extraordinary laws to a people, did not have recourse to God, for otherwise they would not have been accepted, since many benefits of which a prudent man is aware, are not so evident to reason that he can convince others of them.'[23] Though it is his intelligence system that has discovered the plot against him, Henry construes his rescue as miraculous evidence of God's special protection and parlays that evidence into a morale-raising prediction of future success in battle: 'We doubt not of a fair and lucky war, / Since God so graciously hath brought to light / This dangerous treason lurking in our way . . . Then forth, dear countrymen. Let us deliver / Our puissance into the hand of God . . .' (2.2.181-7) Here he follows Machiavelli's advice about the efficacy of miracles in creating the 'synergistic' alliance between divine and human energies. Astute leaders will both try to create miracles and more important will reinforce faith in earlier miracles to buttress belief in their own miraculous powers.[24] In secret, the Archbishops admit that they no longer believe in miracles: 'It must be so, for miracles are ceased, / And therefore we must needs admit the means / How things are perfected.' (1.1.68-70) They nevertheless also construe Hal's conversion as a supernatural transformation: ' . . . a wonder how his grace should glean it / Since his addiction was to courses vain' (1.1.54-5). Their wonder is the outcome intended by Henry's overall strategy of dissimulation. To frustrate expectation either by feigning weakness or bluffing strength is as strategic in politics as in poker. Mystification and hiding is a rhetorical means of amplifying the power of revelation. God's obscurity in the Bible, his invisibility and remoteness, makes his voice that much louder when it speaks, whether in thunder on Sinai, out of a whirlwind in Job, or at those moments in the New Testament when he drops the disguise of mortal poverty and is suddenly recognized as a divine presence.

Such appearances and removals of disguise are experienced by the citizenry as another species of miracle. When Hal unmasks his own knowledge of the traitors' conspiracy, they admit their sins and condemn themselves to death. When he reveals himself after the robbery at Gad's Hill as one of the 'men in buckram', Falstaff manages to cover any trace of wonder, but when finally 'breaking through the foul and ugly mists / Of vapours that did seem to strangle him' (*I Henry 4* (1.2.199-200), Henry takes on the mantle of the true King at the last-judgement-like coronation, even the fat man responds by getting real religion. Both playful and awesome, these are the kind of tricks that Hal, like the God of the Bible, seems never to tire of playing.[25] Shakespeare himself also seemed never to tire of plot incidents about dissimulation and of power figures who use such deceptions to produce belief in order to rule others. Some practitioners of this art, like Iago and Edmund, are evil. But more often, the dissimulator adopts a benevolent stance to improve or educate those who are too corrupt or deceived or stupid to recognize the truth in its own terms. Ranging from Rosalind, Viola, and Paulina to Duke Vincentio and Prospero, what they all have in common, and what perhaps accounts for Shakespeare's fascination with them, is their theatricality, their association with himself as author and dramatist, a figure who like the author of the Bible is identified with the Word as creative principle, human protagonist, and book itself.

But Machiavelli's paradox about truth hidden in the lies of state religion hints at a conception of God richer than mere subterfuge. Though he rejects the Christianity of his own day as 'effeminate . . . due to the pusillanimity of those who have interpreted our religion', he affirms a religion like that of the Romans or Hebrews that 'permits us to exalt and defend the father land . . . and to train ourselves to be such that we may defend it'.[26] Machiavelli's own 'God-Talk' includes serious references to personalized cosmic forces—whether the seductive Fortuna of *The Prince* or the God who is a 'Lover of strong men', or the 'heaven' who involves himself in human history by choosing strong leaders.[27] Seventeenth-century commentators made much of this aspect of Machiavelli's writings, defending him as being a theologian of the Divine Right of Kings whose outlook was perfectly commensurate with the Bible's rather than an atheistic Machiavel.[28] Their interpretation links Machiavelli to the ancient and medieval doctrine of The Mystery of State—the notion that royal dissimulation is not only a requirement for rule but in itself a divine and divinity-generating activity. Kings are in possession of magic powers by virtue of their access to secrets and occult wisdom withheld from their subjects: 'It is specifically the violence, obscurity and ineffable quality of the gods that must be imitated . . . the coups d'etat are princely imitations of all those attributes of divinity that were thought to be either beyond human power (like miracles) or beyond the laws and moral prescriptions that bound men but not God.'[29]

Although he practises dissimulation throughout the play, Henry's most sustained enactment of the Mysteries of State occurs during the moonlit scene before the final battle. The 'ruined band' of the 'poor condemnèd English', who 'like sacrifices, by their watchful fires / Sit patiently and inly ruminate / The morning's danger' (4.0.22-5) are experiencing the dark night of the soul which represents the 'original rendering of "holy war" in Christianity . . . the point at which the devotee is forced to fight with all his strength against despair, against creeping doubts concerning the meaningfulness of his past life and previous sacrifices'.[30] The king, in Godlike fashion, with 'largess universal like the sun . . . thawing cold fear' bestows comfort with 'a little touch of Harry in the night'. But after his morale-raising banter with the lords, Henry's warmth is shown to be a pretence when he asks Erpingham for his cloak and admits that he needs to be alone for a while before he can continue encouraging the other officers.

The cloak's new disguise serves him in several ways. First he uses it to spy on the men, in order to determine the strength of their support and to root out their murmurings and weak morale. This he must do in mufti, for he knows that if he appears as himself, his subjects will tell him, like any higher power, only what they think he wants to hear. Eavesdropping on Pistol, Gower and Fluellen produces evidence of their full support, and so he moves on. The conversation between Court, Bates and Williams is less reassuring and requires intervention. He tries to counter their hopelessness with assurances of the King's exemplary valour and their cynicism with biblical parables and Jesuitical casuistry justifying the righteousness of the war, but none of these efforts works to produce belief.

This is the one time Henry fails, and he is so frustrated that he almost blows his cover with a threat against Williams (4.1.207). The frustration arises not so much from the inconsequential political setback, as from the failure of another motive covered by his cloak: he too needs a little touch of warmth. For Henry himself experiences an interior holy war, his own dark night of the soul. Upon leaving Erpingham, he had admitted that 'I and my bosom must debate awhile' (4.1.32), and to the soldiers he utters a lengthy description of the King's personal vulnerability: ' . . . I think the King is but a man, as I am . . . when he sees reason of fears, as we do, his fears, out of doubt, be of the same relish as ours are. Yet, in reason, no man should possess him with any appearance of fear, lest he, by showing it, should dishearten his army' (4.1.101-12). The disguise here is thinning. Harry Le Roi speaks more frankly than Henry the Fifth ever could, but, ironically, the soldiers react to his plea for their support as if it were only manipulative dissimulation.

During the play's first scene, the Archbishops had used the language of holy war to describe Henry's earlier identity crisis as a scourging crusade: '. . wildness, mortified in him, / Seemed to die . . . Consideration like an angel came / And whipped th' offending Adam out of him, / Leaving his body as a paradise / T'envelop and contain celestial spirits / . . . reformation in a flood . . . scouring faults; / . . . Hydra-headed wilfulness / So soon did lose his seat' (1.1.27-37). According to Canterbury, Henry's motivation and ability as a general/king/god was cultivated through his preparatory defeat of the forces of that Great Satan, Falstaff, in a coup d'état much like the one his father staged to topple Richard and his supporters. Developing the personality of a King required killing, whipping, and a scouring flood. But on this eve of battle we see his internal enemies not as wildness but as fear, doubt and guilt.

As he moves away from the soldiers to confront these opponents, Henry uncloaks himself fully. Heard only by the spying audience, in soliloquy he reveals the mystery of state. His royalty, his godlike divine right, is mere dissimulation performed by monarch-actor and applauded by subjects-spectators. His unceremonious encounter with Williams, Court, and Bates has taught him that he is nothing without ceremony, that ceremony itself is at once king and god, and that all are Baconian idols: 'And what have kings that privates have not too, / Save ceremony, save general ceremony? / . . . What kind of god art thou, that suffer'st more / Of mortal griefs than do thy worshippers?' (4.1.235-9) His acknowledgement resembles the tormented recognitions of other Shakespearian military leaders who have lost faith in their own self projections—tragic protagonists like Hamlet, Lear, Antony and Coriolanus—and it also alludes to the tragic portrait of the suffering servant in Isaiah and the Gospels, in particular the internal struggle of Christ during his vigil at Gethsemane. This identification is itself another Mystery of State, what Donaldson calls 'a royal kenosis':

> The prince, imitating a divinity who put off his divinity in Christ in order to achieve the salvation of the world, puts off an ideal and otherwordly goodness in order to achieve the safety of the people, exchanging contemplative perfection for morally flawed action . . . the idea that the king is an imitator of God . . . includes mimesis . . . of those modes of divine action that entail a lowering of the divine nature . . . 'It is only a good prince who will hazard his own salvation to seek that of the subjects whom he governs'.[31]

Reconceiving his despair and weakness as itself an attribute of divinity, Henry can again dissimulate authority in a brief encounter with Erpingham, who interrupts him for a moment to remind him of his officers' need for the King's presence.

Alone once more, perhaps having returned the cloak to its owner, the King addresses God directly in a mode of discourse even less performative than soliloquy, prayer. We see him encountering the existential reality of God-in-the-trenches rather than projecting the ideological spectacle of 'God for Harry'. And yet what does he seek at this moment of truth? 'Steel my soldiers' hearts, possess them not with fear.' His request is for morale—the very thing that his own public performance is expected to produce, the very thing that the soldiers and the lords ask of him, and that he, as Harry Le Roy, has asked of them. His 'God of Battles' is imagined not as one who will bring victory through a miraculous defeat of the enemy, but rather as one who will succeed where Henry has just failed, in buttressing his men's courage and faith. As if to instruct God, he specifies the means by which this effect can be achieved: 'Take from them now / The sense of reck'ning, ere th' opposèd numbers / Pluck their hearts from them' (4.1.287-9). It is to blind them from the truth, to cloud their thinking, to reinstitute ceremonial dissimulation. This request for falsehood slides into another uncomfortable revelation of truth: 'Not today, O Lord, / O not today, think not upon the fault / My father made in compassing the crown' (289-91). He again begs God to hide the truth, but now from Himself. In other words, Henry prays that God will help him deceive his own conscience, like the King in *Hamlet,* 'a man to double business bound' (3.3.41). But also like Claudius, Henry is again frustrated. Instead of being granted forgetfulness, he is further reminded of his guilt and failure: 'I Richard's body have interrèd new, / And on it have bestowed . . . contrite tears . . . / . . . I have built / Two chantries . . . / More will I do, / Though all that I can do is nothing worth, / Since that my penitence comes after ill, / Imploring pardon' (292-302). No matter how he tries to cover them, the King cannot escape the knowledge of the secrets he keeps, Sanctimonious action, whether in the form of daily penances of solemn priests or the holy war against France, fails to produce a feeling of innocence. Both God and King must rule by the art of dissimulation, and yet never be themselves deceived. This is the burden of the Mystery of State that will keep him forever imploring pardon. But simply setting it down for a moment in private allows him to gather the strength to carry it further. For that burden is also a magic instrument, an occult wisdom that gives him the sense of superiority over all other humans.

Machon illuminates the tension in the closing lines of Henry's prayer with this frank analysis of moral frailty and strength:

> When I hide to attend to my natural functions, is this not to dissimulate the human weakness that is in me? When I do not speak all reveries that are in my mind and the extravagances that present themselves there without any consent, is that not to dissimulate, since my words are other than my thoughts and I reveal only the hundredth part of them? When I deny the vices I am accused of, hide my bad humor, am generous against my will, do not speak to women of the favors which in my heart I desire of them, forget myself before those to whom I owe respect, and since all my life, like those of other men is merely constraint, and ceremony, is it not to dissimulate, is it not in fact to practice what people want me to condemn in words? What would the world be without dissimulation? What would become of prudence, shame, modesty, discretion, reserve, honesty, civility, pleasure, estimation, reputation, honor, glory, reward, love, clemency, compassion, good deeds and all the best virtues that temper our malice and cover up our infirmities and our faults.[32]

Like Machon's true confession that falsehood is necessary, Henry's honest acknowledgement of his secret guilt makes it possible for him to continue dissimulating. Now he can respond to his importunate brother Gloucester by saying, 'I will go with thee. / The day, my friends, and all things stay for me' (4.1.304-5).

The night-time victory in his inner holy war powers Henry's morning speech on St Crispian's Day. So effective is this in awakening faith and producing belief that the men express a sense of privilege in being able to participate in an engagement where they are five times outnumbered. In several ways that speech leads back to the original scene of holy war in the book of Exodus. Promising victory to the frightened Israelites on the night before their departure from Egypt, Moses delivers instructions for celebrating this as a feast day with a blood sacrifice and a shared meal that is to protect, mark and bond them:

> Let every man take unto him a lamb according to the house of the fathers . . . then all the multitude of the congregation of Israel shall kill it at even. After they shall take of the blood and strike it on the two posts, and on the upper doorposts of the houses where they shall eat it. And they shall eat the flesh the same night . . .
>
> (Exodus 12: 3-9)

Likewise, Henry proclaims that 'This day is call'd the Feast of Crispian' (4.3.40) and that ' . . . he today that sheds his blood with me / Shall be my brother; be he ne'er so vile, / This day shall gentle his condition' (4.3.61-3). Both speeches prophesy the participation of future generations in the upcoming events by incorporating instructions for ritual commemoration of the event even before it happens. Thus Moses,

> And this day shall be unto you a remembrance: and ye shall keep it an holy feast unto the Lord throughout your generations: ye shall keep it holy

> by an ordinance forever . . . for that same day I will bring your armies out of the land of Egypt: therefore ye shall observe this day throughout your posterity by an ordinance forever.
>
> (Exodus 12: 14-17)

And thus Henry,

> He that shall see this day, and live t'old age
> Will yearly on the vigil feast his neighbors
> And say, 'Tomorrow is Saint Crispian.'
> Then will he strip his sleeve and show his scars
>
> . . . . .
>
> . . . Then
> shall our names . . .
> Be in their flowing cups freshly remembered.
>
> (4.3.44-55)

Though embedded within their historical narratives, both speeches explain future ritual repetitions with reference to the tale that is about to unfold. Moses says,

> And when your children ask you what service is this you keep? Then ye shall say, it is the sacrifice of the Lord's passover which passed over the houses of the children of Israel in Egypt when he smote the Egyptians and preserved our houses. Then the people bowed themselves and worshipped . . .
>
> (12: 26-7)

And Henry commands,

> This story shall the good man teach his son,
> And Crispin Crispian shall ne'er go by
> From this day to the ending of the world
> But we in it shall be rememberèd.
>
> (4.3.56-9)

Such breaks of the narrative frame—endlessly repeated in the biblical accounts of the Exodus—anticipate what is to come, both within the stories themselves and in their later reception.

The anticipatory breaks in biblical and Shakespearian epics of holy war have complex functions. They recursively include readers and auditors as participants in past actions while at the same time instructing them how to make those actions come to pass in the present and stay alive in the future through imaginative reenactment. These functions are shared by Shakespeare's Chorus in its urgent direct addresses to the audience. The Chorus insists that collaboration between author and auditor 'in the quick forge and working-house of thought' (5.0.23) is required to make the illusion real, thereby producing stronger belief, but also acknowledging the fictive nature of the history. The audience is thus both partaker and participant in the Mysteries of State that are enacted in the play. As opposed to the peasant slave whose 'gross brain little wots / What watch the king keeps to maintain the peace' (4.1.279-80), the 'discerning' reader of both the Bible and of Shakespeare is in on the secret and can share with Harry the power and the guilt of the holy war.

Notes

[1] '"Vile Participation": The Amplification of Violence in the Theatre of *Henry V*', *Shakespeare Quarterly*, 42:1 (Spring 1991): 2-32; p. 2.

[2] Citations in this essay are from *The Geneva Bible: A Facsimile of the 1560 Edition* with an introduction by Lloyd E. Berry (Madison, Wisconsin, 1969). I have modernized spelling.

[3] Referred to by Matthew (26.30) and Mark (14.26) as 'The Passover Hymn'.

[4] Holinshed, Raphael, et al., *The Chronicles of England, Scotland, and Ireland,* 3 vols. in 2, 1587; ed. H. Ellis, 6 vols., 1807-8, p. 555, reprinted in *Shakespeare's Holinshed,* ed. Richard Hosley (New York, 1968), pp. 133-4.

[5] See Gerhard von Rad, 'The Form-Critical Problem of the Hexateuch', in *The Problem of the Hexateuch and Other Essays* (New York, 1966), pp. 1-78, also Martin Noth, *The History of Israel* (New York, 1960), and G. E. Mendenhall, *The Tenth Generation. The Origins of the Biblical Tradition* (Baltimore, 1973).

[6] Phyllis Rackin, *Stages of History: Shakespeare's English Chronicles* (Ithaca, 1990), p. 30.

[7] Much attention has been paid to biblical references in Shakespeare, most recently in a three-volume series, *Biblical References in Shakespeare's Comedies, Biblical References in Shakespeare's Tragedies* and *Biblical References in Shakespeare's Histories,* by Naseeb Shaheen published by the University of Delaware Press. But very little scholarly study is available on the literary relationships between biblical and Shakespearian works. One notable exception is an address by James Black entitled ' "Edified by the Margent": Shakespeare and the Bible', issued by the University of Alberta Press. I have yet to find a scholarly treatment of the manifold connections between biblical and Shakespearian historiography and politics.

[8] See Patrick D. Miller, *The Divine Warrior in Early Israel* (Cambridge, Mass., 1973), pp. 154-5. In *Yahweh Is a Warrior: The Theology of Warfare in Ancient Israel* (Herald Press, Scottdale, Philadelphia, 1989), Millard Lind points out that the identification God,

king and general was a common ancient near east convention, as witnessed in a proclamation by Assurbanipal, King of the Assyrian empire 'Not by my own power / not by the strength of my bow / by the power of my gods, / by the strength of my goddesses / I subjected the lands to the yoke of Assur', p. 30.

[9] Miller, p. 156.

[10] 'When thou comest near unto a city to fight against it, thou shalt offer it peace. And if it answer thee again peaceably and open unto thee, then let all the people that is found therein, be tributaries unto thee and serve thee. But if it will make no peace with thee . . . thou shalt smite all the males thereof with the edge of the sword.' (Deuteronomy 20: 10-13).

[11] See Roland Bainton, *Christian Attitudes toward War and Peace: A Historical Survey and Critical Reevaluation* (Nashville, 1960), pp. 44-50 and David Little, ' "Holy War" Appeals and Western Christianity: A Reconsideration of Bainton's Approach', in *Just War and Jihad,* ed. John Kelsay and James Turner Johnson (New York, 1991), pp. 121-41.

[12] 'Invisible Bullets: Renaissance Authority and its Subversion in *Henry IV* and *Henry V*'. In *Political Shakespeare: New Essays in Cultural Materialism,* ed. Jonathan Dollimore and Alan Sinfield (New York, 1985), p. 2.

[13] DI.12.3, p. 244. Citations of Machiavelli as follows: D = Leslie J. Walker trans. and ed., *The Discourses of Niccolo Machiavelli,* 2 vols. (London, 1950); P = *The Prince. A New Translation with an Introduction* by Harvey C. Mansfield Jr (Chicago, 1985).

[14] 'On the continuity of the Henriad'. In *Shakespeare Left and Right,* ed. Ivo Kamps (London and Boston, 1991), p. 229.

[15] For a discussion of the ways conflicting perspectives and attitudes are juxtaposed in Shakespearian texts, see Louis Adrian Montrose, 'The Purpose of Playing: Reflections on Shakespearean Anthropology', *Helios,* n.s. 7 (1980): 50-73. For a discussion of the debate between pacifist and militarist politics in *Henry V,* see Steven Marx, 'Shakespeare's Pacifism', *RQ,* 45, Spring 1992.

[16] See W. Lee Humphries, *Crisis and Story: An Introduction to the Old Testament* (Mt View, California, 1991, pp. 50-3, 120-1 and Baruch Halpern, *The First Historians: the Hebrew Bible and History* (San Francisco, 1988).

[17] David Scott Kastan, '"The King Hath Many Marching in his Coats", or What Did You Do in the War, Daddy.' In *Shakespeare Left and Right,* ed. Ivo Kamps (London and Boston, 1991), p. 256.

[18] D.I10.1, p. 236.

[19] P. XVII, pp. 65-6.

[20] D. III, 30.4, p. 547.

[21] 'Reprehensible actions may be justified by their effects . . . when the effect is good, . . . it always justifies the action . . . I might adduce in support of what I have just said numberless examples, e.g. Moses, Lycurgus, Solon, and other founders of kingdoms and republics . . . ' D. I. 9.2-5, p. 235.

[22] P. XVIII, pp. 69-70.

[23] D. I. II, p. 237.

[24] 'It was owing to wise men having taken note of this that belief in miracles arose and that miracles are held in high esteem even by religions that are false; for to whatever they owed their origin, sensible men made much of them and their authority caused everybody to believe in them.' D. I. 12.3, p. 244.

[25] Only Michael Williams resists this form of Revelation trick. After the battle, when Henry tries to elicit his awe, repentance and gratitude by disclosing that the 'gentleman of a company' to whom Williams had expressed disbelief in the King was actually the King himself, Williams is not impressed.

[26] D. II.2.6-7, p. 364.

[27] P. XXV, pp. 98-101 ('Fortuna'); Martelli *Tutti gli opera,* p. 626 cited by Anthony J. Parel, *The Machiavellian Cosmos* (New Haven, 1992), pp. 57, 56 ('Heaven'); D. II.29.1, pp. 444-5 ('Lover of strong men').

[28] Peter Donaldson, *Machiavelli and the Mystery of State* (New York, 1988). In his final chapter, 'Biblical Machiavellism: Louis Machon's *Apologie pour Machiavel*', Donaldson unearths and analyses an obscure seventeenth century reading of Machiavelli and the Bible. A work of close to 800 pages commissioned by Cardinal Richelieu, it defends those passages in *The Discourses* and *The Prince* most often attacked for impiety. 'One may cease to be surprised', says Machon, 'that I draw parallels between Holy Scripture and the works of Machiavelli and that I propose that his strongest and most formidable maxims were drawn from the book of books . . . if one considers that this sacred volume, which should be the study and meditation of all true Christians, teaches princes as well as subjects . . .' 1668 preface, pp. 1-2, trans. and cited by Donaldson, p. 188.

[29] Donaldson, p. 172.

[30] James Aho, *Religious Mythology and the Art of War: Comparative Religious Symbolisms of Military Violence* (Westport, Connecticut, 1981), p. 146.

[31] Donaldson, pp. 215-16 summarizing and citing Machon 1668, p. 778.

[32] Machon 640-1, cited by Donaldson, p. 200.

[33] As Altman says, he 'extends the [participatory] relationship of prince and subject as portrayed in [*Henry V*] so that it becomes a relationship between player/king and audience/subject . . .', p. 15.

[34] Both Greenblatt and Altman have drawn attention to some alarming implications of these converging suspensions of disbelief: ' . . . the first part of *Henry 4* enables us to feel . . . we are . . . testing dark thoughts without damaging the order that those thoughts would seem to threaten. The second part of *Henry 4* suggests that we are . . . compelled to pay homage to a system of beliefs whose fraudulence somehow only confirms their power, authenticity and truth. The concluding play in the series, *Henry 5,* insists that we have all along been both colonizer and colonized, king and subject.' Greenblatt, p. 42. ' . . . amplification ambiguously reassuring and threatening, which offers up images of rational accessibility juxtaposed with those of imperial closure . . . revelation and mystification, both the articulated and concealed forms—the exquisition of causes, of effects, and of parallels, the emblems and personifications—fill the imagination only to make more illustrious Harry's darkly enigmatic nature. One must always feel anxious about such a king, since one can never fully possess him . . . From dim and unexpected places he will make claims upon one's mind and body that cannot be eluded.' Altman, p. 24. I believe the mentally colonizing rhetorical strategies discovered by these scholars are modelled in the history of the Bible.

Source: "Holy War in *Henry V,*" in *Shakespeare Survey: An Annual Survey of Shakespeare Studies and Production,* edited by Stanley Wells, Vol. 48, 1995, pp. 85-97.

Pilgrims of Grace: *Henry IV* Historicized

Tom McAlindon, *University of Hull*

PAST AND PRESENT

R. G. Collingwood once remarked that all historical writing is a selective process governed by a sense of contemporary relevance. [1] Most historical critics who have sought to interpret Shakespeare's interpretation of the past in *1* and *2 Henry IV* seem to have been in agreement with this view. There has, however, been remarkable divergence among both recent and not-so-recent historicists on how the play (I shall use the singular term for convenience's sake) connects with sixteenth-century practice and ideas; on how, in other words, we should define the context (or larger 'text') which makes most sense of its conceptual orientation. E. M. W. Tillyard tied the play to the Tudor, providentialist philosophy of history focused on the Wars of the Roses and the birth of the Tudor dynasty. But he saw in it nothing more specific to sixteenth-century political experience than a large, approving picture of Elizabethan England, rendered vivid by its social and topographical detail. Like Tillyard, Lily B. Campbell read the play as an uncomplicated endorsement of Tudor political orthodoxy; she was much concerned, however, to establish a central analogy with the Northern Rebellion of 1569-70 (an idea first advanced by Richard Simpson in 1874), as well as a number of politically significant parallels between some of the *dramatis personae* and contemporary individuals. [2]

The two most self-consciously historicist among recent critics of *Henry IV* have constructed interpretative frameworks which also differ strikingly from each other. For Stephen Greenblatt, the dynastic conflict between the houses of Lancaster and York in fifteenth-century England makes most sense when seen in relation to the treacherous methods used by the Elizabethan ruling classes in securing control over the trusting natives of Virginia and the vagabonds and thieves of the domestic underworld. Graham Holderness shares Greenblatt's preoccupation with power, domination, and class conflict as the key to social and political history, but denies this play any important connection with sixteenth-century politics; instead, he sees in it a genuinely historicist concentration on the contradictions of fifteenth-century feudalism. [3]

The limitation of Tillyard's history-of-ideas approach is not just that it constructed a monolithic Elizabethan world-picture, but that it seems to have distracted his attention from the material realities of sixteenth-century political history. So too the interpretative frameworks created by Greenblatt and Holderness, by excluding the high politics of Tudor England, seem initially implausible and leave an impression of contextual mislocation. Campbell's approach (utilized by Alice-Lyle Scoufos in her study of the Falstaff-Oldcastle problem), [4] although unduly speculative in its pursuit of topical allusions, and insensitive to Shakespeare's political scepticism, seems to me to have pointed in a direction which has not been adequately explored. For as I hope to show, *Henry IV* is shaped by certain patterns of thought, action, and characterization which suggest deep affinities between Henry's reign and the religio-political and cultural experiences of sixteenth-century England. Shakespeare was here viewing the rule of Henry and the rise of Hal through the lens of a century when, in one complex process, the English Reformation was coercively established and the crown finally centralized (and 'southernized') power by subduing the Catholic leaders of the North; and when, too, the Renaissance ideals of civility were enthusiastically embraced by gentry and Court. The basis for this interpretation lies in the play's constellation of motifs and historical analogies centred on a complex theme of immense importance in the sixteenth century, that of grace.

REBELLION

A major historical analogy, as I hope to show, is one linking the rebellions of *Henry IV* with the Northern Rebellion of 1569-70 and, more importantly, with the earlier northern rebellion known as the Pilgrimage of Grace (1536). The latter was the first and most dangerous of the Tudor rebellions, 'the archetypal protest movement of the century'. [5] It acquired its paradoxical name because its leaders wished to emphasize its religious and essentially peaceful nature and their willingness to disband if the King redressed their grievances. Although these grievances were a mixture of the economic, the political, and the religious, recent historians have tended to acknowledge that the major source of discontent was Henry VIII's attack on what was soon to be called 'the old religion'. [6] The religious motive was famously declared in the rebels' banners and badges, relics from a recent crusade against the Moors on which were painted the Five Wounds of Christ. [7] The rebels were presenting themselves as crusading defenders of a wounded Christian nation.

The Pilgrims were defeated in a notorious piece of treachery. [8] Heavily outnumbered by the rebels, Henry's deputy followed his master's advice and temporized with politic promises during his two conferences with their leaders at Doncaster. The rebels disbanded and Henry invited their trusting captain-in-chief, Robert Aske, to London, where he was warmly entertained and honoured with a chain of gold; but within months Henry found a pretext for arresting Aske and the other rebel leaders and executing them on a charge of treason. Among those executed was Sir Thomas Percy, the most warlike member of a family which troubled Henry VIII and Elizabeth I almost as much as it did Henry IV (it was Thomas Percy, seventh Earl of Northumberland, who was to lead the Northern Rebellion of 1569). After the Pilgrimage, there were four more rebellions of substance in the sixteenth century, and the one 'clear theme of national significance' running through them was opposition to the Reformation. [9] Thus the banner and badges of the Five Wounds were used again in the Western Rebellion of 1549 and the Northern Rebellion of 1569, with the addition in the latter of the crusaders' red cross. [10] Because of this recurrent theme and symbolism, the Pilgrimage of Grace understandably acquired archetypal status both in the popular imagination and in the historical thinking of government propagandists.

It might seem implausible to claim that in 1596-8 Shakespeare could rely on his audience recognizing inexplicit allusions to the rebellion of 1569; [11] and much less likely that he could expect anyone to recall the Pilgrimage of Grace. But the facts suggest otherwise. The continuing relevance and essential identity of the major Tudor rebellions was hammered into the consciousness of the Elizabethan citizen; it was intrinsic to the state's self-justifying and self-protective version of history. That most popular of Elizabethan histories, John Foxe's *Acts and Monuments,* included an indignant account of the Pilgrimage of Grace that strongly influenced later propagandists. [12] In Richard Norton's *A Warning against the dangerous practises of Papistes, and specially partners of the late Rebellion* (1569), King John's troubles with the papacy, the overthrow of Richard II (allegedly caused by the Archbishop of Canterbury), the Pilgrimage of Grace, the Western Rebellion, and the contemporaneous rebellion in the north, are all linked in immediate sequence as part of the long history of papal incitement to rebellion against lawful rulers in Europe. [13] So too in the 1570 *Homilie agaynste disobedience and wylful rebellion,* subsequently to become the last and longest in the Book of Homilies ('to be read in euerie Parish Church'), a sweeping history of papally inspired rebellions passes from France and Germany to England, where an account of John's struggle with pope and cardinal proceeds to 'matters of later memory': the rebellions 'in the North and West countries' against Henry and Edward, in Ireland against Elizabeth (1566-7), and 'yet more latelie' among 'Northen borderers'. [14] Wilfrid Holme's lengthy narrative poem on the Pilgrimage of Grace, *The fall and euil successe of rebellion,* although written shortly after the event, was not published until 1572, when it had acquired the merit of underlining the repetitive pattern of history. No doubt this aureate composition was gathering dust when *Henry IV* was first staged. Like the Book of Homilies, however, the popular sermons of the Marian martyr, Bishop Hugh Latimer, were not. They were reprinted four times between 1575 and 1596, and in the last as in the earlier editions the opening sermon was one devoted to the Pilgrimage of Grace. [15]

We have good reason to believe that this Henrician sermon, like the last in the Book of Homilies, was felt to have continuing relevance in the late 1590s. The missionary work of the Jesuits and seminary priests was defined by law as treason, seditious and rebellious in intent; [16] thus it was common for trial judges to compare the priests' 'traitorous' activities with those of the northern rebels decades earlier. [17] The mounting sense of political insecurity which afflicted England in the nineties was due almost entirely to a perceived threat from Catholic forces at home and abroad. [18] From 1595 the Irish earls and bishops were in rebellion and receiving help and encouragement from Philip II, who complimented them on their defence of Catholicism; in 1598 they scored a major victory over the English forces, and in 1599 humiliated Essex. There was constant fear of a Spanish invasion, direct from the peninsula, or from Calais (which fell to Spain in 1596), or from Ireland. When Sir Francis Knyvett wrote his *Defence of the Realm* in 1596, advocating compulsory military training for all men aged between eighteen and fifty, he could not have assumed that the expected Second Armada would, like the first, be scattered by storms (as was the case); and in fact organized defensive measures against invasion were in operation throughout the country until the end of the century. Although inspired by the 1569 rebellion, the final sermon in the Book of Homilies, with its systematic linking of past and present, would not have seemed quaintly out of date in these years; much less would its concluding prayer of 'Thanksgiving for the Suppression of the Last Rebellion'.

It is thoroughly characteristic of Tudor politics that in the great body of propagandist writing denouncing actual and potential rebellion there is an insistent attempt to demystify the religious language and symbolism used by the major rebel movements and to dismiss it as an ideological cloak for political ambition and economic discontent designed to ensnare the ignorant populace. The name of the Pilgrimage of Grace, and the insignia copied from it by the later rebellions, were construed as epitomizing the very nature of papistry. For Foxe, calling insurrection 'a holy pilgrimage' and painting Christ and his wounds on streamers and banners was true to the nature of devilish hypocrisy. [19] For Norton, the rebels' self-presentation was all 'shewes and color'—'plaine counterfeit color'. [20] As a translator of Calvin he was especially offended by the claim to 'grace', insisting that papist rebels were instruments of the Pope's political ambitions and adherents of a religion which draws 'the redemption and iustification of man', which is 'God's greatest honor and dignitie', from 'God to man, from grace to workes . . . denying his graciousness therein'. [21] Echoing Norton, and playing on the different senses of the word 'colour' (a military ensign, a painting, a fraudulent appearance), the homily *Against Disobedience and Wilful Rebellion* declaims: [whereas] 'redress of the commonwealth hath of old been the usual pretence of rebels. . . . religion now of late beginneth to be a colour of rebellion'; 'though some rebels bear the picture of the Five Wounds painted in a clout . . . by some lewd painter', yet they know not 'what the cross of Christ meaneth' and march 'against those that have the cross of Christ printed in their hearts'. Even a mixture of good and bad motives is never conceded: idealistic claims are all 'feigned pretence'; purported 'reformation' of religion and country is actually 'deformation'; [22] grace is disgrace.

GRACE

From a Shakespearian perspective, the name of the 1536 rebellion must have seemed both ironic and prophetic, since the Reformation and the Renaissance combined to create a culture in which everyone was a pilgrim of grace in one or more senses of the word. Grace as the divine gift which redeems sinful mortals, making them pleasing in the eyes of God, was, as Norton sharply implied, a distinguishing and proprietorial concern of Reformation theology. And everything required by Castiglione and his like from the gentleman seeking grace and favour at court—eloquence, wit, versatility, *sprezzatura,* modesty, and an unfailing sense of fitness or propriety—was comprehended in that one word: 'every thing that he doth or speaketh, let him doe it with a grace'. [23] Thus in Elizabethan usage the spiritual and the socio-aesthetic senses of this unusually polysemous word tended to reinforce each other so as to make it an index of supreme value.

Not surprisingly, 'grace' is a conspicuous idea in a number of Shakespeare's plays. It is most obvious in those which concentrate on the nature of kingship and 'the Lord's anointed'. In *3 Henry VI* (in the characterization of Edward), in *Richard III,* and in *Richard II,* the word 'grace' functions primarily as an ironic index of the ruler's unfitness for his office and of a more general sense of lost excellence—honour, civility, moral integrity—in the nobility and the nation at large. The word actually occurs more often in *Richard III* than in *1* and *2 Henry IV;* but as a theme the notion of grace is much more deeply embedded in the two-part play. This is due in the first place to the fact that Shakespeare is here concerned not only with loss and decline but also with the struggle for personal and national renewal (redemption, reformation); and in the second to the way in which he has complicated the meaning of grace by tying it to the notion of rebuke or censure, thus drawing upon a central feature of Calvinist spirituality. Indeed with its complex vision of grace in all its senses and associations—socio-aesthetic, spiritual, and political—*Henry IV* becomes something like a dramatic encapsulation of the Tudor century.

Intemately connected, the concepts of grace (with its antonyms 'disgrace', 'shame', and 'impudence') and rebuke (with its synonyms 'check', 'rate', 'chide', and 'upbraid') dominate dialogue and action in both parts of the play. Since disgraceful conduct invites rebuke, the connection is instantly intelligible; but the prominence and full significance of the twin motif can only be understood in relation to Augustinian and Calvinist theology.

Dealing in the *Institutes* (II.v) with objections to his teachings on grace, free will, and predestination, Calvin refers to the claim that if men are predestined to be saved or damned, then 'exhortations are vainely taken in hande . . . the use of admonitions is superfluous . . . it is a fond thing to rebuke'. Augustine, he replies, wrote his book *De Correptione et Gratia (On Rebuke and Grace)* in answer to this objection; and he proceeds to summarize an argument on 'the medicine of rebuke' to which Augustine often returns in his anti-Pelagian writings. When addressed to the reprobate, rebuke beats and strikes their conscience in this life, and renders them more inexcusable on the judgement day. When addressed to the elect, 'if at any time they be gone out of the way sith they fell by the necessarie weaknesse of the fleshe', it avails much 'to enflame the desire of goodnesse, to shake off sluggishness, to take away the pleasure and venimous swetnesse of wickednesse'. It 'stirreth them to desire . . . renuing', prepares them 'to receiue . . . grace', and 'maketh them a new creature'. Thus the prophets, Christ, and the apostles never ceased to 'admonishe, to exhorte and to rebuke'. [24] Preliminary reflection alone would suggest that all of this resonates through *Henry IV,* a play whose seemingly reprobate and much censured hero was fixed in history as one of the elect. But in order to appreciate just how deeply embedded is this play in the culture of its time, one must note that Calvin's discussion of rebuke and grace is really a preamble to his exposition of church discipline (II.xii), 'whereof the chiefe use is in the censure and excommunication'. This provided the theological foundation for what was arguably the best-known feature of Tudor Puritanism: its censoriousness. Fired with a 'white-hot morality', the Puritan saw himself as 'a prophet in his generation, one who freely rebuked both high and low alike'. [25]

Why the Puritan preoccupation with grace-and-censure should have coloured the whole of *Henry IV* has to be ascribed ultimately to Falstaff's uncensored identity as Sir John Oldcastle or Lord Cobham, the Lollard burned for heresy by his friend Henry V and revered by Puritans as a heroic martyr. Much as Falstaff dominates many a performance of *Henry IV,* so Oldcastle dominates John Foxe's 'ecclesiasticall historie' of Henry V's reign: for him, that was the time when a synod was called 'to represse the growing and spreading of the Gospell, and especially to withstand the noble and worthy Lorde Cobham', chief favourer of the Lollards. [26] Oldcastle, however, was the subject of religious controversy in the sixteenth century and had a dual identity as reckless profligate (the Catholic version) and repentant sinner-turned-saint (the Protestant). [27] Shakespeare's comic debunking (and final 'excommunication') of the Protestant hero counterbalances whatever anti-Catholic attitudes might have been read into his presentation of northern rebellion; and the ideas of sin, rebuke, repentance, and grace which are intrinsic to the fat rogue's characterization are gravely relevant to the uncomic characters on both sides of the political divide.

Examination of the ways in which *Henry IV* is shaped by ideas of grace and rebuke, so that an earlier age seems to disclose the major patterns of Tudor experience, must begin with the associated ideas of pilgrimage, crusade, and reformation. The chroniclers mention that Henry had plans at the end of his reign to go on a crusade to recover Jerusalem from the infidels. Shakespeare seizes on this idea, makes it frame the whole of Henry's reign, and gives it the character of a pilgrimage. Henry's motives in this project combine and confuse the political and the spiritual: he would busy restless minds with foreign quarrels, and he would expiate the murder of Richard II, a shared guilt which he never explicitly acknowledges until the end. Henry's sense of guilt and shame, his feeling that present and impending troubles are retribution for past mistreadings, seems to involve the whole nation, so that his postponed pilgrimage effectively symbolizes a general quest for redemptive grace. As in Holinshed, whose favourite rendering of *anno domini* is 'in the year of our redemption', and above all as in St Paul, who urges the Ephesians to put off the unregenerate old man, 'redeeming the time: for the days are evil' (Ephesians 5.15-16), history here is time conceived as a quest for liberation from the sins of the past and the present. Falstaff, the sensual, time-wasting 'old boar' who feeds 'in the old frank' with pagan 'Ephesians . . . of the old church' (2:2.2.111-14), personifies (among other things) the unregenerate order. [28] It is that order which Hal must reject if he is to redeem time past and present and crown the future with a glittering 'reformation' (1:1.2.201-5), thus fitting the role, given him by the chroniclers, of a madcap prince who miraculously became 'a new man'. [29]

The idea that England is almost hopelessly seeking to recover lost grace is posited in the opening scene of *Part 1.* Westmoreland discloses that Council had to 'brake off' its 'business for the Holy Land' on hearing that 'the noble Mortimer' and his men had fallen into 'the rude hands' of 'the irregular and wild Glendower', and that the corpses of his butchered men suffered 'Such beastly shameless transformation . . . as may not be / Without much shame retold or spoken of' (1.1.38-46). Henry complains that 'riot and dishonour stain the brow' of the heir apparent and that the pride and malevolence of his erstwhile friends compel him to 'neglect / Our holy purpose to Jerusalem' (lines 84-101).

Although the word itself is not introduced until 1.2, this opening scene begins to suggest the wide spectrum of meaning in 'grace'. Initially there is grace in the religious sense, and it refers primarily to the process by which military-political aggression is given supreme justification. In *Part I* the Percys make much of the fact that the 'noble prelate well beloved', the Archbishop of York, 'commends the plot' to overthrow Henry: 'it cannot choose but be a noble plot', concludes Hotspur (1:3.165, 277; 2.3.19). Gadshill's comment on the parallel action to rob royal officers and pilgrims reflects ironically on the northern prelate's blessing (while hinting perhaps at the historical parallel in a characteristically ambivalent manner): the involvement in the action of the 'nobility and tranquillity'—who 'pray continually to their saint, the commonwealth, or rather . . . prey on her'—serves to 'do the profession [of highwaymen] some grace' (1.1.69-78). It is only in *Part 2,* however, that 'The Archbishop's grace of York' (1:3.2.119) becomes actively rebellious. Without him, the people could never have been persuaded to rise with the Percys a second time. 'The gentle Archbishop', reports Morton to Northumberland, binds his followers because he 'Derives from Heaven his quarrel and his cause', 'Turns insurrection to religion', and arms himself with a holy relic, 'the blood / Of fair King Richard, scraped from Pomfret stones' (2:1.1.189-206). That this speech is given in the opening scene to a character called Morton (who never appears again) is adroit. There is no comparable character, and no one of that name, in any of the sources, but it was well known that the Northern Rebellion of 1569 was stirred up by Dr Nicholas Morton, an exiled priest and former Prebendary of York sent by Pius V to foster Catholic resistance to Elizabeth. [30] When the rebels confront the King's deputy at Gaultree, and are defeated in the most elaborately treacherous manner, the word 'grace', both as honorific and as abstract quality, will ring through the dialogue no less than nineteen times; for the historically minded, the Pilgrimage of Grace is vividly anticipated. But Morton's name and role ensure that the insurrection in *Part 2* is implicitly paralleled with the other major rebellion of the Tudor period as well. As we have seen, Shakespeare's audience was familiar with complex historical parallelism of this kind.

The role imputed to the archbishop concurs nicely with the demystifying polemics of Tudor orthodoxy. But of course the eye of the demystifier has settled also on the monarchy from the start, and never leaves it until almost the end. Henry's habitual self-righteousness, his proclaimed desire to 'draw no swords but what are sanctified' (2:4.2.4), Gadshill's 'graced' attack on the pilgrims, and 'his grace' Prince John's smug claim at Gaultree that 'God, and not we, hath safely fought today' (2:4.1.142, 266, 280, 349) complete the picture of a political world where all claims to moral authority must be scrutinized with the utmost care. This is Tudor England as many Protestants and Catholics must have seen it.

Converging on grace in the religious sense is the notion of grace as the quality and title of true royalty: kings being sacramentally exalted, appointed 'by the grace of God', and expected like Him to be bountiful and forgiving as well as just and firm. The 'title of respect' which Henry (in his opening speech) complains he is denied by the Percys (1:1.3.8) is possibly 'Your grace', the honorific first used in England in royal address during the reign of Henry IV. [31] Henry's loyal followers readily grant him this title; in fact Westmoreland, engaging with the Yorkist Mowbray in a bout of partisan historicizing, claims that in Richard's time the people's prayers 'were set on Hereford, whom . . . they blessed and graced indeed more than the king' (2:4.1.136-40). But the key question is whether Hal deserves this title. Symptomatically, Falstaff denies this, dis-gracing the Prince in their first scene together: 'God save thy grace—majesty I should say, for grace thou wilt have none . . . not so much as will serve to be prologue to an egg and butter' (1:1.2.15-20). But it is noticeable that when Falstaff has spoken 'vilely' of him in *Part 2* ('a good shallow young fellow, a would have made a good pantler'), both Doll and Mistress Quickly show a conspicuously different attitude: 'O, the Lord preserve thy grace! By my troth, welcome to London. Now the Lord bless that sweet face of thine' (2.4.193, 236-7). Henry himself endorses this attitude in his dying advice to the Prince's brothers. Although 'being incensed, he is flint', Harry 'is gracious if he be observed', having 'a tear for pity, and a hand / Open as day for meting charity'; they must not 'lose the good advantage of his grace' by ignoring or alienating him (2:4.2.28-33).

Henry's advice introduces the kindred notion of royal 'grace and favour' and what it entails in terms of generosity and indulgence. His politic withdrawal of such from the Percys, his 'first and dearest . . . friends', is a major cause of the civil war. In the parleys at Shrewsbury, Worcester complains that Henry 'turn[ed]' his 'looks / Of favour' from 'all our house' (1:5.1.30-1); Hotspur that he 'disgraced me in my happy victories' (4.3.97). But it is in Falstaff's relationship with the heir apparent that this issue becomes one of major importance, both dramatically and politically. Far from being a herald of democratic republicanism, as Graham Holderness has claimed,[32] Falstaff is from the start wedded in soul to the idea of a monarchical order in which royal grace and favour is entirely at his disposal, to be enjoyed, dispensed, and denied by him as he pleases. In the same opening dialogue where he denies Hal 'his grace', Falstaff (with graceful wit) pleads for the titles of respect which will grace and 'countenance'—the word signifies both favour and patronage as well as pretence—his own and his friends' disreputable activities: 'Marry, then, sweet wag, when thou art king, let not us that are squires of the night's body be called thieves of the day's beauty. Let us be Diana's foresters, gentlemen of the shade, minions of . . . our noble and chaste mistress the moon, under whose countenance we steal' (1.2.22-8). At Shrewsbury, Hal magnanimously accedes in part to this request, allowing Falstaff to steal the credit for killing Hotspur: 'if a lie may do thee grace, / I'll gild it with the happiest terms I have' (5.4.152-3). So Falstaff expects 'to be either earl or duke' (line 158); but *Part 2* tells the familiar tale of court preferment endlessly deferred. On his first appearance here he huffily admits (in effect) that he is now out of favour with Hal: 'He may keep his own grace, but he's almost out of mine, I can assure him' (1.2.20-1).

But he sees himself too in the role of patron. He has his own realm where hopefuls like Justice Shallow believe that 'a friend i' th' court is better than a penny in purse', and where servants like Davy complain that 'a knave should have some countenance at his friend's request' (2:5.1.25-6, 36). Hopes for Falstaff and his followers soar with news of the old King's death. He thinks of himself instantly as 'Fortune's steward' Pistol he will 'double charge with dignities' and 'Lord Shallow' can choose what office he will: 'I will make the king do you grace . . . do but mark the countenance he will give me' (5.3.102-7; 5.5.5-7). The key to his failure lies in the way he approaches the new King. Arriving travel-stained and sweaty to stop the coronation procession with 'God save thy grace, King Hal, my royal Hal' (5.5.36), he publicly dis-graces Henry V and presumes to appropriate his royalty. Falstaff's quest for grace is hilarious to begin with and pathetic in conclusion; but its negative underside has been made clear: in the King's fears that Hal's reign will reenact that of Richard II, when 'sage counsellors' gave way to 'apes of idleness' (4.2.249-51); in Falstaff's promise of revenge on the Chief Justice (5.3.113); and in the conviction of Warwick, Clarence, and John that no one in office can now be 'assured what grace to find' unless he is prepared to abandon his principles and 'speak Sir John Falstaff fair' (5.2.30-3).

Falstaff's performance at the coronation procession is

a highly theatrical and 'jocoserious' example of social impropriety: of disregard, as Castiglione would express it, for the circumstances of time, person, and place;[33] he is rebuked at this point in just such terms by Hal, and earlier by the Chief Justice (2:5.5.44, 2.1.49-50). The dazzling verbal dexterity with which he entertains his prince and fits his holiday mood make him in one sense the perfect Renaissance courtier; but his decline and fall are defined in terms of the courtly code which justifies his 'graceful recklessness'.[34] Even in *Part 1* his sallies can displease because mistimed ('is it a time to jest and dally now?' (1:5.3.54)). In *Part 2* the sheer impudence in his responses to rebuke precludes 'the right fencing grace' to which he still lays claim (2.1.151). His perpetual fooling seeks to impose the timeless world of holiday (where disregard for 'the circumstances' is the norm) upon the timebound world of politics, and to collapse the difference between himself and youth and royalty. Applied thus, the courtly code of social grace is inseparable from a philosophy of natural order and a sense of historical necessity. It is the same philosophy which tells us in *Twelfth Night* that there are times when a joke is not a joke (3.1.59-67), and that the rain it raineth every day.

In the wider perspective, the play's concern with grace in the socio-aesthetic sense seems to reflect a self-conscious, Tudor-establishment contrast between medieval and modern, North and South. The contrast is dramatized in the rivalry between Hal, 'king of courtesy' (1:2.4.10), and 'that same mad fellow of the north, Percy' (lines 324-5)—noble and lovable in his way, but more 'rude', irregular and wild' than his Welsh allies. His 'dearest grace', as his uncle perceives, is his outspoken contempt for falsity; but too often this declines into frenetic bluntness and crude philistinism; and his response to tactful criticism is itself graceless: 'Well, I am schooled. Good manners be your speed!' (3.1.177-85).

Hal by contrast proves himself to be the complete Renaissance man.[35] Witty, eloquent, and adaptable as well as valiant, he is obviously schooled in both 'arts and martial exercises' (2:4.2.203). He is eloquently modest as well as concerned to save lives when he issues his challenge to Hotspur, chiding 'his [own] truant youth with such a grace' as 'became him like a prince indeed' (1:5.2.60-2); and with equal grace he relinquishes the name of victor to Falstaff. There is nothing fraudulent in these gracious gestures; no hint of an unfit relationship between what he seems and what he is. His 'fair rites of tenderness' and 'courtesy' when alone (as he believes) with the dead Hotspur (5.4.93, 97) are one of several indications that he is not the coldhearted 'princely hypocrite' imagined by some critics.

Grace in *Henry IV* also means honour, the respect due to those who live by the knightly code whose cardinal values are valour and fidelity.[36] What most stains Hal's honour in his father's eyes is his surrender of military glory to Hotspur. But although Hal's redemption in *Part 1* depends on his defeat of Hotspur, the value of supreme importance in both parts is not valour but truth. Hal's triumph at Shrewsbury is less crucial as a martial achievement than as the fulfilment of a solemn promise (that he would 'redeem' all his shames by killing the rebel leader or dying in the attempt); it accords with his awareness that 'redemption' also means 'fulfilling a promise' (OED 2), and with his self-conception as 'the Prince of Wales who . . . never promises but he means to pay' (1:3.2.132-59, 5.4.41-2). Feudal England celebrated the verbal pledge of trust as the foundation of society; thus as J. Douglas Canfield has argued, the word as bond and the contest between fidelity and betrayal are central to the representation of conflict in literature from *Beowulf* to Dryden.[37] But this contest acquired a singular intensity and painfulness in the sixteenth century with the coming of the Reformation and the disputes about royal sovereignty and succession. The anguish of conflicting loyalties and mutually contradictory vows is vividly registered in the historical documents of the major rebellions. Precisely the same experience is dramatized in that most overtly topical of Shakespeare's plays, *King John* (probably written just before *Henry IV*), where the conflict between Pope and King intensifies the succession dispute and forces conscientious subjects into humiliatingly repetitive changes of allegiance: setting 'oath to oath', making 'faith an enemy to faith' (3.1.189-90).

In *Henry IV* this characteristically Tudor trauma is echoed in the representation of a crumbling society where the very basis of personal loyalty has been undone, and the original and continuing sin is betrayal, perjury, and a total devaluation of the word: 'What trust is in these times?' (2:1.3.100). Mutual accusations of treachery and perjury, and consequently flawed attempts to claim the moral high ground, characterize the relations of Henry and the rebels in *Part 1*. The first rebellion is motivated by anger and fear; but another motive is the Percys' desire to 'redeem' their family honour and erase from 'chronicles in time to come' the 'detested blot' of regicide in which Bolingbroke's broken vow implicated them (1.3.153-82; 4.3.52-105). Distrust bred by Henry's original 'violation of all faith and troth' (5.1.70) prompts Worcester to lie to Hotspur about the King's conciliatory offer at Shrewsbury. By his stress on location Shakespeare connects this distrust with an archetypal historical event, the treachery practised on the Pilgrims at Doncaster in 1536.[38] Rebuked by Henry for having 'deceived our trust', Worcester insists on the King's perjury as the source of dissension, saying: 'You swore to us, / And you did swear that oath at Doncaster . . . Forget your oath to us at Doncaster' (lines 41, 58). The parallel is sharpened by the fact that the offer which is distrusted is four times defined as 'grace, / Pardon, and terms of love' (5.5.2-3; cf.4.3.30,50,112; 5.1.106). What redeems Shrewsbury from the taint of dishonour which the remembered past introduces is the Prince's fulfilment of his promise, and his closing gesture of freeing 'ransomless' his most valuable prisoner: 'I thank your grace for this high courtesy' (5.5.32).

Part 1's pattern of treachery is re-enacted in *Part 2*. Having broken his word to Hotspur by failing to support him at Shrewsbury, Northumberland now resists the pleas of his wife and Lady Percy to absent himself from the planned uprising, arguing that his 'honour is at pawn' and that 'nothing can redeem it' but his going. But he is induced to betray his friends by the accusing argument of Lady Percy ('new lamenting ancient oversights') that it would dishonour Hotspur's name if his father were to keep his promise to others now (2.3.7-47). Northumberland is trapped by his disgraceful past.

But Northumberland's infidelity cannot match that of Prince John at Gaultree; not even in *King John,* which rings with indignation against 'perjured kings' (3.1.33), is there anything comparable to this act of royal treachery. 'His grace's' offer of pardon and redress is buttressed with oaths by the honour of his blood and upon his soul to boot; and it is solemnized by the public ritual (proposed by himself) of drinking and embracing together in token to the assembled armies of 'restorèd love and amity' (4.1.281-93). This studied act of treachery endows the breaking of the verbal bond with the quality of sacrilege.

Apart from royal treachery and the nineteen uses of the word 'grace', there is much to bring the fate of the Pilgrim leaders to mind and generally stimulate the historical sense. Mowbray predicts that Henry will not forget what they have done and will soon find some trivial cause to exact his vengeance on them (precisely what Henry VIII would do); the prelate responds that Henry, knowing that such executions are always remembered by 'the heirs of life', will rather 'keep no tell-tale to his memory / That may repeat and history his loss / To new remembrance' (lines 200-4). As if predicting the way in which the sons and nephews of the leading Pilgrims (Percys, Nevilles, Nortons, Tempests) would rise again in the rebellion of 1569, Hastings warns that, if the rebels fail, 'heir from heir shall hold his quarrel up / Whiles England shall have generation'. The young Prince retorts that Hastings is 'much too shallow / To sound the bottom of the after-times' (4.1.276-9).

REBUKE

Prince John foregrounds the play's censorious mode. 'Monsieur Remorse', the play's mock-Puritan, points to its theological matrix with pious remarks on 'the spirit of persuasion', the 'ears of profiting' (1:1.2.106, 143-4), and the need for 'the fire of grace' if one is to be properly 'moved' (2.4.370-1). What one should be moved to by rebuke is confession, contrition (asking pardon), and 'a good amendment of life' (1.2.97). But as Calvin acknowledged in his discussion of rebuke and grace (*Institutes,* II.V.5), and as Falstaff habitually demonstrates, evasion is a common response. It is characteristic of the endemic dishonesty of Henry's unregenerate world that almost everyone responds to rebuke by denial, obfuscation, and retaliation in kind. The dialogue of the play, both comic and serious, is substantially built on rebuke, evasion, and counter-rebuke.

Rebuke and evasion explode in the third scene of *Part 1* when Henry berates all the Percys for his 'indignities', and Hotspur in particular for withholding his prisoners. Although he still refuses to surrender them, Hotspur protests in the most tortuous manner that he made no such refusal at all. Henry treats this evasion with contempt, a fierce quarrel erupts, and the scene ends with the Percys planning rebellion. On the battlefield, the initial pattern of rebuke and evasion becomes one of rebuke, evasion, and counter-rebuke. Henry lectures Worcester on his betrayal of trust and on the impropriety of old friends and old men confronting each other in 'ungentle steel' (5.1.9-21). Worcester responds at greater length, blaming the present conflict on Henry's violation of all faith and on his 'ungentle' treatment of his former allies (lines 30-71). Loftily dismissing this justification of rebellion, Henry employs a familiar Tudor discourse:

> These things indeed you have articulate,
> Proclaimed at market crosses, read in
>   churches,
> To face the garment of rebellion
> With some fine colour that may please the eye
> Of fickle changelings and poor discontents,
> Which gape and rub the elbow at the news
> Of hurly-burly innovation.
> And never yet did insurrection want
> Such water-colours to impaint his cause . . .
> (lines 72-80)

Consistently with this discourse, however, Henry presents himself as the instrument of both grace and rebuke, offering pardon and redress if the rebels disarm: 'take the offer of our grace . . . if . . . not . . . rebuke and dread correction wait on us' (lines 106-11). Educated by history, Worcester distrusts his grace's word, lies to Hotspur, and the battle takes place. But Worcester is subjected to another homily on the point of execution: 'Thus ever did rebellion find rebuke. / Ill-spirited Worcester, did we not send grace, / Pardon, and terms of love to all of you? / And wouldst thou . . . Misuse the tenor of thy kinsman's trust?' (5.5.1-5). While there is no suggestion here that rebellion is justified, the ironic inappropriateness in the given circumstances of the King's anti-rebellion rhetoric is unmistakable.

From the start, Falstaff's relationship with the Prince is governed by the same dynamics as that between Henry and the men who had and lost his favour. Most of Hal's speeches to the fat knight are either hilariously devastating criticisms of his self-indulgence and deceit or attempts to make him tell truth and shame the devil. And Falstaff's responses characteristically slide from evasion to counterattack. Hal's opening tirade on Falstaff's time-wasting is dissolved in sinuous wordplay leading to the Puritan-sounding lament that Falstaff himself has been corrupted by Hal's company: 'O, thou . . . art indeed able to corrupt a saint. Thou hast done much harm upon me, Hal, God forgive thee for it' (1.2.87-9). His superb escape from the charge of 'open and apparent shame' after Gad's Hill is followed by his warning that Hal should prepare to be 'horribly chid' (2.4.360) by his father. By playing the part of the rebuking king much to his own advantage, Falstaff provokes the exchange of roles which brings upon Hal and himself a thunderous royal rebuke: 'Swearest thou, ungracious boy? . . . Thou art violently fallen away from grace. There is a devil haunts thee in the likeness of an old fat man . . . ' Falstaff's 'fencing' pretence of innocent and polite incomprehension is perfect: 'I would your grace would take me with you; whom means your grace?' (lines 429-44).

Very different is Hotspur's churlish reply in the next scene to his uncle's kindly rebuke ('You must needs learn, lord, to amend this fault'). And different to both is Hal's response in the ensuing scene to Henry's overblown, self-righteous condemnation of his 'rude' and 'degenerate' behaviour (3.2.14, 32, 128). The scenic juxtapositions are pointed, as is the nodal position given to the father-son encounter in the play's structure; for Hal's reaction to rebuke is designed (like his attitude to promises) to distinguish him from everyone else, marking him out as the figure of redemption and reformation, a man of grace. He is most respectful to his irate father ('my thrice gracious lord'); and while pleading that he is in part the victim of newsmongers, confesses that his 'youth / Hath faulty wandered and irregular', and so begs 'pardon'. Moreover, in making his solemn promise of amendment—that he 'will redeem' his 'shames' by defeating Hotspur—he acknowledges that success will depend on divine grace: 'This in the name of God I promise here, / The which if he be pleased I shall perform' (lines 26-8, 132-3, 144, 153-4). Since the defeat of the rebels effectively depends on the fulfilment of this promise, Calvin's teaching on the benefits of rebuking the elect when they 'be gone out of the way by the necessarie weakness of the fleshe' has been fully justified.

In keeping with its graver mood, *Part 2* shows an extraordinary intensification in the spirit of rebuke. In addition to present rebukes, future rebukes are anticipated (4.2.37-41; 4.2.105-21), and past ones are remembered. Northumberland (says Henry) 'checked and rated' Richard II, who rebuked him and Henry in turn (3.1.67-70). Henry 'had many living to upbraid' his way of gaining the throne (4.2.320). Since Shrewsbury, Hal has fallen from grace again and suffered accordingly—as he recalls in his tactical rebuke of the Chief Justice: 'What! Rate, rebuke, and roughly send to prison / Th' immediate heir of England?' (5.2.69-70). Mistress Quickly too has been reproved by the law—'Master Tisick the debuty'—for keeping uncivil customers (2.4.68).

In her response to rebuke ('You would bless you to hear what he said') the hostess set an example which Falstaff, 'deaf . . . to the hearing of anything good', conspicuously fails to follow (2.4.68-76; 1.2.54-5). He is now being reproved by everyone, from his tailor and his whore to Hal, John, and his dedicated moral 'physician' (1.2.100), the Chief Justice. Falstaff's pretended deafness with the latter emblematizes his chronic problem but is also symptomatic of his new impudence. However, the old tricks of sanctimonious reversal, pious pretence, and righteous indignation are in evidence too: it is not he who has misled Hal but Hal who misled him; he has 'checked' the 'rude Prince' for striking the Justice 'and the young lion repents' (lines 115, 153-4); his replies are not impudent sauciness but honourable boldness (2.1.97); if his manners are foolish and become him not he was a fool that taught them him (lines 150-1); abusing the prince behind his back was the part of a careful and true subject, designed to protect him from the love of the wicked (2.4.259-63); he 'never knew yet but rebuke and check was the reward of valour' (4.1.382-3).

As in *Part 1,* the most entertaining dialogue is woven around Falstaff's evasions. However, the volume and severity of the criticisms, and the waning of 'the right fencing grace' to which he still lays claim (2.1.151), anticipate the moment when he prepares to move from tavern to court, only to be fiercely rebuked ('Make less thy body hence, and more thy grace') and resolutely denied the opportunity to 'Reply . . . with a fool-born jest' (5.5.48, 51). The puritanical harshness of Hal's final rebuke may or may not be justified in the circumstances; but the significance of certain obvious facts is too often ignored. Falstaff's banishment (or 'excommunication') is the fulfilment of a promise ('I do, I will'), and it is not absolute: its harshness is moderated by the promise of a pension designed to keep Falstaff out of mischief and to help him 'reform' and so expect 'advancement' (that he is most unlikely to reform and seems deaf to what has been said is beside the point) (lines 64-6).[39] Hal's promise of a pension is a notably solemn one too: in his very last utterance, he emphasizes his own self-conception as defined at Shrewsbury: 'Be it your charge, my lord, / To see performed the tenor of my word' (lines 66-7). As for Falstaff's subsequent sending to the Fleet by the Chief Justice, that accords with Hal's public recognition that the Justice was right to 'rate, rebuke, and roughly send to prison' the heir-apparent, and with his assurance that he would never interfere with the decisions of this 'bold, just, and impartial spirit' (5.2.115). It has been intimated throughout that if anything will redeem England it will be a strong leader who keeps his word and so inspires trust and loyalty. Thus it can be argued that the nature and circumstances of the final rebuke contribute to the conception of Hal as a redeemed and redeeming prince, one who possesses the major *king*-becoming graces. Clearly, however, the scene is intrinsic to a comprehensive structure of thought founded on Calvin's twin Augustinian themes.

The same thematic twinship governs the two other most important scenes in *Part 2:* Prince John's encounter with the rebels, and the King's with his socially rebellious son. Here too the rhetoric of a censorious throne is turned against those who are thought to threaten its survival; and here too the nature and reception of the rebuke deserve scrutiny. Soundly rated by both Westmoreland and the Prince for taking up arms, 'his grace of York' passes lightly over the motive of personal revenge which initially inspired him to rise against Henry; instead, he justifies his action by reference to unspecified common grievances and in particular to the pressures of 'the time misordered' (4.1.70-85, 261). Quite unlike Northumberland, who declared himself committed to anarchy and bloodshed (1.1.154), he repeatedly insists that he is bent, not on conflict, but on securing a genuine peace. His accent is that of confused sincerity, his manner dignified, and his attitude to his opposites trusting and half-apologetic. All of which serves to intensify the unsettling aspects of the criticism to which he is subjected. What is remarkable in the first place is that he is rebuked at length, in the most orotund manner, and twice over: first by Westmoreland, and later by the youthful Prince: the artifice and the doubling intensifies the sense of hollowness and duplicity. Even the argument is the same in both rebukes: a variation on Henry's attack on Worcester in *Part 1,* suitably adapted to the person addressed, and evocative of the great historical paradigm and all the indignant eloquence it spawned. Both men expatiate on the horrible impropriety of a man of God dressing 'the ugly form / Of base and bloody insurrection' with 'the fair honours' of his calling, perverting 'the grace, the sanctities of heaven', and employing 'the countenance and grace of heaven' in 'deeds dishonourable' (4.1.39-41, 249-54). Given his treacherous intent, the Prince's preachifying shows that he has wholly appropriated 'the counterfeited zeal of God' (line 255) which he imputes to the bishop: an appropriation which sharply interrogates official Tudor attacks on 'the counterfeit service of God', the 'false pretences and shews', whereby the various rebel leaders purportedly deluded their gullible followers.[40]

Henry's 'dear and deep rebuke' of Hal two scenes later is comparable to John's in its excess, and mistaken in its view of Hal as a 'rebel . . . spirit' in deep 'revolt' (4.2.195, 300); but it is at least sincere in its anger and its care for the commonwealth. What matters, however, is Hal's response. He is here reduced to tears by his father's words. When he speaks, he begins with the words, 'O pardon me', explains himself, and eloquently communicates feelings of filial love and duty. The effect of this response, like its counterpart in *Part 1,* is all-important: not, this time, for the commonwealth, but for the King. Reconciled and at one with Hal, Henry confesses his guilt for the first time, and begs pardon. Echoing his earlier and entirely characteristic, 'God knows, I had no such intent / But that necessity so bowed the state / That I and greatness were compelled to kiss' (3.1.71-3), he now says: 'God knows, my son, / By what by-paths and indirect crooked ways / I met this crown . . . How I came by this crown, O God forgive' (4.2.311-12, 346). He then learns that he has been resting in the Jerusalem Chamber, and he is satisfied: 'In that Jerusalem shall Harry die' (line 367). Some critics read this detail as a final sign of Henry's insufficiency. I take it as evidence that his pilgrimage is over; that he has, through his son, found grace. Unlike Falstaff and others, he has stopped wrenching the true cause the false way, has told truth and shamed the devil.

PARDON

The analogies adumbrated by Shakespeare between the reign of Henry IV and the Tudor period indicate that his interpretation of English history is here affected at every level by ideas derived from the major political and cultural experiences of his own time, as well as by notions of historical recurrence long established in western historiography.[41] In particular, those analogies intimate that the bitter intestinal divisions of the later period, with their conflicting loyalties and mixed and confused motivations, contributed much to his sense of the tortuous relationship in political affairs between right and wrong, justice and injustice, morality and expediency, freedom and necessity, present and past. Neither the rebellious bishop nor the regicidal King in *Henry IV* is blameless, but both claim with some sincerity and truth that the strong necessity of the times—the accumulated pressure of events—compelled them to do what they did not want to do. Elizabeth might have said the same about the execution of her Catholic cousin, Queen Mary, and of the eight hundred northerners who supported Mary and 'the old religion'.[42]

For Shakespeare, it would seem, the nature of politics is such that most leaders will necessarily do things they would rather have withheld from 'chronicles in time to come'. But if they are to make peace with themselves and posterity, they must confess and beg pardon and not wrap themselves in the rhetoric of righteousness and evasion. And since no one else is guiltless, they may, if they are lucky, be forgiven. Hardly a theme (either political or literary-critical) for our time; but it was probably Shakespeare's intended, final message from the stage. In the epilogue to *The Tempest,* Prospero, the all-powerful but less-than-perfect ruler, addresses the audience in language of moving simplicity. Like his rude and rebellious subject, Caliban, he humbly 'seek[s] for grace' (5.1.299), reminding the audience of its own faults, echoing the Lord's prayer, and gently recalling the old religion's overly indulgent attitude to forgiveness and redemption:

> And my ending is despair
> Unless I be relieved by prayer,
> Which pierces so, that it assaults
> Mercy itself, and frees all faults.
> As you from crimes would pardoned be,
> Let your indulgence set me free.

Notes

[1] *The Idea of History* (Oxford, 1961), p. xi; cited (approvingly) in Paul Q. Hirst, *Marxism and Historical Writing* (1985), p. 44.

[2] Tillyard, *Shakespeare's History Plays* (1944); Campbell, *Shakespeare's Histories: Mirrors of Elizabethan Policy* (San Marino, California, 1947); Richard Simpson, 'The Political Use of the Stage in Shakespeare's Time', *New Shakespere Society Publications,* series 1, no. 2, part 2 (1875): 371-95. Simpson's claim was casually anticipated by Sir Cuthbert Sharpe in his *Memorials of the Rebellion of 1569* (1840), p. 336.

[3] Greenblatt, 'Invisible Bullets: Renaissance Authority and Its Subversion, *Henry IV* and *Henry V*', in *Political Shakespeare: New Essays in Cultural Materialism,* ed. Jonathan Dollimore and Alan Sinfield (Manchester, 1985), pp. 17-47; Holderness, *Shakespeare Recycled: the Making of Historical Drama* (1992).

[4] Scoufos, *Shakespeare's Typological Satire: a Study of the Falstaff-Oldcastle Problem* (Athens, Ohio, 1979).

[5] Penry Williams, *The Tudor Regime* (Oxford, 1979), pp. 316-17. Scoufos (pp. 125-6) briefly notes a parallel between Henry VIII's suppression of the Pilgrimage of Grace and Prince John's handling of the rebels at the end of *2 Henry IV.* She assumes (wrongly, I believe) that John's treachery is presented in an uncritical fashion.

[6] C. S. L. Davies, 'The Pilgrimage of Grace Reconsidered', *Past and Present,* 41 (1968): 54-75; J. J. Scarisbrooke, *Henry VIII* (1968), pp. 338-9; Scott Michael Harrison, *The Pilgrimage of Grace in the Lake District* (1981), pp. 1-3, 132-6.

[7] Edward Hall, *Chronicle Containing the History of England During the Reign of Henry IV and the Succeeding Monarchs to the End of the Reign of Henry the Eighth* (1548-50; 1809 edn), pp. 322-3; Raphael Holinshed, *Chronicles of England, Scotland, and Ireland,* 6 vols. (1587 edn rept. 1808), vol. 3, p. 800. See also Madeleine Hope Dodds and Ruth Dodds, *The Pilgrimage of Grace 1536-1537 and the Exeter Conspiracy,* 2 vols. (1915), vol. 1, pp. 19, 239.

[8] For evidence of contemporary criticism of Henry's treachery, see William Thomas, *The Pilgrim: A Dialogue on the Life and Actions of King Henry VIII* (1546), ed. J. A. Froude (London, 1861), pp. 11, 50-1. Tudor apologists imputed the bloodless suppression of the rebellion to 'the kynges wisedom and . . . discrete counsayle'. See John Hardyng, *The Chronicle. Together with the Continuation by Richard Grafton* (1543), p. 605; and cf. Hall, *Chronicle,* p. 823.

[9] Antony Fletcher, *Tudor Rebellions* (1968; 3rd edn, 1983), p. 101.

[10] Frances Rose-Troup, *The Western Rebellion of 1549* (1913), p. 128, 257, 411-14; R. R. Reid, 'The Rebellion of the Earls', *Transactions of the Royal Historical Society* (1906): 171-203.

[11] Irving Ribner, *The English History Play in the Age of Shakespeare* (London, 1957; revd edn, 1965), p. 182; David Bevington, *Tudor Drama and Politics: a Critical Approach to Topical Meaning* (Cambridge, Mass., 1968), p. 20.

[12] Edn of 1583, pp. 1086-7.

[13] *All such treatises as haue been lately published by Thomas Norton* (1569), sigs. D5v-C1r. Norton's pamphlets were drawn on by other polemical writers throughout the remainder of the Elizabethan period. See James K. Lowers, *Mirrors for Rebels: a Study of Polemical Literature Relating to the Northern Rebellion of 1569* (Berkeley: Calif., 1953), pp. 36, 55, 64.

[14] *The Two Books of Homilies,* ed. J. Griffiths (Oxford, 1859), pp. 594-5.

[15] *Sermons,* ed. G. E. Corrie (Cambridge, 1844), pp. 25-32 (the Elizabethan editions were entitled *Frutefull Sermons*). Concerning the 1536 rebellion, George Whetstone says in *The English Myrrour* (1586): 'It is yet within the compasse of oure memorie' (p. 167). He gives an account of this and later rebellions and conspiracies against the Tudor monarchy (pp. 24-68).

[16] See the Acts of 1585 and 1593 against priests and recusants, rept. in G. R. Elton, *The Tudor Constitution: Documents and Commentary* (Cambridge, 1960), pp. 424-32.

[17] Richard Verstegan (*c.* 1550-1640), *Letters and Dispatches,* ed. Anthony Petti (1959), p. 145 (trial date, 1593; Catholics and Brownists both likened to 'the rebelles in the northe'; their 'diabolicall perswasions tendeth to plaine insurrection and rebellion . . . clooked under the face of religion'); Christopher Devlin, *The Life of Robert Southwell, Poet and Martyr* (1956), p. 305 (trial date, 1595: 'The Rebellion in the North, by whom was it stirred but by . . . Jesuits and Priests?').

[18] J. B. Black, *The Reign of Elizabeth, 1558-1603* (Oxford, 1936; 2nd edn, 1959), pp. 406-18. Fletcher, *Tudor Rebellions,* p. 100, notes that the years 1595-8—within which period *1* and *2 Henry IV* were probably written—were arguably 'one of the most insecure periods of Tudor government'. In addition to the political-religious threat, there was widespread rioting over enclosures and dearth.

[19] *Actes and Monuments* (1583), p. 1087; he is echoing Hall (*Chronicle,* p. 823), who is copied by Holinshed, *Chronicles,* 3, 800. Cf. the Act of 1593 on 'rebellious and traitorous subjects . . . hiding their most detestable and devilish purposes under a false pretext of religion and conscience' (Elton, *Tudor Constitution,* p. 428).

[20] *To the Quenes Maiesties poore deceiued Subiectes of the North Country, drawen into rebellion by the Earles of Northumberland and Westmerland,* in *All such treatises* [n. 13 above], sigs. A3v, B1r. The figure of the rebels' deceitful 'colours' is used repeatedly in this pamphlet.

[21] *To The Quenes Maiesties poore deceiued Subiectes,* sig. C4v.

[22] *Two Books of Homilies,* ed. Griffiths, pp. 579, 581-2.

[23] *The Book of the Courtier,* trans. Sir Thomas Hoby (1561), Everyman edn (1966), p. 42. The nature of grace, and the means by which it is achieved, preserved, or lost is the subject for discussion in the central part of the book (pp. 42-184).

[24] *Institution of the Christian Religion,* trans. Thomas Norton (1582), pp. 96-8 (II, v. 4-5). For Augustine's *On Rebuke and Grace,* see *The Works of Aurelius Augustine,* ed. Marcus Dods, vol. 15, *The Anti-Pelagian Works,* vol. 3 (Edinburgh, 1876), pp. 68-117.

[25] M. M. Knappen, *Tudor Puritanism* (Chicago, 1939), p. 344. Cf. Patrick Collinson, *The Elizabethan Puritan Movement* (1967), pp. 41, 100-2, 346-7, *The Religion of Protestants* (Oxford, 1982), pp. 105-8, 111.

[26] *Actes and Monuments* (1583), p. 557.

[27] Wilhelm Baeske, *Oldcastle-Falstaff in der englischen Literatur bis zu Shakespeare,* Palaestra 50 (Berlin, 1905); Scoufos, *Shakespeare's Typological Satire,* pp. 44-69. In 'The Fortunes of Oldcastle', *Shakespeare Survey 38* (1985), pp. 85-100, Gary Taylor contends—wrongly, I believe—that because of the name-change forced on Shakespeare (by the Elizabethan Cobhams) when he came to write *Part 2,* Falstaff of the second part is a different character to the re-named Oldcastle of *Part I.* Taylor's reference in the course of his argument (p. 93) to 'the original name of Shakespeare's most famous comic *character*' (my emphasis) indicates how difficult in will be for this view to win acceptance. It has been rejected by the editor of the New Cambridge *Part 2* (below, n. 29) and strongly contested by Jonathan Goldberg: see his 'The Commodity of Names: "Falstaff" and "Oldcastle" in *1 Henry IV*', in *Reconfiguring the Renaissance: Essays in Critical Materialism,* ed. Jonathan Crewe (London and Toronto, 1992), pp. 76-88.

[28] J. A. Bryant Jr, 'Prince Hal and the Ephesians', *Sewanee Review,* 67 (1959): 204-19.

[29] Hall, *Chronicle,* p. 4; Holinshed, *Chronicles,* 3, 61. Shakespearian references in this article are to *Henry IV, Part I,* ed. David Bevington (Oxford, 1987) and *The Second Part of King Henry IV,* ed. Giorgio Melchiori (Cambridge, 1989); and (for other plays) to *The Complete Works,* ed. Stanley Wells and Gary Taylor (Oxford, 1988).

[30] William Cecil, Lord Burghley, *The Execution of Justice in England* (1583), ed. Robert Kingdon (Ithaca, N.Y., 1965), pp. 14, 16; George Whetstone, *The English Myrrour,* pp. 141-2.

[31] William Camden, *Remains Concerning Britain,* rept. from the 1674 edn (1870), pp. 169-70.

[32] *Shakespeare Recycled,* pp. 159-60, 167.

[33] *The Book of the Courtier,* pp. 85, 93-5.

[34] 'Recklessness' is Hoby's translation of Castiglione's *sprezzatura,* signifying the impression of naturalness and careless ease. 'Recklessnesse . . . is the true fountaine from which all grace springeth' (p. 48; cf. p. 99). Somewhat pertinent to Falstaff's decline is Castiglione's remark on the 'noysome sawsinesse' of strained and untimely humour: 'thinking to make men laugh, which for that it is spoken out of time will appear colde and without grace' (p. 93).

[35] Cf. Tillyard, *Shakespeare's History Plays,* pp. 278-80.

[36] Sidney Painter, *French Chivalry: Chivalric Ideas and Practices in Mediaeval France* (New York, 1940), pp. 28-30.

[37] Canfield, *World as Bond in English Literature from the Middle Ages to the Restoration* (Philadelphia, 1989).

[38] Dodds, *The Pilgrimage of Grace,* II, pp. 1-25.

[39] Even when rebuke and censure lead to excommunication, says Calvin, 'such seueritie becommeth the Church as is ioyned with the spirit of mildnes'; 'punish them that are fallen, mercifully & not to the extremitie of rigor . . . hoping better of them in time to come than we see in time present' (*Institutes,* trans. Norton, II.xii.8-9).

[40] *The Two Books of Homilies,* ed. Griffiths, p. 579 ('Against Disobedience and Wilful Rebellion').

[41] See G. W. Trompf, *The Idea of Historical Recurrence in Western Thought: From Antiquity to the Reformation* (Berkeley, California, 1979); Achsah Guibbory, *The Map of Time: Seventeenth-Century English Literature and Ideas of Pattern in History* (Urbana and Chicago, 1986).

[42] I have side-stepped in this article the possibility—persuasively argued by E. A. J. Honigmann in his *Shakespeare: the 'Lost Years'* (Manchester, 1985)—that Shakespeare was brought up as a Catholic and spent his 'lost years' before 1592 working as a schoolmaster and player for a wealthy Catholic landowner in Lancashire. If correct, the argument would certainly be relevant to my interpretation of *Henry IV.*

Source: "Pilgrims of Grace: *Henry IV* Historicized," in *Shakespeare Survey: An Annual Survey of Shakespeare Studies and Production,* edited by Stanley Wells, Vol. 48, 1995, pp. 69-84.

Shakespeare and the End of History

Gordon McMullan, *King's College, Cambridge*

I

The study of a writer's late work as often as not invokes two apparently incompatible models of history, linear and cyclical. The concept of the career (with one possible OED definition humorously quoted by Michael Millgate [in *Testamentary Acts: Browning, Tennyson, James, Hardy,* 1992] as 'a short gallop at full speed') seems to imply a conscious, if imperilled, linearity, within which 'late writing' can be seen either as evidence of decline or as an act of will, a looking forward beyond death, a bequeathing, a rejection of the finality of the final (2). At the same time, this bequeathing can be, and often is, manipulative, a deliberate rewriting of the past for the benefit of posterity. In this sense, the 'testamentary act' can be seen as cyclical rather than linear, a return to the 'early' in order to reshape it for those coming after. In other words, late writing is as much about revision, rethinking, and reshaping for the future as it is about finality.

The peculiar tensions and uncertainties that characterise Shakespeare and Fletcher's *Henry VIII* are, I would argue, the product of its status as just such a 'testamentary act.' [1] Coming as it does at the very end of Shakespeare's career, the play has been seen as a failure or at best a partial success, as evidence of artistic decay or actual illness. Even those who accept that the play is collaborative tend to read the partnership with Fletcher as a possible sign of weakness or lack of interest, begrudging Shakespeare his return to professional activity in the wake of *The Tempest.* Yet it is also possible to see the play's disjunctions as deliberate, and to argue that, in turning back to history thirteen years after *Henry V,* Shakespeare is knowingly returning with experimental motivation to a form associated with the early part of his career in a manner characteristic of the 'testamentary act.'

In his work on late nineteenth-century writers, Michael Millgate notes alternative etymologies for the term 'testament.' Two in particular hold resonances which are curiously apposite for analysis of *Henry VIII.* The word, he observes,

> has popularly taken on something of the aura of its now archaic meaning of 'covenant,' especially as found in scriptural accounts of the Last Supper (according to the Authorized version). Its use in legal contexts may also have tenuously attracted to it the sense of testifying or bearing witness, the word 'testator,' indeed, having historically been used as meaning both 'one who makes a will' and 'one who or that which testifies; a witness'. (Millgate 1992, 186)

The religious significance of 'testament' has immediate relevance for a play which looks back to the time of England's break with Rome and which examines the meaning of the birth of Elizabeth for English history. The play's religious (or perhaps better, ecclesiological) meditations, though, remain unsettling, exploring issues of conscience and motivation at the time of the Henrician schism whilst avoiding representing that schism directly. This evasion of direct representation is itself typical since it is the question of 'testimony,' of pinpointing and recounting the truth, which is repeatedly at stake in the play's uncertainties. The act of witnessing is demonstrated to be essential to the construction of history, and it is history as construct, rather than as event, which is emphasised throughout.

I would argue that an examination of the logic of truth in *Henry VIII* suggests that the play is best viewed as a complex and unsettling meditation on the 'end of history,' simultaneously promoting and denying the possibility of truth at a moment of cultural crisis within which the word 'Truth' held very specific sectarian resonances. In deploying the phrase 'the end of history,' I wish to invoke both eschatology and historiography: on the one hand, the sixteenth and seventeenth century apocalypticism (the End of History) that provided a radical symbolic base for Protestants in their political and aesthetic struggle with the counter-reformation, and on the other, the late twentieth century acknowledgment of the radical textuality of historical representation (the 'end of history'), a recognition whose roots lie in the development of the writing of history—and of 'history plays'—in the early modern period. *Henry VIII* is thus, I would argue, in several senses a 'testamentary act': it is a 'late work' which explores the possibilities and problems of testimony and truth in order to examine the contemporary status of an historical covenant.

II

The word 'truth' turns up no fewer than twenty-five times in *Henry VIII,* along with eighteen appearances of 'true' (nineteen, if you count the title of the play as reported by contemporary observers, *All is True*), six of 'truly,' and one of 'true-hearted.' The Prologue alone offers two mentions of 'truth' and one of 'true,' connecting the concept first of all with a nexus of faith, hope and expenditure ['Such as give / Their money out of hope they may believe, / May here find truth' (Prologue 7-9)], then with a sense of deliberate selectivity or, perhaps, election ['our chosen truth' (Prologue 18)], and finally with the relationship between artistic intention and representation ['the opinion that we bring / To make that only true we now intend' (Prologue 20-21)].[2] The play seems almost to tease its audience with 'truth,' hinting at contemporary relevance while retaining a certain ambivalence: 'Think ye see / The very persons of our noble story / As they were living' (Prologue 25-7), the Prologue demands, though it is not clear whether this is merely an exhortation to forget the time-lapse between the events on stage and the England of the present, or whether it is a broad hint that the characters have their counterparts in contemporary politics. A number of recent critics have opted for the latter, reading the emphasis on 'truth' as a straightforward assertion of the conscious topicality of the play.

The year of first performance of *Henry VIII* was an extraordinary one for English politics and in particular for the politics of English Protestantism. The death of Henry, Prince of Wales, in November 1612 shattered the millenarian hopes that militant Protestants had invested in him, with his passion for military display and his allegiance to the dream of a Protestant Europe. Henry's enthusiasm for the impending marriage of his sister Elizabeth to Frederick the Elector Palatine, the principal Continental Protestant ruler, was taken up with a fervour verging on desperation after his death, with the result that (ostensibly, at least) James and his militant Protestant subjects were in atypical harmony at the beginning of 1613. Henry's death had been a terrible blow, though, and the outpouring of grief for the dead prince was continually in danger of overshadowing the celebrations for the wedding, which was postponed to February. Like its sister collaboration *The Two Noble Kinsmen, Henry VIII* dwells on the mixed negative and positive emotions induced by the rapid succession of funeral and wedding.[3] The Prologue predicts a melancholy play: 'if you can be merry then, I'll say / A man may weep upon his wedding day' (Prologue 31-2). And the two wry choric Gentlemen, commenting on the speed of political and emotional change, capture (as they do throughout the play) the mood of the moment:

> *2 Gent.* At our last encounter
> The Duke of Buckingham came from his trial.
> *1 Gent.* 'Tis very true. But that time offer'd sorrow,
> This general joy.
>
> (IV. i. 4 7)

It is hard not to see a parallel between the emotions expressed on stage at moments such as this and the political situation at the time of composition. And it is not surprising that those critics who concentrate on the topicality of the play are also most closely concerned with its relationship to Protestantism.

R. A. Foakes, in his influential Arden edition, points out that a 'play on the downfall of Wolsey, the last great Catholic statesman of England, on the rise of Cranmer, and the birth of 'that now triumphant Saint our late Queene *Elizabeth'* would have been very appropriate at such a time' (Foakes 1957, xxxi).[4] He suggests that *Henry VIII* may well have been performed for the wedding itself, demonstrating a series of verbal parallels between contemporary descriptions of the occasion and the unusually detailed stage-directions in the Folio text, and emphasising the deliberate parallels drawn between Princess Elizabeth and her earlier namesake in sermons and pamphlets at the time. Frances Yates, in *Shakespeare's Last Plays,* [1975], examines the political effect that nostalgia for Elizabeth exercised in James's reign and notes the focus of Protestant hopes on Prince Henry. For her, *Henry VIII* is an unequivocally Protestant play which 'reflects the Foxian apocalyptic view of English history' (Yates 1975, 70).[5] More recently, William Baillie ["*Henry VIII*: A Jacobean History," *Shakespeare Studies* 12, 1979] has analysed a series of topical motifs in the play which would be of particular relevance to militant Protestants, including 'the expansion of the monarch's personal authority in relation to the law, the sudden fall of a court favorite, and a divorce' (that of the Earl of Essex and Frances Howard) 248). And Donna Hamilton [*Shakespeare and the Politics of Protestant England,* 1992] has extended these claims, the latter in particular, arguing that *Henry VIII* aims specifically to discredit the 'Howard faction at court—a faction dominated by Catholics—by associating their values and projects . . . with Wolsey and the values he represents' (164). The consensus of these views (whatever the flaws of some of the individual arguments) is that *Henry VIII* was involved to a substantial degree in the politics of Protestantism at the time of composition.

'Topical' critics tend to emphasise the very last scene of the play—and in particular Cranmer's prophecy over the child Elizabeth—to support the general principle that *Henry VIII* celebrates and projects a future for English Protestantism under James. Yet curiously, despite the rigorous contextualisation effected by these readings, there is a further broad context which has yet to be acknowledged in topical readings of *Henry VIII,* but which is crucial for any reading which aims to assess the play's claims about truth. For Cranmer's language in the last scene and the many other references to truth in the play belong to an established tradition of sectarian appropriation which has clear associations with the crisis of 1612-13. 'Let me speak sir,' Cranmer demands of the king, 'For heaven now bids me; and the words I utter, / Let none think flattery, for they'll find 'em truth' (V. iv. 14-16). The child Elizabeth, he claims, 'promises / Upon this land a thousand thousand blessings, / Which time shall bring to ripeness' (18-21). In this time of revelation, he tells us,

> Truth shall nurse her,
> Holy and heavenly thoughts still counsel her;
> She shall be lov'd and fear'd: her own shall bless her;
> Her foes shake like a field of beaten corn,
> And hang their heads with sorrow. . . .
> God shall be truly known, and those about her
> From her shall read the perfect ways of honour.
> (V. iv. 28-32, 36-7)

And he goes on to foreshadow James's reign after the 'maiden phoenix' (40) has been called by heaven 'from this cloud of darkness' (44):

> Peace, plenty, love, truth, terror,
> That were the servants to this chosen infant,
> Shall then be his, and like a vine grow to him;
> Wherever the bright sun of heaven shall shine,
> His honour and the greatness of his name
> Shall be, and make new nations.
> (V. iv. 47-52)

This repetition of 'truth,' particularly in the context of revelation, read in tandem with the emphasis on Elizabeth's election, invokes the resurgence in 1612-13 of a sectarian iconography which had developed around the concept in the course of the previous century.

The appropriation of 'Truth' for Protestant iconography has been traced as early as 1521, when John Knoblouch of Strasbourg, printer to a range of advocates of religious reform from Erasmus to Luther, had deliberately used as his printer's mark an image of Truth personified as a harassed woman emerging from a cave. The belligerently anti-Catholic use to which Knoblouch's image was in due course put in England is clear from the titlepage woodcut to William Marshall's *Goodly Prymer in Englyshe,* published shortly after the Henrician schism, in which medieval images of the Harrowing of Hell are reworked to depict 'the liberation of Christian Truth (as seen by Protestant reformers) from her captivity under the monster of Roman hypocrisy.' The introduction here of the figure of Time as Truth's rescuer forcefully appropriates the motto *Veritas Filia Temporis* ('Truth the daughter of Time'), which focusses on the temporal revelation of Truth in the framework of apocalypse. Truth was claimed by both sides in the course of the sixteenth century, acquired for Edward VI, reappropriated for Roman Catholicism by Queen Mary at her accession, and then revived by Elizabeth for Reformed religion. Shortly after she came to the throne, Elizabeth went on a procession through London and was greeted by a figure representing Time leading a white-clad Truth who handed to Elizabeth the *verbum veritatis,* the Bible in English. Keen to confirm her association with Truth, the queen allegedly stopped and cried out, 'And Time hath brought me hither!'

It is this specifically Elizabethan appropriation, best known from the figure of Una in Book One of Spenser's *Faerie Queene,* that is key to the resurgence of the iconography of Truth at the time of the first production of *Henry VIII.* The playwright Thomas Dekker had forcefully dramatised the associations of the Time-Truth image early in James's reign in *The Whore of Babylon* [1607], which Gasper calls 'the definitive militant Protestant play's ([The Dragon and the Dove: *The plays of Thomas Dekker,* 1990], 62). As the play opens, Truth awaits the death of Mary so that she and her father Time can help Elizabeth (in the shape of Titania, the Fairy Queen) defeat the malign forces of the Whore of Babylon. The printers of the 1607 Quarto incorporate marginal glosses to help the reader negotiate the significance of the allegory, but by 1612 such interpretative assistance would have been unnecessary. Two examples of entertainments heavily invested with the iconography of *Veritas Filia Temporis* will serve to demonstrate the status of Truth at the time of Prince Henry's death: the anonymous *Masque of Truth* and Thomas Middleton's *The Triumphs of Truth.*

Middleton's entertainment was the first of his series of six pageants written for mayors of London in the 1610s and 1620s. *The Triumphs of Truth* was, according to David Norbrook ["'The Masque of Truth': Court Entertainments and International Protestant politics in the Early Stuart Period," in *The Seventeenth Century* 1, 1968], the most expensive of all such pageants in the Renaissance: 'for no other state occasion in James's reign did the City summon up so much enthusiasm' (94). It echoes the typology of Spenser and Dekker, presenting a 'lengthy struggle . . . between a female figure representing Truth', who is 'poor, thin, and threadbare,' and 'idolatrous Error' (94) riding in a glorious chariot. The arrival of Time precipitates an apocalyptic scene '[a]t which a flame shoots from the head of Zeal, which fastening upon that chariot of Error, sets in on fire, and all the beasts that are joined to it,' so that, by the close of the pageant, with the help of a few fiery special effects, the 'proud seat of Error' lies 'glowing in embers,' and Truth is triumphant. Middleton here seeks ways to instigate a 'reformation of the masque,' to reform a genre associated by English Protestants with James's unmilitant tendencies: the pageant draws on the Protestant triumphalism revived by the wedding of Elizabeth and Frederick after the shock of the death of Prince Henry, and as such is designed to send a strong message from city to court at a time of sectarian crisis.

It seems that Henry's death had already caused an iconographic reversal in the midst of the wedding celebrations themselves, a dilution of the Protestant fervour Henry had championed in the aesthetic arena, since there is evidence of an overtly apocalyptic masque-project for the wedding—*The Masque of Truth*—which was promoted by Henry but aborted immediately after his death (Norbrook 1986). The cancellation of this masque is of particular note because, where Middleton's pageant serves as an address to the court from outside, *The Masque of Truth* seems to have been initiated and supported from within. In the event, it was replaced by a conservative masque commissioned from Thomas Campion, a client of the Howard family, who (as Hamilton's analysis shows) were decidedly at odds with militant Protestant aspirations. No original text of *The Masque of Truth* is extant, but we do have an outline and partial transcription in French, which makes its apocalyptic allegiances abundantly clear. As the masque begins (or would have begun), Atlas is tired of holding up the world, and has come to England to give up his 'burden to Aletheia (Truth), . . . represented on stage by a huge reclining statue reading a Bible and holding a globe in her left hand' (Norbrook 1986, 83). The Muses call on the various nations of Europe 'to pay tribute to King James for his patronage of the Truth' (Norbrook 1986, 83). Europe and her five daughters—France, Spain, Germany, Italy, and Greece—then bow to Truth and offer tribute to James. At the very end of the masque, 'the globe splits in two and disappears, leaving behind it a paradise guarded by an angel bearing a flaming sword' (Norbrook 1986, 83). Truth invites the various nations to repent and enter paradise, and the gates close behind them.

'Truth' can be seen in this context to be a highly loaded term, a Protestant absolute implying a militant foreign and domestic politics and with a heavy investment in the cult of Henry, Prince of Wales. As a result, the project offers a very different view of the marriage of Elizabeth and Frederick from that promoted by James. It presents the union not as the first of a series of Protestant and Catholic marriages designed to bring Europe together in peace but as a 'confessional alliance': James, as guardian of English Calvinist Protestantism, by uniting with the Protestant Palatinate, will ensure that the other nations bow to Reformed religion. It is clear enough why the masque was never performed: it would not exactly have been a diplomatic coup. But if Prince Henry did have a hand in its design, then its cancellation in the immediate wake of his death underlines the immensity of his loss to English militant Protestants.

III

This context for Truth would seem to confirm readings of *Henry VIII, or All is True* as a firmly Protestant, apocalyptic play. Cranmer's prophetic emphasis on Time and Truth evokes an iconographic tradition central to the representation of Protestant hopes and it provides a resounding resolution to the political dilemmas dramatised in the course of the play. Yet several critics (e.g. [Lee Bliss, "The Wheel of Fortune and the Maiden Phoenix in Shakespeare's *King Henry the Eighth," English Literary History* 42; 1975]) have rejected readings of *Henry VIII* which begin with Cranmer's speech and then look back at previous events in light of that speech. For these critics, there is a strangeness, an uncertainty, about *Henry VIII* which is not resolved by locating the play within a tradition of unquestioning apocalypticism: Cranmer's prophecy may come as a final revelation in the play and it may seem to echo the language of apocalypse, but (*pace* Frances Yates) *Henry VIII* can hardly be called an apocalyptic play. As Clifford Leech pointed out nearly forty years ago [in "The Structure of the Last Plays," *Shakespeare Survey* 11, 1958],

> Of all the last plays [*Henry VIII*] is the one that most clearly indicates the cyclic process. Nothing is finally decided here, the pattern of future events being foreshadowed as essentially a repetition of what is here presented.

Paul Dean similarly suggests [in "Dramatic mode and Historical Vision in *Henry VIII," Shakespeare Quarterly* 37, 1986] that in *Henry VIII* there is no `organic and cumulative movement toward a single concluding point' (178). And for Frank Cespedes ["`We Are One in Fortunes': The Sense of History in *Henry VIII*," in *English Literary Renaissance* 10, 1980], the play, despite its status as a `history play,'

> annuls eschatology and teleology. Against the optimistic principle of providential history invoked by Cranmer, the play emphasises the uncertainties of history in order to question the availability of an omniscient' perspective on historical events.
>
> (416-7)

This suggests a tension (a defining tension, even) within *Henry VIII* between linear and cyclical forces. It is as if the play sets the Protestant teleological vision against a mythic sense of time as a cycle; and the key issue provoked by this linear / cyclical struggle becomes, perhaps oddly, not structure but tone. After all, while apocalyptieism is typically humourless, the cyclical and the ridiculous are rarely far apart: the inevitable repeat and return of serious events makes them more ironic, less serious.

Juxtaposing two examples of testimony—a description within the play of an event prior to the action of the play and a contemporary eyewitness description of a performance of *Henry VIII*—might help to underline the nature of the play's uncertainties. The testimony from the play proper is Norfolk's description of the Field of the Cloth of Gold (I. i. 13-38); the account of the performance is the letter of Henry Wotton which is the principal evidence for the date of first production. Critics seem to agree that the opening scene is in many ways representative of the play as a whole 'in its insistence on the second-hand nature of our acquaintance with historical events' (Dean 1986, 182). It is, as Gasper puts it, 'an artful piece of time-release poetry . . . which appears to be a panegyric of the court, but which reveals more and more scepticism, disgust and ridicule the more often we read it' (Gasper 1993, 208). Initially, though, we take Norfolk's glorious description at face value. He describes himself to Buckingham as 'ever since a fresh admirer' (I. i. 3) of the spectacle put on by the kings of England and France as they met to conclude peace at the Field of the Cloth of Gold:

> To-day the French,
> All clinquant all in gold, like heathen gods
> Shone down the English; and to-morrow they
> Made Britain India: every man that stood
> Show'd like a mine. . . . Now this masque
> Was cried incomparable; and th'ensuing night
> Made it a fool and beggar. The two kings
> Equal in lustre, were now best, now worst,
> As presence did present them: him in eye
> Still him in praise, and being present both,
> 'Twas said they saw but one, and no discerner
> Durst wag his tongue in censure.
> (I. i. 18-22, 26-33)

Yet within a few dozen lines we gather that the whole thing was a waste of time, a temporary peace which 'not values / The cost that did conclude it' (I. i. 88-9). And we recognise, looking back at the speech, that it expressed a kind of relativism. The English and French are each viewed in light of the other, with no firm ground for judgement: 'The two kings / Equal in lustre, were now best, now worst, / As presence did present them' (I. i. 28-30). And we are brought up sharp with recognition of the emptiness of the grand gesture. As Lee Bliss observes, in arguably the best reading of *Henry VIII* to date, '[i]n the beginning all had seemed true to Norfolk and, in his report, to us; only in retrospect can we see how false, how truly unstable . . . that appearance was' (Bliss 1975, 3). And we rapidly come to the conclusion that

> 'admire' did not signify wonder in the sense of approbation, but rather an ironic sense of amazement at the disparity between a dream of transcendent and transforming harmony and the disconcertingly mutable political realities of an impoverished nobility and a broken treaty. (Bliss 1975, 3)

In Norfolk's testimony, then, judgement and therefore truth are seen to be at best contingent. The accolade goes to the champion of the moment, but the decision is arbitrary, the moment fleeting, and the triumph glitteringly hollow.

Sir Henry Wotton's letter describing one of the first performances of the play implies in a different way that grandeur is by definition short-lived. Pomp cannot withstand scrutiny, since familiarity breeds contempt:

> The King's players had a new play, called *All is true,* representing some principal pieces of the reign of Henry VIII, which was set forth with many extraordinary circumstances of pomp and majesty, even to the matting of the stage; the Knights of the Order, with their Georges and garters, the Guards with their embroidered coats, and the like: sufficient in truth within a while to make greatness very familiar, if not ridiculous. ([*The Life and Letters of Sir Henry Wotton,* 2 vols., 1907, edited by Logan Pearsall Smith], 32-3)

Wotton is clearly concerned that pomp without distance becomes revealing and therefore self-defeating. The truth (i.e. the irony) of the accuracy and care with which the play represents royal ceremony seems akin to Toby's efforts in *Tristram Shandy* to explain where he was wounded: the more precisely you show the details, the further from the truth you move and the more ridiculous you seem. In *Henry VIII* this movement is most clearly embodied in the conversations of the two choric Gentlemen, notably in Act IV, as they watch the Coronation procession pass by.

The detailed stage directions in the First Folio are echoed in the Gentlemen's comments:

> *2 Gent.* A royal train, believe me: these I know;
> Who's that that bears the sceptre?
> *1 Gent.* Marquess Dorset,
> And that the Earl of Surrey with the rod.
> (IV i. 37-39)

This detailing is apparently neutral: we simply absorb the display of power without question. Until, that is, the Gentlemen begin to move towards their more usual mode of irony. We have already seen the way in which conscience and lust have become intertwined in the king's manoeuvrings to gain Anne Bullen. The king repeatedly claims it is his conscience about his technically incestuous relationship with Katherine that is driving him to divorce. But the audience's suspicions of his motivations are compounded by his turn of phrase when he speaks of his regret at leaving 'so sweet a bedfellow,' crying 'But conscience, conscience; / O 'tis a tender place, and I must leave her' (II. ii. 142-3).[6] Shortly afterwards, in mocking Anne for disguising ambition within her ostensible modesty, the Old Lady speaks with heavy innuendo of 'the capacity' of Anne's 'soft cheveril conscience' to receive gifts, if she 'might please to stretch it' (II. iii. 31-3). These moments of irony resurface at Anne's coronation. The Second Gentleman seems wholly caught up in the ceremony, but his rhapsody concludes with a suggestive, and politically dangerous, bathos:

> Our king has all the Indies in his arms
> And more, and richer, when he strains that lady;
> I cannot blame his conscience
> (IV. i. 45-7)

His friend ignores this aside, but returns to the topic himself a few lines later. 'These are stars indeed—' says the Second Gentleman, admiring the courtly women, to which the First Gentleman adds, 'And sometimes falling ones,' a remark risqué enough (laying bare, as it does, Anne's perceived route to power) to produce a 'No more of that' from his interlocutor. Detail, then, both of the king's motivations and of the practical staging of royal display, leads directly to ridicule, greatness made thoroughly overfamiliar.

The issue of testimony thus foregrounds the uncertainties of the play. There is no firm basis for the interpretation of events: witnessing and irony become blood-brothers. And it is not just interpretation but events themselves which seem ever more problematic as the play goes on. For Pièrre Sahel [in "The Strangeness of a Dramatic Style: Rumour in *Henry VIII*," *Shakespeare Survey* 38, 1985],

> [m]ost of the events of *Henry VIII* are echoed—more or less unfaithfully—within the play itself. They are not dramatized but reported after having passed through distorting filters. Characters present incidents and occurrences—or, often, their own versions of incidents and occurrences. (145)

The effect of this filtering of events is to sustain a sense of radical uncertainty throughout the play. For Sahel, it is rumour which sets the tone: rumour sometimes as a political tool, sometimes simply as the 'buzzing' (II. i. 148) which seems constantly to be going on in the background of each scene. Despite fears of suppression ['no discerner / Durst wag his tongue in censure' (I. i. 32-3)], rumour is never silenced. The absolute Truth upon which the Prologue seemed to stand and upon which Cranmer's prophecy will depend is rapidly submerged in report and opinion.

The relationship between rumour and truth is overtly questioned at the beginning of Act II in another of the Gentlemen's conversations. '[D]id you not,' asks the Second Gentleman, 'of late days hear / A buzzing of a separation / Between the king and Katherine?' 'Yes,' replies his friend,

> but it held not
> For when the king once heard it, out of anger
> He sent command to the lord mayor straight
> To stop the rumour, and allay those tongues
> That durst disperse it.

To which the Second Gentleman immediately retorts:

> But that slander, sir,
> Is found a truth now; for it grows again
> Fresher than e'er it was, and held for certain
> The king will venture at it.
> (II. i. 147-156)

That clause 'held for certain' neatly captures the tone: certainty occupies the same space as opinion. Truth, in this context, is equated with slander: the two seem interchangeable, dependent simply upon the succession of events and the way things are viewed from moment to moment. Communication thus becomes a process which simultaneously transmits and degrades truth, an organic and inescapable infection: 'it grows again / Fresher than e'er it was.' The build-up to this exchange of rumour is both revealing and complex. The Second Gentleman drops a broad hint of occult knowledge: 'yet I can give you inkling / Of an ensuing evil, if it fall, / Greater than this' (II. i. 140-2). His friend's eager, staccato reply is a masterpiece of contradiction, desiring while denying the desire to know the truth (or, rather, the rumour). It also emphasises faith, not just as trustworthiness but as belief: 'Good angels keep it from us: / What may it be? you do not doubt my faith sir?' To which the Second Gentleman responds, teasingly, 'This secret is so weighty, 'twill require / A strong faith to conceal it.' 'Let me have it,' cries the First Gentleman, 'I do not talk much,' a comment generally guaranteed to raise a laugh in performance, since the only capacity in which we have seen the speaker is as a gossip and rumour-monger.

Faith and truth are thus contiguous, and they are equally abused in the process of communication. In fact, the play seems to move towards a proleptic acknowledgement of current definitions of testimony. For Shoshana Felman and Dori Laub [*Testimony: Crises of Witnessing in Literature, Psychoanalysis, and History,* 1992], testimony is

> not simply (as we commonly perceive it) the observing, the recording, the remembering of an event, but an utterly unique and irreplaceable topographical *position* with respect to an occurrence.
> (206)

Individual testimony becomes not one person's perspective on a single coherent truth of which the witness sees only one facet, but rather 'the uniqueness of the *performance of a story* which is constituted by the fact that, like the oath, it cannot be carried out by anybody else' (Felman and Laub 1992, 206). Certainly, *Henry VIII* seems to dwell on the radical and unbridgeable difference between the perspectives different witnesses have on the same event, to the extent that the event itself cannot clearly be said to have happened. Far from sustaining a sense of Truth as a Protestant absolute, the play makes truth an impossibility. Everyone, from Buckingham and his surveyor to Wolsey and Cranmer, claims a monopoly of truth. They cannot all be right. This is the fundamental problem for any attempt to locate the play's obsession with truth in relation to apocalyptic, militant Protestantism, and it puts intolerable pressure on the last scene. The key question is whether this equivocal mood can be fully transformed by Cranmer's prophecy, whether apocalyptic Truth can assert herself above the arbitrariness of the rumour-ridden political world, and even whether the prophecy is as resolutely apocalyptic as has been claimed.

IV

There is little doubt that, for all the problems of truth and testimony the audience have witnessed by the time they arrive at Elizabeth's christening, Cranmer's prophecy nonetheless has a powerful and direct emotive charge. Foakes is clearly right in arguing that the Jacobean audience would have been attuned to two Elizabeths and two royal ceremonies. The prophecy is thus directed at a series of futures, some already completed by 1613, others still projected. And it depends heavily upon the audience's hindsight for its success. The completed predictions serve to validate those as yet unfulfilled, offering a clear linear dynamic to the eschatological mindset, but it is important both to recognise the play's rejection of direct historical agency and to ponder the expected response to the unproven predictions, in particular the Jacobean audience's reading of the scene's references to and predictions for King James. And I would argue that the play demands the deployment of hindsight as a means to examine the contemporary status of the Reformation in England.

Part of the curiosity of Cranmer's speech is that it seems to ascribe to James imperial aspirations which were associated with militant Protestantism but which were at best marginal to the king's own preferred policies. Apocalypse and Empire have a traditional intimacy: here it is the colonisation of America, promoted by Protestants but viewed with suspicion by the king, which is emphasised in 'predicting' James's achievements ['Wherever the bright sun of heaven shall shine, / His honour and the greatness of his name / Shall be, and make new nations' (V. iv. 50-52)].[7] Moreover, the 'phoenix' metaphor by which Cranmer fudges James's relationship to Elizabeth is shared with that most militant of Protestant plays, Dekker's *Whore of Babylon:*

> [O]ut of her ashes may
> A second Phoenix rise, of larger wing,
> Of stronger talent, of more dreadfull beake,
> Who swooping through the ayre, may with his beating
> So well commaund the winds, that all those trees
> Where sit birds of our hatching (now fled thither)
> Will tremble, . . . yea and perhaps his talent
> May be so bonie and so large of gripe,
> That it may shake all Babilon.
> (Dekker 1607, F2^v

James, however, had little intention of shaking 'all Babilon' his interest was in establishing Continent-wide peace by way of dynastic marriage and in confirming his personal appropriation of the seventh beatitude, *Beati Pacifici.* And of course juxtaposing Cranmer's prophecy with the passage from Dekker simply serves to underline the relative bloodlessness of Cranmer's 'apocalyptic' vision. More to the point, as Julia Gasper observes, it is noticeable that though Cranmer makes several biblical allusions in the course of his prophecy, he refers each time to Old Testament prophets and resolutely avoids the obvious text for apocalyptic visions, the Book of Revelation (Gasper 1990, 97). The relationship between Cranmer's prophecy and Protestant apocalypticism thus begins to seem very uncomfortable, particularly when seen in the particular 1612-13 context. And I would argue that it becomes still more problematic with the recognition that the christening scene invokes powerful visual as well as verbal images, drawing on two separate iconographic traditions, each of which presents Henry VIII in a less than flattering light. The first is the tradition of *Veritas Filia Temporis* which we have already examined as a broad context for the play's obsession with Truth; the second is the iconography of David and Bathsheba.

It is important to remember that, in the christening scene, it is Archbishop Cranmer, not King Henry, who occupies centre stage along with the infant Elizabeth. He stands over the child to make his climactic prophecy, and at this key moment of celebration, the scene, I would argue, evokes in a very specific way the iconography of *Veritas Filia Temporis.* The effect of this evocation is to exclude the king from the sacramental scene: at the precise moment in which Elizabeth inherits the mantle of English Protestantism, she is presented to the audience as the spiritual, if not the natural, daughter of Cranmer rather than of Henry. As we have already noted, the language of the prophecy encourages us to see the future Queen Elizabeth as the incarnation of Protestant Truth ['Which time shall bring to ripeness' (V. iv. 20)], and if, as Judith Doolin Spikes has suggested [in "The Jacobean History Play and the Myth of the Elect Nation," *Renaissance Drama* 8, 1977], the figure of Time in *The Whore of Babylon* informs the portrayal of Cranmer here in *Henry VIII,* then this is confirmed by the iconography 140). With Henry to one side, amazed by the archbishop's words, the audience sees the familiar vignette: Time stands over Truth and rapturously predicts the End of History. The moment serves abruptly to decentre the king, removing him from full paternity and leaving the circumstances of Elizabeth's birth (and consequently her legitimacy) as shrouded as her death in Cranmer's prophecy.

I would thus argue that an iconographic interpretation of this moment, taken together with the ambivalence of the portrayal of the king throughout, rejects the Erastian readings sometimes made of the play, rigorously questioning Henry's spiritual authority and thus by implication (extrapolating from the equation of Queen Elizabeth and Princess Elizabeth noted by Foakes) that of King James. Moreover, a second, more covert layer of iconographic potential at the moment of Elizabeth's christening can be seen to exacerbate the discomfort of this moment for James. The reference to 'Saba' (the Queen of Sheba) in Cranmer's prophecy obliquely associates the young Elizabeth with David's son Solomon, implying her adoption of Solomon's various attributes (notably that of wisdom). But seen in conjunction with the sidelining of King Henry and the absence of Anne Bullen at this key moment of the play, it also offers an additional, politically unsettling possibility.

The story of David's desire for and adultery with Bathsheba, his arrangement for the death in battle of her husband Uriah, and his subsequent repentance following denunciation by Nathan the prophet was one of the best-known of Old Testament stories, and an iconographic tradition had grown up which associated David's 'Penitential Psalms' with the Bathsheba story, particularly the initial image of David watching Bathsheba bathing.[8] Reformation readings of 2 Samuel 11-12 tended to emphasise the story as an example of the inevitability of sin and the necessity of repentance, partly in reaction to a Roman Catholic tradition of fairly breathtaking licence in which David's desire for Bathsheba was interpreted as Christ's desire for his Church, Uriah became the 'Prince of this World,' and David's adultery was conveniently reworked as his rescue of the Church from the Devil. Certainly, the Penitential Psalms, like the image of *Veritas Filia Temporis,* were well-known as a Reformation battleground and were associated with the development of Protestant doctrine. The story had, though, been given a dark political significance during the reign of Henry VIII by Sir Thomas Wyatt, who produced verse-translations of the Penitential Psalms, was rumoured to have had an affair with Anne Boleyn before the king met her, and was imprisoned by the king at the time of her execution.[9] According to Rivkah Zim, Wyatt 'may have seen King David—the royal lover guilty of manslaughter, if not murder, in the pursuit of illicit passion—as representing Henry VIII' (Zim 1987, 73-4; also [Stephen Greenblatt, *Renaissance Self-Fashioning: From more to Shakespeare,* 1980], 115, 146-7). It would be hard to deny the dangerous resonances the story held for King Henry, desperately awaiting the birth of a son. David's penitence is such that God lets him live, but his punishment is the death of his first child by Bathsheba. The conception and birth of Solomon in the wake of this marks the return of God's favour, and is confirmed by an alternative name for the child, Jedidiah, 'beloved of God,' given him through Nathan the prophet.

It is thus possible to read the last scene of *Henry VIII* through an alternative iconographic tradition which associates the birth of Elizabeth and her subsequent life and reign with the return of God's favour to his chosen nation in the wake of sinful and adulterous behaviour on the part of the king. Cranmer's centrality as the counterpart of Nathan the prophet has the effect once more of marginalising King Henry in his uncomfortable equivalence to the easily-tempted David, God's anointed, but not always entirely reliable, king. And this might well have uneasy resonances for 1612-13, particularly if the audience were again to see in the character of Henry VIII a shadowing of King James. In view of Dennis Kay's assertion [in *Melodious Tears: The English Funeral Elegy from Spenser to Milton,* 1990] that the death of Henry, Prince of Wales, was widely represented, in a kind of nationwide act of penitence, as 'divine retribution for the nation's sin' (134), an awkward, and presumably highly dangerous, topical interpretation is on offer. The iconographic retreat from Erastianism we have already registered is thus highly telling. The English Reformation is represented at the climactic moment of the play both as something which has happened and as something which is still to happen, even in the reign of James I.

The last scene thus exemplifies the inherent contradictions of the play. In a practical exposition of the Derridean idea that truth is produced at the moment of the dissolution of truth, it is possible to see that the iconographic triumph of Protestant propaganda is achieved at a moment which highlights the contemporary uncertainties of the claim. The scene is a looking-forward to the future which is also a return to the past, mythologising the transition from Elizabeth to James by way of the (unhistorically direct) transition from Henry to Elizabeth, and at the same time strongly hinting at the ambiguous status of the militant Protestant apocalyptic project under James. *Henry VIII* can thus be seen as a meditation on the state of the English Reformation in 1612-13 which sets linear and cyclical models of history against each other in order to project a future for English Protestantism which is at the same time a return to the past.

V

There is one further level on which *Henry VIII* can be seen as a testamentary act, a very specific act of 'will.' Marking and, I would argue, embracing the transition from Shakespeare to Fletcher (the scene of Cranmer's prophecy is, after all, Fletcher's, not Shakespeare's), *Henry VIII* returns to Elizabeth and to the history play both to mark the genre's roots in Shakespeare's early work and to project its future in Fletcher's post-Shakespearean plays. For Shakespeare to give up this moment to Fletcher (whose usual pattern of collaborative work was to write the central acts of a play and leave the beginnings and endings to his partner) can be read not as a sign of weariness or illness but as a significant gesture, an apparent selflessness which is in fact a projection of self. It is a gesture which looks forward to an ideal future, to a new reign which will be both different and the same, even as it recognises that successors rarely live up to their predecessors' hopes. In other words, Shakespeare's *not* writing the scene of Cranmer's prophecy can in itself be regarded as a testamentary act, disabling all readings of the play which view the scene as a culmination, a conclusion. It is no more final than any of the other episodes that have made up the play. To project a future, it returns to the past, a progression at once linear and cyclical, sustaining the hegemony both of Shakespeare and of the King's company, succession assured. As a memorial to the ending of epochs, *Henry VIII* can thus be seen as both a testamentary act and a self-consuming artifact.

Notes

[1] The evidence for *Henry VIII* as a joint composition by Shakespeare and Fletcher seems to me to be conclusive. See, in particular [Cyrus Hoy, "The shares of Fletcher and his collaborators in the Beaumont and Fletcher canon, VII," in *Studies in Bibliography* 15, 1962]. For a useful recent contribution to the debate, see [Jonathan Hope; *The Authorship of Shakespeare's plays: A socio-linguistic study,* 1994].

[2] All references to *Henry VIII* are to [*King Henry VIII,* edited by R. A. Foakes, 1957] and will be given parenthetically in the text.

[3] *The Two Noble Kinsmen* arguably echoes the prevailing emotions of 1613 by way of its unique tragicomic conclusion (a wedding and a funeral, simultaneously), voiced most succinctly by Palamon: 'That we should things desire which do cost us / The loss of our desire! That naught could buy / Dear love but loss of dear love.' See [*The Two Noble Kinsmen,* edited by Eugene Waith, 1989], V. iv. 110-112.

[4] Julia Gasper, though, disagrees, pointing out [in "The Reformation plays on the public stage," *Theatre and Government under the Early Stuarts,* eds. J. R. Mulryne and Margaret Shewring, 1993] that to perform a play `largely concerned with divorce . . . at a royal wedding would surely have been an offence against taste and decorum' (207).

[5] [Glynne Wickham, in "The Dramatic Structure of Shakespeare's *King Henry the Eighth*: An Essay in Rehabilitation," *British Academy Shakespeare Lectures, 1980-89,* 1993], however, finds a very different aim, arguing that the play was designed to rehabilitate Katherine of Aragon, presumably to pave the way for Catholic matches in the future.

[6] As Judith Anderson and others have pointed out, the phrase 'tender place' is at best ambivalent at this moment. See [Judith H. Anderson, *Biographical Truth: The Representation of Historical Persons in Tudor-Stuart Writing,* 1984], 128-9; also [Peter L. Rudnytsky; "*Henry VIII* and the Deconstruction of History," in *Shakespeare Survey* 43, 1991], 51.

[7] On Apocalypse and Empire, see [Frank Kermode, *The Sense of an Ending,* 1967], 10ff.

[8] The 'penitential psalms' are a traditional grouping of Psalms 6, 32, 38, 51, 102, 130 and 143. On the iconography, see [Inga-Stina Ewbank, "The House of David in Renaissance Drama: A Comparative Study," *Renaissance Drama* 8, 1965, pp. 3-10; Rivkah Zim, *English Metrical Psalms: Poetry as Praise and Prayer, 1535-1601,* 1987, pp. 70-74; M. B. Parkes, *The Medieval Manuscripts of Keble College, Oxford,* 1979, p. 175, plate 88; John Fisher, *Treatyse Concernynge the Fruytfull Saynges of Davyd the Kynge and Prophete in the seven Penytencyall Psalmes,* 1509, aa^{2}r]. I am grateful to Professor Richard Proudfoot for suggesting the relevance of the David and Bathsheba story for the study of *Henry VIII.*

[9] For the poetry of Thomas Wyatt, see [Sir Thomas Wyatt, *Collected Poems,* 1978, edited by R. A. Rebholz].

Source: "Shakespeare and the End of History," in *Essays and Studies,* edited by Laurel Brake, n.s., Vol. 48, 1995, pp. 16-37.

Edward III in *Henry V*

E. Pearlman, ***University of Colorado at Denver***

Shakespeare knew the play called *The Raigne of King Edward the Third* as well as he knew Holinshed's *Chronicle* or North's Plutarch or Ovid's *Metamorphoses*. He might have become intimate with *Edward III* in any of a number of ways, for it was "sundrie times plaied about the Citie of London,"[1] during the early 1590s, and it is hard to imagine that Shakespeare, himself a practitioner of the art of chronicle history, would not have taken the trouble to look in at one of its various performances. Shakespeare might also have laid down his sixpence for a copy of *Edward III,* for the play was readily available, having been published by Cuthbert Burby in 1596 and once again in 1599. There is also the possibility that Shakespeare the actor might have undertaken a role or two as a member of the Earl of Pembroke's Men[2]—the company often thought to have the best claim to *Edward III.* And finally, if an emerging scholarly consensus is to be credited, Shakespeare may very well have written the play in part or even in its entirety[3]. It is not beyond possibility that he would have been familiar with *Edward III* in every conceivable way—as writer, actor, reader, and spectator. But by whatever means Shakespeare came to know the play, he knew it exceedingly well. It was a work that left as profound a mark on his work as any piece of contemporary writing, even including the productions of Kyd and Marlowe. And of all Shakespeare's works, the most surely touched was *Henry V.*

There are sundry points of contact between *Edward III* and Shakespeare, none more suggestive than the case of the "scarlet ornaments." King Edward III, replicating the light of a hundred heroes of romance, has fallen desperately in love with the chaste, married, and moral Countess of Salisbury. Edward's private secretary Lodowick has scrutinized king and countess and has observed that in their embarrassment they share an unusual complexional complementarity—a color morphing that causes the one to grow red as the other grows white. Lodowick confides to the audience that

> . . . when shee blusht, euen then did he looke pale,
> As if her cheekes by some inchaunted power
> Attracted had the cherie blood from his;
> Anone with reuerent feare, when she grew pale,
> His cheeke put on their scarlet ornaments. . . .
> (*sig.* B3v-B4; 341-345)

If Shakespeare did not compose *Edward III,* he must have been taken aback to hear these lines spoken by one of the actors. Would he not have remembered his own Sonnet 142 ("Loue is my sinne, and thy deare vertue hate")[4] where "the speaker" complains that the lips of his faithless mistress have "prophan'd their scarlet ornaments" (6)? Did he know or guess that the author of *Edward III* was one of the private friends among whom his sugared sonnets had circulated? There is yet another possibility: that Shakespeare did not write Sonnet 142 until much later (in the first years of the following century, quite likely) and that *Edward III* precedes the sonnet. Did Shakespeare then take note of the striking phrase and store it away for future use? Or (to shift the ground and give credence to the surmise that Shakespeare was in fact the author of *Edward III*) was it then laziness or self-congratulation (or simply forgetfulness) that caused him to re-use the phrase "scarlet ornaments" in another and very different context?

If such inquiries as these can be triggered by a single repeated phrase, they are provoked all the more by a second encroachment a few scenes further on in *Edward III.* The lustful king is still in hot pursuit of his countess. Now the countess's father, the Earl of Warwick, encouraging his daughter (who in truth needs no encouragement) to slap the hand of the lascivious Edward, reminds her that "[a]n honorable graue is more esteemd / Then the polluted closet of a king" (*sig.* D2r; 767-68). Warwick goes on to launch a fusillade of proverbs and sentences that are intended to fortify his daughter's resolve. The sins of royalty are more heinous than those of commoners, he asserts, because

> That poyson shewes worst in a golden cup;
> Darke night seemes darker by the lightning flash;
> Lillies that fester, smel far worse than weeds;
> And euery glory that inclynes to sin
> The shame is treble by the opposite.
> (*sig* D2r; 784-88)

To stumble upon the radiant line from Sonnet 94 in a dark corner of dramatic history is startling today and must have been even more electric—at least to those in the know—in its own time. Was the line stolen by a rival playwright or was it simply repeated by Shakespeare, and why was it so? Scholars since Steevens in 1780[5] have labored to establish whether the lilies migrated from sonnet to play or from play to sonnet, yet nothing more than the obvious can be confidently asserted: the author of Sonnet 94 knew or was known by, or plagiarized or was plagiarized by, or was identical to the author of the *Edward III.*

The scarlet ornaments and the festering lilies proclaim a suggestive but yet only anecdotal entwining of the play and the sonnet sequence. Far more essential is the bond between *Edward III* and *The Life of Henry the Fift*. For it is demonstrable that while in the roll call of the English kings, Edward is but the great-grandfather of Henry, in the arena of literature, *Edward III* can legitimately claim to have directly sired *Henry V*. There are so many intrinsic similarities between the careers of Edward and Henry, that, considering that Shakespeare knew *Edward III* so exceedingly well, he had to decide very early in the making of his new play whether he was going to ignore, or reproduce, or pillage the previous one.

On the subject of Shakespeare's knowledge of *Edward III* there is an interesting story to be retold: in the second scene of Shakespeare's *Henry V,* the English contemplate an invasion of France. There is a brief debate about the problem of fighting a two-front war: can Henry claim his birthright in France and at the same time protect his Scottish flank? Canterbury, the aggressive archbishop, argues that Scotland is a paper tiger, and as evidence he adduces a moment in the glorious past when England

> . . . hath her selfe not onely well defended,
> But taken and impounded as a Stray,
> The King of Scots: whom shee did send to
> France,
> To fill King *Edwards* fame with prisoner
> Kings.
>
> (1.2.159-162; TLN 305-309)[6]

The capture of the Scottish king appears so unemphatically and is so hemmed in—on the one side by the vast excursus on Salic law and on the other by the elegant but distracting fable of the bees' commonwealth—that it slips by without fixing the attention of either audience or reader. Nevertheless, these few lines testify to the strong tie between the two history plays, for David II's abduction, recounted in chapter cxxxix of Froissart's *Chronicles,* is curiously transformed in *Henry V*. It is historically true that "a squyer called John Coplande" (87)[7] captured David II, the king of the Scots, and that Edward's Queen Phillipa was repulsed when she demanded that the prisoner be surrendered to her; it is true also that an angry Edward summoned Copland to Calais. But in defiance of Canterbury's testimony, it is distinctly untrue that Copland obeyed his monarch and carried the captive king to France. Froissart plainly states that when ordered by Edward to his encampment at Calais, John Copland "dyd putte his prisoner in save kepynge in a stronge castell" (87) (a fact with which Holinshed, Shakespeare's source for *Henry V,* concurs).[8] On what authority, then, does Canterbury make the claim that the King of Scots, on the evidence of the chroniclers languishing at Newcastle, was conveyed to France for the purpose of glorifying Edward's name? Solely, it appears, on the testimony of the play of *Edward III.* When Froissart was translated into chronicle history, the story of the hijacking came to be altered. The situation in *Edward III* was this: Crecy has been fought and won and the king has withdrawn to Calais. Derby heralds an important entrance: "Copland, my lord, and David, king of Scots" (*sig.* 14v; 2317). Copland then embroiders the historical record:

> I tooke the king my self in single fight. . . .
> And Copland straight vpon your highnes
> charge
> Is come to Fraunce, and with a lowly minde
> Doth vale the bonnet of his victory:
> Receiue, dread Lorde, the custome of my
> fraught. . . .
>
> (*sig.* J4v; 2325; 2328-31)

The case is therefore clear: it was not the historical but the player king David who crossed the channel and came to Calais. It is not difficult to imagine what the author of *Edward III* had in mind when he changed the facts: in the early 1590s, there could be no more certain index of the pervasive influence of Marlowe's *Tamburlaine* than the gratuitous humbling of a captive king. When he composed Canterbury's version of events, Shakespeare did not return to the story of David of Scotland as it appeared in Froissart or in Holinshed but instead chose to remind his audience of a triumph of English nationalism as it had already been enacted in a number of theatrical venues about the city of London. Favoring theatrical fiction over historical fact, Shakespeare extracted the humiliation of David II from *Edward III* and slipped it easily and unceremoniously into the later play. The upshot: an historical event dating from the aftermath of Crecy was reported by Froissart, nurtured by Holinshed, altered under the sway of Marlovian drama for enactment on the public stage, and then gathered by Shakespeare to argue in support of an imaginary invasion of France that, dramatized, read, and filmed, would eventually become the centerpiece of a real and fervent English nationalism. Canterbury's tucked-in tale of the impounded Scottish king presents an unusually instructive pedigree. It also confirms, if confirmation is required, that Shakespeare had *Edward III* very much on his mind when he composed these first scenes of *Henry V*. The link between the two plays is at once so obscure and so exact that it must be presumed that Shakespeare had recently reviewed the earlier history—either by attending a performance, or by glancing at his copy of the quarto. It is difficult to imagine that Shakespeare's decision to repeat the account of David II in *Edward III* was taken thoughtlessly; in 1599, any reference, howsoever marginal, to the disgracing of a Scottish king would surely have been subjected to the most intense scrutiny for whatever it might imply about Scotland, or Scottish kings, or monarchical succession.[9]

When Shakespeare took up his pen to compose *Henry V,* he had to make a decision about the challenge posed by a play with which he had such complex relations. *Edward III* would always be there, lurking on his shelf or in his memory or in the collective consciousness of his audiences. For the plain fact is that *Edward III* covers ground very similar to the territory Shakespeare would have to traverse in the new play that he had bound himself (in the epilogue to *2 Henry IV*) to deliver to his company and to his audience. Shakespeare had to confront the intransigent fact that there were undeniable and unaviodable parallels between the careers of Edward III and Henry V and that he would either have to dodge or assimilate the old play when he constructed the new; there was no burying the likenesses. *Edward III* begins when the reigning king of England strides on stage to inquire whether he is morally and legally the heir to the French throne and whether he may invade France to regain his crown. He asks a counsellor if Salic law bars him from an inheritance that he claims through his mother. French history and law are ceremoniously reviewed:

> When thus the lynage of Bew was out,
> The French obscurd your mothers Priuiledge,
> And though she were the next of blood,
> proclaymed
> John of the house of Valoys now their king:
> The reason, was, they say the Realme of
> Fraunce,
> Repleat with Princes of great parentage,
> Ought not admit a gouernor to rule,
> Except he be discended of the male.
> And that's the speciall ground of their
> contempt,
> Wherewith they study to exclude your grace.
> (*sig.* A3r; 18-27)

Fortunately, Edward's legal consultant comes to exactly the conclusion that represents the king's deepest wishes: "But they shall finde that forged ground of theirs/ To be but dusty heapes of brittile sand" (28-29). Inspired by so favorable an analysis, the king decides to go to war:

> Hot courage is engendred in my brest,
> Which heretofore was rakt in ignorance,
> But nowe doth mount with golden winges of
> fame,
> And will approue faire Issabells discent. . . .
> (*sig.* A3v; 45-48)

The French monarch sends a messenger to demand that the English king pay him "lowly homage" (60) and "[r]epaire to France within these forty daies" (62). The king responds that he will come to France not as a dependent, but "like a conquerer to make him bowe" (*sig.* A4r; 57), and that, as for the French king, "[w]here he sets his foote he ought to knele" (81).

It is obvious that the plays cover such similar ground that a summary of the beginning of *Edward III* serves as a summary of *Henry V* as well. But the congruence of the two histories does not lie in the opening scenes alone, but in their coincident design: an energetic English king with a history of irresponsible behavior lays claim to the monarchy of France; he raises an army of patriots, secures his Scottish frontier, fights a series of battles against absurdly overconfident French commanders who continually taunt him with cowardice, and at last, against titanic odds, succeeds in bringing the enemy to heel. At both Crecy in the one play and Agincourt in the other, divine intervention produces miraculous victories. And even at the climax of *Henry V,* when the victorious Harry announces his intention to "call . . . this the field of *Agincourt, / Fought on the day of Crispin Crispianus*" (4.7.89-81; 2619-20), the Welshman Fluellen is there to remind the king (and the Globe audience) of Henry's great antecedent and model:

> Your Grandfather of famous memory (an't please your Maiesty, and your great Vncle *Edward* the Placke Prince of Wales, as I haue read in the Chronicles, fought a most praue pattle here in France.
> (82-82; TLN 2622-25)

The two plays are so similarly grounded that there are occasions when passages echo each other eerily. A good example occurs at Crecy. In *Edward III*:

> *Prince.* Heere is a note my gratious Lord of
> those
> That in this conflict of our foes were slaine;
> Eleuen Princes of esteeme, Foure score
> Barons,
> A hundred and twenty knights, and thirty
> thousand
> Common souldiers; and our men a thousand.
> [*King Edward*]. Our God be praised.
> (*sig.* G2r-G2v; 1606-10)

The comparable event at Agincourt is more familiar:

> *King.* This Note doth tell me of ten
> thousand French
> That in the field lye slaine: of Princes in this
> number,
> And Nobles bearing Banners, there lye dead
> One hundred twentie six: added to these,
> Of Knights, Esquires, and gallant Gentlemen,
> Eight thousand and foure hundred. . . .
> Where is the number of our English dead?

Edward the Duke of Yorke, the Earle of Suffolke,
Sir *Richard Ketly, Dauy Gam* Esquire;
None else of name: and of all other men,
But fiue and twentie.
O God, thy Arme was heere.
(4.8.78-83, 100-104; TLN 2799-2804, 2821-26)

If the account in *Henry V* did not virtually paraphrase Holinshed, it would be tempting to speculate that Shakespeare was leaning directly on *Edward III*—nor is it beyond credibility that even as he turned Holinshed's prose into verse, he had the precedent of Crecy in mind. There are, after all, many instances where the correspondence between an accepted source and one of Shakespeare's borrowings is far slighter than kinship between the note of the Crecy dead and the note of the Agincourt dead. And even though Shakespeare was fully engaged with Holinshed, how could he not have been conscious (especially given his keen and intimate knowledge of the predecessor play) of the spirit of *Edward III* flitting about his page?

To deal with the challenge posed by *Edward III,* Shakespeare seems to have adopted a bifold strategy. Sometimes he tried to overwhelm and obliterate the memory of *Edward III* with far fuller treatments of matters that appear in both plays, but he also incorporated the earlier play on those occasions when it was advantageous to do so. An instance of the first strategy: in the case of Salic law, Shakespeare must have realized that the particulars would be known to at least some members of his audience by virtue of their familiarity with *Edward III.* He might have elected to give Salic law short shrift, but did not, and instead, took the exact opposite tack. While the author of *Edward III* allots fifty lines to the question of legitimate succession, in *Henry V,* Shakespeare considers Salic law so fastidiously and in such keen genealogical detail that some critics and some performers, ill at ease with the stress on lineage in traditional societies, have only been able to conceive of the extended survey as a giant joke. Shakespeare employed this same strategy of obliteration elsewhere. He treated Agincourt, for example, so comprehensively that *Edward III's* Crecy (and its Poitiers as well) seem in comparison impossibly thin and dilute.

But to overwhelm the earlier play with detail was not the only strategy that Shakespeare employed. There were also parts of *Edward III* that were too valuable to ignore and that required assimilation and accommodation. In *Henry V,* when Canterbury sets out to persuade King Henry to reclaim his French possessions, he does so by reminding him of the previous century's successes on the fields of France. Canterbury's strategy is to figure Edward III as Henry's "father" and Edward's oldest son Edward the Black Prince as the type of conqueror whom Henry must aspire to emulate. "Looke back into your mightie Ancestors" (1.2.102; TLN 249), says the Archbishop, working up to one of the play's most resonant and evocative pieces of poetry:

Goe my dread Lord, to your great Grandsires Tombe,
From whom you clayme; inuoke his Warlike Spirit,
And your Great Vnckles, *Edward* the Black Prince,
Who on the French ground play'd a Tragedie,
Making defeat on the full Power of France,
Whiles his most mightie Father on a Hill
Stood smiling, to behold his Lyons Whelpe
Forrage in blood of French Nobilitie.
O Noble English, that could entertaine
With halfe their Forces, the full pride of France,
And let another halfe stand laughing by,
All out of worke, and cold for action.
(103-110; TLN 250-61)

As a contemporary neotype of the Black Prince, Henry was not only the great-grandson of Edward III but also in metaphorical terms the surrogate son and heir of the great conqueror himself. Henry is, or should be, and will eventually "become" the Black Prince when he replicates at Agincourt the events of Crecy. It is a wonderful figure that Canterbury creates, and it is also wonderfully theatrical. Canterbury reminds Henry that King Edward and his son "on the French ground play'd a Tragedie." The words "play'd," "Tragedie," and "ground"[10]—as well as the subsequent "entertaine"—conjoin to construct a vision not of the real geographical Crecy (a plain in France), but of Crecy the stage setting in *Edward III* where fictional battles had been recently and "sundry times" enacted.

Henry V's evocation of the "most mightie Father on a Hill," like the abduction of King David of Scotland, is drawn from the theater and not from the chronicles. Canterbury's description of the scene brings together three distinct elements: the first is that Edward withdrew to an elevated spot while the battle was fought by his son; the second is that he took half his army with him; and the third is that even as the king himself stood "smiling," others in his army were all "laughing" as they tarried to await news of the Black Prince. It is a vivid picture. How was it constructed?

Of its three components, just one, the hill, appears in Shakespeare's source and even then only in a subdued form. In Holinshed, which Shakespeare certainly used for *Henry V* (although there is no reason to believe that he backtracked to search the chronicle account of Edward III for Canterbury's reminiscence), Edward "stood aloft on a windmill hill" while the battle was in progress, and later, at its conclusion," came downe from the hill (on the which he stood all that day with his helmet still on his head)" (Holinshed, ii, 639).[11] The hill is a far more prominent feature in the play of *Edward III.* At Crecy, Edward announces to his compatriots that "whiles our sonne is in the chase, / With draw our powers vnto this little hill, / And heere a season let us breath our selues" (*sig.* G1r; 1513-15). While the clash of metal is heard and the prince labors for his knighthood, three successive messengers climb the hill to report that the prince is in desperate straits; they beg the king to descend in his own person or at least to dispatch a rescue. King Edward rejects the call for help, replying with enormous sangfroid:

> Let Edward be deliuered by our hands,
> And still in danger hele expect the like,
> But if himselfe, himselfe redeeme from thence,
> He will have vanquisht cheerefull death and
> feare. . . .
>
> (*sig.* G1v; 1559-62)

Offstage effects interrupt the conversation between the king and his nobility: "But soft me thinkes I heare,/ The dismall charge of Trumpets loud retreat" (*sig.* G1v; 1568-69). It is reported to Edward that his son—the "Lyons Whelpe," as Canterbury will call him—is "Lion like / Intangled in the net of [French] assaults" (*sig.* G1v; 1540-41). The king is still aloft, or imagined to be so, when Artois tells the king that all is lost "[E]xcept your highnes presently descend" (*sig.* G1r; 527). Just when it is conceded that the prince has been slain, the "hope of chivalry" (*sig.* G1v; 1566) enters below brandishing his "shiuered Launce" (1572). He is accompanied by soldiers who bear the corpse of the Bohemian king whose troops had just recently "intrencht [the prince] round about" (*sig.* G2r; 1586). King Edward then apparently descends to knight his son with the sword "yet reaking warme" (*sig.* G2r; 1601) with Bohemian blood. "This day," he tells the prince, "thou hast confounded me with ioy" (1604). The pageantry, the rhetorical flourishes, the formal handling of properties, the not very subtle tension-inducing devices and the repeated trips up and down from an elevated space all unite to create what must have been an extraordinarily memorable moment, and one that certainly seems to have caught Shakespeare's attention. Surely the hill from which the most mighty father watches and listens for his foraging son is a conspicuous feature in the landscape of *Edward III;* it is no wonder that Shakespeare recalled it in Canterbury's stirring address.

Canterbury also claims that the English fought the battle of Crecy with only half of their army while "another halfe stand laughing by, / All out of worke, and cold for action." This assertion also seems to derive from theatrical performance. There is no mention of idle forces in the chronicles, but in *Edward III,* when the king looks out from where he stands "aloft," he is accompanied by three noblemen—Artois, Audley, and Derby—and also by "his powers," who must include at least two supernumeraries. There are therefore four named and some, perhaps two, unnamed characters on the "hill." If Agincourt was indeed represented, as the Chorus in *Henry V* concedes, "With foure or fiue most vile and ragged foyles, / (Right ill dispos'd, in brawle ridiculous)" (*Chorus* 4, 50-51; TLN 1839-40), then the group of actors assembled on the hill might certainly be allowed to signify the half of the English army that stand idle while the battle of Crecy is audible offstage.

Shakespeare's sources are equally silent on the curious matter of Edward's smiling. Did King Edward smile theatrically while his son was imagined in the field attempting to vanquish "cheerefull death" (*sig.* G1v; 1562)? Evidence is lacking but Shakespeare elsewhere describes not only the smile of amusement but the smile of disdain. There is a parallel in *King John,* where at the French enemy's "unhaired sauciness and boyish troops," it is reported, "[t]he king doth smile" (5.3.134). Amusement, condescension, and disdain are the emotions that King Edward projects in this scene; perhaps he smiled, but perhaps Shakespeare only imagined his amusement retrospectively. Or was it rather that the entire stage echoed with relieved laughter when the prince finally made his long awaited entrance, and when, according to the direction, the watchers "runne and embrace him" (*sig.* G1v; 1571 s.d.)? Despite the gaps in the record, taken all together, it is a very creditable inference that Edward and his fellows not only smiled memorably and disdainfully, but, more importantly, that the whole of Canterbury's address was quite consciously designed to recall the events of Crecy as they had recently appeared on one or another London stage.

In the world of fine gardening, there is a traditional technique known as "captured scenery." If there is a mountain or other striking feature somewhere in the distant prospect, the skillful gardener deploys his berms and shrubs and trees in a design that incorporates or "captures" the mountain thereby draws it into the pattern of his own landscape. When he does so, he borrows but also in effect "owns" a beauty or a majesty that he does not have to construct himself. Shakespeare seems to have aimed for something of this sort in *Henry V.* When Shakespeare contrived that Canterbury would allude so explicitly to *Edward III,* he borrowed and therefore "captured" the magnificence of King Edward's triumph at Crecy as well as the grandeur of the black prince. By alluding so artistically to the "Tragedie" played "on the French ground," to the "most mightie Father on a Hill," and to the amused and idle English forces, Shakespeare incorporated a memorable scene from a predecessor play into his own landscape. He refreshed the memory of his stage-literate audience by reprising thrilling triumphs of chivalry and nationalism; at the same time, he prepared the ground for the far more wonderfully imagined victory at Agincourt still in the offing.

Shakespeare's "capture" of Crecy is one of the ways in which the memory of *Edward III* suffuses *Henry V.* It is an important element of the redefinition of the character of King Henry—a refinement very much influenced by *Edward III*'s presence in the regal landscape. In *1* and *2 Henry IV,* Prince Hal constantly struggles to come to terms with the shame that he is the son of the usurper Bolingbroke. But in *Henry V,* the prince sloughs off his prior identity as the son of his sullied father and is reconstructed as the beneficiary of the great-grandfather's legacy. Shrewsbury and Gaultree Forest are replaced by Crecy and Poitiers. In *Henry V,* Shakespeare metaphorically revises the genealogy of the king in order to create the illusion that Henry is not the heir of internecine squabble and regicide but the great-grandson of glory. So it is notable that the heroic great-grandfather Edward III finds his way into *Henry V* eight separate times, poor tattered Henry Bolingbroke appears only twice. One of these mentions is modest and comic: wooing Katherine of France, Henry bemoans his rough features: "Now beshrew my Fathers Ambition, hee was thinking of Ciuill Warres when hee got me" (5.2.216-218; TLN 3212-14). The one substantial appearance of Bolingbroke takes the form of a lengthy apology. It comes upon Agincourt eve, when the king, wandering among his famished troops, pauses for a moment to pray to the "God of Battailes" (4.1.277; TLN 2141).

> Not to day, O Lord,
> O not to day, thinke not vpon the fault
> My Father made, in compassing the Crowne.
> I *Richards* body haue interred new
> And on it haue bestowed more contrite teares.
> Then from it issued forced drops of blood.
> Fiue hundred poore I haue in yeerely pay,
> Who twice a day their wither'd hands hold vp
> Toward Heauen, to pardon blood:
> And I haue built two Chauntries,
> Where sad and solemn Priests sing still
> For *Richards* Soule.
> (4.1.280-290; TLN 2144-55)

This solicitation is the climactic moment in the long redemptive process by which the English king as well as his armies are cleansed of guilt and sin and made worthy of the divine intervention that is to occur at Agincourt. King Harry becomes, even if only for the instant, reverent, pious, contrite, tearful, and sincere—a critic of ceremony who paradoxically finds himself employing a traditional Roman ceremonial to expiate inherited guilt. In *Henry V,* the king's father Bolingbroke is an unwelcome guest allowed entrance only so he may be repudiated and only so that his repentant son may purge his "fault" (the word "fault" euphemizes usurpation, murder, regicide).

The father's sin and the apologetic manner in which it is introduced in *Henry V* contrast in every particular with the virtual deification of the great-grandshire. Even the king of France knows that he must fear Henry V, not because of the young English king's merits, but because

> . . . he is bred out of that bloodie straine,
> That haunted vs in our familiar Pathes:
> Witnesse our too much memorable shame,
> When Cressy Battell fatally was strucke,
> And all our Princes captiu'd by the hand
> Of that black Name, *Edward,* black Prince of Wales;
> Whiles that his Mountaine Sire, on Mountaine standing
> Vp in the Ayre, crown'd with the Golden Sunne.
> Saw his Heriocall Seed, and smil'd to see him. . . .
> (2.4.51-59; TLN 941-949)

While the tarnished memory of father Bolingbroke can only be redeemed by monkish chanting, the majesty of King Edward is revealed in an extravagant theophanic figure. The "Golden Sunne" with which the father is crowned must be envisioned as a halo of gold leaf,[12] while the phrase "Heroicall Seed" blasphemously conflates Edward's son the Black Prince (and therefore his neotype Henry) and the offspring of divinity itself. Yet even in the very midst of this resplendent imagery, the scene recalls the staging of Crecy in *Edward III.* The little windmill hill has resurfaced as a veritable Alp and Edward's so memorable smiling has expanded into a figure of divine beneficence. While in *Henry V,* the neglected father is a subject of shame, the amused great-grandfather has become celestial, sublime, glowing, numinous. The substitution of Edward III for Henry IV argues for Harry's moral and military pedigree, while the consignment of the usurping father to oblivion carves out a generous space in which the potent myth of King Henry V may flourish. How convenient to overleap troublesome epochs in the history of monarchy and assert a direct line of succession from Edward III to Henry V! The beneficiary: not only Henry V, but English monarchy as an institution—and therefore, it follows, even the monarch at the time of the play's composition, the "gracious empress" Elizabeth herself. The glow of King Edward III as it was reflected in Henry V glorifies English kings and queens and serves to counterbalance the daring and (to some eyes) potentially subversive nod toward Essex that appears in Chorus 5 of the folio text. (In fact, reminiscences of the glory of *Edward III* appear only in those portions of *Henry V* in which the young king is heroized; they disappear whenever he is brutal, machiavellian or opportunistic.)

There is, then, a repeated and fertile interchange between *Edward III* and *Henry V*. Shakespeare recalled specific moments of the earlier play in the later, he "captured" and exploited potent events, and he made use of the play to supply King Harry with an ancestry appropriate to his new mythic stature. *Edward III* is the ground on which *Henry V* is built.

In composing *Henry V,* Shakespeare did not necessarily conceive that his new play brought to a close a "second tetralogy" that began with *Richard II* and followed the careers of Hal and Falstaff. On the contrary, in *Henry V* Shakespeare leapt backward over three preceding plays to respond, both specifically and allusively, to *Edward III.* While there is no doubt that there are important senses in which *Henry V* is the latest of a series of plays that begins with *Richard II,* it is just as true that *Henry V* derives its meaning from a more capacious theatrical environment than from the tetralogy with which it is traditionally associated. It has been proposed that the idea of a tetralogy "is seriously misleading if understood as implying that Shakespeare actually planned in advance to produce sequences of four plays as organic units." However, if *Edward III* is Shakespeare's, and if "we must speak in terms of tetralogies . . . , [then] the second of them [is] formed by *Edward III . . . Richard II, Henry IV,* and *Henry V.*" [13] This is an idea worth thinking about, but perhaps it would even more useful to discard the idea of "tetralogy" altogether. The neat and seductive symmetry of first and second tetralogies was never more than an aesthetically satisfying fictional construction, one that has led to a rigid separation of the early and later histories and to the neglect of *King John.* It is clear that in *Henry V,* Shakespeare responded both defensively and creatively to the fact that *Edward III* lay in his landscape (and it does not matter, in this case, whether he was the author of the play or merely a competing playwright trying to find a place for his own work). It is therefore the case that questions that have customarily been framed in terms of tetralogies can usefully be reframed more broadly. The cost of not doing so is to obscure the filiations that *Edward III* puts forward. *Henry V* responds not only to *Henry IV* but also to *Edward III* (and to *The Famous Victories of King Henry V* as well) just as *Richard II* responds to *Woodstock,* as *King John* responds to *The Troublesome Reign,* and, more specifically and less subtly, as *Sir John Oldcastle* responds to *Henry IV.*

To specify exactly how surely *Henry V* finds itself in the orbit of *Edward III,* it would be convenient to discover that one or another playgoer attended an early performance of *Henry V* and had returned home to write in his diary: "To the Glob to see the new Pistoll plaie with Burbidge as kinge Harey—Shakespeare very much in the debt of the apocryphal *Edward III,* as will someday be noticed." In the absence of such confirmatory testimony, an alternative is to look to the single relevant record that has come down to us. Writing a few years after the heyday of the English history play, Thomas Heywood paid tribute to the power of the theater to inspire patriotism. His examples, *Edward III* and *Henry V*:

> To turne to our domesticke hystories, what English blood seeing the person of any bold English man presented and doth not hugge his fame, and hunnye at his valor, pursuing him in his enterprise with his best wishes, and as beeing wrapt in contemplation, offers to him in his hart all prosperous performance, as if the Personater were the man Personated, so bewitching a thing is liuely and well spirited action, that it hath power to new mold the harts of the spectators and fashion them to the shape of any noble and notable attempt. What coward to see his contryman valiant would not bee ashamed of his owne cowardise? What English Prince should hee behold the true portrature of that [f]amous King *Edward* the third, foraging France, taking so great a King captiue in his owne country, quartering the English Lyons with the French Flower-delyce, and would not bee suddenly Inflam'd with so royall a spectacle, being made apt and fit for the like atchieuement. So of *Henry* the fift: but not to be tedious in any thing. [14]

How remarkable that Heywood juxtaposes *Edward III* and *Henry V* and then, surprisingly, gives pride of place to the work that was for an age and remands to an afterthought the work that was for all time! Moreover, it is also the case that Heywood's memory of *Edward III* was extraordinarily accurate, for elsewhere in the same brief pamphlet he was able to remember that among "[w]omen likewise that are chaste, are by vs extolled, and encouraged in their vertues, being instanced by *Diana, Belphebe, Matilda, Lucrece,* and the Countesse of *Salisbury*" (*sig.* G1v)—the very Countess, that is, whose scarlet cheeks so captivated King Edward. Heywood's recall of *Edward III* seems to be faithful in the details. Does Edward actually add, as Heywood says, the English lion to the French coat of arms and is he to be found "foraging France?" In *Edward III,* an unnamed "mariner" tells the story of an English naval assault. He reports that

> . . . on the top gallant of the Admirall
> And likewise all the handmaides of his trayne
> The armes of England and of Fraunce vnite,
> Are quartered equally by Heralds art.
> (*sig.* E2v; 1078-81)

As to the "foraging," the French confess that "[s]laughter and mischiefe walke within [our] streets / And vnrestrained make havock as they passe" (*sig.* F1r; 1245-46). There is a report that "[f]or so far off as I directed mine eies, / I might perceaue fiue Cities all on fire, / Corn fields and vineyards burning like an ouen" (1249-51). This destruction fulfills the prophecy that "a Lyon rowsed in the west / Shall carie hence the fluerdeluce of France" (1236-37). Heywood is wrong about one detail, for it is not King Edward but his son, the Black Prince, who captures the French king. A stage direction hints at a colorful scene that gave prominence to captured royal insignia:

> Enter prince Edward, king John, Charles, and all
> with Ensignes spred.
> Retreat sounded.
> *Prince*. Now John in France, & lately John of France,
> Thy bloudie Ensignes are my captiue colours,
> And you high vanting Charles of Normandie,
> That once to daie sent me a horse to flie
> Are now the subiects of my clemencie.
> . . . . .
> *King* [John of France]. Thy fortune, not thy force hath
> conquerd vs.
> (*sig.* 12v; 2188 s.d-2193; 2198)

Yet at the same time that Heywood recalls *Edward III* in such particular detail, his account is very obviously filtered through his memory of *Henry V*. His praise of the history play (that it inspires the uninspired, or as Heywood says, "What coward to see his contryman valiant would not bee ashamed of his owne cowardise?") reproduces a sentiment borrowed from Shakespeare's play:

> . . . who is he, whose Chin is but enricht
> With one appearing Hayre, that will not follow
> These cull'd and choyse-drawne Caualiers to France?
> (*Chorus* 3, 23-24; TLN 1066-68)

In essence, Heywood echoes the position that no matter the limits of the theater, art can be so persuasively presented that it can momentarily move a willing audience to patriotic fervor. Just as Canterbury sees *Edward III* in *Henry V*, so Heywood finds the two plays so closely allied that the rhetorical power of the later history spills over to encompass and dignify the earlier. The record therefore reveals that the two plays were linked in the mind of at least one of Shakespeare's most discerning colleagues as well as in the fertile imagination of the playwright himself.

Notes

[1] These words appear on the title page of *The Raigne of King Edward the third* (London: Cuthbert Burby, 1596). I have used the facsimile in the Tudor Facsimile Text series published by J. S. Farmer (Edinburgh and London, 1910). Citations of *Edward III* are identified by the facsimile signatures as well as by the line numbers in Fred Lapides's critical, old-spelling edition (New York and London: Garland, 1980). The punctuation of the 1596 quarto is whimsical and has been silently normalized.

[2] Richard Proudfoot summarizes the argument that *Edward III* was a property of Pembroke's Men on pp. 181-82 of "*The Reign of King Edward the Third* (1596) and Shakespeare," *Proceedings of the British Academy* 71 (1985): 159-85. Proudfoot follows G. M. Pinciss, "Shakespeare, her Majesty's Players and Pembroke's Men," *Shakespeare Survey* 27 (1974); 129-36; Scott McMillin, "Casting for Pembroke's Men," *Shakespeare Quarterly* 23 (1972): 141-59; and MacDonald Jackson, "*Edward III,* Shakespeare, and Pembroke's Men," *Notes and Queries* 210 (1965): 329-31. Proudfoot toys with the "romantic hypothesis" that Shakespeare "may for a time have belonged to the company, long enough to acquire an actor's familarity with their repertoire" (182). It has recently been suggested that the author of *Edward III* read and studied an annotated copy of Froissart in the hand and possession of Henry Carey, Lord Hundson, and that the play was written for Hunsdon's players (Roger Prior, "Was *The Raigne of King Edward III* a Compliment to Lord Hundson, *Connotations* 3 (1993/94): 243-64.

[3] For the authorship of *Edward III,* see Stanley Wells and Gary Taylor with John Jowett and William Montgomery, *William Shakespeare a Textual Companion* (Oxford: Clarendon, 1987), 136-37 and the accompanying bibliography: "of all the non-canonical plays [*Edward III*] has the strongest claim to inclusion in the Complete Works" (136). On the basis of the evidence, Proudfoot does not understand why "single-volume complete works should continue to exclude what has become . . . the sole remaining 'doubtful play' which continues, on substantial grounds, to win the support of serious investigators as arguably the work of Shakespeare" ("Raigne," 185).

[4] *A New Variorum Edition of Shakespeare, The Sonnets,* ed. H. E. Rollins, 2 vols. (Philadelphia: Lippincott, 1944), 1:363.

[5] See Rollins, *Variorum,* 1:234. Lapides discusses these and other parallels, 9-15.

[6] Quotations from *Henry V* are drawn from *The First Folio of Shakespeare* ed. Charlton Hinman (New York: Norton, 1968) and are identified by Hinman's through line numbering as well as by the lineation in Andrew Gurr's New Cambridge edition (Cambridge: Cambridge University Press, 1992).

[7] Froissart's *Chronicle* is cited from G. Harold Metz, *Sources of Four Plays Ascribed to Shakespeare* (Columbia, Mo.: University of Missouri Press, 1989), 43-107.

[8] See Holinshed's *Chronicles* (London, 1807), ii, 645.

[9] See Annabel Patterson, "Back by Popular Demand: The Two Versions of *Henry V,*" *Renaissance Drama* 19 (1988): 29-61. The relation between the drama and things Scottish has been most recently surveyed by James Shapiro, "*The Scot's Tragedy* and the Politics of Popular Drama," *English Literary Renaissance* 23 (1993): 428-49.

[10] Cf. Ben Jonson: "the vnderstanding Gentlemen o' the ground here," *Bartholomew Fair,* "Induction," 49-50, *Ben Jonson,* ed. C. H. Herford and P. and E. Simpson, 11 vols. (Oxford: Clarendon Press, 1927-52), 6:14.

[11] Holinshed slightly embroiders Froissart: in Froissart's *Chronicle,* the King waits out the battle "on a lytell wyndmyll hyll" (cxxx, 80).

[12] See *Henry V,* ed. Andrew Gurr, 2.4.58-59 n.

[13] Giorgio Melchiori, "The Corridors of History: Shakespeare the Re-Maker," *Proceedings of the British Academy* 72 (1986): 167-85. The discussion of tetralogies is on p. 176.

[14] Thomas Heywood, *An Apology for Actors* (1612), ed. R. H. Perkinson (New York: Scholar's Facsimiles and Reprints, 1941), *sig.* B4r.

Source: "*Edward III* in *Henry V,*" in *Criticism,* Vol. 37, No. 4, Fall, 1995, pp. 519-36.

Saints Alive! Falstaff, Martin Marprelate, and the Staging of Puritanism

Kristen Poole, *Harvard University*

In the early fifteenth century, a pious, innocent man was put to a most gruesome death—that, at least, is the story according to his sixteenth-century chronicler, the Protestant bishop John Bale. A faithful follower of John Wyclif and an avid reader of the Scriptures, this gentleman was a "moste valyaunt warryoure of Iesus Christ" who courageously battled that Whore of Babylon, the Roman Catholic Church:

> In all adve[n]terouse actes of wordlye manhode was he ever bolde, stronge, fortunate, doughtye, noble, & Valeau[n]t. But never so worthye a conquerour as in this his present conflyct with the cruell and furyouse frantyck kyngedome of Antichrist. Farre is this Christen knyght more prayse worthye, for that he had so noble a stomake in defence of Christes Verite agaynst those Romyshe supersticyons, than for anye temporall nobylnesse eyther of bloude, byrthe, landes, or of marcyall feates.[1]

Against an onslaught of hostile questions from an archbishop and his prelates, those "spyghtfull murtherers, ydolaters, and Sodomytes," the Christian knight firmly stood his ground, bravely defending the opinions he had gleaned from the Gospel concerning the material substance of the Eucharist (merely symbolic), the sacrament of confession (invalid), and the efficacy of pilgrimages (pointless). But alas, the "bloud thurstye rauenours" that were his opponents sentenced him to death, and not a pretty one at that. The faithful prisoner, bound "as though he had bene a most heynouse traytour to the crowne," was carted from the Tower to St. Giles Field and a new pair of gallows. There he fell to his knees, praying "God to forgeve his enemyes." Standing, he "behelde the multytude" and exhorted them "to folowe the lawes of God wrytten in the scripturs" and to be wary of teachers that are "contrarye to Christ in theyr conuersacyn and lyvynge." Finally, the unfortunate was hung in "cheanes of yron and so consumed a lyve in the fyre, praysynge the name of God so longe as his lyfe lasted. In the ende he commended his sowle into the handes of God, and so departed hens most Christenlye." Adding insult to injury, his ashes, like those of his predecessor Wyclif, were unceremoniously tossed into the Thames.[2]

Writing in 1544, Bale intended to reveal the horrors of this particular inquisition; or, as he put it, to show "by this treatyse what beastlye blockeheades these bloudye bellyegoddes were in theyr unsauerye interrogacyo[n]s." As is evident from his conclusion, Bale also wished to establish this man as a Protestant martyr, one who had "a tryumphau[n]t Victorye ouer his enemyes by the Veryte which he defended," and who "dyed at the importune sute of the clergye, for callynge vpon a Christen reformacyon in that Romyshe churche of theyrs, & for manfullye standynge by the faythfull testymonyes of Jesu."[3]

The subject of Bale's account was the Lollard leader Sir John Oldcastle, Lord Cobham, best known to literary scholars as the model for Shakespeare's Sir John Falstaff. Oldcastle became a popular figure in Elizabethan England, his trial and death recounted in Foxe's *Acts and Monuments,* Stowe's *Annales,* Holinshed's *Chronicles,* and elsewhere.[4] For some, Oldcastle was the valiant, victimized religious martyr we see in Bale's chronicle; for others, he was a devious, schismatic heretic and traitor who betrayed his friend and king, Henry V.[5] Elizabethan puritans hailed Oldcastle as a proto-puritan; as religious reformers traced the progress of their battle against the Antichrist, they frequently claimed Wyclif and his followers as the origin of their movement.[6] Opponents of puritanism also located the source of this evil in the Lollards, using them as an example of puritan subversive heresy and sectarianism.

Shakespeare's audience readily identified Falstaff as a caricature of Oldcastle, and Falstaff appears to have been called "Oldcastle" in early performances of *1 Henry IV.*[7] (The name was subsequently changed in order to placate the outraged Elizabethan Lords Cobham, or to appease a disgruntled Protestant audience that hailed Oldcastle as a hero.[8]) Even after "Oldcastle" was re-dubbed "Falstaff," extensive historical and literary evidence indicates that the public did not quickly forget the character's original and "true" identity. The name "Oldcastle" was retained for private (including court) performances, and many seventeenth-century authors indicate that "Falstaff" was widely understood as an alias for the Lollard martyr.[9] The oft-quoted Epilogue of *2 Henry IV* ("Oldcastle died martyr, and this is not the man" [ll. 31-32]—a protest that conversely indicates audiences *did* identify Falstaff as Oldcastle)—as well as the prologue to Drayton and Munday's 1600 counterrepresentation in *The First Part of the True and Honourable History of the Life of Sir John Oldcastle, the Good Lord Cobham* ("It is no pampered glutton we present, / Nor aged counsellor to youthful sin, / But one, whose virtue shone above the rest, / A valiant martyr, and a vertuous peer" [ll. 6-9][10]) indicate that the Oldcastle-Falstaff transformation was considered common knowledge.

Recently, the decision of prominent editors to reinstate

Falstaff's original name has resulted in significant editorial debate, leading critics to argue the textual ramifications of this "discovery."[11] I must join those who contest this decision, as I do not believe it is the role of the modern editor to "retrospectively save a writer from the censor";[12] the censors *were* there and are as much a part of the text's history and circumstances of production as economic and social factors. If "Oldcastle" were to become the predominant title for this character a hundred years from now, as Gary Taylor desires, the history of repression experienced by the Elizabethan stage (and indeed by the arts in general) could easily be overlooked; calling attention to the name "Oldcastle" while retaining the enforced name-change of "Falstaff," on the other hand, highlights this repressive control.

Such editorial discussions do not satisfactorily address the historical or theoretical implications of Falstaff's Lollard origins. Why, contrary to so many of the contemporary representations, did Shakespeare take the figure of this "noble Christen warryour" and mold him into the Rabelaisian, gluttonous coward of the Henriad? Conversely, why did he deviate so far from the alternative tradition of depicting Oldcastle as a bellicose heretic, a serious martial threat to king and state? Some critics maintain that "Shakespeare simply blundered"[13]—that he more or less picked a name out of a historical hat, a name that happened to have unfortunate political consequences. Others assert (somewhat more plausibly) that Shakespeare intended to satirize the Elizabethan Lords Cobham, Sir William Brooke or his reputedly less competent son and successor, Henry—descendants by marriage of the original Oldcastle.[14] Neither of these answers seems satisfying. The notion of the playwright innocently and ignorantly choosing the name of a figure who had become hotly contested as a cultural icon by competing religious/political factions does not seem likely. And while Elizabethan and Jacobean gossips seem to have reveled in the Falstaffian portrayal of a Lord Cobham, thus far scholars have established no clear motive for personal parody; rather, there were strong reasons to *avoid* conflict with William Brooke, then lord chamberlain and in control of the theaters.[15]

I suggest that we need to broaden the investigation by examining the Henriad in the context of Elizabethan polemical religious discourse. Such an examination reveals that Shakespeare's depiction of the Lollard Oldcastle was not a daring, radical, or innovative departure from the stereotypical image of the puritan, as critics have supposed. Nor is it, as J. Dover Wilson suggested, simply an ingenious modernization of the Vice character from earlier morality plays (although Falstaff's presentation is certainly indebted to this tradition).[16] Rather, I believe that this presentation of Oldcastle is perfectly in keeping with the tenor of the antipuritan literature of the late sixteenth century, especially the anti-Marprelate tracts and the burlesque stage performances of the Marprelate controversy (1588-90), which frequently depicted puritans as grotesque individuals living in carnivalesque communities. Indeed, this lively portrayal of the puritan seems to have been much more popular than the lean, mean Malvolio image that post-Restoration readers and audiences (especially post-Hawthorne Americans) would exclusively associate with the term *puritan,* despite the fact that the official holiday celebrating puritans is one of nationwide gluttony.

In many ways Falstaff epitomizes the image of the grotesque puritan. Shakespeare's representation of a prominent Lollard martyr does not depoliticize Falstaff but transposes him into a register of religious/political language familiar to his Elizabethan audience. Harold Bloom has noted that Falstaff "is given to parodying Puritan preachers."[17] Falstaff does indeed parody such preachers, but not just as an overweight, ungodly knight making barroom jokes about them; rather, the person of Falstaff is in and of himself a parody of the sixteenth-century puritan. Shakespeare's audiences would most likely have recognized Falstaff in the literary tradition of grotesque puritans that would continue with Jonson's Zeal-of-the-Land Busy and Middleton's Plumporridge. (Falstaff's very name, "False staff," could be read as a parody of such puritan names as More Fruit, Faint Not, Perseverance, Deliverance,[18] and Jonson's Win-the-Fight.) In the late sixteenth century, carnival and the grotesque became the terms in which religious tensions between conformist Protestants and nonconformist puritans were constantly played out.

I

The pamphlet war of "Martin Marprelate" and his adversaries marks the entrance of the puritan figure into popular literature. By the late 1580s the puritans' hopes of ecclesiastical reform had faded; "popish" vestments and ceremonies remained an integral part of the English church, and in 1583 the antipuritan John Whitgift had been appointed archbishop of Canterbury. As the desired reforms became more illusory, puritans such as the popular twenty-four-year-old preacher John Penry increasingly went underground, illegally publishing attacks on the bishops and nonpreaching (often nonresident) clergy. The church authorities felt the sting of these attacks and appointed John Bridges, dean of Salisbury, as their spokesman. But his *Defense of the government established in the Church of Englande for ecclesiasticall matters* (1587), a large quarto volume containing 1400 pages of "lumbering orthodoxy," did little to stop the flow of antiprelatical attacks. Early in 1588 Penry sallied forth with the *Exhortation,* a scathing assault on the bishops; in April of the same year the young John Udall challenged the episcopacy with *The State of the Church of England laide open.* The printer for many of these pamphlets was the puritan sympathizer Robert Waldegrave, whose printing press was finally seized and destroyed in the spring of 1588.[19]

According to legend, during the chaos surrounding the destruction of his press Waldegrave managed to escape with a box of types hidden under his cloak.[20] Armed with these types and a newly acquired press, Waldegrave was able to help launch the guerrilla pamphlet war of Martin Marprelate. In October of 1588, Marprelate's first clandestine tract, *The Epistle,* exploded onto the scene, quickly circulating in and around London. Intended as an introduction to *The Epitome* (a critical summary of John Bridges's *Defense of the government*), *The Epistle* hailed the "terrible priests" in a riotously irreverent and comic tone, a stark contrast to the stodgy pedantry of Bridges's work. Martin Marprelate (a pseudonym for one or more undetermined authors, most likely including Penry and/or Udall) informs his readers from the first that he must play the fool to respond appropriately to Bridges's text, "Because, I could not deal with his book commendably, according to order, unless I should be sometimes tediously dunctical and absurd."[21] He asks in *Hay any worke for Cooper:* "The Lord being the author both of mirth and gravity, is it not lawful in itself, for the truth to use either of these ways?" Martin recognizes the public's apathy regarding ecclesiastical controversy, and seeks a means to attract their attention: "perceiving the humours of men in these times . . . to be given to mirth. I took that course."[22]

While the text bursts with laughter—"Ha ha ha!" "So-ho!" "Tse-tse-tse!" "Wo-ho-ho!"—the attack on the bishops is ominously real: "All our Lord Bishops, I say, are petty popes, and petty usurping antichrists," Martin writes in *The Epistle*. Marprelate's chief weapon is rollicking ridicule. Rather than confute the biblical basis and authority of an episcopalian church government (the standard approach of most puritan pamphleteers), he endeavors to mar the prelates with personal insults. He asks Stephen Chatfield, the vicar of Kingston, "And art thou not a monstrous atheist, a belly god, a carnal wicked wretch, and what not?" The personal foibles of parish ministers are related with unmitigated zest and extensive poetic license; Martin promises, "In this book I will note all their memorable pranks." Geoffrey Jones, a priest from Warwickshire and a regular at the local alehouse, became an exemplary victim of Martin's witty, sarcastic narration. Once, while frequenting the alehouse, Jones flew into a rage (Martin speculates that either he had been asked to settle his account or he had lost money gambling) and swore "he would never go again into it." "This rash vow of the good priest" was much to the dismay of the alewife, although Martin adds that "the tap had great quietness and ease thereby, which could not be quiet so much as an hour in the day, as long as Sir Geoffrey resorted unto the house." The priest, repenting his vow of abstinence, took advantage of a specific meaning of *go* as "to move on one's feet, to walk," and arranged to be carried to the alehouse on another man's back—thus circumventing his oath.[23] Not only do Martin's cynical comments on this compromise mock Sir Geoffrey, but this episode becomes an allegory for the bishops' manipulation of Scriptural loopholes.

Martin inflicts the greatest harm on the clergy simply by not taking them seriously; for him nothing in the episcopacy is sacrosanct. He openly scoffs at Archbishop Whitgift (whom he hails with such names as "John Cant," "Dumb John," and "Don John"), accusing him of playing "the fool . . . in the pulpit." He mocks the bishop's miter with parodic titles such as "my horned Masters of the Convocation," and provides the bishops with helpful, moralistic "true" stories:

> Old Doctor Turner . . . had a dog full of good qualities. Doctor Turner, having invited a Bishop to his table, in dinner-while, called his dog, and told him that the Bishop did sweat. (You must think he laboured hard over his trencher.) The dog flies at the Bishop and took off his corner-cap—he thought belike it had been a cheesecake—and so away goes the dog with it to his master. Truly, my masters of the Clergy, I would never wear corner-cap again, seeing dogs run away with them.

With this one tale, Martin inflicts more damage on the bishops' image than tomes of biblical exegesis could have accomplished. Now the bishops had not only egg on their faces but cheesecake on their heads; who could take them seriously? Here, as elsewhere, Martin proves himself a master of timing. With this ridiculous image of dog, priest, and cheesecake before the reader, Martin asks the bishops a pointed and sobering question: "May it please you . . . to tell me the cause, when you have leisure, why so many opinions and errors are risen in our Church, concerning the ministry?"[24] The question becomes rhetorical. The bishops, represented as buffoons, are disempowered and cannot respond.

Martin's charm comes from what Christopher Hill termed a "witty, rumbustious, savage and extremely effective colloquial style."[25] Marprelate has a vivid, first-person voice—part reporter, part neighbor, part preacher, part gossip. *The Epistle* contains abundant anecdotal accounts of the bishops' travesties, from not paying their bills to stealing cloth to bowling on Sundays. He claims to be gathering rumors and the sentiments of parishioners, printing the "reports" in their own words; he records popular opinion about the bishop of Gloucester, for example, who once "was endued with . . . famous gifts, before he was a bishop; whereas since that time, *say they,* he is not able to say `bo!' to a goose." Martin even plays the comedian and does impersonations; here he mimics the bishop of Gloucester preaching on St. John, coming to "the very pith of his whole sermon": "`John, John; the grace of God, the grace of God, the grace of God. Gracious John; not graceless John, but gracious John. John, holy John, holy John; not John full of holes, but holy John.'"[26] One can hardly help hearing the voice of Zeal-of-the-Land Busy.[27]

For the next twelve months, Martin continued to harass the bishops. Like a mosquito in a bedroom on a warm summer night, he could not be found; infuriated, the bishops swatted around the country and organized largescale hunts for the Marprelate press but always arrived just after it had stung and moved on. The Marprelate tracts were on their way to becoming "the biggest scandal of Elizabeth I's reign."[28] *The Epistle* was followed over the next nine months by five equally lively tracts, and the persona of Martin was joined by his sons, Martin Jr. and Martin Sr., who engaged in fraternal bickering after the younger brother took the liberty of publishing one of their father's manuscripts which he had "found" lying under some bushes, dirty, crumpled, and only partially legible.[29]

Judging by the official response, the Marprelate tracts were enormously popular. Christopher Hill observes, "Martin's rude, personalizing style appealed because it was subversive of degree, hierarchy and indeed the great chain of being itself. The shocking thing about his tracts was that their rollicking popular idiom, in addition to making intellectuals laugh, deliberately brought the Puritan cause into the market place."[30] Not everyone, of course, found this an endearing quality; the bishops were confounded and the queen was not amused. Following publication of *The Epitome,* Richard Bancroft preached against Martin Marprelate at Paul's Cross, and Thomas Cooper, bishop of Winchester, wrote *An Admonition to the People of England* (January 1589) defending the episcopate and providing scriptural authority for the bishops' large incomes. Such counterattacks merely became fuel for Martin's fire, and he entitled his next pamphlet *Hay any worke for Cooper* (an echo of the common London street cry "Ha' ye any work for the cooper?"[31]) in the bishop of Winchester's honor. When paternalistic admonitions failed to quench Martin-mania, the tracts were categorically outlawed. Legal measures proved equally futile, however, and even the earl of Essex (known as a puritan sympathizer) allegedly waved a Martinist tract before his queen, demanding "What will become of me?" Martin reveled in the mischief he was causing; Martin Sr. tauntingly mimics the archbishop of Canterbury in *The just censure,* having him lament to his servants, "No warning will serve them; they grow worse and worse. . . . I think I shall go stark mad with you, unless you bring him in."[32]

These tracts confronted the bishops with a new breed of ecclesiastical enemy: the puritan wit. The Martin Marprelate author(s)—fiery young men such as Penry and Udall—were the puritan counterpart to the London wits. Indeed, at least one critic maintains that Martin Marprelate originated the grotesque comic prose of the 1590s.[33] After futile attempts to take the Martinists by force, sermon, or dense theological prose, the bishops finally hired mercenaries who could challenge Martin on his own ground: John Lyly, Robert Green, Anthony Munday, and the young Thomas Nashe (Penry's schoolmate at Cambridge). These new arrivals studied Martin's style and learned to imitate it. For the next six months pamphlets were furiously penned by both sides, as colorful insults flew and each side lampooned the other with zeal and relish. New personae entered the scene (Mar-Martine, Pasquill, Marphoreus, Cuthbert Curryknave, Plaine Percevall the Peace-maker, and the sons of Martin the great, Martin Jr. and Martin Sr.) as the pamphlet war took on a plot of its own. Characters made personal challenges to other characters, formed alliances, and at one point rumors filled London that Martin was dead. (Martin's sons, the creation of the same author(s) as Martin himself, capitalized on these rumors, voicing fears in *Theses Martinianae* and *The just censure* that their father had been imprisoned by the bishops; Martin later reappeared to assure his readership that he was alive and well.) Martin was portrayed on the stage and became the target of broadsides; Mar-prelate was attacked by Mar-Martine, who in turn came under fire from Marre Mar-Martin. The controversy became so heated that Gabriel and Richard Harvey and Francis Bacon entered the fray, defending Martin against the anti-Martinists;[34] and Sir Walter Ralegh, related by marriage to Job Throkmorton, a prominent figure in the Marprelate circle and possibly an author himself,[35] undertook the release from prison of John Udall, who, unfortunately, died a few days later.

The anti-Martinists changed the tenor of the controversy by amplifying the grotesque undertones of the Martinist tracts. Throughout Martin's writing, there are elements of the carnival grotesque; the prelates, those "carnal and senseless beasts," "monstrous and ungodly wretches," revel with their "boosing mates" in a world of social madness and hierarchical inversion, where bishops become common laborers and Martin proclaims himself "the great." In *The Epistle* the bishops are "swine, dumb dogs, . . . lewd livers, . . . adulterers, drunkards, cormorants, rascals . . . [causing] monstrous corruptions in our Church." Martin blasts in *Hay any work,* "Horrible and blasphemous beasts, whither will your madness grow in a while, if ye be not restrained?"[36] In the anti-Martinist tracts, however, elements of the carnival grotesque become explicit and predominant; Martin's own rhetorical strategies are turned against him with full force. In *An Almond for a Parrat* (1590), Nashe overtly asserts that he will attack the puritan "Hipocrites and belli-gods" by "imitating . . . that merry man Rablays."[37] Throughout the anti-Martinist literature, Martin is "the Ape, the dronke, and the madde":[38] he copulates, vomits, drinks, gorges himself, and gives birth.

Martin becomes, then, the Bahktinian grotesque body par excellence.[39] Nashe and Lyly depict Martin and his "neast" as a swarm of monstrous, intertwined beings; death, birth, sex, and bodily functions are often simultaneous and inextricable. Witness Martin's birth, described in *An Almond for a Parrat*: "thinke that nature tooke a scouring purgation, when she voided all her imperfections in the birth of one *Martin*."[40] In *A Countercuffe given to Martin Junior* (1589), the self-proclaimed cavalier Pasquill responds to the rumors of Martin's death: "If the Monster be deade, I meruaile not, for hee was but an error of Nature, not long liued: hatched in the heat of the sinnes of *England*. . . . The maine buffets that are giuen him in euery corner of this Realme, are euident tokens, that beeing thorow soust in so many showres, hee had no other refuge but to runne into a hole, and die as he liued, belching."[41] Dying and hatching, belching at his death in the womblike recesses of a hole: the epitome of the grotesque, in which birth and death intersect. Again, consider Lyly's image of a birthing, dying Martin in *Pappe with an hatchet*:

> I sawe through his paper coffen, that it was but a cosening corse, . . . drawing his mouth awrie, that could neuer speake right; goggling with his eyes that watred with strong wine; licking his lips, and gaping, as though he should loose his childes nose, if he had not his longing to swallowe Churches; and swelling in the paunch, as though he had been in labour of a little babie, no bigger than rebellion; but truth was at the Bishoppes trauaile: so that Martin was deliuered by sedition, which pulls the monster with yron from the beastes bowells. When I perceiued that he masked in his rayling robes, I was so bolde as to pull off his shrowding sheete, that all the worlde might see the olde foole daunce naked.[42]

A man in a coffin, feigning death yet childlike, giving birth through his bowels, masquing in a shrouding sheet: this, to many, was a late-sixteenth-century image of the puritan.

Such caricatures were soon translated onto the stage, much to the shock and disgust of the very bishops and city magistrates who had orchestrated the anti-Martinist attack. While texts for these theatrical entertainments have not survived (if they ever existed),[43] both Martin and his foes repeatedly and pervasively allude to the popular anti-Martinist lampoons. According to *Pappe with an hatchet,* Marprelate was mocked at St. Paul's by the choir children; at the Theater, a playhouse near Finsbury; and at Thomas à Waterings in Southwark.[44] (Ironically, this last location doubled as a common place of execution, and Penry himself was later hanged there, convicted of writing the Marprelate tracts.[45]) Such performances appear to have been in the same tone as the prose tracts. Pasquill writes in *A Countercuffe* of "the Anatomie latelie taken of [Martin], the blood and the humors that were taken from him, by launcing and worming him at *London* vpon the common Stage." In another performance mentioned in *The Return of Pasquill,* the battered and scratched character Divinity is brought forth "holding of her hart as if she were sicke, because *Martin* would haue forced her." Unsuccessful in his rape attempts, Martin then "poysoned her with a vomit which he ministred vnto her." In other shows Martin was depicted as an ape (most likely inspired by the first anti-Martinist broadside, *A Whip for an Ape*) and as Maid Marian.[46]

Martin claims in *Theses Martinianae* not to be disturbed by "the stage-players, poor, silly, hunger-starved wretches" who are willing to play "the ignominious fools for an hour or two together . . . for one poor penny." Indeed, he maintains the position that the "poor rogues . . . are not so much to be blamed, if, being stage-players, . . . they . . . have gotten them many thousand eye-witnesses of their witless and pitiful conceits."[47] But such stage productions probably did not leave the anonymous author(s) of the Martinist tracts unscathed. While these theatricals may have backfired in their intent to squelch Martin Marprelate, they certainly hindered his voicing of serious theological and ecclesiastical concerns. Martin Marprelate was not only physically represented on the stage, but authors such as Lyly invited their readers to imagine Martin as an actor:

> He shall not bee brought in as whilom he was, and yet verie well, with a cocks combe, an apes face, a wolfs bellie, cats clawes, &c. . . . A stage plaier, though he bee but a cobler by occupation, yet his chance may bee to play the Kings part. Martin, of what calling so euer he be, can play nothing but the knaues part. . . . Would it not bee a fine Tragedie, when *Mardocheus* shall play a Bishoppe in a Play, and Martin *Hamman,* and that he that seekes to pull downe those that are set in authoritie aboue him, should be hoysted vpon a tree aboue all others.[48]

Lambasted as a stage-player or "some Iester about the Court," his railings against the church described as mere comical posing, Martin is then easily translated onto the stage and his religious concerns become contained as a part of his "act."[49]

Such containment, however, was soon perceived as subversive in itself. As Charles Nicholl observes, the anti-Martinist productions "were obviously coarse, sensational performances, full of violent antics." This theatrical entertainment was "to the greate offence of the better sorte," as John Harte, lord mayor of London wrote to Lord Burghley.[50] In 1589 Edmund Tilney, as Master of the Revels, closed the theaters on account of the grotesque representations of Martin Marprelate. The Privy Council agreed with this move, and a letter was sent to the archbishop of Canterbury, the lord mayor of London, and the Master of the Revels requesting strict censorship of the theater. The Council wrote to the archbishop that "there hathe growne some inconvenience by common playes and enterludes in & about the cyttie of London, in [that] the players take upon [them] to handle in their plaies certen matters of Divinytie and State, unfitt to be suffered."[51] The antipuritan authorities thus quickly decided to contain the disruption they had orchestrated, much to the annoyance of Lyly, who complained that there were still anti-Martinist plays waiting to be performed.[52]

Even as the bishops were suspending the hired pens of their own anti-Martinists, they succeeded in silencing Martin Marprelate himself. While printing the long-awaited *More work for the Cooper,* the Martinist press—now operated by John Hodgkins—was finally ambushed by the earl of Derby's men, who seized the press, destroyed the tract, and tortured Hodgkins and his assistants. Penry and Throkmorton received news of the discovery and quickly produced a small, error-ridden octavo (most likely printed hastily by these two themselves, inexperienced as they were with the printing press). *The Protestacyon* (mid-October 1589) was the last of the Marprelate tracts; it expressed concern for the captive prisoners and contained arguments against imprisonment and torture which verge on a plea for freedom of conscience. Soon after the suppression of anti-Martinist productions and the capture of the Martinist press, the Marprelate controversy fizzled out. Writing for or against Martin had become a politically dangerous gesture. Martin's hot-blooded challenger, the cavalier Pasquill, reappeared briefly in the summer of 1590—but only to offer *Pasquills Apologie,* in which the tattered knight acrimoniously defends himself against the backlash towards the anti-Martinists, his overzealous attacks on puritanism having earned him accusations of being a Catholic.

II

One of the actors likely to have participated in the staging of Martin Marprelate was Will Kemp, who may also have been the first actor to play Falstaff.[53] The connection is an interesting one and, I believe, more than just coincidence. The Marprelate controversy, which took place a mere six or seven years before the production of *1 Henry IV,* was remembered long after the silencing of the tracts and sensational stage manifestations. Thomas Nashe, for instance, perhaps frustrated by the stifling of the stage and of the pamphlet war, continued to allude to the Marprelate controversy in such popular texts as *Pierce Penilesse* (1592).[54] Indeed, Martin Marprelate appears to have remained a vivid cultural figure for the next fifty years.[55] I believe that Shakespeare revived Martin, or at least relied on his legacy, when introducing Oldcastle/Falstaff to the stage; the presence of Will Kemp would have served as a vivid, visual reminder of the Marprelate connection. Shakespeare's creation was not entirely a "profoundly original . . . representation" or a "daring and provocative inspiration":[56] if Oldcastle was widely identified as an early puritan, and stage puritans were widely expected to be comically grotesque figures, then the depiction of Oldcastle as the grotesque Falstaff was not only natural but even expected. Falstaff, I would argue, thus continues, in part, the burlesque representation of the puritan established in the staging of the Marprelate tracts.

Such a reading, of course, has not been the prevailing understanding of Falstaff, and it may at first seem counterintuitive. Late twentieth-century Americans have learned to identify puritans as dry, dour Casaubon-like figures, an image reinforced every time the word *puritanical* is used. Literary critics are not immune to this pervasive cultural image of the puritan, despite the revisionary work of historians such as Christopher Hill. Certainly scholars of the early modern English stage have much to lose by abandoning the image of the fun-hating, dust-breathing fogy; such a representation enables the complex politics governing the theater and its operation to be reduced to simplistic binary terms. We have been taught automatically to equate puritans with antitheatrical (or antientertainment) sentiments and playwrights with largely antipuritan inclinations. Although scholars are beginning to question these categories and stereotypes, this easy puritan/theater division continues to reinscribe and reinstitutionalize itself in contemporary criticism. In a fascinating footnote (the primary habitat of the puritan in many critical texts), Jonas Barish justifies his choice of the term *puritan* to describe the antitheatrical Stephen Gosson: "I use the convenient shorthand term 'Puritan' despite the fact that not all writers against the stage were Puritans. Gosson, for example, . . . 'was actually a vigorous opponent of Puritanism.'"[57] The conceptual incongruity of an author who is simultaneously writing against the stage and against puritans is awkward and uncomfortable; the knowledge of Gosson's antipuritan writings deconstructs these very categories. This information is therefore textually repressed, becoming (quite literally) marginalized, hidden outside the parameters of the main text. We think of Gosson as allied with the puritans, and that is where he remains—whether he belongs there or not.

This same line of thinking prevents us from viewing Falstaff as a puritan. Falstaff's puritan origins have been consistently resisted, even by critics uncovering and foregrounding those origins. Why are scholars willing to make the radical revision in the character's name but not in his religion? Why read the Falstaff/Oldcastle connection as merely typological satire on an elite Elizabethan family, glossing over the implications of Falstaff's origins in a prominent religious figure? The answer, I believe, is that Falstaff has become such an icon of bacchanalian revelry in our own culture that it is almost inconceivable to equate him with another cultural icon, The Puritan, legendary origin of all that is repressed and repressive in American society and history (an image perpetuated by authors from Nathaniel Hawthorne to William Carlos Williams). Puritans and the carnival grotesque are considered not only distant but also antithetical; this antithesis is fundamental to our way of conceptualizing the world.

As we have seen, however, our current popular image of the puritan was not the only one available to Shakespeare's Elizabethan audience. We have lost sight of the plurality of images used to represent puritans in the late sixteenth and early seventeenth centuries. Certainly one predominant stereotype was the austere, rigid puritan, such as Malvolio or Tribulation Wholesome. But a competing representation (and I would argue a more pervasive one) was the grotesque puritan, such as Zeal-of-the-Land Busy or Plumporridge. I believe that it was this tradition of the grotesque puritan, so graphically realized in the staging of Martin Marprelate, to which Shakespeare turned when depicting the Lollard Oldcastle.

Literary critics have often struggled to find an adhesive label for Falstaff's character, a struggle that has resulted in "the endless litany absurdly patronizing Falstaff as Vice, Parasite, Fool, Braggart, Soldier, Corrupt Glutton, Seducer of Youth, Cowardly Liar."[58] Falstaff is, in fact, all of these and yet none in particular; he both deflects and absorbs such labels. With this awareness of Falstaff's slippery and multifaceted identity, I will venture to add "Falstaff as puritan" to the list. I am not attempting to reduce Falstaff's psychological and cultural complexity—Bloom's "Falstaffian sublimity"—to an easily graspable buzzword. Rather I am attempting, to the degree that it is possible to look back over a four-century divide, to uncover an important context that influenced the ways in which Elizabethans recognized and reacted to Falstaff as a social representation: I am endeavoring to reunite popular religious polemical literature and the stage, strands that have been falsely divorced through a history of critical prejudices and misconceptions.[59] This reunification illuminates and explains aspects of Falstaff which have long remained in the shadows.

Modern editions of the Henriad (such as the Arden, the "New" Arden, the Riverside, the New Folger, the New Variorum, and the New Cambridge Shakespeare) all acknowledge Falstaff's theatrical origins in the character of Sir John Oldcastle from *The Famous Victories of Henry V,* and critics have often commented on Falstaff's "puritanical" characteristics and speech patterns. J. Dover Wilson noted that "traces of Lollardry may still be detected in Falstaff's frequent resort to Scriptural phraseology and his affectation of an uneasy conscience" and that the passages on repentance, "together with the habit of citing Scripture, may have their origin . . . in the puritan, psalm-singing, temper of Falstaff's prototype."[60] Alfred Ainger, one of the earliest twentieth-century critics to discuss the Falstaff-Oldcastle connection, similarly observed, "What put it into Shakespeare's head to put this distinctly religious, not to say Scriptural phraseology into the mouth of Falstaff, but that the rough draft of the creation, as it came into his hands, was the decayed Puritan? For the Lollard of the fourteenth century was in this respect the Puritan of the sixteenth, that the one certain mark of his calling was this use of the language of Scripture, and that conventicle style which had been developed out of it."[61] Falstaff does quote extensively from Scripture; of the fifty-four biblical references identified in *1 Henry IV,* twenty-six "come from the mouth of Falstaff."[62] He quotes indirectly from Genesis, Exodus, 2 Samuel, Psalms, Proverbs, Matthew, Mark, Luke, 1 Corinthians, 2 Corinthians, and 1 Thessalonians (citing from the nonconformist Geneva Bible rather than the officially sanctioned Bishops' Bible[63]). The parables of Dives and Lazarus and the Prodigal Son in particular, as Ainger notes, "seem to haunt him along his whole course."[64]

Editors and critics also note that Falstaff speaks in a "parody of liturgical language,"[65] and that his lengthy speeches often smack of "the Scriptural style of the sanctimonious Puritan."[66] This rhetorical style, employed extensively by early modern puritan preachers, is repetitive, pedagogic, and laced with abundant biblical exegesis, and it often incorporates a question-and-answer format. One example of Falstaff's use of this "precise manner of one of the Covenanting preachers"[67] is his famous meditation on honor:

> What is honour? A word. What is in that word honour? What is that honour? Air. A trim reckoning! Who hath it? He that died a-Wednesday. Doth he feel it? No. Doth he hear it? No. 'Tis insensible, then? Yea, to the dead. But will it not live with the living? No. Why? Detraction will not suffer it. Therefore I'll none of it. Honour is a mere scutcheon—and so ends my catechism.
>
> (*1HIV,* 5.1.134-41)

In addition to biblical allusions and a rhetorical style typical of puritan preachers, Falstaff's speech is also rich in sixteenth-century puritan jargon. He compares himself to a "saint," puritan cant for one of God's elect, being corrupted by the "wicked" (*1HIV,* 1.2.88-93), the puritan word for the damned.[68] He speaks of his "vocation" (ll. 101-2), another popular puritan term, and repeatedly mentions the "spirit," a cornerstone of personal puritan theology of the "light within" (as opposed to the conformist emphasis on ecclesiastical authority): "Care I for the limb, the thews, the stature, bulk, and big assemblance of a man?" he asks, "Give me the spirit" (*2HIV,* 3.2.253-55, echoing 1 Samuel 16:7). In both Parts 1 and 2, Falstaff makes references to psalm-singing, a key element of the sixteenth-century puritan stereotype.[69] He wishes he "were a weaver" so that he "could sing psalms" (*1HIV,* 2.4.130)—weavers, who often sang at their work, being particularly notorious for their puritan psalmody—and later claims, "For my voice, I have lost it with halooing, and singing of anthems" (*2HIV,* 1.2.188-89). As Ainger notes, "the Lollard and the Puritan were alike famous for their habit of chanting or singing," the root of *Lollard* supposedly being the low-German *lollen,* to sing, "just as the Puritan form of religion in much later times has impressed upon the vulgar mind as its most prominent association that of *psalm-singing.*" (Ainger points to the puritan in *The Winter's Tale* "who sang Psalms to hornpipes.")[70] Critics have also commented on Falstaff's reliance on salvation by faith alone and his death-bed reference to the "Whore of Babylon . . . the customary Puritan term for the Church of Rome."[71]

Modern literary scholars are not the only ones to note these puritan allusions; Falstaff's companions also appear to identify him—or mock him—as a man of religion. Hal, who prides himself on his chameleonlike ability to speak to various social groups (such as the drawers) in their own language, repeatedly uses biblical idiom when speaking to Falstaff: since Falstaff (Oldcastle) is a famous puritan, Hal attempts to speak to him in the Lollard's own (biblical) terms. The prince teases Falstaff, whom he calls an "elder" (a well-known term referring to the presbyterian form of church government) with "I see a good amendment of life in thee, from praying to purse-taking" (*2HIV,* 2.4.256; *1HIV,* 1.2.99-100);[72] later Hal angrily challenges Falstaff's Calvinist assumptions: "Is she of the wicked? Is thine hostess here of the wicked? Or is thy boy of the wicked? Or honest Bardolph, whose zeal burns in his nose, of the wicked?" (*2HIV,* 2.4.324-27). "Zeal," of course, is another puritan byword.[73] The puritan rhetoric is neither incidental nor a moment of local humor but constitutes one of the many discursive registers through which Falstaff is constructed.

III

Falstaff's puritan associations, then, are pervasive and unmistakable. Most critics noting Falstaff's tendency to speak in biblical idiom and puritan jargon have assumed that such speech is intended as active mockery of the puritans by Falstaff. They comment that Falstaff himself is a self-conscious satirist making "jibes at the Puritans,"[74] that his part "involves Puritan posturing,"[75] and that "his 'religiousness' is a joke at this stage of his life."[76] Major editors have also held the opinion that Falstaff is repeatedly ridiculing puritans. Samuel Hemingway, who edited *1 Henry IV* for the New Variorum Shakespeare, maintains that "in mimicry of the Puritans Falstaff here uses one of their canting expressions" (a reference to his use of "the wicked"), and that "Falstaff here repeats in ridicule another Puritan shibboleth" (a reference to his use of "vocation"), to cite just two examples.[77] A. R. Humphreys, editor of the New Arden edition of the Henriad, also notes that Falstaff uses "frequent Puritan idiom," "mimics Puritan idiom," and devises "Puritan parody."[78]

But to an audience that identifies Falstaff with Oldcastle, such active, self-conscious puritan parody does not make much sense. The parody would have to be self-reflexive, with Sir John ridiculing his own religious inclinations—those same beliefs for which the historical Oldcastle was martyred. Considering Falstaff as a straightforward satirist, or as merely a Vice figure mocking "precisians," neglects the complex ramifications of his own religious associations and identity. Further, to explain Falstaff's religious language as merely a parody of puritan speech fails to take into account the legacy of the Marprelate tracts, especially the stage lampoons of Martin Marprelate and the precedent established for grotesque representations of the puritan. I believe an audience attuned to such representations, as well as to Oldcastle's own history, would have laughed not only *with* Falstaff but simultaneously *at* him: Falstaff does not simply satirize puritans but in many ways is himself a satiric representation of a famous Lollard martyr.[79]

On a superficial level the discrepancy between Falstaff's gluttonous lifestyle and the more restrained and abstemious conduct expected of a reformist religious leader becomes a basis for satire that runs throughout both parts of *Henry IV.* Although Bale has Oldcastle admitting "that in [his] frayle youthe [he] offended the (lorde) most greuouslye in pryde, wrathe, and glottonye, in couetousnesse and in lechere," in his wiser maturity he abandoned such pursuits;[80] Shakespeare, however, retains this aspect of Oldcastle's personality even as he fills the Lollard's mouth with reformist jargon. This coexistence of debauchery and purity, a typical element of the hypocritical puritan figure, is highlighted in Falstaff's identification with "Ephesians . . . of the old church" (*2HIV,* 2.2.142). The "prime church of Ephesus," as Middleton's stage puritan Mistress Purge notes,[81] was cited by puritans as a model for godly living, established according to the directives set out by St. Paul; the pre-Pauline Ephesians, on the other hand, were used as an example of those leading a wanton, ungodly lifestyle.[82] As a reformed Christian, Falstaff should live (as he claims he is trying to do[83]) according to Paul's guidelines for purity and morality in the "new" church; however, Falstaff and his companions are still the heavy drinkers of the unregenerate "old" church. The duality of this image, with Ephesians functioning simultaneously as a model of Pauline morality and of lascivious living, illustrates both Falstaff's puritan leanings and his failure to maintain lofty standards; this conflict between the "old man" and the "new" he is struggling (or pretending) to be is a major source of the comic satire.

The discrepancy between the belligerent Lollard leader of historical accounts and the coward of the Henriad is just as obvious a source of satire. Before Falstaff can engage in puritan parody or function as a comic figure, he must be disenfranchised as a serious martial threat. In virtually all histories of Oldcastle and Henry V, Oldcastle is a powerful and often dangerous figure.[84] As Holinshed and others report, he intended to lead an army consisting of thousands of commoners against Henry V; the attack was averted, But the threat posed to the throne by fifteenth-century Lollards was daunting. In Shakespeare's account Oldcastle's qualities as traitor and militant religious leader are dispersed among other characters in the plays; the historical Oldcastle is dismembered, his parts scattered, his subversive potential attached to other characters. It is the archbishop of York, not Oldcastle/Falstaff, who leads rebellion and "turns insurrection to religion" (*2HIV,* 1.1.201). Similarly, Oldcastle/Falstaff is not given the role of traitor. Holinshed and other chroniclers implicate Oldcastle in the Scroop-Grey-Cambridge plot, a domestic conspiracy that hinged on competing claims to the throne (rather than on personal greed and payoffs from the French, as Shakespeare portrays it).[85] In *Henry V* Shakespeare completely removes Oldcastle/ Falstaff from this treacherous triad; indeed, we might speculate that Falstaff's premature death is an effort to avoid the awkwardness of the historical alliance of Oldcastle with these traitors. Oldcastle's position as militant and treacherous religious leader is thus categorically emptied out, as the fallen knight Falstaff becomes a parody of the "Christen knyght" described by Bale, who "in all adve[n]terouse actes of wordlye manhode was . . . ever bolde, stronge, fortunate, doughtye, noble, & valeau[n]t." Falstaff does not lead armies against the king (indeed he is incapable of it) but rather directs troops that he himself (again turning to one of his favorite biblical parables) deems "slaves as ragged as Lazarus in the painted cloth, where the glutton's dogs licked his sores" (*1HIV,* 4.2.24-26).

To an audience familiar with Foxe, Holinshed, or *The Famous Victories of Henry V,* Falstaff is easily recognizable as a satiric rendition of Oldcastle—but this is not to say that Falstaff does not also assume the role of satirist. Even as he is disempowered as a religious and military figure, Falstaff becomes a powerful center of carnival and articulates overtly subversive sentiments, freely criticizing—even mocking—king and prince. Through his jests, which respect neither rank nor hierarchy nor social order, Falstaff assumes a voice similar to that of Martin Marprelate. Phyllis Rackin has noted that "Falstaff's irrepressible, irreverent wit epitomizes the unruliness of present oral speech, which, unlike a written text, can never be fully subjugated to official censorship and authoritative control."[86] While the Elizabethan political machinery kept a tight reign on the press, the Marprelate tracts presented an important and, for sixteenth-century English men and women, highly visible exception to this rule: the Marprelate tracts were unruly written texts which *did* evade censorship and authoritative control, at least for a time. Like the texts themselves, Martin's irreverent wit was irrepressible and unruly. Martin's manner of heckling the bishops and kicking away their pedestals enabled him to taunt them as equals; Martin explodes sanctioned hierarchies and pieties, and it is this leveling tendency that makes him so threatening—and so appealing.

Similarly, it is only through Falstaff that the audience comes to know the prince familiarly as "Hal." Falstaff's insults to Henry are just as dismissive of social hierarchy as are those of Martin to the bishops. Falstaff's speech itself reverberates with Martin's own grotesque, carnivalesque tone; indeed, the banter between Falstaff and Hal resounds with the taunting exchanges between Marprelate and his textual opponents such as Cuthbert Curryknave or Pasquill.[87] Falstaff hails the prince as his "dog" (*2HIV,* 1.2.144-45), "the most comparative rascalliest sweet young prince" (*1HIV,* 1.2.78-79), and "a good shallow young fellow" who "would have made a good pantler, a would ha' chipped bread well" (*2HIV,* 2.4.234-35). He also hurls such colorful insults as "you starveling, you eel-skin, you dried neat's-tongue, you bull's-pizzle, you stockfish" (*1HIV,* 2.4.240-41) and tells Hal to "hang thyself in thine own heir-apparent garters" (*1HIV,* 2.2.42). Twice Falstaff even threatens treason: "By the Lord, I'll be a traitor then, when thou art king" (*1HIV,* 1.2.141); "A king's son! If I do not beat thee out of thy kingdom with a dagger of lath, and drive all thy subjects afore thee like a flock of wild geese, I'll never wear hair on my face more" (*1HIV,* 2.4.133-36). In addition to mocking the prince, Falstaff lacks all respect for the lord chief justice and undermines the very code of chivalry ("honour is a mere scutcheon") that was to become so central to the way nostalgic Elizabethans viewed Henry V; at Shrewsbury, Sir John discredits the notion of chivalric honor, and in Part 2 he boisterously sings "'When Arthur first in court'—Empty the jordan.—'And was a worthy king'—How now, Mistress Doll?" (*2HIV,* 2.4.33-34), intermingling allusions to the paragon of chivalry with references to chamber pots and prostitutes. In Falstaff, as in Martin Marprelate, social and discursive orders are undermined and overturned.

Falstaff thus plays the role of satirist even as he is the butt of satire. In this dual and contradictory position, Falstaff reproduces a fundamental dynamic of the staging of Martinism. Such burlesque stagings provided Shakespeare not only with a performative model for representing puritans in terms of the grotesque, but also with a vivid example of the staging of satire and the use of the carnivalesque; Falstaff, like Martin, inhabits a pivotal, liminal position from which he is able to toy with the boundaries of orthodoxy and subversion. The duality as satirist and object of satire that lies at the heart of the Marprelate controversy is largely a function of the indeterminate social boundaries that Martin and his adversaries test and prod. In his irreverent attacks on the bishops, Martin challenged the boundaries defining ecclesiastical hierarchy and organization, thus questioning the episcopalian basis for church government. As Evelyn Tribble has recently noted, Martin's defiance of episcopal borders is mirrored in the tracts themselves, where Martin continually shifts his authorial position from the textual margins to the main body of the text. Tribble writes, "In her proclamation [against "Schismatical Bookes"] Elizabeth characterizes the pamphlets as attacking the bishops and the church as a whole 'in rayling sort and beyond the boundes of good humanitie.' 'Beyond the boundes': these words sum up the nature of the Marprelate threat. The pamphlets enact a grotesque breaking of the boundaries of the text and of conventional ecclesiastical discourse."[88] The broken borders of the text were probably the least of the queen's immediate worries; not only did Martin advocate breaking textual and ecclesiastical boundaries, but the unlocatable, unstoppable production of the Marprelate tracts also revealed a very real breach in the authorities' ability to control discursive territories. The illegal pamphlets that continued to stream forth despite all attempts to stop them at their source became a graphic manifestation of permeable borders and failed efforts at containment.

In commissioning the vicious anti-Martinist attacks, the city magistrates and church authorities made a desperate attempt to demonstrate their control over these social and discursive boundaries. The violent, grotesque stage lampoons concocted by the anti-Martinists can be seen as an attempt to reclaim the system of social borders which Martin threatened; like a public execution, Martin's torture onstage is intended, in Foucault's term, to reactivate power.[89] But in the case of Martin Marprelate, such punishment, although initiated by the city magistrates, quickly became a communal, popular act rather than a display organized by and for the central authority; in the staging of Martinism, the audience became not only spectators but participants. Even as the torture of Martin is turned over to the crowd, it loses its sting; onstage Marprelate is "*drie beaten, & therby his bones broken, then whipt that made him winse,*" but at the same time he is playing a role in "a *Maygame* vpon the *Stage*."[90]

Within the anti-Martinist stage attacks, we can detect a shift from the exclusionary violence of the grotesque to the communal participation of the carnivalesque. In a lampoon known as "The Maygame of Martinism," Martin appears crossdressed as Maid Marian with a cloth covering his beard; still the object of laughter, Martin becomes a participant in communal festival—the focal point of the festivities and a source of carnival energy—not a scapegoat of mob violence. Far from marking his exclusion from the community, the staging of Martinism demonstrated Marprelate's ability to draw others into the terms of his own festive world. Crossing into his territory has perilous political consequences, however: in a debate where laughter becomes the ammunition for attacking political targets, to laugh *with* Martin even as he is supposed to be laughed *at* suggests—or could lead to—sympathies with his anti-episcopalian politics. In the roar of communal laughter, it becomes impossible to distinguish anti-Martinist from antiprelatical sentiment. Indeed, the same chuckle at Martin's stage antics could be simultaneously at and with Martin—or, what amounts to the same thing, at and with the city magistrates leading the attack.

Employing Martin's own carnivalesque terms, the anti-Martinists do not reassert a social boundary so much as they playfully test rhetorical bounds. The line demarcating orthodoxy from heresy, which these authors were hired to enforce, becomes dangerously thin; similarly, the distinction between a mob exacting punishment for subversive activities and a crowd reveling in the possibility of that subversion begins to fade or even disappear. "The representation of disorder threatens to collapse into disorder itself," writes Tribble. The anti-Martinist authors themselves were aware of the boundaries they were dancing along and the dangers of slipping over them. Lyly "goes to some pains to avoid a potential collapse of satirizer and satirized"; Bacon, urging the suppression of the anti-Martinists, also "recognizes the tendency of the satirist and satirized to collapse."[91]

In one anti-Martinist pamphlet, where the anonymous author attempts to mock Marprelate and his readers by depicting the way in which his tracts were received, we can see the ambiguous, slippery terms of this satire. In this vignette one is asked to visualize a riotous tavern scene with an illegal, antiepiscopalian Marprelate tract (perhaps read out loud) providing the evening's entertainment: "[Martin], together with his ribauldry, had some wit (though knavish) and woulde make some foolish women, and pot companions to laugh, when sitting on their Alebenches, they would tipple, and read it, seruing them in steede of a blinde Minstrell, when they could get none, to fiddle them foorth a fitte of mirth."[92] The scene is intended as ridicule, but it is nonetheless attractive; who does not enjoy being fiddled forth into a fit of mirth? The conspiratorial, underground nature of the scenario is also appealing, conjuring images of clandestine camaraderie. The seduction of this scene overwhelms its satiric purpose; even as it ridicules Martin, the passage inadvertently illustrates and effects his popular appeal, drawing the reader into Martin's circle. The anti-Martinist authors themselves seem unable to avoid a sense of community with Martin even as they lambaste his opinions and scoff at his prose style. Using Martin's satiric terms, they are unable to convert him entirely into an object of satire or to maintain the distance required for hostile satire. "Even as he attacks Martin," Tribble writes, "Lyly inadvertently implies a sort of fellowship with him; momentarily they become two ruffians drinking together."[93] Despite his awareness of and resistance to the potential collapse of discursive (and, ultimately, political) boundaries, Lyly (like Nashe) cannot successfully maintain the distance between the satirist and the object of his satire.

The anti-Martinists thus played with, rather than policed, the boundaries they were assigned to defend. The tantalizing appeal of the Marprelate controversy is located along this quivering border between the authoritative and the subversive, the orthodox and the heretical. In this high-stakes game (that is, the secure and stable foundation of church—and hence state—government), the anti-Martinist authors toy with limits, daring themselves and each other to apply more pressure on social boundaries. To bend but not to break; this was the rule. The anti-Martinists sought to employ carnivalesque rhetoric while not fully participating in carnival. The play surrounding these limits created the excitement and the tension of the Marprelate controversy as Londoners followed the course of this pamphlet war with bated breath, the possibility of imminent explosion adding to the agitated, even fearful, pleasure of watching the limits grow transparently thin.

This same play at and with social boundaries infuses the Henriad with much of its dramatic energy. *Henry IV, Part 1* in particular is largely driven by Hal's flirtation precisely with the border between authority and subversion, orthodoxy and heresy. Like the anti-Martinists, Hal enters into the terms of carnival subversion, represented and embodied by Falstaff, while still maintaining his position of authority. The danger, however, is that the tension between these two positions might prove stronger than Hal's ability to control and define his own situation—that the boundary distinguishing the role of the prince from that of the reveler could break before Hal can orchestrate his glorious return to orthodoxy and filial duty. It is just possible—or at least we are invited to entertain the possibility—that "the base contagious clouds" Hal "permit[s] . . . to smother up his beauty from the world" could prove too dense, that his plan to imitate the sun could be thwarted by elements beyond his control, and that "the foul and ugly mists" could indeed strangle him (*1HIV,* 1.2.193-94 and 197-98). The force of carnival community might overcome his intention to step back into his role as king.

In Act 3, scene 2, of *1 Henry IV,* King Henry explicitly warns his son of the dangers of slipping over this line, advocating instead a strict division between community and king and lamenting that Hal "hast lost [his] princely privilege / With vile participation" (ll.86-87). Describing Richard II's fall and his own rise to power, Henry prides himself on not becoming "stale and cheap to vulgar company"; he rather kept his "person fresh and new, . . . like a robe pontifical" (ll. 41 and 55-56). By contrast Richard II, "the skipping King" (l. 60) in Henry's version of events,

> Grew a companion to the common streets,
> Enfeoff'd himself to popularity,
> That, being daily swallow'd by men's eyes,
> . . .
> He was but as the cuckoo is in June,
> Heard, not regarded; seen, but with such eyes
> As, sick and blunted with community,
> Afford no extraordinary gaze, . . .
> Being with his presence glutted, gorg'd, and full.
>
> (3.2.68-84)

By "mingl[ing] his royalty with cap'ring fools" (as Henry says of Richard [l. 63]), Hal risks losing himself in the bowels of the common community, being absorbed so that the distinction between the crowd and the prince is no longer recognizable. Indeed, this breakdown of hierarchical division is precisely what Oldcastle threatened by leading a mob against the king, and in part what Marprelate advocated by seeking to pull down pontifical robes. The ever "glutted, gorg'd, and full" Falstaff thus seems almost to literalize this removal of social, hierarchical boundaries: Falstaff becomes the community which can, through jest, ingest its leaders. His rotund, expansive figure, though emblematic of carnivalesque festivity, potentially signifies absorption and loss of social distinction and hence of political authority.

The Henriad thus reenacts issues of discursive and political control presented by the Marprelate controversy. Within the plays themselves, Falstaff assumes a voice and role similar to that of Martin Marprelate, becoming a swelling carnival force that threatens to consume Hal's "princely privilege"; Falstaff, like Martin, challenges the hierarchies that constitute the very structure of church and state. The presence of the historical Oldcastle infuses Falstaff's festive carnival subversion with the potential of actual violence and upheaval. Like the anti-Martinists, Hal confronts Falstaff's festive social force by engaging in its own terms, reveling for a time in the playful contest of insults. But ultimately the prince, like the London magistrates, discovers that the boundary between authority and subversion is too fragile to be long toyed with in this way, and that hierarchies cannot be restored while the discursive play continues: Falstaff must first be banished and Martin's press must be seized, his printers tortured, and his authors killed.

Beyond the bounds of the stage, the Henriad also recreates the dynamic of the anti-Martinist theatrical lampoons, as Falstaff assumes the qualities of the satirized Martin Marprelate. In the anti-Martinist productions the audience is obviously intended to be ridiculing and laughing at the abused Martin; but, as in the anti-Martinist tracts themselves, the legacy of Martin's popular appeal overwhelms the pressures of satire, and the audience finds itself in the position of laughing with the target of the attack. Similarly, the translation of the martial religious hero Oldcastle into the comic buffoon Falstaff seems to require mocking laughter; but even as a butt of satire, Falstaff exudes such inviting carnival energy that the audience engages with him: he is, in his own words, "not only witty in [himself], but the cause that wit is in other men" (*2HIV,* 1.2.8-9). For a short time the audience becomes Falstaff's "pot companions," and they too are "fiddled forth" into mirth—subversive laughter often at the king's expense. It is this wit that draws the spectators into "vile participation" with a figure who led an army against the king. From the position of the satirized, both Falstaff and Martin Marprelate entice the audience to join their carnival revelries. The spectators simultaneously laugh at and with subversive forces, simultaneously disapproving and participating; this is the play of the play.

Notes

[1] John Bale, *Brefe Chronycle concernynge the Examinacyon and death of the blessed martyr of Christ syr Johan Oldecastell the lorde Cobham* (Antwerp, 1544), fol. 4[v]. All quotations of Bale follow this edition. Bale expands on William Tyndale's account of Oldcastle, *The examinacion of master William Thorpe preste accused of heresye. The examinacion of Syr J. Oldcastell* (Antwerp, 1530).

[2] Bale, fols. 9[r], 13[r], 49[r].

[3] 3[r], 52[r], 53[r].

[4] The most thorough catalogue of sixteenth-century references to Oldcastle can be found in Alice-Lyle Scoufos, *Shakespeare's Typological Satire: A Study of the Falstaff-Oldcastle Problem* (Athens: Ohio UP, 1979). In John Foxe's *Acts and Monuments* (1563), which included Oldcastle's biography (largely lifted from Bale) and a woodcut graphically representing his "horrible and cruell martirdome," Foxe recounts Oldcastle's trial and describes the Lollard insurrection of 1413, led in part by Oldcastle, as "an evangelical meeting of the gospellers." This benign version of his participation in the uprising drew sharp attacks from those who adhered to the image of Oldcastle as heretic and traitor, the representation popular through the fifteenth and early sixteenth centuries. In response to such criticism, Foxe added a thirty-page "Defense of Lord Cobham" in his second edition (1570), further evidence of Oldcastle's popularity, as well as an indication of his controversial position. While Foxe acknowledges that Oldcastle was deemed a heretic for his Wyclifite views, he staunchly denies that the nobleman was a traitor or anything but a loyal subject of Henry V (Scoufos, 60-62, esp. 61).

[5] John Stowe's *Annales of England* (1592) described Oldcastle as a "strong . . . [and] meetely good man of war, but . . . a most perverse enimie to the state of the church at that time" (Scoufos, 65). Stowe's depiction follows the fifteenth-century tradition of portraying Oldcastle as an enemy to church and state; this image had predominated until Tyndale's pamphlet (see note 1). Responding to Tyndale, Sir Thomas More "cites the burning of Oldcastle as an English example of the wise use of fire to control destructive forces" (Scoufos, 56-67, esp. 56).

[6] Stephen Brachlow cites several examples of prominent puritans who claimed a genealogy from the Lollards in *The Communion of Saints: Radical Puritan and Separatist Ecclesiology 1570-1625* (Oxford: Oxford UP, 1988); among these were Walter Travers (81), Foxe (90), William Ames (91), and Robert Parker (91). In an attempt to link the reform movement with the chronology set out in Revelation, "Wyclif and the early reformers" were sometimes "identified with" the three angels in Revelation 14 (89n). See also Anthony Milton, "The Church of England, Rome and the True Church: The Demise of a Jacobean Consensus" in *The Early Stuart Church, 1603-1642,* Kenneth Fincham, ed. (Stanford, CA: Stanford UP, 1993), 187-210, esp. 191-92.

[7] Scoufos provides convincing and extensive evidence that Shakespeare's contemporaries, as well as his eighteenth-century readers, recognized Falstaff as an alias for Oldcastle; see especially Chapter 2 of *Shakespeare's Typological Satire.* See also Gary Taylor, "The Fortunes of Oldcastle," *Shakespeare Survey* 38 (1985): 85-100, esp. 91.

[8] Critics have almost universally claimed that the name-change was the direct result of protests by William Brooke, Lord Cobham; while Brooke does seem to have complained about *1 Henry IV* to Edmund Tilney, we have only circumstantial, secondhand evidence of his opposition. For a persuasive argument that the protesting family member was the tenth Lord Cobham, Sir William Brooke, Lord Chamberlain from 1596-97 (thus dating the play in late 1596), see Robert J. Fehrenbach, "When Lord Cobham and Edmund Tilney 'were att odds': Oldcastle, Falstaff, and the Date of *1 Henry IV,*" *Shakespeare Studies* 18 (1986): 87-101.

Thomas Pendleton provides what seems to me a more thorough explanation for the switch, noting that Shakespeare, a man of seemingly conservative religious inclinations, "must have been surprised to find that his proto-Puritan figure of fun was for much of his audience a proto-Protestant martyr. . . . The change from 'Oldcastle' to 'Falstaff' seems to have been motivated not just by Sir William Brooke's displeasure, but as much—and in the greatest likelihood, much more—by the displeasure of a significant part of Shakespeare's audience at his treatment of a hero of their religion" ("'This is not the man': On Calling Falstaff Falstaff," *Analytical & Enumerative Bibliography,* n.s. 4 [1990]: 59-71, esp. 68-69). The Epilogue to *2 Henry IV* thus becomes more comprehensible: "a public apology implies that at least a considerable part of the public had been offended" (68).

[9] Taylor lists "Thomas Middleton (1604), Nathan Field (*c.* 1611), the anonymous author of *Wandering-Jew, Telling Fortunes to Englishmen* (*c.* 1628), George Daniel (1647), Thomas Randolph (1651), and Thomas Fuller (1655, 1662)" as those noting the original identity of "Oldcastle" (85-86). For evidence of court performances of *1 Henry IV* using the name of "Oldcastle," see Taylor, 90-91.

[10] *A Critical Edition of* I Sir John Oldcastle, ed. Jonathan Rittenhouse, *The Renaissance Imagination,* Stephen Orgel, ed., vol. 9 (New York: Garland, 1984), 104. Robert Wilson and Richard Hathaway also collaborated with Munday and Drayton. Commissioned by Henslowe in the wake of the Henriad, this play testifies to the popular demand for more representations of Oldcastle and to the desire of at least part of the public to see him restored as a Protestant martyr and hero. John Weever's hagiographic poem *The Mirror of Martyrs, or The life and death of that thrice valiant Capitaine, and most godly Martyre Sir Iohn Old-castle knight Lord Cobham* (London, 1601) also illustrates this urge to recover the Lollard as a pious knight. See also Scoufos, 33-35.

[11] Gary Taylor, Stanley Wells, John Jowett, and William Montgomery changed the name of "Falstaff" back to "Oldcastle" in *William Shakespeare: The Complete Works* (Oxford: Clarendon, 1986), 509. Jonathan Goldberg, arguing against the name-change, contends that "these restorations, made in the name of 'the integrity of the individual work of art' and, congruously, 'the integrity of the individual'—call him Oldcastle, or Shakespeare—relentlessly reduce multiplicity to singularity. This text of *1 Henry IV* is the one and only text, unrevised. The character's name is likewise fixed, referring to the real. But in these claims, Shakespeare's hand is being held firmly in the censor's grip, for the exterior has violated the very integrity Taylor wishes to secure; claiming to free Shakespeare—and to allow him artistic autonomy—Taylor ties him to a singular historical referent, and a singular meaning. Through the proper name, all sorts of propriety are secured in the transcendental name of the *logos*" ("The Commodity of Names: 'Falstaff' and 'Oldcastle' in *1 Henry IV*" in *Reconfiguring the Renaissance: Essays in Critical Materialism,* Jonathan Crew, ed. [Cranbury, NJ: AUP, 1992], 76-88, esp. 83). David Scott Kastan, noting that "all the authoritative texts print 'Falstaff' and none prints 'Oldcastle,'" writes: "To disregard this fact is to idealize the activity of authorship, removing it from the social and material mediations that permit intentions to be realized in print and performance. It is to remove the text from its own complicating historicity. The restoration of 'Oldcastle' enacts a fantasy of unmediated authorship paradoxically mediated by the Oxford edition itself" ("'Killed With Hard Opinions': Oldcastle, Falstaff, and the Reformed Text of *1 Heny IV*" in *Textual Formations and Reformations,* Thomas L. Berger and Laurie McGuire, eds., forthcoming). Thomas Pendleton further notes the flaws in the assumption that only the name was changed, without corresponding changes in the text (59-71). David Bevington, first to disagree with Taylor and Wells's decision, keeps the name of "Falstaff" in the single volume *Henry IV, Part I* he edited for Oxford (The Oxford Shakespeare [Oxford: Clarendon, 1987]). For a pointed summation of this editorial "battle" (Bevington's term, v), see the review of Bevington's volume by John W. Velz in *Shakespeare Quarterly* 43 (1992): 107-9.

[12] Taylor, 85. In "The Fortunes of Oldcastle," Taylor defends his decision to reinstate "Oldcastle" as the name of Hal's companion. Taylor argues that "in the mouth of a fictional character called Falstaff, the words lose their historicity and ambiguity. To some extent, this is what happens to the whole character. The name 'Falstaff' fictionalizes, depoliticizes, secularizes, and in the process trivializes the play's most memorable character. It robs the play of that tension created by the distance between two available interpretations of one of its central figures" (95). While I appreciate the impulse to rescue Shakespeare from the evils of sixteenth-century court politics, I must also disagree with Taylor's editorial decision. To annihilate the effects of Shakespeare's contemporary censors is to rewrite history in a disturbingly Orwellian fashion and to deny the text's sociopolitical setting. In addition, if, as Taylor effectively argues, Elizabethan and Jacobean audiences were highly aware of Falstaff's "real" identity as Oldcastle, then part of the pleasure of this theatrical experience would have been the knowledge that one could read the clandestine identity hidden behind the name, much like the intrigue of a *roman à clef.* Since "Falstaff" is the name that was presented to the vast majority of viewers, changing his name would be the equivalent of demystifying allegory; *The Faerie Queene,* for example, would not be nearly as titillating if the veil of allegorical names were stripped away, and Britannia, Britomart, and the Faerie Queen herself were all merely "Queen Elizabeth." In short, rather than depoliticizing the play or robbing it of tension,

the presence of the name "Falstaff" *combined with* the knowledge of the character's "true" identity heightens awareness of the political circumstances of the play.

[13] Fehrenbach, 92. Fehrenbach agrees with S. Schoenbaum (*Shakespeare: A Documentary Life* [Oxford: Clarendon, 1975], 144) that the name Oldcastle was simply a mistake.

[14] See Mark Dominik, *A Shakespearean Anomaly: Shakespeare's Hand in "Sir John Oldcastle"* (Beaverton, OR: Alioth Press, 1991) and E.A.J. Honigmann, "Sir John Oldcastle: Shakespeare's martyr," in *"Fanned and Winnowed Opinions": Shakespearean Essays presented to Harold Jenkins,* John W. Mahon and Thomas A. Pendleton, eds. (London and New York: Methuen, 1987), 118-32. Scoufos repeatedly attributes Shakespeare's transformation of the historical Oldcastle to a desire to satirize the Cobham family: "The poet was concerned with ridiculing the new lord chamberlain through an established dramatic character. . . . [Shakespeare] developed within the chronicle material context a broad comic plot in which the Falstaff-Oldcastle character could be manipulated to reflect not only the image of the ancestral Lollard martyr but certain aspects of the life of the contemporary Lord Cobham, Sir William Brooke" (107). After William's death in March 1597, we find Master Ford assuming the alias of Brook in *The Merry Wives of Windsor,* seemingly an allusion to the new Lord Cobham, Henry Brooke (and here again protests caused the name to be changed to "Broom"). Scoufos goes so far as to state that "*The Merry Wives of Windsor* is a play about the Cobhams" (191), and speculates that Queen Elizabeth's famous request to see Falstaff in love was in direct response to Henry Brooke's amorous (mis)adventures (200-204). The Brooke satire was apparently included for the entertainment of Sir George Carey, patron of the Chamberlain's Men and Henry Brooke's unsuccessful rival for government positions. The Carey-Brooke friction continued to provide satiric fodder for playwrights; Nashe's *Lenten Stuffe,* the lost *Isle of Dogs,* and Jonson's *Every Man in his Humour* all take jabs at the Brooke family. See Charles Nicholl, *A Cup of News: The life of Thomas Nashe* (London: Routledge & Kegan Paul, 1984), 249-55. This satiric naming is superficial, however, in comparison to Oldcastle's thorough conversion into the character of the Henriad's Falstaff. A topical allusion to a relatively minor Elizabethan courtier may be read as personal satire; the transformation of a prominent historical figure, one variously claimed as a cultural icon, transcends the level of personal, local attack.

[15] Scoufos, 35-36.

[16] Wilson, *The Fortunes of Falstaff* (Cambridge and New York: Cambridge UP, 1944), esp. Chapter 2.

[17] Bloom, *Ruin the Sacred Truths: Poetry and Belief from the Bible to the Present* (Cambridge, MA, and London: Harvard UP, 1989), 84.

[18] P. A. Scholes, *The Puritans and Music,* 113-16, cited in Patrick Collinson, *The Elizabethan Puritan Movement* (Berkeley: U of California P, 1967), 370. One of the anti-Marprelate tracts includes the line: "Who trusts a broken staffe, we see, doe fall ere they be ware" ([Sir John Davies], *Sir Martin Mar-People, his Coller of Esses* [London, 1590], sig. A4v).

[19] Nicholl, 64.

[20] William Pierce, *An Historical Introduction to the Marprelate Tracts* (London: Archibald Constable, 1908), 152. See also Nicholl, 64-65.

[21] This and all quotations of the Marprelate tracts come from the most recent modern reprint, *The Marprelate Tracts 1588, 1589,* ed. William Pierce (London: James Clarke & Co., 1911), here, 17.

[22] *Marprelate Tracts,* 239.

[23] *Marprelate Tracts,* 28, 75, and 84-85.

[24] *Marprelate Tracts,* 25 and 86.

[25] Hill, *The Collected Essays of Christopher Hill: Volume One, Writing and Revolution in 17th Century England* (Amherst: The U of Massachusetts P, 1985), 76.

[26] *Marprelate Tracts,* 90 and 91 (emphasis mine).

[27] In *Bartholomew Fair,* Busy exclaims, "I wil remoue *Dagon* there, I say, that *Idoll,* that heathenish *Idoll,* that remaines (as I may say) a beame, a very beame, not a beame of the *Sunne,* nor a beame of the *Moone,* nor a beame of a ballance, neither a house-beame, nor a Weauer's beame, but a beame in the eye, in the eye of the brethren . . . " (*Ben Jonson,* ed. C. H. Herford and Percy and Evelyn Simpson, vol. 6 [Oxford: Clarendon, 1938], 5.5.4-9). Falstaff also employs this comic, repetitious manner of preaching in *1 Henry IV:* "an old lord of the Council rated me the other day in the street about you, sir, but I marked him not, and yet he talked very wisely, but I regarded him not, and yet he talked wisely, and in the street too" (1.2.81-85). This and all subsequent references to the Henriad are from the New Arden edition, edited by A. R. Humphreys (London: Routledge, 1960).

[28] Hill, 75.

[29] The promised *Epitome* of John Bridges's "right worshipful volume written against the Puritans" (end of November 1588) was followed in turn by the broad-

side *Minerall and metaphysicall schoolpoints* (mid-March 1589), *Hay any worke for Cooper* (March 1589), Martin Jr.'s *Theses Martinianae* (22 July 1589), and Martin Sr.'s *The just censure and reproofe* (29 July 1589).

[30] Hill, 77.

[31] *Marprelate Tracts,* 200.

[32] *Marprelate Tracts,* 357n and 359. Martin Sr. has Archbishop Whitgift give orders to search London for Martinist pamphlets: "And mark if any Puritan receiveth anything. Open his pack, that you may be sure he hath no Martins sent him. We will direct our warrants so that you may search all packs at your discretion. We will take order also that the Court may be watched, who dispense or read these Libels there; and in faith I think they do my lord of Essex great wrong, that say he favours Martin" (356-57).

[33] Neil Rhodes, *Elizabethan Grotesque* (London: Routledge & Kegan Paul, 1980), 4.

[34] Nicholl, 74-75. In Bacon's *Advertisement touching the Controversies of the Church of England* (late 1589) Bacon takes on the role of peacemaker, and Richard Harvey takes on the persona of Plaine Percevall the Peace-maker in *Plaine Percevall* (late 1589). Gabriel Harvey's *Advertisement for Papp-hatchett and Martin Marprelate* (November 1589) is in part a response to personal attacks from Lyly. Richard Harvey's "abuse of the anti-Martinists in *Plaine Percevall,* and of Nashe in *The Lamb of God* [1590], was the spark which ignited the Nashe-Harvey quarrel" (Nicholl, 75). Of the popular appeal of this dispute, Neil Rhodes writes: "In the middle years of the decade the literary battle between Nashe and Harvey provided spectacular entertainment of a different kind. It was a re-run of the Marprelate controversy conducted at a more sophisticated stylistic level" (92). C. L. Barber discusses the ways in which those entering the Marprelate fray styled themselves as joining Martin's "May game" in *Shakespeare's Festive Comedy* (Princeton, NJ: Princeton UP, 1959), 55.

[35] See Leland H. Carlson, *Martin Marprelate, Gentleman: Master Job Throkmorton Laid Open In His Colors* (San Marino, CA: Huntington, 1981). J. Dover Wilson also advanced his own theory of authorship for the Marprelate tracts, suggesting that Martin was Sir Roger Williams; Wilson goes on to claim that Shakespeare's character of Fluellen was modelled after Williams, an assertion that seems to me rather dubious. See Wilson, *Martin Marprelate and Shakespeare's Fluellen* (London: Alexander Moring, 1912).

[36] *Marprelate Tracts,* 71, 78, 248, 262, and 279.

[37] Nashe's anti-Martinist tract *An Almond for a Parrat* is found in *The Works of Thomas Nashe,* ed. Ronald B. McKerrow, 5 vols. (Oxford: Basil Blackwell, 1958), here, 3:342 and 374. Other anti-Martinist tracts possibly by Nashe, such as *A Countercuffe given to Martin Junior* (1589), *The Return of Pasquill* (1589), and *The First Part of Pasquills Apologie* (1590), are in Volume 1. McKerrow lists the *Almond* under "Doubtful Works," but Nicholl describes this text as "the one anti-Martinist pamphlet accepted as entirely his," while establishing a collaborative relationship with Robert Greene for the authorship of the Pasquill tracts—with Nashe as the "news-hound" and Greene as the author (71-73, esp. 72).

[38] [Thomas Nashe], *Martins Months minde, that is, A certaine report, and true description of the Death, and Funeralls, of olde Martin Marre-prelate* (London, 1589), sig. A1ʳ.

[39] "Contrary to modern canons, the grotesque body is not separated from the rest of the world. It is not a closed, completed unit; it is unfinished, outgrows itself, transgresses its own limits. The stress is laid on those parts of the body that are open to the outside world, that is, the parts through which the world enters the body or emerges from it, or through which the body itself goes out to meet the world. This means that the emphasis is on the apertures or the convexities, or on various ramifications and offshoots: the open mouth, the genital organs, the breasts, the phallus, the potbelly, the nose. The body discloses its essence as a principle of growth which exceeds its own limits only in copulation, pregnancy, childbirth, the throes of death, eating, drinking, or defecation. This is the ever unfinished, ever creating body, the link in the chain of genetic development, or more correctly speaking, two links shown at the point where they enter into each other" (Mikhail Bakhtin, *Rabelais and His World,* trans. Helene Iswolsky [Bloomington: Indiana UP, 1984], 26).

[40] *Works of Thomas Nashe,* 3:355.

[41] *Works of Thomas Nashe,* 1:59.

[42] [Lyly], *Pappe with an hatchet,* Puritan Discipline Tracts (London, 1844), 37.

[43] Mary Grace Muse Adkins argues that *A Knack to Know a Knave* is a surviving anti-Martinist play; but while this play probably emanates from the Marprelate controversy, it is both too late (1592) and too formally constructed to be one of the grotesque anti-puritan interludes referred to in the tracts themselves ("The Genesis of Dramatic Satire Against the Puritan, as Illustrated in *A Knack to Know a Knave,*" *Review of English Studies* 22 [1946]: 81-95, esp. 81-85).

[44] Pierce, 222. Rhodes notes that an especially violent

anti-Martinist play "was probably acted by Paul's Boys in 1589 and the company closed as a result. The public theatres were also engaged in anti-Marprelate satire, but they managed to escape official sanctions. . . . the most likely explanation of the closure of Paul's Boys in 1590 is that it was considered most unfitting for children to be mixed up in a religious controversy" (66-67).

[45] See *Pappe with an hatchet,* 50.

[46] *Works of Thomas Nashe,* 1:59 and 92; Nicholl, 68.

[47] *Marprelate Tracts,* 330.

[48] *Pappe with an hatchet,* 32.

[49] *Pappe with an hatchet,* 12. We find another intriguing reference to Martin's theatricality in Pasquill's (Nashe's) *Countercuffe to Martin Junior,* in which the speaker affirms: "*Pasquills* experience in thys generation teacheth him, that many of your Bowlsterers may be compared to Bookes that are gilded & trimlie couered, they sette a faire face of Religion vppon your cause, but when they are opened, they are full of Tragedies, eyther *Thyestes* eating vppe the flesh of his owne Children, or cursed *Oedipus* in bed with his owne Mother" (*Works of Thomas Nashe,*) 1:63-64).

[50] Nicholl, 68. The letter is quoted in full in the notes to *Pappe with an hatchet,* 48.

[51] The letter to the archbishop is quoted in full in the notes to *Pappe with an hatchet,* 49.

[52] "Would those Comedies might be allowed to be plaid that are pend, and then I am sure he would be decyphered, and so perhaps discouraged" (*Pappe with an hatchet,* 32).

[53] Nicholl writes: "Will Kemp may also have contributed his famous comic talents: a later Martinist tract mentions a 'Kemp' among the 'haggling and profane' detractors of Martin, and Nashe dedicated his own effort, *An Almond for a Parrat,* to Kemp. Both [John] Lanham and Kemp were old members of Leicester's troupe, which had dispersed on the death of its patron in 1588 and joined ranks with Lord Strange's Men. The latter company was specifically mentioned by Lord Mayor Hart in November 1589, when the authorities were moving to suppress the unseemly plays they had originally encouraged. It seems probable that Strange's Men, including Kemp and Lanham, were responsible for some of these gruesome travesties of Martin" (68). Martin Holmes argues persuasively for Kemp's role as Falstaff in *Shakespeare and His Players* (New York: Charles Scribner's Sons, 1972), 47-50, and Wilson writes: "We know very little about the casting of Shakespeare's plays, but William Kempe was the comic man of the Lord Chamberlain's men, one of the principal sharers, and very popular with the London public; so that it seems natural to assume that the character of Falstaff was written for and, theatrically speaking, created by him. The Quarto of Part II even has a stage-direction, 'Enter Will' early in the Doll scene (2.4) which is paralleled by 'Enter Will Kemp' in the Second Quarto of *Romeo and Juliet* and is best explained, I think, as a Falstaff entry for the same player" (124). Thomas Whitfield Baldwin suggested that Thomas Pope had played the part, based on the assumption that this actor did high-comedy parts, while Kemp took the low (*The Organization and Personnel of the Shakespearean Company* [Princeton, NJ: Princeton UP, 1927], 231-32).

[54] See Nicholl's discussion of the "Tale of the Beare and the Foxe" from *Pierce Penilesse,* which he convincingly reads as antipuritan allegory with pervasive references to the suppressed Marprelate controversy (112-15).

[55] Hill, 78.

[56] Bloom, 86. Taylor states that Shakespeare's "decision to conflate the historical Oldcastle with the theatrical Vice" (Wilson's reading) was a radical innovation (96).

[57] Jonas Barish, *The Antitheatrical Prejudice* (Berkeley and Los Angeles: U of California P, 1981), 82n. Barish, noting Christopher Hill's warning against the indeterminacy of the term *puritan,* states that he is using this term to indicate "a complex of attitudes best represented by those strictly designated as Puritans" (82n)—yet Gosson, whom Barish himself acknowledges is anything but "strictly designated" as a puritan, is soon firmly located in the puritan camp based on his antitheatrical tract, *Plays Confuted in Five Actions* (1582), which was possibly commissioned "by the London authorities" (89-90).

[58] Bloom, 79.

[59] Neil Rhodes is one critic who does examine such pamphlet literature, locating the origins of the English grotesque in the Marprelate controversy and exploring its subsequent evolution, largely in the writings of Thomas Nashe. He positions *Henry IV* in the context of the Marprelate tracts and discusses the influence of Nashe on Shakespeare's earlier writing but does not claim the same direct connection for Falstaff, perhaps because he seems unaware of Falstaff's Lollard origins (89-99).

[60] Wilson, *Fortunes,* 16 and 33.

[61] Ainger, *Lectures and Essays* (London: Macmillan,

1905), 1:141-42. Wilson quotes this essay as his primary reference for comments on Falstaff's puritanism (*Fortunes,* 16 and 21).

[62] Naseeb Shaheen, *Biblical References in Shakespeare's History Plays* (Netwark: U of Delaware P, 1989), 137.

[63] The New Arden edition notes that Falstaff's advice, "Watch tonight, pray tomorrow" (*1HIV,* 2.4.273), not only echoes Matthew 26:41 but perhaps refers to the page heading of "Watch & Pray" that appears above Luke 22 in the Geneva Bible. Later Falstaff refers to "tattered prodigals lately come from swine-keeping, from eating draff and husks" (*1HIV,* 4.2.34-36). According to the New Arden, "Shakespeare recollects the Geneva Bible's 'huskes' (*Luke,* xv. 16) rather than the Bishops' or Great Bible's 'coddes'" (130n).

[64] Ainger, 142.

[65] S. L. Bethell, "The Comic Element in Shakespeare's Histories," *Anglia* 71 (1952): 82-101, esp. 99.

[66] *Henry The Fourth Part 1,* ed. Samuel Burnett Hemingway, New Variorum Shakespeare (Philadelphia and London: J. B. Lippincott, 1936), cited in Humphreys, ed., 15n.

[67] Ainger, 142.

[68] Humphreys, ed., 84n.

[69] Puritans set psalms to music in order to make them easier to memorize, part of their educational agenda to encourage learned Christians (Collinson, 356-71). Yet another example of Falstaff's puritan speech, if a less obvious one, is a reference to "Turk Gregory" (*1HIV,* 5.3.46), "whom Protestant writers cited as a by-word for violence," referred to in both Foxe's *Acts and Monuments* and Martin Marprelate's *The Epistle* (Humphreys, ed., 153n).

[70] Ainger, 145. Giorgio Melchiori, the editor of *The Second Part of King Henry IV* for The New Cambridge Shakespeare (Cambridge: Cambridge UP, 1989) also notes that "Falstaff's hymn-singing is . . . possibly a survival of the caricature of the original Oldcastle, a Lollard, equated by the Elizabethans with the Puritans" (76n).

[71] H. Mutschmann and K. Wentersdorf, *Shakespeare and Catholicism* (New York: Sheed and Ward, 1952), 347; see pages 345-49 for a discussion of Falstaff's status as a puritan. Bethell also discusses Falstaff's "Puritan" dialogue (94 and 98-99).

[72] "Amendment of life" echoes Luke 15:7, Matthew 3:8, and Acts 26:20 (Humphreys, ed., 16n).

[73] Humphreys, ed., 84n.

[74] Christopher Baker, "The Christian Context of Falstaff's 'Finer End,'" *Explorations in Renaissance Culture* 12 (1986): 68-87, esp. 72 and 76.

[75] Goldberg, 77.

[76] Honigmann, 127.

[77] Hemingway, ed., 36, 37, and 38n.

[78] The notes to Humphreys's edition provide fascinating examples of the editorial tunnel vision that results from the denial of Falstaff's associations with puritanism and his origins in a famous reformist religious leader. One instance of editorial inconsistency is the definition given for the terms "not-pated" and "knotty-pated." In a moment of anger, Hal calls Falstaff "thou knotty-pated fool" (*1HIV,* 2.4.222). The Arden footnote for this line glosses "knotty-pated" as "block-headed" (68n). The term "not-pated," however, which the Prince hurls at the unfortunate Francis in a similar tirade (*1HIV,* 2.4.69), is defined as a reference to short hair, "common among the lower and middle classes, and the Puritans got the nickname of round-heads because they for the most part belonged to these ranks" (59-60n). Similarly, "smooth-pates" (*2HIV,* 1.2.38) is defined as "city (Puritan) tradesmen who, despising the long locks of fashion, cropped their hair short; known later as Roundheads" (21n). Hal could also be using the term "knotty-headed" with puritan connotations when he speaks to Falstaff.

[79] In *Part 2* Falstaff is associated with "Ephesians . . . of the old church" (2.2.142), a line to which I will return, which the New Arden glosses as follows: "The allusion is perhaps to the unregenerate Ephesians, with the sensual faults St Paul warns them against (particularly indulgence in wine: *Ephes.,* v. 18) before they 'put off the old man' and put on the new. . . . The Page hardly seems to allude (unless ironically, and the irony would be lost on the stage) to 'the prime church of the Ephesians', whose conditions St Paul laid down, and which was the Puritan court of appeal for purity of life" (57n). This gloss, with its blanket refusal to consider the possibility of puritan overtones ("the Page *hardly* seems to allude"), preempts the valid possibility of irony even as it provides an ironic reading of the (otherwise gratuitous) line. In Falstaff's case, the irony of the phrase—an irony that would have been glaringly obvious to an audience aware of both Falstaff's Lollard origins and his bacchanalian behavior onstage—stems from the coexistence of these diametrically opposed social models in the person of Falstaff.

Falstaff is, indeed, a conglomeration of satires: the fallen Knight of the Garter, a *miles gloriosus,* the Lords Cobham. Falstaff also has associations with Sir John

Fastolfe, who is called "Falstaff" in *1 Henry VI* and who was considered a religious figure. Mutschmann and Wentersdorf write: "The fact that the name chosen by Shakespeare as a substitute for Oldcastle, namely Falstaff, was that of another highly esteemed Protestant aroused the anger of the Puritans still more. . . . The historical Sir John Fastolfe (1378?-1459) was one of the leaders of the English forces fighting in France during the reign of King Henry VI. He allegedly behaved 'with much cowardice' on one occasion, and in *1 Henry VI* (iii.2; iv.I), Shakespeare shows Fastolfe deserting the hero Talbot on the field of battle. The Puritans rejected this as a historical error if not a slander, because they regarded him as a Lollard sympathizer" (348).

[80] Bale, fol. 26[r-v].

[81] Mistress Purge exclaims: "this playing is not lawful, for I cannot find that either plays or players were allowed in the prime church of Ephesus by the elders" (1.3.309-11). Thomas Middleton, *The Family of Love,* ed. Simon Shepherd (Nottingham, UK: Nottingham Drama Texts, 1979).

[82] "I am neither heretic nor Puritan, but of the old church. I'll swear, drink ale, kiss a wench, go to mass, eat fish all Lent, and fast Fridays with cakes and wine, fruit and spicery, shrive me of my old sins afore Easter, and begin new afore Whitsuntide" (*I Sir John Oldcastle,* xiii. 129-33).

[83] While Wilson (*Fortunes,* 17-20) argues convincingly for Falstaff's debt to characters from earlier morality plays (such as Riot in *Youth*), we must also acknowledge that Falstaff himself continually resists such a role, implying that *he* is the "saint" being corrupted by the "wicked," that *he* has been "bewitched with the rogue's company" (*1HIV,* 2.2.17), and that "company, villainous company, hath been the spoil of [him]" (3.3.9-10). Falstaff laments privately that he now lives "out of all order, out of all compass" (ll. 18-19)—more the sentiments of a fallen puritan than of a thriving Vice.

[84] The bland Oldcastle in *The Famous Victories of Henry the fifth: Containing the Honourable Battell of Agin-court* (London, 1598) is a rare exception. The neutrality of this figure perhaps indicates another playwright's uneasiness with Oldcastle and the difficulties of presenting him on the stage in Elizabethan England.

[85] *The Oldcastle Controversy,* Peter Corbin and Douglas Sedge, eds. (Manchester and New York: Manchester UP, 1991), 220. In an instance of historical irony, the Jacobean bearers of the Cobham title would once again become involved in treacherous plots to overthrow the king, but this time the schemes involved *Catholic* sympathizers. Despite William Brooke's loyal service and prestige during the reign of Elizabeth, two of his sons were traitors. Henry Brooke, Lord Cobham, was implicated in the Main Plot to replace James I with Arabella Stuart and (together with Sir Walter Ralegh, whom Brooke accused of being a co-conspirator) was condemned to life imprisonment in the Tower. Henry's younger brother George was less fortunate, being accused of involvement in the Bye Plot and decapitated in 1603 (*Dictionary of National Biography,* s.v. "Brooke, Henry, 1619").

[86] Rackin, *Stages of History: Shakespeare's English Chronicles* (Ithaca, NY: Cornell UP, 1990), 238.

[87] The resonance of these exchanges could result from what some see as the direct influence of Thomas Nashe. Rhodes observes: "In the absence of any considerable drama, bar that of Shakespeare, in the middle years of the decade the literary battle between Nashe and Harvey provided spectacular entertainment of a different kind. It was a re-run of the Marprelate controversy conducted at a more sophistocated level. . . . In these circumstances it is highly improbable that Shakespeare was unaware of what Nashe was doing, and in writing *1 Henry IV* in the winter of 1596-97, with its rhapsodies of grotesque abuse and its splendid evocation of low life in the city, he seems to be deliberately following that lead. After all, his instincts as a writer of comedy before this time were throughly romantic; Falstaff, though not without prototypes, declares a sharp switch of direction. One begins to wonder, thinking again of Nashe's hopes of 'writing for the stage' in autumn 1596, not whether, but how closely, he and Shakespeare were associated" (92). In his edition J. Dover Wilson notes many parallels to Nashe and suggests that Nashe was involved in *The Famous Victories of Henry the fifth (The First Part of the History of Henry IV* [Cambridge: Cambridge UP, 1946], 191-96). Critics have also noted resonances of Nashe and the Marprelate tracts in the Jack Cade scenes from *2 Henry VI;* see, for example, Rhodes, 93-95.

[88] Tribble, *Margins and Marginality: The Printed Page in Early Modern England* (Charlottesville and London: UP of Virginia, 1993), 109.

[89] Michel Foucault, *Discipline and Punish: The Birth of the Prison,* trans. Alan Sheridan (New York: Vintage Books, 1979), 49.

[90] [Nashe], *Martins Months minde,* sig. E3[v]; also quoted in Carlson, 72, and cited in Tribble, 108.

[91] Tribble, 118, 119, and 121.

[92] *Martins Months minde,* sig. D[v].

[93] Tribble, 117.

Source: "Saints Alive! Falstaff, Martin Marprelate, and the Staging of Puritanism," in *Shakespeare Quarterly,* Vol. 46, No. 1, Spring, 1995, pp. 47-75.

The Sentimentalizing of *Communitas* in Kenneth Branagh's *Henry V*

Patricia P. Salomon, *University of Findley*

In *Henry V,* Shakespeare's protagonist takes great pains in the well-known Crispin's Day speech to establish the closest possible rapport with his troops at Agincourt, a communitas in which his comrades of every social rank achieve a privileged moment of parity with the King himself:

> We few, we happy few, we band of brothers;
> For he today that sheds his blood with me
> Shall be my brother; be he ne'er so vile,
> This day shall gentle his condition.
>
> (4.3.60-63)

A close reading of the play, however, shows that until this moment of quasi-liturgical bonding, the Boar's Head Tavern subplot characters—Pistol, Bardolph, and Nym—were in every way inimical to the cause of Henry and his truly loyal "band of brothers." This contrast between Shakespeare's subplot characters and Henry's troops is fully analyzed in Brownell Salomon's "Thematic Contraries and the Dramaturgy of *Henry V,*" [*Shakespeare Quarterly* 31, 1980] which documents how all scenes in the play are connected by a single conceptual framework: private cause versus public good. Pistol, Bardolph, and Nym, who go to France for their own personal gain, are equated with all other characters who act out of similarly "private" or selfish motives: Canterbury and Ely, altogether moral churchmen who, not incidentally, serve their own interest by contributing to Henry's war chest in order to avoid a church tax; Scroop, Cambridge, and Grey, traitors who have sold out their king and country for French gilt; the Dauphin, who puts private enmity and spite above public policy (2.4.127-29); and the French nobles in general, whom their king motivates by appealing to aristocratic self-esteem instead of patriotic zeal (3.5.38-47). As for Pistol and his cronies, Richard Levin, in *The Multiple Plot in English Renaissance Drama* [1971], demonstrates that they are clown-foils whose function in the play is "to contrast with, and so render still more admirable, the exploits of the 'mirror of all Christian kings'" (116).

But, just as Shakespeare took broad liberties with medieval history to work these subsidiary character-creations into his rendition of *Henry V* for the Elizabethan audience, Kenneth Branagh remolds the same Shakespearean characters for his later twentieth-century audience. I hope to show that, by means of additions, editorial omissions, and extra-textual gestures, Branagh both minimizes and sentimentalizes the anti-social behavior of the Boar's Head Tavern characters. What emerges is a distinctly anachronistic, twentieth-century social egalitarian perspective that undermines their primary function in Shakespeare's play, which is to demonstrate how selfish, self-serving opportunism runs counter to the civil virtues that King Henry's brotherly *communitas* would achieve.

The most notable additions Branagh makes to *Henry V* involving the subplot characters are three flashback episodes. The first takes place at the end of the scene introducing the Boar's Head Tavern crew. The Boar's Head itself is dark and filthy, and its inhabitants are unwashed and suffer from disorders of the teeth and skin. Bardolph scavenges for food and scuffles with a cat for the previous night's leftovers while Nym recovers from a hangover. Pistol enters, flirting and laughing with Nell, but the mood soon changes when the Boy comes down to relate the seriousness of Falstaff's illness. Melancholy comes over these characters as the film cuts to a closeup of Falstaff's face. The camera returns to a dewy-eyed Pistol who looks longingly into space. He remembers Falstaff's voice. The camera cuts to Falstaff at his revels. When the young Prince Hal enters, Falstaff runs to embrace him, saying, in words transposed from *1 Henry IV:*

> If sack and sugar be a fault, then God help the wicked. If to be old and merry is a sin, if to be fat is to be hated . . . But no, my good lord, when thou art King, banish Pistol, banish Bardolph, banish Nym, but sweet Jack Falstaff, valiant Jack Falstaff, banish not him thy Harry's company, banish plump Jack and banish all the world.
>
> [*"Henry V" by William Shakespeare: A Screen Adaptation by Kenneth Branagh, London: Chatto & Windus,* 1989, p. 35]

In a voice-over, Henry replies, "I do. I will." As though he has heard Henry's answer, Falstaff's face grows sad, and he adds: "But we have heard the chimes of midnight, Master Harry. Jesus, the days that we have seen." Again in voice-over, Henry responds, using the words spoken in *2 Henry IV* 5.5: "I know thee not, old man." At this point, the episode intervenes in which the traitors—Scroop, Cambridge, and Grey—are condemned to death, after which we return to the Boar's Head to learn of Falstaff's death. A profile of the dead Falstaff appears, and Nell, drained of emotion, leans over him. Pistol, Bardolph, Nym, Nell, and the Boy, grieved and teary-eyed, recall Falstaff and his witticisms and console one another.

It is apparent from these scenes that these are characters who deserve our empathy. Perhaps they drink a little too much to forget their social deprivation; perhaps they wake at the Boar's Head because they have nowhere else to go. The way Branagh's tavern crew mourn the death of their friend humanizes and sentimentalizes them. Even Patrick Doyle's highly emotive music supports the sentimental treatment of these characters. In fact, the same tune that plays for Henry's other troops plays for Pistol, Bardolph, and Nym as they take leave of Nell to join Henry in Southhampton.

The second flashback, Henry's this time, takes place when Bardolph is about to be hanged for stealing the pax, a sequence that is reported rather than depicted in Shakespeare.[1] As the hoist is effected, the camera cuts to the Boar's Head, where Bardolph and Falstaff are engaged in a drinking contest. At a crucial moment, Bardolph digs Falstaff in the ribs, causing him to spill his drink. Bardolph teasingly says to Harry, "Do not, when thou art king, hang a thief." "No, thou shalt," Henry replies. The camera cuts back to Henry's face. Tears well up in his eyes as he painfully gives the order for Bardolph's execution. In an apologetic, raspy voice rather than a firm, decisive one, Henry reminds his men, "We would have all such offenders so cut off. . . . " Tears run down Henry's cheeks. It is as though Henry has the flashback in order to reassure himself that Bardolph, not he, is responsible for his own death. Bardolph knew the consequences, ignored them, and broke the law. Henry's situation is a difficult one: he can't ignore an infraction of discipline just because a friend committed it. At the beginning of this scene, Pistol had tearfully begged Fluellen to intercede on Bardolph's behalf and became visibly upset at Fluellen's negative response. Framing the execution with Pistol's and Henry's reactions to it makes it apparent that Bardolph is as much a personal loss to Henry as he is to Pistol. Thus Branagh's every representation of Henry's old friends tends to be empathically charged with nostalgia or pathos, whereas their anti-social qualities are softened or deleted (e.g., Pistol's opportunism: "profits will accrue," 2.1.115).

The third and final flashback is again Henry's and takes place towards the end of the film when Burgundy gives an account of how France has suffered because of the war. A montage of faces appears on the screen as Henry thinks back to all he has lost: his fallen troops, York, the Boy, Nell, Nym, Bardolph, Scroop, and Falstaff. All losses—common soldiers, men of rank, his Boar's Head friends, and even the traitors—are equally felt.

In the introduction to the published but now out-of-print screenplay, Branagh states that he includes these flashbacks because

> It was important for an audience that might have no previous knowledge of the *Henry IV* plays to have an idea of the background to *Henry V*, and I wanted to achieve the greatest possible impact from Mistress Quickly's speech reporting the death of Falstaff, a character that the audience would not otherwise have encountered.
>
> I constructed this brief flashback from three separate scenes in the *Henry IV* plays. My intention was to give, in miniature, a sense of Falstaff's place among the surviving members of the Boar's Head crew and to make clear his former relationship and estrangement from the young monarch. Both this scene and the flashback during Bardolph's on-screen execution help to illustrate the young king's intense isolation and his difficulty in rejecting his former tavern life. (Branagh 12)

Branagh's final words, "difficulty in rejecting his former tavern life," are significant. Whereas Shakespeare clearly indicates that that rejection was a *fait accompli* at the end of *2 Henry IV* (cf. also *Henry V* 1.1.24f), Branagh manufactures "difficulty" by problematizing Henry's already demonstrated maturity, discipline, and social responsibility. As we saw in the interpolated scene of Bardolph's hanging, Branagh's Henry is sentimentalized, tearily insecure, and "vulnerable" in the latest pop-psychological fashion. Henry *will* know "intense isolation," but he does this later, in his "ceremony" soliloquy (4.1).

In addition to the flashbacks, Branagh alters Shakespeare at times by dramatizing events merely reported in the play, as he does with Bardolph's execution. Shakespeare only briefly mentions that Nym, as well as Bardolph, has been hanged for stealing. Branagh, however, shows Nym on-screen, being stabbed in the back and having his neck broken during the battle while he is taking a purse off a dead French soldier.[2] Branagh here provides yet another invented image of gratuitous emotionality in contravention of Shakespeare's purposes in the subplot: upon finding Nym's dead body, Pistol grieves and weeps as he cradles it in his arms.

Another instance of Branagh's expanding a Shakespearean cue into a full-blown sequence occurs after the battle, when Henry proclaims: "Come, go we in procession to the village; . . . / Do we all holy rites: / Let there be sung 'Non nobis' and 'Te Deum'" (4.8.115, 124-25). Covered with dried blood and mud, Henry carries the body of the Boy across the battlefield in an extended, long-take tracking shot that lasts a full four minutes.[3] With this cinematic decision, Branagh surely verges over the line between heart-tugging pathos and sheer bathos. (Mightn't Henry more appropriately have carried a hand-sized cross in one hand and his sword in the other for this shot?) As the single voice intoning "Non nobis, Domine" slowly grows into a full chorus and orchestra, we see Pistol among the carnage still holding and weeping over Nym, as other soldiers, some also carrying the dead, follow Henry's path. When Henry finally reaches the cart containing Agincourt's losses, he lovingly places the Boy inside it and kisses him farewell. It is a scene to melt our hearts. Contributing to the impact of this scene is, once more, Doyle's musical score. As Chris Fitter observes [in "A Tale of Two Branaghs: *Henry V,* Ideology; and the Mekong Agincourt," in *Shakespeare Left and Right,* edited by Ivo Kamps, 1991], "Deftly ambiguated by its director's hand, instantaneous intelligibility and firmly manipulated empathy are secured by supervening music-over at almost every scene, to aid a pulsing speech or moisten a baffled eye" (273). Social egalitarianism could scarcely be more hyper-emotionalized than by this Branaghian interpolation.

Another aspect of Branagh's sanitizing treatment of the subplot characters is their on-screen placement with Henry and his troops. During Henry's "Once more unto the breach" oration, Pistol, Bardolph, and Nym are right up front cheering him on, crying "God for Harry, England, and Saint George!" Branagh briefly shows Fluellen having to compel these craven hypocrites toward the breach ("you dogs! Avaunt you cullions!" 57), but he excises all verbal references to their thievery and cowardice and the Boy's devastating repudiation of "Their villainy" (3.2.1-55). More significant, when Henry delivers his Crispin's Day speech before Agincourt, it is Nym who assists Henry onto his platform-cart, and, again, Pistol and Nym are right there to cheer their King. These examples give the false impression that the Boar's Head characters are as much contributing members of Henry's community as anyone else, not simply during the Battle of Agincourt but throughout the entire film.

Several deletions from Shakespeare's text also soften, if not white-wash altogether, the anti-*communitas* implications of Pistol, Bardolph, and Nym. In the introduction to his screenplay, Branagh discusses the cuts he made in order to keep his film commercial length. He says of the Boar's Head scenes:

> My own experience of cinema-going convinced me that two hours was the maximum span of concentration that could be expected from an audience for a film of this kind. In any case, the cuts dictated themselves. The more tortuous aspects of the Fluellen/Pistol antagonism, culminating in the resoundingly unfunny leek scene, were the first to go. (Branagh 11)

Accordingly, two scenes which vividly depreciate Pistol are eliminated: first, his self-serving capture of the French soldier le Fer, for whom he demands a ransom of 200 crowns (4.4); and, second, his humiliating confrontation with Fluellen and Gower (virtually the entirety of 5.1), in which Pistol is forced to eat the leek they use to knock him over the head. This farcical scene, which, Branagh to the contrary notwithstanding, can be resoundingly funny in performance, dramatizes tellingly what the filmmaker's own egalitarian tolerance makes him loath to reveal: that Fluellen and Gower cannot allow that villainous social pariah Pistol ("You are a counterfeit cowardly knave") to share their company ("Fare ye well"). In its stead, Branagh shows us Fluellen and Henry embrace after the battle in a laughing, tearful bear-hug (extra-textual, of course) and talk sweetly and sentimentally about the importance of the leek as a Welsh symbol and their pride in their Welsh blood (4.7).

The camera cuts to a broken Pistol leaning against a tree, contemplating his losses and empty future. His wife and all his friends are dead. Although he says he will turn cutpurse, we cannot deny him sympathy because he is obviously pained, and being a cutpurse is no different from his past behavior. Ironically, it was Pistol himself (in a line pointedly deleted by Branagh) who told us that his purpose in going to France was not to do his patriotic duty but rather, "like horse-leeches, my boys, / To suck, to suck, the very blood to suck!" (2.3.56-57).

Peter Donaldson, in "Taking on Shakespeare: Kenneth Branagh's *Henry V,*" [*Shakespeare Quarterly* 42, 1991] attributes the treatment of these characters in Branagh's film to his own Irish working-class background: "Branagh's Irish working-class identity shows through his stage English royal persona at strategic moments, giving depth to the king's identification with the common soldiers, lending credence to his claim to be a work-a-day, plain-style king" (68). Whatever the reasons for Branagh's rethinking these characters, the result of it skews Shakespeare's overall structuring of the play. These characters no longer form a contrast to Henry and his loyal "band"; they actually belong to Henry's community, not only at the Battle of Agincourt, where Henry achieves *communitas* with his men, but throughout the film.

Notes

[1] Hanging Bardolph directly before the eyes of the king is an idea borrowed from Adrian Noble's 1984 Stratford-upon-Avon production, in which Branagh also played Henry V.

[2] Later, following the battle, other men and women are also seen pillaging the corpses, plainly diminishing the criminality of Nym's behavior.

[3] In Olivier's *Henry V,* it is Fluellen who merely holds the body of the Boy in his arms. But Branagh may well have seen the extant publicity still photo showing Olivier's King Henry holding the Boy.

Source: "The Sentimentalizing of *Communitas* in Kenneth Branagh's *Henry V,*" in *Shakespeare Bulletin,* Vol. 13, No. 1, Winter, 1995, pp. 35-6.

Loyal Fathers and Treacherous Sons: Familial Politics in *Richard II*

Sharon Cadman Seelig, *Smith College*

The last act of Shakespeare's *Richard II* contains a pair of scenes that constitute a problem for the director and a puzzle for the critic, material so out of keeping with the rest of the play that even one of the *dramatis personae* is made to remark that difference. In the earlier scene (V.ii) the Duke of York first lamentingly retells Richard's passage through the streets of London and then discovers his son Aumerle's involvement in a plot to assassinate Richard's successor King Henry. In the next scene, which begins with Henry's inquiry after his "unthrifty son," Aumerle, York, and the Duchess of York all plead with the King, with York begging for rigorous and prompt justice, the Duchess and Aumerle, for mercy. These paired scenes, the only funny (if not the only embarrassing) things in this perhaps excessively serious play, contain numerous elements of the absurd: an old man trying to get his boots on while suffering the verbal assaults of his wife, a three-way race to the King, an entire family hobbling about on its knees, refusing to rise until its contradictory petitions are granted.[1] The scenes are so odd that even Henry Bullingbrook, not usually noted for his sense of humor, is moved to comment:

> Our scene is alt'red from a serious thing,
> And now chang'd to "The Beggar and the
>   King."
> My dangerous cousin, let your mother in,
> I know she is come to pray for your foul sin.[2]

In its labeling of this material as a scene, an artificial construction, Bullingbrook's distancing remark provides the kind of explicit reference to the fictional quality of the dramatic illusion that we are accustomed to find in Shakespeare's comedies;[3] in pointing to the comedic nature of the scene the remark answers our immediate question as to whether Shakespeare could have intended anything so silly but leaves us wondering just what his reasons were. V.ii and iii have been variously described as savage farce, as deliberate parody, even as evidence of boredom and fatigue.[4] But these scenes, which indeed differ strikingly from the rest of the play in language and tone, nevertheless form an integral part of it: they underscore an often neglected aspect of the play and demonstrate in parodic fashion the moral and personal consequences of the larger dramatic action.[5]

Richard II, usually seen as a play about the balance of power between king and usurper, about the right and the power to rule, is in a significant sense also a representation of the struggle for power between fathers and sons, an issue that has long been seen in the *Henry IV* plays but that is equally important, though differently presented, here. Most explicitly in the Aumerle scenes but also throughout the play, characters struggle for dominance over others whose differences of attitude or loyalty are sharpened and defined by intimate familial bonds.[6] This emphasis on familial rivalry is linked to another basic fact of human nature—the irreducible human frailty that is stressed from the beginning to the end of the play and that forms a matrix for our judgment of characters and action. *Richard II* frames its discourse in terms of sin, so that both the actors and the commentators are seen to be, as the Queen says of the Gardener, "Old Adam's likeness" (III.iv.73), part of an ongoing cycle of betrayal and death.

I

Shakespeare takes care throughout *Richard II* to stress familial relationships, not only, as one would expect, to establish who the characters are, but more pointedly to emphasize the bonds and the power struggles of their interaction. This is so from the very beginning of the play, when Richard refers to Henry as Gaunt's son, and a few lines later, when Richard establishes his own relationship with Henry in emphatic and convoluted terms, the effect of which is to make the relationship seem even closer than it is, to make Bullingbrook and Richard more like brothers than cousins:

> Were he my brother, nay, my kingdom's heir,
> As he is but my father's brother's son, . . .
> (I.i.116-17)

The Duchess of Gloucester similarly exaggerates the closeness of relationship when she is effect equates the crimes of patricide and fratricide, asserting to Gaunt, "Thou dost consent / In some large measure to thy father's death, / In that thou seest thy wretched brother die" (I.ii.25-27). And of course, given the cast of characters, there are frequent references to cousins and uncles throughout *Richard II.* But nowhere is this familial emphasis more marked than in V.ii and iii.

The repeated references to familial bonds in the Aumerle scenes may recall the opening of *King Lear,* which likewise sacrifices psychological realism in order to represent an almost mythic or paradigmatic familial encounter. In *Lear* we hear of *father, daughter, husband, sister, love,* and *bond;* in *Richard II,* of *father, mother, son, uncle, aunt, king, forgiveness,* and *trespass:* both scenes reiterate the designations of relationship in such stark and simple terms that we cannot miss them. But in *Richard II,* as in *Lear,* once Shakespeare has called our attention to family matters, he deviates from the expected pattern in order to represent disorder within the family and the state.

Although V.ii centers on familial relationships, as prologue to a father's denunciation of his son as a traitor before the King, the father and son never address one another in terms of their kinship roles. This treatment contrasts with that of Holinshed, Shakespeare's main source throughout, who refers to York and Aumerle as father and son, as well as with Shakespeare's representation of the Duchess of York, who although historically only Aumerle's stepmother,[7] explicitly and repeatedly designates Aumerle as "my son." By contrast, York calls his son "boy" or simply addresses him without name or title, and he uses a good many terms of opprobrium and explicit rejection—"Villain, traitor, slave" (V.ii.72).[8] Even before he learns of Aumerle's plot to kill King Henry, York emphasizes Aumerle's name rather than his own paternal relationship to him, stressing Aumerle's trespass against the King and York's obligation to that King. When the Duchess says, "here comes my son Aumerle" (V.ii.41), York replies:

> Aumerle that was,
> But that is lost for being Richard's friend;
> And, madam, you must call him Rutland now.
> I am in parliament pledge for his truth
> And lasting fealty to the new-made king.
> (V.ii.41-45)

York's only expression of his paternity is a subjunctive rejection of that relationship: "Away, fond woman, were he twenty times my son, / I would appeach him" (V.ii.101-2). To a degree that approaches caricature, then, York stresses his fealty to the King over his duty as a father, as he refuses to acknowledge his disobedient son. Whereas the Duchess responds as a mother, York responds as a subject, one whose loyalty to the monarch overwhelms every other consideration.

But York is also a father, and therein lies the conflict dramatized both savagely and parodistically in Act V. In the schematic divergence between mother / son and father/son relationships, Shakespeare gives us a family drama, an archetypal representation of the forgiving, indulgent mother and the rigorously judgmental father. The Duchess is almost willfully naive, suggesting of the hidden document York plucks from Aumerle—"'Tis nothing but some band that he is ent'red into / For gay apparel 'gainst the triumph day" (V.ii.65-66)—while the Duke is rigidly, almost perversely, insistent on his obligation to the King and to the state over his obligation to his son and wife.

In plotting treason, Aumerle threatens not only the King but, as York's reaction implies, also the authority of his father. But rather than emphasizing the son's challenge to that patriarchal authority, as is the case with Bullingbrook and John of Gaunt earlier in the play, Shakespeare stresses here the father's harsh reaction: in the face of the son's still potential disobedience against father and king, it is the father, not the son, who is active and hostile, and his anger and shame at his offspring's transgression threaten, Kronos-like, that heir with extinction.

> *Duch.* Why, York, what wilt thou do?
> Wilt thou not hide the trespass of thine own?
> Have we more sons? or are we like to have?
> Is not my teeming date drunk up with time?
> And wilt thou pluck my fair son from mine age,
> And rob me of a happy mother's name?
> Is he not like thee? Is he not thine own?
> *York.* Thou fond mad woman,
> Wilt thou conceal this dark conspiracy?
> A dozen of them here have ta'en the sacrament,
> And interchangeably set down their hands,
> To kill the King at Oxford.
> (V.ii.88-99)

York's extreme reaction goes beyond simple loyalty to the King to a desire to annihilate the son whose trespass threatens not merely to dishonor but to destroy the father.

> Mine honor lives when his dishonor dies,
> Or my sham'd life in his dishonor lies:
> Thou kill'st me in his life; . . .
> (V.iii.70-72)

The father's horror and revulsion, expressed in a desire to purge his family of guilt and shame, are clearly also related to his concern for the realm: his reference to honor and his plea for his son's death may recall the famous example of Lucius Junius Brutus, a paradigm of loyalty and integrity who killed his own sons in order to preserve the Roman republic (an incident that Shakespeare refers to in *Julius Caesar* I.ii.15-19). But the contrast between the Roman republic which Junius Brutus tried to save and Bullingbrook's own usurped realm may cast York's actions in an ironic light. V.ii and iii clearly manifest the sort of chaos that, Tudor homilists argued, would be created throughout the kingdom by chaos at the top,[9] and the representation of civil war in terms of the family—as in the scenes of *3 Henry VI* in which a son has killed his father and a father his son—here reaches a new kind of specificity and insistence, as the strong and binding duties of parent and subject become mutually inconsistent.

York, not highly developed as a character, functions schematically in the play, revealing in his extreme and divergent reactions the dilemma of the loyal subject. The family farce of V.ii and V.iii, it is important to note, immediately follows York's initial description of the progress into London of Bullingbrook and Richard, a rather schizoid account that arouses pity for Richard upon whose "sacred head" "dust was thrown," but that also expresses admiration for "great Bullingbrook," an "aspiring rider," "mounted upon a hot and fiery steed" (V.ii. 30, 7, 9, 8). Although York describes Richard in pitiful terms, he gives little sign of personal anguish, attributing his own clam resignation to the will of God (V.ii.34-36); for the aged Duke, the choice is already made, fixed, and easily stated in a rhyming couplet:

> To Bullingbrook are we sworn subjects now,
> Whose state and honor I for aye allow.
> (V.ii.39-40)

York appears here as a literalist and something of an amnesiac, one who believes in loyalty to the king, whoever that king may be: the King is deposed; long live the King. His position manifests the absurd consequences of a notion of absolute loyalty divorced from the complexity of human reality and history. The scenes in which York and Aumerle oppose one another are comic, but their dilemma is tragic: the psychic conflict that cannot be expressed in the limited figure of York himself emerges in painful and bizarre dramatic action. York, who has sympathized with Richard, now perversely exercises ruthless authority over his own son even as that son enacts those sympathies.[10] One might argue that York's betrayal of his King leads to the betrayal of his son, that in disavowing his father's brother's son, he also inevitably disavows his own offspring and nearly destroys himself.

Clearly in V.ii and V.iii Shakespeare is at pains to depict a familial structure gone wrong, a hostile and repressive father, but he shows these as deriving from a realm in which questionable authority—in the dual forms of usurpation and treachery—leads to domestic and national chaos. Although York here is savagely authoritarian, exerting a futile, even filicidal, attempt to suppress disorder, his role earlier in the play is that of a more neutral[11] articulator of the principle of primogeniture and of the sanctity of the laws of inheritance—hence his sense that Bullingbrook must not be denied his inheritance and that Richard's sovereignty is to be respected. Initially a guardian of order, a would-be champion of justice, York, like that other articulator of divine order John of Gaunt, is impotent to restrain Gaunt's own son. After some wholly ineffectual blustering, York acquiesces easily to the new order, one in which Bullingbrook maintains a fluid and highly politic relation to principle. It is York who announces to Bullingbrook that Richard "with willing soul / Adopts thee heir" (IV.i.108-9) and he who believes, or at least allows himself to say to Richard, that "tired majesty did make thee offer: / The resignation of thy state and crown" (IV.i.177-78). In Acts IV and V York may be seen as wholly insensitive, a fool and a time-server, or as a more genuinely troubled but impotent father and subject; but however we see him, York's conflicting reactions suggest not simply or even primarily his own folly and weakness but the breakdown of the structure of obligations that appears seriously in Act IV as Bullingbrook becomes king and farcically in Act V as he sits in judgment on the family of York. *Richard II* represents the moral chaos engendered by Bullingbrook's usurpation and the impotence of Richard's articulation of principle without effective action. Henry rules a kingdom in which father must turn against son and son against father; Richard, failing to rule, creates an impossible dilemma for his most loyal subject.

The most striking aspect of V.ii and V.iii, the absurdity of the action, is reinforced by an extreme simplicity of language, which stands in sharp contrast to the ceremonial rhetoric, the "poetry" for which the play is so famous. While Shakespeare uses a narrow range of diction to emphasize the familial tensions at issue, he also uses the few deviations from such simplicity to point up the discrepancy between facade and reality. In a scene in which characters address one another in the simplest of familial and human terms—*uncle, aunt, cousin, woman, boy*—and in the most basic terms of the realm—*King, liege, traitor, villain, true man,* we immediately notice Henry's address to York, which builds from these terms of kinship to a more ornate style:

> O loyal father of a treacherous son!
> Thou sheer, immaculate, and silver fountain,
> From whence this stream through muddy passages
> Hath held his current and defil'd himself!
> Thy overflow of good converts to bad,
> And thy abundant goodness shall excuse
> This deadly blot in thy digressing son.
> (V.iii.60-66)

Such hyperbolic praise applied to York clearly overshoots the mark and thus points up the irony of Henry's words, for if Aumerle is a traitor, so is Henry; so is York. Such a statement might equally well have been addressed to John of Gaunt, the loyal father of a treacherous son, for as the Bishop of Carlisle puts it: "My Lord of Herford here, whom you call king, / Is a foul traitor to proud Herford's king" (IV.i.134-35).

The second noticeable deviation from the stylistic norm occurs when the Duchess of York argues that, although she and York both kneel before the King, her posture is true, whereas York's is hypocritical, a mere gesture not supported by his heart. The speech issues in a quibble on the word "pardon":

> *Duch.* No word like "pardon" for kings'
> mouths so meet.
> *York.* Speak it in French, King, say *"pardonne moy."*
> *Duch.* Dost thou teach pardon pardon to
> destroy?
> Ah, my sour husband, my hard-hearted lord,
> That sets the word itself against the word!
> (V.iii.118-22)

The Duchess's words of course anticipate those of Richard, as he speaks of the "thoughts of things divine [which] . . . intermix'd / With scruples . . . set the word itself / Against the word" (V.v.12-14).[12] But whereas Richard's soliloquy represents the conflict as internal ("*scruples* and *thoughts* of things divine . . . set the *word* against the *word*"), the Duchess's speech suggests a much broader framework in which letter and spirit, loyalty and obligation diverge. The Duchess's assertion that her husband's kneeling before the King is merely an empty gesture, emblem of a petition he would not actually wish to have granted, has its antecedent in the scene in which Bullingbrook kneels before Richard, and Richard comments: "Up, cousin, up, your heart is up, I know, / Thus high at least, although your knee be low" (III.iii.194-95). Henry's empty but politically astute gesture in III.iii not only anticipates but casts an ironic light on the kneeling of his loyal subjects in V.iii, for whereas Henry's kneeling is in show, theirs is in frantic earnest. Whereas Richard judges Henry's kneeling inappropriate because it contradicts the latter's wishes and the actual power relationship (though not the reverence due a king), Bullingbrook is embarrassed by the unseemliness of two figures of age and reverence, aunt and uncle, kneeling before him, acting out the inevitable impiety flowing from his usurpation.

As Henry sits in judgment on Aumerle, with Aumerle's father seeking punishment and his mother seeking mercy, the Duchess invokes a larger realm of judgment with her effusive statement, "A god on earth thou art" (V.iii.136). Gratitude is involved, surely, perhaps flattery; but if the Duchess means to say that the King is God's deputy, her statement is also charged with irony, for this god on earth has usurped that other whose balm could not be washed off; and this god, like his predecessor, will shortly be the instigator of murder. The reference to divine judgment, intended by the speaker to magnify its object, can only point up its frailty and weakness, can only suggest that Henry, though more effective than his kingly cousin, manifests the same human fallibility.

The Aumerle scenes are significant for the rest of *Richard II* in their representation of the structure of political power and in the representation of familial roles, not as separate issues but as inescapably intertwined, and painfully cyclical: to put it unkindly, before Aumerle could be a traitor to York's king, Henry, York must have denied York's and Aumerle's king, Richard. It is also worth noting that the dramatic emphasis in V.ii and V.iii is rather more on the parents, on their reaction to their son's trespass, than on the fault of the son. And it is the parents in this scene, supposed images of justice and mercy, rather than the son, the supposed traitor, who are in danger of appearing absurd; it is the parents who suggest also the link to the past, and hence the long sequence of guilt.

Both in parodic language—either too ornate or excessively simple—and in gestures such as kneeling, imploring pardon, knocking and entering, repeated to the point of farce, V.ii and V.iii transform Henry's new order, his well-managed kingdom, into a comic interlude. Although its language and action seem at first awkwardly out of place in the ceremoniousness of *Richard II,* both gestures and language in fact resonate with the rest of the play, acting in counterpoint to the more obviously serious treatment elsewhere of the central issues of these scenes—the emphasis on guilt and innocence, the relations between fathers and sons, the inseparability of familial and political issues.

II

Although in thinking of *Richard II* we may think first of the central dramatic contest between Bullingbrook and Richard, that central action is in fact framed by conflicts between fathers and sons, between Gaunt and Bullingbrook at the opening of the play and between York and Aumerle at the end, and that action, as we shall see, is articulated by Richard himself as a contest between father and son.

The emphasis on conflicts and contests between male parents and their offspring may be detected from the opening lines of the play, lines in which Shakespeare characteristically anticipates the matter of the whole.[13]

> Old John of Gaunt, time-honored Lancaster,
> Hast thou, according to thy oath and band,
> Brought hither Henry Herford thy bold son,
> Here to make good the boist'rous late appeal,
> Which then our leisure would not let us hear,
> Against the Duke of Norfolk, Thomas
> Mowbray?
> (I.i.1-6)

With swift economy, these lines represent the qualities of both Gaunt and Bullingbrook—the father aged, "time-honored," revered; the son, "bold," "boist'rous," more obviously potent; the father presumed to be in charge even though the action of the son has precipitated the scene; the son the only remaining Lord Appellant against Richard, the father supposed to exert authority *in loco regis*. This opening invokes the line of authority in this patriarchal and monarchical society, in which son is subject to father, and even kings, however they may act at other times, at least pretend to speak respectfully to their fathers' brothers.[14] But these lines also testify to strain within, for Richard appears to assume that the son is subject to the father and that youth reveres age, even though what follows bears out how difficult these principles are to maintain against the rising strength of the son, and even though—or especially since—Richard himself has not honored such principles.

Already in this first scene, we see that precisely the sort of apparently well-ordered relationship here sketched engenders emulation and rivalry. Gaunt clearly asserts the principle of filial obedience as he addresses his son: "When, Harry? when? / Obedience bids I should not bid again" (I.i.162-63). And Bullingbrook, in firmly refusing to withdraw his challenge, gives as one of his reasons his position vis-a-vis his father: "Shall I seem crestfallen in my father's sight?" (I.i.188). The language implies an obligation to maintain the family honor in the sight of the one from whom such obligations are derived, but also a sense of pride verging on rivalry, for it is precisely in his father's sight—or in comparison with his father—that the son must assert his potency.

The quality of the opposition between Gaunt and Bullingbrook is figured in their dialogue in I.iii; as Bullingbrook prepares for exile, father and son take characteristically opposed viewpoints. Gaunt urges mind over matter, the control of one's circumstances by one's attitude to them, asserting in effect the power of the imagination over events, and taking a position on the power of language and naming remarkably like that of Richard, a king who-exerts control not by action but by verbal representation:

> Think not the King did banish thee,
> But thou the King. . . .
> Go, say I sent thee forth to purchase honor,
> And not the King exil'd thee; . . .
> (I.iii.279-80, 282-83)

Bullingbrook energetically and impatiently rejects such counsel, asserting a characteristically pragmatic approach: the power lies not in the mind, not in the name, but in the reality of the event:

> O, who can hold a fire in his hand
> By thinking on the forsty Caucasus?
> Or cloy the hungry edge of appetite
> By bare imagination of a feast?
> (I.iii.294-97)

Given the similarity between Gaunt's and Richard's positions, Henry's preference for action over words is ultimately a matter of opposition to both father and king. Gaunt's final words in this scene—"Come, come, my son, I'll bring thee on thy way" (I.iii.304)—are an affirmation of relationship and support which again reasserts the pattern of authority and dependency, and so underscores both the close kinship and the opposing stances of father and son.

Bullingbrook's farewell to his father before the abortive contest with Mowbray appears more orthodox, as Bullingbrook describes his father as an inspiring force to his labors, but this affirmative language is also tinged with the phallic overtones of war, as the father is made new in the son, as his name and spirit, by implication in decline, are regenerated and refurbished by a son whose accomplishments may well exceed those of his father:

> O thou, the earthly author of my blood,
> Whose youthful spirit, in me regenerate,
> Doth with a twofold vigor lift me up
> To reach at victory above my head,
> Add proof unto mine armor with thy prayers,
> And with thy blessings steel my lance's point,
> That it may enter Mowbray's waxen coat,
> And furbish new the name of John a' Gaunt,
> Even in the lusty havior of his son.
> (I.iii.69-77)

Gaunt's "When, Harry? When? / Obedience bids I should not bid again" (I.i.162-63) meets with failure not only because even in Renaissance England grown men did not obey their fathers' commands like model children,[15] but because Bullingbrook, although in one sense the embodiment of his father's spirit, also occupies an antithetical position in the play. Gaunt is the articulator of a harmonious and providential order, most obviously in his evocation of "This blessed plot, this earth, this realm, this England" (II.i.50), but also in his stern stand against the Duchess of Gloucester's pleas for vengeance for her husband's murder, in his assertion that "God's is the quarrel," and his refusal to "lift / An angry arm against His minister" (I.ii.37,41). And it is Gaunt's son who clearly stands as the force that challenges that order, as the breaker of divinely sanctioned descent, the usurper of the crown from the anointed king. In rising against Richard, Bullingbrook also rises against his own father, for Gaunt supports Richard's kingship, if not his management, and seeks to stand a surrogate father to him, hoping on his death bed to "breathe my last / In wholesome counsel to his unstayed youth" (II.i.1-2), and, loving him, as Richard's other uncle York says, as much as his own son.[16]

Fathers and sons, chiefly represented in this play by York and Aumerle, Gaunt and Bullingbrook, are also joined by others. Gaunt and Bullingbrook have scarcely left the stage when the Earl of Northumberland introduces "my son, young Harry Percy" (II.iii.21); and Bullingbrook himself later inquires, "Can no man tell me of my unthrifty son? / 'Tis full three months since I did see him last" (V.iii.1-2). Hal's prodigality, more fully developed in *Henry IV,* figures here as part of the complex of paternal-falial relationships, for like Bullingbrook before him, Prince Hal has his own notions of honor, an honor that must be maintained vis-a-vis his father, though clearly against his counsel. By placing this scene in the midst of the interaction between York and Aumerle, Shakespeare points up that Henry too has a rebellious son, one who deliberately flouts his father's conception of honor by taking as his lady "the common'st creature" from "the stews" (V.iii.16-17) and so enacts a king of parodic counterpoint to Aumerle's more serious challenge to paternal and kingly authority.

In the early encounters between Gaunt and Bullingbrook, as in the later encounter between York and Aumerle, and even in Bullingbrook's allusion to his own son, we see a father clearly articulating a principle of order—obedience to himself, fealty to the King, submission to God—which he is impotent to enforce, and which also is plainly flawed, in practice if not in theory. The tension between the verbal articulation of these principles on the one hand and the action and characters on the other further weakens any sense that Shakespeare's play might exist simply as an expression of the kind of Tudor doctrines of order described by Tillyard; rather it depicts the flawed quality of human action throughout the generational and social order.

Richard II is filled with rebellious acts, not only of subjects against the King, but of sons against fathers. We may see in such proliferation not simply a spreading of images of disorder but also a prompting to question the basis of order. The rebellion or impudence that so perturbs fathers in this play may be seen as a mimetic exaggeration that points up the falsity of honor as it is defined first by Richard and then by Henry. Even the nature of sonship is somewhat unstable: for all that I have spoken of fathers and sons, it is worth noting that Aumerle appears in the first half of the play as a character in his own right, as an independent supporter and adviser of Richard, and only in Act V emphatically and paradigmatically as a rebellious son, as one whom his father sees as in need of chastisement. Such a transformation makes one question whether the moral chaos of England can convert a grown man into a boy, as his father calls him, whether misrule disorders human development, or whether fathers characteristically view rebellion as regression, a notion supported by Henry's reference to his son as "young wanton and effeminate boy" (V.iii.10).

III

Amid this plethora of fathers and sons, one character stands notably sonless. But it is he who most clearly expresses the connection between such relationships and the heart of the play:

> Cousin, I am too young to be your father,
> Though you are old enough to be my heir.
> (III.iii.204-5)

As his own formulation suggests, Richard is neither wise enough nor potent enough to retain his crown. He has fathered no children, a point underscored by Northumberland's response to the Queen's plea that she and Richard be banished together: "That were some love, but little policy" (V.i.84). Richard's chief reproductive act is to people the little world of his mind with a generation of still-breeding thoughts in little world of his mind with a generation of still-breeding thoughts in the soliloquy of Act V. That his native kingdom is the realm of fantasy is implied by his using the image of physical reproduction to represent what is after all a form of cognitive generation:

> My brain I'll prove the female to my soul,
> My soul the father, and these two beget
> A generation of still-breeding thoughts;
> And these same thoughts people this little
> world.
> (V.v.6-9)

Moreover, the unusual character of Richard's world is shown by his making the brain, the rational cognitive force usually associated with the male, subordinate to the feminine soul *(anima).* Richard appears then not so much as father, as controlling force, but as female, as the maternal figure, who on his return from Ireland kisses the earth: "As a long-parted mother with her child / Plays fondly with her tears and smiles in meeting" (III.ii.8-9).

If Richard, who should be king and father, represents himself as mother to his realm, we might expect Bullingbrook to emerge as father. But characteristic of the schematic parallels and contrasts so common in *Richard II,* it is Bullingbrook who first speaks intimately and lovingly of the earth: "Then England's ground, farewell, sweet soil, adieu; / My mother, and my nurse, that bears me yet!" (I.iii.306-7). Of course Bullingbrook's approach to the ground of England is in general much more vigorous: though he leaves as a son, he returns as a gardener, one whose first action is to deal ruthlessly with "Bushy, Bagot, and their complices, / The caterpillars of the commonwealth, / Which I have sworn to weed and pluck away" (II.iii.165-67). As we see in the Gardener's speech it is precisely Richard's inability to engage in the husbandman's characteristically controlled violence, to "cut off the heads of too fast growing sprays, / That look too lofty in our commonwealth" (III.iv.34-35) that has led to his "fall of leaf" (III.iv.49):

> [We] at time of year
> Do wound the bark, the skin of our fruit-trees,
> Lest being over-proud in sap and blood,
> With too much riches it confound itself;
> Had he done so to great and growing men,
> They might have liv'd to bear and he to taste
> Their fruits of duty.
> (III.iv.57-63)

Wishing that he could "purge this choler without letting blood" (I.i.153), Richard fails to demonstrate the pruning and severing skills necessary to physician, gardener, and king. Having no natural son to challenge him, Richard also lacks the power to dominate his rival; whereas Bullingbrook, Richard's contemporary, is old enough to "know the strong'st and surest way to get" (III.iii.201). Richard has neither the years nor the wisdom to be Bullingbrook's father. Thus Bullingbrook, though not Richard's son, becomes his heir, rising up against him more powerfully and unambiguously than against his own father, with consequences for the whole structure of familial and civil relationships.

For all that *Richard II* raises questions about the right and the power to rule, it does so, as I've been arguing, through relationships between fathers and sons, relationships that are on the one hand starkly schematic and on the other morally and psychologically ambiguous. Shakespeare's play shows us two prodigal sons, King Richard and Prince Hal, prodigal in their wasting of time and resources and in their failure to follow the advice of their elders, and it shows us two rebellious sons, Aumerle and Bullingbrook. It gives us loyal and ineffectual fathers—Gaunt, York, and even in a sense, Richard. Both Aumerle and Bullingbrook are disobedient sons who act out the desires or visions of their fathers: Aumerle, though he is denounced by his father for treason, in fact enacts the kind of loyalty to Richard suggested by York's earlier speech to Bullingbrook ("I am no traitor's uncle" [II.iii.88]) and by his poignant description of the desecration of Richard in V.ii. And Bullingbrook embodies all too clearly Gaunt's fears of the consequences if Richard ignores Gaunt's fatherly advice. This is a play then in which sons are 'disloyal' in a way that their fathers either do or would explicitly disapprove, but in which sons, rising against their aged fathers, nevertheless prove true to their fathers' earlier desires, allegiances, or predictions.

Of the unthrifty prodigals, Hal and Richard, one returns to the fold and ultimately becomes king; the other, following evil counselors, is deposed. Of the rebellious sons who rise against the King, the one, Aumerle, is rejected and chastised by his father; the other, Bullingbrook, is chastised and crowned. Such messages as there are here are surely ironic ones, for the consequences of rebellious acts are sharply divergent.

The very schematic quality of *Richard II* emphasizes its paradigmatic and potentially moralistic aspects; yet despite the clarity of its oppositions—Bullingbrook against Gaunt, Bullingbrook against Richard, York against Aumerle—the play also complicates these oppositions in its intricacies of language and character. Bullingbrook, who in his own person challenges the received order, rising up against the values represented or affirmed by his father, also affirms the principle of orderly descent: "If that my cousin king be King in England, / It must be granted I am Duke of Lancaster" (II.iii.123-24). And Gaunt, the most eloquent spokesman for harmonious order, is also the depicter of disorder and the father of the usurper, a usurper whose first act in returning to England is to claim his father's title. Gaunt's superficially clever manipulation of events through language, more probably a device to comfort his son than the result of conviction, in fact becomes truth:

> Think not the King did banish thee,
> But thou the King.
> (I.iii.279-80)

Bullingbrook, a son who in becoming king achieves the language of paternal authority, points to ways in which the laws of inheritance, of orderly succession, favor him; his father's words show how disorder and incipient rebellion are always with us, in fact or in potentiality. In a complicated passage that suggests an uncanny resemblance between generations, between past and future, Gaunt unwittingly prophesies "how his son's son should destroy his sons" (II.i.105), but not foreseeing by what means, not seeing that the accusation he makes against Richard will serve against his own son as well.[17]

In *Richard II* the issues of filial and paternal conflict are intertwined with questions of political order and power. Shakespeare sets before us in both tragic and comic fashion the effects of rebellion and murder—in the disarray caused by Bullingbrook's rebellion and in the absurd farce of the Langleys' disordered familial structure. Neither 'comic relief' nor comical ineptitude, V.ii and V.iii portray in effect the moral chaos of treachery and rebellion, the results of the getting as distinguished from the begetting of power. Yet while setting such painful consequences before us, Shakespeare does not suggest that it should simply be otherwise or that it could easily have been so. For in representing in parodic form the disorder of the realm, V.ii and V.iii also point to the inevitable quality of human fallibility. King Henry, who seizes effective control of the realm in that great scene in which Richard maintains control of images (IV.i) is, like his predecessor, king over disorder and human conflict.

This truth is borne out not only in the familial scenes of V.ii and V.iii, the absurdity of which Henry alerts us to but cannot transform,[18] but also in IV.i, in which the throwing down of gages likewise threatens to become farce. The accusations against Aumerle by Bagot, Fitzwater, Percy, and yet "Another Lord" recall the mutual accusations of Mowbray and Bullingbrook in Act I, an encounter in which the King has the power to stifle conflict but not to resolve it. The scene suggests not so much a new era as a repetition of the past: Richard attempts to bury the crime of Gloucester's murder, allowing the accusations to be brought to knightly combat and then averting a verdict all too likely to implicate him; Bullingbrook is more eager to reach the truth, but he too finds that the quest ends in a cul de sac, for Norfolk, who might resolve the challenge by speech or action, is dead. In both cases the truth remains hidden, while the act itself, though buried in obscurity (Bagot refers to "that dead time when Gloucester's death was plotted" [IV.i.10]), casts a long shadow.

Our questions, then, about right and wrong in *Richard II* are forced aside by images not of guilt and innocence but of guilt and guilt, images that echo throughout the play. The murder of Richard at Bullingbrook's behest and of Gloucester at Richard's are associated with the primal crimes of fratricide and patricide, by language that recalls the death of Abel at the opening of the play (I.i.104) and the sin of Cain (V.vi.43) at the end,[19] in Mowbray's reference to Henry as of Richard's blood (I.i.58-59) and Henry's attempted disclaimer (I.i.70-71). The ambivalent words with which Henry greets the news of Richard's death are appropriate to such an intimate crime:

> Though I did wish him dead,
> I hate the murtherer, love him murthered.
> (V.vi.39-40)

Although Henry's speech may be read as simple hypocrisy, it also underscores the blood relationship between the two kings and reminds us of the rivalry that forces one to challenge and overcome the origins to which one is inescapably bound:

> Lords, I protest my soul is full of woe
> That blood should sprinkle me to make me grow.
> (V.vi.45-46)

In seizing Richard's crown, Henry has overcome both father and brother, the father whose kingdom he inherits, the brother who is his father's brother's son. He commits an act of obvious impiety, yet also of ritual strengthening, for the blood he sheds makes him grow. In the murder of Richard has he "furbish[ed] new the name of John a' Gaunt . . . in the lusty havior of his son" (I.iii.76-77)?

In using the paradigms of father and son, of brother and brother to represent rebellion in the family and in the state, *Richard II* suggests that the political patterns we see are part of essential, fallen human nature. In language that points to repeating cycles of murder, Bullingbrook begins by accusing Richard indirectly of the murder of a brother and ends, in effect, by committing that act himself. To the perpetrator Exton Henry assigns not only the guilt of murder but also Henry's own guilt of fratricide as he bids him "With Cain go wander thorough shades of night" (V.vi.43). When the Duchess of York ends V.iii by saying, "Come, my old son, I pray God make thee new" (V.iii.146), she not only raises the issues of guilt and expiation, sin and regeneration, which have been present from the first scene of the play; her words also suggest the old Adam, in whose likeness the gardener and we all are made, the "old man" in us that, in the formulation of St. Paul, must be made new by the sacrifice of Christ.[20] In using such theologically weighted language in his concluding scenes, Shakespeare returns this play, with its many configurations of fathers and sons, to the archetypal rivalry between brothers and to the original father and his sons. In so doing he gives us a picture of unchanging, cyclical guilt, of unavoidable human frailty, of the effects of sin, perpetuated through generations. This framework suggests that the king who depicts himself in IV.i as martyr and Christ figure is not sinless but rather involved in an infinitely regressing cycle of blame. And it reminds us that our judgments of the two rulers of the play, balancing authority and acumen, right and obligations, cannot be expected to yield a victim and a perpetrator, but a dynamic relation of guilt and guilt.

The near-tragic farce of V.ii and V.iii, which outlines in parodic form the familial and theological aspects of the conflict, playing them in another key, underscores the centrality of these issues in the play as a whole. The taking of the kingdom and the murder of the king are not just political and moral actions but also familial; they take place not only on the large scale of political power but on the intimate scale of domestic conflict, as figured in the violence York would do to his own son, in the violence he fears his son's actions will do to the kingdom. In this complex of relationships there are no easy answers. Just as it is not clear that the King is right and the usurper wrong, so it is not clear that father or son or brother deserves to dominate, but Shakespeare uses these familial conflicts to enrich and intensify our response to a drama which is political and moral but also deeply psychological, reciprocal, Notesand eternal.[21]

Notes

[1] I acknowledge with pleasure Sheldon P. Zitner's witty

and astute account of these scenes in "Aumerle's Conspiracy," *Studies in English Literature,* 14 (1974), 239-57.

[2] *Richard II,* V.iii.79-82. The text quoted throughout is *The Riverside Shakespeare,* ed. G. Blakemore Evans (Boston: Houghton Mifflin, 1974).

[3] See the discussion of this point by Leonard Tennenhouse, *Power on Display: The Politics of Shakespeare's Genres* (New York: Methuen, 1986), esp. Chap. 1.

[4] Cf. Zitner, 243-44, 253-54; M. W. Black, "The Sources of Shakespeare's *Richard II,*" *John Quincy Adams Memorial Studies,* ed. J. G. McManaway et al. (Washington, 1948), p. 208; *Variorum* edition of *Richard II,* ed. Matthew W. Black (Philadelphia: Lippincott, 1955), p. 216n; and Joan Hartwig, "Parody in *Richard II,*" *Shakespeare's Analogical Scene: Parody as Structural Syntax* (Lincoln: Univ. of Nebraska Press, 1983). Waldo McNeir, "The Comic Scenes in *Richard II,*" *Neuphilologische Mitteilungen,* 73 (1972), 815-22, suggests that these scenes of *Richard II* mark a new level of maturity on Shakespeare's part, an ability to mingle comedy and serious purpose to create meaning. While concurring with McNeir's sense of the importance of V.ii and V.iii to the play, I would disagree with his view of the Duchess as chiefly a figure of fun.

[5] I use the term parody in the sense outlined by Joan Hartwig, who describes scenes that are bound to the rest of the action less by narrative action than by analogy (p.3). She points out that parody, "derived from the Greek word 'paroidia,' . . . originally meant a song placed beside or against" (p. 5), and that, like emblem, parody "simplif[ies] in order to expose complexities" (p.10).

[6] Some attention has been paid to the emphasis on familial relationships by David Sundelson, *Shakespeare's Restoration of the Father* (New Brunswick, N.J.: Rutgers Univ. Press, 1983); Robert B. Pierce, *Shakespeare's History Plays: The Family and the State* (Columbus: The Ohio State Univ. Press, 1971); James Winny, *The Player King* (New York: Barnes and Noble, 1968), pp. 74-82; and Harry Berger, Jr. "Psychoanalyzing the Shakespeare Text: The First Three Scenes of the *Henriad,*" in *Shakespeare and the Question of Theory,* ed. Patricia Parker and Geoffrey Hartman (New York: Methuen, 1985), pp. 210-29. Sundelson, whose chapter is entitled "Fathers, Sons, and Brothers in the Henriad," emphasizes not father-son relationships but rather the quasi-fraternal rivalry of Richard and Bullingbrook; Pierce affirms the importance of familial issues but finds the Aumerle scenes "rather frivolous self-parody" (pp. 157-58); Berger's very helpful essay does not treat the Aumerle scenes but deals with the opening of the play in ways that have contributed significantly to my thinking about it.

[7] *The Riverside Shakespeare,* note to *Richard II* V.ii.90-93.

[8] York places special emphasis on titles and designations of kinship: he calls not only Aumerle but also Bullingbrook "foolish *boy*" (II.iii.97) and denies kinship with him (II.iii.87-88) for presuming to disobey Richard and return to England in the King's absence; Bullingbrook, by contrast, insists on the title and the relationship it implies, repeating "My gracious uncle" (II.iii.85 and 106). York also rebukes Northumberland for omitting Richard's title:

> The time hath been,
> Would you have been so brief with him, he would
> Have been so brief [with you] to shorten you,
> For taking so the head, your whole head's length.
>
> (III.iii.11-14)

[9] See Graham Holderness's discussion in *Shakespeare's History* (New York: St. Martin's Press, 1985), Chap. 1.

[10] Norman Rabkin, *Shakespeare and the Common Understanding* (New York: The Free Press, 1967), pp. 87-88, makes the point that Aumerle acts out his father's sympathies.

[11] York's word, happily for my argument, is "neuter" (II.iii.159); earlier in this scene he verbally asserts the power of the King, but soon admits that he lacks the physical force to do so: "this arm of mine / Now prisoner to the palsy" (II.iii.103-4).

[12] The Duchess's accusation of her husband also points to another central issue of the play—the efficacy of words and of gestures, the question whether, as in Richard's notions of kingship, words are potent, meaningful, and magical, or whether they are merely words, whether such gestures as York engages in are merely superficial verbal formulae, or whether they are the outward signs of an inner reality.

[13] See Berger's discussion of the implications of this opening scene, pp. 214-18.

[14] Berger, p. 215, notes the ironic edge to Richard's language in I.i.1-7, in a speech that balances obvious bluntness against ostensible reverence.

[15] Lawrence Stone, *The Family, Sex, and Marriage in England 1500-1800* (New York: Harper and Row, 1979), pp. 122-34, cites the extraordinary standards of obedience exacted by parents in the sixteenth and early seventeenth centuries; more recently, Bruce Young, "Parental Blessings in Shakespeare's Plays," *Studies*

in Philology, 89 (1992), 179-210, deals with the more positive aspects of the hierarchical relationship between parent and child. The situation which Young describes, in which the parental power to impart blessing "did not necessarily imply unconditional submission to a parent's wishes . . . [nor] that the child's agency and identity were entirely subsumed within those of the parent" (p. 192), closely corresponds to the relationship between Bullingbrook and Gaunt in I.i.

> He loves you, on my life, and holds you dear
> As Harry Duke of Herford, were he here.
> (II.i.143-44)

[16] Gaunt says to Richard:

> O had thy grandsire with a prophet's eye
> Seen how his son's son should destroy his sons,
> From forth thy reach he would have laid thy shame,
> Deposing thee before thou wert possess'd,
> Which art possess'd now to depose thyself.
> (II.i.104-8)

[17] Hartwig argues, p. 119, that Henry, in contrast to Richard, is in control of the scene, but Henry is in fact at the mercy of the insistently kneeling Duchess, whom he repeatedly urges, "Good aunt, stand up." As Hartwig subsequently acknowledges, the only way to get the Duchess to rise is to accede to her request, so that henry is represented "as a ruler whose powers are temporarily contained by comic routine" (p.121).

[18] Bullingbrook's association of Gloucester's blood with Abel's (I.i.104), like his association of Exton's crime with Cain's, implies that the crime was committed by a brother; the first statement indicts Richard, the second, Henry himself. In each case the crime was authorized by a father's brother's son.

[19] See Romans 5:12-21.

[20] My thanks to William Oram and Gillian Kendall for their helpful comments on an earlier version of this essay.

Source: "Loyal Fathers and Treacherous Sons: Familial Politics in *Richard II,*" in *Journal of English and Germanic Philology,* Vol. 94, No. 3, July, 1995, pp. 347-64.

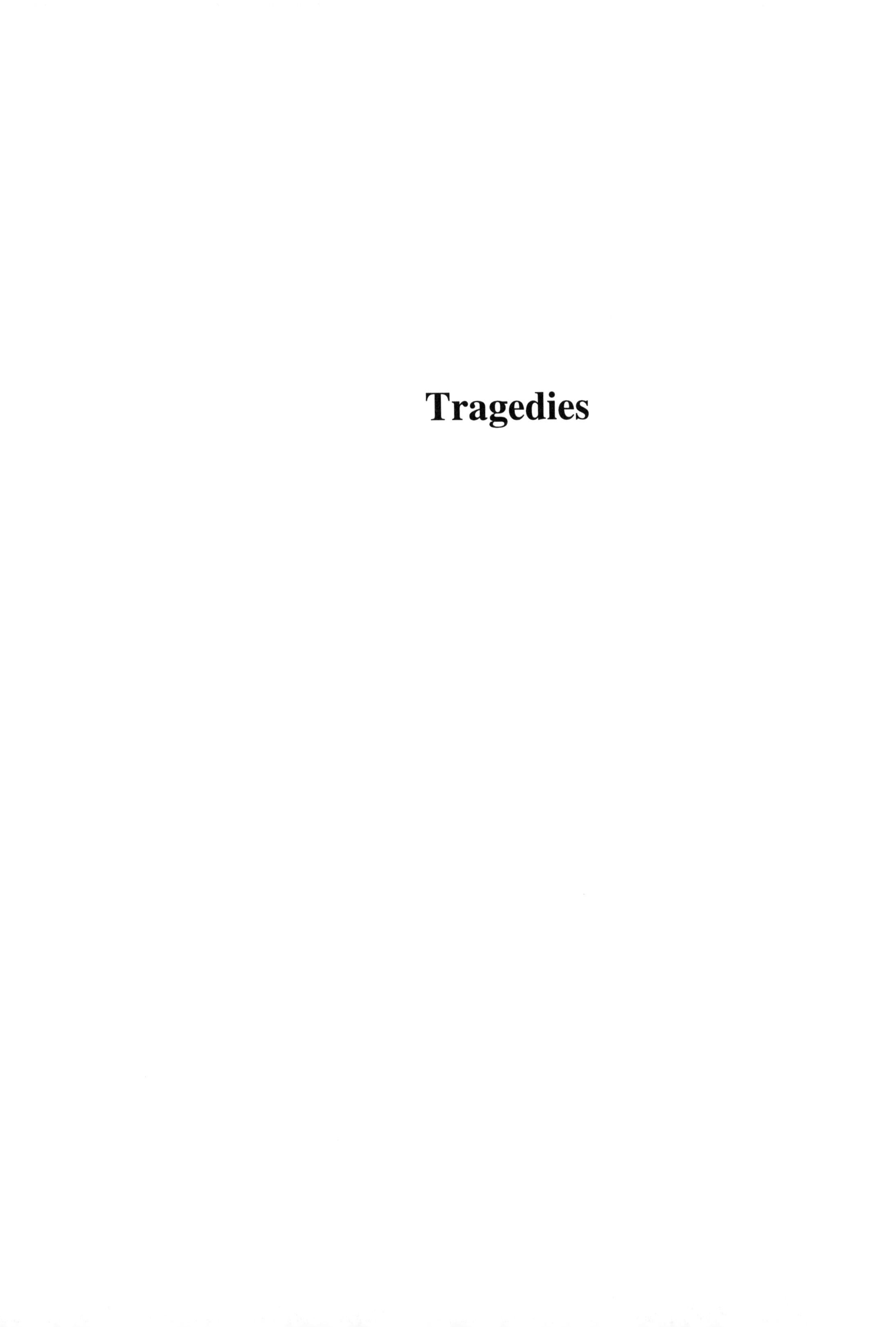

Tragedies

Theatricality and Textuality: The Example of *Othello*

John Bernard, *University of Houston*

Uncle Hilaal pulled at your cheek and teasing you, said, "Askar, where is the *third?* Where's the *other?*"

You looked about yourself, looked here, looked there, looked there and then at the two of them, but remained silent. In the quiet of your daydreams, you asked yourself, *"The third*—who's that?" One, Hilaal. Two, Salaado. Three? What does *the third* mean?

—Nuruddin Farah, *Maps*[1]

I

Is life a game, a stage, or a text? If, as Clifford Geertz has observed, these are the chief paradigms by which the academic discourse of our time has tended to define its agons, no intellectual terrain has proved more receptive to such "refigurations" than the Renaissance.[2] Under the first of these rubrics, studies of courtly behavior have invoked a Burkean or Bourdieuvian practice as the model of both discourse and action in the competition for the favor of princes and patrons.[3] At the same time, critics of a Foucauldian or late-Barthesian bent have investigated how, owing in part to the spread of printing, a consciousness of the possibilities of textual self-construction and self-projection enhanced the authority of the emergent early modern "author."[4] Not surprisingly, the middle branch of Renaissance academic discourse has largely referred itself to the late-Elizabethan and Jacobean public theater, as "metatheatrical" investigations of the art/life ratio in Shakespearean or English Renaissance drama have resonated with sociologically oriented analyses of everyday life.[5]

The links between theater and play are fairly obvious, and those between games and textuality have a special appeal to critics taken with the pleasures of the text. But the kinship of text-centered and stage-centered approaches, both in general and with reference to the Renaissance, has been less well acknowledged.[6] On the whole metanarrative and metatheater remain separate if equal games, though each has come to levy increasingly large claims on our understanding of Renaissance discourse. Yet homologies between theater and text (or stage and page) as modes of discursive production in the Renaissance deserve greater attention than they have received.[7] This is so not only because the material conditions governing productive practices in the two media are often similar, but because those conditions generate analogous consciousnesses—even subjectivities—among producers of discursive and theatrical texts. As Shakespeare studies have lately been emphasizing, the Elizabethan and Jacobean drama betrays an awareness of the theater as a vehicle for the critical evaluation of dominant ideologies, as well as the possible adumbration of emergent ones.[8] This self-consciousness is conveyed especially through the theatrical texts' conscious deployment of space and the attendant antimimetic conventions of the platform stage in constructing a relationship between players and audience.[9] An analogous theatricality has long been noted in Renaissance writers as diverse as Erasmus, Rabelais, and Cervantes, all of whom in different ways seem to willfully defy the logical self-contradictions implied in reifying the metaphor of a textual "audience."[10]

An interesting test of this observation arises in Montaigne, whose distrust of theatricality has been repeatedly noted.[11] I have tried elsewhere to demonstrate a unique aspect of Montaigne's textual construction of his "audience," the practice of representing it within his text, thereby putting into relief the textual *act* of representation itself, a kind of mimesis of mimesis.[12] Under the pressure of a perceived need to open channels of communication with his anonymous reader, Montaigne's *Essays* perform the textual construction of the modern author-as-subject. What is significant about this achievement is the number of explicitly theatrical passages in which Montaigne posits a specular relationship with his reader. This theme is borne out by his somewhat eccentric use of the word *tiers* or "third." On the most basic level, this motif serves to inject a sense of alterity into an original configuration between a subject and an "other" who, in Benveniste's terms, shares a "correlation of personality" with the subject.[13] In contrast to an original relation of self-presence, the self or *moi* becomes a displaced third party objectified so that the subject can speak of it "as a neighbor, as a tree."[14] In more explicitly theatrical passages Montaigne invites his reader to enter as spectator into a three-sided relationship with the speaker (or book) and another, or is encouraged to view such a triangular situation as an analogue to his own relation to the speaker. Hence Montaigne's reader functions less as a voyeur than as a kind of ghost writer of the *Essays,* the indispensable "third" without whom the text cannot mean.[15] Such a conception of the system of author, reader, and other has important implications for the contemporary theater. In the present essay I will try to show that the productive economy of meaning fostered by Montaigne's constructed relationship to his reader is closely paralleled in Shakespeare's *Othello*. Without advancing any claims of source or influence, I will argue that textual and theatrical production are functions of the same cultural situation.

II

Before turning to Shakespeare I want to situate these analogies both in the historical debate about the Renaissance and in the theoretical one about representation.[16] Let me begin by considering briefly the concept of "theatricality" employed in this discussion and to indicate some of its provenances in literary theory. In a series of books and articles on Shakespeare's theater, Robert Weimann has argued for a new kind of theatrical authority in the Renaissance centering on the tension between traditional Aristotelian mimesis and a more subjective form of imitation rooted in a general self-consciousness about representation itself, specifically the actors' representation of the *act* of appropriation.[17] In his earlier work Weimann examines the distribution of space in the late-medieval theater inherited by Shakespeare and his contemporaries, a division that permitted players to break with the mimetic illusion of character and foreground theatrical productivity, that is, "representivity" itself, as a praxis including both actors and audience in the process of creating meaning.[18] Weimann grounds his argument in his own and other scholars' researches into the material conditions of the Elizabethan theater, situated as it was on the margins of late sixteenth- and early seventeenth-century London.[19] But his theoretical model of the theatrical transaction is based on the Marxist concept of *Aneignung* or "appropriation," a reciprocal process whereby the modern bourgeois subject is constituted precisely in the act of making the conditions of his productive labor, in the cultural as well as the material sphere, his own. Applied to literary history, *Aneignung* is "both a text-appropriating . . . [and] a world-appropriating activity," which, "even while it precedes ideology and signification, is not closed to the acts of the historical consciousness of the signifying subject."[20]

Appropriation in this sense clearly transcends the theater. In the fluid social conditions of Elizabethan England, Weimann argues, such acts of "self-authorizing appropriation of language and its media of circulation" reflect a crisis in the authority of traditional vehicles of representation, including literary genres. Out of this crisis is generated a revision of the "modes and aims of representation." Rising in opposition to traditional mimesis, in which actors on the stage transparently represent mythological or historical characters, or narrators in fiction operate as neutral conduits for well-established stories and their meanings, the new mode of appropriation presupposes a representation "not reducible to its mimetic dimension." Instead, "representation (in this historicizing sense) appears as an agency of production and performance, in that it involves such performative action on the level of what is representing as cannot adequately be defined as a mere 'reflection' of the historically given circumstances and ideologies which the act of representation helps to transcribe."[21] Weimann is careful to acknowledge that such appropriative acts "do not serve the free expression of subjectivity" but are conditioned by "discursive usage."[22] Nevertheless, in his quarrel with the poststructuralist tendency to deny all subjectivity in the name of a rigid synchronicity that dissolves representation in "signification" and reduces writing to a subjectless textuality, he locates the limited freedom of the author in this diachronic and "dialogic (or theatrical) dimension in discourse."[23] In the social and historical context of the Renaissance, then, theatricality may be provisionally identified with the (individual or collective) interpretive axis that intersects with language conceived as a fixed and hegemonic system autonomously producing new cultural meanings. In the context of current academic debates, it functions as a counterforce to "textuality," suggesting how appropriating agents query, contest, and sometimes subvert established ideologies, thus effecting cultural change.[24]

This fruitful contamination of textuality by theatricality is exploited by Marie Maclean's performative approach to narrative, which stresses the function of "the reader as spectator." Tracing the traditional enmity of theater and narrative to their common origin—oral narrative at some point splits into theatrical performance and written narrative, ultimately the silent discourse of narrative in print—she identifies the "double nature of speculation, the double bind of spectatorship." By this she means that, like the play-audience, the reader is "tempted by the specularity, the mirroring of identification" with a character in the text addressed directly by the narrator, while retaining the awareness that spectatorship—that is, "the realization that one is a spectator"—entails "critical estrangement, and with it the penalties and pleasures of speculation."[25] For our purposes Maclean's work is most helpful when she comes closest to the psychoanalytic categories of reading, especially those of Jacques Lacan and René Girard. Here Maclean focuses on reading as transgression. Reflecting on the excluded reader and the enforced reader, and their various revenges on their violation by the text, she observes: "Since the reader is always an outsider to the consensus of the text, just as the audience is always an outsider to the consensus of the stage, we must ask if he or she is not always a transgressor, a breaker of boundaries and an intruder into the world of the other. Since the reader's desire is always the desire of the other, which wants what the other wants as much as it wants what the other is, and can never attain either, it must always involve the transgression implicit in the desire of the other." Citing Barthes's *The Pleasure of the Text,* she proposes that to "understand the reader's part in the production of the text" we must analyze his/her "libidinal input," a task she undertakes with respect to Baudelaire.[26]

The view of historians and cultural critics that theatricality is a corrective to textuality is reenforced by theater semioticians.[27] In the present context, what is significant about their approach is the attempt to apply the narratological theory of the *récit* (Propp, Bremond), and specifically actantial theory (Greimas), to the theater. Especially fruitful in this regard is the work of Anne Ubersfeld.[28] If Maclean posits the reader-as-spectator, Ubersfeld's anatomy of the theatrical transaction as a text foregrounds the role of the spectator-as-reader. For her, theatrical discourse is never constative: it "says" nothing about the real, only the imaginary within the mise-en-scène; hence, "the discourse of the play-wright makes sense only as theatricality." In this view theatricality implies a lack of textual subjectivity: the one who speaks is always a personage, embedded in a complex communicative network whose author is always at best a *destinateur* (addresser) and whose address to the spectator/reader/*destinataire* (addressee) is diffuse, dialogic, and plurisubjective.[29]

Ubersfeld devotes special attention to the role of the spectator in the theatrical transaction. In a sequel to her first essay she reiterates a structuralist/semiotic "reading" of theater with a view toward the spectator, analyzing both *représentation théâtrale*[30] and *représentation comme texte* (*ES* 27) on the discursive, narrative, and semic levels (*ES* 37). Like the reader of written texts, the spectator is "the coproducer of the spectacle" (*ES* 304), both *before,* in that it is aimed at her response, and *after,* in that, even more than the reader, she has the task of making sense of it—that is, sense *happens* only in her (*ES* 305f.).[31] As either a witness or the subject of a communication witnessed by others, the spectator is implicated in an "always triangular" relation with various combinations of actor, character, or other spectators.[32] One may quarrel with these particular paradigms, but however this triangulation of theatrical discourse is configured, "the public is the *guarantor* at one and the same time of the reality of the scenic figuration and of the non-verity of the scenic fiction" (*ES* 311). Ubersfeld's semiotics supports and implements Weimann's historicism in treating representation as involving equally the represented and the representing. Her narratological analysis gives a specific theoretical spin to the way in which "the totality of the theatrical representation is inscribed in a psychosocial consensus" (*ES* 311).

Ubersfeld's understanding of the position of the theater spectator, like Maclean's view of the reader-spectator's role as the third party or "outsider" in reading, evokes the familiar Freudian hermeneutic. In his book on jokes, Freud's interest in the role of the "third person" is related primarily to that of the first, the aggressor in a particular kind of social transaction. Freud distinguishes jokework from dreamwork by its social dimension, but ultimately the apparently social nature of the joke triangle—sexual aggressor, target, audience—projects the internal economy of the subject: "The process in the joke's first person produces pleasure by lifting inhibition and diminishing local expenditure; but it seems not to come to rest until, through the intermediary of the interpolated third person, it achieves general relief through discharge."[33] In short, the third person is a catalyst, a cipher or instrument in a circuit of exchange. As such, it is related to the analyst in the transference, a necessary intermediary between the subject and his unconscious. Since it is axiomatic that the subject cannot directly access his unconscious—the residue of his true "self"—through the dreamwork, in the joke as in the dream the execution of the psychic economy by which the inhibitions and potential neuroses resulting from this ban may be overcome always demands this mediation by a third person. As a "reader" of his self, the subject can be constituted only by way of the circuitous interpolation of an other. He can recognize his desire only as the desire of another. His pleasure must be received at the other's hands.[34]

It is this specular element in Freud's "theater of the unconscious" that inspires Lacan's adaptation of Freudian theatricality. In adopting the common economic element of Freud's "dreamwork" and "jokework" Lacan interprets Freud's *Darstellbarkeit* (representability) in explicitly theatrical terms as an "égards aux moyens de la mise en scène" (consideration of the means of staging). Emphasizing the element of distortion (*Entstellung,* or dis-placement), Lacan foregrounds "the intervention of a third party—which Freud calls 'censorship'—in the figuration of the dream, a party that plays the role both of spectator and of judge in the dream-representation."[35] Here again, the explicitly theatrical feature is the triadic structure of dreamer, third party, and addressee, in Lacan's version accompanied by a shift in emphasis from a phonetic to a "scriptural" notation of the dream. In a note explaining how Lacan's theory of enunciation goes beyond the notion of *text,* Samuel Weber writes: "What in Lacan's writings takes the place of textuality is theatricality, and in this respect it anticipates Derrida's own 'pragrammatological turn': each utterance localized in the text, 'in its place,' is determined, post facto as it were—and in this, very much like the dream—by addresses that it did not necessarily intend." Weber links this theatricality with Freud's comments on the third person "upon which the joke depends, and which endows it with its social character." [36]

Psychoanalytic theory, then, supports the semiology of the subject in foregrounding the essential triangularity of both theatrical and textual representation. Both theories, moreover, usefully supplement and revise the materialism of Weimann's account of Renaissance appropriation by narrowing if not annihilating the gap between theatricality and textuality. For Weimann (as for Keir Elam), theatrical *performance* always transcends textuality: the "performance text" includes but supersedes the "dramatic text."[37] Hence the representationality of a Shakespeare play dissolves into a "post-textual future" beyond the play's closure, based on the supplantation (and supplementation) of represented authority in the text's fiction by "the authority of the actor . . . [which] is not that of the text but that of performance itself."

Buttressed by the findings of semiotic and psychoanalytic theorists, we may reasonably assume that in looking at *non*dramatic representations we can identify mediating elements of theatricality in printed texts analogous to those of Weimann's *plataea*-occupying mediators between fiction and audience.[38] Such features would serve the same function of decentering the neoclassical subject as is achieved by Shakespeare's actors as self-conscious representers, or later by Brecht's "alienation effect."[39] Thus Montaigne, for example, is explicitly committed to a nonrepresentational version of mimesis: the unimpeachable flow of time and corresponding multiplicity of perspectives that constitute his shifting "I" contest the representational authority based on a textual monologism parallel to the fixed perspective of High Renaissance art. Specifically, his stagings of audience intrusion into *locus*-like fictions break the representational illusion of textuality by shifting the reader's consciousness from the represented (fiction) to the *act* of representing and to the representing *agent* within the text. Theatricality thus challenges textuality; the dramatic-fictional text becomes a "performance text." In this respect, Montaigne's representations of representation anticipate the metatheatricality of Shakespeare less than a generation later.

III

In *The Notebooks of Malte Laurids Brigge,* Rainer Maria Rilke meditates on the writer's need for "a third person . . . who passes through all lives and literatures," especially drama. In a passage fascinating for its gendering of the various theatrical roles, Rilke speculates that "every playwright up to now has found it too difficult to speak of the two whom the drama is really about":

> The third person, just because he is so unreal, is the easiest part of the problem; they have all been able to manage him; from the very first scene you can feel their impatience to have him enter; they can hardly wait. The moment he appears, everything is all right. But how tedious when he's late. Absolutely nothing can happen without him; everything slows down, stops, waits. Yes, and what if this delay were to continue? What, my dear playwright, and you, dear audience who know life so well, what if he were declared missing—that popular man-about-town or that arrogant youth, who fits into every marriage like a skeleton-key? What if, for example, the devil had taken him? Let's suppose this. All at once you feel the unnatural emptiness of the theatres; they are bricked up like dangerous holes; only the moths from the rims of the box-seats flutter through the unsupported void. The playwrights no longer enjoy their elegant townhouses. All the detective agencies are, on their behalf, searching in the remotest corners of the world for the irreplaceable third person, who was the action itself.[40]

Even without the half-suppressed wish that the devil might take him, this "irreplaceable third person" who both catalyzes and in a sense *is* the play's action might well evoke the powerful presence of Iago.

Iago is the very type of the Rilkean catalyst of the action (or the action itself) and mediator of others' desire. His orchestration of Roderigo's pursuit of Desdemona frames most of the play's action, whose burden is his perversion of Othello's desire for Desdemona. As Edward Snow has noted, through his efforts to thwart the prosperity of the mismatched couple, Iago too "has done the state some service," for that marriage challenges all the ideological hierarchies—of race, class, and gender—of the social system represented in the play.[41] This social role finds its dramaturgical counterpart in the improvisational nature of his stage function. In Weimann's terms, Iago represents precisely the crucial social agency in the self-authorizing appropriation of language by an emerging bourgeois subject. Witness his coy, distorting iterations of common signifiers—"thought," "indeed," "think," "honest"—which Othello mistakes for "close dilations, working from the heart" of a received fund of fixed significations.[42]

As for Weimann's "media of circulation," Iago's dominance of the nonrepresentational mimesis of the *plataea* gradually emerges over the first three acts of *Othello.* From the moment in the first scene when, under cover of darkness, the conspiracy with Roderigo breaks out into furtive appeals to Brabantio's suppressed fears of miscegenation, Iago lurks on the margins of the play's action as both its prime shaper and its interpreter to the theater audience, a position he will retain right down to the threshold of the play's catastrophe (cf. 5.1.11-22 and 128f.). Both in his famous "motive-hunting" soliloquies and in a dozen brief asides, Iago occupies a psychological space belonging as much to the theatrical agency of representation as to the represented social world of the fiction. The asides are especially germane to the present argument. When Iago comments on Cassio's paddling of Desdemona's palm in the "clyster-pipes" speech (2.1.167-78) or the "well tun'd . . . music" of Desdemona and Othello (2.1.199-

201), he is clearly not only inviting the audience to view the ensuing action from his own quasi-directorial perspective but also miming their potential role in constructing the meaning of the dramatic action, a key issue that will peak in the final scene of the play.

The role of the audience is a crucial factor in *Othello* as a theatrical event. And it is mainly through Iago's *plataea* function as presenter and interpreter that the play includes that role in its overall representation. As more than one commentator has noted, the central *anagnorisis* of the play turns on the seemingly unmotivated manifestation by the protagonist of the audience's ideological assumptions. When in the temptation scene Iago wins Othello's concurrence in Desdemona's initial deceit ("And so she did" [3.3.208]) and then elicits his voluntary outburst on "nature erring from itself" in her choice of a black mate (3.3.227), he succeeds in putting into play an anxiety about such social transgressions that embraces all of the principals (except perhaps Desdemona herself) and seems to arise as much from the collective psyche of players, characters, and spectators as from his own discrete subjectivity. This is the fear (and desire) that erupts in the long-deferred scene of the black man and the white woman in the nuptial bed with which the audience as well as Brabantio have been teased since the opening scene.[43] Othello's own internalization of this fear explains both the stern pose of a justicer in the execution scene and the strangely split subjectivity of his final psychomachy, in which the internalized Christian defender of the Venetian state executes vindicative justice against the transgressive Turkish Other.

In the murder scene (5.2), both the protagonist's delusion and its bloody consummation on the conjugal bed are presented without onstage mediation.[44] No one contests Iago's interpretation of Desdemona's conduct, now appropriated by Othello himself, till Emilia enters the scene; and so the theater audience is left briefly to confront directly its own complicity in the communal "bewhoring" of Desdemona. In contrast, through its serial mediations the public finale takes a distinctly metatheatrical turn. From the moment Emilia voices the audience's resistance to Iago's construction of the heroine, the stage in the denouement becomes the site of a contest for the play's meaning. The platform is overrun with interpreters vying to fill the signifying vacuum left by Iago's vow of silence, Iago himself having become at last Rilke's "third person who has never existed, has no meaning and must be disavowed," a theatrical variant on Lacan's purloined letter as floating signifier.[45] The spectators, in turn, are challenged to surrender the unmediated confusions of the murder scene to one or another of the contestants fretting and strutting, in full interpretive regalia, on the stage.

The active judgment demanded of the audience in the finale is not unprepared for in the text. As early as the council scene, a Venetian senator commenting on Turkish obliquity obliquely alerts us to the play's designs on its audience: "'tis a pageant / To keep us in false gaze" (1.3.18-19). Shakespeare's plays from the time of *Othello* on are, of course, full of such pageants: *Troilus and Cressida, Measure for Measure,* and *King Lear* from roughly the same period, and *The Winter's Tale* and *The Tempest* a few years later furnish only the most obvious analogues.[46] Through the first half of *Othello,* this metatheatrical tag may seem to apply solely to the machinations of Iago. In the temptation scene, for example, he skillfully displays his repertory of facial feints and vocal "stops" as an earnest of his interpretive authority regarding the invented pageant of Desdemona's duplicity. But as the play approaches its climax, the phrase's application to the theatricality of the play itself—that is, to the audience's part in the production of its meaning—emerges ineluctably.

This process begins in act 4, scene 1, where Iago sardonically makes good on his promise of "ocular proof," plying Pandarus's instruments of mimetic desire to reduce Othello to murderous infatuation. Unlike the temptation scene, here Iago deploys the basic triangularity of all theatricality, enlarging the pageant to include its audience. As in the notorious scene in the Grecian camp in *Troilus* (5.2), the staged scene with Cassio focuses our attention on the normally unrepresented mediation of meaning by the theatrical producers—playwright, actor, director—to a (normally) equally unrepresented audience. The calculated effects of this pageant on its on-stage spectator, Othello, are duly noted by Iago—who, unlike Pandarus, will also play a part in the pageant—on the threshold of his performance:

> Now will I question Cassio of Bianca
> . . . . It is a creature
> That dotes on Cassio (as 'tis the strumpet's
> plague
> To beguile many and be beguil'd by one);
> He, when he hears of her, cannot restrain
> From the excess of laughter. Here he comes.
> *Enter* CASSIO.
> As he shall smile, Othello shall go mad.
> (4.1.93-100)

The speech of course is not without its ironies. Iago's allusion to the beguiler beguiled not only echoes Othello's word in describing his own ultimately self-destructive persuasion of Desdemona ("I . . . often did beguile her of her tears" [1.3.155-56]) and foreshadows his own situation at the play's end; it also foregrounds the misogynistic construction of women that underwrites the pervasive violence of the action.

This point too is metatheatrically represented in the scene, in a more public sequel to its central mimesis of mimesis. From the outset, the "bewhoring" of Desdemona in her husband's eyes has been the linchpin of Iago's plot. It is the theme of the brothel scene (4.2), one that the women ironically share with Iago afterward: "He hath so bewhor'd her . . . that true hearts cannot bear it" (4.2.115-17). And it motivates Othello's execution of justice: "Strumpet, I come" (5.1.34). But it is in the confusion following the attempt on Cassio that we see how the purely private or personal construction of woman as "strumpet" transcends the individual subject and suffuses the social structure represented in the play—as well, implicitly, as that of the players and audience doing the representing. Iago's scapegoating of Bianca here is based on his persistent construction of her as a whore. Almost immediately on her entrance, he pronounces her a "notable strumpet" to the assembled crowd (5.1.78), confides to the "gentlemen" his suspicion of "this trash" as a party to Cassio's injury (5.1.85), and finally moralizes it as "the fruits of whoring" (5.1.116). So powerful is this argument that even Emilia, a sometime protofeminist who has herself been bewhored by Iago's suspicions of her with Othello, is moved to proclaim, "O fie upon thee, strumpet" (5.1.121). Thus, under the force of Iago's suggestion the patriarchy's severest critic in the play turns against its most blatant victim.[47] My point in this seeming digression is that, like his maddening of Othello through the representation of Desdemona's supposed liaison with Cassio, Iago's public bewhoring of Bianca utilizes the neutral onstage audience—in this instance Emilia in particular—to represent to the theater audience its own susceptibility to false pageants. These scenes lend a metatheatrical twist to the action that prepares the audience for the ultimate challenge of the finale.

Othello's construction of the murder of his wife appropriates and extends Iago's construction of her (and every woman) as a notorious strumpet. The theatricality of this appropriation of his own identity, however, is not created by Iago. Indeed, the warring interpreters of the finale are competing first of all with Othello himself, whose highly theatrical self-representation has earlier persuaded Desdemona to transgress the prevailing code figuratively cross-dressed as his fellow "warrior." Throughout act 5, scene 2, Othello struggles to keep his grip on the version of himself that has been implicit in his character from the outset. In his account of his wooing of Desdemona, for example, Othello betrays a strong sense of theatricality, not only in his pitching his story to the assembled Senators—even the Duke avers that "this tale would win my daughter too" (1.3.171) as it has clearly won himself—but in the calculated effects of what he calls his "process" (1.3.142) on the receptive Desdemona, whose "greedy ear [would] / Devour up my discourse. Which I observing, . . . found good means / To draw from her a prayer" to tell her more (1.3.149-52).[48] In the interim, this self-conception having been subverted by Iago's improvisations, Othello exchanges his role as the exotic outsider whose marginality has convinced her she can break with the norms of Venetian society to share his profession for that of the misogynistic defender of the patriarchy who must sacrifice his strumpet wife lest she "betray more men" (5.2.6). Othello's consciousness of a role asserts itself to the very end, as within a hundred lines the universal justicer who had initiated the scene is transmogrified to an unmanned coward subject to the whim of "every puny whipster" (5.2.244), and again to a loyal patriot who has "lov'd not wisely but too well" (5.2.344).

Vying with Othello's self-definition in the finale are those of Emilia, Gratiano, and Lodovico. It is these *public* mediators of its meaning who keep the play from executing the simple mimetic function of representing the hero's delusion and downfall. The action transcends the represented character, Othello, and embraces the representing theatrical apparatus itself, that is, the entire panoply of production, including the audience, that constitutes the play's ultimate interpretive authority. Othello's interpretive hegemony is first challenged by Emilia's redefinition of his sacrifice of Desdemona as merely another in a succession of "foul murthers" and "filthy deeds" rending the social fabric of Cyprus (5.2.106, 149), and of his noble self as an ignorant "gull," "dolt," and "villain" (5.2.163, 172). Then, as the private site of transgression opens onto a quasi-public determination of a verdict in both the juridical and the characterological sense, Emilia is supplanted (as she must be, her modest authority as a woman being socially limited to the domestic and the erotic) by a chorus of noblemen whose readings of the scene constitute the final agon in the play's self-construal. First Gratiano, whose role in the finale as an *homme moyen sensuel* is signaled twice by an uncomprehending "What is the matter" (5.2.171, 259), registers in a series of banalities the action's openness to interpretation even down to its last hundred lines: "'Tis a strange truth" (5.2.189), "Poor Desdemon" (5.2.204), "[S]ure he hath killed his wife" (5.2.236). It is only in the final lines that this openness is, predictably, foreclosed by Lodovico as the representative of authority in Cyprus-Venice. Lodovico's reconstruction of the events mirrors that of Fortinbras in the last forty lines of *Hamlet,* displaying the same tendency to yoke the dying hero's urge to "tell my story" to the more pressing demands of a political recuperation of meaning. Echoing Othello's self-(re)definition as a man "once so good [but subsequently] / Fall'n in the practice of a [damned] slave" (5.2.291-92), Lodovico (like the triumphant Portia in *The Merchant of Venice*) produces the documentary evidence of Iago's plotting, manna to a starving populace in need of order, and dismisses the private catastrophe while quickly consigning Cassio to the governorship of Cyprus, Iago to a slow and torturous death, Gratiano to the inheritance of Othello's "fortunes," and finally himself to the duty of "relat[ing] to the state / This heavy act" (5.2.370-71).[49]

As at the end of *Hamlet,* the final rhyming of *state* and *relate,* in which the former "dilations" (or "delations") of Othello's contested subjectivity yield to the more public relations or mediations of shared communal discourse, leaves the theater audience in something of a dilemma.[50] As erstwhile spectators to the bloody catastrophe whose identification with the on-stage audience of Cypriots and Venetians is nevertheless strongly solicited, they may be feeling a certain discomfort at the erasure by Lodovico's official version of the more complicated and disturbing one imbricated in the scene they have witnessed. Challenging their potential to be "coproducers of the spectacle" represented in the play's metatheatrical scenes, Lodovico arrogates to himself the function of ideologically authoritative purveyor of meaning found in traditional narrative.[51] For the theater audience to submit to his version of the spectacle is to surrender their part in the production of meaning, which has been foregrounded by the play's persistent theatricality. Conversely, to resist such a surrender is to embrace a metatheatrical subtext of *Othello,* analogous to that in the *Essays* of Montaigne, whose very construction depends on a "sufficient reader" of the theatrical text being interpreted on-stage.

IV

The old chestnut of Montaigne's supposed "influence" on Shakespeare is scarcely germane to the present argument.[32] What is relevant, and deserves to be taken more seriously by cultural critics, are the analogous material conditions of these writers—one writing principally for the printing press, the other for the theater—within the expanding horizons of discourse in the late sixteenth and early seventeenth centuries. Drawing on parallels with the practice of nontheatrical writers like Montaigne, the present study has tried to argue that the Shakespearean text, like the printed one, must be considered with respect to "the printing press and the public theater as unofficial media . . . of self-authorized performance and utterance" at a time when these instruments of cultural production were undergoing rapid and radical change.[53] Within this context *Othello,* like the *Essays,* reveals the textual effects of this change, and of the larger social evolution these texts are part of, in their self-conscious representations of that production. To be sure, the triangular motif of the "third" is but a minor if revealing aspect of this new self-consciousness. But the results of even so preliminary an investigation as this bear out the thesis of a resurgent nonmimetic representation (or nonrepresentational mimesis) and of the increasing sense of literary and cultural authority it implies.

Notes

[1] Nuruddin Farah, *Maps* (New York, 1986), p. 138.

[2] Clifford Geertz, "Blurred Genres: The Refiguration of Social Thought," *The American Scholar,* 49 (1980), 165-79.

[3] Daniel Javitch, *Poetry and Courtliness in Renaissance England* (Princeton, 1978); Steven J. Greenblatt, *Renaissance Self-Fashioning* (Chicago, 1980); Arthur Marotti, "'Love is not love': Elizabethan Sonnet Sequences and the Social Order," *English Literary History,* 49 (1982), 396-428; Frank Whigham, *Ambition and Privilege* (Berkeley, 1984).

[4] Anthony Wilden, "Par divers moyens on arrive à pareille fin: A Reading of Montaigne," *Modern Language Notes,* 83 (1968), 577-97; John Guillory, *Poetic Authority: Spenser, Milton, and Literary History* (New York, 1983); Jacqueline T. Miller, *Poetic License: Authority and Authorship in Medieval and Renaissance Contexts* (New York, 1986); Joseph F. Loewenstein, "*Idem*: Italics and the Genetics of Authorship," *Journal of Medieval and Renaissance Studies,* 20 (1990), 205-24.

[5] On Shakespeare, see esp. *Shakespeare and the Sense of Performance,* ed. Marvin and Ruth Thompson (Newark, N.J., 1989), as well as the works listed in its bibliography (prepared by John Styan). On theater-oriented theories of social behavior, besides Pierre Bourdieu's widely influential *Outline of a Theory of Practice,* tr. Richard Nice (Cambridge, 1977) and Erving Goffman's earlier *The Presentation of Self in Everyday Life* (New York, 1959), see Bruce Wilshire, *Role-Playing and Identity: The Limits of Theater as Metaphor* (Bloomington, Ind., 1983), and Richard Schechner, *Performance Theory* (New York, 1985). For a succinct summary of the claims of "practice"-oriented social theory, see S. P. Mohanty, "Us and Them: On the Philosophical Bases of Political Criticism," *Yale Journal of Criticism,* 2, no. 2 (1989), 19.

[6] Within the field of narratology, Marie Maclean has called for a recognition of "the relationship between those fraternal enemies, narrative and theatre," in her *Narrative as Performance* (London, 1988), p. 17. In Renaissance studies Robert Weimann, who generally treats narrative and theatrical texts separately, has noted the analogous conditions governing sixteenth- and seventeenth-century textual and theatrical production. See, for example, Robert Weimann, "History and the Issue of Authority in Representation: The Elizabethan Theater and the Reformation," *New Literary History,* 17 (1985), 449-75, where he notes that religious pamphlets and drama use the printing press and public theater respectively to circulate new "modes . . . of self-authorized performance" (p. 453). More recently,

however, in his "Representation and Performance: Authority in Shakespeare's Theater," *PMLA,* 107 (1992), 497-510, Weimann draws on Keir Elam's theatrical semiotics to emphasize the "difference . . . between the materiality of theatrical communication and the fictionality of textual configurations" (p. 507). A recent theorist more friendly to crossfertilization is Jonathan Hart, "Narrative, Narrative Theory, Drama: The Renaissance," *Canadian Review of Comparative Literature,* 18 (1991), 117-65. With reference to Chaucer, see Richard Neuse, *Chaucer's Dante* (Berkeley, 1991), pp. 116-21.

[7] In the Shakespearean arena, see the recent writings of Harry Berger, Jr., esp. "Text Against Performance in Shakespeare: The Example of *Macbeth,*" *Genre,* 15 (1982), 49-79 and, in general, his *Imaginary Audition* (Berkeley, 1989).

[8] The terms are Raymond Williams's in *Marxism and Literature* (Oxford, 1977), pp. 121-41.

[9] See, among others, Ann Barton, *Shakespeare and the Idea of the Play* (London, 1962); Robert Egan, *Drama within Drama* (New York, 1975); Garrett Stewart, "Shakespeare's Dreamplay," *English Literary Renaissance,* 11 (1981), 44-69; Ralph Berry, *Shakespeare and the Awareness of the Audience* (London, 1985); and Malcolm Evans, *Signifying Nothing* (Athens, Ga., 1986). On the evolution of spatial conventions in Shakespeare's theater, see Robert Weimann, *Shakespeare and the Popular Tradition in the Theater,* ed. Robert Schwartz (Baltimore, 1978), esp. pp. 143-85 and 208-37. This consciousness, of course, is not limited to Shakespeare: on Marlowe's even greater willingness to have the actor share with the audience his appropriation or "conjuration" of his role—and, by contrast, Shakespeare's characters' relative suspicion of theatrical roles—see Michael Goldman, "Performance and Role in Marlowe and Shakespeare," in *Shakespeare and the Sense of Performance,* pp. 95f.

[10] See Walter Ong, "The Writer's Audience Is Always a Fiction," *PMLA*, 90 (1975), 9-21.

[11] Hugo Friedrich, *Montaigne,* tr. Dawn Eng (1949; Berkeley, 1991), sees Montaigne's confusion about the identity of his audience as confirming his extreme self-orientation and desire to preserve an authentic inner life; hence even the inescapable "communication function of language" is viewed as a "constraint" on his solitary self-exploration (p. 332). For a recent reiteration of Montaigne's distrust of theater, see Joan Lord Hall, "'To play the man well and duely': Role-playing in Montaigne and Jacobean Drama," *Comparative Literature Studies,* 22 (1985), 173-86. Hall asserts that though Montaigne "admires histrionic talent on the stage," he "is not prepared to make a virtue of theatricality" in life and in society (pp. 174, 175). She does, however, concede a "gradual" recognition of its necessity by the author when "writing for the public" (p. 181). Jonas A. Barish, *The Antitheatrical Prejudice* (Berkeley, 1981), p. 112, is one of the few who deny that Montaigne holds such a prejudice.

[12] John Bernard, "Montaigne and Writing: Diversion and Subjectification in the *Essais,*" *Montaigne Studies,* 3 (1991), 131-55. This is close to what Linda Hutcheon calls "process mimesis" (as opposed to "product mimesis"), in her *Narcissistic Narrative: The Metafictional Paradox* (Waterloo, Ont., 1980), pp. 36-47. In a different context, Anthony Wilden has argued that the subject of the *Essais* suffers a "double bind" resulting from the competing demands of an emerging bourgeois notion of autonomy and a residual awareness that the self is capable of definition only within "the collective praxis of human kind." Anthony Wilden, *System and Structure: Essays in Communication and Exchange* (London, 1977), pp. 108f.

[13] See Emile Benvéniste, "Relationships of Person in the Verb," *Problems in General Linguistics,* tr. M. E. Meek (Coral Gables, Fla., 1971), p. 200.

[14] *The Complete Essays of Montaigne,* tr. Donald M. Frame (Stanford, 1965), 3:8, 942c; in the original, *Les Essais de Montaigne,* ed. Pierre Villey, re-ed. Verdun L. Saulnier (Paris, 1978), p. 720.

[15] Bernard, "Montaigne and Writing."

[16] The sources on these debates are both too numerous and too familiar to rehearse here. Besides the works cited elsewhere in this paper, I have found especially illuminating Lucien Dällenbach, *Le récit spéculaire* (Paris, 1977) and Philippe Lacoue-Labarthe, "Mimesis and Truth," *Diacritics,* 8 (1978), 10-23. In the course of critiquing René Girard's view of "representation" (in the theatrical sense of *Darstellung,* presentation/exhibition, as opposed to the philosophical one of *Vorstellung*), Lacoue-Labarthe stipulates a nonrepresentational, self-reflexive conception of theatricality, observing that rather than "covering up or masking mimesis" it always "reveals" it, that is, "defines and 'presents' it as that which . . . it never is on its 'own'" (p. 21).

[17] The most important works in English include Robert Weimann, *Shakespeare and the Popular Tradition*; "Society and the Uses of Authority," in *Shakespeare, Man of the Theater,* ed. Kenneth Muir et al. (Newark, N.J., 1981), pp. 182-99; "Mimesis in *Hamlet,*" in *Shakespeare and the Question of Theory,* ed. Patricia Parker and Geoffrey Hartman (New York, 1985), pp. 275-91; "Bifold Authority in Shakespeare's Theatre," *Shakespeare Quarterly,* 39 (1988), 401-17; and "Representation and Performance." Weimann's view coincides partly with that of Jacques Derrida in "Econo-

mimesis," in *Mimesis des articulations* (Paris, 1975), pp. 57-93, where mimesis is conceptualized not as the representation of something *in* nature (*natura naturata*) but of operations *of* nature (*natura naturans*), that is, a relation not of two products but of two productions. See Hutcheon, *Narcissistic Narrative*.

[18] Timothy Murray has conducted a parallel investigation of theatricality as a "performative mental posture and narrative result" in Baroque theater and theory in his *Theatrical Legitimation: Allegories of Genius in Seventeenth-Century England and France* (New York, 1987), p. 8.

[19] See esp. Steven Mullaney, *The Place of the Stage: License, Play, and Power in Renaissance England* (Chicago, 1988).

[20] Robert Weimann, "'Appropriation' and Modern History in Renaissance Prose Narrative," *New Literary History,* 14 (1983), 465-66.

[21] Weimann, "History and the Issue of Authority," 451.

[22] Robert Weimann, "History, Appropriation, and the Uses of Representation in Modern Narrative," in *The Aims of Representation,* ed. Murray Krieger (New York, 1987), p. 180.

[23] Weimann, "History and the Issue of Authority," 450. Weimann sets his historicizing concept of appropriation between "the classical romantic view of the text as the purely referential activity of some reflecting subject and the (seemingly opposite) view of the text as some autonomous locus of self-determining differentials or epistemes," what he characterizes as the competing hegemonies of "the subject" and "of language itself" in his "Text, Author-Function, and Appropriation in Modern Narrative: Toward a Sociology of Representation," *Critical Inquiry,* 14 (1988), 432. Roger Chartier, *Cultural History,* tr. Lydia G. Cochrane (Cambridge, 1988), drawing on epistemology and the sociology of knowledge to update the traditional French *histoire des mentalités,* arrives at a conception of "representation" and "appropriation," specifically in the textual production of earlier historical periods, that complements Weimann's Marxist approach. Following Norbert Elias and Lucien Febvre, Chartier too rejects "the universal and abstract subject" of both phenomenology and reception-aesthetics in favor of historically grounded "appropriations" of texts' meanings (p. 12).

[24] For a parallel discussion of mimesis and representation that draws on social theorists to define a new nonrepresentational mimesis based on self-alienation and "identification through estrangement" (461), see Luiz Costa Lima, "Social Representation and Mimesis," tr. J. Laurenio de Mello, *New Literary History,* 16 (1985), 447-66.

[25] Maclean, *Narrative as Performance,* p. 34; hereafter cited in text.

[26] Compare Ross Chambers's historically grounded explanation for the shift from "narrative" to "narratorial" authority in *Story and Situation: Narrative Seduction and the Power of Fiction* (Minneapolis, 1984): "When narrative ceases to be (perceived as) a mode of direct communication of some preexisting knowledge and comes instead to figure as an oblique way of raising awkward, not to say unanswerable questions, it becomes necessary for it to trade in the manipulation of desire (that is, the desire to narrate must seek to arouse some corresponding desire for narration) to the precise extent that it can no longer depend, in its hearers or readers, on some sort of 'natural' thirst for information" (p. 11). Though he locates this shift definitively in nineteenth-century narrative texts, Chambers acknowledges earlier adumbrations.

[27] Besides the work of Anne Ubersfeld discussed below, see esp. Keir Elam, *The Semiotics of Theater and Drama* (New York, 1988).

[28] Anne Ubersfeld, *Lire le Théâtre* (Paris, 1977); hereafter cited in text. Translations of quotations from this and other works by Ubersfeld are the author's.

[29] Ubersfeld somewhat naively asserts that theatrical discourse is a "discours sans sujet" in that the author cannot speak in his own voice (p. 264), ignoring the fact that this is equally true of any fictive discourse (or perhaps of any discourse).

[30] Anne Ubersfeld, *L'Ecole du spectateur* (Paris, 1981), p. 22; hereafter cited in text as *ES*.

[31] There is an obvious analogy with, or debt to, Barthes's "writerly" text as aiming to "make the reader no longer a consumer but a producer of the text" (Roland Barthes, *S/Z* [Paris, 1970], p. 10).

[32] For example, the actor addresses the spectator, with the other actors and spectators as witnesses; a character is superimposed on the actor, the spectator being witness; the spectator becomes a character himself, with other characters as witnesses to *their* communication; or, finally, the spectator is the subject of the communication, this time with other spectators, "objectifying" the actor(s) and/or character(s) (*ES* 308-11).

[33] Sigmund Freud, *Jokes and Their Relation to the Unconscious,* tr. James Strachey (New York, 1963), p. 158.

[34] For a critique of Freud's "representative theatricality" based on an attack on the Freudian originary "subject," see Mikkel Borch-Jacobsen, *The Freudian Subject,* tr. Catherine Porter (Stanford, 1988), esp. pp. 26-48, and 117ff.

[35] Samuel Weber, *Return to Freud: Jacques Lacan's Dislocation of Psychoanalysis* (Cambridge, 1991), p. 73; hereafter cited in text. The present paragraph draws heavily on this commentary.

[36] An analogue in the "sociology of discourse" is Volosinov's "third participant" ("the topic of speech" or "hero") in any spoken discourse, who along with the speaker and "listener as ally or witness" imparts to communication its "objective and sociological" character. See V. N. Volosinov, "Discourse in Life and Discourse in Art," in his *Freudianism: A Marxist Critique,* tr. I. R. Titutnik (New York, 1976), pp. 104f. Applied to written discourse specifically, this function is partly shifted to the internal or textual "listener" of a discourse, or "authoritative representative" of the speaker's social group (p. 114), akin to the "implied reader" of narratology. Compare Paul Ricoeur, "The World of the Text and the World of the Reader," in his *Time and Narrative,* tr. K. Blarney and D. Pellaner (Chicago, 1988), 3:157-79.

[37] Weimann, "Representation and Performance," 505; hereafter cited in text.

[38] Compare Paul Ricoeur, "La fonction herméneutique de la distantiation," in his *Du texte à l'action* (Paris, 1986), 3:101-17.

[39] For an exposition of Brecht as an anti-Aristotelian, anti-Freudian, antitheatrical *political* critic of the mimetic category of *catharsis,* see Bernard Pautrat, "Politique en scène: Brecht," in *Mimésis des articulations,* pp. 341-59.

[40] Rainer Maria Rilke, *The Notebooks of Malte Laurids Brigge,* tr. Stephen Mitchell (New York, 1983), pp. 21f. I owe the observation about the gender-specific language of this passage—"man-about-town," "skeleton-key," "dangerous holes," and so forth—to my colleague Professor Ann Christensen.

[41] Edward A. Snow, "Sexual Anxiety and the Male Order of Things in *Othello,*" *English Literary Renaissance,* 10 (1980), 411. In the paragraphs that follow I am especially indebted to this essay and to Stephen Greenblatt, *Renaissance Self-Fashioning,* pp. 232-54.

[42] Act 3, sc. 3, l. 123. Citations of *Othello* are from *The Riverside Shakespeare* (Boston, 1974), hereafter cited in text by act, scene, and line.

[43] Lynda E. Boose, "'Let it be hid': Renaissance Pornography, Iago, and Audience Response," in *Autour d' "Othello,"* ed. Richard Marienstras et al. (Amiens, 1987), pp. 135-43, reads the final scene as "expos[ing] the complicity of [its patriarchal audience's] spectatorship" (p. 136). For a thorough, illustrated survey of the representation of this scene, see Michael Neill, "Unproper Beds: Face, Authority, and the Hideous in *Othello,*" *Shakespeare Quarterly,* 40 (1989), 383-412.

[44] On the question of its bloodiness, and the significance of blood both in this scene and with respect to Desdemona's handkerchief, see Lynda E. Boose, "Othello's Handkerchief: 'The Recognition and Pledge of Love,'" *English Literary Renaissance,* 5 (1975), 360-74.

[45] Jacques Lacan, "Seminar on 'The Purloined Letter,'" tr. Jeffrey Mehlman, *Yale French Studies,* 48 (1972), 39-72.

[46] On the range and function of pageants in Shakespeare see the essays collected in *Pageantry in the Shakespearean Theater,* ed. David M. Bergeron (Athens, Ga., 1985), as well as the earlier works by Withington, Venesky, Orgel, Wickham, Anglo, and Bergeron himself cited in them.

[47] Bianca's spirited defence—BIANCA: "I am no strumpet, but of life as honest / As you that thus abuse me"—evidently provoked only by this betrayal by her fellow victim, and its provoked response—EMILIA: "As I? [Fough,] fie upon thee!"—foreground the mistress/wife dichotomy by which the patriarchy divides its victims (5.1.122-23).

[48] That it is "the story of my life" (1.3.128) *quâ* story that "beguiles" her is underscored by the word's occurrence three times—not counting its variants "history" and "discourse"—in the forty-four-line speech. Ross Chambers, *Story and Situation,* pp. 4-6, sees the passage as a *locus classicus* of the "performative function of story-telling," though he concedes that in the theater words always necessarily occur in a represented context. Hart (see n. 6) distinguishes four functions of narrative in drama: exposition, suggestion, compression, and address (pp. 117f. and 152-62). While all four entail the relation of playwright to audience, the last would seem to be the thrust of most theatrical metanarrative.

[49] Alan Sinfield acknowledges Lodovico's role in telling the official version of Othello's story in *Faultlines* (Berkeley, 1992). As he notes, "The state is the most powerful scriptor" of the stories believed in any society (p. 33). On the relation of Shakespeare's "pageant moments" throughout his oeuvre to the perspectival structure of offstage Elizabethan public ceremonies in which the audience "watched royalty or nobility watch the pageant" (p. 244), see Bruce R. Smith, "Pageants into Play: Shakespeare's Three Perspectives on Idea and Image," in *Pageantry in the Shakespearean Theatre,* pp. 220-46.

[50] For the possibility that "dilations" might also have been heard as "delations" or judicial accusations, see

Patricia Parker, "Shakespeare and Rhetoric: 'Delation' and 'Dilation' in *Othello,*" in *Shakespeare and the Question of Theory,* pp. 54-74.

[51] Robert Weimann, "'Fictionality' and Realism: Rabelais to Barth," in *The Uses of Fiction,* ed. Douglas Jefferson et al. (Milton Keynes, England, 1982), pp. 9-30. Nicholas Potter, in "*Othello* and the Reading Public," *Critical Survey,* 3 (1991), 142-48, makes Lodovico's question, "What should be said to thee?" the basis of Venice's "incapacity for criticism" and judgment, though not that of Shakespeare's audience.

[52] See, most recently, Serena Jourdan, *The Sparrow and the Flea: The Sense of Providence in Shakespeare and Montaigne* (Salzburg, 1983). Jourdan's list of her precursors in the field on pp. 201-4 can be supplemented from Friedrich, *Montaigne,* p. 406. The studies I have personally consulted include Elizabeth Rollins Hooker, "The Relation of Shakespeare to Montaigne," *PMLA,* 17 (1902), 312-66; Alice Harmon, "How Great Was Shakespeare's Debt to Montaigne?" *PMLA,* 57 (1942), 988-1008; Margaret T. Hodgen, "Montaigne and Shakespeare Again," *Huntington Library Quarterly,* 16 (1952), 23-42; and Robert Ellrodt, "Self-Consciousness in Montaigne and Shakespeare," *Shakespeare Survey,* 28 (1975), 37-50. Most of these have been inconclusive, the only hard evidence being still the allusions to "Of cannibals" in *The Tempest.* Friedrich, *Montaigne,* pp. 405f., is particularly skeptical about Montaigne's influence on Shakespeare, concluding that Shakespeare clearly read the Florio translation but that Montaigne functions for him chiefly as a "vehicle" of "commonplace things" that he could have gleaned from other sources. Indeed, Friedrich goes even further and adds that sixteenth- and seventeenth-century readers *read* Montaigne primarily "as a compiler of what was in general circulation" (p. 406).

[53] Weimann, "History and the Issue of Authority," 453.

Source: "Theatricality and Textuality: The Example of *Othello,*" in *New Literary History,* Vol. 26, No. 4, Autumn, 1995, pp. 931-49.

Theatrical *Italics*

Allan C. Dessen, *University of North Carolina, Chapel Hill*

"The Drawer stands amazed, not knowing which way to go"

1 Henry IV, 2.4.76.s.d.

Evidence from the Shakespeare quartos and First Folio suggests the possibility of various forms of onstage juxtaposition, ranging from the early entrances of a Dogberry or Cassandra to the continued presence of a Jaques or Sir Walter Blunt. The resistance to such a practice today by editors, critics, and theatrical professionals acts out a dismissal of a phenomenon that seemingly defies "common sense" but a phenomenon that may equally well signal a gap between the theatrical vocabulary shared then and what is assumed today (or, in some instances, what has been assumed since the eighteenth century). By one set of yardsticks, such juxtapositions can be intrusive and therefore distracting, troubling. But what if such a technique is part of a theatrical strategy designed to highlight a figure or situation so as to make it unmissable? How would (or should) such a strategy predicated upon *italicized* signifiers in their theatrical vocabulary affect interpretation today?

Such questions are part of a larger set of problems (in the broad category of "validity in interpretation") that continue to bedevil literary theorists. To cite one recent formulation, Paul Armstrong posits: "Endless variety is possible in interpretation, but tests for validity can still judge some readings to be more plausible than others." As a pluralist who nonetheless believes in literary criticism as a rational enterprise, Armstrong proposes three such yardsticks for the validity of any interpretation: *inclusiveness, intersubjectivity,* and *efficacy.* For *inclusiveness,* he argues that "a hypothesis becomes more secure as it demonstrates its ability to account for parts without encountering anomaly and to undergo refinements and extensions without being abandoned." Although "as a normative ideal, or principle of correctness," this yardstick by itself may be useless, it can still be valuable "in that it can exclude bad guesses." As to *intersubjectivity* (linked to persuasiveness): "our reading becomes more credible if others assent to it or at least regard it as reasonable," while "the disagreement of others may be a signal that our interpretation is invalid because unshareable." By this criterion, "the ultimate indication" of correctness would be "universal agreement." To invoke *efficacy* is to see whether or not in pragmatic terms an interpretation "has the power to lead to new discoveries and continued comprehension," for "the presuppositions on which any hermeneutic takes its stand are not immune from practical testing" but "must continually justify themselves by their efficacy." If such presuppositions "repeatedly fail to lead to persuasive, inclusive readings, friends as well as foes may conclude that the problem lies not with the limited skills of the method's adherents but with its assumptions."[1]

To apply Armstrong's arguments and distinctions to the many warring approaches to Shakespeare's plays is a daunting task far beyond my province. In terms of recovering a lost or blurred theatrical vocabulary, however, is it possible to single out signifiers or techniques that would make it likely that a given interpretation does or could "work"—whether for a putative playgoer in the 1590s or a playgoer today? To respond to such a question, let me focus upon some onstage moments that not only stand out as noteworthy but actually cry out for interpretation—much like a trumpet or drum roll that in effect says "look at me!" As already noted, my term for such moments or images is *theatrical italics* in that they underscore some effect so as to ensure that a moderately attentive playgoer will recognize that *some*thing of importance is happening. Interpretations of such a moment may vary (in the spirit of Armstrong's pluralism), but, in keeping with his *inclusiveness,* a reading of that play should *some*how incorporate such an italicized moment—at least to be persuasive (or intersubjective) to me. My use of *should* invites a Coriolanus-like rebuke to a "Triton of the minnows" (I claim no moral or legal authority for such a stipulation), but in the search for yardsticks to judge or screen interpretations (or for solid building blocks to create interpretations) I have found few comparable tools that satisfy me.[2]

To apply my yardstick or tool, however, is by no means easy, for . . . many roadblocks prevent today's interpreter from seeing various theatrical effects that would have been obvious to Shakespeare's playgoers. First, given the paucity of stage directions in the original printed texts, the eye of a reader can readily slide over what may have been far more striking to a playgoer. Given various kinds of intervention, moreover, that reader who confronts today's editorial text rather than the original Quarto or Folio version may be spared exposure to such anomalies, just as today's playgoer watching a production may be screened from moments that a director deems unsuitable to our theatrical vocabulary. Since we lack a videotape of the Globe production (and are far removed from their culture and theatrical practice), to determine what was subtle versus what was obvious in *their* terms, in *their* productions, is no easy matter (and may at times be impossible).

Nonetheless, even on the page some images or moments do seem to stand out, to the extent that editors and directors regularly deem them "unrealistic" or offensive and therefore resist them, adapt them, or eliminate them. Here then is promising raw material for this category. What I am proposing, in part, is the converse of what I take to be one common interpretative procedure—to start with an agenda or interpretation and then find ways to realize it. Rather, I am suggesting that interpreters start with odd or extreme moments, assume they are especially noticeable *because* they seem so strident, and then build an interpretation upon them. Again, the apparent anomalies that do not fit "our" ways of thinking or problem-solving often can serve as windows into distinctive Elizabethan-Jacobean procedures. Not all such obvious moments or images are controversial or under-interpreted (e.g., few would disagree that the conjunction of the beautiful Titania and an ass-headed Bottom is both obvious and at the heart of that comedy), but what about equally visible moments that have received little attention or have been altered or suppressed? My goal is not to argue in favor of one obligatory reading based upon such italicized images but rather (in the spirit of Armstrong's *inclusiveness* and *intersubjectivity*) to question interpretations that do not in some way take into account what most would agree to be an unmissable, unforgettable moment in a given play.

As a point of departure, consider the practical joke played upon Francis the drawer by Prince Hal at the outset of the famous tavern scene in *I Henry IV*. Whether owing to a sense of dramatic economy or a distaste for such pranks, this moment is often cut in performance (as in the television production for the BBC's "The Shakespeare Plays"). Nonetheless, the sequence has received its share of commentary, with the focus often upon Francis as an index to the prince's own uneasiness about his truancy or apprenticeship.[3] Indeed, once attended to, this sequence can generate a variety of questions, a situation reinforced when Poins himself asks: "But hark ye; what cunning match have you made with this jest of the drawer? Come, what's the issue?" (2.4.86-8)

What most concerns me here, however, is the stage direction at what I take to be the climax of the trick: *"Here they both call him. The Drawer stands amazed, not knowing which way to go"* (2.4.76.s.d.). Whatever the interpretation, should not the interpreter somehow build upon or take very seriously this highly visible onstage image? For example, what if the frenzied movement of Francis (as he responds alternatively to Poins's offstage calls and the prince's onstage questions) that climaxes in this amazed state would have strongly echoed onstage activity already seen (e.g., of Hotspur in the previous scene) or soon to be seen (e.g., of Falstaff confronted with the truth about his flight at Gadshill)? As I understand the scene, Shakespeare is here setting up for the playgoer a paradigm of the controller and the controlled, the puppetmaster and the puppet, so as to encourage us to recognize what makes Hal so distinctive. That interpretation may or may not satisfy other readers or viewers,[4] but the episode, especially the theatrical punch line signaled in the stage direction, cries out for *some* kind of explanation (as signaled also by Poins's question).

A similar effect is generated by Romeo's attempted suicide in 3.3 where the supposed "good" Quarto of 1599 provides no stage direction, but the "bad" Quarto of 1597 (perhaps based upon an actor's memory of some production) provides: *"He offers to stab himself, and Nurse snatches the dagger away"* (GIV). Some editors incorporate the QI signal into their texts, but New Arden editor Brian Gibbons rejects the Nurse's intervention as "neither necessary or defensible." Rather, for this editor "this piece of business looks like a gratuitous and distracting bid on the part of the actor in the unauthorized version to claim extra attention to himself when the audience should be concentrating on Romeo and the Friar." In the Arden edition the Nurse's intervention is therefore relegated to the textual notes and footnotes.

But, as with other possible examples of theatrical *italics,* what if the strategy behind QI's stage direction is to call attention not to the actor but to the onstage configuration (as with the amazed paralysis of Francis the drawer), a configuration that in turn epitomizes images and motifs enunciated in the dialogue? After Mercutio's death, Romeo had cried out: "O sweet Juliet, / Thy beauty hath made me effeminate / And in my temper soft'ned valor's steel" (3.1.111-13). Then, after Romeo's aborted attempt at suicide, the Friar's long moralization starts:

> Hold thy desperate hand.
> Art thou a man? Thy form cries out thou art;
> Thy tears are womanish, thy wild acts denote
> The unreasonable fury of a beast.
> Unseemly woman in a seeming man!
> And ill-beseeming beast in seeming both!
> (3.3.108-13)

The playgoer who sees Romeo's self-destructive violence interrupted (surprisingly) by the Nurse and then hears the Friar's terms (e.g., "Art thou a man?"; "Thy tears are womanish"; "Unseemly woman in a seeming man") is therefore encouraged to consider: what kind of "man" is Romeo at this point in the play? What by one kind of interpretative logic may seem "gratuitous and distracting" or "out of character" or "unbelievable" may, in the terms of a different logic or vocabulary, prove imagistically or symbolically consistent or meaningful. Indeed, how better act out the ascendancy of the "womanish" or unmanly side of Romeo and call that ascendancy to the attention of a first-time playgoer?

For a third example, consider the context of one of the most famous moments in Shakespeare, Macbeth's "to-morrow, and to-morrow, and to-morrow." Seven lines into the scene a stage direction calls for *"a cry within of women"* (5.5.7), at which point Macbeth asks "What is that noise?" and Seyton responds: "It is the cry of women, my good lord." After a short speech ("I have supped full with horrors") Macbeth asks again: "Wherefore was that cry?" to which Seyton responds: "The Queen, my lord, is dead" (15-16), a revelation that elicits the famous speech. The Folio, however, provides no exit and re-entry for Seyton between his two lines, so the only authoritative text gives no indication how he finds out that the queen is dead. Editors therefore insert an exit for Seyton after his first line and an entrance before his second; a director may have Seyton *exit* or may have him send off a lesser functionary who then returns or may have Seyton walk to a stage door, confer with someone offstage, and return to Macbeth. If the playgoer is to understand that Lady Macbeth has died at the moment of the cry, the announcer of the news presumably must have some means of learning the news; our logic of interpretation or theatrical vocabulary therefore requires an exit or some comparable means of getting that news on stage.

But, again, can today's interpreter conceive of the scene as scripted in the Folio? Macbeth would ask his first question ("What is that noise?") and get the answer ("It is the cry of women"). No one then leaves the stage; Seyton remains by his side. After his ruminations about fears and horrors, Macbeth asks again: "Wherefore was that cry?" and Seyton responds: "The Queen, my lord, is dead." In this literal rendition of the Folio, the playgoer cannot help seeing that Seyton (to be pronounced *Satan?*) has no normal (earthly?) way of knowing what he knows. But he *does* know. Macbeth may be too preoccupied to notice the anomaly, but, if staged this way, the playgoer cannot help being jarred. Indeed, the anomaly then becomes a major part of the context for the nihilistic comments that follow. Such a staging (which adds nothing but rather takes the Folio at face value) strikes me as eerie, powerful, perhaps quite unnerving. A focus upon *how* Seyton knows of the death almost inevitably leads to the addition of stage business that can provide a practical explanation for that "how," but such literal-mindedness may lead to a masking of a truly distinctive Jacobean effect linked to a mystery behind that "how" and may erase today what would have been italicized then.

Such italicized moments can be especially visible in Shakespeare's earliest and least admired plays where such effects are less likely to be screened from view by the poetry or fully realized personae. Let me start with three of the many moments in *Titus Andronicus* that have troubled readers, editors, and playgoers and therefore have often been blurred or eliminated. First, consider the *exeunt* near the end of 3.1 that includes not only Titus, Marcus, and the armless, tongueless Lavinia but also the heads of Quintus and Martius and the severed hand of Titus. The Quarto provides no stage direction here, but the now one-handed Titus stipulates how each exiting figure is to handle an appropriate object:

> Come, brother, take a head;
> And in this hand the other will I bear.
> And, Lavinia, thou shalt be employed in these arms:
> Bear thou my hand, sweet wench, between thy teeth.
>
> (3.1.279-82)

This passage has proved *very* troublesome for editors and directors. Although only one word changes in the Folio (*Armes* becomes *things*, TLN 1430), some editors (most recently Stanley Wells and Gary Taylor in their Oxford edition) have emended line 282 so as to eliminate the hand-in-mouth reference.[5] Readers of an unemended scene may ignore these lines, but directors, unwilling to risk an audience's reaction to the image of Lavinia exiting with the hand like a puppy carrying off its master's slippers, either cut the text or bring on young Lucius to help with the items to be carried.

But consider the *assets* of such an italicized moment. Given the heavy emphasis up to this point upon murder, rape, and dismemberment, how better act out the violation of the personal, family and political body than to have severed heads carried in the hands of the two old men and the warrior's severed hand carried off in the mouth of the violated woman? How better express the Andronici as prey to the wilderness of tigers or the chaotic disorder of the body politic or the failure of traditional norms? In Armstrong's terms, to build an interpretation upon such a strident, evocative onstage image is efficacious and intersubjective. Not to take this *exeunt* into account is to violate the yardstick of inclusiveness and, as with Francis, Romeo-Nurse, and Seyton-Macbeth, to sidestep what many would agree to be an especially noticeable, perhaps unforgettable moment.[6]

Consider next the appearance of Tamora, Chiron, and Demetrius in 5.2 disguised as Revenge, Rapine, and Murder. This lapse into allegory or near allegory poses particular problems in a modern production. The route taken by most actors and directors is to assume a mad or nearly mad Titus and a Tamora so confident in that madness that she is willing to take on a disguise that clearly would not "work" for a sane figure. To enhance the credibility of the moment, today's director will resort to a darkened stage (to heighten the possibility of concealment), heavy make-up, and some kind of outlandish disguise for the three figures so as to diminish Tamora's (and Shakespeare's) apparently anomalous choice of Revenge as a persona for this interview.

But much of the point of the moment as scripted lies not in Tamora's attitude to disguise or Titus' presumed madness (issues crucial to a twentieth-century theatrical vocabulary) but in the "image" of Revenge set up for the playgoer. What Shakespeare provides, at least in 1590s terms, is an individual (here Tamora) who for a moment "becomes" Revenge, a process certainly not irrelevant to Titus himself (whether mad or not) in the last two scenes of this revenge tragedy. Given the fact that in *The Spanish Tragedy* Revenge appears with Don Andrea at the outset and remains onstage throughout the remainder of the play, the presence of a figure of "Revenge" in the "real world" of Titus' Rome was at least possible in the theatre of the early 1590s. Our dominant mode of psychological realism (would such a "character" say or do X in this situation?) does not mesh comfortably with a figure posing as Revenge, even if that pose is to deceive a supposedly deranged figure with "miserable, mad, mistaking eyes" (5.2.66). But given the theatrical vocabulary available in the 1590s, Shakespeare may have had more rather than fewer options than a dramatist confined to "realism."[7]

What then are the assets of having this visible epitome of Revenge announce that she has been "sent from th' infernal kingdom / To ease the gnawing vulture of thy mind / By working wreakful vengeance on thy foes" (5.2.30-2)? Of particular interest here is her demand: "Come down and welcome me to this world's light" and, a few lines later, "come down and welcome me" (33, 43). Here, in a simple yet highly emphatic fashion, Titus' acquiescence to Tamora-Revenge's twice repeated "come down" clearly brings him from some removed position above to her level below. Such a movement downward is characteristic of many Revenge plays (whether that "below" is conceived of as Hell or as subterranean psychological forces) and, moreover, is set up forcefully in this play in the arrow-shooting scene where Publius brings word to Titus that Justice is not available (being employed "with Jove in heaven, or somewhere else") "but Pluto sends you word / If you will have Revenge from hell, you shall." Titus responds that Jove "doth me wrong to feed me with delays"; rather, "I'll dive into the burning lake below, / And pull her out of Acheron by the heels" (4.3.37-44).[8] Titus in 5.2 can therefore act out his literal and figurative descent to the level of Revenge, a descent that, by the end of the scene, yields the bloodiest moment in a bloody play and leads to the ultimate in revenge, the Thyestean banquet of 5.3.

To focus upon Tamora's overconfidence and Titus' madness (or upon darkness and a well crafted disguise), then, is to provide a workable scene in terms that make sense to playgoers today but to diminish the full range of the original effect. The acting out of Revenge as a force that can take over an individual, along with the descent of the title figure to the level of that Revenge, has a stark power and elegant simplicity that anticipates and feeds into the events of the final scene. Like the 3.1 *exeunt* with two heads and a hand, such an italicized effect generates fruitful questions and insights (in keeping with Armstrong's *efficacy*).

As a third example from this early tragedy, consider the signal for Titus to appear *"like a cook, placing the dishes"* (5.3.25.s.d.), an odd costume immediately called to our attention by Saturninus' question: "Why art thou thus attired, Andronicus?" Titus' answer ("Because I would be sure to have all well / To entertain your highness and your Empress") has not satisfied subsequent theatrical professionals, so that today's productions often do not present here a decidedly different image of the revenger. For the original audience, moreover, such a costume (along with *"placing the dishes"*) would have served as part of a theatrical shorthand to denote the "place" (a banquet room) and would have suggested (wrongly) a subservient Titus debasing himself in degree in order best to serve his emperor and empress.

But to ignore this distinctive costume (or to play it for laughs—as in the 1987–88 Royal Shakespeare Company production) may be to blur a climactic image that brings into focus various motifs in the play linked to appetites, feeding, and revenge. Thus, the Folio stage direction for 3.2 indicates *"a banquet"* (TLN 1451), but Titus opens that scene with the order: "So, so, now sit; and look you eat no more / Than will preserve just so much strength in us / As will revenge these bitter woes of ours" (1-3). By the end of the play, however, revenge has become linked not to abstinence but to feeding and appetite, usually in dangerous or self-destructive terms. For example, in her overconfident claims to Saturninus, Tamora promises to "enchant the old Andronicus / With words more sweet, and yet more dangerous, / Than baits to fish or honeystalks to sheep"; the fish, she notes, "is wounded with the bait," and the sheep "rotted with delicious feed" (4.4.88-92). The most potent orchestration of "appetite" or feeding is found in Titus' long speech at the end of 5.2 where the revenger first torments the muted Chiron and Demetrius with a detailed account of what he is going to do to or with them (e.g., "I will grind your bones to dust, / And with your blood and it I'll make a paste"), then promises to "make two pasties of your shameful heads," and finally announces that he will "bid that strumpet, your unhallowed dam, / Like to the earth, swallow her own increase" (186-91). After his command that Lavinia "receive the blood" and a second reference to paste and heads, Titus *"cuts their throats"* and announces "I'll play the cook" so as "to make this banquet, which I wish may prove / More stern and bloody than the Centaurs' feast."

When Titus enters to set up the banquet in 5.3 (with or without a cook's costume), the spectator is therefore well prepared. The savage ironies in his lines, moreover, are anything but subtle: starting with "although the cheer be poor, / 'Twill fill your stomachs; please you eat of it" (5.3.28-9); building to "Will't please you eat? will't please your highness feed?" (54); and climaxing, in response to the emperor's command to fetch Chiron and Demetrius: "Why, there they are, both baked in this pie, / Whereof their mother daintily hath fed, / Eating the flesh that she herself hath bred" (60-2). Indeed, these lines and the overall effect have seemed excessive to many directors and readers.

But what would have been the effect if Titus *does* appear *"like a cook"* (as predicted in the closing lines of 5.2) and, in this odd costume, does call emphatic attention to his culinary role as he hovers around the banqueters? In imagistic terms, what has so far been primarily verbal or aural (animals "rotted with delicious feed") now is being displayed visually, not only in the pasties being consumed by Tamora and others but also in the purveyor of such delicacies, Titus, who sets up the feeding of (and himself feeds upon) his enemies so as to become a visible part of the appetitive revenge process (just as Tamora had "become" Revenge in 5.2). The image of the revenger as cook builds upon what has gone before and, especially as italicized here by both the costume and Saturninus' question, brings to a climax the feed-and-be-fed-upon imagery earlier linked to the hunt and to the "wilderness of tigers" (3.1.54), a wilderness in which *both* families have now become prey. The same man who in 3.2 had urged his family to refrain from eating now sets up the meal for others and feeds upon his revenge. Moreover, if Aaron or Tamora's body is placed in the trap door, this cook-revenger has generated a feast that parallels and supersedes the "detested, dark, blood-drinking pit" and "fell devouring receptacle" (2.3.224, 235) that had claimed Bassianus, Quintus, and Martius. In short, at the climax of this revenge process, *"Titus like a cook"* makes very good sense indeed.

Much of the effect of such italicized moments (whether the *exeunt* with heads and hand, Tamora as Revenge, or Titus as cook) lies in their surprise value or initial illogic, a surprise that is designed to call attention to that moment and, ideally, to tease the playgoer into thought, into making connections. That effect, however, can be undermined, even eliminated entirely, if a subsequent interpreter on the stage or on the page resists such images or such logic of illogic, so that a provocative signpost (at least for the 1590s) is then lost. In such cases, to de-italicize is to diminish the range of possibilities, to weaken the signals, so as to preserve a post-1590s sense of decorum or verisimilitude, principles Shakespeare was aware of but was willing to strain, even violate, to gain his effects.

As a comparable example from another early Shakespeare play consider *I Henry VI* where, at the nadir of her fortunes just before her capture by York, Joan la Pucelle appeals for help to a group of onstage *"Fiends"* (5.3.7.s.d.), but in response these fiends, according to the Folio stage directions, *"walk, and speak not," "hang their heads," "shake their heads,"* and finally *"depart"* (s.d.s at 12, 17, 19, 23). This exchange has not fared well on the page or on the stage, for to deal with this script is inevitably to run afoul of this scene and this appeal-rejection that in several ways tests the notions of today's interpreters. The Folio's call for fiends and for specific reactions is unusually clear (and presumably would have posed few problems in the 1590s for playgoers attuned to *Doctor Faustus*), but Elizabethan onstage presentation of the supernatural repeatedly strains "our" paradigms of credibility (and canons of taste), with this moment (along with the apparitions in the cauldron scene of *Macbeth*) a particular challenge.

Directors have therefore tinkered with the Folio signals. In Jane Howell's rendition for television, Joan speaks her lines while staring at the camera so that no supernatural entities are in sight to walk, refuse to speak, hang their heads, and eventually depart. In Adrian Noble's ninety-minute Royal Shakespeare Company rendition of Part 1 (1987-88), various onstage corpses from the previous battle rose as if animated to provide an onstage audience, but without the reactions to Joan's pleas specified in the Folio. In the Terry Hands 1977-78 Royal Shakespeare Company production, amid the onstage cannons that dominated the battlefield set Joan offered herself to the fiends who appeared suddenly "looking like gas-masked soldiers from the French trenches of the First World War."[9] In contrast, in his ninety-minute English Shakespeare Company production Michael Bogdanov cut the fiends and altered the text, so that, alone on stage and looking at the audience, Joan directed her appeal not to any diabolic entities but rather to the Virgin Mary, a change that eliminated any infernal climax for this sequence.

For generations idealizers of Shakespeare, who have been embarrassed by this play and especially offended by the chauvinistic depiction of St. Joan, have had great difficulty coming to grips with this moment.[10] Such reactions are revealing, for even to a casual reader the interaction between Joan and the fiends leaps off the page in vivid (and to many, offensive) fashion. What then are the advantages of singling out this moment as theatrical *italics?*

As one possible answer, consider Joan and her devils not as a one-shot effect but as the climactic example of a larger progression of images and moments that starts in Act 2. From her first appearance Joan has claimed supernatural powers (see 1.2.72-92), a claim tested in the first meeting between Joan and Talbot that results in a stand-off; still, Joan scorns his strength (1.5.15) and leads her troops to victory at Orleans. Moments later, Talbot, aided by Bedford and Burgundy, scales the walls and regains the town, so that a united English force wins back what had just been lost. The three leaders working together therefore accomplish what Talbot, facing Joan alone, could not. Shakespeare then provides a gloss on both this victory and the larger problem of unity-disunity by means of Talbot's interview with the Countess of Auvergne. Her trap for Talbot fails, as he points out, because she has only caught "Talbot's shadow," not his substance. The set of terms is repeated throughout the remainder of the scene (e.g., "No, no, I am but shadow of myself. / You are deceived, my substance is not here") and is explained by the appearance of his soldiers, at which point he points out: "Are you now persuaded / That Talbot is but a shadow of himself? / These are his substance, sinews, arms, and strength, / With which he yoketh your rebellious necks . . . " (2.3.46-66). The individual standing alone, no matter how heroic (one thinks of Coriolanus), is but a shadow without the substance of his supporters, his army, his country.[11]

This play, however (as two generations of critics have reminded us), is about division, not unity, a division that has already been displayed in the split between Winchester and Gloucester and widens in the Temple Garden scene (that immediately follows Talbot's lecture to the countess), with its symbolic plucking of red and white roses. The figures who had joined Talbot in the victory at Orleans, moreover, soon disappear (Bedford dies, Burgundy changes sides). Factionalism thrives, to the extent that the division between York and Somerset (unhistorically) undoes Talbot himself who, in the terms of 2.3, is denied his substance and must face death (along with his son) as a shadow of his heroic self. Sir William Lucy's listing of Talbot's titles (4.7.60-71) can then be mocked by Joan as "a silly stately style indeed," for "Him that thou magnifi'st with these titles, / Stinking and flyblown lies here at our feet" (72, 75-6).

Joan's scene with her devils then follows less than a hundred lines after her exchange with Lucy. With the French forces fleeing the conquering York, all Joan can do is call upon her "speedy helpers" or "familiar spirits" to help with their "accustomed diligence," but neither the offer of her blood, with which she has fed them in the past, a member lopped off, her body, or even her soul will gain the needed support. She therefore concludes: "My ancient incantations are too weak, / And hell too strong for me to buckle with. / Now, France, thy glory droopeth to the dust" (5.3.1-29).

No one makes grandiose claims for the imagery of this sprawling play. But a verbal patterning involving shadow and substance is clearly set forth in Act 2 (and echoed thereafter—as in Alencon's speech 5.4.133-7); moreover, Talbot eventually falls (and France ultimately is lost to England) because of divisions whereby "substance" is denied and the hero must stand alone as shadow of himself. In her scene with the fiends, Joan too is deserted, denied by those who formerly supported her. Like Talbot, her heroic status cannot exist alone, so she becomes a mere shepherd's daughter, not the figure who raised the siege at Orleans and was a match for Talbot in battle. The denial by the fiends is here equivalent to the squabble between York and Somerset that undoes Talbot, a link that (as with Francis the drawer and Hotspur or Falstaff) can be reinforced through the staging. For example, what if the fiends' scripted reactions to Joan's offer echo similar walking apart, hanging and shaking of heads, and departures by York and Somerset in 4.3-4.4 in response to Lucy's pleas in behalf of Talbot? If so, the playgoer would see two or three parallel failures by first Lucy and then Joan, rejections that visibly set up the deaths of the two previously unbeatable or "heroic" figures. Just as Lucy fails to get the necessary support, a failure that means Talbot must give way to the new factions, so Joan fails to get the support she too desperately needs and must give way to the third Frenchwoman, Margaret (who appears immediately upon Joan's exit with York). However interpreted in theological or political terms, these highly visible fiends can function as part of an ongoing pattern of images or configurations linked to the central themes of the play.

These italicized moments from two early Shakespeare plays (scripts not prized for their complexity or artistry) call attention to themselves and in the process call attention to major thematic or imagistic strands. All four therefore function not as ends in themselves but as indices to a larger network, a network whose presence is heightened by the theatrical italicizing of these images. Such a technique, needless to say, need not be limited to plays from the outset of Shakespeare's career. For some provocative examples, let me now turn to several juxtapositions.

Consider first the question (that turns out to be much trickier than it sounds): when should Macbeth appear on the stage after the murder of Duncan (that occurs between 2.1 and 2.2)? The Pelican editor, like most modern editors, places Macbeth's first line in the scene ("Who's there? What, ho?"–2.2.8) "[*within*]" and then places the stage direction "*Enter Macbeth*" so as to break line 13, the end of Lady Macbeth's second speech (so after " . . . I had done't" and before "My husband!"). The Folio, however, provides a centered "*Enter Macbeth*" at line 8 (TLN 657) after Lady Macbeth's initial speech and before Macbeth's first line in the scene ("Who's there? what hoa?").

Although I have not done an exhaustive search, I have yet to find a modern edition that follows the Folio here. As with the placing of Cassandra *within* in the Trojan council scene (or the repositioning of Gloucester's entrance in 3.6 of the Folio *Lear*), note the logic of verisimilitude at work. How are we to imagine a Macbeth onstage but not noticed by his wife for five lines? In the frenzied dialogue that follows, moreover, she asks "Did you not speak?" and he queries in response "As I descended?" so that Macbeth's earlier half-line ("Who's there? . . . ") can, by this logic, be envisaged as part of an offstage sequence (or onstage in a production with a visible staircase) before his actual entrance signaled by "My husband!" (in the Folio, "My Husband?"). In modern productions, the playgoer often sees Lady Macbeth below and Macbeth above, backing out of Duncan's chamber, then either descending in our sight or reappearing below at the point marked in modern editions when she first sees him. Such an emendation or adjustment seems to fit with the dialogue ("As I descended?") and avoid any awkwardness with Lady Macbeth not seeing her husband for five lines. The Folio, in this instance, is deemed wrong—in a matter of relatively minor consequence.

But . . . the theatrical vocabulary of the 1590s and early 1600s may have included signifiers linked to onstage figures limited in their ability to "see" important things around them. One possible way to signal or heighten such "not-seeing" (as with Claudio-Don Pedro and Dogberry, Gadshill and the chamberlain, the Trojan council and Cassandra, or Macbeth and the ghost) is to use an early stage direction so as to have entering figures onstage (and seen by the playgoer) before those already onstage are aware of their presence. To change the placement of Macbeth's entrance in 2.2 is to produce a much tidier scene, but what about the potential losses? What happens when we stage or imagine the scene as scripted in the Folio?

In practical theatrical terms, the Folio scene can be staged with the two figures facing in opposite directions and therefore backing into each other so as to produce a jolt that fits well with the tensions of the moment. But in terms of my emphasis upon "not-seeing," consider as well the related problem (rarely cited by editors and never, to my knowledge, linked to the early entrance): why does it take so long for Lady Macbeth to notice the bloody daggers (not until line 47), even though Macbeth says "This is a sorry sight" as early as line 20, presumably referring to his bloody hands holding the daggers, and also refers to "these hangman's hands" in line 27? Admittedly, the daggers can be covered (as in the 1988-89 Royal Shakespeare Company production) or somehow hidden—again to satisfy the logic of verisimilitude—but if the daggers were visible to the playgoer but, for some time, were not seen by Lady Macbeth that playgoer witnessed not one but two striking examples of "not-seeing" in the Folio version of this scene. Remember, in a famous speech at the end of the previous scene, Macbeth had seen and described a dagger that was not there: "There's no such thing. / It is the bloody business which informs / Thus to mine eyes" (2.1.47-9). In contrast, for a stretch of time in 2.2, Lady Macbeth does *not* see two bloody daggers that *are* there.

As already noted, an editor or a director can readily "solve" this problem, but what then is the price tag for such a "solution"? If twice in this short sequence Lady Macbeth does not see something that *is* there to be seen by the playgoer (first Macbeth, then the daggers), especially after the dagger speech of 2.1, what kind of "image" or effect is being set up or italicized? Given such a staging of the Folio signals, is not an audience better prepared for the sleep-walking (and her seeing or imagining there) or for the banquet scene when no one but Macbeth sees the ghost? Even here, playgoers may emerge from the Folio version with a different understanding of her "A little water clears us of this deed. / How easy is it then!" if, *twice,* she has *not* seen something they *have* seen. The scene and the tragedy as a whole are about darkness and blindness in various senses, so what happens if the editor, critic, or director trusts the Folio version that, in a curious but potentially telling fashion, italicizes (in symbolic or metaphoric terms) just such darkness and blindness? To filter out this effect is to produce a much tidier scene, especially in terms of verisimilitude, but, in doing so, an interpreter risks translating a rich moment into our (less metaphorical, less symbolic) theatrical language and losing something significant in the process.

An equally provocative juxtaposition is to be found in *As You Like It* where editors and critics continue to puzzle over Duke Senior's "banquet" that, according to the dialogue, is set up on stage in 2.5 (see lines 26-7, 55-6) and then enjoyed in 2.7 with no indication that it is removed for the brief 2.6 (the first appearance of Orlando and Adam in Arden). After reviewing various options (e.g., use of an "inner stage," transposition of scenes) the New Variorum editor (Richard Knowles) concludes: "the early setting of the table seems to me thoroughly puzzling; it is totally unnecessary, for the banquet could have been carried on, as banquets usually were, at the beginning of scene 7." Directors have therefore developed their own strategies for dealing with this anomaly: some transpose 2.5 and 2.6; some cut the offending lines in 2.5 so that the banquet first appears in 2.7; some play the Folio lines and sequence but darken the stage so that neither Orlando or the playgoer can "see" the banquet during 2.6.

As most editors and critics would agree, Shakespeare

did not *have* to introduce a banquet into 2.5. Yet he *did.* The result, moreover, is a clear example of the kind of simultaneous staging often found in earlier English drama that yields for the playgoer a strong sense of overlapping images comparable to that produced by early entrances, by late departures, and by bodies, scrolls, or leavy screens not removed from the stage.[12] What then are the advantages of having such a banquet in full view during the speeches that constitute 2.6?

As one possible answer, consider how the presence of such food affects our reaction to Adam's "O, I die for food" and Orlando's subsequent "if" clauses: "If this uncouth forest yield anything savage, I will either be food for it or bring it for food to thee . . . I will here be with thee presently, and if I bring thee not something to eat, I will give thee leave to die; but if thou diest before I come, thou art a mocker of my labor . . . thou shalt not die for lack of a dinner if there live anything in this desert." What is the effect of such speeches if the food Orlando eventually finds in 2.7 is indeed visible to us while we are hearing these words? What seems anomalous or unrealistic to a reader nurtured upon our theatrical idiom could, in their vocabulary, be one of the striking moments or images in the show (as perhaps with Francis's amazed state, the *exeunt* of the Andronici, Joan and the fiends, or Macbeth's early appearance) if the playgoer somehow gains from the juxtaposition an understanding of the distinctive nature of Arden . . . . To what extent has our sense of "forest" or our resistance to simultaneous staging eclipsed a major signifier in Shakespeare's theatrical vocabulary?

Here, moreover, is where a modern sense of variable lighting and "design" becomes especially important. If interpreters can transcend their theatrical reflexes, they may be able to imagine a Forest of Arden in this instance defined not by onstage greenery but by the presence of food in the background while two figures are starving. Through such juxtapositional staging or signifying, that sense of an option available to be exercised or a potential there (under the right circumstances) to be fulfilled could emerge as the point of the sequence and a major building block for the final three acts. A director in a modern theatre who does introduce the banquet in 2.5 and does not remove it during 2.6 may still be tempted to darken part of the stage and highlight Orlando and Adam, but in a 1590s theatre where that option was *not* available (and where controlling the playgoer's sense of events by means of variable lighting was impossible), the rationale behind this moment and its potential richness—in their terms—could (perhaps) be realized.

The same is true in *King Lear* where, at the end of 2.2, Kent is left alone in the stocks, Edgar enters for a speech of twenty-one lines, and, after his departure, Lear and his group arrive to find Kent. As with my other examples, this sequence has puzzled modern critics, editors, and directors who worry about "where" Edgar is to be "placed." In our vocabulary, the presence of the stocks and the recently completed action involving Oswald, Edmund, Cornwall, and others imply one locale (the courtyard of a castle), but that "place" proves incompatible with a fleeing Edgar (especially given a lapse of time and the pursuit through open country implied in an escape by means of "the happy hollow of a tree"—2.3.2). Editors therefore create a separate scene for Edgar's speech (2.3) and often provide a heading such as "the open country" or "a wood"; directors usually use a lighting change to black out Kent and highlight Edgar during his speech. Clearly, most interpreters would prefer not to have Kent and Edgar visible at the same time.

If Kent is eclipsed by modern lighting, neither Edgar nor the playgoer is conscious of the figure in the stocks (who also has lost his identity and been subjected to injustice). But what about the original production at the Globe where the King's Men had no way to black out Kent? Can the interpreter today at least entertain the possibility that Shakespeare, surveying the various options, *chose* to have these two figures visible simultaneously, not only making no effort to hide the juxtaposition but indeed encouraging a staging that would *italicize* it? On the unencumbered Globe stage with few distractions for the playgoer's eye, such a choice would yield a highly emphatic effect that would strongly enforce any interpretation based upon links between Kent and Edgar—again a form of theatrical *italics* that an attentive viewer would find hard to miss. The original audience would not have been troubled by the imaginary darkness in which Edgar failed to see Kent; indeed, Edgar's stage behavior in itself could have been a major signal for the existence of onstage night. The stocks would then signal not a courtyard or other specific public locale but rather a general sense of imprisonment or bondage (as in such moral plays as *The Interlude of Youth* and *Hickscorner*) or the perversion of an instrument of justice (as developed more fully, again with Cornwall and Regan, when Gloucester is bound to a chair in 3.7), just as Edgar would be assumed to be in flight, anywhere. The chameleon-like flexibility of the open stage here makes possible a juxtaposition rich with potential meanings, a juxtaposition that can easily be blurred or lost (as with *Macbeth,* 2.2 and *As You Like It,* 2.6) when an interpreter translates the scene into our theatrical vocabulary.

Such italicized juxtapositions and configurations that generate fruitful questions for the playgoer recur throughout the Shakespeare canon.[13] In keeping with Armstrong's yardsticks, my purpose in singling out such moments and patterns is to isolate various hit-the-playgoer-over-the-head stage effects that would have been difficult to miss in the original productions but can readily be blurred or lost today. Such a gulf between what was obvious then but can be invisible now raises some troubling questions. What if, as part of an overall strategy, Shakespeare and his fellow players chose to *italicize* X but editors, directors, or critics today ignore or filter out that choice? What is the effect of such filtering upon our interpretations? Given the language barrier that separates us from the 1590s and early 1600s, how are we to recognize when their emphases or theatrical vocabulary diverge significantly from ours (so that a drum-roll or look-at-me effect can be ignored or eclipsed)? Most troubling to me (as one sympathetic to various brands of historicism): are we inferring or creating our "meanings" from the same evidence that was available to the original playgoers? Again, how much is being lost in translation?

Notes

[1] Paul Armstrong, *Conflicting Readings: Variety and Validity in Interpretation* (Chapel Hill: University of North Carolina Press, 1990), pp. ix, 13-16.

[2] In his recent book, Robert Hapgood also raises this issue in the context of a performance-oriented approach to Shakespeare. Citing Stephen Booth's rejection of "either/or" interpretive choices in reading the sonnets, Hapgood suggests that "at an extreme, critical tolerance can mask a failure of nerve, an unwillingness to say: 'this is more likely than that', 'this is given greater emphasis than that', 'this is more central or better balanced than that'." Rather, for him even though Shakespeare's texts "do not provide hard and fast directions for their own interpretation," nonetheless they "do permit such discriminations," for "they do provide guidelines, do set limits to the latitudes they allow." Hapgood concludes that, "although no single reading is definitive, some are downright wrong and among the rest some are in certain respects to be preferred to others." See *Shakespeare the Theatre-Poet* (Oxford University Press, 1988), p. 13.

[3] For example, see S. P. Zitner, "Anon, Anon: or, a Mirror for a Magistrate," *Shakespeare Quarterly* 19 (1968): 63-70. In his *Shakespearean Negotiations* (Berkeley and Los Angeles: University of California Press, 1988, p. 43), Stephen Greenblatt treats the moment as one of "the play's acts of *recording,* that is, the moments in which we hear voices that seem to dwell outside the realms ruled by the potentates of the land."

[4] So Greenblatt (p. 45) concludes his section: "The prince must sound the base-string of humility if he is to play all of the chords and hence be the master of the instrument, and his ability to conceal his motives and render opaque his language offers assurance that he himself will not be played on by another." For my own reading see *Shakespeare and the Late Moral Plays* (Lincoln: University of Nebraska Press, 1986), pp. 69-70.

[5] The Wells-Taylor old-spelling version reads: "And *Lauinia* thou shalt be imployde, / Beare thou my hand sweet wench betweene thine Armes" (*The Complete Works: Original Spelling Edition* [Oxford: Clarendon Press, 1986], lines 1296-7). In their textual note Wells and Taylor build upon an earlier editor's conjecture that someone made the correction "to soften what must have been ludicrous in representation," a correction that in turn led to an error in QI; according to this reconstruction, a scribe then "made sense of the passage by substituting 'things' for 'Armes'" (*William Shakespeare: A Textual Companion* [Oxford: Clarendon Press, 1987], p. 212). "To soften" a "ludicrous" moment, a series of editors have therefore closed down a meaningful option present in the quartos and the Folio. One of these emended editions, moreover (volume 34 in the New Temple Shakespeare, ed. M. R. Ridley [London and New York, 1934]), served as the basis for two landmark productions of this script (Peter Brook's in Stratford-upon-Avon 1955, Gerald Freedman's for the New York Shakespeare Festival in 1967), so that both of these directors could sidestep the problem completely.

[6] For my own treatment of parts of the body in this tragedy, see *Titus Andronicus* (Manchester University Press, 1989), pp. 86-9.

[7] For example, in a dramatic romance published at about the same time as *Titus* (*A Knack to Know an Honest Man*) a banished figure in disguise as a hermit announces his name to be Penitential Experience. In the early 1590s such mixing of allegorical nomenclature and "literal" action, if not widespread, was at least possible. See also the allegorical dumb shows used to make explicit the forces at work behind a contemporary murder in *A Warning for Fair Women* (printed 1599).

[8] Most editors gloss "her" in line 45 as "Justice," but equally likely is a confusion between Justice-heaven and Revenge-Acheron-hell, a confusion that feeds into Tamora's appearance in disguise with her request for Titus to "come down." The link, moreover, can be enforced in the theatre. For example, in the 1988 Shakespeare Santa Cruz production Tamora-Revenge entered bearing an arrow with the message still attached, thereby suggesting that her appearance was in response to his quest in 4.3.

[9] David Daniell, "Opening up the text: Shakespeare's *Henry VI* plays in performance," *Themes in Drama* 1 (1979): 257.

[10] For some recent revisionist interpretations of Joan, however, see Leah Marcus, *Puzzling Shakespeare* (Ber-

keley and Los Angeles: University of California Press, 1988), pp. 51-96; Gabriele Bernhard Jackson, "Topical Ideology: Witches, Amazons, and Shakespeare's Joan of Arc," *English Literary Renaissance* 18 (1988): 40-65; and Nancy A. Gutierrez, "Gender and Value in *1 Henry VI*: The Role of Joan de Pucelle," *Theatre Journal* 42 (1990): 183-93.

[11] For treatments of 2.3, see especially Edward I. Berry, *Patterns of Decay: Shakespeare's Early Histories* (Charlottesville: University Press of Virginia, 1975), pp. 1-28; James A. Riddell, "Talbot and the Countess of Auvergne," *Shakespeare Quarterly* 28 (1977): 51-7; and Alexander Leggatt, *Shakespeare's Political Drama* (London and New York: Routledge, 1988), pp. 1-8.

[12] For the reader skeptical about the juxtaposition of onstage food with starving figures I can offer two comparable examples from plays that antedate *As You Like It* in the 1590s. First, in *Locrine,* with a starving Humber onstage, Strumbo the clown enters saying "it is now breakfast time, you shall see what meat I have here for my breakfast" (1626-8); the stage direction reads: *"Let him sit down and pull out his vittles"* (1629-30). Humber (like Orlando) then has a speech on the fruitless land but does not see the clown or his food; rather, *"Strumbo hearing his voice shall start up and put meat in his pocket, seeking to hide himself"* (1648-9). Eventually, a Humber near death sees Strumbo, asks for meat, and threatens the clown: *"Let him make as though he would give him some, and as he putteth out his hand, enter the ghost of Albanact, and strike him on the hand, and so Strumbo runs out, Humber following him"* (1669-73). Similarly, in *King Leir "Enter the Gallian King and Queen, and Mumford, with a basket, disguised like Country folk"* (2091-2); then *"Enter Leir and Perillus very faintly"* (2109-11) to talk of starving (Perillus goes so far as to offer his own blood to his master, Leir—2128-9). After a long sequence, Perillus calls on God for help (2166-7) and at last sees the food ("Oh comfort, comfort! yonder is a banquet"—2168). Both Humber and Perillus (unlike Adam and Orlando during their brief scene) eventually do see the onstage food, but not until after they have spoken at length about their plight.

[13] Such thought-provoking italicized moments are common in the romances, most notably in *Cymbeline,* 4.2 where Fidele-Imogen awakens next to the headless Cloten whom she mistakes for Posthumus.

Source: "Theatrical *Italics,*" in *Recovering Shakespeare's Theatrical Vocabulary,* pp. 88-108. Cambridge University Press, 1995, pp. 88-108.

Nashe as "Monarch of Witt" and Shakespeare's *Romeo and Juliet*

Joan Ozark Holmer, *Georgetown University*

The general influence of Nashe on Elizabethan literature has long been recognized, but the specific influence of Nashe on Shakespeare's work still remains largely underestimated. This essay will attempt two related tasks: first, the analysis of new evidence for dating Shakespeare's composition of his first romantic tragedy, which helps us to establish Nashe's priority of influence; and second, the exploration of how and why Shakespeare uses Nashe and his work as he does. The latter also reveals new insights about Shakespeare's adaptation of sources as an imaginative act, not merely of reminiscence, but reminiscence with a difference.

1

Some known but misinterpreted facts as well as some overlooked evidence helps to establish the date of composition of *Romeo and Juliet* in the latter half of 1596, a later date than has been traditionally entertained.[1] The evidence now in question revolves around significant verbal parallels, especially the oft-noted important "parallel" between Nashe's lines in *Have with You to Saffron-Walden* (1596)—"not *Tibault* or *Isegrim,* Prince of Cattes, were euer endowed with the like Title" (3.51)[2]—and Shakespeare's description of Tybalt as "more than Prince of Cats" (2.4.17-18). In recorded medieval-Renaissance literature, the name of "Tibault/Tybalt" as a name having feline associations seems to appear *only* in Nashe's and Shakespeare's passages, spelled as "Tibault" in Nashe and as both "Tibalt" and "Tybalt" in the second quarto and first folio texts of Shakespeare's play. Moreover, the precise title, "Prince of Cattes," used in the same passage with the specific name "Tibault/Tybalt" has been found *only* in Nashe's and Shakespeare's passages from works of theirs that are very closely related in time. As G. Blakemore Evans (105) observes, if we can reasonably determine who might be the first to use this unusual language, that would contribute significantly to solving the questions at hand. There is nothing like this "parallel" in the acknowledged literary source for *Romeo and Juliet,* namely Arthur Brooke's *The Tragicall Historye of Romeus and Juliet* (1562). Nor does Brooke present any witty satire like that of Nashe, involving other significant verbal parallels, such as "fiddlestick" (3.1.42). Moreover, Nashe himself and his *Have with You* provide telling hints for understanding how Shakespeare developed Mercutio, one of his most memorable characters, from the minimal reference he found in Brooke.

Have with You to Saffron-Walden is Nashe's long-awaited reply to Gabriel Harvey's attack on him in *Pierce's Supererogation* (1593), and as G. R. Hibbard explains, Nashe's reply is well worth the wait:

> Nashe took his time in order to make something really worth while of his answer, for in its own curious way *Have with You* is a most accomplished piece of writing, a rich mixture of parody, literary criticism, comic biography and outrageous abuse that nevertheless hangs together by virtue of the art that is lavished on it and of the sheer joy in caricature and in linguistic extravagance and inventiveness that informs it from beginning to end.[3]

The quarrel with Harvey was one of the most important events in Nashe's life, and the intensity of that quarrel ultimately prompted the authorities to intervene and recall the works of both Nashe and Harvey. Harvey appears to be the first to use feline allusions, negatively for Nashe but positively for himself, and Nashe quotes Harvey to set him up for his own ridicule: *"But some had rather be a Pol-cat with a stinking stirre, than a Muske-cat with gracious fauour."*[4] In Nashe's satiric dialogue, Harvey is answered through a mockery of his pretentiousness: "I, but not onely no ordinarie Cat, but a Muske-cat, and not onely a Muske-cat, but a *Muske-cat with gracious fauour* (which sounds like a Princes stile *Dei gratia*): not *Tibault* or *Isegrim,* Prince of Cattes, were euer endowed with the like Title."

To begin resolving the question of influence, we must first accurately interpret to whom Nashe's "Prince of Cattes" refers. The traditional reading of the princely title as modifying "Tibault" satisfies logic because in Nashe's "catty" context "Tibault" seems intended to be the name of a cat.[5] Nashe probably has the Reynardian beast epic in mind when he refers to the famous cat properly named "Tibert," despite Nashe's apparently unique use of the name "Tibault."[6] Nashe's recollection of the precise name may be faulty due to witty haste.[7] However, Nashe's own syntax suggests the title is not intended to modify "Tibault" because of its placement; his plural subject ("Tibault or Isegrim") takes the plural verb ("were endowed") so that the singular form for "Prince" appears to be quite intentional on Nashe's part. Nashe's title, however, could syntactically and logically modify "Isegrim" if Isegrim is the name of a cat. One of the main cat characters in William Baldwin's *Beware the Cat* (1570) surprisingly is named Isegrim, surprising because that name is otherwise reserved for the *wolf* in the Reynardian beast epic and because the paucity of references to Isegrim in English literature is striking[8] Therefore, Nashe's "Isegrim" is not a reference to the Reynardian beast epic, as Ronald B. McKerrow glosses it (4:327), but an allusion to Baldwin's cat named "Isegrim." The language for the specific title, "prince of cats," also appears in Baldwin's marginalia; hence, Baldwin's fictitious prose satire proves an overlooked source for Nashe's language.[9]

I suggest Nashe's use of the title "Prince of Cattes" is probably an example of the vocative, not the appositive for either "Tibault" or "Isegrim." The point of his joke on Harvey is that neither of these cats ever was endowed with a princely title that Harvey, the self-styled musk cat assuming princely airs, would arrogantly appropriate to himself. This reading satisfies syntax and logic and reveals Nashe's accurate knowledge of Baldwin's use of this title. Thus, in his parody of Harvey's "flaunting phrases" (3:42), Nashe satirizes Harvey through direct address, giving him a bitter taste of his own medicine through such a mock-heroic title because Harvey had earlier called Nashe's friend, Robert Greene, "the Prince of beggars" (1:170), rallying Nashe to Greene's defense (1:299). There is internal evidence from Nashe's *Have with You to Saffron-Walden* to support an argument for the vocative. Nashe uses the vocative several times, for example, "*goe and prate in the yard,* Don Pedant, *there is no place for you here*" (3:76; cf. 3:49, 118). Nashe's use of the vocative appears in the midst of the sentence, set off by commas or parentheses, as is the title "Prince of Cattes." Nashe also has a stylistic habit of entitling Harvey's metaphors to ridicule them through direct address, the very habit displayed in calling Harvey the "Prince of Cattes."[10]

Shakespeare's use of the princely title in connection with the name of "Tybalt" also captures the spirit of Nashe's vocative usage because Tybalt is directly addressed as "Good King of Cats" (3.1.70). Other aspects of Nashe's passage on Tibault suggest Shakespeare is inventively responding to an *outside* influence. The subject of cats is a given in Nashe's passage as it is not in Shakespeare's. Because Shakespeare inherits "Tybalt" as a proper name for a man as well as a name signifying manliness, what would ever prompt Shakespeare to associate that manly name with cats?[11] The "foreign" nature of Shakespeare's introduction of the "Prince of Cats" title needs to be underscored. This feline satire is a staged "set up" to allow a *jeu d'esprit* for the wittily loquacious Mercutio of Shakespeare's creation. Consider also the "forced" introduction to this passage. It is Benvolio, playing "straight man" as it were to Mercutio, who sets up the fun for Mercutio. Benvolio asks, "What's he [Tybalt]?" (2.4.17) *as if* he does not know Tybalt. Yet this is the same Benvolio who was forced to fight Tybalt in the play's opening scene and who has enough first-hand knowledge of Tybalt's fencing style to satirize it to Lord Montague (1.1.99-104). Shakespeare also responds to the braggadocio spirit of Nashe's satiric one-upmanship. Shakespeare does not merely have Tybalt equated with the Prince of Cats, although later he will call him "King of Cats" and "rat-catcher." Mercutio's response to Benvolio's question is that Tybalt is "*more than* Prince of Cats" (my italics) which is a claim not unlike Nashe's depiction of Harvey as a musk cat pretending to be more than he is by cultivating princely airs. Moreover, the playfully satiric use of the word "prince" in titles is much more characteristic of Nashe than of Shakespeare.[12]

Thus, the merits of the difficult debate over influence regarding the literary use of "Prince of Cattes" as a satiric epithet for an opponent weigh more heavily in favor of Nashe's passage. If Nashe had borrowed from Shakespeare, how can we account for Nashe's knowledgeable use of Baldwin's satire in his borrowing of a name ("Isegrim") and a title ("Prince of Cattes")? On the other hand, Shakespeare's canon reveals no specific knowledge of Baldwin's text.[13] It would seem likely that Shakespeare would borrow and adapt from Nashe what is useful for his own purposes. Shakespeare's conflation of "Tybalt" as "more than Prince of Cats" suggests derivation from Nashe's original rebuttal of the feline satire Harvey initiated against him. The use of animal names and misplaced titles to emphasize false pride informs the entire quarrel between Nashe and Harvey.

What is of particular interest for *Romeo and Juliet* is Nashe's penchant for imagery of the duel and fencing for depicting his quarrel in ink with Harvey, and Nashe's references are of two kinds, literal and figurative. Nashe evidently first accused Harvey of being an "old Fencer" (2:232), at least according to Harvey.[14] Nashe later criticized Harvey for his empty boasting about being a good fencer who will defeat Nashe's sword as well as his pen: "And where he terrifies mee with insulting *hee was* Tom Burwels, the Fencers Scholler. . . . not all the fence he learnd of *Tom Burwell* shall keepe mee from cramming a turd in his jawes" (3:134). Nashe also satirizes the idea that Harvey has an unidentified gentlewoman whom Harvey claims has taken his side in the quarrel against Nashe and who will write against Nashe: "*Tamburlain*-like, hee braues it indesinently in her behalfe, setting vp bills, like a Bear-ward or Fencer, what fights we shall haue and what weapons she will meete me at" (3:121). Finally, the opening of *Have with You* keynotes the imagery we have discussed. Tobin has already noted the passage in which Nashe claims that Harvey and he "*take upon us to bandie factions, and contend like the* Vrsini *and* Coloni *in* Roome" (3:19), observing Shakespeare's echo of *"bandie"* in Romeo's use of "bandying" (3.1.81).[15] But Nashe develops the fight imagery much more specifically and figuratively when he says his satiric dialogue involves real friends bearing pseudonyms, and their "honest conference" can supposed to be held *"after the same manner that one of these* Italionate *conferences about a* Duell *is wont solemnly to be handled, which is when a man, being specially toucht in reputation . . . calls all his frends together, and askes their aduice how he should carrie himselfe in the action*" (3:21). The satirist's metaphoric presentation of a quarrel appeals as well to Shakespeare in his creation of Mercutio's personal satire in his quarrel against Tybalt.

The ingenuity of Shakespeare's use of the feline satire found in Nashe has not been justly appreciated. The title, "Prince of Cats," captures Shakespeare's fancy, and he surpasses Nashe in his brilliant adaptation of the satiric feline title to suit Mercutio's and Tybalt's interest in fencing, a specific focus that is absent from Nashe's "Tibault" passage. Although Nashe uses several different metaphors for a quarrel, such as a cockfight, a catfight, and a pen fight (3:30, 51, 133), he keeps them separate. Shakespeare, however, adroitly *fuses* the two metaphors of the catfight and the sword fight through the means of fighting, namely scratching. The rapier is like the cat's claw because it can literally scratch a man to death, as Mercutio gravely laments (3.1.92). Nashe uses "scratching" to signify "fighting," but he does not take Shakespeare's next step and compare the cat's weapon with man's weapon, claw with rapier.[16]

Hence, Mercutio's feline satire becomes exquisitely appropriate for the punctilious fencer Tybalt. Shakespeare seems ripe to develop such punning because in *The Rape of Lucrece* (1594) his readiness for this imagery is revealed in two passages. The first is typical in that the fighting is portrayed as the scratching normally associated with the human hand or nails. But his next example extends this scratching to a weapon held in the hand—a knife.[17] In our play, Shakespeare develops this weapon imagery further to include the rapier, and one of his tragic points about man's innovative technology for destruction is that the new rapier, unlike the old long sword, does not use so much the edge to cut and kill but the point so that a mere "scratch" can be ironically lethal. Moreover, Shakespeare's associations here find no parallel in any of the generally acknowledged literary sources for his play, especially Brooke's poem that serves as his main source. Little notice has been taken of Shakespeare's emphasis on the duello that he *adds* to his literary sources. In the sources, bands of men fight, but Shakespeare not only cultivates the one-on-one nature of the duel, he also colors it with satiric taunts and name-calling that find an analogue not in Brooke's poem but in the notorious Harvey-Nashe quarrel.

How Shakespeare uses the verbal parallels that abound between Nashe's *Have with You* and his tragedy is revealing for Shakespeare's command of page and stage and particularly for his masterful characterization of Mercutio, who voices the most Nashean echoes in the play. Some new parallels, and the reconsideration of one previously noted, further expose how Shakespeare found Nashe's prose attractive mettle for his verse.

The most important parallel concerns "fiddlestick" and its satiric contexts in Nashe and Shakespeare that associate imagery of dueling and music, and Shakespeare's use of this once again shows how creatively he responds to the Harvey-Nashe quarrel. "Fiddlestick" appears in Shakespeare's canon for the first time in *Romeo and Juliet* (3.1.42) and then reappears only once again in quite a different usage: "the devil rides upon a fiddlestick" (*1H4* 2.4.487). "Fiddlestick" is a crucial insult in the quarrel between Nashe and Harvey. In *Pierces Supererogation* (1593), Harvey mocks Lyly as "the Vice master of Poules, and the Foolemaster of the Theater . . . sometime the fiddlesticke of Oxford, now the very bable of London" (2:212). Earlier in this same work in a remarkably similar string of epithets, he scoffs that Lyly is "a professed iester, a Hickscorner, a scoff-maister, a playmunger, an Interluder; once the foile of Oxford, now the stale of London" (2:132).

In his defense of Lyly, Nashe retorts, "With a blacke sant he [Lyly] meanes shortly to bee at his [Harvey's] chamber window for calling him *the Fiddlesticke of Oxford*" (2:138). Of all Harvey's slurs cited above, the epithet *"the Fiddlesticke of Oxford"* is the one Nashe chooses to counter Harvey's criticism of Lyly's foolish "leuitie" (2:138) by playing on the musical reference of "fiddlesticke" to forecast an ominous retort, Lyly's black sanctus. What is important to note here is that Nashe ingeniously adds the musical nuance basic to the primary meaning of "fiddlestick." Harvey uses "fiddlesticke" solely as a term of contempt in its secondary meaning to signify something insignificant,[18] and his synonyms in parallel constructions indicate this meaning: "bable / foile / stale." The emphasis on music is lacking from Harvey's bashing of the playwright. Moreover, Harvey does not use metaphors of fighting here, although he does elsewhere.

However, Nashe not only adds the elements of music and fighting to his *"Fiddlesticke"* passage but also anticipates these elements with language that echoes in Shakespeare's scene. When Tybalt approaches Mercutio in his search for Romeo and uses the verb "consortest" (3.1.39), Mercutio takes great offense and responds aggressively to what he takes to be demeaning inferences, namely that Romeo and his friends are like common servants rather than gentlemen, a company of "minstrels" (3.1.40) at that. "Minstrel" is a term that can be used disparagingly.[19] Nashe anticipates his *"Fiddlesticke"* allusion with musical imagery that parallels Mercutio's use of "consort." Nashe denounces *"Mounsieur Fregeuile Gautius"* as "one of the Pipers in this consort" who *"befooles and besots"* Nashe in his apology on behalf of Harvey (3:136). Seeing that Nashe has just called Fregeville "that prating weazell fac'd vermin" (3:136), the musical description of him as a piper in Harvey's "consort" strikes the same satiric discord. Indeed, Nashe often uses "piper" and "piperly" to convey the sense of "paltry" (5:320). His "consort" passage is preceded several pages earlier by his assertion: "M. *Lilly* & me by name he beruffianized . . . & termd vs *piperly make-plaies*" (3:130).[20] These are fighting words, as Nashe explains: "[Harvey] bade vs *holde our peace & not be so hardie as to answer him, for if we did, he would make a bloodie day in* Poules Church-yard, & *splinter our pens til they straddled again as wide a paire of Compasses*" (3:130). But Nashe juxtaposes his *"Fiddlesticke"* counterthreat with the triumphant observation that Gabriel Harvey was not "made to hold his peace, till *Master Lillie* and some others with their pens drew vpon him" (3:138).

Shakespeare's response to Nashe's imagery of music and duel is once again imaginative. As with his imagistic fusion of the cat's claw and man's rapier in their lethal scratching, so also he fuses into one wholistic metaphor the music and dueling imagery when Mercutio indicates his rapier and calls it his "fiddlestick" (3.1.42), recalling his initial hostility to Tybalt's opening use of "consortest." Later in *Much Ado,* Shakespeare will again find attractive the imagistic union of opposites (music and sword): "I [Claudio] will bid thee [Benedick] draw, as we do the minstrels, draw to pleasure us" (5.1.128-29). Thus, the satiric use of "fiddlestick" in the Harvey-Nashe quarrel predates Shakespeare's *Romeo and Juliet,* and Nashe's development of the imagery of music and duel in conjunction with this epithet provides one derogatory verbal context that Shakespeare then adroitly adapts for the fatal quarrel midpoint in his play.

At first blush "rat-catcher," noted already by J. J. M. Tobin, looks like too common a word to merit attention. But it is not, and Nashe's satirical use of the term is riveting. Contrary to our modern expectations, "rat-catcher" refers not to an animal but rather to a person who catches rats. The first recorded entry in the *OED* is Shakespeare's use of the term, but the earliest citation for the application of the term to animals dates from the beginning of the eighteenth century. "Rat-catcher" applied to a person, however, is native to Nashe's context, and he may have coined the word.[21] Nashe's context, appearing many lines after his reference to *"Tibault,"* features no feline references, unlike Shakespeare's context. Instead, Nashe is at his funniest in satirizing Harvey as *"a common Mountebanke Rat-catcher"* because Harvey is laughed at for catching a rat, anatomizing it, and reading a lecture for three days on it, and moreover, he *"hanged her ouer his head in his studie, instead of an Apothecaries Crocodile, or dride* Alligatur" (3:67). Tobin has already noted that Shakespeare borrows his unique use of "alligator" from Nashe. I would add here that the fact that the words *"Rat-catcher"* and "Alligatur" occur so closely together in Nashe's passage is revealing for how Shakespeare remembers both words yet uses them at distantly separated points in his text, reserving the alligator reference for his own apothecary episode (5.1.43). Although "rat-catcher" (3.1.68) is unique in Shakespeare, it is ironic that the first citation in the *OED* is Shakespeare's because his is the most innovatively atypical. As with his fused use of cat and rapier, so also Shakespeare weds two associations here in his "rat-catcher": Mercutio's criticizing Tybalt as "a braggart, a rogue, a villain" (3.1.92; cf. Nashe's *"Mountebanke"*) plus Mercutio's feline puns for debunking Tybalt, who as the "Prince of Cats" would catch rats. Shakespeare clearly found arresting Nashe's satiric diction for name-calling.

"Princox" is a verbal parallel that has been overlooked. The term is unique in Shakespeare's canon. Capulet, attempting to ridicule Tybalt into obedient behavior at the feast, calls him "a princox" (1.5.85). This term, however, is a favorite of Nashe's, used at least four times in works that predate *Romeo and Juliet,* including the use of the plural form in *Have with You* in telling conjuction with the verb "consorted":

> Neither of these princockesses (*Barnes* or *Chute*) once cast vp their noses towards *Powles Church-yard,* or so much as knew how to knock at a Printing-house dore, till they consorted themselues with *Haruey,* who infected them within one fortnight with his owne spirit of Bragganisme. (3:109)[22]

In two of his publications in 1593, Harvey offensively borrows Nashe's "princock" to describe the youthful Nashe himself (1:283, 2:7). A good example from Nashe that reveals why the term would be so appropriate for Shakespeare's purposes is the following: "And you shall heare a Cavalier of the first feather, a princockes that was but a Page the other day in the Court . . . stand vaunting his manhood" (1:205). The use of the term is a particularly effective insult for adolescent males, for a "boy" sensitive to becoming a "man." The inflammatory rhetoric colors Capulet's denunciation of Tybalt as "a saucy boy" (1.5.82) and the "boy" insults of the duel scene (3.1.59).

Another probable verbal parallel involves the use and juxtaposition of the words "demesnes" and "adjacent." Mercutio bawdily conjures Romeo by Rosaline's "quivering thigh / And the demesnes that there adjacent lie" (2.1.19-20). "Demesnes" is rather rare in Shakespeare's canon and is used for the first time in *Romeo and Juliet,* once here in a figurative sense, once again in its literal sense of "estates" (3.5.180), and once later in *Cymbeline* (3.3.70). "Adjacent" is likewise uncommon in Shakespeare, and it also appears for the first time in

Romeo and then only once again in *Antony and Cleopatra* (2.2.213).[23] The close juxtaposition of the words "demeanes" and "adiacents," also used in an apparently figurative sense occurs in Nashe's *Have with You* when Nashe, as he often does, jests about Harvey's Latin verses: "The bungerliest verses . . . most of them . . . cut off by the knees out of *Virgill* and other Authors . . . and iumpe imitating a verse in *As in presenti,* or in the demeanes or adiacents, I am certaine" (3:78). McKerrow explains that Nashe's joke is derived from William Lily's Latin Grammar, and Nashe's earlier instance in his *Strange Newes* (1592) of this jest and its pun on "as" for "ass" offers a clearer context for understanding this joke: "Such is this Asse [Harvey] *in presenti,* this grosse painted image of pride, who would faine counterfeite a good witte" (1:282).[24] The coupling of these two terms in figurative wordplay is very unusual in English literature. At any rate, Shakespeare's use of these two terms is more clearly transformed through bawdy innuendo. However, Shakespeare's use of these terms within the context of Mercutio's bawdy verbal conjuring of Romeo may owe something to Nashe's earlier work. Although the idea of conjuring is commonplace, it is not commonplace to summon up a male contemporary through a witty use of the conjuring metaphor. Nashe, a conjurer of words himself, says he would learn any barbarous language "rather than bee put downe by such a ribauldry" as Harvey is: "Heigh, drawer, fil vs a fresh quart of *new-found phrases,* since *Gabriell* saies we borrow all our eloquence from Tauernes. . . . I coniure thee. . . . I drinke to you, M. *Gabriell*" (1:305). He also provides an apropos description of how to become a conjurer (1:363-67).

There are possibly several other overlooked verbal parallels that need to be considered, especially in terms of how they might shed light on Shakespeare's adaptation of his borrowings. Nashe uses "gear" twice, once straightforwardly (3:90) and once bawdily (3:129). Romeo concludes Mercutio's extraordinarily bawdy punning as Juliet's Nurse and her man, Peter, enter: "Here's goodly gear!" (2.4.82). Evans suggests the pun on "gear" revolves around its senses of "rubbish, nonsense" and "the organs of generation" that "link[s] perfectly with Mercutio's wit-play."[25] We might suggest another possibility here. Regardless of whether the stage direction is placed before or after Romeo's line, his line could Janus-like refer before and after, refer back to Mercutio's speech as well as look toward the Nurse and Peter who could be seen approaching Romeo across the large stage platform. I suggest this because Romeo's use of "gear" may well convey another sense, a nautical pun that has gone unnoticed. Romeo's "Here's goodly gear!" is immediately followed by his next line, a curious description of the Nurse indeed: "A sail, a sail!" (2.4.83). "Gear" in its nautical sense refers to rigging of any spar or sail. However, the earliest citations in the *OED* for "gear" in its nautical sense, as well as its slang sense, significantly postdate both Shakespeare's and Nashe's works.[26] Shakespeare's punning, then, is remarkable indeed. His main literary source for his play, Brooke's poem, has several passages of nautical imagery, but perhaps only Shakespeare could fuse so many meanings in one so apparently insignificant term as "gear." Although "gear" in its various senses is a common word in Shakespeare's works before and after *Romeo* and it even appears again at the end of this play (5.1.60), this is the only instance in which he puns on the slang sense of "gear" for genitalia.

In *Have with You,* Nashe has two separate uses of "gear" where he employs the same two senses of "nonsense" and "sexual organs" found in Shakespeare's line, but unlike Shakespeare, Nashe does not fuse the two meanings in one wonderful pun. Nashe's first instance almost parallels Romeo's line when Nashe ridicules Harvey's Latin language as nonsense: "here is such geere as I neuer saw" (3:90). But in a passage we have already noted in relation to *Love's Labor's Lost,* Nashe uses "gear" in its slang sense for his bawdy putdown of Harvey: "let her [Harvey's "gentlewoman"] bee *Prick-madam,* of which name there is a flower; & let him take it to himselfe; and raigne intire *Cod-pisse Kinko,* and Sir *Murdred* of placards . . . as long as he is able to please or giue them geare" (3:129). "Placard/placket," used with sexual innuendo, appears in Nashe for the first time in *Have with You,* here and in a venereal depiction of the Harvey brothers (3:82). It is similarly used for the first time by Shakespeare in *Love's Labor's Lost* and *Romeo* but is not used again until *Troilus and Cressida.*

Finally, Shakespeare's oxymoron, "merry dump," may derive from the surprisingly comical context for "dump" in *Have with You.* Shakespeare's other earlier instances of "dump" for "a mournful tune" employ the term straightforwardly, without any hint of oxymoron.[27] Near the end of Nashe's *Have with You,* in a particularly witty passage featuring facetious titles of works Nashe will write on Harvey, Nashe quips that he will write many comedies on Harvey and one shall be called *"The Doctors dumpe"*: "But wee shall lenuoy him [Harvey], and trumpe and poope him well enough . . . and he will needes fall a Comedizing it. Comedie vpon Comedie he shall haue, a Morall, a Historie, a Tragedie, or what hee will. One shal bee called *The Doctors dumpe*" (3:114).

There is possibly another Nashean verbal influence for how originally Shakespeare uses the rope ladder as a symbolic prop for the stage. Tobin notes that the Nurse talks of "'ropery'/'roperipe' at II.iv.146, and Romeo refers to a rope ladder at II.iv.189." Tobin juxtaposes this with the unique use of the phrase "'with an R'" in both Nashe and Shakespeare, this phrase appearing in Nashe's recurrent attack on Harvey's father for being a ropemaker, a man whose living ironically depends on death, on the gallows and the making of ropes.[28] Nashe himself explains that Harvey told some of Nashe's friends that "the onely thing that most set him afire against" Nashe was Nashe's calling Harvey and his brothers "sonnes of a Rope-maker" (3:56-57).[29] Nashe's emphasis on "the hempen mysterie" behind the names of the Harvey brothers (3:58) and his reiterated wordplay on "rope" cannot be missed (3:57-59). The satirical importance of this matter is highlighted in Nashe's subtitle for *Have with You: "Containing a full Answere to the eldest sonne of the Halter-maker."* Even in his dedicatory epistle, Nashe refers to "the Doctors Paraclesian rope-rethorique" (3:15). Shakespeare, of course, did not need to read Nashe to know the associations between "rope" and "ladder" (the steps of the gallows) in the hangman's profession. But if he were reading Nashe's work, these very associations would be strongly underscored for him because they are so pivotal in Nashe's quarrel.

Shakespeare's "ropery" seems to recall Nashe's, but he newly integrates the verbal nuances in his symbolic use of the rope ladder. Shakespeare had earlier used the prop of a "ladder made of cords" (TGV 2.4.182) in another romantic adventure, and he may have even introduced this lover's prop to the English stage from the Italian *novelle*.[30] The literary tradition of this "lover's ladder" is common in Italy, and the ladder of cords originates as a motif for the Romeo and Juliet story in Boccaccio's *Il Decamerone,* passed down through Shakespeare's possible literary sources.[31] However, no one in Elizabethan literature, other than Shakespeare, forges such a startling paradoxical fusion of meanings in the use of this prop when the instrument for fuller life and love is quickly transformed within the same scene, in keeping with the play's tempo of haste, to an instrument of despair and death (3.2.132-37). As in Shakespeare's transformation of "fiddlestick" from mere word to actual rapier, his finely tuned sense of prop deployment balances Juliet's newly transformed "poor ropes" with Romeo's dagger in a similarly forestalled suicide attempt in the subsequent scene (3.3.108). Neither of these dramatic actions appear in Brooke's poem where Juliet's response to the tragic news is a passive swoon (lines 1159-92) and frantic Romeo falls down and tears his hair (lines 1291-1300); both *wish* for death but do not seek *instruments* to effect it.

Romeo initially describes his ladder as "cords made like a tackled stair / Which to the high top-gallant of my joy / Must be my convoy in the secret night" (2.4.157-59), and herein Shakespeare refashions the much more frankly sexual imagery he found in Brooke's nautical motif: the "betost" ship [Romeus] may "boldly . . . resort / Unto [his] wedded ladies bed, [his] long desyred port" (lines 799-808). Brooke's nautical imagery probably inspired Shakespeare's "tackled stair." However, neither Brooke nor Painter nor Shakespeare himself in *The Two Gentlemen of Verona* ever use the word "rope" to describe this traditional lover's ladder of *cord.* This is understandable because the Italian and French words for "cord" (*corda, corde*) closely approximate the English word. The deadly nuance of "rope" is significantly added to Juliet's perception of this prop as she recasts her epithalamium that opens this scene—"Come, Night, come, Romeo"—to its deadly opposite as the scene closes:

> Take up those cords. Poor ropes . . .
> He made you for a highway to my bed, . . .
> Come, cords, come, Nurse, I'll to my wedding bed,
> And death, not Romeo, take my maidenhead!
> (3.2.132-37)

Romeo's emphasis on joyful ascent becomes tragically ironic for Juliet's intended "ascent" on these ropes by hanging that would result in a permanent and "grave" descent.[32] Shakespeare once again surpasses our expectations in a stunning fusion of meanings that fuel the play's paradoxical incorporation of how "all things change them to the contrary" (4.5.90).

Perhaps some tentative conjectures about Shakespeare's literary imagination are worthwhile here. These examples of Shakespeare's borrowing from Nashe not only are helpful for establishing the direction of authorial influence and the date of composition of *Romeo* but also appear to be illustrative of how Shakespeare's imagination works in transforming his literary sources into his poetic drama. The common bond that unifies these examples is Shakespeare's power of fusing or unifying into a more complex whole that he finds separate or disjoined. In this respect, he is very much an artist of Renaissance temperament. In his pervasive use of sources, Shakespeare upholds the Renaissance rhetorical ideal of *imitatio* whereby the combination of old material with new is expressed uniquely, and he does not seem to favor imaginative creation "ex nihilo." Like one contemporary theory of creativity, namely God's creation of the universe out of the raw materials of the four contraries combined into the four elements, so also Shakespeare's creative art often evolves out of his combination of various elements in the raw materials of his literary sources.

Moreover, Shakespeare seems to adhere to Renaissance critical theory regarding the operation of the poetic imagination, theory that has been elucidated by William Rossky.[33] Although Renaissance psychology views the imagination as necessary but dangerous because of its irrational power, Renaissance apologies for poetry exalt this faculty for its transforming or "feigning" power when imagination is guided by reason to create art.[34] Rossky shows this cooperation between reason and imagination for art's sake is revealed in sixteenth-century descriptions of poetic feigning of images as a process of severing and joining things real to form things imagined). Shakespeare's use of his literary sources to feign his own images may be seen as somewhat analogous to this poetic theory, especially in his joining together of what he often finds severed, or at best loosely associated, in his sources, or in our parlance, perhaps a literary version of fission and fusion. Impressive indeed is how Shakespeare's extraordinarily retentive memory generates his free association of images and ideas to form new combinations. On the basis of the few examples considered here, one aspect of Shakespeare's imaginative genius in his practice of *imitatio* seems to be his ability to forge connections where others, like Nashe, do not, or to see things "whole," resulting in a texture of images with greater verbal and ideational complexity.

2

The importance of Nashe for Shakespeare's composition of his play and for his creation of Mercutio demands further investigation. To Evans's succinct account of dating Nashe's composition of *Have with You,* several points might be added for further consideration. McKerrow suggests that Nashe's allusion to writing for the press in his important letter to William Cotton, "which was evidently written about September, 1596. . . . probably refers to *Have with You,* which cannot yet have been published" (5:28-29). In this letter to Cotton, Nashe also refers to writing for the stage, but his hopes there have been thwarted because London's mayor and aldermen persecute the players who had known better days "in there old Lords tyme." McKerrow annotates this as apparently an allusion to the death of Lord Chamberlain Henry Carey, the first Lord Hunsdon, in July 1596, and he suggests that Nashe was probably associated "with the Chamberlain's men, for these alone would be affected by Hundson's death" (5:194). If so, Nashe's association with Shakespeare's company would increase the likelihood of Shakespeare's access to Nashe's *Have with You.*

Although Nashe's composition cannot be precisely dated and seems to have extended over a considerable period of time,[35] it appears that Nashe probably was busily at work finishing this piece in the late summer of 1596. Another overlooked allusion to Lord Hunsdon, this time not to the father but to the son, may help to substantiate this view. Nashe refers to the work of "a singular Scholler, one *Master Heath,* (a Follower of the right Honorable and worthie *Lord of Hunsdon* that now is)" (3:83). McKerrow explains that Thomas Heath dedicated his work against Harvey that appeared in 1583 to Sir George Carey (Baron Hunsdon) (4:342). But Nashe's explicit phrasing for the Lord of Hunsdon *"that now is"* (my italics) suggests that Sir George Carey is now the new or second Lord Hunsdon. He succeeded his father, Sir Henry Carey, the first Lord Hunsdon, who died on 23 July 1596, but he did not receive the title of Lord Chamberlain until March 1597. Consequently, as E. K. Chambers explains, Shakespeare's company "was properly known as the Lord Hunsdon's men from 22 July 1596 to 17 March 1597; before and after that period it was the Lord Chamberlain's men."[36] Sir George Carey was also a patron of Nashe (5:21). Nashe's reference to the *present* Lord Hunsdon here indicates that at least this passage was written after July 1596, and this reference would accord with the suggestion McKerrow offers from Nashe's letter to Cotton. Evans wisely cautions that the reference to performance of *Romeo and Juliet* by "'the L. of *Hunsdon* his Servants'" on the title page of the first quarto, published in 1597, might be "only a publisher's device to capitalise on the most recent performances and does not prove that the play was not acted earlier when Shakespeare's company was known as the Lord Chamberlain's Men." This reference, however, might also refer to the play's debut and its immediate popularity because the title page advertizes that the play "hath been often (with great applause) plaid publiquely."

Not only do Shakespeare's echoes from Nashe's *Have with You* appear scattered throughout *Romeo and Juliet* from its first to last scene, but also equally important to note is that Shakespeare's references from Nashe are culled from throughout the whole of his *Have with You.* McKerrow thinks that it is "not improbable that all the early part, as far as 33:30, was added just before it was sent to press" (4:302). If so, and if we accept Tobin's evidence from this early part of characterization hints for Shakespeare's Benvolio and Mercutio, then we must conclude that Shakespeare had access to either a nearly complete manuscript version or to its published version.

Several important points concerning Shakespeare's characterization of Mercutio might be added to Tobin's evidence taken from the supposedly latest part of Nashe's composition. Tobin stresses only Nashe's emphasis on "sportive wit" in his characterization of his interlocutor, Don Carneades, the boon companion to Domino Bentiuole, whose name probably serves for Shakespeare's Benvolio because that name appears in no other source.[37] But Nashe also describes Don Carneades as a good fighter—*"who likewise is none of the unworthiest retainers to Madame* Bellona" (3:22)—and there is an aggressive side to Shakespeare's Mercutio. Although McKerrow does not gloss Nashe's use of "Don Carneades," Nashe probably has in mind the famous Greek philosopher, Carneades, because later in *Have with You* Nashe mocks the praise given by Harvey's schoolmaster to Harvey's mind: "O acumen Carneadum" (3:64). Carneades's reputation for skepticism and rhetorical skill would suit Nashe's idea of this interlocutor as well as Shakespeare's own development of Mercutio.

Shakespeare's portrait of Mercutio is not far off the mark from Nashe and his inclination to loquaciousness, his claim to "frolicke spirits" (3:77), his skill in bawdry (3:30-31), his intolerance of vain fencing boasts, his resentment of boyish accusations, and his genius for personal satire replete with inventive name-calling and mock titles, all of which resonate in Nashe's wittiest and most scornful treatment of his quarrel against Harvey, *Have with You to Saffron-Walden*. In his quarrel with Harvey, Nashe opposes, as does Mercutio, airs and newfangledness (3:30-31). Nashe's hatred of fads—the "new fangled *Galiardos* and Senior *Fantasticoes*" (3:31) and Harvey's looking and speaking like an Italian and affecting "Italian *puntilios*" (3:76)—parallels Mercutio's animadversion against the "new tuners of accent," "fashion-mongers . . . who stand so much on the new form, that they cannot sit at ease on the old bench" (2.4.26-30). Like Mercutio's tirade against Tybalt, Nashe denounces Harvey as "idle and new fangled" (3:26), as a "swash-buckler" (3:55) whose "horrible insulting pride" (3:56) needs someone like Nashe *"to humble him"* (3:69). The princely airs of Harvey and Tybalt—that "spirit of Bragganisme" (3:109)—are precisely what Nashe and Mercutio claim to eschew. Mercutio's allegiance to male camaraderie in adopting a friend's cause in a quarrel is especially noteworthy because of the absence of such a motif from Brooke's poem, Shakespeare's chief source. In Brooke the briefly introduced element of youthful male friendship drops out after the unnamed counterpart to Shakespeare's Benvolio offers to Romeus his counsel about the cure for lovesickness (lines 101-48). Yet this very motif of a friend assuming the defense of another friend in a private quarrel undergirds the Elizabethan literary altercation with Nashe defending Lyly against Harvey.

Just as some critics have thought Nashe a model for Moth in *Love's Labor's Lost,*[38] it is tempting to suggest that Nashe, praised by Francis Meres as a "gallant young *Iuuenall*" (5:148), also provides some hints for Mercutio when Shakespeare seeks to enflesh a witty, aggressive, young masculine character who has a personal quarrel with another arrogant, quarrelsome enemy. Nashe's youthfulness was an issue in the quarrel, so that Harvey finds fault with Nashe's "minoritie of . . . beard" and calls him *"Captaine of the boyes"* (3:129). Nashe's reputation, as described by Izaak Walton, for "merry Wit," for being "a man of a sharp wit, and the master of a scoffing, Satyrical Pen" (5:47-48), lingers long after his premature death in 1601. Although Shakespeare inherited the name of "Mercutio" from Brooke's poem, for Shakespeare that name probably conveys nuances of ingenuity and eloquence derived from Mercury. Appropriately enough, mercurial Nashe associates himself especially with the winged Mercury, desiring "*sprightly* Mercury" to be his muse in *Have with You* (3:23-4). Nashe's nimble wit, capable of "a new kind of a quicke fight" (1:283), characterizes that of Mercutio as well, who also employs imagery of the fight in his "wild-goose chase" of matching wits with Romeo when he quips: "Come between us, good Benvolio, my wits faints" (2.4.57-60). Later in this same work, Nashe mocks Harvey's pretense to "attractive eloquence"—"the Mercurian heauenly charme of hys Rhetorique" (3:96)—and spoofs Harvey's desire to "stellifie" himself "next to *Mercury*" (3:107) when Nashe has invoked Mercury *"to inspire [his] pen."*[39]

Nashe's influence on Shakespeare's characterization of Mercutio also has provocative implications for recent critical discourse on Renaissance sexuality. Using mythographic evidence, Joseph A. Porter, for example, links Mercury to Mercutio through homosexuality, emphasizing the strongly phallic character of both. Porter stresses how Mercutio speaks to affirm male bonding against the incursions of women. He speculates that in killing off Mercutio, Shakespeare stifles that spokesman against romantic love as well as overcomes his own anxiety of influence in processing some of what is most disturbing in Marlowe, who can be seen as the embodiment of the Renaissance Mercury and Shakespeare's rival in several respects. Emphasizing what he sees as Mercutio's homosexual bawdry, Porter claims one of the prime textual examples to be what he finds an image of sodomy: "O Romeo, that she were / An open-arse, and thou a popp'rin pear" (2.1.37-38).[40] However, "open-arse" has been more compellingly glossed as an image of the pudendum on the basis of the known anatomical features of the medlar that cause it to be called the open-arse fruit.[41] A definition from a sixteenth-century herbal suggests how this fruit could be so viewed: "the fruite . . . is of a browne russet colour, of a rounde proportion and somewhat broade or flat . . . with a great broade nauel or Crowne at the toppe, or ende. . . . after they haue bene a while kept . . . they become soft and tender."[42] Hence, Mercutio balances the female (medlar) and male (pear) genitalia for intercourse in his "fruitful" wordplay. However, the sense of Mercutio as the arch-advocate of male bonding does indeed pervade the play.

The topic of Mercutio's sexuality and aggression is a complex one. It can be argued that Mercutio's "phallocentrism" is not simply a "scorn of heterosexual love," nor is it simply "light intermittent misogyny," as Porter claims (197-98). Hatred of women is not so much at stake as is the use and abuse of women. Believing a man should "be rough with love," Mercutio advises Romeo: "You are a lover . . . / Prick love for pricking, and you beat love down" (1.4.17, 28), and Mercutio conjures Romeo "in his mistress' name" (2.1.28). Heterosexual activity is upheld as long as it remains at its lowest common denominator, at the brute level, the level of Sampson's and Gregory's sexual tyranny: "I will be civil with the maids; I will cut off their heads. . . . their maidenheads, take it in what sense thou wilt" (1.1.19-20, 22-23).[43] For the audience, the prince's opening denunciation of "mistempered weapons" (1.1.78) through bestial man's misuse of them may refer to more than one kind of foining and recall the "naked weapon" (1.1.29) wordplay that just preceded. Mercutio's preference for rough love serves as a foil to Romeo's romantic love until Romeo tragically adopts Mercutio's view of such love as "effeminate" (3.1.105) and embraces Mercutio's definition of manhood in terms of violence—fight and fury.

In evoking a male-dominance ethos where women are objects for male sexual pleasure and clearly take second place to male bonding, Mercutio differentiates himself from his friends Romeo and Benvolio, both of whom share a similarly described desire for romantic privacy (1.1.110, 117-21). Mercutio is never depicted as desiring such moody solitude, but rather he is ever the hub of his social wheel, the center of male conviviality. He even defines Romeo as becoming his true self once he stops groaning for love and resumes his male sociability: "Now art thou sociable, now art thou Romeo" (2.4.72-73). Mercutio's social definition of selfhood accords well with Nashe's own penchant because, as Hibbard reminds us, Nashe "lives wholly and only in society" (252). Although Porter argues that Shakespeare "conjures the god Mercury and also the raised spirit of Marlowe" (163) in Mercutio, Nashe's essential sociability complements the fraternal spirit of Mercury that Porter emphasizes (32) but that Marlowe does not typically exhibit.[44] Porter also associates Mercury, the classical deliverer of dreams, with Mercutio's Queen Mab so that in this speech "what we have is a kind of possession of Mercutio by the god" (104). But a Mercury-Mercutio linkage through dreams operates not by "possession" but by detachment. Mercutio, as a foil to Romeo, mocks dreams, and as a dream scoffer Mercutio resembles not Marlowe but Nashe who wrote a very clever *jeu d'esprit* on dreams, *The Terrors of the Night* (1594).[45] Shakespeare's emphasis on Mercutio's pugnacity tends to contradict Porter's otherwise richly suggestive argument for Mercutio as an avatar of Mercury because pugnacity is not a trait typical of Mercury, despite the variety of his attributes. Mercutio's quarrelsomeness, so essential to the duels on behalf of friends at the play's tragic turning point, is not unlike Nashe's defensive posture for his friend Lyly. However, Mercutio's comic combativeness—his verbal sparring—does modulate into tragic aggression—his physical dueling—that costs his own life.

Although Nashe's own combative spirit is a quality he shares with his admired friend Marlowe, Shakespeare's particular expression of Mercutio's aggressiveness points to Nashe, who was as quarrelsome as he was witty and who itched to use a sword against Harvey (3:134). Even if we do not overrule but qualify Porter's argument for the influence of Marlowe on Mercutio, it would seem that Nashe makes an equally good, if not better, candidate for real-life influence. Porter claims that "in plot the most striking homology is between Mercutio's death and Marlowe's" (138), and he generates a Romeo-Shakespeare link from his Mercutio-Marlowe association, suggesting that Romeo's indirect responsibility for Mercutio's death presents "a trace of Shakespeare's unconscious assumption of responsibility for Marlowe's death" (141).[46] Mercutio does indeed resemble Marlowe in the fact of early death resulting from a quarrel. But the manner and motive of Marlowe's quarrel is very different from Mercutio's where the language and emphases, as we have seen, indicate Nashean influence. Inside a tavern room, with three other men present, Marlowe dies from a dagger wound during a quarrel with Ingram Frizer over the supper bill. This is no outdoor rapier duel in defense of a friend's reputation against an insulting enemy.

Even Marlowe's earlier duel in Hog Lane, not considered by Porter, might seem more apropos for Mercutio's duel but that it differs from Shakespeare's characterization of an intractable Mercutio who dies as a result of his duel. In this swordfight, Marlowe neither suffers a wound nor dies because he *withdraws* from his combat against William Bradley after his friend Thomas Watson arrives. Responding to the clamor the people raise against the fight, Watson seeks to part the combatants to keep the queen's peace, according to the coroner's jury, but as Mark Eccles suggests, he may also have intended to aid Marlowe against Bradley with whom he already was at odds.[47] Unlike the peacemaker Romeo, Watson does not raise his arm or interpose his body but rather draws his sword. When Bradley sees Watson with drawn sword, he attacks and severely wounds Watson. Defending himself, Watson retreats into a ditch whereupon he finally strikes Bradley a mortal blow. This historic duel is superficially suggestive for the duel in *Romeo and Juliet,* namely, the intervention of a third man to part two combatants with one being killed as a result. However, Marlowe's retirement from this skirmish, despite his bleeding friend's peaceful intervention and posture of self-defense, contrasts markedly with Mercutio's quarrelsome instigation against Tybalt as well as his refusal to withdraw. Nor does "newly entertain'd revenge" (3.1.171) motivate Watson to fight because his friend Marlowe has not been slain, unlike the much more problematic situation the avenger Romeo faces.

If we entertain the possibility that Shakespeare found Nashe suggestive for his characterization of Mercutio, what more might we glean from the Harvey-Nashe quarrel? Unlike Marlowe but like Mercutio, Nashe had a reputation for an effervescent satiric wit and for a decidedly bawdy bent reflected in his life and literature. As Bruce R. Smith has argued, what moderns term "heterosexuality" and "homosexuality" may not have been necessarily opposed categories in

Renaissance England.[48] Nashe, as a possible real-life model for Mercutio, would be an intriguing instance of this idea, and a consideration of him also raises provocative questions about the place of libertine sexuality in Elizabethan London.

Evidence about Nashe as a young rakehell in London who probably engaged with both sexes in wanton behavior parallels the sense of double play that Mercutio seems to convey through his heterosexual bawdry and his possibly implicit homosexual position as the keynoter for male bonds. Some of the evidence comes from Nashe's own pen, but the bulk comes from his adversary Gabriel Harvey. Concerning the latter, we must bear in mind the complex evolution of the Harvey-Nashe quarrel, traced so carefully by McKerrow (5:65-110), and the tendency in such personal satire to hyperbolic invective and fictitious embroidery of skeletal facts. It is worth observing that Harvey initially thought well enough of Nashe to describe Nashe as "a proper yong man if aduised in time" (1:170). Oddly enough in a letter directed against Nashe, Harvey evidently recognized Nashe's talents as a writer to group him with other accomplished writers, like Spenser and Daniel, for "their studious endeuours . . . in enriching, & polishing their natiue tongue, neuer so furnished, or embellished as of late" (1:218-19).[49] Nashe originally counterattacked Richard Harvey, Gabriel's brother, and did not attack Gabriel himself until his *Strange News* (1592), and then he did so violently. After this attack by Nashe, Gabriel begins his leveling of specific sexual accusations against Nashe in his *Pierces Supererogation* (1593) and his *A New Letter of Notable Contents* (1593), the latter being a letter that McKerrow suggests Harvey never intended to publish (5:103-04). Even bearing in mind these provisos, the evidence is telling.

Nashe's *Christ's Tears over Jerusalem* (1593) precedes in print Harvey's attacks and records Nashe's religious "conversion," his turning away from his past "weake . . . deedes" (2:9).[50] Nashe repents his vain writings, including "some spleanatiue vaines of wantonnesse" written to supply his private needs (2:13). In his treatment of London's sins of lust, Nashe laments "this City-sodoming trade" of "priuate Stewes" (2:152-53), upbraiding both woman's self-debasement and man's contribution to that defilement (2:154). In so doing, Nashe reveals his own personal knowledge of such houses, confirming Harvey's accusation (2:91):

> The worlde woulde count me the most licentiate loose strayer vnder heauen, if I shoulde vnrippe but halfe so much of their veneriall machiauelisme as I haue lookt into. We haue not English words enough to vnfold it. Positions & instructions haue they, to make theyr whores a hundred times more whorish and treacherous. . . . I am weary of recapitulating theyr roguery. I woulde those that shoulde reforme it woulde take but halfe the paynes in supplanting it that I haue done in disclosing it. (2:153)

Likewise, Nashe's brothel poem, *The Choice of Valentines* (3:403-16), runs in the same vein of heterosexual bawdiness native to Mercutio. Nashe concludes that "Ouids wanton Muse did not offend"; in following Ovid, his own mind is "purg'd of such lasciuious witt" (3:416). But in considering the bawdry of Nashe's *The Choice of Valentines,* or *Nashe's Dildo,* as it is sometimes entitled, Hibbard is puzzled why this poem acquired so much notoriety so quickly: "Its bawdry is of the elementary, direct, indecent kind. Nashe's attitude to sexual matters is too normal and healthy to be anything but dull" (57). Although Hibbard's assessment of the poem's bawdry is accurate enough, some Elizabethan sensibilities could be aggravated by Nashe's own personal reputation for loose living and his first-person narration of his visit to a brothel on St. Valentine's Day, coupled with his almost journalistic description of detail that is not at all acceptably filtered through any classical myth, such as the stories of Hero and Leander or Venus and Adonis.[51] Hibbard rightly suggests that Nashe's poverty probably constrained him to be a ghostwriter of bawdy verses for other gentlemen, and *The Choice of Valentines* is cited as the surviving example (55). But both Nashe (3:30-31) and Harvey imply that many such rhymes came from Nashe's impoverished pen; therefore, Harvey rails that Nashe has written "his owne vanities in a thousand sentences, and whole Volumes of ribaldry; not to be read but vpon a muck-hill, or in the priuyest priuie of the Bordello" (2:233). Nashe's attitude to sexual matters is anything but dull if we are to accept as even partially true any of Harvey's accusations and Nashe's admissions.

Harvey condemns Nashe's disorderly erotic behavior with men and women. In *Pierces Supererogation,* Harvey indicts Nashe's "brothell Muse" that "needes be a young Curtisan of ould knauery" in writing "bawdye, and filthy Rymes, in the nastiest kind. . . . to putrify gentle mindes":

> Phy on impure Ganimeds, Hermaphrodits, Neronists, Messalinists, Dodecomechanists, Capricians, Inuentours of newe, or reuiuers of old leacheries, and the whole brood of venereous Libertines. . . . the sonnes of Adam, & the daughers of Eue, haue noe neede of the Serpentes carowse to set them agogg: Sodome still burneth; and although fier from heauen spare Gomorra, yet Gomorra stil consumeth itselfe. (2:91-92)

Harvey even objects to the moral harm of "amorous Sonnets," observing that the devil's dam is "an old bawde" who needs not "the broccage of a young Poet" (2:92). Later in this same text, Harvey complains against "the poulkat of Pouls-churchyard" (2:273):

> Agrippa detesteth his [Nashe's] monstrous veneries, and execrable Sodomies. . . . the most-impudent Ribald, that euer tooke penne in hand. . . . the Ring leader of the corruptest bawdes, and miscreantest rakehells. . . . His wanton disciples . . . in their fantasticall Letters, and Bacchanall Sonnets, extoll him monstrously, that is, absurdly: as the onely Monarch of witt. (2:271-72)

In his *New Letter,* Harvey questions the sincerity of Nashe's "conversion" by pitting Nashe's words against his deeds:

> but still to haunt infamous, or suspected houses, tauernes, lewd company, and riotous fashions, as before, (for to this day his behauiour is no turnecoate, though his stile be a changeling). . . . Though *Greene* were a Iulian, and *Marlow* a Lucian: yet I would be loth, *He* [Nashe] should be an Aretin: that . . . discoursed the Capricious Dialogues of rankest Bawdry: that penned one Apology of the diuinity of Christ, and another of Pederastice, a kinde of harlatry, not to be recited. (1:288-91)[52]

Nashe's fantastically satiric wit and extremely bawdy lines are captured in Shakespeare's creation of Mercutio, whereas in Brooke's poem there is no satiric emphasis, and the only sexual clue is that Mercutio is bold among maids (lines 257-59). Nashe's response to Harvey is intriguing because it may also suggest something about the place of libertine sexuality in Elizabethan London. Nashe does not specifically defend his private life against Harvey's charges; perhaps he feared accusations of protesting too much.[53] But what Nashe is concerned about defending is his public image as a man of letters. In the opening pages of *Have with You,* Nashe immediately takes up the glove to rejoice that his poverty compelled him to prostitute his pen in writing bawdry for recompense from some of the "newfangled" gentlemen (3:31). The unidentified author of *The Trimming of Thomas Nashe* mocks Nashe's poverty by telling a story about how Nashe and his "fellow *Lusher*" lay together in coleharbor and had but one pair of breeches between them so that they had to take turns, one lying in bed while the other wore the breeches, to go cony catching for victuals.[54] However, the emphasis in this passage is not on sexuality but on humbling poverty. One could routinely expect charges of loose living in personal satire as vitriolic as the Harvey-Nashe quarrel becomes. But Nashe's own admissions give Harvey's charges particular heft.

However, it would be grossly misleading to intimate that these charges inform the core of Harvey's attack. As Nashe's response indicates, the main thrust of criticism always centers on the major sin of false pride; Nashe's "wild Phantasie," unschooled "in the shop of curious Imitation," needs more acquaintance "at the hand of Art" (2:277). It is "the ignorant Idiot" (2:275), far more than "the bumm of Impudency" (2:273), that galls Harvey, and this accords well with the medieval-Renaissance hierarchy of the seven deadly sins that ranks pride, the perversion of man's godlike reason, as a worse sin than lechery to which man's body so easily falls prey. Thus, of the five senses, the sense of touch is ranked the lowest, and King Lear voices this viable perspective: "Adultery? / Thou shalt not die. Die for adultery?"[55] By the time of the Victorians, however, this hierarchy of vices has been turned on its head, and sins of the flesh ranked most reprehensible. No small wonder then that the rough honesty and graphic articulation of Mercutio's Elizabethan bawdry has been continually cleaned up by later editors who have a new sensibility about such matters.

As bawdy as Mercutio's lines are, and they are probably the bawdiest in all of Shakespeare, Mercutio's nimble wittiness, like Nashe's, raises him up so that he is viewed by his male companions, as Nashe is by his, as a leader, indeed "the onely Monarch of witt," as Harvey complains (2:271). Nashe, who self-consciously imitates the Italian satirist Aretino (3:152), is so outrageously witty that it is hard to out-Nashe Nashe, as Harvey's own effort reveals when he tries that approach (2:275).[56] We need to understand better the emphases of a world where social privilege can outweigh sexual indiscretion, where being poor and breechless or being born the son of a ropemaker levels more shame than being accused of lechery, where the use of one's wit overshadows the use of one's body. The dramatic history of the popular and disturbing Mercutio sheds light on real-life conditions then and now, as we seek to unravel our responses to Mercutio, whose base string of sexuality, like the Nurse's, predominately contrasts with, but also paradoxically parallels at points, the more refined love of Romeo and Juliet. Hibbard does not link Nashe to Mercutio, but his final assessment of Nashe emphasizes traits that are most appropriate to our discussion of Nashe's influence on how Shakespeare characterizes Mercutio: Nashe's impressiveness of personality on his peers; his calculated awareness of his impact on an audience; his sympathy for an audience of young men who, like Nashe, were "hostile to Puritanism and the middle-class ethos, witty, caustic, and dissatisfied"; his "biting satirical wit" in his mastery of burlesque and parody; and his playful fascination with language that renders some of his work a *jeu d'esprit* (250-53). Placing Shakespeare's first romantic tragedy within a historical context is a more complex business than we have usually persuaded ourselves.

It would appear that the burden of proof is rapidly shifting to those who would deny Nashe's influence on Shakespeare, particularly the influence from *Have with You.* The evidence presented here, like the evidence presented earlier by John Dover Wilson, J. M. M. Tobin, and G. Blakemore Evans, demonstrates Shakespeare's enduring interest in and use of

Nashe's works. As a dramatist, Shakespeare would have been reasonably attracted to Nashe as "an improviser" in prose who "works in terms of what may be described as scenes" (Hibbard, 147). Nashe's *Have with You,* which he called a "Comedie" (3:69), is particularly attractive as a conversational script, a self-proclaimed dialogue wherein "Auditors" (3:42) are addressed and Harvey's written "Pedantisme" (3:42) is presented as the "Oration." Shakespeare had good reason to admire Nashe's style. Some of Nashe's talents as a writer include his inventiveness with the English language, his sharp rendering of London life, and his awareness of narrative voice. As a professional controversialist, Nashe cultivated a rich prose vocabulary in a style peculiar to himself—his "fantasticall Satirisme" (2:12). He scorned English affectations and used freely the vernacular for his burlesque effects. But when English monosyllables would not suffice, he compounded his words and coined words from foreign languages in order to create a style that "must bee swelling and boystrous" if it, like a strong wind, is to have "any power or force to confute or perswade" (2:183-84).

What I wish to indicate here is that Shakespeare found Nashe, the man and his work, a creative stimulus for his own artistic imagination. Shakespeare's interest in Nashe goes beyond verbal echoes to include subject matter, stylistic flair, personal attitudes, and even Nashe's self-styled literary role as a professional jester that Hibbard has so aptly analyzed (251-52). It is Nashe's professional performance as the witty jester, always keenly aware of his audience, who could stingingly satirize contemporary types, much as Mercutio depicts the fashionable Tybalt, that contributes most to influencing Shakespeare's creation of his self-conscious performer of verbal acrobatics. Mercutio entertains his audience, much like Nashe, by using his versatile wit to make much of little as he always lands on his feet. But the darker side is also there, and Hibbard rightly notes Nashe's "fascinated interest in the grotesque, not to mention the deep attraction towards violence" (250) that pervades so much of his work. This violent aggressiveness also bonds Nashe and Mercutio.

As Kenneth Muir and G. K. Hunter maintain, Shakespeare's reading is more extensive than has been formerly held, and he generally devotes more careful attention than his contemporaries to the collection of his source material.[57] *Romeo and Juliet* has long been considered one of the few plays that seem to have a single source, but given the pivotal "Prince of Cattes" passage, along with the host of other verbal echoes, the evidence cumulatively and unmistakably points to an important influence of Nashe's *Have with You to Saffron-Walden* on Shakespeare's *Romeo and Juliet,* helping us to date the composition of that play in the last half of 1596. It appears that Nashe also provides for Shakespeare a viable milieu for the combative and sexual male ethos that Shakespeare found especially promising for the mercurial Mercutio he was to create from the barest of hints in his literary source material. Above all, the analysis of borrowings presented here also reveals how fertile is the transformative power of Shakespeare's imagination in shaping "the airy word" (1.1.80) as he unifies disparate elements from Nashe's *Have with You to Saffron-Walden* to create the artistically coherent world of his first romantic tragedy.

Notes

[1] All references are to *Romeo and Juliet,* ed. G. Blakemore Evans, New Cambridge Shakespeare edition (Cambridge: Cambridge University Press, 1984), and are cited parenthetically in my text. Evans examines the question of chronology (4-6), and he favors the case for Nashe's influence on Shakespeare, based chiefly on J. J. M. Tobin's arguments (see Tobin, "Nashe and the Texture of *Romeo and Juliet,*" *Notes and Queries* 27 [1980]: 161-62). To Tobin's list of verbal parallels, Evans adds the word "coying"; see 3 n. 7. See also *William Shakespeare: A Textual Companion,* ed. Stanley Wells et al. (Oxford: Oxford University Press, 1987), 118-19. I am deeply grateful to Franklin B. Williams, Jr., and Bruce R. Smith for their invaluable advice in their reading of this essay.

[2] See Thomas Nashe, *The Works of Thomas Nashe,* ed. Ronald B. McKerrow, 5 vols. (1904-10; rpt. Oxford: Basil Blackwell, 1958), 3:51; hereafter cited in the text.

[3] G. R. Hibbard, *Thomas Nashe: A Critical Introduction* (Cambridge: Harvard University Press, 1962), 221; see also 223-24.

[4] See McKerrow, *Nashe,* 4:327 nn. 29-30. He implicitly entertains the possibility of "savour," but he asserts "favour" is the correct reading.

[5] See McKerrow, *Nashe,* 4:327; Cyrus Hoy, *Introductions, Notes, and Commentaries to Texts in 'The Dramatic Works of Thomas Dekker,'* ed. Fredson Bowers, 4 vols. (Cambridge: Cambridge University Press, 1980), 1:300, 204. If Shakespeare editors cite Nashe's passage as illustrative evidence, they imply or explicitly state that Nashe, like Shakespeare, identifies "Tibault" as "the Prince of Cattes." See, for example, editions of *Romeo and Juliet* by George Lyman Kittredge, John Dover Wilson and George Ian Duthie, T. B. J. Spencer, John E. Hankins, Frank Kermode (Riverside), Brian Gibbons, and G. Blakemore Evans. Cf. also, Tobin, "Nashe and the Texture of *Romeo and Juliet,*" 165, 167, 172; Evans, 2.4.18n.

[6] I am very grateful to three experts in Reynardian literature—Kenneth Varty, Hubertus Menke, and Thomas W. Best—for confirming my findings that neither

"Tibault" as a name for the cat ("Tibert") nor the title "Prince of Cats" appears in any recorded versions of the medieval beast epic. For the misleading conflation of the names "Tibert" and "Tibault" for the Reynardian cat, see Staunton, cited in *Romeo and Juliet,* ed. H. H. Furness, Variorum Shakespeare edition (Philadelphia: J. B. Lippincott, 1899), 119 n. 18.

[7] Nashe quotes extensively, but not always accurately. There is an interesting example from *Have with You* that illustrates this. Despite Nashe's close work with Harvey's text against him, *Pierces Supererogation,* Nashe refers to Harvey's fencing master as "Tom Burwell" (3:134) while Harvey calls him "Tom Burley." See Gabriel Harvey, *The Works of Gabriel Harvey,* ed. Alexander B. Grosart, 3 vols. (1884; rpt. New York: AMS Press, 1966), 2:327; hereafter cited in the text.

[8] See William Baldwin, *Beware the Cat,* ed. William A. Ringler, Jr., and Michael Flachmann (San Marino, Calif.: Huntington Library, 1988); the editors note Isegrim is the wolf in *Reynard the Fox,* but a cat in Baldwin's text (30, 37, 46, 47, 51, 68). All references to Baldwin's pamphlet are to this edition; see "Textual Note," xxix-xxx. I am indebted to Franklin B. Williams, Jr., for bringing this text to my attention. Cf. also, William Baldwin, *"Beware the Cat" and "The Funerals of King Edward the Sixth,"* ed. William P. Holden, Connecticut College Monograph 8 (New London: Connecticut College, 1963), that reprints the 1584 copy at the Folger Shakespeare Library. See *OED,* "Isegrim."

[9] The female cat Isegrim is never ranked a prince; Isegrim is an assistant to the gray cat Grisard, the counselor to Cammoloch, who is identified as *"chief prince among cats."* Later Glascalon is called *"chief prince of the cats"* (see Baldwin, 36-37, 47). Grisard, Pol-noir, and Isegrim are called "the commissioners" (51); for the orderly and courtly world of these cats, see 46, 47, 51. The conversational format of Baldwin's satire also probably influences Nashe's similar framing of his *Have with You* as a dialogue of male friends who use the "oration" of another to mock him with his own words. Nashe admired (3:20) Baldwin's earlier and popular *Treatise of Morall Phylosophye* (1547); Nashe would especially appreciate the blend of fictional prose narrative and religious satire in Baldwin's *Beware the Cat.*

[10] For example, in the lines immediately following Nashe's *"Tibault"* passage, Nashe cites Harvey's *"Muske is a sweete curtezan, and sugar and honey daintie hipocrytes"* and spoofs this by addressing Harvey's metaphors as "Madame Muske, . . . your worships, Master Sugar & Master Honie" (3:51).

[11] For the meaning of "Tybalt" and other related issues, see my article, "'Myself Condemned and Myself Excus'd': Tragic Effects in *Romeo and Juliet,*" *Studies in Philology* 88 (1991): 352-54.

[12] For Nashe's playful use of "prince" and his disdain of princely language, see 3:24, 3:103; *The Unfortunate Traveller,* 2:209-10. Of the many times Shakespeare uses "prince," only once is it meant to be witty, in Berowne's *jeu d'esprit* on the paradoxical giant-dwarf Dan Cupid, "Dread Prince of Plackets, King of Codpieces" (*LLL,* 3.1.184). As Evans (5) notes, this play's revised version of 1597 may be influenced by *Romeo and Juliet.* Moreover, Shakespeare's precise description of Cupid here may be influenced by Nashe's similar description of Harvey in *Have with You* as *"Cod-pisse Kinko,* and Sir *Murdred* of placards" (3:129), a passage to be examined later. See Richard David, ed., *Love's Labor's Lost,* 4th ed. New Arden Shakespeare (London: Methuen, 1951), xxix-xxx, xxxix-xliv, for how *Love's Labor's Lost* also might recall the Harvey-Nashe quarrel.

[13] The mere appearance of the names of "Grimalkin" and "Robin Goodfellow" in Baldwin's text cannot serve as persuasive proof that Shakespeare knew this text; these names are too common by the time of Shakespeare's *Macbeth* (1.1.8, "grey Malkin") and *A Midsummer Night's Dream* (2.1.34). See Ringler and Flachmann, 11, 16, 60; Holden, 31, 35.

[14] I have not been able to locate this reference in Nashe's works.

[15] See Tobin, "Nashe and the Texture of *Romeo and Juliet,*" 169. Nashe also refers to their quarrel as such "bandyings as had past bewixt vs" and his "strappadoing" and "torturing" Gabriel Harvey (3:91).

[16] Nashe uses "scratching" in a general sense to signify fighting, as well as the construction "scratche with" used later in his text (3:92), but no weapons are specified in either of these passages. Shakespeare never uses the construction "scratche with." He does use, however, Nashe's general sense of scratching as fighting but embellishes it.

[17] Cf. *The Rape of Lucrece:* "And was afeared to scratch her wicked foe" (line 1035) with her "poor hand" (line 1030), but "And with my knife scratch out the angry eyes / Of all the Greeks that are thine enemies" (lines 1469-70). See *The Rape of Lucrece,* in *The Riverside Shakespeare,* ed. G. Blakemore Evans et al. (Boston: Houghton Mifflin, 1974), 1733-34, 1738; all quotations from Shakespeare's works, except *Romeo and Juliet,* are to this edition and are cited parenthetically in the text.

[18] See *OED,* "Fiddlestick," sb. 2.

[19] See Evans, 3.1.40n., 4.5.110-11nn.

[20] For the accusation Nashe is a "piperly makeplay, or makebate," see Richard Harvey's *Lamb of God* (1590), in McKerrow, *Nashe,* 5:180.

[21] Baldwin might serve again as an inspiration to Nashe because in his *Beware the Cat* "Catch-rat" is the name of the cat who falsely accuses "Mousesleyer" (51). For a later ballad (1615?) on the foreign travels of the rat-catcher, see STC 207411. We should also note that the word "rat" comes as a surprise in Shakespeare's context because his three other rodent references in the play, both before and after this scene, are to the "mouse" (1.4.40, 3.1.100, 3.3.31). Only through Mercutio, whose satiric vocabulary has been influenced most by Nashe's, is "rat" introduced, in "rat-catcher" and in a list of the animals who fight by scratching (3.1.91). Shakespeare figuratively uses "mouse-hunt" (4.4.11) later, and he might have coined "mouse-catcher" here to serve his needs.

[22] For Nashe's other uses of "princox," see 1:44, 205; 2:309.

[23] Shakespeare's figurative usage of "demesnes," likening Rosaline's sexual anatomy of high and adjacent regions to geographical domains, may recall the spirit of his *Venus and Adonis* (lines 229-40).

[24] I surmise that Nashe's figurative use of "demeanes or adiacents" in parallel construction with his quotation from Lily's grammar means that Harvey abortively imitates verses from that place or from its adjoining places or "domains." But Nashe may also intend a bawdy play on "asse" as "arse."

[25] See Evans's notes on 2.4.77-82. As Evans notes, editors present different glosses for Romeo's line as well as place the stage direction for the Nurse's and Peter's entries either after Romeo's line, as Evans does, or before his line. If the latter choice is adopted, "gear" is usually taken as referring depreciatively to the Nurse's clothes or "stuff" which would accord well with Mercutio's first response to the Nurse and Peter: "Two, two: a shirt and a smock" (2.4.84). Cf. *LLL* 5.2.303: "disguised like Muscovites, in shapeless gear."

[26] See *OED,* "Gear," *sb.* 8, *sb.*5b.

[27] See *The Rape of Lucrece,* "Distress likes dumps when time is kept with" (1127); *Two Gentlemen of Verona,* "To their instruments tune a deploring dump" (3.2.84). Even William Painter's English version of the Romeo and Juliet story from Boaistuau uses "sorrowful dumpes"; see Evans, 174 n. 104.

[28] See Tobin, "Texture of *Romeo and Juliet,*" 166-67, 174 n. 15; "Nashe," 161-62. "Roperipe" appears in Q1; McKerrow notes the possible parallel between Shakespeare's "ropery/roperipe" and Nashe's *"Rupen-rope"* (4.334-35). Evans compares "ropery" (knavery) to "roperipe" ("ready for the hangman"), 112 n. 122. Cf. *The Taming of the Shrew,* 1.2.112; *The Comedy of Errors,* 4.4.90.

[29] Cf. Nashe's use of "ropes" (3:127). Cf. Nashe's *Strange News* (1592) for this motif in his quarrel with Harvey: "Maister *Birdes* Letter shall not repriue you from the ladder. . . . *Ergo,* he is no Rope-maker" (1:274); cf. "the Ladder" (2:304).

[30] I am indebted to Alan C. Dessen for the information that all the references to ladders of cords or ropes in extant English dramatic literature postdate Shakespeare's use.

[31] See Olin H. Moore, *The Legend of Romeo and Juliet* (Columbus: Ohio State University Press, 1950), 77-78, 90, 135. Cf. Brooke's "corden ladder . . . with two strong and crooked yron hookes," in Geoffrey Bullough, *Narrative and Dramatic Sources of Shakespeare* (London: Routledge and Kegan Paul, 1957), vol. 1, lines 775-76, 813-14, 832. Cf. the other possible English source, William Painter, trans., *The Palace of Pleasure,* ed. Joseph Jacobs (1890; rpt. New York: Dover Publications, 1966), "Rhomeo and Iulietta," 3:92-93, 99.

[32] Shakespeare's use of the rope ladder also cultivates directional imagery (ascent/descent) native to the Elizabethan public theater. "Ascent" for the lovers understandably has life-associated connotations, even in Friar Lawrence's knowing "lamentation" for Juliet (4.5.71-74), and "descent" usually conveys death-associated nuances, as in separation and death itself (cf. 3.5.54-56, 5.1.20). Thomas Middleton reveals his understanding of Shakespeare's use of this prop in his own dramatic parody of *Romeo and Juliet,* his play *The Familie of Love* (London, 1608), sig. D3v: "a ladder of Ropes; if she would let it downe; for my life he would hang himselfe in't."

[33] See William Rossky, "Imagination in the English Renaissance: Psychology and Poetic," *Studies in the Renaissance* 5 (1958): 49-73.

[34] Sir Philip Sidney, *A Defence of Poetry,* ed. J. H. Van Dorsten (Oxford: Oxford University Press, 1966), 24, 32, 36. See Rossky, 49-53, 73. Cf. John Milton, *Paradise Lost,* ed. Merritt Y. Hughes (New York: Odyssey Press, 1962), 5.100-21.

[35] For the complicated problem of dating the composition of Nashe's *Have with You,* see McKerrow, *Nashe,* 4:302; cf. Evans, 3. Nashe indicates that he has been gestating this text since "*the hanging of* Lopus [1594]," although not working on it continually (3:18). As Evans

rightly notes, we cannot be certain which Candlemas Term (23 January to 12 February) of what year Nashe has in mind for the projected publication (3:133; Evans, 3 n. 5). However, two other references have gone unnoticed. Nashe declares he is half done with a comedy on Harvey, to be acted "in *Candlemas Tearme*" (3:114), and he concludes by promising "more battring engins" against Harvey that he will *"keepe backe till the next Tearme"* (3:139). Perhaps this comedy is what Nashe intends when he refers to writing for stage (and press) in his letter to Cotton, dated about September 1596 (5:28). Nashe's references, occurring at the end of his text, to anticipated publication in Candlemas Term of different works on the same satiric topic suggest that he has one specific Candlemas Term in mind, probably that of 1596/97. Perhaps Nashe's state of poverty, always a misfortune in his life but particularly acute at the time he writes Cotton, prompted an earlier than anticipated publication of *Have with You,* perhaps shortly after September 1596.

[36] See E. K. Chambers, *The Elizabethan Stage,* 4 vols. (Oxford: Clarendon Press, 1923), 2:195.

[37] Tobin, "Texture of *Romeo and Juliet,*" 167-68, 172.

[38] See David, ed., *Love's Labor's Lost,* xxxix-xliii.

[39] Nashe links himself to nimble Mercury in his critique of Gabriel Harvey's style that Nashe feels is opposite to his own: "his inuention is ouerweaponed; he hath some good words, but he cannot writhe them and tosse them to and fro nimbly, or so bring them about, that hee maye make one streight thrust at his enemies face" (1:282). Nashe's imagery of the fight is again revealed when he declares Harvey is resentful of this Aretine-like "new kind of a quicke fight" because Harvey's "decrepite slow-mouing capacitie cannot fadge with" it (1:283).

[40] See Joseph A. Porter, *Shakespeare's Mercutio, His History and Drama* (Chapel Hill: University of North Carolina Press, 1988), 143-63. For Porter's analysis of Mercury's importance for Mercutio, see pp. 11-94. We should also note that Nashe associates the planet Mercury with nimbleness, such as characterizes his own style. See Nashe, 1:268; n. 39 above.

[41] See Eric Partridge, *Shakespeare's Bawdy,* rev. ed. (New York: Dutton, 1969), "et cetera," 101-02; Evans, 91 nn. 36, 38. Cf. *OED,* "Medlar," 2. Porter says Partridge avoids "mention of even heterosexual sodomy" (161), but in the revised edition of Partridge's book he explicitly analyzes and argues against that.

[42] Rembert Dodoens, trans. Henry Lyte, *A Niewe Herball; or Historie of Plantes* (Antwerp: Henry Loë, 1578), sigs. Ppp-Ppp^{v}. Cf. John Gerard, *The Herball; or Generall Historie of Plantes* (London: John Norton, 1597), 1265-66.

[43] Cf. Nashe's jest about Harvey's bawdy "striking" pun and truculent posture with Queen Elizabeth's "Maids of Honour" (3:75).

[44] Robert E. Knoll, for example, suggests the "only love [Marlowe] knew was self-fulfillment," despite being a cynosure among his contemporaries (see Knoll, *Christopher Marlowe* [New York: Twayne, 1969], 23).

[45] For Nashe's influence on Shakespeare's use of dreams and Queen Mab, see my essay, "No 'Vain Fantasy': Shakespeare's Refashioning of Nashe for Dreams and Queen Mab," in *"Romeo and Juliet": Text, Context, Interpretation,* ed. Jay L. Halio (Newark: University of Delaware Press, 1995).

[46] Regarding the complex issue of tragic responsibility given contemporary duello ethic, see my essay, "'Draw, If You Be Men': Saviolo's Significance for *Romeo and Juliet,*" *Shakespeare Quarterly* 45 (1994): 163-89.

[47] For this combat, see Mark Eccles, *Christopher Marlowe in London* (Cambridge: Harvard University Press, 1934), 9-14, 59-60, 171. Eccles suggests Marlowe was probably fighting Bradley on behalf of his friend Watson (59, 171). Despite the friendship between Marlowe and Watson, Eccles's supposition of this motive seems unlikely because Marlowe desists and does not risk coming to Watson's aid even though his friend is severely wounded because he has intervened, thereby relieving Marlowe. According to the legal proceedings, Watson fights only in self-defense, which is the reason the coroner's jury acquits Watson of murder or manslaughter.

[48] See Bruce R. Smith, *Homosexual Desire in Shakespeare's England: A Cultural Poetics* (Chicago: University of Chicago Press, 1991), esp. chap. 2, "Combatants and Comrades," 31-77.

[49] Cf. McKerrow, *Nashe,* 5:83, 86.

[50] McKerrow argues that Harvey probably knew of *Christ's Tears* but had not actually read it before he penned his most vicious attacks (5:98-102).

[51] I think Hibbard is right to suggest that Nashe's literary model for his only verse narrative is not the Ovidian epyllion, despite his borrowing from Ovid's *Ars Amatoria,* but is rather the racy *fabliaux* in Chaucer's manner.

[52] Cf. Nashe's two other references to "sodomitrie," 3:177, 278. Measuring Nashe's boast about his prolific writing against the size of his printed corpus, McKerrow suggests perhaps much of Nashe's work remained in manuscript and is now lost; see 5:136.

[53] Jonathan Goldberg argues that Gabriel Harvey's homosexuality was an "open secret." See "Colin to Hobbinol: Spenser's Familiar Letters," *South Atlantic Quarterly* 88 (1989): 192-220. When Nashe tenders his apology to Harvey in *Christ's Tears,* however, he acknowledges Harvey's "courteous well gouerned behauior" (2:12). Harvey's Puritanism may have tempered his private life because in *Have with You* Nashe seems delighted to have occasion to twit Harvey about licentiousness by using Harvey's "gentlewoman" against him. Nashe also attempts to ridicule Harvey by claiming his motive for his English hexameters "was his falling in loue with *Kate Cotton,* and *Widdowes* his wife, the Butler of *Saint Johns*" so that "*Gabriell* was alwayes in loue. . . . " (3:81).

[54] Grosart tries to gloss *"Lusher"* as if it were a word (perhaps "lasher") instead of a proper name as the context suggests (3:104). McKerrow suggests the author is not Gabriel Harvey but Richard Lichfield (5:107).

[55] *King Lear,* 4.6.111. However, the mad Lear's perspective on the penalty for adultery is counterbalanced in the play by the punishment inflicted upon his patriarchal counterpart in suffering, Gloucester: "The dark and vicious place where thee [Edmund] he got / Cost him his eyes" (5.3.173-74).

[56] Cf. Nashe's ridiculously funny descriptions of Harvey's book and person (3:36-38). Nashe also accuses Harvey of stealing his railing terms and of rehearsing, but never answering, accusations (3:122-25).

[57] See Kenneth Muir, *The Sources of Shakespeare's Plays* (London: Methuen, 1977), 1; G. K. Hunter, "Shakespeare's Reading," *A New Companion to Shakespeare Studies,* ed. Kenneth Muir and S. Schoenbaum (Cambridge: Cambridge University Press, 1971), 60.

Source: "Nashe as 'Monarch of Witt' and Shakespeare's *Romeo and Juliet,*" in *Texas Studies in Literature and Language,* Vol. 37, No. 3, Fall, 1995, pp. 314-43.

The First Quarto of *Hamlet*: Reforming Widow Gertred

Dorothea F. Kehler, *San Diego State University*

Critics who compare the First Quarto's Gertred with Gertrard of the Second Quarto and Gertrude of the Folio have for the most part found Gertred more "sympathetic."[1] Once informed that her new husband is a murderer, she commits herself unequivocally to Hamlet's cause, promising to keep up connubial appearances only to deceive Claudius. Rather than another variation on the Shakespearean category "woman with divided loyalties," like *King John*'s Blanche, *Antony and Cleopatra*'s Octavia, or *Hamlet*'s Gertrard/Gertrude, Gertred is now all mother. Moreover, throughout the play she has been pious, reserved, passive, unexceptional; who would not have his widow so? Although the First Quarto does not resolve questions about Gertred's sexual behavior or erase the story's inherent misogyny, it does present a queen who differs so significantly from her counterparts that she impresses critics as the site of greatest difference between the variant texts.[2]

Of the three texts, Q1, first discovered in the 1820s, is the most enigmatic, retaining its notorious distinction as the best known of the "bad" quartos, even as that term is challenged.[3] To adumbrate the most problematic features of Q1: signs of proofreading are few and many passages are garbled; prose lines are capitalized, thus suggesting verse; verse lines are frequently mislineated (printing, e.g., two pentameter lines as a hexameter and a tetrameter); the quality of the writing is radically uneven; and plotting is inadequate and inconsistent. When Q1 is compared with the other texts, additional problems appear: it is little more than half the length of F and Q2; names and titles are inconsistent (in the case of Polonius and Reynaldo, entirely different); several scenes differ in placement or content (for example, Hamlet ponders whether "To be, or not to be" and raves at Ophelia before rather than after he first encounters Gilderstone and Rossencraft or the players, and Laertes does not lead a rebellion against the king); and in a scene unique to Q1, the queen learns from Horatio, who trusts her loyalty to Hamlet, of Claudius's attempt on Hamlet's life.[4]

Despite these problematic features, the quarto's title page claims to offer the play "As it hath beene diuerse times acted by his Highnesse seruants in the Cittie of London: as also in the two Vniuersities of Cambridge and Oxford, and else-where." Granted that the title page may be no more than an advertising puff, unacceptable as hard evidence of Q1's performance history;[5] that *Hamlet* on the page can only approximate individual *Hamlet*s on the stage; and that theatrical researchers have yet to discover Q1's performance sites "else-where." Notwithstanding, even in our own time Q1 has proven to be a playable text,[6] and chances are that it was indeed played as the title page claims, not only before but also after publication. But where else besides "the Cittie of London" and the "Vniuersities"? Questions about playing venues for Q1 are, I suggest, linked to the characterization of Gertred, the cultural production of a particular historical moment. To that end, my essay contextualizes Gertred's representation, seeing her as a quasi-allegorical object lesson in the consequences of rejecting celibate widowhood. Hers is a story, I argue, that validates the deeply rooted, lingering prejudice against remarrying widows. Where Q1 was played enters into this story.

I. Widows and Remarriage

Although some twenty-five to thirty-five percent of sixteenth- and seventeenth-century English marriages were remarriages,[7] censuring remarriage was tantamount to a convention for early modern writers. Pernicious clichés about widows (but not widowers) are found in polemics, household manuals, and plays of the period[8] and can be explained politically, in that, of the socially endorsed roles available to women—maid, wife, widow[9]—the last is most perplexing for patriarchal theory. Solanio's quip in *The Merchant of Venice* about a hypocritical widow who "made her neighbors believe she wept for the death of a third husband" (3.1.9-10)[10] reminds us that widowhood is problematic not only because the weaker vessel survives the stronger but because she may remarry, thus, some would say, cuckolding her former husband(s), albeit belatedly. In consequence, remarrying widows are liable to be figured as "lusty widows."

Of some thirty-one widows in Shakespeare, ten remarry—Elizabeth Woodville, Anne Neville, Tamora, Hortensio's wife, Hostess Quickly, Gertrude, Mistress Overdone, Cleopatra, Octavia, and Cymbeline's Queen; one might also include *Lear's* Regan, who intended to remarry. These, lusty or not, were more liable to wed calamity than joy. Six of them die—or seven, if we include Regan. Two of them are killed by their husbands (Anne by Richard III and Gertrude by Claudius), and two die by their own hands (Cleopatra and Cymbeline's Queen). For the survivors the future is less than reassuring: Elizabeth Woodville, widowed yet again, has also lost her sons and brother; Hortensio's wife, having publicly discomfited her new husband, has gotten the marriage off to an unpromising start;

Mistress Overdone, nine times a bride but "Overdone by the last" (*Measure for Measure,* 2.1.202), remains in prison; and Octavia, deserted by Antony, is an object of pity in Rome. Little wonder that Paulina remains silent when Camillo is thrust upon her. Because remarrying widows consistently fare ill, genre as the determinant of their destinies seems less relevant than a residual ideology of revered celibacy which the widows have violated, even though both desire and economics encouraged the Elizabethan social practice of remarriage.

In Chaucer's "Merchant's Tale," while we are invited to scoff at January's wishes for his young wife, May, his words nevertheless voice a widespread medieval ideal of widowhood:

> For neither after his deeth nor in his lyf
> Ne wolde he that she were love ne wyf,
> But evere lyve as wydwe in clothes blake,
> Soul as the turtle that lost hath hire make.[11]

These lines echo Catholic discourse on proper behavior for the devout. Following biblical, apocryphal, and patristic writings, the Church allowed but denigrated remarriage. In Leviticus 21:14 the widow is grouped with the divorced woman, the profane woman, and the harlot as an inappropriate wife. Paul honored pious matrons who were "widows indeed"; those over sixty who had been married only once were deemed fit to join the congregation (1 Timothy 5:3, 5, 9). Asserting that Jerome implied a similar binarism when he wrote "Fly the company of those widdowes, who are widdowes not in will, but of a kind of necessity," Father Fulvius Androtius, a Jesuit, describes "the Mantle and the Ring," a rite honoring the patristic view and celebrated in England from about 660 AD until the establishment of the Anglican Church.[12] In this rite widows who had remained celibate for a number of years after the death of their first husbands knelt before the high alter during the Mass. After vowing never to remarry on pain of punishment by the Church, each widow was clothed by the bishop in a consecrated black mantle. On her fourth finger he placed a silver or gold wedding band, and over her head a veil. The bishop then blessed the widow as a sacred person, and *Te Deum laudamus* was sung before the widow was accompanied to her home by two pious matrons.[13] It is noteworthy that her habitlike apparel did not signify the widow's mourning for the loss of her husband but rather her perpetual mourning for sin—her own and that of others. That the celibacy of a widow who had been unhappily married would be more an act of will than of sorrow presented no problem.[14] Inclusivity promoted participation in the rite.

Both Torquato Tasso and Juan Luis Vives wrote out of this Catholic tradition of celibacy for the widowed. Although unwilling to blame those who remarry, in "The Father of the Family" (1580) Tasso instructs widowers as well as widows that "the happiest are still those who have been bound by the marriage knot only once in their lives"; for Tasso "once the knot that binds a soul to a body is dissolved, that particular soul cannot be joined to any other body . . . and therefore it also seems fitting that the woman or man whose first marriage knot has been dissolved by death should not form a second."[15] Writing under Catherine of Aragon for the edification of Mary, Vives, on this issue a doctrinal conservative, expresses similar sentiments. In his influential *Instruction of a Christen Woman,* written in 1523 and translated from the Latin some six years later, Vives, like Tasso, holds that marriage is a spiritual union continuing after death.[16] A truly Christian widow sought no second husband but Christ. Approvingly, Vives quotes Jerome's advice to Furia "on the Duty of Remaining a Widow," agreeing that lust is the real motive of remarrying widows, whatever other reasons they may allege: "For none of you [widows] take a husband but to the intent that she will lie with him nor except her lust prick her."[17] Unlike the lusty widow, the celibate widow was serviceable to the community both as a philanthropist (if wealthy) and as an intercessor. As Androtius wrote:

> It was an ancient custome in our Iland (and the same continueth in some parts of *Germany* vntill this day) that in tyme of warre, plagues, famyne, or of any publicke necessity, there were in many Citties and Townes a certaine number of widdowes ordayned to watch & pray continually, night and day, in the Churches, by their turnes or courses, one or more togeather: because it was held, that their prayers were of more efficacy, and power with Almighty God, to asswage his wrath, then the prayers of other common people, as persons dedicated wholy to his seruice, by the obseruation of Continency, in their Chaste, and Holy widdowhood.[18]

The Epistle Dedicatory reminds readers that "Virginity, and Widdowhood, haue euer been accounted Sisters, and betroathed to the same Eternall Spouse Christ Iesus,"[19] and Androtius himself, looking back over the past five hundred years, takes pride in the more than thirty widowed English queens who either became nuns or lived the remainder of their lives as secular chaste widows.[20] It is the latter choice that Gertred seems to be gesturing toward once apprised of Claudius's crime.

Even after the Reformation stripped marriage of its status as a sacrament, many sixteenth-century English writers were loath to abandon earlier attitudes. John Webster, the probable author of the thirty-two New Characters appearing in the sixth edition of Overbury's *Characters* (1615), set "A vertuous Widdow" in opposition to "An ordinarie Widdow."[21] Shunning remarriage, the "vertuous Widdow," whose celibacy is a second virginity, garners up her heart in her children and her Maker. Of particular importance to *Hamlet,* neither her children's persons nor their inheritance is at the mercy of a new husband or step-siblings. Several generations after the first edition of Vives's *Instruction* appeared, Middleton wrote *More Dissemblers Besides Women* (c. 1623), in which the Duke of Milan instructs his wife,

> *For once to marry*
> *Is honourable in woman, and her ignorance*
> *Stands for a virtue, coming new and fresh;*
> *But second marriage shows desire in flesh;*
> *Thence lust, and heat, and common custom grows. . . .*
>
> (2.1.76-80)[22]

The Duke may have been self-serving, but he voices persistent conventional sentiments.

Most Protestant thinkers and polemicists, perhaps suspicious of celibacy as smacking of Catholicism, or fearing fornication, or desiring male control over the widow's wealth, knew in principle that they should feel differently. Even while urging remarriage, however, they could not escape its age-old coding as a betrayal of the deceased. The aporia between Sir Walter Ralegh's two statements on this point exemplifies an ineradicable ambivalence within the culture. In 1603, expecting to be executed and realizing that his wife would need protection from his enemies, he advised her to remarry, "for that will be best for you, both in respect of God and the world."[23] But later he was to cringe at the prospect of a Ralegh widow's wedded bliss and counseled his son, as one testator to another, "if she [the son's wife] love again, let her not enjoy her second love in the same bed wherein she loved thee. . . . "[24] Ambivalence toward remarriage was most apt to become condemnation when widows no longer young thought to love again. Their breach of a generational boundary might offend both Catholics and Protestants, but especially the former, taught to prize celibacy. Reformed preachers, on the other hand, devising a theology out of difference, were prone to foster Thomas Becon's belief "that second marriages were never disallowed 'tyl the Deuyl and the Pope began to beare rule, whiche enuye no State so much, as the holy state of honorable Matrimonye.'"[25]

II. The Widow Gertred

Significantly, whatever Q1's relationship to Q2 and F *Hamlet*—whether Q1 was itself re-formed from an early version of the play and precedes Q2 or is a later version of the Q2 or F texts—an early modern audience would find little in Gertred's onstage words or actions to substantiate the prejudice against remarriage. So dependent is Gertred, Claudius's pale accessory and echo, that she appears foreordained to remarry. Her precipitate second marriage casts her as a lusty widow, but despite the stereotype, her speeches and actions are characterized almost exclusively by meekness and silence. For one thing, Gertred is neutralized politically, being largely overlooked by Claudius and slighted by Corambis.[26] Yet silence seems as much native to her as imposed by others' disregard. Gertrard/Gertrude's plea to Hamlet (Q2/F1TLN 248-53 and 255-56) to end his mourning does not appear in Q1;[27] Gertred speaks only two lines in the entire scene, begging Hamlet to stay (Q1CLN 194-95). Her words follow and summarize two longer speeches by Claudius in which he entreats Hamlet to remain in Denmark as "the Ioy and halfe heart of your mother" (Q1CLN 176), this phrase itself underlining Gertred's domestic, maternal role. Welcoming Rossencraft and Gilderstone, Gertred speaks but one line of thanks (Q1CLN 734), echoing Claudius; she greets Corambis's announcement that he has discovered the cause of Hamlet's madness with "God graunt he hath" (Q1CLN 746), a sentiment both exemplary and concise. She urges the same concision on Corambis—"Good my Lord be briefe" (Q1CLN 781)—and exits at his request (Q1CLN 833). When Claudius promises lasting thanks to Rossencraft and Gilderstone, thinking them responsible for Hamlet's high spirits, Gertred again ventures no more than a two-line echo (Q1CLN 1182-83). In another two lines she agrees to see the play, saying "it ioyes me at the soule / He is inclin'd to any kinde of mirth" (Q1CLN 1186-87). At Corambis's and Claudius's request, she also agrees to summon Hamlet and question him while Corambis eavesdrops on his reply: "With all my heart, soone will I send for him" (Q1CLN 1202). No small part of why Gertred impresses us as "a relatively passive mirror of events, a surface without independent motives for action,"[28] is her possessing in quantity the silence thought so proper to womankind: foremost among "The infallible markes of a vertuous woman," writes Barnabe Rich in 1613, are "bashfullnes, [and] silence. . . . She must not bee a vaine talker."[29]

In addition, Rich counsels the virtuous woman to be "tractable to her husband."[30] Her own subjectivity undeveloped, Gertred is scripted as tractable to everyone; she is a peacemaker as well. To placate Laertes, she tries to explain away Hamlet's behavior at Ofelia's grave; she concurs with Claudius's feigned desire that Laertes and Hamlet reconcile: "God grant they may" (Q1CLN 2082). She disobeys Claudius only as she attempts to protect him from Laertes. She does *not* disobey when she drinks from the poisoned cup; in Q1 Gertred drinks *before* Claudius orders her not to:

> *Queene* Here *Hamlet,* thy mother drinkes to thee.
>
> *Shee drinkes.*
>
> *King* Do not drinke *Gertred:* O t'is the poysned cup!
>
> (Q1CLN 2160-62)

Unlike Gertrard/Gertrude of Q2 and F1, Gertred could never be construed as a conscious site of resistance to social expectations.[31] She is not self-willed; she makes no suggestions; and she is quick to fall in with the plans of others. But so tractable a wife to her second husband logically must have been no less compliant as the widow of her first. The virtue of female submissiveness proves itself a two-edged sword when the ideological goal is marital fidelity undaunted by the husband's death. Gertred's behavior throughout the play beckons us to read her acquiescence to a questionable and sudden second marriage as the corollary of an otherwise praiseworthy habit of obedience to male authority.

Just as Gertred's actions are marked by compliance, so her language is informed by piety. She typically alludes to her prayers and her soul, invokes God and heaven, and makes sacred vows. Her protestation of innocence is an oath: "But as I haue a soule, I sweare by heauen, / I neuer knew of this most horride murder" (Q1CLN 1582-83). She calls on God (as Bel-imperia, from whom the lines are lifted, does *not*) to witness her loyalty to Hamlet:

> *Hamlet,* I vow by that maiesty,
> That knowes our thoughts, and lookes into our hearts,
> I will conceale, consent, and doe my best,
> What stratagem soe're thou shalt deuise.
> (Q1CLN 1594-97)

When Claudius hopes "to heare good newes from thence [England] ere long, / If euery thing fall out to our content" (Q1CLN 1678-79), Gertred devoutly observes, "God grant it may, heau'ns keep my *Hamlet* safe" (Q1CLN 1681). In fact, G. B. Shand observes that, "although her role is just over half the size of the Q2/F1 Gertrude, she has three times the number of references to God, heaven, her soul, and prayer, culminating in this vow to Hamlet [at CLN 1594-97]."[32] All these iterations both sanitize Gertred and associate her with a comfit-maker's wife, making it difficult for an audience to believe that she would have committed adultery, and underscoring her innocence but for her misguided remarriage.

Silence, obedience, piety—such qualities become all Elizabethan women; when motherly concern and celibacy (a strong possibility for Gertred after the closet scene) are joined to these virtues, we confront the model Catholic widow, a "widow indeed." Gertred's bland words and actions are always decorous—she describes Ofelia's death with no unseemly references to "long Purples" or "liberall Shepheards" (Q2/F1TLN 3161-62)—and always maternal. Gertred stakes her only claim to importance on her position as Hamlet's mother. In her closet Gertred shows the first signs of self-regard when, in reply to Hamlet's stichomythic "Mother, you haue my father much offended," she demands, "How now boy?" (Q1CLN 1498-99). In other words, her sole demand for respect is for deference to her maternal authority. Again, while Gertred's account of the murder of Polonius is similar to that in Q2 and F1, the unique lines "But then he throwes and tosses me about, / As one forgetting that I was his mother" (Q1CLN 1607-8) intimate astonishment that Hamlet could so disregard her parental status. When Hamlet returns to Denmark, she asks Horatio to "command me / A mothers care to him, bid him a while / Be wary of his presence, lest that he / Faile in that he goes about" (Q1CLN 1826-29).[33] When Gertred learns of the fate of Gilderstone and Rossencraft, she thanks heaven for preserving Hamlet, sending him "thowsand mothers blessings" (Q1CLN 1843). Offering Hamlet her napkin to wipe his sweaty face is another gesture of concern. Gertred toasts her son, saying "Here *Hamlet,* thy mother drinkes to thee" (Q1CLN 2160)—"thy mother" rather than "The Queene" (Q2/F1TLN 3758). Overall Q1 presents a cohesive enough but neutral character who is neither temptress nor villain; she does and says what is expected of her and little more. In this regard Q1 seems less misogynistic than Q2/F1, but because the price of being more "sympathetic" than her counterparts is a lack of vitality and distinctiveness, one might more accurately conclude that Q1 merely wears its misogyny with a difference.

Gertred's behavior may be well intentioned and in keeping with Elizabethan social codes, but it is not entirely appropriate to a queen regnant. Pitying the mad Ofelia, "poore maide" (Q1CLN 1684), Gertred does not at first refuse to see her, as in Q2/F1, or stop to consider the political wisdom of seeing her, as in F1; Gertred is both less tortured and less politically sophisticated than her counterparts. A significant discrepancy between Q1 and Q2/F1 is Q1's omission of the speech in which Claudius describes Gertrude as "Th'Imperiall Ioyntresse of this warlike State" (Q2/F1TLN 179-203), a queen he married while still in mourning but—he claims—with the consent of his advisers. Gertred's rank seems secondary rather than integral to her role; compared with the business of Norway, Claudius's marriage to Gertred seems inconsequential since undeserving of comment. Again, in Q1's prayer scene Claudius does not speak of murdering for "My Crowne, mine owne Ambition, and my Queene" (Q2/F1TLN 2331). Q1's audience would not likely conclude that longing for Gertred led Claudius to kill his brother; rather, she becomes a benefit incidental to the crown. Neither is Q1's Gertred "so coniunctiue [Q2 concliue] to my life and soule; / That as the Starre moues not but in his Sphere, / I could not but by her" (Q2/F1TLN 3022-24). In place of Gertrard/Gertrude's power over Claudius, Q1 Hamlet's description of Claudius's villainous appearance intimates Claudius's power over Gertred: "A looke fit for a murder and a rape, / A dull dead hanging looke, and a hell-bred eie, / To affright children and amaze the world" (Q1CLN 1528-30). Hamlet believes that his mother was cozened by a devil (Q1CLN 1532).

But whether she was cozened or not, Hamlet's soliloquy over "this too much grieu'd and sallied flesh" (Q1CLN 202) and the Ghost's diatribe against his "most seeming vertuous Queene" (Q1CLN 516), although compressed, level every charge against Gertred that is found in the other *Hamlet* texts. Gertred was seduced not by Claudius's "wicked Wit" (Q2/F1TLN 731) but by his "wicked will," his desire—that "and gifts!" (Q1CLN 515). Yet what would a queen lack, what requirements of hers are we to imagine as having been in such short supply, that Claudius's gifts would so easily move her? Surely if we are to believe the Ghost's account of his brother's successful courtship, a courtship in which Claudius "bought" Gertred's love, it is important to note that the gifts in themselves could not matter except as signifiers of Claudius's desire, a reassurance to Gertred that she is not yet the "matron" (Q1CLN 1547; Q2/F1TLN 2458) that in all three texts Hamlet would have her be, whose "appetite . . . is in the waine," whose "blood runnes backeward now from whence it came" (Q1CLN 1544-45). But clinging to youth and marrying while newly bereft and most vulnerable to Claudius's will do not mitigate Gertred's fault. As in Q2 and F1, she is likened to "Lust . . . [that would] prey on garbage" (Q1CLN 519-21). Only if Gertred assists Hamlet's vengeance can her "infamy" die with Claudius (Q1CLN 1593). Yet while the play's audience, familiar with the trope of the lusty widow and positioned to identify with the protagonist, may accede to the assessment of Gertred they hear from Hamlet and the Ghost, the queen they actually witness is apt to strike them as a basically decent, rather ordinary woman, able to accept guidance from her son and willing to mend her ways. In particular this latter response might well prevail with playgoers who—unlike us—do not already know the Gertrard/ Gertrude of Q2/F1 conflations.

Although the character of Gertred appears straightforwardly drawn when compared to the queens in Q2 and F1, her representation is still complicated by underlying sexual issues. Was Gertred—however religious and domesticated—an adulteress? Although Q1's Ghost charges Claudius with "incestuous" acts (Q1CLN 514), he does not, like the Ghost in Q2/F1, immediately follow this adjective with "adulterate" (Q2/F1TLN 729). And yet in his soliloquy Claudius refers to "the adulterous fault I haue committed" (Q1CLN 1462). Does he mean that, as in Belleforest, he slept with the queen before killing his brother or that he merely wished to? Perhaps the king follows the notion of adultery expounded in Matthew 5:28: "But I say vnto you, y[t] whosoeuer loketh on a woma[n] to lust after her, hathe cõmitted adulterie w[t] her already in his heart."[34] Hamlet also admonishes Gertred to "Forbeare the adulterous bed to night" (Q1CLN 1589). This evidence suggests that the Q1 text may be using *adulterous* interchangeably with *incestuous,* an incestuous union being adulterous in the sense defined by the *Oxford English Dictionary* as "spurious, counterfeit, adulterate" or in any way reprehensible.[35]

There is also the question of whether Gertred sleeps with Claudius after the closet scene. Since the *Hamlet* texts don't provide a definitive answer, directors often signify their decisions through costuming; a high neckline and somber gown make one point, décolletage another. Is Gertred, like Richard III's Anne, reluctantly flattered to think, whether rightly or not, that a man would kill her husband to gain her? Does Claudius please Gertred? Hamlet draws him as not only a moral but a physical monster yet insists that Gertred lives "in the incestuous *pleasure* of his bed" (Q1CLN 1535, my emphasis). The paradox is explicated by Steven Mullaney in his analysis of the mother/son dynamics of Q2/F1 *Hamlet.* Mullaney sees Hamlet as obsessively disgusted with "Gertrude's *aging* sexuality, conceived at times as a contradiction in terms, at times as a violation of [Gertrude's] own body akin in its unnaturalness to a rebellion in the body politic: hers is a passion that 'canst mutine in a matron's bones' . . . at once unimaginable and yet impossible not to imagine and visualize in graphic detail."[36] For Hamlet, in all three texts of the play, his mother's sexuality is perverse, hence her perverse pleasure in his monstrous uncle.

Gertred's integrity is also under assault from Q1's unique plot twist. In order to "conceale, consent, and doe my best, / What stratagem soe're thou [Hamlet] shalt deuise" (Q1CLN 1596-97), she must "soothe and please him [Claudius] for a time" (Q1CLN 1820). Compelled to dissimulate, she recalls *Titus Andronicus's* "High-witted Tamora," resolved "to gloze with all" (4.4.35), thus deceiving Titus: "For I can smooth and fill his aged ears / With golden promises" (ll.96-97). In fact, Tamora and Cymbeline's wicked Queen are also remarried widows, reprehensible not least for dissimulating with their husbands in a patriarchal society, with their sovereigns in a monarchical one. Gertred undeniably has need of guile once she knows Claudius to be the murderer of his brother and the potential murderer of her son, but the hypocrisy to which she pledges herself is an unstable indicator of moral fiber. The action of Q1 may be more straightforward than that of the other versions, the queen's role a main cause of Q1's direct telling of the story, but Gertred herself is not represented as direct; the plot allows her repentance but denies her full integrity. The fact that, despite her passivity and blandness, Gertred contains traces of the ambiguity associated with Gertrard/Gertrude demonstrates that the reformed lusty widow is a slippery role. Q1 refuses to negotiate the ramifications of that role, but the tension between the Gertreds of the play's surface and subtext also reminds us that Q1 is a palimpsest in which *Hamlet*'s sources are written over but never entirely obscured.

III. "Else-Where"

From the characterization of Gertred, who behaves much like her counterpart in the play's sources, one might infer that Q1 preceded the later printings of *Hamlet*—the assumption being that the more closely a particular version adheres to its sources, the earlier the text is apt to be.[37] In any event, focusing on Gertred as a step toward unraveling the relationship between the various *Hamlet* texts suggests that wherever else besides "the Cittie of London" and the "Vniuersities" Q1 may have been played, it especially lent itself to performance where ideas about the sacred nature of celibacy and the faithful widow lingered longest. Indisputably, on its surface Q1 holds the queen to a very narrow standard of chastity. Although in all three texts the Dutchesse/Player Queen brands a remarrying widow a murderer—"A second time, I kill my Husband [Q1: Lord that's] dead, / When second Husband kisses me in Bed" (Q2/F1TLN 2052-53; Q1CLN 1327-28)—the Dutchesse's explicit death wish is unique to Q1: "When death takes you, let life from me depart" (CLN 1321).[38] Subject to so demanding a code, Gertred's guilt does not lie in *when* she remarried or *whom* she remarried; that she remarried at all condemns her. By attempting to reform the lusty widow and prodigal mother, by presenting the audience with a good woman gone wrong—"her sex is weake" (Q1CLN 1566)—then showing her the error of remarriage and aligning her with her son, Q1 depicts a queen well suited to audiences dedicated to the old religion and its values, one who could be considered a "Catholic" Gertred.

Keith Wrightson, discussing the general survival of Catholic beliefs and practices in the 1580s and '90s, quotes a Puritan estimate that three out of four English subjects were "'wedded to their old superstition still.'"[39] However exaggerated, given Puritan animosities, that ratio may offer some leads to the locations of "else-where," both before and after the publication of Q1. Whether one favored formal Catholic doctrine or simply craved familiar rites and rituals, nostalgia for the past lent itself to antireform sentiments prepetuating the esteem in which the ideal of celibate widowhood was held. Such sentiments, though shared by people of many shades of Christian belief, were inevitably Catholic in origin, and most likely to appeal to Catholics. Between 1594 and 1603 the Lord Chamberlain's Men are known to have traveled no further north than Cambridge;[40] thus a conservative surmise as to Q1's possible prepublication enactment sites would be confined to those counties in the south and midlands most closely tied to their Catholic past. According to Roland G. Usher, Hereford, Gloucester, Worcester, Cornwall, and southern Wales (Monmouth and Glamorgan) were all heavily Catholic (thirty to forty percent) in 1603.[41] Candidates for "else-where" would include the first four counties, all accessible from London and Oxford, where the title page claims Q1 had been performed.[42] Within those counties, the towns of Gloucester, Worcester, and Leominster had hosted theatrical performances by the Queen's Men between 1583 and 1603. In the last decade of the century, Worcester's Men had also played at Gloucester and Leominster.[43] Could not the Chamberlain's Men have played at one or more of these towns as well?

Also, not without interest is Q1's postpublication history. If the travels of the play were to a marked extent dictated by its affinity with audiences favoring traditional ways of thinking, it would appear likely that Q1 was played in the north, the area of England historically most reluctant to abandon Catholicism. Durham and York were important sites of the 1536 Pilgrimage of Grace; a generation later the peasantry supported the rising of the northern earls—Thomas Percy, seventh earl of Northumberland, and Charles Neville, sixth earl of Westmorland—in another attempt to restore Catholicism. During Elizabeth's reign York could claim more of its sons ordained abroad as priests than any other county; Lancashire, the runner-up, harbored the most recusants.[44] The Corpus Christi play lingered until the 1580s in Newcastle-upon-Tyne,[45] until the end of the century in the Lake District and Lancashire,[46] and until 1605 in Kendal, Westmorland.[47] Westmorland and Cumberland border one of the ecclesiastical divisions of Lancashire, the deanery of Furness; in these counties, as in nearby Durham and Northumberland, many remained if not strongly recusant—a choice that by 1581 nominally entailed impoverishment and imprisonment—minimally Anglican, privately Catholic.[48]

Of course, whether Q1 was acted in the north and, if so, by whom are matters for speculation.[49] Even so, it may be helpful to explore one possibility regarding Q1's provenance by juxtaposing our knowledge of attitudes toward widows against some facts and theories concerning provincial performance. Most companies traveled at least during the summers; outbreaks of plague between 1603 and 1609 compelled the King's Men to travel in 1606, perhaps for as long as half the year. In August of 1606 and again in 1619, the King's Men toured as far afield as Leicester. Between 1609 and 1612 three records attest to their touring further north and west to Shrewsbury, and twice they continued north to Stafford. In 1615 they played at Nottingham and Congleton.[50] While we might expect that, as Shakespeare's company grew measurably more successful, they would have been spared arduous tours to remote locations, the reverse is true. Or rather, as Alan Somerset proposes, touring may have been something of a vacation, and not just a summer one, that paid for itself, as well as a service to the realm which King James expected of "his" players and which the provinces keenly anticipated.[51] REED editor Sally-Beth MacLean concurs: "The appearance, for the first time, of Congleton in Cheshire on the 1615 circuit underlines the addition of a northwestern route through Shrewsbury, which figures frequently in the schedule of the King's Men from 1603 onwards."[52] Regrettably, the titles of the plays the King's Men performed in the north have not survived, and we have no record of any northern productions of *Hamlet*. Yet its performance is not precluded: records are scant, and frequently either the names of the acting companies or the names of the plays performed or both are missing from the municipalities' records.[53] If "strowling" was not necessarily a risky, unpleasant experience that obliged players "to trauel vpon the hard hoofe from village to village for chees & buttermilke,"[54] the King's Men themselves might have taken Q1 *Hamlet* north.

What northern audiences and authorities, by no means monolithic, would have expected of strollers and whether the First Quarto would have succeeded remain subjects for inquiry, but we can be reasonably assured that for nonconformists who remained attached to Catholicism, as opposed to nonconformists of the Puritan persuasion, playgoing was no sin;[55] northern venues inhospitable to Puritan reform persisted in welcoming players well into the 1630s.[56] Thanks to data from the Records of Early English Drama project, we are aware of players traveling north to Carlisle in Cumberland—some thirty-four troupes between 1602 and 1639—and performing at York, Kendal, Durham, Newcastle, and numerous towns and manors in Lancashire, tours in part made possible by the patronage of various noble households (Lowther, Curwen, Howard, and Clifford) that supplemented the payments of town officials.[57] For example, unidentified plays were performed for Richard Shuttleworth in Lancashire's Gawthorpe Hall by Lord Derby's Men in 1609; by Lord Dudley's Men and Lord Mounteagle's Men in 1610, 1612, and 1616; by Lord Stafford's Men (twice), Derby's, and an unknown company in 1617; and by Queen Anne's Men and an unknown company in 1618. The Clifford-family accounts from 1607 to 1639 show the fourth earl of Cumberland and his son Henry, Lord Clifford, being visited by these and other troops of strolling players at their three family seats in the north: Londesborough, slightly east of York; Skipton Castle, not far from Gawthorpe Hall; and Hazelwood Castle, midway between Londesborough and Gawthorpe. Aside from providing room and board, the earl paid £1-£2 to hear a play, and his guests may have added tips; even when he declined performances, he tipped 10s-13s.[58] Gratuities such as these produced further impetus for northern touring. It is true that we have no record of the King's Men going north. But after publication, once in the public domain, Q1 need not have been performed by the King's Men. Rather, any number of companies that customarily toured the north could have played it. Furthermore, the publication of Q2 would not have abrogated the usefulness of Q1 to the King's Men or to any other acting company. The First Quarto is still praised for its theatrical energy despite its pedestrian and often mangled verse; if nothing else, this version of *Hamlet* is fast-moving.

Janis Lull, who accepts the memorial-reconstruction theory, finds that Q1's reporter/author(s), preferring an earlier feudal ethic, were capable of "selectively forgetting parts of *Hamlet* that allude to Protestant ideology."[59] Catholic references common to all the *Hamlet* texts are less problematic in Q1, which seems theologically more of a piece than the other versions of the play. Most Q1 spectators are less bound to feel a Reformation sensibility at war with so important an element as the purgatorial Catholic Ghost, in part because the depiction of the reformed Gertred that an audience most immediately apprehends, the Gertred of the text's surface, is one more aspect of a version of *Hamlet* endorsing an older order of things: the soundness of Pauline doctrine, the wisdom of widowed celibacy. Admittedly, some Catholic playgoers might have preferred a more ambiguous queen on whom they could project the utmost moral deformity, that is, a Gertrard/Gertrude; moreover, to entertain a hypothesis privileging the representation of a single character in order to solve the mystery of an unsupported claim, "acted . . . else-where," requires an act of faith. Nevertheless, if only for lack of sufficient external evidence about Q1, textual critics may find these conjectures useful, Gertred being a focal point of Hamlet's psychic life, and the title-page claim having yet to be disproved. Alan Somerset submits that an important benefit of traveling may have been to free the actors from taking chances on the success of new plays. Instead the actors needed to perform only those plays sure to please.[60] To go a step further, I submit that just as actors may have been typecast, or roles created to suit the talents of specific actors, so playtexts may have been chosen or adapted to "fit" specific audiences. Of course, reforming the lusty widow may not have been a deliberate ploy but rather the inadvertent result of cuts meant to achieve dramatic economy. In such a case we might conclude that if a Catholic audience liked Q1, the (un)reformed Gertred is a prominent part of why they liked it. On the other hand, in light of Gertred's construction and emplotment, together with the selective exercise of forgetting Protestant concepts, it is worth considering the hypothesis that the ideology of Q1 *Hamlet* was strategically finetuned for performance before a particular audience in particular regions.

Notes

My thanks to Professors Alan Dessen, Guy Hamel, and especially Paul Werstine for their responses to an early draft of this paper, written for the session chaired by Kathleen Irace, "Revision and Adaptation in Shakespeare's Two- and Three-Text Plays," at the 1994 annual meeting of the Shakespeare Association of

America, Albuquerque, New Mexico. I am also indebted to my friends Professors Thomas Moisan and Susan Baker for reading my revisions and adaptations.

[1] See, for example, Kathleen Irace, "Origins and Agents Q1 *Hamlet*" in *The* Hamlet *First Published (Q1, 1603): Origins, Form, Intertextualities,* Thomas Clayton, ed. (Netwark: U of Delaware P; London and Toronto: Associated University Presses, 1992), 90-122, esp. 106. Steven Urkowitz finds a more harmonious and trusting relationship between the queen and Hamlet in Q1 than in the alternative texts; see "'Well-sayd olde Mole': Burying Three *Hamlets* in Modern Editions" in *Shakespeare Study Today: The Horace Howard Furness Memorial Lectures,* Georgianna Ziegler, ed. (New York: AMS Press, 1986), 37-70, esp. 48-49.

[2] See, for example, Giorgio Melchiori, "Hamlet: The Acting Version and the Wiser Sort" in Clayton, ed., 195-210, esp. 201; Stanley Wells and Gary Taylor with John Jowett and William Montgomery, *"Hamlet"* in *William Shakespeare: A Textual Companion* (Oxford: Clarendon Press, 1987), 396-423, esp. 398; and Grace Ioppolo, *Revising Shakespeare* (Cambridge, MA, and London: Harvard UP, 1991), 136.

[3] Philip Edwards, editor of the New Cambridge *Hamlet* (Cambridge: Cambridge UP, 1985), describes Q1 as a "bad" quarto: "a corrupt, unauthorised version of an abridged version of Shakespeare's play" (9) and claims, more specifically, that Q1 "inherits the cuts and changes made in the early playhouse transcript, and demonstrates that the transcript was in progress towards the Globe's official promptbook. . . . [Perhaps] it reflects the shortened acting version of Shakespeare's own theatre" (30). In his "Narratives About Printed Shakespearean Texts: 'Foul Papers' and 'Bad' Quartos" (*Shakespeare Quarterly* 41 [1990]: 65-86), Paul Werstine argues against just such a practice of textual constructivism by which scholars mistake dubious hypotheses of origin for historical fact.

[4] G. R. Hibbard mentions all but the omission of the rebellious mob in the introduction to his Oxford edition of *Hamlet* (Oxford: Clarendon Press, 1987), 1-130, esp. 67-74.

[5] The fact that the Privy Council reprimanded Cambridge in 1593 for the ineffectuality of its efforts to suppress dramatic performances within five miles of the university bespeaks play production despite the Council's decree (Alan H. Nelson, ed., *Records of Early English Drama: Cambridge,* 2 vols. [Toronto, Buffalo, and London: U of Toronto P, 1989], 1:348). Moreover, Hibbard's persuasive explanation of the unsuitability of the names *Polonius* and *Reynaldo* for performance at Oxford goes some way toward affirming the title-page performance claims for that university as well (74-75). But see Ioppolo's suggestion to the contrary (135-36). Certainly a play about students on leave from their university who intrigue to catch a murderer before he catches them could hardly fail to appeal to a student audience.

[6] See Bryan Loughrey, "Q1 in Recent Performance: An Interview" in Clayton, ed., 123-36; and Michael Muller, "Director's Notes [on *Hamlet, Quarto 1*]" in the program for the Shakespeare in the Park 1992 production, Fort Worth, Texas, 12.

[7] Vivien Brodsky claims that widows comprised a little over a third of brides marrying by license as opposed to banns in late Elizabethan London (fewer widows may have married by banns); see "Widows in Late Elizabethan London: Remarriage, Economic Opportunity and Family Orientations" in *The World We Have Gained: Histories of Population and Social Structure,* Lloyd Bonfield, Richard M. Smith, and Keith Wrightson, eds. (Oxford and New York: Basil Blackwell, 1986), 122-54, esp. 128. E. A. Wrigley and R. S. Schofield, studying marriage records for both sexes, determined that about thirty percent of mid-sixteenth-century English marriages were remarriages; see *The Population History of England 1541-1871: A Reconstruction* (Cambridge, MA: Harvard UP, 1981), 258. Richard L. Greaves, surveying Elizabethan society overall, estimates death in the first fifteen years of marriage at thirty percent and remarriages of bride or groom at twenty-five percent; see *Society and Religion in Elizabethan England* (Minneapolis: U of Minnesota P, 1981), 191.

[8] For the most recent study of this extensive body of material, see the first three chapters of Elizabeth Thompson Oakes's 1990 Vanderbilt University dissertation, "Heiress, Beggar, Saint, or Strumpet: The Widow in Society and on the Stage in Early Modern England." Three earlier dissertations treat widowlore: Linda Bensel-Meyers, "A 'Figure Cut in Alabaster': The Paradoxical Widow of Renaissance Drama" (University of Oregon, 1985); Roger Alfred MacDonald, "The Widow: A Recurring Figure in Jacobean and Caroline Comedy" (University of New Brunswick, Canada, 1978); and Katherine Harriett James, "The Widow in Jacobean Drama" (University of Tennessee, 1973). Also see Lu Emily Pearson, *Elizabethans at Home* (Stanford, CA: Stanford UP, 1957), 498-516; Ruth Kelso, *Doctrine for the Lady of the Renaissance* (Urbana: U of Illinois P, 1956), 121-32 and 257-58; and Carroll Camden, *The Elizabethan Woman: A Panorama of English Womanhood, 1540 to 1640* (London, New York, and Houston: Elsevier Press, 1952), passim.

[9] This classification scheme is best known from *Measure for Measure* (1604), but Morris Palmer Tilley cites its appearance both earlier and later in Peele's *Old Wives' Tale* (c. 1590) and Rowley's *All's Lost by Lust*

(1633); see *A Dictionary of the Proverbs in England in the Sixteenth and Seventeenth Centuries: A Collection of the Proverbs Found in English Literature and the Dictionaries of the Period* (Ann Arbor: U of Michigan P, 1950), 404, M26.

[10] Quotations of Shakespeare plays other than *Hamlet* follow *The Riverside Shakespeare,* ed. G. Blakemore Evans (Boston: Houghton Mifflin, 1974). Quotations of *Hamlet* follow *The Three-Text* Hamlet: *Parallel Texts of the First and Second Quartos and First Folio,* ed. Paul Bertram and Bernice W. Kliman (New York: AMS Press, 1991).

[11] *The Riverside Chaucer,* ed. Larry D. Benson, 3d ed. (Boston: Houghton Mifflin, 1987), 164 (ll. 2077-80). *Upon My Husband's Death: Widows in the Literature and Histories of Medieval Europe,* Louise Mirrer, ed. (Ann Arbor: U of Michigan P, 1992), demonstrates the continuity of attitudes towards widows between the medieval and early modern periods.

[12] Fulvius Androtius, S.J., *The Widdowes Glasse,* trans. I.W.P. (London, 1621), esp. 290. Androtius's tract is appended to a tract by Leonard Lessius, S.J., *The Treasure of Vowed Chastity in Secular Persons,* reprinted in vol. 214 of *English Recusant Literature 1558-1640,* ed. D. M. Rogers (Ilkley and Yorkshire: Scolar Press, 1974).

[13] The ceremony of the mantle and the ring is described by Androtius on pages 341-48. According to Roger Alfred MacDonald, the ceremony is also alluded to in an anonymous 1525 play titled *The Twelve Merry Jests of the Widow Edyth* (65).

Androtius finds parallel practices honoring chaste widows in pagan Rome:

> . . . when a widdow died, her head was adorned with a Crowne of Continency, and to [i.e., so] caryed in solemne triumph to her graue.
>
> The said Romans did also attribute another honour to the Continency of Widdowhood, which was, That on the wedding day, there were no women suffered to come neere, much lesse to touch the Bride, but only such as had beene the wiues of one husband, to wit, such as had beene but once marryed; comanding all that had beene twice marryed (yea though they were Widdowes) to keep aloofe of, as prophane, impure, and fortelling of an euill fortune to the happynes of marriage.
>
> (322-23)

[14] In *The Treasure of Vowed Chastity in Secular Persons,* Lessius, expounding Paul's dictum that to marry is to have "trouble in the flesh" (1 Corinthians 7:28), depicts marriage as an inevitable disaster for both sexes (94-130).

[15] *Tasso's Dialogues: A Selection, with the "Discourse on the Art of the Dialogue,"* trans. Carnes Lord and Dain A. Trafton (Berkeley: U of California P, 1982), 81. Also see Margaret Lael Mikesell's "Catholic and Protestant Widows in *The Duchess of Malfi,*" *Renaissance and Reformation* 19 (1983): 265-79, esp. 266-67.

[16] *Daughters, Wives, and Widows: Writings by Men about Women and Marriage in England, 1500-1640,* ed. Joan Larsen Klein (Urbana and Chicago: U of Illinois P, 1992), xi. Klein notes that this much-reprinted treatise was also translated into French, German, Italian, and Castilian.

[17] Quoted in Klein, ed., 97-122, esp. 120 and 121, n. 110.

[18] Androtius, 336-37.

[19] From "The Epistle Dedicatory" to *The Treasure of Vowed Chastity in Secular Persons* by the translator, I.W.P.

[20] Androtius, 332.

[21] *The Complete Works of John Webster,* ed. F. L. Lucas, 4 vols. (London: Chatto and Windus, 1927), 4:38-39.

[22] *The Works of Thomas Middleton,* ed. A. H. Bullen, 8 vols. (London: John C. Nimmo, 1885), 6:404.

[23] "Letter to Lady Ralegh, the night before he expected to be put to death, 1603" in *Sir Walter Ralegh: Selected Writings,* ed. Gerald Hammond (Manchester, UK: Carcanet Press, 1984), 276.

[24] *Sir Walter Raleigh's Instructions to His Son and to Posterity,* 2d ed. (London, 1632); rpt. in *Advice to a Son: Precepts of Lord Burghley, Sir Walter Raleigh, and Francis Osborne,* ed. Louis B. Wright (Ithaca, NY: Cornell UP, 1962), 22.

[25] Quoted in Mikesell, 268.

[26] G. B. Shand makes this point in an unpublished paper he kindly shared with me, "Queen of the First Quarto," delivered at the 1991 annual meeting of the Shakespeare Association of America, Vancouver, Canada.

[27] I conflate Q2 and F thus (Q2/F1) when they duplicate each other aside from differences in line arrangement, capitalization, or spelling.

[28] Steven Urkowitz, "Five Women Eleven Ways: Changing Images of Shakespearean Characters in the Earliest Texts" in *Images of Shakespeare: Proceed-*

ings of the Third Congress of the International Shakespeare Association, 1986, Werner Habicht, D. J. Palmer, and Roger Pringle, eds. (Newark: U of Delaware P, 1988), 292-304, esp. 300.

[29] Quoted in Suzanne W. Hull, *Chaste, Silent, and Obedient: English Books for Women 1475-1640* (San Marino, CA: Huntington Library, 1982), 196.

[30] Hull, 196.

[31] Recall that for Carolyn G. Heilbrun, writing in the 1950s, Gertrude is "strongminded, intelligent, succinct, and, apart from this passion [her refusal to abjure sexuality], sensible" ("The Character of Hamlet's Mother," *SQ* 8 [1957]: 201-6; rpt. in Heilbrun's *Hamlet's Mother and Other Women* [New York: Columbia UP, 1990], 9-17). Leslie A. Fiedler categorizes Gertrude as one of Shakespeare's "'antiwomen,' subverters of the role assigned to them by men who seek to naturalize their strangeness to a patriarchal world" (*The Stranger in Shakespeare* [New York: Stein and Day, 1972], 74); and Lisa Jardine calls Gertrude one of Shakespeare's "strong" women, a congener of Desdemona, Cleopatra, and Webster's Duchess of Malfi (*Still Harping on Daughters: Women and Drama in the Age of Shakespeare* [Sussex: The Harvester Press; Totowa, NJ: Barnes and Noble Books, 1983], 69).

[32] Shand, 12.

[33] If Q1's Hamlet is still in his teens, Gertred's protectiveness toward a son new to adulthood is all the more understandable. In Q1, Yoricke's skull "hath bin here this *dozen* [not twenty-three] yeare, / . . . euer since our last king *Hamlet* / Slew *Fortenbrasse* in combat" (Q1CLN 1987-89, my emphasis); however, the gravedigger says nothing about his length of service as sexton or the day of Hamlet's birth.

[34] The Geneva Bible: *A facsimile of the 1560 edition* (Madison, Milwaukee, and London: U of Wisconsin P, 1969), AAiii.

[35] For an early refutation of Gertrude's adultery, see John W. Draper, *The* Hamlet *of Shakespeare's Audience* (Durham, NC: Duke UP, 1938), 109-26, esp. 112-14.

[36] Mullaney, "Mourning and Misogyny: *Hamlet, The Revenger's Tragedy,* and the Final Progress of Elizabeth I, 1600-1607," *SQ* 45 (1994): 139-62, esp. 151. In the First Quarto, Hamlet expresses horror that "lust shall dwell within a matrons breast" (Q1CLN 1547), a sentiment that, like its Q2/F1 counterpart, invites Mullaney's reading of an obscene maternal desire thwarting filial mourning.

[37] Steven Urkowitz advances this argument ("'Well-sayd olde Mole'" in Ziegler, ed., 48). Recognizing the early quality of Gertred, though not of Q1 as a whole, Philip Edwards agrees with George Duthie that Gertred may well be "a recollection of the old play of *Hamlet*" (25).

[38] Juliet actively and *Richard II*'s Duchess of Gloucester passively enact the widow's suicide, a European version of *sati.*

[39] Keith Wrightson, *English Society 1580-1680* (New Brunswick, NJ: Rutgers UP, 1982), 200. He explains that what these traditionalists, particularly the poor, missed most were protective rituals, without which they felt vulnerable and frightened (201). Q2 and F, but not Q1, remind their audiences of such rituals when the Ghost deplores having died "Vnhuzled, disappointed, vnanueld" (Q2/F1TLN 762), i.e., without the Eucharist or the annointing essential to extreme unction. If the average person felt the loss of these rituals—communion in its Roman Catholic form and extreme unction—more than the loss of purgatory, a theological abstraction, it is conceivable that a censor or adapter alert to predictable social irritants may have cut this line from a text apt to be played for an audience dominated by Catholic sympathizers while allowing the Ghost's allusion to his abode, an integral part of the play, to stand. By the same token, could not state- or self-censorship explain the omission of Laertes's insurrection from a text to be played in an area known for its history of Catholic rebellion?

[40] See "Map 6" in Sally-Beth MacLean's "Tour Routes: 'Provincial Wanderings' or Traditional Circuits?" *Medieval and Renaissance Drama in England* 6 (1993): 1-14, esp. 6-7.

[41] See Ronald G. Usher's "Map of the Distribution of Catholic Laymen, 1603" in *The Reconstruction of the English Church,* 2 vols. (New York and London: D. Appleton and Company, 1910), 1:135; and "Note B—Number of Catholic Laity, 1600," which includes the official report of the Anglican bishops in 1603 on Catholic recusants (157-59). Although Usher's conclusions have been questioned (see John Bossy, *The English Catholic Community 1570-1850* [New York: Oxford UP, 1976], 96, n. 36), they have not been superseded.

[42] Although to date REED has found no evidence of the Lord Chamberlain's Men having played in any of these four counties, or, indeed, in any county that Usher estimates as more than fifteen percent Catholic, it should be noted that the REED project is ongoing and that MacLean's maps are part of a progress report rather than a definitive statement.

[43] See "Map 4" and "Map 5" in MacLean, "Tour Routes," 6-7.

[44] Christopher Haigh, *Reformation and Resistance in Tudor Lancashire* (Cambridge: Cambridge UP, 1975), 279 and 275. Bossy notes that William Allen's family belonged to the Lancashire gentry and that under Allen's direction the English college at Douai dedicated itself to educating missionary priests (12).

[45] *Records of Early English Drama: Newcastle-upon-Tyne,* ed. J. J. Anderson (Toronto, Buffalo, London: U of Toronto P, 1982), xi.

[46] Sally-Beth MacLean, "Players on Tour: New Evidence from Records of Early English Drama," *The Elizabethan Theatre* 10 (1988): 55-72, esp. 62.

[47] *Records of Early English Drama: Cumberland, Westmorland, Gloucestershire,* ed. Audrey Douglas and Peter Greenfield (Toronto, Buffalo, London: U of Toronto P, 1986), 18-19.

[48] In *The English Catholic Community 1570-1850* Bossy provides a map showing the distribution of Catholics in 1641-42, in which recusant households exceed twenty percent only in the Welsh county of Monmouth and in the two northern counties of Lancashire and Durham (404).

[49] Such speculations are complicated by the lack of any evidence for specific performances of Q1, despite the general claims of its title page. Additionally, Janette Dillon reminds us that if Q1 is the memorial reconstruction of a performance, "it may in fact be further removed from performance than either the Second Quarto or the Folio texts by virtue of being subject to two degrees of intervention (memory and print) rather than one" ("Is There a Performance in this Text?" *SQ* 45 [1994]: 74-86, esp. 82).

[50] Chambers, 1:78; and Yoshiko Kawachi, *Calendar of English Renaissance Drama 1558-1642* (New York and London: Garland Publishing, 1986), passim. Kawachi charts the travels of the King's Men further: in 1624 they were at Skipton Castle in Craven District; in 1629 and 1631 in York; in 1634 in York and Doncaster; in 1635 in Newcastle; and in 1636 and 1638 again in York. The reference to Congleton is from MacLean, "Tour Routes."

[51] Alan Somerset, "'How Chances it they Travel?': Provincial Touring, Playing Places, and the King's Men," *Shakespeare Survey* 47 (1994): 45-60, esp. 60 and 53-54. Somerset corrects Gerald Eades Bentley's contrary statistics in *The Profession of Player in Shakespeare's Time,* 1590-1642 ([Princeton, NJ: Princeton UP, 1984], 177-84), finding that players were welcomed over ninety-five percent of the time (50).

[52] MacLean, "Tour Routes," 10.

[53] MacLean, "Players," 66.

[54] From Thomas Dekker's *Lanthorne and Candle-light* (1608), quoted in E. K. Chambers, *The Elizabethan Stage,* 4 vols. (Oxford: Clarendon Press. 1923), 1:332.

[55] The propriety of playgoing for priests has, however, been questioned. In his discussion of the theatergoing habits of London Catholics, Alfred Harbage quotes an interchange between Father Harrison and Father Thomas Leke, the one ordering the other to desist from attending the theater (though not necessarily from seeing plays at more respectable venues such as the court). Leke wrote in his own defense, "'Wee knowe, that most of the principal Catholicks about London doe goe to playes, and all for ye most part of my ghostly children do knowe that I sometimes goe, and are not scandalised.' To which Harrison rejoined: 'the Catholicks that use to playes are the young of both sexes, and neither matrons, nor graue, or sage man is there seen'" (*Shakespeare's Audience* [New York and London: Columbia UP, 1941], 72). Harbage doubts the validity of Harrison's observations; in any case, to insist on a distinction between playgoing juniors and stay-at-home seniors would seem less feasible in counties where theater's chief association was religious and where sources of entertainment were few. More likely, then as now, the whole community turned out when the Royal Nonsuch came to town.

[56] MacLean, "Tour Routes," 10-11.

[57] MacLean, "Players," 63-64.

[58] Kawachi, passim; and Lawrence Stone, ed., "Companies of Players entertained by the Earl of Cumberland and Lord Clifford, 1607-39" in *Collections V* (Oxford: The University Press for the Malone Society, 1959 [1960]), 17-28, esp. 19-20. Stone reprints the Bolton Abbey manuscripts in which the play's titles are not recorded.

[59] Lull, "Forgetting *Hamlet:* The First Quarto and the Folio," in Clayton, ed., 137-50, esp. 149.

[60] Somerset, 59-60.

Source: "The First Quarto of *Hamlet*: Reforming Widow Gertred," in *Shakespeare Quarterly,* Vol. 46, No. 4, Winter, 1995, pp. 398-413.

"Come Down and Welcome Me to This World's Light": *Titus Andronicus* and the Canons of Contemporary Violence

Philip C. Kolin, *University of Southern Mississippi*

Early criticism of *Titus Andronicus* tried to come to terms with the violence in the play by confining its horror to Elizabethan England. The bloody grotesqueries in *Titus* were seen as characteristic of Shakespeare's age. In the process, both the times and the mores were indicted; Shakespeare and his Elizabethan audience were tainted. Samuel Taylor Coleridge, for example, pronounced that *Titus* was "obviously intended to excite vulgar audiences by its scenes of blood and horror."[1] In the early 1850s, Georg Gottfried Gervinus similarly attacked *Titus* and accused Shakespeare of pandering to the Elizabethan demand for blood and guts: "If it be asked, how it were possible that Shakespeare with his finer nature could even have chosen such a play even for the sake of love of opportunity . . . we must not forget that the young poet must always in his taste do homage to the multitude, and that . . . he would be stimulated to speculation upon their applause, rather than by the commands and laws of an ideal."[2] A few years later, John Addington Symonds added more coals to the fires over which *Titus* was roasted: "Playwrights used every conceivable means to stir the passions and excite the feeling of their audience. They glutted them with horrors."[3] The editor of the original (1904) Arden edition of *Titus,* H. Bellyse Baildon, credited Shakespeare for writing *Titus* and claimed that he was "afraid of mulcting his audience of the sensationalism they loved."[4]

Some sophisticated readers and playgoers of the twentieth century continue to deprive *Titus* of praise. J. Dover Wilson characterized *Titus* as a foolish parody—the revenge play heaping revenge upon itself. *Titus* was "a huge joke which, we may guess, Shakespeare enjoyed twice over, once in the penning of it, and again in performance, while he watched his dear groundlings, and most of those in the more expensive parts of the theatre also, gaping ever wider to swallow more as he tossed them bigger and bigger gobbets of sob-stuff and raw beef-steak."[5] Similarly, for the novelist Evelyn Waugh, the "text seemed to hold no potentiality save burlesque."[6] Dan Sullivan began his review of a 1967 production noting that "this gory and ungrateful play . . . is so crudely pitched at the lowest element in the Elizabethan audience—what might be called the bear-baiting crowd—that some scholars refuse to believe that Shakespeare actually wrote it, and most wish that he hadn't."[7]

Coleridge's response, or Waugh's, or Sullivan's is culturally myopic. Claiming that *Titus*'s violence is crude and unapplicable to audiences today is misleading and unfair; it depoliticizes any attempt on the part of critic or director to interpret Shakespeare in light of contemporary anxieties and instabilities. The Elizabethan-myopic school of *Titus* criticism by branding the play as sixteenth-century Grand Guignol missed the mark no less than do the suave debunkers who deplore *Titus* as artistically naive or parodic. Recent criticism and production history have attempted to explain and de-marginalize the violence in *Titus* by broadening its focus beyond Elizabethan sensationalism. My goal in this essay is twofold: (1) to show how *Titus* accurately reflects contemporary society's most pressing political and personal horrors and, in the process, (2) to survey ways in which directors have justifiably incorporated contemporary signifiers into the *Titus* script. I hope to challenge "received Shakespeare," what Ron Daniels calls the "thatched cottage Shakespeare" where actors "wear tights and doubtlets and flowing hair, and . . . the idea that this is a classical work and this is the [only] way it should be done. . . ."[8]

In lamenting the ravages of violence, the Age of Elizabeth may not have been as far away from our own as earlier critics believed. Peter Brook, who in 1955 directed a landmark *Titus,* maintained that "this obscure work of Shakespeare touched audiences directly because we had tapped in it a ritual of bloodshed which was recognized as true"; Brook later added, "Everything in *Titus* is linked to a dark flowing current out of which surge the horrors, rhythmically and logically related—if one searches in this way one can find the expression of a powerful and eventually beautiful barbaric ritual."[9] In stylizing, though not minimizing, the violence in *Titus,* Brook emphasized its ritualistic, universal presence. *Titus,* like other Shakespearean plays, holds the mirror up to what is universally abhorrent in nature. It is a blunt steel mirror, terrifying to look into; it is George Gascoigne's steel glass with a vengeance.[10] The closer we look at *Titus,* the greater capacity the play has to reflect the terror embedded in contemporary society.

A catalogue of the horrors in *Titus* is as frighteningly contemporary as it is unmistakenly Senecan. As Brian Cox, who played Titus in the 1987 Stratford-upon-Avon production, rightfully claimed: "This is the most modern of plays."[11] Alan C. Dessen has asked some telling questions about *Titus*'s contemporaneity and how audiences should respond:

> For the playgoer in 1986, this tragedy poses a series of provocative questions. What happens to a society that condones such acts of violence (Tamora calls the public sacrifice of her son "cruel, irreligious piety")? When public justice fails, is private revenge acceptable or is it a form of madness? Can the parts of the body politic indeed be put back together after so many violent terrorist actions, serial murders, and vigilante responses? Is this tragedy indeed an embarrassment to Shakespeare worshippers or does it convey something about us and our world we would prefer not to face? After almost four hundred years, are we finally ready for *Titus Andronicus?*[12]

Dessen's last question needs to be answered in the affirmative. We are not only ready for *Titus* but we have internalized and projected its messages. Murder and Rape have come to visit and, alarmingly, reside in the contemporary world.

In fact, the atrocities acted out in *Titus* correspond to many of horrors that shock America today. Our society, like *Titus*'s, recoils from mass murders. The crimes of the Manson family, Richard Speck's slaughter of student nurses in Chicago, and the multiple assassinations of Son of Sam in New York in the 1960s and early 1970s were unrelentingly gory. The 1980s and 1990s also witnessed brutal crimes spilling across newspapers and TV screens. Two of the most ghoulish criminals of the last few years have been Jeffrey Dahmer of Milwaukee and John Wayne Gacy of Chicago. Dahmer puts Cook Titus's deeds into a twentieth-century context. He slew his victims, then cut them up, and put their body parts in bags and stored them away in his freezer. Gacy sexually abused, tortured, and slowly murdered his victims before interring them beneath the floorboards of his house, almost a parodic travesty of the internment of the Andronici brothers. In the early 1990s, Danny Rolling terrorized Gainesville, Florida much as Tamora's sons did to Rome. Rolling killed his victims and then decapitated some of them. A syndicated story from early February 1994 reported on yet another *Titus*-like ghastly murder case:

> BEAUMONT, Texas—A computer programmer allegedly stabbed his mother more than 100 times and decapitated her, then sat calmly on the living room sofa until police arrived.

The O. J. Simpson murder trial, and all the gore and horror surrounding it, occupied America a great deal in 1994 and 1995. And the atrocities go on.

Yet these heinous acts of individual madmen are, from recent history's perspective, part of a larger global violence in the mid to late twentieth century. Again, *Titus* can reflect the widespread explosion of political violence of our age. "*Titus* is a political play, and Shakespeare is the most political of all dramatists," so correctly asserted Hereward T. Price in 1943.[13] Through its fictional representations, *Titus* offers a deeply political script. I strenuously take issue with Ann Thompson who judges *Titus* as more of a family tragedy than a political one.[14]

Ample justification for twentieth-century parallels with *Titus* is found in a variety of productions. Comments from critics attuned to *Titus*'s strong political warnings in these productions prove instructive. In 1923, Herbert Farjeon likened the play's savageries to the crimes of World War I: "the horribilism has got the old Blue Books on War atrocities beaten hollow."[15] Calling to mind a more recent political agony, William Johnson in his 1987 review of a Santa Cruz production observed: "the cycle of revenge which drives *Titus* throughout is still capable of dictating human behavior—witness the alternating savageries between the United States and Iran."[16] *Titus* holds our conscience hostage still. For the Chinese director Qiping Xu, *Titus* is reminiscent of the horrors from China's cultural revolution.[17] Easily finding contemporary political parallels in *Titus,* Brian Cox persuasively saw reflected in Shakespeare's play the troubles emanating from "the rise of Islamic fundamentalism, the breakdown of social units, . . . the sectarian violence of Northern Ireland. . . . " Further extending the analogues in *Titus* to the tragedies in Northern Ireland, Cox locates in the ritualistic slaughter of Titus's and Tamora's sons reminiscences of the war "with Irish Catholic versus Irish Protestant . . . [where] perhaps—one man's civilized behavior becomes another man's barbarity."[18]

A recent production of *Titus*—set in the Rustaveli Theater in Tbilisi in the former Soviet republic of Georgia—was staged within a charged political context. According to an article in *Izvestia, Titus* played in a "crippled cultural sector that will require much time and energy. The disease has spread too far. Not long ago in Tbilisi supporters of Gamsakhurdia banned books of writers they found objectionable. This is a new low on the gauge measuring the decline of the human spirit."[19] In such a context of political repression, *Titus* was an appropriate choice for the Rustaveli Theater.

One twentieth-century horror that several directors have visualized through Shakespearean plays, including *Titus,* is the scourge of fascism. Margaret Webster's memorable production of *Richard III* in 1953 found that Shakespeare's script easily accommodated several fascist/Nazi myths. She opened her *Richard III* with a swastika and hammer and sickle and swelled the crowd scenes with storm troopers.[20] Fascist imagery also helped to represent Ian McKellen's much-respected *Richard III* at the Royal Theatre in 1992.[21] Many directors of *Titus* see the script justifying the imagery and chants evoking the Age of Mussolini and Hitler. Locating Brook's *Titus* within the political shadows of fascism, Brian Cox pointed out: "In our century the context for this play has never been more powerful. When Peter Brook produced it in 1955 the shadow of totalitarianism was very much upon us: Stalinism and the purges of the thirties, Hitler's Germany and the subsequent revelations of the Nuremberg trials."[22]

In the 1966-1967 production of *Titus* at Baltimore's Center Stage, director Douglas Seale dressed his actors in fascist uniforms—Anthony Brafa's Saturninus was a dead-ringer for Mussolini and Robert Gerringer's Titus was clad in Hitler brown. Wanting his audience to link the atrocities in *Titus* with the horrors of World War II, Seale pointed out marked similarities between Shakespearean fictions and contemporary reality:

> I have chosen to set the play in the mid 1940s in the hope that you will be reminded of the horrors of the concentration camps, the bombing of Hiroshima and the mass executions of Nuremberg and so will be less inclined to dismiss *Titus Andronicus* as a blood bath of horror which might be acceptable to those coarse Elizabethans but hardly to sophisticated, civilized, educated humanitarians like us.[23]

Seale demonstrated how Shakespeare's art foreshadowed/mirrored twentieth-century reality.

Looking at *Titus*'s German stage history, Horst Zander also documents a host of productions that readily saw elements of fascism reflected in the play. For Zander, these productions were not actually interested in a particular historical period (the 1930s, the 1940s) as much as wanting to demonstrate that fascist attitudes are universal, an everlasting phenomenon. Zander points out that Hans Hollmann's *Titus,* done at Basel in 1969, was based upon the belief that fascist attitudes were as prevalent in ancient Rome as in modern Europe. Similarly, Rudolph Seitz's *Titus,* performed at Esslinger in 1987, used fascist costumes to emphasize similarities between classical Rome and Hitler's Berlin.[24]

Perhaps the most significant justification of fascist ideologies in *Titus* was Peter Stein's production in 1989-1990. First done in Germany, Stein's *Titus* traveled to the Stabile de Genova where it became *Tito Andronico.* Stein saw many fascisti reminders into the play. Michael Billington remarked that in Stein's production Titus was "unequivocally a fascist general."[25] However, according to Dominique Goy-Blanquet, Stein broadened the associations of the characters with the mafia or the fascists. "The critics who read fascism in Lucius's elevation to the title of 'benigno duce di Roma' were too simple-minded: the references to modern Italy were not restricted to the 1930s nor to one particular set of politicians, but to more permanent traits like the connections of family and state affairs in a world where dynasties mean business."[26] Though denying particular references to fascism, Goy-Blanquet nonetheless proves my point that *Titus* has irrefutable application for contemporary directors and audiences.

While parallels between events in *Titus* and specific political movements like fascism shows the relevance of *Titus* today, it is not the only way *Titus* speaks to late twentieth-century audiences. Above everything else, *Titus* is most aesthetically relevant in representating urban violence. The play has a strong urban feel; the sense of the city permeates the *Titus* language, the characters' behavior, and even the *mise-en-scène. Titus* overflows with urban associations and structures that contemporary directors have translated visually for audiences. *Titus* begins with references to the Senate house, "the passage to the Capitol,"[27] and the Andronici tomb, all at the center of the city. With its references to the loci of various gods, act 4 arguably might present urban signs, such as those used to mark the houses in *The Comedy of Errors.* Urban danger extends even into the surrounding "ruthless, gloomy woods" (4.1.53), the location of act two. The woods themselves are co-opted into the urban violence in *Titus;* the city's law of the jungle infects the pastoral. The woods in *Titus* like New York City's Central Park offer no sylvan enclave. Recognizing the corruption in city life in *Titus,* Stein gave his audiences a "glimpse [of] the rusting corrugated iron of an urban wasteland."[28]

Titus's urban setting—and the violence it spawns—provides an appropriate landscape for the cultural tensions and anxieties of our society. Much has been written about Titus's Rome. Clearly it is not the glorious Rome of Caesar Augustus, the city closely tied to law, justice, order, and military might; it is the decaying Rome of the fourth century, with the barbaric Goths pouring in at the gates. Just before slaying one of Tamora's sons, Titus advises him, "Look round about the wicked streets of Rome" (5.2.98). Aaron and Tamora, with her sons, invade Rome, and the city becomes less a wilderness of tigers than an urban jungle for all revenging predators to feed in. John P. Cutts goes so far as to say that Titus is one of the tigers.[29] But what is scary about *Titus* is that now that the Goths have come to town, they invade a city that, under Saturninus, is hospitable to their violence. The "warlike Goths" and the "noble Romans" become one force. Goths and Romans try to outdo each other in the urban violence that also afflicts our cities—gang rumbles; rapes; cries of grief-struck parents; extortions and executions; the trampling of victims' rights; a corrupt judicial system and an equally corrupt police force.

In some productions, Tamora's sons are represented as gang members dressed in motorcycle jackets and boots. They are called "cubs," "bear whelps," and a "pair of hellhounds" to situate them in gangs of predators. Derek Cohen even styles them with a reference to a leading gang of our time—they are in a "Hell's Angel's club."[30] Unquestionably, Chiron and Demetrius have a gang-like mentality and code. Ironically, Tamora asks Titus at the start of the play: "But must my sons be slaughtered in the streets?" (1.1.115), a question haunting parents in New York, Detroit, Miami, and Los Angeles. Her remark is prophetic—her sons as well as those of Rome will be slaughtered in Rome's streets, gangland fashion.

The hacking and hewing of Alarbus in act 1 and the decapitations of the Andronici brothers in act 3 also evoke contemporary gang violence. Act 2 even presents a rumble as Bassianus and Lavinia and the Andronici boys, Quintus and Martius, are pitted against Goth mother, her two sons, and her paramour Aaron. Like the present-day gangs who terrorize their rivals, warfare in *Titus* is often based on a battle for turf or territory—Romans vs. Goths (or Hezbollah Palestinians vs. Israelis)—for control of a city. The streets of Titus's Rome are no different from the contemporary turfs of East Los Angeles, Miami, or Harlem where rival gangs spill each other's blood. Worried about order, succession, and assassinations, Elizabethan England was threatened by civil strife just as the world's hot spots are today.

Titus symbolizes another problem in urban life, corruption in city hall and in the courts of justice. "There's as little justice at land" (4.3.9) as there is at sea. The city government of Rome has sold out to the gangland terrorists, the Gothic thugs and their Roman collaborators. Tamora's sons go free for atrocities while Titus's offspring are executed for innocence and Titus loses all his power and control. Under the new Emperor Saturninus, the hoods earn impunity at the victimized men's expense. As Gail Kern Paster observes, Rome's "political processes reveal a predatory savagery that seeks out and destroys the hero at the moment when he most completely embodies the ethos of the city."[31] Saturninus and his regime typify Boss-ism, city corruption through dictatorship and cronyism. Ironically, the cover of Mike Royko's sensational portrait of Chicago mayor, Richard J. Daley, Boss, (1971), presented "His Honor" dressed like a Roman tribune.

Nowhere does *Titus* provide a more scathing indictment of institutionalized crime than in act 3, scene 1. Justice is not blind in *Titus*—it sees only one side of a quarrel—but it is now dumb. Silence in *Titus* is synonymous with corruption at the highest levels. The tribunes to whom Titus justly appeals for his sons' life do not respond; they do not even recognize him: "no tribune hears you speak" (3.1.22), bemoans Lucius to his father. Equivalent to city commissioners, Roman tribunes accompany Roman lawmakers who also turn a deaf ear to Titus's pleas: "*Enter the Judges and Senators (and Tribunes) with Titus's two sons bound, passing over on the stage to the place of execution, and Titus going before pleading*" (3.1).

In a corrupt city government, honest leaders are mocked or, worse yet, wiped out. Aaron boasts of his treatment of the good tribune Marcus: "I brave[d] the tribune in his brother's hearing" (4.2.36). Pitifully, Titus appeals to the authorities but his pleas backfire, and for his attempts Tamora's sons gloat that it is "good to see so great a lord / Basely insinuate and send us gifts" (4.2.37-40). The city expels anyone who would plead justice's cause too loudly. Accordingly, Lucius is banished; the gates of the city have been shut on him (5.3.104). The final victory of the gangs seems to go to "the sons of Rome" led by Lucius, though some critics have labeled Lucius's relatinship with the Goths an unholy alliance.[32]

True to hero mythology, as operative today as when *Titus* was first performed, Lucius can return as the honest cop—the Eliot Ness come to wipe out the Al Capones/Saturnines of the city.[33] Lucius is the G-man (the man sent in answer to Titus's prayers for justice in act 4). The last four lines of the play, found only in the First Quarto, leave contemporary audiences with a clear sense that Lucius is the victorious government (FBI) agent. He returns "To order well the state." Again, as in so many films about urban crime, the cop who succeeds must leave the corrupt city to gather outside additional forces for further strength. Moreover, Lucius is true to the archetype, described by Joseph Campbell's *Hero With a Thousand Faces,* of the hero wandering in the wilderness in preparation for the great victory. It is as old as the Buddha story and as recent as Eliot Ness going to Canada before returning to a decisive victory in Chicago in David Mamet's screenplay *The Untouchables*. Appropriately, Lucius must leave Rome in order to return a hero.

Titus not only depicts the tyranny inflicted upon the state, but the play is particularly prophetic about the dangers engulfing women and children in our society. Women—Lavinia, the nurse, the mid-wife, and even Rome as a feminine presence—suffer heinously from the violence unleashed in *Titus*. In a very contemporary sense, Lavinia's rape, urged on and plotted by the Gothic mother Tamora, is the result of, and staged as if it were, gang warfare. The deed recalls a familiar scene in many gang-soaked movies—the sexual assault on a pristine or innocent woman from the rival gang or other vulnerable group the gang wants to prey upon. One thinks of the assault on Anita in *West Side Story* or the attempted rape of the new school teacher, Miss Hammond, by a student gang member in *Blackboard Jungle,* or the sexual assault of Ally Sheedy's character in *Bad Boys*. Such treatment of women is tragically standard in war reports. Atrocities ravaged the women of the Bosnian Muslims, and Kuwaiti women were allegedly violated by Iraqis.

Lavinia's fate mirrors some of the worst crimes against women. Her rape symbolizes the attempted disenfranchisement of women as well as the empowerment of male violence. Consequently, Lavinia's horror is similar to that many contemporary women face when they seek to bring rapists to trial and punishment. In classical Rome, Lavinia might have had no rights against her assailants. Yet in many ways Lavinia is not simply the male-dominated Lucrece or Ophelia some critics have made her out to be. She defies the masculine code which would have her suffer in silence and retreat into the world of guilt or fear of reprisal. Flying in the face of a corrupt society that wants her to forget about, or worse yet blame her for, the rape, Lavinia valiantly assists in the identification, capture, and punishment of her assailants.

Children in *Titus,* as in our world, are also endangered—Lavinia, Alarbus, Quintus, Martius, Mutius, and Aaron's black baby. Young Lucius in particular witnesses the dismemberment and mutilation of his family, the slaughter of his aunt, and the murder of his grandfather. The young Lucius has many peers in America, and around the world. In November 1994 all America was horrified by Susan Smith's murder of her two young sons in Union, South Carolina. Children of Beirut, Sarajevo, Mogadishu, Belfast, and Johannesburg daily witness the atrocities of gang warfare, the wholesale slaughter of family members, the destruction of a way of life. The lessons of world politics are often written in blood spilled by children. *Titus* could not be more contemporary in depicting this message.

Aaron's black infant is the victim of an especially pernicious attack against children. The child born to Tamora and Aaron has been incorporated into the mandates for revenge of both the law-abiding Romans and the Goths. The "tadpole," like its progenitors, merits death, or so proclaims every character in *Titus,* save Aaron. Certainly, the baby is a dangerous embarrassment to its adulterous mother, eager to keep her sexual transgressions secret. In being implicated in his mother's crime, the child personifies a variety of dangers to children, and on several levels, too, as Cohen explains:

> . . . no crime that Tamora commits in the play causes such universal outrage as her crime of being seen to have betrayed her husband . . . Like a woman, the child cannot survive without a protector. Like a woman it is a necessary nuisance. In this baby are concentrated the various cultural and social stigmas which are placed on the powerless. As a black child, in particular, it stands as a reminder of this masculine society's propensity to stratify all of its elements according to their capacity to command and enforce equality.[34]

Tamora becomes the model for the new, unchaste Roman matron. She is not as kindly to her first Roman-born child (the black baby) as was the wolf Lupus who suckled the twins Romulus and Remus, the former being the founder of the eternal city.

What the child is and will do are conditioned by cultural anxieties grafted onto the babe both by Elizabethans and contemporary Americans. The black child has been co-opted into the aporia of fear in the play. In 1942 William T. Hastings speaking of good guys and bad in *Titus* presented "a world of black and white."[35] Though not focusing directly on racial issues, Hastings nonetheless summarized one kind of prejudice *Titus* represents. Although concerned with the dissolution of distinction of gender and race in *Titus,* Dorothea Kehler still admits that "Like the white Christian spectators watching these later plays [*Merchant, Othello*], *Titus*'s audience, then and now, may be drawn to side with their own kind, their partnership elicited not by the opposition of Roman and Goth *per se* but by the Gothic party's inclusion of an unchaste woman and the black man she empowers."[36]

When seen as a victim of prejudice against race and miscegenation, Aaron's baby is invested with enormous contemporary cultural and political significance. The child is denied its rights, including protection from the white power-based parent who is in a position to insure its welfare. Even more alarming, the treatment of the baby in *Titus* foreshadows, by some four hundred years, the fate of unfortunate American infants born to drug mothers who, like the suspicion-crazed Tamora, see their children as a burden or, even worse, a palpable indictment of their own offense. Abortion is sometimes the most convenient route these mothers take to escape responsibility. But if these drug babies come to term, their mothers frequently abandon them to a welfare system that may want to protect them but is under a stormy siege of protests about diminishing resources. Like the authors of the Elizabethan poor laws, some contemporary reformists want to distinguish between the "deserving" and "undeserving" wards of the state.[37] In the straight, white world, a black child born with a drug addiction can be as endangered as Aaron and Tamora's offspring. The contemporary message that *Titus* sends is that a drug-addicted child, or one with AIDS, is often segregated and denied the protection of family. The baby crystalizes the fate of alienated minorities whether because of race, ethnicity, or disease.[38]

In his review of the Old Vic production of *Titus* in 1923, Herbert Farjeon identified one of the key features of the play that, I believe, makes it so appropriate for twentieth-century audiences. Stressing that he did not "like being disgusted in the theatre," Farjeon conceded: "but this is a disgusting play, and if it does not disgust, it does not achieve its end."[39] Because of its terrifying brutality and senseless crimes against the natural order, *Titus Andronicus* has provided an accommodating script for contemporary directors to share with their audiences. Judging from the number of successful attempts to translate *Titus*'s disgusting horrors into twentieth-century signifiers, directors have been immensely perceptive readers of Shakespeare. Whether in its condemnation of a fascist-like world order or its laments over urban violence, *Titus* is indeed a play for our age.

Notes

[1] T. M. Raysor, ed. *Coleridge's Shakespearean Criticism* (Cambridge, MA: Harvard UP, 1930): II, 31.

[2] "*Titus Andronicus* and *Pericles*." *Shakespearean Commentaries*. Trans. F.E. Bunnett (Rpt. New York: AMS Press, 1971): 102.

[3] "*Titus Andronicus* and the Tragedy of Blood." *Studies in Elizabethan Drama* (New York: E.P. Dutton, 1919): 62.

[4] H. Bellyse Baildon. "Introduction." *The Works of Shakespeare: The Lamentable Tragedy of Titus Andronicus* (London: Methuen, 1904): xxv.

[5] "Introduction." *Titus Andronicus* (Cambridge: CUP, 1948): lxv.

[6] "*Titus* with a Grain of Salt." *The Spectator,* Sept. 2, 1955: 300.

[7] "Papp's Troupe Offers *Titus Andronicus*." *New York Times,* Aug. 10, 1967, 43: 2.

[8] Quoted in Silvana Tropea, "Ron Daniels Finds the Space Inside Shakespeare." *American Theatre,* April 1994: 40.

[9] *The Empty Space*. New York: 1969. 86.

[10] "The Steel Glass." *The Complete Works of George Gascoigne*. Ed. J. W. Cunliffe (Cambridge: Cambridge UP, 1907-1910).

[11] "*Titus Andronicus*." *Players of Shakespeare 3*. Ed. Russell Jackson and Robert Smallwood (New York: Cambridge UP, 1993): 176.

[12] "Why *Titus Andronicus?*" *Oregon Shakespeare Festival Souvenir Program*. Ashland: Summer/Fall 1986. 11.

[13] "The Authorship of *Titus Andronicus*." *JEGP* 42 (1943): 57.

[14] "Philomel in *Titus Andronicus* and *Cymbeline*." *Shakespeare Survey* 31 (1978): 23-32.

[15] "*Titus Andronicus*." *Saturday Review* [London], Oct. 1923.

[16] "*Titus Andronicus*." *Times Tribune* [Santa Cruz, CA], Aug. 14, 1988: 7.

[17] "Directing *Titus Andronicus* in China [1986]." *Titus Andronicus: Critical Essays*. Ed. Philip C. Kolin (New York: Garland, 1995).

[18] Cox, 176.

[19] "Georgia After Gamakhandia." *Izvestia,* April 17, 1992: 3.

[20] Samuel Leiter. *Shakespeare Around the Globe* (Westport, CT: Greenwood, 1986).

[21] See Marjorie Oberlander's excellent review of *Titus Andronicus* in *Shakespeare Bulletin* 11 (Winter 1993): 10.

[22] Cox, 176.

[23] Program, *Titus Andronicus,* Baltimore Center Stage, 1966.

[24] "*Titus Andronicus* in Germany." *Titus Andronicus: Critical Essays*. Ed. Philip C. Kolin (New York: Garland, 1995).

[25] "Connoisseur of Cruelty." *Manchester Guardian Weekly,* Dec. 10, 1989: 27.

[26] "*Titus resartus:* Warner, Stein, and Mesguich Have a Cut at *Titus*." *Foreign Shakespeare: Contemporary Performance*. Ed. Dennis Kennedy (New York: Cambridge UP, 1993): 46.

[27] All citations to *Titus Andronicus* come from *The Complete Works of William Shakespeare*. Ed. David M. Bevington (New York: HarperCollins, 1992).

[28] Goy-Blanquet, 47.

[29] "Shadow and Substance: Structural Unity in *Titus Andronicus*." *Comparative Drama* 2 (1968): 74.

[30] *Shakespeare's Culture of Violence* (London: St. Martin's, 1993): 89.

[31] *The Idea of the City in the Age of Shakespeare* (Athens, GA: U of Georgia P, 1985): 58-59.

[32] The following critics, among others, have serious reservations about Lucius, his motives and his effectiveness: Larry S. Champion, *Shakespeare's Tragic Perspective*. Athens: U of Georgia P, 1976; Henry Jacobs, "The Banquet of Blood and the Masque of

Death: Social Ritual and Ideology in English Revenge Tragedy," *Renaissance Papers 1985* (1985): 39-50; Dorothea Kehler, "*Titus Andronicus*: From Limbo to Bliss." *Shakespeare Jahrbuch* 128 (1992): 125-31; and David Willbern, "Rape and Revenge in *Titus Andronicus,*" *English Literary Renaissance* 8 (1978), 159-82.

[33] Clifford Chalmers Huffman, "*Titus Andronicus:* Metamorphosis and Renewal," *Modern Language Review* 67 (1972): 730-41, also discusses Lucius's return, relating it to a larger Christian message Huffman finds in *Titus.*

[34] Cohen, 90.

[35] "The Hardboiled Shakespeare." *Shakespeare Association Bulletin* 17 (1942): 114-25.

[36] Kehler, "From Limbo," 126.

[37] "The Case for Comparison." *University of Chicago Alumni Magazine,* April 1994: 37.

[38] As with every other character in *Titus Andronicus,* Aaron's baby has elicited a host of contradictory interpretations. Two critics who speak most harshly about the baby as a sign of continuing evil in the play are Douglas F. Green, "Interpreting 'her martyr'd signs': Gender and Tragedy in *Titus Andronicus,*" *Shakespeare Quarterly* 40 (1989): 317-26, and Douglas H. Parker, "Shakespeare's Use of Comic Conventions in *Titus Andronicus,*" *University of Toronto Quarterly* 56 (1987): 486-97. In an earlier essay ("Performing Texts in *Titus Andronicus,*" *Shakespeare Bulletin* 7 [1989]: 5-8), I also cast the child in a negative light, indicating that it was "a child-text" of Aaron's revenge and "a sign of Aaron's lustful conquest of Tamora and the power of his lust in action in ravaged Rome" (7). I now modify my views of the baby; it is important to differentiate Aaron's use of the baby from the infant's own helplessness and total lack of complicity in Aaron and Tamora's designs. It is in such a context that I think the child can, like contemporary drug babies, elicit our sympathy and recruit our energy for Tamora's and Aaron's disclosure.

[39] Farjeon, "*Titus Andronicus.*"

Source: "'Come Down and Welcome Me to This World's Light': *Titus Andronicus* and the Canons of Contemporary Violence," in *Titus Andronicus: Critical Essays,* edited by Philip C. Kolin, Garland Publishing Inc., pp. 305-16.

Tradition and Subversion in *Romeo and Juliet*

Francois Laroque, *University of Paris III, Sorbonne*

Romeo and Juliet, the story of "star-crossed" love, is so well and so deeply rooted in a number of traditions—those of myth, legend, folklore, novella, to name a few—that to present it as a subversive play may appear paradoxical and perhaps even perverse. Yet the play's main polarities that explore the frictions between high and low spheres, public and private lives, age and youth, authority and rebellion, sacred and secular love, generate powerful whirls of energy that partly account for its enduring fascination for world audiences.

To the ebullient atmosphere of erotic drives that is released by the prospect of marriage, by music, dancing, and masquing, as well as by the flares of torches at night and the dog days of early summer in Verona, one must surely add the numerous language games, puns, innuendoes, and paradoxes whose main source is Mercutio, the play's lord of misrule. These witty language games and conceits are all part of a tradition (rhetorical tropes, Petrarchan codes, sonneteering conventions) as well as of the subversion of this tradition. *Romeo and Juliet* introduces us into a world upside down where the ordinary rules—whether they be syntactical, social, or sexual—are temporarily lifted or brushed aside. The violence of the civil brawls is reflected in the violence of the language or rather in the violence imposed upon language. The very genre of the play—a love tragedy—is itself a subversion of tragedy since the first two acts correspond to the structure of Shakespearean comedy until Mercutio is turned into a "grave man," thus causing the play to veer off into tragedy. Gender is also subverted, as Shakespeare plays at presenting an active, almost masculine Juliet against a weak, effeminate Romeo.

The law is subverted by a love that brings about a destabilization of domestic order, thus leading to a world where contraries are reconciled in a series of sublime or grotesque conjunctions (high and low, hate and love, the sacred and the profane, life and death) so as to create a series of discordant fusions. Shakespeare is here influenced by Marlowe, whose heterodox approach to life and love, repeatedly stressed in his plays, allowed the pagan mysteries to displace or subvert the traditional Christian values that were then regarded as the foundation of public order and of household peace.

Young Shakespeare seems to have delighted in delineating the ravages of misrule, of the hurly-burly of love and desire, in a traditional aristocratic society dominated by custom, patriarchy, and well-established wealth.[1] Festivity is not limited to orchestrating the coming of age in Verona or the various rites of passage for young men and women, but it also serves to turn the world upside down, to subvert its rigid hierarchies. United with the subversive power of love, festivity does not only achieve a temporary suspension of social rules and political authority, but it also leads to a radical questioning of traditional patriarchal order.

Following on the dense, syntactically complex and highly contorted sonnet prologue, we are thrust *in medias res* into the verbal sparrings of the two Capulet servants, Sampson and Gregory (1.1.1-30). Theirs is a stichomythic exchange depending on linguistic thrust and parry, on a quick succession of quibbles: *colliers—choler—collar;* of antithesis and paradox: *move—stand.* Although this is unquestionably a type of demotic language that foreshadows the future banter between Romeo and Mercutio (what the latter calls the "wild-goose chase" in 2.4.72), it remains both vivacious and entertaining and serves to strike the keynote, one of aggressive virility and unabashed phallicism, at the outset of the play.[2]

Before going further I should also remark that, on stage, the servants' appearance creates an impression of rapid movements, intense agitation, and a great expenditure of youthful male energy. Sampson and Gregory use a number of telling gestures while they speak to denote outrage, provocation, insult, or mockery; and their mode of expression also depends on body language. So expressions like "we'll draw" (1.1.3), "to stand" (1.8), "women are ever thrust to the wall" (lines 14-15), "'tis known I am a pretty piece of flesh" (line 28), "draw thy tool" (line 30), are all accompanied by specific gestures, some of them probably quite obscene and using all the possibilities offered by the costumes and properties of the set (in particular the bulging codpieces so conspicuous on Renaissance male apparel). So, this mixture of verbal aggressiveness and of "macho" pride (the flaunting of sexual virility traditionally identified with the implements of fight with expressions like "stand" or "tool") has elements of clowning as well as of youth culture with its martial rites that find expression in street brawls as well as in carnival games.[3] This is a sample of what Peter Burke has called "blue-apron culture,"[4] which found expression in riots or on various festive occasions, something quite reminiscent of the French *Sociétés Joyeuses* or "Abbeys of Misrule" described by Natalie Davis.[5] The play thus opens on a combination of popular culture, joyful anarchy, and sexual bravado, an index to festive license or mass rebellion as in the Jack Cade scenes in *2 Henry VI.*

We find here a string of gruesome puns on "cutting off the heads of the maids" (lines 22-23) amounting to taking their "maidenheads," a style of wordplay already found in *2 Henry VI* in a dialogue between Jack Cade and Dick the Butcher (4.7.121-23). In *2 Henry VI* this was followed by the savage farce of showing the heads of Lord Say and his son-in-law, Sir James Cromer, on top of long pikes and then in having them kiss one another in some sinister puppet show. This bloody spectacle may be construed as the unmetaphoring[6] of the latent brutality of the sexual punning (4.7.124-25), and one is reminded of Lavinia's rape and mutilation in *Titus Andronicus*. In the latter, as in the history play, verbal violence is followed by acts of sadism and cruelty that take the form of bloody farce and savagery. In *Romeo and Juliet* subversion is apparently less radical since, on the surface at least, it remains confined to speech patterns and to a series of provoking postures.[7]

Yet if we think of Juliet's ominous threat, " . . . Nurse, I'll to my wedding bed, / And death, not Romeo, take my maidenhead" (3.2.136-37) or of old Capulet's lament in 4.5, when his daughter is discovered apparently dead on the morning of her marriage to Paris, we may see an interesting underground connection between the initial jokes and the belated accomplishment of Juliet's fate:

> O son, the night before thy wedding day
> Hath Death lain with thy wife. There she lies,
> *Flower as she was, deflowered by him.*
> Death is my son-in-law, Death is my heir.
> My daughter he hath wedded. . . .
> (4.5.35-39; emphasis mine)

This association between defloration and death had also been anticipated by Juliet's own fantasies when she said to Friar Laurence:

> O, bid me leap, rather than marry Paris,
> From off the battlements of any tower,
> Or walk in thievish ways, or bid me lurk
> Where serpents are. Chain me with roaring bears,
> Or hide me nightly in a charnel-house
> *O'ercover'd quite with dead men's rattling bones,*
> With reeky shanks and yellow chapless skulls.
> (4.1.77-83; emphasis mine)

These are not only words, as the initial sinister images are acted out in the play's final scene when, after a last kiss to the dead Romeo, Juliet kills herself with a dagger and exclaims:

> O happy dagger.
> This is thy sheath. There rust, and let me die.
> (5.3.167-68)

The act of suicide is a perversion of the act of love since the phallic dagger (Gregory's "tool") is allowed to penetrate Juliet's "sheath," a word that is used instead of the more technical term "scabbard," which is also the exact English translation of the Latin *vagina.* More farfetched but no less intriguing is the possible Latin pun on head/*caput* that refers us directly to the name Capulet, so that the word "maidenhead" could already be an indirect allusion to the play's heroine—Juliet **Capulet**.[8] This type of linguistic juggling, combining two separate signifiers ("head" and "maid") into a component whole ("maidenhead") that radically alters the initial meaning (from cruelty to sexuality) while opening up metaphorical perspectives used later in the play, is an illustration of a form of linguistic subversion characterizing low comedy.

Another example of these subversive language games may be found in the Nurse's soliloquy in 1.3, when she refers to her teeth and exclaims:

> . . . I'll lay *fourteen* of my teeth—
> And yet, to my *teen* be it spoken, I have but *four*—
> She's not fourteen.
> (1.3.12-14; emphasis mine)

A similar pun is found in the scene where Old Capulet is busy preparing the marriage festivities with Peter and the other servants:

> *Cap.* —Sirrah, fetch drier logs!
> Call Peter, he will show thee where they are.
> *2 Ser.* I have a *head,* sir, that will find out *logs* and never trouble Peter for the matter.
> *Cap.* Mass and well said! A merry whoreson, ha.
> Thou shalt be *loggerhead!*
> (4.4.15-20; emphasis mine)

This repeats the type of popular wordplay already indulged in by the servants, male or female, all of them part of the Capulet household, so that it may be regarded as a form of clannish mannerism; the various puns on the word "head" are also indirectly related to the name Capulet.

Such low-life linguistic *bricolage* has its counterpart in the rhetoric of the lovers that places such an emphasis on the oxymoron—the "pretty riddle," as Erasmus calls it.[9] It conveys the extreme tension between polar opposites characterizing such a brief and intense experience, this "prodigious birth of love" where "[their] only love [is] sprung from [their] only hate" (1.5.137).

Contrary to the euphuistic dead language of Lady Capulet comparing Paris to a book (1.4.81-92) and in opposition to Old Capulet's cyclical vision of life and love (1.2.26-30), inscribed within an immemorial and universal tradition of succeeding generations that prompts him to cast a nostalgic backward glance on the lost pleasures of his youth ("Nay sit, nay sit, good cousin Capulet, / For you and I are past our dancing days . . . / Come Pentecost as quickly as it will, / Some five and twenty years: and then we masqu'd"—1.5.30-37), Romeo and Juliet's language of love seems closer to a "misshapen chaos of well-seeming forms" (1.1.177). The simultaneously rapturous and destructive experience of love at first sight, suggested in the French expression *le coup de foundre,* which associates sudden love with a flash of lightning, is rendered in the play's complex and ambivalent light and darkness imagery[10] in repeated allusions to fire, powder, consummation, combustion, explosion, and also in the language of impetuous and rash speed (running, galloping, and so forth). The oxymoron, which can only be reduced, when used mechanically, to a string of dead images as in Romeo's pseudo-Petrarchan ejaculations in 1.1.174-79, "O brawling love, O loving hate . . . ," is bound to produce or to reflect an emotional shock; if antithesis may be defined as a strategy of opposition and paradox as a strategy of inversion, the oxymoron itself is based on a strategy of fusion.[11] The ontology of the oxymoron is in fact close to the neoplatonic concept of *coincidentia oppositorum* as illustrated by Marsiglio Ficino in his commentary on Plato's *Symposium,* where he states that "Love is Desire aroused by Beauty":

> Only by the vivifying rapture of *Amor* do the contraries of *Pulchritudo* and *Voluptas* become united: "Contradictoria coincidunt in natura uniali." But to achieve the perfect union of contraries, Love must face the Beyond; for as long as Love remains attached to the finite world, Passion and Beauty will continue to clash.[12]

An equivalent of this may be seen in some of the love images in the play that both contrast and collapse the opposite ideas of light and darkness, like Romeo's description of Juliet "As a rich jewel in an Ethiop's ear" (1.5.45) or Juliet's description of Romeo as "day in night" (3.2.17). Oddly enough, Puttenham calls this figure "the Crosse-couple" because "it takes [me] two contrary words, and tieth them as it were in a paire of couples, and so makes them agree like good fellowes."[13] So the oxymoron, or "crosse-couple," should indeed be regarded as the emblematic trope of the "pair of star-crossed lovers."

But in the play's dialectics, love is a transcending force that disrupts and subverts the marriage strategies of the establishment but it is itself subverted by Mercutio's wit and by the Nurse's bawdy humor. In creating a multiplicity of perspectives, Shakespeare is able to view the central love story from conflicting and parallel lines and thus to deflate some of its potential pathos and sentimentality. Romanticism is pitted against the cynical view of love as sex, as an affair of a "poperin pear" in an "open arse" (2.1.38), as Mercutio crudely puts it. The voices of tradition and subversion are not one-sided in this play but constantly interact and reflect one another so that they oblige the spectator and the reader to resort to constant realignments of perspective. We find a similar dynamic at the level of social, sexual, and gender roles, as well as of ideological positions in general.

That the Nurse should be regarded as one of the strong voices of tradition in the play seems an undeniable fact. In her long rambling speech about Juliet's age in 1.3 she seems to be the keeper of family memory, reminiscing numerous details about Juliet's infancy and growth to childhood (her weaning, her standing "high lone," her falling forward). For her the past is safely contained within a double calendar—that of an old Celtic holiday (*Lugnasadh*) turned into the agricultural feast of Lammastide celebrating the beginning of harvest and the calendar of her own private memories, the death of her daughter Susan, the earthquake that surprised her while she was "sitting in the sun under the dove-house wall. . . ." If time is associated with the cycles of growth and coming of age, as in the traditional or pastoral notions of time in the Renaissance,[14] her discourse remains predicated on a void, on the dark shadow of death that it simultaneously suggests and screens. It also betrays an insistence on and even an obsession with the body and bodily functions that combines sexuality and death. The Nurse's speech undermines itself since the counterdiscourse of sex and death progressively subverts the surface search for calendar landmarks, thereby destroying the happy remembrance of things past.

The Nurse's way of reckoning time is highly idiosyncratic. The main public event that she recaptures is the earthquake "eleven years before," a phrase she repeats several times. This event coincided with little Juliet's weaning, just before she turned three, an unusually late age for weaning a child, even by Elizabethan standards.[15] This reconstruction of time past is achieved, as it were, by means of her own bodily geography. On several occasions she refers to her "dug" and "nipple" (lines 26, 30, 31, 32), just as earlier she had jokingly mentioned her teeth to count Juliet's age. At this juncture one is reminded of the poetic *blason*—that is, the metonymic game consisting of describing and heraldizing the female body, or rather its naughty parody, the *contreblason,* which both belong to the tradition started by the French poet Clément Marot.[16] Indeed, the Nurse relies on this particular part of her old and ugly body (her sagging breasts or "dugs," otherwise emblematic of her trade) as a piece of evidence to date one particular episode.[17] In spite of the apparent disorder and random associations of her soliloquy,[18] she resorts to *loci memoriae* while her own *ars memorativa* associates past events with bodily pictures. Indeed, hers is an instinctive memory system that works as *memoria rerum* or rather as *memoria corporis*.[19] The weaning of Juliet and the earthquake are a miniature drama encapsulated within her brain ("I do bear a brain," line 29) that she is physically reexperiencing on the stage as she is telling her story. The scene begins as a picture of "childhood recollected in tranquillity" until the idle, lazy "sitting in the sun under the dovehouse wall" (line 27) suddenly quickens into life when the "pretty fool" grows tetchy and falls out with the dug; then the wall shakes with the earthquake, thus obliging the Nurse to "trudge." This gentle, peaceful action appears in strong contrast to Gregory's thrusting the "maids to the wall" (1.1.16). The uncomfortable association of the earthquake and of domestic bliss is accompanied by the darker note of the evocation of the dead figures of Susan and of her "merry" husband. The Nurse's incongruous animation of the dovehouse ("'Shake!' quoth the dovehouse," 1.3.34), a pathetic fallacy combined with *hysteron proteron,* a trope inverting the order of cause and effect, may also be interpreted as just another way of evoking the "shaking of the sheets" in the "love-house." Besides being very common rhymes, love and dove are almost interchangeable words in poetry and Romeo does call Juliet a "snowy dove" when he first sees her (1.5.47); moreover, the traditional Renaissance interconnections between micro- and macrocosm made the earthquake a possible image for the tremors of the belly and of the lower bodily parts. So the reawakening of dead or dormant memories is first and foremost a means or an excuse for the Nurse to bring back to life her extinct sexual life so as to retrieve the happy time when her husband was still of this world. If the sexual allusion is transferred to young Juliet, as may seem appropriate since the business at hand is, after all, her prospective marriage, it can also be understood as an expression of the Nurse's nostalgia for her own married life, now dead and gone with her husband's body.

Indeed, the correspondences between the little world of man and nature's macrocosm made it possible to establish a series of links and analogies between bodily parts, the four elements, and the planets. In this view the earth was quite logically associated with the lower parts so that an earthquake could be interpreted in a sexual or scatological manner as, for instance, in Hotspur's sarcastic remarks to Glendower in *1 Henry IV*:

> Diseased nature oftenti ,es breaks forth
> In strange eruptions,   ɫt the teeming earth
> Is with a kind of colic pinch'd and vex'd
> By the imprisoning of unruly wind
> Within her womb, which, for enlargement striving
> Shakes the old beldame earth, and topples down
> Steeples and moss-grown towers. At your birth
> Our grandam earth, having this distemp'rature,
> In passion shook. . . .
>
> (3.1.26-34)

Hotspur is here bent on sending down the mad pretensions of the Welsh magus but this piece of "Bakhtinian grotesque" reveals that the eruptions of nature were also popularly construed as the release of an unruly wind contained within the womb of "our grandam earth." Scatological allusions being, if one may say so, next door to sexual innuendo, the allusion to the earthquake may be regarded as a kind of double entendre that the gestures of the actress playing the part of the Nurse can always make quite explicit on stage.

In *The Comedy of Errors,* Shakespeare had already developed a string of comic analogies between the female anatomy of Nell, the kitchen wench, and European geography,[20] an idea followed up in *The Purple Island, or the Isle of Man* (1633) by Phineas Fletcher, where the human figure merges into the landscape and the landscape is made to look like a human body,[21] a double conceit that is a verbal equivalent of the art of the "curious perspective" or anamorphosis.

The Nurse's soliloquy can thus be read as a verbal anamorphosis of her own body, where the travel into "the dark backward and abysm of time"[22] provides her with an opportunity to retrieve the map of her female anatomy with its periodic fluxes and shakings.[23] Such powerful corporeal presence is also a screen for an absence and a palimpsest that points to the shadow of death underneath. When one uses the method of "backward reckoning," which seems to have been common practice in the religious and judicial worlds as well as in the popular culture of early modern Europe,[24] one realizes that the reference to "Lammas-eve at night" (31 July) takes us back to the probable date of Juliet's conception, nine months earlier, which corresponds to the night of Hallowe'en (31 October), when the souls of the dead were believed to be roaming about. The Italian historian Carlo Ginzburg has described these Hallowe'en superstitions as the offshoots of a vast corpus of European beliefs in the night battles waged between the living and the dead or between the night walkers, or *benandanti* (children born with a caul and thus with a sign of their gift), and bands of nocturnal demons spreading sterility and death:

> The nocturnal ridings of the women following Diana's cult are no doubt a variant of the 'wild hunt' . . . Diana-Hecate is indeed herself followed in her night peregrinations by a group of disquieted dead souls—the premature dead, children

> having died in infancy, people having died violent deaths. . . . [25]

So even if it is subdued and if it only briefly surfaces in the Nurse's monologue, this association of wintry barrenness and fruition (Lammas and Hallowe'en), of "birthday and deathday,"[26] of breast-feeding, weaning, and burying ("falling backward" is an expression that links copulation and death, a possible proleptic suggestion of Juliet's "death" on the very morning of her marriage to Paris) is both paradoxical and typical of the play's alliance of contraries.

On closer examination, the image of the weaning of Juliet with the laying of wormwood on the dug, which uses what Gail Paster describes as "the aversion technique,"[27] may probably be regarded as a subliminal foreshadowing of Juliet's desperate attempt in the end, when she tries to suck the last drops of poison from Romeo's lips and exclaims:

> Poison, I see, hath been his timeless end.
> O churl. Drunk all, and left no friendly drop
> To help me after? I will kiss thy lips.
> Haply some poison yet doth hang on them
> To make me die with a restorative.
> (5.3.162-166)

The Nurse's smearing her breast with wormwood, a proverbially bitter oil used to discourage the child from breastfeeding, also reinforces the motif of death insofar as the prefix "worm" also looks forward to Mercutio's curse after the fight against Tybalt—"A plague o' both your houses, / They have made *worms' meat* of me" (3.1.109; emphasis mine), and to Romeo's lurid evocation of "worms that are [Juliet's] chambermaids" (5.3.109), both announcing Hamlet's irreverent epitaph for Polonius:

> *King* Now, Hamlet, where's Polonius?
> *Ham.* At supper.
> *King* At supper? Where?
> *Ham.* Not where he eats, but where 'a is eaten. A certain convocation of politic worms are e'en at him. Your worm is your only emperor for diet: we fat all creatures else to fat us, and we fat ourselves for maggots. Your fat king and your lean beggar is but variable service, two dishes, but to one table—that's the end.
> *King* Alas, alas!
> *Ham.* A man may fish with the worm that hath eat of a king, and eat of the fish that hath fed of that worm.
> *King* What dost thou mean by this?
> *Ham.* Nothing but to show you how a king may go a progress through the guts of a beggar.
> (4.3.16-31)

Hamlet's sardonic humor is here at its most savage as it presents an image of royal festivity, of going "a progress" through the empty stomachs and the "guts" of the populace. This is more than the traditional *memento mori* or than the description of death as the great leveler. This provocative vision of a world upside down is a caveat to Claudius, a direct challenge to his authority, a veiled death threat associated to grim apocalyptic visions of social revenge in the form of latter-day cannibalism using the worms as proxies. In the case of *Romeo and Juliet,* things are far from being so clear, and the subversive elements in the Nurse's defense of tradition and memory can only appear through the work of retrospective interpretation (like the Nurse's own serpentine anamnesis) once the play's sequence of unlucky events has been disclosed and the theme of the triumph of death has taken over on the triumph of love. Shakespeare resorts to the power of language and imagery to prepare the audience for the idea and the spectacle of the gradual fusion of eros and thanatos.

Indeed, the reference to the earthquake has the function of a dark saturnalia: it combines the ideas of the dance of sex and of the dance of death and it rolls into one the impressions of catastrophe and ecstasy (other images for this are images of the flash of lightning, of the meteor, or allusions to the myth of Phaëton). Like the Nurse's insistence on her own body, this combination of sexuality and death, of joy and mourning, is a recognizable feature of the grotesque mode with its specific mixture of humor and horror[28] and its foregrounding of bodily organs and bodily functions. This ambivalence is analyzed by Bakhtin in what he calls "grotesque realism":

> Degradation and debasement of the higher do not have a formal and relative character in grotesque realism. "Upward" and "downward" have here an absolute and strictly topographical meaning. "Downward" is earth, "upward" is heaven. Earth is an element that devours, swallows up (the grave, the womb) and at the same time an element of birth, of renascence (the maternal breasts), . . . To degrade is to bury, to sow, and to kill simultaneously, in order to bring forth something more and better. To degrade also means to concern oneself with the lower stratum of the body, the life of the belly and the reproductive organs; it therefore relates to acts of defection and copulation, conception, pregnancy and birth. Degradation digs a bodily grave for a new birth; it has not only a destructive, negative aspect, but also a regenerating one.[29]

The conversion from festival to funeral, therefore, does not only concern Juliet's planned marriage rites. The play negotiates a constant to and fro movement from mirth to lament and vice versa until it becomes itself a dramatic equivalent of Peter's "merry dump" (4.5.105).

Another example of the subversion of the ordinary opposition between life and death may be found in the scene where Juliet is discovered dead on the morning of her marriage to Count Paris. The hysterical nature and the hyperbolic artificiality of the collective lamentations orchestrated by the Nurse and articulated by Old Capulet have often been rightly pointed out. This is all the more visible as the audience knows that Juliet is not actually dead, so that all emotion is drained of the lament and mourning is turned into a hollow performance. As Thomas Moisan writes:

> Shakespeare deliberately undercuts the rhetoric of grief in this scene to underscore, by contrast, the more genuine emotions of Romeo and Juliet . . . the ululant effusions of the mourners, with their "O"-reate apostrophes and expletives undeleted . . . are too "high" and "tragic" for a death that has not actually occurred, while the punning *badinage* between Peter and the musicians is too "low" and "comic" for a death that is *supposed* to have occurred. . . . [30]

So when Paris expresses his grief by exclaiming,

> Beguil'd, divorced, wronged, spited, slain.
> Most detestable Death, by thee beguil'd,
> By cruel, cruel thee quite overthrown
> (4.5.55-58)

he follows suit and amplifies Capulet's most vocal lamentation but he also unwittingly reveals that Romeo, who has taken Juliet away from him and married her in secret, is now identified with the figure of Death. He had already been recognized as such by Tybalt during the masque scene in 1.5, when the latter had described him as "cover'd with an antic face" (the word *antic,* as *Richard II* reveals, was a traditional name for death).[31] So, among the play's supreme ironies and successive reversals we discover that the two rivals for Juliet's love, both unknown to each other, are allowed to be cheated and defeated by a false death. This is the result of Friar Laurence's unfortunate attempt to simulate death to preserve life, which led him to a dangerous transgression with unforeseen consequences.

The subversion of the border between life and death at the initiative of figures that seem hallmarked by tradition and experience follows another subversion, namely that of gender roles in the play. This appears when Romeo compares Juliet with the sun in the "balcony" scene:

> But soft, what light through younder window breaks?
> It is the east and Juliet is the sun!
> Arise fair sun and kill the envious moon
> Who is already sick and pale with grief
> That thou her maid art far more fair than she.
> (2.2.2.-6)

Juliet is placed above him and Romeo hears her from below, unseen in the dark. He is thus spatially dominated by Juliet and this places him in an inferior, passive position, later acknowledged by Romeo himself when he describes the situation in terms of the mystic adoration of a saint:

> O speak again bright angel, for thou art
> As glorious to this night, being *o'er my head,*
> As is a winged messenger of heaven
> Unto the white-upturned wondering eyes
> Of mortals that fall back to gaze on *him*
> When he bestrides the lazy-puffing clouds
> And sails upon the bosom of the air.
> (2.2.26-32; emphasis mine)

Juliet, compared to an angel, is made explicitly masculine here, riding the clouds in the air like the incubus Queen Mab in Mercutio's description "the hag, when maids lie on their backs, / That presses them and learns them first to bear" (1.5.92-93).[32] Furthermore, Romeo is said to be "fishified" by love—that is, emasculated: Mercutio says that he has lost his "roe" and compares him to a "dried herring," an image evoking Lenten fare (2.4.38-39). After Mercutio's death, Romeo will indeed exclaim:

> O sweet Juliet,
> Thy beauty hath made me effeminate
> (3.1.115-16)

Critics have also noted that it is Juliet who is allowed to speak the prothalamic soliloquy in 3.2 ("Gallop apace, you fiery-footed steeds"), thus reversing the traditional sexual roles, since the prothalamion was traditionally sung by the bridegroom on the eve of the marriage night. This detail adds to Juliet's self-confidence, turning her into what a critic has called an "atypical, unblushing, eager bride."[33] The last line of the play, which reverses the order of the appearance of the heroes in the title—"For never was a story of more woe / Than this of Juliet and *her* Romeo"—making Romeo the one who belongs to Juliet rather than the other way around, cannot only express the necessities of the rhyme. It also confirms the subversion of traditional sexual relations and the taking over of initiative and authority by Juliet in the field of love and sex.

The love between the two children of enemy families leads to a reversal of ordinary social and sexual roles and to the subversion of the borders between life and death. The initial transgression lies in the love at first sight experienced during the masque at old Capulet's house, and it will subsequently defeat all the plans worked out by the traditional forces and voices of authority in the play (parents, confessor, Nurse). Paradoxically, the speeches that remind us of times past, of grave customs and ancient power, are laden with ironical foreboding of the inevitable transgression and subversion of tradition that will be allowed to take place. The subversion of life by death is itself an old idea found in morality plays, and it is mainly due to its being placed in a Renaissance context and applied to a pair of young and innocent lovers that it may be regarded as sensational or shocking. More intriguing is the ambiguous game played with the idea and the gruesome representation of death itself, which is responsible for the creation of horror with a sort of morbid, pre-Gothic or even Poesque thrill.[34] The repeated occurrences of the normally rather rare figure of the oxymoron serve to "define the carnal knowledge of a love in which life and death intertwine"[35] and this macabre representation is given pride of place, often with a highly visual emphasis, in important soliloquies (4.3.15-58 and 5.3.75-120).

But this simultaneous expression and subversion of *amour passion* and of Petrarchan love lyrics also corresponds to a particular aspect of the artistic sensibility of the Northern European Renaissance, in a *topos* known as that of the encounter between the Maiden and Death, often found in the works of German artists such as Hans Baldung Grien, Samuel Beham, or Peter Flötner. In this macabre iconography, where a perverse erotic touch is added to the representation of the young woman's naked body, the painters gave birth to a pre-Mannerist *memento mori,* just another melancholy and disturbing variation on the traditional theme of *Vanitas*.[36] Since another of Dürer's disciples, the German painter Hans Holbein, worked for a long time in England, it is quite possible that this Continental motif reached London and the theatrical circles where Shakespeare was working, giving him the idea of a dramatic transposition of these images so as to lend more power to Arthur Brooke's moralizing poem, which he was otherwise using as his main source.

Tradition in *Romeo and Juliet* is certainly seen as a constraint that reduces the freedom of the individuals,[37] obliging them to follow the inherited hatreds of the clannish feud, "the continuance of their parents' rage," as the sonnet Prologue puts it, rather than gratify their own inclinations. On the other hand, the importance or the precedence given to tradition also implies that there is an obligation inherent in ceremony, a respect due to the laws of hospitality that, for instance, leads Old Capulet to curb Tybalt's fury when he recognizes Romeo hiding behind his "antic face" in the ball scene (1.5.53-91).

But Shakespeare treats the whole relation in a more complex, dialectic manner, as tradition in the play combines order and disorder, discipline and disobedience (to the Prince and to the laws of Verona). Moreover, characters like the Nurse and the Friar, who represent the voices of tradition, engage in soliloquies full of subversive potential. Their various attitudes and actions in the play also favor the clandestine resistance of the lovers to their family traditions. Does not Friar Laurence, after all, go far beyond the allowed limits of the church tradition and of his own responsibility as a holy man when he tampers with the forces of life and death and allows Juliet to "continue two and forty hours" in a "borrow'd likeness of shrunk death" (4.2.105-6)? Mercutio is also a highly ambiguous figure who embodies the traditional cynicism of young men's festive societies while simultaneously allowing the darker forces of dream, desire, and death to haunt his eerie Queen Mab soliloquy (1.4.53-94).

By contrasting and combining the voices of tradition and the forces of subversion in his early love tragedy, Shakespeare was in fact still experimenting with the power of dramatic art. Even if the influence of Marlowe is still very much felt in this play, the lovers pay a heavy price in the end and they cannot be said to be "overreachers" like Tamburlaine or Doctor Faustus. They do not set out to conquer the world or engage in black arts and in the quest of forbidden knowledge. They do not pay for their own sins only (impatience, anger, and revolt) or for their own blindness or naiveté, but they are also the victims of the subversive forces let loose by some of the other characters in the play (the Nurse, Mercutio, and Friar Laurence). Their love heroism is certainly misguided and vulnerable, as the recurrent imagery of the tempest-tossed or pilotless ship suggests,[38] but it also reflects the contradictions and clashes in Verona's patriarchal system as well as those inside the world of desire itself.

In the last analysis, their death is the sign of a triumph of sterility over the hope for continuity and regeneration, since it is not the old who die in the play, as tradition and natural laws would have it, but mainly the young (Mercutio, Tybalt, Paris, Romeo, and Juliet). The golden statues raised by the parents to commemorate the two eponymous heroes in the end are a sad and painful tribute, a mourning monument built to remind future generations of the dangers of civil strife and of the triumph of tradition over individual desire with its subversive potential. But, as the play itself plainly shows, this Pyrrhic victory is just another name for disaster since it is achieved at considerable expense, that of the sacrifice of the young and of the forces of life and renewal.

Notes

1 In a study of the early plays, Alexander Leggatt pits Shakespeare's well-known "sense of control" (as illustrated by the tightly knit structure of *A Midsummer Night's Dream*) against what he rightly calls "a fascination with the anarchic" (Alexander Leggatt, *English Drama: Shakespeare to the Restoration, 1590-1660* [London: Longman, 1988], 31).

[2] According to Valerie Traub in *Desire and Anxiety: Circulations of Sexuality in Shakespearean Drama* (London: Routledge, 1992), "each space of transcendent love is ultimately shown to be contained within, and even invaded by, the dominant ideology and effects of masculine violence," 2. Joseph A. Porter insists on the resemblances between Marlowe and the character of Mercutio and writes that "the opening of *Romeo and Juliet* with Sampson and Gregory talking of thrusting maids to the wall . . . is the most relentlessly phallic opening in all of Shakespeare's plays" ("Marlowe, Shakespeare and the Canonization of Heterosexuality," *South Atlantic Quarterly* 88 [Winter 1989]: 134).

[3] See François Laroque, *Shakespeare's Festive World: Elizabethan Seasonal Entertainment and the Professional Stage* (1991); reprint, Cambridge: Cambridge University Press, 1993), 209-10.

[4] Peter Burke, "Popular Culture in Seventeenth-Century London," in *Popular Culture in Seventeenth-Century England,* ed. Barry Reay (1985; reprint, London: Routledge, 1988), 32. See also Barry Reay's essay "Popular Culture in Early Modern England" in the same collection (p. 21).

[5] See Natalie Davis, "The Reasons of Misrule," in *Society and Culture in Early Modern France* (1965; reprint, Stanford, Calif.: Stanford University Press, 1975), 97-123 and Emmanuel Le Roy Ladurie, *Le carnaval de Romans* (Paris: Gallimard, 1979), 249-50, 326-28, 356.

[6] I am here using Rosalie Colie's concept for the deliberate transposition of a conventional stylistic figure to the reality presented on the stage in *Shakespeare's Living Art* (Princeton: Princeton University Press, 1974), 11. In an early tragedy like *Titus Andronicus,* gruesome puns on bodily mutilation and sexual defloration through rape become literally true when they are acted on stage.

[7] The first scene of the play would certainly fit in with C. L. Barber's formula (to describe Cade's rebellion) of a "consistent expression of anarchy by clowning" (*Shakespeare's Festive Comedy* [Princeton: Princeton University Press, 1959], 13). In this connection, see François Laroque, "The Jack Cade Scenes Reconsidered: Rebellion, Utopia, or Carnival?" in *Shakespeare and Cultural Traditions: The Selected Proceedings of the International Shakespeare Association World Congress, Tokyo, 1991,* eds. Tetsuo Kishi, Roger Pringle, and Stanley Wells (Newark: University of Delaware Press, 1994), 76-89.

[8] In this connection, see Pierre Iselin, "'What shall I swear by?' Langue et idolâtrie dans *Romeo and Juliet,*" in *Roméo et Juliette: Nouvelles perspectives critiques,* eds. Jean-Marie Maguin and Charles Whitworth (Montpellier: Collection Astraea, Imprimerie de Recherche, 1993) 174.

[9] See Marjorie Donker, *Shakespeare's Proverbial Themes: A Rhetorical Context for the Sententia as Res* (Westport, Conn.: Greenwood Press, 1992), 31.

[10] See Caroline Spurgeon, *Shakespeare's Imagery and What It Tells Us* (1935; reprint, Cambridge: Cambridge University Press, 1961), 310-16, and François Laroque, "'Cover'd with an Antic Face': les masques de la lumière et de l'ombre dans *Romeo and Juliet,*" *Études Anglaises,* no. 4 (October-December 1992): 385-95.

[11] See Gilles Mathis, "'L'obscure clarté' de *Roméo et Juliette*: les parades du langage," in *Roméo et Juliette: Nouvelles perspectives critiques,* ed. Maguin and Whitworth, 243.

[12] Edgar Wind, *Pagan Mysteries in the Renaissance* (1958; reprint, Oxford: Oxford University Press, 1980), 46-47, 54-56.

[13] Gladys Doidge Willcock and Alice Walker, eds., *The Arte of English Poesie* (1598; reprint, Cambridge: Cambridge University Press, 1936), 216.

[14] See Laroque, *Shakespeare's Festive World,* 74-76. See also Ricardo Quinones, *The Renaissance Discovery of Time* (Cambridge: Harvard University Press, 1972), 442.

[15] See G. Blakemore Evans, *Romeo and Juliet,* The New Cambridge Shakespeare (Cambridge: Cambridge University Press, 1984), 198-99.

[16] See François Laroque, "'Heads and Maidenheads': Blason et contreblasons du corps," in *Roméo et Juliette: Nouvelles perspectives critiques,* ed. Maguin and Whitworth, 189-208. See also Gayle Whittier, "The Sonnet's Body and the Body Sonnetized in *Romeo and Juliet,*" *Shakespeare Quarterly* 40 (1989): 33-35.

[17] See Laroque, "'Heads and Maidenheads,'" 196-97. See also Gail Kern Paster, *The Body Embarrassed: Drama and Disciplines of Shame in Early Modern England* (Ithaca: Cornell University Press, 1993), 205-6.

[18] Lois Potter describes them as "jangled reminiscences" in "'Nobody's Perfect': Actors' Memories and Shakespeare's Plays of the 1590s," *Shakespeare Survey* 42 (1990): 91.

[19] See Frances Yates, *The Art of Memory* (1966; reprint, Harmondsworth: Penguin, 1978), 22-27.

[20] *The Comedy of Errors* 3.2.93-138. In "The letter that

killeth: the Desacralized and the Diabolical Body in Shakespeare," *Shakespeare et le corps* (Paris: Les Belles Lettres, 1991), Ann Lecercle makes the following commentary on this scene:

> Nell's name is her body. . . . The second body is that of a type of representation that reached its apogee between 1550 and 1650, the landscape anamorphosis. For Nell's second body is a *mappa mundi*. . . . (143)

[21] See Andre Topia, "Les liturgies du corps dans *A Portrait of the Artist as a Young Man,*" in *Figures du corps,* ed. Bernard Brugière (Paris: Publications de la Sorbonne, 1991), 164.

[22] *The Tempest* 1.2.50.

[23] Edward Snow, "Language and Sexual Difference in *Romeo and Juliet,*" in *Romeo and Juliet: Critical Essays,* ed. John Andrews (New York: Garland, 1993). Snow says that "the Nurse's memory weaves all this eventfulness into a matrix of primary female experience (birth, lactation, weaning, marriage, maidenheads and their loss)," 388.

[24] In this connection, see for example Rabelais, Book 5, chapter 29:

> . . . by the registers of christenings at Thouars, it appears that more children are born in October and November than in the other ten months of the year, and *reckoning backwards,* it will be easily found that they were all made, conceived, and begotten in Lent.

in *The Complete Works of Doctor François Rabelais,* trans. Sir Thomas Urquart and Peter Motteux, 2 vols. (1653; reprint, London: The Bodley Head, 1926), 2:626-27, my emphasis. See also Laroque, *Shakespeare's Festive World,* 237-39.

[25] Carlo Ginzburg, *Les batailles nocturnes. Sorcellerie et rituels agraires aux XVIe et XVIIe siècles* (Turin, 1966; Paris, 1980; reprint, Paris: Flammarion, 1984), 39. (I translate here from the French edition.) In *Le sabbat des sorcières* (1989; reprint, Paris: Gallimard, 1992), Ginzburg establishes a connection between those nocturnal ridings and Mercutio's description of Queen Mab, 118.

[26] Barbara Everett, *Young Hamlet: Essays on Shakespeare's Tragedies* (Oxford: Clarendon Press, 1989), 115.

[27] Paster, *The Body Embarrassed,* 224.

[28] On this see Neil Rhodes, *Elizabethan Grotesque* (London: Routledge and Kegan Paul, 1980), 49.

[29] Mikhail Bakhtin, *Rabelais and His World,* trans. Hélène Isowlsky (1965; reprint, Bloomington: Indiana University Press, 1984), 21.

[30] "Rhetoric and the Rehearsal of Death: the 'Lamentations' Scene in *Romeo and Juliet,*" *Shakespeare Quarterly* 34 (1983): 390.

[31] *Romeo and Juliet* 1.5.55. See Laroque, "'Cover'd with an Antic Face': Les masques de la lumière et de l'ombre," 390.

[32] In this connection see Ann Lecercle, "Winking in *Romeo and Juliet,*" in *Roméo et Juliette: Nouvelles perspectives critiques,* ed. Maguin and Whitworth, 259.

[33] Whittier, "The Sonnet's Body and the Body Sonnetized in *Romeo and Juliet,*" 33.

[34] See Mario Praz, *The Romantic Agony* (1933; reprint, Oxford: Oxford University Press, 1991), 27-32.

[35] Whittier, "The Sonnet's Body," 32.

[36] See Jean Wirth, *La jeune fille et la mort. Recherches sur les thèmes macabres dans l'art germanique de la Renaissance* (Geneva: Librarie Droz, 1979), 137, 171-73. The rich iconographical appendix, with some 156 black-and-white reproductions of etchings, prints, drawings, and paintings, gives an idea of the diversity and continuity of the theme in Germanic art, from Dürer to Baldung Grien.

[37] At a lecture at the Sorbonne Nouvelle in November 1992, Brian Gibbons spoke of "the Juggernaut of custom."

[38] This contrasts with what happens in *Othello* and *Antony and Cleopatra* where love is presented against a heroic background and where the influence of Marlowe's *Tragedy of Dido* and *Tamburlaine* is visible. See Brian Gibbons, "Unstable Proteus: Marlowe and *Antony and Cleopatra,*" in *Shakespeare and Multiplicity* (Cambridge: Cambridge University Press, 1993), 182-202.

Source: "Tradition and Subversion in *Romeo and Juliet,*" in *Shakespeare's "Romeo and Juliet": Texts, Contexts, and Interpretation,* edited by Jay L. Halio, University of Delaware Press, 1995, pp. 18-36.

Scattered Corn: Ritual Violence and the Death of Rome in *Titus Andronicus*

Naomi Conn Liebler, *Montclair State University*

> [We] never really confront a text immediately, in all its freshness as a thing-in-itself. Rather, texts come before us as the always-already-read; we apprehend them through sedimented layers of previous interpretations, or . . . through the sedimented reading habits and categories developed by those inherited interpretive traditions. Fredric Jameson, Preface, *The Political Unconscious*

"Tragedy conjures the extinction of the human race" (Woodbridge 1994: 179). The ominous loading of the stage at the ends of Shakespearean tragedies encourages the view that tragedy is about death: the death of the body, of the spirit, of the polity. In that sense, *Titus Andronicus* (which rivals *Hamlet* in its final on-stage body count) should be judged one of Shakespeare's most successful tragedies, a *tour de force,* the quintessence of the genre itself. But many critics have argued that it was the least successful of Shakespeare's tragedies (Bevington 1980: 956; Rackin 1978: 10; J. D. Wilson 1948: li-lvi). A notable exception is Maurice Charney's observation that, along with other revenge tragedies of its generation, *Titus Andronicus* "helped to explore the possibilities of tragedy," and "shows the way that leads to greater plays. . . . The greatness of Shakespearean tragedy is already manifest" (1990: 9-10).

It was, however, Terence Spencer who reminded us a generation ago of the context in which an Elizabethan audience would have received *Titus*. Citing Antonio Guevara's *Decada,* translated by Edward Hellowes as *A Chronicle, conteyning the lives of tenne Emperours of Rome* (1577), as an "established" source for the play, he notes that among the "lives" an Elizabethan reader would have found therein,

> appears a blood-curdling life of a certain Emperor Bassianus. . . . [It] is one of almost unparalleled cruelty. . . . I will not say that it is a positive relief to pass from the life of Bassianus by Guevara to Shakespeare's *Titus Andronicus* (and there to find, by the way, that Bassianus is the better of the two brothers). . . . *Titus Andronicus* is Senecan . . . a not untypical piece of Roman history, or would seem to be so to anyone who came fresh from reading Guevara. Not the most high and palmy state of Rome, certainly. But an authentic Rome, and a Rome from which the usual political lessons could be drawn.
>
> (Spencer 1957:32)

The fact that *Titus Andronicus* follows classical models should not be ignored or explained away; neither should the idea that it offered its original audience "the usual political lessons" for which they turned to Roman history in the first place, although Spencer does not say what those were. More recent critics (Miola 1981; Charney 1990) have historicized the play from this hybrid Elizabethan-Roman point of view. This is not easy to do; as Miola says, "any approach which seeks to fit the various incarnations of Shakespeare's Rome to a single political or theological Procrustean bed does violence to the heterogeneity of the city's origins and character" (1981: 95).

The horrors that the play represents, however shocking they may be to the kinder, gentler culture that we think we are, would probably not have shocked an audience regularly entertained by what Steven Mullaney calls the "dramaturgy of the margins," by which "the horizon of the community was made visible, the limits of definition, containment, and control made manifest," and which included "hospitals and brothels, . . . madhouses, scaffolds of execution, prisons, and lazar-houses" (1988: 31), not to mention various animal and human atrocities going on virtually next door to the Theater in bear-baiting and cock-fighting dens, and similarly heterodox, disorderly, or "incontinent" cultural entertainments. As John Velz notes, walls are the most important edifices in Shakespeare's Rome, which is "above all *urbs* in its etymological sense, the enclave of civilization ringed round with a protective wall, outside of which the dark forces of barbarism lurk" (1978: 11). Evidently one did not have to venture very far outside those walls to find lurking barbarism.

A "margin" is not only linear, defining a city's limits, but also spatial, a topology inhabited and informed by a social behavior and a political status. A space that delimits ambiguity and flux, that defines and contains by describing a boundary, a margin is itself a locus for alteration. In the terms by which a *polis* defines itself, "margin" represents the verge, the limits, by which one is citizen or alien, endogenous or exogenous, "one of us" or "one of them." Once again Mary Douglas's observation applies: "all margins are dangerous. If they are pulled this way or that the shape of fundamental experience is altered. Any structure of ideas is vulnerable at its margins" (1966: 121). In *Titus Andronicus,* as in *Othello* and *The Merchant of Venice,* one may live, or be brought to live, within a city's walls, and still be marginalized. That, surely, is one of the play's "usual political lessons."

Titus Andronicus is in many respects a marginal play. As Shakespeare's first tragedy, it was the *terminus a quo,* the initial boundary for the rest of his work in the genre. But most important is the play's concern with marginality and its threat to political identity. Rome in this play is a city of ambiguity, whose cultural identity is challenged from the outset by the incorporation of aliens within its boundaries, by confusion and dissension about its rules of conduct and their consistent applications, and by the hybridization of its central leadership.

Previous attempts to identify the play's sources have yielded a patchwork of less than satisfactory nominations, aside from the usual round-up of Ovidian, Senecan, and Virgilian—that is, literary—analogues. With every suggestion, scholars have noted how little may be said with certainly about Shakespeare's acquisition of the plot concerning the Goths and Aaron, as well as any story about any actual Andronici (Bullough 1973: VI: 3-82; Maxwell 1961: xxvii-xxxii; Charney 1990: 7; D. J. Palmer 1972: 323). The closest parallel texts are a prose story and a ballad printed in an eighteenth-century chap-book owned by the Folger Library, but as Bullough says, these are as likely to have followed Shakespeare's play as to have preceded it. The uncertainty of the date of the play itself (Hill 1957) makes it difficult to determine what Shakespeare knew and how he could have known it. What history of fifthcentury Rome was available to him? All of Shakespeare's usually accepted classical sources significantly antedate the famous Gothic "Sack of Rome." Tacitus's *Histories* and *Annals* (translated into English in 1591 and 1598, respectively), and Pliny's *Natural History* (translated into English in 1566) merely mention among various Germanic tribes the *Gothones* (Tacitus) or *Gutones* (Pliny); in any case both historians wrote during the first century C.E., long before these "Goths" became any sort of threat to Roman borders or territories. Moreover, in Shakespeare's play, it is the Romans who are victorious, and nothing in the play indicates who started the war, or who invaded whose territories.

It may be said with some safety, then, that Shakespeare's "Goths" are not the ones who overthrew Rome in the fifth century, and indeed may not be any particular historical Goths at all. "Goth" may be a generic term for barbarian, especially barbarians of Eastern origin and fierce and bloody reputation: in "A Valediction: Of the Book," Donne employs the image of "ravenous / Goths and Vandals" to signal the end of civilization and especially of literacy and learning. In *As You Like It,* Touchstone compares his displacement in Arden with that of "honest Ovid . . . among the Goths" (III.iii.9), alluding to Ovid's description of his banishment among the Getae (formerly identified with "Goths") in the *Pontic Epistles*. Lear, in banishing Cordelia, compares her to "The barbarous Scythian, / Or he that makes his generation messes / To gorge his appetite" (I.i.116-18), incorporating a reminder of the reputation of invaders from the East for intrafamilial cannibalism that is, of course, reflected in Tamora's unwitting consumption of her children.[1]

The term "Goth" functions in Shakespeare's play as part of a differential economy as the "other" of Roman civilization. In fact, long before any *Gothic* invasions, Rome was nearly destroyed from within by the same Bassianus Spencer mentions. This Bassianus was a Libyan on his father's side (the emperor Septimius Severus) and a Syrian on his mother's (Julia Domna), and converted his court to the manners and customs of Syrian theocracy. His reign and those immediately following constituted a long and bloody period of religious and political instability in Rome. For these events Shakespeare did indeed have a specific source, previously unidentified by the play's editors and critics. That source, which is also the source of Guevara's *Decada* and thus of Hellowes's *Chronicle,* is Herodian of Antioch's *History of the Roman Empire*. Herodian tells of a Rome governed for sixty years by an Afroasiatic dynasty, its religion converted to a Syrian theocracy spearheaded by a politically clever and ambitious *materfamilias* and her two sons, one of whom had the other killed and proceeded to rule as one of the more vicious tyrants in Roman history. There are only two extant contemporary records of this period of internal destruction, this undoing by a marginalized and demonized force ruling from within Roman borders. The Greek Dio Cassius's *Roman History* was not translated into English until the twentieth century. Herodian's *History* was translated into English by Nicholas Smyth and printed by William Coplande *circa* 1550 as *The history of Herodian,*[2] a chronicle, modeled on Plutarch's *Lives,* of the late empire from Marcus Aurelius (161-80) to Gordian III (238-44), including the reign of Bassianus and his successors. Here is the lesson Tudor England would have learned from Herodian.

The historical Rome that later failed to stave off the Gothic invasion had long since already destroyed itself from within. Herodian's claim to the authority of an eye-witness may well be believed, since the Afroasiatic dynasty covers a period of only some sixty years (180-238): "And when by the space of lx. yeres, the Citie of Rome had sustained more gouernours then for the time sufficed, it came to passe, that many straunge thinges and worthy admiracion chanced" (Herodian 1550: sig. B.iv).

The story that interested Shakespeare began under Bassianus's father, Septimius Severus, a Libyan who had gained control of Rome without significant opposition during an interregnum in 193 when Rome had no central leadership. His main rival for control of Rome was one Niger, a former consul and governor of Syria. Niger's belated (and futile) campaign to defeat Severus deployed troops of Moroccan javelin-throwers, famous (says Herodian) for bravery, brutality, and savagery, and in Herodian's account Shakespeare might have found inspiration for his Moor.[3] Severus's most famous exploit was the attempted subjection of Britain, to which Herodian devotes detailed attention. He died in the middle of this prolonged effort, and was succeeded by Bassianus (also known as Caracalla, and as Antoninus, an honorific attached to all Roman emperors from Septimius Severus to his grandson Severus Alexander). Bassianus was preferred to the throne by his Syrian mother, Julia Domna, herself a formidable and assiduous politician, mostly on behalf of her sons but with almost equal dedication to her own licentious and ambitious leanings. Several years before he died, Septimius Severus married Bassianus to the daughter of his Libyan compatriot, one Plautianus. The marriage was far from happy. To avenge his daughter's neglect, Plautianus hired a tribune out of the praetorian guard to kill both Bassianus and Severus, but the plot failed when the tribune betrayed his employer. The tribune's name was Saturninus, and he too was Syrian by birth (sig. M.iii, fol. xlii-xliii).

The historical Bassianus's brother was actually named Geta; perhaps the name Saturninus sounded more "Roman" for the brother of Shakespeare's Bassianus. It is entirely possible, as well, that "Geta" suggested "Goth" to Shakespeare; in fact, early histories of the Goths refer generally to the scattered tribes of Goths as Getae or Geticae.

In Herodian several missing links come together. The matter of religious controversy and Julia Domna's manipulations behind palace doors suggest two of the structural elements of the plot concerning Tamora. If Saturninus is indeed a name-replacement for Geta, Shakespeare simply reversed the personalities of the brothers, for the historical Bassianus killed his brother, annexed his lands, and ruled most tyrannically. In explaining himself to his people, Bassianus cited historical precedents for "kynred"-killers, naming, among others, "Romulus hym selfe, the buylder of this Citye," and Domitian's murder of his brother Titus (there is no connection between Shakespeare's Titus and Domitian's victim, but the name may have stuck in Shakespeare's mind). In the end, having killed too many of his own people—"he began to destroye euery man from the verie bedde syde, as the prouerbe sayth" (sig. N.iii, fol. xlv)—Bassianus was slain by the surviving brother, Martialis, of yet another of his victims. The manner of his death is worth noting: in Mesopotamia, returning from worship at the Temple of Diana, he stopped, as Herodian narrates,

> to do the requisites of nature. Then Martialis, (which awaited euery conuenie~t howre) seyng the Emperour alone, & all other farre of, made haste towardes him asthough he were called for some businesse, & running vpon him unwares, as he was vntrussing his pointes, stabbed him in w~ a dagger, which he of purpose, secretly bare in hys sleaue.
>
> (fol. lv.)

The reign of Bassianus lasted altogether six years, and ended, ironically, in an act of defecation.

The utility of Herodian's narrative to a study of *Titus Andronicus* is not only as a previously unrecognized source for Shakespeare, the only one that links the names of Bassianus and Saturninus. Its special value is in its presentation, certainly available to Shakespeare, of a peculiar period in Roman history when Elizabethan England's favorite cultural antecedent was itself hybridized and feminized. Rome's "Syrian phase" began in 186, when a legion commander married the daughter of a Syrian priest of Elagabalus. In 193, when the Libyan Septimius Severus became emperor, Rome had a Syrian empress, Julia Domna, "the key figure in Rome's Syrian dynasty. . . . A shrewd, highly capable woman [who] assumed imperial responsibility with her husband" (Echols 1961: 4). When Bassianus (Caracalla) became emperor in 211, Rome had a Syrian-Libyan emperor, and when Elagabalus became emperor in 218, Rome had a Syrian emperor. The Syrian domination of Rome continued through the reign of Alexander Severus, a pacifist whose weak military command ultimately led to the return of "European" leadership under Maximinus (235-8), who was born in Thrace.

Thus, in Herodian we find not only some of those names that have baffled *Titus's* editors, but perhaps more importantly, a slice of Roman history which saw Rome dominated from within by "barbarians,"[4] its values compromised and perhaps by Elizabethan standards bastardized and miscegenized,[5] its pollution led and orchestrated by a politically ambitious and calculating matriarch who gave him his model for Tamora, and a dynasty of African rulers. *Titus Andronicus* may be Shakespeare's attempt to accommodate that long and problematic episode in the history of a Rome which England preferred not to recognize. The Roman history that Tudor England read about in Herodian was not the masculine, European Roman history of Marcus Brutus, Julius Caesar, and Marc Antony; it was not the Rome upon which England in part rested its own cultural genealogy. It was a Rome dominated by feminine influence,[6] subverting everything that was understood by the ideology of *romanitas*.

The relation of the cultural displacements in the play, as suggested by Herodian's *History,* to ritualistic action is significantly illuminated by other ancient sources known to Shakespeare. There are certain aspects of

Seneca's *Thyestes* that are undervalued in most criticism of *Titus Andronicus*. The *Thyestes* was already an old Elizabethan story when Shakespeare was born. Jasper Heywood's 1560 English translation was more than twenty years old when Thomas Newton published it in *Seneca His Tenne Tragedies* (1581). More familiar to the Elizabethans than the Aeschylean version preferred today, it told the base legend, the ur-myth, on which classical familial tragedies are modeled. Zeus's son Tantalus kills *his* son Pelops (in Seneca, constructed sentimentally as a baby "running to kiss his father" [1966: TLN 145]) and feeds him to the gods assembled at a formal banquet, with catastrophically inverted results for the entire community: "The consequence of this repast was hunger, / Hunger and thirst for all eternity" (1966: TLN 149-50). Similarly, in the Ovidian source for Lavinia's rape and mutilation, Procne retaliates against her rapist-husband Tereus on her sister Philomel's behalf by killing their son Itys and feeding his baked body to his father. Neither Ovid nor Seneca gives any reason for this originary, causeless infanticide, which in Seneca is reversed when Zeus restores Pelops. Pelops's two sons, Thyestes and Atreus, compete for their father's throne. Thyestes seduces his brother's wife; Atreus retaliates by killing and feeding Thyestes's sons to their father—all except Aegisthus (born of Thyestes's incest with his sister Pelopia), who grows up to seduce Clytemnestra, wife of Atreus's son Agamemnon, who had meanwhile sacrificed his daughter Iphigenia in order (he said) to summon the winds and save his navy. Clytemnestra kills Agamemnon, ostensibly in revenge for Iphigenia's death, and Orestes retaliates by killing his mother Clytemnestra while Electra, the remaining sister, urges him on, pours libations, and curses everyone in her whole sad family.[7]

This dizzying synopsis illustrates a mythic base of infanticide and incest, laundered in the Aeschylean *Eumenides* to suggest an evolution towards "modern" and "humane" systems of justice. Seneca, however, was more interested in the foundational significance of *sparagmos* [ritual dismemberment] and *omophagia* [child-eating] than in institutionalized forms of civil retribution. Foundational stories define a culture to itself, setting standards and parameters by which it distinguishes itself from others. Originary violence, as Girard argues, is a given in foundation myths; it is nonetheless interesting to notice *against whom* and *in whose behalf* that violence occurs. The story of the House of Atreus deals entirely with intrafamilial or endogenous relations; kin-killing and incest are at the heart of both Aeschylean and Senecan versions of the story. The larger political narrative is just barely remembered in the face of these horrors: the Argive victory over Troy; the endless hunger in the aftermath of a banquet at the very beginning, and of course the fact that the "kin" in these stories are royalty (and earlier, deity), and therefore responsible for the welfare of whole polities.

It is worth noting how closely Shakespeare hews to his Senecan antecedent. The Gothic family looks much like the Thyestean side of Seneca's story: although Tamora does not kill her own children, she does, like Thyestes, eat them; the miscegenation of Tamora and Aaron can be seen as an inversion (a radical exogamy) of the incest (a radical endogamy) that produced Aegisthus. Recalling the Atreidan side of the story, Titus kills both a son and a daughter, as Tantalus killed his son and Agamemnon killed his daughter,[8] and plays the role of Atreus in feeding Tamora's sons to her.

The Thyestean pie put before Tamora, however, is more than a Senecan or Ovidian exercise by a novice playwright; it is appropriate justice. From the beginning of his career, Shakespeare understood the resonances of ritualistic action in performance. The baking and serving of Chiron and Demetrius is a fitting response to Lavinia's rape and mutilation. Tamora is literally made to swallow the agents of the grotesque violations she has engineered. A formal banquet is perverted into a mythologically antecedent act of *omophagia,* which in the mythic base devolves to a cycle of revenge with no resurrective or regenerative possibilities. In *Titus, omophagia* repays outwardly directed crimes of mutilation and murder with an inwardly directed pollution. The punctilious design of Titus's revenge reflects the power of inversion as redress.[9]

Jan Kott's investigation of ancient rites involving *sparagmos* and *omophagia* as the cultural context of Euripides's *Bacchae* locates maternal *omophagia* as a structural inversion of incest, and also of giving birth and feeding. It is *"genesis* annihilated, moved back to its origins," negating both time and succession. "This simultaneous fili-, regi-, and dei-cide is the ultimate completion of the cycle. Cosmos has become chaos again so that everything can begin anew. . . . Fertility is mortally wounded in order that it may be renewed" (Kott 1973: 200). Kott's focus on maternal *omophagia* brings us closer to Tamora's punishment in *Titus Andronicus* than does any segment of the Atreus legend, in which all the child-eaters are male. "In such myths and *sparagmos* rites, women are the priestesses. They tear bodies to pieces and partake of the raw flesh. The sacrificial victim is always male: a child of the male sex, or a young man, or a ram, he-goat, or bull" (1973: 199).

Shakespeare aborts the ritual intention of *sparagmos* and *omophagia; Titus* is set not in the world of the Eleusinian rites but in late Imperial Rome as performed for Elizabethan England. In the violent and violational world of Shakespeare's play, cosmos becomes chaos but nothing can begin anew. This is evident from the specific nature of the Gothic family's crimes against the Andronici, which are themselves retaliation for the play's initial *sparagmos,* the "lopping" of Alarbus's "limbs." As Miola notes, "Instead of beginning the

Roman Empire, the rape of Lavinia signals the end of whatever civilization Rome possesses and the triumph of lawless savagery" (1981: 88-9). Her mutilation signals the end of civilization in yet another way: the loss of hands and tongue deprive her of both writing and speech, which Ben Jonson called "the only benefit man has to expresse his excellencie of mind above other creatures. It is the Instrument of Society" (1965: 347). Their deprivation, then, signals the removal of the speechless from the social construct and renders her, by definition, inhuman.

The implication for the larger order of Rome in the play is disastrous: not only is Lavinia dehumanized, but as the only Andronica (and one of only three females in the play, all dead or imminently so by the end), her death, like her silencing and her rape, undermine Marcus's weak charge to the "sad-fac'd *men,* people and *sons* of Rome" (my emphasis) to "knit again / This scatter'd corn into one mutual sheaf" (V.iii.67-71). The phallocentric image of the sheaf, the seminal one of scattered corn, and the address to men and sons are curious. On the one hand, Tamora's feminization of the Roman emperorship figures as the primary source of Rome's destruction,[10] not only as a masculine civilization but as a civilization of any kind. On the other hand, without women, Rome's hopes for renewal reside in an impossible parthenogenesis. The reconstruction of the body politic is highly doubtful after so much dismemberment: the bodies of Lavinia and Titus (and Martius and Quintus Andronicus, and Alarbus) are not the only ones dismantled in the play. The dismemberment of Rome as a polity is declared at the play's outset when Titus is invited by his brother on behalf of "the people of Rome" to accept the emperorship, "and help to set a head on headless Rome" (I.i.186). Shakespeare's pun is clearly intended; Titus's refusal inculpates him in his city's *sparagmos.*

A completed ritual would require both *sparagmos* and *omophagia,* dismemberment *and* ingestion or reintegration in a new body. Shakespeare fragments the ritual process by assigning the agency of *sparagmos* both to Chiron and Demetrius and to Titus, and that of *omophagia* to Tamora. Alarbus's and Titus's respective "lopp'd" limbs and Martius's and Quintus's severed heads all separately and collectively represent fragments of a body of ritual *practice* that in another time and place would have signalled the start of a healing rite. This play's deployment of *disjecta membra* demonstrates the nihilistic impact of ritual gone awry. Consequently, the promised end, the scattered corn knit into one mutual sheaf, is set up as an impossibility. There is no renewal, none is possible, for a Rome so torn apart and so far from the proper management of its foundational ritual practices.

In *Titus Andronicus* Shakespeare does not simply replicate the *Thyestes* or interpellate several foundational stories; he inverts them, foregrounding the political implications for Rome. Beginning with the election of Titus as emperor and his rejection of the honor, this aborted ceremony is immediately conflated with the entry of the Andronicus funeral procession, which takes us immediately to the sacrifice *ad manes fratrum* of Alarbus (D. J. Palmer 1972: 327). The play is arranged as a central story of *sparagmos* (Alarbus, Lavinia, Titus, Martius and Quintus) bracketed by infanticide (Mutius in Act I and Lavinia in Act V) and *omophagia* (Act V). This structuring foregrounds the confusion or interpenetration of political and religious ritual, which makes it much more than a Senecan imitation. It is a dissection of cultural formation and its definition, an interrogation of the inextricable relation between the political and ritual in culture. Ritual becomes not the effective redress for which it is designed but the actual site of contestation (for which there is no redress) and a reminder of the consequences to the polity of ritual violation or neglect.

The play's numerous and various examples of *sparagmos* enact a dissection or anatomy of culture that discloses its fault-lines. The intersections of axes along which culture is produced are also its vulnerable points; what can be joined can also be sundered. Shakespeare's meticulous attention to these junctures might seem remarkable in such an early play. But the discourse of the body that contextualizes this attention was a long-standing and well-known commonplace by the late sixteenth century. The observation that the body is especially vulnerable at its joints and orifices belongs to Sir John Cheke, who noted in *The Hurt of Sedicion Howe Grevous it is to a Commune-wealth* (1549; STC 5109) that, like the natural body, the body politic "cannot bee without much grief of inflammacon, where any least part is out of joynt, or not duely set in his owne natural place" (quoted in M. James 1983: 8n.). The Rome that interested Shakespeare in *Titus Andronicus* was for sixty years a sutured patchwork of European and Afroasiatic population, politics, and religion.

What happens to such a sutured civilization? What specific junctures make it vulnerable? In *Titus,* culture is literally articulated in terms of body parts (D. J. Palmer 1972; Tricomi 1974; Paster 1989; Kendall 1989), which are further arranged into male and female categories. These anatomical assignments are expanded into gendered social roles, which are then undermined by constant inversion and re-inversion in this play. The consistency with which Shakespeare attaches such imagery to Roman history is worth noting; we find it again in *Coriolanus* in Menenius's Fable of the Belly. Remarkably, Shakespeare's first tragedy looks ahead to his final one when, in *Titus,* Aemilius looks "backward" by invoking the "historical" Coriolanus as a model for Lucius's revolt against Rome (IV.iv.68).

A culture defines itself in part by distinguishing self from other, "them" from "us," citizen from alien, and does so along both national and racial lines of demarcation. Out of such defining divisions, or rather to secure them, ideology is formed, and ritual's primary function, after guaranteeing physical survival, is to guarantee the survival of the cultural definition, that is, its ideology. But the Rome of *Titus Andronicus* has no unifying ideology. Titus believes that it does, as we see by his actions in the first moments of the play; but his faith is immediately contested by his sons and further problematized by the union of Tamora, the Asiatic Goth, and the Roman Saturninus.

The combined ritual function of *sparagmos* and *omophagia* belongs to that of the scapegoat or *pharmakos*. Again the matter of cultural distinctions, "them" and "us," is crucial. As Girard has explained, in order for a scapegoat rite to be effective, the *pharmakos* must resemble the rest of the community enough to represent it, and at the same time must be sufficiently alienated, misrecognized as *other,* to be killed with impunity (1977: 13). The opening scene of *Titus Andronicus* positions the political and ritual requirements of the victorious Romans against those of the defeated Goths, thereby interrogating the definitions that distinguish self from other, "Roman" from "Goth."

While I am not arguing that *Titus Andronicus* represents an Elizabethan plea for multicultural tolerance, it does raise questions about the definitions of culture that enable the chain of killing and revenge, and of *sparagmos* and *omophagia* that encircle and define this play. The play begins with a ritual sacrifice, *ad manes fratrum* (I.i.96-101), for Titus's sons who have been killed in battle. This sacrifice is seen as a legitimate demand from the Roman point of view, but not, obviously, from that of the Goths, who (again from the Roman point of view) are both aliens and prisoners of war, and therefore are perfect scapegoats. Their foreign status means that the Roman community is not contaminated by killing or by failing to avenge one of its own. If Alarbus were a solitary prisoner, his sacrifice would have achieved its intended effect, and we would hear no more of him or the Goths. But Shakespeare problematizes the ritual situation by including Tamora and her remaining sons. The "other" that Alarbus represents to Rome is "self" to the Gothic contingent. Moreover, the rite itself is problematic in so far as it is intended as a rite of completion, to answer a killing and to avoid further reprisal; that effect is only possible in the case of communal agreement about its function and operation. For Tamora, it is not a rite but a murder, and therefore demands revenge. Her pleas for Alarbus's life complicate audience response by cutting across national lines of definition: instead of Goths and Romans, the audience is invited by Tamora's lines to consider an undifferentiated human *communitas*:

> Victorious Titus, rue the tears I shed,
> A mother's tears in passion for her son;
> And if thy sons were ever dear to thee,
> O, think my son to be as dear to me!
> Sufficeth not that we are brought to Rome
> To beautify thy triumphs, and return
> Captive to thee and to thy Roman yoke;
> But must my sons be slaughtered in the streets
> For valiant doings in their country's cause?
> O, if to fight for king and commonweal
> Were piety in thine, it is in these.
>
> (I.i.105-15)

Her argument appeals to Titus's sense of piety as well as to the same *romanitas* that informed his own willing sacrifice in war of twenty-one sons for his country. His response turns the argument back upon her.

> Patient yourself, madam, and pardon me.
> These are their brethren, whom your Goths beheld
> Alive and dead, and for their brethren slain
> Religiously they ask a sacrifice:
> To this your son is mark'd, and die he must,
> T'appease their groaning shadows that are gone.
>
> (I.i.121-6)

No compromise is possible: paradoxically, the cycle of revenge that ritual is designed to prevent is inevitable in the circumstances of the play. The hard truth of perspective is brought home: what Lucius calls the "clean" consumption by fire of the *pharmakos* (127-9) is for Tamora nothing but "cruel, irreligious piety!" (130), a definition that contradicts Titus's surname, "Pius," noting the virtue for which he is famous.

These contesting claims for "piety," defined separately by Tamora and Titus in terms of both "vengeance" and proper burial rites, illuminate from the very start of the play the crisis of Roman cultural definition. The question of definitions entailed in ritual clarity immediately spreads to members of Titus's own family when he kills and disowns Mutius. In his refusal to allow Mutius's burial, Titus enacts the definitional crisis, and Marcus identifies it: "Thou art a Roman; be not barbarous" (I.i.378). Roman values are themselves revealed as the site of contestation. Since one of the hallmarks of *romanitas* is filial obedience, Mutius's rebellion against Titus in the matter of remanding Lavinia to Saturninus seems to Titus nothing less than treason. But Rome's belief in its own laws is equally compelling, and Lavinia was contracted to Bassianus. In order to resolve this particular conflict, Titus kills the "traitor" by first disclaiming kinship: Mutius is deliberately misrecognized, made an "other," an alien: "Nor thou [to Lucius] nor he, are any sons of mine. / My sons would never so dishonor me. / Traitor, restore Lavinia to the Emperor" (I.i.294-6). As an alien, Mutius can be denied proper ritual burial in the family tomb (I.i.349-54); but as an Andronicus, he must be so buried, and Titus's refusal is called by his brother Marcus "impiety" (355), the charge now coming not from Tamora but from within the family. The violation of Roman burial rites by a Roman immediately establishes the pattern of ritual perversion and neglect that continues throughout the play to the end, when the belated attempt is made to resurrect Rome from its own scattered seed: Titus and Lavinia are granted proper burial, but Tamora and Aaron will be left to rot at the margins of the city.

The tragedy is set in motion by conflicting ritual observations, a set of relativities, a clash of cultures whose differences reflect their similarities as we can hear in Tamora's pleading. Her maternal plea is dismissed; fittingly she later ignores Lavinia's appeal to "sister-hood." As disturbing as her "unfeminist" treatment of Lavinia is, it is also a strong form of revenge against Titus; as Miola points out, the rape of a daughter "is a flagrant violation of the family and the sacred bonds that tie it together . . . the destruction of her familial bonds has disastrous implications for the order in the city and the hierarchical order in nature itself" (1981: 87). Tamora learns quickly that the Rome Titus embodies has no regard for the feminine (we see this again in Marcus's phallocentric closing invocation), and despite its claims to the contrary, none for the family either unless that family is natively Roman. G. K. Hunter long ago suggested that the "alternative 'household' of Saturninus/Tamora/Aaron with Tamora's assorted children . . . can only be called a 'family' by a radically deformed definition" (1974: 4). However, it should be noted that the vaunted Roman regard for family is shown to be seriously limited in the *paterfamilias* himself. As Shylock says in *The Merchant of Venice,* "The villainy you teach me I will execute, and it shall go hard but I will better the instruction" (III.i.71-3). Since, in this Rome, feminine values are eschewed, Tamora, out of sheer survivalist adaptation, becomes more like the quintessential Roman male, that is, like Titus, one who can kill not only other people's children but his own. Though Tamora never quite manages to kill her own children (she orders her baby's death, but does not execute it), Titus remedies that by making her eat them. In an exchange of behaviors, father-Titus learns to be more like the Gothic (not the neo-Roman) mother-Tamora; his daughter's dismantling teaches him to empathize with the "parents" of a fly. Meanwhile, Aaron, the permanent alien, doubly demonized as "the black man with the Jewish name" teaches everyone what paternity and paternal love really mean when he taunts Chiron and Demetrius about their baby brother and bargains with Lucius to protect his son. Aaron preserves all the characteristics of his theatrical ancestor the Vice (until he steps forward to protect his son); he stays in the margin of Rome and machinates the inversion of all-that-is-Roman to nothing-at-all, an unregeneratable pile of scattered seed.

Rome, as represented by Saturninus, attempted to subvert the alien Goths by incorporating them into Roman citizenship and Roman values by his union with Tamora. But a dismembered polity, "headless Rome" (I.i.186) split from the beginning of the play by opposing brothers, is already fractured beyond any unified set of values. Since gender and racial distinctions are two especially visible options out of a number of tactics for cultural definition, the concretizing of Rome's cultural disintegration in a feminized and racialized dialectic enabled Shakespeare's audience to "see" the consequences to this civilization that allowed itself to let go of its cultural definitions, as Rome indeed had done and as Elizabethan England seemed increasingly in danger of doing (Mullaney 1988: 64; Bartels 1990; Neill 1989).

The definitional crisis spreads in yet another direction when Saturninus establishes Tamora as his empress. Tamora and her sons, former prisoners of war, are absorbed into Roman (or neo-Roman) identity, and the distinction of "Roman" from "non-Roman" is no longer persuasive, no longer even possible. Tamora's empowerment enables her to avenge her son's death, but she does so as a new-made Roman, and the "clean" ritual distinction of *other*ness is obliterated: for the remainder of the play, except for Aaron, all participants in this internecine slaughter are either Romans or neo-Romans by definition, and the entire community, in a chaos of kin-killing and self-mutilation, turns in upon itself in the ultimate pattern of annihilation.

From the start of the play, little more than half way through the first scene, we see the consequences first of contestation between separate communities; then the arena narrows to a specifically Roman venue, and then the circle contracts to the still smaller arena of a single family. Before the play is over, that arena will contract yet further to its most microcosmic version, the individual: Titus himself becomes the site of contestation, and the divisions we have already witnessed between communities, within a community, and within a family, become manifest in the literal dismemberment of the patriarch and his only daughter and the beheading of two of his three remaining sons. Like Alarbus, Martius and Quintus died from their dismemberment; but the mutilated images presented by both Titus and Lavinia are images of life-in-death, terrifying indistinctions that pollute by their failure to separate the living from the dead, which is the aim and the design of properly conducted, unsubverted, burial rites and mourning practices. Critics have struggled to define Titus's killing of Lavinia in a range of meanings from cruelty to mercy; but within the play, even Saturninus calls him "unnatural and unkind" (V.iii.48). Moral evaluations aside (and who among those present, except perhaps for Lucius and Marcus, is qualified to make any?) Titus completes Lavinia's definition as "dead"; and thus he explains it to Tamora: "'twas Chiron and Demetrius. / They ravish'd her, and cut away her tongue; / And they, 'twas they, that did her all this wrong" (V.iii.56-8).

Ironically, the "headlessness" by which Rome is identified at the opening of the play is filled in by the image of Aaron's punishment at the end of the play. Set "breast-deep," "fast'ned in the earth" (V.iii.179, 183), he appears to be a disembodied head; "planted," he epitomizes the paradox of an unregeneratable polity—his is not the corn or seed Marcus hopes to gather, but as he hopes, his seed, half Moor and half Roman-Goth, will eventually destroy what is left of Rome. By that time, and indeed before the play is over, Rome has lost all vestiges of its political identity. Titus had a hand in that too, when he sent Lucius, "the turn'd forth" (V.iii.109), off to rally the Gothic army to march against what was once his city (a reversion also performed by Coriolanus) and against a woman who was once their queen. Throughout *Titus Andronicus,* both Roman and Gothic cultural distinctions are confounded: early on, Demetrius counseled his mother to wait for the "opportunity of sharp revenge" that would "favor Tamora, the Queen of Goths— / When Goths were Goths and Tamora was queen" (I.i.139-40). By the end of the play, Goths are still not Goths (no more than Romans are Romans); they return with Lucius as his allies. Rome, too, is hybridized by Tamora's marriage to Saturninus; she refers to herself as "incorporate in Rome, / A Roman now adopted happily" (I.i.462-3). After this, her coupling with Aaron and the birth of their interracial child simply extends the blurring of distinctions already set in motion.

All cultural definitions are nullified in this play by the confusion or neglect of cultural markers. Rome, which has long since become a "wilderness of tigers," is in the end identified with the incorporated aliens Tamora and Aaron, each of whom is separately (V.iii.5; V.iii.195) called by Lucius a "ravenous tiger" (Loomba 1989: 46). Marcus's "Let me teach you how to knit again" and Lucius's promise "to heal Rome's harms, and wipe away her woe" (V.iii.148) are taken by some critics at face value (Hunter 1974: 6; D. J. Palmer 1972: 338); that is, they assume that Rome will indeed arise from its "scattered corn." Lucius's first act of "healing" is properly constructed as the re-establishment of funeral rites, which return us to the play's beginning. Funeral rites are part of the set of cultural distinctions that separate "Roman" from "other": Lucius buries Titus and Lavinia in the Andronicus tomb while planting Aaron and leaving Tamora "to beasts and birds to prey" (V.iii.198). Aaron and Tamora are denied such rites not only in revenge but also because there are no rites appropriate to them; as incorporated aliens they remain demonized and marginal.

No regeneration is possible in such a fractured polity. Lucius's attempt to restore cultural unity is undermined by the truth about the bodies he would inter in the Andronicus tomb, once the symbol and locus of ritual integrity as Titus had argued in refusing to bury the son he had killed. The bodies of Titus and Lavinia are fragmented; they are missing parts. Despite Lucius's fiat, then, which is too little and comes too late, the Rome of *Titus Andronicus,* like its historical counterpart under Bassianus and his successors, cannot and could not be re-established, and it never was. By the end of the play we know why and how Rome fell.

Notes

[1] Although Scythian invasions of the area around the Black Sea, where the Greeks encountered them, apparently ceased by the end of the second century, *B.C.E.*, their reputation for barbarism was easily conflated with that of the various "Goths" who were active during the first several centuries, *C.E.*

[2] *The history of Herodian.* Subsequent English issues are from 1629 and 1634-5, too late for Shakespeare. The extremely popular, anonymous *Scriptores Historiae Augustae* was known throughout Europe in Latin codices (six editions from 1475 to 1518), including ones owned by Petrarch and Erasmus, but was not translated into English until the twentieth century. Its details differ from those in Herodian: it does not mention Saturninus, it diminishes Julia Domna's role (although she is identified as a notorious adulteress), and it underemphasizes the conversion of Rome to Syrian religion (Magie 1921, 1924: I and II). Herodian's history is the only contemporary record known to have existed in English during Shakespeare's lifetime. For a detailed account of Shakespeare's use of Herodian and its implications for reading *Titus Andronicus,* see Liebler 1994a.

[3] Both Maxwell (1961) in a line gloss at IV.ii.20, and West (1982: 70) note the reference to "Moorish javelins" in the line from Horace's *Odes* that Titus inscribes on the bundle of arrows presented to Chiron and Demetrius, and both think this a glance at Aaron. But it is just as likely that the Moorish reputation for javelin-throwing was already inscribed within Shakespeare's conception of Aaron, derived from Herodian. Horace provided additional support.

[4] Echols reminds us that Herodian was himself a Syrian living in Roman exile (and, interestingly, writing in Greek), and adds that "his early association with the Syrian dynasty at Rome would account for the amazing 'Romanness' of his outlook. Herodian is so thoroughly patriotic and so Romanized that he can speak

of his fellow non-Romans as barbarians, and can offer an analysis of his fellow Syrians that is thoroughly unflattering" (1961: 5).

[5] It is important to recognize that modern interpretations of "Elizabethan" attitudes may be more modern than Elizabethan. As Bernal argues, "For 18th- and 19th-century Romantics and racists it was simply intolerable for Greece, which was seen not merely as the epitome of Europe but also as its pure childhood, to have been the result of the mixture of native Europeans and colonizing Africans and Semites" (1987: I: 2); in the Renaissance, "no one questioned the fact that the Greeks had been the pupils of the Egyptians, in whom there was an equal, if not more passionate, interest" and who were "deeply respected for their antiquity and well-preserved ancient religion and philosophy" (1987: I: 23-4). If Elizabethan England inherited the Classical period's acceptance of the Afroasiatic roots of Greek culture, we may need to re-evaluate our assessments of Shakespeare's representations of his Moors—not only Aaron, but more obviously Othello and Portia's Moroccan suitor in *The Merchant of Venice*—all of whose noble traits are misrecognized by their Italianate fellow characters. Bernal's thesis has been challenged, not only on points of historical accuracy but also on its failure to recognize a distinction between "objective" and "subjective" ethnicity. The former is "a biological category which defines groups of human beings in terms of their shared physical characteristics resulting from a common gene pool," whereas the latter identifies "the ideology of an ethnic group by defining as shared its ancestors, history, language, mode of production, religion, customs, culture, etc., and is therefore a social construct, not a fact of nature" (Hall 1992: 185). Herodian's history (along with Dio's and the *Historia Augusta*) establishes as certain that Rome between 183 and 236 was governed by an Afroasiatic dynasty, in terms that satisfy Hall's important distinctions of "objective" as well as "subjective" ethnicity. How the Elizabethan heirs to this history interpreted that ethnic admixture is a question requiring further careful investigation; see Loomba (1989); Neill (1989); Bartels (1990).

[6] Julia Domma's extraordinary influence during Bassianus's reign is generally acknowledged by historians and translators of Herodian. See Echols 1961: 5, and Whittaker 1969: II: 367n.

[7] Electra's relative passivity is sometimes considered evidence of the "patriarchal" (i.e., misogynist) nature of both Aeschylean and Senecan tragedy (Figes 1990). Presumably a more even-handed treatment of social formations would have allowed Electra to do more than pour libations, curse, and wait for Orestes to do the filthy deed of matricide; but then, a less even-handed treatment would not have allowed Clytemnestra to wield the knife against her husband.

[8] Cox underscores the Stoic Roman nature of Titus's infanticide, arguing that such a view of "romanism" had a long and solid following among Elizabethans (1989: 173-6). This is a fair enough reading, but Titus's extraordinary suffering might have been represented through any of a variety of dramatic events. The play's persistent focus upon violence and ritual, it must be said, figures something else besides a fascination with Roman Stoic values.

[9] Laroque identifies the pie as:

> the transgression of a triple taboo. The first, clearly, is cannibalism; the second and third are indicated by the use of the word "daintily" ["Whereof their mother daintily hath fed" (V.iii.61)]. "Dainty" was also a term currently employed to refer to the testicles, which suggests that two other major taboos have also been transgressed—those of castration and incest, for Tamora has taken in and consumed her own sons' reproductive organs. Born from their mother's body, they re-enter it through a different orifice.
>
> (1991: 275)

This identification of the triple taboo, it seems to me, is a better claim than the limited Freudian one which sees the cannibalistic feast as "oral vengeance" of the "catastrophically perceived preoedipal mother, who threatens total dismemberment and destruction (the devouring mother)" (Willbern 1978: 171). However, the issue of *omophagia* in the context of a formal banquet is more problematic than either Laroque or Willbern represent; it is simultaneously a ritual act of regeneration and an act of pollution, and in its inherent ambiguity it expresses the contestational and contradictory nature of foundation myths in general. For a provocative discussion of *omophagia* in Greek tragedy, see Kott 1973: 186-230.

[10] White argues that Lavinia's rape and mutilation implicitly condemn a Rome where justice is constructed as male, self-destructive, revenge even when instituted by a woman such as Tamora (1986: 26-35; cf. Willbern 1978: 161; Tricomi 1974: 17). However, apart from a brief imagistic suggestion at the beginning (I.i.9-17) and another one at the end (V.iii.73-6), the crisis in Rome is represented throughout the play as a masculine ethos compromised by Tamora's Asiatic feminizing influence, an issue Shakespeare explored again later in *Antony and Cleopatra*.

[11] This is extremely problematic, as both Derrida and his translator acknowledge. Derrida used Robin's "authoritative French translation" (1981: 71) of Plato for most of his essay's quoted material. Derrida's translator, Barbara Johnson, used yet a different edition of Plato in English, with supplemental reference to several different English translations which, she says, she "sometimes partially adopted" (1981: 66n.). Thus the

difficulty of linguistic access is not only thoroughly explored in this essay; it is also thoroughly exemplified.

[12] Lincoln suggests a significantly tangent view of the Fable's referential domain: without mentioning *Coriolanus,* he discusses the narrative from Livy, II.32, the "Apologue of Menenius Agrippa," where, he says, debt and its punishment are the major issues. "Unable to win concessions from the patricians . . . the plebs are said to have physically withdrawn from the city and established themselves as an independent community on the Aventine Mount, leaving the patricians to tend their own needs without the support of plebeian labor" (1989: 145-6). Lincoln argues that Livy's account has been contested as an inflected discourse effacing the dependence of the patricians on the plebs; in Livy, the Fable persuades the plebs to end their secession and return to the city, reconciled. Subsequently and consequently, the office of *Tribuni plebis* was created to provide protection for plebeian interests by officers elected from the plebs themselves. This revisionist reading raises questions about Shakespeare's selection of material: there is no hint in the play of so autonomous a plebeian move as secession, or of a threat of *patrician* starvation without plebeian labor. Apparently unaware of *Coriolanus,* Lincoln concludes his section on Menenius: "this discourse was still being employed as late as 1594, when the lieutenant general of the Cahors court, in condemning the Croquant rebels, posed as a rhetorical question: What would happen if the members of the body should rebel against the stomach and refuse to feed it?" (1989: 148). What makes this interesting for readers of *Coriolanus* is the play's interpretation of the plebs as hungry and complaining, but dependent upon patrician "generosity," and endangered both by its absence and by seditious tribunes. The question of source-reception, the "genealogy" through which the "Apologue" reached Shakespeare—whether directly from Livy, or perhaps via Machiavelli's version in the Discourses, which supported the principle of *vox populi* (Zeeveld 1962: 323-4)—interpellates its appropriation for the play. The idea of a plebeian power to secede, absent from the play, reconfigures the play's initial conflict and raises questions about the scapegoating of Coriolanus to both plebeian and patrician interests.

[13] John Drakakis has very kindly given me permission to quote from his essay on *Coriolanus* (cited above, chapter 1, note 8). Among his valuable interventions in this essay is his suggestion of yet another "body" discourse, the economic body.

[14] In "*Coriolanus* and the Delights of Faction," Kenneth Burke offers an Aristotelian reading of victimage that inculpates any audience watching the play. We (Burke insists on "we," rather than restricting response to a Jacobean collective) "pity him even while we resent his exaggerated ways of representing our own less admirable susceptibilities. . . . Thereby we are cleansed, thanks to his overstating of our case" (1966: 89, but the point is reiterated throughout the essay: 81-94). He reminds us that the play is concerned "drastically" with class distinctions, recalling that "in earlier medical usage, a 'drastic' was the name for the strongest kind of 'cathartic.' Also, the word derives etymologically from the same root as 'drama'" (1966: 82).

[15] The 1607 Midlands Uprising and other revolts against Enclosure Acts, which not only destroyed livelihoods but also re-drew, and in some cases erased, village maps, may have been more a symptom of growing unrest than a cause, "more often to have followed the abandonment of holdings than to have caused it" (Keen 1990: 72); in some cases tenants rather than landlords did the enclosing (Keen 1990: 73). Such enclosures actually began as early as the thirteenth century. Pettet's (1950) essay linking the date of *Coriolanus* with the 1607 Insurrection is now generally dismissed for occluding the long history of enclosures and their pernicious consequences all over England and over several centuries. Pettet seems to have ignored his own cited evidence, relegating to a footnote Stow's report in the *Annales:* "that of very late years there were three hundred and forty towns decayed and depopulated" (quoted in Pettet 1950: 40, n. 6). By Shakespeare's time, enclosure and redistricting had made the metonymy of land as an inviolable integrity (so eloquently lamented in Gaunt's famous speech in *Richard II* II.i.40-66), an illusion, or at least a very distant nostalgia.

[16] As late as the early twentieth century, Sharp noted the "sudden" lack of support for local morris teams in the counties, which he attributed in part to "the enclosure of the common lands, and the creation of a proletariat, which led to a general migration of labouring men from the villages to the towns in search of work, the disruption of the social life of the village," and other ills; but, he added, "Whatever the reason of its decay, the Morris dance . . . flourished almost universally in the Midland counties as recently as fifty years ago" (Sharp and McIlwaine 1912: 19). E. O. James (1961) and Helm (1965) found recent evidence of its survival, although Helm thinks it is finished as a serious endeavor, relegated as it was by the 1960s to entertainment at school-term festivals. Curiously, morris and sword dancing have seen increasing popularity in the United States at festivals celebrating British culture and during intervals at regional performances of Shakespearean plays; there are at present considerable numbers of active professional and amateur morris teams, including an all-female team, the Ring o' Belles, who perform in the New York metropolitan area.

[17] Chambers briefly mentions this text, although his suggestion appears to have been subsequently ignored. He credits Johnson with having "brought together the

scattered legends of the [other six] national heroes" (1903: I: 221), and notes that "the mummers' play follows Johnson" (1903: I: 221, n.2), that is, Johnson supplies an authentic narrative.

[18] The dragon, says Chambers, was probably "the representative of the hardness of the frost-bound earth in winter" (1993: 178); thus the St George play, in his view, adumbrated the old seasonal ritual battle of winter and spring. He implies that the dragon directly symbolizes natural, i.e., climatic, elements that threaten plenitude and fruition, which might seem now to be a naive critical stance. Shakespearean demons are invariably human, and in so far as these cultural figures derive from solidly entrenched customs and practices, it might be more accurately said that the dragon figure, separately and as collapsed into the figures of both George and Coriolanus, represents a range of human and other forces inimical to communal life.

Source: "Scattered Corn: Ritual Violation and the Death of Rome in *Titus Andronicus,"* in *Shakespeare's Festive Tragedy: The Ritual Foundation of Genre,* pp. 131-48, Routledge, 1995.

That Which We Call a Name: The Balcony Scene in *Romeo and Juliet*

David Lucking, *University of Lecce*

The balcony scene in *Romeo and Juliet* lends itself so gracefully to being read simply as a sustained flight of lyricism, as one of the most poignant and intense love duets to be found in English literature, that it might almost seem an act of ingratitude to attend too closely to its more ominous reverberations. The reverberations however are unmistakably present, as intrinsic to the text as the more appealing melodies for which the scene is celebrated, and in their totality impose themselves as an ironic counterpoint to that music. These darker implications are rendered partially explicit in the apprehension that Juliet confesses to Romeo to feeling despite the rapture induced by her nascent passion: 'Although I joy in thee, / I have no joy of this contract tonight' (II.ii.116-17).[1] Juliet accounts for this anxiety at the time by remarking that their love is 'Too like the lightning, which doth cease to be / Ere one can say "It lightens"' (II.ii.119-20), and although this might seem to foreshadow Friar Laurence's troubled estimation of their situation, and lend substance to Caroline Spurgeon's view of the play as depicting 'an almost blinding flash of light, suddenly ignited, and as swiftly quenched',[2] there would appear to be more to the matter than that. What specifically provokes Juliet's comment is Romeo's persistently repeated endeavour to find words commensurate with the intensity of his feelings, a strenuous effort at linguistic formulation that collapses with each renewal into the threadbare commonplaces of amatory rhetoric. Romeo is defeated by the conventions of the very language he seeks to deploy as a notation of private experience, and the point to be observed in this connection is that this, in a sense, is what happens in the play as a whole. Despite its predominantly lyrical tone, in other words, the scene mirrors within its own reduced compass the tensions operating throughout the entire work, tensions that are already latent in the situations depicted in the opening scenes of the drama, and that ultimately erupt in so momentous a form as to make a tragic conclusion inevitable.

Few readers would be likely to dispute that one of the most important thematic motifs developed in the balcony scene in particular is that of language in its relation to what might variously be described as subjective experience, feeling or, more generally, life itself. Commentators have frequently observed that one of the things the young lovers are doing in this scene is repudiating the language of artificial convention they have formerly spoken in favour of a personal language more consonant with the realms of private experience they are beginning to explore.[3] Juliet has just encountered Romeo for the first time, and fallen irretrievably in love with him, only to learn immediately afterwards that he belongs to the detested Montague family and is therefore to be regarded as an enemy. Her initial response to this discovery is one of stunned perplexity at the paradox of her predicament, expressing itself rhetorically in the pointed juxtaposition of contradictory terms which, as has often been pointed out,[4] is a particularly prominent feature of this play:

> My only love sprung from my only hate.
> Too early seen unknown, and known too late.
> Prodigious birth of love it is to me
> That I must love a loathed enemy.
>
> (I.v. 137-40)

Subsequently, however, as Juliet muses on the situation in what she erroneously supposes to be the privacy of a balcony overlooking the family garden, she recognizes the paradox to be a spurious one. It is spurious because it consists exclusively in the fact that the enmity she is expected to feel for Romeo is rooted not in personal experience but in transmitted codes whose authority over the individual is not in the least self-evident. The words in which she formulates this recognition, though specifically referring to the personal name of a single individual, amount in effect to a denial of the constitutive or regulative authority of language in general:

> 'Tis but thy name that is my enemy:
> Thou art thyself, though not a Montague.
> What's Montague? It is nor hand nor foot
> Nor arm nor face nor any other part
> Belonging to a man. O be some other name.
> What's in a name? That which we call a rose
> By any other word would smell as sweet;
> So Romeo would, were he not Romeo call'd,
> Retain that dear perfection which he owes
> Without that title. Romeo, doff thy name,
> And for thy name, which is no part of thee,
> Take all myself.
>
> (II.ii.38-49)

The temptation to contrast this moment with that of Adam's naming of the beasts in another garden is almost irresistible, whatever associations might reasonably be supposed to have been operating in the playwright's mind.[5] Whereas the male compulsion to 'name' is symptomatic of the systematic differentiation of experience that leads ultimately to that estrangement which has its most comprehensive symbol in the Fall, the female gesture of 'unnaming' represents an effacing of divisions and a movement towards the re-establishment of the essential continuum of existence. In a sense the play reflects a struggle between what might therefore conveniently be described as the male and female attitudes with respect to language,[6] with the former asserting its inevitability at the same time as the latter vindicates its independent spiritual validity. Although the Capulet garden seems for a while to hold out the possibility of a prelingual unity analogous to that of Eden before the Fall, it turns out that it is a possibility fatally vitiated by the conditions of its own existence.

What is ultimately at issue, of course, is not only personal names as such, or even the language of which names comprise a crucial element, but the entire network of codes through which experience is mediated and the individual's vision of reality constituted. As Harry Levin argues in his brilliantly concise discussion of the play, Juliet's speech 'calls into question not merely Romeo's name but—by implication—all names, forms, conventions, sophistications, and arbitrary dictates of society, as opposed to the appeal of instinct directly conveyed in the odor of a rose'.[7] The more philosophically farsighted members of Shakespeare's original audience might well have perceived even more radically subversive overtones attaching to Juliet's meditations, pointing the way as they potentially do to an indictment of Authority in its social and political as well as in its purely linguistic aspects. In her classic analysis of Shakespeare's wordplay and its relation to the philosophy of language that was current in his epoch, M. M. Mahood points out that 'to doubt the real relationship between name and nominee, between a word and the thing it signified, was to shake the whole structure of Elizabethan thought and society'.[8] It is the menacing spectre of precisely such a doubt as this that Juliet, however naively and with however little regard for practical implications, is raising in her speech.

At first sight, it might seem that the play is tacitly endorsing Juliet's critique, for the social reality it depicts is one almost petrified in its own formalisms. Not even private experience would seem to escape this general process of schematization, for one of the dominant veins of imagery in the play is that constituted by recurrent allusions to literary codes, allusions suggestive of the reduction of life to aesthetic moulds, the sort of bookish pedantry that is parodied so richly in *Love's Labour's Lost* and elsewhere. This reaches the absurd point that human beings themselves are likened to books, as occurs for instance when Lady Capulet expatiates in an extended and rather laboured conceit on Paris's suitability as a prospective husband for Juliet:

> Read o'er the volume of young Paris' face
> And find delight writ there with beauty's pen.
> Examine every married lineament
> And see how one another lends content;
> And what obscur'd in this fair volume lies,
> Find written in the margent of his eyes.
> This precious book of love, this unbound
> lover,
> To beautify him only lacks a cover.
> The fish lives in the sea; and 'tis much pride
> For fair without the fair within to hide.
> That book in many's eyes doth share the glory
> That in gold clasps locks in the golden story.
> (I.iii.81-92)

Even Juliet is not wholly immune to employing imagery of this sort, although it is to be observed that she does so in one of her least characteristic speeches, that in which she briefly inveighs against the absent Romeo after learning of his responsibility for Tybalt's death: 'Was ever book containing such vile matter / So fairly bound?' (III.ii.83-4). When Romeo uses a related image, towards the end of the play, it assumes a very different connotation. His description of the dead Paris as 'One writ with me in sour misfortune's book' (V.iii.82) transforms the individual from a self-contained volume in himself to the contents of more comprehensive text in which other human beings and their vicissitudes are also inscribed, which is another matter altogether.

This transformation only occurs at the conclusion of the play, after Romeo's own perceptions have been enlarged through personal tribulation. In the scenes of the drama that precede his fateful encounter with Juliet, however, Romeo is himself dominated by what is quite obviously meant to be apprehended as a 'literary' vision of reality. Romeo's conception of love, it is frequently observed, is directly derived from the Petrarchan tradition, and involves all the conventions and devices associated with that tradition.[9] In his studied passion for the apparently unattainable Rosaline he is self-consciously assimilating himself to a stereotyped role, albeit with a touch of saving irony which has prompted Mahood among others to conjecture that he is merely 'posing at posing'.[10] Not only is Romeo's infatuation no more than the function of a literary convention, but he frequently expresses his sentiments in terms that make explicit reference to reading and writing, as when he remarks for instance 'Show me a mistress that is passing fair; / What doth her beauty serve but as a note / Where I may read who pass'd that passing fair?' (I.i.232-4). Friar Laurence is ruefully aware of Romeo's literary bias, and suggests that the reason Rosaline did not requite the passion he professed so ardently was that she too recognized its artificial nature, perceiving that 'Thy love did read by rote that could not spell' (II.iii.84). It is in consequence of this tendency that the first exchange between Romeo and Juliet at the Capulet feast assumes the form of an elaborately contrived sonnet in the composition of which both characters participate on equal terms (I.v.92-105). What occurs subsequently might almost be regarded as an anticipation of the conflict between opposed conceptions of language that develops later. A second sonnet is commenced, but is aborted after the initial quatrain by the interruption of the Nurse, who hints at the existence of other linguistic realities by informing Juliet that 'your mother craves a word with you' (I.v.110). Even before this intervention, however, Juliet, in a manner which we later learn is wholly characteristic of her, makes an apparent effort to shatter the literary spell to which Romeo has succumbed by completing a couplet with the wry observation 'You kiss by th'book' (I.v.109).

In view of Romeo's exaggerated literary proclivities, the tendency to live his own life as a projection of the written word which betrays itself among other things in the Petrarchan idiom he habitually employs, it is significant that the event initiating the action of the drama should be his reading a communication not addressed to himself. It is made perfectly clear in the play that it is Romeo's literacy, and not only chance or destiny, that occasions this incident. Capulet, organizing a feast at his house in accordance with an ancient family custom, has supplied his servant with a list of invited guests, but the servant 'can never find what names the writing person hath here writ. I must to the learned' (I.ii.43-4). When the servant encounters Romeo immediately afterwards the following conversation takes place:

> *Servant:* God gi' good e'en; I pray, sir, can you read?
> *Romeo:* Ay, mine own fortune in my misery.
> *Servant:* Perhaps you have learned it without book. But I pray can you read anything you see?
> *Romeo:* Ay, if I know the letters and the language.
> *Servant:* Ye say honestly; rest you merry.
> *Romeo:* Stay, fellow, I can read.
>
> (I.ii.57-63)

Romeo examines the invitation list, learns that Rosaline will be present at the feast, and allows himself to be persuaded by Benvolio to put in an appearance himself. This is only the first of a number of written communications alluded to in the play, and the point that is perhaps worth noting is that there is not a single instance of one of these missives arriving directly at its intended destination.[11] On a later occasion, for instance, Tybalt sends Romeo a letter challenging him to a duel, a gesture that sparks off the following exchange between Mercutio and Benvolio:

> *Benvolio:* Tybalt, the kinsman to old Capulet, hath sent a letter to his father's house.
> *Mercutio:* A challenge, on my life.
> *Benvolio:* Romeo will answer it.
> *Mercutio:* Any man that can write may answer a letter.
> *Benvolio:* Nay, he will answer the letter's master, how he dares, being dared.
>
> (II.iv.6-12)

In the following encounter between Romeo and Tybalt, however, Romeo does not mention receiving the letter, and it is to be wondered whether he would have shown himself abroad, and run the risk of being embroiled in a quarrel on his wedding day, had he in fact done so. There is proleptic irony in Mercutio's comment that 'any man that can write may answer a letter', for Romeo's conspicuous literacy does not enable him to receive the letter that Friar Laurence sends to inform him of the design he has put into operation to assist the two lovers, and it is this failure to read a letter addressed to himself that annihilates once and for all any possibility of a comic resolution to the play. The symmetry between the letter from Capulet that Romeo reads by chance, and the letter from Friar Laurence that he does not read by chance, is emphasized by the close conjunction of Capulet's instruction to a servant 'So many guests invite as here are writ' (IV.ii.1), which recalls his earlier invitation, and Laurence's promise to Juliet that he will 'send a friar with speed / To Mantua with my letters to thy lord' (IV.ii.123-4). It would perhaps not be too much of an exaggeration to suggest then that it is the miscarriage of letters that both initiates what appears to be the comic trajectory of the play and precipitates its tragic conclusion, and that Romeo's fate therefore lies at the mercy of a world of 'letters' that, for good or ill, manifestly fail to achieve their proposed object. Even the explanatory letter that Romeo himself writes to his father before taking his own life—and it is perhaps significant that one of his first impulses after having taken this drastic decision is to procure ink and paper (V.i.25)—is read by the Prince before arriving at its true destination.

Romeo's subjugation to the world of language, in all its manifestations, is thus a fundamental datum of the play, yet it is precisely this servitude that Juliet calls into question at the beginning of the balcony scene. Names, she reasons, are extraneous to the individual, and it is therefore folly to allow one's response to a human being to be determined by his name. And what is true of names in particular is also applicable to language at large, which encodes and enforces patterns of perception and conduct that, however deeply embedded in the corporate consciousness of the community, are not automatically binding on the individual. But Juliet, it ironically turns out, is no less inextricably immersed in the world of language than Romeo himself. Juliet's endeavour to resolve one paradox, that of loving an enemy, immediately plunges her into another, one hinted at already in her apostrophe to Romeo: 'Romeo, wherefore art thou Romeo?' (II.ii.33). In this question, and throughout the meditations that follow, the name *Romeo* functions in two distinct referential capacities: as a sign for the flesh-and-blood human being with whom Juliet has fallen in love, and as the designation of his position within a social order riven by enmity. As Jacques Derrida points out in his suggestive discussion of the balcony scene, Juliet's injunction to Romeo to 'Deny thy father and refuse thy name' (II.ii.34), brings these two significations into effective contraposition inasmuch as 'it is in his name that she continues to call him, and that she calls on him not to call himself Romeo any longer, and that she asks him, Romeo, to renounce his name'.[12] The irony that derives from this bifurcation of referential function is intensified by the fact that although Juliet believes her meditations to be private, and that her reflections on language take place in isolation from any communicative context, in fact she is being overheard by Romeo himself. The words she speaks are therefore discharging a function within a linguistic community after all, although it is precisely the sovereignty of that community she is implicitly impugning when she muses upon the irrelevance of names to the person.

Carried away by his own feelings, Romeo is at first only too willing to submit to Juliet's decree, permitting her in effect to be the arbiter of language and its meanings. To her invitation to 'doff thy name, / And for thy name, which is no part of thee, / Take all myself' (II.ii.47-9), he replies with a significant play on words:

> I take thee at thy word.
> Call me but love, and I'll be new baptis'd:
> Henceforth I never will be Romeo.
> (II.ii.49-51)

It is perhaps symptomatic of their different attitudes towards language that whereas Juliet wants to divest Romeo of a name that for her is charged with problematic connotations, Romeo himself immediately stakes his claim to a new name appropriate to what he deems to be his new reality. But the futility of the attempt on the part of both characters to dispense with publicly sanctioned names becomes ironically manifest a moment later, when Juliet realizes she is being overheard, and the problem arises of how Romeo is to identify himself if not through his name:

> *Juliet:* What man art thou that thus bescreen'd in night
> So stumblest on my counsel?
> *Romeo:* By a name
> I know not how to tell thee who I am
> (II.ii.52-4)

Although Romeo, taking his cue from Juliet's remarks, refrains from directly pronouncing his own name, the anxious circumlocutions to which he resorts serve nonetheless to identify him in relation to that name, if only in a negative respect:

> *Romeo:* My name, dear saint, is hateful to myself
> Because it is an enemy to thee.
> Had I it written, I would tear the word.
> *Juliet:* My ears have yet not drunk a hundred words
> Of thy tongue's uttering, yet I know the sound.
> Art thou not Romeo, and a Montague?
> *Romeo:* Neither, fair maid, if either thee dislike.
> (II.ii.55-61)

Things go from bad to worse, for in order to communicate their love the two young people are obliged to fall back on the very language whose authority they have effectively denied. At this point Juliet is confronted with the not inconsiderable difficulty of how much she is to believe Romeo in his protestations of passion, and once again the problem resolves into that of whether, and in what sense, one can take another's word for anything:

> Dost thou love me? I know thou wilt say 'Ay',
> And I will take thy word. Yet, if thou swear'st,
> Thou mayst prove false. At lovers' perjuries,
> They say, Jove laughs.
> (II.ii.90-93)

Furthermore, she acknowledges candidly enough that there are circumstances in which she too would be capable of distorting words for her own purposes, and thus of widening still further the rift between verbal statement and subjective truth:

> Or, if thou think'st I am too quickly won,
> I'll frown and be perverse and say thee nay,
> So thou wilt woo . . .
> (II.ii.95-7)

And that this is no empty threat is indicated in the fact that Juliet will later demonstrate herself to be an accomplished prevaricator in her dealings with her family, employing language as an instrument of dissimulation in order to be true to her own emotional world.

The language that the lovers have both, in their different ways, sought to exclude from the garden therefore enters again at their tacit instigation, attended with all the fallibilities, hazards and deceptions inherent in the public use of language. Not only is the language that the lovers themselves use potentially mendacious, but it also imposes its own conventions and its own perverse rules. This becomes ironically apparent when Romeo strives to find adequate expression for his feelings, and notwithstanding what we must suppose to be the sincerity of his sentiments allows himself to be carried away on the flood of his own rhetoric, letting language and its stereotypes assume control once more: 'Lady, by yonder blessed moon I vow, / That tips with silver all these fruit-tree tops—' (II.ii.107-8). When Juliet interrupts him with the injunction not to swear by the moon, depriving him suddenly of the literary coordinates which are all he has to orientate himself by, he is left completely at a loss, and rather pathetically inquires: 'What shall I swear by?' (II.ii.112). Juliet admonishes him not to swear at all, or, at most, to 'swear by thy gracious self' (II.ii.113). But when Romeo attempts to oblige her, he lapses once more into a conventional formula ('If my heart's dear love—' [II.ii.115]), until Juliet brusquely cuts him short once again with 'Well, do not swear' (II.ii.116). Later it looks suspiciously as if Romeo is about to embark on another of his fights when he exclaims 'So thrive my soul—' (II.ii.153), but Juliet puts an end to his verbal flounderings with her terse 'A thousand times good night' (II.ii.154). Not only does the language which Juliet has sought to banish refuse to be banished, but it dominates the proceedings to the point of parodying itself.

The paradox hovering in the background of this scene is not only that the name by which an individual is known belongs to the community rather than himself, but that his personal identity is also, in a more profound sense than can safely be ignored, the possession of that community. Juliet's desire to create a world innocent of names, a private realm of pure essences in which it is the individual alone who can legitimately serve as a sign of himself, implies the abandonment of the world of codified responses which she recognizes to be arbitrary, destructive and inimical to the positive values of life. For his own part, Romeo wants to take Juliet at her word, and assume the name that she is to designate for him at his behest, thus creating in effect the germ of a private language. But, as Coriolanus also learns to his cost, names can never be appropriated by the individual, however acutely conscious he might be of the hazards attendant on the public use of words. Even if language is corrupt and alienating, and in the divisions it encodes potentially destructive, it can neither be dispensed with nor dissociated from the community which is its matrix. As Romeo seems to acknowledge later—'One writ with me in sour misfortune's book' (V.iii.82)—the individual's being is indelibly inscribed in realities that lie beyond his control and as often as not beyond his comprehension. It is the continuing existence of such realities that, at least in their social aspect, makes itself felt towards the end of the balcony scene in the offstage voice of the Nurse summoning Juliet in from the garden: 'I hear some noise within' (II.ii.136). Juliet's physical oscillation between the house interior and the garden, between the promptings of the Nurse's voice and those of Romeo's, is vividly suggestive of the tension between the worlds of public and private identity that have come into collision in this play, a tension which, at least at the overt level of material events, is destined to be resolved in favour of the former.[13]

In view of what I have been saying, there is a considerable irony in the fact that the name whose referential authority Juliet has begun by questioning should be rehabilitated before the scene concludes, though in what at the time might appear to be transfigured form:

> *Juliet:* Hist! Romeo, hist! O for a falconer's voice
> To lure this tassel-gentle back again.
> Bondage is hoarse and may not speak aloud,
> Else would I tear the cave where Echo lies
> And make her airy tongue more hoarse than mine
> With repetition of my Romeo's name.
> *Romeo:* It is my soul that calls upon my name.
> How silver-sweet sound lovers' tongues by night,
> Like softest music to attending ears.
> (II.ii.158-66)

Not only have names been reinstated in all their former potency, but both Romeo and Juliet have deferred, without further protest on the part of either of them, to the sovereignty of other codes as well. In alluding to the story of Echo and Narcissus Juliet is drawing on the Ovidian repertory of mythological precedents which was part of the standard stock-in-trade of Renaissance literature, while the essentially conventional character of the synaesthetic trope that Romeo employs will later be exposed by Peter when he mockingly interrogates a group of musicians as to the significance of the phrase 'music with her silver sound' (IV.v.125-38). In its immediate context such an appeal to traditional formulas might seem innocuous enough, but what is ultimately implied by this unqualified acceptance of names and poetic conventions is the lovers' progressive reincorporation within that structure of conventions which also comprehends, among other things, the feud between the Montagues and the Capulets. To invoke once again one of the more suggestive metaphors of the play, it signifies a gradual return to a world of 'letters' that includes Tybalt's invitation to a duel.

It is the contradiction between the two worlds in which they simultaneously participate, and their incapacity to commit themselves unreservedly to either one or the other, that destroys the lovers in the end. The intermediate stance that Juliet adopts when she stands on a balcony situated on the boundary between the house and the garden, and between the conflicting worlds of value these represent, cannot be sustained. If in chiding Romeo for kissing 'by th'book' (I.v.109) at the time of their initial encounter, and in denying the personal relevance of his name later, Juliet has in effect been contesting the primacy of the word in human affairs, her own practical subjugation to the tyranny of language becomes ironically manifest towards the end of the balcony scene when she urges Romeo to 'send me word tomorrow' in order to clarify his intentions (II.ii.144). No less ironically from this point of view, it is by demanding 'a word with one of you' that Tybalt provokes a confrontation with Romeo's friends (III.i.38), while Romeo's subsequent effort to revaluate public names in the light of private experience by addressing his antagonist as 'good Capulet, which name I tender / As dearly as mine own' (III.i.70-1) is precisely the gesture which Mercutio uncomprehendingly construes as a 'vile submission' (III.i.72), and which triggers the fatal quarrel. After Mercutio's death at the hands of a man who 'fights by the book of arithmetic' (III.i.103-4), and who might be regarded in this respect as the embodiment of the destructive formalism of his society. Romeo himself consciously surrenders to the public codes in which his name is implicated, censuring his own earlier acquiescence before an 'effeminate' vision of reality and deliberately complying with the dictates of a masculine value system based on honour and reputation:

This gentlemen, the prince's near ally,
My very friend, hath got this mortal hurt
In my behalf—my reputation stain'd
With Tybalt's slander—Tybalt that an hour
Hath been my cousin. O sweet Juliet,
Thy beauty hath made me effeminate
And in my temper soften'd valour's steel.
(III.i.111-17)

For a few critical minutes, for as long as it takes for his fortunes to reverse themselves irretrievably, Romeo's being 'Romeo, and a Montague' takes precedence over all other considerations, and he allows his conduct to be determined not by his personal inclination but by what the conventions of his society require of him.

After this dramatic confirmation that personal identity is inevitably a function of a public code, and that one's own name can therefore be the most insidious enemy of the self, the play that has until this moment continued to draw attention to its own comic potentialities gathers inexorable tragic momentum as both protagonists are compelled to contemplate the destructive power of words. Upon being informed of Tybalt's death at Romeo's hands Juliet delivers herself of a distracted tirade against her husband, only to reproach herself a moment later with the reflection 'Ah, poor my lord, what tongue shall smooth thy name / When I thy three-hours wife have mangled it?' (III.ii.98-9). If she has attempted in her garden to forge what is in effect a private language safe from the onslaughts of a hostile world, it is made apparent to her now that public language cannot long be kept at bay:

Some word there was, worser than Tybalt's death,
That murder'd me. I would forget it fain,
But O, it presses to my memory
Like damned guilty deeds to sinners' minds.
Tybalt is dead and Romeo—banished.
That 'banished', that one word 'banished',
Hath slain ten thousand Tybalts . . .
(III.ii.108-14)

Not only does Juliet discover that 'There is no end, no limit, measure, bound, / In that word's death', but she also realizes that 'No words can that woe sound' (III.ii.125-6). The implication would seem to be that language is intractably alien to the realm of interior experience, provoking pain without even affording the consolation of making possible the expression of that pain. Romeo voices a similar consciousness of the power of public words to defeat private meanings when he responds to the Friar's news of his banishment with the question of how he can be so heartless as 'To mangle me with that word "banished"?' (III.iii.51), a term which he insists on equating with death even though the Friar reminds him that the Prince has 'turn'd that black word "death" to banishment' (III.iii.27). Subsequently he expresses the fear that even his own name might have transformed itself into a weapon capable of inflicting harm upon Juliet:

As if that name,
Shot from the deadly level of a gun,
Did murder her, as that name's cursed hand
Murder'd her kinsman. O, tell me, Friar, tell me,
In what vile part of this anatomy
Doth my name lodge? Tell me that I may sack
The hateful mansion.
(III.iii.101-7)

It is intensely ironic that Romeo should here be reverting to the sense of Juliet's remark in the garden that a name is 'nor hand nor foot / Nor arm nor face nor any other part / Belonging to a man' (II.ii.40-42), words that at the time were meant to affirm the fundamental irrelevance of names to the individual. Now words are conceived as being endowed with greater reality than the entities to which they are assigned, invested with the power to mangle and to murder without being themselves in the least subject to human discipline. The phrase 'that name's cursed hand' reverses the relation between the name and its referent as this is customarily envisaged. Not only do names not belong to the individual, but the profoundly disturbing possibility opens up that in a sense it is the individual who belongs to his name.

In *Romeo and Juliet* names, like letters, belong to a world of language which operates according to its own unfathomable logic, a logic which has nothing to do with human reality except insofar as it is capable of fashioning that reality in its own likeness. Letters do not arrive at the destinations that have been designated for them, and names do not mean what the individuals who bear them or pronounce them intend them to mean. Words cannot be excluded from the human domain because humanity realizes itself through language, but words, once admitted, proceed to impose their own laws in defiance of man's private exigencies. Human beings can never be the authors of their own destinies, but are all, as Romeo says, 'writ with me in sour misfortune's book' (V.iii.82), condemned to serve more or less passively as the vehicles of a meaning beyond their comprehension. The one moment in the play in which individuals seem to seize momentary control of the world of words that speaks itself through them is that rendered in the balcony scene. But, as I have been arguing, in this scene epitomizing the lovers' effort to create a private realm for themselves in which only their own dialect has currency they already come up against the contradictions inherent in their enterprise, contradictions that eventually actualize themselves more tangibly, and more destructively, in the external world of material action. In the charmed seclusion of their garden Romeo and Juliet, recognizing the impossibility of dispensing with words altogether, have tried to regenerate language by transforming it into a medium of personal sentiment. If they have failed it is not through any want of emotional sincerity on their own part but because the language they have been obliged to use simply does not lend itself to regeneration in human terms, because in the final analysis that which we call a name, however earnest and even heroic the effort at reformulation might be, by any other name would still be a name.

Notes

[1] All references to *Romeo and Juliet* are to the Arden Edition edited by Brian Gibbons (1980; rpt. London: Methuen, 1983).

[2] Caroline Spurgeon, *Shakespeare's Imagery and What it Tells Us* (1935; rpt. Cambridge: Cambridge Univ. Press, 1965), p. 312.

[3] A representative statement of this view is to be found in Brian Gibbons's Introduction to the Arden Edition of *Romeo and Juliet,* in which it is argued that 'the play progressively distinguishes between characters who contentedly express themselves through received verbal and rhetorical conventions, and the hero and heroine who learn that greater maturity and fulfilment require language true to their own particular selves' (ed. cit., p. 48).

[4] For a discussion of the figure of oxymoron in particular see Robert O. Evans, *The Osier Cage: Rhetorical Devices in Romeo and Juliet* (Lexington: Univ. of Kentucky Press, 1966), especially pp. 18-41.

[5] Barbara L. Estrin suggests that 'in her garden Juliet becomes a kind of Adam in reverse, unnaming the universe, decomposing—in order to recompose—the world'. 'Romeo and Juliet and the Art of Naming Love', *Ariel* 12:2 (April 1981), 31-49 (this quotation p. 37).

[6] The difference between the modes of expression employed by Romeo and Juliet respectively is the subject of an intensive analysis by Edward A. Snow. 'Language and Sexual Difference in *Romeo and Juliet'*, in Peter Erickson and Coppélia Kahn (eds.), *Shakespeare's 'Rough Magic'* (Newark: Univ. of Delaware Press, 1985), pp. 168-92. Snow argues that while Romeo's metaphors 'assemble reality "out there", and provide access to it through perspectives that tend to make him an onlooker rather than a participant' (p. 170), Juliet's "imaginative universe . . . is generated by all the senses, and by a unity of feeling that is more than just the sum of their parts' (p. 173).

[7] Harry Levin, 'Form and Formality in *Romeo and Juliet', Shakespeare Quarterly* 11 (1960), 3-11 (this quotation p. 4).

[8] M. M. Mahood, *Shakespeare's Wordplay* (1957; rpt. London: Routledge, 1988), p. 73.

[9] Petrarch is explicitly mentioned by Mercutio in II.iv.40. For discussions of the Petrarchan elements in this play, see Joseph S. M. J. Chang, 'The Language of Paradox in Romeo and Juliet', *Shakespeare Studies* 3 (1967), 22-42, and Jill L. Levenson, 'The Definition of Love: Shakespeare's Phrasing in *Romeo and Juliet', Shakespeare Studies* 15 (1982), 21-36.

[10] Mahood, op. cit., p. 61. Mahood points out that Romeo's inquiry to Belvolio as to where they are to dine is 'a most unlover-like question which gives the show away' (p. 61).

[11] In more general terms, Gibbons observes that 'Shakespeare makes the plot depend crucially on messages', and that in certain scenes he 'stresses . . . the ease with which messages can go wrong' (ed. cit., p. 41).

[12] Jacques Derrida, 'Aphorism Countertime' (trans. Nicholas Royle), in Derek Attridge, ed., *Acts of Literature* (New York: Routledge, 1992), pp. 416-33 (this quotation p. 425).

[13] The paradox inherent in proper names that I am examining here is somewhat differently formulated by Derrida in his essay cited above: 'detachable and dissociable, aphoristic though it be, his [Romeo's] name is his essence. Inseparable from his being. And in asking him to abandon his name, she [Juliet] is no doubt asking him to live at last, and to live his love . . . but she is *just as much* asking him to die, since his life *is* his name. He exists in his name . . . Romeo is Romeo, and

Romeo is not Romeo. He is himself only in abandoning his name, he is himself only in his name'. Ibid., pp. 426-7.

Source: "That Which We Call a Name: The Balcony Scene in *Romeo and Juliet,*" in *English,* Vol. 44, No. 178, Spring, 1995, pp. 1-16.

Hamlet and "A Matter Tender and Dangerous"

Mark Matheson, ***University of Utah***

I offer this essay as a contribution to a discernible movement in Shakespeare studies which is once again raising the question of the relation of the plays to early modern religious discourse. For a long time this relationship was addressed in the context of biographical criticism, with the texts being read as cryptic testimonials to Shakespeare's Catholicism, his royalist Anglicanism, his agnosticism, his hostility to Puritanism, and so on. In the new assessment of Shakespeare's work and religion, biographical concerns have been displaced by a focus on the texts as part of a broad cultural order and on the great variety of contemporary discourses that nourish the plays and the dramatic conflicts they represent. The interpretive process is complicated by the issue of censorship, a force difficult to assess but undeniable, and, in the case of *Hamlet,* by the existence of three different texts with their vast number of variants. Religious discourse is integral to *Hamlet,* but Shakespeare's representation of religion in the play is oblique and inconsistent, and critics have come to many different conclusions about *Hamlet*'s religious content. The play's inconsistent representation of religion is interesting in itself, and I would argue that to a certain extent the forces producing this instability and the role of religion in the play's ideological drama are accessible to historicist criticism. We can, for example, illuminate the representation of religion in the play by viewing it in relation to Hamlet's subjectivity, which is a principal site of ideological contention. We can also engage with specific religious discourses in the text, among them Roman Catholicism, neo-Stoicism, and Protestantism, and with Shakespeare's representation of their historical and institutional affiliations. To classify Stoicism as a religious discourse is arguable, but it clearly functions as an important constituent in the contemporary synthesis of humanism and Christianity. Considering Stoicism within a religious context illuminates Hamlet's involvement with comprehensive ideological systems and helps to prepare the way for an analysis of his subjective transformation at the end of the play.

The language and theology of Roman Catholicism emerge most clearly in *Hamlet* in the prince's encounter with his father's spirit, where the Christian and specifically purgatorial context that Shakespeare creates for the Ghost is rather surprising. The play contrasts sharply in this respect with *The Spanish Tragedy,* where the ghost of Don Andrea inhabits a classical underworld derived from the sixth book of Virgil's *Aeneid,* a strategy that allows Kyd to avoid the ideological pitfalls of representing a Christian afterlife. The spirit of old Hamlet explicitly identifies his situation beyond the grave, speaking of the "sulph'rous and tormenting flames" to which he must render himself, and of the "certain term" of penance he must endure until "the foul crimes done in my days of nature / Are burnt and purged away" (1.5.3, 10, and 12-13).[1] His complaint that he has gone to his death "unhouseled" and "unaneled" (1.77)—that is, without benefit of the Eucharist and extreme unction—introduces a language that is unambiguously Roman Catholic. The authority of the Ghost's appeal to Hamlet is based in part on a tradition of Catholic discourse in which the power of speech—what Horatio calls "sound or use of voice" (1.1.109)—is given to the suffering dead. In Sir Thomas More's *Supplication of Souls* (1529), for instance, those tormented in purgatory make their appeal to the living:

> If ye pity the blind, there is none so blind as we, which are here in the dark, saving for sights unpleasant, and loathsome, till some comfort come. If ye pity the lame, there is none so lame as we, that neither can creep one foot out of the fire, nor have one hand at liberty to defend our face from the flame. Finally, if ye pity any man in pain, never knew ye pain comparable to ours; whose fire as far passeth in heat all the fires that ever burned upon the earth, as the hottest of all those passeth a feigned fire painted on a wall.[2]

The language that the Ghost uses in his encounter with Hamlet is related to this collective voice of the dead: there is an affinity between More's vocabulary of torment and that found in the play. In a sense the Ghost's "I" is based on the "we" of More's text, deriving part of its authority from the whole community of the dead as identified in a specific dogmatic tradition. What is novel about the Ghost is that it comes not to beg relief for its own pains but to command Hamlet to revenge the death of King Hamlet and to restore order in the temporal political world. But in this displacement the purgatorial context remains pertinent, and the way Hamlet responds to the edict suggests that for him it carries the residual force of a religious obligation.

Emphasis on the torments of purgatory reflects doctrines and practices of late medieval Catholicism which clearly survived into the early modern period in England, but as the sixteenth century progressed, these traditions were steadily undermined by the Reformation. Early Protestants like John Frith and William Tyndale denounced both purgatory and indulgences as priestly stratagems to drain the resources of rich and poor alike. As A. G. Dickens has observed, the government of Edward VI effected in the Chantries Act of 1547 what was in many respects a second Dissolution, taking control of institutions and endowments set aside for prayers for the dead and using them to further secular causes.[3] In contrast to the first Chantries Act of 1545, which stated that the funds from dissolution were needed for the war against France and Scotland, the Edwardian act was aggressively Protestant in doctrine, declaring in its preamble that much superstition and ignorance concerning the true means of salvation had been caused "by devising and phantasying vain opinions of purgatory and masses satisfactory, to be done for them which be departed."[4] The Forty-Two Articles of 1553 and the Thirty-Nine Articles promulgated under Elizabeth denounced the doctrine of purgatory as "a fond thing vainly feigned, and grounded upon no warrant of Scripture, but rather repugnant to the word of God."[5] Thus by the time Shakespeare wrote *Hamlet* 1.5, the religious doctrine it represents had been vigorously rejected by the established church for half a century. References to purgatory in English Renaissance drama are rare,[6] no doubt in part because it was heretical, and Shakespeare shows a certain daring in establishing the context of the Ghost so plainly.

His reasons for establishing this purgatorial context may be associated with his complicated representation of time in the play, which is set deep in the medieval past but which stages the world of a Renaissance court. It may also be related to his portrayal of Hamlet's mind as a sensitive register of social and historical change. In writing this scene, Shakespeare may have been playing with the hidden or vestigial beliefs of his audience in order to establish a sense of distance between the world of old Hamlet and the official ideology of contemporary England. The Ghost's affiliations are clearly with feudalism and the old religion; it thus represents a social order displaced by the early modern state but still exercising an influence within contemporary institutions. This older society solicits Hamlet in the Ghost's appeal for revenge, an appeal that constructs Hamlet not as a self-conscious Renaissance prince but as a son who must fulfill the responsibilities entailed by an older communitarian identity that binds him to both the living and the dead. Shakespeare portrays Hamlet in this scene as powerless to contest the dictates of his father's spirit, and this inability to counter or qualify his father's cultural authority is evident throughout the play. As Jacques Lacan notes:

> There's something very strange in the way Hamlet speaks about his dead father, an exaltation and idealization . . . which comes down to something like this: Hamlet has no voice with which to say whatever he may have to say about him.[7]

Historicist criticism might apply this psychoanalytical insight as follows: Hamlet's awkwardness in the filial role is symptomatic of his ambivalent relationship to the ideological order represented by his father, a culture whose values he consciously embraces but whose established cultural roles he is unable to perform. Shakespeare makes a point of representing Hamlet as a product of humanism and (more cautiously) of the Reformation, and thus of a material history that he cannot simply, as he vows to do, "wipe away" in an act of will (1.5.99). The rest of the play demonstrates the impossibility of fulfilling this idealist intention, which Hamlet seems to make out of a conscious but tormented loyalty to his father and the older culture he represents, in which the prince's roles are not only those of the unhesitant revenger, the son obedient to the patriarchal word, but also the devout Catholic who recognizes his solemn responsibility to the souls of the dead.[8]

But if the spirit of his father intrudes spectacularly to assert the values of medieval society and to impose on his son an older communitarian identity, throughout most of the play Hamlet must negotiate more contemporary political relationships. The central political institution portrayed in *Hamlet* is the Renaissance court, which is represented as the center of an early modern state led by a powerful monarch and deploying the full apparatus of the new diplomacy. It is also a world of humanist learning, secular politics, and religious division. In this postfeudal context the problem of unique individual identity and self-consciousness has arisen: a sense of self for aristocratic men who are not necessarily bound by older ideologies of religious and secular community. Shakespeare's portrayal of Hamlet is sensitive to this cultural development. He makes the same historical point indirectly in his representation of Rosencrantz and Guildenstern, who at first glance seem to belong to patterns of loyalty and group identity specific to the older culture, especially when one considers their devotion to the monarch and their notable lack of individuality. But more careful examination shows that Shakespeare portrays them as thoroughly contemporary, the product of power relations at a Renaissance court. The undifferentiated treatment he gives them is in fact rather novel, and it reveals Shakespeare's awareness of broad historical and institutional change and of the consequences of such change for individual identity. Rosencrantz and Guildenstern seem born at a stroke with the alienated individual subjectivity represented by Hamlet; Shakespeare's conception of their essential sameness is possible only from a perspective in which individual identity has already become a problematic fact. The play suggests that questions of identity never arise for the two courtiers because they are subsumed by the structure of the early modern state. In fact state power accomplishes in their case something similar to what love effects in "The Phoenix and Turtle." In both instances "number" is "slain" ("The Phoenix and Turtle," 1.28), with the difference being that in the play individuality dies not in spiritual union with another but in complete subordination to a newly emerging institutional power.

The play's representation of Rosencrantz and Guildenstern can thus be seen as a testimony to Shakespeare's interest in the power of the early modern state to shape identity, a power that shapes Hamlet's sense of self as well. When Hamlet's place in the state structure becomes vulnerable, his sense of identity is necessarily threatened. Psychological or idealist readings of Hamlet often err by paying insufficient attention to the political position of the prince, who unexpectedly finds himself displaced from the center of the court and regarded as a potential enemy of the state. His introspective brooding and painful sense of individual isolation are in part the result of this sudden estrangement from state power. In attempting to reconcile him to the new reign, Claudius invokes the contemporary humanist discourse of neo-Stoicism, which thus carries with it the institutional authority of the state. Only a few years earlier, in *Julius Caesar,* Shakespeare had treated Roman Stoicism in its original setting, where it had associations with republicanism and anti-imperial politics. In its Renaissance revival Stoicism retained some of its oppositional potential, but more often it performed a conservative ideological function by projecting an unchanging reality to which the individual subject must adapt. Stoicism counseled self-adjustment rather than political activism and was dismissive or condemning of actual efforts to change the social order. This doctrine had certain advantages for the contemporary aristocracy, which was more completely subject to royal control than its progenitors had been.[9] Stoicism could mitigate the pains and minor humiliations of a privileged class for whom the Hotspurian resort to arms was fast becoming a reckless and even futile alternative.[10] Although Hamlet is of royal blood, he occupies a position in the play not unlike that of a nobleman in early modern English society. Claudius in fact attempts to impose such a status on the prince when he describes him as "Our chiefest courtier" (1.2.117). One might then expect that neo-Stoicism would emerge in the play as an ideological alternative for Hamlet, a troubled aristocrat who finds himself thwarted and vulnerable to royal power.

The king would certainly like him to embrace this philosophy. In Claudius's first speech (1.2.1-39) he represents himself as a model of Stoic balance worthy of Hamlet's emulation, and he figures the mind as a place where strong emotions and conflicting forces are balanced and reconciled by the sovereign faculty of reason. The image of a scale functions as the master trope of this speech and of his discourse throughout this crucial public scene.[11] In his efforts to persuade Hamlet, Claudius relies on the Stoic ideology of self-control, invoking its cultural prestige to accuse the prince of immaturity. Speaking like a schoolmaster, he chastens Hamlet for having "A heart unfortified, a mind impatient, / An understanding simple and unschooled" (ll. 96-97). The king's discourse suggests how the Stoic concept of the subject can be used to support a conservative ideology of obedience to the existing order, or even to bolster political quietism.

Hamlet is unpersuaded, but it would be wrong to suggest that Stoic discourse has no authority for him or that he simply dismisses it as part of the king's ploy. He later invokes its terms in his elaborate compliment to Horatio, the extravagance of which is apparently embarrassing to both: "Something too much of this," says Hamlet (3.2.72). Hamlet's praise for his friend has a certain manic edge, an intensity that establishes Stoicism as a philosophy of refuge for aristocrats in the play's dynamic representation of ruling-class ideology. Here he uses the Stoic language that Claudius earlier established as normative discourse among the Danish elite and, in doing so, gives it his implicit endorsement. Nevertheless this discourse proves useless to him as a way of ordering his mind or of assisting him in carrying out the will of his father. In fact the play as a whole represents a society in which the ideology of Stoicism is in crisis. Stoicism cannot control the behavior of the prince, though the king invokes the power of the state in making this attempt; and while Claudius pretends to embody Stoic balance, his self-representations are revealed to be a rhetorical overlay for a subjectivity dominated by aggressive sexual and political drives.

The crisis of Stoicism in the play world emerges interestingly in Hamlet's prescriptions for theatrical art. His aesthetic politics are decidedly aristocratic, as his advice to the Player makes clear (3.2.1-35, 38-45). He sets up rules for the actors, urging them to strike a balance between an overly passionate style and one that is "too tame" (1.16), and he speaks about acting in the theater (and by implication beyond it) with an intensity that suggests a deep connection between aesthetics and ideology. According to Hamlet, those performing the drama must strive for balance and "temperance" (1.8), and in achieving this, their "discretion" can be a helpful "tutor" (ll. 16-17); his diction suggests how closely his aesthetic theory is related to humanist concepts of identity and conduct. Hamlet reaffirms this conservative aesthetic in his final warning that those who play the clowns should "speak no more than is set down for them," adding that to do otherwise is "villainous, and shows a most pitiful ambition in the fool that uses it" (ll. 39 and 43-45). For Hamlet the theater is a polity for which he prescribes an authoritarian government.[12] Because degree must be observed, any self-assertion or departure from one's scripted role is stigmatized as "pitiful ambition." The noun has clear political connotations elsewhere in the play, as when Rosencrantz suggests that it is Hamlet's "ambition" that makes Denmark a prison (2.2.253). Hamlet says that actors who transgress his rules are deserving of punishment, and he specifies the sentence for one who fails to "acquire and beget" the proper temperance: "I would have such a fellow whipped for o'erdoing Termagant" (3.2.7 and 13-14)—surprisingly violent language in a discourse about playacting.

Shakespeare represents Hamlet as craving order and hierarchy in the world of art, perhaps in order to suggest that the prince finds little stability in his own subjective life and in the political life of contemporary Denmark. In the context of the play, Hamlet's theories of acting and playwriting are a reactionary gesture, an attempt to realize or validate in the aesthetic realm a conservative ideology that is failing in his own experience and in the political life of his society. The impossibility of this gesture is made evident by Hamlet's own practice, especially by his antic behavior at the theatrical performance for which he serves as patron. Hamlet there comports himself as he suggests a groundling might, interpreting the action for other members of the audience (Ophelia says he is "as good as a chorus" [3.2.233]); speaking in sexual innuendo during the intervals ("It would cost you a groaning to take off mine edge" [l. 237]); and harrassing the players through sardonic asides and direct address ("Begin, murderer. Pox, leave thy damnable faces and begin" [ll. 240-41]). His obtrusive involvement in the performance violates both letter and spirit of his critical principles, and thus his theory of a decorous aristocratic theater is undermined by his own ebullient practice.

This contradiction helps to confirm that in the world of the play the ideologies of Stoicism and humanism are failing more generally, even if Hamlet's behavior here can be explained to a considerable extent by his stated intention to be "idle" (l. 88). In the sequence of scenes at the center of the play, Hamlet invokes and attempts to conduct himself according to humanist ideals. But he repeatedly subverts them, as in the scene with Ophelia, who, in lamenting Hamlet, sees his role as a "scholar" as an important part of his courtly identity (3.1.154). Hamlet briefly addresses her in the mode prescribed by contemporary aristocratic culture, but he soon assaults her with language based on the concept of original sin: "for virtue cannot so inoculate our old stock but we shall relish of it" (ll. 119-21). Hamlet's language here, with its emphasis on human depravity, may suggest the influence of Protestant culture while containing within it a fundamental challenge to the ideologies of aristocratic humanism. In Act 3 it is clear that Hamlet can no longer inhabit the conceptual order constituted by Stoicism and humanist culture more generally, even though at certain moments of the play, as when he praises Horatio or expounds his program for an aristocratic theater, he is capable of giving its values enthusiastic assent.

Shakespeare thus represents Hamlet in the throes of an ideological unhousing from both the residual and dominant cultural systems of Danish society. Neither the feudal Catholic world nor the humanist Renaissance court can provide him with a secure identity or an ideological basis for action. In the odd locution of Marcellus, which seems to announce the play's interest in the relationship between objective ideological systems and individual consciousness, Hamlet cannot "let belief take hold of him" (1.1.22). As a result Hamlet's relationship to his culture in general becomes highly self-conscious and essentially critical. The ideological voracity of this manic and introspective Hamlet is evident through most of the play, but the critical Hamlet finally passes from the scene during the episode at sea. Two divergent readings of this apparent discontinuity in the representation of Hamlet's character might be cited here. Francis Barker has argued that this shift should be read not in terms of realism or "character development" but rather as a "quasi-Brechtian" device in which a melancholy agnostic is supplanted by a "man of action"; in ideological terms Barker regards this change as basically reactionary. Through most of the play Hamlet has questioned the fundamental beliefs of his society, but for Barker he "goes to his death inserted into the traditional Christian values."[13] In a notable reading Harold Bloom agrees that on Hamlet's return from the sea his character is "radically" changed, but he reads the ideological bearings of this change quite differently than Barker. For Bloom what we "overhear" is "an ethos so original that we still cannot assimilate it." The "urgency" of the earlier Hamlet is gone, and the prince now embodies an "achieved serenity," a "mysterious and beautiful disinterestedness" that cannot be illuminated by references to late Elizabethan culture.[14] For Bloom, Hamlet's newly acquired disinterestedness, far from being a reactionary step, is dazzlingly progressive, effectively transcending both his private disillusionment and contemporary Christianity.

Rather than viewing Hamlet's change as a regressive failure of nerve or a transhistorical advance, I suggest that we investigate more closely the precise nature of this change and evaluate its consequences in the field of early modern ideology. In these terms it can be argued that the impasse in which Hamlet finds himself is broken in the final act by the emergence of a specifically Protestant discourse of conscience and of God's predestinating will.[15] The "mysterious and beautiful disinterestedness" that Bloom finds so striking may be understood in late-sixteenth-century terms as the poise of a soul that has come to know its dependence on the will of an utterly transcendent God. C. S. Lewis rightly emphasized the importance of a specific kind of religious experience in the lives and thought of early modern Protestants. He characterized this experience as one of "catastrophic conversion" in which the gift of faith bestowed by the grace of God results in a buoyant sense of subjective liberation, a "farewell to the self with all its good resolutions, anxiety, scruples, and motive-scratchings."[16] Lewis's description of the mental state that precedes the experience of regenerating grace might also serve to describe Hamlet as Shakespeare represents him through the first four acts of the play. Lewis's account may exaggerate the emotionalism and suddenness of the early modern conversion experience, which in orthodox terms was usually conceived as the dawning of grace, the culmination of a gradual process of spiritual discipline.[17] Nevertheless, a rhetoric of the utopian liberation of the spirit can be found in the classic Protestant texts, a liberation that could not always be circumscribed by qualifying theological commentary.[18] That the play implicitly represents such a conversion or regeneration is a plausible hypothesis. Even if one rejects this reading, there remains substantial evidence for a change corresponding with such an experience in Shakespeare's representation of Hamlet in the final act.

Earlier passages in the play establish Protestantism as a relevant discourse, and they suggest that Hamlet's transformation may develop out of the ideological preoccupations of the text as a whole. Consider for instance the conspicuous references to Wittenberg in the first act. That Hamlet should be educated at Wittenberg may be Shakespeare's original contribution to the story, since there is no mention of this in the surviving sources. The role of this university as a cradle of religious revolution would likely be a significant part of its identity for a contemporary audience. By making a point of giving the prince this experience, Shakespeare places him at the source of radical Protestantism. Shakespeare may also show a knowledge of recent history in associating the university with sixteenth-century Danish politics. After spending time at Wittenberg, the Danish monk Hans Tausen returned home to preach Lutheran doctrine in 1525, and the Reformation movement in Denmark was furthered by King Christian II (another visitor to Wittenberg), who ordered the production of a Danish Bible. Christian III had attended the Diet of Worms and had become a devotee of Luther, and he summoned an envoy from Wittenberg to perform his coronation in 1536. Luther himself approved the ordinance of 1537 which ultimately created a Protestant national church in Denmark.[19] Shakespeare may thus refer his audience to a contemporary society in which the established church was thoroughly reformed and evoke Protestant associations against the medieval Catholic traditions still alive in the play.

One can argue further that the history of Protestantism functions as a kind of subtext in *Hamlet,* surfacing occasionally in ways that are barely articulate. One such moment occurs when Hamlet, brought before Claudius to explain the whereabouts of Polonius, tells the king he is "At supper . . . Not where he eats, but where a is eaten. A certain convocation of politic worms are e'en at him. Your worm is your only emperor for diet" (4.3.18 and 20-22). As many critics of the play have noted, these lines seem to contain a scrambled allusion to the Diet of Worms, convened by the Emperor Charles V in 1521. Luther was called to be examined before this "convocation," at which he upheld the authority of his own experience against the assembled powers of the Holy Roman Empire and the Catholic Church. Hamlet is under guard here, and his allusion to this famous confrontation might be stimulated by his own encounter with the power of Claudius and by a deep identification with the figure of an individual confronting the institutional establishment. His image of the imperial worm, suggesting the devouring nature of established power, follows very closely in stage time the eating metaphor he uses to describe the king's cynical manipulation of Rosencrantz and Guildenstern: "He keeps them, like an ape an apple in the corner of his jaw, first mouthed to be last swallowed" (4.2.16-18). The imagery of eating and swallowing links these passages with other Shakespearean evocations of tyrannical power and may suggest that Hamlet's perception of his struggle with Claudius is growing less personal and increasingly political.

Shakespeare's emphasis on individual conscience also contributes to the Protestant character of Hamlet's religion in the last act. As it developed in Protestant thought, the term *conscience* came to mean not just a faculty of moral censorship but a medium through which the individual could receive the revealed truth of a distant God. In the Protestant understanding it became less a severe judge keeping the subject timid and fearful and more an alternative authority that could function as a source of moral justification. The Puritan theologian William Perkins, following Calvin, elevated conscience to a position above human law and beneath God; in doing so, he provided a theological argument capable of undermining his basic social conservatism.[20] David Little has written that in Perkins's system it is the genuine Christian who grasps what the ends of earthly law actually are, since the consciences of the elect stand above this law in a new order where the aims of human law will ultimately be fulfilled. He goes on to say that this position is fundamentally at odds with the views of contemporaries like Whitgift, Hooker, and Coke, for whom human and divine law more nearly coincide.[21] In England the Puritan emphasis on the ability of the individual to criticize or oppose the state was based in large measure on this new discourse of conscience. Christopher Hill has argued for the progressive political effects of this discourse but has also noted that the idea of a "priesthood of all believers . . . was logically a doctrine of individualist anarchy," with reformed churches having no external checks against the authority of the individual conscience they otherwise served to encourage.[22]

In Shakespeare's representation of Hamlet's subjective history there is a recapitulation of this broad historical movement from a medieval to a Reformation concept of conscience. Interest in this change is evident in the play as a whole, with the term *conscience* appearing more often in *Hamlet* than in any other Shakespeare tragedy. In the course of the play, conscience ceases to be an impediment to the prince and becomes an authority that licenses him to think and act with greater freedom. The Hamlet who, after contriving the deaths of his former friends, can say "They are not near my conscience" (5.2.59), or who can say that it would be "perfect conscience" (1.68) to kill Claudius, is clearly speaking from a different subject position than the speaker who earlier says that "conscience does make cowards of us all" (3.1.85).[23] His concept of conscience as an empowering force seems to derive from a general subjective transformation consistent with Protestant experience, and one important consequence of this change is Hamlet's summary abandonment of *reason* as a crucial ideological term. The "sovereignty of reason" (1.4.54) over the political microcosm of the mind simply ceases to be an issue, because the Stoic and more generally humanist concept of identity on which this view of reason is based is an ideological casualty in the play. Up until Act 5 *Hamlet* depicts a society in which the official ideology holds that an individual is defined by his or her place in a rationally ordered universe and by relation to a God whose being and law are accessible to human reason—an ideology of human identity that had just received full expression in the work of Hooker.[24] But the final act of the play represents this Christian-humanist ideology as exhausted; Hamlet passes beyond it into a new cultural paradigm, one in which a Protestant concept of conscience supplants reason as the crucial human faculty.

In a parallel change, Hamlet's new perception of the scope and power of providence becomes evident in the graveyard scene. Of one of the skulls tossed up by the gravedigger, he says, "This might be the pate of a politician which this ass o'er-offices, one that would circumvent God, might it not?" (5.1.77-79). By implication, the living politician's self-interested plotting had no more chance against the designs of God than his remains now have against the rough treatment of the sexton. In 5.2, when Hamlet recounts to Horatio the episode at sea, he describes a subjective experience profoundly changed by his newly acquired concept of divinity, as in the speech that Bloom finds particularly important:

> . . . Methought I lay
> Worse than the mutines in the bilboes.
> Rashly—
> And praised be rashness for it: let us know
> Our indiscretion sometime serves us well
> When our dear plots do pall, and that should teach us
> There's a divinity that shapes our ends,
> Rough-hew them how we will. . . .
> (ll. 5-11)

This celebration of "indiscretion" contrasts sharply with Hamlet's earlier counsel of "discretion" to the player. In humanist discourse reason is the faculty crucial to understanding divine precepts, but in 5.2.6-11 there is a strong association of rashness with divinity: Hamlet suggests that following his impulses serves to connect him with the divine purpose, and this altered perspective seems to liberate him from debilitating subjective constraints. Later, when Horatio asks him how the new commission was sealed, he replies, "Why, even in that was heaven ordinant" (l. 49), indicating his conviction that providence directed the entire episode.

Hamlet sounds the same new note in refusing to allow Horatio to postpone the fencing match with Laertes:

> Not a whit. We defy augury. There's a special providence in the fall of a sparrow. If it be now, 'tis not to come. If it be not to come, it will be now. If it be not now, yet it will come. The readiness is all.
> (ll. 165-68)

In Matthew 10:29, Christ tells his disciples that a sparrow "shal not fall on the ground without your Father."[25] By alluding to this text, Hamlet projects the vision of a creation governed in every detail by the divine will. Contrary to the argument of Bloom, who maintains that it would be a mistake to regard Protestantism as an important context for this speech, Hamlet's citation of the biblical text has everything to do with the relationship between the individual and God in Reformation Christianity. That Protestantism is relevant here is supported by the First Quarto, which reads "theres a predestinate prouidence in the fall of a sparrow."[26] A good case can be made for regarding this adjective as Shakespeare's, rather than as the invention of a hypothetical reporter of the 1603 text. He had used it very recently in *Much Ado about Nothing* (1.1.128), and it was thus part of the vocabulary he was currently employing. In an analysis of the dialogue leading into this speech, Steven Urkowitz finds one of many instances in which "three different alternative readings appear in equivalent spots in all three versions of *Hamlet*."[27] He goes on to argue that such instances imply authorial "tinkering," a position which adds support for the view that Shakespeare is responsible for "predestinate." It may also be pertinent that the title page of the First Quarto advertises the play as having been acted by Shakespeare's company in the two universities. *Predestinate* would be a resonant word in those settings—particularly at Cambridge, where advanced Protestant views were common. The speech can be regarded as another moment in the play when the radical Protestant subtext surfaces quite clearly, with the term *predestinate* being generated by the specific ideological and dramatic moment Shakespeare represents.[28]

Shakespeare wrote *Hamlet* at a time when the political consequences of Protestant doctrine were receiving sustained attention. During the 1590s the civil and ecclesiastical establishment in England debated the potential for dissent inherent in predestinarian theology, and many found such potential dangerously high. They feared that if subjects believed themselves to be saved or damned by God's eternal decree, which they could not alter through personal effort, then a great incentive for living a godly and obedient life was lost. That the doctrine of predestination was common knowledge compounded the political problem. An Italian visitor to England in the 1580s reportedly observed that "the very *Women* and *Shopkeepers*" were capable of discussing predestination.[29] In the last decades of Elizabeth's reign the established church was orthodoxly Calvinist on this point, but many feared the political consequences of Calvin's teachings if they were not carefully interpreted. The bishop of London, Richard Bancroft, endorsed absolute predestination as a theological principle, but over the course of his career he deplored what he regarded as its perversion into a basis of support for oppositional political movements. In 1593 he wrote a tract charging that a group of millenarians, who had recently announced the return of Christ and attempted to seize power for the godly, based its actions in predestinarian theology. Archbishop Whitgift supported the Calvinist Lambeth Articles of 1595, but he may have overestimated the strength of reformed feeling at court and in the church: in December of 1595 Robert Cecil wrote him to say that the queen "mislikes much that any allowance hath been given by your Grace and the rest of any point to be disputed of predestination being a matter tender and dangerous to weak ignorant minds and thereupon requireth your Grace to suspend them."[30] Elizabeth had probably been briefed on the Lambeth Articles by Burghley, who objected to them on the same political grounds. A group of Cambridge divines wanted the Lambeth Articles to be given confessional status (to be incorporated with the Thirty-Nine Articles), but there was no support for this at court. The proposal remained on the agenda, however, until the Hampton Court Conference of 1604, when it was effectively defeated. Bishop Bancroft used the occasion to repeat his warning to the king against the political danger of those who lay "all their religion upon predestination."[31] James was later advised on this point by his chaplain, Benjamin Carier, who argued that radical Protestant beliefs were unfit "to keepe subjects in obedience to their soveraigns"; he feared the subjects would soon "openly maintayne that God hath as well pre-destinated men to be trayters as to be kinges."[32]

Hamlet's remark on the fall of the sparrow could thus have touched a sensitive political nerve, especially since in the play he has a plausible claim to the throne and is "loved of the distracted multitude" (4.3.4). The possibility emerges that the Q1 reference to a "predestinate" providence is absent from the Second Quarto and the Folio through self-censorship or even censorship by the government. A reference to predestination in a play about regicide would likely attract attention at a time when the queen and her closest advisors had been ordering the church authorities to suppress any discussion of the issue and when the religiously more conservative reign of James was getting underway.[33] Hamlet realizes a measure of the potential for dissent inherent in the Protestant doctrines of conscience and predestination, and to that extent he illustrates the case made by contemporary authorities who feared the political consequences of reformed theology. The argument that his Christianity in the last act is "traditional" is accordingly incorrect, though this adjective does describe other aspects of his ideological orientation. According to the Protestant concept, the human subject of God's grace was in fact less likely to be politically passive than to be active in the service of causes ratified by individual conscience, an activism evident in the careers of militant Protestant aristocrats like Leicester, Sidney, and Greville. The lives of these men also make it amply clear that members of the elite could hold radical Protestant beliefs and still be social conservatives.

This combination of religious radicalism and social conservatism characterizes Hamlet's position in the final act of the play. Mixing a royal or aristocratic sense of self with radical Protestant beliefs in providence and the authority of conscience was likely to produce volatile results, and Hamlet's religion in Act 5 clearly functions as an oppositional discourse supporting his struggle with the king. But the utopian promise of his subjective transformation remains mostly unfulfilled. The daring he displays in associating rashness with divinity and his radical transcendence of egocentric concerns in the "readiness is all" speech are signals of a subjectivity liberated from the constraints of conservative Renaissance ideology. But the radicalism of his religion in Act 5 also ends up subserving sharp political practice while stabilizing his conventional aristocratic sense of self. This paradox explains the difficulty of trying to establish the political bearings of Hamlet's change, in which a revolution in the order of subjectivity assists him in bringing down a corrupt government but nevertheless confirms him as a defender of traditional aristocratic society. The possibility of a political union with the people, which Claudius fears and which Laertes manages so easily, is never realized. But Hamlet's ultimate conservatism should not be allowed to obscure what the play represents in the final act: a glimpse of a radical relocation of the human subject beyond both the static identities of the feudal order and the self-centeredness demanded by Renaissance politics. It would, in fact, be surprising if there were no evidence of Protestantism and its powerful redefinition of the place of the subject in a play so thoroughly engaged in testing the ideological resources of contemporary culture. That predestination and its worldly consequences were tender political matters may be an important reason for Shakespeare's rather oblique and suggestive handling of Hamlet's transformation.

Notes

[1] Unless otherwise noted, all quotations of *Hamlet* and of all other Shakespeare plays and poems follow *William Shakespeare: The Complete Works,* ed. Stanley Wells and Gary Taylor with John Jowett and William Montgomery (Oxford: Clarendon Press, 1986).

[2] Quoted in A. G. Dickens, *The English Reformation* (London: B. T. Batsford, 1989), 29.

[3] See Dickens, 230-33.

[4] Quoted in Dickens, 230.

[5] Quoted in Dickens, 281.

[6] See Arthur McGee, *The Elizabethan Hamlet* (New Haven, CT, and London: Yale UP, 1987), 39-41. For a recent discussion of government censorship of plays, see Richard Dutton, *Mastering the Revels: The Regulation and Censorship of English Renaissance Drama* (Iowa City: U of Iowa P, 1991).

[7] Jacques Lacan, "Desire and the Interpretation of Desire in *Hamlet,*" *Yale French Studies* 55-56 (1977-78): 11-52, esp. 49.

[8] Of course this older ideological synthesis was not without its contradictions. Medieval Catholicism prohibited revenge, but this Christian prohibition was sometimes superseded among feudal aristocrats by their intense allegiance to a secular code of honor. For a discussion of this code and of how the early modern state, in asserting its exclusive right to judge disputes and mete punishment, attempted to alter and subsume it, see Mervyn James, *Society, Politics, and Culture: Studies in Early Modern England* (Cambridge: Cambridge UP, 1986), 11ff. James makes an important distinction between the "lineage" society of feudalism and what he calls the "civil" society of the emerging Renaissance state. His discussion helps to clarify the extent to which Shakespeare represents King Hamlet and his son as the products of very different cultural orders.

[9] In "Shakespeare and the Stoicism of Seneca" T. S. Eliot argues for the broad influence of Stoic ideology on Elizabethan and Jacobean drama. He suggests that Stoicism is an attractive philosophy for those who find themselves in "an indifferent or hostile world too big for [them]" and implies that the political and religious turmoil of Shakespeare's England created an environment favorable for its reception (*Elizabethan Essays* [London: Faber and Faber, 1934], 33-54, esp. 41). For a relevant and more specific discussion of the cultural issues challenging contemporary aristocratic men, see Mervyn James's analysis of the multicultural situation that complicated the experience of Essex and others (460).

[10] On the tensions between the traditional aristocracy and the growing power of the state, see Joan Kelly-Gadol, "Did Women Have a Renaissance?" in *Becoming Visible: Women in European History,* Renate Bridenthal, Claudia Koonz, and Susan Stuard, eds., 2d ed. (Boston: Houghton Mifflin, 1987), 175-201, esp. 184ff. Kelly-Gadol offers a reading of *The Courtier* as a text that assisted the European aristocracy in adapting to its changing relationship with royal power. See also Richard C. McCoy, "'A dangerous image': The Earl of Essex and Elizabethan chivalry," *Journal of Medieval and Renaissance Studies* 13 (1983): 313-29.

[11] Claudius first uses this trope in referring to the sensitive issue of his marriage to Gertrude:

> Therefore our sometime sister, now our queen,
> Th'imperial jointress of this warlike state,
> Have we as 'twere with a defeated joy, . . .
> In equal scale weighing delight and dole,
> Taken to wife.
>
> (1.2.8-14)

[12] It is also true, however, that Hamlet does not want the clowns to prevent the audience from hearing "some necessary question of the play" (3.2.42-43), indicating that he associates drama with an interrogative and possibly progressive function. To a certain extent the early modern closet drama actually performed this role, and the "question" such a play might consider could be as politically sensitive as the issue of tyrannicide.

[13] Francis Barker, *The Tremulous Private Body: Essays on Subjection* (London and New York: Methuen, 1984), 40.

[14] *William Shakespeare's* Hamlet, Harold Bloom, ed., *Modern Critical Interpretations* (New York: Chelsea House, 1986), vii and 2.

[15] For another reading interested in the relevance of Protestantism to *Hamlet,* see Kenneth S. Rothwell, "Hamlet's 'Glass of Fashion': Power, Self, and the Reformation" in *Technologies of the Self: A Seminar with Michel Foucault,* Luther H. Martin, Huck Gutman, and Patrick H. Hutton, eds. (Amherst: U of Massachusetts P, 1988), 80-98.

[16] C. S. Lewis, *English Literature in the Sixteenth Century Excluding Drama* (Oxford: Clarendon Press, 1954), 33.

[17] For a discussion of this point with respect to Calvin, see William J. Bouwsma, *John Calvin: A Sixteenth-Century Portrait* (New York and Oxford: Oxford UP, 1988), 12.

[18] Calvin speaks of the "spiritual freedom" of the elect and of how this freedom comforts and raises up "the stricken, prostrate conscience, showing it to be free from the curse and condemnation with which the law was pressing it down, bound and fettered. When through faith we lay hold on the mercy of God in Christ, we attain this liberation and, so to speak, manumission from subjection to the law. . . ." (John Calvin, *Institution of the Christian Religion,* trans. Ford Lewis Battles [Atlanta: John Knox Press, 1975], 44).

[19] On the Reformation in Denmark and its relationship to Wittenberg, see A. G. Dickens, *Martin Luther and the Reformation* (London: The English Universities Press, 1967), 114-16; and *Reformation and Society in Sixteenth-Century Europe* (London: Harcourt, Brace, and World, 1966), 87-88. See also Ole Peter Grell, "Scandinavia" in *The Reformation in national context,* Bob Scribner, Roy Porter, and Mikulas Teich, eds. (Cambridge: Cambridge UP, 1994), 111-30.

[20] For Perkins's assertion that the conscience is above human law, see "A Treatise of Conscience" in *The Workes of . . . William Perkins,* 3 vols. (London, 1612), 1:529-30.

[21] David Little, *Religion, Order, and Law: A Study in Pre-Revolutionary England* (Oxford: Basil Blackwell, 1970), 125.

[22] Christopher Hill, "The Problem of Authority," *The Collected Essays of Christopher Hill,* 3 vols. (Amherst: U of Massachusetts P, 1986), 2:37-50, esp. 38.

[23] In reading Hamlet's use of "conscience" in the 3.1 soliloquy, I agree with Catherine Belsey's view that the meaning of the term is not just awareness but also the faculty of moral judgment; see her "The Case of Hamlet's Conscience," *Studies in Philology* 76 (1979): 127-48.

[24] See, for example, Book 1, chapter 8, of Hooker's *Laws of Ecclesiastical Polity* (1593), in which he asserts the "force of the light of reason, wherwith God illuminateth every one which commeth into the world, men being inabled to know truth from falshood, and good from evill. . . . " (*Of the Laws of Ecclesiastical Polity,* ed. Georges Edelen, Vol. 1 of *The Folger Library Edition of The Works of William Hooker,* W. Speed Hill, gen. ed. [Cambridge, MA, and London: Harvard UP, 1977], 84).

[25] The Geneva Bible: *A facsimile of the 1560 edition* (Madison, Milwaukee, and London: U of Wisconsin P, 1969), BBii^v.

[26] Hamlet: *First Quarto, 1603,* ed. W.W. Greg, Shakespeare Quarto Facsimile No. 7 (London: Sidgwick and Jackson, 1951), 12^v and 13^r.

[27] Steven Urkowitz, "'Well-sayd olde Mole': Burying Three *Hamlets* in Modern Editions" in *Shakespeare Study Today: The Horace Howard Furness Memorial Lectures,* Georgianna Ziegler, ed. (New York: AMS Press, 1986), 37-70, esp. 55 and 62. Paul Werstine suggests that, rather than being preoccupied with the problem of a single authoritative text, we should closely examine "what we have—namely, the early printed texts themselves" ("The Textual Mystery of *Hamlet,*" *Shakespeare Quarterly* 39 [1988]: 1-26, esp. 2).

[28] Even the term *special,* found in both Q2 and F, has possible associations with Protestant discourse. In *Measure for Measure,* a play that seems to have been written at almost the same time as the publication of the Second Quarto of *Hamlet,* Shakespeare has the Duke use an oddly Protestant discourse when explaining his decision to confer power on Angelo: "For you must know we have with special soul / Elected him. . . ." (1.1.17-18).

[29] This observation is reported in Izaak Walton's "Life of Hooker" and is quoted here from *The Compleat Walton,* ed. Geoffrey Keynes (London: Nonesuch Press, 1929), 350. For a discussion of the wide dispersion of predestinarian thought, see Nicholas Tyacke, *Anti-Calvinists: The Rise of English Arminianism c. 1590-1640* (Oxford: Clarendon Press, 1987), 1-2; Tyacke notes that "between 1579 and 1615 at least thirty-nine quarto editions of the Genevan Bible, *all* printed in England, had a predestinarian catechism bound with them" (2).

[30] Quoted in Peter Lake, *Moderate puritans and the Elizabethan church* (Cambridge: Cambridge UP, 1982), 228.

[31] Quoted in McGee, 169.

[32] Quoted in Tyacke, 6.

[33] It is tempting to speculate that the First Quarto's "predestinate" reflects the language of a performance text and that it was prudently omitted when the text of Q2 was prepared for the press. The government's scrutiny of drama seems to have been unusually intense during the period in which the first two quartos of *Hamlet* appeared. Richard Dutton notes that in 1597 the Privy Council began to monitor drama with increased vigilance, often becoming directly involved in issues ordinarily handled by the Master of the Revels. Robert Cecil, who was actively involved in suppressing the discussion of predestination and was

responsible for orchestrating the transition of power from Elizabeth to James, directly intervened in the investigation of Samuel Daniel's *Philotas* in 1604. Ben Jonson was required to appear before the Privy Council for *Sejanus,* and Dutton speculates that this summons may have resulted not from the acting of the play in 1603 but from its printing in 1605 (109-10 and 164-65). The political atmosphere suggested by these incidents may thus be seen as unfavorable to the inclusion of "predestinate" in the Second Quarto of *Hamlet,* published in 1604. David Ward has recently argued that the publication of Q2 might have been a "pointed intervention" by Shakespeare's company in the political situation created for the company by James's accession. He suggests that Q2 is a text in some ways tailored to the interests and views of the new king, who had recently become the patron of Shakespeare's company and whose works were being published voluminously in London. Ward's hypothesis is relevant here, since James's opposition to radical Protestantism and to any justification for revenge against a royal figure might have made Q1's reference to "predestinate prouidence" unacceptable; see Ward's "The King and *Hamlet,*" *SQ* 43 (1992): 280-302.

Source: "*Hamlet* and 'A Matter Tender and Dangerous'," in *Shakespeare Quarterly,* Vol. 46, No. 4, Winter, 1995, pp. 383-97.

Venetian Culture and the Politics of *Othello*

Mark Matheson, *University of Utah*

In *Othello* Shakespeare represents a society in many ways fundamentally different from his own, and rather than minimizing or obscuring these differences he explores them in a politically creative way. The play is a powerful illustration of his ability to perceive and represent different forms of political organization, and to situate personal relationships and issues of individual subjectivity in a specific institutional context. Here and in much of his other work Shakespeare displays what might be described as a sociological imagination. He portrays in *Othello* not a feudal monarchy or Renaissance court but an enduring Italian city-state, a republic which continued to survive despite growing Habsburg domination in the rest of the peninsula. Taken in the context of his career as a whole the play is a fascinating example of Shakespeare's interest in republicanism, which is evident from 'The Rape of Lucrece' to *The Tempest.* It provides clear evidence that he was neither an uncritical advocate of conservative Tudor ideology, as an older critical tradition maintained, nor a writer materially unable to think and imagine beyond the monarchical paradigm, as a more recent historicist criticism has sometimes suggested. In the English context the act of representing a republican culture was itself a progressive gesture, since Venice offered an existing and stable alternative to the 'natural' and 'eternal' order of monarchy. In addition to this, and to a degree not usually recognized, Shakespeare represents the city's institutions exercising a shaping influence on personal relationships and individual experience. These institutions inform and complicate the ongoing process of cultural exchange at the heart of the play, which is Othello's attempt to thrive in the foreign cultural world of an aggressive European power, and they also influence the representation of women's experience, which the play suggests would be different in a patriarchal but non-monarchical culture. The play is itself the product of cultural exchange, and Shakespeare's imaginative sensitivity to the ways of a different society generates political energies in the text which carry it beyond the ideological boundaries of official English culture.

The extent of Shakespeare's interest in the institutional life of Venice can be suggested by a comparison with contemporary playwrights. John Marston's *Antonio's Revenge* (*c.* 1600) is set in the city but offers little sense of its specific social and political practices. Jonson's *Volpone* (1605) reveals a much greater interest in particular Venetian institutions, and Daniel C. Boughner has argued that Jonson's research for the play was stimulated in part by Shakespeare's recent portrayal of Venice in *Othello*.[1] Shakespeare had probably read Lewes Lewkenor's *The Common-Wealth and Government of Venice* (1599), a translation of Contarini's laudatory exposition of the Venetian state.[2] Those who wrote dedicatory poems for this volume include Edmund Spenser, who praises not only the beauty of Venice but its 'policie of right', and John Harington, who compares it 'For Freedome' with the Roman republic.[3] Jonson read Contarini for *Volpone,* in which Sir Politic Would-Be reveals that he has hastily studied 'Contarene' in order to pass himself off as a Venetian citizen (4.1.40). Boughner has argued that in this play Jonson deliberately undercuts the idealized portrait of Venice in Contarini's work and Lewkenor's introduction. This is a plausible view, since the Venice of *Volpone* is a greed-driven city where predatory relations are the norm, where the citizens take a Machiavellian attitude toward religion (4.1.22-7), and where the supposedly democratic law courts are venues in which 'multitude' and 'clamour' overcome justice (4.6.19).

Shakespeare's more favourable representation of Venice may suggest an imaginative willingness to explore the strengths of a republican culture, and may also reflect a sympathy with the political interests of the Sidney and Essex circles, with which of course he had some connection. Members of these aristocratic circles were interested in the mixed government of the Venetian republic, and as Protestants they approved of its steadfast opposition to the authoritarianism of the Counter-Reformation. Some took a specific interest in the work of Lewkenor, who in his address to the reader describes the Venetian state as comprising monarchical, aristocratic, and democratic elements. The prince has 'all exterior ornamentes of royall dignitie' but is nevertheless 'wholy subiected to the lawes'; the 'Councell of Pregati or Senators' is invested with great authority but has no 'power, mean, or possibility at all to tyranize'; and a 'Democrasie or popular estate' is evident in the existence of a 'great councell, consisting at least of 3000. Gentlemen, whereupon the highest strength and mightinesse of the estate absolutely relyeth.'[4] Lewkenor's adverb in this final clause demonstrates how terms usually associated with monarchy could slip from their ordinary usage in descriptions of a state with a mixed constitution, and his account is an example of how cultural exchange could destabilize and enrich conventional English political discourse. There is unquestionably a degree of idealization in Lewkenor's discussion of Venice, just as there is in the text of Contarini, but the enthusiasm he reveals is itself suggestive of the political interest the city was generating in England at the end of the sixteenth century.

The governmental structure of Venice may seem to be of only incidental importance to *Othello,* but in fact it is indispensable for generating the basic dramatic situation, and it influences every personal relationship in the play. In the first act Shakespeare offers a compelling representation of the city's political and cultural life, and his interest in its institutional structure is evident in a variety of ways. There is a notable shift, for instance, to a more explicitly republican discourse than he had used in *The Merchant of Venice*. In part this might be due to his intervening work with Roman republicanism in *Julius Caesar,* which seems to have influenced the later play. The councilmen who were simply 'magnificoes' (4.1.1 stage directions) in *The Merchant* have become 'Senators' in *Othello* (1.3.1 stage directions). Other traces of a discourse associated with republican Rome include Iago's early reference to 'togaed consuls' (1.1.24), with whom he compares Cassio for their common lack of military experience. Iago may be making a vague reference to classical culture, but he is probably referring instead to the current members of the Venetian council, as becomes clear in the next scene when Cassio uses the republican term 'consuls' for the senators who are meeting with the Duke (1.2.43). Iago's words may glance at Rome but can also be read as referring to a specifically Venetian practice. It was widely known that the members of the Venetian council had no military pretensions, and Lewkenor finds it extraordinary that these 'vnweaponed men in gownes' should give direction to 'many mightie and warlike armies'.[5] The practice of employing foreign mercenary officers and generals—by law no Venetian citizen could have more than twenty-five men in his command—was also based on republican principle. Contarini writes that Venetian leaders and armies involved in long wars on land would inevitably fall into 'a Kinde of faction' against the other 'peaceable citizens'. This could easily lead to civil war, and he notes in an analysis identical to Machiavelli's that this problem helped to undermine the Roman republic, since Caesar drew the loyalty of his men away from the state and to himself, and this permitted him 'to tyrannize ouer that commonwealth to which hee did owe all duty and obedience'.[6] The Venetian policy designed to prevent any conquering Caesar from turning against the republican state opened the way for men like Othello, and owing to its setting in this particular city the play has genuine plausibility.

Perhaps the character most clearly shaped by the institutional life of Venice is Desdemona. In part this influence is traditional, since Brabanzio's household functions on a typical patriarchal model. His rule seems to have been mostly benign, but a specifically political idiom emerges in his spontaneous laments over Desdemona's behaviour: 'O heaven, how got she out? O, treason of the blood!' (1.1.171). After he learns that she has willingly married Othello he employs the same political language:

> I am glad at soul I have no other child,
> For thy escape would teach me tyranny,
> To hang clogs on 'em.
>
> (1.3.195-7)

Throughout Act I Brabanzio speaks the language of fatherly ownership with a frightening intensity, and he has inculcated in Desdemona obedience to the father's word. But Brabanzio's absolutist regime at home exists in tension with the government of the state, which as the council scene attests is based on debate and consultation. His household is built on the older political model of a *corpus,* of which he is unquestionably the head, but it exists within a larger political order based on the more progressive model of a *res publica,* whose participants are citizens rather than subjects, and whose leaders conduct affairs of state on a generally equal footing.[7]

In the council scene Brabanzio uses a kind of absolutist discourse in his address to Desdemona, asking if she knows where most she owes 'obedience', and she replies by saying that what she owes her father is 'respect' (1.3.179, 183). Desdemona's response represents a cultural shift away from her father's conception of the family, with her carefully chosen term 'respect' indicating in part the degree to which she has been shaped by the relatively liberal institutions of Venice. It seems to be a word in some ways specific to the republican context, where it characterizes the tenor of relations among members of the council, and this government has certainly made Desdemona aware of alternatives to the royalist doctrine of unquestioning obedience. Desdemona herself introduces the concept of a broader cultural order in her reply to Brabanzio before the senators, in which she makes repeated mention of her 'education' (1.3.181)—the only time this word appears in Shakespearian tragedy. This education is partly responsible for her independence, and for the verbal agility with which she disengages herself from the identities constructed for her by her father. The most striking line by which she accomplishes this is 'I am hitherto your daughter' (1.3.184), in which she brings out an instability in the word 'daughter' itself, using it to designate not the natural bond she refers to earlier when she says she is 'bound' to Brabanzio for 'life', but rather a relationship of power in which the daughter is the father's possession as guaranteed by a specific set of cultural arrangements. By using the word in this second sense she implicitly asserts the role of culture in establishing such identities, and thus disturbs Brabanzio's simple distinction between a nature which cannot 'err' and the supernatural order of 'witchcraft' (1.3.62, 64).

The problem for Brabanzio is that the progressive political and economic life of Venice is at work beneath his conservative ideology of gender and paternal relations, and Shakespeare's broad representation of Venetian political life makes Desdemona's capacity for independent judgement and action more convincing. A comparison with the sexual politics of *The Merchant of Venice* can be instructive here. As Walter Cohen has pointed out Belmont functions in that play as a 'green' world inhabited by a traditional landed aristocracy, who in the course of events are brought into contact with the commercial and urban world of contemporary Venice.[8] The central figure of this green world is Portia, 'a living daughter curbed by the will of a dead father' (1.2.23-4), and one who completely accepts that her father's word has taken away her choice in marriage. As witty and resourceful as she is Portia never contemplates the transgression of the patriarchal decree, and even allowing for the difference in genre her behaviour makes a notable contrast with that of the city-dwelling Desdemona, who does something incomparably more daring. It also happens that Portia is visited by the Moorish Prince of Morocco, who comes in suit to her for marriage, and of whom she says 'If he have the condition of a saint and the complexion of a devil, I had rather he should shrive me than wive me' (1.2.126-8). The first thing Morocco says to her is 'Mislike me not for my complexion' (2.1.1), and when he has departed after failing to choose the correct casket Portia says 'Let all of his complexion choose me so' (2.7.79). Next to Desdemona's cosmopolitan openmindedness Portia's response looks very provincial, a predictable reaction to cultural otherness from the daughter of a traditionalist aristocracy. Portia lives idly in her great house on inherited wealth, with perhaps the nearest neighbour a 'monastery two miles off' (3.4.31); by contrast Desdemona lives in the city which Contarini describes as 'a common and generall market to the whole world', its streets thronging with a 'wonderful concourse of strange and forraine people'.[9] In this setting the traditionalist gender and racial ideologies of Belmont are on rather more shaky ground, subjected as they are to the pressures of a society moved by the concerns of commercial exchange and with a practical-minded government ready to reward merit rather than birth.

Shakespeare thus represents Desdemona's self-confidence as partly a product of the progressive Venetian culture he portrays in the play. Othello comes to this culture as an outsider, and his association with the city is based on both the government's republican principles and its readiness to seek out those with merit and to pay for their services. Much of Othello's relationship with Venetian culture is determined by the racial prejudice (like Portia's) he encounters there, which Shakespeare makes a deliberate point of portraying in the opening scenes of the play. This prejudice surfaces repeatedly, as in Brabanzio's insistence that the case be heard that very night:

> For if such actions may have passage free,
> Bondslaves and pagans shall our statesmen be.
> (1.2.99-100)

This is one of the earliest recorded uses of 'statesmen', a noun which evokes the republican setting of the Italian city-state. (Jonson had used it a few years earlier to name a category of men typified by Machiavelli.)[10] The limits to popular participation in contemporary republican government are abundantly clear in Brabanzio's speech, in which he apparently alludes to the period when Othello was 'sold to slavery' (1.3.137). He also leaves little doubt about his view of Othello's conversion to Christianity, which he evidently regards as a flimsy overlay for an essentially pagan nature. It seems to be Shakespeare's imaginative sympathy for the experience of the cultural outsider, particularly in the hostile environment often created by natives like Brabanzio, which enables him to move beyond the stereotypical images of Moorish people retailed in plays and pageants in England throughout his lifetime.[11] He created this highly original character by imagining Othello in a concrete social situation, and by permitting him to bring to Venice an ideological orientation formed under a different set of cultural institutions.

If one judges this orientation in the context of the Venice Shakespeare represents, Othello emerges as arguably the most conservative character in the play. The rich portrayal of his conservative sensibility seems to be generated in part by Shakespeare's interest in liberal Venetian institutions, and in the contrasts which accordingly emerge as Othello's relationship with Venice unfolds. He finds a model for his personal and political relationships in the tradition of monarchy, and in his first appearance he offers an indication of the degree to which his sense of self has been shaped by this tradition: 'I fetch my life and being / From men of royal siege' (1.2.21-2). Among the things to which Othello will later bid farewell is 'the royal banner' (3.3.358), a detail suggesting once again his experience of a political order remote from the republican institutions of contemporary Venice. Othello's language before the council in Act I tends to obscure the economic basis of his relationship with the state, which is accurately described by Iago's reference to their employment in 'the trade of war' (1.2.1).[12] Othello has a more nearly feudal conception of this relationship, which he speaks of in terms of duty and religious devotion. He conveys this in his first address to the senators—'Most potent, grave, and reverend signors, / My very noble and approved good masters' (1.3.76-7)—where his devotional attitude contrasts with the practical tone of the council's deliberations. Othello positions himself here in the role of devoted servant, and interestingly to the men themselves rather than to the state as an institution. His sense of his relationship with Venice as a personal tie rather than a contractual agreement is also evident when he prefaces a request to the council with 'Most humbly therefore bending to your state' (1.3.234), where 'state' slips from its usual sense of designating the Venetian republic and refers instead to the personal status of the senators. At one point he likens their council to the judgement seat of the Christian God:

> as truly as to heaven
> I do confess the vices of my blood,
> So justly to your grave ears I'll present
> How I did thrive in this fair lady's love,
> And she in mine.
>
> (1.3.122-6)

Some have read this as an ominous passage, as perhaps revealing an unconscious identification in Othello's mind between sexual vice and his love for Desdemona,[13] but more plainly it indicates the hierarchical understanding he has of both political and religious institutions. The deep identification Othello makes in these lines would seem to be between Roman Catholicism and political absolutism, a conceptual integration roughly on the Habsburg model.

The council acts in a way which contrasts sharply with the political world as understood by Othello. Shakespeare represents them as a functioning participatory government, with a large measure of equality among aristocratic peers. Brabanzio makes reference to 'my brothers of the state' (1.2.97), an unusual locution which recalls the republican rhetoric of *Julius Caesar,* in which the anti-imperial faction employs the metaphor of fraternity in regarding themselves as the true sons of Rome. The members of the council make no sweeping ideological claims about what is at stake, but engage instead in a business-like attempt to calculate the number of ships in the Turkish fleet. In denying the accuracy of a certain report the First Senator says ''tis a pageant / To keep us in false gaze' (1.3.19-20), which suggests the deliberative nature of their government, and their ability to see through theatrical displays of power associated in contemporary culture (and in present-day criticism of Renaissance texts) with imperial and absolutist governments. The practical-mindedness of the council was objected to in the late seventeenth century by Thomas Rymer, who found that Shakespeare's presentation lacked sufficient nobility:

> By their Conduct and manner of talk, a body must strain hard to fancy the Scene at *Venice;* And not rather in some of our Cinq-ports, where the Baily and his Fisher-men are knocking their heads together on account of some Whale, or some terrible broil up the Coast.[14]

What Rymer sees as a fault (and exaggerates to make his point) can also be read in terms of Shakespeare's awareness of different political cultures. He may have thought it fitting that the senators of this commercial republic should be less concerned with shows of worldly greatness than with shrewd calculation and getting their figures right.

Certainly the religious character of Othello's devotion to the Venetian cause cannot be found among members of the council, who make no plea of any kind for Christendom. In fact in the context of Venetian culture Othello's religious sensibility seems rather antiquated. More than any other character he invests the Turkish-Christian conflict with spiritual significance, as his attribution of the Turkish defeat to God's will and his plea for 'Christian shame' among the victors makes clear (2.3.163-5). His piety seems to belong more to the era of the Crusades than to the increasingly secular world of sixteenth-century politics, when the powers of Europe were sometimes willing to ally themselves with the Ottoman empire to gain an advantage over other Christian states. Desdemona's sensitivity to this aspect of her husband's character may emerge when she tells Emilia that instead of losing the 'handkerchief' she would rather have lost her purse 'Full of crusadoes' (3.4.26). This is Shakespeare's only reference to this coin, which was stamped with a cross and current in contemporary England, and its name evokes the larger context of religious war in which Othello is involved, and perhaps also his tendency to regard the Christian-Turkish conflict in heroic and romantic terms. Desdemona's reference to 'crusadoes' might thus be read as an involuntary testimony to her sympathetic understanding of Othello's motives.

The character most aware of how Othello's traditionalist perspective makes him vulnerable to exploitation in Venice is Iago. Shakespeare makes a point of emphasizing Iago's role in the Venetian army, whose rigidly hierarchical relations contrast markedly with those within the state government, where the rule is consultation among equals rather than a structure of command and obedience. Like Brabanzio's household, the army and the martial law government in Cyprus have absolutist associations. Marguerite Waller has pointed out how Iago derives a sense of his own value from the military hierarchy—'I know my price, I am worth no worse a place' (1.1.11)—and that what he regards as the intrusion of Othello and the Florentine Cassio helps to create the 'obsessive energy' with which he plots their ruin.[15] Othello and Cassio are also incorporated into the structure of the army in a way which shapes their subjective experience, but their concept of this institution lacks the commercial connotations of Iago's view. Both tend to regard the army as an instance of the organic community envisioned by the ideology of contemporary monarchy, and the politicized language of love which typifies political discourse in absolutism comes easily to them both. Cassio reveals this in his fall from Othello's favour, particularly in his request to Desdemona to intercede on his behalf:

> I do beseech you
> That by your virtuous means I may again
> Exist and be a member of his love
> Whom I, with all the office of my heart,
> Entirely honour.
> (3.4.108-12)

Cassio's identity is dependent on his place within the institution, though he figures this not in practical political or economic terms but in the language of love, with the term 'member' recalling the traditional monarchical rhetoric of the 'body' politic and the organic community. Shakespeare may represent Cassio in this way partly because he is a product of the absolutist government of Florence, which had reverted from its earlier republicanism to the autocracy of the later Medici. In any case the crucial role played by the army in supporting Cassio's sense of self is evident in his use of the surprisingly strong verb 'Exist', and in its prominent placement. The play offers an analysis of male identity within the army as profoundly dependent on place and hierarchical relations, and as being distinct in this way from the system of relative equality among members of the Venetian governing class. In the speech quoted above Cassio's discourse of love and duty is suggestive of the personalized politics of absolute monarchy, and at odds with the legalism and practical business relationships of Venetian society as a whole. As a product of this society Desdemona is influenced by these more progressive conditions, and the legal or contractual basis for relationships in the city is evident in her language. She tells Cassio 'If I do vow a friendship I'll perform it / To the last article' (3.3.21-2).

Othello prefers to conduct his political relationships in the older language of loyalty and loving service, and Iago plays on this idealistic and somewhat dated vocabulary to exploit him. In the central scene of the play (3.3) he is attuned to Othello's habit of viewing power relations in terms of devotion and love. When Othello threatens to kill him he projects indignation at his general's ingratitude: 'I'll love no friend, sith love breeds such offence' (3.3.385). At this Othello retreats, and presently Iago swears himself to 'wronged Othello's service':

> Let him command,
> And to obey shall be in me remorse,
> What bloody business ever.
> OTHELLO I greet thy love,
> Not with vain thanks, but with acceptance
> bounteous.
> (3.3.470-3)

In the speech partly quoted Iago never mentions love, and that Othello interprets his promise of devoted obedience in this way reveals the politicized nature of 'love' in his discourse. The extent to which Othello's mind is imbued with the monarchical is evident in the despairing language he uses after falling to Iago's treachery. It emerges in his vow of revenge, 'Yield up, O love, thy crown and hearted throne / To tyrannous hate!' (3.3.452-3), in which Othello represents his own subjective world as an absolutist political order. The following image in which he compares his 'bloody thoughts' to the rushing Pontic Sea is a remarkable intensification of a conventional Renaissance metaphor for tyranny, in which the boundless ocean is used to figure engulfing despotism.

There is also a religious element in the political discourse Othello uses at this point in the play, as in his accusation that Desdemona's hand is 'moist':

> This argues fruitfulness, and liberal heart.
> Hot, hot and moist—this hand of yours
> requires
> A sequester from liberty; fasting, and prayer,
> Much castigation, exercise devout,
> For here's a young and sweating devil here
> That commonly rebels. 'Tis a good hand,
> A frank one.
> DESDEMONA You may indeed say so,
> For 'twas that hand that gave away my heart.
> OTHELLO
> A liberal hand. The hearts of old gave hands,
> But our new heraldry is hands, not hearts.

It is typical of Othello's deeply conservative notions of service and heroism that he praises the 'old' ways and speaks of infidelity in love in terms of the debasement of heraldic signs. His speeches here are an interesting mix of political and sexual discourse, in which he conflates the Venetian tradition of political liberty with sexual licence—another tradition for which the city was widely known.[16] Othello uses the term 'liberty' to imply sexual indulgence, and the remedy he prescribes is the very un-Venetian practice of authoritarian religious discipline, indicating once again the distance of his sensibility from the religion and politics of Venice.

One further aspect of Othello's ideological orientation needs to be mentioned: he has no conception of a world divided into public and private spheres. This is manifest when Iago impugns the fidelity of Desdemona, and Othello responds by bidding farewell to his career in war, uttering in a painful lament that his 'occupation's gone' (3.3.362). Michael Neill has noted Othello's tendency to make no distinction in his life between public and private roles, and that his reference to 'occupation' can be read at a variety of levels both political and sexual.[17] The play seems to suggest in fact that the domestic or private sphere is in the process of evolving as a practical and conceptual category within the broader institutional life of the Venetian state. Francis Barker has argued that a conception of the public and private as autonomous spheres developed mostly after Shakespeare's work in the theatre, and he cites the second scene of *Hamlet* to support his point.[18] He suggests that in that scene the looming war with Norway, Laertes' intention to return to France, and Hamlet's melancholy are all represented as continuous issues within a single conceptual and political order. The scene which invites comparison in *Othello* is the gathering of the council, in which the Duke responds tellingly to the question of whether Desdemona should be permitted to accompany Othello to Cyprus: 'Be it as you shall privately determine' (1.3.275). In *Hamlet* Claudius involves himself much more conspicuously in the familial debate over whether Laertes should return to France.[19] What Shakespeare seems to suggest in *Othello* is that the distinction between public and private is more developed in the context of a commercial and republican society. If it is less evident in *Hamlet* this is probably because in that play he represents a monarchy in which the traditions of feudalism continue to exert an influence. In royalist countries the corporate ideology which Barker finds in *Hamlet* may have inhibited any sharp distinction between the domestic and public spheres, but Shakespeare's treatment of the issue in his play about Venice suggests his ability to think beyond the social practices of monarchy, and perhaps also his awareness of how the conceptual order would be different in a commercial state based on citizenship rather than on the older notion of membership in a body politic.

As the play develops Shakespeare shows an increasing interest in the association of Venetian women with the private sphere, and in the different roles they play there. In part this seems to be because the domestic sphere is charged over the course of the play with the displaced energies of state politics, and this politicizes the language of this sphere and the actions and speech of women to an unusual degree. The relative equality of Desdemona and Othello in their marriage is evident in the encounter when she first pleads Cassio's 'cause', in which she adopts the part of a 'solicitor' and establishes the setting for debate and persuasion (3.3.27). Both the legalism of Venice and its consultative government are influences here, and Desdemona brings a consciousness shaped by republican traditions to both her marriage and the more conservative institutional setting of Cyprus. After speaking her mind freely throughout this scene she exits telling Othello 'Whate'er you be, I am obedient' (3.3.90), and thus uses a traditional discourse of submission to male authority only when she has already succeeded in creating a space for negotiation. Much more oppressive is the marriage between Iago and Emilia, in which the husband exerts a despotic control over his wife's actions and speech. In this relationship Shakespeare portrays the private sphere as a place of privation, with Emilia deprived of any broader agency or public role. Her plight reflects Iago's virulent misogyny and his obsession with hierarchical relations, and perhaps also a contemporary republican tendency to masculinize the state and to confine women exclusively to the private order. That Iago believes Emilia has no role in the public world is evident in his rebuke to her for suggesting that some 'villainous knave' is poisoning Othello's mind: 'Speak within door' (4.2.148). But Shakespeare also shows an interest in the private order as the place of women's collective experience, and this is most clearly evident in the 'willow' scene (4.3). Desdemona and Emilia experience solidarity and freedom of speech in this setting, and in the absence of male controls they touch issues of power and desire beyond the range of ordinary discourse.[20] Shakespeare represents them developing a collective consciousness by quietly exploiting the limited freedom of the private sphere, and this scene clearly generates some of the political energy Emilia displays in the final act.

In the last scene Othello is moved not only by his desire for revenge but by what he regards as the requirements of 'Justice' (5.2.17). As it opens he is still the military governor of Cyprus, and he evidently believes the murder of Desdemona to be within the purview of his powers under martial law. Desdemona may refer to his status as the ruler of the island when she says 'O, banish me, my lord, but kill me not' (5.2.85). Othello is thus guilty not only of murder but of the arbitrary exercise of power, and Shakespeare represents his actions as both morally wrong and tyrannical. Othello has himself been tyrannized by Iago, and the character responsible for overthrowing both these tyrannies is Emilia. That Shakespeare chose her as the agent responsible for breaking her husband's domination can be regarded as the fulfilment of a certain logic in the play in which a relationship develops between the women of Venice and the city's tradition of political liberty. The aspect of this tradition focused on in the text is the idea of free speech, which is defined not in terms of modern liberalism but in the contemporary context of monarchical and patriarchal restrictions on utterance, an absolutist context in which political speech is made 'tongue-tied by authority' (Sonnet 66). Desdemona's candid political and sexual discourse before the council is the first evidence of this relationship between women and the city's traditions, and she is associated with such discursive freedom repeatedly in the play, as when Othello says (approvingly) that his wife is 'free of speech' (3.3.189), and when she later tells Cassio that she stands in the blank of her husband's displeasure for 'my free speech' (3.4.127).

In the final scene Emilia uses much the same discourse to bring down the tyranny of her husband. Shakespeare's interest in Emilia in the context of the relationship between Venetian women and political speech emerges much earlier in the play. When Iago implies in Act 2 that his wife is a scold Desdemona defends her by saying 'Alas, she has no speech!' (2.1.106). This is a rather unusual phrase for making the point, and its oddity signals the gradually developing connection between the women of Venice and political expression. When Emilia's speech threatens him at the end of the play Iago tries to return her to the private sphere: 'I charge you get you home' (5.2.201). Having already spoken without male permission in interrupting Montano's address to Othello, Emilia asks the representatives of the Venetian state for 'leave to speak':

> 'Tis proper I obey him, but not now.
> Perchance, Iago, I will ne'er go home.
> (5.2.203-4)

What Emilia announces in these lines is a political revolt: in this context 'going home' has both its literal meaning and the political sense of returning to a state of complete subordination. Emilia's disobedience of her husband's authority will likely have radical consequences, as she is well aware. When Iago again tells her to be silent she again rejects him:

> 'Twill out, 'twill out. I peace?
> No, I will speak as liberal as the north.
> Let heaven, and men, and devils, let 'em all,
> All, all cry shame against me, yet I'll speak.
> (5.2.225-8)

In Emilia's use 'liberal' is completely without the sexual connotations it had in Othello's discourse, and suggests a freedom exercised with great effort in the face of traditional male authority. Her image of the north wind for the force of a woman's speech in the public sphere summons up other Renaissance usages in which storm and tempest are metaphors for political upheaval and revolution. And the emerging emphasis late in the play on the solidarity of women makes it possible to take her reference to 'men' as designating not humankind but the ruling gender. Like the Venetian woman she serves Emilia seems to be an agent for realizing the city's political ideals of justice and liberty. Her last words are 'So, speaking as I think, alas, I die' (5.2.258), a line which foreshadows Edgar's closing speech in *King Lear,* in which he says that the witnesses to the catastrophe must 'Speak what we feel, not what we ought to say' (5.3.300). Emilia's words endow what Edgar says with a significance more clearly political, and they may suggest that Shakespeare regarded such speech as a recourse against both loss and tyranny.

Critical awareness of Shakespeare's interest in fundamentally different forms of social organization allows this kind of political content in his work to emerge more clearly. Certainly this interest informs *Othello,* and the tension between monarchy and republicanism charges its language with nuance and political significance. Shakespeare's representation of a non-European's life in Venice and of women's experience in the city is creatively influenced by his awareness of these different systems, and his encounter with the foreign political culture of Venice produces a play that explores and at times subtly endorses ideological perspectives outside the framework established by the monarchical and patriarchal traditions of contemporary English politics.

Notes

[1] Daniel C. Boughner, 'Lewkenor and *Volpone*', *Notes and Queries,* n.s. 9 (1962): 124.

[2] For discussions of Lewkenor as a source for *Othello* see Kenneth Muir, 'Shakespeare and Lewkenor', *Review of English Studies,* n.s. 7 (1956): 182-3; William R. Drennan, '"Corrupt Means to Aspire": Contarini's De *Republica* and the Motives of Iago', *Notes and Queries,* n.s. 35 (1988): 474-5; and David McPherson, 'Lewkenor's Venice and Its Sources', *Renaissance Quarterly,* 41 (1988): 459-66.

[3] Gasparo Contarini, *The Common-wealth and Gouernment of Venice,* trans. Lewes Lewkenor (London, 1599), 3v, A4.

[4] Contarini, *The Common-wealth and Gouernment of Venice,* A2v.

[5] Contarini, A3.

[6] Contarini, pp. 130-I.

[7] For a discussion of these contemporary political models see J. G. A. Pocock, *The Machiavellian Moment: Florentine Political Thought and the Atlantic Republican Tradition* (Princeton and London: Princeton University Press, 1975), pp. 339ff.

[8] Walter Cohen, '*The Merchant of Venice* and the Possibilities of Historical Criticism', *ELH* 49 (1982): 777. Cultural historians have pointed out that in contemporary Italy the countryside became a prime area for the investment of urban capital, and this was especially true of the region around Venice. Powerful families who made their fortunes in banking or trade bought estates in the country, and city interests dominated the rural economy. Partly as a result there was a revival of the pastoral genre and older aristocratic ideals, a 'refeudalization' similar in some respects to what was happening elsewhere in Europe. Cohen is right to stress the conservatism of aristocratic culture in the 'green' world of the play, though in actual historical terms it was often an instance of the 'new' traditionalism. See Lauro Martines, *Power and Imagination: City-States*

in Renaissance Italy (Harmondsworth: Penguin, 1979), pp. 221-9.

[9] Contarini, *The Common-wealth and Gouernment of Venice,* p.1.

[10] See *Every Man Out of His Humour,* 2.6.168.

[11] For discussions of the representation of Moors and other non-Europeans in contemporary English culture see Samuel C. Chew, *The Crescent and the Rose: Islam and England during the Renaissance* (New York: Oxford University Press, 1937); Eldred Jones, *Othello's Countrymen: The African In English Renaissance Drama* (London: Oxford University Press, 1965); and Geoffrey Bullough, *Narrative and Dramatic Sources of Shakespeare,* vol. 7 (London: Routledge and Kegan Paul, 1973), pp. 207ff.

[12] Barbara Everett has noted the conflict between Othello's romanticized view of war and the fact that he is paid to fight by a city known for commerce and secularism. See her '"Spanish" Othello: The Making of Shakespeare's Moor', *Shakespeare Survey* 35 (1982), p. 112.

[13] See Stephen Greenblatt, *Renaissance Self-Fashioning: From More to Shakespeare* (Chicago and London: University of Chicago Press, 1980), p. 245.

[14] From his *Short View of Tragedy* (1693); quoted in G. R. Hibbard, '*Othello* and the Pattern of Shakespearian Tragedy', *Shakespeare Survey* 21 (1968), p. 41.

[15] Marguerite Waller, 'Academic Tootsie: The Denial of Difference and the Difference It Makes', *Diacritics,* 17.2 (1987): 17.

[16] For a discussion of how contemporary observers of Venice found it difficult to distinguish between the political freedom fostered by the city's institutions and its reputation for sexual indulgence see William Bouwsma, 'Venice and the Political Education of Europe', in *Renaissance Venice,* ed. J. R. Hale (London: Faber, 1973), p. 461.

[17] Michael Neill, 'Changing Places in *Othello*', *Shakespeare Survey* 37 (1984), p. 127.

[18] Francis Barker, *The Tremulous Private Body: Essays on Subjection* (London and New York: Methuen, 1984), pp. 30ff.

[19] The practice of Shakespeare's own culture was closer to that represented in *Hamlet.* On 29 June 1601 William Herbert, third earl of Pembroke, asked the queen through Robert Cecil for permission 'to go abroad to follow mine own business'. He was still asking for this permission two months later. At Elizabeth's court such royal control over the travels of the nobility was the general rule, and Shakespeare was thus departing from the custom of his own society in imagining a different political practice for contemporary Venice. See 'William Herbert, third Earl of Pembroke', *Dictionary of National Biography,* vol. 9, p. 678.

[20] Carol McKewin has noted that the women's friendship in this scene is an 'implied rebuke' to relationships between men in the play. See her 'Counsels of Gall and Grace: Intimate Conversations between Women in Shakespeare's Plays', in *The Woman's Part: Feminist Criticism of Shakespeare,* ed. by Carolyn Ruth Swift Lenz, Gayle Greene, and Carol Thomas Neely (Urbana: University of Illinois Press, 1980), p. 128.

Source: "Venetian Culture and the Politics of *Othello,*" in *Shakespeare Survey: An Annual Survey of Shakespeare Studies and Production,,* Vol. 48, 1995, pp. 123-33.

The Adaptation of a Shakespearean Genre: *Othello* and Ford's *'Tis Pity She's a Whore*

Raymond Powell, ***University of Reading***

Othello's popularity in the early seventeenth century is indicated both by the frequency of its revival and by its influence over many of the dramatists of the period.[1] It seems to have exerted a lasting hold over Ford's imagination, the effects traceable in three plays written at different stages in his career: *The Queen,* published anonymously in 1653 but now generally reckoned to be an early work, *Love's Sacrifice* (1633), and *The Lady's Trial* (1638). The extent and significance of the influence of *Othello* on *Love's Sacrifice* has been much discussed.[2] In the words of one commentator, "So close are the parallels with *Othello* in the middle scenes of the action that it is tempting to imagine that Ford wrote with a copy of the play at his side."[3] Ford's Shakespearean borrowings are not, however, confined to *Othello,* and there is even more general acknowledgment of the influence of *Romeo and Juliet* on the structure, characterization, and detail of *'Tis Pity She's a Whore.*[4] What I want to argue here is that *'Tis Pity* owes some of its distinctive qualities not merely to *Romeo and Juliet* but also to the Shakespeare play that occupied Ford's mind throughout his career, and that *'Tis Pity* received from both plays an important creative stimulus. In the progression from *Romeo and Juliet* to *Othello,* Shakespeare greatly enlarged the scope of the tragedy of love, emphasizing the tendency in romantic love to an unbalanced destructive excess. In taking the visible imprint of both plays *'Tis Pity* became both a record and an extension of what Ford had learned from Shakespeare.

Evidence of a line running through from *Romeo and Juliet* and *Othello* to *'Tis Pity She's a Whore* can be detected in Ford's presentation of the relationship of Annabella and Putana. This portrayal, it is often pointed out, derives from that of Juliet and her Nurse. What needs adding is that in *Othello* Shakespeare, with characteristic economy, reworked his earlier creations; as a result the relationship of Annabella and Putana looks back not merely to Juliet and the Nurse—and since these are stock characters, more distantly to a host of earlier versions—but also to Desdemona and Emilia. There is a similar contrasting pattern in all three: between, on the one hand, a high-minded, self-authenticating romantic idealism that defies both worldly prudence and the constraints of family and social position, and, on the other hand, the voice of a coarser-grained, pragmatic realism in varying degrees sympathetic, skeptical, and compromised.

Elsewhere the influence of *Othello* is traceable in the characterization of Bergetto and Vasques and, with greater significance for the play as a whole, of Giovanni and Annabella. Bergetto, as well as deriving in part from the gross and simple-minded Ward of *Women Beware Women,*[5] has a clearer origin in Shakespeare's Roderigo. Like his predecessor, Bergetto is shallow and foolish, but he is both more comic and more gently humanized than Roderigo; for all his gaucheries he seems genuinely to win the love of Philotis, and his death prompts from Donado the tearful comment, "Alas poor creature, he meant no harm, that I am sure of" (3.9.8-9). The main structural similarity between Bergetto and Roderigo is that each is linked with ludicrous inappropriateness to a woman who, even without the counter-attraction of respectively Othello and Giovanni, would scarcely have favored him with a second glance. The situation is one with considerable potential for comedy of social embarrassment that, although no more than hinted at textually in *Othello,* is often exploited in performance; Robert Lang's lugubrious face and Andrew Aguecheek-like wig in Olivier's film version is a memorable example. Ford develops Shakespeare's sketch of a comically inept suitor in Bergetto's unconsciously self-revealing narration of his first meeting with Annabella, an account that leaves Donado holding his head in his hands ("O gross! . . . This is intolerable," 1.3.64, 68). Both dramatists dismiss them to the same fate: each is killed ignominiously in a brawl.

Vasques's malignity, although not motiveless, is something of a puzzle, and its origin lies in the not-fully-absorbed influence of Shakespeare's Iago. Vasques is set apart from Soranzo, Hippolita, and Grimaldi, all of whose murderousness is readily explicable in terms of sexual jealousy. His dominating passion, by contrast, as he himself tells us in the final scene, is his devotion to Soranzo and before that to Soranzo's father (5.6.115-21). A combination of loyalty to Soranzo and some excessive zeal may explain much of what he does on his master's behalf; it does not account for the evident pleasure he takes in his ingenious stratagems and the gleeful self-hugging delight in what they reveal ("Better and better . . . Why, this is excellent," 4.3.217, 236). The dominant impression is less that of devoted loyalty than of a man who, like Iago, is shrewd, without scruple, and above all self-contained. He keeps his own counsel, confides in no one, and, like Iago, his greatest pleasure derives from the fact that he is an extremely deft, plausible, and successful manipulator. Just as Iago wins the confidence of those he seeks to entrap, so too does Vasques, with the result that Hippolita is betrayed to her death and Putana to a vicious blinding. The pleasures of the puppet-master seem to affect even his exertions on Soranzo's behalf. He instructs his master how to feign reconciliation with Annabella; and later, as part of his plan to "tutor him better in his points of vengeance" (4.3.240), he inflames Soranzo's imagination against his wife in exactly the same way that Iago does Othello's. There is even the suggestion of a malicious pleasure in goading his master further than his purposes strictly require:

> *Vasques*: Am I to be believed now? First, marry a strumpet that cast herself away upon you but to laugh at your horns? To feast on your disgrace, riot in your vexations, cuckold you in your bride-bed, waste your estate upon panders and bawds?
>
> *Soranzo:* No more, I say no more!
> *Vasques:* A cuckold is a goodly tame beast, my lord.
> *Soranzo*: I am resolved; not another word.
>
> (5.2.1-8)[6]

Vasques is not an entirely satisfactory dramatic creation, less successful on the whole than Ford's unambiguous Iago-figure D'Avalos in *Love's Sacrifice,* for whom in some respects Vasques may have constituted a preliminary sketch.[7] The reason is that Iago calls into play the tradition of the murderous machiavel, scheming, self-delighting, wittily inventive in his villainy; and such a conception is difficult to harmonize with the even more familiar but dramatically less arresting stereotype of the virtuous, loyal servant. Iago's devotion to Othello is a façade, a part of his comprehensive wickedness; Vasques's to Soranzo is meant to be genuine. Because Vasques's dedication to his master's well-being is never more than an inert *donnée* of the plot, the theatrical emphasis is all on his monstrous villainy, and he departs the play on what is, in the circumstances, a justified note of triumphant self-assertion: "this conquest is mine, and I rejoice that a Spaniard outwent an Italian in revenge" (5.6.145-46). If Vasques was indeed motivated all along by no more than a disinterested concern for his master's best interests, all one can say is that his concern proved to be a means of achieving an enviably high level of job satisfaction and personal fulfillment.

It is in the handling of the love theme, where the effect of *Romeo and Juliet* has long been acknowledged, that the further influence of *Othello* is detectable. There are suggestions, mainly though not exclusively in the closing movement of the play, of a correspondence between Giovanni and Othello and between Annabella and Desdemona. The last scene contains several verbal echoes, the clearest one accompanied by a partial correspondence in terms of physical action. Giovanni's words when he stabs his sister echo in syntax, rhythm, rhyme—indeed in choice of rhyme—those of Othello when he stabs himself:

> *Giovanni*: One other kiss, my sister.
> *Annabella:* What means this?
> *Giovanni*: To save thy fame, and kill thee in a kiss.
>
> (5.5.83-84)

> *Othello*: I kiss'd thee ere I kill'd thee. No way but this—
> Killing my self, to die upon a kiss.
>
> (5.2.361-62)[8]

The correspondence here is sufficiently strong to lend weight to others in the same scene which might otherwise seem tenuous or coincidental:

> *Giovanni*: Fair Annabella, should I here repeat
> The story of my life . . .
>
> (5.5.52-53)

> *Othello*: Her father lov'd me, oft invited me;
> Still question'd me the story of my life.
>
> (1.3.128-29)

> *Giovanni:* Give me your hand; how sweetly life doth run
> In these well-coloured veins! how constantly
> These palms do promise health!
>
> (5.5.73-75)

> *Othello:* Give me your hand. This hand is moist, my lady . . .
> This argues fruitfulness and liberal heart.
>
> (3.3.33, 35)

Verbal correspondences of this closeness point to a deeper level of connection between the two protagonists: both, in their different ways, love not wisely but too well. The phrase is, of course, a benign understatement of the nature and consequences of Giovanni's passion, but that is precisely the point. With its connotations of excess and imbalance, loving not wisely but too well was the initial stimulus that Ford derived from *Othello* and exploited and enlarged in *'Tis Pity She's a Whore*.[9]

Othello's manhood, life as a soldier, and deepest sense of self now rest on the absolute nature of the love between himself and Desdemona. "When I love thee not, / Chaos is come again" (3.3.92-93), and if not Chaos, then at least the certainty that "Othello's occupation's gone" (3.3.361). Giovanni's feelings for his sister are not just inherently unbalanced; they are also of such all-consuming intensity that nothing else merits attention, least of all his studies. Both protagonists believe themselves betrayed, and the effect on them of this realization is as extreme as their earlier love. After a descent into a temporary distraction in the case of Othello, or as part of a deeper and more lasting derangement in the case of Giovanni, they each decide to kill the woman they love. The circumstances of the killing are similar in both cases. They both pause, momentarily affected by her beauty.[10] Both indeed weep at what they feel constrained to do, and both seek to conduct the murder at a level of high-minded disinterestedness ("To save thy fame" [*'Tis Pity* 5.5.84]; "else she'll betray more men" [*Othello* 5.2.6]). The reality is very different. Othello's invocation of "Justice" conceals only briefly a craving for personal vengence, and though he claims he "would not kill your soul" (5.2.33), he in fact smothers Desdemona before she has time to pray. Giovanni's mind is darkened in even greater moral confusion, and his motive for murder seems less that of saving Annabella's fame than the combination of a desire to preserve eternally in death their early love ("If ever aftertimes should hear . . ." [5.5.68-73]), of bitterness at her proving "treacherous / To your past vows and oaths" (5.5.4-5), and of a triumphant forestalling of his hated rival ("Soranzo, thou hast missed thy aim in this, / I have prevented now thy reaching plots" [5.5.99-100]). Finally, the element of posturing and self-dramatization, arguably present in Shakespeare's depiction of Othello, is a discernible feature of Giovanni's view of himself at the close ("this act / Which I most glory in . . . and boldly act my last and greatest part" [5.5.90-91, 106]). His "last and greatest part" turns out to be his entrance into Soranzo's feast with the heart of Annabella impaled on his dagger.

In his portrayal of Annabella, Ford seems to have taken over from *Othello* the heroine's rejection of the social conventions and expectations that bear upon an unmarried, attractive, well-born young woman. Desdemona has turned down all the eligible Venetian bachelors—just as Juliet, though with rather more reason, turned down Paris—and in the end, prompted by her own judgment and feelings, she contracts a clandestine marriage with a black man. As an act of social defiance based on love, it is surpassed only by Annabella's love affair with her brother. The difference is that Desdemona's act is an affront to propriety and fatherly authority, whereas Annabella's is a defiance of morality and religion. In one respect at least the effect is the same. Both daughters' actions eventually cause their fathers' deaths of a broken heart, Brabantio's unobtrusively reported (5.2.207-209), whereas Florio's takes place on stage in the final scene.[11] For the bulk of the play Desdemona and Annabella's paths diverge, and while one remains a chaste and loving wife, the other progresses from incest to adultery. At the end of the play, however, Ford's treatment of Annabella seems to have the purpose of preparing for a death scene that will echo Desdemona's both in its manner and in the emotions aroused.[12] Act 5, scene I reveals Annabella as remorseful and penitent, and in her last meeting with Giovanni she displays a self-forgetful tenderness and concern as she urges him to save himself while at the same time talking to him in the sisterly tones of their earlier affection, delicately attempting to establish the necessary distance between them. As with Desdemona, the innocence, selflessness, and piety of Annabella's feelings make the murder, when it comes, particularly dreadful. Fearful of death at the hands of one they love, both women seek refuge in their religious faith ("Ye blessed angels, guard me!" [*'Tis Pity,* 5.5.67]; "Then Heaven / Have mercy on me" [*Othello,* 5.2.34-35]). Both die forgiving their murderer, Desdemona implicitly in her vain attempt to take the blame for her death upon herself and Annabella explicitly ("Forgive him, Heaven—and me my sins" [5.5.92]), though one may add that, unlike Desdemona, Annabella does not attempt to deny what Giovanni has done (she is given no opportunity to do so), and her religious pieties at the moment of death combine with a final rebuke and even occusation ("Brother, unkind, unkind" [5.5.93]).[13] The threat to her very life that Giovanni has come to represent is shadowily anticipated in a further echo from *Othello.* The moment at the beginning of *'Tis Pity* when Giovanni and Annabella kneel to each other in mutual dedication is a distant reworking of that other quasi-religious ceremony in *Othello,* itself sometimes referred to as a symbolic marriage, in which Othello and Iago kneel together and Iago makes his sinister pledge, "I am your own for ever" (3.3.483).[14]

For the full significance of all these apparently opportunistic and ad hoc echoes and borrowings from *Othello,* one needs to view *'Tis Pity She's a Whore* in the context of the rest of Ford's work. What sets him apart from his contemporary dramatists is an interest in genres and their potential for transformation. Anne Barton has discussed *Perkin Warbeck* and *The Broken Heart* as modifications and reconstitutions of, respectively, the history play and the revenge tragedy.[15] In *'Tis Pity She's a Whore* Ford, drawing upon *Othello* as well as *Romeo and Juliet,* appears to be rethinking the Shakespearean tragedy of love. He is doing more than effecting a shift from an idealized romanticism to a love that is corrupted and sinful, a view that is generally accepted as the main significance of his reworking of *Romeo and Juliet.* What seems to have struck him about the depiction of romantic love in both Shakespeare plays—the later even more than the earlier—is its fragile instability, the way its narrow intensities can so easily be diverted into hysteria, derangement, and destructive monomania.

The nature of the progression from *Romeo and Juliet* to *'Tis Pity* can be traced most economically by looking backwards and forwards from Othello's lines, quoted earlier: "I kiss'd thee ere I kill'd thee. No way but this— / Killing my self, to die upon a kiss" (5.2.361-62). In these lines Othello recalls the beginning of the final scene when he kissed the sleeping Desdemona ("O balmy breath" [5.2.16]), a kiss he repeats now as his final act. Romeo, too, had kissed Juliet as he killed himself: "Here's to my love! [Drinks] O true apothecary! / Thy drugs are quick. Thus with a kiss I die"

(5.2.119-20). The poignancy of this moment, however, is that although, like Othello, Romeo believes his wife to be dead, in reality Juliet is still alive. She is sleeping, just as Desdemona is when Othello kisses her at the beginning of the last scene. Romeo here kisses his wife simultaneously alive and "dead," whereas in Othello's farewell to Desdemona, what the earlier play had concentrated in one stage action is now expanded into two, linking the beginning and end of the final scene. The similarities and differences go further. Othello's death, like Romeo's, is a suicide, and he too flings himself in despair across the body of his dead wife. But it is the body of a wife innocent and chaste like Juliet whom he has murdered. His own death expresses not just grief but also belated horror, remorse, and the need for self-punishment to expiate a terrible wrong. What meager consolation this act of restitution may represent for the audience is completely absent from the corresponding scene in *'Tis Pity.* Othello's repeated kisses on the sleeping Desdemona occur here too, but Giovanni's are received by the now-penitent Annabella in a different spirit from that in which they are offered, and the coercive insistence that informs them causes her increasing apprehension about what they portend. Romeo's—and Othello's—lines undergo their final transformation, this time as an accompaniment not to suicide but to murder:

> *Giovanni:* One other kiss, my sister.
> *Annabella:* What means this?
> *Giovanni:* To save thy fame, and kill thee in a kiss.
> (5.5.83-84)[16]

Unlike Othello's, this killing leads to no remorse; Giovanni is triumphant to the end in the absoluteness of his sexual conquest and control; and Annabella's / "sad marriage bed" (5.5.97) becomes the site of the final atrocity of her evisceration.

There is one final aspect of the murder that is perhaps worth briefly remarking on. Ford took from *Othello* a hint of what was to become a familiar theme of seventeenth-century tragedy, the conflict of love and honor.[17] As he kills Annabella, Giovanni asserts that "honour doth love command" (5.5.86), and in this he is echoing Othello's claim to be an "honourable murderer" (5.2.297). Othello's blend of self-deluding moral elevation and savagery is grotesquely magnified in the circumstances of Giovanni's murder and mutilation of Annabella. As in *Othello,* it is both the notion of honor and the quality of that love that Ford's play calls in question.

Bibliography

Anderson, Donald K., Jr. *John Ford.* New York, 1972.

Barton, Anne. "He that plays the King: Ford's *Perkin Warbeck* and the Stuart History Play." In *Drama: Forms and Development,* ed. M. Alston and R. Williams, 69-93. Cambridge, 1977.

———. "Oxymoron and the Structure of Ford's *The Broken Heart.*" *Essays and Studies* 33 (1980): 70-94.

Bradbrook, M. C. *Themes and Conventions of Elizabethan Tragedy.* 2d ed. Cambridge, 1980.

Brodwin, Leonora Leet. *Elizabethan Love Tragedy 1587-1625.* New York and London, 1972.

Butler, Martin. "*Love's Sacrifice:* Ford's Metatheatrical Tragedy." In *John Ford Critical Re-Visions,* ed. Michael Neill, 201-31. Cambridge, 1988.

Champion, Larry S. "Ford's *'Tis Pity She's a Whore* and the Elizabethan Tragic Perspective." *PMLA* 90 (1975): 78-87.

Dent, R. W. *John Webster's Borrowing.* Berkeley and Los Angeles, 1960.

Farr, Dorothy M. *John Ford and the Caroline Theatre.* London, 1979.

Ford, John. *'Tis Pity She's a Whore,* ed. Derek Roper. Manchester, 1975.

Frost, David L. *The School of Shakespeare.* Cambridge, 1968.

Gentleman, Francis. *The Dramatic Censor* I. London, 1770.

Gurr, Andrew. "Singing Through the Chatter: Ford and Contemporary Theatrical Fashion." In *John Ford Critical Re-Visions,* ed. Michael Neill, 81-96. Cambridge, 1988.

Homan, Sidney J., Jr. "Shakespeare and Dekker as the Keys to Ford's *'Tis Pity She's a Whore.*" *Studies in English Literature* 7 (1967): 269-76.

Leech, Clifford. *John Ford and the Drama of His Time.* London, 1957.

Lomax, Marion. *Stage Images and Traditions: Shakespeare to Ford.* Cambridge, 1987.

Neill, Michael, "'What Strange Riddle's This?': Deciphering *'Tis Pity She's a Whore.*" In *John Ford Critical Re-Visions,* ed. Michael Neill, 153-79.

Oliver, H. J. *The Problem of John Ford.* Melbourne, 1955.

Putt, S. Gorley. *The Golden Age of English Drama.*

London and Totowa, NJ, 1981.

Ribner, Irving. "'By Nature's Light': The Morality of *'Tis Pity She's a Whore.*" *Tulane Studies in English* 10 (1960): 39-50.

Rosenberg, Marvin. *The Masks of Othello.* Berkeley and Los Angeles, 1961.

Sargeaunt, Joan M. *John Ford.* Oxford, 1935.

Shakespeare, William. *Othello,* ed. Peter Alexander. London and Glasgow, 1951.

———. *The Rape of Lucrece,* ed. Peter Alexander. London and Glasgow, 1951.

———. *Romeo and Juliet,* ed. Peter Alexander. London and Glasgow, 1951.

Smallwood, R. L. "*'Tis Pity She's a Whore* and *Romeo and Juliet.*" *Cahiers Élisabétains Études sur la Pré-Renaissance et la Renaissance Anglaises* 20 (1981): 49-70.

Stavig, Mark. *John Ford and the Moral Order.* Madison and London, 1968.

Notes

[1] Frost, 110. See also Dent passim, which establishes the taste for *Othello.* Webster was particularly influenced by *Othello,* and he, in his turn, proved a direct influence on Ford. "Ford's admiration for [*The Duchess of Malfi*] is a matter of record: he contributed encomiastic verses upon its publication in 1623; and that it was among the many plays in his mind as he worked on *'Tis Pity* has already been demonstrated through the various verbal echoes noted by Dorothy Farr." Neill, 169. It is possible, therefore, that *Othello,* in addition to bearing directly on *'Tis Pity,* may have had a second, more indirect effect as a result of its earlier absorption by Webster. See note 14 below.

[2] Sargeaunt, 127; Oliver, 80-81; Leech, 78, 110, 119; Stavig, 89, 133; Frost, 160-63; Anderson, 110-11; Farr, 58-78; Putt, 161-63; Butler, 216-19.

[3] Farr, 67.

[4] In addition to the critics above passim, see also Ribner, 47-48; Homan, 269-73; Champion, 81-84. The fullest discussion is contained in Smallwood, 49-70.

[5] Noted by Roper in Ford, xxxiii. Smallwood, 52, sees Bergetto as a reworking of Mercutio, "the principal comic character of *Romeo and Juliet.*" In presenting "the horrible accident of the death of Bergetto, the principal comedian of his drama, [Ford] removes the comic element from the play and points unequivocally toward its tragic conclusion." Although there is a parallel here in terms of dramatic structure, Mercutio (as Smallwood later acknowledges) is no buffoon, unlike Roderigo and Bergetto; and the tragic outcome of *Othello* and *'Tis Pity* scarcely requires the removal of either Roderigo or Bergetto to signal something that is apparent from the very start.

[6] An example of someone who is trapped into marrying a prostitute and is gleefully mocked for his pains is Old Hoard in Middleton's *A Trick to Catch the Old One.* A less genial instance of malicious taunting, which conceals itself behind a mask of servantlike concern, is that of Mosca in Jonson's *Volpone.*

[7] Dating is still to some extent uncertain, but Gurr, 93, has made a strong case for 1630 as the date for *'Tis Pity* and 1631 as that for *Love's Sacrifice.*

[8] Recorded without comment by Roper in Ford, 114. Lomax, 171, suggests "Ford fuses metaphor and stage action in a reversal of Othello's 'Killing myself, to die upon a kiss' (V.ii.360). In *'Tis Pity,* Giovanni stabs Annabella 'To save thy fame, and kill thee in a kiss' (V.v.84) which recalls the friar's words to Annabella, describing hell: 'Then you will wish each kiss your brother gave / Had been a dagger's point,' (III.vi.27-8)."

[9] Brodwin provides an extensive treatment of the tragic confusions of romantic love from *Romeo and Juliet* to *'Tis Pity.* While her categorization of love tragedies in terms of Courtly Love, False Romantic Love, and Worldly Love makes possible certain suggestive connections, the terminology used, involving three different modes for each category, forms a complex schema which is not readily transferable to the discussion pursued here.

[10] There is a transformation here of a common source: Romeo's final pause as he contemplates Juliet's beauty for the last time before he kills himself. An echo of a different sort, which has nevertheless a greater direct kinship with that of Othello and Giovanni, is Tarquin's delay before his assault on Lucrece: "Here with a cockatrice' dead-killing eye / He rouseth up himself, and makes a pause" (*The Rape of Lucrece,* 540-41).

[11] Lomax, 173, relates the death of Florio to those of Romeo and Juliet. "The discovery of their forbidden relationship also occurs when it is too late to save it, but their deaths bring about understanding and reconciliation between the two families. In *'Tis Pity* the opposite occurs—a previously loving father dies renouncing his children in horror."

[12] "In that scene Annabella's wry reference to her 'gay

attires' (V.v.20) makes it clear that she faces death in the bridal robes which Soranzo commanded her to put on (V.ii.10-11); like Desdemona's wedding sheets, they provide a bitterly ironic visual commentary on a murder." Neill, 163.

[13] Bradbrook, 259, has argued, not entirely convincingly, that Annabella's dying words here are an inversion of the last words of Desdemona, "Commend me to my kind lord." More plausibly, she draws attention to the way that variations of this striking phrase occur in *The Broken Heart* and *The Lady's Trial,* the significance of which is further developed in Gurr, 92.

[14] This moment in *Othello* may have been recalled by Ford directly. It is equally possible, however, that its effect may have been transmitted indirectly through a work which had been itself influenced by *Othello,* Webster's *The Duchess of Malfi*. "Bradbrook notes that the improvised marriage ceremony in *The Duchess of Malfi* might have been the model for Ford's ritual. She does not comment further, but in both cases the couples kneel, the ritual is quickly improvised in an atmosphere of tension, and a kiss plays a significant part in the ceremony. If Ford is deliberately recalling Webster's scene, the kiss with which Giovanni and Annabella seal their relationship can also be seen as a *Quietus est*—not only sealing their relationship, but also their doom." Lomax, 170.

[15] Barton, 1977 and 1980.

[16] These lines constitute a link in a process of influence from *Romeo and Juliet* to *'Tis Pity* that would not otherwise be readily apparent, and it is therefore unsurprising that Smallwood, the fullest and most assiduous commentator on the relation of *Romeo and Juliet* to *'Tis Pity,* makes no mention of them.

[17] The characteristic form of the conflict between love and honor in seventeenth-century heroic drama involved a generally different emphasis in terms of plot from that in either *Othello* or *'Tis Pity*. Nevertheless, the theatrical fate of *Othello* suggests that with only modest editing it could readily gratify the taste of the time as a play about a man of absolute honor experiencing the tragic consequences of passionate love. The cuts in the one surviving Restoration text have the consistent purpose of emphasizing the hero's dignity, nobility, and poise. Rosenberg, 24-25, notes, "After Othello has killed Desdemona and learned how wrong he was, in his volcanic outburst, after 'Cold, cold my girl' (338), lines are cut that we know offended a century later by their 'extravagance,' and apparently were already in bad taste: 'Even like thy chastity. O cursed, cursed slave! Whip me, ye devils! Wash me in steep-down gulfs of liquid fire! . . .' (339-43) . . . The altered text tries to make him die as it made him live: somewhat less human than Shakespeare's Othello, even greater of heart, closer to Decorum's idea of a hero." That this conception of Othello survived well into the eighteenth century is indicated by the following comment in Gentleman, 149: "There is something very noble in reminding the state of Venice with almost his last words, that he finished his life in the same manner, which he had once used to vindicate the public honour of his masters."

Source: "The Adaptation of a Shakespearean Genre: *Othello* and Ford's *Tis Pity She's a Whore,*" in *Renaissance Quarterly,* Vol. XLVIII, No. 3, Autumn, 1995, pp. 582-92.

The Integrity of *King Lear*

Sidney Thomas, *Syracuse University*

In a brief article published a decade ago, I ventured to challenge the then relatively new theory of a two-text *King Lear,* hoping that by calling attention to some of the theory's weaknesses and exaggerations, I could help to prevent it, as I said then, from hardening into 'a new orthodoxy'.[1] What I anticipated has now happened: not only, as Jay Halio has recently observed, has 'strong support for a revision hypothesis [. . .] grown among scholars',[2] but the new orthodoxy I feared has proved to be even more rigid and uncompromising in its assertion of the absolute truth of its position than any one could have expected, and what I half-jokingly predicted, the metastasis of the two-text theory of *King Lear* to other plays in the canon, has taken place with a vengeance.

Thus, in the latest and most extensive treatment of the revisionist theory, Grace Ioppolo recommends that 'the Quarto and Folio texts of *Hamlet, Troilus and Cressida, Othello,* and other plays should also [in addition to *King Lear*] be printed in separate versions if scholars are ever to come to terms with all that they offer'.[3]

The adherents of the revisionist hypothesis have now proclaimed victory. In the approving words of Ioppolo, 'the new revisionists have achieved a *coup d'état* which offers a new constitution for how scholars read, study, and teach Shakespeare's canon and also redefines the canon itself' (p. 3). I am therefore impelled to take up once again the argument for a *King Lear* conceived and written by Shakespeare as an integral work, and left untouched by him except for minor changes made *currente calamo,* or in the course of rehearsal or initial staging.

To begin with, there is not a shred of external evidence to support the notion that Shakespeare revised any of his plays after its first performance except, perhaps, to correct an obvious gaffe. Significantly, the very Oxford editors who argue for the hypothesis of Shakespearean revision in one passage of their *Textual Companion*[4] take a very different tack in another passage. Referring to the contention that Shakespeare's plays might have been posthumously revised, they declare:

> Most obviously, Shakespeare could not veto or influence any changes imposed upon his plays in the theatre after his death. Fortunately the economics and mechanics of the pre-Restoration repertory system made it impractical to reshape a play every time it was revived; when later adaptation did occur, it usually involved the addition of discrete chunks of material. Therefore the number of changes affected by such intervention should be small. (p. 15)

But if the economics and mechanics of the repertory system made posthumous revision unlikely, did they not also make revision by Shakespeare himself equally unlikely? The very same article cited by the Oxford editors as a basis for their dismissal of the probability of posthumous revision provides strong evidence against the theory of authorial revision. Rosalind Knutson, after a careful and thorough analysis of Henslowe's theatrical records, concludes:

> For the last decade of the Elizabethan period, for the one company with a playhouse document that shows patterns of revival *and* the commercial value of plays in the repertory, the assumption that revision accompanied revival cannot be supported. Furthermore, the assumption that revision was necessary to make old plays profitable cannot be supported. [. . .] Only in a few isolated cases is there evidence that the plays being revived were also revised. [. . .] On the basis of evidence in *Henslowe's Diary,* therefore, revision for the occasion of revival was neither commonplace nor economically necessary.[5]

But, it may be objected, the evidence of *Henslowe's Diary* need not apply to Shakespeare's company or to Shakespeare himself. There is, however, a striking piece of evidence to suggest that for the management of the King's Men, as well as for Henslowe, revival did not necessarily entail revision. In an often-cited 1604 letter from Sir Walter Cope to Robert Cecil, Lord Cranborne, Cope reports his efforts to arrange a theatrical performance for the Queen, and after detailing his frustrations, records his success: 'Burbage ys come, & Sayes ther ys no new playe that the queene hath not seene, but they have Revyved an olde one, Cawled *Loves Labore lost,* which for wytt and mirthe he sayes will please her excedingly.'[6] Surely, if the 'old play' being revived (the most topical of Shakespeare's comedies) had been revised to bring it up to date, Burbage would have mentioned it to Cope, and Cope would have reported it to Cecil. We can be virtually certain, therefore, that the play revived in 1604, was basically identical with the play written and first acted about 1594, and published in 1598. Moreover, if there had been a new version produced in 1604, we would expect the 1623 Folio text to embody that version, rather than the 1598 text, as it essentially does.

Of course, the example of *Love's Labour's Lost* proves nothing about the text of *King Lear*. Shakespeare may have chosen not to revise the one, but to revise the other. It does, however, induce us to question Gary Taylor's 'obvious conclusion, that Shakespeare occasionally—perhaps if we could only see it, habitually—revised his work'.[7] So far from being obvious, the theory of habitual, or even occasional, Shakespearean revision has nothing to support it. No play in the canon, it is safe to say, more desperately needed revision to make its wealth of topical allusions (many still a mystery to us) meaningful to an audience after the passage of ten years than *Love's Labour's Lost*. That it seems not to have received such revision should make us cautious about any theory of habitual revision.

What we know, from contemporary references, about Shakespeare's creative processes and relationship to his own work also militates against the theory of authorial revision. Heminge and Condell, who were Shakespeare's close colleagues for many years, provide in their address 'To the great Variety of Readers' (whether written for them by Ben Jonson does not matter) in the 1623 Folio (A3) a picture of a man from whom they never received a blot in his papers, who unfortunately never lived to oversee the publication of his plays, and whose work they were now presenting to the reader in its perfect form, free of the corruptions of previous unauthorized publications. All these statements emphasize one thing: as editors, Heminge and Condell were giving the public what Shakespeare had written once and for all, restored to its initial perfection as it had originally existed. There is no mention, not even a hint, that they were presenting what Shakespeare himself had revised and presumably further 'perfected', certainly an effective selling-point if they could have made it. To claim that what they did say is meaningless hyperbole, not to be taken seriously (though I do not believe this to be so) ignores the fact that a more useful hyperbole was available to them, if the revisionists are right.

If the external evidence for revision is nonexistent or dubiously conjectural, on what, then, do the proponents of the two-text *Lear* mainly rely? It is the so-called internal evidence of the texts themselves, the revisionists assert, that overwhelmingly supports their theory that the Q and F *Lears* are two separate plays that must be printed, staged, and studied as independent entities. One of the basic underpinnings of this theory (the argument that the characterization of Edgar and Albany, as well as their relationship to each other, is radically different in F from what it is in Q) was first elaborated by Michael Warren in a pioneering essay some years ago and has remained an article of faith for the revisionists ever since.[8] If, therefore, Warren's thesis can be shown to rest on unfounded assertions and assumptions, as I believe it does, the two-text theory of *Lear* can be seriously questioned. Here is Warren's principal argument in detail:

> The elevation of Edgar at the close and relative reduction of Albany that distinguish F from Q can be documented from three other places. At 5.3.229 [V.3.204; TLN 3180] in Q, Edgar says to Albany 'Here comes Kent sir', but 'Here comes Kent' in F. The transfer of the command 'Hast thee for thy life' (5.3.251 [V.3.225; TLN 3209] from Albany in Q to Edgar in F gives Edgar a more active role in the urgent events; indeed, Q may indicate that it is Edgar who is to run. [. . .] In Q [. . .] Edgar concludes the play stunned to silence by the reality of Lear's death, a very young man who does not even answer Albany's appeal 'Friends of my soule, you twaine / Rule in this Realme' (5.3.319-20) [V.3.293-94; TLN 3294/95]. [. . .] This characterization of Edgar is a far cry from the Edgar of F who comes forward as a future ruler when he enables Albany to achieve his objective of not ruling. (pp. 104-05).

I begin with Warren's first piece of documentation, the omission of 'sir' in F. Leaving aside the distinct possibility that the omission of 'sir' in F is a compositorial error, and accepting for the moment the authenticity and intentionality of the F reading, it is still possible to reject it as 'documentation' of the argument that Edgar in F is deliberately made more assertive and less deferential to Albany than he is in Q. For, some fifty lines earlier in the scene (v.3.169; TLN 3141) Edgar has addressed Albany in F (as in Q) as 'Worthy Prince'; and a few lines later in F as 'my Lord' (v.3.172; TLN 3144), and again in F (v.3.223; TLN 3206) as 'my Lord'. Above all, there is Edgar's reference in F (as in Q) to Albany as 'this high illustrious Prince' (v.3.125; TLN 3090). To claim, as against these examples of Edgar's proper deference to Albany, that the absence of 'sir' at the end of a casual observation (incidentally, not directly addressed to Albany in F) is crucial evidence of a change in the relationship between Edgar and Albany in F is making far too much of very little.

Even less convincing is Warren's second piece of documentation. 'The transfer of the command "Hast thee for thy life" (5.3.251) [v.3.225; TLN 3209] from Albany in Q to Edgar in F gives Edgar a more active role in the urgent events; indeed, Q may indicate that it is Edgar who is to run', says Warren. But what Warren neglects to point out is that it is Albany who gives the first decisive command, in F (as in Q) 'Run, run, O run' (v.3.221; TLN 3205) and that Edgar's words merely echo Albany's. Moreover, throughout v.3 it is always Albany who is in command, and directs the necessary action. To claim that 'in F Edgar grows into a potential ruler, a well-intentioned, resolute man in a harsh world, while Albany, a weaker man, abdicates his responsibilities' (p. 105) is to fly in the face of the evidence. Against Warren's sweeping statement may be placed R. A. Foakes's acute and, in my opinion, demonstrably correct comment on 'the new toughness and independence shown by Albany in the later scenes of the play'.[9] At the very least, Albany is no weaker a character in F than he is in Q. Again and again in his exchanges with Edmund, Albany shows his resoluteness, his determination to assert his authority and control. At his first entrance in v.3, he makes it clear, in his exchange of words with Edmund, that he will brook no challenge to his own primacy:

> Sir, you have shew'd to day your valiant
> straine
> And Fortune led you well: you have the
> Captives
> Who were the opposites of this dayes
> strife:
> I do require them of you so to use them,
> As we shall find their merites, and our
> safety
> May equally determine.
> (v.3.394; TLN 2984)

After Edmund's attempt to justify his action in disposing of his prisoners come Albany's curt dismissive words:

> Sir, by your patience
> I hold you but a subject of this Warre,
> Not as a brother.
> (v.3.53; TLN 2997)

Further, to speak of Albany in F as 'a weaker man' who 'abdicates his responsibilities' is manifestly untenable in the light of the ringing accusatory and condemnatory speeches he addresses to Edmund in F (as in Q):

> Stay yet, heare reason: Edmund, I arrest
> thee
> On capitall Treason; and in thy arrest,
> This guilded Serpent: for your claime faire
> Sisters
> I bare it in the interest of my wife,
> 'Tis she is sub-contracted to this Lord,
> And I her husband contradict your Banes.
> If you will marry, make your loves to me,
> My Lady is bespoke.
> (v.3.76; TLN 3027)

Continuing after Goneril's contemptuous interjection, 'An enterlude':

> Thou art armed *Gloster,*
> Let the Trumpet sound:
> If none appeare to prove upon thy person,
> Thy heynous, manifest, and many Treasons,
> There is my pledge: Ile make it on thy heart
> Ere I taste bread, thou art in nothing lesse
> Then I have heere proclaim'd thee.
> (v.3.84; TLN 3035)

In these two successive speeches, it is not only their content that shows Albany as a strong, self-assured leader. It is their poetic force, the sardonic wit of the first speech, the hammer blows of the second speech, that project a mature and powerful personality, no less so than in Q. If he abdicates his responsibilities in F at the end of the play when he asks Kent and Edgar to 'Rule in this Realme, and the gor'd state sustaine' he does no less in Q in virtually identical words. Nor do I think any significance should be attached to the fact (Warren's third piece of 'documentation') that the final speech, given in Q to 'Duke' or Albany, is given to Edgar in F. I believe that Q is in error here and that the speech with its clear emphasis on 'we that are yong' (in both F and Q) belongs to Edgar, the one survivor of the new generation.

Not only does the attempt to make the Albany of the closing scene of the play in F a differently conceived and developed character from the Albany of Q fail: the similar attempt by Steven Urkowitz to present the Albany of the earlier scenes of the play in F as a morally ambiguous figure, in contrast to the morally assured Albany of Q, is also unsupported by the evidence, as I have argued before.[10] But if the case for a major revision of Albany in F collapses, what then is left of the overall argument that the F text of *Lear* is a substantial authorial reworking of the play embodied in the Q text, and that the two texts represent two independent works that must be printed, studied, and produced as separate entities? For it is the supposed change in the characterization of Albany in F on which the two-text theory of *Lear* largely rests, since, as Gary Taylor, one of the principal revisionists, concedes, 'the Folio-only passages do not include new narrative material or major, structurally important incidents; they do not consist of new scenes, but of alterations here and there'.[11]

The argument for supposed changes in characterization between Q and F, while one of the main props of the two-text theory, is not, however, the only one on which the revisionists depend. Equally important to their thesis is the treatment of all substantive differences in wording between Q and F, except for the most obvious compositorial errors, as evidence of authorial revision, designed to change or modify the dramatic impact or significance of a particular speech. In what the General Editors describe as 'the first fully annotated, critical edition of *King Lear* to appear for forty years' (p. i), Jay Halio gives, in support of 'the revision theory on which this edition is based' (p. 81), the most detailed, well-argued, and lucid account of the presumed evidence for revision found in the linguistic variants between Q and F that has yet appeared.

None the less, I find the case for revision, as he presents it, no more convincing than that earlier made by Warren, Urkowitz, and others.

It is impossible, in this article, to deal with all of the presumed evidence for revision presented by Halio in his textual analysis. I deliberately select his discussion of one of the key speeches in the play, Lear's opening statement:

Q

LEAR. Attend my Lords of France and Burgundy, *Gloster*.
GLOST. I shall my Leige.
LEAR. Meane time we will expresse our darker purposes,
The map there; know we have divided
In three, our kingdome; and tis our first intent,
To shake all cares and busines of our state,
Confirming them on yonger yeares,
The two great Princes *France* and *Burgundy,*
Great ryvals in our youngest daughters love,
Long in our Court have made their amorous sojourne,
And here are to be answerd, tell me my daughters,
Which of you shall we say doth love us most,
That we our largest bountie may extend,
Where merit doth most challenge it,
Gonorill our eldest borne, speake first?

F

LEAR. Attend the Lords of France & Burgundy, Glouster.
GLOU. I shall, my Lord.
LEAR. Meane time we shal expresse our darker purpose.
Give me the Map there. Know, that we have divided
In three our Kingdome: and 'tis our fast intent,
To shake all Cares and Businesse from our Age,
Conferring them on yonger strengths, while we
Unburthen'd crawle toward death. Our son of *Cornwal,*
And you our no lesse loving Sonne of *Albany:*
We have this houre a constant will to publish
Our daughters severall Dowers, that future strife
May be prevented now. The Princes, *France & Burgundy,*
Great Rivals in our yongest doughters love,
Long in our Court, have made their amorous sojourne,
And heere are to be answer'd. Tell me my daughters
(Since now we will divest us both of Rule,
Interest of Territory, Cares of State)
Which of you shall we say doth love us most,
That we, our largest bountie may extend
Where Nature doth with merit challenge. *Gonerill,*
Our eldest borne, speake first.

Halio's comments, summarizing arguments made by Thomas Clayton, Urkowitz, and others on what he considers F's 'additions of entirely new material' (p. 72) in the speech deserve to be quoted in full, since they state what not only he but other revisionists consider one of the strongest pieces of evidence for the two-text theory:

> The complex effects of this amplification (in F) are essentially threefold: (1) anticipation of Lear's firmness, as in the alteration of Q 'our first intent' to F 'our fast intent' (line 33), and the added 'We have this houre a constant will' (line 38); (2) provision of more detailed and rational-sounding motives for abdication, as in the desire to confer responsibility of the realm on 'yonger strengths' (line 35) and the wish to prevent 'future strife' by immediately publishing the daughters' dowries (lines 38-40); (3) contributions to the patterns of imagery involving clothing and nakedness, as in the announcement that Lear will 'divest' himself of rule, territory and responsibility for the state (lines 44-5). Careful comparison of the entire speech in F with its shorter—and different—form in Q, combined with other changes later in the Folio version of the play that Clayton notes, strongly suggest, though they cannot prove, authorial second thoughts and subsequent revision. (pp. 72-73)

No one has better stated the case for revision than Halio has in the above paragraph. And it must be said that if his analysis of the F 'amplifications' in this speech is correct, then we cannot dispute his conclusion. But the fatal flaw in Halio's discussion of the differences between Q and F here, as elsewhere in the play, is his total disregard of an alternate (and, in my opinion, a more satisfactory) explanation for these differences. In my earlier article, I suggested that the so-called amplifications in F were part of the speech as Shakespeare first wrote it, and that Q's text represents not an earlier state of the speech, but a corrupt and truncated version of it. What we are dealing with are not F's 'authorial second thoughts' but Q's omissions. Shakespeare could never, even in a first draft, have omitted all reference to Cornwall and Albany and their role in the division of the kingdom. That lines 35-40 (beginning 'while we' and ending 'may be prevented now') have simply dropped out of the Q text, thereby creating the false apposition, 'Confirming them on yonger yeares / The two great princes *France* and

Burgundy', is in my opinion a far more likely supposition than that they were added in F. Significantly, as I pointed out in my earlier article, the metrically incomplete Q line, 'Confirming them on yonger yeares', is completed in F by 'while we', the first two words of the omitted passage.

That the difference between Q's 'first intent' and F's 'fast intent' is a Shakespearean amplification designed to create an 'anticipation of Lear's firmness' is a baseless assumption. 'First intent' makes no sense in the context of the speech and the scene, which deals with Lear's *fast* intent to divest himself of rule and to divide his kingdom. Even Halio, having cited the difference between the two readings, as part of his 'threefold' argument for revision here, admits in a footnote (p. 72) that 'first' may simply be a misprint for 'fast', corrected in F. To even grant the possibility, as Halio does here, that a variant reading in Q may be an error is to violate one of the basic stratagems of the revisionists. For to the adherents of the two-text theory, beginning as they do with the *a priori* conviction that Shakespeare revised *King Lear,* every verbal difference between Q and F is seen as evidence of deliberate authorial tinkering, and any other explanation for such differences is dismissed out of hand. Thus, Randall McLeod, commenting on the difference between Q's 'great pallace' and F's 'grac'd Pallace' (I.4.201; TLN 755), concedes that 'one must admit the ease of phonetically or graphically confusing "grac'd" and "great"', but then goes on to assert that 'the issue is whether one need postulate error in either text'.[12] But I would maintain that to postulate revision here, or elsewhere, is to take a far greater leap into conjecture than to postulate error.

The presence of error in Q is not simply a possible alternative hypothesis to that of revision; it is a demonstrable fact, and the kind and number of errors are such as to destroy the theory that Q was printed from an authentic Shakespeare manuscript, no matter how illegible it is presumed to have been. The assumption of compositorial misreading cannot explain the overwhelming number of errors of mishearing, mislineation, and mispunctuation that again and again destroy the sense of what Shakespeare must have written, and what is correctly given in F. Nor can these errors represent Shakespeare's first thoughts, later revised in F; rather, they are clearly corruptions of the text preserved in F.

The first two acts of the play alone provide a number of examples of errors (almost certainly mishearings rather than misreadings) that turn F's sense into nonsense:

Q. She is her selfe and dowre.
F. She is herselfe a Dowrie.
(I.1.236; TLN 264)

Q. [. . .] epicurisme and lust make more like a taverne
or brothell, then a great pallace
F. [. . .] Epicurisme and Lust
Makes it more like a Taverne, or a Brothell,
Then a grac'd Pallace.
(I.4.199; TLN 753)

(Despite McLeod, 'grac'd Pallace', a necessary antithesis to the squalid, ungraced "Taverne or a Brothell', is obviously right here, and 'great pallace' is in error).

Q. with accent teares, fret channels in her cheeks
F. With cadent Teares fret Channels in her cheekes
(I.4.240; TLN 799)

Q. 'striving to better ought, we marre what's well.
F. Striving to better, oft we marre what's well.
(I.4.300; TLN 870)

Q. You should doe small respect, shew too bald malice
Against the Grace and person of my maister,
Stobing his messenger.
F. You shall doe small respects, show too bald malice
Against the Grace, and Person of my Master,
Stocking his Messenger.
(II.2.119; TLN 1209)

'Stobing', in uncorrected copies of Q, is an obvious error and was changed by the press corrector to 'stopping', an intelligent guess but one that proves he cannot have consulted an authentic manuscript, since the F reading, 'stocking', is, as the context makes clear, what Shakespeare must have written in the first place.[13]

Q. nothing almost sees my rackles
But miserie
F. [. . .] Nothing almost sees miracles
But miserie.
(II.2.148; TLN 1242)

Here again, the Q press corrector, desperately guessing, without recourse to a genuine manuscript, has changed 'my rackles' to 'my wracke'. Nothing in Q, incidentally, is more certainly a mishearing than 'my rackles'.

Q. Why the hot bloud in *France,* that dowerles
Tooke our yongest borne
F. Why the hot-blooded *France* that dowerlesse tooke

Our yongest borne
(II.4.205; TLN 1505)

These examples of simple mishearing in Q, not only in the first two acts of *Lear,* but in other acts as well, could be further expanded. But it is sufficient to cite, in addition to those already given, the most notorious error in the Q text, occurring in the great confrontation scene between Lear and Gloucester in the latter part of the play:

Q. see how yon Justice railes upon yon simple theife, harke in thy eare handy, dandy, which is the theefe, which is the Justice, thou hast seene a farmers dogge barke at a begger. [. . .]

And the creature runne from the cur, there thou mightst behold the great image of authoritie, a dogge, so bade in office.

F. See how yond Justice railes upon yond simple theefe. Hearke in thine eare; Change places, and handy-dandy, which is the Justice, which is the theefe: Thou hast seene a Farmers dogge barke at a Beggar? [. . .]

And the creature run from the Cur: there thou might'st behold the great image of Authoritie, a Dogg's obey'd in Office.
(IV.5.145-51; TLN 2595-2603)

I have put the ludicrous Q reading 'a dogge, so bade in office', in its context, not merely to show how Q mangles one of Shakespeare's most powerful images but also to reveal the presence of other errors, of dropped words or phrases, of reckless mispunctuation, as here, that are endemic throughout Q, and that cannot be explained away as compositorial misreadings of a Shakespeare holograph.

It is such errors, as well as those of mislineation, to which I now turn. As early as the first scene, we find what is a pervasive characteristic of the Q text: a running together of phrases that belong in F to separate clauses or sentences, and that in F are properly set off by necessary marks of punctuation. Regan's first speech in Q begins:

Sir I am made of the self same mettall that
my sister is,
and prize me at her worth in my true heart,
I find she names my very deed of love, only
she came short

The corresponding lines in F read:

I am made of that self-mettle as my Sister,
and prize me at her worth. In my true heart,
I find she names my very deede of love.
(I.1.64; TLN 74)

I cannot here list all the instances of such sense-destroying mispunctuation, but I give some of the more flagrant examples. In Q, Goneril says:

His Knights grow ryotous, and him selfe
obrayds US,
On every trifell when he returnes from
hunting,
I will not speake with him, say I am
sicke.

The corresponding passage in F reads:

His Knights grow riotous, and himselfe
upbraides us
On every trifle. When he returns from
hunting,
I will not speake with him, say I am sicke.
(I.3.7; TLN 513)

In Q, Lear's outburst at Goneril reads:

Doth any here know mee? why this is not *Lear,* doth *Lear* walke thus? speake thus? where are his eyes, either his notion, weaknes or his discernings are lethergie, sleeping, or wakeing; ha! sure tis not so, who is it that can tell me who I am?

The corresponding lines in F read:

Do's any heere know me?
This is not *Lear:*
Do's *Lear* walke thus? Speake thus? Where
are his eies?
Either his Notion weakens, his Discernings
Are Lethargied. Ha! Waking? 'Tis not so?
Who is it that can tell me who I am?
(I.4.185; TLN 738)

Later in this scene, we have a complete breakdown of sense in another of Lear's passionate outbursts in Q:

We that too late repent's, O sir, are you
come?
Is it your will that we prepare any horses,
ingratitude! thou marble harted fiend.

Compare this gibberish with the corresponding lines in F:

Woe, that too late repents:
Is it your will, speake Sir? Prepare my horses.
Ingratitude! thou Marble-hearted Fiend.
(I.4.212; TLN 769)

Even more corrupt is the continuation of Lear's speech in Q: 'detested kite, thou list my traine, and men of choise and rarest parts, that all particulars of dutie know'. In F, these lines form the beginning of a new speech, after Albany's interjection, 'Pray, sir be patient':

Detested Kite, thou lyest.
My traine are men of choice, and rarest parts
That all particulars of dutie know.
(I.4.217; TLN 775)

Still another example of Q's transformation of sense into nonsense is found later in Regan's speech, which reads in Q:

It was great ignorance, Gloster's eyes being out
To let him live, where he arrives he moves
All harts against us, and now I thinke is gone
In pitie of his misery to dispatch his nighted life,
Moreover to discrie the strength at'h army.

The absurdity of Gloster's having gone to descry the strength of the army vanishes when we turn to F's version of these lines:

It was great ignorance, Glousters eyes being out
To let him live. Where he arrives, he moves
All hearts against us: Edmond, I thinke is gone
In pitty of his misery, to dispatch
His nighted life: Moreover to descry
The strength o' th' Enemy.
(IV.4.11; TLN 2394)

I find it hard to believe that any compositor, no matter how bungling, could have misread 'Edmond' as 'and now'. The error is far more likely to be due to a lapse of memory, by whoever prepared the copy for Q, as with other errors in the Q text.

One more example of memorial distortion must suffice. Edgar's description to his blind father of the imagined heights on which they stand reads thus in Q:

[. . .] the murmuring surge
That on the unnumbered idle peeble chaffes
Cannot be heard, its so hie ile looke no more

Compare the same lines in F:

The murmuring Surge,
That on th'unnumbered idle Pebble chafes
Cannot be heard so high. Ile looke no more
(IV.5.20; TLN 2455)

One of the most conspicuous features of the Q text is its frequent inability to reproduce the verse lineation of the original text. Either the attempt is given up as hopeless, and verse is simply broken down into prose, as in virtually all of the first half of the first scene of Act II, or the verse is nonsensically mislined, resulting in such absurdities as these lines of Lear's in Q:

The art of our necessities is strange that can,
Make vild things precious, come you hovell poore,
Foole and knave, I haue one part of my heart
That sorrowes yet for thee.

Compare F:

The art of our Necessities is strange,
And can make vilde things precious. Come, your Hovel;
Poore Foole, and Knave, I have one part in my heart
That's sorry yet for thee.
(III.2.68; TLN 1725)

I find it difficult to believe that the Q compositor is here following an authentic manuscript, embodying a first version of the play by Shakespeare. It is, of course, just possible that someone in the printing-house dictated these lines to the compositor, who was unable to read a badly illegible manuscript. But I think it far more likely that the manuscript was already corrupt when it reached Okes's print shop, as the memorial errors I have already cited demonstrate.[14]

In any case, this is not an isolated example of mislineation in Q, with attendant damage to punctuation and sense. At the beginning of III.3, there is a futile attempt by Q to make verse out of the prose preserved in F as in the opening lines of Gloucester's speech:

Alacke alacke Edmund I like not this,
Unnaturall dealing when I desir'd their leave
That I might pity him, they tooke me from me
The use of mine owne house.

Compare F:

GLOU. Alacke, alacke Edmund, I like not this unnaturall dealing; when I desired their leave that I might pity him, they tooke from me the use of mine owne house.
(III.3.1-3; TLN 1753-55)

Another example of mislineation combined with mispunctuation in Q is found in Edgar's reply to Albany's wondering question, 'Where have you hid your selfe? / How have you knowne the miseries of your Father?':

By nursing them my Lord,
List a briefe tale, and when tis told
O that my heart would burst the bloudy proclamation
To escape that followed me so neere,
O our lives sweetnes, that with the paine of death,
Would hourly die, rather than die at once
Taught me to shift into a mad-mans rags

To assume a semblance that very dogges
disdained
And in this habit met I my father with his
bleeding rings,
The precious stones new lost became his
guide,
Led him, beg'd for him, sav'd him from
despaire.

F here reads:

By nursing them my Lord. List a breefe tale,
And when 'tis told, O that my heart would
burst.
The bloody proclamation to escape
That follow'd me so neere, (O our lives
sweetnesse,
That we the paine of death would hourely
dye,
Rather than die at once) taught me to shift
Into a mad-mans rags, t'assume a semblance
That very Dogges disdain'd; and in this habit
Met I my father with his bleeding Rings,
Their precious stones new lost: became his
guide,
Led him, begg'd for him, sav'd him from
dispaire.
(v.3.172-82; TLN 3144-54)

The various Q errors that I have cited, mishearings, omissions, mispunctuation, mislineation, are all characteristic features of so-called 'bad' quartos, texts that have long been considered the products of memorial reconstruction, whether put together by renegade actors or playhouse note-takers, or assembled for provincial performance by a company lacking its playbooks. The theory of 'bad' quartos needs and has received some modification in recent years, most impressively in an important article by Paul Werstine.[15] I do not maintain that Q of *Lear* is corrupt throughout; as Greg himself emphasized, no simple explanation can account for all the textual features of Q, not least the obvious rightness of many passages, particularly in the middle scenes of the play.[16] But, as I have tried to demonstrate, there are many clear errors of a sort that can only be due to some form of oral transmission, and that are difficult to reconcile with the hypothesis of an authentic Shakespeare manuscript as the copy for Q.[17]

If I am right in believing that both the absence of any external evidence for Shakespearean revision of *Lear,* and the weakness of the internal evidence, make it improbable, to say the least, that Q represents a first version of the play, the question remains: why has the theory of a two-text *Lear,* enshrined as it has been in two prestigious editions, the one-volume Oxford *Complete Works,* and the New Cambridge *King Lear,* won such widespread acceptance? The answer to this question involves a number of factors.

First of all, there is the complete assurance, the categorical dismissal of all alternative hypotheses, with which the theory is presented by its adherents. Warren, for example, concludes his influential article with the following words: '[Q and F] must be treated as separate versions of *King Lear,* and [. . .] eclecticism cannot be a valid principle in deciding readings. Conflated texts such as are commonly printed are invalid, and should not be used either for production or for interpretation [. . .]. [The conflated text is] a work that has no justification for its existence' (pp. 104-05). It is no wonder that many scholars, confronted with such absolute certainty, should accept the two-text theory as proved beyond a doubt.

Even more important in muting possible criticism of the two-text theory has been the constant iteration, by some of the more active revisionists, of their theatrical expertise, which has enabled them to discern major differences of dramatic emphasis and staging to which Greg, Duthie, Alice Walker, and others were presumably blind.[18] Most Shakespeare scholars, with some notable exceptions (such as G. Wilson Knight and Kenneth Muir), have had little or no experience as actors or directors, and are reluctant to challenge the confident assertions by revisionists that transform palpable errors into heavily charged markers of changes in stagecraft.

Above all, the two-text theory has flourished because it has lent support to, and been supported by, the deconstructionist emphasis on textual indeterminacy, and the virtual disappearance of the creative autonomy of the author, what R. A. Foakes has characterized as 'the new enthusiasm for cutting Shakespeare down to size' (p. 9). The idea that *King Lear,* arguably the greatest literary work in English, is not one play, 'absolute in [its] numbers, as he conceived them', but at least two separate plays, has had a powerful appeal, especially for younger scholars. Thus, we have been told by a respected scholar, 'Shakespeare was a reviser of scripts subject to numerous contingencies; there never was *a King Lear*'.[19] And Leah Marcus, arguing that Shakespeare may have revised his plays for different audiences and different venues, observes: 'We may find ourselves gravitating towards a multiple editorial presentation of the plays that allows us and our students to explore deviations between texts not as symptoms of corruption but as signs of local difference.'[20]

What I am concerned to affirm is the integrity, the oneness of *King Lear* as a coherent vision of life and human relationships. There are not two *Lears,* or as some would have it, an indefinite number of possible *Lears,* but one supreme masterpiece, that like Rembrandt's sublime painting of 'The Return of the Prodigal Son', with its *Lear*-like theme of reconciliation and mutual forgiveness, convinces us, despite the apparent bleakness and nihilism of the close, that something can come of nothing.[21]

Notes

[1] 'Shakespeare's Supposed Revision of *King Lear'*, *Shakespeare Quarterly,* 35 (1984), 506-11 (p. 506).

[2] *King Lear,* p. 69. All act, scene, and line references are to the New Cambridge *King Lear,* ed. by Jay L. Halio (Cambridge: Cambridge University Press, 1992). Even those few scholars who remain unconvinced that Q and F *King Lears* are separate and independent plays accept, for the most part, the idea that it is a revised version of Q. Thus, in his excellent recent book, '*Hamlet* versus *Lear*' (Cambridge: Cambridge University Press, 1993), R. A. Foakes concludes: 'What I take to be the revised *King Lear* of F is thus significantly different from Q, though not as radically different as the authors of *The Division of the Kingdoms* would have us think' (p. 212).

[3] *Revising Shakespeare* (Cambridge, MA: Harvard University Press, 1991), p. 184.

[4] Stanley Wells and Gary Taylor, with John Jowett and William Montgomery, *William Shakespeare: A Textual Companion* (Oxford: Clarendon Press, 1987).

[5] '*Henslowe's Diary* and the Economics of Play Revision for Revival, 1592-1603', *Theatre Research International,* 10 (1985), 1-18 (p. 1). Knutson effectively confutes G. E. Bentley's conclusion (heavily relied on by the revisionists) that 'almost any play [. . .] kept in active repertory by the company which owned it is most likely to contain later revisions by the author or, in many cases, by another playwright working for the same company' (*The Profession of Dramatist in Shakespeare's Time, 1590-1642* (Princeton, NJ: Princeton University Press, 1971), p. 263).

[6] E. K. Chambers, *William Shakespeare: A Study of Facts and Problems,* 2 vols (Oxford: Clarendon Press, 1930), II, 332.

[7] *Textual Companion,* p. 17.

[8] 'Quarto and Folio *King Lear* and the Interpretation of Albany and Edgar', in *Shakespeare: Pattern of Excelling Nature,* ed. by David Bevington and Jay L. Halio (Newark: University of Delaware Press, 1978), pp. 95-105. Warren's essay has, since its publication, served as one of the cornerstones of the two-text theory of *Lear,* and its conclusions have never been seriously challenged.

[9] '*Hamlet* versus *Lear*', p. 208.

[10] 'Shakespeare's Supposed Revision', p. 510.

[11] '*King Lear*: The Date and Authorship of the Folio Version', in *The Division of the Kingdoms: Shakespeare's Two Versions of 'King Lear',* ed. by Gary Taylor and Michael Warren (Oxford: Oxford University Press, 1983), p. 376.

[12] '*Gon.* No more, the text is foolish', in *The Division of the Kingdoms,* p. 176. The refusal to see corruption rather than revision as the explanation for differences between Q and F is even shared by Foakes. He speaks, for example, of 'the *conversion* [my emphasis] of Lear's "Who is it that can tell me who I am? Lear's shadow" (Q) into a dialogue with a mocking retort by the Fool: "*Lear.* Who is it that can tell me who I am? *Fool.* Lear's shadow" (F)' (p. 101). I believe that F is clearly right here and represents what Shakespeare must have written in the first place, whereas Q corrupts the meaningful dialogue of Lear's anguished question and the Fool's bitter response into a meaningless rhetorical question that Lear immediately answers.

[13] See Peter W. M. Blayney, *The Texts of 'King Lear' and their Origins* (Cambridge: Cambridge University Press, 1982-), Vol. I; *Nicholas Okes and the First Quarto,* 'The variants in *Lear* are of many different kinds. Some of the substantive alterations suggest, with varying degrees of probability, that the copy was consulted and that its readings were correctly restored. Others appear to reflect nothing more reliable than the corrector's wrong guesswork' (p. 219). See also W. W. Greg, *The Shakespeare First Folio* (Oxford: Clarendon Press, 1955), 'Some of [the press alterations in Q of *Lear*] were correct, some were not: for some it is clear that he consulted the copy, some are obviously guess-work' (p. 384).

[14] As Greg observed in *The Shakespeare First Folio,* p. 387, note B: 'It looks as though the copy for Q had been written continuously, without line division, and without punctuation, and that it had been left to the compositor to punctuate the text and identify and divide the verse as best he could.' But if Greg's conjecture is correct (as I believe it is), then we must reject the assumption of the revisionists that the copy for Q was an authentic Shakespeare manuscript. There is no evidence to suggest that Shakespeare, or any other Elizabethan dramatist, ever wrote, even in a first draft, without line division or punctuation. On the other hand, this is precisely what we would expect of an orally transmitted play text.

[15] 'Narratives About Printed Shakespeare Texts: "Foul Papers" and "Bad Quartos"', *Shakespeare Quarterly,* 41 (1990), 65-86.

[16] *First Folio,* p. 383.

[17] I have by no means, in this article, exhausted the list of palpable errors that betray the surreptitious origins of Q, and which have been catalogued and analysed by such scholars as Greg, G. I. Duthie, Alice Walker, and others, to whose work I am deeply indebted.

[18] See, for example, Steven Urkowitz, '"Well-sayd olde Mole": Burying Three *Hamlets* in Modern Editions', in *Shakespeare Study Today,* ed. by Georgianna Ziegler (New York: AMS Press, 1986), p. 39.

[19] Jonathan Goldberg, 'Textual Properties', *Shakespeare Quarterly,* 37 (1986), 213.

[20] 'Levelling Shakespeare: Local Customs and Local Texts', *Shakespeare Quarterly,* 42 (1991), 169.

[21] Michael Warren's invaluable *The Parallel King Lear* (1608-1623) (Berkeley and Oxford: University of California Press, 1989), has been a major resource in the writing of this article.

Source: "The Integrity of *King Lear,*" in *The Modern Language Review,* Vol. 90, No. 3, July, 1995, pp. 572-84.

Romances and Poems

Lucrece's Gaze

Stephen J. Carter, ***York University***

I

In Shakespeare's *The Rape of Lucrece* Tarquin's and Lucrece's acts of seeing precede their speaking. I shall argue that a specific, constructed experience of social space *produces* their ability to speak through a sequence of narratable actions. This spatial figuration projects along gender lines. How vision is socially put together reveals the linguistic means by which Lucrece, Tarquin, 'their' narrator, and the narrative's audience come to be screens for the imaginal projection of gender.

A useful beginning may be to investigate the phenomenological acquisition of sight as documented in clinical situations. When patients who had been blind from birth first started receiving cataract operations, records of the doctors' reports on the patients' progress were collected in a study by Marius von Senden.[1] As it turned out, such "newly sighted" patients were not merely confronting a surfeit of new, different data. Their task was to learn a thoroughly new intellectual skill: how to put together the vast sensory experience contained in even the simplest, smallest movement of one's body through space. Their experience constitutes persuasive evidence that we are "taught" to posit not only an objective world outside ourselves, but also, and perhaps more importantly, a curiously objective gender inside, inseparable from our experience of being subjects. "I showed her my hand," wrote one of the doctors of a patient,

> and asked her what it was; she looked long at it, without saying a word; I then took her own hand and held it before her eyes, she said with a deep sigh: 'That's my hand.' A blind person has no exact idea even of the shape of his own body; so that I first had to hold her own hand before her in order for her to recognize mine as a hand also.[2]

The patient could be described as passing through Lacan's mirroring ego-ideal stage; she *emerges* on this side of what she sees, as a subject—opposite to and abstracted from a constructed tableau. To see, in a sense, is to be the author of oneself. Another patient described seeing

> an extensive field of light, in which everything appeared dull, confused, and in motion. He could not distinguish objects.[3]

In the course of time, however, by trial and error s/he learns to pick out such static patterns of nonmovement from the swirling of forms and colors: objects. This, as noted above, can be interpreted as the initiating, establishing event in subjectivity, setting in motion all of a life's subsequent events. Like vision, then, *being* a subject is an acquired mental process, a process of mirroring. A subject/object grid is deployed between observer and observed, such that vision does not merely interpret, but organizes, in effect produces, our social, gendered reality.

This process of linking with one's reality effects a cognitive "lack of being," the recognition that one's "realization lies in another actual or imaginary space."[4] Such a patient, like Lacan's infant,

> only sees [his] form as more or less total and unified in an external image, in a virtual, alienated ideal unity [. . .][5]

—in a mirror. The "gendered Other" gazes at his/her untouchable virtuality. Male/female as Other only knows itself by the mediating image(s) it has of the mirror-subject. It knows what it is by what it is not. This "lack of being" is initiated by, produced, and grows with one's capacity for sight. A patient's lack—this "rushing in" of gender—occurs in the act of making himself real in an imaginary space.

In *The Rape of Lucrece* this spatial metaphorizing of gender is apparent in the linguistically partitioned actions, and therefore the identities, of the two primary characters, Lucrece and Tarquin. I shall focus primarily, though not exclusively, on the scene of Lucrece "reading" the wall painting in which Troy's defeat is depicted. I shall argue that in her surveying of the painting—in her return from a journey into sightedness—she constructs herself as a rhetorical, gendered Other, whom she then projects back into herself as subject. As a subject she becomes a "newly sighted" space that frames what might be termed her former feminine unseen-ness. By examining the tension between the rhetorical and painterly registers in this passage (spoken by Lucrece and the narrator), in the context of its ordering of narrative voices, I shall reconstruct the means of her transformation.

II

The story of Lucrece would have been well-known to Elizabethan audiences. Its passive/active linking of her rape/suicide was left largely unquestioned. The presumed choice presented in the poem between death or shame was a foregone conclusion. The theological position counseled choosing shame, of which one could be shriven, over suicide, a mortal sin. Preferring death implied that rape was necessarily, regardless of the purity of mind, a pollution of the *body's* chastity, an effect which could not be undone. The Elizabethan audience could imagine, and perhaps praise, a woman's choosing a public transformation of unchastity through death, over the private shame of bodily pollution, however technically virtuous of mind she remains. A gap opens up here socially between an audience's deploying of a secular discourse within the larger theological context. The former produces a reading of female space as that which needed to be kept enclosed, unseen, pure—within a larger, allegedly protective male space. The latter, however, produces a reading that condemns Lucrece's actions as, in St. Augustine's view, a failure to see

> that while the sanctity of the soul remains even when the body is violated, the sanctity of the body is not lost; and that in like manner, the sanctity of the body is lost when the sanctity of the soul is violated, though the body itself remains intact.[6]

Shakespeare's text intriguingly anticipates and conflates these two readings. Lucrece's choice of suicide is *not* presented as the automatic secular choice it was assumed to be. The process of her reaching her decision is represented as a discursively critical task in which she challenges the casting of her rape as bodily pollution. The Elizabethan audience was potentially being made aware of its emphatically split reading: that she courageously chose and acted on a theologically incorrect reading, for which she could not be held responsible given the Roman setting of the story.

III

The activity of her "looking at" the wall painting occurs within a larger terrain of envisioning modes. These take many forms in the poem: the mutable register of Tarquin's gaze at Lucrece and Collatium's interior, and similarly of Lucrece's "regard" (for Tarquin, the Apostrophic objects, and the painting); the mind's eye of lust and shame, which as signifieds, look inward at their objects; the varied surfeit(s) of what is seen (focalized); and the presence of "painted" eyes within, and looking back from, the painting.

The narrator gradually escalates the activity of Tarquin's 'seeing' of Lucrece: from his "wanton sight,"[7] to "lustful eye" (179), to "greedy eyeballs" (368), to "willful eye" (417), to "a cockatrice' dead-killing eye" (540). Such rhetorical anaphora proliferate in tandem with the violent expansion of Tarquin's envisioning space; his license to "look," to penetrate with ever greater intensity, inscribes his movement across and into the female space of corridors, doorways, and the bedchamber of Collatium, which enclose the chaste, untrespassed inner female space of Lucrece's body. The nature of his seeing—surveying and violently reaching out—is being employed here to construct a version of incursive male space.

Female space is possessed within the envisioning male, whether Collatine or Tarquin. As the signified within Tarquin's mind's eye, she contracts.

> Within his thought her heavenly image sits,
> And in the self-same seat sits Collatine.
> That eye which looks on her confounds his
> wits:
> That eye which him beholds, as more divine,
> Unto a view so false will not incline [,]
> (288-92)

Her eye (as his signified) "which him beholds" proceeds *to, but not beyond* the boundary of his inner gaze.

> But she that never cop'd with stranger eyes,
> Could pick no meaning from their parling
> looks,
> Nor read the subtle shining secrecies
> Writ in the glassy margents of such books.
> She touch'd no unknown baits, nor fear'd no
> hooks,
> Nor could she moralize his wanton sight,
> More than [that] his eyes were opened to the
> light.
> (99-105)

Her enclosed passivity here seems to preclude any worldly understanding of what waits there to be read (or not) in his eyes and looks. Imposed chastity works to contain vision; it reverses the seeing/speaking progression for the female such that Lucrece literally does not see Tarquin's lust until he speaks it. Tarquin however is allowed to cross the boundary of his gaze, to pierce his own inner outrushing "look."

> Then looking scornfully, he doth despise
> His naked armor of still-slaughtered lust [,]
> (187-88)

An ineffectual armor against fear, his lust self-reflexively slaughters even as he inwardly gazes on its self-replenishing object.

Who does Tarquin rape? He rapes Collatium, the home and room, as female space. His vision precedes his movement through its corridors and doorways, pushing him steadily deeper into "her." He proceeds "As each unwilling portal yields him way" (309); he forces "The locks between her chamber and his will" (302); he ignores that "The threshold grates the door to have him heard" (306). He rapes as he sees.

> Now is he come unto the chamber door
> That shuts him from the heaven of his
> thought,
> Which with a yielding latch, and with no
> more,
> Hath barr'd him from the blessed thing he
> sought.
>
> (337-40)

What he sees/rapes is nothing less than the patriarchically programmed, enclosed, inrushing space of the constructed feminine. Georgianna Ziegler[8] draws on Peter Stallybrass's useful analogy between Bakhtin's notion of the grotesque, and the Renaissance reading of female vision—the grotesque as transgressive, antihierarchical, unfinished, obscene.[9] Such potentiality within female space is normatively constrained by patriarchy—"her signs are the enclosed body, the closed mouth, the locked house."[10] Rape becomes a rending of gendered space; what undergoes pollution is not a body, but a patriarchal construction of female space her "body" occupies.

IV

What is our response upon viewing an effectively conceived and executed visual representation? Writing on narrative painting, Leonardo da Vinci states that if the work

> represents terror, fear, flight, sorrow, weeping, and lamentation; or pleasure, joy, laughter and similar conditions, the minds of those who *view* it ought to make their limbs *move* so that they seem to find themselves in the same situation which the figures in the narrative painting represent.[11] (italics mine)

As an *audience* before the Troy painting Lucrece herself does this, and more. We need to observe, however tritely, that she must have walked by this artwork, glanced at it, and doubtless viewed it at length on countless occasions during the years she lived at Collatium. Yet on this occasion she deliberately seeks it out. Faced by a representation-as-event, one that exerts a gradually intensifying, cathecting hold on her, she experiences herself mimicing and voicing the physiological and emotional states of its varied characters. In doing so she temporarily *steps into* the representation. Not surprisingly, the meaning she makes of herself in the painting is to a considerable degree determined by the remembered image of the violence of her rape—an image, some critics argue, unduly "stimulated" by her own language.

"Narratives," as R. Rawdon Wilson claims, can "catch, hold, illude, and frequently delude their narratees."[12] The painting-as-narrator tells Lucrece her own story. Moreover, being "caught" by an ostensible illusion can work no less genuine a transformation on a viewer/listener than that worked by a real sight. The Trojan figures she moves among open up and frame Lucrece's own narrative, that is the internal struggle between the two poles of violence she endures, rape and suicide. The gaze of the text-as-narrator at the painting (over Lucrece's shoulder) directs, constructs, and contains her (and our) gaze.

Let us take a brief, initial "wide-angle" look at the sweep of narration, Apostrophic address and prosopopoeic voice that speak in this scene of the "skillful painting." First the narrator throws his peripatetic, focalizing eye here and there over the painting in a cinematic manner—panning, cutting, tracking in and back, tilting—that gradually escalates. The linguistic effect of installing vision in this way intensifies the very reality (not the realism) of the representation, opening up a space in her own enclosed image of self.

It is during *her* first narration of (and address to) the painting that Lucrece, in effect, crosses over into what she sees, and also into herself as representation (Other). Indeed, the rhetorical features of her speech in this passage emphasize an emerging detachment from female space.

In the narrator's second passage, half the length of the first, Lucrece's impassioned response from within the painting is narrated. The text implements Simonides's aphorism mentioned earlier when Lucrece prosopopoeically gives language to the silent, painted figures, who in turn give to her her own movements and expressions. The narrator's language rearranges Lucrece's reality within her reading of the painting and herself. However, in her second passage, in which Lucrece responds emphatically to the artist's perjury of Sinon's face (linking Sinon to Tarquin), she takes control of her own seeing by the linguistic rearranging of what she sees.

In the narrator's third passage Lucrece is represented as having pulled back from her former rage, directed not only at Sinon/Tarquin, but also at the circumstances of her own (now oblique) "story."

The possibility of conferring worldhood on her own story, a place to which she returns from the embedded narrative of the painting, undergoes an anachronic shift. The space Lucrece's newly sighted eyes now project has little in common with her former world. At the moment of her death her language, actions, and seeing have a curious unity that allows us in, while holding back the males present in the scene.

V

Let us now "track in" for a closer look at the rhetorical, visual, and narrative components of each of these passages in the wall painting scene. In the narrator's first passage (1366-1463) we are gradually introduced to the "skillful painting." The narrator's initial, tentative address to the reader, "These *might* you see [. . .] / " (1380), "That one *might* see [. . .] / " (1386), and "You *might* behold [. . .] / " (italics mine) acknowledge the painting as "mere" representation, of which we are rightly to be skeptical. By the midpoint of this passage, however, by a grammatical shifting from the conditional to the simple past, the language inserts us into that representation.

This process is emphasized in the cinematic movement of narrative focus. Whom and what do we see? The most visual sequence within this passage directs our eye as follows: a "medium shot" on

> Ajax and Ulysses, O what art
> Of physiognomy might one behold!
> (1394);

CUT to a "close shot" on

> The face of either cipher'd either's heart
> (1396);

CUT to an 'extreme close' on

> Ajax' eyes blunt rage and rigor roll'd
> (1398);

PAN to

> the mild glance that smiling Ulysses lent.
> (1399);

CUT to a "medium" on Nestor; PULL BACK to a "long" to bring into frame the silent, listening faces of the soldiers; and follow with a slow "pan" among

> The scalps of many, almost hid behind,
> To jump up higher seem'd to mock the mind.
> (1413-14)

With this there is a shift back, in language, from what occurs in the painting-as-narrative to a look at the painter's technique itself. A subsequent description of the painterly device of *overlap* intensifies this:

> That for Achilles' image stood his spear,
> Grip'd in an armed hand, himself behind
> Was left unseen, save to the eye of the
> mind[:]
> (1424-26)

Space, in effect, is being constructed through an acknowledgement of what perception contributes—our learning to view the real in fragments. Fragments imply gaps; the text signals that what is "left unseen" is where the reader's role enters, to fill in such space. A whole is merely a consensus among the senses of a thing "they" willfully put together. From the poem's above-noted technical description of painterly special effects there is a further shift to the description of the Trojan mothers' contradictory spectatorship:

> And from the walls of strong-besieged Troy,
> When their brave hope, bold Hector, march'd
> to field,
> Stood many Troyan mothers, sharing joy
> To see their youthful sons bright weapons
> wield,
> And to their hope they such odd action yield
> That through their light joy seemed to
> appear
> (Like bright things stain'd) a kind of heavy
> fear.
> (1429-35)

We are compelled to read in both directions here. Our line of sight travels to the walls, and from there to the field, simultaneously reflected back from the "light" of the "bright weapons" to the mothers' eyes. Is vision an intersubjective agency, or an activity by which space invents itself between two sites of seeing? It would seem that we learn not to see how we have learned to see.

This progress of the first passage—a pull back from the painted representation as deep cinematic reality, to a framing of technique, and back again to a framing of the problematics of vision itself—leaves the reader at a considerable distance from Lucrece. We hear and see her identification with Hecuba, yet cannot follow her as she crosses over.

Escalating rhetorical density has a stroboscopic effect on the space this passage produces, as demonstrated in: the piling on of anaphora (1467-8) in her first stanza, the chiasmus (1475-6) in the second, an epanalepsis (1480) in the third, and the combined anaphora and assonance (1487-8) in the fourth, each involving variations on the strategic repetition of key words. Critical opinion has often tended to resist the reflexivity of rhetorical forms, arguing that rhetoric closes down the possibilities for the development of narrative and character otherwise present in a scene. All language, however, has a rhetorical dimension, of which audiences choose to be aware. Lucrece's rhetoricity can perhaps best be read as her awareness of her own transformation. She *knows* she can step outside her ideologically grounded female space, yet she also knows she cannot escape the similarly grounded expectations her social frame places on her.

The chiasmus of her second stanza warrants more specific attention.

Thy eye kindled the fire that burneth here,
And here in Troy, for trespass of thine eye[,]
(1475-76)

It is Paris's inescapable, space-making eye that activates lust and destruction (of Helen and Troy), piercing, penetrating, fixing on its object: spatial absence as allotted the female. She sees that it is male envisioning that frames a woman's seeing and speech.

In the narrator's second passage Lucrece's intense sorrow over Troy's destruction is initially foregrounded. The literal sympathetic exchange between the silent painted figures and her rhetoricizing voice, "She lends them words, and she their looks doth borrow" (1498-9), removes her even further from our view. Her identification with the painting as embodying the Real, as being more than representation, reaches the stage where "Such signs of truth in his [Sinon's] plain face she spied" (1532) are such "That she concludes the picture was belied." (1533) She is seeing, in effect, two paintings—one she assembles in her mind (of which she is a part), and another she can designate as merely "the picture." The emphasis here on separating the painting (as embedded narrative) from Lucrece's viewing of it incites her to momentarily rescript Sinon's role in Troy's defeat. In the last stanza of this passage language rearranges both itself and Lucrece within what is (and is not) spoken.

"It cannot be," quoth she, "that so much guile"—
She would have said, "can lurk in such a look";
But Tarquin's shape came in her mind the while,
And from her tongue "can lurk" from "cannot" took:
"It cannot be" she in that sense forsook,
And turn'd it thus, "It cannot be, I find,
But such a face should bear a wicked mind.
(1534-40)

The active past tense is parried by the conditional past, what was spoken by what nearly was, the unspoken "can lurk" by the sense of the spoken "cannot." By the last two lines she recursively participates in the rearrangement of her own speech. With these spoken/unspoken phrases she gasps out her incredulity, her struggle with herself as narratee (after the spatial stroboscopy of the painting).

In her second narrative passage she responds directly to Sinon's treason, and commands herself to

Look, look how list'ning Priam wets his eyes,
To see those borrowed tears that Sinon sheeds!
(1548-49)

By the end of this passage she is no longer having her speech rearranged *for* her, she actively rearranges what she says and sees in a complex series of inversions:

Such devils steal effects from lightless hell,
For Sinon in his fire doth quake with cold,
And in that cold, hot burning fire doth dwell;
These contraries such unity do hold
Only to flatter fools, and make them bold:
So Priam's trust false Sinon's tears doth flatter,
That he finds means to burn his Troy with water.
(1555-61)

She takes a certain distracted enjoyment in her ability to manipulate the painting's reality.

In the narrator's third passage her language and sight collide, as

She tears the senseless Sinon with her nails,
Comparing him to that unhappy guest
Whose deed hath made herself herself detest.
(1564-66)

The violence of her action returns her to 'herself'; she collapses back into the world of *her* narrative. Space contracts as, with the arrival of Collatine, Lucretius, and Brutus, the narrator pulls back slightly. A period of time is elided, "But now the mindful messenger, come back" (1583), until Collatine "[. . .] finds his Lucrece clad in mourning black." (1585) When she speaks next, it is to address her husband and his guests.

She has stepped back into her former space, but with a difference. She looks ahead to her suicide from a vantage in which the text conflates the pagan Roman and Augustinian readings of her story.

Though my gross blood be stain'd with this abuse,
Immaculate and spotless is my mind;
That was not forc'd, that never was inclin'd
To accessary yieldings, but still pure
Doth in her poison'd closet yet endure.
(1655-59)

She has come to see her pollution in Augustinian terms, that her virtue is untouched, yet the text acknowledges that this is still governed, framed by, her society.

She does not escape through death; nor does she become a symbol of Chastity for others to follow; nor indeed does she become an ironized subject in the text. Her suicide is a reassertion of the differently constructed space she sighted within the painting, and from which she returns, transformed.

Notes

[1] Marius von Senden, *Space and Sight* (London: Methuen & Co. Ltd., 1960).

[2] Ibid., 109.

[3] Ibid., 130.

[4] Bice Benvenuto and Roger Kennedy, *The Works of Jacques Lacan: An Introduction* (New York: St. Martin's Press, 1986), 55.

[5] Senden, *Space and Sight,* 130.

[6] *A Select Library of the Nicene and Post-Nicene Fathers of The Christian Church,* Vol. II, "St. Augustin's [*sic*] City of God and Christian Doctrine" Philip Schaff, ed. (Grand Rapids, Mich.: Wm. B. Eerdmans Publishing Co., 1956), 13.

[7] William Shakespeare, *The Riverside Shakespeare,* ed. G. Blakemore Evans (Boston: Houghton Mifflin, 1974), 1. 104. All subsequent references to the poem will appear in the text of the paper.

[8] Georgianna Ziegler, "My lady's chamber: female space, female chastity in Shakespeare" *Textual Practice* 4.1 (1990): 73-90.

[9] I partially concur with the position Ziegler argues with reference to Stallybrass, however in her conclusion regarding "these two female poles" she seems to essentialize the female grotesque as the authentic pole opposite female enclosure as a constructed normative. Rather, both "poles" are equally such constructions.

[10] Peter Stallybrass, "Patriarchal territories: The body enclosed", in *Rewriting the Renaissance,* ed. Margaret W. Ferguson (Chicago: University of Chicago Press, 1986), 124.

[11] Leonardo da Vinci, *Treatise on Painting,* trans. by A. Philip McMahon (Princeton, N.J.: Princeton University Press, 1956), 110.

[12] R. Rawdon Wilson, "Shakespearean Narrative: *The Rape of Lucrece* Reconsidered," *Studies in English Literature* 28 (1988): 55.

Source: "Lucrece's Gaze," in *Shakespeare Studies,* Vol. XXIII, 1995, pp. 210-21.

Truth and Decay in Shakespeare's Sonnets

James Dawes

For sweetest things turn sourest by their deeds;
Lilies that fester smell far worse than weeds.

Howsoever it may pique the reader with its opacity,[1] sonnet 94 achieves a concussive conclusion through its evocation of a rarely used sense: the poem terminates in thick smell. Shakespeare evokes smell, briefly, in only nine of the 154 sonnets. Sight, a sense that the poet can control, is preferred. One can close one's eyes or turn one's head, one can manipulate and sculpt the visual world; but invisible smell assaults and surprises the body, delivering a shock commensurate only to the shock of seeing an ideal down-razed, or a faith forsworn. The jarring couplet of 94 alludes, of course, to the beloved's alleged moral turpitude.[2] Infidelity is so pungent here because, as John Bernard argues, the young man is not merely a representation of an ideal Platonic form but the ideal itself, 'not the mere shadow but the very substance of the divine.'[3] The young man is a figure for the very possibility of belief, and hence allegations of his moral failure threaten to shatter not only the speaker's heart, but also his capacity for faith. The speaker's cosmology is knitted into the very flesh of his beloved—but like the lily, skin rots.

The fallibility of the speaker's ideals and the 'wantonness' (96) of his beloved (the two, I argue, are the same) provide the sequence with one of its central fixations: constancy. Critics have taken various positions on the matter: John Bernard, for one, dismisses the young man's sins as 'mortal accidents.' Denying Shakespeare's sense of the perfidious mutability and slippage of language, as well as the speaker's parallel anxiety over the undependability of the young man, Bernard insists that Shakespeare's ironclad faith in 'the Logos, the Name of names by which the Godhead reveals itself to men' engenders a verse which is as 'unique and unchanging' as the object of its praise: hence what he calls the 'predictable sameness' of the sonnets.[4] On the other hand, Lars Engle insists that the sonnets are the harbinger of the fragmented modern psyche. Shakespeare, he claims, is not only aware of but also comfortable with the economic flux and inconstancy of all forms and values.[5] Aligning himself with Anne Ferry and Joel Fineman,[6] Engle offers a comfortably 'antifoundationalist' Shakespeare, a Shakespeare modeled upon Wittgenstein, Rorty and Lacan.[7] These are plausible but also, I believe, desiccated readings. By over-emphasizing the speaker's faith on the one hand, and by underestimating his *desire* for faith on the other, both groups of critics thereby deny the speaker's torment and doubt, his simultaneous need and inability to believe in the constancy of Love, the beloved, and the poetry which alone can represent them.

The 'monumentalizing' sonnets engage the dialectic of the speaker's faith most explicitly: 116 (the constancy of love), 55 (the constancy of poetry), and 105 (the constancy of the beloved). The disagreements among critics on these sonnets reproduces the interior dynamic of each poem: at any given moment the speaker may believe with desperate faith, or undercut himself with detached cynicism.[8] Rather than adding to the daunting amount of criticism on these particular sonnets, however, I will investigate representations of constancy by tracing the development of specific word clusters and images throughout the sequence as a whole. I will read the sonnet sequence *as* a sequence—a move of faith for which I can provide no justification other than the agnostic's: my belief cannot be disproved even if it cannot be proved.[9] Shakespeare, intuition tells me, was well aware of the potential for reverberation between the parts of his sequence; he was cognizant of the resonance certain phrases or ideas might accumulate throughout. The sequence as a whole, then, dramatizes the mind's *endurance* of love, its struggle over time between desire and disgust, between philosophical idealism and the dictates of the corporeal. By following the narrative of Shakespeare's clauses and the plot of his images, I hope to provide a theoretical framework for understanding both the compelling faith of the 'monumentalizing' sonnets and their critically revealed potential for self-consumption. I hope to provide a more complicated understanding of Shakespeare's notion of belief, and a deeper appreciation of his idea of constancy, which thrusts to the heavens as 'truth,' and crumbles into the earth as 'decay.'

'In all external grace you have some part, / But you like none, none you, for constant heart' (53). A close cousin to 105, sonnet 53 deploys the rhetoric of Platonic forms to commemorate the constancy of the beloved.

What is your substance, whereof are you made,
That millions of strange shadows on you tend?
Since everyone hath, every one, one shade,
And you, but one, can every shadow lend.
Describe Adonis, and the counterfeit
Is poorly imitated after you;
On Helen's cheek all art of beauty set,
And you in Grecian tires are painted new.
Speak of the spring and foison of the year;

The one doth shadow of your beauty show,
The other as your bounty doth appear,
And you in every blessed shape we know.
In all external grace you have some part,
But you like none, none you, for constant heart.

Many critics accept the straightforwardness of this convention, attributing to the speaker a votary's ingenuous faith, and an infatuate's hyperbolic ebullience. Of 53 Murray Krieger writes: 'the friend is the one final reality . . . the single Platonic perfection.'[10] I believe, however, that Shakespeare has too complicated an awareness of the duplicity of man and language for such an un-selfconscious faith, for a faith blind to the possibilities of its own betrayal. Doubt does not begin, however, until the sonnet closes, until the reader breathes the very last words of the terminal couplet. According to Stephen Booth, 'for constant heart' may have been pronounced much the same as 'for constant art'[11]—that is, perpetual artifice, counterfeit honesty. If the sonnet is first read as a celebration of constancy, a rereading based upon this potential phonetic misprision would reveal the denotative duplicity of much of the imagery deployed throughout. Line 7, for example, reads thus when paraphrased: 'When one describes Helen's ideal beauty.' But the tortuous line can also suggest, as Booth notes, Helen's 'cosmetic deceit'[12]—a deceitfulness which affects our reading of the beloved's participation in 'external grace,' and more importantly, a deceitfulness in which the essence of the beloved is 'painted new.' Similarly, the 'counterfeit' of Adonis, like a crystal which casts new light with each perspectival change, may one moment signify a portrait, and the next a painted fraud—the word nimbly traverses the borders between representation and deceit, between fiction and fraud. If one emphasizes 'counterfeit' (two of its three syllables are stressed), then the sentence can indeed suggest that it is the very *counterfeitness* of the description which is 'imitated' after the beloved. And indeed, if *portrait* accumulates connotations of falseness upon rereading, then 'shadows' and 'shade,' which can signify both images and portraits, may as well. The 'strange shadows' prefigure the slanders which 'tend' to the beloved in sonnet 96, as well as the darkness cast against the beautiful sky by the crow in 70. By line 4 of sonnet 53, the beloved has become a merchant in such shadows: shadows which produce darkness, change form and obscure meaning—shadows which 'mask' (54) the canker embedded in the rose. 'What is your substance?' the speaker asks. 'Whereof are you made?' It is a plea for access to truth, for a glance behind the beloved's plenitude of masks, his bewitching 'millions.'

On one level then, sonnet 53 is a poem about blinding proliferation, about impossible multiplicities of form and meaning, and the slippage of an infinitely permutable language. The Platonic convention itself may have arisen in response to such anxiety. It sets limits to the possibility of metamorphosis, rooting polyform materiality in changeless origin: the ideal Form is the constant One at the same time that it generates the fluid Many. Appropriating this model, the speaker insists that the young man is constant, even as he participates in an unending flux of 'external grace.' With the rereading I have posited, however, this paradox would prove untenable: the embodied Platonic ideal would prove *in*constant, wilting before our very eyes like a flower sapped of its vitality.

A master of wordplay, Shakespeare surely must have anticipated this possibility—he must have known that words, like men, are mutable and inconstant, and that poems thus contain within themselves the possibility of their own destruction, like the canker roses which, in the very next sonnet, die sadly alone.[13] In the end, the best that Shakespeare can do is to hold off the bloom of decay for as long as possible. This poem is meant to celebrate flexible constancy, the fluid repetition of a stable beauty. Shakespeare guarantees this by inhibiting the swerve of language, hemming in his words. The octave proceeds in units of two: lines 1 and 2 form a unit, as do 3 and 4, 5 and 6, and 7 and 8. Lines 9 to 12 form a unit of four, and the sonnet concludes, of course, with a couplet. I re-quote the poem for convenience:

What is your substance, whereof are you made,
That millions of strange shadows on you tend?
Since everyone hath, every one, one shade,
And you, but one, can every shadow lend.
Describe Adonis, and the counterfeit
Is poorly imitated after you;
On Helen's cheek all art of beauty set,
And you in Grecian tires are painted new.
Speak of the spring and foison of the year;
The one doth shadow of your beauty show,
The other as your bounty doth appear,
And you in every blessed shape we know.
In all external grace you have some part,
But you like none, none you, for constant heart.

The six clausal units each proceed rhythmically: lines 1 and 2 come in three breaths (What is your *substance,*—whereof are *you* made,—That millions of strange *shadows* on you tend?); lines 3 and 4 each repeat, through the use of caesura, the triple breath (Since *everyone* hath,—*every one,*—one *shade,* / And *you,*—but *one,*—can every *shadow* lend). Lines 5 and 6 vary the rhythm slightly with two breaths (Describe *Adonis,*—and the *counterfeit* is poorly imitated after *you*), and 7 and 8 become the second beat of this new two-breath rhythm (On Helen's *cheek* all art of *beauty* set,—And *you* in Grecian tires are painted new). Line 9 prepares for the return to the triple breath (Speak of the *spring* and *foison* of the *year*), which manifests itself in the unit of three lines which follows—a pattern reproduced in the couplet, whose unbroken first line introduces the three-breathed finale (But you like none,—none you,—for constant heart). Finally, included within each of these units of the poem are three moments of emphasis, three objects of attention (see previous emphases). The formal structure of the sonnet thus reproduces its content: it achieves constancy through repetition, and fluidity through rhythm, as if embodying the Form itself. By arranging the poem in this way—by *breathing* it thus—Shakespeare most effectively 'transfixes' his slippery words, locking them into place and thereby creating a truly 'constant art.'

On the other hand, it is also possible that Shakespeare designed the poem to maximize the potential for semantic drift. The sonnet would thereby enact the process of decay which the sequence so consistently laments. Like the young man or the rose, the sonnet blossoms forth into beauty, into a ringing declaration of faith and love. But after the final words of the terminal couplet, after time with subsequent rereadings begins to pass, the poem begins to wither into cynicism and self-consuming irony. 53 is embedded, after all, between sonnets emphasizing betrayal, alienation, and the failures of love (40-42, 49, 54, 56-58). As Shakespeare writes:

> *Nativity, once in the main of light,*
> *Crawls to maturity, wherewith being crowned,*
> *Crooked eclipses 'gainst his glory fight.*
> (60)

Without wishing to close off this potential reading, I nonetheless believe it is more plausible to read 53 as the material manifestation of the speaker's kinetic faith. Its violent compression of constancy and mutability, certainty and doubt, bodies forth the speaker's complex attitude toward his language and his love. His is not an ingenuous faith, a faith blind to its own rational impossibility. Nor is it, on the other hand, a sham of faith, a cynical mockery of a lover's belief. The speaker does not fluctuate between these poles, nor does he come to rest in a nullifying middle ground; rather, he *simultaneously* believes and disbelieves, each moment. Indeed, his faith is fortified by his very doubt. The steely-eyed conviction which informs the couplet of 116, for example, is engendered by the *subversion* of his belief: it is his desperate defiance of a reality which proves that love does indeed decay. And the confident grandeur of 55, likewise, is a product of his *inability* to believe fully in his own words, to accept rationally their truth and permanence. But love insists, and the speaker thus surrenders to the irrationality of his faith with a proselyte's hopeless, hyperbolic energy. It is a faith which derives its energy from its desperation; it is a faith that is forever shoring itself up against its own decay.

Decay—the failure of constancy—is one of the sequence's central fixations. The speaker images decay in two primary ways: as corruption from within, best symbolized by the cankered rose, and as corruption from without, best symbolized by the assault of an external, frequently personified Time. The actuality of decay is not so interesting to Shakespeare, however, as the *representation* of decay: Shakespeare uses his persona to explore the difficulty of perceiving that which must not be perceived, of speaking that which must not be spoken (the smell that cannot be smelled, the thought that cannot be thought). In most relevant poems, the image which predominates is that of decay as an external force which assaults a separate and pure beauty (e.g., 11, 13, 15, 16, 23, 64, 65, 71, and 100). The speaker, apparently, hesitates before evoking the lurid imagery of corruption from within: it is easier to imagine decay as a contest between two clean bodies than as the noisome suppuration of flesh feasting upon itself.[14] In 73 for example, the word 'decay' is never spoken, and self-consumption—'Consumed with that which it was nourished by'—is deferred until the climax, as if the speaker needs to muster up courage to speak its possibility. Even as the 'it' is spoken, however, *it* is denied: the perceptual experience of rot (the smell that cannot be smelled) is reconceived as a clean burning, and thereby made speakable, thereby made bearable. Indeed, the surprising reversal of the couplet, in which the dying speaker becomes the forsaken rather than the forsaker, the jilted lover rather than the decaying corpse, resonates with and hence reasserts the model of decay posited in the first two quatrains—namely, the assailant-victim model rather than the self-consuming model: love is ruined by the action of an external agent rather than a natural law of internal disintegration.

Internally generated corruption horrifies the speaker for metaphysical as well as corporeal reasons: if rot can generate itself from within beauty, from an invisible, interior source, then the trusted may prove false, and the ideal of purity itself might prove a mere illusion (the thought that cannot be thought). In 35, the speaker once again must gather momentum, accumulating images of extrinsic and identifiable imperfections—'Roses have thorns, and silver fountains mud, / Clouds and eclipses stain both moon and sun'—before invoking the shocking images of rot from within, of invisible interior consumption—'And loathsome canker lives in sweetest bud.' Suddenly aware that he has gone too far, the speaker silences himself. Quatrain two begins gently, after a pause, with the calm language of aphorism ('All men make faults') and a rejection of what has been asserted in quatrain one ('and even I in this . . . Excusing thy sins more than thy sins are'). The speaker cannot deface his own Ideal; he cannot infect his beloved with the imagery of the cankered rose. In the final ten lines the speaker tries frantically to deflect his hasty words, finally absorbing the stain of his miasmic language by standing in for the young man as the figure of the self-consuming cankered rose: 'corrupting' himself (7), working ''gainst' himself (11), the speaker 'robs' (14) himself of his own vitality in a vicious, self-consuming 'civil war' (12).

The sequence as a whole reproduces this pattern of assertion and erasure: the speaker invokes the disruptive imagery of internal decay only to quickly extinguish it, to overwhelm it and subsume it into the totalizing image of decay as the assault of Time. The speaker's nervous stewardship over his own words evinces Shakespeare's belief in the palpability and viscerality of language, its almost material power. Words of true faith inscribe the young man into the rock of the earth, into the flesh of the unborn (55, 81). As if absorbing their power to endure, the beloved with such words will pace forth against death like a body resurrected. But the language of decay stains and infects; the very act of speaking corruption may itself corrupt. In 95, for example, decay infects the hand which writes it; rot eats through the speaker's words even as he inscribes them.

How sweet and lovely dost thou make the shame
Which, like a canker in the fragrant rose,
Doth spot the beauty of thy budding name!
O in what sweets dost thou thy sins enclose!
That tongue that tells the story of thy days,
Making lascivious comments on thy sport,
Cannot dispraise but in a kind of praise;
Naming thy name blesses an ill report.
O what a mansion have those vices got
Which for their habitation chose out thee,
Where beauty's veil doth cover every blot,
And all things turns to fair that eyes can see!
Take heed, dear heart, of this large privilege;
The hardest knife ill used doth lose his edge.

In line 3, the rot of the canker *spots* the beauty of the budding rose; in line 6, this 'spot' of corruption begins to eat its way through the word 'sport.' In line 11, the spot has become a 'blot,' which then infects line 9 ('got'), line 7 ('Cannot') and poses like a hungry mouth at the beginning of lines 4 and 9 ('O'). Like the rose, the poem is consumed from within, by the very canker it names: it is left tired, blemished, and 'ill' (14).

Of course, when restricted to its surface context, the 'ill' of the couplet denotes only the 'misuse' ('ill' use) of a knife. However, it graphically doubles and therefore throws us back to the 'ill' of line 8, which signifies the sickening, staining effect of rumor upon reputation. It is the very subtlety of this associational trace, the very nearly unidentifiable 'spot' embedded in the final 'ill,' which most horrifies the speaker. Furrows in the brow are the gradual, steady, and immediately recognizable work of a wasting Time (e.g., 2, 12, 22, 60, 62, 63, 77, 104), but the rose's small external blot is a discontinuity, a sudden tear in the surface of beauty which may simply be an accident of environment, or, like the first dark teardrop of melanoma on fair skin, may be the first and last warning of a ravaging, internally fed cancer.

The speaker well knows, then, that the smallest of spots can lead to eventual ruin. He deploys the infectious images of interior decay more hesitantly, encodes them more subtly in the rest of the sequence. In 92, the speaker suspects that the young man is 'inconstant.' 'What's so blessed-fair that fears no *blot*?' he asks, not quite daring to speak the word of corruption, but nonetheless aware that the association will give force to his complaint. His criticism of false beauty in sonnet 68, likewise, gathers its intensity from an association with decay. Here the speaker criticizes the 'bastard signs of fair': cosmetics, wigs, and other 'ornament'—such pleasant surfaces often mask a repugnant interior. Indeed, wigs are the 'golden tresses of the dead, / The right of sepulchers.' These indignant verses criticize what is, essentially, an act of robbery; but they also jam together the images of cosmetics and tombs, of surface beauty and the meat of coffins. If cosmetics *are* the beauty of those the speaker castigates, and cosmetics are also 'the right of sepulchers,' then for these men and women of 'false art,' beauty is itself a form of decay. Cosmetics will show the blot of this startling association henceforth: make-up is the two-dimensional analog of the cankered rose.

Sonnet 68, of course, echoes the 'infection' of 67: together they invest a specific cluster of images with contagious energy: the beauty of the cheek, painting and ornament, theft from the tomb, and the imbrication of the dead and the living. This imagery is invoked most noticeably in relation to the rival poet, whose adaptability to fashion contrasts unfavorably with the more constant style of the speaker: 21 criticizes the 'painted beauty' and 'ornament' of the rival ('painted beauty,' as Booth points out, may be a painting, a poem, or a person whose beauty is 'cosmetically achieved' [15]); the 'compounds strange' of 76 recall the cosmetics of 68, just as 76's 'dressing old words new' recalls 68's 'robbing no old to dress his beauty new'; in 79 the rival 'robs' beauty from the young man's 'cheek,' and in 82 the speaker criticizes the rival's 'gross painting,' along with the deathly pale 'cheeks' which 'need blood'; 83 again criticizes the rival's 'painting,' and together with 86 emphasizes the exchange between the dead and the living ['when others would give life, and bring a tomb' (83), 'their tomb the womb' (86)].

If the speaker attempts to stain the rival poet's work by associating it with interior rot, he runs the risk of likewise infecting his own poetry. As with 95, so with the sequence as a whole: after all, what's so blessed fair (what young man, what sonnet, what sequence?) that fears no blot? Anne Ferry writes that the friend's falseness destroys the speaker's ideals *and* his poetry: his love makes him a liar. The speaker's warnings to the young man may thus reveal something of his own anxieties: 'After my death, dear love, forget me quite / . . . lest your true love may seem false in this, / That you for love speak well of me untrue' (72). If the speaker's sonnets memorialize an essentially 'fraudulent world,' then his sequence can achieve integrity only by entering into a 'parodic' relationship with itself.[16] By thus giving the lie to its own proclaimed eternizing powers and constancy (as Ferry claims), the sequence enacts the very self-consumption and decay which it criticizes: it eats itself up like the cankered rose.

Even Bernard speaks of the 'falsity of his art.'[17] The 'lie' of the speaker's poetry, which Bernard cites from 115, is of course only a trope which allows the speaker to praise his beloved in ever more hyperbolic terms. However, when this 'lie' is read against 106, the implications are potentially disturbing. If the speaker can appropriate the verse of an 'antique pen,' if he can rob the 'dead,' using their beauty to dress new his beloved, then certainly the same can be done with his own poetry. Thus, not only is his poetry tainted by its implicit association with the grave-robbing censured in 68, but also it is logically possible that the young man himself can be typologized, hierarchically subordinated to the beauties of later generations, just as easily as those 'fairest wights' memorialized in 'old rhyme.' The sequence would then seem to hold within itself the possibility of its own subversion, its own hungry canker.

But this last rhetorical gesture, of course, fails, and in its failure reveals the limitations of the models of decay thus far presented. Embedding within itself the pattern of its own abnegation, the sequence would seem to prefigure its own demise, to mime self-consumption; but on the other hand, by implicitly predicting that it will be consumed and discarded by later writers, the sequence posits itself as a victim-to-be of external action rather than of internal logic. The easy slippage between these possibilities, between the external and the internal, between foreknowledge and complicity, decomposes the model of decay thus far presented.

A closer look at 95 will clarify the issue. The sonnet begins by comparing the young man to the cankered rose, but quickly modulates the invaded rose out of its degenerative materiality into an assortment of 'sins' and 'vices.' Alluding to the New Testament story of Legion, a man possessed by devils, Shakespeare writes: 'O what a mansion have those vices got / Which for their habitation chose out thee.' Here, at the beginning of the third quatrain, the speaker replaces the model of the cankered rose with the model of a body possessed by demons, and in so doing finally *displaces* the canker, removes it from the body it inhabits and destroys: the fire of 73 may indeed feed upon itself, but the canker is as foreign to the rose as spirit is to matter. Internal decay is distinguished from self-consumption.

The speaker, however, relies upon the easy confusion of the two even as he emphasizes their difference. To the imperfect human eye the cankered rose does indeed appear to eat itself: filth and decay seem part of its very nature. But as the speaker here emphasizes, it is human vision which is inherently flawed—not the cankered rose. Thus even if to the entire world the young man appears wanton (96) or lascivious (95), even if the speaker himself cannot wish away the visible moral decay of his beloved, Faith will not be shaken. At the apogee of horror, when the speaker has imagined his love as a lurid self-cannibalizing shame, the model of self-consumption dissolves and the speaker realizes with a faith strengthened by doubt overcome that beauty is forever pure, vices are always external, and decay is *athwart* rather than *of* beauty, like ravaging Time against a poor, sweet flower. As the logic of the canker rose shows, the speaker can deny his eyes, and maintain his Ideal.

The speaker's model of faith-shattering decay enacts its own displacement, and thereby most powerfully reaffirms the constancy of the beloved: the more withering the power of the canker rose metaphor, the more powerful the speaker's faith. However, the blindness of this faith raises troubling questions about belief, agency, and representation. Does the centrality of the *act* of faith occlude its referent? And does belief in an ideal (Poetry, Love, or a Beloved) marginalize the importance of the real (poetry, love, or a beloved)? The sequence asks but does not answer.

As the troubles accumulate, the rot continues. The speaker hence must do more than negate his doubt—he must justify his belief. He must contend with the reality of decay, whatever its sources, and offer an alternative to the ease and inevitability of decrepitude. The dichotomy between external and internal decay roughly corresponds to the opposition between the decay of sweet tissue ('sweet issue,' 13) and the decay of spirit, between the assault of Time upon the fragile body, and the interior, moral waste of the 'loathesome canker' (35). If reproduction is the primary means of defying the decay of flesh (1-17), then the spiritual analog of reproduction is the cultivation of spiritual constancy. The poet offers a model of such constancy with his 'true plain words' (82). Truth, in the end, is the only effective talisman against decay (e.g., 123).

For the speaker, the True manifests itself variously, as veracity, fidelity, and constancy: respectively, truth of proposition (I speak the truth when I say I love you), truth of representation (my poetry depicts the truth of my beloved), and truth of essence (my beloved appears beautiful because his nature is and always will be beautiful). Upon this latter form of truth—constancy—all other forms depend: the truth of essence is the essence of truth, for there is nothing true which does not overcome the caprice of environment, which does not endure. Veracity and fidelity are, so to speak, only *symptoms* of truth: by speaking true and by representing his beloved in 'true plain words,' for example, the speaker reveals his constancy, the truth of his love.

Unfortunately, the communicative epiphenomena of truth, veracity and fidelity, are problematic concepts at best. In the sonnets dedicated to the young man, the speaker's visual relationship with such truth is contorted: propositional and representational truth are always veiled, always misperceived (e.g., 17, 72, 110, 113, 114, 21, 24, and 62). The effect is insidious. Like an inverted canker rose, truth decays from the outside in: the uncertainty of the signs of truth infects the certainty of truth itself. In other words, if we cannot conclusively identify those things which are ultimately the *only* visible signs of essential truth, then what of the *truths* which sustain us? If truth cannot be known, does it exist? Is it a usable concept? For the speaker, such questions always translate back into the body of the beloved: if the young man is both the sign and the essence of truth, and, like all signs of truth, the young man is open to misreadings, then is his truth identifiable, or perpetually fluxing? Is constancy itself unreliable?

The speaker's desperate desire to believe in a truth which he cannot fully see generates great anxiety. In 82 'true,' which here signifies veracity and fidelity as well as constancy, is rhymed both with 'hue' and 'new' (embedded within 'anew'), and is thereby associated with the 'gross painting' of cheeks which 'need blood'—with ornament, cosmetics, and decay. The speaker's inability to distinguish fully between the 'hue' and the 'true,' between cosmetic beauty and true beauty, between the canker and the pure rose, is ultimately the inability to distinguish between the nausea of decay, and the truth which alone can defy it. The coincidence between the two is striking. Like decay, truth is invisible, an essence that must be inferred from a collection of slippery signs. But unlike decay, which finally reveals itself positively as rot, truth can never be known (e.g., 92, 93). Constancy achieves certainty only through its own negation: a truth sustained is always only a potential, but a faith forsworn is a certainty.

The negative character of truth generates in the speaker an enervating doubt, but nevertheless does not obviate his belief. Rather than abandoning truth the speaker mourns its misperception, offering it a faith which is as desperate as it is strong. In 105 the speaker repeats 'fair, kind, and true' like an anthem, or an incantation: if he says it enough, perhaps it will come true. The aggressive couplet of 125 best expresses the quality of the speaker's faith: 'Hence, thou suborned informer! A true soul / When most impeached stands least in thy control.'

This desperately defiant tone is completely absent from the Dark Lady sequence. Indeed, truth as a concept is frequently effaced, stated only through its negation: sonnets 127, 130, 142, and 152 engage the issue of truth only through reference to the 'false,' and in 131 a logically expected *true* is expressed instead as 'not false' ('And to be sure that is not false I swear / A thousand groans but thinking on thy face'). The speaker has no doubt, no anxiety—he knows that the Dark Lady lies, that the 'truth' he sees is false. Truth is not veiled or distorted, but simply wrong, deliciously and terribly wrong. Because the constantly, visibly false approximates an identifiable truth, the speaker, finally, can revel in certainty (e.g., 137, 138, 147, 148, 150, 152).

> *Therefore my verse to constancy confined*
> *One thing expressing, leaves out difference*
> (105).

If the speaker cannot have dependable truth, then he will choose dependable lies.

Significantly, the speaker's fixation with death and decay vanishes in the Dark Lady sequence—indeed, it vanishes *because* of the Dark Lady sequence. There is nothing at stake in her physical or moral decay, no cosmological crisis. The speaker has moved from an economy of constancy and eternal memorialization to an economy of lust and momentary gratification. It is a progression as natural as the progression from youth to age, strength to weakness, motion to rest. The indeterminacy of the young man, the passionate conflict of belief and disbelief, has simply exhausted the speaker. He now prefers the woman who will each day send him into the storm, rather than the young man who might one day surprise him thus. He prefers the ease of disbelief and cynicism to the terror of an Ideal, the realization of pain rather than the lingering threat. With the dark lady the speaker suffers the frustration and shame of lust, and the anguish of spiteful cruelties; and he must struggle for her, hold desperately to her, lest he lose even this last, crude pleasure. But in this torment he has found a certain grim exhilaration—the exhilaration of a man who no longer has much to lose.

Notes

[1] Thomas P. Roche, for example, calls it the 'most perplexing of all the sonnets . . . a paradigm devoid of

meaning' (*Shakespeare and the Sonnet Sequence, in English Poetry and Prose, 1540-1674,* vol. 2, ed. Christopher Ricks, New York: Peter Bedrick Books, 1981, p. 87). For a concise bibliography of work done on 94, see Anthony Easthope, 'Same Text, Different Readings: Shakespeare's Sonnet 94,' *Critical Quarterly,* vol. 28, nos. 1 & 2.

[2] As W. G. Ingram and Theodore Redpath explain, one can read this allusion in any number of ways: for example, as an ironic dismissal of such slanders against the young man, or perhaps as a none-too-subtly veiled warning against the probability of such behavior. *Shakespeare's Sonnets* (London, 1967), 214. See also Philip Edwards, *Shakespeare: A Writer's Progress* (New York: Oxford University Press, 1986), 66.

[3] John D. Bernard, "To Constancie Confin'd': The Poetics of Shakespeare's Sonnets,' *PMLA,* January 1979, 94(1), p. 83.

[4] Bernard, 84; 88; 81. The conflation of author and speaker is Bernard's. 'As the friend is one so is the poet's style, and so the poet himself in his metaphysical posture. The series of equations is virtually endless: you = love = I = words' (82). Contrast Bernard's insistence upon the *oneness* of Shakespeare's words with Howard Felperin: 'What with its demonumentalization of fixed or 'natural' meaning, Shakespeare's wordplay would seem to be the ultimate 'figure of disorder'.' *Beyond Deconstruction: The Uses and Abuses of Literary Theory* (Oxford: Clarendon Press, 1985), 188.

[5] Lars Engle, 'Afloat in Thick Deeps: Shakespeare's Sonnets on Certainty,' 833.

[6] Fineman, for example, claims that Shakespeare anticipates both Derrida and Freud. *Shakespeare's Perjured Eye: The Invention of Poetic Subjectivity in the Sonnets* (Berkeley: University of California Press, 1986), 46-48.

[7] Engle, 833.

[8] For Lars Engle, sonnet 116 reveals that love is 'contingent,' while for Murray Krieger it displays the 'eternal fixity of love.' E. S. Bates claims that sonnet 55 reveals Shakespeare's deep faith in 'the permanence of poetry'—but Stephen Booth points out that even as the speaker asserts the immortality of poetry he reminds us of the 'flimsiness and vulnerability of anything written on paper.' Of 105 Bernard writes that the beloved reproduces the 'ultimate Christian mystery of the three persons of the Godhead in one 'seate',' while Booth reads the sonnet as a 'playful experiment in perversity.' Engle, 840; Murray Krieger, *A Window to Criticism* (Princeton: Princeton University Press, 1974), 148; E. S. Bates, *The Sonnets of Shakespeare,* ed. Raymond Macdonald Alden (New York: Houghton and Mifflin Company, 1916), 141; Stephen Booth, *Shakespeare's Sonnets* (New Haven: Yale University Press, 1977), 229, 336; Bernard, 85.

[9] Katherine Duncan-Jones, for one, argues for the 'integrity' of the 1609 Quarto. 'Was the 1609 *Shake-Speares Sonnets* Really Unauthorized?' *The Review of English Studies,* May 1983, vol. XXXIV, no. 134, pp. 154-155.

[10] Krieger, 176-177. Bernard writes that Shakespeare's friend is the material embodiment of eternal and 'divine beauty' (80-81), and Germaine Greer insists that 'Shakespeare's persona continues to project the ideal of diamond-hard constancy.' *Shakespeare* (New York: Oxford University Press, 1986), 114.

[11] Booth, 226.

[12] Booth, 225.

[13] For a list of works which attribute to Shakespeare a distrust of language, see Margreta De Grazia, 'Shakespeare's View of Language: An Historical Perspective,' *Shakespeare Quarterly,* Summer 1978, vol. 29, no. 3, p. 374. De Grazia insists, however, that this assumption is fallacious: it was not until the seventeenth century, she writes, that writers began to distrust language (379). In any case, De Grazia admits that Shakespeare was in all likelihood experimenting with the imperfections of language through the imperfections of his speaker (383).

[14] The speaker, of course, aggressively employs images of self-consumption in the first seventeen sonnets. However, he is not representing decay so much as he is attempting to denigrate the young man's abstinence by associating it with the lurid imagery of cannibalism and self-consumption.

[15] Booth, 166.

[16] Anne Ferry, *All in War with Time* (Cambridge: Harvard University Press, 1975), 59, 50.

[17] Bernard, 85.

Source: "Truth and Decay in Shakespeare's Sonnets," in *Cahiers Elisabethains,* No. 47, April, 1995, pp. 43-53.

The Shapeliness of *The Tempest*

Peter Holland, *Cambridge*

When in 1667 Sir William Davenant turned his attention to adapting Shakespeare's *The Tempest,* he found a play that seemed to him in need of something more. The story is familiar: the addition of Hippolito to balance Miranda, Dorinda to balance Hippolito, Caliban's sister Sycorax to balance both the others and, to crown it all, Ariel's sweetheart Milcha to balance all the others. The process even involved the doubling of authorship as Davenant called in Dryden to balance himself.

What Dryden and Davenant did to *The Tempest* was a response, however excessive, to something about the nature of the play, an implication of mirroring and reflection, a suggestion of pattern and parallel, an understanding of the peculiar dramatic form of the play they are transforming. They took much further the play's own possibilities of mirroring, implied by such well-recognised features as the parallel openings of successive scenes of Shakespeare's play, 2.2 and 3.1, both beginning with a character carrying on logs, Caliban and Ferdinand.

Dominated by Kermode's 1954 Arden edition, criticism of *The Tempest* seemed for a long time concerned with little but nature and nurture. Just when it looked as though we had escaped that, there is now a concern bordering on obsession with the play as the epitome of the tensions in colonialism. This trend in academic criticism had been anticipated in adaptations like Aimé Césaire's *Une Tempête* (1969) or in productions like Jonathan Miller's at the Mermaid Theatre in 1970 which made of Ariel and Caliban the contrast between house-nigger and field-nigger of much recent black analysis of the structures of colonial power. An even earlier, if surprising, comprehension of the model comes in a letter by Eric Gill when he was carving his powerful stone sculpture of Prospero and Ariel to go on the BBC's Broadcasting House:

> 'Prospero and Ariel'. Well, you think. *The Tempest* and romance and Shakespeare and all that stuff. Very clever of the BBC to hit on the idea, Ariel and aerial, Ha! Ha! And the BBC kidding itself, in the approved manner of all big organizations . . . , that it represents all that is good and noble and disinterested—like the British Empire or Selfridges.[1]

Nevertheless, there is still a need to attend to the play's form, its dramatic structure, its scenic method, to work, that is, unfashionably close to the play as a theatrical object, to respond as Davenant and Dryden did to its odd shape, its strange shapeliness. For not only does *The Tempest* observe the unities of time and place in a way unprecedented in Shakespeare—a familiar fact about the play, echoing and intensifying the formal tightness he had explored as early as *The Comedy of Errors* and hardly again thereafter—but its scenic form is original, innovative and, above all, curious in its shapeliness.[2]

The study of scenic form in Shakespeare to explore his dramaturgy is still a comparatively new discipline. It effectively begins with Emrys Jones's *Scenic Form in Shakespeare* (1971) and with Mark Rose's *Shakespearean Design* (1972). Identifying it as 'one of the most disciplined, most severely controlled plays in the canon',[3] Rose points out that *The Tempest* has fewer scenes than any Shakespeare play since A *Midsummer Night's Dream,* only nine in all. He then defines, with the help of a diagram, a remarkable feature of that sequence. The middle scene of the nine, the fifth, is 3.1, in which Ferdinand carries logs with Miranda and with Prospero watching. The scene before this, 2.2, has Caliban, Stephano and Trinculo and so too does the sixth scene, 3.2. The scene before that, the play's third, 2.1, is a 'lords' scene for Alonso, Antonio and Sebastian; so too is the seventh, 3.3. The scene before that, 1.2, ends with Prospero, Ferdinand and Miranda and the eighth scene, 4.1, starts with the same group of characters. As Rose sums it up, "Surrounding the centrepiece, and accounting for almost the entire play, is thus an extraordinary triple frame comprised of distinct character groups' (p. 173).

In fact, we can go even further than Rose, for the play's opening scene introduces as the first two characters brought onstage the ship's Master and Boatswain, two people who will not reappear again until the end of the play's last scene, providing another 'distinct character group' marking another outermost frame to the play. This turns Rose's triple frame into a quadruple one, which, although slightly blurred around the edges, now accommodates all the play's scenes and all its characters bar one, predictably Ariel. That even Prospero is held within this pattern seems highly significant.

Rose, with engaging honesty, admits to being unsure what to make of this shape he perceives, a shape that is architectural in the extreme. He describes it as having 'little dramatic function' and comments that 'it seems to be merely a display of virtuosity, a pyrotechnical grand finale from the age's most accomplished dramatist on the eve of his retirement' (p. 174). 'Alternatively', he hesitantly adds, 'both the unities and the design can be regarded as the structural correlative to the central theme—discipline. Like Prospero, Shakespeare derives the authority to preach self-control from his own practice' (p. 174). One line of argument emanating from such a position would be that Prospero himself is thus subject to discipline and Ariel's indiscipline, his status as free floater, defines his ambiguous relation to authority.

I have myself to admit that I have no idea how Rose's extraordinary perception of this 'extraordinary triple frame' (now a quadruple frame in my extension of it) can be demonstrated in performance. Throughout his book, Rose sets out simpler architectural shapes operating through time, diagrams of spatial interconnectedness that seem to defy the temporal unfolding of theatre. The realisation of visual diagrams in time is mysterious and, when I have described the pattern of *The Tempest* to directors they have been initially fascinated and then frustrated, unable to suggest how to make an audience see this in the course of production. However, neither of Rose's explanations—virtuosity and the virtues of discipline—seem satisfactory or sufficient, the former too straightforwardly aesthetic, the latter far too simplistic in its response to the play's stresses and strains.

Rose's pattern of characters emphasises *The Tempest's* nine-scene form but it is also clearly a play written in five acts, a structure that, apart from *Henry V,* had not engaged Shakespeare significantly. At the end of Act 4, Prospero and Ariel leave the stage, having seen the spirits disguised as dogs start hunting Caliban, Trinculo and Stephano; at the beginning of Act 5 they re-enter. This is the only time in Shakespeare's works, according to the best authorities, that the so-called 'law of re-entry', the putative law that says a character cannot exit and immediately re-enter at the start of the next scene, is unequivocally broken.

Prospero's opening lines here define the moment of climax, the play's action coming to its close: 'Now does my project gather to a head' (5.1.1).[4] The opening dialogue of this act also marks the crucial movement of Prospero's own intentions from revenge to forgiveness, to 'virtue', as Prospero himself defines it, as Ariel describes the effect of the spectacle of the three madmen: 'if you now beheld them, your affections / Would become tender' (5.1.18-19). 'Tender' is a word that was earlier used by Adrian to describe the island itself, a place that seems 'to be desert . . . Uninhabitable, and almost inaccessible . . . Yet . . . It must needs be of subtle, tender, and delicate temperance' (2.1.37-45), terms that might now almost be applied to Prospero whose inaccessibility to some other affections will be transformed to tender temperance. The exit and re-entry, the gap where nothing happens save the performance of act-music, are the precondition of change, of the alteration of Prospero's fixed purpose to the possibility of a different action. As Margreta de Grazia remarks, 'Prospero decides to take the action that will free him and his enemies to move and act again'.[5]

The change comes about, as de Grazia points out, 'from no prior action' (p. 249), but from Ariel's description of an action or rather a sight of immobility, a spectacle of magical imprisonment, for the lords are 'confined together' (5.1.7) just as Sycorax 'did confine' Ariel (1.2.275), or Caliban was 'deservedly confined into this rock' by Prospero (1.2.363). The lords have been trapped in 'the lime-grove which weather-fends your cell' (5.1.10),[6] the same grove of limes or lindens as that in which Caliban and his co-conspirators are tempted by the finery of clothes, hung 'on this lime' (4.1.193, in F 'this line')—the word suggesting here lime-tree more than clothes-line and inducing in Stephano a heavy fit of punning. The grove is as completely a place of confinement as a rock or a cloven pine.

The play has explored a whole series of means of release from imprisonment and oppression,[7] such as the false freedom that Ariel found from the cloven pine to Prospero's service, the one Sebastian suggests Antonio will find if he kills Alonso ('One stroke / Shall free thee from the tribute which thou payest', 2.1.297-8), and Caliban's drunken freedom-song with Trinculo and Stephano. From the opening of Act 5 on, *The Tempest* will define a new series of releases: the lords from the spell of madness, Caliban and company from the spell of pursuit, Ariel from the spell of service. Each release will now be from Prospero's magic, the thing he will in Act 5 promise to abjure, rather than the release of the usurping, murderous freedoms previously envisaged.

This change is only possible through the freeing of Prospero himself at the start of Act 5, the change recognised in the promise to 'break my staff' (5.1.54) and bury it in the earth and 'deeper than did ever plummet sound' to 'drown my book' (5.1.56-7). 'Plummet' is an unusual word in Shakespeare's vocabulary, two of its three occurrences are in this play. Earlier Alonso had wanted to search for his missing son 'deeper than e'er plummet sounded' (3.3.101); now the same phrase is used for Prospero's magic book. The place where Ferdinand is wrongly thought to be is now the place where the source of the magic that lead to that false assumption will lie. The movement from fantasy to normality is charted in the sea-change the phrase undergoes in its repetition.

The freeing of the characters is inagurated by the unprecedented dramaturgy of re-entry, the freeing of characters from an assumed rule. I am not suggesting that the theatrical device embodies a simple meaning of enfranchisement from dramaturgical law transferred metaphorically to the rest of the action but rather that the extraordinary dramatic event in *The Tempest's* form emphasizes the transition, calls attention to that which too will be unprecedented, liberating and transforming, a turning away from the confinements of Prospero's magic.

The visible marks of that magic reside in three objects, three props repeatedly present on stage: the staff, the book and the robe. With the first he can conjure storms or draw a circle to define a holding-place, a space of imprisonment onstage; with the second he has the source of his power's action, the knowledge of possibility that a book of spells provides; the third is defined from the beginning as the emblem of his power and status as magus, the cunning and unnaturalness of the magus's control, announcing 'lie there, my art' (1.2.25), as, in a well-known analogue, 'at night when [Lord Burleigh] put off his gown, he used to say, Lie there, *Lord Treasurer'*.[8]

In suggesting that all three objects are present onstage I have gone slightly further than the evidence will warrant, for while the staff and robe are certainly used by Prospero, the book may not be. Those books which Prospero prized 'above my dukedom' (1.2.169) are, according to Caliban, in Prospero's cell and he repeatedly advises Stephano and Trinculo to grab them before attacking Prospero: 'Having first seized his books . . . Remember / First to possess his books . . . Burn but his books' (3.2.90-6). Perhaps Prospero was never meant to be seen to carry the book on stage, though so many images of the magus in the period and so many productions of the play have found it appropriate to show him carrying book as well as staff. Where the book is certainly seen is in its comic and distorted version, Stephano's bottle, the object Caliban and Trinculo are told to kiss ('kiss the book', 2.2.129) so that it becomes both a parodic bible but also a parodic book of power, alcohol as a form of social control, a religion enshrined in its book, the bottle. Prospero's book is the magus's bible, an object which tells him how to perform acts that are themselves distortions of religious actions, an appropriation of acts that belong orthodoxly only to Christ, 'graves at my command / Have waked their sleepers, oped, and let 'em forth / By my so potent art' (5.1.48-50).

These objects of power enable Prospero to engineer many of the play's spectacles. In one of the play's three most spectacular moments, the appearance of Ariel as harpy, Shakespeare creates for the only time in his work a three-level vertical image, with Ariel descending and with Prospero, watching as so often in the play but placed this time, as Folio's stage-direction states, *'on the top'* (3.3.19.1-2), the level above the gallery. In 1938, in a speculative article examining the complex problems of staging this scene, John Cranford Adams, while describing Prospero as 'like some god of Olympus surveying mortals on the earth',[9] suggests that Prospero is there partly to control the mechanics of the theatre action, to cue the music for the entrance and exit of the spirits and the machinists to operate the descent and ascent of Ariel. In modern terms we might want to think of Prospero as a visible director, like the Polish director Tadeusz Kantor who was onstage throughout his productions, moving the actors, controlling the process of the performance. In Giorgio Strehler's famous version of *The Tempest* for the Piccolo Teatro in Milan in 1978 Prospero became quite explicitly the play's director, as he did for Yukio Ninagawa's production in 1992. But in renaissance terms, if the concept of the stage's controller has resonance, it can have no overtones of the modern director; instead the cueing of the action was the prerogative of the prompter or, as he was always known, the book-holder. In Ninagawa's brilliant production of the play, the book that Prospero promises to drown became quite naturally the script of *The Tempest,* the sheets fluttering from their holder at the end. This is to make literal what is implicit, that the book controls the production, that Prospero is both playwright and book-holder, since the play's scenic form, the creation of separate character groups that enables Rose's pattern to exist, is the direct result of Prospero's power, his instruction that Ariel has fulfilled: 'And, as thou bad'st me, / In troops I have dispersed them 'bout the isle' (1.2.220-1). As book-holder Prospero is of course displaced from the normal invisibility of book-holder to audience; his stage placing here, 'on the top', marks his position of power, visible and emphatic beyond a book-holder's wildest dreams, but precisely aligned with the power of the magus as holder of magic books.

The harpy costume of this scene is the second of Ariel's three disguises in the play. The Puck of *A Midsummer Night's Dream,* Ariel's precursor and the greatest of Shakespeare's metamorphic figures, is never seen transformed. Though we hear of him as crab-apple, headless bear, gossip's stool and a whole host of other guises, only Bottom in the play will change shape. But, while Ariel says he has been invisibly and metamorphically present in the storm disguised as fire, where he 'flamed amazement' (1.2.199), that was not a stage effect which the Blackfriars or the Globe could run to.

Ariel's long dialogue with Prospero in 1.2, the rehearsal of his history, the monthly repetition of the story of his torment, makes clear the close and complex analogy between Prospero and Sycorax, both powerful magicians, both banished, both stuck on the island with their child, both enslavers of Ariel, an analogy which is another of the play's mirrors. After this, Prospero instructs Ariel to 'make thyself like to a nymph o'th'sea. Be subject / To no sight but thine and mine, invisible / To every eyeball else' (1.2.303-5). It is a passage that troubles editors since it is metrically corrupt, but the costume-change is itself odd, for, if Ariel is to be invisible to Ferdinand, the sea-nymph costume is 'logically pointless', as the play's most recent editor, Stephen Orgel, puts it.[10] As with Feste as Sir Topas appearing to Malvolio in prison, who, as Maria says, 'mightst have done this without thy beard and gown, he sees thee not' (4.2.64-5), only the watchers will appreciate the appropriateness of the change. Prospero and the audience will enjoy the effect; its point is the charm of its visible harmony with the song.

Such pleasures of costume are genuine but Ariel's re-entry in disguise is another of the play's odd moments of dramaturgy. Prospero and Miranda have, by this stage, gone to 'visit Caliban my slave' (310), Prospero has called and Caliban growled back. Prospero calls on him to enter—'Come forth, I say! There's other business for thee. / Come, thou tortoise! When?' (317-18)—and then, *'Enter Ariel, like a water-nymph'* (318.1).

Ariel has had barely a dozen lines to make the change, a remarkably short period; by comparison he has seventy lines to change into the harpy costume, though that may be more elaborate, and twenty-seven lines to change into Ceres in the masque, his third and final change. In Peter Hall's production at the Old Vic in 1973 Ariel entered from the point at which Prospero, Miranda and the whole audience were staring, waiting for the first appearance of Caliban. This seems to me brilliantly right; we expect Caliban and we get a water-nymph. We do not expect Ariel to be back so quickly and Miranda cannot, in any case, see this 'Fine apparition', as Prospero calls him (319). Even Prospero must be surprised. Prospero's indulgence in the disguise, his pleasure in the theatrical appropriateness of the switch, becomes unexpected. But it is also part of the curious lurches that can occur when Ariel is onstage. Miranda may indeed be used to the way that her father talks to invisible spirits but the effect of Ariel's presence, particularly on Ferdinand, is to produce jumps in the continuity of such scenes for both Ferdinand and Miranda. What do they do when Prospero talks to Ariel? The problem is much more extreme than in the comparable case of Oberon and the Puck. For while Robin can only talk to Oberon when both are onstage, Oberon is himself invisible. The twin perspective, the super-imposed double scene, Prospero and Miranda, Prospero and Ariel, is unique to this play. Its disconnections are a mark of the island's strangeness, of the odd canons of realism appropriate to this world. The oddity of the sea-nymph costume is only a part of this effect.

Costume changes and the state of one's clothes are a peculiar trademark of *The Tempest.* Something about the island results in quick-drying fabrics. The wedding-clothes that Alonso and his party are wearing, the ones they put on 'in Afric, at the marriage of the King's fair daughter Claribel to the King of Tunis' (2.1.74-6), though they were, as Gonzalo remarks, 'drenched in the sea, hold notwithstanding their freshness and glosses, being rather new-dyed than stained with salt water' (67-9). Elsewhere Prospero will put on and off the robe of invisibility and of power: Henslowe's list of costumes belonging to the Admiral's Men in 1598 included 'a robe for to go invisibell'.

There are three sets of noble or monarchical costume in the play: alongside the first, the clothes that the lords group wears throughout, must come those, the second, that tempt Stephano and Trinculo. Prospero describes the *'glistering apparell',* as the Folio stage-direction has it, as 'The trumpery in my house' (4.1.186). Editors have a tough time with the phrase and when Orgel suggests, rather desperately, that 'Prospero, suiting his art to his audience, produces carnival costumes from his cell',[11] I am not sure what he is thinking of. Of course the costumes must be the sort that would attract Stephano and Trinculo and divert their attention from the plot in hand but what would Prospero be doing with carnival costumes in his cell in the first place? It seems unlikely that they were put in the boat by Gonzalo. Stage responses have recently tended to be extreme, producing gold cloaks and ermine collars in abundance, pantomime theatre costumes that have no connection with the language of costume in the play.

What would Prospero see as 'trumpery' and what would impress Stephano and Trinculo? It is quite conceivable that the wedding finery of the lords might rate the comment 'trumpery' from Prospero and the gowns and jerkins specifically mentioned might well be versions of the lord's costumes. This would tie their fascination for the drunks more directly to their perception of aristocratic style—about which a butler and a jester might be presumed to know something and with which they might well be fascinated—and would then become a structural mid-term leading to the third aristocratic costume, Prospero's dressing in the hat and rapier from his cell so that he can 'myself present / As I was sometime Milan' (5.1.85-6).

The worldly costume of a prime duke, itself the sort of trumpery that Prospero disdained when for him his library was dukedom large enough, is rather unremarkable onstage. The final costume change, which one might reasonably expect to be triumphant and climactic, serves only to make Prospero rather insignificant. I am always struck in performance by the way that Prospero as Duke, shorn of the magic robe, becomes oddly unimportant and strangely easy to ignore. An ordinary man, in normal doublet and hose, hat and rapier, Prospero's ordinary ducal clothes may be less gaudy, less fine than the festive wedding-clothes of the lords. After the initial recognition, Alonso and the others seem just as interested in Ferdinand and Miranda, in the master and boatswain, in Stephano and Trinculo, and, above all, in Caliban, as in Prospero. They can treat him rather too much like an equal.

In fact, dressed like or less well than the others, Prospero is not recognisably the magus who has controlled the play. I am not convinced, for instance, that even Alonso suspects what Prospero has done to them. When they were held in their distraction in the magic circle, that strange moment when they are each analysed and defined by Prospero, they cannot hear him (for it is only at the end of the speech that, as he says, 'Their understanding / Begins to swell', 5.1.79-80). Prospero's speech is, in effect, a soliloquy. Harry Berger goes so far as to see the speech as a rehearsal: 'It is as if he hesitates to put on the real scene without one more dress rehearsal; or as if he is primarily aiming the words at himself, reminding himself of the part he has decided to play, and of the parts he has written for them, as penitents'.[12] But, if Berger is right, this proves to be a dress rehearsal without a performance, with the actors, especially Antonio and Sebastian, prone to refuse this casting against type.

Alonso, amazed by the sailors, wonders

> This is as strange a maze as e'er men trod,
> And there is in this business more than nature
> Was ever conduct of. Some oracle
> Must rectify our knowledge.
>
> (5.1.245-8)

His words pick up the maze that Gonzalo had earlier described as 'trod indeed' (3.3.2), all the amazement that has gone through the play from the point when Ariel flamed amazement in the first scene onwards, through Miranda's 'amazement' that Prospero calms (1.2.14), and all the 'strangeness' that has beat over and over again in the lines—26 times in all its cognate forms (strange, strangely, strangeness, stranger), many more if one adds in Folio's stage-directions. Some Alonsos direct the lines very pointedly at Prospero, identifying him as the oracle who can 'rectify our knowledge' but Prospero's reply, 'Sir, my liege, / Do not infest your mind with beating on / The strangeness of this business' (248-50), suggests that Alonso is worrying about how he can explain it, not waiting for Prospero to provide the explanation. There is, after all, no reason for Alonso and the others to think that Prospero can explain it or that he has unusual powers—they cannot see Ariel, have not yet seen Caliban—and Prospero, who has spent so much of the play invisibly watching others, becomes in the end too ordinarily visible to be credited with them.

Ariel's final costume was as Ceres in the masque, the third of the play's spectacular scenes. Complex and dense in its iconology, rich in its allusions and implications for the play as a whole, the masque is a vision of a world that might have been, a golden world like Gonzalo's fantasy, but one that cannot be achieved. Its idyll of abundance and perfection, present both in Juno's song and in the dance of nymphs and reapers, cannot reach the proper conclusion of masque, that moment of structural necessity in the form when the masquers take the members of the audience into the masque-world, combining the image and reality in dancing. Instead, *'To a strange, hollow, and confused noise,* [the spirits] . . . *heavily vanish'* (4.1.142.1-2).

The Folio text of *Tempest* derives, it is generally agreed, from a Ralph Crane transcript. Some have argued, most particularly John Jowett, that its stage directions have large quantities of Crane added to briefer putative Shakespeare originals; Jowett indeed claims to be able to define word by word which bits of the stage directions are Shakespeare's and which Crane's.[13] He may well be right but, as Greg observed, the style of the stage directions 'is the language of a spectator recording with appreciation the ingenuity of the staging, and there is no reason why Crane should not have seen *The Tempest'*.[14] Even so, the language of the stage directions has such remarkable and unusual resonance within the structure of the play and such coherence that, if not Shakespearean, they can quite reasonably be taken to record Shakespearean stage effects. They are integrated within and integral to the nature of the only early text of *The Tempest* we have.

It is justifiable, then, to investigate this 'strange, hollow and confused noise'. Orgel, following *OED*, finds the sound 'sepulchral' and compares the sounds of birds in Strachey's letter, one of Shakespeare's sources. But, although no-one appears to have noticed it, there has already been both another confused noise heard and a second strange, hollow noise heard or at least described in the play. One of the Folio directions for the sounds of the ship-wreck in the first scene—the sound that makes the mariners assume the ship has split or the sound of the mariners making that assumption—is described as *'A confused noise within'*. When Ariel wakes Alonso and the other sleepers as Antonio and Sebastian are about to strike, the sound of the song is described by Sebastian: 'Even now we heard a *hollow* burst of bellowing, / Like bulls, or rather lions' (2.1.316-17, my emphasis). Sebastian is probably lying, of course; the sound he describes is part of his excuse for having drawn his sword. Antonio, predictably, expands on the idea: 'O, 'twas a din to fright a monster's ear, / To make an earthquake! Sure it was the *roar* / Of a whole herd of lions' (319-21, my emphasis).

The change from the music of Ariel's song to the conspirators' description of it as noise is much like the change from the music of the masquers' dance to the 'confused noise'. The hollow bellow, the din, the roar connects with a whole series of sounds heard through the play, for if the isle is full of noises a surprising number of them are roars, from the sound of the tempest onwards: the 'roarers' who disdain the name of king (1.1.16-17), the 'roar' into which Prospero's magic has put 'the wild waters' (1.2.2), the 'sulphurous roaring' of Ariel's thunder and lightning (1.2.205) which will lead to the 'confused noise' as the ship breaks but which is also the sound that accompanied Prospero's and Miranda's journey to the island, when the sea 'roared to us' (1.2.149).

Roaring is also the sound that Caliban will produce if he suffers the 'old cramps' that Prospero threatens him with, they will 'make thee roar' (1.2.371-2). After the end of the masque, brought about by Prospero's forgetfulness of the 'foul conspiracy', he will plague the conspirators 'Even to roaring' (4.1.193) and, as they are chased offstage by the spirit-dogs, Ariel will hear them crying, fulfilling now Prospero's threat to Caliban in 1.2, 'Hark, they roar!' (259). The sounds of the tempest and the sounds of people in pain are the same sounds. The last description of roaring links to the sound that awakened Alonso and the others, for when the Boatswain tries to describe the sound that he and the other sailors heard, the sound that made *them* wake up, he speaks of 'strange and several noises, / Of roaring, shrieking, howling, jingling chains, / And more diversity of sounds, all horrible' (5.1.235-7).

Jonson's *Masque of Queens* was performed on February 2nd 1609. It contains his first great antimasque, his response to the queen's instruction to 'think on some dance or show that might precede hers and have the place of a foil or false masque', the performances of the witches that stand, says Jonson, 'not as a masque but a spectacle of strangeness'.[15] The end of the antimasque is cataclysmic:

> In the heat of their dance on the sudden was heard a sound of loud music, as if many instruments had made one blast; with which not only the hags themselves but the hell into which they ran quite vanished, and the whole face of the scene altered, scarce suffering the memory of such a thing.
>
> (p. 134)

Orgel, in editing *The Tempest,* rightly points to the rich connections between Prospero's speech 'Our revels now are ended' and the common comments on the ephemerality of masques, those pageants which so often displayed 'The cloud-capped towers, the gorgeous palaces, / The solemn temples, the great globe itself' (4.1.152-3).

Masques may indeed fade but the way that Prospero's 'insubstantial pageant' vanishes suddenly to the accompaniment of a confused noise is remarkably like the transition from anti-masque to masque in Jonson's form, performed a couple of years before *The Tempest* and in the same place, Whitehall, where Shakespeare's play would, by chance, be similarly presented. For Prospero's masque is a vision of perfection as unattainable and as ineffective as the imperfect world of Jonson's anti-masque. In some sense Prospero's masque can only be a 'foil or false' show, not a true one, for the meeting of worlds in *The Tempest* will not be and cannot be between masquers and spectators but a reunion of people on an island that is itself by turns real and unreal.

Orgel suggests three possible antimasques to Prospero's masque: the opening storm, the harpy's banquet and the personified abstractions that would destroy the union of the marriage-bed, 'barren hate, / Soureyed disdain, and discord'.[16] The witches of the antimasque in *The Masque of Queens* gather 'fraught with spite / To overthrow the glory of this night',[17] their dances and songs are charms of opposition and chaos. Their world is a combination of magic and conspiracy and I cannot help but be struck by the resonance with *The Tempest,* for the masque which is created by Prospero's magic is disrupted by a conspiracy designed to 'overthrow the glory' of Prospero's day. It is as if the masque must halt and disappear because the anti-masque's action now, through Prospero's forgetfulness, follows the masque rather than preceding it, leaving it coded by its opposition (anti) rather than its sequence (ante), the binary structure of Jonsonian masque irreparably and impossibly reversed. It makes Prospero's masque a premature event, too early for a celebration of union, something that must wait for Act 5 and, in particular, the moment when Ferdinand and Miranda, spectators to the earlier masque, themselves become actors in the emblematic action of the chess-game, presented to spectators with whom they as actors will join to ask for blessing.

The most significant moment of spectacle and dramaturgical oddity, is the tempest itself. As Anne Barton and Andrew Gurr have shown,[18] Shakespeare is responding in the scene to two contradictory impulses. The first is the frequent and conventional acknowledgement that showing sea-storms was beyond the stage's capabilities. Part 1 of Heywood's *The Fair Maid of the West,* for instance, first performed just before or just after *The Tempest,* has the Chorus announce 'Our stage so lamely can express a sea / That we are forc'd by Chorus to discourse / What should have been in action'. In his earlier play, *The Four Prentices of London,* Heywood takes the equally conventional next step, suggesting that the audience's imagination must create what cannot be shown, relying on the language to represent as vividly as possible the scene that cannot be seen:

> Imagine now yee see the aire made thicke
> With stormy tempests, that disturbe the sea:
> And the foure windes at warre among
> themselves:

> And the weake Barkes wherein the brothers saile,
> Split on strange rockes, and they enforc't to swim.[19]

Shakespeare had demonstrated the same technique in *Henry V* and had returned to it in *Pericles,* recognising the dramatic potential of the ambiguous event, the event that defies performance and tensely opposes the stage's own show. In many ways, the virtuoso handling of the opening scene of *The Tempest,* its extraordinary demonstration of the limits of stage realism, of the potential for show, suggests a master-dramatist showing off, that 'pyrotechnical grand finale' Mark Rose describes.[20] Accompanied by the roaring sound, the *'tempestuous noise of thunder and lightning'* described in the Folio stage-direction, the mariners' nautical jargon quickly conjures up the storm, the frenetic activity of efficient seamen working fast under stress, the variety of survival measures they take and their failure, as well as their arguments with the aristocratic passengers.

But, as Peter Hall discovered when rehearsing the scene for his production at the National Theatre in 1988, mere activity is not the answer. After several rehearsals, Hall gloomily muttered 'The scene is becoming what it always is, just a lot of desperate noise'.[21] Hall's solution was to underplay the realism, to adopt 'a more formalized approach'. Beginning the scene in a 'deadly quiet that seemed much more dangerous', Hall made 'the sounds punctuating the scene . . . more surrealistic—and much more disturbing—than the usual violent storm which drowns everything'.[22] Interestingly, both Nicholas Hytner in his production for the RSC in 1988 and Peter Brook in his version, *La Tempête* (1990), adopted similarly eerie solutions to the problem of staging the storm.

The second impulse that Shakespeare was responding to is the one technique for the representation of the consequences of shipwreck that the renaissance stage regularly employed, the entrance of characters 'wet'. In The *Thracian Wonder* (1599), for instance, comes the direction 'Enter old Antimon bringing in Ariadne shipwrecked, the Clown turning the child up and down, and wringing the Clouts . . . Enter Radagon all wet, looking about for shelter as shipwrecked'.[23] Each of the shipwrecked brothers in Heywood's *The Four Prentices,* cast away in France, Ireland and Venice, duly enters 'all wet'. The Folio stage direction in the storm at the start of *The Tempest, 'Enter Mariners wet',* was, as Anne Barton has said, 'clearly designed to make the calamity as convincing and tangible as possible, for characters and audience alike' (p. 45).

The revelation that Prospero created the storm and that no one was harmed startlingly denies the first scene's realism; the common mistake in productions from at least William Poel onwards of having Prospero and Miranda on stage to watch the storm works directly against everything which that realism aims to achieve, refuting the threat of the sound of the ship splitting and the desperation of the offstage cries, 'Mercy on us! / We split, we split! Farewell, my wife and children! / Farewell, brother! We split, we split, we split!' (1.1.57-9). It also undermines the confidence trick, for the audience will see, once it knows Prospero's part in all this, that the shipwrecked people do not enter wet, that the lords' clothes are fresh and glossy, and that, although Ferdinand is 'something stained', it is 'With grief' not with water (1.2.417-18).

The audience, knowingly unsurprised, will not share Gonzalo's surprise. From Prospero's explanation of the storm onwards, they will be unable to share the characters' endless amazement. Theatrical thrift creates the exact and careful definition of the stage direction: it is the mariners who enter wet for all the others who appear onstage in the first scene; master and boatswain, Alonso, Sebastian, Antonio, Gonzalo and the rest will all have to appear subsequently in the same costumes bone-dry. The mariners will not be back even in act 5; indeed I assume the actors will reappear transformed into the spirits of the island. The entry of wet characters is here a feature of the process of a shipwreck that is not a shipwreck, not the consequence of one, being in the middle of a shipwreck rather than having been shipwrecked.

The storm, the most vigorous moment of stage realism in the play, is not realism at all. It is as artifical, formal and theatrical as the harpy or the masque. Its disorientation is disturbing but not sustained. No wonder then that Kemble's production in 1807, keen to make all clear, altered the sequence of the scenes so as to play the storm *after* Prospero's account of it and to have songs by a chorus of 'spirits of the storm'.[24] No wonder that Hazlitt described this version as 'travestie, caricature, any thing you please, but a representation'.[25] The wet actors, both bearing a mark of the real and standing as a theatrical sign for something beyond, prove to have poured water over themselves for no purpose; they are wet but prove not to be, they convince us they are shipwrecked but are in no danger. The forms of performance apply even here; this storm too is structured.

Rose's triple frame with which I began breaks down at the moment of the end of the masque, for instead of seeing only Caliban, as the mirroring pattern would prescribe, we are now shown Stephano and Trinculo as well. It breaks down when Prospero loses control, forgets something, allows the conspiracy to fall outside his consciousness, the power that has so far defined the sequence of the play. But if the play starts with a storm which is not a storm, it ends with a reconciliation which is not a reconciliation, a pattern which is not a pattern. The pattern of the play's structure completes itself, not with the last scene but with the epilogue, an action that, asking for applause, seeks to conjure up its own particular noise, a storm of clapping, that makes it into its own transformed echo of the play's opening storm-scene. We might even contemplate thinking of the storm as prologue, the journey to the island balancing the epilogue which asks for help to make the journey away from the island, 'the thunder and lightning' becoming 'Gentle breath' (Epilogue, 11).

Whatever the complexities and difficulties of the end of the play, I want to focus finally on the formal importance of the play's middle scene, so often undervalued. When Ferdinand enters bearing a log, we should catch the deliberate echo of the opening of the preceding scene when Caliban enters bearing a *'burden of wood'*. Both are defined in relation to Miranda: Caliban bears wood because he has become Prospero's slave after trying to have sex with Miranda by raping her; Ferdinand bears wood because he has become Prospero's slave so that he can have sex with Miranda by marrying her (though, as Prospero insists, not before marriage). Attempted sex leads to slavery; slavery will lead to achieved sex. The pattern is neat.

The scene with Miranda is played out with Prospero watching. He had of course planned the dynastic marriage from the beginning but what Prospero had not expected is that the two would fall so immediately and wondrously in love. Emotions are beyond Prospero's control—as he will find with Antonio in the last scene—however cleverly he may, like a god or a playwright, engineer the movement of bodies round the stage. Prospero's pleasure in their love is immense and positive: 'So glad of this as they I cannot be, / Who are surprised with all; but my rejoicing / At nothing can be more.' (3.1.93-5). Wearily unsurprised though he may be, there is a natural easy affection exuded by the young couple that is engaging.

It is also, I want to suggest, triumphant. Alistair Fowler has argued for the significance in Elizabethan writing of the notion of the triumphant centre.[26] Even when the details of his argument became excessively immersed in numerology, his analysis of 'structural patterns in Elizabethan writing poetry', the subtitle of his book *Triumphal Forms,* powerfully suggested that the centre, the sovereign centre of triumph, is often at least as important as the end of a work of defiantly abstract form. In pageants and processions, triumphs and displays, the sovereign is centred. Only occasionally does this seem to be a shape that interested Shakespeare. After all, drama is defiantly linear, its narrative working so strongly against the architectural patterns of the kind of sequences that Fowler detects.

But in Banquo's triumph at Macbeth's feast and here in *The Tempest,* the play's centre does indeed offer a triumph. In Miranda's and Ferdinand's love we might find the epitome of the structural form, the shapeliness of the play that no amount of disturbance, ambiguity, cynicism or incompletion that the ending can generate can quite overwhelm or even significantly harm. Even if Miranda is naive, even if the world is not as brave or as new as she sees it, yet when informed that 'To th'most of men [Ferdinand] is a Caliban' she is modestly and comically satisfied: 'My affections / Are then most humble. I have no ambition / To see a goodlier man' (1.2.483-6). As the slightly pompous and self-important Ferdinand of 1.2, the man wrapped up in the virtues of his courtly language, sets to his task of shifting the logs so his language takes on a new sincerity, tutored by hers, another mirror of reversal, here of her previous success as a tutor when her teaching Caliban language has only resulted in his learning how to curse.

We may wish to distrust the false play of their game at chess, for their entry as a couple into a social world is hedged around with the dangers of that threatening and deceitful world that Ferdinand's false play suggests he already shares in.[27] But their love in 3.1 is an image of a world of feeling beyond any control of magic, dramaturgy and shapeliness that *The Tempest* can impose. Its triumph is both the central panel of a formal structure and a denial of that structuring. In that tension, it defines in more ways than one, the heart of the play.

Notes

[1] Quoted by Fiona MacCarthy, 'The word became flesh', *TLS,* 25th December 1992, p. 15.

[2] For a different recent approach to *The Tempest*'s dramaturgy, see Stanley Wells, 'Problems of Stagecraft in *The Tempest*', *New Theatre Quarterly* 10, (1994), pp. 348-57.

[3] Mark Rose, *Shakespearean Design,* (Camb., Mass., 1972), p. 173.

[4] All quotations from *The Tempest* are from William Shakespeare, *The Complete Works,* ed. Stanley Wells *et al.,* (Oxford, 1986).

[5] Margreta de Grazia, *'The Tempest:* Gratuitous Movement or Action without Kibes and Pinches', *Shakespeare Studies* 14, (1981), p. 249.

[6] F reads *'Line-groue'* here and, while Wells-Taylor rightly modernises to 'lime-grove', F's reading points up the echo I find below.

[7] On such echoes, see Jan Kott, 'The Tempest, or Repetition' in *The Bottom Translation,* (Evanston, Ill., 1987), pp. 91-3.

[8] Quoted in William Shakespeare, *The Tempest,* ed. Stephen Orgel, (Oxford, 1987), p. 103.

[9] John C. Adams, 'The Staging of *The Tempest,* III.iii', *RES* 14 (1938), p. 415.

[10] Orgel, p. 117.

[11] Orgel, p. 183.

[12] Harry Berger, Jr., 'Miraculous Harp: A Reading of Shakespeare's Tempest', *Shakespeare Studies* 5, (1969), p. 276.

[13] See John Jowett, 'New Created Creatures: Ralph Crane and the Stage Directions in *The Tempest' Shakespeare Survey* 36, (1983), pp. 107-20.

[14] W. W. Greg quoted by Orgel, p. 58.

[15] Ben Jonson, *The Complete Masques,* ed. Stephen Orgel, (New Haven, 1969), pp. 122-3.

[16] Orgel, p. 47.

[17] Jonson, *Masques,* p. 126.

[18] See Andrew Gurr, *'The Tempest*'s Tempest at Blackfriars' *Shakespeare Survey* 41, (1989), pp. 91-102 and Anne Barton, '"Enter Mariners, wet": Realism in Shakespeare's Last Plays' in Nicholas Boyle and Martin Swales, eds., *Realism in European Literature,* (Cambridge, 1986), pp. 28-49. See also Louis B. Wright, 'Elizabethan Sea Drama and its Staging', *Anglia* 51, (1927), pp. 104-18.

[19] Both passages quoted by Gurr, pp. 91-2.

[20] Rose, p. 174.

[21] Quoted by Roger Warren, *Staging Shakespeare's Late Plays,* (Oxford, 1990), p. 160.

[22] Warren, p. 160.

[23] Quoted Barton, p. 44.

[24] John Philip Kemble, *Prompt-books,* ed. Charles H. Shattuck, 11 vols., (Charlottesville, Virginia, 1974), vol. 8, p. 16.

[25] Quoted Orgel, p. 68.

[26] See in particular, *Triumphal Forms,* (Cambridge, 1970).

[27] See Bryan Loughrey and Neil Taylor, 'Ferdinand and Miranda at Chess', *Shakespeare Survey* 35, (1982), pp. 113-18, but see also Maynard Mack's comment on chess as 'a *mimic* war . . . to channel our aggressions into art and play', *Everybody's Shakespeare,* (1993), p. 9.

Source: "The Shapeliness of *The Tempest,*" in *Essays in Criticism,* Vol. 45, No. 3, July, 1995, pp. 208-29.

The King and the Poet: *The Tempest*, Whitehall, Winter, 1613

Alvin Kernan

The fall and winter of 1612-13, probably the last of Shakespeare's tenure as resident playwright with the King's Men, were disturbed times at Whitehall. Robert Cecil, the real power behind the throne and the most farsighted politician in England, had died on May 24, 1612, aged forty-nine. The court, mean as ever, buzzed with the news that he had died of syphilis. Arbella Stuart, melancholy and with a streak of willfulness, was also gone from the court, having tried the king's patience too far at last. Her story is pure Shakespearean romance from beginning to end. She had a claim to the throne, as good in law as that of James, who kept her at court like Hamlet in Claudius' Elsinore, so that he could keep an eye on her and prevent her marriage, which might have produced a dangerous heir. Life at court kept Arbella broke, as it did most courtiers, and she played the marriage card, her only trump, more than once, in order to extract money and gifts from James. In 1610 she seems to have been carried away by her own game and fell in love with William Seymour, the second son of Lord Beauchamp, descended through Catherine Grey from Henry VII, and the one man whom James could not allow her to marry. Seymour's claim to the throne combined with Arbella's held the possibility of political mischief, if anyone cared to make it—as someone always did. Nervous about the legitimacy of his own claim to the throne, and brokering every court marriage to prevent rivals, James questioned the lovers, separately and together, about their relationship.

The scene intrigued the Venetian ambassador for its undercurrents, and his report is worth repeating for what it tells us about the way in which the king interacted with his courtiers, particularly about marriage:

> As we reported, the King is anxious that the marriage of the lady Arabella [*sic*] with the nephew of the Earl of Hertford should not go forward, so as to avoid the union of the claims of these two houses, who are the nearest to the Crown. After examination separately they were both summoned before the King, the Prince and the Council and ordered to give up all negotiations for marriage. Lady Arabella spoke at length, denying her guilt and insisting on her unhappy plight. She complained again that her patrimony had been conceded by the King to others. She had sold two rings he had given her. She was then required to beg the King's pardon, but replied that seeing herself deserted she had imagined that she could not be accused if she sought a husband of her own rank. All the same, if error she had made she humbly begged pardon. This did not satisfy the King; he demanded an absolute confession of wrong and an unconditional request for forgiveness. That she complied with, and received fresh promises of money and leave to marry provided the King approved. (*Calendar of State Papers and Manuscripts Relating to English Affairs, Existing in the Archives and Collections of Venice and in other Libraries of North Italy,* 37 vols., ed. R. L. Brown et al., 1864-1947, XI, p. 439)

Money was the king's usual way of patching up quarrels, and Arbella took it, but she went on to marry Seymour secretly in the spring of 1610. The king was furious when he heard, exclaiming that a woman with royal blood had no right to live or marry as she wished. James then played the role of the villainous king of romance, like Leontes in *The Winter's Tale* (which, with its obvious connections to Arbella, was performed in court on November 5, 1611), confining Seymour to the tower and trying to send Arbella to Durham in 1611, although he got her no farther than Highgate. Arbella dressed as a man, in black wig, long cape, and rapier—just like Portia or Rosalind—and fled to France, whither William also went. At the last moment Arbella's ship was captured, and she was returned to England and the Tower, where, still like some heroine of romance—Hermione, say—imprisoned by a cruel tyrant, she lingered until 1614 and then died. James remained unrelenting to her pleas to be reunited with William, responding only with a stern Calvinist message, "Ye had eaten of the forbidden tree" (David N. Durant, *Arbella Stuart, a Rival to the Queen*, 1978, p. 184).

In a better world, 1613 would be best remembered as the year in which the last heretic was burned in England, when the wretched Bartholomew Legate died at Smithfield on March 18 and a few days later Edward Wightman suffered the same fate at Lichfield for no better reason than to affirm the authority of an ecclesiastical court to inflict capital punishment. But no one cared much for the suffering of these unknowns in the crowded time when over the course of a year the scandalous divorce of Frances Howard from the earl of Essex was pushed by the king, Cecil died, Arbella went to the Tower, the princess Elizabeth was betrothed, and Henry, prince of Wales, died after a long and mysterious illness in the fall of 1612, leaving his brother, the unpromising Charles, the successor to the throne.

There was always bad blood between the prince and his father, and the court had been scandalized years earlier when James hit his son with a tennis racket for some minor irritation. In a scene that sounds like something out of *Lear,* the king's fool, Archie Armstrong, "was after every night they could meet him tossed like a dog in a blanket" (Francis Osborne, *Historical Memoirs on the Reigns of Queen Elizabeth and King James*, 1658, p. 269) by Prince Henry's men, simply for pointing out to King James that his son was becoming more popular and had a larger retinue than he. This fool, despite accumulating a fortune by selling his influence in the court, seems in the end to have been entirely fool, for he later, in Charles' time, had "his coat pulled over his head" and was banished from the court for some unhelpful remarks to the archbishop of Canterbury about high church policy. Henry's death was inevitably viewed by many at court as highly suspicious. Historians have concluded that Henry died of typhoid, but during his long, painful, and undiagnosed sickness, some of the court gossips, according to Sir Simond D'Ewes, recalled Tacitus' description of the poisoning of Germanicus. Others saw in the prince's death a Catholic plot linked with the assassination in 1610 of the prince's model, Henri IV. It was even said that if James had not poisoned his son, nonetheless the physicians feared to treat the disease lest they "might possibly offend no lesse by his recovery then death" (Osborne, 269). Chief Justice Coke, by then on the outs with the king, was less circumspect, voicing the suspicions of many when he said darkly, "God knows what became of that sweet babe, Prince Henry, (but I know somewhat)" (Anthony Weldon, *The Court and Character of King James*, 1649, vol. I, p. 427).

The prince was dead, but arrangements were already forward for the marriage of his sister Elizabeth to Frederick of Heidelberg, Elector of the Rhineland Palatinate, and it was decided not to allow mourning to interrupt this state marriage. James intended to play a hand in Continental religious politics, which were then working up to the Thirty Years' War, and the marriage would establish an English base on the Continent. A formal betrothal was celebrated on December 27, 1612, and the wedding took place, prettily, on Valentine's Day 1613. In the period between the engagement and the wedding, the palace was busy with various festivities, and the King's Men, one of four royal companies providing plays, were paid for twenty performances, the largest number they had yet given in a single season, from Christmas through May 20. The royal pair passed their days before the wedding riding, boating, playing cards, hunting, and attending plays and other court entertainments. Frederick was made a member of the Order of the Garter in St. George's Chapel at Windsor. Rich gifts were exchanged as expressions of esteem and worth—spurs set with diamonds, a bottle cut out of a single agate, a chain of diamonds and a tiara (G. P. V. Akrigg, *Jacobean Pageant, or The Court of King James I*, 1962).

The court buzzed about James's "desire to be rid of [the Princess Elizabeth] with least expense" and said maliciously that the match was made only "to render himselfe the umpire of all Christian differences" (Osborne, 282). The queen was snippy. Jealous of her daughter's being the center of attention, she referred to her as "Goodwife Palsgrave," to make certain that no one missed the fact that the princess was marrying down. But whatever the family may have felt privately, James spared no expense publicly, spending £50,000, which he could ill afford, on the festivities and £40,000 more on his daughter's dower. The Thames opposite Whitehall was packed with boats of all kinds, and a model of Algiers was built on the south bank, while a display of fireworks was loosed from barges, showing Saint George battling the dragon in a setting of castles, rocks, bowers, and forests. Oohs and ahs greeted squibs ignited to create a pack of hounds chasing a deer through the air, "making many rebounds and turns with much strangeness, skipping upon the air as if it had been a usual hunting upon land" (Akrigg, 237). The coup was a naval battle in which an English fleet flying the red cross of Saint George attacked a Turkish fleet, with much mock cannon fire—and many real accidents—until the Turks surrendered and were brought by the English admiral to the Whitehall stairs, where they submitted to the royalty assembled there to watch the fete.

After these festivities, the great show of the marriage itself began. The procession took the long way to the royal chapel in Whitehall in order that as many as possible might see the bride, with her golden hair hanging loose to her waist—a sign of her virginity—and interwoven with "a roll or list of gold-spangles, pearls, right stones and diamonds" (Akrigg, 242). Her coronet alone was said, by her father, who had commissioned it, to be worth a million crowns. On a stage in the royal chapel, Elizabeth, wearing a white satin gown and jewels valued at £400,000, was joined by her mother and took a seat opposite Frederick and her father, the latter covered with rich gems said to be worth £600,000. An anthem was sung and then the dean of the Chapel preached a sermon on the wedding at Cana in Galilee. The ceremony itself was performed by the archbishop of Canterbury, attended by a bishop, both in splendid vestments. The Elector mumbled his vows in broken English. Benediction was pronounced, and another anthem, composed by Dr. John Bull especially for the occasion, was sung, after which the Garter King of Arms proclaimed to the audience the new titles of the royal couple. The royal party took communion before they withdrew from the chapel.

A state dinner was followed by Thomas Campion's *Lord's Masque,* set by Inigo Jones on a stage with two levels, the first for the anti-masque danced by twelve "franticks" representing various kinds of unsocial behavior. This was followed on the second stage by Prometheus fixed against a background of stars, along with eight dancing lords attended by sixteen pages. Amid "pilasters all of gold, set with Rubies, Saphyrs, Emeralds, Opals and such like," the lords moved toward silver statues that turned into living ladies. When the masque ended and the revels began, from the audience Frederick and Elizabeth were taken out to dance by the masquers first, and as the dancing began, golden statues of the bridegroom and bride flanking a silver obelisk were revealed on stage.

John Donne, long seeking a place at court but destined to dangle for a time longer, composed an *Epithalamion* describing the extended day and the sexual climax toward which it slowly moved:

> And why doe you two walke,
> So slowly pac'd in this procession?
> Is all your care but to be look'd upon,
> And to be others spectacle, and talke?
> The feast, with gluttonous delaies,
> Is eaten, and too long their meat they praise,
> The masquers come too late, and'I thinke, will stay,
> Like Fairies, till the Cock crow them away. . . .
> But now she is laid; What though shee bee?
> Yet there are more delayes, For, where is he?
> He comes, and passes through Spheare after Spheare,
> First her sheetes, then her Armes, then any where.
>
> (1.61)

Donne's witty freedom with the royal privy parts was matched by the interest of the king, who, with his usual frank curiosity about such matters, called on the couple after their first night and, bouncing up and down on the bridal bed, asked for explicit details of the consummation. He need not have worried, for it was a love match between the sixteen-year-olds from the start, and before its tragic end it would produce thirteen children, including Prince Rupert of the Rhine and the Princess Sophia, the progenitress of the Hanoverian kings of England.

The celebration was by no means over with the ceremonies and royal bedding, for on the next night the gentlemen of the Middle Temple and Lincoln's Inn marched by torchlight down the Strand to Whitehall to present a masque by George Chapman, the dead Prince Henry's playwright. Small boys were dressed as baboons, musicians rode in cars, the masquers were costumed like the Indians of Virginia, accompanied by Moors and followed by floats and two hundred halberdiers. The next night still another masque, prepared this time by the gentlemen of Grey's Inn and the Inner Temple with Sir Francis Bacon serving as producer and master of ceremonies, arrived by water in illuminated boats. Never did Bacon experience more painfully the truth of his mot "rising into place is laborious." Nothing went well from the beginning. The masquers had trouble getting ashore at Whitehall because of the tide, and when all was ready the king was so exhausted and out of sorts that he put off the performance until another time. The masquers were despondent, feeling that, as John Chamberlain wrote (on February 18, 1613, in *The Letters of John Chamberlain*, Vol. I, ed. N. E. McClure, 1939), "the grace of theyre maske is quite gon when theyre apparele hath ben alredy shewed and theyre devises vented so that how yt will fall out God knowes, for they are much discouraged, and out of countenance, and the world sayes yt comes to passe after the old proverb, the properer men, the worse luck." Bacon's essay "Of Masques and Triumphs" takes the high philosophic view that "these things are but toyes," but when his own reputation was involved, he was unable to take them so lightly. He pleaded with the king, begged really, and even the king's promise to watch the masque four nights later could not repair the shattering loss of face he suffered, no matter what the reason, in having his entertainment publicly refused after such extensive and expensive preparations and, as Chamberlain understood, in having all the surprise of the masque's devices lost.

Few weddings can have been celebrated by so much artistic talent as this—Campion, Donne, Shakespeare, Bull, Chapman, Jones, Bacon, Beaumont, and Fletcher—a master demonstration of art in the service of the prince. The King's Men had to reach deep into their repertory for some of their older plays to fulfill the needs of the festivities, performing *Much Ado about Nothing* twice, if *Benedick and Betteris* is, as seems likely, *Much Ado*. With its war between the sexes and multiple marriages it would have been an obvious repeat during the celebration of a wedding. Altogether the plays for which they were paid were: *Philaster, Knot of Fools, Much Ado about Nothing, The Maid's Tragedy, The Merry Devil of Edmonton, The Tempest, A King and No King, The Twins' Tragedy, The Winter's Tale, Falstaff, The Moor of Venice, The Nobleman, Caesars Tragedy, Love Lies a Bleeding, A Bad Beginning Makes a Good Ending, The Captain, The Alchemist, Cardenio, Hotspur, Benedick and Betteris*. The Beaumont and Fletcher team was taking Shakespeare's place by now as the resident playwrights of the King's Men, and their recent plays, *A King and No King* and *Philaster,* were the newest offerings of the season.

Still, Shakespeare remained the staple when his company played at court, and six of his plays, possibly seven, if *Caesars Tragedy* be taken for his *Julius Caesar,* were performed. So great was the need for plays that Shakespeare's recent pieces, *The Winter's Tale* and *The Tempest,* which had been performed at court the year before at Hallowmas, were performed again. Bacon may not have been the only disappointed producer at these celebrations, for it is likely that an unnamed "stage play to be acted in the Great Hall by the King's players," which aroused "much expectation" on February 16, the second night after the wedding, but was then dropped because "greater pleasures [a masque] were preparing" (Edmund K. Chambers, *The Elizabethan Stage*, Vol. II, 1923, p. 213), was Shakespeare's new play of the season, *Henry VIII,* possibly written in collaboration with John Fletcher. The play was designed as a tribute to Elizabeth Stuart, climaxing in the triumphant birth of the great queen after whom she had been so hopefully named. It is impossible to understand why *Henry VIII,* so suitable for the occasion, was not put on in place of one of the older plays in the spring of 1613. Something must have gone badly wrong, for the first known performance was downtown, and in June 1613 the Globe burned down during a performance of the play when cannons, fired to announce the birth of Elizabeth Tudor, ignited the thatch roof of the theater.

But the older plays served, and by the spring of 1613 Shakespeare's *Tempest,* perhaps reworked, some have said, to add the betrothal masque that Prospero provides for Ferdinand and Miranda, suited the occasion on which it was performed somewhat more shrewdly than could have been anticipated when it was first played at court about a year and a half earlier. Prospero instructing his daughter and her prospective husband in the duties of marriage, and providing a magnificent betrothal masque for them, fit very nicely with the Solomonic James lecturing his children, spending a fortune displaying them to the public eye, and providing numerous amusements.

Claribel, daughter of Alonso, the play's king of Naples, in sailing to her wedding in Tunis journeyed no farther than did Elizabeth when she sailed out of the Thames shortly after her own wedding. The beautiful and prolific Winter Queen went first to Heidelberg and then to Bohemia, where she was crowned queen. She and her husband were deposed in 1620, after which she remained in exile, not to return to England for fifty years. And then only after her beloved brother Charles, although defended by her remarkable sons, Prince Rupert of the Rhine and Prince Maurice his faithful companion, had been executed, and her nephew Charles II had at last been restored to the English throne. The Stuarts, by no means excluding the stodgy but still quirkily interesting James I, are surely the most romantic of the European royal families. The Romanovs cannot match them. From Mary, queen of Scots, and the martyr king, Charles I, to the Old Pretender and Bonny Prince Charlie, the Stuart family underwent a journey from Holyrood Palace to the back street in Rome where the dissolute Young Pretender died and suffered a "sea change" no less total than those sung of in *The Tempest,* where the skeletons of drowned men turn to coral and their eye sockets fill with pearls.

Before so sea-changed a family, *The Tempest* opened appropriately, though ominously, with a spectacular scene of falling yardarms, wildfire, a great storm, and a ship striking rocks, which much resembled a recently printed description of a wreck in the Bermudas of ships on their way to the new Virginia colony. The survivors in the play are cast up on a desert island, similar to the brave new worlds that Englishmen on the eve of empire were at that time encountering in Asia, Africa, and America. The courtiers were naturally curious about what went on in these far places, and especially what the natives were like—were they cannibals or noble savages? There was money involved as well, for the court was investing heavily in these new ventures. The earl of Northampton, who after Cecil's death had become the real power in the government, invested a good deal in the Irish plantation in Ulster—the native Irish being thought of as aliens at least as strange as the Indians of North America—in the Hudson Ventures in 1610, in the Northwest Passage Company of two years later, and in a Newfoundland plantation intended to trade fish with the Mediterranean. Salisbury, Pembroke, Shakespeare's old patron Southampton, and 650 other members of the highest levels of society had put large sums into the Virginia project.

The Tempest projected the freshness and excitement of the newfound lands where the courtiers were investing their surplus capital. Springs and brine pits, berries and trees, fish and birds, pignuts and filberts, untrodden beaches where the "printless foot" flies across the yellow sand and the flats of oozy tidal mud, a sky "full of noises, Sounds and sweet airs, that give delight and hurt not." The courtiers' conflicting expectations of the natives—hard and soft primitivism at once—were confirmed by the aborigines who appeared on the stage. Caliban (an anagram of *cannibal*), repellent and fishlike, all earth and water, is the savage of hard primitivism, lusting to rape white women, good only for menial work, controlled by superior intelligence and force. Ariel is the more delicate and playful side of uncivilized life, a fanciful and obedient noble savage, treading "the ooze Of the salt deep," running "upon the sharp wind of the North," doing his master's "business in the veins o' th' earth When it is bak'd with frost" (1.2.255). The emerging image of the white man's burden was loaded on Prospero, the patriarchal ruler of the island, whose magical knowledge and stern moral sense give him absolute power over the untrustworthy aborigines, as well as over the female of his own family, his daughter Miranda.

Humanist artist that he always was, Shakespeare once again stooped to truth and moralized his song, dramatizing for the court not only the wonders of the brave new world of overseas colonies, but the various ways that their European discoverers could and did conceive of their new possessions and subjects. For the old courtier Gonzalo, as for those who would later settle the many utopian communities of America, the new world offers the opportunity to recover the lost Eden where, freed of the weight of European society, human nature will be purified and the sins of the old world left behind:

All things in common nature should produce
Without sweat or endeavor: treason, felony,
Sword, pike, knife, gun, or need of any
engine,
Would I not have; but nature should bring
forth,
Of its own kind, all foison, all abundance,
To feed my innocent people.
(2.1.160)

If for some the new world is potentially John Winthrop's "City on a Hill," to others it is imperialism's city of gold, Cortez's Mexico, Pizarro's Peru, a fountain of eternal youth, to be taken by those bold enough to seize and hold it. The drunken servingmen Trinculo and Stephano find on the island an opportunity to plunder and rape; they enslave the one native they encounter and treat him as a monster to be taken home and displayed in a sideshow. To the courtiers Antonio and Sebastian the island is the heart of darkness, with no policeman around the corner, a place to kill their king, Alonso, and seize power for themselves.

To others, the encounters with the vastnesses of an untouched nature bring profound psychological changes. Loss, and his helplessness within it, engender in the king of Naples remembrance and repentance for old wrongs he has done. His son, the youthful Ferdinand, finds the wonder of love in his new condition of freedom. Prospero, who preceded all these visitors to the island, has found in his exile a close encounter with his own person, body, and appetite in the form of Caliban, his imagination and creation in Ariel, and he has developed as a result a new sense of self and his magical powers over the world.

The primary work of the Renaissance artist was to create the lavish displays of wealth and grandeur required by noble patrons to spectacularize their authority, wealth, and power. This was as true for Shakespeare as it was for other artists who worked in the palace, the church, and the great houses. *The Tempest* supplied his noble audience with images of the expansion of empire: into the religious politics of the Continent and into the conquest of the new world. But from time to time the artist took a place in his art, along with his patrons and their interests.

Even some workaday Renaissance painters and sculptors began to think of themselves in time as artists rather than simple craftsmen and servants of their patrons. They asserted their improved social status by cultivating good manners, stressing their intellectual attainments, and, in Italy, organizing painting fraternities like the Academia di Santa Luca. Concepts of "the artist" and "the work of art," especially in Italy and even more especially in the fine arts, began to take rough shape, usually in connection with the greatest artists. Giorgio Vasari wrote stories of their lives in the 1550s and 1560s, and by the 1600s a mythology of the artist had already taken shape. The Holy Roman Emperor, Charles V, was said to have handed brushes to Titian as he painted and, in a different version of the same story, Cardinal Barberini was described as holding the mirror for Bernini as he chiseled his self-portrait in the face of David. Although only the statutes of Moses and of the two slaves were completed, the myth of Art created a pretty picture of Michelangelo and Pope Julius II, artist and patron together, sitting in a marble quarry planning for the pope a tomb of such previously unknown beauty that it would realize the human dream of perfection in art. The paintings by towering figures like Titian were sought without regard for subject or size, and as early as around 1520 works were commissioned "for no other reason than the desire of the patron to have, for example, *a Michelangelo:* that is to say, an example of his unique *virtù,* or his *art;* the subject, size or even medium do not matter" (John Shearman, *Mannerism*, 1967, p. 44).

The success of art increasingly "led to two results in the mind of the artist, . . . the concept of the work of art as an enduring virtuoso performance ('something stupendous') and the concept of the 'absolute' work of art" (Shearman, 44). More and more, artists asserted their social dignity and the importance of the artist and his work in cultural life. By the mid-seventeenth century the painter Salvator Rosa could boast to a would-be patron in a high romantic fashion that "I do not paint to enrich myself, but purely for my own satisfaction. I must allow myself to be carried away by the transports of enthusiasm and use my brushes only when I feel myself rapt" (Francis Haskell, *Patrons and Painters: A Study in the Relations between Italian Art and Society in the Age of the Baroque*, rev. ed., 1980, p. 22). Rosa refused to set a price for his pictures beforehand on the grounds that he did not know how his work was going to turn out. "I can see," said an agent, "that he would rather starve to death than let the quality of his produce fall in reputation" (23).

This elevated status and increased sense of dignity registered itself in various ways—self-portraits of the artist, for example, which were becoming commonplace; or the inclusion of art within the artwork, like the play within the play. Artist figures moved among their social superiors inside the work, like the poet in Shakespeare's sonnets and the painter in Velázquez's *Las Meninas*. Michelangelo painted an image in *The*

Last Judgment of himself sitting woefully holding his skin as the flayed Marsyas, who contested with the god of art, Apollo, on oboe against the flute and lost.

Nowhere does Renaissance art speak of its powers with more confidence than in *The Tempest,* where its greatest dramatic poet, figured as an exiled duke-magician instructing kings and their heirs on a desert island, proudly catalogues the accomplishments of his theatrical magic in a list that invokes with eerie memories the entire Shakespearean oeuvre:

> I have bedimm'd
> The noontide sun, call'd forth the mutinous winds,
> And 'twixt the green sea and the azur'd vault
> Set roaring war; to the dread rattling thunder
> Have I given fire, and rifted Jove's stout oak
> With his own bolt; the strong-bas'd promontory
> Have I made shake, and by the spurs pluck'd up
> The pine and cedar. Graves at my command
> Have wak'd their sleepers, op'd, and let 'em forth
> By my so potent art.
> (5.1.41)

In the play, Prospero's magic is the magic of the theater, his power the theatrical one of staging illusions that deeply move and teach his audience. Compared to the rough actualities of production and performance on the Bankside and even in Whitehall, the circumstances on the island stage of *The Tempest* are ideal for the exercise of Prospero's art. Whatever the playwright-magician conceives is performed instantly by Ariel and his "meaner fellows." The skill of Ariel's spirit-actors transfixes his noble audiences, renders them "spellbound," totally absorbed in the tableaux put before them, something a court dramatist must have dreamed of more often than he achieved it. And though the theatrical experiences are intensely real to the stage audiences, they are never in physical danger. The clothes which the travelers wear in the shipwreck are not stained by seawater and lose no color. The great storm and the destruction of the ship that seem catastrophic to them are only illusions, done and undone with the wave of a wand.

After experiencing wreck and immersion, the travelers straggle ashore in three groups at different points of the island, each thinking the others dead. Ferdinand, the young prince of Naples, comes out of the waves first, alone and utterly despairing, "Sitting on a bank, Weeping again the King my father's wrack." But then Prospero's art begins to work on him positively, as it already has negatively by stripping him of his social identity, and the music of Ariel's song creeps by him upon the waters, "Allaying both their fury and my passion With its sweet air" (1.2.393). The strange promise of the song means nothing to Ferdinand, but it is intriguing enough to get him up on his feet and moving off the beach toward the center of the island. Life is renewed at once by the sight of Prospero's daughter, Miranda (whose name means "wonder"), already in love with him, as he is with her, at first sight. But Prospero's and Shakespeare's art is moral as well as erotically stimulating, and Prospero freezes Ferdinand when he advances with sword uplifted—like the "hellish Pyrrhus" in *Hamlet*—and then puts him to the hard Calibanish work necessary to keep the world going.

Miranda has previously been instructed by her father, who recounted for her how they came to the island and what they experienced there. The engaged couple is later instructed in the necessity of premarital chastity, after which they are treated to a celebratory masque, "a most majestic vision," written by Prospero and executed by Ariel and his actors. The ballet is danced by country nymphs and swains, while the goddesses Juno and Ceres invoke the fertility of a bursting world of plenty to bless the plighted pair:

> Honor, riches, marriage-blessing,
> Long continuance, and increasing,
> Hourly joys be still upon you!
> (4.1.106)

At the play's end Ferdinand and Miranda are at the center of the island and are there revealed by the drawing of a theatrical curtain, engaged in a game of chess, a play within a play, life and marriage as an intricate artwork. At every stage of their journey the young lovers have been instructed and controlled by Prospero's art, arriving at a point where social life becomes an art form, a combination of game and theater.

If art in the Ferdinand and Miranda plot shows "virtue her feature," the Trinculo-Stephano plot shows "scorn her own image." These servants come to the island like some group of Conrad's thugs—say, Mr. Brown and his gang in *Victory*—debarking in paradise to pollute it. Intoxication is their passage into the illusion of the island, and they ride ashore on a cask of wine, which they begin to imbibe at once. They see not the wedding masque but Caliban's Hollywood adventure of killing Prospero, taking over the island, and raping Miranda. "O brave monster," says Stephano, "lead the way," as he introduces the monster to liquor and to the possibility of an anarchic freedom: "'Ban, 'Ban, Ca-Caliban, Has a new master, get a new man."

Prospero's art controls these comic conquistadors, and as they move on his cell planning gory mayhem, he has Ariel put in their way a heap of colorful theatrical costumes and gilded props. Much to Caliban's disgust,

Stephano and Trinculo immediately begin looting these tinsel fineries, losing sight of their plan. These are children, capable of viciousness but easily diverted and amused by any kind of gaudy spectacle and by fantasies of dressing up as great nobles and bold heroes. Theater is crude and its audiences often vulgar, and the playwright manages the appetites he encourages by fear, as well as pleasure. As the servants root around among the bright clothes, putting on a colorful coat, belting on a sword, trying on a plumed hat, Prospero calls up a pack of dogs. They come yelping and roaring through the woods, like some obligatory ending of a cheap crime movie, to chase Stephano, Trinculo, and Caliban through brambles and briars, driving them at last into a foul pond where they stand mired up to their chins in mud and rotting matter.

Prospero's art does not address these groundlings—"capable of nothing but inexplicable dumb shows and noise"—through their reason, but deters them from mischief by amusing them at times and frightening them at others. The groundlings are, however, apparently capable of learning something, for after he gets out of the pond Stephano mumbles, "Every man shift for all the rest, and let no man take care for himself" (5.1.256). But no real regeneration takes place, and Stephano and Trinculo are sent back, along with Caliban, to menial work once more, which they are glad to accept to escape the freedom which has been so disappointing and painful.

Theater shows the very age and body of the time his form and pressure to the court group gathered around Alonso: his counselor Gonzalo; Antonio, who usurped Prospero's dukedom; and Sebastian, brother to the king of Naples. The habits of life in all these older men are deeply ingrained, not easily changed, and the men are, with the exception of Gonzalo who is incurably innocent, inured to their guilt. The journey to the center of the island, which represents geographically the change of heart that Prospero's art works toward, is therefore more lengthy and painful for them, and their transformation less complete, than it is for Ferdinand. Alonso's immersion in the ocean of an indifferent and violent nature in the opening shipwreck, and the loss of his son, Ferdinand, overwhelm the king with despair, but Sebastian and Antonio are unmoved by the storm. The island is for them an opportunity to seize power. When Prospero's art produces before the famished wanderers a rich banquet and then causes it to disappear to remind them of their sins and to show them the necessity of "heart's sorrow," the effect is less than complete. Sebastian and Antonio refuse to acknowledge any guilt, and, drawing their swords, they race through the island striking at the air, like the passion-mad lovers pursuing one another in the forest of *A Midsummer Night's Dream*. Alonso, however, is more deeply touched, and the banquet tableau opens up a buried memory of the old wrong that he had done Prospero. But the beginnings of repentance at first drive him only deeper into despair and thoughts of suicide.

In their different ways these older courtiers are "spell-stopped," locked in their reactions to the knowledge of guilt that the island and Ariel's production has made them know and unable on their own to take the next step. In this condition they are brought to Prospero's cell at the center of the island where, in the words of the original stage direction, "all enter the circle which Prospero has made, and there stand charm'd" (5.1.56). In the "O" of this ultimate magical theater, Prospero makes himself known, forgives those who set him adrift so long ago, draws the curtain to reveal Miranda and Ferdinand, and reunites the royal family. Ariel's song symbolically foreshadows the transformation that is the central plot of all the Shakespearean comedies and tragedies and is the ultimate form of the sea change that Prospero's art works on the visitors to his theatrical island:

> Full fadom five thy father lies,
>   Of his bones are coral made:
> Those are pearls that were his eyes:
>   Nothing of him that doth fade,
> But doth suffer a sea-change
> Into something rich and strange.
>
> (1.2.397)

As usual in Shakespeare, not everyone shares in the regeneration and community that the end of the play brings. Antonio and Sebastian refuse the feast of life, speaking no word in the last scene until the end, when they recover their bravado enough to snarl at the offered forgiveness. The "thing of darkness," Caliban, remains unregenerate (to become the darling of late twentieth-century anticolonialists), and Prospero has to acknowledge his inescapable involvement with him. The art of theater can work its magic on some but not all, change some things but not everything. But for those who open themselves to its spell and allow their feelings to flow with it, it provides a renewal after all seems lost, a feeling of union with the rest of being, "a sea-change Into something rich and strange." Even the sailors on the king's ship who sleep out the time of the action are brought to the stage at the center of the island to share in the general reunion and forgiveness with which the play ends.

The artist-magician of *The Tempest* is the leading character in a sketchy version of "The Growth of a Poet's Mind," in which the artist is very much made, not born. Once Prospero was the great duke of Milan—non sanz droit?—athirst with a desire for knowledge, who avoided the practical responsibilities of life to bury himself in his study with his books. His magic is founded on the lore preserved in arcane volumes like the work of Paracelsus or "thrice-great Hermes," but the written word cannot alone give him the power to work his will upon the world by means of art. Experience finally gives him that power. Only after having been betrayed and deposed by his brother and set adrift in the open sea in a leaking boat with his infant daughter, Miranda, and only after living long years in exile on a desert island, working with Ariel and Caliban, does the scholar develop the magical skills of the artist. Only, that is, after going through the standard journey of Shakespearean tragedy, like that of Lear in his movement from the castle to the heath, is the artist able to work his magic. Theatrical magic is not, in the Shakespearean art myth, some supernatural gift but wisdom about life acquired only after long study and painful experience.

Prospero's art is not finally perfected until he encounters and masters those mirrors of the division in his own nature, the physical Caliban (body) and the delicate Ariel (fancy). But Prospero's ego-control of these two components of his art, sensual appetite and playful inventiveness, is never complete. In an artistic psychomachia, both body and spirit continue throughout the play to long for the freedom to live their own lives exempt from work in one case, confinement or limitation in the other. The education of the Shakespearean artist is no Wordsworthian election by higher powers, as in *The Prelude*—"I made no vows, but vows Were then made for me"—but a much more realistic and painful training involving hard study, disillusionment, isolation, and a painful process of learning how to master the basic powers out of which the creating reason, or the romantic imagination, makes art.

The purpose of art is never so unambiguous for Prospero as it would be for the romantic Wordsworth. In the first exercise of his art, the illusion of a shipwreck with which the play opens, the powers of the artist are used for the intensely personal end of revenge against those on board, Prospero's brother, Antonio, and Alonso, king of Naples, who set him and his daughter adrift in the open sea to die. And as Prospero uses his art to manipulate the feelings and manage the wanderings of the castaways throughout the play, his heart remains hard toward them. But when at the end of the play Ariel reveals the suffering of his old enemies, he is, like Lear in similar circumstances, made pregnant to good pity:

> Hast thou, which art but air, a touch, a feeling
> Of their afflictions, and shall not myself,
> One of their kind, that relish all as sharply
> Passion as they, be kindlier mov'd than thou
> art?
> Though with their high wrongs I am strook to
> th' quick,
> Yet, with my nobler reason, 'gainst my fury
> Do I take part. The rarer action is
> In virtue than in vengeance.
>
> (5.1.21)

Art, as Shakespeare depicts it, begins as a satiric art to hurt and instruct enemies, but ends in comic identification and sympathy with the audiences it manipulates.

If there is some piece of Shakespearean biography in this, the key is unfortunately lost forever, though it would be easy enough to contrive parallels. But art is longer than life, and in the Shakespearean view it apparently transforms its practitioners as well as its audiences, moving them from narrow purposes to larger understanding, and from self-serving interests to broadly shared humanitarian concerns.

The Tempest makes the proud humanistic claims of pleasing and instructing that were standard for the Renaissance. But immediately after boasting of the magical powers of his theater to work sea changes without risk to its audience, the magician-dramatist Prospero, like some medieval poet—Petrarch or Chaucer—writing his palinode, abjures his "rough magic," breaks and buries his staff, and "drowns" his book "deeper than did ever plummet sound" (5.1.56). Shakespeare, soon to leave the theater and return to Stratford, had made no arrangements to publish *his* book. More than half his plays remained unprinted until the 1623 folio published after his death. He had a mixed attitude toward theater, partly a proud insistence on its ability to get at the truth of things and partly a feeling of shame about the crudities and deceits of its methods. Whenever players appear as characters on his stage they are bumbling, like Bottom and company in *A Midsummer Night's Dream,* or lower-class and hammy, like the Wittenberg troupe in *Hamlet.* The limitations of theater are discussed openly in *Henry V,* written about 1599, where, at the height of Shakespeare's powers, the Chorus apologizes for a "bending author" and the "flat unraised spirits" who "force a play," "in a little room confining mighty men," on the "unworthy scaffold" of a "wooden O," where "time . . . numbers, and due course of things, . . . cannot in their huge and proper life Be . . . presented." The references here are to the public theater on the Bankside, but the concerns about the limitations of theatrical pretense would apply as well to theater at court, if not to the masques, then surely to the plays performed there on the temporary trestle stages erected at the end of the hall.

These uneasy feelings about the inadequacy of theatrical spectacles are still present in *The Tempest,* where even the great masque of Juno and Ceres is spoken of slightingly by its creator as no more than "some vanity of mine art," its characters only "spirits" who when the performance is over "are melted into air, into thin air." The play's flimsy pretense is easily destroyed by the appearance of the drunken servants, who lack the imagination to comprehend it. In the end, having held the stage for only a brief moment and then disappeared into the nothingness where all plays go after the performance is over, "the baseless fabric of this vision" becomes no more than an "insubstantial pageant faded," leaving not even a wisp of cloud behind to mark where and what it once was.

The greatest of the world's playwrights was apparently unable to shake off his knowledge that the theater even at its best was only greasepaint trumpery, magic in its most trifling sense of prestidigitation, a few words, some stock jokes, a couple of costumes, a prop or two, music, and a dance. Here for an illusory moment, then gone forever. But then, Prospero reminds us, the great world itself is in the long run little more substantial and enduring than the brief tinseled moment of the play:

> The cloud-capp'd tow'rs, the gorgeous palaces,
> The solemn temples, the great globe itself,
> Yea, all which it inherit, shall dissolve,
> And like this insubstantial pageant faded,
> Leave not a rack behind.
>
> (4.1.152)

Whitehall and Westminster endured longer than *The Tempest*'s two hours' traffic on the stage that evening in the palace in the late winter of 1613, when King James and his court watched the play as part of the wedding celebrations of Princess Elizabeth. But now these, too, have gone, leaving perhaps fewer traces behind—an empty banqueting hall, gossip about the king's sex life—than *The Tempest*. Our playwright was right: the transitoriness of the theater is its final comment upon the great globe itself and all that is in it. "All the world's a stage" was a familiar trope, and one that Shakespeare used often in his long career, and now he used it one last time to justify an art that had its force not in its permanence, as he had once boasted in Sonnet 55—"Not marble nor the gilded [monuments] Of princes shall outlast this pow'rful rhyme"—but in its evanescence.

As Prospero sailed away for Milan after breaking his staff and drowning his book, so Shakespeare about the time of *The Tempest* left a stage where he had performed for his royal patron for years and went back to the country town from which he came. It must have been one of the great moments of English theater when Prospero turned that night to the king and queen sitting in their State, their two remaining children beside them, and to the glittering court watching the performance, to speak one last time for the bending author and ask his royal patron for his release from service. Whatever transcendent claims his play may have made for his art, Shakespeare, like the professional court playwright he had become, deferentially asserted at the end no more than that during all these years he had sought only to amuse his royal patron and his court:

> Let me not,
> Since I have my dukedom got,
> And pardon'd the deceiver, dwell
> In this bare island by your spell,
> But release me from my bands
> With the help of your good hands.
> Gentle breath of yours my sails
> Must fill, or else my project fails,
> Which was to please.

Under the patronage of kings and their nobility, the arts flourished in the Renaissance, not as "art-for-art's-sake," but as a part of the process of legitimating the state and its monarchs. Architects built great palaces, artists painted portraits of the aristocracy, sculptors made equestrian statues, historians narrated the story of the nation, poets sang the praises of the kings in epic poetry, and theatrical designers and dramatists created spectacular performance settings for divine-right ideology. Although England lagged behind the Continent in fostering the arts, the Stuarts were extraordinarily sensitive to the uses of art for the purposes of the state, and after their arrival in England, the cultural budget increased many fold. Inigo Jones worked for King James as an architect and theatrical designer, while Shakespeare enjoyed the patronage of the earl of Southampton and in time became the king's official playwright. His sonnets offer an in-depth picture of the patronage relationship.

The Stuart court was in advance of the rest of Europe in its theatrical resources, and the public theaters of London provided the court with actors and playwrights of unparalleled ability. The skills of the architect-designer Inigo Jones transformed the Great Halls of the Stuart palaces into theaters of miraculous illusion. Shakespeare's Stuart plays are one of the great patronage oeuvres of the Age of Kings, comparable to such master works as Michelangelo's Medici Chapel at San Lorenzo in Florence, and the court paintings of Velázquez for the Spanish ruler, Philip IV.

Source: "The King and the Poet: *The Tempest,* Whitehall, Winter, 1613," in *Shakespeare, the King's Playwright: Theater in the Stuart Court, 1603-1613,* Yale University Press, 1995, pp. 150-69.

Death by Rhetorical Trope: Poetry Metamorphosed in *Venus and Adonis* and the Sonnets

Pauline Kiernan

Shakespeare's careful insistence that *Venus and Adonis* is 'the first heir of my invention' has been frequently explained away as the playwright's attempt to dismiss the worth of his dramatic achievements to date, fearful of offending the poem's dedicatee by a reference to his vulgar craft. According to this view, the narrative poems published in 1593 and 1594 become testimony to a quickly abandoned flirtation with literary, as distinct from dramatic, ambitions, and are taken to represent either a desire to begin a new career as a narrative poet or an enforced momentary departure from a lifelong commitment to dramatic art.[1]

The practical reason offered by most commentators that the poems were written in a period of enforced idleness when the theatres were closed, as a precaution against the plague, between August 1592 and the end of 1593 does not, of course, explain what kind of artistic motivations were occupying the writer's mind during their composition.[2] There has, however, been a tendency for critics to suppose that financial considerations were primary determinants in the choice of form and subject and this has, perhaps, helped to prevent us from exploring fully their precise significances as a dramatist's responses to Renaissance concerns with literary imitation. F. T. Prince, for example, seems happy to conclude that if we accept that these poems were written to help compensate for losses incurred by the theatre shutdown, 'we have an explanation both of why the rising young dramatist turned to "narrative" verse, and of why he chose first such a subject as that of Venus and Adonis'.[3] Shakespeare successfully gauged the taste of his readers by producing a risqué Ovidian romance he knew would be a best seller and, along with Marlowe, started the popular craze for erotic epyllion. All of which is probable, and embarrassing for those critics who have had trouble reconciling their image of the great artist happy to starve for his art with the idea of a commercial writer responding to market forces.[4] The problem that arises from this kind of righteous sensitivity is that it muddles critical judgement. Commentators have sought to find ways of defending the poem by concentrating on the beauty of the language and verse as if this will somehow compensate for the unseemly reason it was written, only to find themselves feeling uncomfortable with its rhetorical excesses.

It has long been recognized, if not always approvingly, that *Venus and Adonis* possesses a high degree of self-conscious artistry and elaborate rhetoric. Richard Wilbur concedes that its 'main and steadiest sources of pleasure' are 'its elaborate inventiveness, its rhetorical dexterity, its technical éclat', and in the next sentence regrets that 'mostly one is reacting to an ostentatious poetic performance' of 'artful variety'. F. E. Halliday complains that the stanzas are 'rigid with rhetorical constructions and studded with compound and decorative epithets', and the diction 'studiously artificial and "poetical"'. Robert Ellrodt thinks that "Through the poem the artist seems at once hesitant about tone and too confident in the power of rhetoric.'[5]

Richard Lanham has provided a helpful corrective to such discomfort with the poem's rhetorical artifice, in arguing that *Venus and Adonis* and *The Rape of Lucrece* 'are poems about rhetorical identity and the strategies of rhetorical style'. Shakespeare, he says, 'often describes and exemplifies at the same time; he writes about the form he writes in.'[6] I should like to pursue this point further and consider why the dramatist seems to have felt it important to conduct his interrogation of rhetorical poetics employing rhetorical strategies in a narrative form, and to prepare this written narrative poem for the press. Is there some further, and related significance in his choosing to foreground the literary and textual status of rhetorical poetry, and the medium of print to 'write about the form he writes in'?

Before we can begin to explore the ramifications of the dramatic consciousness working in a narrative, non-dramatic form, perhaps we need to look again at the problematic status of the statement that *Venus and Adonis* is the first heir of Shakespeare's invention, and try to work out a more satisfactory explanation than the 'dyer's hand' theory: the 'vulgar' playwright aspiring to coterie literary fame, which assumes a primary narrative impulse behind the poem at odds with an essentially dramatic creative urge.[7] Both the narrative poems have tended to be placed in a marginalized position in relation to the main body of Shakespeare's work, but even when critics have argued that the poems possess pivotal importance in his development as a dramatist, they have usually been content to examine their relation to the plays in terms of technical experimentation.[8]

The statement begins to invite a quite different reading if we can ignore—for the moment—questions of chronology, of whether or not it means the poem is a first composition or a first published work, and start by trying to take it at face value.[9] We would then have to ask different questions about this poem. Is it about origins? In what way does its author see it as being seminal? Is the dramatist announcing his intention, in this poem, to deliver an original self-created authority, uncontaminated by the seminal disorder of previous literary conceptions? If he regards it as the first heir of his invention, why does he choose an 'overhandled theme', and one, moreover, that has received an apparently definitive treatment by the classical poet with the greatest influence on the Renaissance, and which has itself engendered imitative texts? Spenser's treatment of the myth, for example, had been published as recently as 1590 when the first three books of *The Faerie Queene* appeared in print. If we now reinstate the importance of chronological considerations and assume, for our present purposes, that four history plays and three comedies precede the writing of *Venus and Adonis,* we may become yet more sceptical of taking the statement at any kind of literal level, but our refusal to do so is dependent upon a prior assumption that the author is aspiring to a specifically literary fame.[10] Confronted with the statement's stubborn insistence that it is there, uncharacteristically carefully prepared for publication and bearing its author's signature, loudly proclaiming his debut in print, we would seem to have conclusive evidence that the poem represents a new ambition to achieve recognition as a literary poet who would not want to draw attention to his presumed ignominious status as a dramatist. But what if we attend to the artistic concerns which the poem itself examines? What I want to argue is that in *Venus and Adonis* Shakespeare is conducting a highly self-conscious exploration of the nature of poetic identity, and of his own role as a dramatist in literary history.

That Shakespeare chose the consummate practitioner of rhetorical poetics to be the source inspiration for what he himself describes as this seminal moment of his career has, I suggest, a significance beyond that which the poem's criticism traditionally acknowledges.[11] That most imitators of Ovid in the Renaissance seem to have been primarily concerned with emulating the classical poet's wit and style and/or exploiting his amatory themes is borne out by criticism's use of the term 'Ovidian' (taking its cue from Francis Meres's famous comparison of Shakespeare and Ovid) as a convenient and loose definition of a poetic style to cover almost any example of mellifluous rhetoric and verbal wit, and often one, or more, or all of the following: self-conscious artistry, an ostentatious disregard for structural and formal narrative continuity, a particular tone of detachment, moral levity, psychological realism, titillating eroticism, and metamorphic transformation.[12]

But Shakespeare's narrative imitations of Ovid, I suggest, involve a complex set of responses, requiring a more carefully delineated definition of the term 'Ovidian', and less willingness to assume that his poems register the same kind of responses to the style and content of Ovid's work as the poems of his literary contemporaries do.[13] The most significant Ovidian presence which underlies *Venus and Adonis* is acting in response to certain, specific implications which its artistic and thematic concerns offered to a dramatist who is exploring questions of aesthetic theory and the workings of literary imitation; in particular, the self-proclaimed originality and immortality of the *Metamorphoses* and the way in which the poem explores the problematic relations of insubstantial image and corporeal substance.

. . . . .

Shakespeare's *Venus and Adonis* begins, as it were, where Ovid's story ends. The classical writer's story *ends* with Venus turning the *dead* body of Adonis into a flower. Shakespeare's poem *begins* with Venus turning the *living* body of Adonis into a flower.

In Ovid, Venus finds Adonis 'lying lifeless and weltering in his blood', and then tells his corpse that her grief shall have an 'enduring monument':

> 'luctus monimenta manebunt
> semper, Adoni, mei, repetitaque mortis imago
> annua plangoris peraget sumulamina nostri;
> at cruor in florem mutabitur.'
> (x. 725-8)

('My grief, Adonis, shall have an enduring monument, and each passing year in memory of your death shall give an imitation of my grief. But your blood shall be changed to a flower.')

She sprinkled the blood with sweet-scented nectar, and a flower of blood-red hue sprang up (732-5). The blood of Adonis is replaced by a symbol, an imitation (*simulamina*). In Shakespeare, Venus' first metaphor turns the flesh and blood of Adonis into a flower three times more beautiful than herself. This second stanza is packed with hyperbolic comparisons, her characteristic wooing mode throughout the poem. Shakespeare turns Ovid's happily compliant Adonis into a recalcitrant love object who refuses to mate with a poet who can offer only the praise of 'false compare' in 'strainèd touches' of derivative rhetoric:

> 'Thrice fairer than myself,' thus she began,
> 'The field's chief flower, sweet above
> compare;
> Stain to all nymphs, more lovely than a man,
> More white and red than doves or roses are:'
> (7-10)

The succeeding stanzas begin to suggest why such 'couplement[s] of proud compare' must be resisted. She threatens to smother him with kisses, make his lips red-sore, and drain them of their colour ('Making them red, and pale, with fresh variety'), so that a summer's day will seem but short: 'Being wasted in such time-beguiling sport' (21-4). 'Being' suggests that Adonis himself, as well as the day, will be 'wasted', spent, sapped of strength. Here, the narrator interrupts Venus to insist on the boy's organic corporeality and to mock the enervating effect of her metamorphic displacement which robs the human body of its energy and strength:

> With this she seizeth on his sweating palm,
> The precedent of pith and livelihood,
> And trembling in her passion, calls it balm.
>
> (25-7)

Prince's gloss on 'pith and livelihood' reads: 'strength and energy. "Pith" means "marrow", the full development of which signifies maturity and hence strength.'[14] What is being presented here is not the simple paradox of an immature, coldly chaste young virgin bearing what is traditionally thought of as the physical mark of sexual desire. The flesh that is sweating, which arouses Venus' desire and makes her flesh tremble with passion, prompts her to use a language which robs the object of her desire of the very organicism and physicality which has made it desirable, and which has set in motion an organic process in her own body. The biological movement of sweat coming through the pores of Adonis' flesh which, by definition, is subject to time and process and change, is arrested in a stopped momentum by the metaphor 'balm', and turned into a senseless, lifeless figure of speech.

It is a technique which is repeated throughout the poem. Two kinds of language are juxtaposed, placed in conflict with each other, to point up the contrast between a poetry which stresses corporeal substance and seeks to accommodate organic process, mutability, and time, so that the body may be summoned into something like an immediate physical presence; and a poetry which dematerializes flesh and blood and seeks to transcend time and change and therefore succeeds only in making the body absent, lost to the present. Here is the narrating voice again stressing the biological, dynamic process of Adonis' body to demonstrate how Venus' use of metaphor deprives fleshly existence of its vital principle:

> Panting he lies and breatheth in her face,
> She feedeth on the steam as on a prey,
> And calls it heavenly moisture, air of grace.
>
> (62-4)

Venus' rhetoric disembodies the body she desires: a metaphor has taken Adonis' breath away. But when this heavenly goddess praises her own body to Adonis, it is the sensuous warmth and life of her flesh which her words emphasize:

> Mine eyes are grey and bright and *quick* in turning.
> My beauty as the *spring* doth yearly *grow,*
> My *flesh* is *soft* and *plump,* my *marrow* burning.
> My smooth *moist* hand, were it with thy hand felt,
> Would in thy palm *dissolve,* or seem to *melt.*
>
> (140-4; my italics)

Fluidity and change, organic process, physical growth and renewal, all that she has removed from Adonis' body in the metaphor 'air of grace' are here brought into a visual and sensual immediacy. Several stanzas later, she accuses Adonis of being a lifeless image:

> 'Fie, lifeless picture, cold and senseless stone,
> Well-painted idol, image dull and dead,
> Statue contenting but the eye alone,
> Thing like a man, but of no woman bred!'
>
> (211-14)

But it is Venus who has turned Adonis' flesh and blood into a cold and senseless statue, she who has turned life into art. Ovid's story of Venus and Adonis is placed in a sequence in which an artist, prompted by a revulsion against the real bodies of women, creates a cold and senseless statue of his ideal woman's body. In the *Metamorphoses,* when Pygmalion becomes inflamed with desire for this semblance of a body, *simulati corporis* (x. 253), he prays to have a wife like his statue. And it is important to notice the precise use Ovid makes of his expressions of similitude and corporeal substance:

> 'si, di, dare cuncta potestis,
> sit coniunx, opto,' non ausus 'eburnea virgo'
> dicere, Pygmalion 'similis mea' dixit 'eburnae.'
>
> (x. 274-6)

> ('If ye, O gods, can give all things, I pray to have as wife—' he did not dare add 'my ivory maid,' but said, 'one like my ivory maid.')

But Venus, Ovid says, knew what the prayer really meant, and brings the statue to life. When Pygmalion returned from the altar of the goddess, he sought once again the 'image of his maid' (*simulacra suae petit ille puellae*) and, bending over the couch, he kissed her:

> visa tepere est;
> admovet os iterum, manibus quoque pectora temptat:
> temptatum mollescit ebur positoque rigore
> subsidit digitis ceditque, ut Hymettia sole
> cera remollescit tractataque pollice multas
> flectitur in facies ipsoque fit utilis usu.

dum stupet et dubie gaudet fallique veretur,
rursus amans rursusque manu sua vota
retractat.
corpus erat! saliunt temptatae pollice venae.
(281-9)

(She seemed warm to his touch. Again he kissed her, and with his hands also he touched her breast. The ivory grew soft to his touch and its hardness vanishing, gave and yielded beneath his fingers, as Hymettian wax grows soft under the sun and, moulded by the thumb, is easily shaped to many forms and becomes usable through use itself. The lover stands amazed, rejoices still in doubt, fears he is mistaken, and tries his hopes again and yet again with his hand. Yes, it was real flesh! The veins were pulsing beneath his testing finger.)

In Shakespeare, Venus' hand touches the malleable cheek of Adonis and turns active, fleshly warmth into a passive, cold whiteness:

Now was she just before him as he sat,
And like a lowly lover down she kneels;
With one fair hand she heaveth up his hat,
Her other tender hand his fair cheek feels:
His tend'rer cheek receives her soft
hand's print,
As apt as new-fall'n snow takes any dint.
(349-54)

The simile of the last line jars, as it is intended to. It demonstrates the mimetic inadequacy of figurative similitude by giving a particularly lame and inappropriate example of such literary poetic expression (the use of 'apt' here wittily reinforces the point). It is an example of how Shakespeare in this poem makes an implied criticism of the way the poetic written word turns everything which has life, warmth, and movement in its immediate presence into an iconographical stasis, irretrievably lost to the present. Adonis' life, in Venus' hands, becomes a dead, literary image so that the only progeny he will be capable of begetting is sterile rhetorical tropes. For a stanza later not just the cheek, but Adonis' hand has become a metaphor, then his whole body. The supplicating Venus kneeling before him like a lowly lover is now overpowering him. Adonis himself becomes an inaccessible original, trapped inside a literary device:

Full gently now she takes him by the hand,
A lily prison'd in a gaol of snow,
Or ivory in an alabaster band:
So white a friend engirts so white a foe.
(361-4)

A lily, or ivory—it does not matter which. Choose whatever tired trope comes to mind, and simply tack it on to the subject. A lily? That will do. The poem already has Venus turning Adonis into a cold, senseless statue: when her 'arms infold him like a band' he struggles to be gone, and she 'locks her lily fingers one in one', so that two lines later her linked arms become a 'circuit' of 'ivory pale' (225, 228, 230). Before that, she has described her encircling arms making Mars 'a prisoner in a red rose chain' (110). Adonis' cheek has just been turned into 'snow' so: 'A lily prison'd in a gaol of snow, / Or ivory in an alabaster band.'

So this is how rhetorical poetry gets written. Take a conceit from Spenser, a figure from Marlowe, a hyperbole from Lyly and Sidney, and the poem has begun. Turn hot, pulsating cheeks into a rose, compare them with the 'purple-coloured face' of the sun taking his leave of 'the weeping morn' (1-3).[15] Metamorphose the beloved into the field's chief flower whose superior beauty casts a 'stain' on all others (8, 9).[16] Say, as everyone else does, that the face is 'More white and red than doves or roses are' and there are your first two stanzas. But once you start you find you cannot stop. Make human sweat a 'balm' (27) and hot breath an 'air of grace' (64). Turn a blushing cheek into a 'crimson shame' and cold anger into something 'ashy pale' (76); tumescent female pudenda and pubic hair into 'Round rising hillocks, brakes obscure and rough' (237).[17] Make eyes 'two blue windows' up-heaved so that they may be compared to the sun at dawn (482-6).[18] Play with an extended metaphor which makes lips red sealing-wax and a thousand kisses the price of a human heart (511-22). Turn all that is red, which you make not red, but something else such as 'ruby-colour'd portal' or 'red morn' instead of a mouth, into white. But make sure you do not simply say white. Flesh can be a dove, a lily, white sheets, alabaster, or snow. What it cannot be is . . . flesh.

Take the human body and turn it into something being written in a poem, and the poet's writing hand seems to find itself involuntarily steeped in rhetorical dyes:

The forward violet thus did I chide:
'Sweet thief, whence didst thou steal thy
sweet that smells,
If not from my love's breath? The purple
pride
Which on thy soft cheek for complexion
dwells
In my love's veins thou has too grossly dyed.'
The lily I condemnèd for thy hand,
And buds of marjoram had stol'n thy hair;
The roses fearfully on thorns did stand—
One blushing shame, another white despair;
A third nor red nor white, had stol'n of both,
And to his robbery had annex'd thy breath,
But for his theft in pride of all his growth
A vengeful canker ate him up to death.

> More flowers I noted, yet I none could see
> But sweet or colour it had stol'n from thee.
>
> (Sonnet 99)[19]

Here, the Friend is made an original, a kind of seminary of all created forms and their substances, as he is in Sonnets 98 and 53. As Sonnet 98 insists: the lily's white and the deep vermilion in the rose were 'but figures of delight, / Drawn after you, you pattern of all those' (9-12). But Shakespeare exploits this sonneteering convention to introduce the idea that when the Friend is absent, the original of the world's beauty is inaccessible. The odour and hue of all the flowers means it must be summer—'Yet seem'd it winter still' (13)—and the Poet has to make do with looking at poor imitations of the original: 'and, you away, / As with your shadow I with these did play' (13-14).

If we pause now to examine Sonnet 98 in relation to Sonnet 53, we may begin to detect how Ovid's preoccupation with the relations of image and substance, unreal and real, helps to shape Shakespeare's exploration into the mysterious workings of poetry's rhetorical dyeing process both in the Sonnets and in *Venus and Adonis*. We may also begin to discover some further significance in why the forward violet is so firmly castigated in Sonnet 99. Here is Sonnet 53 quoted in full:

> What is your substance, whereof are you made,
> That millions of strange shadows on you tend?
> Since every one hath, every one, one shade,
> And you, but one, can every shadow lend:
> Describe Adonis, and the counterfeit
> Is poorly imitated after you;
> On Helen's cheek all art of beauty set,
> And you in Grecian tires are painted new:
> Speak of the spring and foison of the year,—
> The one doth shadow of your beauty show,
> The other as your bounty doth appear;
> And you in every blessèd shape we know:
> In all external grace you have some part,
> But you like none, none you, for constant heart.

This seems to be peculiarly responsive to the exactness of Ovid's expressions of corporeal substance and false semblance, and their problematic relations to individual identity. In Ovid's story of Narcissus and Echo, Narcissus *spem sine corpore amat, corpus putat esse, quod umbra est,* falls in love with that which is *imaginis umbra . . . nil habet ista sui* (*Met.* iii. 417-35). He falls in love with that which is but the shadow of a reflected form and has no substance of its own. Ingram and Redpath's gloss on shadows in lines 2 and 4 of Sonnet 53 reads: 'Here . . . presumably not *umbrae,* in which colour, texture and detail are absent, but *imagines,* as the examples in lines 5ff show, though the phrase "on you tend" would more naturally apply to *umbrae.*'[20] But if the central idea of this sonnet is approached with Ovid's extremely precise sense of something doubly unreal in mind, we can see that it is *because* the Friend's substance, the 'colour, texture and detail' of his living body are absent in *umbrae,* and because all other beauty is but a bodiless semblance of the Friend's substance, that the word *shadows* is used. The shadows are bodiless, false illusions of the real thing, like the reflection in the pool upon which Narcissus gazes and which Ovid calls *imaginis umbra* and *sine corpore.*

Similarly, in answer to Ingram and Redpath's question about the use of the word *shade* at line 3—'Does the word here mean *umbrae* or *imago,* or neither with any precision? It is hard to say'—I would want to argue that each shade is both *umbra* and *imago* in the Ovidian sense of it being a likeness of a form in which the body is absent. We need to reassess criticism's traditional view that in this sonnet, Shakespeare is deliberately employing such vocabulary without precise connotation and comprehensiveness.[21] When we examine just a few of the ways in which Ovid, throughout the *Metamorphoses,* exploits the words *umbra, imago,* and *corpus* to explore distinctions between that which has corporeality and is real, and that which is without bodily substance and is unreal, it becomes clear that Shakespeare's use of substance, shadow, and shade, far from being vague and undelineated, is both precise and paradoxical in the strictly Ovidian sense found in the Latin which describes Narcissus's falling in love with that which is *imaginis umbra* and Phaethon being puffed up with *imagine falsi* which has the precise connotation of something doubly unreal. Ovid's Venus, we remember, replaces the blood of Adonis with a *simulamina,* an imitation of her grief, an *imago* of his dead body. Pygmalion asks for a wife who is like his *false semblance* of a body (*Met.* iii. 434-5; i. 754; x. 253).

It is significant that in Sonnet 53 nature's organic renewal process and its fruitful progeny, 'the spring and foison of the year', are made but shadows of the Friend's beauty (9-11). As Ingram and Redpath point out, 'the antithesis is not between Spring and Autumn simply as seasons of the year, but between the *active* properties which characterise them, *the concreteness of association* being characteristically Shakespearean. The "spring" is freshness and vitality, as the "foison" is abundance of produce' (my italics).[22]

If the Friend's beauty is the source of nature's beauty and its powers of renewal and fecundity, it must not be allowed to fade until its life-giving essence is distilled by something that will ensure its perpetual presence and immortality. Nature cannot do this: though it is summer when the Friend is absent, 'Yet seem'd it winter still'. The flowers are merely reminders of what is absent, and the world has to make do with a semblance of the original: ' . . . and, you away, / As with your *shadow* I with these did play' (Sonnet 98, 13-14; my italics). Indeed, nature's flowers are castigated for being passive dissipators of the Friend's strength and vital energy, and the repeated insistence in Sonnet 99 that the conventions of poetic similitude and comparison are pointless because the Friend's beauty cannot be compared to anything but itself takes on a new and sinister significance.

In Sonnet 21 another Muse is described as 'Making a couplement of proud compare / With sun and moon, with earth and sea's rich gems, / With April's first-born flowers and all things rare' (5-7), and is accused of merely repeating what others have said before: 'And every fair with his fair doth rehearse' (4). But the other poet's praise becomes an act of double theft. He steals someone else's words and because such praise has already been bestowed on other subjects, it robs the subject of present praise of his individuality and true worth—something which Adonis seems particularly enraged by when he condemns Venus' 'device in love / That lends embracements unto every stranger' (789-90). This is why the Poet keeps insisting that his verse is 'so barren of new pride, / So far from variation or quick change', why he keeps 'invention in a noted weed' (Sonnet 76, 1-2, 6), and why the Friend must be 'most proud of that which I compile, / Whose influence is thine and born of thee' (Sonnet 78, 9-10).

The 'rival' poet in Sonnet 79 is accused of robbing the Friend in order to give back what the Friend already possesses: 'Yet what of thee thy poet doth invent, / He robs thee of, and pays it thee again . . . beauty doth he give, / *And found it in thy cheek'* (Sonnet 79, 7-8, 10-11; my italics). The 'true plain words' of the Poet are explicitly contrasted with the 'gross painting' of other poets:

> yet when they have devis'd
> What strainèd touches rhetoric can lend,
> Thou, truly fair, wert truly sympathiz'd
> In true plain words by thy true-telling friend;
> And their gross painting might be better us'd
> *Where cheeks need blood*—in thee it is abus'd
> (Sonnet 82, 9-14; my italics)

Such poets, then, are like the violet chided in Sonnet 99 who is 'forward', which suggests precocious, presumptuous, but also flowering before its time; forced, because fed on the blood and breath it has stolen from the fecund source of the world's organic growth. The violet has 'too grossly dyed' (5) the fresh blood flowing through the veins of the Friend's cheek, and what is being suggested here is that the violet causes the Friend's blood to 'die'—to stop flowing through the veins, with the same enervating effect of the rhetorical dyes in which the rival poets *grossly* paint the beauty of the Friend in Sonnet 82. Ingram and Redpath gloss 82's 'gross painting': 'In addition to the obvious sense of "laying it on thick" . . . there may also be a reference here to "larded" rhetoric. Cf. "Colours" = rhetorical figures.'[23] This idea that rhetoric's gross painting stops the life flow of the human body is made explicit in Sonnet 83 which begins: 'I never saw that you did painting need, / And therefore to your fair no painting set' (1-2). There is more glory, the Poet says, in his silence, 'being dumb' (9-10), because when the 'rival' poets try to capture the vital presence of the Friend's beauty, their painting 'kills' it:

> For I impair not beauty, being mute,
> When others would give life and bring a tomb.
> *There lives more life* in one of your fair eyes
> Than both your poets can in praise devise.
> (11-14; my italics)

In Sonnet 99 all the flowers of nature are implicated in the life-destroying theft. 'The roses fearfully on thorns did stand', because conscious of their guilty thefts, but the pink rose is the most guilty because not showing shame like the red, nor despair like the white, it steals the Friend's breath as well as his colour ('And to his robbery had annex'd thy breath', 11). The pink rose is punished for robbing a living human organism of its life-force: 'But for his theft in pride of all his growth / A vengeful canker ate him up to death' (12-13), so that, in the words of Sonnet 54, nothing of the original vital essence can now be distilled.

It is significant that the Sonnet which claims that the Poet's verse will immortalize the Friend's truth and beauty associates the life-preserving effect of the verse with the sweet odour of the rose, whose essence may be preserved when the rose perishes, in contrast to the canker blooms which have no perfume, to make a distinction between that which has colour and an essence which can be made to live on after death, and that which has 'as deep a dye' (Sonnet 54, 5), but nothing that can be made to last once it has decayed. The verse of the 'rival' poets is like the canker bloom: 'But for their virtue only is their show / They live unwoo'd and unrespected fade— / Die to themselves' (Sonnet 54, 9-11). The 'rival' poets of Sonnet 82 cannot make the Friend live after death: their rhetorical dyes 'kill' him while he still is alive. Their verse is like the pink rose which, in feeding on the Friend's flesh and blood, deprives him of the very thing which could ensure the survival and prepetuation of his vital essence (Sonnet 99). The verse of these other poets is like both the canker, the pale pink dog-rose, whose colour is a short-lived display and has no potentially enduring essence, and the canker-worm which eats up its blossoms (Sonnet 54). The 'rival' poets, then, eat up the Friend 'to death', like the vengeful canker-worm who eats up the pink rose 'to death', because the shameless pink rose had robbed the Friend of his colour and his breath (Sonnet 99). Being both canker and canker-worm, the other poets are responsible for the decay of their own verse.

This, then, is the price poets have to pay for turning flesh and blood into a rhetorical trope. This is why the Poet keeps defending the 'poverty' and 'silence' of his Muse, insisting that his 'argument all bare is of more worth / Than when it hath my added praise beside!' (Sonnet 103, 3-4). 'I think good thoughts, whilst others write good words . . . In polish'd form of well-refinèd pen' (Sonnet 85, 5, 8). Throughout the Sonnets which ridicule the painted rhetoric of other poets, we find an almost obsessive concern with the idea of *writing, pen, quill, pencil* being repeatedly used to suggest that it is the colours of rhetoric *written down* which deserve the greatest condemnation.[24] It is a 'modern quill' ('*modern:* "commonplace, trite, ordinary", as always in Shakespeare') which comes too short of the Friend's worth in Sonnet 83, where, as we have seen, the writers who 'would give life . . . bring a tomb'.[25] Transcription thus becomes equated with death of the subject, with destroying life. The only way to summon that life into presence is to compare it to nothing else, since it exceeds the 'barren tender' (fruitless offering) of a poet's debt (Sonnet 83, 3-4), and simply say 'you are you':

> Who is it that says most which can say more
> Than this rich praise,—that you alone are you,
> In whose confine immurèd is the store
> Which should example where your equal grew?
>
> (Sonnet 84, 1-4)

Ingram and Redpath think that the image in lines 3-4 here 'certainly seems to be biological rather than that of a treasury. The sense would be that the only stock from which one could learn under what conditions a person of the Friend's excellence could develop is to be found in the Friend himself.'[26] The only way we can understand how the Friend developed his unique excellence is to attend only to what we see now: the biological physical presence of what he *is*. This is why we find, in *Venus and Adonis,* so many passages itemizing parts of the body in 'true plain words': why, for example, we find a conventional extended metaphor being paradoxically employed for a bare, literal description of the different parts of Adonis' face:

> Even as an empty eagle, sharp by fast,
> Tires with her beak on *feathers, flesh and bone,*
> Shaking her wings, devouring all in haste,
> Till either gorge be stuff'd or prey be gone:
> Even so she kiss'd *his brow, his cheek, his chin,*
> And where she ends she doth anew begin.
>
> (55-60; my italics)

When Venus feigns death, Adonis 'wrings her *nose,* he strikes her on *the cheeks,* / He bends her *fingers,* holds her *pulses* hard, / He chafes her *lips*' (475-7; my italics). It is why, in the poem's description of the horse, each part of the animal's body is carefully delineated:

> Round-hoof'd, short-jointed, fetlocks shag and long,
> Broad breast, full eye, small head, and nostril wide,
> High crest, short ears, straight legs, and passing strong,
> Thin mane, thick tail, broad buttock, tender hide:
> Look what a horse should have he did not lack,
> Save a proud rider on so proud a back.
>
> (295-300)

Dowden, in his famous comment on this passage, spoke truer than he knew when he asked with heavy sarcasm: 'Is it poetry or a paragraph from an advertisement for a horse sale? It is part of Shakespeare's study of an animal and he does his work thoroughly.'[27] Touchstone could have told him that the 'truest poetry (that which is most poetic) is the most feigning' (*As You Like It,* III. iii. 16). Such a reversal of the poetry of false compare is placed in the poem in order to demonstrate that the poet who can say a horse is a horse is a horse is the one who tells the truth. As the Poet of the Sonnets says: 'he that writes of you, if he can tell / That you are you, so dignifies his story' (Sonnet 84, 7-8), unlike Venus who, far from making Adonis 'the onlie begetter' of her poetry, succeeds only in saying that Adonis is everything but *himself.* She has no power to preserve Adonis' distilled self because like the pink rose in Sonnet 99 she feeds on his flesh and blood. It is the threat of the self being overwhelmed in a plethora of derivative rhetorical tropes that Adonis, in refusing union with Venus, is trying to resist. When she traps him within her 'circuit of ivory pale' so that he becomes 'a lily . . . / Or ivory in an alabaster band', the now inaccessible original essence that was Adonis has been turned into a literary figure borrowed from a prior literary text, so that Adonis is no longer *Adonis* as an ideal poetry would present him—a unique, original essence capable of being perpetually renewed like the rose essence which endures after the rose perishes, but the Hermaphroditus of Ovid's poem, trapped in Salmacis' enervating pool, flashing with gleaming body through the transparent flood, *ut eburnea si quis / signa tegat claro vel candida lilia vitro* (*Met.* iv. 354-5), 'as if one should encase ivory figures or white lilies in translucent glass'. Venus is like the rival poet who 'every fair with his fair doth rehearse'. She merely repeats what other poets have written and deprives Adonis of his individuality and vital presence.

But Shakespeare's use of Ovid here is characteristically more complex than even this. Adonis, in Venus' entrapping and paralysing embrace, becomes Ovid's Hermaphroditus to provide a paradigm for the poet confronted by a seductive enervating other which threatens to overwhelm, enfeeble, and emasculate his fertile powers of invention:

> Was it the proud full sail of his great verse,
> Bound for the prize of all-too-precious you,
> That did my ripe thoughts in my brain
> inhearse,
> Making their tomb the womb wherein they
> grew?
> Was it his spirit, by spirits taught to write
> Above a mortal pitch, that struck me dead?
> No, neither he, nor his compeers by night
> Giving him aid, my verse astonishèd:
> He, nor that affable familiar ghost
> Which nightly gulls him with intelligence,
> As victors of my silence cannot boast,—
> I was not sick of any fear from thence:
> But when your countenance fill'd up his
> line,
> Then lack'd I matter; that enfeebl'd mine.
> (Sonnet 86)

The Poet's verse, ripe for birth, dies unborn, is forever buried in the womb where it was conceived. Why? The Poet takes eight of the sonnet's ten remaining lines to say what has *not* aborted this embryo. But we find that the false starts and changes of direction in this sonnet lead us to believe that it is the other poet's verse which killed the Poet's embryonic thoughts. We do not know *as we read* lines 5 and 6 that the answer to the questions in lines 1 to 6 will be 'No'. We are made to imagine the Poet's verse dying before it is born, buried by the verse of another poet which is itself an imitative text ('his spirit, by spirits taught to write') and this remains in our minds even after line 7's refutation 'No, neither he', because 'compeers by night' in that line has the effect of reinforcing the image of the *spirits* in line 5. The other poet, aided by *compeers,* other books or their authors, and/or a coterie of literary associates has *astonished,* paralysed, his verse into silence.[28] Trope begets trope, literary text begets literary text. Line 12 obliterates all that has preceded it, so that the concluding couplet can reveal what has really struck him dead. But the couplet does not fully contradict all that has been said before. The Friend's countenance 'fill'd up his line' takes us back to 'the proud full sail of his great verse' in the opening line, and we imagine the Friend's countenance swelling the sails of the other poet's verse. 'Then lack'd I *matter*' faintly recalls, by contrast, 'his *spirit,* by spirits taught to write', and the Friend's countenance is something being written in a poem which itself is swelled with the written words of other poets. By the time the Poet comes to write his verse, there is no substance of the Friend left for him to write about. The line which would have been able to bring 'all-too-precious you' into being cannot now be born.

That is why Shakespeare's Venus must be punished, why Adonis resists her enfeebling rhetoric, is determined not to be crushed in the huge expanse of her bosom ('Fie, fie, fie . . . you crush me; let me go', 611), which is the rhetorical excess of other poets and their books, the surfeit of literary texts which 'fill up' the space where new poetic creation should take place. Venus is denied any part in Adonis' metamorphosis because she has been made to function as a poet whose 'gross painting' turns life into art, by robbing flesh and blood, as the forward violet and pink rose steal the colour and odour of the Friend's beauty. Her verse cannot bring fleshly existence into an eternal present. She cannot renew him because all along her rhetoric has turned its object into a literary figurative device, as Adonis well knows: 'I hate not love, but your device in love' (789); and she must make way for the dramatist who alone can reverse the flesh-and-blood-into-symbol process of such sterile rhetoric. Venus' kisses will destroy time itself, 'A summer's day will seem an hour but short, / Being wasted' (23-4). But it is time itself that Adonis needs if he is to reach maturity with his fertility intact. Venus repeatedly tries to persuade him that it is his duty to procreate and fructify the world when it is her persuasion, her rhetoric itself, which is threatening to emasculate his potential fecundity. The sterile fate which she prophesies will befall him if he does not mate with her, is precisely what will happen to him if he does:

> 'What is thy body but a swallowing grave,
> Seeming to bury that posterity,
> Which by the rights of time thou needs must
> have,
> If thou destroy them not in dark obscurity?
> . . . . .
> So in thyself thyself art made away.'
> (757-63)

But, as her subsequent list of conceits testifies once again, it is Venus' self-propagating proliferation of figurative devices that has 'made' Adonis 'away'. Adonis resists what by this stage of the poem have become heavily ironic entreaties to 'Be prodigal' in 'despite of fruitless chastity' (755, 751), because copulation with her will prove a fruitless union. It is her rhetoric, which, as Adonis points out, is merely a sterile imitation of another poet's words, that must be rejected if he is to produce a fertile language of his own. Venus warns him that his body and all the life that it is capable of reproducing will be buried in a grave of his body's own making, which is '"Foul cank'ring rust the hidden treasure frets, But gold that's put to use more gold begets"' (767-8). Adonis recognizes Venus' last metaphor as deriving from another text. She has turned him into Marlowe's Hero and once again, he is tossed on to the vast stock-pile of literary convention to be buried in what is his real *swallowing grave:* '"Nay then," quoth Adon, "you will fall again / Into your idle over-handled theme"' (769-70).[29] We might note in passing how this allusion to the interchangeability of Renaissance poetic texts is associated with the idea of 'foul cank'ring' which 'frets', *eats away,* 'hidden treasure', in the way that the pink rose of Sonnet 99 is eaten away by the canker.

The Adonis who keeps disappearing under the weight of Venus' rhetorical glut is allowed to re-emerge to utter an impassioned critique of her kind of poetry, and by one revealing word, explains why the reader of Shakespeare's poem is so easily seduced by it—such poetry is *bewitching.* Adonis must not allow the goddess's words to enter his ear, fearing contamination:

> 'If love have lent you twenty thousand tongues,
> And every tongue more moving than your own,
> Bewitching like the wanton mermaid's songs,
> Yet from my heart the tempting tune is blown:
> For know, my heart stands armed in mine ear,
> And will not let a false sound enter there;'
>
> (775-80)

He knows that the 'false sounds' of Venus' poetry will not be true to *him,* because they are used on everyone else:

> 'I hate not love, but your device in love
> That lends embracements unto every stranger.
> You do it for increase.'
>
> (789-91)

Breeding with Venus promises only an infinite proliferation of the eloquent 'figures' beloved by the Renaissance rhetoricians: the increase they meant by the term *copia.*[30] If, at this point in the poem, readers begin to find Adonis' expressions of earnest refusal reaching their most poetically dull, perhaps it is because we are being admonished, too. If we find ourselves thinking that Venus is entertaining, and Adonis too often a 'killjoy', then the goddess has succeeded in bewitching us. We have been made to experience for ourselves the irresistible allure of rhetoric's flattering colours. We are preferring painted rhetoric to true plain words: Adonis' distinction between love and lust is a plea for poetic chastity which can produce a perpetually renewing truth with the power to bring forth new life after the surfeit of rhetorical images has gorged itself to death.

> 'Love's gentle spring doth always fresh remain,
> Lust's winter comes ere summer half be done;
> Love surfeits not, lust like a glutton dies;
> Love is all truth, lust full of forged lies.'
>
> 'More I could tell, but more I dare not say:
> The text is old, the orator too green.
> Therefore in sadness, now I will away;
> My face is full of shame, my heart of teen,
> Mine ears that to your wanton talk attended,
> Do burn themselves, for having so offended.'
>
> (801-10)

In trying to express the difference between a poetry which is bred by a union with the rhetorical past which is doomed to perish, and a poetry which is self-created and uncontaminated by such rhetoric and which will, therefore, 'always fresh remain', *Venus and Adonis* seems to be going beyond a pointing to the inadequacy of rhetorical strategies to reproduce an object, to consider what means a poet might use to ensure that his invention possesses its own powers of self-renewal. Adonis demands to be allowed to ripen in his own good time:

> 'Who plucks the bud before one leaf put forth?
> If springing things be any jot diminish'd,
> They wither in their prime, prove nothing worth.'
>
> (416-18)

'If the first heir of my invention prove deformed,' William Shakespeare writes in the poem's dedication, 'I shall be sorry it had so noble a godfather, and never after ear so barren a land, for fear it yield me still so bad a harvest.' The truly dangerous threat which Venus poses is that of the proud full sail of the 'rival' poet in Sonnet 86 which buries the ripe thoughts in the Poet's brain 'Making their tomb the womb wherein they grew'. Adonis is identified as both poet and poem. He is the poet's embryonic poem 'springing', growing, in the creative womb which Venus is threatening to 'diminish' by stunting its growth. But he is also the poet trying to protect the embryonic heir of his invention from anything that might cause it to be deformed at birth. Venus' rhetoric, like the 'gross painting' of the 'rival' poets in the Sonnets, who 'would give life' but 'bring a tomb', robs him of the biological, organic processes needed for the creation of new life. Her 'tedious' song that outwore the night because spent with 'idle sounds resembling parasites, / Like shrill-tongu'd tapsters answering every call, / Soothing the humour of fantastic wits' (841, 848-50), is merely second-hand rhetoric, stolen from other literary texts, and used indiscriminately to lavish praise on everyone.[31] Her 'compeers by night' have given her aid, taught her to write her 'idle over-handled theme' in the 'strainèd touches rhetoric can lend' 'unto every stranger'.[32] The neighbouring caves 'Make verbal repetition of her moans; / Passion on passion deeply is redoubled.' Twenty times she cries '"Woe, woe," / And twenty echoes twenty times cry so' (831-4). The night resounds with a cacophony of shrill parasitic sounds and becomes a nightmare vision of poetry's incestuous interchangeability. Union with Venus would produce only one more parasitic echo of other poets' words, and merely add to the seminal contaminated mess of previous literary conceptions.

> If there be nothing new, but that which is
> Hath been before, how are our brains beguil'd,
> Which labouring for invention bear amiss
> The second burthen of a former child!
> (Sonnet 59, 1-4)

The image of pregnancy and birth has remarkably close affinities with the way Shakespeare describes *Venus and Adonis* in the dedication to Henry Wriothesley, and perhaps we can now suggest why. We might begin by noting that Sonnet 59 opens with a conditional *If* to suggest that novelty is not a certain impossibility. But *if* repetition is all that a poet can hope for, how are our brains beguiled when they labour for invention, the first process of rhetoric defined in the Renaissance as 'the finding out of apt matter . . . a searching out of things true or things likely; the which may reasonably set forth a matter'.[33] Shakespeare uses 'beguile' elsewhere to mean: (1) to deprive or rob of; (2) to cheat, disappoint (hopes); (3) to divert attention in some pleasant way from (anything disagreeable); to while away (time); and (4) to disguise.[34] In this sonnet, the primary sense is of disappointed hopes, being cheated or deluded, but perhaps there is also a suggestion of the brain being robbed of something *and* of sense 3, whiling away time, which, incidentally, is a Shakespearian neologism, and could therefore be a subtle refutation of the idea that there is nothing new, reinforcing the conditional 'If'. In *Venus and Adonis,* as we have seen, the goddess tells the youth that her kisses will make the summer's day but short, 'Being wasted by such time-beguiling sport', which the poem presents as a threat, something that will *rob* Adonis of his vital strength and energy.

The image in Sonnet 59 of labouring to carry out the first of rhetoric's five processes, *inventio,* becomes, as we reach *bear,* an image of pregnancy, and imaginative creation is now the dominating sense of *invention,* so that at *amiss* we are holding in our minds the idea of an embryo growing in some way imperfectly inside the womb. At line 4 the sense of the pain of a heavily pregnant womb is doubled by the word *second* but then we are confronted with the mental exertion of trying to grasp the sense of 'The *second* burthen of a *former* child' (my italics). Ingram and Redpath think that without the word 'amiss' the sense would be perfectly clear: '"If everything is merely a repetition of what has happened before; how our brains are deluded, when they toil and labour to give birth to new matter, and only bring forth what has been created before!"' They go on to ask: 'But what is the sense of the word "amiss", modifying "bear"? If we took it to mean "wrongly", then "bear amiss" might suggest an abortion, which clearly does not fit the sense, since if there is an exact repetition, either the new birth is not an abortion or the old one was also.'[35]

But what if we imagine the embryo being deformed as it develops in the womb because there is not enough space there for its body to be perfectly formed? 'If springing things be one jot diminish'd,' Adonis says, 'They wither in their prime, prove nothing worth.' Is the 'former child' the heir of some other poet's invention, squashing the embryo, restricting and stunting its growth, so that what is being carried in the womb is an unwelcome extra weight, a second burden which should not be there? What is being borne 'amiss', *wrongly,* is this second burden which itself was once a child. The sense would then be: 'If everything is a repetition of all that has been before, how are our brains deluded, when they try to originate new matter, and find that their thoughts are being stifled by the oppressive weight of all that has been created before. Our brains, being filled up with what has already been reproduced by others, are deprived of the means of creating anything that *is.*'

Perhaps what is being suggested in this quatrain is the idea of a poet trying to create a new and original poetry in biological process by making that which is *is,* and not lost to the present, but who is confronted by the *seminal* mass of literary imitation where nothing new can be born because that which is hath been before. The Poet tries to bring something into being for the first time, but before it can get born it is crushed under the weight of previous creations. The Poet then has to carry a double weight in the creative womb: his own embryonic thoughts, and the second burden, another poet's poem which was once a child being borne in another womb. When it is time for the new child to be born it has been deformed, like the Poet's verse in Sonnet 86—enfeebled and paralysed.

When Adonis finally manages to break from Venus' paralysing embrace, he runs 'homeward through the dark laund' (813). *Laund* is an open space of untilled ground in a wood, land that has not yet been cultivated for the raising of crops—virgin ground where new seeds can be sown uncontaminated by previous crops. There, in the 'pitchy night', Adonis is safe from this predatory wooer. The night did 'Fold in the object that did feed her sight' (821-2). Now it is Venus' turn to be paralysed:

> Whereat amaz'd, as one that unaware
> Hath dropp'd a precious jewel in the flood,
> Or 'stonish'd as night-wand'rers often are,
> Their light blown out in some mistrustful
> wood:
> Even so confounded in the dark she lay,
> Having lost the fair discovery of her way.
> (823-8)

In the words of Sonnet 86, the proud full sail of Venus' great verse, bound for the prize of all-too-precious Adonis, is astonished. She has never been capable of saying to him 'You alone are you', but has kept turning him into a precious jewel—decorporealized inert matter. But the poem now reverses the effect of those 'glutton-like' kisses insatiably feeding on his flesh and blood to 'draw his lips' rich treasure dry' (548, 552), when she finds Adonis' blood on the boar and is made to confront the stark physicality of a 'frothy mouth bepainted all with red, / Like milk and blood mingled both together' (901-2). Venus had turned the living flesh and blood of Adonis into an image 'dead and dull' when she steeped him in rhetoric's colours to make him 'too grossly dyed'. We remember how the sweat on Adonis' palm made her body tremble with passion, the biological process of his body setting in motion an organic change in her own, and how her metaphor 'balm' stopped time, process, and change and turned organic substance into a senseless figure of speech. Now she must be made to suffer the sight of the truly gross dye of real blood, and her 'gross painting' poetic techniques must be replaced by a poetic language which can accommodate time, process, and change. The narrating voice takes over to demonstrate how poetry can be made to *reinstate* the body in all its sensuous and organic power. The language which tells us that the blood which Venus sees makes her body tremble with fear becomes an active moving process summoning the goddess's fear into a physical presence: 'A second fear through all her sinews spread' (903).

> A thousand spleens bear her a thousand ways,
> She treads the path that she untreads again;
> Her more than haste is mated with delays
> Like the proceedings of a drunken brain.
> (907-10)

It has the power to move nature's beasts into an immediate present. Here is the narrator's true, plain words describing the animals Venus encounters:

> And here she meets another sadly
> scowling,
> To whom she speaks, and he replies with
> howling.
> When he hath ceas'd his ill-resounding noise,
> Another flap-mouth'd mourner, black and
> grim,
> Against the welkin volleys out his voice;
> Another and another answer him,
> Clapping their proud tails to the ground
> below,
> Shaking their scratch'd ears, bleeding as
> they go.
> (917-24)

Venus finds terrible omens in 'these sad signs', and is prompted to 'exclaim on death' (925-30). She 'chides' death:

> Grim-grinning ghost, earth's *worm,* what dost
> thou mean,
> To *stifle beauty and to steal his breath?*
> Who when he liv'd, his breath and beauty set
> Gloss on the *rose,* smell to the *violet.*
> (933-6; my italics)

But it is Venus who stifled Adonis' beauty and stole his breath when he lived, just as the forward violet and the pink rose, chided in Sonnet 99, robbed the Friend of his beauty and breath.

When Venus finds Adonis dead, the eyes which had fed on his living flesh and blood are unable to bear the sight of the substance her kind of rhetoric has turned into lilies and roses, doves and ruby-coloured portals, red sealing-wax and snow:

> her eyes as murder'd with the view,
> Like stars asham'd of day, themselves
> withdrew.
> Or as the snail, whose tender horns being hit,
> Shrinks backward in his shelly cave with pain,
> And there all smother'd up in shade doth sit,
> Long after fearing to creep forth again:
> So at this bloody view her eyes are fled
> Into the deep dark cabins of her head.
> (1031-8)

The punishment for turning the human body into a literary stylistic trick must be a *prolonged* torture. When she opens her eyes again the cruel light shows the wound in shocking and vivid immediacy. Rhetoric's colours are now made to reinstate corporeal substance to stress what Venus' eyes must be opened to:

> And being open'd threw unwilling light
> Upon the wide wound that the boar had
> trench'd
> In his soft flank, whose wonted lily-white

With purple tears that his wound wept, was
drench'd.
No flower was nigh, no grass, herb, leaf
or weed,
But stole his blood and seem'd with him
to bleed.
(1051-6)

Venus' eyes are so dazzled, her sight 'makes the wound seem three . . .' and 'makes more gashes, where no breach should be. / His face seems twain, each several limb is doubled' (1064-7). And at once, Venus starts to use language which brings the uniqueness and individuality of Adonis to life, to capture the freshness and vitality she had taken from him when he was alive. 'The flowers are sweet, their colours fresh and trim, / But true sweet beauty liv'd and died with him' (1079-80). When Adonis lived, 'sun and sharp air / Lurk'd like two thieves to rob him of his fair' (1085-6). All of nature, she says, responded to his presence. The sun and wind would compete for the privilege of drying his tears, the lion would walk behind a hedge so that he could see Adonis without frightening him. Adonis' song tamed tigers. To hear him speak, wolves would leave their prey.

In Ovid, it is Venus who transforms Adonis into a flower, but Shakespeare's Adonis, having the power of the primordial poet, Orpheus, to make the birds and the beasts and the trees move, can effect his own metamorphosis:

By this the boy that by her side lay kill'd
Was melted like a vapour from her sight,
And in his blood that on the ground lay
spill'd,
A purple flower sprung up, checker'd with
white,
*Resembling well his pale cheeks and the
blood*
Which in round drops upon their
whiteness stood.
(1165-70; my italics)[36]

This purple flower will *not* be 'too grossly dyed'. Its colour and odour have not been stolen from the blood and breath of another. The false rhetorical exercise of comparing Adonis to a flower, with which Venus opened the poem, to produce a sterile, lifeless image, that could beget only barren verse, has undergone an exact reversal. Adonis has refused to be compared to anything else, an insistence paralleled by the Poet of the Sonnets, who spurns couplements of 'proud compare' (Sonnet 21, 5) in repeated refusals to compare his subject with anything else and in reiterated injunctions that everything else must be compared to his subject. The blood with which Venus has smeared her cheeks is no metaphor, but the congealed substance that once flowed through the veins of Adonis' body (she 'stains her face with his congealed blood', 1122), and which is now flowing as nourishing green sap through the stalk of the flower. Comparing the flower to Adonis' flesh and blood is no rhetorical exercise. The 'new-sprung' flower has grown to vigorous strength from an original seed sown in an open space of untilled ground, fed by its own vital body fluid. If it is picked, the self-renewing power which has created it can produce another.

She bows her head, the new-sprung flower to
smell,
Comparing it to her Adonis' breath,
And says within her bosom it shall dwell,
Since he himself is reft from her by death.
She crops the stalk, and in the breach
appears
Green-dropping sap, which she compares
to tears.

'Poor flower,' quoth she, 'this was thy father's
guise,—
Sweet issue of a more sweet-smelling sire,—
For every little grief to wet his eyes;
To grow unto himself was his desire,
And so 'tis thine; but know, it is as good
To wither in my breast as in his blood.'
(1171-82; my italics)

Venus may place the self-created heir of Adonis in her bosom where it will wither, but its vital essence has been distilled. Her sterile rhetoric has been metamorphosed into an organic language that can bring everything into new life. She hies home to Paphos, where she 'Means to immure herself and not be seen', taking the flower with her—but leaving Shakespeare's poem behind.

Notes

[1] e.g. F. T. Prince in his introd. to the Arden edn. writes: 'Shakespeare's own description of the poem offers an apparent difficulty, since he had already begun to make his name as a playwright; but Lord Southampton would not have been flattered, and might even have been annoyed, by a reference to the vulgar dramatic successes of the young writer: such works were not considered to fall into the category of literature' (*The Poems,* ed. F. T. Prince (London, 1960; repr. 1982), p. xxvi). All quotations from *Venus and Adonis* are from this edn. All quotations from other Shakespeare works are from the Arden edns., gen. eds. H. F. Brooks, H. Jenkins, and B. Morris, unless otherwise stated. G. Bullough writes: 'The style, so much richer and more glowing than that of the earliest Histories and comedies, suggests either a new literary discipleship or some recent enrichment of personal experience, perhaps both. . . . Shakespeare seems to

be making a bid for court approval by writing in the lavish manner of the urbaner classicists who took Ovid for a model' (G. Bullough (ed.), *Narrative and Dramatic Sources of Shakespeare* (London and New York, 1977), i. 161).

[2] The Oxford Shakespeare editors suggest that Shakespeare 'probably' wrote *Venus and Adonis* at this time, 'perhaps seeing a need for an alternative career' (*The Complete Works,* ed. S. Wells and G. Taylor (Oxford, 1986), 253).

[3] *The Poems,* ed. Prince, p. xxvi. Marlowe's fragment *Hero and Leander* was entered in the Stationers' Register in 1593, the same year *Venus and Adonis* was published, although *Hero* was not published until June 1598. We do not know which influenced which. Lodge's *Scillaes Metamorphosis* was published in 1589 and can claim to be the first English epyllion, but *Hero* and *Venus* seem to have been responsible for the outburst of Ovidian epyllia in the years 1593-8. Since the influence of Marlowe on these is clearly apparent, it is generally assumed that Hero was known almost from the date of entry. See M. C. Bradbrook, *Shakespeare and Elizabethan Poetry* (London, 1951), 57, 226.

[4] Note the unspoken assumption that concerns with artistic development and financial gain are mutually exclusive motivations in Prince's statement: 'Despite the presentation of *Venus and Adonis* and *Lucrece* as the works of a conscious artist, Shakespeare probably sat down to write them in the hope that they would bring him some immediate practical reward' (*The Poems,* ed. Prince, p. xxvi).

[5] R. Wilbur, 'The Narrative Poems: Introduction', in *William Shakespeare: The Complete Works,* gen. ed. A. Harbage (New York, rev. edn., 1969; repr. 1977), 1403; F. E. Halliday, *The Poetry of Shakespeare's Plays* (London, 1954; repr. 1964), 62; R. Ellrodt, 'Shakespeare the Non-Dramatic Poet', in S. Wells (ed.), *The Cambridge Companion to Shakespeare Studies* (Cambridge, 1986), 45.

[6] R. Lanham, 'The Ovidian Shakespeare: *Venus and Adonis* and *Lucrece*', in his *Motives of Eloquence: Literary Rhetoric in the Renaissance* (New Haven and London, 1976), 82.

[7] Traditional editorial glosses on the meaning of Sonnet 111 (following Shelley's, that Shakespeare is complaining of the ignominy of writing for the public stage) have encouraged the plausibility of this view.

[8] In an essay on *Venus and Adonis,* N. Lindheim has sought 'to place a seemingly marginal or curious specimen of [Shakespeare's] work in fruitful relation to the canon' for purposes different from my own. Lindheim argues that the poem is Shakespeare's 'earliest poetic *or* dramatic exploration of the nature of love', and that it shows 'the poet's very early attempts to manage considerable tonal complexity . . . [which] is not conspicuous in the stage works that probably precede *Venus and Adonis*' (my italics) (N. Lindheim, 'The Shakespearean *Venus and Adonis', Shakespeare Quarterly,* 37 (1986), 190-203, at pp. 190, 191).

[9] E. K. Chambers quotes Sidney Lee's theory that there is 'reason to believe that the first draft lay in the author's desk through four or five summers and underwent some retouching before it emerged from the press in its final shape', in order to counter it with his own suggestion that it 'need mean no more than that it was his first published work' (E. K. Chambers, *William Shakespeare* (Oxford, 1930), i. 545).

[10] *Henry VI, Parts One, Two, and Three; Richard III; The Taming of the Shrew; The Comedy of Errors; The Two Gentlemen of Verona.* Dating of the early plays is, of course, problematic. For the purpose of this present study I wish merely to support the supposition that Shakespeare is already an experienced playwright at the time of his writing *Venus and Adonis,* and to 'place' the poem within a period of imaginative genesis to which these early plays belong.

[11] The poem explicitly draws on three stories from Ovid's *Metamorphoses:* 'Venus and Adonis' (*Met.* x. 519-59; 705-39); 'Salmacis and Hermaphroditus' (*Met.* iv. 285-388); and 'Narcissus and Echo' (*Met.* iii. 339-510). The epigraph is taken from Ovid's *Amores* I. xv. 35-6. All quotations from Ovid's works are from the Loeb Classical Library. *Metamorphoses,* trans. F. J. Miller, rev. G. P. Goold (Cambridge, Mass., vol. i, 3rd edn. repr. 1984; vol. ii, 2nd edn. repr. 1984).

[12] 'As the soule of *Euphorbus* was thought to liue in *Pythagoras*: so the sweete wittie soule of *Ouid* liues in mellifluous & hony-tongued *Shakespeare,* witnes his *Venus and Adonis,* his *Lucrece,* his sugred Sonnets among his priuate friends, &c.' (Francis Meres, *Palladis Tamia: Wits Treasury* (London, 1598), 281-2).

[13] e.g. C. Martindale states that the 'extreme literariness' of Ovid's work was seen as a virtue 'to Shakespeare and the Elizabethans' (C. Martindale (ed.), *Ovid Renewed: Ovidian Influences on Literature and Art from the Middle Ages to the Twentieth Century* (Cambridge, 1988), 14).

[14] *The Poems,* ed. Prince, 5.

[15] 'Now when the rosy fingered morning faire / Weary of aged Tithones saffron bed, / Had spred her purple robe through deawy aire' (Spenser, *FQ* I. ii. 7); 'Rose-cheek'd Adonis' (Marlowe, *Hero and Leander,* i. 93).

[16] Prince's gloss on stain (*The Poems,* 4) cites Pooler quoting Lyly: 'My Daphne's beauty staines all faces' (*Works,* ed. Bond, iii. 142); and Sidney's 'sun-stayning excellencie' (*The Countess of Pembrokes Arcadia,* ed. A. Feuillerat (Cambridge, 1912), 7).

[17] Discussing Spenser's Garden of Adonis in *The Faerie Queene,* J. Nohrnberg notes the well-known physical allegories of Adonis which characterize him as a 'genital field', and the traditional *mons veneris* 'with its uncut foliage and enclosing grove [which] stands for the female pudenda' (J. Nohrnberg, *The Analogy of 'The Faerie Queene'* (Princeton, 1976), 526).

[18] As Shakespeare wrote elsewhere: 'My mistress' eyes are nothing like the sun' (Sonnet 130).

[19] The present study follows the 1609 Q order of the Sonnets.

[20] *Shakespeare's Sonnets,* ed. W. G. Ingram and T. Redpath (London, 1964), 122. All quotations from the Sonnets are from this edn.

[21] See *Shakespeare's Sonnets,* ed. Ingram and Redpath, 122.

[22] Ibid.

[23] *Shakespeare's Sonnets,* ed. Ingram and Redpath, 188-9.

[24] See esp. Sonnets 78, 79, 83, 85, 101. The 'rival' poets of Sonnet 85 write 'In polish'd form of well-refinèd pen', in contrast to the Poet who is silent: 'Me for my dumb thoughts, speaking in effect.' The mistrust of polished written poetry evident in these sonnets suggests that what appears to be merely the conventional 'modesty' of a poet in Shakespeare's dedication in *Venus and Adonis*—'I know not how I shall offend in dedicating my *unpolished* lines to your Lordship' (my italics)—is more an ironic claim to the poet's truthfulness rather than prompted by a fear of offending the dedicatee because the poem's author is a 'vulgar' playwright. That the lines are 'unpolished' is, then, a virtue. Speaking in effect, Shakespeare is implicitly criticizing the polished form of the well-refined pens of other poets whose work Henry Wriothesley would have been used to reading.

[25] The gloss on *modern* is that of *Shakespeare's Sonnets,* ed. Ingram and Redpath, 190.

[26] *Shakespeare's Sonnets,* ed. Ingram and Redpath, 192.

[27] Quoted in *The Poems,* ed. Prince, 19.

[28] The gloss on *compeers* is that of *Shakespeare's Sonnets,* ed. Ingram and Redpath, 197.

[29] Prince's gloss reads: 'Venus is recurring to commonplace arguments for enjoying beauty, her "idle over-handled theme". Her last metaphor had been used in *Hero and Leander,* I. 232-6' (*The Poems,* ed. Prince, 44).

[30] Falstaff and Hal will exceed the limits of Erasmian *copia* with a comparative hyperbole contest in a hilarious send-up of the rhetoricians' ideal text:

> *Prince.* I'll be no longer guilty of this sin. This sanguine coward, this bed-presser, this horse-breaker, this huge hill of flesh,—
>
> *Falstaff.* 'Sblood, you starveling, you eel-skin, you dried neat's-tongue, you bull's-pizzle, you stock-fish—O for breath to utter what is like thee!—you tailor's-yard, you sheath, you bow-case, you vile standing tuck!
>
> *Prince.* Well, breathe awhile, and then to it again, and when thou hast *tired thyself in base comparisons,* hear me speak but this.
>
> (1*HIV,* II. iv. 237-47; my italics)

[31] Ellrodt provides an interesting example of criticism's failure to respond to the presence of Shakespearian irony in matters theoretical: 'One would like to think the poet mocked the Elizabethan partiality to *copia* when he compared the "tedious" lament of Venus to "copious stories" that "End without audience and are never done". Vain wish, since wordiness grew worse in *Lucrece*!' (Ellrodt, 'Shakespeare the Non-Dramatic Poet', 45-6).

[32] Sonnet 86, 7; *Ven.* 770; Sonnet 82, 10; *Ven.* 790.

[33] Quoted in *Shakespeare's Sonnets,* ed. Ingram and Redpath, 90.

[34] C. T. Onions, *A Shakespeare Glossary* (Oxford, 2nd edn., repr. 1980), 15.

[35] *Shakespeare's Sonnets,* ed. Ingram and Redpath, 138.

[36] Bradbrook notes that 'Though a goddess, Venus has no supernatural powers . . . She is not responsible for his metamorphosis into a hyacinth: it seems to be spontaneous. Shakespeare abandoned the supernatural: his gods are identified with Nature, physically one with it, enmeshed in its toils even more firmly than Marlowe's.' She goes on to say that Venus's 'inappropriate conceits' are an attempt to convey her grief by 'fantastic elaborations. Yet the horror of the blank glazed stare of the corpse is *physically realised'* (my italics) (*Shakespeare and Elizabethan Poetry,* 62-3). J. Pitcher argues that in *Venus and Adonis,* Shakespeare makes his own poetry 'breed inwardly' so that the red and white trope 'breeds out of itself a riot of colours, comparisons, and metaphors, and eventually, in climactic moments, it meets with the real: red and white are

literally on the boar's mouth' ('Tudor Literature (1484-1603)', in P. Rogers (ed.), *The Oxford Illustrated History of English Literature* (Oxford, 1987), 101).

Source: "Death by Rhetorical Trope: Poetry Metamorphosed in *Venus and Adonis* and the Sonnets," in *Review of English Studies,* Vol. XLVI, No. 184, November, 1995, pp. 475-501.

The Tempest and Cultural Exchange

Jean-Marie Maguin

Looking at commercial exchange may prove a convenient way of approaching the problem of cultural exchange in general, for commerce is steeped in all sorts of constraints and traditions and, pragmatic though it appears, still measures desire as much as reason, and reflects an estimated balance of power between seller and buyer. The proverb 'exchange is no robbery' (Heywood, 1542) is significant of a conceptual impediment. No less significant is the adjectival crutch it often uses in order to reassure itself and us that 'a *fair* exchange is no robbery'. Yet what is a 'fair' exchange? At one end of the scale, exchanging or bartering one necessity for another—so long as the need for the things exchanged is similarly pressing for both parties—may in all likelihood be accounted fair. At the other end of the scale, trading one luxury for another may be found fair as long as it suits the whims and plans of the exchanging parties. The trickster king, Richard III, exclaims 'A horse! A horse! My kingdom for a horse' (5.7.7). It is Shakespeare who adds the exchange suggestion. All that the source (Hall) says is that when they see that the battle is lost, the king's party 'brought to hym a swyfte and a lyght horse to convey hym awaie'. Are we to understand that Shakespeare's Richard is pinning a low price on his kingdom and a high price on a horse? As we laugh at Richard's desperate offer, are we to ponder also over the well-known fact that 'necessity's sharp pinch', according to Lear's phrase (*King Lear* 2.2.384), works a strange arithmetic or that need, as Lear puts it more generally some time later (438), is simply not to be reasoned at all? The truth here is more simple. Richard is trying to barter what is no longer his for what may still save his life. Here is the disproportion that goads the audience into smiling or laughing. In this battle scene, poles apart from epic or tragic grandeur, the cheekiness of the character, drawing close to his last gasp, is still in the spirit of farce, but his ultimate deceitful offer, though repeated (5.7.13), will not save him from death.

Less pragmatic, though hardly less artful in its desire to move the listener, is Richard II's exchange programme, carefully built on the rhetorical pattern of *gradatio:*

> I'll give my jewels for a set of beads,
> My gorgeous palace for a hermitage,
> My gay apparel for an almsman's gown,
> My figured goblets for a dish of wood,
> My sceptre for a palmer's walking staff,
> My subjects for a pair of carvèd saints,
> And my large kingdom for a little grave.
> (3.3.146-52)

Apart from the revealing—nay, poignant—symbolism of each proposition, the general truth applies to the beginning of the wars of the Roses as it did to the end of them at Bosworth: lost kingdoms go cheap enough.

All exchanges are marked by a triple uncertainty. They bow to circumstances that may suddenly transform a needle into the most precious thing on earth. They defer to subjective preferences whatever those may be. They reflect cultural traits. No two cultures rate their values according to the same scale. The scarcity of a particular product is a local factor and unless it proves a common denominator between the exchanging parties—which virtually precludes exchange of that product—it will lead to mutual misapprehension. To exchange a handful of glass-beads for an ingot of gold arguably sets up each party of that exchange as the other's laughing-stock, if the respective cultural backgrounds are not thoroughly known and mastered. In this respect, all exchanges, commercial bargains included, are coloured by culture.

As a story of visitors setting foot successively on an inhabited island, albeit singly, *The Tempest* addresess very plainly the problems that arise from cultural difference, and influence exchanges between men, and also, as it turns out, exchanges with supernatural entities. Although the story line adopted by Shakespeare does not appear indebted to any main narrative or dramatic source, *The Tempest,* for all its low level of intertextuality, still manifests a diversity of cultural exchanges. There is what Stephen Greenblatt has described in terms of 'negotiation'. To quote him, 'works of art, however intensely marked by the creative intelligence and private obsessions of individuals, are the products of collective negotiation and exchange'.[1] The formula is deceptively unassuming and one immediately thinks this is nothing but the foreseeable return of a once fashionable socio-historical approach. And it is, in a way. Yet everything in Greenblatt's successful analysis is idiosyncratic, and, in the case of *The Tempest,* the measure of his mastery is demonstrated in proving—odds-against, as far as I am concerned—that the play is partly the result of a negotiation between representatives of two London joint-stock companies with Shakespeare standing for the King's Men's venture and Strachey for the Virginia company. The substance of the fascinating demonstration need not be summed up here; I shall accept it as defining a new type of cultural exchange, infinitely more subtle and important than the commercial negotiation whose pattern I initially borrowed to explore the concept of exchange.

While in material and commercial exchanges we can always trace a cultural element, in the cultural negotiation or exchange there is no swapping of objective goods, neither need there be an awareness of mutual enrichment on the part of the participants. Cultural exchange is primarily communication but this need not be reciprocal, and certainly not so *hic et nunc*. What did Shakespeare give Strachey, a friend of friends and a Blackfriars neighbour, in exchange for the yet unpublished account of his shipwreck and of the state of the Virginia colony? Put in this way, the question is badly formulated. What did Strachey receive in exchange for his information? Only Strachey knows. Perhaps nothing that he was conscious of, bar the pleasure he must have felt as a keen follower of the stage, of making conversation with the greatest dramatist in London—that is, assuming that the two men communicated verbally. Shakespeare may simply have read a copy of Strachey's manuscript letter, if the letter was circulated in this form, as we think it was. Even in this form, cultural exchange did take place. In exchange—but by now it is plain that strictly measured reciprocity and mutual advantage are no longer defining features—Strachey, like ourselves, received *The Tempest*. Adaptation, appropriation, deviation according to whatever set of pressures is at work on the body and the mind that receive the cultural implant take precedence as far as the literary scholar is concerned. The phenomenon is still akin to intertextuality even though the hypotext may not be a text at all. None of those who imitated, adapted, or stole from Homer could repay him, naturally. The type of cultural exchange I am describing is no longer reciprocal but one-sided and outward bound. Its progress is comparable to that of wine in a still. Substantial changes take place in the process. 'Exchange' and 'change', understood as 'transformation' become equated (as in the *Oxford English Dictionary,* 'exchange' 1.1.6.)

The play's plot successively portrays two pseudo-colonial situations, the first with the relationship between Prospero and Miranda on the one hand and Caliban on the other, the second between Stefano and Trinculo on the one hand and Caliban again on the other. No structure could invite us more clearly to establish comparisons than does this parallel between two separate and successive representations of intercultural exchange. Such are the givens of the dramatic work that we are made to react to situations in different and often contradictory ways according to whether we pay attention to macro- or micro-elements in the play's structure. The parallel instituted between the three sets of pseudo- or would-be planters (Prospero, Gonzalo, and Stefano) depends on macro-elements. While keeping them separate until the very end in order to allow independent and sharper focus, the play reflects here the contacts established between Europeans and Indians in the new world since the end of the fifteenth century. The spectrum of European society is reduced to its two extremes with at one end the gentility of the prince and his fair daughter, or the political philosophy of Gonzalo, and, at the other end, the vulgarity of the jester and the drunken butler. On the indigenous side, Shakespeare simplifies the social picture by giving us only one savage. Caliban's singularity possibly emblematizes an undifferentiated European vision of the savages as 'other'. Gonzalo and Caliban never meet to talk but exchanges between savage and prince, savage and rag-tag crew members pass through two distinct and opposed phases of friendship and hatred. The prince's gift of language and amity is reciprocated by the savage's gift of knowledge of the isle and worship. I stress *knowledge* of the isle for it seems to me that Caliban's gift is not simply practical. He has shown Prospero 'all the qualities o' th' isle, / The fresh springs, brine-pits, barren place and fertile' (1.2.339-40). The proposition he makes later to Stefano, while starting more or less in the same fashion, soon bottoms out with mere ancillary services:

> I'll show thee every fertile inch o' th' island,
> . . . . .
> I'll show thee the best springs; I'll pluck thee berries;
> I'll fish for thee, and get thee wood enough.
> . . . . .
> I prithee, let me bring thee where crabs grow,
> And I with my long nails will dig thee pig-nuts,
> Show thee a jay's nest, and instruct thee how
> To snare the nimble marmoset. I'll bring thee
> To clust'ring filberts, and sometimes I'll get thee
> Young seamews from the rock . . .
> (2.2.147-71)

In this passage are found micro-elements whose presence, as they raise echoes, modifies the more immediate response to macro-structural features. We are referred to an earlier moment when Caliban nostalgically remembered how, in the friendly phase of their relationship, Prospero would reward him by giving him 'Water with berries in't . . .' (1.2.336), a diet whose simplicity is reminiscent of the golden age. Not so the diet Caliban is planning for Stefano in exchange for wine from the wicked, inexhaustible bottle. Amongst the nuts and berries, there lurks food of the iron age. The flesh of the marmoset testifies to competition between the species and brings feeding disturbingly close to cannibalism since the victim belongs to the animal family closest to man. Are we to understand that the more varied and sanguinary diet is innate, that Caliban did all these things for Prospero too, and from the first, though we are not told in so many words, or are we to believe that Caliban's fishing and hunting skills grew from Prospero's teaching? The question obviously cannot be answered but the difference between the two discourses on food, the allusive and the detailed, is sufficiently marked to arrest us in this exploration of cultural exchange. From the innocence of water and berries we have passed to wine—the imported curse of colonized New-World populations—and blood, an ominous association. Caliban's other intended gift to Stefano is also stained with blood. It is political power in exchange for the killing of his present tyrant.

The second phase in each relationship is one of hatred. Slavery and incarceration are the price paid by Caliban for his attempted rape on the person of Miranda. In exchange for this hardship, all he can repay Prospero and his daughter with are the curses which witness to his acquired linguistic capacity. This new type of exchange, using the word in the flattest sense of 'reciprocal giving and receiving' (*Oxford English Dictionary,* 1.1.d), has two main characteristics: (a) unbalance resulting from Prospero's position of power, and (b) the fact that it is no longer intercultural but becomes intracultural. Slavery and curses, meaningless in Caliban's original isolation on the island, are two evils that belong in Prospero's world. What Caliban has lost is a capacity to exchange with his visitor, and now master, anything of his own tradition. He is the exemplary subject of violent and total assimilation. The second phase of the relationship between the two drunkards and Caliban is also placed under the auspices of contempt, and curses are exchanged. While the balance of power is in this case satisfactory, Caliban is still shown wanting, as he was in his later dealings with Prospero and Miranda, in anything original to exchange.

It seems important not to restrain the meaning of Caliban's remark 'You taught me language, and my profit on't / Is I know how to curse' (1.2.365-6) to something which one could gloss as 'and now I am capable of verbal violence or vulgarity'. The play's strategy encourages such a limitation, in a sense, since a curse in the most common acceptation of the word is made to follow immediately: 'The red plague rid you / For learning me your language!' (366-7). Caliban's own account of the initial teaching process—he learned to name the sun and the moon—suggests that 'your language' does not mean the play's English, or its Milanese referent, but 'that thing which you call language'. In Prospero's laboratory an extraordinary experiment has therefore been attempted which consisted not so much in teaching someone to speak as in humanizing a 'freckled whelp' (1.2.284), a less than human creature accidentally found in the natural environment. In his original state, Caliban is like Chaos, which is not the world at all, but capable of becoming the world if it meets its god. What Prospero and Miranda teach Caliban is to conceptualize, and whether or not Caliban is 'A devil, a born devil, on whose nature / Nurture can never stick' (4.1.188-9), Caliban is stuck with language, or more essentially, as intimated earlier, with the power to conceptualize without which misery is nothing but an experience of the moment, and with which misery and loss of liberty become subjects of endless woeful meditation that aggravate the fate of the sufferer. What Caliban chiefly deplores is the step he was made to take into the human condition. He was taught language and the only profit he finds is a capacity to curse his fate.[2]

The Tempest is a play which capitalizes on contradiction, and commentary is bound to reflect this. Thus do I follow Shakespeare's example in simultaneously setting up Caliban as subhuman—therefore as incapable of culture—and analysing his initial exchanges with Prospero as evidence of an original culture. We should be careful, however, of possible dangers arising from the fact that our notion of culture is quite different from the Elizabethan concepts of the development of mental faculties, of manners, or education. Although the *Oxford English Dictionary* records one occurrence of the word 'culture' in the modern sense about 1510, all other illustrations are post-Shakespearian. Shakespeare never uses the word either in this sense or any other. Modern usage has certainly stretched the concept to take in manifestations which, even recently, ethnocentric prejudice would have pushed far below the level of the cultural. No matter how ferocious the contempt of the conquistadors for the people whose lands they were taking over, the very ferocity of their persecution is proof that, in most if not in all cases, they were eliminating a recognized competitor. The ardour to Christianize the savages meant that although occasionally deemed not to own a soul, they were thought capable of acquiring one through the mystic operation of baptism, just as subhuman Caliban is capable of receiving the language of man. When and where the indigenous populations were thought to be the children of the devil this did not preclude conversion. Their barbarity was only strangeness, pleaded some humanists and a few, like Montaigne, radically deconstructed the prevailing contempt for the savages by holding them up as an enviable cultural model. They formed a society closely mirroring the famed Golden Age which we could describe through an oxymoronic phrase as a 'natural culture'. This paradox, or seeming paradox, is not the product of modernity. It is embedded in the very myth of the Golden Age where Saturn gives man a sickle, a symbol that the natural fertility of the soil can still be improved. In the Judeo-Christian world, the garden of Eden has pitfalls of its own but no agricultural implements.

There are two main borrowings from Florio's translation of Montaigne's essays in *The Tempest*. They concern Gonzalo's daydreams about a Utopian government of the island (2.1.149-70) inspired by Montaigne's essay 'Of the Caniballes', as well as Prospero's statement that 'The rarer action is / In virtue than in vengeance' at the beginning of Act 5 (5.1.27-8).[3] Montaigne's influence on the latter passage was identified by Elizabeth Prosser in 1935.[4] It poses little or no difficulty. Shakespeare simply makes Prospero adopt, in his renouncing vengeance, Montaigne's sentiment that flawless and unshakeable goodness is as unheroic as it is incomprehensible, and that the voluntary domination of his passions and overcoming of temptation is a rarer virtue. The flow of moral philosophy from Montaigne to the play's character-philosopher is straightforward and unencumbered. The problem offered by Gonzalo's Utopian enthusiasm is different. Although it is well known I shall cite the passage in full since I intend to scrutinize it. I omit the courtiers' quizzing interruptions:

> GONZALO (*to Alonso*)
> Had I the plantation of this isle, my lord,—
> . . . . .
> I' th' commonwealth I would by contraries
> Execute all things. For no kind of traffic
> Would I admit, no name of magistrate;
> Letters should not be known; riches, poverty,
> And use of service, none; contract, succession,
> Bourn, bound of land, tilth, vineyard, none;
> No use of metal, corn, or wine, or oil;
> No occupation, all men idle, all;
> And women too—but innocent and pure;
> No sovereignty—
> . . . . .
> All things in common nature should produce
> Without sweat or endeavour. Treason, felony,
> Sword, pike, knife, gun, or need of any
> engine,
> Would I not have; but nature should bring
> forth
> Of it own kind all foison, all abundance,
> To feed my innocent people.
> . . . . .
> I would with such perfection govern, sir,
> T' excel the Golden Age.
> (2.1.149-74)

This, now, is how Florio translates the imaginary conversation carried out by Montaigne with Plato about the population discovered by Villegagnon in 'Antartike France':

> It is a nation, would I answer Plato, that hath no kinde of traffike, no knowledge of Letters, no intelligence of numbers, no name of magistrate, nor of politike superioritie; no use of service, of riches or of povertie; no contracts, no successions, no partitions, no occupation but idle; no respect of kindred, but common, no apparell but naturall, no manuring of lands, no use of wine, corne, or mettle. The very words that import lying, falshood, treason, dissimulations, covetousnes, envie, detraction, and pardon, were never heard among them.[5]

Montaigne had introduced this description by deploring the fact that neither Lycurgus nor Plato could know of the existence of such peoples:

> for me seemeth that what in those nations we see by experience, doth not only exceed all the pictures wherewith licentious Poesie hath proudly imbellished the golden age, and all her quaint inventions to faine a happy condition of man, but also the conception and desire of Philosophy.[6]

Shakespeare appears to be working with Florio's Montaigne at his elbow and reproduces the list of twelve or thirteen characteristic features whose lack negatively defines the state of happiness experienced by these Antarctic populations. Illiteracy and lack of political hierarchy, which take second and third places in Montaigne's list, are quoted in reverse order in *The Tempest*. Lack of occupation and lack of metal, respectively number seven and number twelve of Montaigne's declension are switched about and figure as number nine and number seven in Shakespeare. Lack of corn and wine are given a higher priority in the play, figuring as number eight instead of number eleven in Montaigne. The prohibition of weapons is original to Gonzalo's speech, and he is made to interject a remark about the innocence and purity of women which is perhaps an interpretation of Montaigne's statement of the fact that 'the women lie from their husbands'[7] and that the husbands are constantly reminded to observe 'an inviolable affection to their wives'.[8] None of these differences however are very significant, apart from the emphatic ban on arms, and they would pass unnoticed in the theatre by anyone who does not happen to know Florio's text by heart.[9] The manipulation lies elsewhere and is most evident whatever the capacity of one's memory.[10] Whereas Montaigne is indirectly describing a state of affairs existing in the new world, Gonzalo is talking about (re)creating such a state of affairs: nature and lack of artifice on the one hand, artifice in imposing a return to nature on the other. Gonzalo is running head first into the perverse old paradox of pacifism and tolerance only ever enforceable by dint of war and intolerance. The best of intentions are often the nearest way to the devil. In this connection Gonzalo's most reassuring quality is his ineffectuality for we have met such fundamentalists before. Jack Cade and his crew are against possessions, partitions, and the knowledge of letters, and the rope and knife make short shrift of lawyers and schoolmasters. The courtiers are quick to underline the contradictions in Gonzalo's speech: 'GONZALO No sovereignty—SEBASTIAN Yet he would be king on't.' (162). Although the courtiers are cynical villains this does not detract from the fact that their logic is not only valid but establishes the truth. Although the fact that they are right does not make them better characters in the appraisal of the spectators, the effective invalidation of Gonzalo's reasoning by an arrogant couple of blackguards seriously undercuts the attraction of his Utopian zeal.

The question that interests us here is whether the manipulation of Montaigne's essay by Shakespeare is made solely at the expense of Gonzalo or also at the expense of Montaigne's philosophy. The answer is not easy to determine. It remains a general truth that the ridicule of the exponent of a theory—here Gonzalo—will, up to a point, rub off on the theory itself and its original proponent. Nowhere is Gonzalo more ridiculous or naive and unrealistic than in the introduction of his argument when he announces that his commonwealth would do 'all things by contraries'. We are free to imagine what Swift might have constructed on the basis of such an extreme proposition. Nowhere is Gonzalo less convincing than in the summation of his argument when he smugly remarks that he would govern with such perfection 'T' excel the Golden Age'. The statement is markedly different from Montaigne's. The French writer uses the regular contempt of the philosopher for poetic imagination to announce to the world that the blissful state of existence of the savages actually outdoes all those excessive accounts of the Golden Age found in poetic tradition. He then proceeds to hoist himself with his own petard by furthermore assuring the reader that the savages have actually outdone 'the conception and desire of Philosophy'. Two things here would have ruffled Shakespeare's sense of the relative and his spirit of tolerance: (a) the philosopher's bad faith in accepting poetic symbols literally, and (b) the excessive claim in making experience the be-all and end-all, feigning thus to put matter so much over mind only to validate paradoxically what remains an *intellectual* operation, his philosophizing. In *Shakespeare and Ovid,* Jonathan Bate makes the point that 'Shakespeare denies the myth of the Golden Age restored in a New World peopled by noble cannibals',[11] and that Caliban's fallen state, whether innate or not, is apparent in his claim of the island as his heritage. I fully concur in this judgement and refer here to the Golden Age as a myth respected as such by Shakespeare but rather affectedly spurned by Montaigne in a conventional instance of philosopher disparaging poet. The confrontation between Shakespeare and Montaigne, as I see it, is anything but a head-on collision. It is rather in the nature of an abrasion of Montaigne's philosophy by Shakespeare concerning the point of knowing whether the savages' existence is perfect or not. At first sight, we might have thought primarily of Gonzalo as a man hopelessly exposed, a sort of *enfant perdu* shot at by his own camp, by the Antonios and the Gonzalos. Instead we discover that Gonzalo is, practically speaking, a mask from behind which Shakespeare is vigorously teasing Montaigne for his radicalism.

The last manipulation relevant to the problem of cultural exchange that I wish to look at here is apparent in Miranda's famous appreciation of the men she discovers: 'O wonder! / How many goodly creatures are there here! / How beauteous mankind is! O brave new world / That has such people in't!' (5.1.184-7). The traditionally observed inadequacy of the remark can hardly be overrated, Miranda looking as she does upon usurpers and would-be murderers. Although Shakespeare is not above a joke at the expense of his characters, I do not think irony *ad feminam* to have been his main motivation in this case. The colonial analogy developed in the play with varying degrees of accuracy and varying urgency, seems to take over here. We have hundreds of accounts by Europeans of Europeans discovering 'savages', but how many accounts do we have, recorded by savages themselves, of their discovery of Europeans? By the time Miranda discovers the Neapolitans, we have already seen Caliban, the play's single aborigine, worship a couple of newly arrived drunken aliens, a mistake he readily acknowledges and one that is a repeat of his initial adulation of Prospero. Miranda, since she has only a few memories of Milan, could almost be considered as a near aborigine, but is the category admissible at all? It is clear that the education received at the hands of her father disqualifies her as a 'savage' commenting on her discovery of a new race of men. Why then does Shakespeare choose her to repeat Caliban's mistake in a register totally different from the grotesque farce of Prospero's slave? Beyond the comedy of misplaced praise, the pressure of contemporary colonial history introduces graver and disturbing echoes in her words of welcome. They ring with the fatal error made by all the New-World people who judged us on our fair looks and declared good intentions only to be rapidly subjected or wiped out by alcohol, disease, and main force. In the circumstances, Prospero's warning to Miranda ''Tis new to thee.' (187) is one of those hushed, subdued asides that hold the promise of ulterior explanations ('Can't tell you now, not in this company'). The shift from 'savage' to 'civilized' is momentous. It implies that the error of the 'savage' in welcoming the colonists is not, as might have been thought, the unavoidable fault of brutish brains, a natural defect. European culture, represented in Miranda, is prone to a similar failure. The parallel between Caliban and Miranda is Shakespeare's deft way of putting the New World on the same fragile footing as the Old. Humanity is shared equally between them because both worlds are shown to have an identical potential for erring in judgement.

Curiously, Miranda's exclamation about that 'brave new world' is close in sentiment to a Latin quotation added in the 1595 posthumous edition of Montaigne's *Essays*—the one that Florio translates—and omitted in the English translation. In the French book it occurs rather awkwardly just before another Latin quotation from Virgil's *Georgics,* already present in the 1588 edition. The Latin phrase that Florio leaves out is taken from Seneca's 'Epistle xc': *viri a diis recentes* (men fresh from the hands of the gods). Montaigne applies the phrase to the savages, Miranda's salutation is aimed at the sophisticated, and perverse Old-World race as it appears before her. Could Shakespeare have had access to a copy of the 1595 edition of Montaigne's *Essays* in French? If he knew Florio personally—as it is quite possible he did since the two men shared the same patron in Southampton—he could have looked at the copy from which Florio translated. Would the difference, would the omission have caught his eye? It is impossible to say. The beautifully clipped Latin phrase has a magic appeal and would understandably invite memorization and re-use or adaptation in a different cultural environment.

There is on the periphery of any critical problem a zone of grey shadow whose status is ambiguous and uncomfortable for while it still invites attention and probably belongs to the ground explored, analysis seems to lose its leverage here, and demonstrates its power of persuasion. One should not be shy of stepping into this area but retreat should always be kept in mind. In this last instance, we are perhaps facing no more than the ghost of cultural exchange and must perturb the spirit no further, but rest content with the more corporeal instances previously encountered.

Notes

[1] Stephen Greenblatt, *Shakespearean Negotiations* (Oxford, 1988), p. vii.

[2] In 'Learning to Curse: Aspects of Linguistic Colonialism in the Sixteenth Century' (Freddi Chiapelli, ed., *First Images of America: The Impact of the New World on the Old,* 2 vols. (Berkeley, 1976), vol. 2, pp. 561-80), Stephen Greenblatt appears fleetingly to move towards this conclusion but the problematics of his paper work against it since, rejecting the animal-man dichotomy which I retain as one of the issues here, he chooses to look instead at multiple degrees of humanity, as they seem to emerge from the discourse of some of the early colonists.

[3] On these, and other similarities in thought and phraseology which he identifies, Arthur Kirsch comments in 'Montaigne and *The Tempest*' (in Gunnar Sorelius and Michael Srigley, eds., *Cultural Exchange between European Nations during the Renaissance* (Uppsala, 1994), pp. 111-21).

[4] 'Shakespeare, Montaigne, and the "Rarer Action"', *Shakespeare Studies,* 1 (1965): 261-4.

[5] 'Of the Caniballes', *The Essayes of Michael Lord Montaigne, translated by John Florio,* 3 vols. (London, 1904), vol. 1, p. 245.

[6] Ibid., p. 245.

[7] Ibid., p. 246.

[8] Ibid., p. 247.

[9] In '"The Picture of Nobody": White Cannibalism in *The Tempest*', David Lee Miller, Sharon O'Dair, Harold Weber, eds., *The Production of English Renaissance Culture* (Ithaca and London, 1994), pp. 262-92, Richard Halpern, also attentive to alterations of Montaigne's thought and phraseology by Shakespeare, sees a major instance in Gonzalo's use of the word 'plantation' 'which unambiguously signifies an exclusively European colony. Hence the "innocent and pure" subjects of Gonzalo's imagined polity are not Montaigne's Indians but white Europeans who now somehow occupy an American Indian arcadia' (p. 268). The whole essay contributes to greater awareness of multiple and subtle forms of cultural manipulation in *The Tempest.*

[10] In *Shakespeare and Ovid* (Oxford, 1993), Jonathan Bate claims that 'Sixteenth-century models of reading were always purposeful' (p. 9) rather than mere stylistic imitations and therefore meant to be noticed. The problem is an interesting one.

[11] Bate, p. 257.

Source: "*The Tempest* and Cultural Exchange," in *Shakespeare Survey: An Annual Survey of Shakespeare Studies and Production,* edited by Stanley Wells, Vol. 48, 1995, pp. 147-54.

The Masculine Romance of Roman Britain: *Cymbeline* and Early Modern English Nationalism

Jodi Mikalachki

The birth of the English nation was not the birth of a nation; it was the birth of the nations, the birth of nationalism.

Nations have no clearly identifiable births.[1]

It is somewhat misleading to put the above quotations together, since the first describes the birth of nationalism in England at a specific historical moment (the sixteenth century), while the second invokes the (usually imagined to be) ancient origins of something that has come to be called a nation. I juxtapose them here not simply to imply a wide divergence of scholarly opinion but also to suggest that any discussion of nationalism and early modern England necessarily involves both ways that these quotations read the phenomenon they describe: one places the origins of English nationalism (and perhaps of nationalism more generally) in the early modern period; the other recognizes early modern England's own perception of its national origins in antiquity. The quotations do nevertheless represent opposite poles in theories of nationalism. The first introduces Liah Greenfeld's recent study of early modern England as the world's first nation; assuming the causal primacy of ideas, Greenfeld argues for the idea of the nation as the constitutive element of modernity. The second quotation virtually concludes the last appendix to Benedict Anderson's influential *Imagined Communities,* a study that famously rejects ideological definitions of nationalism, considering it instead alongside anthropological terms like *kinship* or *religion,* and arguing strongly for its emergence in the eighteenth-century Americas. Both works participate in the new social, political, and historical interest in nationalism that developed during the 1980s, just as its subject seemed about to become obsolete.[2]

My own approach emphasizes the interplay between historical obsolescence and continuity with the past in the recovery of national origins. I am less concerned to establish whether nationalism did indeed originate in sixteenth-century England (believing, as I do, that nationalism, too, has no clearly identifiable birth) than I am to explore the complexities of early modern attempts to recover English national origins. The tensions of this sixteenth-century project of recovery—its drive, on one hand, to establish historical precedent and continuity and, on the other, to exorcise a primitive savagery it wished to declare obsolete—inform virtually all expressions of early modern English nationalism. These tensions derive from the period's broader social tensions about order, manifested most acutely in anxiety over the nature of familial relations and the status of the family as a model for the order of the state.[3] The centrality of the family and the church to early modern English articulations of the nation suggests that Anderson's anthropological focus might be particularly appropriate to the study of English nationalism in this period. His understanding of nationalism as aligned "not with self-consciously held political ideologies, but with the large cultural systems that preceded it, out of which—as well as against which—it came into being,"[4] informs my own understanding and guides my consideration of how perceptions of national origins reflected and shaped early modern concepts of the English nation.

Greenfeld's intellectual history is not without interest, however, particularly given the prominent role of early modern intellectuals—scholars, poets, visual artists—in developing nationalist icons and narratives in England. One of the great intellectual stumbling blocks to the recovery of national origins in sixteenth-century England was the absence of a native classical past on which to found the glories of the modern nation. Worse yet, the primitive British savagery that purportedly preceded Roman conquest proved antithetical to a fundamental principle of hierarchy in early modern England, for the Britons made no distinction of sex in government.[5] Powerful females loomed large in early modern visions of national origins, from the universal gendering of the topographical and historical "Britannia" as feminine to the troubling eruptions of ancient queens in the process of civilization by Rome. Like the unruly women who challenged the patriarchal order of early modern England, these powerful and rebellious females in native historiography threatened the establishment of a stable, masculine identity for the early modern nation.

Recent work on the mutually informing constructs of nationalism and sexuality has defined the former as a virile fraternity perpetuated by its rejection of overt male homosexuality and its relegation of women to a position of marginalized respectability.[6] I would argue that this gendering and sexualizing of the nation, generally presented as having emerged in the eighteenth century, had become current by the early seventeenth century in England and involved both an exclusion of originary female savagery and a masculine embrace of the civility of empire. Jacobean dramas set in Roman Britain often conclude with a masculine embrace, staged literally or invoked rhetorically as a figure for the new relation between Rome and Britain. These concluding embraces depend on the prior death of the female character who has advocated or led the British resistance to Rome. The exorcism of this female resistance, constructed as savage, grounds the stable hybrid that crowns these plays with a promise of peace for Britain and wider membership in the Roman world of civilization. And yet it is precisely the savage females banished from the conclusions of these dramas—ancient queens like Fletcher's Bonduca or the wicked Queen of Shakespeare's *Cymbeline*—who articulate British nationalism and patriotism.

In the following account I shall read Shakespeare's romance of Roman Britain in terms of these issues of gender and sexuality, taking both as constitutive of the nationalism the play articulates. In doing so, I hope not only to revise twentieth-century readings of *Cymbeline* as a nationalist drama but also to explore Renaissance anxiety about native origins and the corresponding difficulty of forging a historically based national identity in early modern England.

I

The Queen's great patriotic speech in 3.1 has long been a stumbling block in interpretations of *Cymbeline*. Combining appeals to native topography, history, and legendary origins, it recalls the highest moments of Elizabethan nationalism:[7]

> . . . Remember, sir, my liege,
> The kings your ancestors, together with
> The natural bravery of your isle, which stands
> As Neptune's park, ribb'd and pal'd in
> With rocks unscaleable and roaring waters,
> With sands that will not bear your enemies' boats,
> But suck them up to th' topmast. A kind of conquest
> Caesar made here, but made not here his brag
> Of "Came, and saw, and overcame:" with shame
> (The first that ever touch'd him) he was carried
> From off our coast, twice beaten: and his shipping
> (Poor ignorant baubles!) on our terrible seas,
> Like egg-shells mov'd upon their surges, crack'd
> As easily 'gainst our rocks. For joy whereof
> The fam'd Cassibelan, who was once at point
> (O giglot fortune!) to master Caesar's sword,
> Made Lud's town with rejoicing-fires bright,
> And Britons strut with courage.
>
> (3.1.17-34)[8]

The Queen's opening command to remember invokes the restitutive drive of early modern English nationalism. The nation's glorious past—its resistance to the great Julius Caesar, its ancient line of kings, and the antiquity of its capital—depends paratactically on this command. emerging in the incantatory power of names like "Lud's town" and Cassibelan and in the powerful icon of native topography.[9] Moved by this nationalist appeal, Cymbeline refuses to pay the tribute demanded by the Roman emissaries, thus setting Britain and Rome at war.

As the last of the play's many reversals, however, Cymbeline agrees to pay the tribute and announces his submission to the Roman emperor. In place of the bonfires of victory remembered by his queen, he commands that "A Roman, and a British ensign wave / Friendly together" as both armies march through Lud's town (5.5.481-82). This volte-face is the more remarkable in that the Britons have just defeated the Romans in battle. Honor, not force, dictates Cymbeline's decision, as he invokes the promise made by his uncle Cassibelan to Julius Caesar, from which, he recalls, "We were dissuaded by our wicked queen" (l. 464). Despite everything else the Queen does to earn this epithet, Cymbeline accords it here in the context of her opposition to the Roman tribute, her disruption of the masculine network of kinship, promises, and honor that binds Cymbeline to Rome. In this final assessment of the political plot, the king's full censure falls on the radical nationalism articulated by "our wicked queen."

Critics who wish to read *Cymbeline* as a straightforward celebration of national identity dismiss the Queen's motivation as mere self-interest.[10] By doing so, they fail to interrogate the corporate self-interest that animates nationalism. They further marginalize the Queen by focusing on the oafish Cloten as the main proponent of an objectionable patriotism, thus avoiding the problem of how to interpret her delivery of one of the great nationalist speeches in Shakespeare. Even those who do acknowledge the interpretive difficulties of this scene find ultimately that the patriotic voices of the Queen and Cloten must be rejected in order to effect the play's romance conclusion.[11] G. Wilson Knight's masterful account of Shakespeare's use of Roman and British historiography remains the most instructive in this regard. Knight casts Cymbeline's refusal to pay the tribute, the pivotal national action in the play, as a "question of Britain's islanded integrity." While noting Posthumus's early description of British virtue in his reference to Julius Caesar's respect for British courage (2.4.20-26), Knight nevertheless recognizes that the Queen expresses it much more satisfyingly in 3.1. He argues, however, that the Queen and Cloten are types Britian must ultimately reject in order to recognize freely her Roman obligation and inheritance. Writing shortly after the Second World War, Knight comments that the national situation in *Cymbeline* serves, "as often in real life, to render violent instincts respectable."[12]

George L. Mosse's argument about nationalism and sexuality, which culminates in an analysis of Nazi Germany, also rests on the term *respectable*. Indeed, in Mosse's analysis an alliance between nationalism and respectability is crucial to the formulation and dissemination of both. He traces naturalized concepts of respectability to the eighteenth century, when modern nationalism was emerging, and finds both to be informed by ideals of fraternity for men and domesticity for women. Men were to engage actively with one another in a spirit of brotherhood, while women were to remain passively within the domestic sphere, exercising a biological maternal function that in no way challenged the spiritual bonding of adult males. "Woman as a national symbol was the guardian of the continuity and immutability of the nation, the embodiment of its respectability," Mosse observes, adding that the more respectable nationalist movements become, the more respectable their feminine icons look.[13] When Knight notes in 1947 how the national situation in *Cymbeline* serves "to render violent instincts respectable," he intuits the naturalized alliance between nationalism and respectability that Mosse theorizes forty years later.

Cymbeline's Queen is hardly a figure of national respectability. Even her maternal devotion to Cloten can be censured,[14] and the rest of her career as evil stepmother, would-be poisoner, and finally suicide fully earns Cymbeline's concluding approbation of the "heavens [who] in justice both on her, and hers, / Have laid most heavy hand" (5.5.465-66).[15] Yet Cymbeline's insistence on her political intervention as the mark of her wickedness per se suggests a critique of the nationalism she articulates. This convergence of national and personal wickedness indicates the difficulty of forging national identity before the eighteenth-century alliance of nationalism and respectability. Indeed, the complex and somewhat clumsily resolved romance of *Cymbeline* dramatizes the immediate prehistory of that alliance and its constitutive elements. Early modern England certainly had an ideal of respectable womanhood. one that (as in the eighteenth century) rested on the chastity and subordination of women within the patriarchal household. Susan Amussen has demonstrated, however, that the terms of this ideal were not so clear nor so universally accepted in the seventeenth century as has often been suggested. Definitions of wifely obedience in particular were contested by seventeenth-century English women, despite their general acquiescence to the principle of female subordination. Only by the late seventeenth and early eighteenth centuries are these challenges muted, suggesting that the naturalized ideal of feminine respectability Mosse invokes as an element of nationalism had been fully internalized by women.[16] The difficulties of constructing and ensuring this sexual ideal in the early seventeenth century reveal themselves in the complex formation of a national identity in *Cymbeline*.[17] If respectable nationalism depends in part on respectable womanhood, someone other than the wicked Queen must embody it. Imogen, so beloved of the Victorians for her wifely devotion and forbearance, might figure as the wicked Queen's respectable double, and she does indeed come to represent an alternative nationalism.[18] Her progress through a series of disguised identities and alliances, not all of them British, indicates the amount of work needed to construct a national icon of feminine respectability, just as the messages from and about the Queen in the final scene assert the impossibility of resolving the drama without invoking her feminine wickedness. This duality of feminine respectability and wickedness reveals how fraught early modern English nationalism was with fears of the unrespectable, or, in the language of the period, the uncivil or barbaric. It also indicates how important gender was as a category for working out these fears.[19] Work that applies Mosse's analysis of nationalism and sexuality to the early modern period notes the identification of the feminine with the barbaric in nationalist discourse. Jonathan Goldberg's reading of *Plimoth Planation* as the inaugural text of a national American literature notes its persistent alignment of Anglo women with Indians. Although not precisely identical, he argues, they must both "be effaced in order for history to move forward as the exclusive preserve of white men."[20]

The collapse of the categories of "woman" and "savage" also informs *Cymbeline*. Anxiety about gender, given a nationalist inflection, haunts the drama, emerging particularly in contests over Roman-British relations. If it is most apparent in the caricature of feminine wickedness represented by the Queen, who tries to come between Britain and Rome, it also informs masculine characters in all-male settings. After the Queen's intervention in 3.1, British articulation and enactment of male bonding become increasingly important, from Belarius's reconstitution of an all-male family in the Welsh cave to the princes, further bonding with Posthumus on the battlefield and the ultimate reconciliation of Rome and Britain in the final scene. Although Imogen appears in all these settings, she does so only in boy's dress, a costume she retains to the play's conclusion. I shall discuss the implications of her disguise more fully below but would point out here that it shifts not only her gender but also her status and age from married adult to single youth.[21] These shifts make more apparent the exclusion of adult women, particularly mothers, from the scenes of male bonding in *Cymbeline*.[22] An historiographical concern over originary females seems to be enacted here in familial terms. The construction of the Queen as a figure of savage excess, even if not especially with regard to her maternity, recalls Goldberg's formulation of the necessary effacement of women and savages "in order for history to move forward as the exclusive preserve of white men."[23] In the context of *Cymbeline,* one might alter his last words to read "civilized" or perhaps "Romanized men." All roads of male bonding lead to Rome in this play and, correspondingly, to a place in the exclusive preserve of Roman history.

Critics reading *Cymbeline* from the perspective of early modern historiography are divided on the question of Rome's role. Those who identify the play's romance resolution with the Romans cite the importance of Rome in British chronicle history and Jacobean enthusiasm for Augustan analogies.[24] Others argue that in *Cymbeline* Shakespeare exorcises his fascination with Roman history in favor of a more humane British national ethic.[25] Early modern responses were not so one-sided. In their attempts to reconcile ancient British patriotism and a civilized union with Rome, English historians acknowledged and developed a hybrid nationalist response to the Roman Conquest. Violently patriotic queens played an important role in negotiating this hybrid. The hierarchical binarism of gender, fundamental to the construction of early modern society, also governed that period's construction of the ancient British relation to Rome. In the section that follows, I shall examine this phenomenon through the early modern historiography of two ancient Britons, Boadicea and Caractacus. Although separated historically by almost twenty years, these two figures of ancient British patriotism appear side by side in early modern accounts of Roman Britain. Their dramatic juxtaposition reveals much about the gendering and sexualizing of national origins and identity in early modern England.

II

Cymbeline's Queen has no direct source in Holinshed's reign of Kymbeline. She bears a striking resemblance, however, to Voadicia, or Boadicea, who appears in Holinshed's narrative of Roman Britain roughly sixty years after the events depicted in Shakespeare's play.[26] Like Cymbeline's Queen, Boadicea opposed the Roman conquerors but ultimately failed to free Britain of the imperial yoke, taking her own life (or dying of "a natural infirmity") after a conclusive battle. Also like the wicked Queen, she was famous for her nationalist stance, especially her great speech on British freedom and resistance to tyranny, where she opposed the payment of tribute to Rome and invoked the same topoi of the island's natural strengths and the glorious history of Britain's people and kings. Ultimately, Boadicea, too, suffered condemnation for her ruthless defense of this position. Although Holinshed acknowledges the legitimacy of her initial grievance (the Romans had seized her late husband's kingdom, raped her daughters, and had her flogged), he finds that her female savagery carried her too far in revenge. Showing no mercy, Boadicea led the "dreadful examples of the Britons' cruelty" until her undisciplined army of women and men finally met defeat at the hands of a smaller, well-organized band of Romans under the leadership of Suetonius. The editorial summary of her revolt makes explicit both the cause of her failure and the reason for her condemnation: "the chief cause of the Britons insurging against the Romans, they admitted as well women as men to public government."[27]

Caractacus, on the other hand, wins unqualified historiographical praise for both his initial resistance and his eventual submission to Rome. In 43 AD he led the western tribe of the Silurians in revolt against Rome. Although he, like Boadicea, was defeated, he did not end his life but was taken to Rome to be led as a captive in the Emperor Claudius's triumphal procession. There he so distinguished himself by the dignity of his speech and bearing that he won freedom and commendation of his manly courage from Claudius himself. Caractacus's manliness, his Roman *virtus*, is the focus of early modern accounts of his uprising. The patriotic oration Caractacus delivers before Claudius is never condemned. On the contrary, the 1587 Holinshed cites it as both laudable and successful, calling it the "manly speech to the Emperor Claudius, whereby he and his obtain mercy and pardon." The term *manly* draws an implicit contrast with the earlier condemnation of Boadicea's revolt as an example of feminine government.[28]

The distinction between Caractacus's manly *romanitas* and Boadicea's female savagery became a standard feature of early modern accounts of Roman Britain. Camden begins his collection of "Grave Speeches and Wittie Apothegmes of woorthie Personages of this Realme in former times" with a thirteen-line citation of the "manly speech" of Caractacus before Claudius. He follows this with a three-line speech from Boadicea, after which, he reports, she lets a hare out of her lap as a token of the Romans' timidity. This superstitious piece of barbarism meets with the fate it deserves, for "the successe of the battell prooved otherwise."[29] As late as Milton's *History of Britain* in 1671, the distinction was maintained. Milton cites in full Caractacus's manly speech and offers him as a classic exemplum of masculine virtue. When he comes to Boadicea's rebellion, however, he refuses to include her oration, saying that he does not believe in set speeches in a history and that he has cited Caractacus only because his words demonstrate "magnanimitie, soberness, and martial skill." In fact Milton accuses his classical sources of having put words into Boadicea's mouth "out of a vanity, hoping to embellish and set out thir Historie with the strangness of our manners, not caring in the meanwhile to brand us with the rankest note of Barbarism, as if in *Britain* Woemen were Men, and Men Woemen."[30] In this standard pairing of the male and female British rebels against Rome, then, Boadicea represented "the rankest note of Barbarism," that state in which gender distinctions are collapsed. Caractacus, on the other hand, was a figure of exemplary manliness, invoked to counterbalance the overwhelming female savagery of Boadicea and to reestablish British masculinity.[31]

Fletcher seems to have followed this pattern in composing his drama *Bonduca.* Although he derived most of his historical information from classical sources and Holinshed's *Chronicles,* he also included a character named Caratach, Bonduca's cousin and general of the Britons.[32] Caratach conducts the war by Roman rules, for which he expresses great admiration. He even chastises Bonduca for her extravagant speeches against the Romans, thus anticipating Milton's rejection of her feminine oratory. Because she defied Caratach's order to return to her spinning wheel and instead meddled in the affairs of men, Bonduca is made to bear full responsibility for the Britons' eventual defeat. Despite her eponymous role in the drama, she dies in Act 4, leaving the "Romophile" Caratach to represent Britain in the last act. During that act he earns the further admiration of the Roman soldiers, who publicly honor and praise him for his Roman virtues. The play ends with his embrace by the Roman commander Swetonius and the latter's words: "Ye shew a friends soul. / March on, and through the Camp in every tongue, / The Vertues of great *Caratach* be sung."[33]

Other plays of the period which deal with British rebellion against Rome end with the same masculine embrace. In *The Valiant Welshman,* a dramatization of Caractacus's rebellion, the character "Caradoc" is betrayed into Roman hands by the duplicitous British queen Cartamanda and brought before the Emperor Claudius. Claudius then recalls Caradoc's valor in battle, lifts him up from his kneeling posture, and celebrates his valiant name.[34] In William Rowley's *A Shoemaker, a Gentleman,* a disguised British prince twice saves the life of the Emperor Dioclesian and rescues the imperial battle standard in successive clashes with Vandals and Goths.[35] On resigning his trophies to Dioclesian in the next scene with the words "Now to the Royall hand of Caesar I resigne / The high Imperiall Ensigne of great Rome," the prince is bidden by the emperor to "Kneele downe, / And rise a Brittaine Knight" (3.5.17-49).[36] *Fuimus Troes, or the True Trojans,* a play about Julius Caesar's conquest, ends in a metaphorical embrace of empire, with the words "The world's fourth empire Britain doth embrace."[37] With the exception of Rowley's *Shoemaker,* these plays work toward a reconciliation between Rome and Britain that is exclusively masculine.[38] Any women who might have figured in the action (and they usually do so in invented love plots) have been killed off, leaving the stage free for men to conclude matters of true historic import. With the exclusion of women from the action, the stage of Roman Britain becomes the "exclusive preserve" of men, both British and Roman. This triumph of exclusion is figured in the masculine embrace that is the dominant trope of these final scenes, invoked as a metaphor of empire and embodied in the stage embraces of male Britons by Roman commanders and in the symbolic merging of their national emblems.[39]

If the masculine romance of Roman Britain delivers Britain from the self-destructive violence of the wicked Queen, however, it also defines the province of Britannia as the passive object of Roman desire. Mosse emphasizes the fear of male homosexuality that haunts the fraternal bonding of nationalism.[40] Goldberg expands on this idea in his analysis of *Plimoth Plantation,* citing William Bradford's need to separate the pervasive homosociality of his founding American fantasy of all-male relations "by drawing the line—lethally—between its own sexual energies and those it calls sodomitical." Commenting on Bradford's reluctant inclusion of "'a case of buggery'" because "'the truth of the history requires it.'" Goldberg sets the unrealizable desire to distinguish originary male bonding from sodomy at the heart of Bradford's history: "The truth of the history, as I am reading it, is the entanglement of the 'ancient members' with and the desire to separate from the figure of the sodomite who represents at once the negation of the ideal and its literalization."[41] Fear of homosexuality is neither so clear nor so lethal in early modern constructions of Roman Britain, where female savagery is the primary object of revulsion. When Fletcher and Shakespeare attempt the literalization of this masculine ideal in terms of a purely British nationalism, however, they produce scenes of male bonding characterized by feminine and domestic behavior.[42]

The assumption of women's work, speech, and familial roles characterizes male bonding among Britons in *Bonduca* and *Cymbeline.* Wales, the last preserve and final retreat of pure Britishness, provides the setting in both cases.[43] In *Bonduca* this nationalist male bonding dominates the last act, where Caratach, hiding from the Romans, cares for his nephew Hengo, last of the royal Iceni after the deaths of Bonduca and her daughters. In doing so, Caratach takes on the maternal role that Bonduca, in her unfeminine lust for battle, has refused to exercise. His whole concern in this last act is the nursing and feeding of the boy Hengo, who is dying of sickness and hunger after the British defeat. Caratach's language to the boy is tender and protective: he tries to shield him from the knowledge of their loss and soothes him with such endearments as "sweet chicken" and "fair flower" (5.1.27; 5.3.159). Hengo's name (Fletcher's invention) points to Hengist, the first Saxon ruler in Britain, often used in early modern iconography as the representative of England's Saxon heritage.[44] The moving spectacle of the old warrior nursing the last sprig of British manhood might thus suggest an imaginative attempt to construct a native masculine genealogy proceeding directly from ancient Britain to the Saxon heptarchy, and excluding both women and Rome from the national past. The death of Hengo signals the failure of this fantasy. Only after the collapse of this last hope for the continuation of the British line does Caratach allow himself to be won over by the brave courtesies of the Romans, who promise the boy honorable burial (5.3.185-88). Caratach's embrace by Claudius follows the failure of this domestic interlude, in which Caratach tries to keep alive the generative fantasy of a purely masculine Britain.[45]

The experiment in an all-male British world is more developed in *Cymbeline*. In the middle of Act 3, after ties with Rome have been broken, Shakespeare introduces the Welsh retreat of Belarius, Guiderius, and Arviragus. This idyll represents as full a return to unmitigated Britishness as the wicked Queen's opposition to the payment of tribute. Just as her resistance to Rome fails, causing (in Cymbeline's view) her own death and that of her son,[46] so, too, does the primitive fantasy of the Welsh cave fail to stave off the ultimate embrace with Rome. In the latter case it is not the death of the British heirs that ends this hope but rather their fear that they will lack a historical afterlife. When Belarius praises the purity of their Welsh retreat, contrasting it with the tales he has told the boys "Of courts, of princes; of the tricks in war" (3.3.15), the elder son responds: "Out of your proof you speak: we poor unfledg'd, / Have never wing'd from view o' th' nest; nor know not / What air's from home" (ll. 27-29). He concedes that the quiet life of their retreat may be sweeter to Belarius than the court but asserts that "unto us it is / A cell of ignorance" (ll. 32-33). His younger brother then adds:

> What should we speak of
> When we are old as you? When we shall hear
> The rain and wind beat dark December? How
> In this our pinching cave shall we discourse
> The freezing hours away? We have seen
> nothing:
> We are beastly.
>
> (ll. 35-40)

What the brothers protest is their exclusion from history. They have seen nothing; they are barbaric. Confined to their pinching cave in Wales, they have, quite literally, no history to speak of. This conflict between the princes and their presumed father comes to a head when the brothers want to enter the battle against the Romans. Belarius takes their zeal as an irrepressible sign of their royal blood, which longs to "fly out and show them princes born" (4.4.53-54). It is equally, however, a sign of their desire to enter the world of history. Belarius's own sense of having been painfully shaped by a wider experience only fuels this desire. "O boys, this story / The world may read in me: my body's mark'd / With Roman swords," he claims (3.3.55-57), as though his body were a literalization of the Roman writing of ancient British history. Without fighting the Romans, the princes will have no such marks to read by the winter fire when they are old. The masculine rite of passage such scars represent for them personally is a version of the national entry into history by means of the Roman invasion. For early modern historiographers Britain, too, would have remained outside history had she never entered into battle with the Romans.[47]

This convergence of the personal and the national in the forging of masculine identity offers the possibility of reconciling two of the most important interpretive traditions of *Cymbeline:* the psychoanalytic and the historicist. Where historicists find the battle and its aftermath puzzling and inconclusive in terms of the play's treatment of Roman-British relations, psychoanalytic critics focus on the battle as the play's central masculine rite of passage, interpreting it in archetypal terms that ignore its historiographical complexity.[48] The approach I have been advocating, developed from Mosse's insight about the interrelatedness of nationalism and sexuality, historicizes the development of sexual and national identities as it demonstrates their interdependence. Janet Adelman, while recognizing the historiographical complexity of Cymbeline's submission to Rome, interprets it in psychoanalytic terms as a result of "the conflicted desire for merger even at the root of the desire for autonomy."[49] In historiographical terms, I would argue that in early modern England an originary engagement with Rome was necessary for the formation of an autonomous national identity. Roman Britain came to play a foundational role in the recovery of native origins not only because it provided a context for the male bonding that characterizes modern nationalism but also because it enabled exorcism of the female savagery that challenged both the autonomy and the respectability of nationalism.

Engagement with Rome also brought Britain into the masculine preserve of Roman historiography. It is battle with the Romans that affords Cymbeline's sons, the male Britons of the next generation, that historical identity they lacked in their pastoral retreat. In the dramatization of this episode, they achieve historical status instantly, not because they rewrite Roman history, or win a lasting victory, but rather because that victory is immediately described and preserved in historiographical forms. As soon as the princes' stand with Belarius has been presented dramatically, Posthumus recapitulates it as a historical battle narrative, complete with citations of brave speeches and descriptions of the terrain and deployment of troops (5.3.1-51). His interlocutor responds by producing an aphorism to commemorate their action, "A narrow lane, an old man, and two boys" (l. 52), which Posthumus improves into a rhymed proverb: "Two boys, an old man twice a boy, a lane, / Preserved the Britons, was the Romans' bane" (ll. 57-58). The transformation of the dramatic stand in 5.2 into narrative, aphorism, and proverb in 5.3 represents instant historicization. This making of history issues directly from engagement with the Romans, which also leads to the princes' restoration as Cymbeline's male heirs. Both the continuance of the masculine British line and the entrance of its youngest branches into written history require abandonment of the purely British romance of the cave in Wales.[50]

III

Imogen alone remains as a possible icon of pure Britishness in the complex of gender, sexuality, and nationalism I have been describing. Surely in her we have an early version of Mosse's icon of respectable womanhood to bless the virile bonding of nationalism.[51] She, more than her father or brothers, presents and experiences Britain, wandering through it, calling up its place names, and describing its natural situation. Imogen's name, invented by Shakespeare for the heroine he adds to his historical material, is derived from that of Brute's wife, Innogen, mother of the British race.[52] And like other ancient queens, Imogen, too, voices a lyrical celebration of the island: "I' th' world's volume / Our Britain seems as of it, but not in't: / In a great pool, a swan's nest" (3.4.138-40). The image of the swan's nest is as evocative of national identity as that of Neptune's park in the Queen's speech, suggesting among other things Leland's great chorographic song of the Thames, *Cygnea Cantio*.[53] The context of the speech, however, is quite different from that of the Queen's national celebration in 3.1. In contrast to the Queen's radical "Britocentrism," Imogen asserts in 3.4 that Britain is only a small part of a larger world, a world from which it is in fact separate. Her line "Our Britain seems as of it, but not in't" raises the historiographical question of Britain's isolation from the civilized world. At least one critic has suggested that Imogen's line is a version of the Vergilian verse *"Et penitus toto diuisos orbe Britannos,"* cited in Holinshed's *Chronicles*.[54] Whether the image is derived from a Roman source or not, it perpetuates the imperial view of Britain's separation from the world identified with civilization. Rather than lauding this separation, as would Boadicea or the wicked Queen, Imogen suggests that there is a world outside Britain where she may fare better than she will at the hands of the Queen and her son.

As in early modern accounts of ancient Britain, this flight from native isolation leads inevitably to Rome, for Pisanio answers Imogen's speech with the words: "I am most glad / You think of other place: th' ambassador, / Lucius the Roman, comes to Milford-Haven / To-morrow" (3.4.141-44). Lucius the Roman and Milford Haven will together shape Imogen's identity for the rest of the play. The mutuality required for them to do so signals how British national identity is formed from the interaction of the Roman invaders with the native land. If there is a magic of place in *Cymbeline,* it is in Milford Haven. The place name takes on an almost incantatory power as Imogen and the other characters make their way to the haven of final recognition and reconciliation.[55] Critics since Emrys Jones have stressed the importance of Milford Haven in Tudor mythography as the place where Henry Tudor landed before marching to defeat Richard III at the Battle of Bosworth Field.[56] They have built on this historiographical reading a sense of Milford Haven as a sacred or enchanted place that saps the strength of Britain's enemies and grounds the resistance of her true defenders. This is very satisfying in terms of Tudor-Stuart mythography, with its claims of Arthurian and British precedence, but it does not explain why Lucius the Roman, rather than Cymbeline, lands at Milford in anticipation of the future Henry VII of England.

The first Britons Lucius encounters on landing are the disguised Imogen and the headless corpse of Cloten in Posthumus's clothes. Lucius's attempt to reconstruct the story of the figure sleeping on the "trunk . . . / Without his top" issues in a series of questions that demand a recapitulation of the play's action which no single character can articulate (4.2.353-67) and which will occupy much of the lengthy recognition scene at the play's conclusion. The unreadability of this tableau of headless masterlessness emphasizes the confusion of British national identity at this moment, with Cymbeline under the domination of his wicked Queen, Cloten dead in Posthumus's dress, the princes in hiding and ignorant of their royal identity, Imogen disguised and believing Posthumus to be dead, and Posthumus himself at large and still deceived as to his wife's fidelity. Imogen voices this confusion in response to Lucius's final, blunt question, "What are thou?":

> I am nothing; or if not,
> Nothing to be were better. This was my
> master.
> A very valiant Briton, and a good,
> That here by mountaineers lies slain. Alas!
> There is no more such masters: I may wander
> From east to occident, cry out for service,
> Try many, all good: serve truly: never
> Find such another master.
> (4.2.367-74)

Recalling medieval laments over the dead body of a feudal lord, Imogen presents herself as a youth who has lost all status or place after the death of the "very valiant Briton" "he" calls master. In this invented identity she gives voice to the inner despair of her presumed widowhood—her sense of being nothing at the seeming death of her husband—in terms of a nationless wandering from east to west. As in the princes' entry into battle, the personal and the national intersect in Imogen's crisis in Wales.

The upward turn of Imogen's fortunes, and those of her nation, is not far to seek. If there is any straightforwardly respectable character in *Cymbeline,* it is the Roman commander and emissary Lucius. He conducts himself with honor in the council scenes of 3.1 and 5.5 and succors the disguised Imogen with grace and generosity in 4.2. He is also resolutely masculine, deriving his identity from military and political functions, and appearing in such masculine contexts as the council chamber, the march, and the battlefield. Here indeed is a virile antitype of Henry Tudor at Milford, and an ancient predecessor on which to found a stable masculine identity for the nation. When Lucius questions the disguised British princess about her dead "master's" identity, she gives the latter's name as "Richard du Champ" (4.2.377), suggesting an analogy between his body and the ground. Without putting undue pressure on this analogy, I would suggest that Lucius, in raising Imogen from the ground, also releases her from her quest to reach Milford Haven, from her ritualized laying out by the princes and Belarius, and from her second "death" on the body of "du Champ." In taking her from this multiply constructed British ground, he gives her a new identity in his Roman entourage.

The only constant of Imogen's shifting identity in this scene is her assumed name, Fidele. It is her proper epithet, and yet, for a personification of unwavering marital fidelity, Imogen changes allegiance a remarkable number of times. Her initial defection from her father precedes but informs the play's action; one might even read in her decision to reject the death planned by Posthumus, or in her mistaken abandonment of her marriage while her husband yet lives, a kind of defection from absolute fidelity to him also.[57] Certainly she moves from one allegiance to another in the middle acts of the play, where she leaves the princes and Belarius, abandons the seeming corpse of Posthumus, and ultimately betrays Lucius himself when she refuses to plead for his life before Cymbeline (5.5.104-5). Both in this series of shifts between British and Roman identifications and in the wager plot, the question of Imogen's fidelity is of central importance. Posthumus reviles Imogen and all women for faithlessness when he believes she has betrayed him (2.5.20-35), and Lucius makes a similar generalization about those who place their trust in girls and boys when she abandons him to his fate (5.5.105-7).[58] By the conclusion of the play, however, Imogen reconciles all her conflicting fidelities. Cymbeline is again her father; Posthumus, her husband; and the princes, her brothers. Last of all these bonds, she restores her relation to Lucius, to whom she says, "My good master, / I will yet do you service" (ll. 404-5).

This restoration immediately precedes the final reversal of the play, in which Cymbeline restores Britain's tributary relationship to Rome and blames its earlier disruption on the nationalism of his "wicked queen." Imogen's final act of fidelity, like her father's, is an acknowledgment of Rome as master, even in defeat.[59] The Latin name Fidele that she assumes as a badge of her wifely constancy suggests the general importance of Rome in the construction of *British* faithfulness. Imogen's quest to prove her marital fidelity becomes involved in the complex question of national fidelity when she decides to follow Lucius. It is Lucius who raises her from ritualized death and failure in 4.2, and he who gives her the context in which to reconstruct her identity as Fidele when she acknowledges herself reduced to nothing by the apparent death of Posthumus. Even when she seems to deny Lucius, Imogen reaffirms the Roman bond, telling Cymbeline, "He is a Roman, no more kin to me / Than I to your highness" (5.5.112-13). While she is disguised, she is constituted as her Latin name Fidele, as though her disgrace could only be lifted, her fidelity reconstructed, in Roman terms.

The role of Fidele involves a shift not only in national identity but also in gender, Lucius's generalization about those who put their trust in girls and boys being truer than he realizes. Her relationship with Lucius thus becomes a version of the other bonds between male Britons and Roman commanders. Like Caractacus, she is lifted from the ground by a Roman leader who celebrates her virtue, and in Lucius's redefinitions of their hierarchical relationship, she becomes increasingly the object of his love, not his mastery. The masculine embrace of Roman Britain is thus figured in the relationship of the disguised Imogen and the Roman Lucius even before the Roman and British ensigns "wave friendly together" at the play's conclusion. The complexity of what Imogen represents in this embrace, in terms of both gender and sexuality, illustrates the complicated nature of British national identity in the play. Neither her imagined female body nor her boy's disguise offers a stable masculine identity for Britain.[60] The instability of the gender, status, and national identities represented in this figure of disguise and much-questioned fidelity precludes the construction of any stable identity, personal or national.

The resolution of the play's many riddles of identity depends on the deus ex machina of the oracle Posthumus finds on his bosom after dreaming of his family and lineage in 5.4. This restoration of personal identity has its national analogue. The Roman Soothsayer who explicates the oracle of Posthumus's identity is the same who prophesied the merger of Cymbeline's emblem of the radiant sun with the Roman eagle, as he recalls in the penultimate speech of the play (5.5.468-77). When he reads Imogen into the oracle, he identifies her as "The piece of tender air . . . / Which we call *mollis aer:* and *mollis aer* / We term it *mulier:* which *mulier* I divine / Is this most constant wife" (ll. 447-50). This display of pseudo-etymology recalls the involved and equally fanciful antiquarian derivations of the name *Britain.* (Except for its context, it would stand as a parody of such pedantry, in the style of a Don Armado or a Fluellen.) Camden begins the *Britannia* with a survey of such theories, including Humfrey Lhuyd's derivation of *Britain* from the Welsh *Prid-Cain,* meaning a "pure white form," a phrase that resonates with the Soothsayer's "piece of tender air" in its attempt to articulate an ethereal purity.[61] As in the Soothsayer's derivation of *mulier* from *mollis aer,* it also works to disembody and desexualize the loaded term *Britannia.* Even so, by presenting Imogen as a piece of tender air, the Soothsayer completes the separation from the earth begun by Lucius when he lifted her from the ground of Wales and the body of "du Champ." This fancy antiquarian footwork restores Imogen to her husband by reconstituting woman, strongly identified with the land in both Imogen and the wicked Queen, as air so that she might take her place in the prophetic new order of Roman Britain.[62]

Imogen never regains the visual trappings of her femininity. If she represents a version of ancient British respectability, it is one riddled with the problems of gender and sexuality which characterize the British relation to Rome. To the extent that she reemerges as a respectable ideal at the end of the play, it is through a series of alliances with the male characters, both British and Roman, from whom she derives her identity. Cymbeline's daughter, Posthumus's wife, the princes' sister, and the servant of Lucius, she does not raise the specter of female autonomy and leadership suggested by the wicked Queen's machinations and the example of Boadicea. The anxieties provoked by these ancient British queens are thus ultimately defused in the series of bonds Imogen has established by the end of the play. These bonds emphasize the necessary subordination of the feminine within the patriarchal structures of marriage and empire. The fact that Imogen reestablishes these bonds while still in her boy's disguise indicates the degree of anxiety about female power to destroy them. Like *Bonduca, The Valiant Welshman,* and *The True Trojans, Cymbeline* concludes with the image of an exclusively male community.

I would like to close with a word about the relative roles of homophobia and misogyny in early modern constructions of national origins. In Mosse's formulation the greatest threat to the male bonding of nationalism is overt male homosexuality, an anxiety Goldberg discovers as early as the 1630s in *Plimoth Plantation.* Both theorists emphasize the interrelatedness of homophobia and misogyny in the formation of masculine national identity. In the masculine romance of Roman Britain, fears of effeminacy and of women are also interwined. It strikes me, however, that the latter are much more explicit than the former. A fear of originary female savagery consistently drove early modern historians and dramatists of ancient Britain to find refuge in the Roman embrace. The complexities of Britain's position in this embrace certainly raise issues of sexuality, but these seem to me to be subordinated to an overriding concern about the gender of national origins. British origins in all these works emerge as unavoidably feminine, either in the savagery of a wicked queen or in the feminized domesticity and submission of the British male to the Roman embrace. I take the violence with which early modern dramatists and historians rejected the figure of the ancient British queen as an indication of how thoroughly their failure to transform the femininity of national origins disturbed them. Their attempts to avoid this originary femininity led them ultimately to embrace a subordinate status in the Roman empire. While this new status also consigned Britain to a feminized role, it avoided the savagery of the purely British nationalism articulated by ancient queens. It also allowed for a historical afterlife for Britain. In contrast to the ancient queen's savage refusal of empire, the masculine embrace of Roman Britain became the truly generative interaction, producing a civil masculine foundation for early modern English nationalism.

Notes

[1] Quotations are taken respectively from Liah Greenfeld, *Nationalism: Five Roads to Modernity* (Cambridge, MA: Harvard UP, 1992), 23; and Benedict Anderson, *Imagined Communities: Reflections on the Origin and Spread of Nationalism,* rev. ed. (London and New York: Verso, 1992), 205. Anderson's formative study was first published in 1983.

[2] For their respective theoretical positions, see Greenfeld, 17-21; and Anderson, 1-7. Anderson's preface to his second edition provides a useful summary (c. 1991) of changes in the study of nationalism during the 1980s and the ironies of the global political transformations that defined the early 1990s.

[3] The historical bibliography for this "crisis of order" in early modern England is a long one; the model has received some recent challenges from within the ranks of social historians (who largely developed it). For studies emphasizing the issues of gender and sexuality I take up in this article, see Susan Dwyer Amussen, *An Ordered Society: Gender and Class in Early Modern England* (Oxford: Basil Blackwell, 1988); Amussen, "Gender, Family and the Social Order, 1560-1725," and D. E. Underdown, "The Taming of the Scold: the Enforcement of Patriarchal Authority in Early Modern England," both in *Order and Disorder in Early Modern England,* Anthony Fletcher and John Stevenson, eds. (Cambridge: Cambridge UP, 1985), 196-217 and 116-36. For a broader Continental perspective, see Natalie Zemon Davis, "Women on Top." *Society and Culture in Early Modern France* (Stanford, CA: Stanford UP, 1975), 124-51. For a recent critique of the historiographical use of the term *crisis* and a call for

greater attention to the disorder of masculinity as well as femininity in the period, see Lyndal Roper, *Oedipus and the Devil: Witchcraft, sexuality and religion in early modern Europe* (London and New York: Routledge, 1994), 37-52.

[4] Anderson, 12.

[5] In his description of the revolt led by the Iceni queen Boudicca, Tacitus notes this political equality of the sexes and identifies it as one of the defining features of British barbarism: *"neque enim sexum in imperiis discernunt"* (see Tacitus, *Agricola,* trans. M. Hutton, Rev. R. M. Ogilvie, in *Agricola, Germania and Dialogus,* 5 vols., Loeb Classical Library [Cambridge, MA: Harvard UP, 1970], Vol. 1, Bk. 16.1-3). For corroboration of this assessment in early modern English historiography, see the discussion of Boadicea below, p. 309.

[6] The most elaborate articulation of this model is George L. Mosse, *Nationalism and Sexuality: Respectability and Abnormal Sexuality in Modern Europe* (New York: Howard Fertig, 1985). Sexuality is also implicit in much of Anderson's study and emerges explicitly in the closing pages (199-203), where Anderson posits two versions of eroticized nationalism that also consider how attitudes to race and miscegenation figure in this complex. See also Carole Pateman, "The Fraternal Social Contract" in *Civil Society and the State: New European Perspectives,* John Keane, ed. (London and New York: Verso, 1988), 101-27. While Pateman does not examine sexuality, she usefully describes how the fraternal pact that excludes women from power remained constant in the transition from patriarchal to social-contract theories of government in seventeenth-century England.

[7] For the historical and land-based nationalism developed by Elizabethan antiquarians, see Richard Helgerson, "The Land Speaks," *Forms of Nationhood: The Elizabethan Writing of England* (Chicago, IL, and London: U of Chicago P, 1992), 105-47. G. Wilson Knight includes this Jacobean speech with other Shakespearean examples of what he calls Elizabethan post-Armada sentiment: Hastings's short invocation of the impregnable isle in Act 4 of *3 Henry VI:* John of Gaunt's speech in Act 2 of *Richard II;* and Austria's description of the kingdom he promises to the young Lewis of France in Act 2 of *King John.* (This last is a somewhat equivocal appeal to nationalism, given its context.) See *The Crown of Life* (London: Oxford UP, 1947), 136. Indeed, this Elizabethan sentiment persisted into James's reign, when many of its more accessible monuments were first published; e.g., the first English translation of William Camden's *Britannia* in 1610; Part 1 of Michael Drayton's chorographical epic *Poly-Olbion* in 1612, along with John Speed's *Theatre of the Empire of Great Britain,* the first fully developed county atlas of England. Saxton's 1579 atlas, often combining several counties to a sheet, and not including inserts of county towns, represents a less fully realized version of what came to be the county-atlas genre.) J. M. Nosworthy's dating of *Cymbeline* as probably 1609 puts it at the peak of popular interest in national history and topography (The Arden Shakespeare *Cymbeline,* ed. J. M. Nosworthy [London: Methuen, 1955], xiv).

[8] All quotations of *Cymbeline* follow Nosworthy's Arden edition.

[9] For a rich account of nostalgia in Shakespearean appeals to national history and topography, see Phyllis Rackin, "Anachronism and Nostalgia," *Stage of History: Shakespeare's English Chronicles* (Ithaca, NY: Cornell UP, 1990), 86-145. Rackin notes the receding horizon of nostalgia in John of Gaunt's "scepter'd isle" speech in *Richard II,* where the nineteen-line accumulation of appositive noun phrases grammatically constructs the desired past "as an ideal substance beyond the reach of historical process," a changeless prehistory that syntactically resists narrative (122-23).

[10] Alexander Leggatt, "The Island of Miracles: An Approach to *Cymbeline."* *Shakespeare Studies* 10 (1977): 191-209; Leah S. Marcus, "*Cymbeline* and the Unease of Topicality" in *The Historical Renaissance: New Essays on Tudor and Stuart Literature and Culture,* Heather Dubrow and Richard Strier, eds. (Chicago, IL:U of Chicago P, 1988), 134-68; Robert S. Miola, *Shakespeare's Rome* (Cambridge: Cambridge UP, 1983), 206-35; Joan Warchol Rossi, "*Cymbeline*'s Debt to Holinshed: The Richness of III.i" in *Shakespeare's Romances Reconsidered,* Carol McGinnis Kay and Henry E. Jacobs, eds. (Lincoln: U of Nebraska P, 1978), 104-12; Warren D. Smith, "Cloten with Caius Lucius," *Studies in Philology* 49 (1952): 185-94.

[11] Geoffrey Hill, "'The True Conduct of Human Judgment': Some Observations on *Cymbeline*" in *The Lords of Limit: Essays on Literature and Ideas* (London: André Deutsch, 1984), argues that although Shakespeare ultimately rejects the "ferocious insularity" of 3.1, most of his original audience would have applauded it (55-66). J. P. Brockbank, in "History and Histrionics in *Cymbeline*" (*Shakespeare Survey* 11 [1958]: 42-49, esp. 44 and 47), characterizes Cloten and the Queen as "hypostatized versions of the arbitrary spleen and malevolence that Geoffrey [of Monmouth] often found antecedent to the rule of law," yet he ultimately argues that their "minimal virtue of defiant patriotism" is never allowed to menace seriously the natural integrity of the British court.

[12] Knight, 136. For his full reading of *Cymbeline* in this regard, see 129-67.

[13] Mosse, 18. As France settled into the bourgeois early nineteenth century, for instance, the revolutionary icon of Marianne, once depicted half-naked and leading men into battle, became a fully clothed, seated figure. For Mosse's full argument about respectability, see his "Introduction: Nationalism and Respectability," 1-22; for the development of woman's role in this alliance, see chap. 5, "What Kind of Woman?" 90-113.

[14] Knight regards the Queen as an extreme figure of motherhood, "a possessive maternal instinct impelling her violent life" (132).

[15] It is not quite clear that the Queen dies by her own hand. As in the historiography of Boadicea described below, the Queen might also be said to have succumbed to an excess of savage emotion. Cornelius's response to Cymbeline's question "How ended she?" bears both interpretations: "With horror, madly dying, like her life, / Which (being cruel to the world) concluded / Most cruel to herself" (5.5.31-33).

[16] Amussen, *Ordered Society,* 118-23. Literary challenges to the ideal of wifely subordination persist into the eighteenth century, notably in Restoration and Augustan comedy. Within a Lockean context of the family as private, however, these challenges no longer represent the same disruptive force to society that they did earlier in the seventeenth century. Indeed, one might argue that wifely insubordination (and adultery) figures as largely as it does in Restoration and eighteenth-century comedy precisely because it was no longer perceived as a social threat. For the perceived threat of feminine insubordination to earlier seventeenth-century English society, see the bibliography incorporated into note 3, above.

[17] The kind of complex prehistory to Mosse's model of nationalism that I develop in this article is what gives meaning, I think, to the term *early modern,* i.e., the broader field of less-developed alternatives to the naturalized constructs of modernity, from nationalism to psychic or sexual identity. I invoke the term *prehistory* here in the spirit of Stephen Greenblatt's essay "Psychoanalysis and Renaissance Culture" in *Literary Theory/Renaissance Texts,* Patricia Parker and David Quint, eds. (Baltimore, MD: Johns Hopkins UP, 1986), 210-24. Greenblatt's assertion that "psychoanalysis is, in more than one sense, the end [purpose? goal? final point?] of the Renaissance" (210) can be adapted to nationalism, or the kind of respectable nationalism whose birth Mosse, Anderson, and others locate in the eighteenth century. The "compulsive cultural stabilizing" of individual identity that Greenblatt finds "unusually visible" in the story of Martin Guerre (218) is also remarkable in the construction of national identity in this period. I explore its specificities here in the case of English recovery of native origins, working on the assumption that the quest for national identity, like psychoanalysis's quest for the individual, is (in Greenblatt's words) "the historical outcome of certain characteristic Renaissance strategies" (224). In my discussion of masculine historical identity below, I suggest ways in which historicist and psychoanalytic readings of early modern texts need not be mutually exclusive.

[18] For an account of Imogen as the pattern of conventional Elizabethan womanhood, see Carroll Camden, "The Elizabethan Imogen," *The Rice Institute Pamphlet* 38 (1951): 1-17.

[19] Helgerson points in this direction in his brief afterword to *Forms of Nationhood,* "Engendering the Nation-State," 295-301. For a more developed discussion of how gender anxieties figure in early modern English nationalism, see Jean E. Howard, "An English Lass Amid the Moors: Gender, race, sexuality, and national identity in Heywood's *The Fair Maid of the West*" in *Women, "Race," & Writing in the Early Modern Period,* Margo Hendricks and Patricia Parker, eds. (London and New York: Routledge, 1994), 101-17.

[20] Jonathan Goldberg, "Bradford's 'Ancient Members' and 'A Case of Buggery . . . Amongst Them'" in *Nationalisms and Sexualities,* Andrew Parker, Mary Russo, Doris Sommer, and Patricia Yaeger, eds. (New York and London: Routledge, 1992), 60-76, esp. 63-64. Goldberg acknowledges here the pioneering work of Ann Kibbey on the collapse of Pequots and Anglo women in (masculine) Puritan accounts of the Pequot War; see her chap. 5, "1637: the Pequot War and the antinomian controversy" in *The interpretation of material shapes in Puritanism: A study of rhetoric, prejudice, and violence* (Cambridge: Cambridge UP, 1986), 92-120.

[21] Indeed, even before she assumes her boy's disguise, Imogen's status and authority as a married woman are not clear. Anne Barton, in *Essays, Mainly Shakespearean* (Cambridge: Cambridge UP, 1994), has recently pointed to numerous ambiguities in the play's references to the union of Imogen and Posthumus, suggesting that it might have been an unconsummated precontract rather than a solemnized marriage (19-30). Janet Adelman, in *Suffocating Mothers: Fantasies of Maternal Origin in Shakespeare's Plays,* Hamlet *to* The Tempest (New York and London: Routledge, 1992), notes the degree to which Imogen's disguise disempowers her, in contradistinction to the ways it enabled the selfhood of Shakespeare's earlier comic heroines (210).

[22] Cymbeline's first queen, mother to Imogen and the lost princes, leaves no other trace in the play than the diamond Imogen gives Posthumus (1.2.43). Belarius's wife, Euriphile, nurse to the young princes and mourned by them as a mother, also seems to have been dead for some time (3.3.103-5). Adelman comments on the need

to efface the maternal in the all-male pastoral of Wales (202-4).

[23] Goldberg, 63-64. Rackin elaborates how women function as "antihistorians" who resist patriarchal structures of masculine history-writing in Shakespeare's histories ("Patriarchal History and Female Subversion," 146-200). For the particular danger posed by mothers in this regard, see 190-91.

[24] Brockbank, 44-45; David M. Bergeron, "*Cymbeline*: Shakespeare's Last Roman Play," *Shakespeare Quarterly* 31 (1980): 32-41. Bergeron expands his reading of the play's Augustan elements in *Shakespeare's Romances and the Royal Family* (Lawrence: UP of Kansas, 1985), 136-57. For other accounts of the idealization of Augustus as a context for *Cymbeline,* see J. Leeds Barroll, "Shakespeare and Roman History," *Modern Language Review* 53 (1958): 327-43; and T.J.B. Spencer, "Shakespeare and the Elizabethan Romans," *SS* 10 (1957): 27-38. See also Knight, who notes that symbols of English patriotism in Shakespeare's medieval histories often have Roman origins, as in Julius Caesar's supposed erection of the Tower of London, which stimulates nationalist expressions in *Richard III* at 3.1.68-93 and *Richard II* at 5.1.2 (166).

[25] Robert S. Miola articulates the most radical development of this position in two essays: "*Cymbeline*: Shakespeare's Valediction to Rome" in *Roman Images: Selected Papers from the English Institute, 1982,* Annabel Patterson, ed. (Baltimore, MD: Johns Hopkins UP, 1984), 51-62; and "*Cymbeline*: Beyond Rome," *Shakespeare's Rome,* 206-35. See also Leggatt, 192 and 204; and William Barry Thorne, "*Cymbeline*: 'Lopp'd Branches' and the Concept of Regeneration," *SQ* 20 (1969): 143-59. Both "pro-British" and "pro-Roman" historiographical readings of *Cymbeline* have trouble placing Iachimo and the scenes in Rome in a first-century Roman-British context. The only historiographical sense critics have made of Iachimo is to read his symbolic rape of the sleeping Imogen in 2.2 as a figure for the Roman invasion of Britain. Like the Romans at Milford Haven, Iachimo fails to achieve his conquest yet collects his "tribute." The anachronistic intrusion of Renaissance Italy in all its degeneracy may also provide an outlet for anti-Roman sentiment by invoking the early modern context of Rome as the Papacy rather than as the ancient seat of empire. For a brief discussion of 2.2, see note 51 below.

[26] Raphael Holinshed, "Historie of England" in *Chronicles of England, Scotland and Ireland,* (London, 1587), 32-33 and 42-46. Spelling of quotations from Holinshed has been modernized throughout. Brockbank cautiously suggests a resemblance between Cymbeline's Queen and Boadicea (49, n. 20).

[27] Holinshed, "Historie of England" in *Chronicles,* 44 and 42. Abraham Fleming added moralizing headnotes to chapters and episodes in the 1587 Holinshed. These headnotes seem designed both to summarize the narrative and to influence reader response to it. My references to "Holinshed" imply the multiply-authored 1587 text, as opposed to the individual named Raphael Holinshed. For a recent account of the "syndicate" that produced the 1587 edition of the *Chronicles,* see Annabel Patterson, *Reading Holinshed's* Chronicles (Chicago, IL, and London: U of Chicago P, 1994), 1-70.

Throughout his account of the uprising, Holinshed emphasizes the presence of British women in battle as well as government. To introduce Voadicia's oration, set off with its own subtitle in the 1587 edition, he describes the Iceni queen as wearing "a thick Irish mantle" and carrying a spear (43). Ann Rosalind Jones and Peter Stallybrass, "Dismantling Irena: The Sexualizing of Ireland in Early Modern England" in Andrew Parker et al., eds., discuss how the Irishwoman wearing the mantle became an icon of disorder, confusing gender, class, and political categories in early modern English accounts of Ireland (165-69). They also comment on the conflation of mantled Irishwomen and vagrants (158-59). In Holinshed's account Boadicea cites such a conflation in her own case to inflame her troops against the Romans, whose "cruelty showed in scourging her like a vagabond" (45).

[28] Holinshed, "Historie of England" in *Chronicles,* 39. Both evaluations were added to the 1587 edition by its editor, Abraham Fleming.

[29] Camden, *Remains Concerning Britain,* ed. R. C. Dunn (Toronto: U of Toronto P, 1984), 205-6. Dunn uses the 1605 *editio princeps* as his basic text but notes revisions and additions to the 1614 and 1623 editions, also prepared by Camden. The accounts of Caractacus and Boadicea date from the first edition and were neither revised nor expanded in 1614 and 1623. In addition to the *Agricola,* Bks. 15-16, the classical sources for Boadicea's revolt were Tacitus, *The Annals,* trans. John Jackson, in *The Histories and The Annals,* 4 vols., Loeb Classical Library (Cambridge, MA: Harvard UP, 1937), Vol. 4, Bk. 14.30-36; and Dio Cassius, *Dio's Roman History,* trans. Earnest Cary, 9 vols., Loeb Classical Library (London: William Heinemann, 1935), Vol. 8, Bk. 62.1-12.

[30] Milton, *History of Britain,* ed. French Fogle in *Complete Prose Works of John Milton,* Don M. Wolfe, gen. ed., 8 vols. (New Haven, CT, and London: Yale UP, 1971), 5:70-72 and 79-80. Camden, while giving a truncated speech in *Remains,* omits Boadicea's oration from any edition of the *Britannia* published in his lifetime, perhaps for reasons similar to Milton's. Camden mentions Boadicea in conjunction with Camalodunum, London, and Verulam, the three settlements she sacked,

gradually increasing the amount of information and detail in each Latin edition of the *Britannia* (1586, 1587, 1590, 1600, 1607), until she plays a major role in the historical narrative of Roman Britain in the first English-language edition (*Britain,* trans. Philemon Holland [London, 1610], 49-52).

[31] Rackin describes a similarly gendered antithesis between Talbot and Joan of Arc in Shakespeare's first Henriad (151).

[32] In this, Fletcher also drew on the account of Voada, a northern queen, which includes a British leader named Caratake; see Holinshed, "Historie of Scotland" in *Chronicles,* 45-50.

[33] John Fletcher, *Bonduca,* ed. Cyrus Hoy, in *The Dramatic Works in the Beaumont and Fletcher Canon,* Fredson Bowers, gen ed., 8 vols. (Cambridge: Cambridge UP, 1979), Vol. 4, 5.3.201-3

[34] R. A., *The Valiant Welshman, or The True Chronicle History of the life and valiant deeds of Caradoc the Great, King of Cambria, now called Wales.* ed. Valentin Kreb (Leipzig: Georg Bohme, 1902), 5.5.39-58.

[35] William Rowley, *A Shoemaker, a Gentleman in William Rowley: His "All's Lost by Lust," and "A Shoemaker, A Gentleman,"* University of Pennsylvania Series in Philology and Literature 13, ed. Charles Wharton Stork (Philadelphia: John C. Winston Co., 1910), 3.4.

[36] The defeated Vandal Prince Roderick kneels in turn at the end of this scene, promising to confine his people to Germany, to which Dioclesian responds, "And that obedience Roderick weele imbrace" (3.5.64). *Cymbeline*'s combination of British victory with submission to the embrace of empire is thus refracted through a third nation in this probably contemporaneous drama of Roman Britain. (Stork dates *Shoemaker* to 1609 [162]. Bergeron notes the contemporaneity and relevance of this play to *Cymbeline* [*Shakespeare's Romances,* 140].) Despite an unusual emphasis on Roman atrocities (invoked throughout in the context of Christian persecution), Rowley's play too presents a Roman emperor praising the valor of a British prince in the final scene, with Dioclesian's words: "It is a man, whose Fate / Vpheld the glory of the Roman State" (5.2.22-23). I am grateful to an anonymous *SQ* reader for bringing this intriguing play to my attention.

[37] Jasper Fisher, *Fuimus Troes, or the True Trojans* in *A Select Collection of Old Plays,* ed. Robert Dodsley, 12 vols. (London: Septimus Prowett, 1825), 7:456.

[38] The masculine embrace of *Shoemaker* takes place in the third act rather than at the play's conclusion. Several outspoken female characters, British and Roman, take part in the conclusion to this play, distinguishing it from the all-male reconciliations of the other Roman-British dramas. Indeed, the embrace that closes the play is performed by the newly liberated British queen and her recently restored sons.

[39] Just as the Roman and British ensigns "wave friendly together" at the conclusion of *Cymbeline,* so, too, Cymbeline's emblem of the radiant sun is said to merge with the Roman eagle in the Soothsayer's interpretation of his vision before the battle (5.5.468-77). In this interpretation, the meeting of the emblems becomes the symbol of the right relation between Britain and Rome, vested with the force of destiny, and presented as the key to understanding the play's peaceful resolution. The implicit embrace of national emblems in *Cymbeline* is made explicit at the conclusion of *The True Trojans.* There another soothsayer, the Druid Lantonus, describes the new device of Roman Britain, in which the British lion and the Roman eagle are surrounded by two semicircles, representing the double letter C from the names Caesar and Cassibelan: "the semicircles, / First letters of the leader's names, we see, / Are join'd in true love's endless figure" (453). In Lantonus's description of their meeting, "true love's endless figure" represents the embrace of the names Caesar and Cassibelan, even as "The world's fourth empire Britain doth embrace."

[40] See Mosse, chap. 2, "Manliness and Homosexuality," 23-47.

[41] Goldberg, 67-68.

[42] Jones and Stallybrass comment on early modern antiquarian assumptions about national character that linked barbarism with effeminacy in descriptions of the "Scythian disease," a condition of masculine effeminization that included impotence and the assumption of women's work, clothing, speech, and other forms of behavior, represented in national terms by the hereditary effeminacy of the Scythian royal family. Noting the derivation of Irish origins from the Scythians in some late-sixteenth-century apologies for Irish colonization, Jones and Stallybrass argue for the English need to distinguish their own national identity from this barbaric effeminacy (158-65).

[43] For Wales as a place of geographical and sexual liminality in Shakespeare's histories, as "a scene of emasculation and female power, . . . the site of a repression in the historical narrative," see Rackin, 170-72.

[44] Hengist was the architect of the Saxon heptarchy, or seven minor kingdoms, that introduced Saxon rule to Britain. Holinshed chronicles his ascendancy and how as a result "the Saxons come over by heaps to inhabit

the land" ("Historie of England" in *Chronicles,* 78-86, esp. 78). Hengist appears with Brute, Julius Caesar, and William the Conqueror, representing England's Saxon heritage on the title page of Drayton's *Poly-Olbion.* A similar figure entitled "A Saxon" appears with a Briton, a Roman, a Norman, and a Dane on the title page of Speed's *Theatre of the Empire of Great Britain.*

[45] Sharon Macdonald, in "Boadicea: warrior, mother and myth" (*Images of Women in Peace and War: Cross-Cultural and Historical Perspectives,* Sharon Macdonald, Pat Holden, and Shirley Ardener, eds. [London: Macmillan, 1987], 40-61, esp. 49-50), also notes the emphasis on manliness and homoeroticism in *Bonduca.*

[46] See, for instance, 5.5.462-66, where Cymbeline attributes the deaths of the Queen and her son to divine retribution for her interference in the proper submission of Britain to Rome.

[47] The Welsh retreat of the princes has in fact led some critics to conclude that the setting of *Cymbeline* has no historiographical importance and merely enhances the play's romantic qualities. I would argue that the Welsh setting of these scenes is of historical importance precisely because it dramatizes the anxiety of being excluded from history. For the opposing readings, see Irving Ribner, "Shakespeare and Legendary History: *Lear* and *Cymbeline*." *SQ* 7 (1956): 47-52; and Arthur C. Kirsch, "*Cymbeline* and Coterie Dramaturgy," *ELH* 34 (1967): 288-306.

[48] In a recent historicist account, Leah Marcus highlights the battle as an essentially mysterious and unassimilable episode, recapitulated four times in forms that exemplify the insoluble nature of the play's many riddles of interpretation (139-40). Most psychoanalytic critics interpret the Welsh cave as a form of maternal protection from which the princes must emerge into battle with the Romans, which restores them to their father and their patrilineal identity. Caesar functions in these readings as the ultimate father, with whom Britain works out its relationship through the Roman conflict and its resolution. See Meredith Skura, "Interpreting Posthumus' Dream from Above and Below: Families, Psychoanalysts, and Literary Critics" in *Representing Shakespeare*, Murray M. Schwartz and Coppélia Kahn, eds. (Baltimore, MD: Johns Hopkins UP, 1980), 203-16, esp. 209-14: D. E. Landry, "Dreams as History: The Strange Unity of *Cymbeline*," *SQ* 33 (1982): 68-79; and Murray Schwartz, "Between Fantasy and Imagination: A Psychological Exploration of *Cymbeline*," *Psychoanalysis and Literary Process,* ed. Frederick Crews (Cambridge, MA: Winthrop, 1970), 219-83, esp., 250-59. In contrast, Adelman regards the Welsh retreat as an exclusively male preserve where Belarius can raise Cymbeline's sons free from the tainted maternity that haunts masculine imagination in the play (203-4). David M. Bergeron, while not discussing the battle, notes that the Welsh retreat affords the princes no opportunity for sexual experience, arguing that their seclusion is another version of the play's sterile or incomplete sexuality; see his article "Sexuality in *Cymbeline*," *Essays in Literature* 10 (1983): 159-68, esp. 167.

[49] Adelman, 207. Although I disagree with her reading of Wales as an unproblematically masculine sphere, I find Adelman's general discussion of *Cymbeline* (200-219) insightful and persuasive, particularly in her insistence that masculine anxiety about gender and sexuality informs both the marriage plot and what she calls "the Cymbeline plot" (the question of British autonomy and the relation to Rome).

[50] Rackin notes the nostalgic longing in *Richard II* for an all-male past where heroic deeds of warfare conferred meaning and value (191). Her historicist reading of masculine longing in *Richard II* complements and reinforces psychoanalytic analyses of the princes' entry into adult masculine identity in *Cymbeline.*

[51] Imogen's identity with Britain has been commented on from a variety of critical perspectives, especially regarding the analogy between the Roman invasion of Britain and Iachimo's invasion of Imogen's bedchamber; see Leggatt, 194; Schwartz, 221; and Skura, 210. Robin Phillips's 1986 production at Stratford, Ontario, indicates the staging possibilities of this scene within the culminating period of Mosse's argument. Phillips set the play in twentieth-century England between the two world wars, with Iachimo as an Italian fascist whose invasion of Imogen's bedchamber enacted fascist intrusion into and regulation of private relations. His monologue was delivered in an amplified whisper, recalling the role of radio in bringing fascist "morality" literally into the home. I am indebted to Elizabeth D. Harvey for suggesting the radio analogy.

[52] Indeed, some recent editors have made a strong argument for "Innogen" as Shakespeare's intended form of the name. For a summary of this argument, see Roger Warren's *Shakespeare in Performance:* Cymbeline (Manchester and New York: Manchester UP, 1989), viii.

[53] But see Nosworthy's note to this image in the Arden edition, where he surveys critical concern about the image as undignified or degrading.

[54] Brockbank, 48; Holinshed, "Description of Britaine" in *Chronicles,* 2. The line is from the First Eclogue, translated by H. Rushton Fairclough as "wholly sundered from all the world"; see *Virgil,* 2 vols., Loeb Classical Library (Cambridge, MA: Harvard UP, 1950), 1:36.

[55] Simon Forman, who saw a performance of *Cymbeline* in 1611, mentions Milford Haven several times in his account as the place toward which all the action tends. Nosworthy prints Forman's account in full in the introduction to the Arden edition (xiv-xv).

[56] Emrys Jones, in "Stuart Cymbeline" (*Essays in Criticism* 11 [1961]: 84-99), presents the original and most elaborate reading of the historiographical importance of Milford Haven (93-95). For discussions of the power of Milford developed from Jones's argument, see Landry, 71-73; Leggatt, passim; Marcus, 148-51; and Frances A. Yates, *Shakespeare's Last Plays: A New Approach* (London: Routledge and Kegan Paul Ltd., 1975), 47-52.

[57] In the medieval ballads her lament of masterlessness invokes, her role would have been to remain by her dead master's body until she herself died (e.g., like the "fallow doe/lemman" in "The Three Ravens").

[58] One might even suggest that Posthumus provides a needed vent for the collective masculine anxiety about Imogen's fidelity when he unwittingly strikes his disguised wife onstage (5.5.228-29).

[59] Cymbeline's earlier recollection (3.2.69-73) of having served as a page in Augustus's household (a courtly anachronism culled from Holinshed, "Historie of England" in *Chronicles,* 32) strengthens this parallel.

[60] The boy's disguise adds a further complication in that it foregrounds the theatrical convention of boy actors playing female roles.

[61] See Holland's translation of this passage in Camden, *Britain,* 5-6.

[62] Adelman reads the Soothsayer's linguistic transformation of Imogen as an unmaking of her sexual body that "does away with the problematic female body and achieves a family and a masculine identity founded exclusively on male bonds" (218). Rackin, noting the importance of Elizabeth of York, Katherine of France, and the infant Elizabeth at the end of Shakespeare's two Henriads and *Henry VIII,* argues that "the incorporation of the feminine represents the end of the historical process . . . [and] can only take place at the point where history stops. A world that truly includes the feminine is a world in which history cannot be written" (176). From my analysis of *Cymbeline,* I would agree. I would suggest that the converse is also true, that in the romance of national origins, the dis-incorporation of the feminine is the place where history starts.

Source: "The Masculine Romance of Roman Britain: *Cymbeline* and Early Modern English Nationalism," in *Shakespeare Quarterly,* Vol. 46, No. 3, Fall, 1995, pp. 301-22.

Jacobean Muscovites: Winter, Tyranny, and Knowledge in *The Winter's Tale*

Daryl W. Palmer

Muscovy matters to the English imagination in ways that have scarcely been remarked. To some observers in Jacobean England, mention of the place would have conjured up stories of wintry exploration and icy imperialism, beginning, no doubt, with the image of Sir Hugh Willoughby, frozen along with his company in a Lapland river. Sailing north for Cathay in 1553, Willoughby gave new meaning to the telling of tales in winter. The note detailing his final ice-bound days in the month of September, discovered in one of his two ships, inscribes the event: "Thus remaining in this haven the space of a weeke, seeing the yeare farre spent, & also very evill wether, as frost, snow, and haile, as though it had beene the deepe of winter, we thought best to winter there."[1] Here is a story of winter coming before winter, of winter as fate and alien world, a narrative that breaks off because no one survives to finish it. The cold destruction of this winter's tale meshes in fascinating ways with the narrative of Richard Chancellor, who, having become separated from Willoughby in a tempest, voyaged on to make contact with Ivan the Terrible, emperor of Russia and the embodiment of rough, cold extremes. Chancellor, it was said, had discovered Russia.[2] A flourishing trade developed alongside fragile diplomatic ties. Russian ambassadors visited London in 1557, 1569, 1582, and 1600. A little group of Muscovite students came in 1602 to study at Winchester, Eton, Cambridge, and Oxford.[3] And tales proliferated, so that the mere mention of Muscovites would have brought to mind a picture of this terrible Ivan IV,[4] the burly ruler who proposed marriage to one of Elizabeth's ladies and subsequently chastised the queen for allowing men to rule in her place, for ruling "'in your maydenlie estate like a maide.'"[5] Muscovy would have suggested the famously unhappy Boris Godunov. It would have triggered images of the wintry port of Archangel, a stormy place of tentlike encampments and of reindeer pulling sleds. Above all, it would have suggested the many narratives of Muscovy Company agents, rehearsed in the pages of Hakluyt and Purchas: stories of the emperor, his customs, jealousies, and violent deeds; accounts of Russian households and ceremonies; chorographies of Russian landscapes; and so on into a wintry prose that stands, I think, as prologue to Shakespeare's *Winter's Tale*.[6]

The play encourages such associations even when it seems focused thematically and geographically elsewhere. When the king of Sicilia accuses his queen "of high treason, in committing adultery with Polixenes, king of Bohemia' (3.2.14-15),[7] Hermione's defense, remarkable both for its pertinence and eloquence, nonetheless exceeds the local terms of Leontes's Sicilia and King James's London. As the court waits breathlessly for the oracle's word, Hermione adds,

> The Emperor of Russia was my father:
> O that he were alive, and here beholding
> His daughter's trial! that he did but see
> The flatness of my misery, yet with eyes
> Of pity, not revenge!
>
> (ll. 119-23)

In the note to line 119 of his Arden edition of the play, J.H.P. Pafford echoes H. B. Charlton, who believes that the Muscovite reference lends "'a sense of majesty and pathos'" to Hermione's plight. Peter Erickson has proposed that "this recourse to the benign father provides a microcosm of the play's resolution."[8] But in its particularity the passage surely demands more aggressive questioning, especially since we know that Shakespeare went out of his way to alter his source so that it was Hermione who would have a Russian father. In Greene's *Pandosto,* the main character contemplates the obstacles to his revenge: "yet he saw that Egistus was not only of great puissance and prowess to withstand him, but had also many kings of his alliance to aid him, if need should serve, for he married *to* the Emperor's daughter of Russia."[9] In Greene's story, that is, the Russian connection is to the Polixenes character and matters incidentally, but Shakespeare keys Hermione's public display of innocence and outrage to the invocation of Russia.

What difference do trace elements of faraway cultures, their climates and their rulers, make to a grand and complex romance meant for the stage? *Topicality, intertextuality,* and *influence* are but a few of the terms scholars have traditionally employed in answering this kind of question; and the choice of rubric indicates a corresponding emphasis on culture, textuality, and the author, respectively. Regardless of the emphasis, the scholar's work depends on a process of identification whereby equivalent patterns are uncovered. For Glynne Wickham and David M. Bergeron the investigation of a topical *Winter's Tale* leads them, despite differing theoretical orientations, to identifications of the play's characters with the Stuart royal family.[10] Similarly, when Leah Marcus reads *Measure for Measure,* she pursues an identification of Vienna with London.[11] Louise Schleiner, following Julia Kristeva's subtle formulation of intertextuality, sees an identification between Greek versions of the *Oresteia* and *Hamlet.*[12] In *The*

Winter's Tale "Autolycus may incarnate the unemployed vagrant" of the period's pamphlet literature for Barbara Mowat.[13] For Howard Felperin the old codes of the morality play and the early revenge play influence vestigially key scenes in *Hamlet*.[14] In each case the process of identification seems to authorize the scholar's retelling of the Shakespeare story. In each case the question is not whether identifications can be avoided but whether the scholar's descriptions of these identifications can admit obvious gaps and contradictions and still have value as interpretive enterprises.[15] Marcus offers cautions on this score, noting that "the meanings generated by a given text may well be multiple or self-canceling, or both. Instead of striving for a single holistic interpretation of a text, we may find ourselves marking out a range of possibilities or identifying nexuses of contradiction."[16]

In light of these precedents, taking up Hermione's reference to the emperor of Russia becomes a precarious business for several reasons, the most important being that, unlike Schleiner or Felperin, I have no one or two rich texts to hold up against Shakespeare's play. Instead, my proposed mode of attenuated reading actually leads to a scattering of identifications between and among dozens of jostling texts born of decades of English contact with Russia. Such reading ensures that I will not be able to tell Shakespeare's tale anew and whole.[17] This apparent diffuseness will prove unsettling to some, reassuring to others.[18] But ultimately the issue has less to do with my ability to account for Shakespeare's play than with my responsibility to that play's dialogue with its culture of origin. If the play dangles identifications of Jacobean Muscovites in front of me, then I want to be able to describe what made those identifications provocative. When, for instance, Shakespeare invokes a Russian ruler, he encourages his audience to undertake a fleeting albeit bracing "passage from one sign system to another," from English questions about kingship to Russian queries on the same theme.[19] Marking these passages, I can give shape to my reading by respecting fields of cultural doubt, regions of common anxiety, what Marcus calls "nexuses of contradiction."[20] In the pages that follow, I attend to three such fields—winter, tyranny, and knowledge. At the end of the essay, neither the play nor these fields will be reduced to neat individual tales; instead I shall have mapped a series of entertaining and half-fulfilled identifications that played out with urgency for a Jacobean audience.

The fact that any careful observer could have noticed certain resemblances between the apparently disparate worlds of England and Muscovy seems to have encouraged certain habits of analysis in the pages of Hakluyt and Purchas. To be sure, voyaging led English writers into a host of alien worlds where they developed and refined rhetorical strategies for constructing—even consuming—otherness.[21] Nevertheless, Muscovy posed a special challenge because the region always appeared uncomfortably similar to England; indeed, from their first contact in 1553, English merchants and diplomats asked their readers to understand Muscovy as an imperfect analogue to England. This analogical thinking underlies both the composition and the reception of Shakespeare's romance. Richard Chancellor inaugurates the convention: "Mosco it selfe is great: I take the whole towne to bee greater then London with the suburbes: but it is very rude, and standeth without all order." Following the same rhetorical plan, he begs his reader to see the emperor of Russia in terms of the English monarch: "then I was sent for againe unto another palace which is called the golden palace, but I saw no cause why it should be so called; for I have seene many fayrer then it in all poynts: and so I came into the hall, which was small and not great as is the Kings Majesties of England."[22] Invoking a favorite notion of the age, we might say that Russia existed as a kind of looking-glass for England and its ruler. The land and its people seemed to encourage projection. So when John Merrick, chief agent for the Muscovy Company, returned to England in the autumn of 1612, he asked James I to envision Russia as his own. Less than a year earlier Shakespeare had toyed with such identifications in *The Winter's Tale*. Now Merrick was proposing that the king make Russia a protectorate, and James fancied the notion.[23] "A King," James asserted, "is trewly *Parens patriae,* the politique father of his people."[24] Perhaps, with his noble prince Henry taken ill, James found comfort in imagining his fatherly duties elsewhere: he would be imposing parental order on the orphaned country. James was still contemplating the project when *The Winter's Tale* was performed at court on the occasion of Princess Elizabeth's wedding in February 1613. For a brief moment it seemed that the English monarch might actually take the place of the emperor of Russia, that the world of fractured courts might merge with the world of happy plays: but the election of Michael Romanov later that same year put an end to this fantasy of Jacobean Muscovites. James never saw his daughter again and hardly spoke to his wife. Any careful observer could have pointed out that none of these reflections had ever been stable.

What unsettled these reflections more than anything else was the famed Russian temperament, made available (as such notions often are) through an atmospheric discourse of season and place. Shakespeare could hardly have avoided the influence of this seductive matter.[25] When Clement Adams set down Chancellor's account, he tried to capture the environment in a paradoxical scene of wonder:

> The north parts of the Countrey are reported to be so cold, that the very ice or water which distilleth out of the moist wood which they lay upon the fire is presently congealed and frozen: the diversitie

> growing suddenly to be so great, that in one and the selfe firebrand, a man shall see both fire and ice.[26]

The idea of winter in Russia gave Englishmen a profoundly concrete way of writing about the yoking of elemental opposites. Accounts published in the decades preceding composition of *The Winter's Tale* nurtured the extraordinary vernacular of ice and fire. Giles Fletcher put the evolving aesthetic succinctly: "The whole countrie differeth very much from it selfe, by reason of the yeare; so that a man would mervaile to see the great alteration and difference betwixte the winter and the sommer in Russia."[27] Here was a Russian world whose climate modeled the unstable psychologies of its inhabitants and also of the characters of English romance, who very often differ from themselves.

Then, in the 1590s, the Dutch explorer William Barents undertook three voyages to a string of islands off the northern coast of Russia, a region known as Nova Zemlya. On the third voyage, in 1596, the expedition found itself trapped in the thickening ice. Against incredible odds, the party survived the winter there. In 1598 Gerrit De Veer published his account of Barents's voyage in Dutch; Latin, French, and German editions of De Veer soon circulated throughout Europe. An English translation, by William Phillip, appeared in 1609. In a 1942 article Sarah M. Nutt recounts this publishing history and describes the resemblances between Claudio's "Thrilling region of thick-ribbed ice" in *Measure for Measure* and De Veer's narrative. Nutt characterizes the narrative as possessing

> that quality of interest and enthusiasm which might have served as a model for Claudio's delighted spirit. At times his descriptions of nature become intensely poetic. He often speaks of the terrific movements of the pack-ice and the strength of tremendous polar bears as "admirable."[28]

In the same essay Nutt catalogs the variety of icy allusions in seven other plays by Shakespeare, pointing out that

> the year 1609 saw a revival of interest in the search for a northeast passage. The Dutch East India Company had persuaded Henry Hudson to leave the employ of the Muscovy Company to make a new trial for them and a rival group of Dutch merchants immediately sent out another expedition. The open-polar-sea theory gained new adherents. Thomas Pavier finally printed Phillip's translation of De Veer's narrative; it was dedicated to the governor of the Muscovy Company.[29]

As Shakespeare composed his romance for staging in 1611, *winter* and *Muscovy* were in fashion. Moreover, Nutt correctly suggests that this language of alien winter could function quite effectively for a playwright interested in the extremes of romance characters.

A decades-old dialogue between poetry and commerce affirmed that great profits were to be made by moving between England and Russia as long as Englishmen were prepared for the attendant risks—both physical and political. In fact, the published communications between England and Muscovy suggested an evolving language of suspicion, secrecy, and spying. On the one hand was the court of Ivan IV, where the ruler so distrusted his subjects that he wrote to Elizabeth in 1565 of "'the perverse and evill dealinge of our subjects, who mourmour and repine at us; forgettinge loyall obedience they practice againste our person.'"[30] This distrust gradually extended to the English queen herself. By 1568 the emperor had become so frustrated with Elizabeth's inattention to his overtures for greater princely intimacy that Thomas Randolph, the queen's ambassador, met with royal suspicion on his arrival in Moscow. He complained of being "'straightlie kepte prisonere with suche uncourtoyse usage of the sergeaunt that kepte them, as worse coulde not have byn shewed to an eniemy.'"[31] On the other hand was Richard Eden, who described the English "discovery" of Muscovy "by the direction and information of the sayde master Sebastian who longe before had this *secreate* in his minde."[32] During the 1550s and 1560s this single English secret grew into a distinctive mode of operation for Cabot's company. As part of their instructions to the purser and other servants of the third voyage to Muscovy in 1556, the Company commanded the men to "spie and search as secretly as you may," probing for abuses by Englishmen and Muscovites alike. These merchants were asked to have "Argos eyes" and to "keepe a note thereof in your booke secretly to your selfe."[33] Refining these aims in a letter to their agents in Russia in 1557, officials of the Muscovy Company noted the emperor's mistrust of the ambassador and reminded the agents to write in "cyphers."[34] Such examples, drawn from the actions of Muscovites and Englishmen alike, could be multiplied many times over. Taken together, they amount to a veritable code of diplomatic interaction between two kingdoms whose rulers never forgot to address each other as "sister" and "brother," where travelers could never be certain of the line between "prisoner" and "guest."

From within a context of suspicion and spying, contemporary observers began to compare the two realms in order to articulate a virulent notion of tyranny. Writing of his journey to Muscovy in 1557, Anthony Jenkinson explains that "This Emperour is of great power: for he hath conquered much, as well of the Lieflanders, Poles, Lettoes, and Swethens. . . . He keepeth his people in great subjection: all matters passe his judgement, be they never so small. The law is sharpe for all offenders."[35] George Turberville devotes one of his verse letters to a description of Russia as the

> . . . savage soyle,
> where lawes doe beare no sway
> But all is at the King his wil,
> to save or els to slay.
> And that saunce cause God wot,
> if so his minde be such
> But what meane I with kings to deale
> we ought no Saints to touch.
> Conceave the rest your selfe,
> and deeme what lives they leade:
> Where lust is law, and subjectes live
> continually in dread.[36]

The poet's couplets suggest that "the emperor of Russia" was synonymous with arbitrary and extreme violence. To the English mind the emperor of Russia meant torture. Purchas relates how Ivan's own brother was "put to exquisite tortures first, and after to death; his wife stripped and set naked to the eyes of all, and then by one on horse-backe drawne with a rope in to the River and drowned." Purchas also tells how Ivan's "Chancellor Dubrowsti sitting at table with his two Sonnes, were also upon accusation without answere cut in pieces, and the third sonne quartered alive with foure wheeles, each drawne a divers way by fifteene men." Purchas describes Ivan's dissatisfaction with his supreme notary, whose "wife was taken from him, and after some weeks detayning was with her hand-maid hanged over her husbands doore, and so continued a fortnight, he being driven to goe in and out by her all that time."[37] Writing directly to Elizabeth, Giles Fletcher explains that "In their [the Russians'] maner of government, your Highnesse may see both a true and strange face of a tyrannical state (most unlike to your own), without true knowledge of God, without written lawe, without common justice."[38] In his "Maxims of State," Sir Walter Ralegh emphasizes the need for "proportion" in the government of a nation, a balance of power, "so that a monarch be not too monarchical, strict, or absolute, as the Russe kings."[39] At the end of James's reign, Purchas concludes: "We Englishmen under the government of his Majestie, have enjoyed such a Sunshine of peace, that our Summers day to many hath beene tedious," while the Russian emperors have engendered a "Hellmouth centre, there pitching the Tents of Destruction, there erecting the Thrones of Desolation."[40] In the manifold elaboration of these comparisons, the writers have begun to use the idea of the emperor of Russia and his propensity for violence in their measurements of early modern England. We can certainly imagine, I think, a mature Shakespeare musing over Turberville's couplets and their sense that "lust is law." In crafting the unstable blank verse of Leontes, the playwright simply extends a poetic assay that was decades in the making.

At this juncture it ought to be apparent that Hermione's invocation of a Russian father resonates with far more specificity than the play's critics have previously noted. In her awful moment of persecution, Hermione appeals to a land famous for subjection. In their imaginations the English audience might remember Ivan IV for many things, certainly for revenge; but pity would not be the obvious choice.[41] So the daughter of the Russian emperor turns out to be what we would call an "expert witness." She testifies:

> if I shall be condemn'd
> Upon surmises, all proofs sleeping else
> But what your jealousies awake, I tell you
> 'Tis rigour and not law.
> (3.2.111-14)

Hermione can grasp the difference between rigor and law in such clear monosyllabic terms—"I tell you"—because her own father epitomizes its abuse. I suggest that her search for pity from the Russian emperor marks the extremity of Leontes's tyranny; or else, perhaps even at the same time, it marks her great capacity for hope. The queen knows the emperor of Russia and still imagines a sympathetic gaze.

What I want to emphasize here is the extraordinary way that identifications multiply in light of Hermione's paternal invocation. For instance, Bergeron has shown in convincing detail how this mimetic relationship translates in *The Winter's Tale* into an emphasis on fathers and royal succession, re-presenting the ongoing conflict between James and his son Henry, suggesting to a courtly audience in 1613 "Henry's death painfully fresh in their minds."[42] In Shakespeare's play, of course, Leontes exceeds Jacobean fury by angling for the destruction of his own newborn child: "Go, take it to the fire" (2.3.140). Having lost both his wife and son, Leontes listens to the oracle define the crisis: the king of Sicilia "shall live without an heir, if that which is lost be not found" (3.2.135-36). So the Sicilian problem is a Jacobean concern is a Russian fate, because, as Turberville puts it, "best estates" have "none assurance good / Of lands, of lives, nor nothing falles / unto the next of blood."[43] As in Shakespeare's play, the emperor of Russia also had to endure the effects of his own tyranny. On 9 November 1581 Ivan entered his daughter-in-law's chamber and began to rebuke her for her attire. When his son. Ivan, answered his wife's cries, the father and son fought and the son was killed.[44] Jerome Horsey relates the course of events, how Ivan

> strake him in his furie a box on the ear; whoe toke it so tenderly, fell into a burninge feavour, and died within three daies after. Wherat the Emperor tore his hear and byrd like a madd man, lamentinge and morninge for the loss of his sonn. But the kingdom had the greatest loss, the hope of their comfortt, a

wise, mild and most woorthy prince, of heroicall condicion. . . .[45]

When Ivan died in 1584, disputed successions rocked his empire. The "Thrones of Desolation" described by Purchas were, in part, attributable to the emperor's violence against his own offspring. Of equal importance for our understanding of the Russian emperor's relation to Shakespeare's play is the way that, over time, the historical specificity of Ivan's familial violence collapsed into a simple notation of psychological extremes. By 1674 a historian writing about Muscovy could conclude that Ivan killed his son "upon no other provocation than that of his violent Temper."[46] Hermione's "father" had already become an archetype.

Finally, if we are to understand something of English theatrical pleasure and its relation to Ivan's cruel ways, then we must confront the bear's part in Shakespeare's romance. Many critics have noted, as Nutt does, that "there was really no necessity for this scene; Antigonus could just as easily have been taken out of the action by the shipwreck."[47] So why the bear? In part, as Sir Walter Raleigh pointed out at the beginning of this century, the creature functions as a bridge, leading the audience toward the spring world of comedy.[48] And, in part, Shakespeare surely understood that the bear carries symbolic and cultural associations: ideas of winter and tyranny mingled with his audience's taste for bearbaitings.[49]

I want to suggest that the bear alludes here (as it always did in sixteenth-century Moscow) to Ivan and the play's investment in notions of kingship. By 1603 this connection could be dealt with in shorthand by Purchas: "Cutting out tongues, cutting off hands and feet of his complayning Subjects, and other diversified tortures I omit; as also the guarding his father in lawes doores with Beares tyed there." Ivan, he explains, liked "recreating himselfe with letting Beares loose in throngs of people."[50] As it did for the common audience in early modern London, the bear embodied for Muscovites Ivan's particular tastes in sport. Nowhere is this ursine association more telling than in Fletcher's narrative about Ivan's "private behavior":

> One other speciall recreation is the fight with wilde beares, which are caught in pittes or nets, and are kepte in barred cages for that purpose, against the emperour be disposed to see the pastime. The fight with the beare is on this sort. The man is turned into a circle walled round about, where he is to quite himselfe so well as he can, for there is no way to flie out. When the beare is turned loose, he commeth upon him with open mouth. . . . But many times these hunters come short, and are either slaine, or miserably torne with the teeth and talents of the fierce beast. If the party quite himselfe well in this fight with the beare, he is carried to drinke at the emperour's seller door, where he drinketh himselfe drunke for the honor of *Hospodare*. And this is his reward for adventuring his life for the emperours pleasure. To maintaine this pastime the emperor hath certein huntsmen that are appointed for that purpose to take the wild beare. This is his recreation commonly on the holy daies.[51]

Fletcher's formula is seductive: know the tyrant through his "recreation" and the origins of his "pleasure." I would, in turn, apply this formula to Shakespeare's theater and suggest that we understand the romance of tyranny as a psychological triumph in which the audience learns how to take pleasure from cruel re-creation.[52] Traces of violence from alien cultures contribute to this end because they can be mingled with native tastes while retaining an aura of alterity, of "not us."

Shakespeare manages this negotiation with dexterity. Near the end of the play, Autolycus has the Clown by his ears, regaling him with Polixenes's planned barbarities against the Shepherd's son. "who shall be flayed alive, then 'nointed over with honey, set on the head of a wasps' nest, then stand till he be three quarters and a dram dead . . ." (4.4.785-88). But most fascinating, the narration of tyranny (Paulina's old task) has been taken over by the fooling thief and ballad-hawker. At this distance, near the play's end, a tyrant's atrocities become the stuff of "merrie tragedie,"[53] leading the frightened Clown to seek out Autolycus's help and to spell out a marketable version of kingship: "and though authority be a stubborn bear, yet he is oft led by the nose with gold" (ll. 803-4). The Clown's proverbial wisdom sharpens the significance of the Russian emperor in Shakespeare's vision of royal romance. The existence of Ivan and Muscovy allowed English writers to imagine authority as a wild, raging bear, a creature of spectacle that entertained both kings and commoners alike. The trope of Ivan as beast fable enabled the English audience to become fanciful when thinking about political exigencies, to imagine that courtly capacities for envy and cruelty belonged to old tales from faraway lands of winter. So the detail that startles and makes us question its necessity actually leads toward a more thoughtful consideration of the royal households on which succession depends.

Both the historian Felicity Heal and I have argued that the idea of hospitality exists as a profound nexus for English Renaissance thought.[54] In one prose tract after another, writers shaped evolving humanist ideals in terms of household structure and management. But the impulse to define the household that inspired Tasso flowed through Muscovy as well. In Shakespeare's day the grand Muscovite text on the subject was the *Domostróy,* compiled during Ivan's reign. In a distinctly Muscovite fashion, the *Domostróy* codifies household discipline and punishment. It advises: "Punish your son in his youth, and he will give you a quiet old age" and "If you love your son, punish him frequently."[55] Expanding the uses of familial rigor, the book codifies hospitable conventions in an explanation of the wife's discipline. We find an uncanny prologue to the matter of *The Winter's Tale:* "Let her be sure that her husband wants her to keep company with the guests she invites, or the people she calls upon." In this context the household text enjoins, "A woman ought to talk with her lady-friends of handwork and housekeeping."[56] The husband's control of the woman's company and talk are absolutely crucial to the life of the household. In his account Jenkinson confirms this fact: "The women be there very obedient to their husbands, & are kept straightly from going abroad, but at some seasons."[57] To these bits of cultural proscription, I would append a scene of Muscovite hospitality.

In his account of Chancellor's arrival in Muscovy, the schoolmaster Adams pays special attention to the Russian emperor's hospitality, his royal "Cupboorde," "the vessels, and goblets" of gold. Adams notes how "the ghests were all apparelled with linnen without, and with rich skinnes within, and so did notably set out this royall feast."[58] Adams notices many things, but Ivan's handling of the bread fascinates him most:

> . . . and before the comming in of the meate, the Emperour himselfe, according to an ancient custome of the kings of Muscovy, doth first bestow a piece of bread upon every one of his ghests, with a loud pronunciation of his title, and honour. . . . Whereupon al the ghests rise up, and by & by sit downe againe.[59]

Adams goes on with his narration, but this ceremony so catches his imagination that he returns to it once more: "The Russes tolde our men, that the reason thereof, as also of the bestowing of bread in that maner, was to the ende that the Emperour might *keepe the knowledge of his owne houshold:* and withal, that such as are under his displeasure, might by this meanes be knowen."[60] I find in this account the kind of cultural motive that ties the many foregoing scenes of Muscovite life together. The emperor's practice and his ordinance come together as a special version of Renaissance government. Whereas the traditional ideal of "the Renaissance" is absolutely defined by the humanist impulse to recover, translate, and share knowledge, Muscovy in the same age is positively defined by the keeping of knowledge. Royal displeasure is taken for granted. Talk and company must be controlled and limited. The ruler must be able to name and summon servants at will. Men keep knowledge, while women simply take their disciplined place under male confinement.

With its strange cartographic accretions and what Stephen Orgel has dubbed its "incomprehensibility,"[61] *The Winter's Tale* makes sense in terms of this alien model. Since Chancellor's first voyage to the frozen land of Ivan IV, English writers had probed this kind of linkage. I suggest, then, that we might *place*—if not understand—Leontes's jealousy. The king inhabits a world of secrecy, suspicion, and spying that has no proper name until the playwright asks his audience to think on the emperor of Russia. When Leontes confronts Camillo, he complains of his servant's powers of observation: "not noted, is't, / But of the finer natures?" (1.2.225). The Sicilian king is trapped in a Muscovite bind, struggling to control wife's talk in (what seems to him) a precarious court while attempting to be hospitable. He tells her to speak, so Hermione pleads with Polixenes: "How say you? / My prisoner? or my guest?" (ll. 54-55). As in Muscovy, the difference between prisoner and guest is dangerously ambiguous. The ruler's mounting jealousy over her winning conversation comes in an aside: "O, that is entertainment / My bosom likes not, nor my brows" (ll. 118-19). Leontes struggles to put into public speech what the factors of the Muscovy Company committed to "cyphers": the need to discipline talk and negotiate suspicion. This leads the king aggressively toward his son and heir and on toward a nearly incomprehensible rage. In lines that recall Fletcher's poetical account of fire and ice in the Russian winter, Camillo describes Leontes as "one / Who, in rebellion with himself, will have / All that are his, so too" (ll. 354-56). Seen from a Muscovite perspective, the Sicilian predicament is clear: they can fathom neither the ways nor the consequences of keeping knowledge. Shakespeare's romance is, among many other things, a grand interrogation of competing versions of how human beings ought to treat knowledge.[62]

The playwright has Polixenes announce the theme in straightforward terms when he presses Camillo: "If you know aught which does behove my knowledge / Thereof to be inform'd, imprison't not / In ignorant concealment" (ll. 395-97). "Ignorant concealment" stands as a wonderfully crabbed epither for what the rest of the play is about. By the end of *The Winter's Tale,* all of the major characters have engaged in a version of this practice. Polixenes, Camillo, Florizel, Perdita, Autolycus, Paulina, and Hermione—all conceal knowledge in order, for better and for worse, to breed ignorance in their relations with others. Along the way, each character attempts to assert a distinctive mastery over the others, that special prerogative that Ivan so violently protected. In this spirit Leontes complains, "Alack, for lesser knowledge!" (2.1.38). The king then returns to the language of hospitality to explain his sense of betrayal, invoking the fanciful notion of the cup poisoned by the spider which cannot kill if the spider is unseen because the drinker's "knowledge / Is not infected" (ll. 41-42). Properly kept knowledge, we may presume, would make the keeper inviolable, but Leontes confesses with fury: "I have drunk, and seen the spider" (l. 45). Weakened by infected knowledge, the king is vulnerable to the challenges of the women. When Leontes accuses Hermione of being a "bed-swerver" and cohort in the escape of Polixenes and Camillo, the queen chides, "No, by my life, / Privy to none of this. How will this grieve you, / When you shall come to clearer knowledge . . ." (ll. 93 and 96-97). Hermione's innocence is founded on honest ignorance, and her retort has authority because she discriminates between kinds of knowledge. From the same solid ground, Paulina challenges the king's anger, obtaining the baby daughter by command: "The keeper of the prison, call to him; / Let him have knowledge who I am" (2.2.1-2). Informed of the woman's arrival, Leontes's bitter, perhaps comic conclusion sums up his tangled position of knowing and commanding: "I charg'd thee that she should not come about me. / I knew she would" (2.3.43-44).

Lest we miss the ubiquity of the problem Shakespeare is dramatizing and casually attribute the whole question to the failings of the Sicilian king, we need to look ahead into the springtime world of Bohemia, where Florizel is contemplating marriage to Perdita. When the disguised Polixenes questions Florizel about the absence of the father, the son replies: "for some other reasons, my grave sir, / Which 'tis not fit you know, I not acquaint / My father of this business" (4.4.412-14). In ways familiar from the preceding discussion, we find the prince keeping knowledge and the father spying out his suspicions. With an eye toward dramatic intensity, the playwright modulates this confrontation by constructing a series of shared verse lines in which the stakes become explicit before the recognition occurs:

> POLIXENES Let him know 't.
> FLORIZEL He shall not.
> POLIXENES Prithee, let him.
> FLORIZEL No, he must not.
> SHEPHERD Let him, my son: he shall not need to grieve
> At knowing of thy choice.
> (ll. 414-17)

The urgency of this pleading heightens the king's anger, a rage quite akin to Leontes's wrath in its violence and origin. "Know't" and "not," "know" and "no," knowledge and negation collapse in similar sounds, in a way of being in the world. Polixenes tells Perdita: "I'll have thy beauty scratch'd with briers and made / More homely than thy state" (ll. 426-27). He threatens the Shepherd with a "cruel" death and threatens to deny his son's claim to the throne. Florizel accepts the doom and, like Leontes, the king is without an heir because of the way men keep knowledge.

Tyranny is always about the control of knowledge, but what moved early modern audiences most, as it still does today, is tyranny's endlessly expanding ripples of violence, a movement that begins in *The Winter's Tale* with Leontes's entrance in 2.1 and achieves extraordinary closure with the Clown's description of the bear's feast in 3.3. Ironically, Leontes tries to restrain his ranting when addressing the emperor of Russia's daughter lest he become the very "precedent" of "barbarism" (2.1.84). Leontes, in other words, is fearful of exchanging places with Hermione's father. Perhaps it is too late. For the king's rage breeds, even in the best-intentioned of his servants, a crude language of reciprocal ferocity. Antigonus both pleads and threatens: "If it prove / She's otherwise, I'll keep my stables where / I lodge my wife; I'll go in couples with her" (ll. 133-35). Reducing his own family to hounds and horses, Antigonus seems transported by the possibility of violent punishment for offending women, so that he promises: "Be she honour-flaw'd, / I have three daughters . . . If this prove true, they'll pay for 't" (ll. 143-44, 46). When the mother of these three daughters rebukes Leontes, he simply spins the rage to new heights: "Hence with it, and together with the dam / Commit them to the fire!" (2.3.93-94). In the face of so much fury, Paulina has the courage to invoke the term "tyranny" (l. 119), only to have Leontes pose a question that would have puzzled even the observers of Ivan's court: "Were I a tyrant, / Where were her life? she durst not call me so, / If she did know me one" (ll. 121-23).

Solving the problem of knowledge in this play means, from the outset, that Leontes will never become Ivan. As Dion puts it, Leontes's request for the truth of the oracle ensures that "something rare / Even then will rush to knowledge" (3.1.20-21). In Sicilia things "rare" still have the force of sudden, public discovery, a poetics not admitted in Ivan's world. It is at the early spectacle of revelation that Hermione wishes her father present as spectator, a whimsically appropriate thought since the superstitious Ivan might well have contributed to such a spectacle. Leontes submits but quickly discounts the revelation as "mere falsehood" (3.2.141). And it is here, in this moment of analogy, that the king's son dies and Hermione dies (it seems), too. But unlike Ivan, who seems to have waded through great scenes of death with little recognition, Leontes reckons the impact immediately: "the heavens themselves / Do strike at my injustice" (ll. 146-47). By letting go of the private domain of suspicion and admitting the public rush to knowledge, Leontes has allowed himself a conversion. The playwright seems to be suggesting, as he so often does, the positive effects of spectacle in relation to personal and communal knowledge.

Finally, though, we must notice the difference gender makes to this troubled state of knowledge. Shakespeare proposes a decidedly female and English solution, precisely the kind of thing that infuriated Ivan in his dealings with Queen Elizabeth decades before. On the heels of Leontes's epiphany, Paulina steps forward in a way no Russian woman would ever have dared: "What studied torments, tyrant, hast for me? / What wheels? racks? fires? what flaying? boiling . . . ?" (ll. 175-76).[63] Leontes permits the rough speech and more, for Paulina has been keeping her own knowledge of the king's household. She reports of the queen, "I say she's dead: I'll swear 't" (l. 203). Under the cover of her chiding, Paulina keeps the knowledge of the royal family, of Leontes's wife and queen, at her "poor house" (5.3.6). In the wake of the reunion that Shakespeare chooses to report rather than stage,[64] the First Gentleman agrees that the spectators ought to hurry to Paulina's house, where the families have gathered: "Every wink of an eye, some new grace will be born: our absence makes us unthrifty to our knowledge" (5.2.110-12). As everyone gathers around the queen's statue, it is Paulina who speaks:

> So her dead likeness, I do well believe,
> Excels whatever yet you look'd upon,
> Or hand of man hath done; therefore I keep it
> Lonely, apart.
>
> (5.3.15-18)

It is a thrifty Elizabethan solution to a Muscovite problem: women keep the house of knowledge where their labors do excel what the "hand of man hath done."

The Winter's Tale, as Autolycus puts it, ends "When daffodils begin to peer" (4.3.1). We may hearken back to the words of Clement Adams: "When the winter doth once begin there it doth still more & more increase by a perpetuitie of cold: neither doth that colde slake, untill the force of the Sunne beames doth dissolve the cold, and make glad the earth, returning to it againe."[65] In Shakespeare's hands the English dramatic plot has resolved itself in the manner of a Russian spring, in what Purchas called "the Sunshine of peace" under James. Theater concludes with such resolutions; discussions of knowledge, as every English commentator on Russia well understood, do not. Writing to Elizabeth in 1589 about the decay of the Russian trade, Fletcher complained of the Company's servants, the "lack of good discipline among them selves, specially of a preacher to keap them in knowledge and fear of God, and in a conscience of their service towards their Maisters."[66] In a curious set of objections that will serve as epilogue for my own reading of Shakespeare's romance, Purchas complains most vociferously about the interaction of Englishmen and Muscovites. It seems that Ivan's

> love to our Nation is magnified by our Countrimen with all thankfulnesse, whose gaines there begun by him, have made them also in some sort seeme to turne Russe (in i know not what loves or feares, as if they were still shut up in Russia, & to conceale whatsoever they know of Russian occurrents) that I have sustayned no small torture with great paines of body, vexation of minde, and triall of potent interceding friends to get but neglect and silence from some, yea almost contempt and scorne.[67]

This is what happens when England meets Russia: seeming conversion and concealed knowledge; Englishmen "turne Russe" and hide "whatsoever they know."[68] What began in 1553 as an adventure of exploration and contact has become a problem of "no small torture," a problem of knowledge and its oblique ethnographic consequences. Englishmen have become what they meant to probe: Jacobean Muscovites.

For this reason Shakespeare's romance may be seen as marking an epoch of sorts, a new age of dispute that even Shakespeare's contemporaries could recognize. Indeed, even as the playwright was busy with his romance, Sir William Lower, having heard of Galileo's experiments, wrote to Thomas Hariot: "'Me thinkes my diligent Galileus hath done more in his three fold discoverie than Magellane in openinge the streightes to the South sea or the dutch men that were eaten by beares in Nova Zembla. I am sure with more ease and saftie to him selfe and more pleasure to mee.'"[69] Here were brave empirical options, the roots of modern disciplinary division, new born, knowledge derived from the calculation of distant bodies as opposed to knowledge gleaned through contact with different cultures. Shakespeare's romance stands as a provocative assay of the latter, with all its attendant pleasures and strains, knowing and negation, bears and reunions.

Notes

[1] This poignant document appears in Richard Hakluyt's *Principal Navigations, Voyages, Traffiques, and Discoveries of the English Nation,* 8 vols. (London: J. M. Dent, 1932), 1:253. Unless otherwise stated, subsequent references to English descriptions of Muscovy will come from this edition of Hakluyt and be cited parenthetically in the text. For a discussion of Hakluyt's handling of materials in the two major editions (1589 and 1598-1600) of his project, see J. S. G. Simmons, "Russia" in *The Hakluyt Handbook,* ed. D. B. Quinn, 2 vols. (London: The Hakluyt Society, 1974), 1:161-67.

[2] Francesca Wilson, in *Muscovy: Russia Through Foreign Eyes, 1553-1900* (London: George Allen and Unwin, 1970), describes quite succinctly the exceptions to this English perception (19-20). As imperial ambassador, Sigismund von Herberstein saw the coun-

try firsthand in 1517 and 1526. The ambassador's account, *Rerum Moscoviticarum commentarii,* was published on the Continent in 1551; the first English translation did not appear until 1576.

[3] John Chamberlain, "To Dudley Carleton," 4 November 1602, *The Letters of John Chamberlain,* ed. Norman Egbert McClure, 2 vols. (Philadelphia: American Philosophical Society, 1939), 1:169.

[4] Samuel Purchas, in *Purchas His Pilgrimes* (20 vols. [Glasgow: James MacLehose, 1906]), gives the reader a sense of how archetypal "Ivan Vasilowich, the Great Great Muscovite," had become, describing him as a ruler who had earned "supersuperlatives of crueltie" (14:110).

[5] Quoted in H. G. Koenigsberger and George L. Mosse, *Europe in the Sixteenth Century* (London: Longmans, 1968), 196.

[6] Two studies have documented the major points of contact between English literature and Muscovy: Robert Ralston Cawley, *The Voyagers and Elizabethan Drama* (Boston: D. C. Heath, 1938), 253-71; and Karl Heinz Ruffmann, *Das Russlandbild in England Shakespeares* (Gottingen: Wissenschaftlicher Verlag, 1952).

[7] William Shakespeare, *The Winter's Tale,* Arden edition, ed. J.H.P. Pafford (London: Methuen, 1963). Quotations of this play and of its source. Robert Greene's *Pandosto,* follow Pafford's edition.

[8] Peter Erickson, *Patriarchal Structures in Shakespeare's Drama* (Berkeley: U of California P, 1985), 152.

[9] Quoted here from Pafford, ed., 191.

[10] Glynne Wickham's argument develops over three essays: *"The Winter's Tale:* A Comedy with Deaths" in *Shakespeare's Dramatic Heritage: Collected Studies in Mediaeval, Tudor and Shakespearean Drama* (London: Routledge and Kegan Paul, 1969), 249-65; "Shakespeare's Investiture Play: The Occasion and Subject of 'The Winter's Tale,'" *Times Literary Supplement,* 18 December 1969, 1456: "Romance and Emblem: A Study in the Dramatic Structure of *The Winter's Tale"* in *Elizabethan Theatre III,* David Galloway, ed. (Toronto: Macmillan of Canada, 1973), 82-99. David M. Bergeron develops his approach to Jacobean topicality in *Shakespeare's Romances and the Royal Family* (Lawrence: UP of Kansas, 1985), 1-25.

[11] Leah S. Marcus, *Puzzling Shakespeare: Local Reading and Its Discontents* (Berkeley: U of California P, 1988), 162.

[12] Louise Schleiner, "Latinized Greek Drama in Shakespeare's Writing of *Hamlet,"* *Shakespeare Quarterly* 41 (1990): 29-48, esp. 29.

[13] Barbara A. Mowat, "Rogues, Shepherds, and the Counterfeit Distressed: Texts and Infracontexts of *The Winter's Tale* 4.3," *Shakespeare Studies* 22 (1994): 58-76, esp. 69.

[14] Howard Felperin, *Shakespearean Representation: Mimesis and Modernity in Elizabethan Tragedy* (Princeton, NJ: Princeton UP, 1977), 44-48.

[15] That critics have been carried away in the past with such projects is the subject of Richard Levin's famous attack on "The King James Version" of *Measure for Measure* and what he calls "occasionalism" in *New Readings vs. Old Plays* (Chicago, IL: U of Chicago P, 1979), 171-93. For admirable defenses of topical readings that respond to Levin's objections, see Bergeron, 12-13; and Marcus, 164.

[16] Marcus, 37-38. Marcus enacts this more subtle method as she investigates the identification of Vienna with London in *Measure for Measure:* "What Shakespeare accomplished through the play's restlessly oscillating topicality was the initiation of a theatrical event which could be taken as Stuart propaganda, or as the expression of a contemporary nightmare, or most likely as both together" (200). Mowat concentrates on the same kinds of instabilities when describing "the struggle between infracontexts" (69).

[17] Particularly relevant to my predicament is Bergeron's representation of the royal family as a text among texts: "No privileged texts, absolutely ruling out competing texts, exist; nor are there autonomous texts; all are dependent on pre-texts, written or observed" (21). Marcus aptly categorizes the kinds of topical effect in such a system as either scattering "interpretation in a number of directions" or narrowing "it along a single axis of political allegory" (109).

[18] Marcus, for instance, is relentless in her urging that topical reading always de-essentializes (38). For a cogently argued exception to Marcus's commitment on this account, see Michael D. Bristol's review of *Puzzling Shakespeare* in *SQ* 41 (1990): 375-79. esp. 379.

[19] The quoted phrase originates with Julia Kristeva, *Revolution in Poetic Language,* trans. Margaret Waller (New York: Columbia UP, 1984), 59.

[20] In his brilliant work on *Measure for Measure,* Jonathan Goldberg, in *James I and the Politics of Literature: Jonson, Shakespeare, Donne, and Their Contemporaries* (Baltimore, MD: Johns Hopkins UP, 1983), establishes a precedent for what I propose by concen-

trating on how the play "manages to catch at central concerns" (235).

[21] See, for example, Steven Mullaney's notion of "the rehearsal of cultures" in *The Place of the Stage: License, Play, and Power in Renaissance England* (Chicago, IL: U of Chicago P, 1988), 69.

[22] Hakluyt, 1:255-56.

[23] Inna Lubimenko, "A Project for the Acquisition of Russia by James I," *English Historical Review* 29 (1914): 246-56; Chester Dunning, "James I, the Russia Company, and the Plan to Establish a Protectorate Over North Russia," *Albion* 21 (1989): 206-26.

[24] Quoted in Bergeron, 28.

[25] Commentators' explanations of Mamillius's winter tale-telling in 2.1 of *The Winter's Tale* have depended on this connection between temperature and temperament; see *A New Variorum Edition of Shakespeare,* ed. Horace Howard Furness (Philadelphia: J. B. Lippincott, 1898), 72-73.

[26] Adams's account was published in London in 1554 in an edition no longer extant; I quote this passage from Hakluyt, 1:278-79.

[27] Giles Fletcher, *Of the Russe Common Wealth* in *Russia at the Close of the Sixteenth Century,* ed. Edward A. Bond (New York: Burt Franklin, 1963), 1-152, esp. 5.

[28] Sarah M. Nutt, "The Arctic Voyages of William Barents in Probable Relation to Certain of Shakespeare's Plays." *Studies in Philology* 39 (1942): 241-64, esp. 246. Perhaps the most comprehensive discussion of this sphere of exploration is found in Sir Clements R. Markham's *The Lands of Silence: A History of Arctic and Antarctic Exploration* (Cambridge: Cambridge UP, 1921).

[29] Nutt, 260.

[30] Quoted in Bond, ed., xxxviii-xxxix.

[31] Quoted in Bond, ed., xxv.

[32] Richard Eden, *The Decades of the Newe Worlde* (London, 1555), 256 (my emphasis).

[33] Hakluyt, 1:332.

[34] Hakluyt, 1:389-90.

[35] Hakluyt, 1:416.

[36] George Turberville, "The Author Being in Moscovia," *Epitaphes, Epigrams, Songs and Sonets (1567) and Epitaphes and Sonnettes* (1576), intro. Richard J. Panofsky (Delmar, NY: Scholars' Facsimilės and Reprints, 1977), 442.

[37] Purchas, 14:111.

[38] Fletcher in Bond, ed., cxxxvii.

[39] Sir Walter Ralegh, "Maxims of State," *Works of Sir Walter Raleigh,* 8 vols. (Oxford: University Press, 1829), 8:5.

[40] Purchas, 14:108-9.

[41] Koenigsberger and Mosse make this point in passing; see 196, n. 2.

[42] Bergeron, 163.

[43] Turberville, 442.

[44] Robert O. Crummey, *The Formation of Muscovy 1304-1613* (London: Longman, 1987), 175-76. Ivan's motives have been disputed. See note 45, below.

[45] Jerome Horsey, *Travels* in Bond, ed., 153-266, esp. 195. Horsey says that Ivan was angry with the prince for showing mercy to some of Ivan's Christian victims, and other minor offenses (195). For further discussions, see Koenigsberger and Mosse, 202-3. A Jacobean frame for these events comes from Purchas: "His last crueltie was on himselfe, dying with griefe, as was thought, for the death of his eldest sonne Ivan, whom falsly accused he struck with a staffe wrought with Iron, whereof he dyed in few dayes after" (Purchas, 14:112-13).

[46] M. R., *The Russian Impostor: or, the History of Muskovie* (London, 1674), 2.

[47] Nutt, 260. Decades before Nutt, Sir Arthur Quiller-Couch, in *Shakespeare's Workmanship* (New York: Henry Holt, 1917), called the bear a "naughty superfluity" (264). As Nutt acknowledges, Chambers suggested long ago (1:489) that there were two white bears in London and that Jonson may have used them in his *Masque of Oberon.*

[48] Sir Walter Raleigh, *Shakespeare* (New York: Macmillan, 1907), 138.

[49] For the best surveys of these interpretations, see Dennis Biggins, "'Exit pursued by a Beare': A Problem in *The Winter's Tale,*" *SQ* 13 (1962): 3-13; Michael D. Bristol, "In Search of the Bear: Spatiotemporal Form and the Heterogeneity of Economics in *The Winter's Tale,*" *SQ* 42 (1991): 145-67, esp. 159-60. Bristol connects these complex significations in a fascinating examination of space and time in the romance. Identi-

fying Shakespeare's bear with the myth of Callisto opens up a range of interpretations for Jonathan Bate in *Shakespeare and Ovid* (Oxford: Clarendon Press, 1993), 225-27.

[50] Purchas, 14:112.

[51] Fletcher in Bond, ed., 143. Horsey provides a distinct version of this spectacle in his narrative. When Ivan demanded great sums of wealth from the religious houses in his country, he met with resistance. So he summoned twenty of the organizers: "About seaven of those principall rebellious bigg fatt friers were brought forthe, one after another . . . and, through the Emperowr's great favour, a bore spare [spear] of five foate in length in the other hand for his defence, and a wild bear was lett lose, rainginge and roaring up against the walls with open mouth, sentinge the frier by his fatt garments, made more mad with the crie and shoutinge of the people, runs fearsly at him, catches and crushes his head, bodie, bowells, leggs and arms, as a cate doth a mous, tears his weeds in peces till he came to his flesh, bloud and bones, and so devours his first frier for his prey" (Bond, ed., 178).

[52] Rebecca W. Bushnell, in *Tragedies of Tyrants: Political Thought and Theater in the English Renaissance* (Ithaca, NY, and London: Cornell UP, 1990), describes what Sidney calls the "sweet violence" of tragedy: "What Foucault does not discuss is what Sidney recounts, the possibility that the audience enjoyed the spectacle for its own sake, whether for the pleasure of sorrow or pity, or more cynically, for the pleasure of seeing blood or watching the elaborate ritual that let that blood" (4). It should also be pointed out that the playful waywardness of identification makes this kind of pleasure possible. Bears devour but they also dance. So Chamberlain wrote to Carleton on 27 May 1601 that the "Moscovie ambassador [who] tooke his leave at court on Sonday was sevenight like a dauncing beare" (1:123).

[53] The phrase is used by Horsey when he introduces his own narrative of "death by bear" (Bond. ed., 178).

[54] See Heal's *Hospitality in Early Modern England* (Oxford: Clarendon Press, 1990); and Daryl W. Palmer, *Hospitable Performances: Dramatic Genre and Cultural Practices in Early Modern England* (West Lafayette, IN: Purdue UP, 1992), 1-49.

[55] *Domostróy* in *Anthology of Russian Literature: From the Earliest Period to the Present Time,* ed. Leo Wiener, 2 vols. (New York: G.P. Putnam's Sons, 1902), 1:127.

[56] *Domostróy* in Wiener, ed., 1:128-29.

[57] Hakluyt, 1:417.

[58] Hakluyt, 1:281.

[59] Hakluyt, 1:281-82.

[60] Hakluyt, 1:282 (my emphasis).

[61] Stephen Orgel, in "The Poetics of Incomprehensibility" (*SQ* 42 [1991]: 431-37), argues that a certain obscurity, appropriate to the action of *The Winter's Tale,* indeed to any Shakespeare play, cannot be escaped. Orgel points out that "modern interpretation represents an essentially arbitrary selection of meanings from a list of diverse and often contradictory possibilities and does not so much resolve the linguistic problem as enable us to ignore it" (432).

[62] Stanley Cavell, in *Disowning Knowledge in Six Plays of Shakespeare* (New York: Cambridge UP, 1987), is surely right when he suggests that the play "is understandable as a study of skepticism" (198).

[63] There did exist a precedent for this kind of rebuking of royal authority, in the Muscovite notion of "the fool in Christ (*iurodivyi*)." Jerome Horsey describes the extraordinary confrontation at Pskov between Ivan (who intended to destroy the city) and "an impostur or magician, which they held to be their oracle, a holly man, named Mickula Sweat, whoe, by his bold imprecacions and exsorsims, railings and threats, terminge him the Emperour bloudsuccer, the devourer and eater of Christian flesh, and swore by his angell that he should not escape deathe of a present thounder boltt" (Bond, ed., 161).

[64] Shakespeare's play concludes with reunions not unlike those described by Gerrit de Veer, who explains that it was "as if either of us on both sides had seene each other rise from death to life again" (Purchas, 13:159).

[65] Hakluyt, 1:279.

[66] Fletcher to Queen Elizabeth, *The English Works of Giles Fletcher, the Elder,* ed. Lloyd E. Berry (Madison: U of Wisconsin P, 1964), 377.

[67] Purchas, 14:113.

[68] Purchas continues in the most resonant terms: "This for love to my Nation I have inserted against any Cavillers of our Russe Merchants: though I must needs professe that I distaste, and almost detest that (call it what you will) of Merchants to neglect Gods glorie in his providence, and the Worlds instruction from their knowledge; who while they will conceale the Russians Faults, will tell nothing of their Facts; and whiles they will be silent in mysteries of State, will reveale noth-

ing of the histories of Fact, and that in so perplexed, diversified chances and changes as seldome the World hath in so short a space seene on one Scene" (14:114).

[69] Quoted in Nutt, 249.

Source: "Jacobean Muscovites: Winter, Tyranny, and Knowledge in *The Winter's Tale,*" in *Shakespeare Quarterly,* Vol. 46, No. 3, Fall, 1995, pp. 323-39.

Idealization and the Problematic in *The Tempest*

Joseph Westlund, ***Northeastern University***

For a very long time *The Tempest* was perceived as an idealistic romance about a benevolent prince who by means of his art inspires repentance in his enemies and creates a better world; that critics perceived an identity between Prospero and Shakespeare reinforced the view. This comfortable and rather sentimental interpretation no longer prevails. In the most striking instance of the present shift in attitude, Stephen Orgel has written the first introduction to a play by Shakespeare devoted entirely to the discovery of problematic aspects, with the inevitable result of undermining traditional idealizations about the play.[1] With similar effect, new historicist readings treat *The Tempest* as part of the discourse of English colonialism; from such a perspective idealization is always suspect as a political act.[2] Psychoanalytic interpretations (such as my own) also take an increasingly skeptical view of Prospero and his efforts to control others.

These recent developments rescue *The Tempest* from some of the most enervating effects of overidealizing Prospero—and behind him, Shakespeare, patriarchy, and colonialism. To assume that the central character and his "project" are entirely selfless, benevolent, and successful runs contrary to the text in crucial ways. However, one unfortunate effect of this revision is that it denigrates the response of people who, like many before them, find something extremely good in Prospero and in the overall effect of *The Tempest.* In the iconoclastic mood of the day critics run the risk of fitting themselves with a new set of ideological blinkers when they deny that the play creates the illusion of an intensely subjective character, Prospero, with whom members of the audience find it difficult not to identify and—to some degree—idealize.

I want to concentrate upon problematic aspects of the play that center around Prospero, who until recently was thought the obvious center of attention. That some critics now find Caliban an almost equally important figure reveals their own impulse to idealize, to elevate to a standard of perfection. Caliban is of late portrayed an innocent, peaceful native dweller on the island; Prospero is the colonist. However, Caliban and Sycorax are themselves not native to the island and are indeed vigorous colonists; that this is so would seem to be the point of Caliban's attempt to rape Miranda.[3] Present-day critics often find Caliban a representative Native American, a noble savage, an idealized victim of colonialism. Yet, as Vaughn points out, "if Shakespeare, however obliquely, meant Caliban to personify America's natives, his intention apparently miscarried almost completely."[4]

Caliban performs a function that Prospero previously served: both characters assist interpreters in their idealization of a view of the world that they themselves bring to the play—in this case, anticolonialism. Here, too, the play undermines their attempts. For instance, Caliban is so comically subservient to his European coconspirators that he abandons liberty before he even gets it. Or, if he hopes to rule, he would simply replace Prospero as head of a colonialist state. That Caliban's characterization involves so many self-contradictions makes the idealization of his role even more precarious than is the case with similar attempts with regard to Prospero. My point is that the play both problematizes and idealizes Prospero, and that the idealization survives *because* it is tempered with the anomalous, discordant aspects. They ground the idealizations in a realistic world of self-contradiction and limitation. By problematizing central aspects of the play—at the same time as exalting them—*The Tempest* offers the audience an idealization that becomes more believable and thus more usable.

In psychoanalytic theory, and within Western culture as a whole, many people lose sight of the value of idealization. We define "idealization" as "the representation or exaltation of someone or of something to a state of perfection not found in actuality." Although this seems to be a neutral definition, it masks a prejudice against looking for something not present in the world—against longing for something better. Utopian literature often gets similarly bad press, and for much the same reason. An individual's ability to create and discover something extremely good beyond what is expectable, seems essential not only to our feeble attempt to make a better world but to maintaining a viable sense of self-esteem.

Nevertheless, psychoanalytic critics themselves often find idealization suspect because it often results from "splitting" (over-simplifying things into what is entirely good or entirely bad). Splitting not only distorts reality but impoverishes a person's range of feelings. On the other hand, idealization is central to human development—for instance, in the way children imagine their parents perfect, then temper this idealization as they realize that even they have feet of clay. It seems that we have to pass through a stage in which we can participate in their magnificence and then differentiate from our exalted view. Idealization adds zest, vitality and purpose to life. That this is so may account for why some critics now idealize Caliban. It may also account for why literary theory now raises indeterminacy as a standard of perfection.

The early psychoanalyst Melanie Klein was unusual in her insistence that people idealize because of an innate need to feel that something extremely good exists. She argues that this feeling "leads to the longing for a good object [an internalized benign aspect of other persons] and for the capacity to love it. This appears to be a condition for life itself."[5] Klein argues that this longing is what motivates "reparation," a continual attempt to repair real or imagined destructive attacks on the "good object" outside us (say our parents or our internalized sense of ourselves). Her theory of reparation puts the Christian view of sin, guilt, grace and repentance into psychoanalytic terms (although she seems not to have realized this).[6] J. O. Wisdom adds philosophical support to Klein's view. He notes the importance of reparation as "essentially a theory of emotional integration centering around ambivalence." Reparation allows the idealization to retain its perfection unblemished: "in the state of ambivalence, the desired object is attacked; this attack is not canceled, but redressed by reparation."[7] Wisdom concludes that the neutralization by reparation "relieves the desired object of all diminution of good quality"; yet this idealized state is not split-off from reality—as would be the case in pathological idealization—but results instead from "neutralization of its bad part" through reparation.[8]

From this psychoanalytic perspective, we can see how the problematic aspects of *The Tempest* serve to keep the audience in touch with the complexities of reality—including anger, aggression, and loss of self-esteem. The play draws us into its idealized world and yet admits destructive feelings of various sorts that are then neutralized by their relation to the good object: the idealized ruler, parent, and magician/scientist. Like Shakespeare's own audience, we find ourselves at a historical moment in which we must negotiate some course between skepticism and its opposite pole, a viable idealization. The play assists this process, I think, by implicating the ideal in a problematic context that adds plausibility.

I want to discuss a few specific instances in which this delicate process occurs. As Orgel remarks, editors have for a long time tended to ignore the play's ambivalences, to "sweeten and sentimentalize it, to render it altogether neater and more comfortable than the text that has come down to us."[9] He points out numerous examples in which interpreters perfect the play by "correcting" manifest contradictions, by smoothing over disparities, and by making Prospero thoroughly laudable.

In the simplest instances editors correct the text in ways that sentimentalize characters and undermine the text's hold on reality. Take the case of Miranda. Editors have often transferred her violent rebuke of Caliban to Prospero:

> Abhorred slave,
> Which any print of goodness wilt not take
> Being capable of all ill!
>
> (1.2.350-52)

As Orgel notes, "from Dryden to Kittredge, this speech was almost always reassigned to Prospero, its tone being considered inappropriate to Miranda's character." Orgel concentrates on the energy she displays. I would emphasize her anger: Miranda rebukes Caliban not only for his attempted rape but for his ingratitude and lack of repentance. The text prevents us from imagining Miranda a pallid idealized creature; from the very start she comes across as not only forceful but highly skeptical about her father's intentions. Indeed, it is through her that the audience first learns that it may be wise to question Prospero's good intentions, for it is she who confronts him for raising the tempest that sank the ship and "the fraughting souls within her" (1.2.1-13). At every step, the play encourages members of the audience to balance positive and negative views of the same character.

The play's treatment of magic is another instance of this process. Magic often strikes modern readers as a rather quaint and largely irrelevant factor in the play, even though footnotes alert us to its serious implications and to its historical relation to modern science. That Prospero is a magician is one of the play's most problematic idealizations of knowledge and power. That he should *choose* to be a magician—on top of being a patriarch and omnipotent ruler—emphasizes his quest for absolute supremacy in all spheres of life.[10]

Frank Kermode follows a long line of interpreters who obscure this issue by trying to validate Prospero's elaborate—and largely spurious—distinction between white magic and black magic.[11] As Orgel demonstrates, such distinctions simply do not convince us unless we want to be convinced.[12] For instance, the play sets up a strong correlation between Prospero's magical powers and those of his predecessor on the island, Sycorax. Prospero alleges that Sycorax is a witch, but he also demonstrates that they share strikingly similar powers. For instance, he threatens to punish Ariel in exactly the way Sycorax punished him in the past (a twelve-year spell of imprisonment in a tree)—and for exactly the same offense (being too fastidious to carry out the magician's commands). Given such details as these, it is difficult to accept his claim that his magic differs from hers. If it differs at all, it is in benign intent, but he undermines this assumption by furious outbursts and threats. In addition, he gratuitously claims the black-magical power of necromancy in his valedictory speech beginning "Ye elves of hills, brooks, standing lakes, and groves"—a speech based on Medea's in Ovid's *Metamorphoses*. Why does Shakespeare have Prospero crib from this infamous practitioner of black magic? And why have Prospero claim necromancy when it is irrelevant? It is difficult not to conclude that the character is designed to create an ambivalent response; there is something prohibited and dangerous about Prospero's magic—and something devious about his claim to be entirely above suspicion.

Prospero continually tries to idealize himself, to conceive of himself as a standard of perfection—not only as magician with impeccable credentials and goals, but as an ideal ruler. The play assiduously undermines his attempts. For instance, he clearly feels that he himself was in no way to blame for losing his dukedom, but in so doing reveals his irresponsibility:

> The government I cast upon my brother,
> And to my state grew stranger, being
> transported
> And rapt in secret studies.
>
> (1.2.74-76)

"Rapt" is an ominous term in the context of "secret studies," for it is one used to describe the effect of the Witches upon Macbeth. No ruler can safely cast his power on another, particularly on a brother next in line for the throne. Prospero exalts himself as blameless and wronged, but in so doing the text allows us to realize that he is idealizing himself in a defensive maneuver. He cannot admit that he was partly to blame for the conspiracy against him.[13]

The play's single most vexing problem is that he never fully achieves his "project," which is to make his enemies repent. It is not for want of trying to do so, for he bends his energy toward this goal from the start. The goal of repentance and regeneration is central to the whole play—as critics have for a long time agreed. It is only quite recently, however, that they have become skeptical about his success. Neither his brother Antonio, nor Alonzo's brother Sebastian give any sign of repenting in the final scene. Only Alonzo does so, and in a speech whose fullness and clarity makes the silence of the two chief malefactors all the more startling. Since the entire plot is devoted to this goal, its failure can hardly be the result of Shakespeare's oversight; he might have wrapped up the matter in a couple of lines. Yet none exists; nor do we have reason to believe that a speech dropped out of the play as we know it, for the Folio is an exemplary text.

Therefore, it is wonderfully strange that critics have only recently begun to note that the wicked brothers fail to repent. For an astonishingly long time interpreters simply could not see that the text refuses to support Prospero's claim that he succeeded in his grand design. In one scholarly publication after another it was assumed that repentance, forgiveness, and reconciliation are achieved at the end of the play. Indeed, so certain were critics of Prospero's success that they conceived of *The Tempest* as an allegorical drama on the Christian pattern of sin, repentance, and reconciliation.

The failure of the wicked brothers to repent alters the achievement at the end of *The Tempest*. For instance, Antonio seems not to have repented, and yet Prospero forgives him. Why does he do so? Perhaps we are supposed to conclude that Prospero is so very good—so full of the rarer virtue—that he forgets his brother's cruel deed and forgives him despite the fact that there is no sign of contrition. Such a reading makes Prospero benign beyond all measure, a perfect ruler and Christian. But such a reading is given the lie by his contemptuous and uncharitable speech:

> For you, most wicked sir, whom to call
> brother
> Would even infect my mouth, I do forgive
> Thy rankest fault—all of them—and require
> My dukedom of thee, which perforce, I know
> Thou must restore.
>
> (5.1.130-34)

Prospero "requires" his dukedom in such a way as to freeze any penitence that might be stirring in his brother. Critics therefore had to ignore the speech or excuse Prospero's tone. Still, the tone is stunningly contemptuous; that the word "brother" "Would even infect my mouth" undermines a term central to all discussions of Christian charity; and it seems spiteful to say, "Thy rankest fault—all of them."

Yet many critics want to subordinate this harsh tone to Prospero's essential goodness. I would agree with their impulse and carry the matter a bit further. His tone is at odds with his profession that he will not be vengeful. On the other hand, he does not punish Antonio and Sebastian for their treason when he captures them. Prospero's forgiveness is not the free and charitable gift he led us to expect when he said:

> . . . the rarer action is
> In virtue than in vengeance: they being
> penitent,
> The sole drift of my purpose doth extend
> Not a frown further.
>
> (5.1.27-30)

But he does not have them drawn and quartered as a ruler under similar circumstances in Shakespeare's day would surely have done.

What are we as members of the audience to make of this curious blend of good and ill? The play seems to offer three main options. We can emphasize either of two potentially split-off approaches: Prospero is a paragon, an idealized father, ruler and magician; or, he is an irascible, omnipotent despot. Over the years, most critics have fallen into one camp or the other. However, since both approaches are manifestly present—and manifestly inadequate—I suggest that we simply admit the problematic nature of the play and its central character. Over the past twenty years Shakespeareans have grown more comfortable with the lack of consensus among critics about what the plays mean and they are ready for such a response.[14]

By admitting the problematic nature of the play we should not, however, ignore its strong idealistic bent. Prospero is neither so successful nor so benevolent as he would have us believe, but he manages to defeat the conspirators without bloodshed. He has also taken steps to ensure his hold over them in the future by means of a dynastic marriage that excludes his brother from succession, and by his threat to reveal that Sebastian and Antonio plotted to kill Alonzo. Prospero has been "forgiving" and he has been provident. As a result, the play offers members of an audience *usable* idealizations about key issues: power, control, rule, vengeance, forgiveness, and repentance. The results are usable because they are implicated in the actual world by means of such realistic emotions as grandiosity, spite, contempt and deviousness. These color the ending so strongly that it cannot be called "ideal." *The Tempest* presents a world firmly grounded in the anomalies, self-contradictions and problems attendant upon everyday reality.

The play can serve as a warning to anyone who seeks a perfect ruler of the sort Prospero pretends to be—yet it seems overhasty to insist that all values represented by the play are vitiated. To modern critics Prospero may seem tyrannical, patriarchal, colonialist and pathological in his obsession with control. In a way, he is. Nevertheless, in character, intelligence, and temperament he is a distinct improvement over most of the world's rulers from the time of James I to the present. It is difficult for modern audiences to make such comparisons given the enormous difference in forms of government, but the play reminds us of alternatives: Antonio, Sebastian, Alonzo, and the drunken conspirators.

Notes

1 Stephen Orgel, Introduction to the Oxford Shakespeare edition of *The Tempest* (1987), 1-87. I cite this text for quotations.

2 For an important critique of new historical readings of the play—along with an extensive psychoanalytic interpretation—see Meredith Ann Skura, "Discourse and the Individual: The Case of Colonialism in *The Tempest,*" *Shakespeare Quarterly* 40 (1989): 42-69. Curt Breight offers an excellent historical argument in which he argues that the play demystifies official strategies designed to deal with treason—and thus makes Prospero a problematic figure, a creator and manipulator of conspiracy; see Breight, "'Treason doth never prosper': *The Tempest* and the Discourse of Treason," *Shakespeare Quarterly* 41 (1990): 1-28.

3 See Orgel, Introduction, 25.

4 Alden T. Vaughan, "Shakespeare's Indian: The Americanization of Caliban," *Shakespeare Quarterly* 39 (1988): 137-53. This is quoted in Skura's discussion of colonialism in the play, "Discourse and the Individual," 45-57.

5 Melanie Klein, "Envy and Gratitude" (1957) in *"Envy and Gratitude" and Other Works: 1946-1963* (New York: Dell, 1975), 193.

6 I discuss this cultural aspect and its implications in "Some Problems with Klein's Theory of Reparation," *Journal of The Melanie Klein Society* 6 (1988): 68-80. Heniz Kohut offers a more complicated, and in many ways more convincing, account of why people idealize; see his important *The Restoration of the Self* (Madison, Conn.: International Universities Press, 1977). In brief, Kohut argues that we idealize others as a way of endorsing our idealization of ourselves as centers of vigor, strength, and perfection.

7 J. O. Wisdom, "Freud and Melanie Klein: Psychology, Ontology, and *Weltanschauung*" in *Psychoanalysis and Philosophy,* ed. C. Hanley and M. Lazerowitz (New York: International Universities Press, 1970), 350.

8 Ibid., 350-51.

9 Orgel, Introduction, 10.

10 For the cultural and psychological significance of attempts to control others, see Alice Miller, *For Your Own Good,* trans. H. and H. Hannum (New York: Farrar, Straus, Giroux, 1983).

11 Frank Kermode, Introduction to his Arden Edition of *The Tempest* (sixth edition, 1961). The makers of the Hollywood science fiction movie *The Forbidden Planet* (1955) were not taken in by this fastidious distinction, and as a result the movie is probably the first thoroughly skeptical response to Prospero in the last few hundred years.

12 Orgel, Introduction, 19-23; I follow this account for the rest of my paragraph.

[13] See my article "Omnipotence and Reparation in Prospero's Epilogue," in *Narcissism and the Text: Studies in Literature and the Psychology of Self,* ed. Lynne Layton and Barbara Schapiro (New York: New York University Press, 1986). I explore some of the theoretical basis for idealization in "Idealization as a Habit of Mind in Shakespeare: *The Tempest,*" *Melanie Klein and Object Relations* 7 (1989): 71-82.

[14] Norman Rabkin's *Shakespeare and The Problem of Meaning* (Chicago: University of Chicago Press, 1981) was probably the first book to establish this trend.

Source: "Idealization and the Problematic in *The Tempest,*" in *Subjects on the World's Stage: Essays on British Literature of the Middle Ages and the Renaissance,* edited by David G. Allen and Robert A. White, Associated University Presses, 1995, pp. 239-47.

Cumulative Index to Topics

Topic Index

The Cumulative Index to Topics identifies the principal topics of discussion in the criticism of each play and non-dramatic poem. The topics are arranged alphabetically. Page references indicate the beginning page number of each essay containing substantial commentary on that topic.

As You Like It

The Comedy of Errors

Coriolanus

Cymbeline

Hamlet

Henry IV, Parts 1 and 2

Henry VIII

Julius Caesar

King John

King Lear

Love's Labour's Lost

Topic Index

The Merchant of Venice

The Merry Wives of Windsor

A Midsummer Night's Dream

Much Ado about Nothing

Richard II

Richard III

Romeo and Juliet

Sonnets

Topic Index

The Taming of the Shrew

Topic Index

ISBN 0-8103-9978-4
90000
9 780810 399785